Stymphalos: The Acropolis Sanctuary

Volume 1

The buildings and artefacts uncovered by Canadian excavations at Stymphalos (1994–2001) shed light on the history and cult of a small sanctuary on the acropolis of the ancient city.

The thirteen detailed studies collected here illuminate a variety of aspects of the site. Epigraphical evidence confirms that both Athena and Eileithyia, goddess of childbirth, were worshipped in the sanctuary between the fourth and second centuries BCE. The temple and service buildings are modest in size and materials, but the temple floor and pillar shrine suggest that certain stones and bedrock outcrops were held as sacred objects. Earrings, finger rings, and other jewellery, along with almost 100 loomweights, indicate that women were prominent in cult observances. Many iron projectile points (arrowheads and catapult bolts) suggest that the sanctuary was destroyed in a violent attack around the mid-second century, possibly by the Romans.

A modest sanctuary in a modest Arcadian city-state, the acropolis sanctuary at Stymphalos will be a major point of reference for all archaeologists and historians studying ancient Arcadia and all southern Greece in the future.

(Phoenix Supplementary Volumes)

GERALD P. SCHAUS is a professor in the Department of Archaeology and Classical Studies at Wilfrid Laurier University.

PHOENIX

Journal of the Classical Association of Canada

Revue de la Société canadienne des études classiques

Supplementary Volume LIV

Publications of the Canadian Institute in Greece

Publications de l'Institut canadien en Grèce No. 7

Lake Stymphalos by Edward Dodwell, 1806

EDITED BY GERALD P. SCHAUS

STYMPHALOS: THE ACROPOLIS SANCTUARY

Volume 1

with contributions by

Sandra Garvie-Lok
Christopher Hagerman
Monica Munaretto
Deborah Ruscillo
Gerald P. Schaus
Peter Stone
Mary Sturgeon
Laura Surtees
Robert Weir
Hector Williams
Alexis Young

UNIVERSITY OF TORONTO PRESS
Toronto Buffalo London

Toronto Buffalo London
utorontopress.com

Reprinted in paperback 2015

ISBN 978-1-4426-4529-5 (cloth)
ISBN 978-1-4875-2042-7 (paper)

Library and Archives Canada Cataloguing in Publication

Stymphalos : the acropolis sanctuary. Volume 1 / edited by Gerald P. Schaus ; with contributions by Sandra Garvie-Lok, Christopher Hagerman, Monica Munaretto, Deborah Ruscillo, Gerald P. Schaus, Peter Stone, Mary Sturgeon, Laura Surtees, Robert Weir, Hector Williams, Alexis Young.

(Phoenix supplementary volumes ; LIV)
Includes bibliographical references and index.
ISBN 978-1-4426-4529-5 (bound). – ISBN 978-1-4875-2042-7 (paperback)

1. Stymphalos Site (Greece). 2. Temples – Greece – Stymphalos Site. 3. Arkadia (Greece) – Antiquities. 4. Excavations (Archaeology) – Greece – Arkadia. I. Schaus, Gerald P., 1950–, editor of compilation, author II. Garvie-Lok, Sandra, 1966–, author III. Williams, Hector, 1945–, author IV. Series: Phoenix. Supplementary volume (Toronto, Ont.) ; LIV

DF221.S79S79 2014 938′.8 C2013-908071-6

This book has been published with the help of a grant from the Canadian Federation for the Humanities and Social Sciences, through the Aid to Scholarly Publications Program, using funds provided by the Social Sciences and Humanities Research Council of Canada.

This book has been published with the help of a grant from the Canadian Institute in Greece.

University of Toronto Press acknowledges the financial assistance to its publishing program of the Canada Council for the Arts and the Ontario Arts Council, an agency of the Government of Ontario.

Conseil des Arts du Canada

Funded by the Government of Canada Financé par le gouvernement du Canada

CONTENTS

TABLES AND CHARTS

TABLES

CHARTS

ILLUSTRATIONS

ABBREVIATIONS

AA	*Archäologischer Anzeiger*
AAA	*Analecta Archaiologika Athenon*
ActaLund	*Acta Universitatis Lundensis*
AfrIt	*Africa Italiana*
Agora XXVI	See Works Cited
Agrinion	See Works Cited
AJA	*American Journal of Archaeology: The Journal of the Archaeological Institute of America*
AJPA	*American Journal of Physical Anthropology*
AM	*Mitteilungen des Deutschen Archäologischen Instituts, Athenische Abteilung*
ANSMN	*American Numismatic Society Museum Notes*
AnthPal	*Palatine Anthology*
AntK	*Antike Kunst*
AntP	*Antike Plastik*
AntW	*Antike Welt: Zeitschrift für Archäologie und Kulturgeschichte*
AR	*Archaeological Reports* (supplement to *JHS*)
Archaeology	*Archaeology: An Official Publication of the Archaeological Institute of America*
ArchDelt	*Archaiologikon Deltion*
ArchEph	*Archaiologike Ephemeris*
ArchJ	*Archaeological Journal*
AttiMGrecia	*Atti e memorie della Società Magna Grecia*
BABesch	*Bulletin antieke beschaving: Annual Papers on Classical Archaeology*
BAR	*British Archaeological Reports*
BAR-IS	*British Archaeological Reports, International Series*
BCD Pel.	See Works Cited
BCH	*Bulletin de correspondance hellénique*
BCH supp.	*Bulletin de correspondance hellénique*. Supplément
BdA	*Bollettino d'arte*
BÉFAR	Bibliothèque des Écoles françaises d'Athènes et de Rome
BMC	See Works Cited
BMFA	*Bulletin of the Museum of Fine Arts, Boston*
BSA	*Annual of the British School at Athens*
Bull. ROMA	*Bulletin of the Royal Ontario Museum of Archaeology*
BurlMag	*The Burlington Magazine*
CJ	*Classical Journal*
EchCl	*Echos du monde classique. Classical Views*

Expedition	*Expedition: Bulletin of the University Museum of the University of Pennsylvania*
GR	*Greece and Rome*
Hesperia	*Hesperia: The Journal of the American School of Classical Studies at Athens*
IG	*Inscriptiones graecae*
IGCH	C. Kraay, O. Mørkholm, and M. Thompson, *An Inventory of Greek Coin Hoards* (New York, 1973)
IstMitt	*Istanbuler Mitteilungen*
JdI	*Jahrbuch des Deutschen Archäologischen Instituts*
JGS	*Journal of Glass Studies*
JHS	*Journal of Hellenic Studies*
LIMC	*Lexicon iconographicum mythologiae classicae* (Zurich and Munich 1974–)
Mnemosyne	*Mnemosyne: Bibliotheca classica batava*
MonAnt	*Monumenti antichi*
NumAntCl	*Numismatica e antichità classiche*
OJA	*Oxford Journal of Archaeology*
ÖJh	*Jahreshefte des Österreichischen archäologischen Instituts in Wien*
OlForsch	*Olympische Forschungen*
OpAth	*Opuscula Atheniensia*
PBF	*Prähistorische Bronzefunde*
PECS	R. Stillwell et al., eds., *Princeton Encyclopedia of Classical Sites* (Princeton 1976)
Phoenix	*Phoenix: The Classical Association of Canada*
Prakt	*Praktika tes en Athenais Archaiologikes Etaireias*
RA	*Revue archéologique*
RDAC	*Report of the Department of Antiquities, Cyprus*
RE	A. Pauly and G. Wissowa, *Real-Encyclopädie der klassischen Altertumswissenschaft* (1893–1978)
RÉG	*Revue des études grecques*
RN	*Revue numismatique*
RömMitt	*Mitteilungen des Deutschen Archäologischen Instituts, Römische Abteilung*
SIMA	*Studies in Mediterranean Archaeology*
ThesCRA	*Thesaurus Cultus et Rituum Antiquorum*
ZPE	*Zeitschrift fur Papyrologie und Epigraphie*

Stymphalos: The Acropolis Sanctuary

Volume 1

INTRODUCTION

Stymphaleia is a term used today to denote the beautiful green valley with a small lake tucked away in northeast Arkadia below the southern and eastern slopes of Mt Kyllene. Canadian excavations at Stymphalos, at the Lower Town site (eastern lakeside area of the ancient city) and in the sanctuary near the summit of the low acropolis (fig. 0.1), began in 1994 as a result of several earlier seasons (1982–4, 1989) of geophysical investigation carried out by Hector Williams of the University of British Columbia. Initially, the goal of the investigation was to discover the plan of the ancient city, since casual observation of anomalies in vegetation growth in the flat areas near the lake at the east end of the acropolis ridge suggested an orthogonal grid layout for the streets and housing units. During these early field seasons, geophysical methods, including proton magnetometer and electrical resistivity metering, both still in a nascent stage of use in Greece, were employed to produce a plan of the sub-surface features of the area. This was done in conjunction with the Archaeological Society at Athens, represented by Mr John Travlos, which still had rights to the site as a result of archaeological work conducted by Anastasios Orlandos in the 1920s for the Society.[1] Once the results of the geophysical work were known, and clear evidence for streets and houses was discovered just below the surface, Williams's intention was to confirm these results with excavation of certain areas having the most promise, and easy access. One important goal was to obtain dates for the development of this orthogonally planned town, one which Pausanias (8.22.1) noted as a new location, it having moved from an earlier site somewhere else in the valley where there seemed still in his time to be three sanctuaries of Hera. Pausanias gave no indication of the date for this move to a new site. The orthogonal plan certainly suggested that the site close to the modern lake at the foot of the acropolis ridge was the new site rather than the old one to which Pausanias alluded.

In 1990, the Archaeological Society transferred all rights to the site to the Canadian Archaeological Institute at Athens (now the Canadian Institute in Greece), and thereafter Williams began planning for a series of campaigns aimed at exploring features of the ancient city. In 1993, approval was obtained from the Byzantine Ephoreia for Williams and Sheila Campbell of the Institute for Mediaeval Studies at St Michael's College, Toronto, to begin archaeological investigations of the Cistercian monastery near the north end of Stymphalos' fortified circuit, close to the modern road where it passes the section of Stymphaleia called Kionia. It was the following year that permission was received from the Archaeological Service of the Ministry of Culture and Sciences to begin investigation of the Classical antiquities. Most of the focus in the first season of excavations was in the lakeside area at the east end of the acropolis ridge, to try to uncover elements of the street plan; however, a small team directed by Kimberley Wooten made an initial test of the acropolis Sanctuary with seven shallow sondages of the enigmatic building, now called Building A, which Orlandos had called the "priests' house." This is located to the northeast of the temple explored from 1924 to 1926 and identified as a temple of Athena Polias by Orlandos, on the basis of an inscription found there.

Expectations of major discoveries in this Sanctuary were not high when Canadian work first began. Orlandos had suggested in his reports in *Praktika* of the work on the acropolis that he had excavated much of the Temple if not the whole Sanctuary, first in a larger campaign in 1924, and then with follow-up work in 1926 when the inscription was found. From this work, however, he only published a plan of the Temple walls, with a small part of the southwest corner of Building A (see chapter 1 below, fig 1.10), his so-called priests' house, and a description of the one-word inscription identifying the Sanctuary, "ΠΟΛΙΑΔΟΣ" ("Poliados" – "belonging to Polias," the very common epithet of Athena, protectress of the city) (see chapter 1 below, fig. 1.8). Beyond this, nothing was known about Orlandos' finds, since his notebooks were not yet accessible to us. If the Sanctuary were indeed completely excavated as he intimated in his reports, further work might only marginally enlighten and improve on the earlier results. At the very least, a complete plan of the "priests' house" (Building A) might be made, and any unexcavated areas, if found, might provide a sampling to elucidate Orlandos' earlier, presumably unpublished, material. In any case, it was thought that the most significant discoveries had probably occurred seventy years before.

This, however, turned out to be far from the case. It became clear on the first day of excavation that the Sanctuary had not been completely excavated, and that many important discoveries remained to be made. Over the course of seven seasons of excavation and study, the site has provided a wealth of material far beyond our hopes, illuminating the cult practices of the Sanctuary and its history, and indeed aspects of the city's history as a whole.

My own association with the project began in 1995, when I was invited by Williams to bring a group of archaeology students from Wilfrid Laurier University specifically to receive training in archaeological field methods. Dr Williams offered me the responsibility of supervising the acropolis Sanctuary excavations begun the year before by Wooten. This was the first of five campaigns that I supervised. There was no fieldwork on the site in 1998, and excavations in 1999 were supervised by Dr Yannis Lolos, while I occupied myself with writing a site description and beginning a study of the architecture. Major excavations in the Sanctuary ended in 2000, although some limited testing and cleaning continued in 2001.

Before any soil was excavated in that 1995 season, a piece of marble sculpture belonging to the arm of an Archaic kore was discovered during weed removal along the south wall of the Temple. It was then that we realized what potential the excavations of the Sanctuary still held. The next day, the first trench was laid out inside the Temple along the south side of the cella. Topsoil was removed, and as work proceeded in a second pass from east to west, numerous small fragments of marble sculpture began to appear. Whatever ideas we had of the extent of excavations by Orlandos were quickly set aside, and new plans were made for a thorough exploration of the site. Besides the Temple, trenches were laid out eventually in all parts of the Sanctuary, and along the City Wall running across the upper south edge of the acropolis. Important finds were made of building materials, weapons, sculpture, coins, pottery, cult implements, and votives including a fine array of jewellery and terracotta figurines. The discovery of a shrine area with five broken tetragonoi (rectangular stelae) and two late graves, one in the Temple and one just outside, was completely unexpected. In sum, despite its modest size and unimpressive appearance, this Sanctuary has now yielded rich evidence for its own history and that of the city, including cult practices, external contacts beyond the polis's restricted boundaries, and the basic architecture of the site. A large first volume of this material is presented here, while we hope that a second volume will follow in due course that will include the terracotta figurines, a more complete study of the pottery, some minor classes of small finds, and an important discussion of the overall results focusing on the cult, the history of the Sanctuary, its place within our understanding of Arkadian religious practices, and its contribution to the history of Stymphalos.

There are many individuals whose contributions to the acropolis Sanctuary excavations must be acknowledged and gratefully thanked. The first of these is Professor Hector Williams, whose overall direction of the Stymphalos project allowed us to complete work in the Sanctuary expeditiously and with remarkable results. Next are the field assistants, Michael Patience, Christopher Hagerman, Monica Munaretto, Laura Surtees, and Holly Lutomsky, whose help in supervising workers and volunteers, as well as keeping the notebooks and recording finds, was vital to the success of the field seasons. Sue Millar, Wendy Porter, and Kathleen Sherwood organized operations in the work and storage area in different years, Olympia Theofanopoulou, Georgina Garrett, Eric Nordgren, and Lisa Bengtson were our conservators, Andrew Price and Susan-Marie Cronkite Price set up the computer database for the finds, Thomas Boyd, Steven Copp, Mark Campbell, and Ben Gourley served as site architects. A host of students from Canada, Great Britain, the United States, Greece, and elsewhere contributed many long, hot, dusty hours of labour to the success of the campaigns with remarkable good cheer, as did also a devoted group of workmen from Stymphaleia and Pheneos who added their own expertise to the efforts of the team.[2] Special thanks also must be extended to the Goubatsos family, who fed and accommodated the team every season at Hotel Stymphaleia. Since excavations ended, other Wilfrid Laurier University students have assisted us in various ways, including Michelle Gamble, Roxann Bruder, Erika Nitsch, Lianne Maitland, and Kate Tyka.

Most important to acknowledge are the individual authors who have contributed to this volume, without whom the site could not properly have been studied and the results published. Their important contributions are much more easily appreciated by readers who can judge for themselves the significance of the material presented in these careful studies.

It would be remiss of me not to mention the family members who felt our absence each summer for long periods over the course of the project. In my case, my wife, Pamela, and our children had to cope without me and often went without a real summer vacation. Many others on the team were no doubt in the same position.

1

Stymphalos: Ancient Sources and Early Travellers

Gerald P. Schaus

"Stymphalos" is the name most commonly used of the town which lies on and around a southerly spur of Mt Kyllene in the most northeastern of the Arkadian city-states.[1] Corinth is 45 km to the east northeast; Sikyon is 35 km to the northeast; Argos is 45 km to the southeast, and Mantineia is 25 km directly south, in straight line measurements. It lies in a small valley about 600 m above sea level, the floor of which is approximately 12 km long (southwest to northeast) by 1.5 wide, though the entire territory may have been about 180 square kilometres (fig. 1.1a–b). At times it has had up to a third of its plain covered by a shallow lake; at other times the lake has almost dried up when thoroughly drained through a natural katabothros on its south side at the foot of a cliff of Mt Apelauron, but since the late nineteenth century through a man-made water channel at the east end of the valley.[2]

BRONZE AGE, CLASSICAL, AND EARLY HELLENISTIC STYMPHALOS

In antiquity, the small city-state was surrounded by Sikyon to the north, Phlious to the east, Alea to the southeast, Kaphyeia and Orchomenos to the south, and Pheneos to the west. Pellene lay directly to the north on the other side of Mt Kyllene.

Stymphalos was mentioned quite commonly in ancient sources, at least more so than its somewhat larger neighbour Pheneos, perhaps in part because it lay on routes through northern Arkadia from Sikyon on the north coast, from Argos and Nemea (Kleonai) eastward, from Orchomenos and the southern Arkadian cities, and from Olympia and Elis in the western part of the Peloponnese. It is normally associated in Greek art with the sixth (sometimes listed as the fifth) labour of Herakles, the killing or scaring away of the Stymphalian birds. The earliest finds from the site, besides a possible Upper Palaeolithic hand axe (on display in the new Stymphalos Museum of the Environment), include two or three Early Bronze Age (or earlier) polished stone celts (fig. 1.2a–b),[3] and several pieces of Mycenean pottery (fig. 1.3).[4]

There must have been Mycenean inhabitants in this valley, just as there were in neighbouring valleys to the east where Mycenean remains have been found: for example, at Aidonia, Aghia Sotira, and Tzoungiza, and to the south, where a large Mycenean tholos tomb is known at Arkadian Orchomenos. The so-called throne at Kionia, about half a kilometre from the acropolis of Stymphalos, has a megalithic lintel block raised above an odd cavelike indentation in the bedrock and a niche ("throne") carved in the bedrock above it (fig. 1.4a–b).[5] There is also a pair of deep rectangular shafts cut into bedrock with longer and wider cuttings around each shaft closer to the surface, which are likely for stone slab lids. These are located on the lower terrace of the acropolis (fig. 1.5) with a north-south orientation towards the lake and Mt Kyllene. They are similar to Mycenean shaft-and-pit tombs at Kambi on Zakynthos, for example, though not well paralleled on any closer Mycenean sites, it seems.[6] Since they were missing their lids, and were empty of any objects that could be securely associated with them, it is impossible to date them, but they have a greater resemblance to Mycenean shaft grave construction than any similar shaft and lid construction that can be associated with Greek or Roman period Stymphalos.

A small, well-preserved tholos with a small corbelled opening (like a relieving triangle) (fig. 1.6a–c) exists in the side of a seasonal stream bed near Lafka at the west end of the Stymphalos valley, not far from a low hill, called Aghia Triadha after its chapel, which has fortification walls of rough, almost Cyclopean masonry and distinct offsets reminiscent of Mycenean walls (fig. 1.7).[7] There is, however, a notable lack of Mycenean pottery on the surface of this site and no other ancient building foundations, so the purpose and date of the walls are not clear.

The earliest mention of the area in Greek literature is found in Homer's Catalogue of Ships (*Il.* 2.608), where Stymphalos is noted as having provided men for the war against Troy. This and the well-established myth of Herakles' visit to rid the valley of its troublesome birds are the best literary indications of a Bronze Age presence in the valley.[8] Pindar (*Ol.* 6, 99–100) calls Stymphalos the metropolis or mother of Arkadian towns.[9] According to Pausanias (8.4.4,6), it was founded by Stymphalos, who was the son of Elatus and grandson of Arkas, and he (8.22.2) also tells us that according to tradition the goddess Hera was educated here by Temenos, son of Pelasgos, who upon Hera's separation from Zeus and return to Stymphalos was honoured by Temenos with three sanctuaries, one to her as a maiden ("Partheneian" Hera), one as a bride ("Teleian"), and one as a widow or, more properly, divorcee. These sanctuaries were said to be at the old site of Stymphalos, which Pausanias did not describe and so presumably did not see. The original settlers in the area are associated with the Pelasgians by Pausanias and others,[10] and the worship of gods who were represented by tetragonoi is believed to be connected with Pelasgian tradition according to Herodotus (2.51.1), although Pelasgians in the region of Attica were supposed to have passed on the practice first to the Athenians.[11]

Besides the mention of three cults of Hera at the older site of Stymphalos, Pausanias (8.22.7–9) describes a temple and sanctuary of Artemis, whose cult was strengthened or rejuvenated by a divine sign shortly before his visit in the mid-second century CE. This may or may not be the same sanctuary, identified as that of Brauronian Artemis, mentioned in an inscription found at Stymphalos before the Second World War that directs a memorial plaque to be set up in the agora of Elateia and in the sanctuary of Brauronian Artemis at Stymphalos to commemorate assistance given by the Stymphalians to people of Elateia seeking refuge after being expelled from their homes by the Romans or the Aetolians.[12] The date for the inscription is ca. 189–185 BCE, when the Elateians were allowed to return to their homes by the Roman consul, Acilius, after their period of exile between 197 and 189 BCE. There is also evidence for the worship of Hermes from an inscription with his name[13] and Demeter from an inscribed spear butt of the fifth century,[14] as well as Athena Polias from the inscription in the acropolis Sanctuary found by Orlandos (fig. 1.8).[15]

There are no Geometric or early Archaic remains found to date on the present site of Stymphalos. A few pieces of pottery from the Sanctuary and Lower Town may be late Archaic in date, and the marble kore found inside the acropolis Temple dates ca. 500–490 BCE, though it may have been brought to the acropolis later from Old Stymphalos or elsewhere.[16] We learn of two Olympic champions from Stymphalos in the first half of the fifth century. Pindar (*Ol.* 6) praises the accomplishment of Hagesias, citizen of Stymphalos and Syracuse, winning the Olympic mule chariot race (*apene*) in 468 BCE or shortly before, and Pausanias (6.7.10) tells us of the double periodoniketes (Circuit victor, of all four Panhellenic games), Dromeus, champion in the *dolichos* (long distance foot race), whose victories at Olympia are more likely dated 460–456 BCE than 484–480 BCE.[17] Both winners may come from some other part of the Stymphalos valley rather than a major town called Stymphalos within it, though the performance of Pindar's ode at Stymphalos must have occurred at the old site of Stymphalos town, given the fourth-century date posited for the new, orthogonally planned Stymphalos. The performance took place under the direction of Aineas (a possible relative of the victor from Stymphalos), possibly at the festival of Hera Partheneia, the maiden, since this goddess is said in the poem to be honoured first (Pindar, *Ol.* 6, 88).[18] This would seem to be the location where the three Hera sanctuaries, for Hera as maiden, bride, and "widow" (divorcee), were to be found. The chorus then, to judge from the closing lines of the ode, sailed to Sicily to offer the same performance at Syracuse as well.

The second Olympic victor from Stymphalos was one of the greatest runners from antiquity. Pausanias (6.7.10) noted the appropriateness of his name ("Dromeus" means "runner," though one wonders if this were a nickname), and that besides winning twice at the quadrennial games of Olympia and Delphi, he also won three times at the biennial games of Isthmia and five times at the fourth Panhellenic games site, Nemea, just east of Stymphalos. Pausanias tells us that his statue in the Altis at Olympia was sculpted by Pythagoras, who is among the five best-known sculptors of the era.[19] We may speculate that the costs for such a statue were out of reach for most Stymphalians, but such a successful runner must surely have made an impressive income from victories in generously funded prize games throughout Greece. Pausanias, perhaps erroneously, credits Dromeus with the introduction of a meat diet for athletes rather than fresh cheese. One may also speculate whether this great runner benefited from the higher altitude of Stymphalos (ca. 600 masl) for his training.

Already by the end of the fifth century, men from Arkadia, including Stymphalos, were finding employment as mercenaries, as we learn from Xenophon's *Anabasis*.[20] A captain named Agasias, the Stymphalian, was among the Greek mercenaries in Cyrus' army and from Xenophon's account, he was clearly one of the bravest, most respected of all the soldiers in the expedition.[21] A few coins from distant places found at Stymphalos from the fourth century on suggest that local men sent or brought home money from such foreign expeditions.[22] One native son, Aineias of Stymphalos, served as general of the Arkadian League in 367 BCE (Xen. *Hell.* 7.3.1). This is presumably the same Aineias, called *Taktikos* (the "Tactician"), who wrote a still extant book (*Poliorketika* or *Siegecraft*) on city siege tactics (hence his epithet), which among other things focuses on how defenders may counter the threat of betrayal by rival parties within the city.

The refounded town of Stymphalos was occasionally the object of attack, first perhaps by the Athenian Iphikrates, more likely in 370/69 BCE than in 391 (Xen. *Hell.* 4.4.16 and 6.5.49; Strabo 8.8.4; Diodorus 15.63.2 and 65.6; Cornelius Nepos, *Iphicrates* 2.5; possibly also Polyainos, *Strategemata* 3.9.28).[23] This presumed attack on Stymphalos by the Athenians under Iphikrates, during which the purported attempt at blocking the katabothros with sponges may have taken place, seems to be in odd juxtaposition with a rare *symbola* document, an interstate agreement between the Athenians and the Stymphalians, dated about 368 BCE.[24] This agreement has been preserved in a very fragmentary marble inscription found in Athens. Its purpose was to provide avenues of equal justice for citizens of the two states in whichever state they brought their suits, particularly in commercial dealings.[25] But in Stymphalos' case, trade must have been minimal with Athens, and instead, the agreement may have been prompted more by sentiment or religious interest, suggests Walbank.[26] He points to the later inscription (noted above) which mentions a sanctuary of Brauronian Artemis at Stymphalos and says that this suggests family or religious ties between the two states. Walbank also wonders whether an infusion of settlers, including exiles from Attica, may have prompted the refounding of the town at its new location and the building of strong fortification walls.[27]

On the other hand, because Athens made similar agreements at this time with several other states, including Troizen and Knossos, Woodhead suggested that such agreements may be part of Athenian foreign policy, in creating different levels of relationships with other city-states.[28] The first level, he points out, was membership in the Second Athenian Confederacy. The second level was one in which allies were less closely bound to Athens and were not actually members of the Confederacy. The third level, represented by these *symbolai*, was one in which bilateral agreements were reached with states not wishing to be allies of Athens but still wanting to have good relations with her, to protect citizens' commercial activities and legal rights in both states. The agreement between Stymphalos and Athens is an indication of the rapprochement between Athens and the Arkadian League which led to the treaty between Athens and the League in 366 BCE. Clearly, the hatchet bared by Iphikrates against Arkadian cities in 370/369 BCE was very quickly buried. The rapprochement between Stymphalos and Athens, however, seems to have been closer than Woodhead might have anticipated. Shared cults bear this out.

Williams and Gourley speculated that the refounding of Stymphalos was part of a concerted effort to contain Sparta, with the establishment of strong cities at Messene, Mantineia, and Megalopolis.[29] The establishment of a cult of Athena Polias on the acropolis of Stymphalos may thus have been an integral part of the establishment of the new town having undergone an amalgamation of villages, or *synoikism*. One can only suggest that a recently established sanctuary of Athena Polias at Stymphalos also had ties with Athens' patron goddess, and that the link could have been cemented by the appearance of the marble kore, a product of Athens, it appears, found in the acropolis Temple, whether it was simply moved from old Stymphalos or elsewhere in the valley, or, perhaps unlikely, was a gift from Athens or an Athenian.[30] The provision for weaving within the Sanctuary (below) only seems to strengthen the possibility of such a link between Athens' and Stymphalos' cults of Athena Polias.

Half a century after Iphikrates' attack, Stymphalos was the object of a night-time assault by Kassander's general, Apollonides, in 315 BCE (Diod. 19.63.1).[31] What damage this may have done and whether this led immediately to a Macedonian garrison being left in the town is not known. It is fairly probable, based on coin evidence, for example, and ancient sources, that the Macedonians did occupy the town for a time in the late fourth to early third century.[32] Stymphalos was also close to the location of a skirmish between the Macedonian king, Philip V, and a small army of Eleans abandoned at the last moment by their leader, Euripidas, in 219/18 BCE (Polyb. 4.68–9). Polybius (2.55.8) says that Stymphalos was the only Arkadian city besides Megalopolis in which King Kleomenes of Sparta could find neither a partisan to work for him nor a single traitor during the Kleomenian War (228–222 BCE).

After the fourth century, the archaeological evidence suggests a much lower level of cultic activity in the Sanctuary, with many fewer votives being left by worshippers. One explanation may be the effect of Macedonian attacks and occupation, but a more serious factor may be a general trend across Arkadia of population decline in the third and second centuries, caused by such things as emigration, service as mercenaries, and soil erosion.[33] B. Forsén believes that Bintliff's "Upland Boom-bust Model" for population variations in mountainous areas applies to Arkadia, with a peak of population in the fourth century but a serious decline in the Hellenistic period.[34]

Stymphalos was presumably an object of attack by the Romans in lengthy mopping-up operations after the fall of Corinth to Mummius in 146 BCE (see below).[35] Pausanias (7.16.9) mentions the concerted efforts that the Romans made after the fall of Corinth to deal with the resistance among the other Achaian League cities.[36] It has long been puzzling to readers of Pausanias that he says specifically that the resistance only came to an end in 140 BCE (160th Olympiad), six years after the fall of Corinth.[37] Why should it have taken so long unless perhaps the resistance was particularly fierce?

Strabo (388, 8.8.2) in the late first century BCE/early first century CE lists Stymphalos as one of the cities in the area that had ceased to exist, or had only traces of remains, along with Mantineia, Orchomenos, Heraea, Kleitor, Methydrion, Kaphyeis, Maenalos, Kynaetha, and Pheneos.[38] Strabo, who is, however, not very reliable as a source on this topic and who never, it seems, visited the area, nevertheless also says, "In consequence of the complete devastation of the country, it is unnecessary to give a long description of it. The cities, although formerly celebrated, have been destroyed by continual wars" (Loeb trans.) Certainly by the time that Pausanias (8.22.7) visited the town of Stymphalos, he found only a temple of Artemis still in working condition to comment on.[39]

POST ROMAN CONQUEST

Coins and pottery suggest that habitation at Stymphalos continued through the second and first centuries BCE though at a much reduced level. Building A within the acropolis Sanctuary may have been restored to working order, but there is no evidence of regular worship in the Altar area or the Temple. Only a few lamps from the later first or second centuries CE bear witness to the occasional visitor. On the Lower Town site, however, substantial houses were occupied in the early first century CE with impressive remains of pottery, a sword and shield, marble table feet, wall plaster, and a door leaf decorated with large bronze bosses. This occupation ended in a serious destruction thought to be in the reign of Tiberius and caused by an earthquake.[40] After this, there is little evidence for life in the town.

By the fifth or sixth century CE, burials were being dug on the acropolis ridge, reusing ancient stone blocks to line graves and terracotta roof tiles to cover them. These are found all along the ridge in small numbers, from the acropolis bastion on the summit, to the acropolis Sanctuary, to the lower terraces. To judge from the layout of the graves, with heads to the west for the adults, and head to the north for an infant, presumably unbaptized, these should belong to an early Christian population in the valley. So few burial goods accompany the graves that it is hard to date them. They are presumed to belong to the fifth or sixth century, but without strong support. Two dog burials in the same style of cist graves are worth noting. After this, there is little evidence of habitation till the thirteenth century when Cistercian monks came to Greece following the conquests of the Frankish knights and built a monastery using much ancient building material for their impressive basilica and gatehouse at Zaraka. This was occupied by the monks for a short period, perhaps fifty years, before it was abandoned, and the church burnt. It is possible that the monks faced significant challenges from malaria, though this is far from confirmed.[41] There is a little glass from the acropolis Sanctuary which seems to be Medieval in date, and a coin of Manuel I (1143–80 CE) has also been found there.[42]

Pausanias's reference to an older site (where the three sanctuaries of Hera are presumed to be) and a newer one, where he saw the Artemis temple, has confused early European travellers visiting Stymphalos. Since the remains of a large temple were still to be seen in the nineteenth and early twentieth century beside the Cistercian monastery, commonly called by the travellers the "Katholikon,"[43] which itself is not far from the substantial spring that served as the main source for the lake (identified as the ancient "Metopa" spring), it was thought that the newer site of Stymphalos was around Kionia, and that the older site lay in ruins at the time of Pausanias on the spur of Kyllene beside the lake.[44] This idea, however, must certainly be set aside now, since excavations on the acropolis ridge and in the area beside the lake have confirmed that the main period of habitation only begins in the fourth century BCE, and after a significant, if not total, break in the second and first centuries BCE, some reoccupation occurred again in the first century CE. The older site referred to by Pausanias should be elsewhere in the valley.[45] The large temple seen by the nineteenth- and early twentieth-century visitors near the Cistercian monastery cannot now be located definitely. Its identification as the Artemis temple seen by Pausanias rests both on its impressive size and on an inscription found in the vicinity which mentions the Artemis sanctuary and which seems to have been set up in it.[46] The ancient city wall loops far enough to the north from the acropolis to encompass an area reaching the Cistercian monastery. The large temple ruins still seen a century ago in massive stone foundations just east of the basilica might just have been incorporated within this circuit.[47] There are no other foundations in the vicinity of Kionia, other than the column drums and marble roof tiles already mentioned well to the northeast (near the north end of Stymphaleia), which can be associated with an Archaic or Classical period town.

Strabo (389, 8.8.4) notes that when the katabothros was blocked up, the lake swelled so that the town was situated on its edge, but that in his time, the lake had drained and the town of Stymphalos was 50 stades away (from the katabothros presumably). Edward Dodwell was first to note that this must have been an error by Strabo's transcribers, and that 5 stades was more correct.[48]

Stymphalos is rarely noticed during the Roman period, except for Hadrian's aqueduct and Pausanias' visit, and likewise through the Byzantine. The Cistercian monastery founded at Zaraka after the Frankish conquest of Greece likewise has left few records about life in the valley.[49]

EARLY EUROPEAN TRAVELLERS

Earlier travellers who visited Stymphalos noted the presence of the Temple on the terrace below the summit of the acropolis. Dodwell visited the site on 12 March 1806 and described the acropolis Temple as follows: "Nearer the lake the brow of an impending eminence is characterized by the ruins of another temple, the lower part of the cella of which is still visible."[50] Colonel Leake seemed to have identified two temples on the acropolis. He first talks about "the vestiges of a temple on the summit of the projection"[51] but later mentions, "on the cape, perhaps, stood a temple of Neptune, for he was the favourite deity among the Arcadians, and his temples often occupied such projecting heights."[52]

Equally brief though interesting for suggesting that the Temple was an *in antis* one is Ludwig Ross's description when he passed through the valley: "Östlich unter der Akropolis auf dem niedrigeren Rücken sind die Fundamente eines Tempels in antis."[53] Ernst Curtius provided the first sketch plan of the city, done by H. Strack in Curtius's day book, and on it the Temple is shown as distyle in antis. Curtius provides dimensions for the Temple, but gives the wrong unit of measurement: "Oestlich unter dem höchsten Thurme erkennt man die Grundlagen eines Tempels von fünfzehn Fuss Lange und neun Fuss Breite."[54] Curtius's error was caught by Wilhelm Vischer, who gave his own measurements of the Temple and his support for the hypothesis that it was an *in antis* temple. "Curtius ... giebt die Länge des Tempels auf 15 Fuβ, die Breite auf 9 Fuβ an. So ist das ohne Zweifel nur ein Schriebfehler für eben so viele Schritte. Ich fand die Cella 10 Schritt lang, die Vorhalle (es ist ein Tempel in antis) 5 Schritt."[55]

Conrad Bursian was another who regarded the remains as belonging to an *in antis* temple, and he could not resist the temptation to connect it with Pausanias's mention of an Artemis temple in the city. "Auf dem Felsboden erkennt man noch die linien einiger Strassen, im westlicheren theile die Fundamente eines kleinen Tempels in antis (vielleicht des von Paus. VIII, 22, 7 erwähnten alten Tempels der Artemis Stymphalia, die als Hauptgöttin der Stadt jedenfalls in der Oberstadt ihr Heiligthum hatte) und besonders an der Südostseite, gegen den See zu ..."[56]

An early guidebook for travellers to Greece provided remarkably good dimensions for the Temple, and seems to have noted the remains of the Altar without identifying it: "La première terrasse s'étend jusqu'à la 5e tour ronde, qui mesure 6 mèt. de diamètre. On y remarque les fondations d'un temple de construction presque polygonale, long de 11 mèt. 30 c. et large de 5 mèt. 75 c., avec une division intérieure, qui laisse au parvis une longueure de 4 mèt. A côté est une autre ruine de 15 pas de long, dont la nature n'a pas été déterminée."[57] The plan of the city accompanying the guide's description is the same as that published by E. Curtius forty years earlier. J.G. Frazer saw the Temple ruins and gave rough dimensions for it: 6 paces wide, 8 paces long for the cella and 4 feet (paces?) deep for the pronaos. He says that only "the outer foundation walls are preserved."[58]

F. Hiller von Gaertringen was the first scholar to describe the antiquities of Stymphalos in greater detail and include photographs, basing his article on notes made by Heinrich Lattermann during a visit to the site in mid-June 1910.[59] Two photographs of the Temple itself were published.[60] In the better of the two, taken from the west southwest, the surface of the ground reaches almost to the top of the Temple's west wall, and the pronaos cross wall is clearly visible, covered to within about 20–30 cm of the tops of the blocks on both sides of the central doorway. In the distance, one can see the tops of the Altar blocks, and the east wall, part of the south wall, and even a section of the middle dividing wall of Building A. The other photograph is from a greater distance, although the same details can be made out of the Temple, Altar, and Building A. The southeastern corner of the Temple is better seen in this photograph and already it had one less course preserved than other parts of the structure.

Anastasios Orlandos, during several seasons of work in the 1920s at Stymphalos, identified this Sanctuary as belonging to Athena on the basis of an inscribed stele found in a small section of the temenos next to Building A ("priests' house") which had been left undug in 1924 but then excavated in 1926. The so-called horos stone provided only the name ΠΟΛΙΑΔΟΣ (POLIADOS).[61] Orlandos published another photograph of the remains (fig. 1.9a) (two other photographs are in the Archaeological Society of Athens archives – figs. 1.9b–c) and the first state plan of the Temple (fig. 1.10).[62]

His claim to have carried out excavations within the Temple has already been discussed. No evidence of trenches or backfilled areas could be isolated when new excavations were carried out from 1995 to 1997, so one has to assume that any actual dirt removal in the Temple area involved clearing of the tops of walls. No finds from the Sanctuary were ever mentioned in his reports, nor was there any record of finds in his field notebooks, other than the inscription just mentioned. It is also not clear on what basis Orlandos identified the building lying beside the Temple as a priests' house. No attempt was made at reconstructing the plan or elevation of the Temple, or discussing the present remains. Orlandos' plan makes it clear that three orthostate blocks of the cross wall separating the pronaos from the cella were still preserved *in situ* at that time. Orlandos also made a rough plan of the visible remains of his so-called priests' house (Building A), but it was not published (see fig. 1.11). It provides a better understanding of what he could discern at the time in the Sanctuary. Most of the west wall of Building A, as well as part of the north wall and interior dividing wall of the original structure, must have been covered with soil, while the West and North Annexes were unknown to him.

No scholarly work had been done on the Sanctuary since Orlandos' time. Whenever the Sanctuary was referred to, it was only in the briefest terms without discussion. Orlandos' published plan of the Temple was used as recently as 1980 in N.D. Papahatzis' commentary of books 7 and 8 of Pausanias.[63] To this point, no one has discussed either the Altar or the building close beside the Temple which we briefly called the Tripartite Building but now call Building A. Five preliminary reports on recent excavations in the Sanctuary have appeared, as well as a preliminary study of the jewellery finds, and a summary article of results to date.[64]

2

The Sanctuary: Site Description

Gerald P. Schaus

Located on a sloping terrace just east of the summit of the acropolis of Stymphalos, the Sanctuary opens eastward with a view towards the pass leading to Phlious and Nemea and southward with a view of Lake Stymphalos at the foot of the acropolis ridge. It is sheltered below the highest point of the acropolis, which lies 140–50 m west of the Temple and about 25 m higher (see fig. 2.1).[1] The Sanctuary terrace slopes down from northwest (640.5 masl) to southeast (637.4 masl) across outcroppings of bedrock in an area measuring roughly 43 (east-west) × 44.5 m (north-south) (fig. 2.2a–b). Old photographs (e.g., Orlandos' from about 1924) and descriptions by early travellers show that the Temple and other walls were readily visible and that the terrace was clear of any major bushes or trees. This may partly have been due to cultivation, since Williams was told by a local man that the terrace had been ploughed with a mule by the landowner some time in living memory. This must not have been done around the Altar, or within the Temple or Building A, since a mule and plough could not make any progress here, but the soil below the large terrace wall on the east and south side of the Altar may have been turned over on occasion, and this would have disturbed the first two, or possibly three, levels of soil discerned in excavations here. One of the two landowners who claim the Sanctuary terrace as theirs appeared one day during the 1999 season and expressed concern with our work, but did not return.

Three main structures are found within the Sanctuary: a modest temple, an altar, and a larger auxiliary building, called here Building A. A fourth structure, called Building B, lies just below the Altar Terrace wall but apparently was used in association with the Sanctuary (figs. 2.3–2.4, fig. 2.6). The Temple measures 6.0 × 11.5 m and is situated at the western edge of the Sanctuary at the foot of the more steeply sloping bedrock leading up to the acropolis summit. Both the Temple and the Altar, 5 m east of the Temple entrance, are oriented 80° E. of magnetic north, towards the double peak of a low mountain, called Gavrias, on the far side of the lake which separates the valley of Stymphalos from that of Phlious (fig. 2.5). Whether it was this peak, or the rising sun on a given day, or another cause, the reason for the orientation is speculative.

The Temple had two rooms, cella and pronaos; there is no evidence to indicate that columns stood in the pronaos, despite early travellers who identified it as a distyle in antis temple.[2] The pronaos was accessed by a narrow set of stairs at the east. The Altar, built of large, roughly cut rectangular blocks, presently measures 1.65 × 2.4 m; it was surrounded by an open court whose surface is covered with small stones preserved only in rough patches in a radius of no more than about 4 m away from the Altar. Just below the Altar to the east is a line of large fieldstones running roughly north-south which seems to have been deliberately laid in order to hold back earth around the Altar Court.

Building A was originally built with dimensions 10.7 (east-west) × 8.8 m (north-south) and an orientation of 60° E. of magnetic north for the line of its south façade. Its main entrance in the middle of this façade opened towards the Altar Court. The southwest corner of Building A comes to within one metre of the northeast corner of the Temple. Two rooms were later added to this building. The North Annex, 3.95 m wide, was added along the full length of the north side (10.7 m), while the West Annex is 3.6 m wide but only 4.85 m in length, overlapping both the original part of Building A and the North Annex. The original foundations of Building A are similar to those of the Temple: large, square-cut limestone blocks; the foundations for the two annexes are unworked fieldstones.[3]

Building B has only been partially excavated, so the plan is incomplete. Wall foundations were built of fieldstones with upper walls no doubt of mudbrick. It must have had at least three rooms originally, of which only one has been completely uncovered. This room's dimensions are 5.0 × 5.4 m with a door in the middle of its west wall and two steps leading down to its floor surface. The orientation of Building B is closer to that of the City Wall and Building A than to the Altar, Terrace, and Temple.

In 1926 Anastasios Orlandos returned to the Sanctuary, previously identified as Hera's,[4] and discovered an inscribed stone located somewhere close to the Temple and beside Building A which he believed was a boundary stone ("horos lithinos").[5] The stone was broken at one end, but still had a preserved length (or height) of 56 cm; its width and thickness were 29 and 21 cm respectively. It bore a single, complete word, POLIADOS ([- ? -] ΠΟΛΙΑΔΟΣ), in fourth-century BCE lettering according to Orlandos, on its narrower (21 cm) face (see chapter 1 above, fig. 1.8). There are two possible ways that this inscription was displayed. Either it was laid flat with the inscription stretching horizontally and right side up, presumably built into a wall, or it was set up as a vertical stele with the writing being read top to bottom. There is no noticeable bulge at the unbroken end of the stone in Orlandos' drawing to suggest that this end was once inserted into the ground and meant to stand vertically like many horoi or like the other stelae in the Sanctuary which bulge out in their lower ends. Also the space between the end of the inscription and the end of the block is only 20 cm, which hardly allows enough clearance for the full inscription to be read easily if the block were set in the ground vertically. If it were set up vertically, it seems more likely that it was set on top of a stone base perhaps with a small inset. On the other hand, this stone may not readily have been built into the wall of either the Temple or Building A, since both structures have a tall, wide orthostate course on top of which mudbrick walls were laid. For both buildings the width of the orthostates is approximately 40 cm, while the inscription is only 29 cm wide. On balance, it seems slightly more likely that the unbroken end of the inscribed stone was placed on a stone base, with the other end being broken off like all the stelai in situ in the Sanctuary whose top ends have been lost at varying heights. (Because all the stelai in the Pillar Shrine area had lost their tops, it may not be proper to call them "aniconic," since it is possible, though perhaps not likely given the quality of the stone, that images [i.e., heads] once decorated their tops, like examples in the Tegea museum.)

Most of the horos stones from the Athenian Agora are vertical stelai inscribed horizontally near or at their tops, but for the few examples where the inscription is written vertically, the writing is always from top to bottom, as the Poliados inscription would be with this assumption about the unbroken end being in the ground.[6] Orlandos' drawing shows a 20-cm gap between the end of the word "Poliados" and the end of the stone, which is barely enough room for the stone to be set firmly in the ground with the inscription still clear and visible.

According to Orlandos' notebook drawing, there was a 6-cm gap between the break of the stele and the beginning of the preserved lettering. If the drawing is accurate on this face of the stone, it is enough to suggest that there was no other word written before ΠΟΛΙΑΔΟΣ, although horoi commonly had clearly separated words, normally on different lines. The 6 cm-gap does not exclude entirely the possibility that there was another word, such as "ΗΟΡΟΣ" ("horos"), written before "ΠΟΛΙΑΔΟΣ" and perhaps even perpendicular to it, such as is found on two of the horoi from the Agora.[7] Another possibility is "ΑΘΕΝΑΣ" as a second word in front of ΠΟΛΙΑΔΟΣ, similar to the stele from Delphi (below) with ΔΙΟΣ ΠΟΛΙΕΟΣ.

The dimensions of the Poliados stone are close to sanctuary horoi from the Agora, e.g., H8 (H 0.77 × W 0.27 × Th 0.16 m) and H19 (H 0.58 × W 0.38 × Th 0.185 m), both complete,[8] but writing on the narrower side is not normal for such horoi. While the genitive case of the inscription clearly was meant to identify something, presumably an area (temenos) or object, as "belonging to Polias," it is not certain that the Poliados inscription is a horos in the normal sense of a boundary stone. It is possible that it was a dedication belonging to Athena, or indeed yet another Arkadian stele of the "aniconic" type, and was inscribed as much for identifying purposes as to mark a spot for worship of this particular deity, like the stelai in the Pronaia sanctuary at Delphi (below). In any case, "Polias" is the epithet commonly given to Athena in Arkadia as elsewhere in Greece.[9] The association with this goddess therefore seems secure.

Another stele, narrow and about a metre in length, discovered in 1983 built into a stone wall in the central part of the ancient city, north of the acropolis, bore a one-word inscription "along one edge": EPMAC. It was suggested that it was part of a herm, or alternatively a boundary marker for the temenos of a Hermes sanctuary somewhere close by.[10] The fact that the name is in the nominative case may better support an identification of it as a herm, or an "aniconic" pillar representing the god himself, similar to the five stelai found in the small "Pillar Shrine" area of the acropolis Sanctuary. "Aniconic" pillars having a pyramidal top in the Tegea museum occasionally have inscriptions, including one (Tegea museum 1437) with "ΑΡΤΕΜΙΣ" written horizontally on the front face and the dedicant's name on the side ("ΚΛΗΝΙΑΣ ΑΝΕΘΗΚΕ" "Klenias anetheke"), and another (Tegea museum 220) with "ΛΕΟΙΤΑΣ ΑΓΑΘΟΙ ΘΕΟ ΑΝΕΘΗΚΕ" "Leoitas agathoi theo anetheke" (presumably an error, for "to the good god," dative "ΑΓΑΘΟΙ ΘΕΟΙ" "agathoi theoi") horizontally on the front face.[11]

The discovery of four or more objects in the Sanctuary with partial inscriptions, apparently dedications to Eileithyia (inv. 27 – Sikyonian silver coin; inv. 503 – Corinthian potsherd; inv. 2909 – terracotta loomweight; and inv. 2525 – a bronze rim fragment), provides an identification for another deity worshipped in the Sanctuary.[12] Eileithyia, a goddess of childbirth and child rearing, was prominently worshipped at nearby Kleitor in Pausanias' day (Paus. 8.21.3), but otherwise is not very commonly attested in Arkadia.[13]

An unusual parallel for the Stymphalos Pillar Shrine can be found in the Athena Pronaia sanctuary at Delphi (Marmaria).[14] Here as many as five stelai, three of which were inscribed with the names of deities while two others were either uninscribed or the inscriptions have disappeared, were discovered close to the Archaic altar and temple of Athena. Two other inscribed names of deities on the nearby retaining wall seem to identify worship places with altars or offering tables in front of the wall.[15] The stelai were dated to the late sixth century, while the names on the wall were thought to belong to the fifth century, although the letter forms are similar.[16] The stelai bear the names respectively of Athena Ergane, Athena Zosteria, and Zeus Polieos, the first two in the dative case, the last in the genitive. The goddesses honoured on the retaining wall with an "altar" in front of each are Eileithyia and Hygieia, both in the genitive case. While such stelai have been considered altars by some (νηφάλιοι βωμοί – for libations without wine), they have also been considered simply as dedications rather than altars.[17] The association of Athena with Eileithyia, the use of stelai simply inscribed with the names of gods and goddesses in different cases, the placement of an altar or offering table in front of an inscribed retaining wall block or in front of stelai, and the date of the inscriptions will be part of a later discussion.

It is likely that the main access to the Sanctuary was from the east. A well-built, in part terraced, road leads up to the acropolis from the lake to the south of the Sanctuary. It rises diagonally from west to east along the acropolis flank until it passes through a gate high on the acropolis slope, and then reaches one of the acropolis terraces about in the middle of the ridge. From there, a smaller road may have led along the inside of the City Wall westward to the Sanctuary. This smaller road probably forked, with a western prong leading into the Sanctuary, and a second prong leading further north across the terrace to the north flank of the acropolis. The main line of this small road presumably continued along the line of the City Wall, but it could not have been more than a footpath when it climbed steeply toward the summit of the acropolis to the west. A modern goat path also leads into the northwest corner of the Sanctuary from the western heights, but there is nothing to suggest that this path was used in antiquity.

EXCAVATIONS

While nineteenth- and early twentieth-century travellers took measurements of the Temple, drew rough sketches of it, and even published two photographs, the first excavator of the acropolis Sanctuary was Anastasios Orlandos.[18] In 1924, he wrote that he carried out a small excavation that included work on both the temple and the "priests' house" (Building A). In 1926, he returned and noted that he dug a small area that was unexcavated in 1924, near the priests' house. No plan of his trenches, nor a description of any of his finds other than the inscription, ever appeared in his brief reports (*Prakt* 1924–30), nor was anything recorded in his notebooks other than the plan of the Temple, Sanctuary, and again a sketch of the inscription. It was puzzling, and indeed a surprise, when excavations resumed in 1994 in Building A and in 1995 in the Temple, that no evidence could be found of any earlier excavation. There was one small, irregularly shaped area in the middle of the cella of the Temple which was "soft" and filled with dark earth almost to bedrock, but this could have been created by the roots of a tree or bush which once had grown there, or indeed could have been part of a medieval intrusion, based on some finds of glass in the vicinity. In an excavation of a room at the foot of the acropolis to the east of the Velitsouri area in 2001 (Stym XIV), there were very clear indications of earlier trenches along the inside of the well-built walls. No similar indications could be discovered in the acropolis Sanctuary. This has led to the assumption that Orlandos' work was confined to cleaning along the tops of walls, and that he did not excavate to any depth in areas which were tested in the 1995–2000 excavations. The three early photographs taken of the Temple show approximately the same amount of wall exposed as was found when the new excavations commenced in 1995 (see chapter 1 above, fig. 1.9a–c).

STRATIGRAPHY

Scarp drawings from three trenches (97.9, 00.5, and 00.4) provide a fair sample of the stratigraphy in the Sanctuary (fig. 2.7 a–c). Surfaces at or just above bedrock inside the Sanctuary structures, including the Temple, Building A, and Building B, were kept well swept, without any significant build-up of soil or debris until their destruction. Once they were burned and allowed to collapse, there is a thin layer of ash and charcoal sometimes mixed with or immediately covered by a thick layer of decomposed mudbrick and broken tile fall. Some salvaging must have been done over the subsequent years, since most of the unbroken roof tiles had been removed, leaving only smaller pieces of tiles. The upper layers were more disturbed than the lower layers, perhaps partly through vegetation and burrowing animals, though partly through human disturbance.

One exception to this general pattern may have occurred with Building A, where there is evidence for reoccupation for a short period after its destruction. The destruction layer seems to have been levelled, the threshold in the interior doorway between main rooms appears to have been raised, and some first- or second-century CE objects were left there, before the building was abandoned.

Outside the Sanctuary structures, there is more evidence of occupation material which built up over bedrock before the Sanctuary was destroyed. In Trench 97.9 (south scarp) near Building B, this can be seen in Level 5 with reddish soil, some rocks and tile fragments as well as occasional discarded votives and mostly fourth-century BCE pottery. In Trench 00.5 (north scarp) just outside Building A, it can be seen in Level 4 with reddish soil and smaller stones which fill in the foundation trench for the east wall of the building. In Trench 00.4 (east scarp) beside the City Wall, this occupation material built up more substantially, in Levels 5, 6, 7, and 8 once the Wall was constructed.[19]

The destruction, salvaging, and abandonment levels can be seen in these same trenches, undergoing different degrees of disturbance over time, but normally containing a mixture of stones, roof tiles, pottery, and occasional votives such as terracotta figurines, pieces of jewellery, or coins. The iron projectile points are normally found in these layers. In all three of the trenches, this can be seen in Levels 1, 2, and 3.

An intrusive pit (Level 4) was identified in Trench 00.4 through some of this destruction material. Pits, perhaps where fires were made at a later time, were also found towards the middle of the Temple cella and in the southeast area of Building A. The most important pit, though, was found in Trench 96.15, just to the south of the West Annex and right against the original west wall of Building A. Clearly this pit was used to bury votive debris and other sweepings from the Sanctuary towards the end of the fourth century. It was dug after the completion of the main part of Building A, and probably closed and sealed shortly afterward with a layer of stones and some plaster fragments. The ground surface of the West Annex, including its floor, was prepared over top of the sealed pit. How long the West Annex was built after the pit was closed is not known. Some pottery evidence found in the floor of the West Annex suggests it occurred very shortly after the pit was filled and sealed, but if the floor were also generally kept well swept and otherwise held material from the time that the pit was dug in the fourth century, it is possible that the West Annex was built later. It certainly is later in date than the North Annex, since it depends on the west wall of the North Annex for part of its own east wall.

THE TEMPLE

A very modest structure both in its dimensions and its building materials, the Temple once had mudbrick walls set on a solid orthostate course which in turn rested on bedrock or on rough lower foundation courses over bedrock (fig. 2.8). The roof was made of terracotta tiles supported by wooden beams. There is some evidence to suggest that the walls were reinforced by vertical posts, since two votives were found with nail holes through them, presumably for nailing up on the Temple walls. (See figs. 2.9–2.10 for elevations and reconstructed views and cross-section.)

The interior was divided into two rooms, a cella with inside dimensions 5.2 × 6.3 m, and a pronaos measuring 5.2 × 3.9 m. Surprisingly, there is no evidence for a floor, at least within the cella. Instead, the outcroppings of bedrock were roughly chiselled down to a more or less even surface, but as far as the evidence demonstrates, the areas and crevices around these outcroppings were never filled in with dirt to bring them up to the level of the top of the flattened outcroppings. This is unusual, though not without precedent.

Two other structures with a rocky interior surface are the Altar Court in the Sanctuary of the Great Gods on Samothrace and the Artemis Temple at the Letoon near Xanthos.[20] The Altar Court at Samothrace has been restored as an open structure built by Phillip III Arrhidaios enclosing a large built altar which sat over top of an outcrop of porphyry and boulders used in the Archaic period as a rock altar. This interpretation was rejected by Oscar Broneer in favour of a roofed building, though he was rebutted by Phyllis Lehmann.[21] In either interpretation of the unusual structure, the massive pile of bedrock and boulders bears no resemblance to the chiselled bedrock outcrops left in the floor of the Stymphalos Temple.

The Letoon, however, presents a more interesting and perhaps significant situation. All three temples, to Leto, Artemis, and Apollo, from the fourth century or a little later, show evidence that earlier cult buildings or sacred locations were left visible inside their cellas. The Temple of Artemis has an 18.2 × 8.7 m foundation with an Ionic crowning moulding "couronnement ionique" on at least three sides. The larger northern room has a large outcrop of bedrock left exposed and a separate pronaos.[22] The second Temple of Leto has no cella floor in order to leave visible an earlier structure within.[23] The earlier temple, on the other hand, has evidence for a floor, but this is only partially preserved, and below this is an uneven surface with low bedrock outcrops, similar to the interior of the Stymphalos temple. Likewise for the Apollo temple, there is evidence for an earlier structure at a different orientation, apparently made of timber, and this was also still visible inside the cella of the later temple.[24] The floor of the earlier timber temple was decorated with a mosaic having three separate panels in the mid-second century BCE. Des Courtils explains this unusual discovery by saying, "The first temple, built with local traditional architecture, is conserved as a holy relic and sheltered within a new temple built with Greek inspiration and model."[25] This is reminiscent of the preservation of the older cult spot and building within the cella of the Apollo Temple at Didyma. The unusual outcropping of bedrock in the middle of the Artemis Temple, and the unusual lack of floor in the Temple of Leto, are explained along the same lines by Laroche: "La réexamen du rocher conservé à l'intérieur de la *cella* montre que, comme au temple de Létô, le bâtiment hellénistique a été conçu comme un écrin autour d'un lieu de culte archaïque, conserve dans sa forme naturelle primitive."[26]

If these explanations for the unusual lack of a flat floor surface at the Letoon are correct, they offer credible reasons for a similar lack of floor surface within the Temple at Stymphalos. The interior could easily have been filled with dirt up to the level of the chiselled-down bedrock, but there might have been a shrine here, or at least an image, perhaps with an offering place, that was preserved when the Temple was built in the first half of the fourth century. The late Archaic kore found inside the Temple (chapter 3 below) and the different orientation of the square base also found in the cella (see below) both suggest that the Temple was built on a spot already set aside for religious reasons.

Since the Temple is placed where the bedrock rises from east to west at the west edge of the Sanctuary, the builders chiselled away a section of bedrock at the west end of the Temple for placement of the foundations. They also left a narrow space (as little as 0.7 m near the northwest corner) for labourers to manoeuvre blocks between the Temple west wall and the steeply rising bedrock. Here at the west end and for a short distance along the north and south walls, a euthynteria or string course, with a height of 0.28–0.31 m, rested directly on the roughly chiselled bedrock, except where bedrock itself rose high enough to be used in place of blocks for the string course (figs. 2.9, 2.11a–b). In this case, the bedrock was cut so that a "shelf" was created that rose up about 5 cm above the rest of the chiselled bedrock. The euthynteria or string course was approximately 10 cm wider than the ca. 0.40 m wide orthostates, which were centred over this course, giving a margin of about 5 cm on each side. The remainder of the north and south walls as well as the entire east wall of the structure needed the support of foundation walls since the bedrock sloped away here. The course of square-cut foundation blocks directly below the euthynteria also projected out about 5 to 7 cm wherever it was preserved.

Two partial courses of roughly cut blocks with irregular dimensions were placed either on the bedrock where it could be found, or on smaller rocks, or on the hard red clay above the bedrock to form foundations for the orthostates. The lowest of these two courses varies in height from 0.20 to 0.45 m and is found along the entire east side and a short distance on the north and south sides. At least seven blocks of the second course have been displaced since Orlandos' time at the east end of the temple, exposing the upper surfaces of the blocks from the lower course. Their upper surfaces and exterior faces have been roughly chiselled; otherwise, the joints are careless, only being consistently tight near or on the exterior faces. The depth of the blocks varies, and there is no concern with squaring off the interior sides. Directly behind this lowest course near the southeast corner, outcroppings of bedrock have been exposed which rise to the top of the course and have been chiselled off at this height.

The stones of the second course also vary in height, from 0.25 to 0.40 m along east, north, and south sides, but their upper surfaces are more carefully chiselled flat in order to receive the string course. Neither of these two lowest courses was meant to be seen, presumably being covered with earth. The same can be said for the four westernmost blocks of the euthynteria course on the south side (2.2 m in length). They have a more carefully chiselled margin for 0.05–0.08 m along their upper edges, but the rest of their exterior face is only partly finished. The westernmost of these blocks has a large "pillow" below its drafted margin. From this we can reconstruct approximately the ancient ground level outside the Temple.

The "floor" level within the pronaos was raised by filling the sloping ground behind the two lowest foundation courses with medium-sized rocks, some at least of which must have been chiselled from nearby bedrock. In this rocky packing, a little black-painted pottery was found, not much of which is distinctive in shape, but the majority of the pottery is of Corinthian miniature kotylai, coarsely made and not closely datable. No clearly defined "floor" surface was distinguished within the pronaos, perhaps owing to the fact that blocks were removed from both the pronaos cross wall and the Temple east façade in the past seventy years.[27] This allowed natural erosion and possibly some human earth removal to occur, so destroying evidence for an occupation surface. An artificially raised surface should have existed within the pronaos; otherwise there would have been a large step down from the threshold of the Temple entrance and another step back up to the threshold of the cella door.

Inside the cella, however, where bedrock rises higher than in the pronaos, outcroppings of bedrock rose up to and indeed higher than the ancient occupation surface (fig. 2.12). Despite great care in trying to distinguish floor surfaces once the chiselled tops of the bedrock outcroppings were found, no such surface could be located. Instead, the destruction material, including much evidence for burning, especially in the northwest quadrant of the cella, continued down into the areas between the outcroppings until dark red, sterile clay was reached just above bedrock. Evidence for possible placement of floor beams also could not be found, especially above the string course blocks, which tend to project inward below the orthostates of the Temple walls. The interior faces of the string course blocks are entirely undressed and irregular. Furthermore, the bedrock outcroppings within the cella are roughly dressed down to the level of the top of the string course (bottom of the orthostates), except where the string and orthostate courses rise 0.233 m higher at the west end of the temple (see below). Here at the west wall in fact the string course blocks were dressed, and sections of red-painted lime plaster were still preserved adhering to the interior of the string course blocks (mentioned again below).

The lack of finish on the string course blocks of the flank walls and the dressing of bedrock just to this level suggests that a floor, probably of earth, may have been planned. There is, however, no good reason to believe that such a floor existed, at least at the time of the Temple's destruction. If there were no even floor surface, earthen or otherwise, then there must have been a certain awkwardness in trying to walk around inside the room, causing, one supposes, some stumbling and stubbed toes. Unless rugs or sheepskins or reed mats were laid down over the rocky surface, one must have had to exercise caution while walking inside the cella.

One piece of evidence which supports this hypothesis is the large ashlar block carefully laid just to the north of the largest outcropping of bedrock within the cella (fig. 2.13 a–c). This puzzling block (length 0.64–0.67, width 0.59–0.62, height approx. 0.26 m), placed off centre, off axis, and with a different orientation from the Temple, was nevertheless set deliberately at this spot. (The block's orientation is 54° east of magnetic north, and its centre is 0.95 m north of the main east-west axis of the temple and 1.4 m west of the north-south axis of the cella.) Its stone is a fine, pebbly conglomerate. The bedrock outcropping beside it appears to have been cut away on its north side in order to fit a corner of this block tightly against it. The block's upper surface rises about 26 cm from the sterile red clay and barely reaches to the level of the dressed bedrock outcropping's upper surface. If a dirt floor had been put into the cella up to the level of the dressed bedrock, then this carefully placed ashlar block would have been almost completely covered. See figs. 2.12–14.

A second piece of evidence has already been mentioned. No occupation surfaces were found at the level of the dressed bedrock outcroppings, and instead destruction material, including areas of intense burning, was found without interruption right down to the sterile red clay in the gaps and crevices between sections of bedrock. Down low, just above the sterile red clay, close to the ashlar block, was found a large fragment of a figured Hellenistic mould-made bowl amid the heaviest of the carbonized remains from the temple's destruction. This supports coin evidence from the Temple suggesting that the latest period of use was the mid-second century BCE (Weir's **II-73**, coin of Sikyon ca. 196–146 BCE) and that at the time of destruction there was no dirt floor acting as a level surface within the cella.

A third piece of evidence should be considered. A narrow row of stones was found lying on the sterile red clay between the ashlar block and the interior of the north wall of the Temple (see fig. 2.13a–c). It seems to have been laid there deliberately, but before or at the time of the Temple's destruction. Evidence for burning was particularly intense over and around this narrow row of stones (figs. 2.14–16). This could not have happened if a dirt floor had been in place here.

One of the stones in this narrow row is a very finely chiselled rectangular block ("tetragonos" with dimensions 0.19 × 0.18 m, max. pres. length of 0.41 m), about the same size as the rectangular pillars located in a row outside the Temple to the north. It is more finely finished than those pillars, but having been burnt inside the Temple, it is badly calcined so that large fragments split off its corner edges when it was excavated. (The outside surface is white, but the breaks at the ends show a light grey-blue colour.) The fact that it is about the same size and shape as the vertical pillars, if more finely worked, and that it was found within the Temple, indeed close to the only possible base which might have served for a cult statue, is certainly suggestive. This will be discussed further below. (There is one place on the spur of bedrock near the middle of the back of the cella where the rock is more carefully chiselled flat and at a slightly lower level. If there were any other spot where an image might be displayed, this seems to be the most likely.)

At this point, it is worth mentioning that there is one other stone "base" in the vicinity of the Temple. It is located directly behind the Temple in the centre of the west exterior façade, almost touching the Temple wall (figs. 2.11a–b, fig. 2.13a). The block is roughly rectangular, measuring 0.54–0.56 × 0.43–0.46 m with a height that varies from 0.26 to 0.31 m. It has split down the middle into two pieces, and settled somewhat. Like the block inside the cella, this stone has no cuttings or depressions on the upper surface to indicate what might have been set on top of it. Its placement in the narrow space between the rising bedrock and the back of the Temple is odd, since it is so inaccessible to view. Whatever it supported must have been visible only to determined visitors. On the other hand, Pausanias (8.22.7) makes a point of telling his readers about the statues of maidens with birds' feet which he saw behind the Temple of Artemis at Stymphalos, a temple which he describes as "old" ("archaion"). This at least makes one wonder whether it predated the establishment of the new Stymphalos. This temple has not yet been located (unless it was indeed that structure that Lattermann saw being destroyed by locals at the time of his visit),[28] so it is impossible to make a comparison between the two other than to note the common local practice apparently of placing objects behind the temple.

The orthostate course has a height of 0.68–0.69 m. and a thickness of 0.41–0.42 m. The blocks vary in length (see fig. 2.9). The orthostates are still in place in the western half of the Temple, where eroding soil from the hill to the west built up and protected them. In the eastern ends of the north and south walls as well as the entire east wall, the orthostates as well as many euthynteria blocks have been pushed over and a good number lost. Much of this damage occurred since Orlandos' work in the 1920s, as a glance at his plan of the Temple shows. At the west end of the Temple and for a single block on the north (length 1.28 m) and south (length 0.95 m) sides, although the orthostates themselves are the same height, they are set on a bed of chiselled bedrock or, where there are gaps in the bedrock, on a total of seven low blocks of varying lengths, called here a string course. This raised bed for the orthostates is 0.23–0.24 m in height, meaning that the upper surface of the orthostates here at the rear of the temple is 0.23–0.24 m higher. One can only speculate as to the reason for this. Perhaps it was felt that a little added strength was needed here in case of flooding or erosion down the steep slope directly behind the Temple. If it were for any aesthetic reason, it was likely simply to expose the full height of the orthostates along the entire length of the Temple. The ground level rises from east to west, covering at least four blocks of the string course, and then threatening to cover the lower part of the orthostates at the west. Indeed the bottom corner of the second orthostate block on both south and north sides may well have been partly covered by earth. By raising the orthostates 0.23–0.24 m, the architect perhaps felt that the Temple looked more firmly based throughout. This small rise in the back orthostates provides the only clue regarding the possible height of the courses of mudbrick in the walls of the Temple (see below).

The orthostate blocks were cut from the same local bedrock as the other blocks of the Temple foundations, as well as the blocks used in the nearby City Wall. It is a brittle grey limestone that weathers poorly, especially from the effects of rainwater, which seems to act to "dissolve" the stone. The most obvious source for this material is the very prominent quarry located less than 400 m away to the east on the lakeside edge of the acropolis just above the fountain house. Evidence of the quarriers' long chisels is still clearly seen along the entire vertical face of the quarry. If this is indeed the source, workmen had only a short distance to transport the blocks, albeit uphill, along a road built on the south edge of the acropolis ridge. A second type of local stone, used for some of the blocks of Building A and the pillars in the Shrine area, was not used in the Temple; this is a hard, gravelly conglomerate.

An interesting feature of the masonry is that the orthostates are often not joined along vertical lines. Rather it is common for the blocks to join each other along shallow diagonal lines (see fig. 2.9). This of course increased the problems for masons in fitting blocks closely together. On the other hand, it may have strengthened the rather tall orthostate course, and perhaps helped maximize the area of the quarried stones actually used in the finished blocks. On the second block from the northwest corner on the north side, a repair was made to one corner (see fig. 2.17a–b), most likely at the time that the Temple was constructed. Presumably the block was cracked or chipped or otherwise damaged after it had reached an advanced stage in the finishing process.[29] It was decided that it was worth salvaging the block rather than replacing it or ignoring the damaged spot, so a small wedge-shaped stone was carefully cut to fit the broken corner. No clamps were used to hold it in place, and unless some type of binding material held it, it must have depended on gravity or the pressure of the neighbouring block, as well as the mudbrick above it, to keep it in place.

The exterior face of the orthostates was given a medium-fine chiselled finish. The interior face of these blocks was left more roughly chiselled. One might expect that both interior and exterior faces would be covered with plaster. There is, however, no evidence that the exterior face of the orthostate course was covered. If a fine mud plaster were once used, it simply has not been preserved. The interior face, on the other hand, was clearly finished with a very fine white lime plaster which was then painted a deep red colour. Hundreds of fragments of this plaster were recovered in excavations, mainly within the Temple, but also outside the Temple and even within Building A (fig. 2.18a–b). Small sections of this plaster were found still adhering to the lower parts of the interior west wall. Larger sections were found towards the northwest corner, and here, where evidence for the destruction of the building was clearest, there were several large pieces of plaster lying face down on the bedrock "floor" amidst much charcoal and other debris. A large deposit of white lime, 50 × 35 cm with a thickness of 5 cm, was found in Trench 96.11 (Level 6 Pail 7) amidst the rocky packing to the south of the later grave in the pronaos (below the measuring stick in fig. 2.29a). It is possible that this was left by the plasterers when they finished doing the Temple walls.

The dividing wall between pronaos and cella was much better preserved in Orlandos' day. His plan (see fig. 1.10) shows the entire lower course still preserved, and three blocks belonging to the orthostate course, if we can judge from his shading. Now only one block of the lower course is left next to the Temple north wall (dimensions, length 0.60 × width 0.53 × height 0.28 m) laid on chiselled bedrock with small fieldstones between it and the string course block of the Temple north wall (fig. 2.19a–b). On the orthostate block of the Temple north wall right beside this low pronaos block, there is a clearly visible vertical division between the roughly chiselled surface like that of the other orthostate blocks inside the cella and a less chiselled-down "cushion" corresponding to the line of the pronaos dividing block. This division or line is most clearly visible in the raking sunlight of late mornings in the summer. The cushion is almost 2 cm thick where it is best preserved. This indicates that a final chiselling of the faces of the orthostates only occurred once they were set in place, and that because of the line of this dividing wall between pronaos and cella, the masons were not able to finish the orthostate any further. Outside the Temple to the north, a somewhat thick layer of limestone chips was found, perhaps from this very final chiselling.

On the south wall of the Temple, both the string course and the orthostate blocks are missing where the pronaos wall would have met the south wall; however, on the ground just to the south of the Temple is an orthostate block which must have been tipped over right here from the south wall. On the east end of this block one can clearly make out a similar "cushion" as was observed on the Temple's north wall. The thickness of this block over the "cushion" is approximately 0.445 m, while on the west side of the block, the thickness is only 0.40 m. In other words, the "cushion" in places is 4.5 cm thicker. (Measurements are inexact because of the rough chiselled surface, the brittle nature of the stone, and damage both human and natural to the exposed surface.) The distance from the edge of the "cushion" on the north wall orthostate to the east façade of the Temple (second foundation course) is 4.35 m. On the south wall, the distance from the east Temple façade to the first in situ orthostate block is 5.25 m. The distance from the west-facing edge of the orthostate lying on the ground to the line of the "cushion" on this block is 0.91 m. So subtracting 0.91 m from 5.25 m one arrives at 4.34 m, almost perfectly matching the measurement on the north wall.

Although the pronaos cross wall is now missing entirely on the south side of the Temple, several blocks were still visible to Orlandos (see fig. 1.10). Below this cross wall, however, on the south side, four large, relatively flat fieldstones have been discovered carefully laid over bedrock with several smaller rocks laid between the south foundation blocks of the Temple and the larger fieldstones. The upper surface of the fieldstones is 0.13 m lower than the upper surface of the in situ ashlar cross wall block. Orlandos shows an ashlar threshold block in his 1924 plan, which is now missing. It does not fill the opening between the central second-course pronaos blocks, though. Presumably the cross wall rose to the same height as the orthostate course (no elevations are found on Orlandos' plan). How that 0.13 m difference in height between fieldstones and ashlar block was made up is now lost to us, though one might suppose there was a narrow string course, below an orthostate course of uniform height. At least two of the fieldstones show evidence of chiselling or at least hammering on their upper edges in order to fit them tightly into place. These were used as a foundation for the cross wall, but it is not clear that this was their first purpose. It is hard to judge the alignment of this "foundation" on the basis of the four stones, but it is not clearly the same alignment as the pronaos cross wall. It is possible, though not strongly supported by evidence, that these stones were a base for some structure in the Sanctuary prior to the building of the Temple. A little pottery evidence, and the fragments of marble sculpture, suggest activity here in the Sanctuary by the early fifth century, but the Temple itself was more likely constructed before the mid-fourth century, perhaps in the second quarter. This is the date when pottery and terracotta figurines become much more numerous. Evidence from coinage is somewhat helpful. There are only a few coins which may date as early as the late fifth century, and they are heavily worn, indicating that they were in circulation for some time before coming to ground. There are enough coins from the first half of the fourth century to suggest that the Sanctuary was vibrant by that time. This is close to the presumed date of the laying out of the new city of Stymphalos, implicit from the mention in Pausanias of an earlier place where there were three sanctuaries of Hera, and the orthogonal plan of the Lower Town.[30] The acme of Sanctuary activity, based on coins, was from ca. 350 to 270 BCE.[31] A silver coin was found in the rocky packing of the pronaos behind the Temple foundations. It was issued by Megalopolis on behalf of the Arkadian League (inv. 915) and is dated by Weir ca. 330–275 BCE.[32] This date roughly coincides with a small hoard of six silver coins found in Trench 99.13 to the south of the Altar; as a group they argue for a deposition date within the range ca. 330–310 BCE.[33]

The walls of the Temple were made of mudbrick set on top of the orthostate course, in a similar way, for example, to the temple of Hera at Olympia. The modest width of the Temple (6.0 m) meant that its roof could easily span this distance without the need for interior columns or posts. Much material from the mudbrick walls was found in excavations of the Temple interior where it had collapsed following the Temple's destruction. Most of the bricks had long ago "dissolved," leaving only the reddish-yellow claylike dirt, but in some areas where burning was more evident, chunks of burnt mudbrick with impressions of the straw used for reinforcement were found. None of these were larger than about 10 cm in length. There were also a few chunks with more regular striations on their surfaces, perhaps to hold a layer of plaster more firmly (see fig. 2.20).

Nevertheless, we may hypothesize what the normal dimensions of the mudbricks were.[34] If we assume that the mudbricks were laid in pairs, alternating between headers and stretchers, along the top of the orthostate course, which is one method to minimize cracks in a mudbrick wall due to settling, then knowing that the width of the Temple wall is 0.41–0.42 m, we can suppose that the standard length of the mudbricks was 0.41–0.42 m (headers), and that the standard width was half that, 0.205–0.21 m, in order to fit a pair of stretchers on top of the orthostates. Only the standard height of the mudbricks is still needed. Although not certain, there is at least a clue even for this dimension. As was mentioned already, the orthostates along the west wall of the Temple, and the first ones returning along the north and south walls, have been raised to a height 0.23 m above the rest of the orthostates in the Temple. The builders must have felt some pressure to even out the courses of mudbrick all around the Temple, even with this rise in the western orthostates. This could have been done easily by laying either one or two courses of bricks over the east, north, and south walls first in order to reach the level of the western orthostates. If only one course of bricks were used, then it would be 0.23 m in height. If two courses were used, as is somewhat more likely given normal mudbrick production practices, then each course would have been about 0.115 m in height. As was mentioned previously, these walls may well have been reinforced with posts set into the walls, as the nail holes on two votives from the Temple suggest.

The roof of the structure was covered with terracotta tiles, supported by wooden beams which themselves were presumably held in place by cuttings and/or with iron nails. Hundreds of pins, nails, and spikes made of iron have been found throughout the site, though no significant pattern has been distinguished as yet from their findspots. The Temple was one area where iron nails were less common on the site. As an alternative to nails and notched cuttings, wooden pegs might be considered, such as are commonly used to tie together beams in modern timber frame construction; however, there is no evidence that this strong but more difficult technique was used here.

At least some evidence for the roof beams was found while digging in the cella, in the northwest corner, where at least one significant line of burning must reflect a burnt beam which collapsed here. How the roof beams were laid out exactly can only be surmised, but there cannot have been much room to vary from the most practical system of horizontal wall plates or beams along the top of the mudbrick walls, horizontal tie-beams spanning the distance between north and south Temple walls, diagonal rafter beams running up to a ridge beam from the walls, smaller cross boards or sheathing over the diagonal rafters to tie the whole system together and provide a bedding for the roof tiles themselves, perhaps with some reinforcing horizontal beams between the two flank walls.[35]

In the Lakonian system for tiling roofs, both pan tiles and cover tiles are curved, with the pan tiles being much larger.[36] Both types have a narrower end, but they are placed on the roof in opposite ways. The pan tiles have their narrower ends lower on the sloped roof, while the cover tiles have their narrower ends higher on the slope. Many more fragments by far of curved pan tiles have been found in the Sanctuary than of curved cover tiles. If this is an accident of preservation, it might be explained at least in part by the possibility that when the roof collapsed, the much larger pan tiles below the cover tiles suffered greater rates of breakage, perhaps being more fragile, and therefore were not salvaged by later local inhabitants in the same quantities as the cover tiles. On the other hand, R. Catling offers a different, and probably better, explanation, since the same phenomenon of pan tiles without cover tiles was discovered in a survey of Lakonia, and that is that the common practice was not to have two types of tiles, cover and pan, but rather to use the pan tiles also as cover tiles.[37] Two broken but complete rounded cover tiles were found just outside the Temple to the west and south (fig. 2.21a–b). They have roughly the same dimensions: length 0.94 m; width 0.24 to 0.18 m.[38] With so few other cover tiles, if Catling's explanation is correct, perhaps these preserved cover tiles had a special use, such as to cover the ridge of the building.[39]

The best-preserved examples of pan tiles (curved) came from Building A; they were found in 1996, and may belong to that building: one has a length of 1.00 m and width (narrower end) 0.42 m, (wider end) 0.48 m; thickness 0.024–0.028 m (fig. 2.22). Another has a preserved length of 0.765 m; width (narrower end) 0.395 m, (wider end) 0.44 m; thickness 0.0195–0.022 m.

Another complete pan tile, found in the West Annex (loomweight room) of Building A (Tr. 96.8 Level 3 Pail 4 – SF X81) is of quite different shape (fig. 2.23a–b). It is shorter than the curved pan tiles but much thicker. Its upper surface is only slightly curved; however, it has raised edges which would be overlapped by cover tiles on both sides. Its lower surface is flat. Along one of the short ends, the flat surface abruptly changes to become slightly convex. This presumably allows for 8.5 cm of overlap from another large pan tile with a curved upper surface below it on the roof: length – 0.737 m; width – 0.567 m; thickness – middle 0.048 m, edge 0.068 m. This would only work to shed water efficiently from a roof if this pan tile lies higher on the roof, and the pan tile sitting below its overlap edge is lower on the roof. What purpose it serves to have a flat-bottomed pan tile other than in the lowest position on the roof is hard to judge.

One other flat pan tile is half preserved and has a wide groove on its underside presumably to be held in place over a wooden beam (about 0.065 m wide) along the edge of the roof, above the mudbrick wall (fig. 2.24a–c). It has a 0.03 m lip which hangs at the eaves, and raised edges on the upper surface (preserved length 0.45; width 0.60). These two flat pan tiles are much heavier and suggest that perhaps the two courses of pan tiles lying lowest on the roof were of this thicker type, while above them were the thinner curved pan tiles.

THE STAIRCASE AND TEMPLE DESIGN

In front of the east façade of the Temple, where one expects its main entrance, is a well-built foundation, approximately 1.7 m square (see figs. 2.25a–d), consisting of a combination of ashlar blocks for the three outer faces (north, east, and south sides), and carefully placed fieldstones filling the central area. The three fieldstones directly behind the two eastern ashlars have been roughly chiselled on their upper surface as if for the placement of a block on top of them. Furthermore, barely visible on the upper surface of these two eastern ashlars is a line running parallel to their eastern edges but set back 0.33 m. This line distinguishes a more carefully finished, or perhaps worn, eastern section on the upper surface from a less carefully finished western section. This faint line is best seen in the early morning sunlight and doubtless indicates the setting line for a second step. If we can take the width of the first step, i.e., 0.33 m, as the standard for all the steps in this small staircase, then it becomes evident that there were five steps altogether, and that the average width of the steps was 0.34 m.

The next question concerns the height of the steps (see fig. 2.10). The rise to a threshold block can only be judged by the height of the Temple foundation, presumably being at least to the height of the second foundation course, but not any higher than the top of the string course. We may assume, though it is not certain, that a person took a sixth step up to the Temple threshold from the top step of the staircase, rather than assuming that the top step of the staircase was at the same level as the threshold. The height of the two eastern ashlar blocks in the stair foundation (at least 0.32 m) cannot be used to estimate the height of the other steps because the ground level around these blocks likely reached part way up the blocks and we do not know exactly where the ancient ground level was. If the threshold of the Temple was at the top of the second foundation course, its presumed minimum height, then the rise from the surface of the first step of the staircase to the top of this foundation course is 0.91 m. Assuming then four more steps and a similar riser from the top step to the threshold, i.e., five risers, then each step would be 0.182 m (0.91 m ÷ 5). If the threshold of the temple was at the top of the string course, its presumed maximum height, then the rise from the first step to the threshold would be 1.22 m, and this, divided by five risers, would mean that each step was a maximum of 0.244 m (1.22 ÷ 5). The former height per step (0.182 m) is quite comfortable; the latter (0.244 m) is still in the range of comfort, but certainly approaching steep, especially for descending the steps. It is also possible that a special threshold block once existed which was of greater length in order to span the entire doorway, but also lower than other blocks of the string course to allow for a less steep staircase. There is only one suitable block which would fit this hypothetical threshold, and it is not clear whether this block in fact belongs here on the Temple or with the Altar where it now rests, though certainly no longer in situ (fig. 2.26). The block is 0.18 m thick in its inset portion, but 0.20–0.21 m thick otherwise. Its total width is 0.66 m, of which 0.44 m is "inset" or chiselled down by 2 cm (i.e., with a thickness of 0.18 m). It is broken, so its original length is not known. Its present location may suggest that this block was once a capping stone for the Altar, but it could easily have been pushed downhill from the Temple and come to rest here beside the Altar. If so, and if it once served as the Temple door threshold, then it would seem to be upside down, with the inset portion meant to lie over top of the second foundation course and the thicker portion of the block lying towards the inside of the pronaos. Hypothetically, this would give four risers of 0.227 m (0.91 ÷ 4), and the fifth step up to the threshold of 0.18 m. If this were part of a threshold block, one would expect to find a round hole or depression near one edge (the other edge being broken and lost) to act as the pivot point for the door so it could be swung open and closed as needed. There is no evidence for such a depression on this block. It seems less likely that this block was once part of one step, although its thickness is suitable for one.

It is worth noting that the three blocks of the first foundation course directly west of the staircase platform are particularly poorly laid and finished. Virtually no effort was put into providing a surface flush to the Temple façade. On the other hand, the other three blocks on each side of the stair platform do show greater effort in placement and finish. This observation confirms that the stair platform was planned and in place right from the beginning of the Temple's construction.[40]

That there was a staircase built here at the front of the Temple should not be a surprise, given the sloping ground level leading up to the building. The foundation of the Temple was laid at the west end of the sloping terrace, just to the east of the acropolis height, with substantial chiselling away of the bedrock at its west end just before the steep rise in elevation begins towards the summit of the hill. There was a corresponding building up of the Temple foundation towards its east end in order to produce a suitable length for the Temple, and to include a pronaos; however, this also meant that the height of the threshold at the entrance to the Temple was elevated well above the ground surface, and the only easy solution to the difference in elevation between threshold and ground level was to build this small set of stairs.

The tradition of building a simple rectangular structure to house a cult statue goes back to the Geometric period at least. The approach to the entrance of such structures is not often known, though in most cases, on even surfaces in front of the structure, no special arrangement was needed. The creation of a ramp to reach the level of the entrance is a feature of several temples in the Peloponnese, Delphi, and Aigina, most notably in the temple of Zeus at Olympia. One may suggest that it is in this same tradition that the stairs leading up to the Temple at Stymphalos lie, but in truth, there were already stairs as part of the common two- or three-step krepidoma of temples, and the ramp served a different function to facilitate entry. The Stymphalos Temple is such a modest building in every way – size, materials, design – that it is hardly surprising to find such a simple solution to the problem of accessing the building from the ground below.

The length to width ratio of the structure (approx. 6:11) may be as much a function of the chosen location and practicality as it is of contemporary architectural fashion. Stone temples of the fourth century, the presumed date for its construction, began to shrink from fifth-century proportions (6:13), so the Ionic temple of Athena at Priene, the Doric temples of Asklepios at Epidauros, of Zeus at Nemea and at Stratos, and the Metroon at Olympia were somewhat shorter in proportion to their width compared to fifth-century examples.[41] Again, the limited space at the west side of the terrace at Stymphalos would have caused substantially more effort to overcome, due to the sloping bedrock from west to east, if the Temple had been increased in length. Such effort was likely reserved for the cult of more significant deities in the city, in particular that of Artemis, which attracted Pausanias' attention still in the mid-second century CE.

For building materials and construction methods of this rather simple structure – rubble stone socle, large finished orthostates covered in painted lime plaster, mudbrick walls presumably reinforced with wood, and a wooden roof with terracotta roof tiles – some information may be gleaned from clay and stone house models.[42] If vertical and horizontal wooden beams were used to reinforce the walls and support the roof, there is no evidence for them on the stone orthostates, for example. The discovery in the northwest corner of the cella of a bronze patera with a nail hole driven through it, presumably for hanging on a wall, is the best evidence for a solid wooden beam against which the nail might have been driven. A silver coin found right outside the south wall of the Temple (Weir's **II-51**) likewise has a nail hole through it. If vertical beams were used, they must have been placed directly on top of the orthostates without being tied any further into the structure. Diagonal beams between the vertical ones, such as is suggested by the temple model for Sparta, may also have been used, though such diagonal supports would be less conducive to the use of mudbrick than perhaps other types of wall construction. Catling, however, suggested clay in combination with wooden battens as a possibility.[43]

The "house models" consistently demonstrate a square or rectangular structure with a large door on one of the short ends and featureless walls on the other three sides. No windows or other openings are found in most cases other than the one door.[44] Almost all of them are one-room structures, but some have either prostyle columns or antae, forming a porch or pronaos in front of the cella.[45] Ceiling beams project prominently between the tops of the walls and the roof on some of the models.[46] Evidence for a two-panel door exists on just one of the models, but no details are given of the hardware that should go with it, including bosses, or a locking device, such as is likely to have been found on the Stymphalos Temple, judging from the hook-keys and bronze bosses that have been found.[47]

The best evidence for a roof is found on a well-preserved clay model from the Sanctuary of Athena at Mazi near Skillous in Triphyllia, south of Olympia, which shows four rows of narrow curved cover tiles over five rows of broad flat pan tiles, wide raking cornices, and disk acroteria at the ends of the ridge beam (fig. 2.27).[48] It also has a pediment which seems to be completely open. For the roof at Stymphalos, there is likely an important variance from information provided by the models, since they display disk acroteria, antefixes, and projecting eaves, none of which are found among the tiles recovered from the Stymphalos Temple.[49] The impression one is left with at Stymphalos is basic simplicity, with little added expense, for example, to create an unusual effect on the visitor. The roof tiles indicate that the roof was sloped, and with no other bases for posts, one may assume that the weight of the central ridge beam was carried by the walls at the narrow ends of the structure.

As for the proportions of the building, in particular its height, again we may turn to these Archaic "temple" or "house" models for an impression.[50] Judging from the proportions, they imitate quite small structures, perhaps little more than a naiskos, three or four metres on a side, allowing for 4 to 7 rows of cover tiles, and a door which fills most of one of the narrow ends. The impression from the Skillous models is that the walls were plastered so that details of the structure and materials are not evident. All these examples are earlier in date, from the

Geometric and Archaic periods, than the presumed date of the Stymphalos Temple, but they still provide valuable evidence for a building type which in its simplicity could not have changed much in the Classical period.

A partly restored marble or fine limestone model, likely of a temple, is on display in the Kavalla museum. It is quite high in proportion to its length and width with a tall broad doorway. No information is provided about it in the museum, though it seems more advanced than the clay models. It exhibits the simple doorway (restored with raised threshold) on the short end of the structure, featureless walls, a projecting cornice on all four sides, a prominent ridge beam, possibly with central and corner acroteria on the side with the door (broken at all three spots where acroteria would be on this side), and somewhat recessed pediments. It sits on a thickened raised base carved all in one piece with the structure, but without a floor.

A simple doorway in a solid wall at the east end of the Temple at Stymphalos is probable, rather than a porch with two columns in antis, on the basis of the stairway directing visitors only to a central entrance.

Schattner, in studying the "house models," commented on the frequency of these models in sanctuaries of female deities, in particular Hera but also Athena, concerned with the home and family.[51] Since there is some evidence for such a role in the Stymphalos cult, including a marble statue of a "temple boy," one may also consider the possibility that the design of the Temple deliberately echoed that of a simple Greek house with that aspect of the deity in mind. There were three shrines to Hera, as maiden, wife, and "widow," at the old location of Stymphalos, suggesting a role for her as wife, with concern for the household. Here in the city's new location, some similar aspect for a goddess, whether Athena or Eileithyia or some other, might have been reflected in the simple design chosen for this Temple, although in the end it is just as likely that the design arose out of well-established, modest, and affordable practices for this region, especially appropriate in the confined, sloping location chosen for it.

Perirrhanterion Base

Directly to the north of the first step of the staircase is an almost square base made of the local conglomerate. (See fig. 2.25a–d) Its width is 0.488 m, but the length varies from 0.497 to 0.504 m on its upper surface; its height is at least 0.32 m. On its upper surface is a round cutting set into the block to a depth of 2.0 cm; its diameter is 0.405 m. The southeast corner has been chipped, and the outline of the circular inset also has been partly lost where it reaches the middle of the north and east sides of the block. The block has been somewhat tilted out of its original position, so that its north edge is now 4.0–4.7 cm higher than its south edge, which is flush with the first step of the staircase. This base clearly once held something, but the object could not have been particularly valuable, nor particularly unstable, since the cutting for it is so shallow and no clamps were used. An initial thought was that it held a statue or a very large terracotta figurine, types of which have turned up in the Sanctuary in fragments. Stone statues, however, normally are set much more deeply and securely on their bases, often with iron clamps sealed with lead to keep them in place. There is little evidence from other sites to suggest that terracotta figurines or indeed terracotta statues were ever set on special stone bases, no matter the depth of their setting. More probable, given the location at the steps leading up to the Temple and the perfectly circular cutting, is that the base held a perirrhanterion for visitors to the Temple to cleanse themselves ritually before entering the building (fig. 2.28a–b).[52] Such cleansing is well known; a good example is found on a Roman-period inscription listing proscriptions against visitors found at the propylaea of the sanctuary of Athena Lindia on Rhodes, and at the same time mentioning the existence of perirrhanteria nearby.[53] A good number of fragments of large terracotta perirrhanteria have been found in the Sanctuary excavations, including a large base with a diameter of about 0.38 m discovered in Trench 99.1, indicating the importance of ritual cleansing as part of the local cult practice.[54]

THE GRAVE

Situated against the north wall of the pronaos is a shallow cist grave, partially disturbed so that its covering was not preserved (fig. 2.3, fig. 2.29a–c).[55] It did not appear in Orlandos' plan of the Temple. Evidence for this grave first appeared when fragments of a disarticulated human skeleton, or skeletons, began to turn up in the soil above the grave. It was only then that the outline of the north side of the grave was identified among the scattered blocks lying close to the northeast corner of the Temple. Further digging soon revealed the full outlines of the grave, as well as more disarticulated bones, and finally the articulated skeleton of a young girl, as well as the lower legs of an earlier adult burial still in place.

The grave was constructed from reused ashlar blocks,

fieldstones, of which some showed signs of chiselling, and broken roof tiles. The main axis of the grave is very close to the orientation of the Temple, about 83° east of magnetic north. The last burial in the grave was laid with its head at the west end, on its side with legs partly bent. The earlier burial, for which we have only the extended legs in place, had its feet to the east, and was lying on its back.

The interior dimensions of the grave are: length 1.74 m, maximum width 0.52 m (at the "shoulders"), width at the "ankles" 0.37 m. The south side of the grave wall is virtually straight, while on the north side, the wall curves in at the legs. The largest block, along the top course of the north side, is similar in dimensions and finish to the rectangular pillars in the Pillar Shrine area. Its preserved length is about 0.74 m, its width is 0.25 m, and it has a thickness of 0.23 m. There is a taper towards the "east" end as it lies in the grave wall, like the best preserved of the pillars outside the Temple. One difference, however, is that the surface finish on this block is roughly chiselled instead of the more finely chiselled final surface found on the other tetragonoi.

The grave was used perhaps as many as six times, since besides the articulated remains of a juvenile and the legs of an adult (male?), there were also bones of an infant, an older juvenile, and two other adults found in fill around the grave.[56] Apparently, the bones of earlier burials were haphazardly gathered and set aside to make room for later burials, except that the latest burial only made use of about two-thirds of the grave, so the legs of a previous interment were left in place.

Since only some common earrings[57] and a simple necklace of tiny beads were found with the latest burial, it is difficult to propose a date. One would like to connect this grave with the small grave of a baby just outside the Temple's northeast corner, and also with the more numerous graves laid in the foundations of the Tower at the summit of the acropolis just to the west and with other burials along the acropolis ridge, some of which have burial goods of the fifth to sixth century CE.[58] Since they are laid with their heads to the west, except for the baby in the little grave outside the Temple, whose head is to the south, one supposes that these are early Christian burials. The baby in grave 2 was not given the usual west-east orientation. There are several possible explanations for this. One is that the baby was not yet baptized, and so was not expected to receive salvation, or alternatively, that unbaptized infants benefited from special divine protection.[59] Another is that infants were buried in certain places somewhat apart from adults, though the reasons are hard to specify. It may at times have been a factor of the available burial space (within churches sub-adult burials tend to be towards the right wall, closer to the baptismal font area, or near the entrance in the narthex).[60] In any case, the presence of full-term infant remains in the fill above grave 1 inside the Temple, if they were not still in the womb of one of the female burials, may suggest that being unbaptized at death was not a deciding factor for burial location or orientation here. Burial practices in the Early Byzantine (Proto-Byzantine) period seem to have been less fixed than in later times.[61]

Indications of later human presence in the Sanctuary include 15 Early to Middle Roman lamps, one of which was complete, dating to the first century CE, found against the interior of the south wall of the cella.[62] One fragment of a sixth-century CE North African type lamp was found in Building A.[63] Two coins have tentatively been thought to belong to the fifth/sixth century CE, along with one of the twelfth century (Manuel I), while a few fragments of what has been identified by John Hayes as fifteenth-century Venetian (?) glass have also been found within the Temple.[64]

THE ALTAR AND COURT

The Sanctuary's Altar lies a little more than seven metres to the east of the Temple, in the middle of an open court whose surface was covered in places by a thin layer of small fieldstones (fig. 2.30a–d). There are six ashlar blocks in and around the Altar, of which four are still in situ. These four are numbered here 1–4, from north to south (right to left in photo). Block 5 has split into two pieces and fallen away from the Altar a little downhill to the south. Block 6 is resting near the top of the west side of the Altar. These will be discussed in more detail and some comments made about their original appearance.

Block **1** forms the north side of the Altar. It is a large ashlar block (dimensions: length 1.44 m, height 0.85 m, thickness 0.31 to 0.34 m) which leans slightly to the north, but otherwise is in its original position. The surface has been roughly chiselled; there is no evidence for plaster or other finish. The coarse stone "paving" of the court has been well preserved, especially around the northeast corner of northeast corner of this block. It is worth noting that the paving rises almost 30 cm up against this corner of the Altar, suggesting a later date for its deposition, certainly later than the Altar itself.

Block **2** projects further to the east than **1** by as much as 20 cm. It has a roughly chiselled north face, but it is not parallel to the south face of **1**. In other words, it seems to have shifted from its original placement, allowing dirt fill to penetrate between the two blocks. Blocks **3** and **4** once joined, but are now about 14 cm apart. The "S" curve representing the break between the two is pronounced; the correspondence of the two opposing faces to each other is striking.

If one accepts that blocks **3** and **4** once joined, as seems certain, and notes that block **4** has a roughly chiselled flat south face, while block **2** has a roughly chiselled flat north face, then it seems clear that the explanation for the lack of any finish on the surfaces between blocks **2** and **3** is that these two blocks also originally joined. The correspondence of the south face of **2** with the north face of **3** is close, but not nearly as striking as the faces between **3** and **4**. Still, there is no reason to think that they did not fit together; weathering over the years is the probable cause for the present lack of close correspondence.

If blocks **2**, **3,** and **4** all once joined to make a single block, we have here the largest single block in the Sanctuary. Its dimensions (estimated by assuming that blocks **3** and **4** have separated by about 14 cm, and blocks **2** and **3** have separated by 6.5 cm) must have been approximately 1.605 m long (N-S), 0.87 m wide (E-W), and 0.70 m high. It has slipped downhill out of its original position by at least 16 cm, as seen by the back corner piece of block **4** which broke off and rests this distance apart now, but more likely by 20 cm or more, which is the distance that the east face of blocks **2**, **3**, and **4** is out of alignment with the east face of block **1**.

Block **5** has broken into two pieces and now lies on its side between 0.70 and 1.60 m from the south face of **4**. Not enough of either piece is preserved to give a length or height measurement; however, the thickness is 0.31–0.33 m, which matches very closely with the thickness of block **1** and suggests that block **5** must have formed the south end of the Altar and had the same dimensions overall as block **1**. One reconstruction of the Altar then would have blocks **1** and **5** form the north and south sides respectively, while blocks **2**, **3**, and **4** form the core of the structure, possibly with one or two blocks of the same thickness as **1** and **5** forming the east and west sides of the Altar, and thus surrounding the core. This would create an Altar that had a north-south length of about 2.25 m, an east-west depth of 1.44 m, and a height of at least 0.85 m.

There is still the question whether there was a block which capped the entire Altar, or perhaps only the core area over blocks **2**, **3**, and **4**. It is worth looking again at block **6**, mentioned previously as a possible threshold block for the Temple. Its thickness varies from about 0.18 m, where a 0.44 m wide inset has been cut 2 cm in depth down the length of the block, to about 0.21 m for the remainder of the length of the block. The width of the block is 0.66 m; its original length is not preserved. Since the width of block **6** (0.66 m) does not match the height of block **1** (0.85 m), it would not be suitable for either the east or west façade of the Altar. Nor does it seem to fit as a capping stone over the core, since the width of its inset (0.44 m) does not closely match the thickness of block **1** or **5** (0.31–0.34 m). If block **6** belonged to the Altar, its original position is not evident.

No evidence has been found to suggest that either the Altar or the Temple had any architectural ornament associated with it, whether in stone or terracotta. This is something worth noting, and perhaps in some way reflects the poverty of the city or the lack of interest in any decorative effect. One supposes that the discovery of marble sculpture inside the Temple is indicative of some level of wealth, and the votive offerings also give support for the notion that people were willing to offer items of worth to the deity, but there is no architectural extravagance shown either here in the Sanctuary or in the city in general. A quick look at the fine altar constructed in front of the similarly sized temple of Asklepios at Alipheira in southwestern Arkadia, a town which could hardly have been larger than Stymphalos, demonstrates this point. The altar is 2.18 × 5.36 m, and is made from a very fine local limestone, having carefully carved orthostate blocks with drafted borders, and on the short ends, a crowning block decorated on the raking geison with an excellent anthemion motif.[65]

Patches of rocky paving in the court around the Altar at Stymphalos appear to have been deliberately laid, but with little care (figs. 2.30a, d, 2.31a–c). The rocks are unworked fieldstones, generally no more than 15 cm in length. In some places they are very thinly scattered, while in others, for example on the west and north sides of the Altar, there is a thicker strew. This has caused problems in excavation, since the paving was dug through without being recognized at times, especially to the east of the Altar. The paving was probably a late addition to the court, since, as was mentioned, at the northeast corner of the Altar it rises almost 30 cm up against the Altar blocks.

Outcroppings of bedrock around the Altar show clearly that their upper surfaces have been chiselled away to create a more regular surface in the Altar court. It is not clear, however, when this done. It is possible that it was part of a project to harden the surface of this high-volume traffic area, since votive material and other occupation debris were found below the level of the "paving" and tops of the outcroppings, but it is also possible that the bedrock was chiselled away even before the paving of the court occurred. Since several iron projectile points were found embedded in the rocky "paving," and even below it, the whole issue of dating will be discussed again in the study of the projectile points.[66]

BUILDING A

Building A was originally constructed with outside dimensions of 10.7 m (east-west) by 8.8 m (north-south) on square-cut stone foundations 0.41–0.42 m thick. An equally thick, well-built wall divided this structure in an east-west direction into two unequal halves (fig. 2.32). The southern section (Front and Southeast Rooms) was entered from the Altar Court and had an interior width of 2.8 m (north-south). The northern half was entered from the Front Room likely through a single opening, and had an interior width of 4.75 m (north-south). At some date, perhaps still in the fourth century, the "North Annex" was added along the full length of the building's north side with a width of 3.45 m (north-south), and a second smaller room, 4.9 by 3.6 m, was added to the west side ("West Annex").

The east-west long axis of Building A is toward the southeast (149° from magnetic north), with its main entrance facing southward toward the Altar (fig. 2.33a–b). While the Temple's orientation to the east is easy to understand, it is less easy to understand that of Building A. Perhaps the simplest explanation is that it follows the slope of the hill here so there is less incline from one side to the other. It also faces out to the Altar Court and the lake (or dry plain when the lake had contracted or disappeared), and is more or less perpendicular to the line of the City Wall below the Sanctuary. In other words, it fits the topographical setting.

The walls of the original structure's foundations are built with blocks of different sizes and shapes, though most are square-cut and rectangular. The width is very close to that of the Temple's orthostates, approximately 0.41 m, and this is perhaps as good a reason as any to suggest that Building A was built at the same time as the Temple, perhaps even using blocks rejected for the Temple. The foundations are preserved to no more than two courses. The blocks of the first course only have a standard thickness, not a standard length or height. Most blocks are laid lengthwise, but others have their long sides extending vertically. The second course is still preserved only on the west wall, the interior dividing wall, and the north wall of the original structure. Virtually the whole second course is preserved on the north wall, but it has been shifted southward, downslope, by the pressure of eroding soil from the north. The second course of the north wall and the northern part of the original west wall have regular, flat upper surfaces on which to lay mudbrick courses. Further to the south on the west wall, the second course of blocks produced an irregular upper surface, suggesting that some few third course blocks were laid here. Several blocks have been deliberately cut in order to receive blocks above them, whether or not those blocks are now still preserved. A few instances show that blocks were carefully cut so that small blocks could be fitted tightly into gaps. In other places, the joins are careless and haphazard so that gaps are only filled carelessly with rough fieldstones.

Possibly at the time of construction of the building, a small room was created in the southeast corner of Building A, called here the Southeast Room (interior dimensions: 2.95 × 2.8 m) (fig. 2.34a–b). Two short spur walls, each about 0.8 m long, were built, abutting the south wall and the main dividing wall of Building A respectively, leaving a 1.2 m doorway between them. Both spurs were built from squared but irregularly shaped blocks, to a height of two courses. Inside the Southeast Room, a clear floor surface was discovered, characterized by six or seven flat tiles set into the surface and then broken into smaller pieces through foot traffic. There were also patches of burning with much charcoal, and in the corners and edges of the room were pieces of cooking pots which had been broken into smaller pieces, again presumably by foot traffic. Evidence for the use of this room as a kitchen is reinforced by the discovery of pottery in Trench 96.3 (Level 3) just to the south in the Altar Court that also included many cooking wares. The richest of this material was very close to the south wall of Building A.

Two half-metre-wide test trenches were dug below the floor in the Southeast Room along the north and south sides (fig. 2.34b). Signs of cooking quickly gave out, and instead an unusual number of terracotta figurine fragments were found, including the torso of a so-called Tanagra figurine type and the torso of a standing naked boy, perhaps an "Eros" (see fig. 3.44).[67] These may provide evidence for the use of this area during the first phase of the structure.

The main entrance to this large building in the Sanctuary was always in the middle of its south side, facing the Altar. The door, at least in the second phase of the structure, was accessed by a two- or three-step stairway, which led into the first interior room, the Front Room, occupying about two-thirds of the east-west length of the building. The other third, in the east end, was occupied by the Southeast Room as mentioned. A doorway then led off-centre through the thick east-west central wall into the Middle Room, which ran uninterrupted for the full east-west length of Building A. This was the original design of the structure. After an apparent destruction and rebuilding, this doorway had its threshold raised to the level of the new floor. It seems that both North and West Annexes were added well before this destruction and rebuilding, but it is not known whether they survived the destruction. The entrances to these two additions were from the outside, since no interior doorways exist to access them from the Middle Room.

A large ashlar block, length 0.91–0.94, width 0.395–0.41, height 0.20–0.25 m, lies in situ close to the middle of the south foundation wall of Building A (fig. 2.33a–b). A setting line for a second block is visible on the upper surface of this block but set back 0.28–0.29 m from its south edge. Clearly this is the first step of a small stairway leading to the main entrance of the building. Two smaller flat stones have been set on top of each other between the ashlar block and the wall of Building A to help support a now missing second step.

There is a problem regarding the existence of a threshold block. The preserved ashlar step has shifted somewhat so that its top surface is no longer horizontal, rising about 5 cm from west to east. It is also not parallel to Building A, varying from 17 cm (northeast corner of block) to 29 cm (northwest corner) from the line of the exterior south face of Building A. A second step clearly existed, but if it had the same height as the first step, it would have taken the stairs to a level well above the presently existing, only roughly cut block in the foundation behind it. This would therefore necessitate a threshold block. Now this hypothetical threshold block would be high enough to match the level of the second floor surface in the Front Room, but it would be much too high for the original floor level found within the building.

One is forced to consider whether the two- or three-step stairway was installed in conjunction with the rebuilding or second phase of Building A, and not with the original construction. The present main doorway with step in front of it is not centred along the south wall. The building is 10.7 m long, and yet the middle of the presumed doorway with step is placed 6.0 m from the southwest corner, or 0.65 m off centre to the east (i.e., 10.7/ 2 = 5.35. 6.0 – 5.35 = 0.65). One might expect the original doorway to be located at a break in the line of the stone foundation wall. A close examination reveals a wider opening between the two taller square-cut foundation blocks on this side. This wider opening not only aligns better with the doorway (possibly a divided or double doorway) leading from the Front into the Middle Room, but the centre of this wider opening is shifted westward from the presumed door with steps in front by about 0.4 m, bringing it much closer to the centre of this south wall of Building A.

Is there any indication of the threshold block or blocks for this wider opening that would correspond with the original phase? In fact, the opening contains a section of chiselled bedrock in place of square-cut foundation blocks. The builders must have decided to chisel the outcrop here to follow the line of the foundation. At its tallest point, the bedrock rises to about 30 cm in height, but its upper surface then declines diagonally to the west to meet the next large foundation block. This means that a block or blocks must have fitted above the bedrock outcrop to produce a flat surface. Just to the east of the bedrock outcrop in the foundation (behind the preserved step) is a square-cut block with rough surfaces and some deep holes in it, but whose upper surface aligns with the top of the bedrock outcrop in the foundation wall beside it. This block and the outcrop may be the best evidence for the level of the threshold of the original entrance to the building. The two- or three-step stairway leading to the entrance of Building A would then belong to the second phase when the threshold was raised to the level of the new floor in the Front and Middle Rooms.

The thick dividing wall between north and south "halves" of the original building was interrupted either by one or less likely two openings divided by a single square-cut foundation block at least in the building's first phase (fig. 2.35). The more eastern (right) opening is wider, and aligns quite well with the steps and evident doorway into the building from the Altar Court. The narrower more western opening in this wall dividing the Front from the Middle Room, if it existed, leads neither to a separate room nor from a separate room. The Middle Room is a single large interior room, while the Front Room has a low line of stones running north-south almost along the line of the block dividing the two openings, but if this line of stones is anything, it is not a room divider. It would appear more to fit as a base for a low platform or bench. This, however, seems to be impractical in terms of traffic flow between the doorways and within the room, especially when a bench could be placed more efficiently against one wall. The two openings or "doorways" in the central wall, again if the western one ever existed, were blocked up almost to the same height, although the western doorway, raised by a preserved height of 0.37 m, may have lost some of its original stones. The eastern doorway is blocked up to a height of 0.48 m. Several roof tile fragments have been used to fill small spaces in blocking the eastern opening, along with large and small rocks set in a clay mortar. No roof tiles were used for the western "doorway."

It is possible that only one doorway existed here, and that the second, western one is a phantom, giving the impression of a raised doorway from the use of smaller fieldstones between two larger square-cut blocks. It seems much more likely that there was a single doorway into the Middle Room from the Front Room. One should not, however, dismiss the possibility that a wider opening between the Rooms was interrupted by a vertical post resting on a sturdy foundation block to help support the central ridge beam. The dividing wall must have served the purpose of supporting the roof at least partly through the use of vertical posts. In order to have a wider opening between the Front and Middle Rooms for air and light to reach the interior, the opening may well have been divided in two by a post. In a second phase of the Building, when the floor was raised, the opening was partly filled in with smaller stones and the odd tile to raise the threshold (divided in two by the base for a post?).

If the dividing wall provided support for the ridge beam, as seems necessary, then the two sides of the roof were of unequal width, and possibly also of different slopes, especially once the North Annex was built. Since not only would the northern half of the roof be wider but also because the natural ground level sloped up to the north, it can be imagined that the builders faced a problem with roof height here towards the north edge of the building. This must have been made even more pronounced when the North Annex was constructed, since its roof likewise must have slanted down to the north. Somehow it would have to be overlapped by the roof sloping down from the original part of Building A, if it were not simply a continuous roof line. Two readily available solutions to the problem here are to raise the roof of Building A somewhat, or to make the slope of the roof to the north less steep. Perhaps both were tried, although no evidence of either has been left. (See figs. 2.36 and 2.37.)

At present there is only a little dating evidence to suggest when the apparent change of floor levels and raising of the doorway threshold between the Front Room and Middle Room occurred. A fragment of a mouldmade bowl was found in the thick deposit of tile fragments below the upper "floor" level of the Front Room (Trench 95.2 Level 4 Pail 9) and a couple of others were found below the floor in the Southeast Room (see below, Trench 96.12 Level 4 Pail 4, incl. inv. 1683) together with both an "Eros" terracotta figurine (pudgy standing boy, fig. 3.44) and a "Tanagra"-type cloaked female figurine, which suggests that this change of floor levels occurred at least after ca. 200 BCE.[68] A Broneer Type 16 lamp fragment from the first century CE was found in the upper floor surface, along with two or three Broneer Type 27 fragmentary lamps from the second century or so CE, and two coins were found in the thick deposit of tile fragments below the upper floor of the Middle Room.[69] One is a fourth-century coin of Phlious (Weir, **II-43**), but Weir suggests that the other is a first-century BCE coin of Sikyon (75–50 BCE), based on a revised chronology by Warren.[70] This is not much to go on in dating the later floor level and raising of thresholds, but perhaps it is enough to suggest that some reoccupation occurred with repairs to Building A in the first century CE. Certainly there is enough pottery evidence now to demonstrate that the Sanctuary as a whole suffered a substantial destruction and probable abandonment for a lengthy period about the middle of the second century BCE, but there are also enough lamp fragments to suggest that the site was visited in the first and second centuries CE, at the same time as and also later than the reoccupation of houses at the lakeside Lower Town of Stymphalos.[71]

There was a good amount of charcoal and some ash on the surface of the lower floor in the Front Room, but more clear evidence that the changes occurred due to a destruction was the quantity of large roof tile fragments which were used as fill between the earlier and later floors (figs. 38–9). This is most evident in the Front Room where the tiles were piled up by the hundreds amid the otherwise rather clean yellow-red dirt.[72] There was a thick deposit of tiles in the Middle Room as well, including some of the largest tile fragments found on the site.

In the second phase of Building A, the low north-south row of stones in the Front Room was covered over, the steps to the main entrance seem to have been put in place, and the threshold of the door leading to the Middle Room was raised with a new floor for both Middle and Front rooms made at the level of the raised doorway.

The large Middle Room of Building A, 9.75 × 4.75 m, provided very few clues about its use or whether it was ever subdivided. Neither floor level produced the quantities of cooking pottery or fine wares that one might expect if ritual dining occurred here. Nor was the room rich in votives or any other common type of object found in a sanctuary. The use of the Middle Room is therefore uncertain, though proximity to cooking done in the Southeast Room would argue for food and drink consumption in it. The only unusual feature found here was a very large square-cut block (0.82 m long, 0.48 m high, and 0.41 m thick) set on its side against the eastern part of the main dividing wall between the Middle Room and the Southeast Room. Its upper surface was badly worn or weathered so that edges were chipped away, giving it a pronounced curve. Its thickness suggests that it was cut to fit the foundations of the building, but for some reason was not needed. It obviously served some function, given its worn upper surface.

North Annex

The North Annex had foundation walls built of unworked fieldstones laid with clay mortar on its west, north, and east sides (fig. 2.32, fig. 2.40). Its south side was the north wall of the original Building A. Many of the foundation stones on the east and north sides are large, providing the full width of the wall. On the west side, the wall is more often two smaller stones wide. The foundations are two courses in height. Against the north face of the original north wall of Building A, the dirt fill rises to a height of 0.55 m. Most of this dirt must have accumulated or been deposited before the building of the North Annex. The bottom of the lowest course of the North Annex wall closest to the northeast corner of the original Building A is, however, only about 0.20 m above the bottom of the foundation of the original building. There is no evidence for foundation trenches for the North Annex walls, but it is possible that they once existed in order to strengthen the walls.

The fact that the West Annex uses the west wall of Building A including the North Annex for its east wall strongly suggests that the West Annex was built after the North Annex. But the West Annex may have been built as early as the late fourth century, according to Stone's analysis of the pottery associated with its floor. If this evidence is trustworthy, then the North Annex should be fourth century as well. There is reason to be cautious about this dating, though, as will be discussed below (West Annex).

No clear threshold for a doorway into the North Annex exists, but there is a gap in the second course of the foundation at its southeast corner. The gap is 1.35 m wide. A second opening, although perhaps an accidental one, is located 2.75 m from the northwest corner along the north wall; it is almost 1.0 m wide. At the east side of this second opening directly adjacent is the largest and most carefully cut block in the entire foundation of the North Annex. On the floor just to the south of this large block is a narrow stone foundation. If this were deliberately laid, it appears more like a low bench than the remains of a dividing wall.

In the middle of the North Annex, towards its east side, a pit was discovered in the Annex floor, filled with a thick deposit of ash and charcoal, among which was mixed the heaviest scattering of mould-made bowl fragments found anywhere in the Sanctuary, and also fragments of many clay lamps as well as two iron projectile points. This discovery suggests a use for the room and also provides dating evidence for a major destruction of the Building, and also, it seems, for an end to the active use of the Sanctuary for cult purposes.

West Annex

The West Annex, as mentioned, was the latest structure built within the Sanctuary (fig. 2.32). It depends for its east wall on the west wall both of the North Annex and of the original part of Building A. In other words, the North Annex must have been standing so the West Annex could use its west wall for its own east wall. The floor level of the West Annex towards its south side has been raised from the natural ground level by approximately 0.45 m. A pit was dug into soil that had built up in this area against the exterior west wall of Building A, and into it were dumped stones, broken roof tiles, Sanctuary votive refuse, and other cast-off material. It was then covered with a layer containing scattered pieces of lime plaster, and levelled with a layer of dirt.

In studying the pottery from this refuse pit (Tr. 96.15 Level 5), Peter Stone noted that there was an inordinate number of miniature votives (over 300), especially cups, most as fragments. Even more significant was that there were no fluted kantharoi in the deposit. The significance of this is that virtually all other levels have these kantharoi, which seems to suggest that the deposit was made before the fluted kantharos was introduced to the site. Such kantharoi were introduced in Athens early in the fourth century, and at Corinth they are known before the middle of the fourth. With so many drinking cups in the deposit, mostly skyphoi or kotylai (and the miniatures are also drinking shapes), but no fluted kantharoi, it would seem that the pottery supports a rather early date for the refuse pit, perhaps by the mid-fourth century, or at the latest, the third quarter. The fact that the deposit is placed right up against the west wall of Building A means that Building A is earlier than the deposit. Depending on the final date for the material of the refuse pit, a *terminus ante quem*, likely in the first half of the fourth century, can be established for Building A. This has an effect on the date of the Temple as well, since it has been assumed that Building A is quite close in date to the Temple, and if anything, the Temple should be earlier, since it is a more important building for the cult.

The foundation walls of the Annex were built of relatively small, unworked fieldstones laid with a clay mortar. Two courses are preserved on the north side, only one on the west and south. The best indication of a door is the gap in the south wall close to the original exterior wall of Building A. This gap is now 2.45 m, but part of the south wall has been lost. The length of the West Annex is 4.9 m; its width varies from 3.3 m at the north to 3.6 m at the south side. On the floor of this room, mostly towards its south end, were found 20 conical loomweights, of which 19 were the normal standard size, and one was much smaller (figs. 2.41 a–c). These provide evidence for a specific activity within the room.[73]

The pit that was dug against the west exterior wall of Building A produced by far the richest deposit of votive material from the Sanctuary (Tr. 96.15) (fig. 2.32).[74] As soon as this level was reached, all soil was carefully sieved to maximize recovery of artifacts. The date of all the material in the refuse pit is earlier than at least ca. 300 BCE; as was mentioned, the lack of fluted kantharoi may put the pit's date in the mid to third quarter of the fourth century or so. Rather surprisingly, the pottery found associated with the floor of the West Annex also is consistently fourth century. So unless there is a misunderstanding of the chronology caused by the predominance of fourth-century pottery in the Sanctuary, and a general lack of identifiable third- to second-century material, it appears that an explanation is in order. It is hard to believe that the West Annex was built after the votive refuse pit was covered over and the North Annex was constructed, then had a brief use in the late fourth for weaving and perhaps storage, and was destroyed and abandoned as a pile of rubble close to the Pillar Shrine area, while the rest of the Sanctuary continued in use till the middle of the second century.[75]

Since fourth-century pottery so dominates the finds of virtually every trench and level, it is possible that later pottery or other dating evidence for a feature or level has been missed. Even more important, however, the floor surface of the West Annex was not so easily distinguishable, except directly below where the groups of loomweights lay. It is therefore hard to say exactly what pottery rested on the floor, what lay below the floor surface, and what material may have filled in from around and above when the West Annex was destroyed. In any case, it is unlikely that the floor surface contained much pottery directly on it, since we presume that there was a loom in the room, and that weavers generally should have kept it well swept so that broken sherds did not get underfoot.

The West Annex is certainly later than the material from the refuse pit, since the level of the floor in the West Annex extends southward to cover it. The pit itself contains much material from the mid- to late fourth century. The West Annex is also later than the construction of the North Annex which it is built up against. It is evident that the West Annex is the latest construction in the Sanctuary, except for the rebuilding of the main part of Building A after its mid-second-century BCE destruction. It seems more likely that the West Annex was destroyed at the same time as the rest of Building A, and that because its floor was well swept at the time of destruction, there was only fourth-century material at or just below its surface instead of the second-century material found in the North Annex and Building A.

INFANT'S GRAVE

A small grave was discovered against the exterior of the west wall of Building A, close to its southwest corner (fig. 2.42 a–b).[76] It measures approximately 0.3 × 0.6 m, and is constructed of small fieldstones and a broken roof tile set on their edges and sloping inward around a shallow pit. The floor of the grave was the bare dirt at the pit's bottom. In the grave were found the skeletal remains of an infant, lying on its back, with head to the south. From head to foot the skeleton measured 0.48 m, and across its chest, including its arms, the measurement was 0.17 m. Indications from the bones are that the baby died close to birth. No grave goods were found with the burial, so that a date can only be suggested based on the other grave nearby, found within the Temple. Since that was identified as an early Christian grave based on the placement of the skeletons with head to the west, as well as a single fifth- to sixth-century CE lamp found in the Temple, one may propose a similar date for the baby's grave, recognizing that unbaptized infants need not be buried with heads to the west in early Christian practice.[77]

PILLAR SHRINE AREA

Tucked away in the northwest corner of the Sanctuary between the Temple and the West Annex is a row of five rectangular pillars ("tetragonoi") (numbered 1 to 5, from

Table 2.1. Locations and dimensions of the six *in-situ* pillars in the Sanctuary

	Distance from ext. W wall of W Annex	Distance from neighbour to south	Preserved height above base	Width near base	Thickness near base
Pillar 1. flat stone	2.7 m 1.55 m	–	0.21	0.245	0.195
Pillar 2. flat stone	2.55 m 1.1 m	1.52	0.24	0.25	0.16
Pillar 3. flat stone	2.25 m 0.76 m	1.12	0.49	0.275	0.192
Pillar 4. flat stone	2.8 m 1.5 m	2.14	0.26	0.25	0.18
Pillar 5. bedrock outcrop	2.8 m 1.8 m	0.57	0.32	0.26	0.18
Pillar 6	N of N Annex	0.11	0.16	0.09	

south to north) (fig. 2.43, fig. 2.44, table 2.1). They are carved out of local breccia (conglomerate), still in situ and upright, although numbers 1, 4, and 5 were found tipped towards the east (downhill), number 2 was tipped towards the north, and number 3 was tipped slightly towards the west (uphill). All of them are missing their tops; they were carefully chiselled on three sides, with the western face left with a rougher finish. A bulging lower element was set into the ground to give the pillars a stable base. Their placement is in a rough north-south line parallel to the west wall of the West Annex among the outcrops of bedrock where the ground begins to slope more steeply towards the height of the acropolis. To the east of each of the first four pillars is a large, unworked fieldstone with a relatively flat upper surface. Each of these fieldstones has now broken into two or more pieces, but they were found in situ closely associated with the pillars. The fifth pillar has a large outcrop of bedrock to its east, but this has been somewhat chiselled flat on its upper surface, perhaps to serve the same purpose as the squarish fieldstones in front of the other pillars.

These pillars were not exactly rectangular, but rather tapered upwards, as is seen by the best preserved of them, Pillar 3. Furthermore, it is clear that the five in the Pillar Shrine area were deliberately meant to face eastward. Their north-south line with rising bedrock behind them to the west is one indication of this. Even more indicative, though, is the fact that their west-facing surfaces were not chiselled as smooth as the other three sides, and their east-west faces are wider than their north-south faces. Also, of course, the fieldstones associated with each pillar are set to the east of them. The pillar bases are merely unshaped extensions of each tetragonos, forming a heavy, bulbous foundation for the pillar meant to be set into surrounding soil. It is worth noting that the square stone base set close to a bedrock outcrop inside the cella of the Temple roughly follows the alignment of these five pillars although somewhat farther to the west, and the orientation of this base is closer to the orientation of the five pillars in the Shrine area and to Building A than it is to the Temple itself. The fact that all the pillars are placed very close to bedrock outcrops may have some significance.

A sixth pillar still in situ was discovered a short distance away, 2.8 m north of the northwest corner of the North Annex (fig. 2.45). It was much smaller, however, just 0.16 × 0.10 m, and preserved to a height above the bulbous base of 0.10 m. Its smaller size and placement away from the row of other pillars suggests either another use, for example as a horos stone, or less importance.

There is one other pillar (now lost) worth mentioning again here, which has always been taken as a horos stone identifying the divinity worshipped in this Sanctuary (see chapter 1 above, fig. 1.8). This is the ΠΟΛΙΑΔΟΣ ("belonging to Polias") inscription found by Orlandos in the 1926 season near Building A.[78] The block's width and thickness are close to the dimensions of the five pillars in a row, and one might consider whether it too was in fact one of these rectangular pillars rather than a horos stone. The word ΠΟΛΙΑΔΟΣ is in the genitive rather than the nominative case as one might otherwise expect of such Arkadian pillars, but one of the inscribed stelai in the Athena Sanctuary on the Marmaria terrace at Delphi is also in the genitive case – ΔΙΟΣ ΠΟΛΙΕΟΣ (fig. 2.46).[79]

As discussed briefly earlier, there is some inscriptional evidence for the worship of Eileithyia in the Sanctuary. This goddess is mentioned on three occasions by Pausanias in his description of the towns of Arkadia. These are at Megalopolis, Tegea, and Kleitor. At Megalopolis, Pausanias (8.32.4) says that in the southern sector of the city, east of the theatre, there is a hill with a temple of Artemis Agrotera, to its right there was a sacred enclosure to Asklepios, and just down from this there were quadrangular images (σχῆμα τετράγωνον) of gods, called the Ergatai, which he then identifies as Athena Ergane, Apollo Agyieus, Hermes, Heracles, and Eileithyia. For the last of these, Pausanias notes that in Homer (*Il.* 16.187, 19.103) she presides at childbirth. These five divinities, the Ergatai, did not have a sanctuary of their own, just quadrangular pillars to represent them. Each may have had a sculpted head on top to help differentiate it.[80] Pausanias is able to identify each god represented by these pillars quite precisely, but does not say how this was done. Heads by themselves are not enough to differentiate Athena Ergane from another aspect of Athena, or Apollo Agyieus from another aspect of Apollo, so presumably there were inscriptions, whether engraved or painted. Quite a number of such pillars either with a pyramidal crown or with sculpted heads have been found in Arkadia and elsewhere, and some are known from vase representations.[81]

There were five pillars in the group seen by Pausanias at Megalopolis, and there are three inscribed stelai near two "altars" with associated identification inscriptions at the east end of the Delphi Marmaria terrace for a group of five gods worshipped together. The appearance of five such pillars in a row, in situ, in the Pillar Shrine area at Stymphalos therefore seems at first glance to be more than mere coincidence, but the coincidence likely has no significance. In the Tegea museum there are two groups of six such pillars, one of which has six pyramidal crowns and the other six sculpted heads, in both cases on top of a single rectangular block with vertical lines to divide one "herm" from its conjoined neighbour(s). Two other "groups" in the museum have three, one with a dedication to the Nymphs, and the other identified with the names Zeus, Poseidon, and Demeter.[82] In the sanctuary of the Great Goddesses at Megalopolis, Pausanias says there was a group of six such tetragonoi – listed as Hermes Agetor, Apollo, Athena, Poseidon, Helios Soter, and Herakles – and he (7.22.4) also mentions a much larger group of 30 tetragonoi, each of which is called by the name of a different god, in the agora of the Achaian city of Pharai well to the northwest. He adds (7.22.5) that in the remote past, all the Greeks worshipped uncarved stones ("argoi lithoi") rather than "agalmata." So the number does not seem to have significance. In the Sanctuary at Stymphalos, while there are five in a row in situ in one area, there is another by itself to the north of Building A, yet another possible one found in fill behind the Temple (fig. 2.47), and a probable one found inside the Temple cella.

More important, though, at Megalopolis and at the Marmaria in Delphi is the identification of one of the five deities as Eileithyia. This of course is only circumstantial evidence for the identification of one of the Stymphalos stelai as a representation of the same goddess, but the votives with partial inscriptions certainly suggest that this deity either was worshipped in the Temple itself or may have been recognized in one of the five stelai. Pausanias' identification of the other four pillars at Megalopolis offers even less helpful evidence for the Stymphalos stelai, but it should not be overlooked entirely. Certainly Hermes would be a prime candidate for worship at Stymphalos, as the pillar inscribed with ΕΡΜΑC (mentioned above) found north of the acropolis ridge suggests. According to myth, Hermes was born in a cave on Mt Kyllene to the north of Stymphalos. A cave has been found on the north slope of Kyllene with ancient inscriptions which have helped identify the place as his supposed birthplace.[83] Pausanias (8.17.2) says that there was a large wooden statue of him in a ruined temple on the summit of the mountain. Also, neither Apollo nor Herakles would be out of place for veneration in the acropolis Sanctuary. Athena, of course, is already identified in the Sanctuary by the "Poliados" inscription.

Pausanias (8.48.7) mentions that in the agora of Tegea there is a temple to Eileithyia which has in it a statue identified as Auge on her knees, in a position of birthing.[84]

At Kleitor, quite close to Stymphalos to the west, the Eileithyia sanctuary is third in order, after those of Demeter and Asklepios, says Pausanias (8.21.3), and he adds that Olen, the Lykian poet, composed some hymns for the Delians among which was one to Eileithyia, where she is called the "fine weaver"[85] and is thought to be more ancient than Kronos.[86]

Finally, Pellene, Stymphalos's neighbour to the northwest, on the other side of Mt Kyllene, also had a temple of Eileithyia, according to Pausanias (7.27.8). It might be argued that the Temple on Stymphalos' acropolis was in fact dedicated to Eileithyia and not Athena Polias, but the evidence is not yet sufficient to determine this.

Although aniconic pillars, including inscribed ones, are common in Arkadia, there are no good Arkadian parallels for the large flat stones found in front of the pillars at Stymphalos. These stones, ranging in size from approximately 75 × 50 cm to approximately 43 × 39 cm, seem clearly to be associated with the pillars. If the pillars are representations in aniconic form of deities, then it would certainly be appropriate to have small offering tables, like altars, in front of each image where a small gift might be left by worshippers of the deity. The two small "altars" or offering tables in the Marmaria area at Delphi, sitting in front of the inscriptions for Hygieia and Eleithyia in the large terrace retaining wall (the "altar" in front of the Eleithyia inscription is barely visible at ground level), provide a closer parallel to the Stymphalos pillars and fieldstones.[87]

With respect to the Pillar Shrine area, the builders of the West Annex may have faced a small dilemma. If the pillars were already in place before the West Annex was added to Building A, they all should have been visible from the Altar Court through the narrow gap between the Temple and Building A. Obviously there must have been access to this shrine area so worshippers could honour the gods represented by the pillars. Presumably it would be regarded as worthwhile for worshippers to be able to see the pillars from the main traffic area in the Altar court. Those controlling the Sanctuary, perhaps just one priest or priestess, decided that a room, apparently for weaving, was desirable, close to Building A. We do not know why the more isolated west side of Building A was chosen, rather than the east side. Certainly the north side would be a problem, because of the rising ground, and the difficulty of extending the roof of Building A any further to the north. In any case, the west side was chosen so that the west wall of Building A could be used for the east wall of the new Annex. The builders, however, could not extend the room for the full length of Building A, as they had for the North Annex, since the Temple was in the way at the south and it would completely block off the view of the Pillar Shrine area. Furthermore at the north end, there was the difficulty of trying to fit a westward slanting roof of the new West Annex underneath the northward slanting roof of Building A and the North Annex. So, the West Annex was built, blocking off all view of the northern two pillars (Pillars 4 and 5) from the Altar Court; even the middle pillar (3) could barely be seen, since it is aligned with the northeast corner of the Temple and the southwest corner of the West Annex.

Two large unworked stones lie in a line to the west of Pillar 1, between outcrops of bedrock. They look suspiciously as though they were placed here deliberately. If so, they might have acted as a boundary for the Pillar Shrine area, or might have been meant to protect the shrine area from soil eroding down the hill from the west.

AREA EAST AND SOUTH OF THE ALTAR: TERRACE WALL

During the 1997 and 1999 seasons, two noteworthy structures were uncovered to the east and south of the Altar. The first is a line of very large, unworked rocks, roughly parallel to the east face of the Altar and the Temple, but 5 m to the east of the Altar. The second is a small room just southeast of this line of rocks whose most notable feature is a tile-lined basin in the southeast corner which drains towards the City Wall (fig. 2.48).

The line of very large rocks runs northeast-southwest for a distance of 10.5 m or more. There may be a return to the west from the south end of this line of rocks, but it is not a clear and distinct one, nor does it continue for any more than about 4 m. In places where the line is two or three rocks across, it reaches a width of 1.3 m. Several of these large rocks rise to a height well above the "paving" around the Altar Court, the biggest being 30 to 35 cm above the Court level. Smaller though still substantial rocks fill the gaps between the bigger stones. All seem to be placed in a very haphazard manner, although as a whole, the line appears to be created deliberately. There is no question of this being the foundation for a roofed structure, especially given the irregularities of the rocks and their placement. Rather it appears to be a terrace wall with two possible functions, either to keep back soil and the rough cobbling around the Altar Court and so level the ground somewhat, or to act as a kind of peribolos wall marking off the temenos proper of the Sanctuary. A few of the large stones have been dislodged and so slid a short distance down the slope, giving the wall a more irregular appearance; nevertheless, it looks as though its builders decided to gather large rocks from around the Sanctuary area and put them to use by lining them up in front of the Altar. Smaller stones were thrown in behind the larger ones, and then the area behind was filled in with dirt, including fragments of pottery and figurines of fourth-century date. At some point, a rough stone "paving" was laid over the Court surface, but for the moment, it is impossible to be precise as to when this occurred.

In favour of the Terrace Wall also acting as a peribolos for the Sanctuary is the fact that the one supposed horos stone, found by Orlandos, was said to have come from beside the "priests' house," i.e., Building A, but his brief mention of it suggests that it was found in the space between Building A and the Temple rather than anywhere close to the Wall. There is a gap of about 3 m between the north end of the Terrace Wall and the southeast corner of Building A. This would seem to be the most suitable location for an entranceway into the Sanctuary. If indeed the boundaries of the Sanctuary were as close as the walls of Building A, then this Terrace Wall may well have formed a kind of boundary to the south and east of the Altar, as well as acted as a guide for visitors coming into the Sanctuary through a defined entrance.

BUILDING B AND THE TILE-LINED BASIN ROOM

The small room with tile-lined basin is part of a larger complex whose other rooms are suggested by wall segments that run off into still unexcavated areas to the north and east (figs. 2.48 and 2.49). The interior dimensions of the room are 3.9 m (east-west) × 4.1 m (north-south). Its foundation walls (thickness 0.35–0.40 m) are constructed of small unworked fieldstones laid in two rows to a height of two courses, and held in place with clay mortar. Several larger blocks are used near the basin's drain, as well as in the west wall just south of the doorway, and at the northwest corner. The doorway is in the middle of the west wall, where there is a gap of 0.8 m. A carefully chiselled surface in the bedrock just inside the door served as a threshold from which a person could step down to the floor of the room.

The tile-lined basin (roughly 0.9 × 0.8 m) was built using large pieces of broken pan tiles laid on their flat sides for the floor of the basin, and on their edges for the walls. Many other large pieces were piled in the middle of the basin when the feature was excavated, far more tiles than were needed to line the sides. The basin floor was slanted towards the south where a narrow gap, like a simple drain, exists between large stone blocks forming the southeast corner of the room. At its deepest point close to this apparent drain, the basin was 0.35 m deep. The simple basin must have been used to gather some liquid. It is not lined or watertight, so any liquid would appear to drain out through the gap in the wall. Traces of charcoal were found on the floor outside the basin; otherwise there is little evidence for the use of the room from the objects found within it.

Outside the room, in the narrow space between the trench wall (Tr. 97.9) and the exterior of the south wall of this small room, a deposit of animal bones was discovered. Although found in a very confined area, this was the largest single deposit of bones found anywhere in the Sanctuary. Most of the bones belonged to young caprids, and these could be identified further from the five or so young goat horns found in the deposit. The proximity of this deposit of bone and horn to the Tile-lined Basin Room is suggestive of a function for the room, though confirmation is lacking. Certainly a basin is useful in the normal butchering of animals, since the carcass is regularly hung up to drain blood. Also suggestive is the proximity of the Sanctuary's Altar, where portions of sacrificed animals would be burnt as offerings to the god. Again, confirmation that these three elements – Altar, basin, and bones – are linked still waits.

CHANNEL CUT THROUGH BEDROCK

A final puzzling feature in the Sanctuary area is a deep channel cut through an outcrop of bedrock about 10 m to the south of the Temple's west end (fig. 2.50). This channel has a length of about 1 m, and is 41 to 48 cm wide with a minimum height of 40 cm (east wall) and maximum height of 60 cm (west wall). Nothing else is preserved to suggest its use. It might have anchored a wooden beam for a structure of some sort, for example, but this is speculation.

3

Sculpture[1]

Mary Sturgeon

During the 1995 and 1996 excavations in the Temple, parts of two marble statues were discovered, coming to light primarily in the back of the cella. Some surfaces of the marbles were blackened or had a "fried" appearance, which appears to result from proximity to intense fire. Most segments of the statues were found within or beneath a layer of broken roof tiles from the building, which was destroyed in the mid-second century BCE.[2] There are no signs of intentional breakage of the sculptures, and so it seems likely that the statues were damaged by the weight of the roof tiles and mudbrick walls falling on them, which caused them to break into large chunks and small chips. The portions of the statues that are now missing were probably removed by looters when they took roof tiles and other elements from the building for reuse in other contexts.

The marble fragments derive from a standing female figure and a male child in a sitting/leaning pose. Pieces are associated with a specific statue due to the similarity of the subject, size, and proportions. In both sculptures the marble is white, relatively fine grained, and heavily weathered from fire. Provenance tests on a fragment from each sculpture have been conducted by Yannis Maniatis and Demetris Tambakopoulos. The results of this analysis show that the kore (**3.1**) is most likely made of Parian marble and the child (**3.2**) is certainly Parian Lychnites.[3]

FEMALE FIGURE

The more significant sculpture from Stymphalos is the standing draped female figure in Late Archaic style that holds an animal forward in its left hand (**1**; figs. 3.1–30). The Archaic sculpture was found, anachronistically, in the cella of a fourth-century BCE temple, and evidence for earlier activity at the Temple site is limited.[4] The Sanctuary was destroyed in the mid-second century BCE,[5] and there is no sign of later construction or significant use of the Temple afterwards.[6] Hence, it is unlikely for archaeological reasons that this is a Roman archaizing sculpture. In addition, as we shall see, the style of the sculpture is purely Archaic, not a mixture of Archaic and later elements, which would indicate a fourth-century BCE or later date. Thus, the statue was originally used in another religious context, possibly one nearby, and appropriated for reuse within the fourth-century BCE Temple, where it would have served as a cult statue or an offering. The use of an earlier-style statue in a fourth-century context would have emphasized the figure's age and venerability. The animal held by the figure, which is probably a hare, is commonly associated with Artemis and with Aphrodite, and so the statue may have been dedicated to one of these deities when it was first set up, and possibly also in its secondary use, although another possibility, Eileithyia, must also be considered based on several dedicatory inscriptions in the Sanctuary.

Reconstruction and pose

The draped figure is preserved in fragments that represent the neck to mid-calf areas, including the right shoulder and upper arm, **1A**; the left shoulder, **1B**; the left breast, **1C**; the left arm, **1D**; the left hand holding an animal, **1E**; the draped legs, **1I**; and drapery fragments of varied sizes, **1F, 1G, 1H, 1J, 1K, 1L, 1M, IN, IO, IP**. The larger pieces are combined in a reconstruction drawing (fig. 3.1). Missing are the head, the right hand, most of the torso, the thighs, the lower calves, and the feet. The figure would have stood with both arms extended forward, holding a small animal in the left hand. Two features indicate that the subject is female: the rounded breast, **1C**, and the long slender proportions of the hand, **1E**.[7]

Small details help formulate the reconstruction. The vertical hang of the central pleat, paryphe, on **1I** shows that the figure does not pull her skirt aside, even though the right leg is somewhat advanced. The diagonal folds on the side of the right lower leg, **1I**, show that the right leg was advanced, and the straight folds beside the left leg indicate that it is treated as the weight leg. On the back of this piece, the diagonal pull of drapery to the lower right also reflects the advanced position of the right leg. The left arm, **1D**, is bent forward and worked in the round, and so both hands were free. Hence, the figure may have held an attribute or a phiale in the right hand. A small portion of the hair remains on the back of **1A**, but there are no hanging locks in front, on the right shoulder, or over the left breast, **1C**. In addition, there is no joining surface on the inner break of the right shoulder piece, **1A**, and so the head may have been carved in one piece with the body. The figure's height is estimated as ca. 1.40 m.

Garments

The figure wears three garments, a thin veil or scarf, epiblema, a short mantle, himation, and an underlying tunic, chiton. The veil is draped around the shoulders and under the hair, and is gathered into a bunch of narrow folds around the neck. The veil would have hung beside the breasts, where it would have been covered by the mantle. A large portion of the veil remains on **1A**, and a small area on **1B**, where it crosses the left shoulder.

The himation was worn diagonally in front, as suggested by three folds that emerge from beneath the right shoulder at the neck on **1A**. One edge of the mantle was probably anchored under the left arm. Portions of the mantle's hanging folds, which would have hung against the body, are preserved, as in **1G**, and beneath the arms, as in **1F** and **1H**. The tip of the swallowtail fold that is missing below the drapery in **1G** probably reflects the pointed shape of the break over the right knee. The thick material of the himation is contrasted with the thin quality of the veil.

On the right upper arm, **1A**, the chiton sleeve emerges from under the epiblema, and a portion of the chiton sleeve also remains over the left elbow, **1D**. These sleeves, which end just beneath the elbow on **1D**, do not have carved folds. Part of the chiton would also have been visible on the chest, and it is probably depicted over the legs, **1I**, unless the garment shown there is a "skirt." There are no flat surfaces or stylization on the back of the lower leg segment.

On other korai that wear three garments, the arrangements vary. Acropolis 615, ca. 490 BCE, for example, wears a chiton and a short himation, draped asymmetrically from the right shoulder to under the left arm, on top of which is an epiblema, which hangs over the left shoulder, around the back and right hip, across the front, and around the left lower arm.[8] Acropolis 684, ca. 500–490 BCE, wears an epiblema symmetrically over the back and shoulders, while the himation crosses the chest diagonally, which appears to be the arrangement here.[9]

The Stymphalos figure is one of several Late Archaic korai that do not pull their skirts to one side. This group includes Acropolis 671, ca. 520 BCE, Acropolis 615, ca. 490 BCE, Acropolis 685, ca. 500–490 BCE, and Acropolis 688, the Propylaea Kore, ca. 475 BCE.[10] This pose, which leaves both hands free to hold objects, is a transitional feature of Late Archaic korai.

As with other Archaic Greek sculptures, the garments of the Stymphalos kore would have been enhanced by colourful painted decoration. Possible traces of pigment survive on some fragments, **1A**, **1B**, **1C**, **1E**, **1F**, **1G**, **1H**, and **1O**.

Metal attachments

The use of metal attachments is indicated by two small holes above the breast, on **1C**, and one hole on the right shoulder-to-arm piece, **1A**. These attachments probably took the form of two metal chains, each affixed at the side of the chest. As such they would recall the chains, carved in marble, that are worn by the over-life-size statue of "Leto" from Delos. The objects attached to the Stymphalos figure may have been created in metal because of the statue's smaller size.[11] In addition, a circular shadow around the proper right hole on the breast fragment, **1C**, suggests that the chain was suspended from a metal disk affixed to the torso. The male torso found near the Ilissos River also has small holes on each side of the chest to receive metal attachments, two on the left and one on the right.[12] On the Leto, decorative elements were attached by small metal pins in the centre of the two lower chains. If the Stymphalos kore had worn such elements, they would have been attached directly to the metal chains.[13]

Piecing

In the animal's head, **1E**, the cutting for a vertical pin indicates the attachment of something above the head, most likely its ears. The dowel cutting, which is slanted somewhat towards the front of the head, probably indicates the backward slant of the ears. The vertical cutting is pierced by an even narrower cross-pin, which may have acted as a pour channel for lead. The lead would have helped insulate the metal and secure the attached object into its relatively small base.[14] The use of such cross-pins occurs in some korai in Athens, such as Acropolis 680 and 685, and it appears to be a feature of Late Archaic sculpture.[15] Here, the attachment by means of dowel and cross-pin has been employed in a very narrow area. The use of such a complex join in this location demonstrates the sculptor's high degree of skill. It probably served as a means of reducing the risk of damage to the statue if the ears had been in one piece with the head, though it could also have resulted from damage during carving. Notably, the ears of the animal held by the Laurion kore were carved in one piece with the animal, but the kore's arm was attached.[16] The corrosion from the metal pin that remains on the top of the Stymphalos animal's head occurs only at the line of the join, where the metal would have been exposed. This exposure would have occurred when the statue was set up out of doors during its first phase of use. The corrosion does not occur within the entire cutting, so the metal would not have remained in the cutting after the head was broken.

No trace of attachment is preserved for either arm. The right arm, **1A**, which is bent forward at the elbow, is broken through the forearm. Thus, it seems that the forearm was not attached separately, since such an attachment would have been inserted into the statue at the edge of the drapery, judging by the many indications of attached forearms among the Acropolis korai.[17] The extended left forearm, **1D**, was carved in one piece with the upper arm, which seems surprising, considering the weight that was supported by the left hand. The left arm could have been attached to the side of the torso in the middle of the upper arm, but no trace of a joining surface or dowel cutting remains. Arms could be attached to smaller figures in the middle of the upper arm without using a dowel, however, as shown by the upper arms of the Late Archaic seated figure from Rhamnous.[18]

Marble

The Stymphalos sculpture appears to be made of Parian marble, based on scientific analysis conducted by Maniatis and Tambakopoulos. The white colour, fine grain size (1 mm), sparkling aspect, and the cubic appearance of the grains on heavily weathered surfaces correspond to sculptures found on Paros that are made of local marble.[19] Parian marble begins to be employed for sculpture in the late seventh to early sixth centuries BCE. The use of Parian marble expands in the later sixth century, when it appears in abundance in Attica.[20] The Peloponnese has yielded only a few pieces of marble sculpture from the Archaic period, as is discussed below.[21] The Stymphalos statue could have been transported up to Stymphalos from the Gulf of Corinth.

Hand-held animal

The Stymphalos figure belongs to a well-established tradition of Archaic female statues holding objects. Many of these statues have been found in religious sanctuaries, where their hand-held objects would convey meaning about the recipient of the dedication, whether the figure represents the giver or the receiver. Fruits and birds, especially doves, are common hand-held objects among the korai found in the sanctuary of Athena on the Athenian Acropolis.[22] A number of hands from Acropolis statues, some of which are preserved separately from their statues, hold apples or pomegranates, birds, flowers, and possibly pieces of meat.[23] Hares are held by two statues from the Heraion on Samos,[24] while at Miletus figures hold birds and staffs which are possible offerings to Artemis.[25] In addition, several large terracottas from the Archaic period held objects in both hands, which were extended forward.[26] On Cyprus, a number of Archaic korai hold flowers, while some later statues hold bulls.[27] Some figures on Classical funerary reliefs carry hares as well.[28] Following in this tradition, some archaistic statues from the Roman period hold flowers and animals.[29] Overall, the number of Archaic-style figures that carry quadrupeds is relatively small.

The species of a hand-held quadruped can be difficult to identify, since such animals are often fragmentary. The Stymphalos quadruped lacks the features of a deer, since its forefeet are clearly articulated as paws, rather than hooves. In addition, the lower part of a deer's ear is narrow, and the tail emerges from the upper part of the rump, not the lower, as here.[30]

Greek hunting dogs are often depicted with slender necks and bodies, as here.[31] Artemis is frequently represented with a hunting dog, and terracotta figurines of Artemis with a dog have been found at Stymphalos.[32] The way that our animal reclines, however, with its legs held close to the body and the forepaws curving down over the statue's fingers, shows a greater similarity to felines and hares.[33] In addition, depictions of hunting dogs from the early fifth century show the ears starting far back on the head, which is not the case here.[34] Moreover, when Artemis is shown with her dog, it is beside her, where it functions as her hunting companion. It is not held in her hand, as a protected animal.

The Stymphalos animal resembles members of the cat family – including the short-haired domestic cats, cheetahs (hunting leopards), leopards, and panthers – with regard to the square shape of the back of the head, the prominent jaw, and the long tubular body. Many animals identified as panthers occur on vases from the sixth and fifth centuries BCE.[35] Heads that are turned, which is the case here, are conventionally termed panthers, as with a reclining figure of terracotta in Boston,[36] but the head direction itself is not always diagnostic. The body of the Stymphalos animal, which is more slender and graceful than that of a lion, is longer and thinner than that of a domestic cat, and even the hunting cats and cheetahs are stockier.[37]

The Stymphalos quadruped can be best interpreted as a hare.[38] In *On Hunting* Xenophon devotes a full chapter to the hare, and the similarity between his description and the Stymphalos animal is striking. As he says, when she sits she puts the hind legs under the flanks and usually keeps the forelegs close together and extended (*Cyn.* 5.10). The head is light, small, and narrow in front; the ears are upright; the neck is thin, round, and long; the forelegs are close together; the chest is not broad; the hind legs are much longer than the forelegs and turned outwards slightly; the coat is short (5.30). The fastest are the hares that live in the mountains (5.17). Their conformation makes them strong and very agile (5.31). Hares do not walk, but spring forward, and are capable of covering long distances at great speed (5.32). The conformation of the hare is well illustrated in bronze and terracotta figurines, on Greek vases, and on coins of Messana in Sicily, and hares are represented as gifts on Egyptian paintings.[39]

Hares are carried by statues in various ways. The kore from the Samos Heraion in Berlin, of ca. 560 BCE, holds the hare against the chest in her open left hand; the paws curve down over her fingers.[40] A smaller statue from the Samos Heraion similarly holds a hare against the breast on her left hand.[41] In both, the hare's long ears rest along its back, and the head faces forward. In the Classical period some hares recline on the bearer's hand and arm with their ears adhering to their back, as in the fourth-century statue of a girl from the Sanctuary of Artemis at Brauron,[42] but in other examples the animal is carved more independently from the hand, as at Stymphalos. On the funerary relief from Laurion, for example, the hare's ears are raised from the body and the head is turned outward in three-quarter view.[43] A hare may even sit upright in the bearer's hand, as on a relief in Paris.[44] The long, slender body of the Stymphalos animal lacks the muscular shoulders and haunches often shown with hares, probably because the animal is meant to be quite young.[45] The Stymphalos sculpture seems to be a three-dimensional version of its two predecessors from Samos, with later developments. The animal does not recline; its torso is completely separated from the kore's palm, as in the Classical reliefs in Athens and Paris just mentioned. The Stymphalos animal is perched on its legs, and yet it is not restrained by the bearer, making it appear tame, as in some vase depictions.[46]

With Attic korai the arm that holds an offering is generally the right, but in a statue of ca. 530–520 BCE said to come from the Laurion area, near Brauron, the hare is held in the extended left hand, as here.[47] In the Laurion animal, which is part of an ancient reworking of the sculpture, the ears project straight back without touching the animal's back. Samian and East Greek korai also carry their animals in their left hands, as at Stymphalos. The animal's placement in the left hand may result from the figure holding an object such as a bow or libation bowl in the more active, right hand. Holding two sets of objects becomes possible when garments are more naturally sized, so that the korai do not need to lift their skirts in order to walk forward.

Small quadrupeds are held by various deities and mythological figures, including Apollo, Artemis, and maenads, but the species of animal held by a certain figure may vary and therefore does not by itself provide a certain means of identifying the holder. Apollo holds a deer in his right and a bow in his left hand on an archaistic relief from the Miletus theatre, thought to reflect the Archaic statue of Apollo Philesios once in his temple at Didyma,[48] and a similar bronze statuette in London holds a small faun in its right hand.[49] On the other hand, a marble hand from Tralles, which holds a small reclining deer,[50] has been associated with Apollo through comparison with the Miletus relief,[51] but Artemis would also be possible. Maenads who carry small animals can be distinguished from Artemis by their animal-skin garb, as with the archaistic maenad in the Palazzo Altemps in Rome.[52] Other possibilities occur: a female figure holding a hare on her hand on a bell krater from Nola is identified by inscription as Tragoidia.[53] It should be pointed out that none of the hand-held objects from the Athenian Acropolis can be identified as a quadruped.

Artemis is one of the few female deities that carries an animal.[54] An archaistic statue of Artemis in London, of Early Imperial date, for example, holds a quadruped on her left hand, which Fullerton identifies as a small stag.[55] An over-life-size statue of Artemis in the Villa Albani, which reflects an Early Classical sculpture, similarly supports a small fawn on her left hand.[56] These retrospective works appear to reflect a Late Archaic to Early Classical tradition. In fact, in contemporary terracotta figurines Artemis is shown with various animals, holding a fawn, or less commonly a lion,[57] and she may have a panther or even a lion walk beside her.[58] As for other female deities, Hera may carry a lion, Aphrodite may receive a kitten as a gift, and piglets are the favourite of Demeter/Ceres, as on a cup in Berlin.[59] On this cup the lion perches on Hera's hand and wrist in a pose analogous to the Stymphalos animal.

Hares are associated with Aphrodite because they are a symbol of fertility.[60] Hares may be depicted as love gifts.[61] A Roman terracotta figurine of Aphrodite in Athens includes Eros holding a hare.[62] Interpretation of the two Samian korai that carry hares is uncertain, since they were found in a sanctuary of Hera. Blümel considered the larger figure a dedication to Aphrodite, or possibly a depiction of the goddess herself, since a building near the Heraion was considered a temple to Aphrodite, of ca. 560–555 BCE, but this identification is no longer maintained.[63] Freyer-Schauenberg, however, points out that the dedicatory inscription on this sculpture says only "to the goddess" and that the hare has no special connection to Hera.[64]

Hares are linked to Artemis because they are a popular animal to hunt, and so they become a symbol of the hunt, a trophy of the sport, and an indication of the countryside.[65] Xenophon states that Apollo and Artemis invented game and hounds (*Cyn.* 1.1), and they are often depicted in this context. On a red-figure Apulian krater in Paris, Apollo hands a hare to Artemis Bendis,[66] and a bronze hare from Priene bears an inscribed dedication to Apollo.[67] On a tin medallion from Eretreia, ca. 420 BCE, Artemis is shown with four animals: a dog, deer, bird, and hare, the hare strung up, as if a recent catch.[68] A young animal may also symbolize Artemis' kourotrophic aspect.

On present evidence Artemis seems the most likely association for the hand-held animal at Stymphalos. This view is supported by a related figural type that is popular in small terracottas from the Late Archaic period and later. In these figurines Artemis is depicted carrying in one hand a small animal, such as a deer or a hare,[69] and a bow in the other. The animal is carried against the body, a configuration that is necessitated by the figurines' small size and by the fact that they are mould-made. The Stymphalos statue seems to be a three-dimensional depiction of the same concept. Also similar are the dress of the figurines, the pleated Ionic chiton, and often the lack of hair locks on the chest. This type has been found over a broad area, in especially large quantities on Corfu, and at Argos, Athens, Brauron, Corinth, Delphi, Lousoi, Olynthos, Perachora, Taranto, Thespiae, and Volos. Of Late Archaic style, most figurines of this type are dated to the late sixth to early fifth century BCE due to their facial features and costume.[70] Among the approximately 5000 terracotta figurines of Artemis that were found in 1889 in the small sanctuary of Artemis on Cape Kanoni, Corfu, the goddess holds various animals, including a stag, doe, hare, lion, panther, wild boar, and less frequently, a bird, and a cock.[71] In some of these figurines, the hand-held animal (a deer) is large and covers the entire chest, in others (also deer) it stands in front of the deity, as if drawing a chariot.[72] In one of the Kanoni terracottas Artemis carries a hare against her chest, in four she carries a bow and a hare, and in twenty she holds a hare by its paws; clearly, the hare is one of the animals associated with Artemis in the early Classical iconographical tradition.[73] Artemis is also depicted on some "Melian" reliefs with a deer standing beside her and a hare perched on one arm.[74] In fact, the pose of this hare, which rests on its legs with its body separate from the arm, is very similar to that of the Stymphalos sculpture. Finally, Xenophon (*Cyn.* 5.14) says that newborn hares are not killed but are given to the goddess, since she protects the young. In the Stymphalos statue her gift is displayed announcing the realm that she watches over.[75]

These widely dispersed Late Archaic and Early Classical terracotta representations of Artemis carrying an animal are important for our understanding of the Stymphalos kore. They indicate that the statue found at Stymphalos presents an image type of Artemis holding an animal that was well known in certain parts of the Greek world in the early fifth century BCE. Two larger-scale examples in limestone occur on Cyprus from the second quarter of the fifth century BCE,[76] and other versions or variations of these types probably once existed in marble.[77]

Certain bronze statuettes from the Peloponnese reinforce the theme of Artemis carrying objects in her hands. An Archaic figure from Mazi (Elis), which bears an inscribed dedication to Artemis Daidale, holds a bow in her left hand and probably once carried an arrow in the hole behind it. It is suggested that she held the legs of a small animal in her lowered right hand.[78] An Early Classical bronze acquired in Kalavryta and possibly from Lousoi held a torch in her right and a long-stemmed poppy in her left hand.[79] The Mazi figure, as it stands on a three-stepped base, appears to reflect a larger figure, possibly a cult statue; the attributes and stool that she stands on suggest the same for the figure from Kalavryta.

Also from the Peloponnese are a group of Late Archaic bronze statuettes of Hermes or a shepherd carrying a ram in the left arm. Identification as the deity for some of these figures is confirmed by the presence of winged boots.[80] Hence, the Stymphalos figure can be seen to fit comfortably in another way into a Peloponnesian artistic context.

Age of the subject

An age of the subject of about 12 to 14 years is suggested by several features. The long, unbound hair and the small breast indicate that the sculpture depicts an adolescent girl of marriageable age. Such "budding breasts" are understood as a symbol of early adolescence.[81] Athena and Artemis, as unmarried deities, wear their hair down, as here, not rolled up or covered in the manner of brides or married women, such as Aphrodite and Hera. Further, the statue's estimated height, ca. 1.40 m, would be appropriate for a figure who is not yet fully grown. In addition, Evelyn Harrison has shown that veils are an indicator that their wearers are young women of marriageable age, rather than married women.[82] The subject of the Stymphalos sculpture could be an adolescent girl who is shown as an initiate or votary of a cult, or a deity of the same age. There is no sign of an aegis that would indicate Athena, and so from the standpoint of its age and iconography also the statue can most likely be associated with Artemis.

Date

A number of features suggest a Late Archaic date of ca. 490–480 BCE for the Stymphalos statue. The wave pattern of the hair is similar to the kore Acropolis 615, the tight zig-zags of earlier figures' hair having given way to looser waves.[83] Separations between the waves are cut more sharply in Acropolis 615, and individual hairs are not incised on either piece. The Stymphalos kore's loosely waving hair also resembles the back hair of the Amazon from metope 9 of the Athenian Treasury at Delphi, ca. 490–480 BCE, the hair of a youthful head from Corinth, from ca. 490 BCE, and that of Acropolis 615 and the Propylaea Kore, both dated ca. 480 BCE.[84] Most Archaic korai have three or four tresses hanging down each side of the chest, but the Stymphalos figure, like two small Attic korai from Eleusis[85] and the young girl on the "brother-sister stele" in New York and Berlin, shows no sign of this feature.[86] Moreover, the absence of side tresses in front forms part of the change to a new hair arrangement in the early fifth century BCE in which the hair projects in two bunches before the ears, then is hooked over the ears and hangs as a single mass down the back, as illustrated by the head NM 60, from Eleusis.[87]

The manner in which the epiblema is stacked in folds around the neck and shoulders corresponds with sculptures dated to the early fifth century BCE: note especially the folds about the neck of Acropolis 684, the Propylaea kore Acropolis 688, the Acropolis Charioteer relief, and the male torso from the Ilissos.[88] The low relief of the overlapping sections of the epiblema is also similar to overlapping drapery on the neck and shoulders of the "Leto" from Delos, dated ca. 500 BCE.[89] In the Stymphalos kore the absence of carved folds in the chiton sleeves recalls the left chiton sleeve of the Euthydikos kore.[90] The way the chiton sleeves hang behind the elbow is also congruent in these figures. The lower edges of hanging folds, as on **1F**, **1G**, **1L**, **1N**, have undulating surfaces similar to a number of Late Archaic Acropolis korai,[91] figures from the East pediment at Aegina,[92] the Kallimachos Nike, and the colossal statue of Artemis on Paros, ca. 490–480 BCE.[93] The way the material is folded upward where it crosses the arm below the biceps also finds companions among Late Archaic statuary, such as the Leto from Delos, in the folds at the shoulders.[94] The low, flat folds over the right shoulder of Acropolis 684, ca. 490 BCE, have an equally "soft" appearance, as does the mantle folded back at the shoulders on the Ilissos torso.[95]

A few other details are congruent with late Archaic work as well. For example, the unweathered and unburned surfaces, such as the back of the left hand, **1E**, and one corner of the left shoulder, **1B**, display extremely finely polished surfaces of the sort that is characteristic of much Late Archaic sculpture. Also, the sharp creases in the thumb are similar to those on the left hand of Athena from the West pediment of the Aphaia Temple on Aegina, as well as on some Acropolis korai.[96]

Based on its modelling and volume, the back of the kore's draped legs, **1I,** would likely be interpreted as deriving from an Early Classical statue if the front had not survived. This back area resembles the drapery of Angelitos' Athena, ca. 480 BCE, the soft, undulating folds on the back of the running maiden from Eleusis, ca. 485–480 BCE, the Propylaea Kore, of ca. 480 BCE, and a statue from Xanthos, ca. 470 BCE.[97] Hence, the Stymphalos kore appears to be a transitional figure that displays many Late Archaic features, but also anticipates some developments of the Early Classical period.

On the other hand, neither the archaeological context of the kore nor the style suggests that it was made after the Archaic period, in an archaizing or archaistic style. The sculpture fragments were found in association with the burned destruction debris and the collapsed roof tiles of the fourth-century BCE temple, and they display signs of burning in the same conflagration. In addition, the sculpture lacks features that regularly appear in archaistic works, such as carved crinkly chiton folds, stylized ends of drapery folds, and some illogicality of drapery arrangement, and the pinhole attachments for metal jewellery are not a feature of archaistic sculpture.[98]

Regional affiliation

In general, the Stymphalos kore is related to the Attic-island styles of sculpture in contrast to those of East Greece/Ionia. It exhibits, for example, volume in the draperies and a delicacy of carving that is analogous to figures on the east and north friezes of the Siphnian Treasury at Delphi, in contrast to flatter and more schematic renderings in the west and south friezes.[99] In more specific terms, the style and format of the Stymphalos kore find good comparisons with sculptures from Attica and the Cyclades,[100] enhanced by some iconographic and technical relationships with Attic and East Greek statuary.

Island features include soft, billowing folds in back, fine surface decoration in the hair and in drapery folds on the back, and the use of metal attachments. The rendering of drapery combines fine, delicate ridges in some areas with three-dimensional modelling in others. The folds crossing the back are formed by particularly low, narrow ridges. These resemble fine ridges in the hair and drapery folds of the Apollo from Delos of ca. 500 BCE and across the lower back of the later sixth-century kore in New York, thought to be from Paros.[101] In contrast, in the Acropolis korai folds that cross the arms are typically thicker and rendered as a change in plane, usually with a groove to emphasize this change. A similar effect is created in the grave relief of the warrior Aristion, ca. 510 BCE.[102] None of the Acropolis korai has soft, undulating folds in back that resemble those of the Stymphalos kore, for which good comparisons are seen in the statue of Phrasykleia, by Aristion of Paros, the front of the Xanthos figure previously mentioned, and the Nike from Paros of ca. 470 BCE.[103] The preference for catenary folds, as suggested in the right side of the Stymphalos kore's back, is seen, however, in some Acropolis korai, such as nos. 684 and 594, and on the Charioteer relief, Acropolis 1342.[104]

With regard to the manner of attaching jewellery, none of the Acropolis korai has small holes on the chest for metal attachments, and none wears ornaments attached to the necklace by small metal pins, as does the "Leto" from Delos. In addition, metal buttons were added to the chiton sleeves of korai from Delos.[105] The Ilissos kouros from the early fifth century BCE, which also has small holes for metal attachments on the chest, combines East Greek (drapery) with Attic features (anatomy).[106]

East Greek traits comprise the pose, which is the reverse of most korai, with the left hand holding the object and the right leg forward. Samian and Milesian offering bearers similarly carry the attribute in the left hand rather than the right.[107] One figure from the Acropolis, number 672, also walks with the right leg advanced rather than the left.[108]

The hare as the hand-held attribute finds good comparisons outside Attica, as with the statues from the Heraion on Samos and the terracottas from Corfu. Hares are also held by Classical sculptures from the Sanctuary of Artemis at Brauron. Hares seem appropriate to Artemis because of her association with wild animals and the hunt, and their relationship to Aphrodite is also clear, due to their fecundity. The significance for Hera is less clear, but two marble hares were dedicated to Hera on Samos in addition to those carried by the Archaic statues previously mentioned.[109] In addition, a hare is carried by the fifth-century terracotta sculpture of a youth that was found in the Sanctuary of Demeter and Kore on Acrocorinth.[110]

Like the Late Archaic korai from Attica, the Stymphalos kore displays a simplification of Archaic stylization in hair and drapery, lacks incised chiton folds on the arm, and drops the gesture of the raised skirt. Thus, the sculptor of this piece seems to speak an artistic language in keeping with that of the Cyclades, but he is also well aware of stylistic and iconographical developments in Attica and East Greece as well as on Corfu.

Primary and secondary functions

The Stymphalos Archaic kore was found in the back of the cella of a fourth-century BCE Temple, where it appears to have stood at the time of the Temple's destruction. The manner in which the statue was shattered into segments of various sizes, including small bits, and was greyed from burning is consistent with this interpretation. Furthermore, there are no signs on the fragments that the sculpture was intentionally broken apart. Such signs would consist of deep marks from a hammer and cracks radiating outward from these points, as exemplified by sculptural fragments found in the Sanctuary of Palaimon at Isthmia, which were intentionally broken up.[111] The missing portions of the Stymphalos statue and the statue base were probably exposed when some of the temple's roof tiles were carried off, and hence they were also carried away. The find spot suggests that the statue was an offering, placed, like the temple boy, inside the fourth-century temple. The hare that the figure carried and the statue's earlier, Archaic, style could have led to its reinterpretation as a deity. Two features – the statues' find context in the cella, and the use of the Archaic style to depict older statues in the fourth-century BCE Peloponnese, as discussed below – suggest its interpretation as a deity in its secondary use.

Primary use

The significance of the statue in its primary use is unknown. There is no evidence for an Archaic temple on the Stymphalos acropolis,[112] but some finds from the early fifth century have been identified.[113] It seems likely, however, that the first use of the kore was not far from the Stymphalos acropolis. The location of the old town of Stymphalos of the sixth and fifth centuries is not known, but that one existed is made clear by sources such as Pindar (*Ol.* 6.84–90, 472 BCE ?), who refers to the grandmother of Agesias of Syracuse as coming from Stymphalos, and Pausanias (8.22.2,3), who states that Temenos established three sanctuaries of Hera in the old town, which had disappeared by his day. In addition, Pausanias (8.22.7) refers to a wooden statue mostly gilded in the old sanctuary (ἱερὸν ἀρχᾶιον) of Artemis Stymphalia.[114] Pausanias' statement indicates that the sanctuary of Artemis Stymphalia was still active in the second century CE, and, therefore, this is not the identity of the Acropolis sanctuary, which exhibits no significant religious activity in the Roman period.[115] Further, Williams and his colleagues have noted architectural fragments from one Ionic and at least five Doric buildings (one of Late Archaic to Early Classical date) in various parts of the Stymphalos valley.[116]

The primary location of the Archaic marble statue, judging by the presence of considerable weathering over the upper surfaces, as on the shoulders, would have been out of doors. The statue would have survived relatively undamaged and been available for reuse, perhaps because the sanctuary where it had previously been dedicated had fallen into disuse and disrepair or had problems with flooding. Williams has suggested that the statue was brought from Attica in the fourth century BCE, but Archaic statues that were set up in Attica were buried in association with the Persian invasion of 480 BCE, as were the kore and kouros found at Merenda,[117] or reused as building material.[118] Long-distance transport of earlier art works does not appear characteristic of the fourth century BCE, as it was to become in later periods. The sculpture may initially have been dedicated in a sanctuary at or near Stymphalos, possibly on the Stymphalos acropolis itself.

As previously discussed, if the hare serves an attributive function, it suggests that the sculpture was initially dedicated to a female deity, most likely Artemis, as a gift or as a representation of the goddess. The pose with the hand forward and the palm up may imply that a gift was expected, recalling a passage in the *Ecclesiazusae* of Aristophanes (ll. 777–83). If the animal's size in relation to that of the girl can be understood as natural, then the animal depicted is young and possibly newborn. The presentation of a newborn recalls the custom of sacrificing young animals to other deities, such as Demeter.[119] If the statue were a votive, it might have been dedicated by a successful hunter.[120]

Secondary use

At the time of its reuse in the Stymphalos Temple, the viewing context of the statue was changed, and so its function may also have changed. All pieces of the kore were found in the rear of the cella, many near the west wall, so it seems likely that it stood in the cella. In this location it could have served either as a cult statue or as a votive.

During the late fifth to early fourth centuries BCE, interest in Archaic-style sculpture is also demonstrated in other parts of the Peloponnese. Archaistic images form part of three sets of architectural sculptures from this period – the frieze of the Temple of Apollo at Bassai,[121] one of the pediments of the Temple of Hera at Argos,[122] and the East pediment of the Temple of Asklepios at Epidauros.[123] In these sculptural assemblages, the style of an earlier period may have been chosen to signify a specific early statue, the Palladion from Troy (Epidauros), or the venerability of the image (Bassai). The idol in the Bassai frieze depicts a small statue of Artemis Orthia in her rural, outdoor sanctuary.

A full contextual interpretation of the sculpture would depend on how the various parts of the acropolis sanctuary functioned and whether cults of different deities were honoured there. One inscription known to come from the sanctuary records the name Poliados. This inscription was not found inside the Temple, but between the Temple's northeast corner and Building A, and indicates the worship of Athena Polias on the acropolis. In addition, three partial inscriptions, one on a bronze rim fragment, one on a silver coin, and one incised on a Corinthian red-figure calyx krater (?), appear to indicate that Eileithyia was worshipped in the sanctuary.[124]

The presence of multiple deities may also be indicated by a row of stelai found west of Building A in the Pillar Shrine area, which are discussed further in the conclusion. The stelai tops are missing, but the flat stones found in front of them suggest that the stelai were aniconic images of deities and the flat stones were designed to receive offerings. A similar stele, also missing the top, was found within the cella. It has been conjectured that it acted as an aniconic cult statue.[125]

A substantial number of small finds from the Stymphalos acropolis are associated with female deities. These include bronze jewellery (such as earrings, finger rings, bracelets, and necklaces) and objects used in weaving (20 loomweights from the West Annex of Building A and 80 from elsewhere in the sanctuary).[126] It is even possible to conjecture that some of the jewellery, for example buttons and chains, may have decorated the statue itself. Other finds, such as terracotta figurines and the marble sculpture of a "temple boy" (here, no. **2**), specifically suggest a kourotrophic deity.[127]

C. Morgan suggested that the main shrine on the acropolis was dedicated to Artemis.[128] A few finds from the acropolis may suggest the presence of this goddess; in addition to the hare held by the statue, two bronze figurines of hares came to light, one of them in the Temple; however, if these were mirror attachments, they cannot be associated with a specific deity.[129] Whether the kore was intended to depict a deity or an offering bearer,[130] the hare indicates that in the statue's primary use, it was more likely dedicated to Artemis than another deity; the same association probably continued in its secondary use.

Archaic marble sculpture in the Peloponnese and abroad

Arkadia, like the rest of the Peloponnese, is not known for having marble sculptures of the human figure in the Archaic period, and so the appearance of an Archaic kore on the Stymphalos acropolis is unusual. The Stymphalos kore is not the only example of an Archaic sculpture made of good quality white marble that has been found in the Peloponnese, but the numbers are small and the examples mostly fragmentary. Fragments of a Late Archaic kore have been found in the Argive Heraion,[131] for example; the vertical folds over the right leg of the Argos figure resemble the folds over the Stymphalos kore's breast, **1C.** In eastern Achaia at Mamousia, ancient Keryneia, fragments of two Late Archaic marble sculptures are identified as pedimental sculptures. Of Parian marble, they include part of a helmeted head and the lower drapery and feet of a walking female figure, a very carefully finished piece in which the folds are rendered with some volume.[132]

At Asea in Arkadia south of Tripolis a life-size seated statue of Athena was found amid traces of a sanctuary.[133] As with the Stymphalos kore, the small, high breasts reflect her youth. The sculpture has four large holes on each side of the chest, probably to affix locks of hair. Beneath these are four small holes, similar to those on the Stymphalos kore, which probably received metal pins for attaching decorative objects. The style of the Tripolis statue has been connected with that of East Greek workshops, and the format is associated with the seated Athena on the Athenian Acropolis of ca. 530–520 BCE, attributed to Endoios.[134] For Tegea, Endoios was commissioned to make a statue of Athena Alea out of ivory (Pausanias 8.46.5).[135] Pausanias mentions it because the use of ivory was unusual. Less unusual probably was the hiring of an artist from another city when a city or a member of the elite wanted to commission a special statue for an important dedication.

The number of marble statues of the human figure from the rest of the Peloponnese is equally small and shows a preference for the male figure. The Tenea kouros of ca. 550 BCE, which comes from a cemetery outside Athikia (Corinthia), is the best preserved and the best in quality.[136] No draped female figures have been found at Corinth, but a number of kouroi survive, if partially. These include a Late Archaic head of a youth with a krobylos hairdo, which was found in a funerary area, and an early Classical head of a youth.[137] Other sculptures are represented by smaller fragments: a knee from an Archaic kouros of Naxian marble in Corinth and legs of at least three kouroi from the Sanctuary of Poseidon on the Isthmos.[138] Parts of Archaic kouroi of white marble have also appeared at Asine (?), Epidauros town, Ligourio, and Phigaleia,[139] a male head of the late seventh century BCE comes from Lepreon in Arkadia,[140] and a bearded head of blue-grey marble was found at Meligu in the Thyreatis.[141] The head and upper torso of a warrior, "Leonidas," from the acropolis of Sparta is a fine, Late Archaic to Early Classical sculpture in Parian marble.[142] A marble head in a private European collection has recently been attributed to Sikyon, and a headless kouros is a recent find from Figareto on Corfu.[143] Amid all these male figures, female figures from the Peloponnese occur largely in the form of perirrhanteria supports from the mid to second half of the seventh century.[144] In addition, fragments of two korai made of local marble come from Geraki, south of Sparta, pieces from a kouros from Aigies, and from Sparta an inscribed marble shield with reliefs of an Amazonomachy would have been held by a statue of Athena.[145] Dated ca. 510–490 BCE, the helmet and eyes on the shield reliefs are East Greek in style.

Increased ease of long-distance transport allowed Archaic statuary to be introduced into areas far from the primary marble sources in Attica and the Cyclades. Many of these sculptures are isolated examples, and they were probably specially commissioned for a specific use. Due to their spotty survival, it is difficult to tell whether the present picture is representative, but, again, the male figure seems preferred. In Sicily and southern Italy, a number of marble kouroi are well known, which come from Leontini, Locri, Metapontum, Megara Hyblaea, and Terravecchia di Grammichele, and an unusual one recently found in Reggio.[146] An unfinished kore from ca. 500 BCE was found outside ancient Tarentum and a second kore at nearby Satiro.[147]

In the Aegean, a substantial amount of Late Archaic marble sculpture has been found. Keos and Aegina, which have important temples and architectural sculpture, have produced a certain amount of free-standing statuary,[148] and two korai from the west central acroterion of the Temple of Aphaia on Aegina are especially well preserved.[149] Marble korai have appeared on Andros, which has also yielded one kouros, and on Skyros.[150] From more distant locations, a fragmentary kore and a kouros have appeared at Istros (Histria) in Romania, a fragmentary kouros was found in a funerary context at Olbia, and a kore at Odessa on the north coast of the Black Sea.[151] From various locations, new publications and new excavations bring new material into view all the time.[152]

This brief overview of the distribution of marble kouroi and korai outside the marble-bearing areas makes it evident that in the Peloponnese and the west there is a strong preference for dedications of male sculptures. One should ask not only why the Stymphalos kore is one of the few marble korai from the Peloponnese, but also what causes people to commission marble sculptures, especially korai, in areas distant from the marble sources where the practice of setting up marble sculptures is infrequent. It seems that particularly in the Late Archaic period, the mobility of sculptors had increased to the extent that a person of some means who lived in a remote area could contact a workshop and commission a sculpture for a truly special purpose. The very factors that allow scholars to speak of an International Style in the Late Archaic period also make it possible for marble sculptures of high quality to appear in widely distant areas.[153]

In summary, the kore from Stymphalos may be understood as one of many sculptures of the Late Archaic period that were commissioned by wealthy individuals at some distance from the primary artistic centres. Even though such sculptures may occur far from the major sources of material and workshops, this distance does not necessarily have an impact on artistic quality, as the kore from Stymphalos attests.

CHILD, "TEMPLE BOY"

The statue of a young boy is partially preserved together with most of its plinth (**2**; figs. 3.31–41). The right foot is flat on the plinth, and so the right knee would have been up and sharply bent. Hence, the figure can be visualized in a sitting position, with the left leg bent and on the ground, the left foot resting on its side. The boy supported himself on his hands, since both are spread palms down at the edge of the plinth. He would have leaned strongly to his left, in a combined sitting/leaning position.

The head was at first thought to belong to the female figure from Stymphalos,[154] but its cubic proportions, lack of hair, and the naturalistic rendering of the ear make association with the child more likely. The head is poorly preserved, but the original width, part of the crown, and the crease of the neck survive. The crease suggests that the figure probably looked up and to its right.[155] The head exhibits a cubic shape that is quite different from the elongated oval heads of most Archaic korai.[156] If this head were from such a kore, hair would appear immediately before and behind the ear, reaching the ear's lower tip in back, and the figure would have worn earrings.[157] In this piece, however, the flesh on both sides of the left ear is bare. In addition, the ear differs markedly in shape from ears of the Archaic period. With the ear of the kore, Acropolis 674, for example, the helix forms a high curve above the tragus, but in the ear of the Stymphalos head the helix curves downward immediately. Further, in the boy's head the deeply carved area of the ear's centre is wider than in Archaic ears, as in Acropolis 674.[158]

The head, body, and possibly the left leg and foot would have been carved as a separate piece. This mode of construction is indicated by the upper surface of the plinth, which contains continuous tool marks between the foot and the hands and no sign of breakage. The body may have been attached by means of the dowel hole in the centre of the plinth. Most sculptures of children in sitting/leaning positions are carved in one piece with the plinth, as with the seated figures from the healing sanctuary of Eschmun in Lebanon and the statue of a girl with a goose from Isthmia.[159] The Stymphalos boy may have been pieced because of a fault in the stone or a mistake in carving. The wide, irregular plinth was shaped to conform to the figure's pose and could have been inserted into an appropriate cutting in a statue base. Typically, lead would be used to secure such a sculpture to its base, perhaps assisted by a metal clamp.[160] If a clamp had been used in this case, the cutting for it would have been on the missing portion of the plinth in back. No block was found in the Temple with a cutting for a statue, and so either the statue base was removed later or the statue was set up on the Temple floor or possibly on the block set at an angle in the north side of the cella.

The type

The pose of the Stymphalos child is a variation on the popular type of seated boy. Many sculptures of this type have been found in temples or sanctuaries; hence, they have acquired the nickname "temple boy." Such young children are frequently represented sitting or crawling, but the Stymphalos figure combines the popular seated pose with one knee up and a sideways leaning position, the head looking upward. This pose may depict the child as it is about to walk, as on a red-figure pelike in London.[161] Many statues of children hold one or two objects, even when both hands are on the ground, but here the child's hands are empty.

One of the earliest examples of the seated male child in marble is a boy from the Eschmun Sanctuary at Sidon in Lebanon, whose pose approximates that of the Stymphalos child. This boy is stretched out on a plinth facing our right, with his right foot flat on the plinth pointing left and both hands on the plinth at right; the main difference is that the right foot faces the side, not the front, of the plinth.[162] The Sidon figure, which is draped from the waist down, is dated by its Phoenician inscription ca. 430–420 BCE.

On Cyprus, many examples of temple boys occur on a large scale in limestone, beginning in the late sixth century and extending through the Hellenistic period.[163] Comparable to the Stymphalos boy is a limestone figure from a temple at Kourion, which presents a similar pose in reverse: both hands rest on the ground (holding objects), the right leg, covered by drapery, is kneeling, and the left leg is stretched out to the side.[164] A limestone child in Nicosia reproduces the position of the Stymphalos figure's legs, in which the right foot is flat on the ground and the left leg is kneeling, but the torso is vertical and the hands were not on the ground.[165] Other limestone figures from Kourion have the right foot flat on the ground and the leg bent and on the ground in front, but both hands typically hold a pet.[166] The first two Cypriot figures mentioned are dated between the third quarter of the fourth and the early third centuries BCE.

The age of the Stymphalos child is probably nine months to one year, based on the plumpness of the neck, arms, and hands, which indicate that the subject is not yet walking. The proportions of the head and hand and the plumpness are similar to a baby boy from Ephesus, which Rühfel defines as barely one year old.[167] The lack of hair on the head is typical of children of this age, while children who are somewhat older, such as the youth from Lilaia, thought to be three to four years old, wears his hair cut short behind the ears.[168]

Marble sculptures of seated children are also popular in Attica. A nude seated-leaning boy comes from the Asklepieion in Athens, and a seated-leaning girl derives from the sanctuary of Eileithyia at Agrai by the Ilissos, dated to the late fourth to early third centuries BCE.[169] In addition, seated boys are cited from the Sanctuary of Artemis at Brauron, one occurs on Paros, and another in the Kavalla Museum derives from Himeros.[170] Few stone figures of temple boys are known from the Peloponnese, but one was found in the Sanctuary of Artemis at Lousoi in Arkadia.[171] Terracotta versions are popular at various sites in Greece, such as Rhodes and Corinth,[172] as well as in the west at Taranto and in the Malophoros Sanctuary at Selinus.[173] One of these was found in the Sanctuary, but a second may be an Eros rather than a temple boy (see figs. 3.43–4). In light of the popularity of marble statues of children of similar pose and style from Attica, the artist of the Stymphalos boy seems familiar with Attic production, but the use of Parian Lychnites marble may indicate that the workshop is Parian.

Date

The features that help determine the date of the Stymphalos child are the pose with both hands on the plinth, the plumpness, and the proportions and realistic features of the head. Sitting or crawling children that are supported by both hands are known from the mid-fifth century BCE, as illustrated by a bronze figurine from Delphi and a terracotta figurine from Corinth.[174] The pose is also paralleled by a terracotta from Olynthos, dated before 348 BCE.[175] Large, cubic heads and large features are displayed by the children from the Eschmun sanctuary in Sidon, dated from the late fifth to fourth centuries BCE. The cubic head, natural ear, and overall plumpness are also seen in the boy from the Athenian Asklepieion and the girl from the sanctuary of Eileithyia, already mentioned, from the later fourth to third centuries BCE, and in a baby boy with a goose from Ephesus, which is a second-century CE version of a third-century BCE sculpture.[176] Although the popularity of seated or crawling boy sculptures extends from the late fifth to the early third centuries BCE, the best comparisons for the Stymphalos boy's natural features and the pose with both hands on the plinth suggest a date in the mid- to late fourth century BCE.

Significance

Figures in temple boy format have appeared in sanctuaries, graves, and domestic contexts. They occur in sanctuaries of deities that are associated with children and are related to fertility and child care, such as Artemis, Asklepios, Demeter and Kore, Eileithyia, the Kabeirii at Thebes, Athena Lindia on Rhodes, and on Cyprus in sanctuaries of Aphrodite, Apollo Hylates, and the Mother of the Gods.[177] One terracotta figurine in the seated format has come to light near the Stymphalos acropolis Temple (fig. 3.43).[178] When statues of young boys are found in sanctuaries of Asklepios, they may be interpreted as the young Asklepios, but when found in sanctuaries of female deities, they appear to depict real children. In such contexts they may represent a prayer or thank offering for the birth or good health of a boy child.[179] It seems likely that the Stymphalos figure was set up in the acropolis Temple as a dedication to a female deity concerned with children.

THE STYMPHALOS SCULPTURES: CONCLUSIONS AND QUESTIONS

Destruction

The two sculptures found in the acropolis Temple were probably broken by the weight of the heavy roof tiles and collapsing mudbrick walls, and they were partially burned from proximity to the wooden elements of the temple (see fig. 3.45). The child has sustained significantly more calcification than the kore, and so it appears to have been closer to the hottest parts of the fire, or possibly some of the burning timbers of the building fell directly on it.

Much of the Temple debris was robbed out, probably long before the first mention of the Temple in the early nineteenth century. Similarly, parts of each statue were carried off, either as trophies, for reuse in building, or for burning in a lime kiln. In fact, the excavators noted that the fill beneath the destruction layer appeared churned up, since a mould-made bowl probably from the first quarter of the second century BCE was found on the Temple floor, and fourth- to third-century BCE pottery appeared at a higher level.[180]

The face of the hare appears to have broken off at its weakest point, along the line of the dowel. This could have occurred when the statue fell. As for the missing head of the kore, it may have been buried or thrown down an unused well or pit, an act that may be related to fear of incurring the wrath of a deity or of the spirit inhabiting the sculpture.[181] So, for example, at Isthmia the colossal upper torso of the figure of Amphitrite was abandoned where it had fallen, in the opisthodomos of the Temple of Poseidon, but the head had disappeared.[182] The eye from a colossal sculpture was thrown into one of the sacred pits in the adjoining sanctuary of Palaimon.[183] Likewise, three Roman heads from the sanctuary of Demeter and Kore on the slopes of Acrocorinth were found at the bottom of a well.[184] The head of the Stymphalos child has survived, possibly because it is so battered as to be almost unrecognizable as such.

Setting

Pieces from both statues were found inside the Temple cella, mostly in the southwest quadrant of the cella. Their find locations do not indicate their precise locations, but the cella is relatively small.[185] A large, nearly square base (L 0.64–7, W 0.59–62, H 0.23–5 m) was discovered in the cella next to a section of bedrock, located approximately in the centre of the room, which was roughly worked to form a flat surface.[186] The bedrock was cut down to about the upper level of the square block, and so the square block and the cut bedrock appear to have had a related function, but neither has setting lines or cuttings that might indicate a use as statue supports.[187] The square block is not aligned with the axis of the Temple, but is set at an angle to it, and it appears to have been wedged in as close to the bedrock as possible. If the statues had been set up on statue bases, these have long disappeared, but the form of bases for statues in temples has been shown to vary by region; thus, the original disposition remains unclear.[188]

The lower part of a finely worked stele was also found in the cella (L 0.19, W 0.18, p.H 0.41 m), north of the square base and amid a row of medium-sized stones.[189] The excavators have suggested that this stele may have served as an aniconic cult statue, and it may have rested on the nearly square base, or on the cella floor. The two statues may have been displayed inside the Temple as impressive votives, or the female statue may have been set up as a depiction of Artemis and the boy to symbolize a primary area of her concern. If the latter, the combined image is that of a kourotrophic deity. Other signs of such a deity have also been found in the acropolis sanctuary.[190] The possibility of the statue representing Eileithyia should also be considered.

A gold rosette, with parts of two gold spirals, dated to the late fourth to early third century BCE, was found near the back wall of the temple.[191] It has been proposed that it once formed part of a wreath or diadem.[192] It is tempting to suggest that this gold wreath formed part of the adornment that was added to the Archaic statue in its secondary phase of use. Whether a separate gift or an addition to the figure's costume in the later fourth century BCE, such a wreath may have helped identify the statue as a representation of the deity, much as wreaths and head decorations would have done in the Archaic period and in archaistic renderings.[193]

The size of the female figure would not be unusual for a cult statue in a small temple of the fourth century BCE. The fourth-century statue of Artemis from the Delion on Paros, for example, was found in the temple and is 1.28 m tall.[194] Notably, with the Paros temple there is also a disjunction between the date of the temple, ca. 550 BCE, and the date of the statue, ca. 360 BCE, though the chronological relationship is the reverse of that at Stymphalos. The statue on Paros is considered to be the cult statue, based on its find spot and the inscription on the base that records its dedication to Delian Artemis. Moreover, its archaizing features, such as the high polos, long hair locks, and lack of contraposto stance, underscore the idea that Archaic or archaizing features were considered appropriate for religious statues in the mid-fourth century BCE.

At least parts of the walls of the Temple were coated with plaster. Traces of red plaster show that the walls were painted, but not enough survives to indicate whether red was used as baseboard decoration or for the entire wall.[195]

Deity

Interpretation of the sculptures is related to the identification of the deity that was worshipped in the Stymphalos Temple and other deities worshipped within the Sanctuary. The presence of Athena is indicated by the fourth-century inscription with Poliados previously mentioned.[196] It was found, Orlandos says, near the "priests' house," now known as Building A, but it is not known whether it referred to the entire Sanctuary area or simply to the stele itself. Orlandos thought it identified the Sanctuary as Athena's.[197] The three partial inscriptions possibly referring to Eileithyia on small finds (mentioned above), one found just south of the Temple, one near the Altar, and one just east of the Terrace Wall, as well as the row of aniconic stelai, suggest that other deities were also worshipped in the Sanctuary. This information will be reviewed again to indicate its relevance to the sculpture under discussion.

Sources speak of a number of female deities at Stymphalos, without specifying particular locations. These include Artemis Brauronia, Artemis Stymphalia, Athena, Demeter, and Hera. Sanctuaries of Hera and of Stymphalian Artemis are mentioned by Pausanias in his section on Arkadia (8.22.2, 7). Artemis Brauronia at Stymphalos is mentioned in an inscription found at Stymphalos, published by Mitsos.[198] A second inscription, carved on two sides of a large stele, mentions a decree placed in the Artemision.[199] This stele, which was found near a Doric temple close to the "Byzantine basilica," led to an identification of the Doric temple as that of Artemis Stymphalia. A dedication to Demeter Stymphalia is recorded on a fifth-century BCE spear butt in Athens.[200] The lack of a certain location for worship of the other deities mentioned makes the presence of some of them (not Artemis Stymphalia) on the acropolis a possibility. In addition, as already mentioned, the stelai found west of Building A and in the cella may have functioned as representations of diverse deities.

Finds uncovered on the acropolis seem to indicate one or more female deities. Besides the large sculptures discussed above, objects found in the Temple include animal rim attachments from bronze mirrors. Many complete bronze mirrors from the late sixth to early fifth centuries have animals, like those from the Stymphalos Temple, attached to the rim.[201] Mirrors themselves are cited as gifts to Cyprian Aphrodite, and they appear in scenes that show the bride being adorned for her wedding.[202] In addition, a marble statuette of Aphrodite (no. **3**), which probably dates to the late fourth to early third century, was discovered inside the cella. Further, finds from Building A consist of many loomweights, which suggest a goddess that is associated with weaving. Athena Polias, usually connected to the Poliados inscription, is typically thought of as a war deity, but she also has other associations, such as weaving and the protection of heroes.[203] Finally, a coin with two letters pricked into its surface, a vase graffito, a loomweight with an incised letter, and a careful inscription on a bronze rim may record dedications to Eileithyia, the goddess of childbirth. These dedications recall the sanctuary of Eileithyia that Pausanias records at the nearby site of Kleitor (8.21.3).[204] In connection to finds from the Stymphalos acropolis, it is interesting that at Kleitor this deity is referred to as the "clever spinner" or "skilful weaver." In addition, many of the terracottas found on the Stymphalos acropolis depict female figures, and some holding doves indicate Aphrodite. Other figurines are "priestess types," but none have been identified as Artemis or Athena.[205] A significant amount of jewellery is also suggestive of a female deity.[206]

The Poliados inscription was found outside the Temple, but since it may represent one of several such stelai, it does not necessarily identify the deity of the Temple. This would not be the only temple for which the residing deity is unclear, even with the presence of an inscribed stele. At Paestum, for example, the worship of Hera in the sixth century BCE "Basilica" is made evident by the appearance of her name on a number of objects found in or near the temple. These include inscriptions on a silver disk, on pottery, on terracotta figurines representing the *hierogamia*, and on a silver object dedicated to Zeus. In the precinct, however, a large cippus found near the altar is inscribed vertically with the name Chironos. This inscription appears to indicate a cult, but not the deity of the temple.[207]

As we have seen, varied evidence suggests the worship of multiple deities on the Stymphalos acropolis. The hare carried by the female statue that stood in the cella, whether the statue functioned as a cult statue or a votive, suggests Artemis as a figure of worship in the Temple. In addition, animal bones found in the Sanctuary include those of young goats and wild boars, adult as well as newborn and young, and wild boar is not attested for Athena.[208] Hence, on several grounds, Artemis seems a likely deity for worship, and her location on the acropolis seems appropriate.[209] If this identification could be accepted, it would strengthen the thesis that the kore functioned as a cult statue in the fourth-century BCE Temple. Xenophon (*Cyn.* 5.14) even says that hunters leave the very young hares to the goddess, and he specifies that the deities that are associated with game and the hunt are Apollo and Artemis (*Cyn* 1.1). The major objection to this identification, however, is that the primary sanctuary for Artemis was located elsewhere in the city, where it was seen by Pausanias. Perhaps the hare, especially its early age, as well as the temple boy statue, is as indicative of the worship of Eileithyia as Artemis, but comparative evidence from cults of Eileithyia is scarce.

The cult of Artemis Brauronia is cited at Stymphalos in the inscription mentioned above, and so it seems appropriate to consider possible relationships between statues of Artemis in Athens, Brauron, and Stymphalos. From studying inscriptions from Brauron and the Athenian Acropolis, Despinis has shown that the statues mentioned therein refer to statuary in the sanctuary at Brauron rather than the one on the Acropolis, as had previously been thought.[210] Despinis has identified five fragmentary acrolithic statues (one of colossal size); four of these, which date to the fifth and fourth centuries BCE, are possible cult statues.[211] Thus far, no evidence for acrolithic sculpture has been located at Stymphalos, however.

CONCLUSION

The discovery of two marble sculptures in the Temple at Stymphalos makes an important contribution to our knowledge of the use and reuse of marble statuary in remote, mountainous areas of southern Greece. The female figure is a rare example of an Archaic kore found in the Peloponnese, an area in which free-standing marble sculpture from the Archaic and Early Classical periods is not common. The Stymphalos kore is an exponent of the delicate and decorative Attic-island style and an important transitional work from the Late Archaic to Early Classical period. The statue's hand-held offering, a hare, whether it is being given or received, relates this piece to Archaic marble statues from Samos that carry hares and to a substantial tradition of animal-bearers among Archaic terracotta figurines from the early fifth century BCE. It also establishes a link with female statues of Archaistic style in Rome holding quadrupeds, which may be directly inspired by such Archaic statues.

As with the kore, the temple boy was found in the Temple cella. Temple boys made of marble are rare in the Greek mainland, but a companion has been found at the Sanctuary of Artemis at Lousoi in Arkadia, west of Stymphalos. A sitting/leaning child made of marble is also uncommon in the Peloponnese, and it is a type with Attic and eastern connections. The statue of a boy helps characterize the deity of the acropolis Temple at Stymphalos as kourotrophic, and its find context inside the Temple indicates one function of such sculptural dedications, which may serve as a physical "prayer" as well as an attribute of a deity.[212] It also illustrates where such votive sculptures may be displayed. The two figures may be visualized as being displayed in the context of a small cella with brightly painted walls.

CATALOGUE

L	length
NB	notebook
GS	G. Schaus
S	sculpture
SF	small find
St.	storage
PH	preserved height
PL	preserved length
PTh	preserved thickness
PW	preserved width
W	width

1 Female figure (figs. 3.1–30)

Thirteen non-joining pieces of varying sizes can be associated with the statue of a draped female figure. The original height of the statue is estimated as ca. 1.40 m, based on comparison of the length of the right arm with the proportions of the kore Acropolis 685.[213] Comparison with the same statue yields a width at the shoulders for our figure of ca. 0.286 and ca. 0.424 m at the widest point. A reconstruction drawing, fig. 3.1, should help visualize the piece. All pieces were found in the Temple.

1A. Right shoulder and upper arm. **Figs. 3.2–4**
Temple, near west wall. Tr. 95.1.8.14, NB GS-Stym II 95, pp. 14, 15. SF 1995.61
PL 0.295; L upper arm and shoulder 0.238; W upper arm 0.074 m
Draped right shoulder and upper arm to elbow, including part of the chest, the back, and the hair hanging down the back; composed of two joining fragments, with some restoration at the join. The upper surfaces of the shoulder and back are heavily weathered and chipped, the lower areas of the arm are not. The conservator of the Corinth Excavations of the American School of Classical Studies, Stella Bouzaki, applied paraloid to the drapery on the back of the arm, where pigment may survive.

The figure wears three garments, each rendered in low relief, which are therefore difficult to distinguish. A veil or epiblema of a thin fabric was once wrapped around both shoulders. It is characterized as very thin by five low, ridged folds that are suspended from the right shoulder and appear to have crossed the back symmetrically (fig. 3.4). Part of the epiblema is pulled up about the neck, against which it rests in five closely stacked folds, which overlap the same garment at the shoulder. Over the upper arm one edge of the epiblema is folded upward and lies smoothly.

The subject also wears a short, Ionic himation that was draped diagonally across the torso. The diagonal arrangement is indicated by parts of three folds that are faintly visible near the neck, where they emerge from under the veil (fig. 3.2).

Part of the chiton sleeve is visible over the upper arm. This sleeve does not have crinkly folds, but lies smoothly across the arm in front. It has four wide folds in back, and appears to have ended in a V pattern shortly beneath the elbow. The arm and shoulder are naturally modelled.

In back, long, unbound hair hangs over the himation in loose waves, rendered as thin ridges. No locks appear on the chest. A small dowel hole (W 0.001, D 0.003 m) above the breast denotes an attachment.

Some painted decoration is preserved on the chiton folds on the back of the arm. Traces of a row of triangles appear in one area and curvilinear elements filled with dots in another. A white area on the flat portion of the chiton sleeve may be surrounded by a reddish yellow area, Munsell 7/5 YR 6/6. The hair, which is heavily weathered, has a reddish-yellow tone similar to that of the upper back. Indeed, much of the fragment has a reddish-yellow colour, which may derive from the soil.

1B. Left shoulder. **Fig. 3.5**
Temple, near west wall. Tr. 95.1.5. SF 1995.21
PH 0.075; PW 0.087; PTh. 0.029 m
Two joining fragments, preserving part of a draped shoulder. Part of the surface is grey, the rest is reddish brown, Munsell 7.5 YR 7/6.

Three narrow folds in low relief cross the outer portion of the left shoulder along the upper edge of the piece. The folds probably derive from the thin epiblema that is wrapped around the shoulders, as shown on **1A**. Dots from a painted pattern may survive near the folds, possibly from the edges of the sleeve.[214]

1C. Left breast. **Fig. 3.6**
Temple, near west wall. Tr. 95.1.8.14. SF 1995.60
PL 0.096; PW 0.068; PTh. 0.023 m
Single fragment, preserving most of a breast. The surface is grey and white from exposure to burning; cracked near one edge and missing a few chips.

The small, pointed breast is the figure's left, as indicated by the side of the torso which curves back towards the underarm. Four folds of a relatively thick garment, probably the himation, hang vertically, one folded backward. The folds vary in width from 0.01 to 0.019 m, widening towards the centre of the chest. The nipple is rendered through the drapery. Two drill holes (D 0.001, PL 0.008 m) occur at the upper break. These holes appear too small to attach marble locks of hair, and so they probably attached objects by means of metal pins.[215] The hole at proper right is surrounded by a dark circle. The area around the holes is not roughened or concave, as would be the case for a marble attachment. Shadows from painted decoration may survive; in the fold at proper right a row of squares with central dots is suggested.[216]

1D. Left arm. **Figs. 3.7–9**
Temple, 3.76 m from east wall. Tr. 95.1, surface, NB GS Stym II 95, p. 6. SF 1995.1
PL forearm 0.134; PL upper arm 0.104; arm at elbow: Th. 0.068, W 0.063 m
Single fragment, preserving part of draped upper arm and forearm, and missing a large chip from the outer side of the elbow. Outside of forearm and break are heavily weathered and chipped.

The left arm, bent at the elbow, was held relatively close to the torso. The garment it wears is less well preserved than that on **1A**, but the conformation is similar, and so the fabric here can be identified as a chiton. The chiton sleeve lies smoothly across the inside of the elbow. In back, three straight folds (W 0.013–0.022 m) extend to the elbow, where the drapery is undercut with a small drill.

1E. Left hand holding an animal. **Figs. 3.10–15**
Inv. 0856, St. S 0045, finger section. Temple. NB GS-Stym II 96, Tr. 95.4+1.2.2. SF 1995.59
Left hand, palm section. Temple, near west wall, Tr. 95.1.8.14. SF 1995.68
Inv. 0708, St S 0007, thumb and animal. Temple. Haunch, near west wall, Tr. 95.1.5. SF 1995.23; body, Stym II.96, Tr. 95.4+1.2.4. SF 1996.249; neck, Tr. 95.4+1, 1996, near southwest corner of cella
PL hand and wrist (if it were straight) 0.17; L hand from wrist 0.12; L third finger 0.064; Max. W palm 0.064 m
PL animal 0.125; L torso 0.101; Max. W 0.042 m
Six joining fragments. Most of left hand in three joining segments, tip of thumb and first finger chipped; restoration in cracks; palm blackened from fire. Reddish-yellow substance, Munsell 7.5 YR 7/6, that resembles paint remains on fingertips and the animal's forepaws.
Animal: most of the figure is preserved in three joining sections, missing front of head, end of tail, and chips from the haunches. The right side is black, the head grey from exposure to fire. The upper and right surfaces are weathered, the left are not. Dark discolouration at the mouth of the vertical dowel hole shows the effect of weathering and corrosion of the metal pin. A red vertical line above the tail and a short diagonal line to left of the tail remain from painted decoration, both Munsell 5 YR 4/6.

A woman's left hand is open and the fingers, long and delicately modelled, curve upward, loosely holding an animal. The inside of the figure's wrist was probably level, the forearm straight or slightly raised near the hand. The elbow was probably held relatively close to the torso in order to help support the animal's weight. The crevices between the fingers are worked with a fine chisel as a V-shaped channel. The nails are wider at the tip than the base. Two deep creases mark the first digit of the thumb, but the digits of the fingers are not incised. The outside of the hand is carefully smoothed, as if it would have been seen.

A quadruped is perched on the hand, turning its head three-quarters to proper right. The animal sits on the palm, is partially supported by the figure's thumb, and curls its forepaws, with individually rendered toes, over the tips of the statue's fourth and fifth fingers. The animal's ears were made as a separate piece and attached by a vertical metal dowel (L 0.017, D 0.005 m) and secured by a metal cross-pin (PL 0.01, D 0.002 m). The back of the rectangular jaw is slightly raised from the neck. Part of the left side of the face and the junction with the chin is preserved. The tip of the tail, which emerges from the lower part of the rear end, is missing. The long, narrow body and forelegs as well as the inside of the hand are carefully modelled and smoothed.

1F. Fragment of hanging drapery. **Fig. 3.16**
Inv. 0709, St. S 0008-B. Temple. Stym II.96, Tr. 95.4+1.2.2. SF 1996.126
PL 0.085; PW 0.061; Th. 0.018 m
Segment of hanging folds, broken on three sides. Surface somewhat greyed, whitened along the worked edge from burning; edge of one fold missing a long chip.

Hanging drapery with four narrow folds of a himation on the front. The back is smoothly finished, and so the piece would have hung free. The edges of the folds retain traces of reddish-yellow pigment, Munsell 7/5 YR 6/6, possibly in decorative patterns.

1G. Segment of two swallowtail folds. **Fig. 3.17**
Temple
PL 0.17; PW 0.13; PTh. 0.042 m
Five joining fragments with segment of hanging folds. Some edges are chipped and discoloured from exposure to fire. The marble of this piece was analysed to determine its provenance (see note 3).

Large segment of drapery with two overlapping edges of a himation, hanging symmetrically in overlapping folds, narrowing to a missing tip or swallowtail fold. The curve of the piece reflects the right side of the figure, and so only part of the fragment would have been visible in front. The centres of the folds appear soft and undulate gradually. The soft undulation resembles that of the undulating folds on the draped legs, **1I**. One side of the fragment is heavily weathered, the other is not. This piece was probably located directly above the missing right knee of **1I**, and the folds would have curved around the side of the right thigh.

Traces of a reddish-yellow pigment, Munsell 7/5 YR 6/6, may survive in the centres of the two lowest folds, possibly indicating scattered rosettes or larger floral designs.

1H. Segment of hanging drapery. **Fig. 3.18**
Temple, near west wall. Inv. 0709, St. S 0008-A. One section: Tr. 95.1.8.13. SF 1995.54; second section: Stym II.96, Tr. 95.4+1.2.2. SF 1996.126
PL 0.188; PW 0.08; Th. 0.017 m
Segment of hanging drapery composed of five joining fragments, broken at top and on right side, the edges of some folds chipped. Surfaces are white, grey, and reddish-yellow.

Lengthwise section from the himation, smooth in back, which would have hung free from the statue. It contains four stacked folds to viewer's right and one to left of a central pleat. A zigzag lower edge is partially preserved. The piece resembles **1F** and **1G**. This group can probably be restored hanging at the figure's left. A painted line appears to indicate the hem along the lower edge and along one side of the central pleat. One or two grey areas on the central pleat may reflect scattered patterns, possibly in the form of rosettes.

1I. Draped legs. **Figs. 3.19–22**
Temple, near west wall. Tr. 95.1. 1995
PL 0.278; W top 0.214; W bottom 0.197; Th. upper right side 0.141; Th. left side 0.112 m
Seven joining fragments, preserving the draped lower legs. The front surface of the left leg is chipped off from above the knee to just above the ankle, and a large section of the projecting right knee is missing. Part of the front surface is blackened, the back is not.

Preserved are the legs from the knees to the ankles draped in a chiton, the thicker right side showing that the right leg was advanced. Small sections of folds have been split off the front of the left leg. Folds over the side of the right leg are sharp-edged, resulting from the forward position of the right knee; the undulating folds over the left leg hang vertically at the side. The fold lines show that the right hand did not pull the drapery back or up from the right leg. Correspondingly, the central fold, *paryphe*, flanked by two narrower folds, hangs vertically, widening towards the bottom. The paryphe is flat, with slightly tubular edges.

In back, the drapery is characterized by soft, gradual undulations. One projecting segment is pulled to the left from bottom to top. No fold edges are depicted on the back, so the thicker area represents a raised swath of material that flows behind the figure.

1J. Fragment of hanging drapery. **Figs. 3.23 and 3.24**
Temple. Inv. 0852, St. S 0042. Stym II 96, Tr. 95.4+1.4.4. SF 1995.66
PL 0.054; PW 0.05; Th. 0.157 m
Single fragment of drapery, broken on three sides. Surfaces are greyed, and the worked edge is white from calcification.

Fragment of drapery with folds carved on both sides. The piece derives from a projecting segment of drapery that has three relatively flat, straight folds on one side, and three narrower, curved folds of a lighter material on the other. The garment on one side derives from the hanging edges of the himation, while the garment on the other side probably represents the edge of the veil; hence, the piece was located just beneath the (right) arm. The curve of the veil suggests that this piece, and the other hanging folds that have smooth backs and similar thickness, **1F** and **1H,** derive from the sides of the statue.[217]

1K. Fragment of hanging drapery. **Fig. 3.25**
Inv. 860 P1. Temple. Tr. 1996.111.1 (NE cella)
PL 0.043; PW 0.042 m
Single fragment with three drapery folds on the front face, smoothly finished on back.

These regular folds come from a garment hanging freely at the figure's side, because the back side is worked. The curve of an adjacent fold is preserved next to the break. This piece may derive from the end of the mantle hanging under the figure's right (?) arm.

1L. Fragment of hanging drapery. **Fig. 3.26**
Temple
PL 0.07; PW 0.083; PTh. 0.033 m
Single fragment of hanging drapery with parts of two fold systems, broken vertically from the statue at back. Edges of folds chipped and discoloured.

The fragment contains part of a wide, overlapping fold next to the lower edge of a smaller, stacked fold. The piece has a slight curve, as if it derives from the side of the statue's front. The wider fold resembles the folds on **1H,** and so it probably comes from the himation, possibly below the arm and close to **1H**. The surfaces undulate vertically within the fold.

1M. Fragment of mantle. **Fig. 3.27**
Inv. 860c. Temple. Tr. 1996.11.1.1 (NE cella)
PL 0.095; PW 0.058 m
Single fragment, broken all around.

This piece seems to derive from the hanging folds of a heavy garment such as a himation. Although its length corresponds to the gap above the figure's right knee, the horizontal upper break precludes its connection with that part of the statue. It probably represents a tip of the mantle hanging farther back on the figure's right side.

1N. Small segment of overlapping fold. **Fig. 3.28**
Temple
PL 0.083; PW 0.058; PTh. 0.015 m
Single piece, broken vertically at back, preserving the end of one fold. Edges chipped, surfaces weathered.

This broad fold resembles the overlapping folds of a himation, as on **1H**, and it probably stems from the same segment of hanging drapery. Within the fold, the surface undulates vertically.

1O. Small segment of overlapping fold. **Fig. 3.29**
Temple
PL 0.079; PW 0.048; PTh. 0.012 m
Two joining fragments, broken vertically at back, with the end of one fold. Edges chipped, surfaces weathered.

This wide fold resembles the overlapping folds of a himation, like those of **1H**, and it probably formed part of the same fall of drapery. The fold surface undulates vertically. A light brown substance that remains over much of the surface is possibly residue from pigment, Munsell 7.5 YR 6/6.

1P. Fragment, possibly drapery. **Fig. 3.30**
Inv. 882. Temple. Tr. 95.4+1.2.5
PL 0.023; PW 0.022 m
Small piece from a marble statue, preserving two and a half folds of a fine garment.

In this piece the slightly roughened surface contains faintly worked zigzags. These zigzags are tighter than the more elongated zigzags of the kore's hair. Thus, this pattern, together with the roughened surface, is more suggestive of the crinkly material of the chiton, such as the folds that lie bunched together around the shoulders.

Bibliography: Williams, Cronkite Price and Schaus 1996, 80–3, pls. 4 (fragments of the statue), 5 (hand with animal); Williams et al. 1997, 49, pl. 4 (draped legs); Williams et al. 1998, 297, pl. 8, previous reconstruction (note that this preliminary reconstruction was done as a photo montage and a number of inaccuracies have been changed in the present reconstruction: notably, the left arm and hand, **1D**, **1E**, now face forward, the large draped segment, **1F**, has been lowered from the thighs to the lower legs, and the lowest drapery section, **1I**, which is carved on the back, has been treated as hanging drapery); Williams and Schaus 2001, 85; Williams et al. 2002, 151.

2 Statue of a male child, "Temple boy" (figs. 3.31–41)

Eight non-joining pieces remain from a male child. Both hands and the right foot were carved in one piece with the plinth, but the head-and-body section was attached separately. The maximum width of the figure with its plinth is estimated as ca. 0.52 m, the figure's height, in its sitting/leaning pose, ca. 0.35–0.40 m.

2A. Head. **Figs. 3.31–3**
Temple, near west wall. Tr. 95.1.5. SF 1995.22
PH 0.101; W 0.121; PTh. 0.085; W head behind ears 0.105; ear: L 0.041, W 0.025 m
Single fragment of a head, preserving the left ear and small portions of the left, right, and rear surfaces. The broken surfaces are heavily weathered and damaged from burning; the edge of the ear is white from calcification; the outer surface of the helix is chipped.

Part of a head survives, including the left ear, part of the cheek, and the outline of the back of the right ear. The head is short and square, and the line of the break above the left ear probably reflects the hairline. The ear is natural in proportions and rendering; the interior is relatively deep and simple, and the three drill holes that shape it are smoothly hollowed out. The neck behind the ears has no hair, and the back of the head has little hair, if any. The roll of flesh on the right side indicates that the head was turned upward and twisted to proper right, and the horizontal crease on the left of the neck suggests that this side of the neck was stretched.

2B. Fragment of neck or torso. **Figs. 3.34 and 3.35**
Temple. Tr. 95.4+1.2.2. SF 1996.96
PH 0.053; W 0.126; PTh. 0.059 m
Single fragment from a nude figure. Surface greyed and calcified from exposure to burning.

Fragment with preserved surfaces on opposite sides. It may derive from the neck, with the depression between the clavicles at the front and a horizontal crease at the back. There is no hair at the back, so this piece comes from the child, rather than the female figure. It might be located at the neck, but the more likely location may be an area near the lower torso/buttocks segment, **2C**, since the thickness of this fragment corresponds, although it does not join. The crease would then belong to the child's plump legs or to a fatty section of the torso, and the indented area to the front or side.

2C. Buttocks and left thigh. **Figs. 3.36 and 3.37**
Temple, near west wall. Tr. 95.1.8.13. SF 1995.53
PL 0.162; PW 0.15; PTh. 0.107 m
Single fragment of nude anatomy, broken irregularly on top and bottom; front surface badly abraded. The back is white from calcification; broken edges are heavily weathered.

Preserved is a portion of a nude figure, possibly from the buttocks and left thigh, with no trace of genitalia. A small depression on the front of the left thigh may indicate an indentation at the base of the thigh that results from its being outstretched. No trace of a dowel hole remains for attachment to a plinth. A crease between the legs rises to mark the left side of the groin. The left thigh was down, as if the figure was kneeling on the left knee or crouching. Creases in back mark the vertical separation and lower outline of the buttocks.

2D. Fragment of a limb. **Fig. 3.38**
Temple, near west wall. Tr. 95.1.8.13. SF 1995.48
PL 0.038; W 0.049; PTh. 0.042 m
Single fragment of a limb, broken diagonally at both ends. The surface has a brown residue on one side, possibly from pigment, Munsell 7.5 YR 5/4. The remaining surfaces are white from calcification.

A portion of an arm survives from a small figure. The brown substance on one side, which is aligned with a shallow groove, emphasizes the child's fleshy arm. This non-joining piece represents the left forearm, including the crease at the elbow.

2E. Fragment of curved skin. **Fig. 3.39**
Temple, near west wall. Tr. 95.1.8.14. SF 1995.73
PL 0.092; PW 0.088; PTh. 0.028 m
Single fragment, broken around a curved surface, vertically at back, worked surface is cracked near one end. Surface somewhat greyed; possible traces of reddish-yellow pigment, Munsell 7.5 YR 7/6.

A portion of a broadly curving skin surface remains, possibly from the child's face or torso. Undulations of the surface are suggestive of the area under the chin, a depression around the edge of the mouth, or possibly a location on a nude torso. The broad, continuous curve seems more appropriate for the child than for the female figure.

2F. Plinth fragment. **Figs. 3.40 and 3.41**
Temple. Tr. 95.4+1.2.2. SF 1996.120
PL 0.124; PW 0.097; Th. 0.045 at break to 0.026 at end
Single fragment, broken at an angle. Surface greyed.

The piece preserves the curved, left end of the plinth. The upper surface has a scar indicating where a long, narrow object has broken away. This scar may represent a thin edge of drapery (L 0.075, W 0.015 m), such as a small cloak, that trails on the ground behind the child, or the lower edge of a toy or animal.

2G. Right arm, right hand, right foot on plinth. **Figs. 3.40 and 3.41**
Temple. Arm. Inv. 0858, St. S 0046. Stym II.96, Tr 95.4+1.2.4. SF 1995.56
Plinth section with toes. Inv. 0864, St. S 0048. Temple. Stym II 96, Tr. 95.4+1.2.2. SF 1995.120
Plinth with left part of hole (23). Inv. 0858, St. S 0046. 1995
Right hand. Temple. Tr. 95.1.8. 1995
Plinth: PL 0.377; W 0.226; H 0.034 front, 0.048 rear; hand: PL 0.088; W 0.054; foot: PL 0.124; W 0.054; D hole in plinth 0.01 m
Most of a plinth, in eight joining pieces, and part of the adjoining statue, including the right hand, right forearm, and right foot. The marble of this piece was analysed to determine its provenance (see note 3).

Right hand, forearm, and right foot from the statue of a young child, carved in one piece with the plinth. The open right hand rests flat on the plinth, and the plump forearm rises sharply at the wrist. The right foot faces forward, and the heel is flat on the plinth. There is no trace of the left leg or foot.

The upper part of the statue was possibly attached by the dowel cutting in the plinth. Within 0.03 m of the left front edge, beside the right hand and behind the right heel, the upper surface of the plinth is carefully smoothed. The central area has a worked surface, but it has tooling that is set at a sharp diagonal to the front edge, which differs in direction and smoothness from the rest. This roughly tooled area provides the approximate size and shape of the figure's lower body, L 0.27, W 0.14 m.

2H. Left hand on plinth. **Figs. 3.40 and 3.41**
Temple, near west wall. Tr. 95.1.8.14. SF 1995.67
Hand: PL 0.076; W 0.057; plinth: PL 0.086; PW 0.080; Th. 0.037 m
Single, non-joining fragment, with left hand broken through the wrist, carved on the plinth. The hand and edge of the plinth are white from calcification due to intense heat.

The left hand is open and rests flat on the plinth, with the fingers curving over the edge. The missing forearm would have risen sharply at the wrist just before the break. The short proportions and fleshy, dimpled knuckles are those of a young child.[218]

Bibliography: Williams, Cronkite Price and Schaus 1996, 81 (head), 83, 84, pl. 6 (plinth with two hands and right foot) 84 (buttocks, referred to as possibly from a kouros); Williams and Schaus 2001, 85, 86; Williams et al. 2002, 151.

3 Fragmentary figurine of Aphrodite (fig. 3.42)

3. Fragmentary figurine of Aphrodite. **Fig. 3.42**
Inv. 0854, St. S 0043. SF 1996.75
Found 29 June 1996, in Stym II 96. Tr. 95.4 +1.2.2
A. Base: PH 0.049; PW 0.061; Th. 0.046 m
B. Right leg, joins at back of leg (not mended): PL 0.047; W 0.016; Th. 0.23 m
Marble, white, medium grained, probably Parian. Heavily greyed and calcined from proximity to fire. A. Left leg broken below knee, missing front of calf and foot; front of base broken away; B. Right leg broken through ankle and knee and vertically at back.

Base and lower legs of a marble figurine depicting a standing Aphrodite. Folds of a long himation hang behind the goddess, leaving the legs bare. The figure's legs are positioned somewhat apart, with the left leg, which is farther back, acting as the weight leg, the right leg, in a forward position, being the free leg. Such a configuration occurs in several types of Aphrodite statues of Hellenistic to Roman date, e.g., the Aphrodite Syracuse type and the related Aphrodite from Italica type. The Stymphalos figurine is too fragmentary to be certain of the type.[219] At Corinth a marble figurine of a nude Aphrodite is similarly set off by the backdrop of a hanging mantle. The Corinthian figure, which was found in a well, is dated by its context to the Hellenistic period, which also seems appropriate for the Stymphalos piece.[220]
Date: early Hellenistic: late fourth to early third century BCE.

4

Coins[1]

Robert Weir

Canadian excavations in the Sanctuary on the acropolis at Stymphalos between 1994 and 2000 uncovered 98 coins of silver, bronze, and iron that range in date from the fifth century BCE through the twelfth century CE.[2] After cleaning and conservation, over 90% of the coins were legible, and even some illegible ones were attributable in a general way. Study of the Sanctuary coins begins with an inclusive catalogue and continues with brief discussions of interesting features and individual details. It concludes with some observations about the usefulness of the coins for interpreting the life of the Sanctuary in general.

CATALOGUE

The catalogue has been arranged in the traditional order for Greek numismatics, namely a geographical progression from west to east, then north to south, with further subdivisions by chronology in the case of coins of the same city or dynast. Most categories of information are self-explanatory, though a few points are worth clarifying.

- Catalogue numbers have been given the format **II-xx** so that future publications of the coins from other parts of Stymphalos (Stym **I** and **III** through **XV**) can easily fit into the same scheme.
- Although ongoing scholarship is gradually clarifying the face values represented by Greek bronzes, I have not ventured to suggest denominations in all cases.
- Sizes and weights are given in millimetres and grams respectively.
- Die-axis ("Axis") is the relative orientation of one face of a coin to the other expressed as a position on a clock face (e.g., 3, or three o'clock, equals a rotation of 90° to the right from obverse to reverse, or from reverse to obverse). The die-axis of any one coin is insignificant, but this information is supplied as an aid to future researchers who might want to test specific issues for consistency of production. For instance, the fact that Phlious seems to have struck its coins so that the orientation of one side relative to the other was always some multiple of 90° allows for the possibility that obverse and reverse dies were routinely hinged together.
- Because a coin's degree of wear is in some fashion proportionate to its circulating life,[3] the number of years that elapsed between its striking and its joining the archaeological record, I give a rough assessment of this characteristic under the rubric of "Wear." The abbreviations here denoting wear are the same as those used by numismophiles worldwide; they run in the following descending order: EF (=Extremely Fine, i.e., mint state, or virtually so), VF (=Very Fine), F (=Fine), VG (=Very Good), G (=Good), and P (=Poor, i.e., worn practically smooth). The letter "a" (=about) before a grade indicates that the coin's condition falls a little short of the standard, but the symbol "+" after the grade indicates the opposite: thus, for instance, aF, "about Fine," falls in the low end of the Fine range, but F+, "Fine plus," is one step below aVF, "about Very Fine." Two different grades separated by a slash denote the different conditions of obverse and reverse sides respectively.
- Stratigraphic data is included for each coin, but two concordances placed immediately after the Catalogue furnish cross-references to both this information and excavation catalogue numbers.[4]

- Wherever possible, there are multiple references for each coin because not all readers will have access to all works. In such a list the first work to be cited is the preferred reference, either because it is the most recent, most authoritative, or both.
- All illustrations have been enlarged to 300% of actual size to show details better.

Sicily: Syracuse (1)

Date: 410–400 BCE

II-1 Denom.: hemilitron. Metal & Size: Æ 18. Weight: 3.2. Die-Axis: 5. **Fig. 4.1**
Wear: VF. Inv. 2261. SF 1999.98, 17/07/99. Tr. 99.6.1.1
Obverse: female head to left, hair in sphendone; behind, spray of olive
Reverse: dolphin leaping to right above scallop-shell; ΣΥΡ̣Α̣ between
Reference: Calciati 1986, 55–8, no. 24; *Agora* XXVI, no. 425; *SNG Copenhagen* no. 697–9; *BMC 2* no. 301
Notes: Pottery context fourth to second century BCE

Macedonian Kingdom: Alexander III (1)

Date: 336–323 BCE

II-2 Denom.: —. Metal & Size: Æ 20. Weight: 7.2. Die-Axis: 12
Wear: F+/aVF. Inv. 2899. SF 2000.52, 25/06/00. Tr. 00.2.3.3
Obverse: head of beardless Herakles to right wearing a lion's skin
Reverse: ΑΛΕΞΑΝΔΡ̣Ο̣Υ̣ across field; above, club to right; below, bow in case; in upper field, K on its side
Reference: sim. Price 1991, no. 316 (slightly different symbol);[5] sim. *Agora* XXVI, no. 490–1
Notes: Pottery context fourth century BCE

Macedonian Kingdom: Kassander, as king (3)

Date: 305–297 BCE

II-3 Denom.: —. Metal & Size: Æ 20. Weight: 4.3. Die-Axis: 11
Wear: G+. Inv. 439. SF 1996.356, 16/07/96. Tr. 96.95.6 ext.1.1
Obverse: head of beardless Herakles to right wearing a lion's skin
Reverse: jockey on horse stepping to right; no lettering visible
Reference: *SNG Copenhagen* no. 1142–53;[6] *Agora* XXVI, no. 500

II-4 Denom.: —. Metal & Size: Æ 19. Weight: 5.1. Die-Axis: 12
Wear: aG/G. Inv. 1150. SF 1997.191, 08/07/97. Tr. 97.4.4.6
Obverse: as **II-3**
Reverse: as **II-3**
Reference: as **II-3**
Notes: Pottery context 350–200/150 BCE

II-5 Denom.: —. Metal & Size: Æ 19. Weight: 4.8. Die-Axis: 9. **Fig. 4.1**
Wear: VG/aF. Inv. 2291. SF 1999.109, 20/07/99. Tr. 99.1.4.4
Obverse: as **II-3**
Reverse: as **II-3**, but [B]AS[ILEΩS / KASSANΔPOY] and Λ or A beneath horse
Reference: *SNG Copenhagen* no. 1147; *Agora* XXVI, no. 500a
Notes: Pottery context fourth to second century BCE

Macedonian Kingdom: Demetrios Poliorketes (2)

Date: ca. 300–295 BCE

II-6 Denom.: —. Metal & Size: Æ 14. Weight: 2.6. Die-Axis: 9. **Fig. 4.1**
Wear: VF. Inv. 1085. SF 1997.155, 04/07/97. Tr. 97.4, L 3, P 4
Obverse: beardless male head (Demetrios?) wearing crested Corinthian helmet to right
Reverse: prow of galley to right; BA above; double-headed axe to right; AP monogram below
Reference: *SNG Copenhagen* no. 1185 ("Carian mint?", 306–285 BCE);[7] *SNG Alpha Bank* 956–61 (Carian mint, after 290 BCE); Newell 1926, 149, no. 163, pl. xvii.2 (Carian [?] mint, before 294 BCE)
Notes: Pottery context late fourth century to 150 BCE

II-7 Denom.: —. Metal & Size: Æ 14. Weight: 3.1.Die-Axis: —
Wear: aF. Inv. 2449. SF 1999.208, 28/07/99. Tr. 99.1.5.8
Obverse: as **II-6**
Reverse: as **II-6**, but no monogram or symbol visible
Reference: probably as **II-6**

Epeiros: Korkyra (1)

Date: 300–229 BCE

II-8 Denom.: —. Metal & Size: Æ 14. Weight: 1.6. Die-Axis: 12
Wear: aG. Inv. 559. SF 1996.537, 24/07/96. Tr. 96.5 ext, 6.9
Obverse: forepart of cow standing to right
Reverse: bunch of grapes; Ϙ to right
Reference: probably as *SNG Copenhagen* no. 178–9 (Σ - Ω in reverse fields)
Notes: Pottery context fourth to third century BCE

Thessaly: the Ainianes (1)

Date: late fourth century BCE

II-9 Denom.: hemidrachmon. Metal & Size: AR 15. Weight: 2.6. Die-Axis: 11. **Fig. 4.1**
Wear: VF+. Inv. 2535. SF 1999.270B, 31/07/99. Tr. 99.13.2.2
Obverse: laureate head of Zeus to left
Reverse: AINIAN / ΩN; facing warrior, his body leaning to the left and looking to the right, hurls javelin with his right hand while holding a *petasos* (or small shield?) in his left hand[8]
Reference: *SNG Copenhagen* no. 1, *SNG Dewing* no. 1376, *SNG Lockett III* no. 1545, *Agrinion* nos. 150–51; sim. *BMC* 7 no. 1
Notes: This coin was found bonded to **II-48** in a bedrock crevice near the Altar, along with **II-35** and **II-53**; see also **II-12** and **II-49**. Pottery context 350–250 BCE

Boiotia: Boiotian League (Thespiai?) (1)

Date: 338–315 BCE

II-10 Denom.: hemidrachmon. Metal & Size: AR 14. Weight: 2.5. Die-Axis: 5/11. **Fig. 4.1**
Wear: EF. Inv. 2889. SF 2000.37, 23/06/00. Tr. 00.3.2.2
Obverse: Boiotian shield with no ornamentation
Reverse: BO - I on either side of kantharos; club above; bunch of grapes to right

Reference: *Agrinion* no. 129; sim. *SNG Copenhagen* no. 174 (B – OI, 338–315 BCE); sim. *SNG Dewing* nos. 1508–9 (BOIΩ, no grapes 379–371 BCE);[9] sim. *BMC* 8 no. 36
Notes: Pottery context late fourth to late second century BCE

Opuntian Lokris: Lokrian League (Opous) (1)

Date: 338–300 BCE

II-11 Denom.: —. Metal & Size: Æ 13. Weight: 1.7. Die-Axis: 12. **Fig. 4.1**
Wear: aVF. Inv. 2611. SF 1999.335, 05/08/99. Tr. 99.1.5.10
Obverse: head of Athena in crested Corinthian helmet to right
Reverse: ΛOK / PΩN; bunch of grapes
Reference: *Agora* XXVI, no. 581; *BMC* 8 nos. 57–68
Notes: Pottery context 350–300 BCE

Euboia: Chalkis (3)

Date: 338–308 BCE

II-12 Denom.: drachme. Metal & Size: AR 16. Weight: 3.5. Die-Axis: 12. **Fig. 4.1**
Wear: VF+/aVF. Inv. 2612. SF 1999.333, 05/08/99. Tr. 99.13.3.3
Obverse: head of Hera with rolled hair to right
Reverse: ҲAΛ (retrograde); as last, but with TH monogram above eagle
Reference: Picard 1979, 32–41, no. 8 (die combination 76co);[10] *Agrinion* no. 89–99; *SNG Dewing* no. 1537; *SNG Lockett III* no. 1786
Notes: This coin perhaps belongs to the same hoard as **II-9**, **II-35**, **II-48**, **II-53**, and **II-49**.

II-13 Denom.: —. Metal & Size: Æ 13. Weight: 1.6. Die-Axis: 6
Wear: F+. Inv. 364. SF 1996.138, 02/07/96. Tr. 96.95.6.5.8
Obverse: facing head of Hera, wearing diadem surmounted by five disks
Reverse: ҲAΛ, eagle flying to right, carrying snake in talons and beak; symbol not visible
Reference: Picard 1979, 46–54, nos. 31–41;[11] *Agora* XXVI, no. 616; *SNG Copenhagen* no. 443 (369–313 BCE)

II-14 Denom.: —. Metal & Size: Æ 12. Weight: 1.5. Die-Axis: 3
Wear: aF. Inv. 372. SF 1996.135, 30/06/96. Tr. 96.3.2.3
Obverse: as **II-13**
Reverse: as **II-13**, but ҲA[Λ]
Reference: Picard 1979, 46–54, nos. 12–22; *Agora* XXVI, no. 616; *SNG Copenhagen* no. 443 (369–313 BCE)
Notes: Pottery context sixth century BCE to first century CE

Euboia: Histiaia (2)

Date: 338–late third century BCE

II-15 Denom.: —. Metal & Size: Æ 14. Weight: 2.1. Die-Axis: 9
Wear: VF+. Inv. 3247. SF 2000.209, 08/07/00. Tr. 00.4.7.7
Obverse: head of Maenad or nymph Histiaia to right, her hair wreathed with vine and rolled; star behind
Reverse: IΣTI; forepart of cow standing to right; caduceus above
Reference: *Agora* XXVI, no. 629; sim. *SNG Copenhagen* no. 510 (whole cow standing before grapevine, 369–338 BCE) and *BMC 8* nos. 10–20
Notes: Pottery context early fifth to late fourth century BCE

II-16 Denom.: —. Metal & Size: Æ 14. Weight: 2.8. Die-Axis: 12. **Fig. 4.1**
Wear: VF. Inv. 3274. SF 2000.216, 12/07/00. Tr. 00.4.7.7

Obverse: as **II-15**, but no star
Reverse: as **II-15**
Reference: as **II-15**
Notes: Pottery context early fifth to late fourth century BCE

Attica: Salamis (1)

Date: 350–318 BCE[12]

II-17 Denom.: chalkous.[13] Metal & Size: Æ 13. Weight: 2.7. Die-Axis: 10. **Fig. 4.1**
Wear: VG+. Inv. 405. SF 1996.258, 10/07/96. Tr. 96.5 ext.3.4
Obverse: head of Demeter or Kore to right, wreathed with wheat
Reverse: ΣΑΛΑ; shield of Ajax
Reference: *Agora* XXVI, no. 642; *BMC 11* no. 9; sim. *SNG Copenhagen* no. 455 (dichalkon, 400–330 BCE)
Notes: Pottery context fourth century BCE to second century CE

Corinthia: Corinth (17)[14]

Date: late fifth century to ca. 355 BCE

II-18 Denom.: —. Metal & Size: Æ 13. Weight: 2.0. Die-Axis: 6. **Fig. 4.2**
Wear: VF. Inv. 3051. F 00.106, 30/06/00. Tr. 00.4.5.5
Obverse: Pegasos flying to left, koppa (Ϙ) visible beneath
Reverse: ornamented trident head, cap or helmet to left
Reference: Price 1967a, 115–16, pl. 6: Group 1, no. 6
Notes: Pottery context fourth to third century BCE

Date: ca. 340–335 BCE

II-19 Denom.: —. Metal & Size: Æ 10. Weight: 1.2. Die-Axis: 4
Wear: G/VG. Inv. 426. SF 1996.381, 16/07/96. Tr. 96.95.1+4.2.4
Obverse: as **II-18**, but no koppa (Ϙ) visible
Reverse: as **II-18**, but E to left
Reference: Price 1967a, 121–3, pl. 7: Group 4, no. 40
Notes: Pottery context sixth century BCE to first century CE

Date: ca. 335–306 BCE

II-20 Denom.: —. Metal & Size: Æ 12. Weight: 1.8. Die-Axis: 1
Wear: VG/VF. Inv. 462. SF 1996.437, 18/07/96. Tr. 96.95.5.6.7
Obverse: as **II-19**
Reverse: as **II-18**, but Δ to left, uncertain letter/symbol to right
Reference: Price 1967a, 123–6, pl. 8: Group 5, nos. 44–51; *Agora* XXVI, no. 667g; *BMC 12* no. 453

II-21 Denom.: —. Metal & Size: Æ 13. Weight: 2.3. Die-Axis: 11
Wear: F/F+. Inv. 877. SF 1996.548, 25/07/96. Tr. 96.10.3.3
Obverse: as **II-19**
Reverse: as **II-20**
Reference: as **II-20**

II-22 Denom.: —. Metal & Size: Æ 12. Weight: 1.2. Die-Axis: —
Wear: aG. Inv. 1264. SF 1997.243, 15/07/97. Tr. 97.5.4.7
Obverse: as **II-18**
Reverse: as **II-18**, but trident flanked by letters, perhaps Α - Δ

Reference: probably as **II-20**; cf. *Agora* XXVI, no. 667f, m, and n; *BMC 12* nos. 446–7
Notes: Pottery context mid- to late fourth century BCE

II-23 Denom.: —. Metal & Size: Æ 13. Weight: 2.2. Die-Axis: 3
Wear: F+/VF. Inv. 3069. SF 2000.118, 01/04/00. Tr. 00.4.5.5
Obverse: as **II-18**
Reverse: as **II-18**, but Δ to left, crescent to right
Reference: Price 1967a, 123–6, pl. 8: Group 5, no. 49
Notes: Pottery context fourth to third century BCE

II-24 Denom.: —. Metal & Size: Æ 12. Weight: 2.3. Die-Axis: 11
Wear: VF. Inv. 3061. SF 2000.120, 01/07/00. Tr. 00.4.5.5
Obverse: as **II-18**
Reverse: as **II-23**
Reference: as **II-23**
Notes: Pottery context fourth to third century BCE

II-25 Denom.: —. Metal & Size: Æ 13. Weight: 1.6. Die-Axis: 5
Wear: F. Inv. 2149. SF 2000.29, 09/07/99. Tr. 99.3.3.3
Obverse: as **II-18**
Reverse: as **II-18**, but Δ to left, oinochoe and Ω to right
Reference: Price 1967a, 123–6, pl. 8: Group 5, no. 55
Notes: Pottery context third to second century BCE

Date: ca. 306–303 BCE

II-26 Denom.: —. Metal & Size: Æ 12. Weight: 2.0. Die-Axis: 10
Wear: F+/F. Inv. 599. SF 1996.479, 20/07/96. Tr. 96.4.6.9
Obverse: as **II-19**
Reverse: as **II-18**, but I to right
Reference: Price 1967a, 126–8, pl. 9: Group 6, no. 66

II-27 Denom.: —. Metal & Size: Æ 11. Weight: 1.5. Die-Axis: 10
Wear: G/F. Inv. 577. SF 1996.550, 25/07/96. Tr. 96.5.6.6
Obverse: as **II-19**
Reverse: as **II-18**, but I(?) or T(?) to right
Reference: as **II-26**
Notes: Pottery context fourth to early third century BCE

II-28 Denom.: —. Metal & Size: Æ 13. Weight: 1.9. Die-Axis: 5
Wear: VF. Inv. 1334. SF 1997.259, 17/07/97. Tr. 97.95.9.7.7
Obverse: as **II-19**
Reverse: as **II-18**, but T to left
Reference: as **II-26**
Notes: Pottery context fourth century BCE

Date: late fifth century to ca. 248 BCE

II-29 Denom.: —. Metal & Size: Æ 11. Weight: 1.1. Die-Axis: 11
Wear: VG. Inv. 581. SF 1996.501, 23/07/96. Tr. 96.95.1+4.2.4
Obverse: Pegasos flying to right, nothing beneath
Reverse: as **II-18**, but no letters or symbols visible
Reference: Price 1967a, 115–37, pl. 6–10: Groups 1–7; *Agora* XXVI, no. 667; *SNG Copenhagen* no. 169; *BMC 12* nos. 423–71
Notes: Pottery context sixth century BCE to first century CE

II-30 Denom.: —. Metal & Size: Æ 12. Weight: 1.6. Die-Axis: 3
Wear: VG. Inv. 362. SF 1996.38, 22/06/96. Tr. 96.3.2.2
Obverse: as **II-19**
Reverse: as **II-29**
Reference: as **II-29**

Notes: Pottery context sixth century BCE to first century CE

II-31 Denom.: —. Metal & Size: Æ 11. Weight: 2.0. Die-Axis: 1
Wear: F. Inv. 400. SF 1996.361, 16/07/96. Tr. 96.9.1.1
Obverse: as **II-19**
Reverse: as **II-29**
Reference: as **II-29**
Notes: Pottery context fourth to third/second century BCE

II-32 Denom.: —. Metal & Size: Æ 12. Weight: 1.6. Die-Axis: 9
Wear: G. Inv. 900. SF 1997.22, 25/06/97. Tr. 97.96.13.4.7
Obverse: as **II-19**
Reverse: as **II-29**
Reference: as **II-29**
Notes: Pottery context fourth century BCE

II-33 Denom.: —. Metal & Size: Æ 13. Weight: 1.8. Die-Axis: 8
Wear: aVF. Inv. 436. SF 1996.357, 16/07/96. Tr. 96.95.1+4.2.4
Obverse: as **II-18**
Reverse: as **II-29**
Reference: as **II-29**
Notes: Pottery context sixth century BCE to first century CE

II-34 Denom.: —. Metal & Size: Æ 14. Weight: 2.1. Die-Axis: —
Wear: P/G. Inv. 1382. SF 1997.289, 22/07/97. Tr. 97.96.12.4.5
Obverse: nothing visible
Reverse: as **II-29**
Reference: probably as **II-29**
Notes: Pottery context 350/325 to third century BCE

Phliasia: Phlious (9)

Date: ca. 400–350 BCE, or later[15]

II-35 Denom.: obolos. Metal & Size: AR 12. Weight: 0.8. Die-Axis: 5/11. **Fig. 4.2**
Wear: VF+. Inv. 2538. SF 1999.273, 31/07/99. Tr. 99.13.2.2
Obverse: forepart of bull butting to left
Reverse: large Φ surrounded by four pellets
Reference: *BCED Pel.* no. 103 (early–mid-fourth century BCE); *SNG Dewing* nos. 1829–30 (ca. 400–360 BCE, described as a trihemiobolon); *SNG Sweden II* no. 1617 (fourth century BCE); *BMC 10* nos. 9–10 (ca. 431–370 BCE)
Notes: Found in crevice in bedrock near Altar; along with **II-9**, **II-48,** and **II-53**; see also **II-12** and **II-49**; pottery context 350 to 250 BCE

II-36 Denom.: chalkous.[16] Metal & Size: Æ 12. Weight: 1.2. Die-Axis: 6/12
Wear: VG/aVF. Inv. 1368. SF 1997.281, 19/07/97. Tr. 97.8.1.1
Obverse: bull butting to left
Reverse: large Φ surrounded by four pellets (not always all visible)
Reference: Mac Isaac 1988, 49–53: Issue 1, Type A; *BCED Pel.* nos. 106–11
Notes: Pottery context fourth to early third century BCE

II-37 Denom.: chalkous. Metal & Size: Æ 13. Weight: 2.3. Die-Axis: 3/9
Wear: F/F+. Inv. 2157. SF 1999.32, 10/07/99. Tr. 99.1.2.2
Obverse: as **II-36**
Reverse: as **II-36**
Reference: as **II-36**
Notes: Pottery context third century BCE (?)

II-38 Denom.: chalkous. Metal & Size: Æ 11. Weight: 1.9. Die-Axis: 3/9. **Fig. 4.2**
Wear: aVF/VF. Inv. 2522. SF 1999.262, 29/07/99. Tr. 99.1.5.9
Obverse: as **II-36**
Reverse: as **II-36**

Reference: as **II-36**
Notes: Pottery context fourth to third century BCE

II-39 Denom.: chalkous. Metal & Size: Æ 12. Weight: 1.6. Die-Axis: 6/12
Wear: F+/VF. Inv. 2751. SF 1999.413, 06/08/99. Tr. 99.1.6.12
Obverse: as **II-36**
Reverse: as **II-36**
Reference: as **II-36**
Notes: Pottery context of fifth through late fourth or early third century BCE

II-40 Denom.: chalkous. Metal & Size: Æ 14. Weight: 1.9. Die-Axis: 6/12
Wear: F+. Inv. 2984. SF 2000.89, 29/06/00. Tr. 00.4.4.4
Obverse: as **II-36**
Reverse: as **II-36**
Reference: as **II-36**
Notes: Pottery context fourth to third century BCE

Date: 350–320 BCE

II-41 Denom.: chalkous. Metal & Size: Æ 13. Weight: 2.1. Die-Axis: 3/9
Wear: G. Inv. 389. SF 1996.332, 13/07/96. Tr. 96.95.1+4.2.4
Obverse: bull butting to left
Reverse: large Φ flanked by two pellets (not always both visible)
Reference: Mac Isaac 1988, 53–4: Issue 2, Type G; *BCED Pel.* no. 129
Notes: Pottery context sixth century BCE to first century CE

II-42 Denom.: chalkous. Metal & Size: Æ 15. Weight: 1.7. Die-Axis: 6/12. **Fig. 4.2**
Wear: VF. Inv. 383. SF 1996.306, 12/07/96. Tr. 96.7.2.2
Obverse: as **II-41**
Reverse: as **II-41**
Reference: as **II-41**

II-43 Denom.: chalkous. Metal & Size: Æ 14. Weight: 2.3. Die-Axis: 3/9
Wear: F+/VF. Inv. 1387. SF 1997.290, 22/07/97. Tr. 97.95.7.5.11
Obverse: as **II-41**
Reverse: as **II-41**
Reference: as **II-41**
Notes: Pottery context mid- to late fourth century BCE

Sikyonia: Sikyon (37)[17]

Date: 420/400 BCE

II-44 Denom.: hemiobol. Metal & Size: Æ 14. Weight: 1.1. Die-Axis: 12?
Wear: P. Inv. 380. SF 1996.314, 13/07/96. Tr. 96.95.1+4.2.4
Obverse: dove flying to left
Reverse: dove flying to right
Reference: Warren 1983, 26–8, pl. 5: Group 1; sim. *BCED Pel.* nos. 209–10

II-45 Denom.: hemiobol. Metal & Size: Æ 13. Weight: 1.4. Die-Axis: 6
Wear: G/VG. Inv. 2163. SF 1999.33, 11/07/99. Tr. 99.3.3.3
Obverse: dove standing to left
Reverse: dove flying to left within circular incuse
Reference: Warren 1983, 26–8, pl. 5: Group 1B
Notes: Pottery context Hellenistic

Date: late fifth century BCE[18]

II-46 Denom.: chalkous. Metal & Size: Æ 12. Weight: 1.1. Die-Axis: 11. **Fig. 4.2**

Wear: F. Inv. 620. SF 1996.511, 23/07/96. Tr. 96.8.3.4
Obverse: dove flying to right
Reverse: large M (san); below, wreath; above, A
Reference: Warren 1983, 28–33, pl. 6: Group 2.19; *BCED Pel.* no. 277.6

Date: 345/325 BCE

II-47 Denom.: hexachalkon. Metal & Size: Æ 17. Weight: 5.6. Die-Axis: 2. **Fig. 4.2**
Wear: VF. Inv. 45. SF 1995.35, 20/07/95. Tr. 95.9.1.
Obverse: laureate head of Apollo to right
Reverse: Σ within wreath
Reference: Warren 1983, 34–6, pl. 6: Group 3A.1–2; *BCED Pel.* no. 281
Notes: Pottery context fourth century to Hellenistic

Date: ca. 330 BCE[19]

II-48 Denom.: obolos. Metal & Size: AR 12. Weight: 0.8. Die-Axis: 11
Wear: VF. Inv. 2534. SF 1999.270A, 31/07/99. Tr. 99.13.2.2
Obverse: laureate head of Apollo to right
Reverse: dove flying to left; no lettering in fields
Reference: *BCED Pel.* no. 262; *BMC 10* no. 163; sim. *SNG Copenhagen* no. 66 (dove flying to right), *SNG Sweden II* nos. 1636–7 (dove flying to right, ΣI in rev. field), and *SNG Lockett IV* no. 2346 (as last)
Notes: This coin was found bonded to **II-9** in a bedrock crevice near the Altar, along with **II-35** and **II-53**; see also **II-12** and **II-49**. Pottery context is 350–250 BCE.

II-49 Denom.: obolos. Metal & Size: AR 12. Weight: 0.8. Die-Axis: 12. **Fig. 4.2**
Wear: VF. Inv. 3059. SF 2000.119, 01/07/00. Tr. 00.99.13.0.0
Obverse: as **II-48**
Reverse: as **II-48**
Reference: as **II-48**
Notes: This coin perhaps belongs to the same hoard as **II-9**, **II-35**, **II-48**, and **II-53**; see also **II-12**.

II-50 Denom.: obolos. Metal & Size: AR 12. Weight: 0.8. Die-Axis: 6
Wear: VF+/aVF. Inv. 3435. SF 2000.310, 18/07/00. Surface near Tr. 99.10
Obverse: as **II-48**
Reverse: as **II-48**, but dove flying to right
Reference: *BCED Pel.* nos. 257–61; *SNG Copenhagen* no. 66; *BMC 10* nos. 163–6; sim. *SNG Lockett IV* no. 2346 and *SNG Sweden II* nos. 1636–7 (both with ΣI behind dove)

Date: ca. 330–ca. 251 BCE[20]

II-51 Denom.: hemidrachmon. Metal & Size: AR 15. Weight: 2.6. Die-Axis: 1. **Fig. 4.2**
Wear: F+. Inv. 27. SF 1995.26, 13/07/95. Tr. 95.5.1.1
Obverse: Chimaera standing to left; ΣI beneath; EΛ pricked into upper field
Reverse: dove flying to left
Reference: *BCED Pel.* nos. 283–4; *Agrinion* nos. 2–8; *SNG Copenhagen* nos. 57–8; *SNG Sweden II* nos. 1629–35; *SNG Lockett IV* no. 2344; *SNG Dewing* no. 1834
Notes: A square nail hole is punched through the coin from obverse to reverse; pottery context Hellenistic

II-52 Denom.: hemidrachmon. Metal & Size: AR 15. Weight: 2.8. Die-Axis: 5
Wear: EF. Inv. 395. SF 1996.113, 29/06/96. Tr. 96.4.2.3
Obverse: as **II-51**, but without graffito
Reverse: as **II-51**, but one pellet to right
Reference: *BCED Pel.* nos. 292–93.2; *SNG Copenhagen* no. 65; *SNG Lockett IV* no. 2341; *SNG Sweden II* nos. 1627–8; *Agrinion* nos. 18–28
Notes: Pottery context fourth to third century BCE.

II-53 Denom.: hemidrachmon. Metal & Size: AR 15. Weight: 2.7. Die-Axis: 9

Wear: VF+. Inv. 2541. SF 1999.277, 31/07/99. Tr. 99.13.2.2
Obverse: as **II-52**
Reverse: as **II-52**
Reference: as **II-52**
Notes: Pottery context 350–250 BCE; found together with **II-9**, **II-35**, and **II-48** in a bedrock crevice near the Altar; see also **II-12** and **II-49**.

Date: 330/320 BCE?

II-54 Denom.: trichalkon. Metal & Size: Æ 14. Weight: 1.9. Die-Axis: 6
Wear: VG/aVF. Inv. 962. SF 1997.20, 24/06/97. Tr. 97.96.10.2.2
Obverse: dove flying to left; no lettering visible
Reverse: tripod-lebes within wreath that ties below
Reference: probably as Warren 1983, 52–6, pl. 8: Group 6A; sim. *BCED Pel.* no. 313.

Date: 330–290 BCE?

II-55 Denom.: dichalkon. Metal & Size: Æ 15. Weight: 4.0. Die-Axis: 12
Wear: aF/F+. Inv. 929. SF 1997.46, 26/06/97. Tr. 97.96.13.4.7
Obverse: dove flying to left
Reverse: wreath with uncertain letter within
Reference: probably as Warren 1983, 44–52, pls. 7–8: Group 5; sim. *BCED Pel.* nos. 305–12
Notes: Pottery context of fourth century BCE

II-56 Denom.: dichalkon. Metal & Size: Æ 17. Weight: 3.8. Die-Axis: 6
Wear: aF/F+. Inv. 1299. SF 1997.265, 17/07/97. Tr. 97.7.1.1
Obverse: dove flying to right
Reverse: Θ within wreath
Reference: Warren 1983, 44–52, pl. 7: Group 5.6i; *BCED Pel.* no. 307.7

II-57 Denom.: dichalkon. Metal & Size: Æ 15. Weight: 3.4. Die-Axis: 9. **Fig. 4.2**
Wear: VF+. Inv. 2559. SF 1999.289, 03/08/99. Surface, Tr. 99.96.6.0.0
Obverse: as **II-55**
Reverse: EY within wreath
Reference: Warren 1983, 44–52, pl. 6: Group 5.4a; *BCED Pel.* no. 306

Date: ca. 330–270 BCE

II-58 Denom.: chalkous. Metal & Size: Æ 11. Weight: 0.6. Die-Axis: 6. **Fig. 4.3**
Wear: F/aF. Inv. 2488. SF 1999.240, 28/07/99. Tr. 99.1.5.9
Obverse: dove flying to left
Reverse: Σ[ ]; wreath not visible
Reference: Warren 1983, 36–43, pl. 6: Group 4A; sim. *BCED Pel.* no. 304.1–7
Notes: Pottery context fourth to third century BCE

II-59 Denom.: chalkous. Metal & Size: Æ 13. Weight: 2.4. Die-Axis: 9
Wear: VG/VF. Inv. 879. SF 1996.517, 24/07/96. Tr. 96.95.1+4.2.4
Obverse: dove flying to right(?)
Reverse: Σ within wreath that ties below
Reference: probably Warren 1983, 36–43, pl. 6: Group 4A.5 *BCED Pel.* no. 304.5
Notes: Pottery context sixth century BCE to first century CE; reverse legend may be ΣI (thus 4C.5), if the I is not simply a longer olive leaf.

Date: ca. 270–200 BCE

II-60 Denom.: chalkous. Metal & Size: Æ 13. Weight: 2.1. Die-Axis: 2
Wear: P/F. Inv. 397. SF 1996.285, 11/07/96. Tr. 96.95.1.9.15

Obverse: as **II-58**
Reverse: ΣΙ within wreath
Reference: probably Warren 1983, 36–43, pl. 7: Group 4C; *BCED Pel.* no. 316–17

II-61 Denom.: chalkous. Metal & Size: Æ 16. Weight: 2.5. Die-Axis: 3
Wear: F+/VF. Inv. 2609. SF 1999.328, 04/08/99. Tr. 99.1 (baulk).3.3
Obverse: dove flying to right
Reverse: as **II-60**, but wreath ties to right
Reference: Warren 1983, 36–43, pl. 7: Group 4C.1; *BCED Pel.* nos. 316.1–2, 317.1–3
Notes: Pottery context fourth century to 150 BCE

II-62 Denom.: chalkous. Metal & Size: Æ 15. Weight: 3.1. Die-Axis: 10
Wear: VF. Inv. 403. SF 1996.202, 05/07/96. Tr. 96.3.3.5
Obverse: as **II-61**
Reverse: as **II-60**, but wreath ties beneath
Reference: Warren 1983, 36–43, pl. 7: Group 4C.5; *BCED Pel.* no. 317.7
Notes: Pottery context fourth to third century BCE

II-63 Denom.: chalkous. Metal & Size: Æ 12. Weight: 1.7. Die-Axis: 12
Wear: VG. Inv. 1435. SF 1997.309, 24/07/97. Tr. 97.11.3.4
Obverse: as **II-61**
Reverse: as **II-62**
Reference: as **II-62**
Notes: Pottery context probably fourth century BCE

II-64 Denom.: chalkous. Metal & Size: Æ 12. Weight: 1.5. Die-Axis: 12
Wear: F/VF. Inv. 657. SF 1996.601, 26/07/96. Tr. 96.13.2.4
Obverse: as **II-58**
Reverse: as **II-62**
Reference: Warren 1983, 36–43, pl. 7: Group 4C.6; *BCED Pel.* no. 317.8–10

II-65 Denom.: chalkous. Metal & Size: Æ 14. Weight: 1.9. Die-Axis: 3. **Fig. 4.3**
Wear: F+/VF. Inv. 1084. SF 1997.141, 04/07/97. Tr. 97.4.3.4
Obverse: as **II-58**
Reverse: as **II-62**
Reference: as **II-64**
Notes: Pottery context late fourth century to mid-second century BCE

II-66 Denom.: chalkous. Metal & Size: Æ 14. Weight: 2.0. Die-Axis: 2
Wear: F+. Inv. 2809. SF 1999.426, 07/08/99. Tr. 99.1 (baulk).4.4
Obverse: as **II-58**
Reverse: as **II-62**
Reference: as **II-64**
Notes: Pottery context fourth to third century BCE

II-67 Denom.: chalkous. Metal & Size: Æ 16. Weight: 2.6. Die-Axis: 12
Wear: F/aG. Inv. 3536. SF 2000.350, 20/07/00. Tr. 00.97.5 (baulk).5.5
Obverse: as **II-59**
Reverse: as **II-62**
Reference: as **II-64**
Notes: Pottery context late fourth and third century BCE

II-68 Denom.: chalkous. Metal & Size: Æ 15. Weight: 1.5. Die-Axis: 12
Wear: aVG/F. Inv. 2222. SF 1999.65, 15/07/99. Tr. 99.1.3.3
Obverse: as **II-61**
Reverse: as **II-60**
Reference: Warren 1983, 36–43, pl. 7: Group 4C.7; *BCED Pel.* no. 317.11–14
Notes: Pottery context fourth century BCE to second century CE

Date: late third century BCE[21]

II-69 Denom.: chalkous. Metal & Size: Æ 11. Weight: 1.6. Die-Axis: 1
Wear: VF. Inv. 361. SF 1996.245, 10/07/96. Tr. 96.95.1+4.2.4

Obverse: Dove flying to left
Reverse: ΣΙ within olive wreath that ties above
Reference: Warren 1983, 36–43, pl. 7: Group 4C.8; *BCED Pel.* no. 317.15–16

II-70 Denom.: chalkous. Metal & Size: Æ 15. Weight: 1.9. Die-Axis: 12
Wear: aF/F+. Inv. 2209. SF 1999.59, 15/07/99. Tr. 99.2.3.3
Obverse: as **II-69**
Reverse: as **II-69**
Reference: as **II-69**
Notes: Pottery context early fifth through fourth century BCE

II-71 Denom.: chalkous. Metal & Size: Æ 13. Weight: 2.1. Die-Axis: 6
Wear: F+/aF. Inv. 2345. SF 1999.136, 22/07/99. Tr. 99.6.4.4
Obverse: as **II-69**
Reverse: as **II-69**
Reference: as **II-69**
Notes: Pottery context fourth century BCE

Date: ca. 330–200 BCE?

II-72 Denom.: chalkous. Metal & Size: Æ 13. Weight: 1.6. Die-Axis: ?
Wear: P. Inv. 3116. SF 2000.137, 05/07/00. Tr. 00.4.6.6
Obverse: dove to left (?, traces)
Reverse: lettering within wreath (?, traces)
Reference: possibly Warren 1983, 34–43, pls. 6–7: Group 4 or 5
Notes: Pottery context fourth to second century BCE

Date: 196–146 BCE[22]

II-73 Denom.: chalkous. Metal & Size: Æ 20. Weight: 2.8. Die-Axis: 3. **Fig. 4.3**
Wear: VF. Inv. 369. SF 1996.183, 04/07/96. Tr. 96.95.1+4.2.3
Obverse: dove flying to left; ΦΙ above tail
Reverse: ΣΙ within wreath that ties above
Reference: Warren 1984, 6–10, pl. 1: Group 8A.2a; *BCED Pel.* no. 328.5
Notes: Pottery context fourth to first century BCE

II-74 Denom.: chalkous. Metal & Size: Æ 15. Weight: 2.3. Die-Axis: 6
Wear: aVF. Inv. 1128. SF 1997.164, 06/07/97. Tr. 97.96.3 (baulk).1.1
Obverse: as **II-73**, but Δ̣Γ above tail, indistinct monogram below tail
Reverse: ΣΙ within wreath
Reference: Warren 1984, 6–10, pl. 1: Group 8A.11; *BCED Pel.* no. 328.10
Notes: Pottery context fourth century BCE

II-75 Denom.: trichalkon. Metal & Size: Æ 17. Weight: 3.4. Die-Axis: 6
Wear: VG. Inv. 2293. SF 1999.112, 20/07/99. Tr. 99.7.2.2
Obverse: dove feeding to right; ΣΙ above; indistinct lettering below
Reverse: tripod-lebes within wreath
Reference: Warren 1984, 11–14, pl. 2: Group 9; *BCED Pel.* nos. 332–3
Notes: Pottery context sixth to fourth century BCE

Date: possibly second to first century BCE[23]

II-76 Denom.: trichalkon. Metal & Size: Æ 17. Weight: 4.9. Die-Axis: 12?
Wear: P. Inv. 1023. SF 1997.108, 02/07/97. Tr. 97.5.1.1
Obverse: dove feeding to right(?)
Reverse: tripod-lebes(?)
Reference: possibly Warren 1984, 11–14, 17–18, pls. 2–3: Groups 9 or 11
Notes: Pottery context fourth to third century BCE

Date: early first century BCE[24]

II-77 Denom.: chalkous. Metal & Size: Æ 18. Weight: 3.7. Die-Axis: 12
Wear: F/aG. Inv. 1090. SF 1997.142, 04/07/97. Tr. 97.4.3.4
Obverse: dove flying to left; above, ΠΡ[Ο]Μ[ΑΧ]|Δ[Α]
Reverse: [ΣΙ] within wreath that ties below
Reference: Warren 1984, 14–17, pl. 3: Group 10.2; *BCED Pel.* no. 338.3
Notes: Pottery context late fourth to mid-second century BCE

Date: 75–50 BCE[25]

II-78 Denom.: trichalkon? Metal & Size: Æ 12. Weight: 1.0. Die-Axis: —
Wear: F. Inv. 1388. SF 1997.293, 22/07/97. Tr. 97.95.7.5.11
Obverse: laureate head of Apollo to left
Reverse: dove flying to left; no lettering visible
Reference: Warren 1984, 18–22, pl. 3: Group 12; *BCED Pel.* nos. 352–3
Notes: Pottery context mid- to late fourth century BCE

Date: possibly 75–50 BCE[26]

II-79 Denom.: trichalkon? Metal & Size: Æ 20. Weight: 2.9. Die-Axis: —
Wear: P/VG. Inv. 64. SF 1995.72, 27/07/95. Tr. 95.3.5.9
Obverse: nothing visible
Reverse: bird to right (?); Π above
Reference: possibly Warren 1984, 18–22, pl. 3: Group 12; *BCED Pel.* nos. 352–3
Notes: Pottery context second century BCE

Date: unknown

II-80 Denom.: —. Metal & Size: Æ 15. Weight: 3.4. Die-Axis: ?
Wear: F/P. Inv. 359. SF 1996.261, 10/07/96. Tr. 96.7.1.1
Obverse: dove flying to left
Reverse: nothing visible
Reference: cf. Warren 1983 and 1984
Notes: Pottery context fourth to third century BCE

Achaia: Aigeira (1)

Date: ca. 360s–330s BCE

II-81 Denom.: chalkous. Metal & Size: Æ 13. Weight: 2.1. Die-Axis: 12. **Fig. 4.3**
Wear: VF. Inv. 3270. SF 2000.219, 12/07/00. Tr. 00.5.5.5
Obverse: head of Athena in crested Athenian helmet to right
Reverse: ΑΙΓ[Ι] forepart of goat to right; all within wreath
Reference: Hainzmann 1997, 44: Type 1A; *BCED Pel.* nos. 392–5; *BMC 10* no. 1
Notes: Pottery context third century BCE (?)

Achaia: Pellene (3)

Date: ca. 350–300 BCE

II-82 Denom.: tetrachalkon. Metal & Size: Æ 17. Weight: 3.9. Die-Axis: 12. **Fig. 4.3**

Wear: VF/VF+. Inv. 458. SF 1996.405, 17/07/96. Tr. 96.95.1+4.2.4
Obverse: laureate head of Apollo to right
Reverse: ΠΕ monogram above ram's head to right; all within laurel wreath
Reference: *BCED Pel.* nos. 595.1–97.1; *Agora* XXVI, no. 743; *BMC 10* nos. 10–12
Notes: Pottery context sixth century BCE to first century CE

II-83 Denom.: tetrachalkon. Metal & Size: Æ 15. Weight: 3.6. Die-Axis: 12
Wear: F-VF. Inv. 465. SF 1996.427, 18/07/96. Tr. 96.8.3.3
Obverse: laureate head of Apollo to left
Reverse: as **II-82**
Reference: *BCED Pel.* no. 592, 594.1; *BMC 10* nos. 8–9; sim. *Agora* XXVI, no. 743
Notes: Pottery context fourth to third century BCE

II-84 Denom.: dichalkon. Metal & Size: Æ 17. Weight: 2.5. Die-Axis: 1
Wear: F/F+. Inv. 2245. SF 1999.91, 16/07/99. Tr. 99.1.3.3
Obverse: as **II-82**
Reverse: as **II-82**
Reference: *BCED Pel.* nos. 595.2–97.2; *Agora* XXVI, no. 743; *BMC 10* nos. 10–12
Notes: Pottery context possibly third century BCE

Achaia: Achaian League (Argos) (1)

Date: 191–146 BCE[27]

II-85 Denom.: tetrachalkon. Metal & Size: Æ 19. Weight: 4.6. Die-Axis: 12. **Fig. 4.3**
Wear: aVF. Inv. 2933. SF 2000.65, 27/06/00. Tr. 00.3.3.3
Obverse: Zeus Amarios standing to left holds Nike and sceptre; no obverse legend
Reverse: ΑΧΑΙΩΝ / ΑΡΓΕΙΩΝ; Achaea (or Demeter Panachaea?) seated to left holds wreath and sceptre; ΦΑΗ / [ΝΟ] Σ to left of goddess
Reference: *BCED Pel.* no. 1132; *SNG Copenhagen* no. 336 (ca. 228 BCE); *BMC 10* no. 155
Notes: Pottery context fourth to second century BCE

Achaia: Achaian League (Stymphalos) (1)

Date: 191–146 BCE

II-86 Denom.: tetrachalkon. Metal & Size: Æ 19. Weight: 4.6. Die-Axis: 1. **Fig. 4.3**
Wear: VF. Inv. 885. SF 1997.1, 22/06/97. Surface, Tr. cleaning
Obverse: as **II-85**, but ΠΥΘΩΝ down right side
Reverse: ΑΧΑΙΩΝ / ΣΤΥΜΦΑΛΙΩΝ; Achaea (or Demeter Panachaea?) sitting to left holds wreath and sceptre
Reference: *BCED Pel.* no. 1708; *BMC 10* no. 170

Argolid: Argos (1)[28]

Date: ca. 425–375 BCE

II-87 Denom.: —. Metal & Size: FE 23. Weight: 8.8. Die-Axis: 5? **Fig. 4.3**
Wear: P/G. Inv. 51. SF 1995.38, 22/07/95. Tr. 95.7.3.6
Obverse: uncertain [forepart of wolf to left?]
Reverse: large A
Reference: Oikonomides 1993; Price 1968, 100; Knapp and Mac Isaac 2005, nos. 1595–1600
Notes: Pottery context second century BCE

Argolid: Hermione (1)

Date: ca. 360–320s/310s BCE

II-88 Denom.: chalkous. Metal & Size: Æ 15. Weight: 2.0. Die-Axis: 12. **Fig. 4.3**
Wear: aVF. Inv. 1522. SF 1997.334, 26/07/97. Tr. 97.5.6.11
Obverse: head of Demeter to left wreathed with wheat
Reverse: E - P on either side of torch, all within wheat wreath
Reference: Grandjean 1990, Groups I-II (375–350 BCE); *BCED Pel.* nos. 1297–8.3; *Agora* XXVI, no. 792; *BMC 10* nos. 2, 8–13, 15
Notes: Pottery context late fourth century BCE

Arkadia: Kleitor (1)

Date: ca. late fourth century–ca. 270s/260s BCE

II-89 Denom.: chalkous. Metal & Size: Æ 13. Weight: 2.1. Die-Axis: 12. **Fig. 4.4**
Wear: VF+. Inv. 3541. SF 2000.359, 20/07/00. Tr. 00.97.5 (baulk).5.5
Obverse: radiate head of Helios facing
Reverse: KΛH monogram; two pellets between uprights of the H
Reference: sim. *BCED Pel.* no. 1434.1–2; *Agora* XXVI, no. 805; *BMC 10* nos. 12–13
Notes: Pottery context fourth century BCE

Arkadia: Mantineia (1)

Date: ca. 330s–320s/310s BCE

II-90 Denom.: chalkous. Metal & Size: Æ 14. Weight: 3.2. Die-Axis: 7. **Fig. 4.4**
Wear: G/F. Inv. 3300. SF 2000.258, 13/07/00. Tr. 00.4.7.10
Obverse: head of Athena (?) to right wearing Corinthian helmet
Reverse: trident head; MẠN to left
Reference: *BCED Pel.* no. 1485.3; *Agora* XXVI, no. 806; *BMC 10* nos. 20–3
Notes: Pottery context fourth century BCE

Arkadia: Arkadian League (Megalopolis) (2)

Date: ca. 320s–275 BCE

II-91 Denom.: obolos. Metal & Size: AR 12. Weight: 0.7. Die-Axis: 6. **Fig. 4.4**
Wear: F/aVF. Inv. 803. SF 1996.635, 27/07/96. Tr. 96.14.2.2
Obverse: horned head of young Pan to left
Reverse: large APK monogram above syrinx; to left, I
Reference: *BCED Pel.* nos. 1517–18; *SNG Dewing* no. 1945 var.; *BMC 10* no. 58
Notes: Pottery context late sixth to mid-fifth century BCE; attributed to Megalopolis mint; same APK monogram, along with a seated Pan, occurs on some early hemidrachms of Megalopolis (e.g., Thompson 1968, nos. 199–201)

II-92 Denom.: obolos. Metal & Size: AR 13. Weight: 0.7. Die-Axis: 12
Wear: F/aVF. Inv. 915. SF 1997.31, 25/06/97. Tr. 96.14.2.2
Obverse: as **II-91**
Reverse: as **II-91**, but ΔY monogram in left field
Reference: *BCED Pel.* no. 1531.2; *SNG Dewing* no. 1945 var.; *BMC 10* no. 57 var.
Notes: Pottery context fifth century to early fourth century BCE; see **II-91**

Ptolemaic Kingdom: Ptolemy III (2)

Date: 246–221 BCE

II-93 Denom.: hexachalkon? Metal & Size: Æ 20. Weight: 4.8. Die-Axis: —. **Fig. 4.4**
Wear: aF/G. Inv. 2150. SF 1999.30, 09/07/99. Tr. 99.3.3.3
Obverse: bust of King Ptolemy to right, wearing fillet and aegis
Reverse: ΠΤΟΛΕΜΑΙΟΥ / ΒΑΣΙΛΕΩΣ; eagle standing to left on thunderbolt
Reference: *SNG Copenhagen* nos. 193–5; Svoronos 1904, no. 1000; *Agora* XXVI, no. 1007; *SNG Ptolemies* nos. 192–5
Notes: Pottery context third to second century BCE

II-94 Denom.: hexachalkon? Metal & Size: Æ 19. Weight: 4.7. Die-Axis: 10?
Wear: G/P. Inv. 3067. SF 2000.115, 01/07/00. Tr. 00.4.5.5
Obverse: as **II-93**
Reverse: probably as **II-93** (traces only)
Reference: as **II-93**
Notes: Pottery context fourth to second century BCE

Roman or Byzantine Empire: uncertain (2)

Date: fifth–sixth century CE

II-95 Denom.: —. Metal & Size: Æ 6. Weight: 0.1. Die-Axis: ?
Wear: P. Inv. 8. SF 1995.15, 08/07/95. Tr. 95.1.2.4
Obverse: nothing visible
Reverse: vertical or horizontal bar across flan
Reference: —
Notes: Pottery context third to second century BCE; reverse "type" may be part of an emperor's monogram, or simply an artifact resulting from the corrosion

II-96 Denom.: —. Metal & Size: Æ 10. Weight: 0.5. Die-Axis: ?
Wear: P. Inv. 2540. SF 1999.276, 31/07/99. Tr. 99.8.3.3
Obverse: beaded border or wreath (traces)
Reverse: Latin lettering (?, traces)
Reference: —
Notes: Pottery context fourth to third century BCE; attribution is based more upon the coin's fabric than anything visible on its surface

Byzantine Empire: Manuel I (1)[29]

Date: 1143–80 CE

II-97 Denom.: half-tetarteron. Metal & Size: Æ 13. Weight: 0.5. Die-Axis: 12. **Fig. 4.4**
Wear: P/VG. Inv. 365. SF 1996.44, 25/06/96. Tr. 96.4.2.2
Obverse: facing bust of Manuel I
Reverse: monogram of Manuel I
Reference: Hendy 1969, pl. 18.1–2; Wroth 1908, nos. 79–82
Notes: Attributed to an uncertain mint in Greece

Unknown Issuing Authority and Date (1)

II-98 Denom.: —. Metal & Size: Æ 11. Weight: 2.5. Die-Axis: —
Wear: P. Inv. 377. SF 1996.243, 10/07/96. Tr. 96.95.1+4.2.4

Obverse: nothing visible
Reverse: nothing visible
Notes: Pottery context sixth century BCE to first century CE; perhaps an unstruck blank?

COMMENTARY

Bronze of Syracuse (II-1)

This coin is anomalous, for being both especially early and the only representative of the Greek West found at Stymphalos. Calciati's chronology for this hemilitron overlaps the reign of Dionysios I of Syracuse (406–367 BCE), which may be significant for the fact that Dionysios commonly employed mercenaries to do his fighting (e.g., against eastern Sicily in 402–399 BCE).[30] The mercenary phenomenon, arguably Arkadia's biggest industry, may explain why unexpected coins such as this one and others (e.g., of Carthage, of Seleukos I) reached Stymphalos.[31] Perhaps a returning mercenary dedicated the coin to Athena or another deity in the Sanctuary as a thank-offering for a safe homecoming. Its condition seems rather too fresh to be the result of years of circulation that eventually fetched it up in southern Greece, especially when one considers that the plentiful bronzes of Syracuse are very rarely found in southern Greece in any case.[32]

Bronzes of the Macedonian kingdom (II-2 to II-7)

Macedonian bronzes, particularly of Demetrios Poliorketes, are generally not found in the Peloponnese, but the stray examples occur in seemingly military contexts.[33] Some Demetrios bronzes were excavated at Nemea, but they account for only about 0.5% of all the Greek coins found there, whereas the proportion for Stymphalos is much higher (4%).[34] The Macedonian monarchy took an active interest in the Nemean Games in the late fourth century when Kassander presided over the festival of 315 BCE and Demetrios held meetings of the League of Corinth there in 311 and 303 BCE.[35] If such visits by the king and his entourage did not translate into a lot of Macedonian coins lost at the site, one can only suppose that the much higher proportion of Macedonian coins at Stymphalos was the result of a garrison. In the case of Stymphalos, we may have evidence for the presence of Antigonid forces, perhaps to rebuild the town's fortifications after the attack of 315 BCE and to garrison the town, but surely posted there to counter the threat from Sparta.[36] In 303 BCE, Demetrios Poliorketes was able to capitalize on Athenian support to expand his interests in mainland Greece, an expansion that included the capture of both Corinth and Sikyon and the resettling of the latter farther inland. That same year he extended his influence into the Stymphalos region when he "liberated" Achaia, Argos, and Arkadia as far south as Mantineia.[37] We know that Demetrios maintained a strong hold on Arkadia partly to contain the threat of Sparta, which in fact made trouble for him in 293 by inducing Thebes to revolt.[38] Even Antigonid policy after Demetrios, at least until it was challenged by the Achaian League's growing power in the years after 250 BCE, required comprehensive control of the cities of the Peloponnese, whether that took the form of garrisons or pro-Macedonian tyrannies. In such a climate, even Stymphalos would have been a strategically desirable stronghold, given its location on a major natural route from Lakonia and the central Peloponnese to the Corinthian Gulf at Sikyon. Interestingly enough, the same variety of Demetrios bronze coins as **II-6** and **II-7** is commonly encountered at Stymphalos and elsewhere in Arkadia (Orchomenos and Tripolis), though Newell long ago attributed them to a mint in southwest Asia Minor.[39] Not only was Arkadia heavily garrisoned by Demetrios' forces in the 290s, but these soldiers seem likely, from the coins they left behind, to have been recruits from his power base in southwest Asia Minor.[40]

A silver hoard? (II-9, II-12, II-35, II-48, II-49, and II-53)

On 31 July 1999 excavators discovered four silver coins in a bedrock crevice located in trench 99.13 a few metres south of the Altar. Six days later, they found a fifth silver coin (**II-12**) in the same shallow trench. A sixth silver coin (**II-49**) was found during cleaning in the same trench at the beginning of the following season. Trench 99.13 comes down on the Terrace Wall that may have demarcated the Sanctuary's edge.[41] If the location was indeed outside the Sanctuary, there is no particular reason to consider the coins a votive offering. Conversely, if the coins were deposited inside the temenos, there is no good reason to suppose that we have a foundation

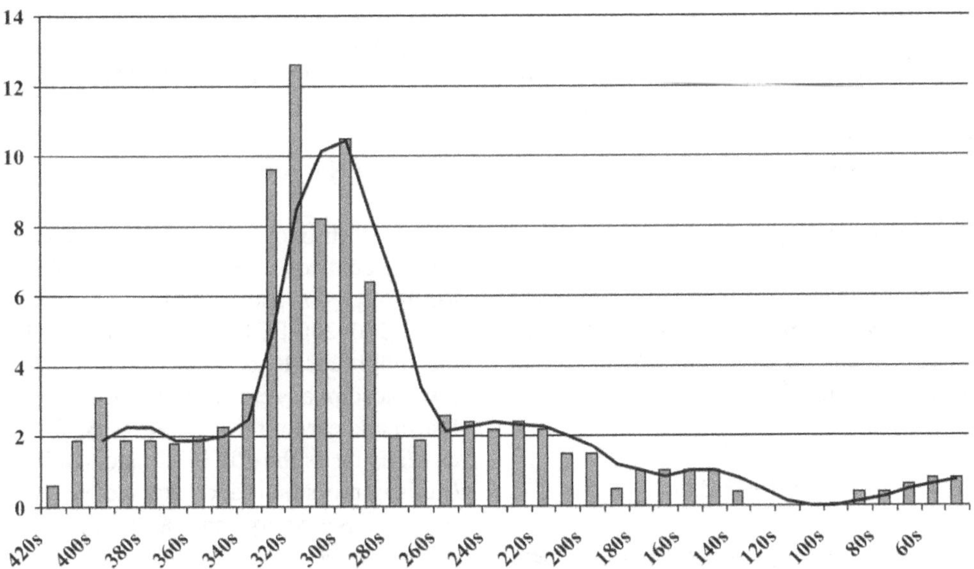

Chart 4.1. Coin loss at Stym II by decade

deposit. Two of the coins (**II-9** and **II-48**) were in fact found bonded to one another, and the fresh condition of all six pieces could indicate that we are dealing with a hoard, probably a savings hoard of the best-condition coins that someone could afford to set aside in the (vain) hope of eventual recovery. Given that the silver pieces of Sikyon (**II-48**, **II-49**, **II-53**) and of Chalkis (**II-12**) have firm dates in the second half of the fourth century, and that the silver coin of Phlious (**II-35**) has the same types as that city's fourth-century bronzes,[42] the almost mint condition of the fifth piece (**II-9**), the hemidrachm of the Ainianes, a Thessalian *ethnos*, encourages a downward revision of its hitherto impressionistic date. A wide range of coinages from various cities and tribes of Thessaly have traditionally borne a date of 400–344 BCE, for which the *terminus post quem* is a matter of stylistic evolution and the end date is made to coincide with Philip's subjugation of Thessaly.[43] Not only has more recent scholarship thrown into doubt any connection between a state's political autonomy and its ability to strike coins, particularly in the case of Thessaly under Philip, but also the hoards that contain these coins of the Ainianes recommend a lower dating.[44] At Stymphalos there are further arguments for a lower dating. For one thing, there is the hoard's pottery context of ca. 350–250 BCE. Secondly, the Ainianes hemidrachm was found bonded to **II-48**, which is a Sikyonian obol with slightly more wear and a date no earlier than about 330 BCE.[45] Roughly contemporary Sikyonian hemidrachms (ca. 330/320s–280s BCE) with a similar amount of wear feature in a hoard recovered from the foundations of the Stym V artillery tower on the city's west side. In this case, the hoard has been dated to ca. 290 BCE and has been associated with a Macedonian intervention at Stymphalos.[46] Because the Stym II area had apparently suffered a decline in activity in the early third century BCE (see chart 4.1) it possibly made it the ideal place, both conveniently accessible and largely unfrequented, for concealing a few coins.

On the other hand, the presence of silver coins together in a bedrock crevice, not to mention the especially high proportion of Stym II coins, especially silver coins, from trenches to the south and southeast of the Altar, could fit another kind of hoard, namely an open votive deposit to which pilgrims would add a coin or two (compare the modern wishing well).[47] Any such deposit at Stym II would have been located somewhere to the south of the Altar, though clean-up operations after the close of the Sanctuary could have scattered some of its contents into fill that ended up beyond the Sanctuary's south edge.[48]

Bronzes of Histiaia (II-15 and II-16)

Coins of Histiaia, a town on the north end of Euboia, were quite common at Stymphalos, though in every other instance it is the later, silver tetrobols that one encounters. The bronzes **II-15** and **II-16** are further distinguished by their relatively slight degree of wear and their having been found so close to one another. Although one would like to call these two coins another votive offering, their discovery in a trench some distance away, along the north side of the southern city wall, does not necessarily connect them with the Sanctuary itself. A more likely scenario is that they were lost more or less simultaneously and in connection with work on the Wall, perhaps a repair of damage to the Wall after the attack of 315 BCE.[49] The large amount of regal Macedonian bronze coinage at Stymphalos holds out the possibility that Macedonian troops or their agents did the reconstruction, and the owner of **II-15** and **II-16** could have been one of them.[50]

Bronzes of Corinth (II-18 to II-34)

The only study of Corinth's plentiful Pegasos/trident bronzes is Martin Price's elusive dissertation.[51] Thanks, however, to the subsequent publication of numismatic finds from Corinth, one can be sure that Price's original chronology spanning the late fifth through mid-third centuries BCE is correct in at least its broad outlines.[52] Furthermore, a number of the Stymphalian examples come from pottery contexts that support his chronology.

Coins of Phlious (II-35 to II-43)

A new, somewhat lower date has been suggested for the silver trihemiobol **II-35**.[53] Otherwise, these coins retain Mac Isaac's chronology since the pottery contexts do not appear to contradict it. Phlious was Stymphalos's neighbour to the east and produced a modest coinage of silver and bronze in the fourth century. Results from Stymphalos, Nemea, and a handful of hoards clearly show how limited its sphere of circulation was. About 9% of the coins recovered at Stymphalos, both at Stym II alone and the city as a whole, are Phliasian, comparable to the 7% proportion from Nemea, which lay at approximately the same distance from Phlious as Stymphalos but in the opposite direction.[54] By the time one goes a little farther east to Mycenae and a large hoard of silver fractions found there in 1895, the Phliasian presence falls below 4%.[55] West of Stymphalos there is no significant Phliasian presence in Arkadia; no examples are known from hoards to the south of Phlious itself, and only a few specimens apparently circulated as far north as the Gulf of Corinth.[56] Such a pattern of limited circulation was surely typical of scores, perhaps even hundreds, of emitters in the Greek world – no systematic study of minor mints' circulations has yet been done – but even the Phliasians could take pride in their success: at Stymphalos itself, for instance, issues from its own mint account for just 1% of all coins recovered there!

Coins of Sikyon (II-44 to II-80)

Warren's chronology is generally consistent with the pottery contexts of Sikyonian coins found at Stymphalos, though one should probably narrow the broad span of ca. 330–200 BCE for her Group 4 when considering the subgroups 4C.5, 4C.6, and 4C.8. The pottery contexts accompanying these subgroups tend to the later fourth and earlier third centuries BCE but seldom come down as far as the 200 BCE date that Warren proposed. If this impression is accurate, there is very little coinage from the Sanctuary that can be dated after about 280 BCE, and the sudden decline in the Sanctuary after the early third seems ever more likely.

The deliberate defacement of **II-51**, a silver hemidrachm, and its find spot at the Temple's south edge strongly suggest a votive dedication, one evidently nailed either to the Temple itself or to one of its furnishings.[57] It is clear enough from the ragged metal edges surrounding the hole that the coin was not pierced for jewellery but was roughly treated with little regard for its future utility. The letters ΕΛ pricked into the coin's surface may represent part of the dedicator's name, though a reference to Eileithyia or Athena is not impossible.[58] Because the coin had seen quite a lot of circulation prior to its being pierced, it can hardly have been dedicated before the early third century BCE.

Bronzes of the Achaian League (II-85 and II-86)

Bronze coins struck by the member states of the Achaian League are not only rarer than the silver hemidrachms but also more interesting for their inclusion of the name of the responsible magistrate at each mint. One of the two, Phaënos of Argos, is not otherwise attested, though he did sign Argive silver as well as bronze issues.[59] The magistrate for Stymphalos is named simply Python, but he could be the same Python who was the father of Theondas, one of three delegates charged in about 189 BCE with commemorating a friendship between Elateia and Stymphalos on stelai at these cities.[60] If the two Pythons are indeed one, it is one of our few pieces of prosopographic information for Stymphalos and evidence that it was the elite of member cities who took responsibility for the league coinage.

Iron coin of Argos (II-87)

It seems that only one of these curiosities has been found at the Sanctuary. Five other iron disks recovered in 1994 and 1995 from trenches in and around the Temple were once thought to be coins, but since then, they have been recognized as more likely to be the heads of iron nails. For now, these disks are excluded from consideration on the grounds that they are too small, too light, and without any discernible type.[61] Whereas Sparta is reputed to have used iron money, and while iron spits (*obeloi*), an Archaic means of storing and exhibiting wealth,[62] may have been the etymological root for silver obols (*oboloi*), Argos's use of iron coins in the Classical period is more suggestive of experimentation with token currency after the precedents set by bronze coins in fifth-century Sicily.[63] Regardless of interpretation, all iron coins are rare (about two dozen examples are known), and fewer still come from an archaeological context.[64]

Bronzes of Ptolemy III (II-92 and II-93)

Worn Ptolemy III hexachalka of the type of Svoronos 1904, no. 1000 were prevalent in both third-century Stymphalos and the Peloponnese as a whole.[65] Ptolemy III's sponsorship, first of Aratos of Sikyon, then of King Kleomenes III of Sparta, with a view to destabilizing Antigonid control in the region is well known from the sources,[66] and the coins are a physical manifestation of his policy.[67] It is worthy of note that all the Ptolemy III bronzes recovered from Stymphalos are heavily worn: whereas most bronze coins from the site do exhibit a lot of wear, one does encounter a sizeable minority of fresh-looking pieces. On the other hand, all but one of the Ptolemy III bronzes are so heavily worn as to hamper early efforts at attribution. The obvious conclusion is that these coins were all issued at once and circulated until they wore out. Had Ptolemy been issuing them sporadically over the years, one would expect to find examples with varying degrees of wear.

CONCLUSIONS

The grand conclusions that one can draw from a corpus of only 98 coins are necessarily possibilities, or even probabilities, but not certainties. Nevertheless, it is only human to push the boundaries of our competence by flying high (hopefully not too close to the sun), because an assemblage of facts and figures without some attempt at interpretation is usually not worth the time, neither the writer's nor the reader's. This final section will attempt to place the coins in the context of the acropolis Sanctuary.

The spatial distribution and chronological spread of coins found in Stym II suggest that cult activity was centred on the Temple and its Altar in the fourth century BCE. The accompanying graph (see chart 4.1) shows the average coin-loss per decade at Stym II, which gives one some idea of how much coin was in circulation when. The chart does not distinguish between dates of production (i.e., the earliest that the coins can have circulated) and when they went to ground, which is generally impossible to determine, though the amount of wear a coin receives is in some way proportionate to its circulating life.[68] If one had a reliable formula to equate wear with time in circulation, one could draw a more accurate graph with peaks that slump further to the right. The black line added to the graph is a three-point moving average, included purely *exempli gratia*, that approximates what a revised graph accounting for circulating life might look like. Despite the uncertainties, a few things seem clear. Most apparent is the Sanctuary's acme between about 340 and 270 BCE. A few coins minted in the late fifth and early fourth centuries BCE could indicate that the Sanctuary was already vibrant before 350 BCE, though this is by no means certain. For one thing, coins minted in the late fifth century could have remained in circulation for decades before coming to Stymphalos and getting lost in the Sanctuary. Indeed, of the five coins dated as early as the late fifth century BCE, all except **II-1**, which may be a memento of mercenary service under Dionysios of Syracuse, are heavily worn.[69] Coins dated to the first half of the fourth century exhibit much less wear and obviously did not circulate as long before going to ground in the Sanctuary, which probably means that they are closer in date to its floruit.[70] On the other hand, bronze coins of token value were not common in southern Greece before the second quarter of the fourth century, and any early worshipper who had dropped a relatively precious silver coin would have made some effort to find it. High Classical coins would thus be underrepresented in a record that consists of what people have lost or neglected to pick up.

In the 280s and 270s BCE, the volume of coin in circulation, thus the volume of traffic, seems to have dropped off significantly and decisively, possibly after a Macedonian intervention in connection with rebuilding the fortifications.[71] It is also apparent that the attack and capture of 315 BCE left a distinctive mark in the numismatic record with a deep notch in the graph line between 320 and 310 BCE. For a period of a few years there was a drop in the number of coins being lost at the Sanctuary, which leads one to suppose fewer visitors there, perhaps as a result of destruction. Regardless of the precise nature of the disruption, economic activity apparently recovered within a few years and stayed high until the early third century BCE, which means that the attack of 315 BCE did not directly cause the apparent decline of the Sanctuary. The Hellenistic and early Roman prosperity of other parts of Stymphalos, most notably the domestic quarter near the lake (Stym I), has no real analogue at Stym II, and from the coins' point of view it seems that the acropolis Sanctuary was largely abandoned in the early third century.

On the other hand, an analysis of the pottery record has revealed that around 300 BCE there was a clean-up of older votive material and that Stym II entered a new phase of its life (Phase 4). Whereas the coins suggest a steep decline in activity at the Sanctuary, the pottery record does not support such a theory.[72] If one discounts a reduction in cult activity, there must have been some change in practice to account for far fewer coins entering the archaeological record. For instance, visitors perhaps no longer offered a coin to the goddess.

In terms of spatial distribution, the greatest concentration of coins recovered from within the temenos is to be found inside and around the edges of the Temple (18), followed by the area around the Altar, particularly just to its south (10).[73] Incidentally, the Temple and Altar areas are also the only locations within the temenos where silver coins were found.[74] The concentration of coin finds falls off to 10 in the trenches of Building A, and to 5 around the row of stelai just north of the Temple.

So far we may be dealing only with casual and unintentional losses by visitors. If so, it is significant that 45% (44) of Stym II coins came from trenches beyond the Terrace Wall that apparently bounded the Sanctuary to the south and southeast.[75] They include an unusually high proportion (7, 64%) of the silver coins found at Stym II.[76] This concentration of coins, particularly the more precious silver coins, may indicate some sort of votive deposit.[77] Any change in practices at the Sanctuary at the end of the fourth century may have included a less diligent sweeping up of litter and the occasional scattered coin. Indeed, most (69%) of the coins from Stym II that postdate the early third century BCE and that can be assigned to a specific trench were found inside the Sanctuary (i.e., inside the Temple, inside Building A, or near the Altar), which may be evidence for decline in the Sanctuary. The corollary is that the fills beyond the terrace wall to the south and east of the sanctuary saw relatively few additions of coins postdating 300 BCE, which suggests a clean-up at about that time.

The latest coins, nine bronze pieces of Sikyon and the Achaian League (**II-73–9**, **II-85–6**), are few in number and do not seem to indicate any especial significance for the Sanctuary beyond the normal "background noise" of casual losses that one finds elsewhere in Stymphalos in the second and first centuries BCE. None of these coins are silver pieces that might have been pilgrims' gifts to the goddess, and the heterogeneity of the earlier coins that were arguably left by such visitors is also absent. These final coins are almost always later than the pottery contexts in which they were found, which suggests that the former were most likely later intrusions that had little bearing on Stym II's actual period of use.

The sorts of coins present at Stym II give some indication of both the town's economic connections and the Sanctuary's draw. Silver coins are equally common at both the acropolis Sanctuary and the town as a whole (11%), though this proportion is high by most standards.[78] The three nearby mints of Sikyon (37, 38%), Corinth (17, 17%), and Phlious (9, 9%) also dominate the currency pool at both the Sanctuary and the town, and in this way the Sanctuary is numismatically typical of all Stymphalos.[79] What distinguishes the Sanctuary before ca. 270 BCE from other parts of Stymphalos is both an emphasis on specifically fourth-century coins and the presence of certain mints that are not otherwise represented in the corpus. Although the Sanctuary accounts for only about one-fifth of all the coins excavated at Stymphalos, it has a number of *hapax legomena*, so to speak: Syracuse (**II-1**), Korkyra (**II-8**), the Ainianes (**II-9**), the Lokrian League (**II-11**), Salamis (**II-17**), Argos (**II-87**), Hermione (**II-88**), and Mantineia (**II-90**).[80] Whereas some discrepancies are bound to occur coincidentally and may not have any particular significance, the acropolis Sanctuary does seem to have received a wider variety of visitors and their coins up to the early third century than other parts of the town did.[81] Besides the good view of the lake from its terrace, another draw could have been a particular connection that Athena had with Herakles' slaying of the Stymphalian Birds.[82]

If the Sanctuary did attract out-of-town visitors, one's first impression is that its draw was probably quite local. By comparing the mints in central and southern Greece that did mint bronze in the fourth century with the mints represented by the finds at Stym II, one can get some idea of the pilgrims' origins.[83] Besides the issues of Sikyon, Corinth, and Phlious, which were the standard currencies of the northeast Peloponnese in the fourth century, one generally sees coins from elsewhere in the northern and eastern Peloponnese (Pellene, Aigeira, Argos, Hermione, Mantineia), a few representatives of central Greece (Salamis, Boiotian League, Lokrian League, Chalkis, Histiaia, southern Thessaly), and some Macedonian regal imports. As previously noted, the presence of Macedonian coins may be connected to a military presence at Stymphalos ca. 300 BCE,[84] but coins from places like Boiotia, Euboia, Lokris, and Korkyra seem a little far-fetched, both literally and figuratively. Perhaps one is dealing in these cases with bonds of kinship between Stymphalos and communities in central Greece, bonds now entirely unknown to us except in the case of Elateia.[85]

What is absent from Stym II, provided that one is sufficiently cautious about conclusions derived from only 98 coins, is potentially more instructive. Most of Stymphalos's Arkadian neighbours are missing, though many of them (e.g., Pheneos, Orchomenos) were never prolific issuers. Nor is there any coinage from Elis or Messenia (Lakonia did not strike coins until the third century). Also absent are any bronze coins from Crete, the Aegean Islands, or the Ionian Islands. In central Greece, one conspicuous absence is Athens. Some of these areas and cities find representation among the almost 400 coins recovered from other parts of the city, but it is interesting to note that none of them arrived at Stymphalos before the early third century.[86] To take one example, all twelve of the Athenian coins found at Stymphalos are either Hellenistic issues of the third to first centuries, or they are very worn fourth-century issues that show up in Hellenistic contexts.[87] The Stym II corpus, although a small one, is evidently an accurate reflection of the city's trading connections and visitors up to the early third century BCE. Coins from other parts of the site help relate its subsequent history; e.g., there is no coin evidence of Romans at the acropolis Sanctuary when troops apparently passed through the lower town in the 140s.[88]

Concordance I: Trench Numbers

Trench	Cat. no.
Tr. 95.1, L 2, P 4, SF 15	= **II-95**
Tr. 95.3, L 5, P 9, SF 72	= **II-79**
Tr. 95.5, L 1, P 1, SF 26	= **II-51**
Tr. 95.7, L 3, P 6, SF 38	= **II-88**
Tr. 95.9, L 1, P 1, SF 35	= **II-47**
Tr. 96.3, L 2, P 2, SF 38	= **II-30**
Tr. 96.3, L 2, P 2, SF 135	= **II-14**
Tr. 96.3, L 3, P 5, SF 202	= **II-62**
Tr. 96.4, L 2, P 3, SF 113	= **II-52**
Tr. 96.4, L 2, P 4, SF 44	= **II-97**
Tr. 96.4, L 6, P 9, SF 479	= **II-26**
Tr. 96.5, L 6, P 6, SF 550	= **II-27**
Tr. 96.5 ext, L 3, P 4, SF 258	= **II-17**
Tr. 96.5 ext, L 6, P 9, SF 537	= **II-8**
Tr. 96.7, L 1, P 1, SF 261	= **II-80**
Tr. 96.7, L 2, P 2, SF 306	= **II-42**
Tr. 96.8, L 3, P 3, SF 427	= **II-83**
Tr. 96.8, L 3, P 4, SF 511	= **II-46**
Tr. 96.9, L 1, P 1, SF 361	= **II-31**
Tr. 96.10, L 3, P 3, SF 548	= **II-21**
Tr. 96.13, L 2, P 4, SF 601	= **II-64**
Tr. 96.14, L 2, P 2, SF 635	= **II-91**
Tr. 96.95.1, L 9, P 15, SF 285	= **II-60**
Tr. 96.95.1+4, L 2, P 2, SF 314	= **II-44**
Tr. 96.95.1+4, L 2, P 3, SF 183	= **II-73**
Tr. 96.95.1+4, L 2, P 4, SF 517	= **II-59**
Tr. 96.95.1+4, L 2, P 4, SF 243	= **II-98**
Tr. 96.95.1+4, L 2, P 4, SF 245	= **II-69**
Tr. 96.95.1+4, L 2, P 4, SF 332	= **II-41**
Tr. 96.95.1+4, L 2, P 4, SF 357	= **II-33**
Tr. 96.95.1+4, L 2, P 4, SF 381	= **II-19**
Tr. 96.95.1+4, L 2, P 4, SF 405	= **II-82**
Tr. 96.95.1+4, L 2, P 4, SF 501	= **II-29**
Tr. 96.95.5, L 6, P 7, SF 437	= **II-20**
Tr. 96.95.6, L 3, P 8, SF 138	= **II-13**
Tr. 96.95.6 ext., L 1, P 1, SF 356	= **II-3**
Tr. 97.4, L 3, P 4, SF 141	= **II-65**
Tr. 97.4, L 3, P 4, SF 142	= **II-77**
Tr. 97.4, L 3, P4, SF 155	= **II-6**
Tr. 97.4, L 4, P 6, SF 191	= **II-4**
Tr. 97.5, L 1, P 1, SF 108	= **II-76**
Tr. 97.5, L 4, P 4, SF 243	= **II-22**
Tr. 97.5, L 6, P 11, SF —	= **II-88**
Tr. 97.7, L 1, P 1, SF 265	= **II-56**
Tr. 97.8, L 1, P 1, SF 281	= **II-36**
Tr. 97.11, L 3, P 4, SF 309	= **II-63**
Tr. 97.95.7, L 5, P 11, SF 290	= **II-43**
Tr. 97.95.7, L 5, P 11, SF 293	= **II-78**
Tr. 97.95.9, L 7, P 7, SF 259	= **II-28**
Tr. 97.96.3 (baulk), L 1, P 1, SF 164	= **II-74**
Tr. 97.96.10, L 2, P 2, SF 20	= **II-54**
Tr. 97.96.12, L 4, P 5, SF 289	= **II-34**
Tr. 97.96.13, L 4, P 7, SF 22	= **II-32**
Tr. 97.96.13, L 4, P 7, SF 46	= **II-55**
Tr. 99.1, L 2, P 2, SF 32	= **II-37**
Tr. 99.1, L 3, P 3, SF 65	= **II-68**
Tr. 99.1, L 3, P 3, SF 91	= **II-84**
Tr. 99.1 (baulk), L 3, P 3, SF 328	= **II-61**
Tr. 99.1, L 4, P 4, SF 109	= **II-5**
Tr. 99.1 (baulk), L 4, P 4, SF 426	= **II-66**

Concordance I: Trench Numbers (*Concluded*)

Tr. 99.1, L 5, P 8, SF 208 = **II-7**
Tr. 99.1, L 5, P 9, SF 240 = **II-58**
Tr. 99.1, L 5, P 9, SF 262 = **II-38**
Tr. 99.1, L 5, P 10, SF 335 = **II-11**
Tr. 99.1, L 6, P 12, SF 413 = **II-39**
Tr. 99.2, L 3, P 3, SF 59 = **II-70**
Tr. 99.3, L 3, P 3, SF 29 = **II-25**
Tr. 99.3, L 3, P 3, SF 30 = **II-93**
Tr. 99.3, L 3, P 3, SF 33 = **II-45**
Tr. 99.6, L 1, P 1, SF 98 = **II-1**
Tr. 99.6, L 4, P 4, SF 136 = **II-71**
Tr. 99.7, L 2, P 2, SF 112 = **II-75**
Tr. 99.8, L 3, P 3, SF 276 = **II-96**
Tr. near 99.10, SF 310 = **II-50**
Tr. 99.13, L 2, P 2, SF 270A = **II-48**
Tr. 99.13, L 2, P 2, SF 270B = **II-9**
Tr. 99.13, L 2, P 2, SF 273 = **II-35**
Tr. 99.13, L 2, P 2, SF 277 = **II-53**
Tr. 99.13, L 3, P 3, SF 333 = **II-12**
Tr. 99.96.6, L surface, P —, SF 289 = **II-57**
Tr. 00.3, L 2, P 2, SF 37 = **II-10**
Tr. 00.2, L 3, P 3, SF 52 = **II-2**
Tr. 00.3, L 3, P 3, SF 65 = **II-85**
Tr. 00.4, L 4, P 4, SF 89 = **II-40**
Tr. 00.4, L 4, P 4, SF 106 = **II-18**
Tr. 00.4, L 5, P 5, SF 115 = **II-93**
Tr. 00.4, L 5, P 5, SF 118 = **II-23**
Tr. 00.4, L 5, P 5, SF 120 = **II-24**
Tr. 00.4, L 6, P 6, SF 137 = **II-72**
Tr. 00.4, L 7, P 7, SF 209 = **II-15**
Tr. 00.4, L 7, P 8, SF 216 = **II-16**
Tr. 00.4, L 7, P 10, SF 258 = **II-90**
Tr. 00.5, L 5, P 5, SF 219 = **II-81**
Tr. 00.97.5 (baulk), L 5, P 5, SF 350 = **II-67**
Tr. 00.97.5 (baulk), L 5, P 5, SF 359 = **II-89**
Tr. 00.99.13, L 0, P 0, SF 119 = **II-49**
Tr. cleaning, L surface, P —, SF 1, 22/06/97 = **II-86**

Concordance II: Excavation Inventory Numbers

8 = **II-95**
27 = **II-51**
45 = **II-47**
51 = **II-88**
64 = **II-79**
359 = **II-80**
361 = **II-69**
362 = **II-30**
364 = **II-13**
365 = **II-97**
369 = **II-73**
372 = **II-14**
377 = **II-98**
380 = **II-44**
383 = **II-42**
389 = **II-41**
395 = **II-52**
397 = **II-60**
400 = **II-31**
403 = **II-62**
405 = **II-17**
426 = **II-19**
436 = **II-33**
439 = **II-3**
458 = **II-82**
462 = **II-20**
465 = **II-83**
559 = **II-8**
577 = **II-27**
581 = **II-29**
599 = **II-26**
620 = **II-46**
657 = **II-64**
803 = **II-91**
877 = **II-21**
879 = **II-59**
885 = **II-86**
900 = **II-32**
929 = **II-55**
962 = **II-54**
1023 = **II-76**
1084 = **II-65**
1085 = **II-6**
1090 = **II-77**
1128 = **II-74**
1150 = **II-4**
1264 = **II-22**
1299 = **II-56**
1334 = **II-28**
1368 = **II-36**
1382 = **II-34**
1387 = **II-43**
1388 = **II-78**
1435 = **II-63**
1522 = **II-88**
2149 = **II-25**
2150 = **II-91**
2157 = **II-37**
2163 = **II-45**
2209 = **II-70**
2222 = **II-68**
2245 = **II-84**
2261 = **II-1**
2291 = **II-5**
2293 = **II-75**
2345 = **II-71**
2449 = **II-7**
2488 = **II-58**
2522 = **II-38**
2534 = **II-48**
2535 = **II-9**
2538 = **II-35**
2540 = **II-96**
2541 = **II-53**
2559 = **II-57**
2609 = **II-61**
2611 = **II-11**
2612 = **II-12**
2757 = **II-39**
2809 = **II-66**
2889 = **II-10**
2899 = **II-2**
2933 = **II-85**
2984 = **II-40**
3051 = **II-18**
3059 = **II-49**
3061 = **II-24**
3067 = **II-94**
3069 = **II-23**
3116 = **II-72**
3247 = **II-15**
3270 = **II-81**
3274 = **II-16**
3300 = **II-90**
3435 = **II-50**
3536 = **II-67**
3541 = **II-89**

5

Weapons: Catapult Bolts, Arrowheads, Javelin and Spear Heads, and Sling Bullets

Christopher Hagerman

INTRODUCTION*

Excavations in the Sanctuary on the acropolis have yielded the remains of 198 projectile weapons. This corpus comprises one of the more remarkable and unexpected outcomes of work in the Sanctuary.[1] Similar pieces have appeared on a wide range of sites across the ancient world, but rarely has such a large collection appeared in so confined an area. Naturally, the projectiles have been of special interest to the excavators. Their presence has significant implications for our understanding of the Sanctuary as well as the history of ancient Stymphalos. For, while some may have been votive offerings, there is good reason to attribute the majority to an attack or attacks on Stymphalos between the late fourth/early third and mid-second century BCE. The assemblage also adds to our understanding of ancient projectile points during the Late Classical and Hellenistic periods. Most important in this regard, the finds from Stymphalos shed new light on the development of specialized points for catapult bolts.[2]

The projectiles recovered from the Sanctuary fall neatly into five classes: heads from catapult bolts (83), arrowheads (108), a javelin head, a spear head, and sling bullets (5).[3] The catapult-bolt heads are somewhat heavier than the arrowheads and more uniform in shape and material. All of the catapult-bolt heads are iron and all but one have a large conical socket and a heavy, square-sectioned, pyramidal head. The lone outlier also has a conical socket, but differs in the shape of its head, which is flat and leaf-shaped. Projectile points of this type have elsewhere simply been labelled "ad hoc," since it is presumed they were made in an emergency; however, they may simply represent a less popular type, or perhaps even a small javelin.

Four distinct types of arrowheads were recovered from the Sanctuary. The most numerous is the so-called *bodkin* variety (92), characterized by a long, pyramidal or "bodkin" head, and a long tang. The next most numerous type (13) also has a tang but the head is a two-edged, leaf-shaped blade with a hemispherical boss at the base. They are commonly called *Cretan* and are the heaviest of the arrowheads found in the Sanctuary. A pair of small, bronze arrowheads of trilobate design comprises yet another category. Each has three barbed blades springing directly from a central socket. This type, the only bronze variety found in the Sanctuary, is most commonly labelled *Scythian*. Finally, there is a single, small, iron arrowhead, which conforms to Walters' Type H. It has a three-bladed head atop a conical socket.

The javelin head is of the usual form, with a conical socket and a flat, leaf-shaped blade. Only the tip of the spear head survives, comprising no more than one-third of the blade's original length. The surviving portion suggests a typical, leaf-shaped blade with a pronounced riser, or midrib.

Four of the lead sling bullets are symmetrical and three of these carry raised letters on their flat sides. The fifth sling bullet is amygdaloid. It bears both a relief inscription and a stylized scorpion as well as another, less easily identifiable symbol, which should perhaps be taken for a highly stylized wasp.

PRESERVATION

Preservation varies considerably across the corpus. Many pieces are fragmentary, and some degree of surface corrosion is normal. Nevertheless, numerous examples of each type have survived in surprisingly good condition.[4] Of these the lead sling bullets and bronze arrowheads are the best preserved. Four of the five bullets are complete in terms of dimension, while one has lost a point. Likewise, four of the five show only minor surface oxidation. Neither of the two Scythian arrowheads has suffered much corrosion, though one has lost part of a barb and the other has a hole in the wall of the socket.

The iron projectile points, on the other hand, are not so well preserved. Corrosion varies from moderate to extreme. In part because of the generally heavy oxidation, losses in dimension are very common. Among the catapult-bolt heads, which are very heavily corroded, portions of socket walls are commonly missing, as are tips. Though two of the Cretan arrowheads are nearly complete, the rest are fragmentary. The most common losses for this type of point are portions of tangs and barbs. Several also have broken tips. An even higher proportion of the bodkin points are only partially preserved. Only the javelin head and the spear head, both of which are fragmentary, are more poorly preserved as a class. With a very few exceptions the bodkin arrowheads have partial tangs and/or broken tips. Nearly 20% have bent, twisted, or crushed tips or tangs, either from accidental damage or intentional destruction. Just under 10% of the catapult bolts show similar damage.

DISTRIBUTION

At first glance, the projectiles do not appear to have an identifiable pattern of distribution within the Sanctuary (see fig. 5.1). They do not cluster around particular features or in particular trenches; examples have been recovered from more than 40 trenches. This impression of random scatter seems to hold whether one examines particular types or the corpus as a whole. Individual trenches have yielded examples of bodkin and Cretan arrowheads as well as catapult-bolt heads; sling bullets have been found along with catapult-bolt heads and bodkin-style arrowheads.

On closer examination, however, several tendencies are noticeable. The most obvious is the much higher concentration of projectiles recovered from trenches located outside of buildings. There are also significant concentrations of projectiles on the Altar Terrace, downslope from the Terrace, in the northwest corner of the site, and within and beneath the Annexes of Building A.

A similar situation obtains with respect to the projectiles' stratigraphical distribution. They are not confined to a particular site-wide stratum. Some trenches have yielded projectiles consistently from topsoil to levels just above bedrock. Relative dating based on coins and pottery appears to confirm the chronological scope of the projectiles, with examples associated with levels ranging from the late fourth century to the mid-second century.[5] As a result it is difficult to associate the entire corpus with a particular era, much less a particular event. However, numerous individual pieces and concentrations of pieces come from better-understood contexts within the Sanctuary. Combined with the trends visible in the distribution of projectiles across the site and a study of comparable artifacts from other sites and other collections, these pieces make it possible to draw some tentative but significant conclusions with regard to the history of the Sanctuary and the development of ancient projectiles. The prerequisite to any such analysis is a detailed catalogue and discussion of the artifacts themselves.

CATALOGUE

Inv.	Inventory
L	length (in centimetres)
M	mass (in grams)
Y.T.L.P.	Year.Trench.Level.Pail

Catapult bolts (figs. 5.2, 5.3b)

Pyramidal, bodkin head with socket (1–82)

Eighty-three of the weapons found in the acropolis Sanctuary have been identified as heads from catapult bolts. The type is usually distinguished by a conical socket or shank meant to receive the shaft of the bolt, and a heavy, pyramidal point (**3**, **7**, **11**, and **48**, fig. 5.2). One of the catapult-bolt heads (**83**, not shown) deviates from this form and will be discussed separately below. Elsewhere in Greece similar pieces have been identified as ferrules or arrowheads. While this remains a possibility, it is a remote one. The size of these points and their close resemblance to catapult-bolt heads recovered from Roman contexts make their identification quite secure.

Many of the catapult-bolt heads recovered from the Sanctuary are missing tips or portions of sockets. This is largely caused by oxidation; however, a reasonable number have survived more or less intact with only moderate corrosion. Where sockets have been well preserved, as in the case of **12**, **13**, and **38**, they often reveal traces of the seam created during manufacture, when a flat sheet of iron at the base of the head was hammered into a conical shank.[6] In one case, **41**, traces of mineralized wood were found embedded in the top of the socket; however, in no case has the pin/rivet hole for fastening the head to the shaft been perfectly preserved. Several of the catapult-bolt points also show ancient damage, most commonly bent or crushed tips (**38**, fig. 5.3a). While some of this damage may be indicative of impact with unyielding surfaces, in some cases (**16**, **20**, **22**, **27**, **33**, **38**, **44**, and **66**) it is suspiciously regular, so that one must consider whether there was a deliberate attempt to decommission the projectile point.

The fair preservation and substantial number of catapult-bolt heads have made it possible to identify minor variations in form, to permit detailed comparisons with examples from different sites, and even to establish the most likely calibre of the pieces. Most of the catapult bolts show a pronounced neck where the socket meets the head, though a few have an almost straight-sided profile from base to tip. A comparison of numbers **15** and **29** with numbers **18**, **33**, **35**, and **38** illustrates this distinction. The heads of the points likewise vary in shape and size. Some are quite long and have a gradual taper from neck to tip, while others are shorter and have a much more precipitous taper. As a general rule, however, the heads constitute one-quarter to one-third of the entire length of the points. The best-preserved examples indicate an original overall length ca. 8.0–9.0 cm. Socket diameters fall between ca.1.2 and 1.6 cm, a variation in part attributable to corrosion. Similarities in the mass of the best-preserved catapult-bolt heads lend further weight to this impression of overall consistency. A best estimate, given the degree of corrosion, is that the pieces originally weighed ca. 20 to 25 grams.

These relatively small differences in shape, proportion, and size may indicate differences in date or origins. Alternatively, they may simply indicate different manufacturers. One would expect to find measurable differences even among projectile points made in the same workshop, and while consistency was surely a goal in the manufacture of all components of ancient projectiles, it stands to reason that "consistency" meant falling within certain tolerances rather than producing absolutely identical items. Other collections of projectiles linked to a single historical event demonstrate inconsistencies in form, size, and weight similar to those seen in the Stymphalian assemblage.[7] With this in mind, the overall consistency of dimensions among the catapult-bolt heads recovered from the Sanctuary implies a common calibre. Given the dimensions in question, it seems safest to conclude that they were intended to be fixed to bolts fired from the two- or three-span anti-personnel machines common from the fourth century.[8]

The most numerous and best-known comparisons for the catapult-bolt heads from the Sanctuary are of Roman provenance. They have been found from Britain, where dates span the duration of the Roman occupation, to Dura-Europos. The third-century CE catapult bolts recovered from the latter site are a particularly important point of comparison; they include our only extant example of an intact bolt.[9] Only slightly less important are the points recovered from Gimla in Israel, which date to the Roman sack of that city in 67 CE. Those from Hod Hill and Maiden Castle in Great Britain, which have been linked to the Roman invasion of 43 CE, and those attributed to Caesar's assault on Alesia in 52 BCE are also useful for comparisons.[10] Some of these pieces, particularly those from Dura-Europos, are slightly larger and somewhat heavier than the examples from the Sanctuary.[11] In the case of the points from Dura-Europos, this difference is possibly attributable to increases in the power of catapults ca. 100 CE traced by Marsden.[12] Some of the Roman examples also have shorter, flat-bottomed heads and more pronounced necks than the majority of pieces from the Sanctuary. Nevertheless, many later Roman catapult-bolt heads are all but indistinguishable from those recovered in the Sanctuary.

These similarities are especially important because no other iron catapult-bolt heads have been identified on Greek sites. Initially, it suggests that the catapult bolts at Stymphalos are Roman. However, such a conclusion would be precipitous and potentially misleading. In fact, the examples from the Sanctuary are not entirely exceptional. Similar pieces in iron have been found at Kalapodi and New Halos; however, at the latter site they were identified as ferrules.[13] Several examples at New Halos dating between 302 and 265 were recovered from domestic contexts. They were originally identified as arrowheads, but were subsequently labelled ferrules (i.e., *sauroteres*: spear butts) albeit with the qualification that they might well be javelin points, or tips of agricultural implements such as pitchforks or cattle prods.[14] While these identifications are doubtless correct for some of the larger pieces and those with very blunt tips and very wide sockets, the four illustrated examples show that at least two of the 21 pieces classified as "ferrules" bear a striking resemblance to the Stymphalian and Roman catapult-bolt heads.[15] At New Halos, the pieces in question measure 7.0 and 6.6 cm in length and 1.5 cm at the base of their sockets. Both have square-sectioned, pyramidal heads separated from the socket by a very slight indentation rather than a distinct neck. Even the V-shaped seams where the two walls of the socket were joined during manufacture are identical to those on the pieces found at Stymphalos.

At Olynthos, among the iron projectile points with pyramidal heads and tangs, one example (Robinson 1941, 393 no. 1983 pl. 123) seems to show the remains of a socket, separated from its head by a distinct neck. At 7.2 cm in length, this artifact is a close match for those from the Sanctuary.[16] It is not surprising that this piece was not identified as a catapult-bolt point. There was no reason for Robinson to expect catapult bolts in an assemblage of projectile points. There was no precedent for such finds on sites of similar date and relatively little was then known about the development of ancient artillery. That is why he identified the large bronze points inscribed with Philip's name as arrowheads, though they have since been reclassified as catapult-bolt heads.[17] Moreover, this was a solitary piece in a collection comprising more than 230 projectile points, of which ca. 20% were iron, and which included 18 distinct types (labelled A–G with sub-classes).

Some of the same factors surely influenced the identification of the pieces from New Halos as ferrules. Aside from the much later Roman examples mentioned above, there was nothing to suggest the possibility that iron artifacts of this type might have been the heads of catapult bolts. The excavators discounted the possibility that they were arrowheads on the basis of weight and socket diameter, both of which exceeded typical dimensions for arrows.[18] It must also be said in defence of this identification that iron catapult-bolt heads do bear a certain resemblance to some types of small ferrules;[19] however, the pieces in question are much closer in shape to known catapult-bolt heads than to the majority of iron ferrules recovered from Greek sites. Such pieces tend to be much longer and narrower, or conversely, much shorter, with a squat, conical profile.[20] Reservations regarding mass and socket size present no obstacle to the hypothesis that such pieces are the heads of catapult bolts, which are typically heavier than arrowheads and also intended to fit on shafts of somewhat larger diameter.[21] Bearing all this in mind there seem to be grounds to suggest a reidentification of the pieces from New Halos as points from catapult bolts.[22]

These tentative reidentifications, if accepted, considerably broaden the chronological range of preserved iron catapult-bolt heads, extending it back from the first century into the fourth century and moving the cultural locus from Rome to Greece.[23] This is not as surprising as it might seem initially. First, it is known that the Romans borrowed artillery design and terminology, not to mention actual machines, from the Greeks.[24] There is no reason to assume that they failed to borrow the design of projectiles as well. Literary sources provide clear evidence that the Romans adopted Hellenistic Greek calibres for their artillery. This testimony is confirmed by the bolts from Roman sites as late as Dura-Europos.[25]

As for chronology, there are good reasons to look to the fourth century for the appearance of specialized points for catapult bolts. Thanks in great part to Marsden's excellent study of ancient artillery, we have a solid understanding of the origins and evolution of bolt-firing catapults. Artillery of this sort was invented in Syracuse in 399, and two years later Dionysios I employed it for the first time in his attack on Motya.[26]

At its inception, artillery was relatively unsophisticated. The very first ancient artillery piece, the *gastraphetes*, resembled a crossbow, and the larger machines that followed close on its heels were essentially scaled-up versions of the same mechanism. In brief, non-torsion artillery consisted of outsized bows mounted on frames and equipped with winches and triggers. Small machines like the gastraphetes may have fired missiles indistinguishable from arrows; larger, more powerful machines naturally fired larger, purpose-built projectiles.[27]

In short order artillery became increasingly sophisticated and effective until about the mid-fourth century, when a quantum leap occurred with the introduction of the torsion spring as the means of propulsion. Marsden argued that this advance might have been the brainchild of Polyidos of Thessaly between 353 and 341. Polyidos was chief engineer to Philip of Macedon, a well-known artillery aficionado.[28] Regardless of the precise timing, it seems clear that as artillery evolved through trial and error in the first years after its introduction, thought must also have been given to the design of projectiles. Eventually, the proportional relationship between bolt length and torsion spring diameter became the guiding principle of bolt-firing catapult design,[29] but even at this relatively early juncture there would have been an awareness that getting the most out of a catapult depended in part on the missiles it fired. Bolts had to manage forces of a different order from those transmitted to arrows. The practical solution was to make the shafts thicker relative to their length and to develop larger points designed for maximum shock and penetration of armoured targets.

Working from a reference by Diodorus to catapult bolts of all kinds and other missiles being readied as part of Dionysios' armament, Marsden placed the appearance of specially designed bolts at the very outset of artillery development in 399.[30] Further literary evidence of specialized missiles comes from Plutarch's *Pelopidas*. Plutarch relates an anecdote from the siege of Samos in 366/5, centred on the Athenian general Timotheus' near-death experience with a "bolt" fired from the walls of the city.[31] Against the possibility that these sources may be guilty of anachronisms, there is epigraphic evidence for the existence of such artifacts as early as the second quarter of the fourth century. The inventory from the Chalkotheke on the Athenian Acropolis confirms the existence of specialized catapult bolts, as distinct from arrows, no later than 363/2.[32] Unfortunately, there is no way to know what distinguished the two classes of missile at this time. The distinction may have been based on size, on design, on material, or on some combination of these factors.

Given the limitations of the literary and epigraphic evidence, we return to the archaeological record and note again that catapult-bolt heads first appear half a century after the invention of artillery, with Philip's siege of Olynthos.[33] Originally identified as arrowheads, six large, bronze, trilobate points with sockets were subsequently identified by Snodgrass as points from catapult bolts.[34] All have been attributed to Philip's attack on the city in 348, thanks in part to the fact that five of them carry Philip's name. These points bear no resemblance to any of the pieces from Stymphalos, much less to the later Roman catapult-bolt heads. They are in fact scaled-up versions of a relatively common type of bronze arrowhead.[35] If not for the presence of what appears to be the earliest iron catapult-bolt head[36] in the same collection, this would suggest that all catapult bolts were simply enlarged arrows. Instead, the only reasonable conclusion to draw is that a varied approach to catapult-bolt head design existed at the time. One would expect the first generation or two of catapult-bolt heads to include a variety of designs based on existing technologies and styles of projectile points and perhaps other weapons or tools. On the other hand, the type of point used for this purpose may have been in transition. This shift could be connected to the appearance of the first torsion-powered artillery.[37] The power of such machines may have necessitated changes in the proportions of bolts, which may in turn have led to experimentation with both the material and the design of points.

The iron pyramidal point that became the standard for catapult bolts seems to have been a hybrid, which provided the strength and penetrating power necessary to withstand and exploit the mechanical power imparted by the catapult.[38] It coupled the socket common to many types of bronze and some iron arrowheads, not to mention javelin heads and spear heads, with the "bodkin" style of point used on some arrowheads since at least the fifth century. Interestingly, the end result was something very like the spear butts or sauroteres that have been recovered from a variety of Greek sites, particularly Olympia and Olynthos.[39] Designed to balance the weight of the spear head and to allow the spear to be driven into the ground, sauroteres were often used for the secondary purpose of delivering the *coup de grâce* to fallen enemies. The sharp, square-sectioned (bodkin) tips on the spear butts gave them excellent penetrating power, which allowed them to be driven through the armour of fallen foes even in the press of a hoplite battle. Cuirasses with square punctures dedicated by victors testify to their effectiveness in this regard.[40] So it may be that the ultimate form of the catapult-bolt head owes as much or more to spear butts as it does to pre-existing projectile points.[41]

The precise moment when this type of catapult-bolt head first appeared remains uncertain, as does the period when it triumphed over rival designs. Nor is it certain that either milestone relates to the change from non-torsion to torsion spring propulsion. Moreover, the apparent absence of stylistic development from the earliest appearance of iron catapult-bolt heads until at least the second half of the third century CE makes it impossible to date the Stymphalian points on such grounds. At most, the existing comparanda suggest that such artifacts were present in Greece by the middle years of the fourth century, though they are much more common on later sites with Roman connections.

Pyramidal, bodkin head with socket

Cat. no.	Inv.no.	Y.T.L.P.	L[42] (cm)	W (cm)	M (g)	Condition
1	9	95.3.1.1	6.6	1.5	16	Good: near complete
2	49	95.7.2.4	6.0	1.3	16	Fair: missing part of socket
3	50	95.8.3.9	7.7	1.0	24	Excellent: near complete

Pyramidal, bodkin head with socke (*Continued*)

Cat. no.	Inv.no.	Y.T.L.P.	L[42] (cm)	W (cm)	M (g)	Condition
4	70	95.7.4.9	7.2	1.3	16	Fair: missing some of socket
5	130	95.9b3.3	7.1	1.3	22	Good: missing part of socket, blunt tip
6	135	96.3.3.5	6.1	1.6	16	Good: near complete
7	139	96.5ex.1.1	4.6	1.4	8	Good
8	140	96.4.2.3	4.7	1.6	10	Good
9	142	96.3.3.5	5.5	1.5	NA	Poor: missing much of socket, broken tip
10	147	96.6.2.3	5.9	1.3	14	Fair: missing part of socket, crushed tip
11	149	95.8.4.12	7.2	1.3	26	Excellent
12	151	95.6.5.8	6.9	1.4	16	Good: missing part of socket, blunt tip
13	218	96.3.3.6	7.1	1.4	14	Good: near complete
14	219	96.3.3.5	6.0	1.8	18	Good: missing part of socket
15	432	96.9.1.1	6.8	1.1	14	Very good: near complete
16	441	96.11.1.1	5.1	1.2	12	Fair: bent tip
17	479	96.8.3.3	7.4	1.5	16	Good: near complete, blunt tip
18	524	96.8.4.5	8.6	1.6	22	Excellent: near complete
19	546	96.9.3.3	4.4	1.1	6	Poor: missing most of socket, broken tip
20	664	96.5ex.10.7	6.3	1.1	18	Good: bent tip
21	811	96.15.3.3	7.0	1.6	20	Excellent: near complete
22	825	96.9.3.3	5.9	1.4	12	Fair: significant bend
23	899	96.9.3.3	5.2	1.5	18	Fair: missing part of socket, bent tip
24	901	96.3.scarp	5.8	1.3	18	Poor: missing tip and much of socket
25	904	96.5ex.10.2	5.6	1.6	16	Poor: missing much of socket, broken tip
26	956	96.13.5.8	6.2	1.3	12	Good: missing part of socket
27	970	95.2.4.8	6.4	2.0	20	Fair: crushed tip, missing part of socket
28	985	97.2.3.3	6.5	1.4	20	Good: missing part of socket
29	1012	97.2.3.3	5.5	1.3	18	Very good: near complete
30	1079	96.8.5.6	5.0	1.2	NA	Poor: missing much of socket, bent tip
31	1080	96.8.5.6	6.6	1.3	20	Fair: heavy corrosion, broken tip
32	1089	97.4.3.4	6.4	1.6	16	Very good: clear socket crease, broken tip
33	1239	97.6.2.2	6.7	1.5	16	Excellent: bent crushed tip
34	1267	97.6.2.2	6.2	1.5	22	Very good: near complete
35	1268	97.6.2.2	7.6	1.6	20	Very good: near complete
36	1367	97.7.3.3	6.4	1.4	16	Good: missing part of socket, broken tip
37	1384	97.7.scarp	6.2	1.3	18	Very good: near complete
38	1385	97.7.3.3	6.2	1.6	22	Very good: tip bent 90°
39	1410	97.10.1.1	6.7	1.5	18	Very good: near complete
40	1562	97.11.5.6	7.1	1.3	18	Very good: near complete
41	1616	97.11.scarp	5.8	1.7	10	Fair: wood fragment preserved in socket
42	1621	95.3.6.11	6.1	1.1	20	Poor: missing most of socket, bent, partial tip
43	2103	97.12.surface	6.0	1.0	20	Fair: missing part of socket
44	2114	96.13.0.0	5.0	1.1	16	Fair: missing part of socket, tip bent 90°
45	2145	96.6.scarp	6.0	0.9	14	Excellent
46	2147	97.12.00	6.2	1.1	20	Fair: missing some of socket
47	2234	99.1.3.3	5.6	1.1	14	Fair: missing much of socket, broken tip
48	2237	99.1.3.3	6.4	1.1	12	Very good: missing some of socket
49	2239	99.5.2.2	5.3	1.4	NA	Poor: split and broken socket
50	2326	99.10.3.4	4.2	NA	10	Fair: missing part of socket
51	2400	99.1.5.7	4.9	1.5	12	Fragmentary: split into 2 pieces
52	2412	99.1.5.7	4.5	1.0	NA	Fair
53	2442	99.10.3.4	7.0	1.4	16	Very good
54	2451	99.1.5.8	5.1	1.0	12	Fair: missing most of socket, blunt tip
55	2481	99.1.5.8	6.9	1.1	12	Poor: missing some of socket
56	2517	99.6.6.6	6.6	1.8	22	Excellent
57	2650	97.5b.3.4	6.2	1.2	18	Good
58	2653	99.1.5.10	6.1	0.9	18	Fair: missing some of socket, broken tip
59	2661	97.5b.4.5	7.4	NA	26	Fair: missing much of socket

Pyramidal, bodkin head with socke (*Concluded*)

Cat. no.	Inv.no.	Y.T.L.P.	L[42] (cm)	W (cm)	M (g)	Condition
60	2745	99.1.6.12	6.0	1.1	14	Good: missing some of socket, blunt tip
61	2807	99.1.6.12	7.5	1.5	26	Excellent
62	2982	00.4.4.4	6.2	1.2	22	Poor: broken tip, missing quite a bit of socket
63	3107	00.scarp	6.0	1.4	18	Good: missing lower part of socket
64	3156	00.3.6.6	6.3	1.6	14	Fair: broken tip
65	3193	00.5.2.2	6.3	1.2	12	Fair: missing part of tip and much of socket
66	3198	00.5.2.2	6.9	1.2	16	Good: bent, crushed tip
67	3205	00.6.2.2	6.3	1.2	14	Poor: missing much of socket
68	3253	00.6.2.2	6.6	1.3	16	Fair: broken tip
69	3254	00.6.2.2	6.6	1.3	18	Fair: missing part of socket and tip
70	3255	00.5.3.3	6.7	1.5	16	Good: missing part of socket
71	3272	00.6.2.2	9.3	1.5	42	Good: missing part of socket
72	3548	00.6.3.3	6.9	1.5	28	Fair: missing part of tang
73	3576	00.6.3.3	5.6	1.4	12	Poor: missing most of socket
74	3612	00.6.4.4	6.6	1.3	14	Fair: missing part of socket
75	3641	00.6.3.3	5.5	1.8	14	Good: broken tip
76	3665	00.6.4.4	7.5	1.5	24	Good: near complete
77	3666	00.6.4.4	6.7	1.4	16	Poor: missing half of socket
78	4288	00.surface	5.8	NA	NA	Poor: broken tip, heavy corrosion
79	No number[43]	95.7	NA	NA	NA	Poor: missing much of socket,
80	No number	95.7	NA	NA	NA	Good: missing part of socket
81	No number	95.7	NA	NA	NA	Poor: missing much of socket, broken tip
82	No number	95.7	NA	NA	NA	Poor: missing much of socket

"Ad hoc" catapult bolt or arrowhead (83)

This class of iron projectile point combines a socket with a leaf-shaped blade. It is represented by a single piece, **83**. The piece is identical to the balance of the catapult-bolt heads from socket base to neck, but the point on **83** takes the form of a flat, leaf-shaped blade, with a pronounced midrib.

Eight similar pieces were found in the Sanctuary of Artemis and Apollo at Kalapodi. Schmitt identified them as arrowheads and their contextual dates ranged from the Late Geometric through the Early Classical periods.[44] **83** may well be an arrowhead of this type, dating perhaps as early as the Late Classical period, given the range of material found in the Sanctuary. However, it is also very much reminiscent of the "ad hoc" catapult bolt points identified by Bishop and Coulston, who believed that such artifacts were made during an emergency when supplies of standard bolts had run out.[45] In light of this and its similarities to the catapult-bolt heads, it seems safest to identify this piece as a catapult-bolt head, while acknowledging the possibility that it may be an arrowhead.

"Ad hoc" catapult bolt or arrowhead

Cat. no.	Inv. no.	Y.T.L.P	L (cm)	W(cm)	M (g)	Condition
83	1190	97.3.5.6	5.5	.9	NA	Poor: missing part of socket and half of blade

Arrowheads

"Scythian" arrowheads (84–5; fig. 5.2)

The only bronze projectiles from the acropolis Sanctuary are two arrowheads of the "Scythian" type, which Robinson labelled Type G at Olynthos.[46] One (**84**) (fig. 5.2) has three convex blades that spring from a central socket and run the full length of the piece. Each blade has a barb on its trailing edge. The other (**85**) (fig. 5.2) is also trilobate, but the blades are somewhat straighter and shorter relative to the overall length of the piece, comprising only about two-thirds of the total. Both are nearly complete and in near perfect condition.

A very slight point, favoured by the lightly armed archers of the Scythian steppes and the Persian Empire, these arrowheads were designed to be fitted to cane shafts. Though capable of very long ranges and doubtless very effective against lightly armed opponents, projectiles of this sort may have been less effective against heavily armed infantry. Similar arrowheads have been recovered from a wide variety of Greek sites, including Athens, Corinth, Kalapodi, Marathon, Nemea, Olympia, Olynthos, and Thermopylae, to name the best known.[47] Olympia and Olynthos, in particular, produced artifacts identical to the Stymphalian examples in every detail.[48] These pieces are common from the sixth century, but appear to have fallen out of favour towards the end of the fourth century, after which they all but disappear from Greek sites.

Arrowheads: Scythian arrowheads

Cat. no.	Inv. no.	Y.T.L.P	L (cm)	W (cm)	M (g)	Condition
84	920	96.10.6.2	2.42	0.9	less than 1g	Excellent
85	2888	00.3.2.2	2.0	0.6	less than 1 g	Excellent

Type H, in iron (86)

One iron point from the Sanctuary has a socket and three-bladed head. The socket is cylindrical, flaring slightly at the base, which is only partly preserved. No identical piece in iron with Greek provenance has been published, it seems, though much later pieces with Romano-British provenance are extant.[49] On the other hand, numerous bronze arrowheads from Olympia and Nemea are similar in general form.[50] Walters labelled bronze examples of this point "Type H."[51] The difference in material makes it impossible to draw conclusions from these pieces with respect to the date of the example from the Sanctuary.

Arrowhead: Type H, in iron

Cat. no.	Inv. no.	Y.T.L.P	L (cm)	W (cm)	M (g)	Condition
86	2219	99.1.3.3	3.0	0.5	1.0	Good: missing part of socket base

Cretan arrowheads (87–99; figs. 5.2 and 5.3b)

The twelve leaf-shaped Cretan points comprise the second most numerous type of arrowhead from the Sanctuary.[52] All are iron. Several are extremely well preserved, while others are missing tangs, tips, and barbs. As a group they are remarkably consistent in form, with a long tang and a flat, leaf-shaped head. **90**, **92**, and **94** are particularly fine examples. Raised bosses at the base of both faces of the head provided a seat for the shaft. Barbs are preserved at the trailing edges of each blade on **90**, **93**, **94**, and **95**. The most complete examples range between 8.0 and 8.6 cm in length, weigh between 12 and 14 g, and are 1.6 to 1.8 cm wide at the broadest part of the head.

This type of projectile point is often called Cretan from the ancient belief that it originated on that island.[53] Similar pieces, most commonly in bronze, have been found elsewhere in Greece, with Olympia, Olynthos, Delphi, Delos, Kalapodi, Lindos, Nemea, Perachora, and Cyrene (Libya) providing examples.[54] In bronze, this type is known as early as the Mycenaean period. The Persians made great use of it before and during their invasions of Greece.[55] It remained popular throughout the Hellenistic period and into the Roman era.[56]

By 500 this type had made its first appearance in iron, as indicated by examples from Olympia dating to the late sixth century.[57] By the late fifth century, iron had become much more common, if the pieces from Nemea, all in iron, are any indication.[58] Even so, bronze continued to be a popular choice for such projectile points beyond this date, as is clear from the pieces recovered at Olynthos, all of which were bronze.[59]

The apparently long transitional period in which bronze and iron examples of this type coexisted makes it impossible to narrow significantly the date of the uniformly iron collection recovered from the Sanctuary. The presence of a bronze example of this type in the domestic quarter of Stymphalos underscores this problem.[60] What can be said on the basis of style and material is that the iron "Cretan" points from the Sanctuary must fall between the early fifth century and the Roman era.

Cretan Arrowheads

Cat. no.	Inv. no.	Y.T.L.P	L (cm)	W (cm)	M (g)	Condition
87	34	95.3.1.3	NA	NA	12	Fair: missing part of tip
88	192	96.3.3.6	5.8	1.7	8	Poor: missing most of tang and part of blade
89	220	96.4.4.7	3.2	1.7	4	Poor: missing tang and part of tip
90	224	96.6.1.2	8.0	1.8	12	Very good
91	225	95.6.5.7	7.2	1.8	14	Fair: missing part of tang and tip,
92	639	96.15.1.1	8.0	2.0	14	Very good
93	1238	97.5.3.6	5.6	1.8	NA	Fair: missing part of tang, tip, and one barb
94	1240	97.6.2.2	8.7	1.8	14	Very good: missing tip and one barb
95	1456	97.9.5.5	5.3	1.6	12	Poor: missing tang and part of blade
96	2126	96.3.1.1	5.0	1.5	6	Poor: missing part of tang
97	2356	99.11.2.2	4.7	1.8	8	Fair: missing tip and part of tang
98	2929	00.2.2.2	6.1	1.9	14	Good: missing part of tang
99	3302	00.6.2.2	7.1	1.6	14	Fair: missing tang

"Bodkin" arrowheads (100–91; figs. 5.2 and 5.3a–b)

By far the largest class of arrowheads recovered from the acropolis Sanctuary is the so-called bodkin type, classified by Robinson as "Type E."[61] At first glance, the 92 bodkin points appear fairly homogeneous in form, each having a long tang and a square-sectioned, pyramidal head. In most cases where the piece has been fully preserved, the tang and head are approximately equal in length. Leaving aside size for the moment, the only point of distinction among the bodkin points is in the shape of the head. On some the sides taper evenly from base to tip. Others taper steeply, giving the base of the head a pronounced bulge, from which emerges a long, narrow tip.

The majority of the bodkin points are consistent in size, at least in terms of the maximum preserved dimension at the base of the head. According to this criterion, most of the points cluster between 0.8 and 1.1 cm. Similar trends are visible in the weights of well-preserved pieces, which tend to fall between 10 and 12 g. That said, four of the bodkin points (**103**, **120**, **163**, **180**) are much smaller than the others, though not small enough to be considered miniature. One (**145**) is considerably larger and, although it is not too large to be an arrowhead, it may be a small javelin head.

As might be expected, tips and portions of tangs are most susceptible to damage. In certain cases, this is attributable to corrosion, but in others it is ancient damage. Some of this appears to be the result of impact; in other cases, it can only be explained by attempts to free a projectile from being embedded in a solid object, or else deliberate attempts to render the projectile point useless. Apparent impact damage can be seen on **38**, **114**, **118**, and **135** (fig. 5.3a), as well as on **149** and **156**. What appears to be secondary or decommissioning damage can be seen on **101** and **164** (fig. 5.2), **118** (fig. 5.3a), and **131** (fig. 5.3b) as well as on **138** and **182**.[62]

The "bodkin" type, traditionally considered to be Cypriot in origin, has a very long history.[63] Remarkably similar points of Bronze Age date were found at Asine (on display in the Nauplion museum), and two bronze examples of indeterminate date have been found at Olympia.[64] The closest comparisons to the Stymphalian examples in material and date again come from Nemea, Olympia, and Olynthos, with Kalapodi and Pylos also contributing important finds. The examples from Olympia and Nemea demonstrate the appearance of this type in iron no later than the fifth century. One of the four iron bodkin points found at Olympia came from a well dated to the first quarter of the fifth century, while the five Nemean examples have been convincingly, if tentatively, linked to a late fifth-century destruction.[65] From this period the type seems to have become more widespread. At Kalapodi some 17 iron bodkin points have been recovered in the sanctuary of Artemis and Apollo. Two of these were found in a fifth-century pit.[66] Pylos yielded six iron bodkin points from domestic contexts, all of which have been securely dated to the site's Classical phase, ca. 425–365/4.[67] The 55 iron examples recovered from Olynthos, all of which have been attributed to Philip's siege in 348, are indicative of the type's apparent popularity in the fourth century.[68] Kalapodi also offers evidence of this type in the later Hellenistic period. Three of the 17 bodkin points found there came from a context which may be as late as the late second or early first century.[69] The Roman period presents many examples of the type, though sometimes with a socket rather than a tang. It survived into the Medieval period, since an example from Corinth is dated to the eleventh century CE.[70] Thus, as with the types already discussed, comparative stylistic analysis provides only a broad chronological range for the bodkin points, a range which spans the entire occupation of the Sanctuary.

"Bodkin" arrowheads

Cat. no.	Inv. no.	Y.T.L.P	L (cm)	W (cm)	M (g)	Condition
100	11	95.3.1.3	4.7	0.9	10	Poor: missing tang, broken tip
101	52	95.8.2.3	4.6	1.0	10	Fair: missing part of tang, tip bent 90°
102	89	95.6.4.5	NA	NA	12	Fair: missing part of tang
103	132	96.1.1.1	4.3	0.6	2	Very good: missing tip
104	133	96.6.2.3	6.3	1.0	10	Good: missing part of tang and tip
105	134	96.6.2.3	8.2	0.9	NA	Very good: near complete
106	137	96.4.3.5	7.5	0.8	8	Good: near complete
107	138	96.3.3.5	3.9	1.0	NA	Poor: missing most of tang and much of tip
108	141	96.3.3.5	5.0	1.1	NA	Fair: missing part of tang and tip
109	143	96.6.2.3	4.9	1.1	10	Fair: missing most of tang and part of tip
110	144	95.9b.3.4	4.5	0.9	4	Poor: missing most of tang and part of tip
111	145	96.6.2.4	4.5	0.9	10	Fair: missing most of tang and part of tip
112	146	96.3.1.1	6.6	0.7	8	Fair
113	148	96.3.3.5	5.3	1.1	10	Fair: missing tang
114	152	96.6.2.3	8.0	1.1	10	Good: bent and broken tip
115	153	96.6.2.3	6.7	0.8	6	Good: slight bend in tang and tip
116	154	96.3.2.2	5.7	1.2	8	Fair: missing most of tang, broken tip
117	191	96.7.1.1	5.7	1.0	10	Poor: fragmentary
118	212	96.8.1.1	4.5	0.8	NA	Good: bent tang and tip
119	214	96.8.3.3	6.2	1.0	8	Fair: partial tang, broken tip
120	215	96.7.2.2	4.9	0.8	6	Very good
121	216	96.3.4.7	5.6	1.0	10	Fair: missing tang
122	217	96.7.1.1	4.2	0.8	NA	Poor: fragmentary
123	221	96.3.3.6	6.2	1.1	10	Fair: missing much of tang and part of tip
124	222	96.8.2.2	5.0	0.5	4	Poor: fragment
125	223	96.1.9.10	3.9	1.0	8	Poor: fragmentary
126	226	96.6.2.4	8.5	1.0	12	Very good: broken and bent tip
127	417	96.8.3.3	9.3	1.1	10	Very good: near complete
128	424	96.9.1.1	6.6	1.0	10	Very good
129	431	96.11.1.1	6.0	0.7	4	Good: missing part of tang and tip
130	480	96.8.3.3	5.1	1.2	8	Poor: missing most of tang and part of tip
131	526	96.13.2.3	6.2	0.9	6	Good: broken and bent tang
132	527	96.8.4.5	8.4	0.9	6	Good: near complete but 2 pieces
133	535	96.8.3.4	5.5	1.1	8	Fair: missing much of tang and part of tip
134	539	96.13.2.3	4.3	0.9	8	Poor: missing tang and part of tip
135	547	96.9.3.3	6.1	1.0	6	Fair: partial tang, tip bent 90°
136	553	96.8.4.5	6.1	1.0	10	Fair: missing part of tang and tip
137	555	96.9.4.4	4.0	0.8	NA	Poor: missing tang and most of tip
138	602	96.5ex.6.8	5.9	0.8	6	Good: bent tang and tip
139	632	96.13.2.4	5.3	0.9	6	Good: missing part of tang and tip
140	634	96.13.2.4	4.4	0.9	6	Poor: missing most of tip
141	715	96.15.3.3	10.1	0.9	10	Excellent: complete
142	717	96.5ex.7.10	3.7	0.8	6	Poor: fragmentary
143	719	96.13.2.5	5.2	0.9	6	Fair: missing part of tang and tip
144	861	96.10.4.4	4.7	1.2	6	Poor: missing most of tang and tip
145	923	96.10.5.1	6.0	1.2	22	Poor: missing tang and part of tip
146	930	96.13.4.7	6.0	0.9	10	Fair: missing much of tang and part of tip
147	950	95.2.4.8	6.4	1.2	10	Fair: missing much of tang, tip bent
148	971	96.13.6.10	7.4	1.0	8	Very good

"Bodkin" arrowheads (*Concluded*)

Cat. no.	Inv. no.	Y.T.L.P	L (cm)	W (cm)	M (g)	Condition
149	1062	97.1.2.3	5.0	0.9	8	Fair: missing most of tang and part of tip
150	1132	97.4.4.6	4.1	0.7	2	Poor: fragmentary
151	1149	97.5.2.4	5.0	0.9	6	Fair: missing much of tang, broken tip
152	1174	96.3nb.3.3	5.2	1.1	10	Poor: missing most of tang and much of tip
153	1186	97.4.5.7	4.5	0.9	8	Fair: missing most of tang and part of tip
154	1200	97.4.5.7	5.4	0.9	8	Fair: missing much of tang and part of tip
155	1211	97.5.3.6	5.0	1.1	8	Poor: missing tang, split and bent tip
156	1236	97.4.5.8	5.8	0.8	6	Fair: missing part of tang, tip bent 90°
157	1269	97.6.1.1	9.4	1.0	10	Excellent
158	1539	97.8.2.3	10.3	0.8	14	Excellent
159	1666	94.6.2.2	5.3	0.8	10	Fair
160	1668	96.surface	5.3	0.8	8	Fair: missing most of tang, bent and broken tip
161	2146	96.3.3.5	5.5	0.6	10	Fair: missing most of tang, bent tip
162	2151	99.1.1.1	5.8	0.9	10	Fair: missing part of tang and tip
163	2216	99.1.3.3	3.3	0.5	less than 1	Poor
164	2235	99.1.3.3	5.0	1.0	8	Fair: tang bent 360°, broken tip
165	2394	99.10.3.4	5.1	1.5	NA	Poor: bent tang, broken tip
166	2407	99.6.5.5	5.3	1.0	8	Poor: fragmentary
167	2441	99.8.3.3	5.5	0.9	8	Fair: missing most of tang, tip blunted
168	2454	99.10.4.5	4.4	1.3	NA	Poor: missing most of tip
169	2530	99.1.5.9	5.5	1.1	10	Poor: missing much of tang, broken tip
170	2543	99.1.5.10	6.1	1.1	8	Fair: missing much of tang, broken tip
171	2660	97.5b.4.5	4.9	1.0	8	Poor: missing most of tang, broken tip
172	2668	99.1.5.10	9.7	1.0	14	Excellent
173	2723	97.5b.4.5	5.6	1.1	6	Poor: missing most of tang
174	2732	97.5b.4.5	8.3	1.2	10	Fair: missing much of tang, slight bend in tip
175	2743	99.1.5.11	5.7	1.0	10	Poor: missing tang
176	2811	99.1b.4.4	5.4	1.0	10	Poor: missing most of tang, broken tip
177	2893	00.3.2.2	4.5	0.9	10	Poor: missing tang, tip bent 90°
178	2928	00.99.10.cleaning	6.6	0.8	8	Fair: missing part of tang and tip
179	2934	00.3.3.3	3.9	0.9	NA	Poor: missing most of tang and part of tip
180	2941	00.2.3.3	3.9	0.9	6	Poor: missing most of tang, bent tip
181	2969	00.2.3.3	NA	NA	NA	Poor: fragmentary
182	2971	00.2.3.3	5.3	1.0	12	Good: tang and tip bent 90°
183	3103	00.4.6.6	4.4	0.9	6	Poor: missing most of tang and tip
184	3141	00.4.6.6	6.7	0.9	8	Fair: missing part of tang and tip
185	3160	00.4.7.7	5.7	0.9	6	Poor: missing most of tang and tip
186	3215	00.5.3.3	8.5	1.0	12	Good: missing part of tang
187	3450	00.3.6.6	5.7	0.9	8	Poor: missing most of tang and part of tip
188	3454	00.97.4.1.cleaning	7.2	0.9	10	Fair: missing part of tang and tip
189	4289	01.surface	NA	NA	NA	Fair: missing part of tang
190	No number[71]	95.7	NA	NA	NA	Fair: broken tang
191	No number	96.8	7.0	1.0	NA	Fair: missing most of tang

Javelin head (192; fig. 5.2)

One piece recovered from the Sanctuary has been identified as a javelin head. Though corroded and missing the tip of the blade, which was evidently broken in antiquity, it is well enough preserved to permit study. It has a conical socket and a bi-lobed, leaf-shaped blade, with a strengthening riser or midrib. Length, mass, and socket diameter place this piece in a category distinct from the catapult bolts, even the "ad hoc" piece (**83**) that it most closely resembles. It seems too small for a thrusting spear head, but it would suit a throwing spear or javelin.

A favourite weapon of *peltasts*, javelins have a long history. Similar points in both iron and bronze have been recovered from several Greek sites. The assemblage from Olynthos included several that seem similar to **192**.[72] They were originally identified as spears, and may have been, though, as Snodgrass pointed out, they seem too small to have been effective in that role.[73]

At Olympia, 18 iron javelin heads (*wurfspeerspitzen*) have been identified, several of which are very close in shape and size to **192**.[74] Without a thorough typological study of javelin heads, it is impossible to date **192** stylistically.[75]

Javelin head

Cat. no.	Inv. no.	Y.T.L.P	L (cm)	W (cm)	M (g)	Condition
192	2296	99.5.3.3	8.5	2.0	30	Poor: missing half of blade

Spear head (193; fig. 5.2)

A fragmentary spear head was recovered from the Sanctuary, with only a fraction of the tip preserved. The surviving portion suggests that it was fairly typical of the hoplite spear, with an elongated, teardrop-shaped blade, incorporating a pronounced central riser or midrib.

Comparable examples are extant at Olympia, Olynthos, Nemea, and many other sites.[76] While the stylistic development of spear heads is better known than that of iron projectile points and javelin heads, **193** is too badly preserved to allow any meaningful conclusions.

Spear head

Cat. no.	Inv. no.	Y.T.L.P	L (cm)	W (cm)	M (g)	Condition
193	99	95.6.4.5	7.6	3.1	22	Poor: fragmentary

Sling bullets (194–8; fig. 5.3c)

All five of the lead sling bullets from the Sanctuary are well preserved. Only **195** suffered ancient damage, the loss of a tip. Four of the five are symmetrical and almond shaped. They are therefore typical of ancient examples in both form and material.[77] The fifth piece (**198**) is less typical: only one end comes to a pronounced point. While all five measure approximately 3 × 2 cm, **198** is markedly lighter, weighing 25 g, whereas the others weigh 40 to 44 g. These differences suggest that **198** is from a different source, though whether this also means from a different era, different state, or simply a different mould is impossible to say.

Sling bullets ("glandes") have a long history. Inscribed lead bullets similar to those recovered from Stymphalos appear on Cyprus as early as the twelfth century,[78] though they are not mentioned in literary sources until Xenophon's *Anabasis* (3.3.16, battle of Cunaxa). Examples have been recovered in large quantities from a variety of Greek and Roman sites.[79] As a general rule, sling bullets vary in their proportions even when originating from the same state or army, though the overall shape remains consistently amygdaloid or ovoid. Published examples range in weight from 20.7 g to 136.8 g, with the majority falling between 30 and 40 g.[80] A great many of the published examples bear raised letters and/or decoration on their sides. These "inscriptions," which are often abbreviations, customarily take the form of a general's or monarch's name or that of a city or manufacturer, an insult to the intended recipient, an invocation of the gods, or an exhortation to the missile itself.[81] Several of the Torone sling bullets have legends on both sides. These seem to be meant to be read together to give a full name, so NA/MER (Namertas or Namertidas are possibilities); MIKI/NAS (Mikinas, unusual nominative case); OR - - DAS/KALOS (possibly Orestadas or Orphondas, nominative case); and KLEO/BOULO (Kleoboulo, should be genitive case Kleoboulou).[82] Decorative symbols are rarely subtle, with thunderbolts, spear heads, scorpions, and wasps being particularly popular choices.[83]

As is typical with Greek sling bullets, four of the five examples from the Sanctuary bear symbols and/or letters, though none has an exact parallel among previously published bullets. The simplest of these is a decorative dot rosette on **197**. The asymmetrical, ovoid bullet (**198**) bears the most complex markings. On one side a scorpion sits beneath the inscription KOYX. On the other side, an unidentifiable symbol – perhaps a winged insect (wasp?) – sits beneath the inscription ΣΑΙ or ΣΑΟ. ΚΟΥΧ may be an acronym and has proven difficult to decipher (a crasis of καί and οὐχ might be possible, indicating an emphatic negative; another possibility is an abbreviated form of κοχύζω, a variant of κοκκύζω, the cry of a cuckoo or cock, to crow; a third possibility is an abbreviation of a name Κουχ(- - -).[84] The other inscription, if read as ΣΑΙ, is perhaps an abbreviation of ΣΑΙΝΩ (σαίνω). This can carry the meaning of cringing or fawning like a dog or shrinking from death, and should probably be considered an exhortation to cower before the missile. If so, it would be perfectly in line with other inscriptions directed at the intended recipient of the bullet and with the symbolism of the scorpion on the opposite side of the bullet. Alternatively, if read ΣΑΟ, then σαόφρων (= σωφρῶν) might fit the context, ironically suggesting that the missile might render its target "of sound mind."[85] In any case, it does not seem to produce any viable name if the two sides are put together like the Torone sling bullets.

The other two inscribed bullets carry only letters. One of these (**196**) preserves a clearly legible KA. The letters on the final inscribed bullet (**195**) are nearly illegible, but appear to be a retrograde version of the same inscription. Alternatively they may represent an AI or even an A followed by a retrograde P. The KA inscription links **196** to a cache of 32 sling bullets recovered from the Artillery Bastion west of the Sanctuary, 12 of which carried the same letters. Contextual dating places this deposit between the early third century, when the Bastion was constructed (over a pre-existing tower) and the late third to mid-second century, when it was abandoned.[86] The latter date, towards the mid-second century, would explain this cache of sling bullets quite well, since it provides a good reason both for the creation of the cache in the first place and for its loss, that is, an attack on the city which led to its destruction. This would also explain the appearance of the sling bullets in the Sanctuary, which would inevitably have been touched by any military action in this part of the city.

Nevertheless, it is tempting to consider a link between the KA inscribed bullets and Kassander. Diodorus Siculus recounts that one of Kassander's generals, Apollonides, took Stymphalos during an attack into Arkadia by night in 315.[87] Kassander himself may have passed through Stymphalos later in 315 on his way from Kenchreai to Orchomenos.[88] He and his generals retained control over much of the area down to 303, despite challenges from Polyperchon and his son Alexander, as well as from Aristodemos of Miletos, Telesphoros, and Ptolemaios, all of whom worked in concert with Antigonos the One-eyed at one time or another.[89] By 303, Demetrios Poliorketes controlled all of Arkadia except Mantinea.[90] This was short-lived. Following the disaster at Ipsos in 301, which claimed his father's life, Demetrios' preoccupation with survival allowed Kassander to reassert his control over the Peloponnese until 297, when Demetrios again turned his attention to the region.[91] The presence at Stymphalos of a garrison or garrisons with connections to the Diadouchoi, including Kassander, is indicated by many Macedonian coins dating between 336 and 288.[92] One of these garrisons was likely responsible for the renovation of the city's fortifications in the early third century.

Nineteen of the bullets in the Bastion cache carried the letters API, which might, for example, be linked to Aristodemos of Miletos. He and his army of local mercenaries fought alongside Alexander, son of Polyperchon, who later in 315 went over to Kassander and became general of his forces in the Peloponnese.[93] In this case, the bullets from the Artillery Bastion might represent a fusion of Kassander's troops with those elements of Aristodemos' mercenary army who followed Alexander into Kassander's service.

Just to speculate for a moment, if the KA association with Kassander were correct, the bullets could have been fired into the Sanctuary during the 315 attack or a later one (i.e., after 301) by Kassander's forces not specified by Diodorus, but probable considering his account of the period. This, however, would not easily explain why similar KA bullets were gathered together within the Bastion in a place where the defenders would be, not the attackers. Another scenario, given the presence of the cache of bullets in the Bastion, is that they were carried into Stymphalos by the garrison which Apollonides surely left there after his night attack, by troops moving through the city at any time when it was subject to Kassander, or by Stymphalian mercenaries returning from employment with Kassander. In this view, the bullets found in the Sanctuary would have to be considered votives or losses. If the sling bullets were deposited towards the end of the Bastion's occupation in the mid-second century, it is much harder to see a connection with Kassander; however, it is at least possible that these pieces, which were found in the basement of the structure, were mislaid and forgotten long before the collapse of the tower.

All that being said, it is important to bear in mind that Greek names beginning with KA and API are very common. Neither Kassander nor Aristodemos can be securely linked with the sling bullets. And on the basis of stylistic and epigraphical evidence alone, **195** and

196, like **194**, **197**, and **198,** cannot be securely associated with either figure. Indeed, an explanation connecting the sling bullets found in the Bastion and in the Sanctuary with an attack on the city between the late third and the mid-second century suits the contextual evidence better.

Sling Bullets

Cat. no.	Inv. no.	Y.T.L.P	L (cm)	W (cm)	M (g)	Inscription
194	316	95.4+1.2.4	3.3	1.8	40	Blank
195	931	96.13.4.7	3.3	1.9	44	A (ret.)K; or A I; or A (ret.) P
196	952	96.13.4.7	3.1	1.9	40	KA
197	2130	96.3.2.2	2.7	1.7	40	Dot rosette
198	2649	99.97.5b.3.4	2.7	1.6	25	A: ΚΟΥΧ (KOUX) and Scorpion B: ΣΑΙ (ΣΑΟ) and symbol (bee?)

CONTEXTUAL ANALYSIS AND HISTORICAL SIGNIFICANCE

While projectiles have often piqued the interest of classical archaeologists, particularly when they could be attributed to a historical event, they have not been the subject of systematic study and comprehensive classification.[94] Broneer lamented the absence of such a treatment of projectiles while discussing the arrowheads recovered from the north slope of the Athenian Acropolis. His call has yet to be answered. This neglect clearly derives from the utilitarian nature of such artifacts. Designed and manufactured with efficiency and economy as guiding principles, ancient projectiles demonstrate little in the way of remarkable stylistic change, much less artistic or epigraphic embellishment.[95]

Sling bullets provide a very important exception to this general rule. Most notably, they receive comprehensive treatment in Pritchett's *The Greek State at War*. The attention paid to sling bullets is partly the result of large-scale survivals and excellent preservation; however, it is no less a consequence of the inscriptions they commonly bear – inscriptions that sometimes provide important links to identifiable individuals and events.

The absence of such inscriptions, relatively poor preservation, and a tendency to privilege bronze over iron may have limited coverage of ancient Greek projectile points in general studies. It is unfair to criticize such early and important contributions as Walters' *Catalogue of the Bronzes, Greek, Roman, and Etruscan*, in the British Museum, Richter's *The Metropolitan Museum of Art: Greek, Etruscan & Roman Bronzes*, and Snodgrass' much later *Arms and Armour of the Greeks* for doing precisely what they set out to do. Yet the parameters these scholars set in their studies reflect a broader tendency to focus only on the materials and periods they considered exemplary of the acme of Greek civilization. This enabled Walters and Richter to establish useful typologies of bronze projectile points and Snodgrass to provide a handy summary of the origins and general chronological parameters of the most common types of projectile points found in Greek contexts down to the close of the fifth century.[96] The end result, however, is something like complete neglect of later Classical and Hellenistic projectile points, especially iron examples, in general studies of Greek metalwork.

The same cannot be said of iron projectile points with Roman provenance. Bishop and Coulston cover Roman projectiles quite thoroughly in their *Roman Military Equipment*, which is particularly strong on artillery ammunition.[97] The long-term consistency in many varieties of projectile points makes Roman parallels potentially useful for the study of pieces with Greek provenance; however, the lack of scholarly interest in projectile points from the Late Classical and Hellenistic Greek contexts creates problems in understanding the precise relationship between Greek and Roman projectiles.

Archaeological reports and publications that give projectiles special attention are ultimately more useful for present purposes than general studies. Since this attention most often results from a well-known historical association, such publications are vital in establishing fixed chronological points for particular types of projectiles encountered elsewhere. As has been seen already, Robinson's *Excavations at Olynthus* is particularly important for the breadth of material published and the similarities with objects from Stymphalos. There are other publications that present useful comparanda with reliable dates. The most important of these are for Dura-Europos, Nemea, New Halos, Olympia, and Pylos.[98]

To address questions of how, why, and when projectiles entered the Sanctuary, it is important to integrate stylistic analysis of the artifacts with the information gleaned from contexts and known events from Stymphalos' history. Beginning with contexts, there are five distinct areas in the Sanctuary where projectiles were found in sizeable numbers: 1) the northwestern corner of the Sanctuary, including the West Annex to Building A, 2) the area just north of the North Annex to Building A, 3) the areas east of the Terrace Wall or original retaining wall for the Altar Court, 4) the Altar Court itself, and 5) Building A, including its North Annex.[99]

Northwest corner – Pillar Shrine and West Annex

The northwest corner of the Sanctuary is delimited by the north wall of the Temple, the western walls of the Annexes to Building A, and the rising ground of the acropolis peak to the north and west. This area contains an important concentration of twelve projectile points, six of them catapult-bolt heads (**17–18, 28–9, 30–1**) and six of them bodkin type arrowheads (**119, 127, 130, 132–3, 136**).[100] These pieces were recovered from Trenches 96.8 and 97.2 and in layers related to the West Annex. Two catapult-bolt heads (**30** and **31**) were recovered from the floor of this room, whereas four bodkin arrowheads (**119, 127, 130**, and **133**) and a single catapult-bolt head (**17**) came from destruction material immediately above the floor of the West Annex.[101] The remaining projectile points in this group (**18, 28–9, 132,** and **136**) came from contexts associated with this same destruction material above the floor. Analysis of the ceramics found associated with the floor suggests a late fourth-century date for the floor and, by extension, for the destruction of the West Annex. This is the strongest evidence in the Sanctuary for a fourth-century context for the projectile points. Stone's study of the pottery from this floor and its overburden suggests that although the quantity of material is limited, it must be dated ca. 300 BCE or earlier.[102]

Nevertheless, there are some reasons to treat this evidence with caution. First of all, the West Annex is certainly built over a refuse deposit (Trench 96.15.5 and below) from a clean-up of the Sanctuary which has also been dated to the second half of the fourth century. Secondly, the West Annex is the latest addition to Building A (later even than the North Annex, the western wall of which it depends on for part of its eastern wall). The main part of Building A with large ashlar foundation blocks was built first, presumably by the mid-fourth century, then the North Annex was added, and finally the West Annex was built. The North Annex continued in use till the mid-second century, which does not preclude the West Annex from being built in the late fourth century, and destroyed a short time later, still in the late fourth century, but the chronology is unusually telescoped. Thirdly, the destruction material above the West Annex floor was left untouched after the destruction of this Annex, since a large group of loomweights was left resting on the floor. The Sanctuary was certainly used down into the second century, which makes it difficult to explain why the West Annex, based on the consistently fourth-century material on and above the floor, seems to have been left as a pile of destruction material for 150 years (300–150 BCE) instead of being cleaned up. The North Annex, constructed earlier than the West Annex, certainly continued in use. It had a floor surface and hearth with material from the first half of the second century.

One explanation for this anomalous fourth-century floor material has already been offered by Schaus (chapter 2 above). The floor of the West Annex may have been swept clean of any second- or even third-century BCE material while it was being used for weaving. There was certainly no scattering of pottery on an easily distinguishable floor surface as was found in the Southeast Room of Building A, for example, or around the hearth in the North Annex. Only the groups of loomweights could be recognized as lying right at this floor level when the area was dug. This would help to explain why the pottery associated with the floor level in the West Annex seems to be purely fourth-century in date, but the destruction and abandonment of the Annex more logically would seem to belong with the destruction of the Sanctuary as a whole.

North of the North Annex

The second general area of interest is in Trenches 99.10 and 00.6, just north of the North Annex. It yielded 15 projectile points: twelve catapult-bolt heads (**50, 53, 67–9, 71–7**), one Cretan arrowhead (**99**), and two bodkin arrowheads (**165** and **168**).[103] Dating evidence is ambiguous. Pottery recovered from the area suggests a date for the associated material in the fourth century.[104] The fact that pottery from Trench 00.6 in particular was somewhat better preserved may indicate that this area was used as a *bothros* for votives in the late fourth or early third century.[105] On the other hand, this is not a sealed deposit and may not represent undisturbed occupation material. The presence of broken roof tiles and burnt mudbrick in these levels suggests the possibility that all the material in question, including the projectile points, is post-destruction fill. As a result, these projectile points may date as late as the mid-second century, though there is no direct contextual evidence to indicate such a date.

East of the Terrace Wall

The third general area for contextual analysis of the projectiles comprises the ground immediately east and south, i.e., down-slope of the retaining wall (Terrace Wall) that supports the Altar Court, which may have marked the southeastern boundary of the Sanctuary. The best-understood portion of this area is Trench 99.1, which has produced building debris in addition to significant amounts of votive material such as miniature vessels, bronze trinkets, and loomweights, as well as a high concentration of projectile points. This area appears to contain two distinct layers with substantial numbers of projectile points in each. The distinction was first noticed in 99.1 Level 5 Pail 11, which was then continued as Level 6 Pail 12 during excavation (supervised by Y. Lolos in 1999). However, retrospective analysis of the ceramics suggests that the distinction occurred even higher, most likely in Level 5 Pail 9. All in all, this lower layer (Level 5 Pails 9–11 and Level 6 Pail 12) contained three catapult bolts heads (**58**, **60**, and **61**), four bodkin arrowheads (**169**, **170**, **172**, and **175**), and two ferrules (**209–10**). The majority of associated pottery was fourth century, but the best diagnostic ceramics and the latest associated coin suggest a date range from the very late fourth through the third century.[106] That said, projectile points unquestionably continue in Pails 9 and 10 of Level 5, which is lower than indicators (mould-made bowls and West Slope ware) of later date are found in this particular trench. This prospective layer may represent an extension or cleaning of the Altar Terrace by dumping debris and other fill over its edge.[107] Terracotta figurines also appear in greater numbers in this layer than the one overlying it.

One must again be cautious here, however, since the distinction between layers was not very clear to the excavators. Neither was the material associated with any architectural feature other than the terrace itself. Moreover, in many areas of the Sanctuary there are only a few scattered fragments of third- or second-century vases, such as mould-made bowls, or other archaeological evidence to provide a date for the destruction/abandonment of the Sanctuary. Some of the projectile points do seem to lie in fourth-century levels, but there is a question of the reliability of the evidence.

This same "early" layer appears to continue into adjacent trenches standing in a similar relationship to the Altar Terrace Wall.[108] Projectiles from the levels which seem to correspond to this layer in Trenches 97.4 (Level 5 Pail 8), 99.6 (Levels 5 and 6), 00.3 (Level 6), and 96.13 (Levels 4–6) numbered ten in all and included catapult-bolt heads (**26**, **56**, and **64**), sling bullets (**195–6**), and arrowheads of the bodkin (**146**, **148**, **156**, **166**, **187**) and "Cretan" (**93**) varieties.[109]

The layer immediately above this apparently late fourth- through early third-century level included Trenches 99.1, 96.13, 97.4, 97.5, 97.5 baulk, and 00.3.[110] Again, 99.1 provides the best picture. Analysis of ceramic remains from the upper levels of this trench indicates a clear layer of material dating from the second half of the third century through the middle years of the second century.[111] Levels 3 and 4 (Pails 3–4) in Trench 99.1 had a small number of mould-made bowl fragments from as late as the mid-second century as well as a possible Type 27 lamp base from the second century CE in Level 3, indicative of the destruction and Roman-residual phase of the site. In this material there were two catapult bolts (**47–8**), a Type H arrowhead (**86**), and two bodkin arrowheads **163–4**. To these should be added the four projectile points from Level 5 Pails 7 and 8 (**51–2**, **54**, and **55**). These findings are echoed in 96.13, 97.4, and 00.3, which yielded in their upper levels nine more projectiles, including a catapult-bolt head (**32**), and bodkin (**131**, **134**, **139–40**, **143**, **177**, and **179**) and Scythian (**85**) arrowheads.[112] Further evidence appears in 97.5 Levels 2 and 3 and 97.5 baulk Levels 3 and 4, where five bodkin arrowheads (**151**, **155**, **171**, **173**, **174**), one catapult bolt (**59**), one Cretan arrowhead (**93**), and one sling bullet (**198**) appeared in association with mould-made bowl fragments.

Altar Court

The fourth general area of note is the Altar Court, which is bounded on the west by the Temple and on the north by Building A. While projectiles were not as numerous here as in the previous two areas, they do appear in significant numbers and in what appear to be two distinct layers. The key feature in this area is an expanse of patchy stone packing or cobble paving to the north and west of the Altar. The date of this feature is uncertain. One possibility is that it ought to be associated with the renovations that appear to have taken place in the Sanctuary ca. 300. A small sondage beneath this feature, due west of the Altar in Trench 96.9 (Level 4), yielded no material dating later than the fourth century. It contained a fragmentary bodkin arrowhead (**137**). The level immediately above the sondage, i.e the "paving/packing" itself (Level 3), contained one bodkin arrowhead (**135**) and three catapult-bolt heads (**19**, **22**, and **23**). The accompanying pottery in Level 3 suggested a date in the late fourth/early third century. Significantly, two other projectiles, one "Cretan" arrowhead (**88**) and one catapult-bolt head (**13**), were found directly beneath this same feature north of the Altar (Tr. 96.3 Level 3 Pail 6).[113] This is another instance where projectile points seem to be found in later fourth- or third-century contexts, but as with other examples, caution must be exercised since the dating evidence is so tenuous.

The discovery of two mould-made bowl fragments and several moulded-rim bowls/lekanai fragments at or below the level of this feature (e.g., 96.3 Level 4 Pail 7) suggests the alternate possibility that the layer of stone "packing/paving" may in fact post-date the mid-second-century destruction of the Sanctuary. However, it is not clear that these ceramic remains were sealed by the "packing/paving" in the way that the projectiles were.[114] What is clear from this ceramic evidence is the presence of a layer of material in this area ranging in date from the last quarter of the third century through the middle years of the second century. This layer is best understood in those areas of Trench 96.3 (Levels 3 and 4) where the "paving/packing" did not extend, and in 96.4 (Levels 3 and 4). Eleven projectiles emerged from this layer: three catapult-bolt heads (**6**, **9**, and **14**), seven bodkin arrowheads (**106–8**, **113**, **121**, **123**, and **161**), and one "Cretan" arrowhead (**89**).

Building A

The fifth and final general area of note is Building A, especially its North Annex. The original floor in the southern or Front Room of Building A was covered by a substantial layer of broken roof tiles and other debris associated with a destruction/collapse. The upper part of this layer included one catapult-bolt head (**27**) and one bodkin arrowhead (**147**). Associated ceramic finds place this layer ca. 150.[115] The Middle Room of Building A was rather more disturbed than the Front Room, but it too preserves traces of destruction, which included a pair of catapult-bolt heads (**4** and **40**). Just as important is a pair of projectiles, a fragmentary bodkin arrowhead (**110**) and a catapult-bolt head (**5**), found in the North Annex. These were recovered from a hearth in the eastern half of the Annex that also contained large numbers of mould-made bowl fragments, dated to the late third through mid-second century.[116] Another catapult-bolt head (**1**) found above the floor level should probably also be dated to this period.[117] A single, fragmentary catapult-bolt head (**42**) was found beneath the floor level in the North Annex with material of fourth-century date.[118]

In addition to these five important areas within the Sanctuary, there were three finds on other sites in Stymphalos with bearing on the Sanctuary projectiles. One poorly preserved bodkin arrowhead (**125**) was found amid fill in the stone foundation of the Hexagonal Artillery Tower just south of the Sanctuary.[119] This fill was part of a reconstruction and expansion of the tower which is thought to have occurred in the early third century. A catapult-bolt head from the Artillery Bastion at the top of the Acropolis just west of the Sanctuary was likewise found in the rubble foundation of the Bastion's western or outer wall. It was sealed by seven courses of intact mud brick.[120] Like the Hexagonal Artillery Tower, the Bastion appears to have undergone a significant reconstruction shortly after 300. As already discussed, the Bastion also yielded a cache of 32 lead sling bullets, twelve of which carry a KA inscription identical to that found on one of the sling bullets (**194**) from the Sanctuary. This cache, along with a bodkin arrowhead and a catapult-bolt head, was found on the floor of the Bastion's basement, beneath the accumulated debris from the tower's collapse. Although this collapse was originally dated to the second half of the fourth century, evidence has since emerged which suggests that the collapse may have occurred as late as the mid-second century and be coeval with the destruction and abandonment of the Sanctuary.[121] For present purposes, the key is that these pieces must have entered the site in the period between the Bastion's reconstruction in the very early third century and its abandonment and subsequent collapse sometime during the period from the later third to the mid-second century.

The conclusion that naturally follows from the preceding survey of contexts is that it is difficult to link all of the projectiles to a single period, much less a single event. Catapult-bolt heads, and bodkin and Cretan arrowheads, have been found in what seem to be late fourth-century contexts and in mid-second-century contexts. As a result any answer to the vital question of how the projectiles entered the Sanctuary would seem to have to consider both possibilities, if not others as well.

Four possible answers to this question are offered here. The first two are suggested by the analogy of the Chalkotheke on the Athenian Acropolis, where surviving inventories include both arrows and catapult bolts.[122] Their presence has been variously interpreted as military stockpiles and as dedications.[123] Both of these hypotheses could explain the presence of the projectiles in the Sanctuary at Stymphalos. The third possibility is that they may have been carried into the Sanctuary along with fill used to level the ground during construction and/or renovation. Fourth, they may have been fired into the Sanctuary during an attack or series of attacks.[124] Leaving aside for the moment the possibility that a combination of these factors will be needed to understand the presence of the collection as a whole, it is appropriate to look at each hypothesis in turn.

Of the four possibilities, the first and third are the least convincing. While the hypothesis that the projectiles were stored in the Sanctuary makes perfect sense given the nature of Athena Polias as one deity worshipped here, and the location of the Sanctuary vis-à-vis the city's fortifications, it does not fit the contexts of the artifacts. Even if we ignore the projectiles which were embedded within the floors of the West and North Annexes of Building A and those recovered from beneath the "paving/packing" on the Altar Terrace, it is still difficult to believe that the remainder came from a stockpile within the Sanctuary. An arsenal or stockpile would surely have been indoors, in order to protect weapons from the elements. Consequently, it would not have been susceptible to extreme soil movement any more than the cache of sling bullets recovered from the Artillery Bastion west of the Sanctuary.[125] Yet, the sling bullet (**194**) found relatively deep in Trench 95.4+1 and the bodkin arrowhead (**125**) deep in 96.1 are hardly evidence of mass storage in the Temple.[126] The same could be said of the handful of projectiles recovered in or immediately below the destruction layer of Building A and its North Annex, not to mention those in the West Annex.[127] Nor is it possible to explain the spread of projectiles across the site by recourse to a nearby storage facility, from which all or even a large portion of the projectiles later washed into the Sanctuary. No such building has been discovered; nor is there room for anything of the sort upslope of the Sanctuary. Finally, the severe damage evident on a substantial number of the projectiles, which would have rendered them useless, makes their inclusion in any stockpile highly unlikely.[128]

The hypothesis that the projectiles entered the site amid fill used for construction or renovation also presents problems. A few projectiles were found amid fill, particularly on and around the Altar Terrace. As noted earlier, the archaeology in this area was confused by bedrock outcroppings and intermittent patches of loose fill and stone "packing/paving." However, three projectiles were recovered from beneath the feature around the Altar. These included the fragmentary bodkin head (**137**) recovered from the sondage in 96.9 and a Cretan arrowhead (**88**) and catapult-bolt head (**13**) found north of the Altar in 96.3. Another bodkin arrowhead (**135**) and three catapult-bolt heads (**19**, **22**, and **23**) appeared amid the intermittent "packing/paving" west of the Altar in 96.9. A further fragmentary catapult-bolt head (**42**) was found beneath the floor in the North Annex to Building A. Finally, there is the large collection of projectile points found beyond the Altar Terrace. The earlier of the two layers in this area may have been fill used to extend the Altar Terrace to the south and east, perhaps as part of a renovation or cleaning of the Sanctuary. No fewer than 17 projectiles, including catapult-bolt heads, bodkin and Cretan arrowheads, and sling bullets, were found in contexts associated with this layer.[129]

Adjacent sites within Stymphalos provide additional examples of projectiles appearing in construction material. As we have seen, in both the Hexagonal Artillery Tower south of the Sanctuary and the Artillery Bastion to the west, a few projectiles were found in material that appears to date to reconstruction in the very early third century. It is possible that at least some of the projectiles found on the Altar Terrace and beyond its eastern and southern limits, as well as around Building A, were also deposited amid imported rubble/debris used as fill during renovation or reconstruction.[130] All this being said, a great many projectiles were discovered in contexts that cannot be linked to construction and/or renovation, and even the projectiles found amid fill and beneath ancient surfaces need not necessarily be identified as material brought into the Sanctuary from elsewhere.

This brings us to the more plausible hypotheses, that the projectiles were dedications, or that they were fired into the Sanctuary during one or more attacks. The former fits nicely with the presence of projectiles in contexts spanning the entire period of activity of the Sanctuary *per se*, that is, from the fourth century through the mid-second century. In general terms the distribution of the projectiles across the site also fits the votive hypothesis. The distribution of projectiles across the site and through practically all identified strata is consistent with the distribution of votive material. Moreover, the material in the lower layer beyond the Altar Terrace, which of course included a large number of projectiles, may represent a clean-up of Sanctuary material. So too the deposit in Trenches 00.6 and 99.10 north of the North Annex, with its fifteen projectiles, may include the remains of dumped votive material. The relatively good preservation of the associated ceramics here suggests that this material may have been deposited against the north wall of the North Annex quite soon after its entry into the Sanctuary. On the other hand, as noted earlier, this deposit may simply be destruction debris.

The fact that some of the projectiles appear to preserve traces of deliberate destruction also suits the votive hypothesis.[131] Numbers **38, 44, 101, 118, 135, 156, 164, 177**, and **182** in particular have tangs and/or tips that were bent between 90 and 360 degrees. Many more demonstrate less significant damage, which still seems somewhat too regular to be the result of impact.[132] Even where damage seems consistent with normal use, it is important to remember that military dedications were commonly in "used" condition and could have been damaged prior to dedication.

Finally, the presence of weapons as votive offerings would be nicely in line with finds from many other Greek sanctuaries. Olympia, of course, provides a particularly famous and extensive example of military dedications, but votives of this sort were a commonplace in Greek sanctuaries.[133] Dedications of arms and armour, whether the property of the dedicator or trophies taken from defeated enemies, served as offerings of thanks for victory or as attempts to secure continued success in battle. At Bassai, in southwestern Arkadia, not only were a variety of bronze and iron weapon heads left in the Archaic sanctuary, but miniature bronze breast plates, helmets, greaves, and shields were also left there, and these could only have been votives.[134] Dedications of personal military gear could also serve to mark a "retirement" from active participation in martial life.[135] If, as seems likely, Stymphalos was as heavily involved in mercenary employment as the rest of Arkadia, such dedications seem particularly appropriate.[136] Men embarking on or returning from mercenary service abroad are likely candidates to have left votives of this sort in the Sanctuary. The same might be hypothesized for citizens concerned with the well-being and/or success of loved ones involved in mercenary or indeed any other form of military service.[137]

Athena sanctuaries especially attracted numerous military dedications. Simon has concluded that in the Archaic period at least, Athena was more likely to receive military dedications than any other deity.[138] Nor is there reason to presume that this trend changed dramatically in subsequent centuries. Sites where military dedications have been found in Athena sanctuaries include Athens, Emporio, Erythrai, Elateia, Lefkas, Lindos, Kamiros, Philia, Smyrna, Sounion, Syracuse, and Tegea.[139]

While the best-known examples of military dedications tend to be impressive items such as the shields, helmets, spears, spear butts, and cuirasses recovered from Olympia, there are numerous examples of projectiles in sanctuaries.[140] At Olympia itself, large numbers of projectiles were dedicated.[141] The votive assemblages of five of the sites mentioned above (Athens, Emporio, Erythrae, Lindos, and Tegea) also included arrowheads.[142] Votive finds from the acropolis of Kamiros included lead sling bullets.[143] And, as noted above, there is evidence at Athens for catapult bolts among the property of Athena held in the Chalkotheke.[144] The sanctuary of Athena in Pergamon offers yet another useful piece of evidence for the dedication of projectile weapons. The balustrades from the stoa surrounding the temple include catapults in their relief representations of dedicated weapons and armour.[145]

The Sanctuary on the acropolis at Stymphalos, which Orlandos identified as Athena's based on the "Poliados" inscription, is not entirely bereft of more impressive material, though by comparison with some of the aforementioned sites, the list is meagre: fragments of perhaps two bronze shield rims were found, presumably but not certainly dedications, as were the remains of a javelin and a spear head.[146] Yet the really remarkable thing about the assemblage from the Sanctuary is the ratio of such items to projectiles. The overwhelming preponderance of projectiles, if they were dedications, might reflect a special interest of the dedicators. As has already been noted, the importance of mercenary service to the citizens of Stymphalos might have made military dedications of all sorts entirely appropriate; however, the relative poverty motivating them to seek mercenary employment might also have made them reluctant to offer more substantial and much more expensive types of arms and armour. They may also have been inclined to pass on the more substantial "tools of their trade" to subsequent generations upon retirement.[147] This of course is speculative, without much support at other Arkadian sanctuaries.

It is also possible that projectiles were chosen without any concern for cost. For instance, their popularity might be indicative of contemporary attitudes to the importance of projectile weapons in siege warfare. Sieges had taken on an increasingly important role in warfare during the fourth and third centuries, spurring tremendous advances in fortifications and in siege tactics.[148] It is reasonable to suggest that mercenaries were very responsive to such developments. If the Aineias Taktikos who wrote a treatise on surviving sieges was in fact the Aineias of Stymphalos mentioned by Xenophon, then there would be even more reason to expect the people of Stymphalos to be well versed in military developments.[149] Stymphalos' own history of fourth-century siege and attack, as well as the renovation of the city's fortifications early in the next century, ought to have driven the point home, so to speak.

This defensive concern may in turn afford a connection to one particular deity in the Sanctuary, Athena Polias. Given the importance of projectile weapons to the defence of the city, they would seem especially appropriate dedications to her. On the other hand, they may reflect another, more unique aspect of the Stymphalian persona of Athena.[150] A recent interpretation of the metope from the Temple of Zeus at Olympia representing Herakles' Stymphalian labour provides the vital link in a possible connection between projectiles and the cult of Athena Polias at Stymphalos. Schaus suggested that the rock outcropping, on which the goddess sits to receive the dead birds from the outstretched hand of the hero, might represent the acropolis of Stymphalos.[151] Though judiciously tentative in advancing this hypothesis, he nonetheless illuminated a possible connection between Herakles' labour and the acropolis Sanctuary. The potential link becomes even more interesting when we recall that Herakles traditionally employed a projectile weapon – either a bow or sling – to kill the troublesome birds.[152] The majority of literary sources that speak explicitly of Herakles killing the birds – as opposed to merely frightening them away with a rattle or drums – indicate that he used a bow.[153] The nexus among Herakles' labour, projectile weapons, Athena, and the Sanctuary on the Stymphalian acropolis must remain conjectural; nevertheless, it presents an interesting possibility: a local variety of the Athena Polias cult in which offerings of projectiles played a particularly important role.

Ultimately there is no need to choose between the personal interests of the dedicator/worshipper and the attributes of the deity in explaining the dedications of projectiles. Far from being mutually exclusive, these explanations ought to be considered complementary. If anything, the potential confluence of personal significance and suitability to the patron deity of the cult makes the case for the votive hypothesis even stronger.

Despite all these arguments in favour of identifying the projectiles as votives, there are also reasons to question this hypothesis. First, there is no precedent for such a high percentage of projectiles in an assemblage of military dedications – though, in view of the mounting evidence for local and/or regional idiosyncrasies in cult practice, this alone is hardly reason to discount the votive hypothesis.[154] Second, the projectiles might also seem a poor fit with the votive assemblage as a whole. The large volume of miniature vessels, terracotta figurines, and jewellery seems much more indicative of a cult devoted to traditionally female concerns than one with military associations.[155] Even so, as Simon noted, there are many examples of sanctuaries with a mix of what appear to be "female" and "male" dedications very similar to what has been found in the acropolis Sanctuary.[156] Then there is the evidence of fourth-century prohibitions against bringing weapons into certain sanctuaries.[157] However, there is no persuasive evidence that such prohibitions were anything but local and specific.

There are other, more serious, arguments against identifying the projectiles as dedications. First, the recovery of similar projectiles from other areas within the city implies the need for a rather more far-reaching explanation of their presence than one focused entirely on cult activity.[158] Second, the presence of projectiles in what might have been votive deposits north and west of the North Annex and beyond the Altar Terrace does not necessarily mean they were themselves votives. Material gathered during a clean-up or renovation of the Sanctuary could conceivably have included projectiles and other debris from a siege or demolition, in addition to aging votive material. Finally, and most importantly of all, not a single projectile was recovered from the only sealed votive deposit discovered in the Sanctuary, which was in Trench 96.15 beneath the West Annex to Building A.

Although these objections are not sufficient cause to abandon completely the hypothesis of projectiles as votives here, they inspire enough doubt to require consideration of the fourth possibility: that the projectiles entered the Sanctuary during one or more attacks on the city. Now, it may not immediately be apparent why projectiles would be fired into the Sanctuary during an attack. The explanation lies in the Sanctuary's proximity to key elements of the city's defences. The city wall that runs along the southern edge of the acropolis is less than 10 m from the southern edge of the Altar Terrace. The Hexagonal Artillery Tower, which dominates this stretch of wall, is also very close, only 20 m to the southeast. Then there is the large Artillery Bastion atop the Acropolis some 70 m distant and at much higher elevation. It is due west of the Sanctuary, at the juncture of the city's southern and western curtain walls. Either of these artillery towers would have been a prime target for suppressing fire during an attack from the south or the west. Missiles fired from the south could have reached the Sanctuary very easily if they missed their intended mark. Missiles fired from the west might also have done so, considering the difference in elevation between the Sanctuary and the peak of the acropolis, which would have added to their range. It must be said, however, that this last possibility seems unlikely, given the topography and the likely location of besieging forces.

The possibility that the projectiles were fired into the Sanctuary during an attack or attacks on the acropolis has the undeniable attraction of attributing their appearance in the archaeological record to them fulfilling their intended purpose. It is also consistent with the small number of projectiles recovered from within buildings, and with their otherwise seemingly random distribution across the site. There is also the matter of the damage visible on many of the projectiles, which in some cases seems more indicative of impact with unyielding surfaces than of deliberate attempts to decommission the projectile. Indeed, some of the more severe damage, such as tangs and tips with dramatic bends, could be the result of attempts to free projectiles from objects in which they were deeply embedded.[159]

The fact that literary sources preserve references to two known attacks on the city and suggest the possibility of several more such incidents adds to the plausibility of the siege(s) scenario. The events in question range from the early fourth century through the mid-second century, covering the whole of the Sanctuary's active life.

The earliest possibility is an unsuccessful siege of Stymphalos conducted by the Athenian general Iphikrates in either 392 or 370/69 BCE and described by Strabo.[160] The balance of scholarly opinion currently inclines to the later date.[161] In any event, Strabo's account makes it clear that Stymphalos was on its present site near the lake when Iphikrates' attack took place. Strabo tells of Iphikrates' attempt to block the katabothros (sinkhole) that drained the lake, presumably in hopes of damaging the city's walls and bringing his so far futile siege to a successful close.[162] Strabo's testimony further suggests that Iphikrates had tried and failed to take the city using conventional means, which might have included the use of projectiles shot into the Sanctuary. While there is not much archaeological evidence of activity in the Sanctuary earlier than the middle years of the fourth century, it is likely that the Temple and Building A were present by the second quarter of the century at the latest;[163] however, no projectile points have been found in contexts definitively linked to this era. Indeed none of the projectiles found in datable contexts within the Sanctuary can be securely linked to the first half of the fourth century. As we have seen, there is good reason to doubt that iron catapult bolts of the type found so frequently in the Sanctuary even existed as early as 370.

Diodorus Siculus provides an account of an assault on the city with a date more suited to some of the archaeological evidence from the Sanctuary. He indicates that one of Kassander's generals, Apollonides, made a night raid into Arkadia from the Argolid and took Stymphalos in 315.[164] Diodorus provides no tactical specifics indicative of a link between the projectiles and Apollonides' action. If anything, the implication of his account is that the city was taken by surprise during a night assault. This negates the sort of prolonged assault in which large numbers of projectile weapons would have been employed. Moreover, the Sanctuary seems an unlikely target for a surprise attack of any sort, given its relatively inaccessible location. On the other hand, Diodorus specifies subsequent attempts by Polyperchon's son, Alexander, and his sometime ally, Aristodemos of Miletos, to root out garrisons that Kassander had installed throughout the Peloponnese, as well as campaigns in the area by two other agents of Antigonos Monophthalmos, Telesphoros and Ptolemaios, in 313 and 312.[165] In fact, Diodorus' account of the military activity in Arkadia during this tumultuous period suggests that Stymphalos may have been attacked and even changed hands more than once between 315 and 308. It had certainly done so again by 303, when Demetrios Poliorketes was in control of the whole of Arkadia except Mantinea. Following the defeat of Antigonos and Demetrios in 301, Kassander reasserted his control, only to have Demetrios return and reconquer the area between 297 and 295, after which the situation in Arkadia became more stable.[166]

This general period of upheaval suits the date for the ceramics associated with the floor in the West Annex, where 12 projectiles were recovered, although an explanation has been offered for the earlier ceramics in what otherwise might be part of the larger second-century Sanctuary destruction.[167] The deeper of the layers east of the Altar Terrace might also be linked to this period. As we have seen, analysis of associated ceramics and coins suggested a date for this layer in the early third century. It contained 17 projectiles, including examples of the three main types present in the assemblage: sling bullets, arrowheads (Cretan and bodkin), and catapult-bolt heads. The concentration of 15 projectile points north of the North Annex might be associated with this general period. In both these cases it is necessary to hypothesize that the concentrations of points were the result of cleaning after an attack(s); however, since neither of these concentrations was sealed, or part of a distinct feature, any link between the projectiles found there and the era of unrest inaugurated by Apollonides' attack rests entirely on a reconstructed stratigraphy determined by the associated pottery.[168]

Nevertheless, there is some corroborating evidence linking these projectiles to this particular period. First, as noted several times already, analysis of the coins found in the Sanctuary and elsewhere in Stymphalos suggests a significant change ca. 300. This is indicated most clearly by the sudden appearance of good numbers of Macedonian issues minted between 336 and 288, which has been taken as evidence of a Macedonian garrison.[169] Second, three projectiles recovered from other sites within Stymphalos have been associated with the reconstruction of the fortifications, which has in turn been linked to the arrival of the proposed Macedonian garrison.[170] Third, the "inscriptions" on one or two of the sling bullets found in the Sanctuary, like 12 of the 32 lead sling bullets from the deposit in the Artillery Bastion west of the Sanctuary, bear the letters KA. Such inscriptions were often abbreviations of a commander's name, which suggests the possibility that the KA referred to Kassander. As noted earlier, however, this link is tenuous. Finally, external evidence suggests that the particular combination of predominantly iron projectile point types recovered in the Sanctuary would likely have been possible by the end of the fourth century, though not perhaps much earlier.

Olynthos provides a useful archaeological *terminus post quem* for catapult bolts. Numerous bronze examples and a single iron example of the type found at Stymphalos were recovered there in contexts linked to Philip's siege in 348. Olynthos is also the earliest example of a corpus of projectiles including both iron catapult-bolt heads and iron bodkin arrowheads.[171] However, the relative scarcity of the former seems to suggest that iron catapult-bolt heads had not caught on to any great extent as of 348; indeed they may have been a new development linked to the first appearance of torsion-powered artillery. Regardless, the prevalence of iron catapult-bolt heads in the corpus from the Sanctuary and the total absence of bronze examples suggests that the Stymphalos collection – if indeed it is a collection linked to a single event – is likely later. How much later is difficult to say on this basis alone.

The ratio of iron to bronze projectile points is similarly suggestive but inconclusive. At first glance the adoption of iron for projectile points seems fairly linear. At Olympia the ratio of bronze to iron was 483:6. At Nemea it was 58:16. At Olynthos it was 186:55. At New Halos, which dates to the first half of the third century, it appears to have been 1:11. At the Sanctuary the ratio is 2:196.[172] This would seem to put the Stymphalos corpus not only later than Olynthos but also perhaps later than New Halos. However, given the differences in these sites' histories, and lacking a clear understanding of the process by which iron supplanted bronze as the metal of choice for projectile points, it is impossible to use the ratio of bronze to iron as a basis for dating the collection after the mid-fourth century. At this point the most that can be said from the design and material of the projectile points from the Santuary is that they are not likely to be early fourth century and thus not likely to be from the attack by Iphikrates.

Of course, on these bases the projectiles may be slightly more likely to be post-fourth century than late fourth century. In fact, the third and second centuries provide two potential historical associations for the projectiles. The later third century saw considerable military activity in Arkadia. Kleomenes campaigned extensively in the region during the 220s, since his plan to restore Spartan primacy in the Peloponnese brought a collision with the Achaian League under Aratos.[173] For his part, Aratos repeatedly attacked Arkadia in retaliation for its partiality towards Kleomenes and Sparta.[174] In 223/2 Kleomenes was in turn forced to relinquish control of the Peloponnese by the forces of Antigonos III, to whom Aratos and the Achaians had turned for aid.[175] Then, in 219 the army of Philip V swept through the area, defeating Euripidas' forces on the road to Sikyon just ten stades from Stymphalos, at a place called Apelauros.[176]

While neither Plutarch nor Polybius mentions an attack on Stymphalos in his narrative of these years, it must be considered a possibility for three reasons. First, the city's position along the important communication route linking Lakonia to points north and east made it strategically significant and tactically problematic for armies marching through the region. It is no coincidence that both Philip and Euripidas chose the same route and collided near Stymphalos. Second, Polybius relates that only the citizens of Stymphalos and Megalopolis had been immune to Kleomenes' threats and blandishments, and had thus earned his special hatred.[177] This implies both well-known attempts by Kleomenes to dominate Stymphalos and active resistance on the part of its inhabitants. Kleomenes' typical *modus operandi* in such cases was to combine intrigue and military demonstrations to cow his opponents into submission, though where necessary he was willing to resort to main force. Finally, the presence of silver tetrobols from Histiaia in the numismatic assemblage from Stymphalos suggests the possibility of Philip's presence. This was a type of coin he commonly used to pay his troops.[178] With all this in mind a later third-century attack or attacks on the city must remain a consideration. While such attacks would not explain the presence of projectiles in apparent fourth-century contexts, they could account for some of the pieces with late third- to mid-second-century contexts, particularly those in the upper layer to the south and east of the Altar Terrace, and even more importantly the points recovered from the second-century destruction layer within Building A.

The final historical possibility, however, would seem a better fit for these particular concentrations of projectiles. It would also account for several other important finds. Pausanias' description of Mummius' campaign against the Achaian League, of which Stymphalos was then a member, indicates that all the cities that had taken part in the struggle against Rome were disarmed and their walls demolished following the sack of Corinth in 146.[179] He makes no specific mention of Stymphalos. Yet the knowledge that Mummius' forces were active in the area, in conjunction with the archaeological evidence that the Sanctuary and perhaps even elements of the city's fortifications were abandoned in the middle of the second century, makes a Roman attack between 146 and 140 a strong possibility.

There is some archaeological evidence from the Sanctuary to support this hypothesis. Viewed in plan, the distribution of projectiles across the site certainly appears consistent with a siege that caused the site to be abandoned. Indeed one of the problems with arguing for an earlier siege(s) is explaining why such a large number of projectiles had not been cleaned up even though the Sanctuary was still in use down to the mid-second century. In the case of a successful assault that led to the abandonment of the site, however, one would certainly expect to find only a few projectiles within buildings, which is precisely the case in the Sanctuary. At both Olympia and Nemea, projectiles found within sanctuaries have been linked to military action: the fight between the Eleans and Arkadians in 364 and the Argive seizure of Nemea in the late fifth century, respectively.[180] In both cases aggregate numbers of points and concentrations were much lower than at Stymphalos. Since occupation on both of these sites continued, the assumption is that projectiles there had been recycled. Obviously nothing of the sort took place in the Sanctuary at Stymphalos after its apparent destruction and abandonment. In this respect the Sanctuary appears to offer a much closer parallel to Olynthos, where large numbers and heavy concentrations of projectiles were recovered because the site was never reoccupied after Philip sacked it.[181]

Even better evidence of a mid-second-century attack comes from the seven projectile points recovered from the final destruction/collapse layer in Building A, which has been dated to the mid-second century. Then there is the pair of projectiles recovered from the hearth area in the North Annex to Building A. They were found in close association with the latest pottery from the Sanctuary: mould-made bowls, which on comparison with Corinth suggest a latest possible date of ca. 146. The 24 projectiles found in the later third- to mid-second-century layer of material beyond the Altar Terrace, which has been interpreted as post-destruction fill, may provide further corroboration for this hypothesis.

Additional support for the link to Roman activities against the Achaian League derives from a counterfeit denarius dating to 149 found in the lower town area of Stymphalos. Though only a single piece, this coin suggests the presence of Roman troops in Stymphalos during Mummius' war on the Achaian League.[182] Finally, there is nothing about the projectile points that obviates a potential link to Mummius' campaigns. The prevalence of iron in the assemblage of projectiles presents no obstacles to a mid-second-century date. In fact, the similarity of the catapult-bolt heads found at Stymphalos to later Roman artifacts of this type would appear to add further weight to this hypothesis.

Pausanias' reference (7.16.9, above note 179) to the demolition of fortifications in cities that had resisted the Romans might be combined with the apparent archaeological evidence that elements of Stymphalos' fortifications collapsed and were abandoned in the middle of the second century. While Pausanias' account could support such an interpretation, there is little to indicate a deliberate destruction of the walls then.

It is asking too much of the archaeological contexts in the Sanctuary to expect that all the projectile points would be found in a single consistent level. The site was looted, abandoned, scavenged for building materials, and occasionally revisited in later centuries. All this must have caused disturbances even in deeper levels. No single attack can be isolated and argued to have accounted for all the projectile points with complete confidence. In order to accept only an early siege, the projectiles in later contexts must be dismissed as detritus that had not been cleared from the Sanctuary in 50 or even 150 years. Likewise, to argue for a single siege in the mid-second century requires a good explanation for the projectiles found in contexts with fourth-century pottery. An alternative hypothesis, that Stymphalos, and more particularly the fortifications adjacent to the Sanctuary, experienced two or more sieges between the late fourth and the mid-second centuries, also is not very satisfactory. Evidence for even a single siege is very rare on Greek sites; why should Stymphalos have evidence for two or more? Could one siege even be distinguished from another? Evidence of violent conflict has not been clearly recognized elsewhere in Stymphalos, though the high point of the acropolis is where it should be most expected.[183] One thing beyond doubt though is that Stymphalos was virtually abandoned for a century and a half after the mid-second century BCE. This is best explained by a catastrophic event, and projectile points are telling signs of a violent attack.

CONCLUSION

The remarkable collection of projectiles from the Sanctuary on the acropolis at Stymphalos stands alongside only a handful of similar collections in the Greek world. While other sites have yielded larger numbers of projectiles, none can match the concentration of such artifacts encountered in the Sanctuary. The collection is likewise unparalleled in terms of the particular combination of types represented. Its real significance, however, may lie in its contribution to our understanding of the development of catapult-bolt heads. Contextual analysis of the Stymphalos assemblage suggests the possibility that iron points of this type were in use by the close of the fourth century, though there are no closed deposits within the Sanctuary to confirm this. When combined with the evidence from Olynthos and New Halos, and with Marsden's outline of the historical development of artillery, the finds from the Sanctuary help demonstrate the development of what later became the standard iron catapult-bolt point. The Romans borrowed it, along with artillery technology and expertise, during the Hellenistic period. The subsequent development of Roman arms ensured that such projectiles were scattered to the four corners of the Empire.

APPENDIX A

Ferrules

A significant number of ferrules appeared in the acropolis Sanctuary. Initially they caused some confusion because of their resemblance to catapult-bolt heads; however, closer analysis revealed subtle but important differences between the two classes of artifacts. First, the ferrules from the Sanctuary typically have a circular section over their entire length. They taper evenly from tip to base, rarely displaying a "neck" between point and socket. They are also somewhat shorter, rarely more than 4.2 cm, which gives them a stocky, conical shape quite distinct from the catapult-bolt heads. In addition, the ferrules from the Sanctuary tend to be considerably lighter than the typical catapult-bolt head.

Artifacts of this type are often identified as sauroteres, that is, spear or javelin butts, which are relatively common finds; however, spear butts are usually much larger than the pieces from the Sanctuary, a fact explained by the need to balance the weight of the spear head. Javelin butts would better fit the dimension of the pieces in question.[184] On the other hand, the 17:1 ratio between ferrules and javelin heads recovered from the Sanctuary argues against this possibility. All things considered, it seems more likely that these artifacts were protective tips for walking sticks, shepherds' crooks, or agricultural implements such as cattle prods, picks, or pitchforks. Comparable pieces have been recovered in New Halos.[185]

Ferrules

Cat. no.	Inv. no.	Y.T.L.P	L (cm)	W (cm)	M (g)	Condition
199	75	95.9.5.7	4.3	1.5	10	Fair: missing part of socket
200	150	96.4.3.5	4.6	NA	8	Fair: bent tip
201	1101	96.8.6.7	5.3	1.7	12	Fair
202	1189	97.5.2.4	5.3	1.7	12	Poor: missing part of socket
203	1202	97.4.5.7	4.1	1.4	6	Poor: missing much of socket
204	1298	97.7.1.1	4.1	1.6	6	Good
205	1370	97.9.1.1	2.9	1.0	NA	Poor: fragmentary
206	2388	99.12.2.2	4.1	1.7	6	Good
207	2392	99.11.2.2	4.0	1.7	10	Good
208	2403	99.10.3.4	4.0	1.8	6	Good
209	2659	99.1.5.10	4.1	1.6	NA	Good
210	2746	99.1.6.12	3.0	1.5	NA	Poor: fragmentary
211	3142	00.6.1.1	4.1	1.6	10	Fair
212	3195	00.6.1.1	4.6	1.8	NA	Fair
213	3301	00.4.7.9	4.9	1.9	10	Fair
214	3378	00.6.3.3	4.4	1.7	10	Fair
215	3832	01.4.2.2	3.3	NA	NA	Fair
216	No number[187]	NA	NA	NA	NA	Poor: missing most of socket
217	No number	NA	NA	NA	NA	Good: missing base of socket

6

Jewellery

Alexis Young

Over 325 jewellery votives from the Late Classical and Hellenistic periods were excavated from the Sanctuary on the acropolis, of which 246 are described in the Catalogue. The jewellery is arranged according to number, type, and function.[1]

Jewellery was one method of displaying status and wealth; thus it was meant to be visible.[2] Accordingly, primary or personal jewellery adorned the body, head, ear, neck, arm, finger(s), ankles, and feet, whereas secondary jewellery adorned and fastened clothing.[3] The majority here are earrings for pierced ears (**1–96**) and finger rings (**97–147**), mainly of bronze, with a few of silver and gilded silver, or of iron. There are also beads (**148–77**), mostly of bone, but some of bronze and one a glass eye-bead, pendants, mostly of bronze (**178–84**), bronze and iron pins (**185–215**), glass "gems" (**216–21**) probably used as insets like the figured glass ring bezel (**136**), a bronze gaming piece (**222**), a gold rosette (**223**), gilded silver medallions (**224–5**), a gold sheet fragment (**226**), bone buttons (**227–33**), bronze snake bracelets (**234–8**), bronze hair rings (**239–41**), bronze diadems (**242–3**), and bronze fibulae (**244–6**). Although buttons are not classified as jewellery, they are also included in the Catalogue.

Discussion of chronology, materials, technique, and iconography follows the Catalogue, with analysis of the jewellery as votive offerings, and comments on the placement of jewellery votives in the Sanctuary conclude the study.

The measurements and weight of each piece of jewellery are included where possible.

CATALOGUE

D	Diameter
L	Length
W	Width
H	Height
Th.	Thickness
Wt.	Weight

All measurements are in centimetres; weights are in grams.

Earrings (1–96)

Earrings were the most popular form of jewellery votive in the Sanctuary. One hundred and twenty-two were recorded, representing almost 40% of the total finds of jewellery in the Sanctuary. Ninety-six of these are included in the Catalogue, divided into ten distinct types: lunates (**1–31**), hoops with decorative bands (**32–4**) and balls (**35–6**), pyramidals (**38–68**), semi-spirals (**69**), spirals (**70–5**), twisted wire hoops (**76–84**), and penannular hoops (**85–96**). The penannular hoops have either plain circuits (**85–8**), circuits with stylized snake's head terminals (**89–92**), or circuits with collars (**93–5**), one of which has a spiral attachment (**96**). Another thus far unique earring is **37** with a hoop in the shape of a fishhook and a spiral attachment on one end. The 26 earrings not described in the Catalogue include three pyramidals,[4] 11 half-sections of lunates,[5] and 12 suspension hooks for pyramidal earrings; these are listed in Appendix I.

The most common shapes, lunates (**1–31**) and pyramidals ("inverted pendants in the form of pyramids") (**38–68**), were also two of the main types from the Classical period throughout the Greek world.[6] Apart from these, all other types were found in small numbers. Four of the nine twisted wire hoops (**81–84**) terminate on their larger end in lion heads, a popular type of the late fourth to early third century. With the exception of one plain silver circuit (**88**) and one rare amber pyramidal earring (**67**), the rest are bronze. Most of the earrings are fourth century in date when the Sanctuary was at its peak, with a few spiral ones perhaps dating to the late fifth and the lion-head earrings likely belonging to the early third century BCE.

Type A: Lunate (1–31)

The lunate earring, also known as the boat-, ascus-, or leech-shaped earring, is the most popular type in the Sanctuary. It is also one of the oldest in Greece, beginning with Mycenaean examples discovered in Cyprus.[7] Bronze lunate earrings are known from Lefkandi in the ninth century BCE,[8] and gold ones from the eighth–seventh centuries at Ephesus.[9] The type was very popular throughout the Greek world in the Classical period, but apparently became rare in Hellenistic times.[10] Gold examples from graves in the Greek mainland and northern Greece, Thrace, the Crimea, and Southern Italy are especially elegant, decorated with filigree, rosettes, disks, hanging pendants, and figural decoration.[11]

Excavations at the Sanctuary uncovered 42 plain, bronze lunate earrings, of which 31 were catalogued.[12] Bronze lunates are common in sanctuaries and graves in the Peloponnese and mainland Greece, ranging in date from the seventh to the fourth centuries BCE.[13] The Stymphalian examples fit with those of the fourth century. Plain lunates (**1–24**) were cast as one solid piece. No seam lines can be seen where two halves might have been soldered together if cast in halves. Several of these plain lunates also have a visible ridge on either side of the contoured form, apparently flattened slightly from the shape of the mould. Better-preserved examples have thickened terminals and part of the plain curved wire for insertion into the pierced ear. **18** has most of its wire preserved. Four lunates (**1, 5, 8–9**) have a small petal-shaped clasp on their terminals opposite the curved insertion wire, while other examples have flattened terminals. **10** and **11** may have formed a pair, since they were found in the same trench, although in different levels.

Seven lunates (**25–31**) and 11 other fragments[14] were made in two separate hollow halves from sheet bronze and then soldered together, although no traces of solder remain. **25–31** are more decorative than the other plain lunates, with tiny loops or parts of loops preserved along the outer seam where the two lunate sections joined. One lunate (**26**) was found with a tiny acorn-shaped pendant (**178**), no longer attached.[15] Quite likely some of the other small pendants found at the site also once adorned this type.

A.I: Plain lunates (1–24)

1. Bronze, cast. Inv. 177. Tr. 95.4+1.2.4. Temple. **Fig. 6.4**
D 2.0 to 2.1; Th. 0.6; Wt. 4.1
In good condition. Small thickened terminals. Above one terminal is a petal-shaped clasp; the wire is preserved for 0.3 cm above the other terminal. Distinct ridged body.

2. Bronze, solid cast. Inv. 187. Tr. 95.4 +1.2.4. Temple
D 2.1; Th. 0.6; Wt. 3.4
Some surface corrosion. Ridged body with thickened terminals; part of the insertion wire is preserved for 0.3 cm.

3. Bronze, cast. Inv. 194. Tr. 95.4+1.2.4. Temple. **Figs. 6.4 and 6.14**
D 2.1–2.3; Th. 0.7; Wt. 5.4
Very good condition; some surface corrosion. Ridged body with two thickened terminals; part of the insertion wire is preserved for 0.3 cm.

4. Bronze, cast. Inv. 195. Tr. 95.4+1.2.4. Temple. **Fig. 6.4**
D 1.7–1.93; Th. 0.4; Wt. 2.6
Good condition, slight surface corrosion. Two thickened terminals on either end of the ridged crescent shape. The wire is missing; a petal-shaped clasp, similar to **1**, is preserved above one of the terminals.

5. Bronze, cast. Inv. 202. Tr. 95.4+1.2.4. Temple
D 2.1–2.25; Th. 0.65; Wt. 4.9
Fair condition, with major surface corrosion and some accretions. Both thickened terminals are preserved and 0.3 cm of the insertion wire.

6. Bronze, cast. Inv. 598. Tr. 95.4+1.2.4. Temple. **Figs. 6.4 and 6.14**
D 2.2–2.9; Th. 0.7. Wt. 5.6
Good condition with slight surface corrosion. Both thickened terminals are preserved and 1.2 cm of the wire. Body is ridged.

7. Bronze, cast. Inv. 737. Tr. 95.4+1.2.4. Temple
D 1.8–2.2; Th. 0.6; Wt. 5.1
Good condition. A tiny part of the petal-shaped clasp and wire is preserved above each thickened terminal; ridged body.

8. Bronze, cast. Inv. 180. Tr. 95.6.5.11. Temple
D 1.6–2.2; Th. 0.6; Wt. 2.1
Very good condition. Two flattened terminals have

a pierced hole for the attachment of the wire and the clasp, now missing. Ridged body.

9. Bronze, cast. Inv. 807. Tr. 96.13.2.5. S of Altar
D 2.1–2.15; Th. 0.6; Wt. 3.9
Good condition, with some surface corrosion on body. Both thickened terminals, a petal-shaped clasp, and 0.6 cm of the wire are preserved.

10. Bronze, cast. Inv. 913. Tr. 96.13.4.7. S of Altar. **Fig. 6.4**
D 1.8–2.2; Th. 0.6; Wt. 3.3
Fair condition, with surface corrosion and accretions. Both thickened terminals are preserved and 0.2 cm of the wire. Possibly a pair with **11**.

11. Bronze, cast. Inv. 1847. Tr. 96.13.3.6. S of Altar. **Fig. 6.4**
D 1.85–2.1; Th. 0.6. Good condition. Both thickened terminals are preserved and 0.3 cm of the wire. Possibly a pair with **10**.

12. Bronze, cast. Inv. 1027. Tr. 97.4.2.2. S of Altar
D 1.0–1.2; Th. 0.2; Wt. 0.4
Fair condition, with surface corrosion. Very small earring with both thickened terminals preserved and 0.5 cm of the wire.

13. Bronze, cast. Inv. 1091. Tr. 97.4.3.4. S of Altar
D 2.1–2.2; Th0.7; Wt. 4.8
Good condition. Both thickened terminals are preserved and 0.55 cm of the wire.

14. Bronze, cast. Inv. 2218. Tr. 99.1.3.3. E of Altar. **Figs. 6.4 and 6.14**
D 1.7–1.8; Th. 0.4; Wt. 1.5
Good condition. Very small example with narrow body. Both thickened terminals are preserved and 1.0 cm of the wire.

15. Bronze, cast. Inv. 2445. Tr. 99.6.5.5. E of Altar. **Fig. 6.4**
D 1.9–2.2; Th. 0.6; Wt. 4.2
Good condition, with warts of corrosion. Both thickened terminals and a tiny part of the clasp and wire are preserved. Body has a pronounced ridge.

16. Bronze, cast. Inv. 2453. Tr. 99.6.5.5. E of Altar
D 2.2–2.7; Th. 0.6; Wt. 5.9. Fair condition, with surface corrosion. Both thickened terminals are preserved and 0.8 cm of the wire. Body is lopsided in appearance.

17. Bronze, cast. Inv. 2607. Tr. 97.5 baulk.3.4. E of Altar. **Fig. 6.4**
D 1.8–2.3; Th. 0.6; Wt. 3.9
Good condition. Both thickened terminals are preserved above the ridged body, including a tiny part of the wire.

18. Bronze, cast. Inv. 203. Tr. 96.6.5.11. W of Bldg. A. **Figs. 6.4 and 6.14**
D 1.5–1.6; Th. 0.35; Wt. 1.4
Very good condition. Very small earring almost completely preserved except for the end of the wire.

19. Bronze, cast. Inv.1033. Tr. 97.2 + 96.15.5.5. Bldg. A
D 1.5–2.2; Th. 0.6; Wt. 4.2
Good condition; some surface corrosion. The wire and one terminal are missing above the ridged lunate body.

20. Bronze, cast. Inv. 1363. Tr. 95.9.7.7. Bldg. A
D 2.0–2.3; Th. 0.7; Wt. 5.1
Good condition. Both thickened terminals are preserved above the ridged lunate body and 0.5 cm of the wire.

21. Bronze, cast. Inv. 1207. Tr. 97.6.1.1. W of Bldg. A
D 2.0–2.2; Th. 0.55; Wt. 4.2
Good condition, with some pitting and corrosion. Both thickened terminals are preserved and 0.15 cm of the wire.

22. Bronze, cast. Inv. 1262. Tr. 97.6.2.2. W of Bldg. A
D 1.3–2.02; Th. 0.6; Wt. 3.8
Good condition. Both thickened terminals are preserved above the ridged lunate body; missing the wire.

23. Bronze, cast. Inv. 3106. Tr. 99.9 scarp cleaning. Near City Wall
D 1.5–2.2; Th. 0.6; Wt. 3.3
Fair condition, with some surface corrosion and pitting. Missing both terminals and wire.

24. Bronze, cast. Inv. 179. Surface
D 1.9 × 2.1; Th. 0.7; Wt. 3.9
Fair condition with many cracks along the ridged lunate body. One thickened terminal is preserved, as well as a tiny piece of the wire.

A.II: Lunates with loops for pendants (25–31)

The following seven bronze lunates have the addition of tiny loops or parts of loops preserved along their outer seam for hanging pendants. **26** was found alongside an acorn pendant (**178**), no longer attached. There appear to be no parallels in bronze for this type, although examples of gold lunates with pendants are known from the fifth and fourth centuries BCE.[16]

25. Bronze, cast. Inv. 227. Tr. 95.4+1.2.4. Temple. **Figs. 6.4 and 6.14**
D 2.0–2.2; Th. 0.6; Wt. 4.2
Good condition. Parts of three tiny loops preserved along the outer casting seam. Both thickened terminals are preserved and 0.5 cm of the wire.

26. Bronze, cast. Inv. 748A. Tr. 95.6.5.8. Outside of Temple. **Figs. 6.4 and 6.14**
D 1.1–2.15; Th. 0.7
Fair condition. The lunate body is composed of two separate, hollow fragments. Both terminals and wire are missing. Found with a miniature acorn pendant (**178**), which probably once hung from one of the partially preserved loops.

27. Bronze, cast. Inv. 199. Tr. 96.4.2.2. Altar. **Fig. 6.4**
D 1.6–2.2; Th. 0.8; Wt. 1.6
Poor condition, with the lunate body split along upper and lower casting seams. Missing both terminals and wire. Traces of loops preserved along the outer casting seam.

28. Bronze, cast. Inv. 469. Tr. 96.4.6.9. Altar. **Fig. 6.4**
a) D 1.1–1.6; b) D 1.1–2.0 ; Th. 0.7; Wt. 0.5. Poor condition; in two fragments.
Missing terminals and wire, as well as fragments from both sections of the lunate body. Traces of loops along the casting seam.

29. Bronze fragment, cast. Inv. 1290B. Tr. 97.4.7.11. S of Altar. **Fig. 6.4**
MPD 0.7–1.05; Th. 0.7; Wt. 0.2
Very poor condition. Missing terminals and wire. One tiny loop is completely preserved and parts of another. Found with a pyramidal earring, **52**.

30. Bronze fragment, cast. Inv. 644. Tr. 96.8.3.4. Bldg. A. **Fig. 6.4**
D 1.8–2.1; Th. 0.8; Wt. 0.7
Cast. Fair condition, with surface corrosion and splitting along seams. Missing terminals and wire. One loop is preserved and parts of two others along the casting seam.

31. Bronze, cast. Inv. 996. Tr. 97.2.3.3. Bldg. A. **Fig. 6.4**
D 1.6–1.9; Th. 0.8; Wt. 0.5
Fair condition with surface corrosion and splitting along seams; one half and part of the other half preserved. Both terminals and wire are missing. Two loops are preserved and part of a third loop along the casting seam.

Type B: Crescent-shaped hoops with triple band decoration (32–4)

A narrow crescent shape, likely derived from lunate earrings, characterizes this type. The hoops are decorated with two or three raised bands of decreasing size at each end, as well as a transverse band flanked by a narrow fillet around the central part of the crescent. Four examples were discovered in the Sanctuary, all quite small, and close in size (D 1.0–1.1 to 1.05–1.1). One pair (**32**) is preserved, of which one earring preserves the complete insertion wire. A pair of earrings from the Korykian Cave is a close parallel.[17]

32. Bronze pair, cast. Inv. 712. Tr. 96.11.3.3. Temple. **Figs. 6.4 and 6.14**
a) D 1.1–1.05; b) D 0.7–1.05; Th. 0.4; Wt. a) 0.4, b) 0.4
Very good condition. Earring A is almost completely preserved, while earring B is lacking its wire. Hoops are decorated with three raised bands in the centre and at each end.

33. Bronze, cast. Inv. 2100. Tr. 96.11. Surface cleaning. Temple. **Fig. 6.14**
D 1.0–1.05; Th. 0.39; Wt. 0.9
Good condition, with slight corrosion. 0.2 cm of the wire is preserved.

34. Bronze, cast. Inv. 3409. Tr. 96.15.5.5. Refuse pit outside Bldg. A. **Figs. 6.4 and 6.14**
D 1.0–1.1; Th0.3; Wt. 0.3
Good condition. Wire is half preserved. Two raised bands at each end.

Type C: "Fibula-type" hoops (35–6)

Two small earrings have a semicircular bow-shaped hoop, decorated with three or four moulded globes, flanked by a thin fillet. A round bead terminates one end of the hoop, while the other end has a plain wire to pierce the ear. This earring type may have developed in the north, since several silver and bronze examples from the sixth to the fourth centuries BCE were found in the Chalkidike, as well as in Lokris and Phokis.[18] The type is also similar in technique and form to fourth-century fibulae from a Peloponnesian workshop, of which a similar specimen (**244**) was found in the Sanctuary.[19] Remarkably, both earrings from the Sanctuary are completely intact. They are almost identical in size and shape, suggesting that they are a pair, although **35** was found in a fourth/fifth-century CE (?) grave within the temple, while **36** was discovered in the refuse pit (Tr. 96.15) outside Building A. Most likely, **35** was discovered while the grave was being dug, as was another earring (**85**) and an iron pin (**192**), and was buried along with the body.

35. Bronze, solid cast. Inv. 1237. Tr. 96.11.4.5. Temple (fourth/fifth century CE (?) grave of a young girl). **Figs. 6.4 and 6.14**
D 1.5–1.56; Th. 0.3; Wt. 0.6
Intact; in good condition, with some corrosion on the

wire and balls. Bow-shaped hoop has four moulded globes, framed by fillets with a rounded knob on one end. 2.2 cm of the wire is preserved. Found near the head of the skeleton, but well below the chin. Also found with a plain circuit earring (**85**) and an iron pin (**192**).

36. Bronze, cast. Inv. 3440. Tr. 96.15.5.5. Refuse pit outside Bldg. A. **Figs. 6.4 and 6.14**
D 1.5–1.6. Wt. 0.9
Intact; in good condition with some surface corrosion. 2.5 cm of the wire is preserved.

Type D: Crescent-shaped hoop with spiral finial (37)

37 is the only example of its kind from the Sanctuary and has no close parallels.[20] This large earring has a crescent shape, although one end is much longer than the other and curves outwards. The lower end is split into two tips, where the spiral finial at the earlobe was once placed.

37. Bronze, cast. Inv. 2167. Tr. 99.2.3.3. Temple. **Figs. 6.4 and 6.14**
D 2.5–3.1; Th. 0.5; D of spiral 0.4; Wt. 5.6
Good condition, with some surface corrosion and broken at both ends. Missing its ear wire. The lower end is split into two tips for inserting the spiral finial. **96** also has a spiral finial. Very fine lines are incised on the crescent-shaped section.

Type E: Pyramidal earrings (38–68)

The most common type of earring in the Sanctuary after the lunate is the pyramidal. This type, shaped like an inverted pyramid, is known already in bronze, bone, and gold at Perachora and Argos during the seventh century BCE.[21] Pyramidals were prevalent from the sixth to the fourth centuries BCE throughout the Greek Mediterranean.[22] Silver pyramidal earrings were discovered in Classical graves at Isthmia and Halai.[23] Several very elaborate examples in gold have separately attached disks, rosettes, and pendants; unfortunately, these earrings are mostly from uncontrolled contexts.[24] Gold pairs found in graves in Macedonia and the Crimea are mid- to late fourth century in date.[25] Generally, bronze pyramidal earrings lack the separate decorative attachments seen on the gold and silver examples. Bronze pyramidal earrings from graves at Olynthos provide evidence for dates ranging from the late fifth century to 348 BCE, when the city was destroyed by Philip II.[26] Bronze pyramidal earrings have been found in many Peloponnesian and mainland Greek sites, with dates ranging from the sixth to the late fourth centuries. A terracotta mould to manufacture one was found on the Pnyx in Athens.[27]

Thirty-four bronze pyramidal earrings were found in the Sanctuary.[28] They are closely comparable to those from other Greek sites made of bronze dating from the late fifth to late fourth centuries.[29] The bronze type consists of a pendant in the form of an inverted pyramid with a suspension wire attached to the four-sided top by means of a rivet. **52** and **54** are the only two pyramidal earrings with their suspension wires preserved. These wires have flattened, rounded ends, resembling a stylized snake's head.[30]

Pyramidal earrings have three sections: the upper part with suspension wire is in the form of a four-sided top, often with a tiny boss in each corner; the middle section has two levels of four globes each, divided by a thin strip of metal between the pairs of globes; and the lower section has an inverted cone which tapers to a plain or crested globe. **52** and **54** have an inverted tapered cone impressed with a pattern of beaded wire, imitating the coiled, beaded wire found on examples in gold.[31] In contrast, the inverted tapered cones on the remaining pyramidal earrings have thicker coil decoration.

One unique discovery is a pyramidal earring fragment (**67**) carved in amber. Most amber in Greece came from the Baltic, although some also came from Sicily. Amber, apparently prized for its magical, amuletic, and medicinal qualities, was popular in Greece during the late eighth and seventh centuries for pins, fibulae, beads, pendants, and decorative inlay.[32] After the sixth century BCE, it was apparently not used much for decorative purposes, although there was always some available.[33] No other example of the shape in amber is known to me.[34]

38. Bronze, cast. Inv. 607. Tr. 95.4+1.2.4. Temple. **Fig. 6.5**
H1.6; W 1.0; Wt. 4.3
Good condition, with some corrosion on the globes. Found beside another pyramidal earring (SF 1996.493; now missing).

39. Bronze, cast. Inv. 1386. Tr. 96.11.5.6. Temple. **Figs. 6.5 and 6.14**
H 1.35; W 0.55; Wt. 1.4
Fair condition with corrosion on the four-sided top and lower globe. Tiny bosses are preserved on three corners of the base. Four coils on cone, ending in a partially preserved, crested ball. The small size suggests that it is either a young girl's earring or a miniature votive.

40. Bronze, cast. Inv. 1439. Tr. 96.11.5.6. Temple
H 1.8; W 0.7; Wt. 2.9
Fair condition with surface corrosion. One row of moulding is between the four-sided top and two levels of four globes, similar to **60**. Four imitation coils on cone terminating in a large flattened bead with a tiny stemlike granulation.

41. Bronze, cast. Inv. 1461. Tr. 96.11.5.6. Temple
H 2.0; W 0.75; Wt. 4.2
Fair condition with surface corrosion, especially on the globe. Four-sided top has a tiny boss in each corner. Four coils on cone ending in a large, partially crested globe.

42. Bronze, cast. Inv. 1462. Tr. 96.11.5.6. Temple
H 1.3; W 0.65; Wt. 1.3
Fair condition. Three coils on a small cone terminating in a small bead with a tiny stemlike extension.

43. Bronze, cast. Inv. 1551. Tr. 96.11.5.6. Temple
H 1.6; W 0.7; Wt. 2.3
Fair condition. Four coils on cone ending in a small bead with a thick stemlike extension.

44. Bronze, cast. Inv. 1561. Tr. 96.11.5.6. Temple. **Fig. 6.5**
H 0.35; W 0.5; Wt. 1.2
Fair condition. Very small size. **44** varies from others in having two rows of moulding on the upper outer edges of the four-sided top. Below, only one level of globes on each side, rather than the usual two. Four coils on cone, ending in an oblong bead with a tiny granulation.

45. Bronze, cast. Inv. 1587. Tr. 96.11.6.7. Temple
H 1.5; W 0.67; Wt. 1.8
In good condition. Three coils on a small cone terminating in a small, partially preserved crested globe.

46. Bronze, cast. Inv. 2173. Tr. 99.4.1.1. Temple
H 2.0; W 0.75; Wt. 3.1
Fair condition, with corrosion on the four-sided top and the bottom globe. Five coils on cone ending in a small, crested globe.

47. Bronze, cast. Inv. 3060. Tr. 00.2.5.5. Temple. **Fig. 6.5**
H 1.9; W 0.7; Wt. 2.5
Good condition with some corrosion. The base has a tiny boss in each corner. Six coils on cone ending in a globe.

48. Bronze, cast. Inv. 948. Tr. 97.3.3.3. Altar. **Fig. 6.5**
H 1.95; W 0.74; Wt. 3.4
Good condition. Six coils on cone terminating in a globe with a thick rounded stem.

49. Bronze, cast. Inv. 892. Tr. 96.13.4.7. S of Altar. **Fig. 6.5**
H 1.36; W 0.63. Wt. 1.7
Good condition. The two levels of globes are oblong rather than round. Five coils on a small cone ending in a large globe.

50. Bronze, cast. Inv. 1201. Tr. 97.4.5.7. S of Altar
H 1.23; W 0.6; Wt. 1.1
Poor condition with surface corrosion. Tiny coiled cone, ending in a small partially preserved crested globe.

51. Bronze, cast. Inv. 1290. Tr. 97.4.7.11. S of Altar. **Fig. 6.14**
H 2.3; W.1.1; Wt. 7.7
A large specimen, in very good condition. Found with a lunate earring fragment (Inv. 97.262B). The upper edges of the four-sided top have traces of filigree decoration; below is a row of incised semicircles, like those on **53** and **54**. Eleven coils on an elongated cone ending in a crested globe.

52. Bronze, cast. Inv. 641. Tr. 96.8.5.6. W of Bldg. A. **Figs. 6.5 and 6.14**
H 4.1; L of pendant 2.7; W 1.2; Wt. 10.3
Large specimen, in excellent condition. The suspension wire terminates in the form of a flattened snake's head. The other end of the wire, attached to the four-sided top with a rivet, has a V-shaped clasp, now fused together in the form of another snake's head. The thick four-sided top has three tiny bosses preserved. Sixteen coils of fine beaded wire pattern on a tapered cone ending in a crested globe. Found with a lunate earring, **29**.

53. Bronze, cast. Inv. 48. Tr. 95.2.1.1. Bldg. A. **Figs. 6.5 and 6.14**
H 2.0; W. 0.9; Wt. 6.5
Good condition, with some corrosion on the four-sided top. Outside upper edges of the four-sided top are incised with two rows of five semicircles, similar to **51** and **54**. Below are two rolls of oblong balls, like **49**. Twelve coils on cone ending in a globe.

54. Bronze, cast. Inv. 997. Tr. 97.2.3.3. Bldg. A. **Figs. 6.5 and 6.14**
H 3.1; L of pendant 2.0; W 0.95; Wt. 4.0
Good condition, except for slight wear at the four-sided top where it joins the suspension wire. The suspension wire is similar to **52** with a snake's head on the end that pierces the ear and a fused V-shaped clasp riveted to the base. Tiny bosses on three corners of the four-sided top; semicircles decorate the outer edges of the top, similar to **51** and **53**. Seventeen coils of fine beaded wire pattern on a tapered cone ending in a crested globe, close to **52**. Very similar to a bronze pair with silver wires, believed to be from a tomb in Same, Cephalonia, in the British

Museum, ca. 400 BCE, although **54** is larger and lacks the silver wires.[35]

55. Bronze, cast. Inv. 1034. Tr. 97.2 + 96.15.5.5. Bldg. A. **Fig. 6.14**
H 1.82; W 0.85; Wt. 3.6
Good condition. A row of filigree decorates the four-sided top, similar to **51**. Five coils on cone ending in a globe with a stemlike granulation.

56. Bronze, cast. Inv. 1039. Tr. 97.2 + 96.15.5.5. Bldg. A
H 1.93; W 0.8; Wt. 3.6
Good condition. One corner of the four-sided top has a tiny boss. Four coils on cone terminating in a globe with a tiny stemlike granulation.

57. Bronze, cast. Inv. 1044. Tr. 97.2 + 96.15.5.5. Bldg. A
H 1.3; W 0.7; Wt. 2.1
Good condition. Three coils on a small cone ending in a small bead.

58. Bronze, cast. Inv. 2508. Tr. 94.9.6.3. Bldg. A. **Fig. 6.5**
H 1.65; W.0.7; Wt. 3.2
Good condition. The four-sided top has a tiny boss in each corner. Five coils on cone terminated by a globe.

59. Bronze, cast. Inv. 3332. Tr. 96.15.5.5. Refuse pit outside Bldg. A
H 2.4; W 1.0; Wt. 5.7
Fair condition, with some corrosion on the four-sided top, inverted tapered cone and lower globe. Part of the four-sided top is separating from the upper row of balls on one side; the top has partially preserved bosses in each corner. Seven coils on cone ending in a large globe.

60. Bronze, cast. Inv. 3334. Tr. 96.15.5.5. Refuse pit outside Bldg. A
H 1.6; W 0.7; Wt. 2.1
Fair condition. The four-sided top and two levels of globes are separated by one row of moulding, similar to **40**. Two coils on a small cone ending in a globe with a thick, stemlike granulation.

61. Bronze, cast. Inv. 3341. Tr. 96.15.5.5. Refuse pit outside Bldg. A
H 1.3; W 0.4; Wt. 1.0
Good condition. Two coils on a small cone ending in a crested globe.

62. Bronze, cast. Inv. 3463. Tr. 96.15.5.5. Refuse pit outside Bldg. A. **Fig. 6.5**
H 1.46; W 0.6; Wt. 1.8
Good condition with slight corrosion. Tiny bosses are preserved on three corners of the four-sided top. Five coils on cone ending in a small bead with a small, stemlike granulation on the bottom.

63. Bronze, cast. Inv. 3467. Tr. 96.15.5.5. Refuse pit outside Bldg. A
H 1.2; W 0.65
Fair condition with slight corrosion on the four-sided top. Thin strip of metal between two levels of globes has a beaded pattern. Three coils on a small cone ending in a little globe.

64. Bronze, cast. Inv. 3525. Tr. 96.15.5.5. Refuse pit outside Bldg. A
H 1.75; W 1.0; Wt. 2.7
Fair condition. Six coils on cone ending in a globe.

65. Bronze, cast. Inv. 3586. Tr. 96.15.5.5. Refuse pit outside Bldg. A
H 1.65; W 1.0; Wt. 3.8
Fair condition with surface corrosion. The four-sided top has a tiny boss in each corner. Six coils on cone ending in a crested globe with a small granulation.

66. Bronze, cast. Inv. 3669. Tr. 96.15.5.5. Refuse pit outside Bldg. A
H 1.2; W 0.7; Wt. 1.6
Fair condition with surface corrosion. The four-sided top has a tiny boss in each corner. Two coils on cone; the lower globe is missing.

67. Amber fragment, carved. Inv. 3394. Tr. 96.15.5.5. Refuse pit outside Bldg. A. **Figs. 6.5 and 6.14**
H 1.3; W 0.6; Wt. 0.2
Very worn and only partially preserved. The upper broken-off section is quite glossy and polished looking. Missing suspension wire and four-sided top. Three rows of globes are preserved on one side. An inverted tapered cone has three or four rows of beading; the lower globe is missing.

68. Bronze fragment, cast. Part of the wide, square base of the earring
Inv. 3583. Tr. 96.15.5.5. Refuse pit outside Bldg. A.
L 1.1; W 1.1; Wt. 3.4
Fair condition. Tiny boss preserved in each corner. Traces of silver-coloured tin solder used to attach the suspension wire to the top.[36] A similar example was found at Olympia.[37]

Suspension loops of pyramidal earrings (Appendix I)

Twelve pieces of jewellery listed in Appendix I have penannular suspension loops, varying in diameter from 0.8 to 2.6 cm, with ends either tapered and pointed or in the form of a flattened, stylized snake's head.[38] Since these loops are very similar to the loops on preserved examples of pyramidal earrings (**53** and **54**), and since the rest of the pyramidal earrings are missing their suspension loops, it is reasonable to assume that at least some were once attached to pyramidal earrings left in the Sanctuary. The one end is flattened where it is attached to the four-sided top of the earring by means of a rivet or solder. Two examples have a rivet hole, indicating that they were once attached to the base by means of a rivet. In addition, several of the loops have a V-shaped clasp on the flattened end.

Type F: Loop with overlapping ends (69)

One earring from the Sanctuary is in the form of a loop with overlapping ends which bend upwards as if forming the beginning of a spiral. Robinson identified close parallels from Olynthos as earrings, although a silver example found near a skull in a late sixth-century BCE grave in Corinth is classified by Blegen as a "spiral hair coil or earring."[39]

69. Bronze. Inv. 1004. Tr. 96.13.6.11. S of Altar. **Figs. 6.5 and 6.14**
D 1.3; Th. 0.2; Wt. 0.6
Intact, in good condition, with slight surface corrosion. One end of the semicircular loop is flattened into a snake's head, while the other end is pointed.

Type G: Spiral or omega-shaped earrings (70–5)

The spiral or omega-shaped earring has a tightly wound oval spiral in the form of a curved bar with a moulded collar and decorative terminals.[40] Although simple forms were discovered in Iron Age graves at Lefkandi,[41] the spiral with decorated finials was quite popular on Rhodes during the seventh century BCE, where the elongated spiral was likely developed and used alongside the oval type.[42] Bronze and silver oval spiral earrings with moulded collars and budlike finials were popular in the Classical period, judging from finds in graves and sanctuaries in Thessaly, Chalkidike, Macedonia, Lokris, and Crete.[43] Variations in gold and silver have a rosette, in a simplified form of the seventh-century Rhodian type, or sometimes a disk covering the top of the curve.[44] Other versions include pyramidal finials, animal-head finials, and female-head finials.[45]

Six oval spiral objects with moulded collars and decorative finials (**70–5**) were found in the Sanctuary. **70** and **71** have thicker wires (0.4 cm) and simpler finials than the more elongated examples (**73–5**). **70** and **72** have the plainest finials, consisting of a moulded collar, surmounted by a globe. **71** has more elaborate finials consisting of a band of four small globes with a transverse disklike band and rounded globe on top. **73–5** have collars with long, narrow bud-shaped finials.

It is unclear whether these objects were earrings or hair rings (sometimes "hair spirals") or whether some were indeed neither.[46] Because both spiral earrings and hair rings were worn around the head, their location in graves is not helpful in distinguishing function;[47] however, the spiral type was certainly one used for earrings. Lykian coins of the mid-fifth century BCE clearly show examples inserted through a large hole in the earlobe.[48] On the other hand, vase paintings and sculpture show that the omega-shaped earring also hung from a smaller hoop which pierced the ear, or it was worn over the upper earlobe instead, either singly or in a group.[49] The six spiral examples from Stymphalos were not found near supplementary rings that may have passed through the ear. Indeed, their bud-shaped finials are narrow enough to pass through a modest hole in the earlobe (even **70** and **71**) and so were probably worn this way.

70. Bronze, cast. Inv. 2182. Tr. 99.4.1.1. Temple. **Figs. 6.5 and 6.14**
H 1.8; Th. 0.4; Wt. 2.7
Intact with spots of corrosion. Thick spiral, terminated at both ends by a moulded collar and rounded globe.

71. Bronze, cast. Inv. 1041. Tr. 97.2 + 96.15.5.5. Bldg. A. **Figs. 6.5 and 6.14**
H 1.95; Th. 0.4; Wt. 4.8
Good condition with some surface corrosion. Thick wire spiral with both finials preserved. Finials have a thick band of four small globes, a disk-shaped band, and a rounded globe on top.

72. Bronze, cast. Inv. 2887. Tr. 00.2.2.2. Temple. **Fig. 6.5**
D 1.0 × 1.65; Th. 0.1; Wt. 0.3
Intact in two fragments. Fair condition with surface corrosion. The thin bronze wire is bent into a very small flattened loop with overlapping ends that form a spiral. Simple collar terminated by a rounded globe. Possibly a child's hair coil because of its small size.

73. Bronze, cast. Inv. 594. Tr. 96.8.3.4. W of Bldg. A. **Figs. 6.5 and 6.14**
H 2.7; Th. 0.2; Wt. 3.1
Excellent condition. This earring (?) is much larger than **70** and **71**, the wire is thinner, and the ends of the spiral are terminated by an elaborate moulded collar. The collar consists of two transverse bands surmounted by two globes with a long, narrow, angular, budlike finial and two globes.

74. Bronze, cast. Inv. 575. Tr. 96.13.2.3. S of Altar. **Fig. 6.5**
H 2.5; Th. 0.2; Wt. 1.7
Good condition with some corrosion. The budlike finial lacks the moulded collar of **73**.

75. Bronze, cast. Inv. 2736. Tr. 99.1.5.11. E of Altar. **Figs. 6.5 and 6.14**
H 2.0; Th. 0.1; Wt. 1.0
Partially preserved, in good condition. One budlike finial is preserved above two transverse bands. The spiral on the other end is broken off below the finial.

Type H: Twisted wire hoop (76–84)

Nine bronze earrings have a thick, circular hoop, twisted when heated to form a series of parallel ridges. This technique imitates gold earrings formed of thick strands of wire twisted together. **76–80** have a collar on one end. **77** and **78** have a long narrow wire tapering from the hoop to a narrow, flattened stylized snake's head to pierce the ear. Similar twisted wire earrings of bronze have been found in graves at Olynthos, although the preserved wires terminate in a point.[50]

The other four twisted wire bronze hoops have a very worn finial in the form of a lion's head (**81–4**). From the end of the fourth century BCE to the first century CE, twisted wire hoops, with one terminal in the shape of an animal head, were the most popular type of Greek earring.[51] Lion-head earrings were especially fashionable during the late Classical period in Macedonia, where the earliest known examples of gold were found in a grave dating to the mid- to third quarter of the fourth century BCE.[52] Lion-head earrings have also been found in late Classical contexts in sanctuaries and graves in the Peloponnese, northwestern Greece, the Greek East, and Taranto, Italy.[53]

The four bronze lion-head earrings from the Sanctuary are at least late fourth century or early third century in date. They lack the elaborate collars seen on gold examples, with simple indentations for the eyes, snout, and mouth, the mouth being generally open. Flecks of gold and traces of gilding were found on **81** and on one of the plain twisted wire hoops (**77**). The small size of **82** and **83** suggests that they were either votive offerings of young girls, perhaps of marriageable age, or miniature votives of adult females.

H.1: Twisted wire hoops with plain collar (76–80)

76. Bronze. Inv. 471. Tr. 95.4+1.2.4. Temple
D 1.1–1.5; Th. 0.4; Wt. 1.8
Fair condition. Thick twisted wire hoop, with one thick blunted end, and one end that tapers to a point.

77. Gilded bronze. Inv. 2966. Tr. 00.2.3.3. Temple. **Figs. 6.5 and 6.14**
D 1.6; Th. 0.4; Wt. 2.3
Excellent condition, with traces of gilding on the hoop. The pointed end of the wire to pierce the ear is flattened into a small snake's head. A V-shaped clasp forms the other terminus.

78. Bronze. Inv. 979. Tr. 96.13. Scarp. S of Altar. **Figs. 6.5 and 6.14**
D 1.67–2.45; Th. 0.4; Wt. 2.6
Excellent condition. A tapering pointed terminus is slightly flattened into a snake's head while the other terminus forms a V-shaped clasp.

79. Bronze. Inv. 3072. Tr. 00.3.4.4. S of Altar. **Fig. 6.14**
D 1.2–1.6; Th. 0.3; Wt. 1.9
Poor condition. One end has a small collar while the other blunt end is missing the tapering point to pierce the ear.

80. Bronze. Inv. 3673. Tr. 99.1. Surface. E of Altar
D 0.9–1.3; Th. 0.25; Wt. 0.5
Poor condition with surface corrosion. One end has a small collar, while the other end is missing the tapered point.

H.2: Twisted wire hoops with lion-head finials (81–4)

81. Gilded bronze, cast. Inv. 176. Tr. 95.4+1.2.4. Temple. **Figs. 6.5 and 6.14**
D 1.7–1.8; Th. 0.4; Wt. 2.0
Good condition, with flecks of gilding on the twisted wire. There are also flecks of silver, although it may have rubbed off from something else. Thick hoop of twisted wire has a narrow collar with a very worn lion's head on the thickest end; its eyes, muzzle, and mouth are barely visible. The other end of the hoop tapers to a now blunt point to pierce the ear.

82. Bronze, cast. Inv. 463. Tr. 95.4+1.2.4. Temple. **Figs. 6.5 and 6.14**
a) D 1.1–1.9; b) D 0.3–0.8; c) 0.15–0. 7; Th. 0.5; Wt. 2.5
Poor, fragmentary condition, broken in three parts. The tip of the wire is broken off. The lion's crude, bulbous head consists of an open mouth, square snout, and only one eye marked by an indentation.

83. Bronze, cast. Inv. 614. Tr. 95.4+1.2.4. Temple. **Figs. 6.5 and 6.14**

D 1.15–1.3; Th. 0.35; Wt. 0.9
Poor condition; part of the band is missing from the tapered end. What looks like a very worn lion's head on one end with a pointed snout and wide open mouth is likely just a coincidence of breakage at this end.

84. Bronze, cast. Inv. 2740. Tr. 97.5 baulk.4.4. E. of Altar. **Figs. 6.5 and 6.14**
D 1.7; Th. 0.4; Wt. 0.7
Very good condition. Rounded disklike collar; lion's head with a square snout and a large circular indentation for the eyes. The long, tapering pointed end is flattened to form a snake-head.

Type I: Plain circuits (85–96)

Twelve objects having either a plain open circuit of thin wire or an open circuit with a collar on one end have been classified as earrings from their size, narrow thickness, and either pointed or snake's head terminals. The large open circuit (**85**) is likely an earring, judging from its burial context beneath the head of a girl. **89–91** have a snake's head on one end and a V-shaped clasp on the other, features found on other earring types. **89** and **90** are wider than most wires which pierced the ear, but are still narrow enough to pass through an earlobe. It is also possible that these two objects are hair rings, although their diameters and decoration are similar to suspension hoops on pyramidal earrings. The only silver earring (**88**) has tapered ends, indicating its use. **95** may be a precursor of the crescent-shaped hoops with triple band decoration (**32–4**). **93** and **94** are lacking suspension wires, but have a collar on one end like **95**. Other open circuits (e.g. Inv. 650, 1204, 1271) included in Appendix II might also be earrings from their shape and thin wires.

I.1: Plain circuits (85–8)

85. Bronze, cast and hammered. Inv. 1297. Tr. 96.11.4.5. Temple (fourth/fifth century CE (?) grave of young girl). **Figs. 6.5 and 6.14**
D 2.1–2.4; Th. 0.2; Wt. 1.2
Good condition. Large, plain open circuit with blunt ends. Found directly below the skull of a young girl. Because of its context, the earring may be Late Roman, unless it came to be mixed into grave fill by chance. More likely it was discovered while the grave was being dug and was reburied along with the child. In addition, Roman-period bronze plain circuit earrings, such as those from Isthmia and Olympia, tend to have ends twisted into hooks to form a clasp.[54] Found with a "fibula-type" earring (**35**) and an iron pin (**192**).

86. Bronze, hammered. Inv. 2217. Tr. 99.1.3.3. E of Altar
D 1.2–1.8; Th. 0.1; Wt. 0.2
Fair condition with surface corrosion. Fine semicircular wire. One end is hammered flat and the other end has half a broken prong remaining of a V-shaped clasp.

87. Bronze, cast and hammered. Inv. 1048. Tr. 97.2 + 96.15.5.5. Bldg. A
D 1.7; Th. 0.3; Wt. 0.3
Partially preserved, with surface corrosion. One end is broken off, while the other end terminates in a V-shaped clasp.

88. Silver, cast and hammered. Inv. 1182. Tr. 96.8 (scarp cleaning). W of Bldg. A. **Figs. 6.5 and 6.14**
D 1.9–2.0; Th. 0.2; Wt. 1.2
Good condition. Hoop with tapered ends, now bent from its original shape and split at one point. Tapered silver hoops were popular at Cyrene during the late seventh or sixth centuries BCE. The type apparently went out of fashion there by the fifth century BCE. Some of these hoops are decorated with granular clusters, although one is undecorated like **88**.[55]

I.2: Plain circuits with snake's head terminals (89–92)

89. Bronze, cast and hammered. Inv. 190. Tr. 95.6.5.7. Near Temple. **Fig. 6.5**
D 2.0 ; W 0.6; Th. 0.2; Wt. 2.0
Fair condition with surface corrosion. The exterior profile is slightly convex with sharp but uneven edges. One end terminates in a flattened snake's head while the other terminates in a V-shaped clasp.

90. Bronze, cast and hammered. Inv. 418. Tr. 95.1.10.16. Temple
D 2.1; W 0.4; Th. 0.3; Wt. 2.1
Fair condition with surface corrosion, causing uneven thickness and surface. Ring-shaped circuit, with a flattened snake head on one end, while the other end terminates in a V-shaped clasp similar to **89**.

91. Bronze, cast and hammered. Inv. 953. Tr. 97.3.2.2. Altar
D 2.0; Max. Th. 0.21; Wt. 1.1
Fair condition, with surface corrosion. Open circuit with overlapping end. One end is flattened slightly to form a snake head, while the other has a V-shaped clasp, similar to **89** and **90**.

92. Bronze, two fragments. Inv. 1258. Tr. 97.4.6.9. S of Altar. **Fig. 6.5**
a) D 1.1–1.55; b) D 1.0; Th. 0.1; Wt. 0.2

Fair condition with surface corrosion. Thin wire hoop preserved in two fragments. One end is flattened into a small snake's head, while the other end on the smaller fragment is blunt.

I.3: Plain circuits with collar (93–5)

93. Bronze, cast. Inv. 647. Tr. 96.13.2.3. S of Altar. **Fig. 6.6**
D 1.1; Th. 0.2; Wt. 0.3. Fair condition, with surface corrosion. Small, thick semicircular circuit with a thick collar on one end; missing wire.

94. Bronze, cast. Inv. 958. Tr. 96.13.5.8. S of Altar. **Fig. 6.6**
D 1.2; Th. 0.2; Wt. 0.4
Good condition. Same as **93**, although the end which pierces the ear is flattened into a snake's head.

95. Bronze, cast. Inv. 3681. Tr. 96.13. Surface (scarp cleaning). S of Altar. **Fig. 6.6**
D 1.0; Th. 0.1; Wt. 0.3
Good condition. Intact with wire preserved. Same type as preceding.

I.4: Circuit with spiral finial (96)

96. Bronze. Inv. 3617. Tr. 96.15.5.5. Refuse pit outside Bldg A. **Figs. 6.6 and 6.14**
D 1.7; Th. 0.1; Wt. 0.3
Fair condition with surface corrosion. Open circuit with a small spiral attachment (D 0.4 cm) at one end and a curved prong on top. Another spiral was likely once attached to the other prong. The other end tapers to a blunt point. **37** also has a spiral finial. A similar spiral is attached to an earring from Lousoi, and to a circular earring from Perachora, although neither is very similar to **96**.[56]

Distribution of earrings

Thirty-eight earrings, nearly 40% of the total from the Sanctuary, were found in the Temple cella. The largest concentrations occur in the northwestern (Tr. 95.4 +1 Level 2) and northeastern parts of the cella (Tr. 96.11 Levels 3, 4, 5 and 6). Lunates, pyramidals, and lion-head earrings were found in the northwestern part, while pyramidals predominate in the northeastern part, as well as the only pair of earrings (**32**) found together, which are of extremely small size. Of the 47 earrings found in and around Building A, 21 were found in the refuse pit (Tr. 96.15 Level 5), where again pyramidals predominate. Only one lunate earring[57] was found in the immediate vicinity of the Altar (Tr. 96.3 scarp), while the remaining 36 were found scattered to the south (Tr. 96.4 Levels 2 and 6, Tr. 96.13 Levels 2, 5, and 6, Tr. 97.4 Levels 2, 3, and 7, Tr. 00.3 Level 4) and east (Tr. 97.5 baulk Levels 3 and 4, Tr. 99.6 Level 5) of the Altar, including the rectangular room below the Altar Terrace Wall to the east (Tr. 99.1 Levels 3 and 5). (See figs. 6.1 and 6.2.)

Finger rings (97–147)

Fifty-two finger rings were discovered in the Sanctuary; all but one are included in the Catalogue.[58] Forty have bezels (**97–136**). Others include a snake ring (**137**), one with floral attachments (**138**), a similar one without the attachments (**139**), and nine plain hoops (**140–7**). The 40 rings with bezels include one of silver (**103**), two of silver with gold overlay (**100, 110**), one of silver with a gold stud (**115**), one with a glass bezel (**136**), 18 of bronze (**97–9, 101–2, 104–9, 111–14, 116–18**), and 17 of iron (**119–35**). Most of the non-iron bezels are intaglios; only two (**103, 118**) are undecorated.

No doubt the rings with intaglios were worn for decorative purposes, but they may also have been used by women as part of their household provisions. The iron signet rings are in very poor condition, with heavy corrosion, so any decoration has been lost. It is surprising to have nearly as many iron signet rings as bronze. The iron rings have thick stirrup-shaped bands and thick oval bezels. The bronze signet rings are more varied with both thin and thick bands on those of the better-preserved examples. The bronze bezels range from small, narrow ovals forming a point at either end to large and wide ovals; some appear almost circular in shape. The silver and gold signet rings are more finely made with either narrow oval or circular bezels that have more decorative details and design than those in bronze.

Plain hoops (**140–7**) are catalogued as finger rings where their size is appropriate (D 1.6–2.36 cm). These hoops include one of gold (**140**), one of silver and gold (**141**), and six cold-worked, very finely hammered bronze hoops with squared edges (**142–7**). Nevertheless, a bezel is the only accurate indication that a circular band was used as a finger ring.[59] Other larger or smaller rings are listed separately in Appendix II, since they are unsuitable as finger rings.

Boardman's typology of Classical and Hellenistic finger rings with bezels has been followed wherever possible, although not all the rings here can be assigned readily to his types.[60] Ring shapes at Stymphalos indicate a range in date possibly from the late sixth (narrow oval bezels) to the third century BCE, with the majority from the fourth and early third (larger, flat oval bezels and small, round bezels). A ring with a leaf-shaped bezel and stirrup (**97**) is likely the earliest, similar to Boardman Type N of Late Archaic date and Boardman Type I of Early to Mid-Classical date.[61] A massive stirrup ring (**118**) is likely the latest, similar to Boardman Type XVI, of Ptolemaic date. In addition, the thin overlay of gold on either silver or bronze jewellery appears to have been especially popular during the fourth century BCE,[62] so it is very likely that the gilded silver rings at Stymphalos belong then.[63] None of the bronze rings provide evidence of being gilded. Since a number of ring types preserved at Olynthos (mostly destroyed in 348 BCE by Philip II) are similar to ones from the acropolis Sanctuary at Stymphalos, they help provide an important fixed point for dating.

More unusual is the ring with floral attachments and double hoop with snakes' head terminals (**138**) from the refuse pit in the West Annex of Building A, as well as another ring (**139**) similar to it, missing its hoop and floral attachments. Floral attachments were common on other fourth-century BCE types of jewellery such as earrings and necklaces.

Gilded silver and bronze, with bezels (97–118)

97. Bronze, cast. Inv. 742. Tr. 96.4.6.9. Altar. **Figs. 6.6 and 6.15**
D 2.1; Th. 0.4; D (bezel) 0.6 × 1.8; Th. (bezel) 0.4; Wt. 4.1
Well preserved, intact. The stirrup hoop widens towards the leaf-shaped bezel forming a flattened snake-head on either side. Three circular indentations are on one side of the bezel. Sea creature, likely a triton, in profile, facing left, with human head and arms, fish-tail, and a trident extending from its back. Facial features cannot be distinguished. There are no known close contemporary parallels, suggesting another archaizing motif like the siren engraving on **102**. A mid-seventh-century BCE Corinthian (?) bronze band from Corfu depicts a bearded triton, although it lacks the trident.[64]
Late sixth–early fifth century; bezel and hoop are similar to Boardman Type I, which continues from the Late Archaic form, Boardman Type N.

98. Bronze fragment, cast. Inv. 76. Tr. 95.4+1.1.1. Temple. **Figs. 6.6 and 6.15**
D 1.9; Th. 0.2; D (bezel) 1.2 × 1.65; Th. (bezel) 0.2; Wt. 2.2
Poor condition with surface corrosion. Badly worn oval bezel, with a tiny part of the hoop preserved on either side. Female figure (?), facing left, with raised right arm and bent upper body. There appears to be a deep round impression on the edge of the bezel, which may have held a silver stud, like **101** and **105**. See also **115**.
Late fifth century; bezel and hoop resemble Boardman Type II (mid- to late fifth century BCE).

99. Bronze, cast. Inv. 95. Tr. 95.4.4.4. Temple. **Figs. 6.6 and 6.15**
D 2.1; Th. 0.2; D (bezel) 1.2 × 1.8; Th. (bezel) 0.2. Wt. 1.8
Fair condition. The narrow hoop is broken below the bezel, otherwise complete. Surface corrosion and a small hole pierce the centre of the bezel. The narrow oval bezel has a flat surface surrounded by beaded border. Pegasos, facing left, in low relief. The horse is running at full gallop, with outstretched forelegs, uplifted tail, and pointed wing. Small, curved lines below the horse's jaw and above its head may depict reins. Similar depictions have been found on fifth-century rings from the Korykian Cave and Nemea, as well as on fifth- and fourth-century coins from Corinth and Stymphalos.[65] There seems to be an object below the horse's belly, possibly a fish or dolphin, rather than just the extension of its back leg. See also **112** for the motif.
Fourth century, based on the pointed, rather than curved, earlier wing seen on Corinthian coins depicting Pegasos. The thin leaf-shaped bezel and slim hoop resemble Boardman Type II.

100. Silver and gold bezel. Inv. 2911. Tr. 00.2.3.3. SE outside Temple. **Fig. 6.6**
D (bezel) 1.0 × 1.55; Th. (bezel) 0.2; Wt. 0.9
Fair condition. Silver, pointed oval bezel with hatched border. Small bezel covered with gold foil and chased, with a section missing on one end. Worn surface.
Motif of a partially draped, standing woman, possibly holding an infant. The woman is missing most of her head and facial features. The infant (?), balanced on her left hip, faces left, in profile, with head, body, and one bent leg visible. Another figure may stand on the left, partially behind the woman and infant, since a drapery-clad leg may be seen on the lower left, as well as an arm (?); the figure's head is missing. The female figure and infant may represent Aphrodite and Eros, although motifs of women and children appear on fourth-century rings, such as that of a woman suckling a child, which appears on a ring from a tomb in Sedes.[66] If, however, the second figure is male, the depiction of a family scene on **100** would be unique.
Fourth century based on style; the bezel resembles Boardman Type II.

101. Fragmentary bronze, cast. Inv. 2944. Tr. 00.2.3.3. SE outside Temple. **Figs. 6.6 and 6.15**

D 1.9; Th. 0.3; D (bezel) 0.7 × 1.2; Th. (bezel) 0.2. Wt. 1.1
Fair condition. Oval bezel with tiny hole pierced at the woman's chest; small chip missing from the upper left edge. There is a rim around the hole, likely where a silver or gold stud was placed. Part of the hoop is preserved on both sides, widening where it meets the bezel. Draped female, head facing right, seated on the lap of a bare-chested male, head facing left. His left arm is hidden, behind her back. This motif is found on two fourth-century bronze rings from the Korykian Cave and an unprovenanced, late Classical/ Hellenistic ring in the British Museum.[67]

Fourth century based on style; the hoop resembles Boardman Type II.

102. Fragmentary bronze, cast. Inv. 743. Tr. 95.4+1.2.4. Temple. **Figs. 6.6 and 6.15**
D 2.1; Th. 0.3; D (bezel) 1.0 × 2.0; Th. (bezel) 0.3. Wt. 2.6
Poor condition. Very worn, flat, oval bezel; most of the hoop is missing. Silver stud along one edge. Hybrid figure to right with a human head and large, birdlike body, in profile, with wings depicted in frontal view; likely a siren. The siren motif was popular on Archaic gems, although there are a few fifth-century examples in private collections.[68] This motif on a ring was presumably worn to ward off evil. The hybrid figure on **102** could also represent a harpy, similar in appearance and apotropaic function to the siren.[69]

Late fifth century?; the preserved hoop resembles Boardman Type IV (late fifth century).

103. Silver, cast. Inv. 3581. Tr. 96.15.5.5. Refuse pit outside Bldg. A. **Figs. 6.6 and 6.15**
D 1.9; Th. 0.2; D (bezel) 0.8 × 1.9; Th. (bezel) 0.3; Wt. 2.5
Intact, although the hoop is detached from the bezel on one side. The surface of the flat, oval, undecorated bezel has a small round hole on one side and a similar-sized opening that is filled in on the opposite side of the bezel, to anchor a separate silver (? or gilded silver?) bezel. Similar holes are also seen where the bezel meets the hoop on both sides. Thus four anchor points are provided. This ring resembles three plain silver rings found in a fourth-century funeral pyre in Thasos.[70]

Fourth century based on style; the bezel resembles Boardman Type IV.

104. Bronze bezel, cast. Inv. 1088. Tr. 97.4.3.4. S of Terrace Wall. **Figs. 6.6 and 6.15**
D 0.7 × 1.0; Th. 0.1. Wt. 0.7
Very worn, in fragile condition. Small oval bezel with most of the hoop missing. Male (?) head, in profile, facing left, with indistinct features.

Fourth century?

105. Bronze, cast. Inv. 3860. Tr. 96.8 ext.8.11. Near City Wall. **Figs. 6.6 and 6.15**
D 2.2; Th. 0.2; D (bezel) 1.0 × 1.7; Th. (bezel) 0.2. Wt. 2.8
Fair condition. Most of the hoop is missing. A tiny silver stud is inset on the left side of the bezel, with a second small hole on the other side where another silver stud was located. These studs may have anchored a separate silver bezel or overleaf. The oval bezel depicts a dancing female, in three-quarter view, with profile head, facing right, raised right arm, left hand on the hip, swirling short chiton and bare legs. The nearest parallel is found on an early fourth-century gold ring from Taranto, portraying a dancing girl with a short, swirling chiton.[71]

Fourth century; preserved hoop resembles Boardman Type VI (fourth century).

106. Bronze, cast. Inv. 2898. Tr. 00.2.3.3. SE outside Temple. **Figs. 6.6 and 6.15**
D 1.8; Th. 0.2; D (bezel) 0.9 × 1.6; Th. (bezel) 0.1; Wt. 1.7
Fair condition with surface corrosion. Wide oval bezel with slightly bent, faceted hoop. Nude male figure, in three-quarter view, barely visible head in profile, facing left, holding a club or staff (?) in his left hand and a shield in his right. The nearest parallel, on an unprovenanced, fourth-century bronze ring in the British Museum, depicts a young nude male, tentatively identified as Herakles, standing, holding a club in his left hand and shield in his right.[72] Perhaps as much as any signet ring, these examples demonstrate the importance of the impressed image that these ring designs make on a soft substance like wax, since the actual ring image shows a warrior with a shield on the right arm, whereas the impressed image will depict the warrior in the proper way with the shield on the left arm. This reinforces the obvious. The intaglio design on the ring is created as the negative of the intended image for viewers.

Fourth century; the hoop resembles Boardman Type VII (fourth century).

107. Bronze, cast. Inv. 2589. Tr. 97.5 baulk.3.4. E of Terrace Wall. **Figs. 6.7 and 6.15**
D 2.0; Th. 0.2; D (bezel) 1.5 × 2.0; Th. (bezel) 0.25; Wt. 3.8
Fair condition. The hoop is intact, although broken and bent inwards along one side. The large broad oval bezel depicts a slim female figure dressed in a chiton and himation, seated on a stool, facing left, with rounded shoulders and curved back; facial features are obscured. The figure is looking at a round object held at eye level in both hands. The object has two incised lines below, resembling streamers, perhaps representing a tambourine or mask.[73]

Mid- to late fourth century; close to Boardman Type IX (mid- to late fourth century).

108. Bronze with double band, cast. Inv. 229. Tr. 96.3.2.4. Altar. **Figs. 6.7 and 6.15**
D 1.9; D (bezel) 0.92; Th. (bezel) 0.15; Wt. 3.2
Well preserved with slight corrosion on band and bezel. The hoop is formed of two overlapping wires terminated by flattened snake heads, which curve upwards on either side of the bezel (0.5 cm. below bezel). The hoops also form snake heads where they join the bezel. The circular bezel is divided into four in a cross pattern with prominent centre, surrounded by four round petals, one in each quandrant, in a stylized floral pattern. There is no close parallel for this ring.
Mid- to late fourth century; bezel similar to Boardman Type X.

109. Bronze and copper, cast. Inv. 696. Tr. 96.13.2.4. S of Altar. **Figs. 6.7 and 6.15**
D 2.3; Th. 0.3; D (bezel) 0.8; Th. (bezel) 0.3; Wt. 2.3
Small round bezel in good condition. The hoop is broken on one side, otherwise intact. The hoop widens where it joins the bezel and is incised with a scale pattern to simulate snake heads. The bezel with a rope border is divided into four sections, forming a cross pattern similar to **108** with a small copper rosette in the centre. There is no apparent parallel for this motif.
Mid- to late fourth century; bezel similar to Boardman Type X.

110. Silver and gold. Inv. 3620. Tr. 96.15.5.5. Refuse pit outside Bldg. A. **Figs. 6.7 and 6.15**
D 1.5; Th. 0.2; D (bezel) 0.7; Th. (bezel) 0.2; Wt. 1.0
Intact, in fair condition. Small, narrow silver hoop with circular bezel, inlaid with gold foil; a strip is missing. Thick silver wire is wrapped around the ends of the band where they join the bezel. The bezel has a thick, raised, rounded border with some cracks. The bezel portrays a rounded human face in repoussé: large almond-shaped eyes, a few preserved snakelike locks of hair above the missing strip of gold foil, and an outstretched tongue. The projecting tongue and snakelike hair identify the face as the gorgon Medusa, although the projecting tongue is an Archaic motif seldom seen in the Classical period,[74] and the round bezel is typical of the fourth century BCE. This motif most resembles a fourth-century gold disk with Medusa head and four holes for attachment, of unknown provenance, as well as numerous examples on terracotta-gilt disks/buttons from mainland Greece and Asia Minor.[75]
Fourth century; bezel resembles Boardman Type X.

111. Bronze, cast. Inv. 2927. Tr. 99.10 Surface find. N of Bldg. A. **Figs. 6.7 and 6.15**
D 2.3; Th. 0.2; D (bezel) 0.9; Th. (bezel) 0.2; Wt. 2.1
Intact, in good condition. Small, nearly round bezel with a beaded border motif. The engraving portrays a muscular, nude, winged male figure, wearing a wreath, likely Eros. The figure faces right in profile, in either a kneeling or running position, with right leg forward. The pose is standard for runners, although Eros is usually shown running in scenes of pursuit or simply flying.[76] His wing takes the place of his right arm. He holds a circular object, possibly a wreath or crown, in his left hand.[77] He does not seem to hold an iunx wheel twirled around on a long rod, a motif found on other fourth-century rings, since no rod can be seen on the bezel of **111**.[78] An unprovenanced cornelian ring from the British Museum, ca. 400–350 BCE, portrays on the back plate a frontal figure of Eros kneeling on his right knee, somewhat similar to the Eros on **111**. He also has a wing instead of a right arm, although his left forearm and hand rest on his bent left knee, rather than holding an object.[79]
Late fourth–early third century; bezel resembles Boardman Type XV (Hellenistic).

112. Bronze, cast. Inv. 994. Tr. 97.2.3.3. W of Bldg. A. **Fig. 6.7**
D 2.0; Th. 0.2; D (bezel) 1.1 × 1.5; Th. (bezel) 1.0; Wt. 1.4
Intact with very corroded, convex oval bezel. The decorative engraving is badly worn, but Pegasos can be made out. The winged horse gallops left, its body is more compact than **99**. A small object is visible below the horse's belly.
Late fourth century; close to Boardman Type XVI (fourth century or later).

113. Bronze, cast. Inv. 1081. Tr. 96.8.5.6. West Annex. **Figs. 6.7 and 6.16**
D 1.87; Th. 0.2; D (bezel) 0.7 × 1.5; Th. (bezel) 0.3; Wt. 1.1
Poor condition. Finely made hoop missing its lower third. Small, narrow, convex oval bezel. The worn engraving depicts two opposing crescent shapes, possibly representing a very stylized eye.
Third century; close to Boardman Type XVI.

114. Bronze, cast. Inv. 186. Tr. 95.4+1.2.4. Temple. **Figs. 6.7 and 6.16**
D 2.0; Th. 0.2; D (bezel) 0.7 × 1.4; Th. (bezel) 0.3; Wt. 2.1
Intact, with little corrosion. Very worn, slim oval bezel with a large piece of solder on one side. Unidentified motif, possibly a figure in a garment draped to the knees holding an object.
Late fourth century; the hoop widens to accommodate the small oval bezel, as seen on Boardman Type XIV rings.

115. Silver bezel with gold inlay. Inv. 2585. Tr. 99.9.4.4. SE of Terrace Wall. **Figs. 6.7 and 6.16**
D 1.1 × 1.6; Th. 0.1; Wt. 1.1
Fair condition. Small, narrow, oval-shaped silver bezel. Seated figure of a female deity, dressed in a chiton and himation with delicately incised folds. Facing right in profile, holding in her outstretched left palm a nude, winged figure possibly with a wreath, facing left in profile. The deity sits on a stool with a prominent circular gold stud inserted below the seat. Her right hand rests on the upper edge of the stool. Facial features include a prominent nose, deep-set eye, and pursed mouth. Because the top of the figure's head meets the outer edge of the bezel, it is uncertain whether she has rolled hair or is wearing a stephane. The word ΚΑΛΟΣ is inscribed along the outer edge of the bezel below the winged figure.

The seated female deity may represent Aphrodite or Athena; the winged figure either Nike or Eros. The motif is similar to a seated Aphrodite being crowned by Eros on an unprovenanced gold bezel in London, dating to the first quarter of the fourth century BCE.[80] The draperies of both deities are similar, as well as the placement of the arms not holding the winged figures. This motif of Aphrodite and Eros recurs on other fourth-century rings of silver, bronze, and iron from Greek sanctuaries, such as the Korykian Cave, Olympia, and Knossos, possibly also on another bronze ring from the Sanctuary (**116**) and on one from a tomb at Halieis.[81] The winged figure of Eros on these examples is shown as holding a wreath, an object also likely held by the small winged figure on the Stymphalian bezel. Moreover, the word *kalos* on the Stymphalian bezel, if it refers to the winged figure, clearly suits Eros, rather than Nike.[82]

The motif on **115** also may portray a seated Athena holding a Nike. Although Athena in art is often shown in a standing or striding stance, she is also portrayed as a seated goddess on terracotta statuettes and Attic red-figure vases.[83] Pausanias (1.26.4) mentions a seated statue of Athena on the Athenian Acropolis near the Erechtheion.[84] Some representations of Athena also show her wearing a stephane rather than her usual helmet. Stephanai adorn some Late Archaic terracotta seated figurines of Athena from the Acropolis, and even the ancient cult statue of Athena Polias from the Erechtheion wore one, according to fourth-century inventories.[85] In addition, the Archaic cult statue of Athena Nike from the temple on the Athenian Acropolis may have been seated and not wearing a helmet, the helmet being held instead in her left hand.[86]

A representation of a seated figure of Athena holding Nike is found on a large gold ring from the Chersonesos, ca. 300–280 BCE. This composition repeats the reverse of tetradrachms of Lysimachos, ruler of Macedon and much of Asia Minor, 306–281 BCE.[87] In these examples, Athena is shown wearing her Corinthian helmet, her spear rests at an angle against the circle of the gold bezel and coins, and her shield with a lion-head device sits on its edge behind her stool. Although Athena lacks her helmet[88] and spear on the Stymphalian bezel, the gold stud does call to mind her shield. The stud was inset with a rimmed border, like that of an actual shield. The stud also resembles closely the shield held by a naked youth on an unprovenanced Hellenistic onyx scarab.[89] In other examples of silver rings and bracelets with a gold stud, the stud apparently was added for an amuletic rather than ornamental purpose.[90] Perhaps the gold stud represented Athena's shield at the same time as it served an apotropaic function. The Nike figure on the gold ring from the Chersonesos also holds a wreath, like the Eros figures shown with Aphrodite and likely the winged figure on the Stymphalian bezel; however, in the Chersonesan example, Nike faces away from Athena rather than towards her.

Late fourth century.

116. Bronze, cast. Inv. 2734. Tr. 99.1.5.11. SE of Terrace Wall. **Figs. 6.7 and 6.16**
D 0.8 × 1.1; Th. 0.2. Wt. 0.5
Poor condition with surface corrosion on the bezel. Missing most of its hoop. A raised ridge on the back of the bezel indicates that the band was attached separately. Small, nearly circular bezel with traces of silver leaf on the bezel surface. Draped female, facing left, seated on a klismos, holding a winged figure in her right hand. Seated animal (?) beside the leg of the klismos. Aphrodite (?) being crowned by Eros (?). See **115.**

117. Bronze bezel of uncertain shape, cast. Inv. 430. Tr. 95.4+1.2.4. Temple. **Figs. 6.7 and 6.16**
D 0.8 × 1.5 × 0.8; Th. 0.2. Wt. 0.8
Very poor condition, badly worn along the edges. Narrow, eye-shaped, concave bezel depicts a draped figure, likely female, in three-quarter view, head facing right, with partially raised arms.

118. Bronze, cast. Inv. 14. Tr. 95.3.2.5. Bldg. A. **Fig. 6.8**
D 2.5; Th. 0.4; D (bezel) 1.3 × 2.0; Th. (bezel) 0.5; Wt. 8.3
Intact, corrosion on the hoop and bezel. The thick hoop has a heavy stirrup-shaped outline with large flat, oval-shaped, undecorated bezel.

Third–second century; Boardman Type XVII (Ptolemaic).

Iron signet rings (119–35)

Iron finger rings must have been much more popular

than the archaeological record suggests simply due to preservation issues. In Pliny's (NH 33.9) day, we are told that the Lakedaimonians continued to wear iron rings. They must have put up with the inconvenience of corrosion in order to enjoy the symbolic value they held. One method used to overcome the corrosive effect of skin salts was to plate them with silver or gold. At least seven iron finger rings were found in the Demeter Sanctuary at Knossos, one of which had a gilt bezel.[91] Temple inventories list other examples, both plain iron ones and plated ones.[92] Gilded iron rings were apparently called "Samothracian," but more significantly, they had a certain magical importance in the cult of the Great Gods at Samothrace having to do with magnetism.[93]

119. Iron, forged. Inv. 934. Tr. 97.3.2.2. Altar. **Figs. 6.8 and 6.16**
D 2.1; Th. 0.35; D (bezel) 1.0 × 2.0; Th. (bezel) 0.3; Wt. 2.1
Very poor condition, heavily corroded with accretions. Slim oval bezel with part of the hoop missing.
Late fifth–early fourth century; similar to Boardman Type IV.

120. Iron, forged. Inv. 188. Tr. 95.4+1.2.4. Temple. **Fig. 6.16**
D 2.3; Th. 0.2; D (bezel) 1.0 × 1.9; Th. (bezel) 0.4; Wt. 2.8
Very poor condition. Very worn, narrow oval bezel with heavily pocked and discoloured surface; hoop intact. Plain bezel with raised edges and a flat exterior surface.
Fourth century; close to Boardman Type VII.

121. Iron, forged. Inv. 233. (96.368). Tr. 95.4+1.2.4. Temple. **Figs. 6.8 and 6.16**
D 2.25; Th. 0.2; D (bezel) 1.0 × 1.8; Th. (bezel) 0.3; Wt. 3.7
Poor condition with thick accretions. Intact. Plain, narrow, oval bezel.
Fourth century; close to Boardman Type VII.

122. Iron, forged. Inv. 1159. (97.186). Tr. 95.1 surface cleaning. Temple. **Fig. 6.16**
D 2.3; Th. 0.5; D (bezel) 0.85 × 1.7; Th. (bezel) 0.3; Wt. 3.2
Very poor condition. Very corroded, narrow oval bezel. The hoop is broken with a separate, curved lower part.
Fourth century; close to Boardman Type VII.

123. Iron, forged. Inv. 237. Tr. 96.4.2.3. Altar. **Fig. 6.16**
D 1.7; Th. 0.2; D (bezel) 0.7 × 1.4; Th. (bezel): 0.25; Wt. 1.4
Poor condition with surface corrosion on the bezel. Slim, flat, oval bezel with small convex hoop; small piece missing in its lower section.
Fourth century; similar to Boardman Type VII.

124. Iron, forged; of uncertain shape. Inv. 1440. Tr. 96.11.5.6. Temple. **Fig. 6.16**
D 2.36; Th. 0.15; D (bezel) 1.1 × 2.2; Th. (bezel) 0.2; Wt. 2.8
Very poor condition. Large oval bezel, now slightly bent with thick accretions and corrosion. Most of the hoop is missing.

125. Iron, forged. Inv. 231. Tr. 96.4.3.6. Altar. **Fig. 6.16**
D 2.3; Th. 0.3; D (bezel) 1.4 × 2.0; Th. (bezel) 0.4; Wt. 3.9
Very poor condition. Large, oval bezel, now bent, with corrosion and thick accretions on the bezel and hoop. The hoop is broken but complete.
Mid- to late fourth century; close to Boardman Type IX.

126. Iron, forged. Inv. 242. Tr. 96.9.1.1. Altar. **Fig. 6.16**
D 1.8; Th. 0.3; D (bezel) 0.7 × 1.5; Th. (bezel) 0.3; Wt. 2.5
Poor condition. Slim, oval bezel with surface corrosion; part of the hoop is missing.
Fourth century; similar to Boardman Type VII.

127. Iron, forged. Inv. 927. Tr. 96.13.4.7. S of Altar. **Fig. 6.16**
D 2.25; Th. 0.5; D (bezel) 0.9 × 1.4; Th. (bezel) 0.5; Wt. 2.4
Poor condition. Intact, with thick accretions and corrosion on the slim oval bezel and hoop.
Fourth century; close to Boardman Type VII.

128. Iron, forged. Inv. 2450. Tr. 99.1.5.8. SE of Terrace Wall. **Fig. 6.17**
D 2.2; Th. 0.4; D (bezel) 0.9 × 1.6; Th. (bezel) 0.3; Wt. 2.9
Poor condition. Corroded oval bezel; the lower part of the hoop is missing.
Fourth century; resembles Boardman Type VII.

129. Iron, forged. Inv. 692. Tr. 96.8.3.4. West Annex. **Fig. 6.17**
D 1.9; Th. 0.2; D (bezel) 0.8 × 1.6; Th. (bezel) 0.3; Wt. 1.8
Poor condition. Part of the hoop is missing. Corrosion and accretions on the hoop and narrow, slightly convex oval bezel.
Fourth century; simple version of Boardman Type VII.

130. Iron, forged. Inv. 975. Tr. 97.2.3.3. W of Bldg. A. **Fig. 6.17**
D 1.82; Th. 0.4; D (bezel) 1.25 × 2.0; Th. (bezel) 0.3; Wt. 3.3
Poor condition. Corroded, wide oval bezel, with a small part of the hoop on one side.
Late fourth century; similar to Boardman Type IX.

131. Iron, forged, and bronze. Inv. 2406. Tr. 99.10.3.4. SE of Terrace Wall. **Figs. 6.8 and 6.17**
D 2.1; Th. 0.2; D (bezel) 1.2 × 1.8; Th. (bezel) 0.7; Wt. 4.5
Poor condition with surface corrosion and accretions. Intact; hoop broken with one separate fragment. On the underside of the oval bezel is a piece of bronze cut to fit the size of the bezel. This piece was added later either to strengthen the iron ring that was perhaps corroded from perspiration or to size the ring to fit a person's finger. As yet, I know of no other parallels for this odd feature.
Mid- to late fourth century; similar to Boardman Type IX.

132. Iron, forged. Inv. 2604. Tr. 97.5 baulk.3.4. E of Terrace Wall. **Fig. 6.17**
D 2.2; Th. 0.4; D (bezel) 0.8 × 1.7; Th. (bezel) 0.3; Wt. 4.0
Poor condition, with thick accretions on bezel and hoop. Two fragments. Wide oval bezel with most of the hoop.
Mid- to late fourth century; Boardman Type IX.

133. Iron fragment, forged. Inv. 235. Tr. 96.10.1.1. City Wall. **Fig. 6.17**
D 2.0; Th. 0.2; D (bezel) 1.2 × 1.7; Th. (bezel) 0.3; Wt. 2.1
Poor condition. Large, corroded oval bezel, with the start of its hoop.
Mid- to late fourth century; Boardman Type IX (?).

134. Iron, forged; of uncertain shape. Inv. 236. Tr. 95.4+1.2.4. Temple. **Fig. 6.17**
D 2.9; Th. 0.4; D (bezel) 1.1 × 2.1; Th. (bezel) 0.5; Wt. 5.4
Very poor condition. Thick accretions on the long, thick, oval bezel and hoop. The hoop is broken; one non-joining fragment.

135. Iron, forged; of uncertain shape. Inv. 890. Tr. 95.4+1.2.4. Temple. **Fig. 6.17**
D 2.1; Th. 0.5; D (bezel) 1.1 × 2.0; Th. (bezel) 0.3; Wt. 3.0
Very poor condition. Very worn, wide oval bezel, corroded; part of hoop.

Glass bezel (136)

136. Translucent violet glass. Numerous bubbles produce a pitted surface. Cast. Fragile condition, chipped. Oxidized surface has flaked from the upper side. Inv. 690. Tr. 95.4+1.2.4. Temple. **Figs. 6.8 and 6.17**
D 1.35 × 1.6; Th. 0.25; Wt. 0.5
Shallow body modelling. Convex, upright oval intaglio with flat underside. Incuse design of a standing woman; the head is indistinct but probably turned to right. A few thick, rounded grooves render her drapery. Part of her left foot may be visible below the garment. She holds a long, narrow rectangular object, possibly a vase (bowl or phiale), in her left hand, at shoulder height. Her right arm is extended downward, likely leaning on a column.

Very similar to a glass intaglio in London (British Museum 1234), made in the same coarse linear style, which Plantzos groups in his Class of Late Hellenistic Intaglios, suggesting a date in the second century for some at least in the group, perhaps from a workshop in Greece proper.[94] Another example, of better workmanship, in the Ernesto Wolf collection, likewise has a woman, suggested to be a muse, leaning on a column and holding an object in her left hand.[95]

A coin of Aigion which depicts a woman of rather columnar appearance wearing a polos and carrying two long narrow objects, one outstretched (downward appearing) in her left hand and the other upward in her right, has been identified as Eileithyia. The objects are thought to be torches; see *LIMC* III s.v. "Eileithyia" p. 695, especially nos. 94b, 95–6, p. 699; no. 94b, a xoanon at Aigion by Damophon of Messene (first half of the second century BCE) described by Pausanias (7.23.5), had a wooden body but head, hands, and feet of Pentelic marble and was completely covered with a finely woven garment; nos. 95 and 96 are coins of Aigion, the first (146–131 BCE) depicting Eileithyia with a torch in one hand, the other (Antoninus Pius 138–161 CE) with a torch in both hands. Paus. 7.23.6 attempts to explain the torch as an attribute in depictions of Eileithyia, suggesting either that it represents the pangs of childbirth, which are like fire, or that it may imply that this goddess brings children into the light. The similarity to the pose on **136** is noteworthy, even if the objects cannot be easily identified; other goddesses, such as Demeter, are sometimes shown holding torches as well.

Second century (?)[96]

Decorative rings (137–9)

137. Bronze spiral, hammered. Inv. 2879. Tr. 97.5 Surface. E of Terrace Wall. **Figs. 6.8 and 6.17**
L 9.7; Th. 0.3; Wt. 3.0

Fair condition. Mostly uncoiled, plain spiral ring. There are remains of silver-coloured solder on one face of each of the hammered ends. One end is flattened into a very rudimentary snake head. Rings in the form of a spiralled snake started in the Classical period but were extremely popular in the Hellenistic period.[97] This simplified version lacks the scales and realistic heads seen on other examples.

138. Bronze, hammered, with double hoop and floral attachments. Inv. 3438. Tr. 96.15.5.5. Refuse pit outside Bldg. A. **Figs. 6.8 and 6.17**
D 2.0; Th. 0.2; Wt. 2.8
Fair condition. Preserved in six parts: narrow double hoop with snake-head terminal; wire with snake- head terminal that once was attached to the other side of the hoop; two small four-petal flowers; and two tiny pieces of wire attachment. The snake heads are similar to those seen on **108**. At the midpoint of the ring, the hoop splits on each side of the square centre part; the splits widen where the two small flowers were once attached. The larger flower, measuring 0.7 cm in diameter, has tiny balls on the underside of the petals; the smaller flower measures 0.6 cm in diameter. Both flowers have an iron rivet that once secured them to the hoop; iron corrosion is visible in the centre of each flower and in the centre of the ring bezel. Remains of silver-coloured solder on the hoop where the flowers were once attached. A third flower may be missing from the centre. There are no close parallels for this ring with separate floral attachments or for **139**.
Likely mid- to late fourth century, when floral attachments became common on other types of jewellery, such as earrings.

139. Bronze, hammered. Inv. 4287. Surface find. **Figs. 6.8 and 6.17**
D 2.3; Wt. 1.3
Poor condition. Similar to **138** with square centre and wide splits to hold the attachments, although the hoop and attachments are missing.

Plain hoops (140–7)

140. Gold. Inv. 3319. Tr. 97.2 + 96.15.4.4. S of West Annex. **Figs. 6.8 and 6.18**
D 2.0; Th. 0.15; Wt. 0.7
Good condition. Thin gold circular wire, now slightly bent. This ring is similar to plain gold finger rings from Perachora, Sindos, and Knossos, ranging from the Geometric to the Classical periods.[98]

141. Silver and gold. Inv. 3488. Tr. 96.15 (scarp cleaning). S of West Annex. **Figs. 6.8 and 6.18**
D 1.9 ; Th. 0.1 ; Wt. 0.3
Good condition. A thin silver wire forms a circular ring, with faint traces of raised concentric and diagonal decoration. A small rectangular piece of gold sheet covers where the ends join.

142. Bronze, hammered. Inv. 181. Tr. 95.1.9.15. Temple. **Figs. 6.8 and 6.18**
D 2.0; W 0.5; Th. 0.1; Wt. 2.1
Good condition. Thin, plain circular hoop. Slightly concave contour; flattened inside with squared edges. Similar examples have been found in Argos and Isthmia.[99] Compare also **143–7**.

143. Bronze, hammered. Inv. 198. Tr. 95.4+1.2.3. Temple. **Figs. 6.8 and 6.18**
D 2.16; W 0.5; Wt. 3.3
Good condition. Finely hammered wide hoop of even thickness.

144. Bronze, hammered. Inv. 320. (96.276). Tr. 96.6.4.10. W of Bldg. A. **Figs. 6.8 and 6.18**
D 1.6; Th. 0.2; Wt. 1.4
Good condition. Small in size; perhaps a child's ring if it is meant as jewellery.

145. Bronze. Inv. 1051. Tr. 97.2 + 96.15.5.5. West Annex. **Fig. 6.18**
D 1.9; Th. 0.1; Wt. 0.8
Poor condition. Broken in three pieces, but complete.

146. Bronze. Inv. 1371. Tr. 95.7.5.11. Bldg. A. **Figs. 6.8 and 6.18**
D 2.36; Th. 0.2; Wt. 2.3
Very good condition.

147. Bronze. Inv. 2913. Tr. 99.10 (winter wash in). Bldg. A. **Fig. 6.18**
D 1.9; Th. 0.2; Wt. 0.9
Surface corrosion.

Distribution of rings

The heaviest concentration of rings (31%) was found in the northwestern part of the Temple cella (Tr. 95.4 +1 Levels 1 and 2). Four rings came from the refuse pit on the west side of Building A (Tr. 96.15 Level 5), while two rings were found within the main walls of this structure (Tr. 95.3 Level 2, 95.7). Rings were found to the west (Tr. 97.2 Level 3, Tr. 96.8 Levels 3 and 5) and north (Tr. 99.10 surface) of the main walls of Building A. Only one signet ring was found near the Altar (Tr. 96.3 Level 2), while the remainder were scattered to the south (Tr. 96.4 Levels 2, 3 and 6, 96.13 Levels 2 and 4), west (Tr. 96.9 Level 1, 97.3 Level 3), and east (Tr. 97.5

baulk Level 3) of the Altar, as well as in the rectangular room to the east (Tr. 99.1 Level 5). (See fig. 6.3.)

Beads and pendants (148–84)

No complete necklaces were discovered in the Sanctuary, although the variety of beads and pendants indicates that necklaces were a popular votive. Beads are generally defined as ornaments, often of the same type, that are threaded through a string hole onto one or more cords (*linon*).[100] Pendants are also usually repeated ornaments, but they have a suspension loop so that they hang individually on the necklace. Bead and pendant necklaces were usually worn close about the throat or more loosely around the base of the neck. During the Classical period, finds from graves in the Crimea and Southern Russia indicate that beads and pendants in the form of fruit, seeds, and buds were popular, as well as rosettes alternating with palmettes.[101] Elaborate beads in gold were often decorated with granulation, filigree, or semiprecious stones.[102]

Beads (148–77)

Thirty-eight glass, terracotta, bronze, and bone beads were found, of which bone was the most popular. Ten different types can be discerned: barrel-shaped (**148**), cylinder (**149–51**), disk (**152–60**), eye-bead (**161**), lenticular (**162**), spherical (**163–4**), melon (**165**), rounded with relief ring ends (**166–71**), tubular (**172–6**), and triple ring collar (**177**). Beck's classification is followed where possible;[103] exceptional variations are noted. Occasionally a more detailed classification is used.

Type A: Barrel-shaped (148)

148. Terracotta barrel-shaped, handmade and fired. Inv. 228. Tr. 95.4+1.2.4. Temple. **Figs. 6.9 and 6.18**
L 0.9; D 0.7; 0.5 (string hole); Wt. 0.4
Good condition. Small, plain, barrel-shaped terracotta bead with a string hole pierced lengthwise.

Type B: Cylinders (149–51)

Nine cylinder type bone beads were discovered, corresponding to Beck I.C.2.b. The beads are mostly blackened in colour, suggesting that they were burnt. **150** contains pieces of possible plaque fragments while **151** has fragments of burnt frets, so these two cylinders probably served a decorative function other than as beads for a necklace.

149. Bone cylinder, carved. Inv. 54. Tr. 95.4.2.2. Temple. **Figs. 6.9 and 6.18**
D 1.1; 0.35 (string hole); Th. 0.7; Wt. 0.9
Fair condition, mostly burnt black, with flecks of white material concentrating around the holes and on the sides. Small centre piercing.

150. Bone cylinder and plaque (?) fragments, carved. Inv. 749. Tr. 95.4+1.2.3. Temple. **Fig. 6.18**
Beads: D 1.2; Th. 0.6. Largest plaque frag.: 0.3 × 2.9; Wt. total of all 4.7
Fragmentary and burnt condition. Pieces include two fragments of cylinder beads of which one is badly burnt, as well as 31 small, elongated pieces of carved bone (plaque fragments?), which vary in size and shape.

151. Bone cylinder and fret fragments, carved. Inv. 783. Tr. 95.4+1.2.3. Temple. **Figs. 6.9 and 6.18**
Intact beads: D 1.2; 0.3 (centre); Th. 0.75
Poor condition, burnt and fragmentary. Eight pieces, including two tiny pieces of burnt fret, one intact cylinder bead, another cylinder bead with a chip missing along one edge, and four half-preserved cylinder beads.

Type C: Disk beads (152–60)

The simplest type of bead from the Sanctuary is the disk. Nine plainly carved ones are preserved, of which eight are of bone and one of stone. The eight bone disks have a large string hole, much too small to allow their use as finger rings. It is difficult to discern whether they may have been beads or buttons. They have been classified as both depending on sites: buttons – Corinth and Athens, beads – Cyrene.[104] These disks also resemble bone eyelets for the thongs of sandals and boots, such as those found in the shop of Simon the shoemaker in the Athenian Agora.[105] The stone disk (**157**) is quite tiny, although similar examples are found at Perachora made of faience and glass.[106]

152. Bone, carved. Inv. 617. Tr. 95.4+1.2.4. Temple. **Fig. 6.18**
D 1.4; 0.5 (centre); Th. 0.4; Wt. 0.3
Poor condition. Badly worn and chipped around the outer edges.

153. Bone, carved and polished. Inv. 763. Tr. 95.8 scarp cleaning. Outside Temple. **Fig. 6.18**
D 1.6 ; 0.51 (centre); Th. 0.65; Wt. 1.1

Poor condition. Outer edge on one side is chipped and broken. Surface is scratched in places.

154. Bone, carved and polished. Inv. 183. Tr. 96.4.3.5. Altar. **Figs. 6.9 and 6.18**
D 2.1; 0.6 (centre); Th. 0.7; Wt. 2.9
Good condition. Thick disk with a small ridge around outer diameter.

155. Bone fragment, carved. Inv. 653. Tr. 96.3.3.5. Altar. **Fig. 6.18**
D 1.9.0; Th. 1.1; Wt. 1.6
Fair condition with chips along the outer diameter. One half of a very thick disk is preserved.

156. Bone, carved. Inv. 738. Tr. 97.11.1. Altar. **Figs. 6.9 and 6.18**
D 2.1; 0.7 (centre); Th. 0.5; Wt. 1.5
Fair condition with cracks and chips along the outer diameter; a small green stain from touching a bronze object; reddish-brown in colour.

157. Bone, carved and polished. Inv. 470. Tr. 96.8.3.3. W of Bldg. A. **Fig. 6.18**
D 1.7; 0.6 (centre); Th. 0.5; Wt. 1.3
Good condition.

158. Bone fragment, carved and polished. Inv. 762. Tr. 96.7.2.2. City Wall. **Fig. 6.18**
D 1.9; 0.3 (centre); Th. 0.7; Wt. 0.5
Poor condition. Half of the disk is preserved.

159. Bone, carved and polished. Inv. 232. Tr. 96.7.2.2. City Wall. **Figs. 6.9 and 6.18**
D 2.0; 0.8 (centre); Th. 0.7; Wt. 1.7
Good condition with some pitting on the surface. **158** and **159** were found in the same trench and level, so may belong together.

160. Stone, carved and polished. Inv. 24. Tr. 95.3.1.1. Bldg. A. **Figs. 6.9 and 6.18**
D 0.5; 0.1 (centre); Wt. 0.1
Fair condition. Tiny black stone disk with carved string hole.

Type D: Eye-bead (161)

One large, glass, stratified eye-bead was discovered in Building A.[107] Stratified eye-beads were produced in Phoenicia and possibly Carthage from ca. 600 BCE to the end of the third century.[108] Both imports and locally made imitations have been found throughout the Mediterranean, as well as in England and Central Europe.[109] **161** is very similar to Group C II cylindrical beads with layered eyes from either Phoenicia or possibly Carthage, as classified by Tatton-Brown.[110] It therefore appears to be an import rather than of Greek manufacture.[111] Group II beads are assigned to the fourth and third centuries. The eyes on this type are believed to be reduced versions of the faces on face beads and on pendants in the form of heads; the eyes are talismanic, to ward off the evil eye.[112] Since only one eye-bead has been found in the Sanctuary rather than several as part of a complete necklace, it may represent either a curio or an amulet that was dedicated to the goddess.

161. Glass stratified eye-bead. Inv. 1111. Tr. 95.2.4.9. Bldg. A. **Figs. 6.9 and 6.18**
D 2.23–2.9 (at hemisphere); inner D 1.2 (string hole); W 18.1
Fairly well preserved, although the surface is weathered and dull. Wound and tooled on a rod. Fused-on elements: monochrome beads and sections of overlay canes. Cylindrical bluish-green eye-bead with a large, longitudinal string hole. Five stratified eyes are composed of four progressively smaller beads of alternating blue and white on top of each other. Five iridescent blue glass fused-on beads border one edge of the circumference; two are preserved along the other edge. Between the eyes and blue glass beads are ten orange-yellow spherical fused-on beads. Fairly similar eye-beads were found in graves in Corinth and Macedonia.[113]

Type E: Lenticular (162)

162. Blue glass. Inv. 184. Tr. 95.4+1.2.2. Temple. **Figs. 6.9 and 6.18**
L 1.5; W 1.4; Th. 0.5; inner D 0.2 (string hole); Wt. 0.4
Good condition, slightly pitted with one chip. Coiled and cut from a solid rod. Cobalt blue, lenticular shape corresponding to Beck 4.C.1.a; nearly circular, with a convex rounded top and flat bottom. The string hole pierces the bead lengthwise on a diagonal.

Type F: Spherical (163–4)

Two bronze spherical beads of identical size and appearance were found, one in the Temple and one in Building A. Other spherical beads have been found in sanctuaries at Perachora, Chios, and Cyrene, although they are Archaic in date.[114]

163. Bronze, cast. Inv. 69. Tr. 95.3.2.5. Bldg. A. **Figs. 6.9 and 6.18**
D 1.4; 0.2 (string hole); Wt. 12.9

Very good condition. Plain, heavy spherical bead with a small string hole.

164. Bronze, cast. Inv. 429. Tr. 95.1.9.15. Temple **Figs. 6.9 and 6.18**
D 1.4; 0.2 (string hole); Wt. 11.8
Good condition with surface corrosion. Similar to **163** although the surface is more uneven.

Type G: Melon (165)

One bronze melon bead was found, possibly once part of a necklace. The shape can be traced to prototypes in faience from New Kingdom Egypt.[115] Examples in faience, glass, terracotta, and bronze have been found in Greek sanctuaries at Perachora, Corinth, Knossos, Chios, and Cyrene, and range from Minoan to Roman in date.[116] There do not appear to be any other melon beads from Late Classical or Hellenistic contexts in the Peloponnese, although a necklace composed of 77 gilded terracotta melon beads was found in a fourth-century BCE grave in Sedes, Macedonia, and nearly 700 glass melon beads were discovered in the third-century BCE glass factory at Rhodes.[117]

165. Bronze, cast. Inv 193. Tr. 95.1.9.15. Temple. **Figs. 6.9 and 6.18**
D 1.6; Wt. 18.3
Good condition with minimal corrosion. Melon-shaped bead divided into eight striated segments, and pierced longitudinally with a small string hole.

Type H: Rounded with relief ring ends (166–71)

Type H has a short, bulbous shape with a flattened relief ring or collar at each end. Fourteen bone beads of this type were discovered, of which ten came from the refuse pit (Tr. 96.15), perhaps once strung on the same necklace. These beads are very similar to numerous ivory beads found in a fourth-century BCE grave in Thasos.[118] They also somewhat resemble Archaic biconical bronze beads from sanctuaries at Argos, Tegea, and Olympia, although the beads here are shorter in length, narrower in diameter, and lack the pronounced sharp ridge of the cast bronze examples.[119] Two bronze biconical beads of the type were discovered in a fifth-century BCE grave at Olynthos.[120] Examples are also known from graves in Macedonia, where the type appears to be especially common, as well as in the Demeter Sanctuary at Cyrene.[121] Warden suggested that the type is common enough to have been made locally at most sites.[122]

166. Bone, carved and polished. Inv. 1538. Tr. 96.11.5.6. Temple. **Figs. 6.9 and 6.19**
L 0.55; D 0.63; 0.3 (string hole); Wt. 0.2
Good condition. Bulbous-shaped bead with a flaring relief ring on each end; the surface of each end is flat.

167. Bone, carved and polished. Inv. 611. Tr. 96.9.4.4. Altar. **Fig. 6.19**
L 0.6; D 0.85; 0.25 (string hole); Wt. 0.4
Good condition with small chips on the surface. Traces of two carved lines around the centre of the bulbous body.

168. Bone, carved and polished. Inv. 2484. Tr. 99.6.6.6. E of Terrace Wall
L 0.8; D 0.6; 0.2 (string hole); Wt. 0.3
Fair condition with a large jagged crack on the body. One of the longest examples.

169. Bone, carved and polished. Inv. 1181. Tr. 96.8 scarp cleaning. West Annex. **Fig. 6.19**
L 0.65; D 0.55; 0.2 (string hole); Wt. 0.2
Fair condition with a large chip missing from one of the relief rings.

170. Bone, carved and polished. Inv. 3595. Tr. 96.15.5.5. Refuse pit outside Bldg. A. **Fig. 6.9**
L 0.7; D 0.6; 0.2 (string hole); Wt. 0.2
Intact with a long crack across the body on one side.

171. Bone, carved and polished. Inv. 3621. Tr. 96.15.5.5. Refuse pit outside Bldg. A. **Fig. 6.9**
L 0.6; D 0.7; 0.25 (string hole); Wt. 0.2
Good condition.
Eight others were found in the refuse pit (Tr. 96.15.5.5).[123]

Type I: Tubular (172–6)

Two bronze tubular beads (**172–3**) made of coiled bronze strips, one terracotta triangular tubular bead (**175**), and two bone tubular beads (**176–7**) were found in the Sanctuary. Similar ones in bronze came from earlier Geometric and Archaic deposits in sanctuaries at Sparta, Aigina, Knossos, Chios, and Cyrene.[124] A bronze bead (**174**), which properly may be called a "cylinder" in line with similar bronze objects used to anchor loop handles on vases and other objects (see Schaus, chapter 7 below, 155–6, **34**, **37–43**), is included here rather than with Type B bone cylinder beads. It was found together with two other fragments of beads of an unknown material which also preserved a piece of twisted cord used to string the beads together.

172. Bronze, hammered. Inv. 1273. Tr. 97.6.3.3. Pillar Shrine. **Fig. 6.9**
L 0.65; D 0.45; Wt. 0.1
Fragile condition with a crack along one edge. Lengthwise seam of the elliptical tubular bead does not join and is folded back on one side.

173. Bronze, hammered. Inv. 3461. Tr. 96.15.5.5. Refuse pit outside Bldg. A
L 0.8; D 0.4; Wt. 0.2
Fragile and corroded condition. Thin strip wrapped in a tubular shape with a lengthwise seam.

174. Bronze cast cylinder, found with two other pieces that are not bronze, but possibly another metal, and two pieces of the string or cord, which are twisted and still attached in one of these latter pieces. Inv. 914. Tr. 97.96.11.4.5. Temple. **Fig. 6.9**
Bronze cylinder L 1.6, W 0.4; other cylinder a) L 0.9, b) perhaps joining a) L 0.5, D 0.3; Wt. bronze cylinder 0.5, Wt. other two frags. 0.1; total Wt. 0.7
The bronze cylinder has four double raised cords dividing it into three central parts and the two ends. It is hollow all the way through to take a string. The other two fragments do not have the green oxidized bronze. They are dull grey in colour. The strings must have been preserved through being coated with the grey metal, since they are not green either, but they are not stiff from the metal. They are still very flexible.

175. Terracotta, fired. Inv. 3771. Tr. 95.3.4.7. Bldg. A. **Fig. 6.19**
L 2.1; D 0.4; Wt. 0.6
Good condition. Long tubular, terracotta bead with three sides forming a triangular string hole.
Beck Group 8, C.2.b

176. Bone, carved and polished. Inv. 1040. Tr. 97.2 + 96.15.5.5. Bldg. A. **Figs. 6.9 and 6.19**
L 0.75; D 0.4; Wt. 0.1
Good condition. Small tubular bead with three carved bands around the outer circumference. A string hole pierces the bead lengthwise.

Type J: Triple ring collar (177)

177. Bone, carved and polished (bead?). Inv. 182. Surface cleaning. Temple. **Figs. 6.9 and 6.19**
L 1.0; W 0.5; Th. 0.15; Wt. 0.2
Good condition, although split in half lengthwise. The preserved half is rectangular with three rings carved on either end. The back of the "bead" is flat with no evidence of a string hole, suggesting that it might simply be a piece of decorative inlay.

Distribution of beads

Of the 12 beads found in the Temple, eight were discovered in the west part of the cella (Tr. 95.4 +1 Level 2, 95.1 Level 9) and one in the northeast (Tr. 96.11 Level 5); one was a surface find within the Temple walls, and two were found outside the walls on the northeast (Tr. 95.8 scarp) and northwest (Tr. 99.2 Level 3). Two beads were discovered near the Altar (Tr. 96.3 Level 3, 96.4 Level 3), while four others were found in the trenches to the west (Tr. 97.1 Level 1, 96.9 Level 4) and east (Tr. 99.6 Level 6, 96.8) of this structure. Of the 15 beads found within the main walls (Tr. 95.2 Level 4) and the Annexes (Tr. 95.3 Levels 1, 2, and 4, 97.2 Level 5) in Building A, 10 were discovered in the refuse pit (Tr. 96.15 Level 5), likely from the same necklace. Three other beads were uncovered to the west of this (Tr. 96.8, 97.6 Level 3). Two beads were found near the City Wall (Tr. 96.7 Level 2).

Pendants (178–84)

Of the seven small pendants from the excavations, five are bronze, one is bone, and one is gold foil. Pendants are designed with a suspension loop to hang singly on a necklace, often in multiple groups or strung along with beads. Two pendants are acorn-shaped (**178–9**), a popular form for necklaces and earrings.[125] **178** was probably once attached to the lunate earring (**26**), while **179** once adorned a necklace made of bronze wire. Two pendants (**181–2**) are shaped like small amphoras, another popular type of repeating pendant for necklaces.[126] Another resembles a round-mouthed oinochoe without the handle (**180**). A smaller version of **180** was found in the lower town site at Stymphalos.[127] The finely made gold foil leaf pendant (**183**) also likely came from a necklace, although there are no means of attachment preserved. The tiny size of the bronze droplet (**184**) suggests that it once attached to a lunate earring with loops.

178. Bronze, cast. Inv. 748B. Tr. 95.6.5.8. Outside Temple. **Fig. 6.9** (see **26**, fig. 6.4 and fig. 6.14)
H 0.9; D 0.4; Wt. 0.3
Good condition. The acorn-shaped pendant consists of a wide cap and a curved shell with a pointed end. It was found with the lunate earring **26** and might be an attachment. Part of the tiny loop and attachment wire of the acorn is preserved.

179. Bone, carved and polished. Inv. 3755. Tr. 96.15 surface find. Outside Bldg. A. **Figs. 6.10 and 6.19**

H 1.09; W 0.6; Wt. 0.4
Good condition. The cylindrically shaped string hole is discoloured green from a copper/bronze wire once strung through it. The acorn-shaped pendant has a wide cap incised with cross-hatching. The curved shell has a tiny knob on the bottom. The back of the pendant is flat. Probably from a necklace. Comparable is a glass acorn pendant from the Mausoleum at Halikarnassos, ca. 350 BCE; however, that acorn is fully rounded and the string hole is spherical.[128]

180. Bronze, cast (pendant?). Inv. 196. Tr. 96.4.2.2. Altar. **Figs. 6.10 and 6.19**
H 1.9; D0.7; Wt. 3.4
Excellent condition. It resembles a round-mouth oinochoe without the handle; wide base with a flattened bottom. No evidence for attachment.

181. Bronze, cast. Inv. 1061. Tr. 97.1.2.3. NW of Altar. **Figs. 6.10 and 6.19**
H1.05; D 0.4; Wt. 0.4
Good condition. Mostly intact, missing most of the suspension loop. Elongated, plain amphora-shaped body, with a small ball on the bottom. This pendant is similar in shape to the terracotta-gilt amphora pendants from a necklace of unknown provenance (ca. fourth to second centuries BCE) in the British Museum.[129]

182. Bronze, cast. Inv. 2240 (99.86). Tr. 99.1.3.3. Building B. **Figs. 6.10 and 6.19**
H 1.2; D 0.5; Wt. 1.1
Good condition with some surface corrosion. Similar to **181**, although the body is more oval. The upper end is disk-shaped, with the lower part of the suspension loop preserved.

183. Gold foil, hammered. Inv. 1063. Tr. 97.4.2.3. S of Terrace Wall. **Figs. 6.10 and 6.19**
L 1.1; W 0.5; Wt. 0.1
Good condition. Very finely hammered, tiny leaf-shaped droplet. The upper end has two small discoid globes of receding size. No evidence for attachment.

184. Bronze, cast. Inv. 2297. Tr. 99.6.3.3. E of Terrace Wall. **Fig. 6.19**
H 0.6; Th. 0.4; Wt. 0.2
Fair condition with some surface corrosion. Tiny droplet consists of two small spheres on top of each other of receding size. Traces of suspension loop preserved.

Distribution of pendants

One pendant was found outside the northwest wall of the Temple (Tr. 95.6 Level 5), five others were scattered near the Altar (96.4 Level 2, 97.2 Level 2) or below the Terrace wall to the south and east (99.1 Level 3, 97.4 Level 2, 99.6 Level 3), while one was a surface find outside Building A (96.15).

Pins (185–215)

Clothing pins have a long history in Greece to fasten drapery, notably at the shoulders of the Doric peplos.[130] Greek sanctuaries have yielded the greatest number of Archaic pins, with 700–800 found in the Argive Heraion alone.[131] Quite often they were dedicated along with clothes,[132] although storage space for bulky items such as clothes was probably limited in small sanctuaries like that on the acropolis at Stymphalos.

After the sixth century BCE, clothing pins are less common in the Peloponnese, as indicated by the small number found in graves from the first half of the fifth century BCE, or among finds in sanctuaries.[133] In the fourth century, Olynthos likewise produced few pins.[134] Their use declined because the Ionic chiton, with its sewn sides and buttoned arms, replaced the peplos as the prevalent form of dress.[135] Nevertheless, depictions of pins on women's clothing on vases and the inclusion of pins in temple inventories indicate that these objects were still being used in the Early to Late Classical period and likely later.[136]

Thirty-eight bronze and iron pins were found in Stymphalos' Sanctuary on the acropolis, of which six poorly preserved ones are omitted from the catalogue.[137] These include nineteen of iron, twelve of bronze, four with bronze pinheads and iron shafts, two of bone, and one glass pinhead. Finds of iron pins are generally uncommon, and those that have survived are heavily corroded, with details of their shape now lost.[138] The bronze pins from the Sanctuary for the most part are missing their shafts.[139] Classification is therefore difficult at times. Nevertheless, eleven different types can be discerned. These include pins with disks and rings (**185–7**), disks and knobs (**188–90**), round (**191**), round heads with rings (**192–7**), biconical knobs (**198–200**), bud-shaped finials (**201–2**), and pomegranate finials (**203–7**), including more rare forms such as lion-head (**208–11**), snake-head (**212**), and roll-top pins (**213–14**). One partly preserved Illyrian double-shafted pin (**215**) is an import from the north.

Comparisons for most of the pins from the Sanctuary can be found in Kilian-Dirlmeier's typology of Peloponnesian pins from the Archaic period.[140] In contrast, the majority of the jewellery from the Sanctuary is Late

Classical or Early Hellenistic. Only a small number of terracotta figurines and vases, and some metal objects including iron spits, can be assigned to the fifth century or earlier. To these may be added the Late Archaic kore found in the temple, ca. 490 BCE. This, however, is scant evidence for an Archaic phase for the Sanctuary.[141] It does not seem likely that the pins, made of inexpensive bronze and iron, were heirlooms when they were dedicated as votives at the Sanctuary. It is more credible that the types were Archaic ones that continued to be made and used at Stymphalos into the fifth and fourth centuries BCE.

Type A: With disk-heads and rings (185–7)

One bronze pinhead (**185**) and two iron pin fragments (**186–7**) are decorated with a disk on top and small crowning globe, followed by compressed rings below. The heavily corroded iron pins have no close parallels. A pin found in the lower town at Stymphalos is very similar to **185,** although the finial is smaller.[142]

185. Bronze, cast. Inv. 234. Tr. 96.3.4.7. Altar. **Figs. 6.10 and 6.19**
L 2.2; D 1.5 (disk); 0.3 (shaft); Wt. 10.1
Good condition with surface corrosion. Large thick disk with a wide, flat crowning knob. The disk is incised around its upper edge, dividing it into two sections of decreasing diameters. Below are four rings of decreasing diameter, so that the shape resembles an inverted bell. The middle ring is thicker than the others. A small piece of the shaft is preserved below the lowest ring. Close parallels for **185** are difficult to find, although the finial resembles an Archaic pin from Argos, classified as Type A IIc by Kilian-Dirlmeier.[143] The Argive finial has the same wide, flat crowning knob, inverted bell shape, and wide middle projecting ring.

186. Iron, forged. Inv. 721. Tr. 96.13.3.6. S of Altar. **Figs. 6.10 and 6.19**
L 5.2; 3.75 (shaft); D 0.95 (disk); 0.4 (shaft); Wt. 3.6
Poor condition with surface corrosion and accretions on pinhead and shaft. The shaft is broken in two sections, missing its point. Small upper disk with two rows of incision around the outer edges and a crowning globe followed by two compressed rings.

187. Iron, forged. Inv. 2567. Tr. 97.5 baulk.3.3. E of Terrace Wall. **Fig. 6.19**
L 3.5; 2.2 (shaft); D 1.3 (disk); 0.4 (shaft); Wt. 7.3
Very poor condition with corrosion and thick accretions on the pinhead and shaft. Squarish disk with no crowning globe; two, possibly three compressed rings below.

Type B: With disk- and knob-heads and rings (188–90)

Three iron pin fragments have an upper disk, followed by one or more knobs and compressed rings. These pins are poorly preserved, but appear similar to Archaic pins from Peloponnesian sanctuaries.

188. Iron, forged. Inv. 741. Tr. 95.4+1.2.4. Temple. **Figs. 6.10 and 6.19**
L 5.1; D 1.5 (disk); 0.4 (shaft); Wt. 10.2
Poor condition with surface corrosion and accretions on pinhead and shaft. The shaft is broken, two pieces, missing its point. Large disk, lacking a crowning knob, followed by a flattened sphere, then one or two adjoining compressed rings that decrease in size towards the shaft. The disk is incised around the middle diameter. **188** is similar to ones from Perachora, Argos, and Mycenae, Kilian-Dirlmeier's Type A IIb, where the disk sits directly on the globe, which, in turn, rests on two narrow rings;[144] however, Type A IIb pins are seventh century and their pinheads are much smaller than here.

189. Iron, forged. Inv. 1024. Tr. 97.4.2.2. S of Terrace Wall. **Figs. 6.10 and 6.19**
L 4.72; D 1.35 (disk); 0.4 (shaft); Wt. 4.9
Fair condition with surface corrosion. Thin, flattened disk with small crowning knob, followed by a flattened knob, narrow cuff, and two narrow compressed rings. The shaft is slightly bent, missing its point. **189** most resembles two Archaic pins from a sanctuary in Mantinea, Type A Ib.[145]

190. Iron, forged. Inv. 2242. Tr. 99.5.2.2. Pillar Shrine. **Figs. 6.10 and 6.19**
L 2.30; D 1.1 (disk); Wt. 3.0
Poor condition with surface corrosion and accretions. Most of the thick shaft is missing. Flat disk with small crowning knob, followed by two knobs and two or three compressed rings. Although very corroded, this pin most resembles two Archaic pins from Sparta, Type B IIa.[146]

Type C: Round glass pinhead (?) (191)

191 is a tiny, dark blue glass globe attached to a fragment of a very narrow iron shaft. Parallels for a pinhead in glass are hard to find.[147] Bronze pins with plain, round heads have been found in sanctuaries at Corinth, Nemea, Isthmia, and Olympia; however, their contexts are either too early or too late for close comparison.[148]

191. Glass and iron fragment. Inv. 2127. Tr. 99.3 L 2 P 2. Bldg. A. **Figs. 6.10 and 6.19**

L 1.1; D 0.7 (globe); 0.12 (shaft)
Fair condition with slight surface weathering. Most of the shaft is missing. A small, solid globe of dark blue glass with part of an iron shaft is preserved.

Type D: With round heads and rings (192–7)

Six pins have round heads, ranging in diameter from 0.7 to 1.0 cm.[149] The pinheads are surmounted by a crowning knob, with one or more rings below. **194** has a bronze pinhead and broken iron shaft; the other five are iron. Poorly preserved, these pinheads are difficult to classify. Somewhat similar is Kilian-Dirlmeier's Archaic Type D II, with one or two rings between the globe and the shaft, although the Stymphalos examples have larger, rounder globes for the most part.[150]

192 was discovered in the northeastern quadrant of the Temple, in a grave of a young girl presumed to date between the fourth and sixth centuries CE, along with two Late Classical bronze earrings (**35, 85**). The pin is likely contemporary with the other examples listed below since it is similar in type. **192** was likely discovered along with the earrings while the grave was being dug, and was reburied along with the body.

192. Iron, forged. Inv. 1353. Tr. 96.11.4.5. Temple (girl's grave; fourth/fifth century CE (?) **Fig. 6.19**
L 2.4; D 0.8 (head); 0.4 (shaft); Wt. 1.9
Very poor condition with severe corrosion and a large accretion on top of the flattened, rounded head. Below are perhaps two projecting rings. Also found with a bronze "fibula-type" earring (**35**) and a plain circuit earring (**85**).

193. Iron, forged. Inv. 1460. (97.312). Tr. 96.11.5.6. Temple. **Figs. 6.10 and 6.19**
L 5.1 a) 2.8, b) 2.3); D 0.8 (head); 0.3 (shaft); Wt. 1.8
Poor condition with corroded sphere and shaft. Preserved in two fragments, with a crack along one side of the sphere. Sharpened tip of the shaft is missing. Round head with a small crowning knob on top and a narrow projecting ring below. Possibly two small compressed rings on the upper shaft above the break. The pinhead is similar to an Archaic example from Perachora.[151]

194. Bronze, cast and iron, forged. Inv. 1465. Tr. 96.11.5.6. Temple. **Figs. 6.10 and 6.19**
L 2.2; D 0.8 (head); 0.3 (shaft); Wt. 2.1
Fair condition with surface corrosion and accretions. The shaft is iron and the globular finial is bronze; most of the shaft is missing. The finial consists of a slightly flattened, biconical sphere with a large crowning knob. Three projecting rings below. A smaller Archaic version of this pin was found at Olympia, in addition to a closer sixth/fifth century BCE parallel from Halai.[152]

195. Iron, forged. Inv. 1466. Tr. 96.11.5.6. Temple. **Fig. 6.19**
L 2.6; D 0.7 (head); 0.2 (shaft); Wt. 0.9
Poor condition with heavy corrosion. Broken shaft with blunt edge. Small globular head, with a projecting ring.

196. Iron, forged. Inv. 174. Tr. 96.4.2.3. Altar. **Fig. 6.19**
L 4.95; D 1.0 (head); 0.4 (shaft); Wt. 5.2
Fair condition with surface corrosion. Broken shaft is now slightly bent. Small round head with crowning knob and two projecting rings.

197. Iron, forged. Inv. 723. Tr. 96.13.2.5. S of Altar. **Fig. 6.19**
L 2.8; D 0.7 (head); 0.3 (shaft); Wt. 1.6
Poor condition with surface corrosion. Large accretion along one side of the pinhead. Broken shaft with blunt end. Small round head with a tiny stemlike top and one or two projecting rings below.

Type E: With grooved, flattened spheres (198–200)

Three bronze pinheads have two flattened or biconical spheres, decorated with short vertical grooves and divided by a small cuff. The knobs have a loop on top and are flanked by narrow projecting rings of smaller diameter. These pins resemble Kilian-Dirlmeier's Archaic Type E IVb, of which the closest parallels are from a sanctuary in Mantinea.[153]

198. Bronze, cast and iron. Inv. 704. (96.475). Tr. 96.9.3.3. Altar. **Figs. 6.10 and 6.19**
H 1.75; Max. D 0.8; Wt. 2.8
Good condition, with slight surface corrosion. Two flattened spheres decorated with vertical grooves divided by rings and the start of the iron shaft. The top of the loop has been broken and lost.

199. Bronze, cast and iron, forged. Inv. 1092. Tr. 97.4.3.4. S of Terrace Wall. **Figs. 6.10 and 6.19**
H 1.7; Max. D 0.8; Wt. 2.2
Good condition, with some surface corrosion on the flattened spheres and loop; start of the iron shaft.

200. Bronze, cast. Inv. 2814. Tr. 99.1.6.12. Building B. **Figs. 6.10 and 6.19**
H 1.4; Max. D 0.8; Wt. 2.5
Good condition with slight surface corrosion. The loop is open; the start of the iron (?) shaft is preserved.

Type F: With bud-shaped finials (201–2)

Two pins have finials resembling buds and decorative rings below, corresponding to Kilian-Dirlmeier's Type F Ib. Other Peloponnesian specimens come from Olympia, Perachora, and Corinth.[154] Another example turned up in a looted grave near Corinth, with fifth–fourth century BCE pottery.[155]

201. Iron, forged. Inv. 968. Tr. 97.3.2.2. Altar. **Figs. 6.10 and 6.19**
L 3.03; D 0.72 (finial); 0.3 (shaft); Wt. 1.3
Forged and hammered. In poor condition with corrosion and accretions. Shaft broken off and very fragile. The budlike pinhead consists of a crested upper part followed by three disklike rings.

202. Iron, forged. Inv. 645. Tr. 96.13.2.4. S of Altar. **Figs. 6.10 and 6.20**
L 3.1; Max. D 0.9 (finial); Wt. 4.8
Forged and hammered. In poor condition with corrosion and accretions, missing most of the shaft. Stepped conical top, with small crowning knob, widens to its maximum width with two rows of dots then three stepped sections declining in size, each decorated with a row of embossed dots between raised lines.

Type G: Pomegranate pinheads (203–7)

Four bronze pins (**203–6**) and one of bone (**207**) have heads in the form of a pomegranate, globular in shape with a flaring stem above and compressed rings below. The pomegranate is associated with myths concerning Aphrodite and Persephone; its multiple seeds serve as a symbol of fertility.[156] The examples from the Sanctuary appear to belong to Kilian-Dirlmeier's Type F IIb, found at Lousoi, Perachora, Olympia, Mantinea, Corinth, and Argos. A few examples from Argive burials have contexts of the fifth century BCE.[157] Kilian-Dirlmeier suggests the sixth to the early fifth centuries BCE for the type in the Peloponnese.[158] Pomegranate pins from Stymphalos may extend this chronology at least to the late fifth and more likely into the fourth century BCE.

203 and **204** have plain bronze, cubic-shaped heads and fragments of iron shafts,[159] while **205** and **206** have globes with decorated, incised bands. **206** also has beaded decoration around the top of the globe and on the upper ring, as well as incised V's on the globe above and below the incised band. **207** is a version of a pomegranate in bone, with a globular body and four wilting leaves (sepia). It is included here because it has a small hole on the rounded end, which partially pierces the axis. **207** may have decorated the shaft of a pin but it lacks a cross-hole for a rivet to hold the pin in place, as is found on seventh-century BCE bone pinheads from Sparta.[160]

203. Bronze, cast and iron. Inv. 698. Tr. 96.4.5.8. Altar. **Figs. 6.10 and 6.20**
H 1.6; D 1.2; Wt. 3.6
Fair condition with surface corrosion. Traces of iron suggest that its missing shaft was made of this. Cubic-shaped head, two compressed rings below. A bronze and iron example came from a sanctuary in Mantinea.[161]

204. Bronze, cast and iron. Inv. 805. Tr. 96.9.3.3. Altar. **Figs. 6.10 and 6.20**
H 2.2; D 1.3; Wt. 10.9
Good condition. Small piece of the iron shaft. Similar to **203** but larger. Cubic-shaped head, three compressed rings below, of which the middle ring is incised with a pattern of vertical lines.

205. Bronze, cast. Inv. 2930. Tr. 00.4.1.1. City Wall. **Figs. 6.10 and 6.20**
H 1.85; D 1.15; Wt. 6.5
Missing shaft. As **203** and **204.** An incised band with beading decorates the globe. One compressed ring is preserved below. Compare ones from Corinth, Tiryns, and Perachora.[162]

206. Bronze, cast. Inv. 3520. Tr. 96.15.5.5. Refuse pit outside Bldg. A. **Figs. 6.10 and 6.20**
L 1.25; D 0.53
Fair condition with surface corrosion. Missing its shaft. Globe with incised band around its widest diameter, decorated with vertical grooves. Diagonal lines above and below the band decoration form incised V's; a row of beading decorates the upper edge. Two or three rows of compressed rings below; a piece of wire (?) is wrapped around the lower end of the finial, possibly part of a chain.[163] The upper ring is beaded. Pins with pomegranate finials from graves in Halieis and Argos have a similar diagonal V pattern and decorated compressed rings, but lack the vertically grooved bands around their widest diameters.[164]

207. Bone, carved and polished. Inv. 1010. Tr. 96.13.6.11. S of Altar. **Figs. 6.10 and 6.20**
H 0.93; D 0.8; Wt. 0.5
Very good condition. Globular shape with four wilting sepals on top. A hole partially pierces the rounded end of the fruit.

Type H: Lion pinheads (208–11)

Three bronze lion's heads (**208–10**) were likely attached to the shaft of pins, although **208** has a hole through its axis, possibly for a wire attachment to a matching pin or for stringing on a necklace, like a bead. Kilian-Dirlmeier lists only four lion-head pins in her Type F IV, found in sanctuaries at Argos, Corinth, and Mantinea, as well as on the Greek mainland.[165] Also worth noting are two barrel-shaped, hollow bronze lion's heads which are said to be clasps for closing the necklace.[166] Thus the examples from Stymphalos add significantly to the small Peloponnesian corpus, which otherwise has been dated to the late sixth–early fifth centuries BCE.[167] The detailed manes of the Stymphalian lion heads, as well as the bone insets in the eyes, suggest a later date, perhaps early fourth century BCE, when lion's head earrings came into vogue.

A small, carved bone lion (**211**) is included in this section, since traces of iron are visible on its underbelly, suggesting a pin. No parallels for such a bone lion could be found, however, so **211** may once have served a decorative function other than jewellery.

208. Bronze, cast. Inv. 2290. Tr. 99.6.3.3. E of Terrace Wall. **Figs. 6.11 and 6.20**
L 2.9; Max. D 1.1; Wt. 8.4
Good condition with pockets of corrosion. Missing shaft. The lion's head has socketed eyes with bone insets, an open mouth with visible tongue, and a mane, arranged on three levels, incised in straight lines. The head is attached to a collar consisting of a thick projecting ring and amphora-shaped stem incised with two narrow bands. The head has a hole through its mouth, exiting the other end.

209. Bronze, cast. Inv. 3436. Tr. 96.15.5.5. Refuse pit outside Bldg. A. **Figs. 6.11 and 6.20**
L 2.3; Max. D 1.0; Wt. 4.6
Good condition, with surface corrosion. Lion's head has socketed eyes filled with bone inlay, an incised snout, and open mouth with a less distinct tongue than **208**. The mane, arranged on two levels, is incised in a zigzag pattern. The collar has a thick, grooved projecting ring, followed by a narrower, smaller band, which narrows to a plain stem, then flares out to three thin rings, followed by another plain section that tapers to a rounded point. A thin wire is wrapped around the finial between the mane and the large projecting ring, with a piece protruding out one side. Most of the shaft is missing, but a little evidence suggests it was iron. Compare an example from Mantinea.[168]

210. Bronze, cast. Inv. 3622. Tr. 96.15.5.5. Refuse pit outside Bldg. A. **Figs. 6.11 and 6.20**
L 1.6; Max. D 0.7; Wt. 2.4
Good condition with surface corrosion. Missing shaft. This example is smaller than **208** and **209**. The lion's head has eyes inset with bone, an open mouth with bone inset for teeth, and a mane, arranged on two levels, incised in a zigzag pattern. The collar consists of a projecting ring, followed by two smaller rings.

211. Bone, carved. Inv. 3664. Tr. 00.6.4.4. N of Bldg. A. **Figs. 6.11 and 6.20**
L 1.9 ; Max. D 0.9; Wt. 0.9
In worn condition, with chips missing from body and tail. Simply carved tiny lion in a crouching stance. The lion has a blunt snout and six deeply incised lines to delineate the mane, decorated with cross-hatching. The remnant of a thin iron shaft is visible on the stomach between the hind legs.

Type I: Snake's head (212)

One pin with a plain shaft has one end flattened like a stylized snake's head. The type is rare in the Peloponnese; three sixth-century pins are known from Olympia, and a fourth-century silver snake pin came from Halieis.[169]

212. Bronze, hammered. Inv. 1002. Tr. 96.13.6.11. S of Altar. **Figs. 6.11 and 6.20**
L 3.4; D 0.2 (shaft); Wt. 0.3
Intact with surface corrosion. Bent. Small pin with a narrow shaft tapering to a point at one end, flattened at the other end into a stylized snake head without distinguishing features.

Type J: Roll-tops (213–14)

Two roll-top pins have their upper part hammered flat and bent forward into a loop and the other end tapered to a point. The roll-top pin was used in Greece from the Bronze Age to the Roman period, although few are from securely dated contexts.[170] One example, found beside the left shoulder of a skeleton in a grave at Olynthos, attests to its function to secure clothing.[171]

213. Iron, forged. Inv. 354. Tr. 96.5.4.6. City Wall. **Figs. 6.11 and 6.20**
L 5.3; D 0.8 (loop); 0.4 (shaft); Wt. 2.3
Poor condition with corrosion and accretions on the loop terminal and shaft; missing its sharpened point.

214. Bronze, hammered. Inv. 1583. Tr. 97.9.5.7. S of Terrace Wall. **Figs. 6.11 and 6.20**

L 5.7; D 0.7 (loop); 0.4 (shaft); Wt. 1.9
Good condition with slight surface corrosion. The shaft is now bent backwards at the open loop.

Type K: Illyrian double-shafted (215)

One iron pin has a loop which curves around to form a down-swinging second loop. This is a half-preserved example of a double-shafted, Illyrian omega class, Trebenishte type pin.[172] This type is formed by a single piece of wire bent at the top to form two up-swinging loops, joined by a third down-swinging loop. Bronze pins of this type were discovered at Olympia and Nemea, while two similar gold pins came from Patras.[173] It is possible that the pin reached Stymphalos through a Macedonian connection. Pins of Trebenishte type are dated from the late sixth to the third centuries BCE.

215. Iron, forged. Inv. 2812. Tr. 99.1.4B.4. Building B. **Figs. 6.11 and 6.20**
L 4.1; D 1.0 (loop); 0.1 (shaft); Wt. 0.8
Fragmentary condition with surface corrosion. One long thin piece of iron bent into an up-swinging loop and a down-swinging loop, now corroded together; missing the other up-swinging loop, the shaft, and its point.

Distribution of pins

Only five pins were found within the Temple; of these, four were discovered in the northeast part (Tr. 96.11 Levels 4 and 5), and one in the west part (Tr. 95.4+1 Level 2). Of the six pins from Building A, one was found on the east side of the main room (Tr. 99.3 Level 2), four from outside the main west walls (Tr 99.5 Level 2), of which three were from the refuse pit (Tr. 96.15 Level 5), including two of the four lion's head pins (**209–10**), and one from outside the north wall (00.6 Level 4). Another pin was found west of Building A, near the Pillar Shrine area (Tr. 99.5 Level 2). The remaining 23 were scattered in trenches to the south (Tr. 96.4 Levels 2 and 5, 96.9 Level 3, 96.13 Levels 2, 3, 4, and 6, 97.4 Levels 2 and 3, 97.9 Level 5, 00.3 Level 2), west (Tr. 97.3 Level 2), and east (Tr. 97.5 baulk Level 3, 99.6 Level 3) of the Altar, including Building B to the east (Tr. 99.1 Levels 4 and 6). Two others were discovered near the City Wall (Tr. 00.4 Level 1, 96.5 Level 4).

Gems or gaming pieces (216–22)

Seven small disklike objects were found in the Sanctuary. Most have a flat undersurface and convex upper surface, with the exception of **220**, which has a flat upper surface. Six are made of glass and one of bronze. The glass disks are monochrome in colours such as opaque white, yellow, and green. They are included with the jewellery, especially since traces of gold have been detected on two of them, although their function is difficult to determine. Elsewhere they are called "gems" or "gaming pieces."[174] If gems, they could have been used as insets in the bezels of rings, especially **216** with its cone shape and tapered sides. **222**, made of bronze, is likely a "gaming piece."

216. Glass. Inv. 243. Tr. 96.4.2.2. Altar. **Figs. 6.11 and 6.20**
D 1.2; Th. 0.7 (top of cone to flat back)
Very good condition. Opaque white, circular disk possibly with a gold flake on the bottom. Flat undersurface with straight sides on the lower part, tapering upwards into a cone.

217. Glass. Inv. 1094. Tr. 97.5.2.2. E of Terrace Wall. **Figs. 6.11 and 6.20**
D 1.00 × 1.25; Th. 0.5
Very good condition. Opaque white, oval disk. Flat undersurface with traces of gold flake; convex upper surface.

218. Glass. Inv. 925. Tr. 96.13.4.7. S of Altar. **Figs. 6.11 and 6.20**
D 0.8; Th. 0.4
Very good condition. Circular disk, with a slightly green tint. Shape as **216**.

219. Glass. Inv. 1257. Tr. 97.4.6.9. S of Terrace Wall. **Figs. 6.11 and 6.20**
D 1.2; Th. 0.57
Surface is slightly pitted. Circular disk; opaque with slight yellowish tint. Shape as **216** and **218**.

220. Glass. Inv. 1405. Tr. 95.7.5.11. Bldg. A. **Figs. 6.11 and 6.20**
D 0.9; Th. 0.45
Circular disk with burnt and blackened surface. Shape as **216, 218,** and **219**.

221. Glass. Inv. 239. Tr. 96.6.2.4. W of Bldg. A. **Figs. 6.11 and 6.20**
D 1.3; Th. 0.5
In poor condition, with surface corrosion. Circular disk with yellowish tint. Shape as **217**.

222. Bronze, cast. Inv. 329. Tr. 96.9.1.1. Altar. **Figs. 6.11 and 6.20**
D 1.3 × 1.7; Th. 0.2

Oval disk with a groove lengthwise down its centre. Excellent condition.

Distribution of gems

One gem was discovered in the main room of Building A (Tr. 95.7 Level 5) and another, west of Building A near the Pillar Shrine area (Tr. 96.6 Level 2). The remaining five were found to the west (Tr. 96.9 Level 1), east (Tr. 97.5 Level 2), and south (Tr. 96.4 Level 2, 96.13 Level 4, 97.4 Level 6) of the Altar.

Attachment (223)

Rosette (223)

One gold rosette (**223**) was found in the Temple's cella. It is exquisitely made and one of the finest objects in the collection of jewellery from Stymphalos.[175] It must have broken off a larger piece, either a necklace or diadem, when the Sanctuary was looted and destroyed about the mid-second century BCE.[176]

223. Gold sheet, hammered. Inv. 185. Tr. 95.4+1.2.4. Temple. **Fig. 6.11**
H 3.1; D 2.3
Well preserved. Some petals are slightly bent; the spiral volute is partially unrolled. The two-tiered rosette has an outer ring of 12 rounded, convex petals and an inner ring of eight slightly flattened petals. Each petal is hammered and bordered by thin twisted gold wire. The back of the rosette is attached to a small cylinder decorated with two wire bands at the top and bottom to resemble a flower sitting in a vase. Another thicker gold wire is twisted into a spiral volute on one side of the cylinder; the wire on the other side is unwound. The rosette was attached to a larger piece of jewellery by means of this twisted wire.[177] There are no apparent close parallels, though comparisons can be made with rosettes on a gold wreath from the woman's larnax in the antechamber of the royal burial at Vergina, and on a late fourth-century BCE necklace from a grave at Homolion.[178]
Late fourth–early third century

Medallions (224–5)

Two gilded silver medallions were found in the Sanctuary, **224** in the northeast part of the Temple (Tr. 96.11) and **225** from east of the Terrace Wall (Tr. 99.1). Their function as adornment is uncertain. **224** has a hole for attachment, perhaps to a necklace or a box, whereas no means of attachment is preserved for **225**. It seems unlikely that they decorated clothes, since appliqués usually have three or more holes for attachment.[179] The exquisite detail and workmanship of the two figures on **225**, depicting either Eros and Aphrodite or Psyche, suggest that this scene was copied from a larger work of art, perhaps even a wall painting.

224. Gilded silver, die-formed or punched. Inv. 933. Tr. 96.11.4.5. Temple. **Figs. 6.11 and 6.21**
D 2.2; Th. 0.8 mm; Wt. 2.3
Very good condition, some surface corrosion. Hole in the centre at the top of the head for attachment. Silver face has blue/black silver oxide on it; the underside does not. Thin, finely hammered disk in the form of a human head, with well-defined eyebrows, large, deep-set eyes, straight, squared-off nose, rounded cheeks and chin, and pursed mouth. The hair is gilded and very wavy. The gender is not certain, nor is there a close parallel. If female, it might represent Aphrodite, or a maenad or even a "beautiful Medusa"; if male, it perhaps depicts Dionysos, Apollo, or Orpheus.[180]

225. Gilded silver, hammered and chased. Inv. 2549. Tr. 99.1.5.10. E of Terrace Wall. **Figs. 6.11 and 6.21**
D 1.6 × 2.2; Wt. 0.4
Very fragile, fragmentary condition. Four fragments are joined together, preserving about half the medallion. No evidence for attachment. A guilloche band encircles part of the outer edge.

The medallion depicts a rather dramatic motif of a young, winged male embracing a semi-draped female, who reclines in his arms. The female figure's upper body is bare, while diaphanous folds of drapery, chased in fine lines, cover her lower extremities. Her left hand is raised, cradling the male's head, while he bends over, gazing into her upturned face. Her loose, wavy locks of hair appear to be wind-blown over his right arm. The upper body of the male figure is also undraped. He has chubby features and a full head of curly hair. His partially preserved wings are extended as if in flight and the feathers are finely chased.

There are no close parallels for this motif. The handsome winged male is most likely Eros, and the semi-draped female should represent either his mother Aphrodite or his lover Psyche. There are a few representations of Eros, either nude or draped, in a face-to-face embrace with either a nude or a draped Aphrodite.[181] In these scenes, either Aphrodite or Eros is seated. Although Eros' lower extremities are missing on the Stymphalian medallion, it is possible that he too was seated; however, the laid-back reclining posture of the female is very different from other representations.

The two figures embracing recall the second-century

CE love story *Amor and Psyche* by Apuleius. Although this story has no known earlier literary versions,[182] Psyche appears in the Classical period as a young maiden with butterfly wings, representing the Greek notion of the winged soul, moving towards immortality and perfection;[183] however, because of the Stymphalian medallion's fragmentary condition, it is unknown whether the female figure, if meant as Psyche, also had butterfly wings. The reclining female's partially covered lower torso is found on examples of Psyche from the third century BCE on,[184] yet representations of Eros and Psyche embracing from the Hellenistic period typically show Psyche as standing, rather than reclining.[185]

Decorated gold sheet fragment (226)

The small, nearly square fragment of gold sheet, decorated with a row of punched circles, is from a larger piece of jewellery, such as a stephanos, like a late fourth-century BCE one from the Santa Eufemia Treasure in Calabria. The strap on the Calabrian diadem has more decoration, with three rows of punched circles and three rows of grooves.[186] If not a stephanos, it may have been part of a strip diadem or taenia used to bind the hair.[187]

226. Gold sheet fragment, hammered. Inv. 976. Tr. 97.2.3.3. West Annex. **Figs. 6.11 and 6.21**
H 1.5; W 1.6; Wt. 0.1
Fragile condition, missing a large jagged piece. Very thin, small fragment of gold sheet with a rounded end and a border of punched circles.

Buttons (227–33)

Seven circular bone buttons with convex tops were found in the Sanctuary. They are included here since they served both a decorative and a practical function as clothing fasteners. Six of them look like mini-shields (**227–32**), while the seventh is dome-shaped (**233**). By the end of the sixth century BCE, buttons appear to have replaced pins as the main clothing fasteners.[188] Small buttons generally fastened one side of the sleeves of Ionic chitons, while large buttons fastened Doric peploi, one on each shoulder.[189] There are far fewer buttons than pins at the Sanctuary, likely because pins were a popular votive offering, while individual buttons were not, except when they adorned an item of clothing offered as a dedication. Four buttons (**227, 229, 231–2**) have traces of bronze or iron tacks in their attachments, as part of a loop for fastening to clothes.

Mini-shield buttons (227–32)

This type is circular and convex, with a shieldlike design. All six buttons have a small centre piercing, of which two are only partially pierced through their axes (**229, 232**). Four buttons (**228–31**) have two circular rows of incised decoration around the centre piercing. Their diameters range between 1.5 and 2.7 cm. A raised rectangle, with a hole through it for purposes of attachment, is carved on the flattened back of all the buttons except **228**. Other contemporary examples were discovered in a fourth-century BCE grave in Sedes, in Macedonia.[190] Hellenistic and Roman parallels for the type have been found in Lousoi and Mantinea, Corinth, Athens, Delos, and Cyrene.[191] These fourth-century examples from Stymphalos are therefore some of the earliest found in the Peloponnese.

227. Bone, carved and polished and bronze tack. Inv. 326. Tr. 95.4+1.2.4. Temple. **Fig. 6.12**
Button: D 1.5; Th. 0.3; Tack: D 1.0, L shaft 0.7; Wt. bone button 0.6; bronze tack 0.4
Button in good condition, but missing a chip from one edge. Flat, oval disk with convex upper part and centre piercing. Thin bronze tack with narrow shaft which fits through the bone disk for attachment.

228. Bone, carved. Inv. 689. Tr. 95.4+1.2.4. Temple
D 2.6; Th. 0.4; Wt. 2.1
Two joining fragments, in poor condition with chips missing from both pieces. Dark brown in colour. Centre piercing is larger than those preceding, and lacks the carved rectangle for attachment on the back of the button.

229. Bone, carved and polished. Inv. 466. Tr. 95.8.4.12. W of Temple
D 1.95 ; Th. 0.3; Wt. 0.9
Good condition. Convex upper part with a thin flattened outer rim; two rows of circles incised around the centre piercing. A hole partially pierces the centre. Flat back surface has a raised rectangle with a hole through both long sides for attachment.

230. Bone, carved and polished. Inv. 1516. Tr. 96.11.5.6. Temple. **Fig. 6.21**
D 2.7; Th. 0.4; Wt. 1.6
Fair condition with chips missing from the outer rim. The centre is pierced entirely from front to back. Flattened back has raised rectangle with part of an iron tack for attachment.

231. Bone, carved and polished. Inv. 1082. Tr. 96.8.5.6. West Annex. **Figs. 6.12 and 6.21**

D 2.65; Th. 0.4; Wt. 2.8
Very good condition. The centre is not entirely pierced. Tiny fragment of iron is preserved in the carved rear piece for attachment.

232. Bone, carved and polished. Inv. 3578. Tr. 96.15.5.5. Refuse pit outside Bldg. A. **Figs. 6.12 and 6.21**
D 2.4; Th. 0.4; Wt. 2.0
Very good condition. This example varies from **227–31**; the edge of the outer rim is scalloped in a V-shaped wedge pattern. Small centre piercing, with traces of bronze. Flattened back with cube-shaped part and hole for attachment.

Domed-type button (233)

233. Bone, carved and polished. Inv. 802. Tr. 96.8.3.4. West Annex. **Figs. 6.12 and 6.21**
D 2.35; Th. 1.1; Wt. 4.8
Well preserved. Large, circular, dome-shaped button. On the underside is a raised carved circular piece of bone with a hole pierced through it for attachment.

Distribution of buttons

Of the four buttons found in the Temple, two were discovered in the west part of the cella (Tr. 95.4 +1 Level 2), one was found in the northeast quadrant (Tr. 96.11 Level 5), and one was found outside the northwest wall (Tr. 95.8 Level 4). Two other buttons were found outside the west wall of the West Annex of Building A (Tr. 96.8 Levels 3 and 5), while the remaining button came from the refuse pit beside Building A (Tr. 96.15 Level 5).

Bracelets (234–8)

One complete snake bracelet (**234**)[192] and fragments of four others (**235–8**) were found in the Sanctuary excavations. Bracelets are not as common in the archaeological record as other types of jewellery, although vase-paintings and sculpture show women wearing them commonly.[193] The earliest known pair of snake bracelets in Greece from a burial in Spata has flattened snake-head terminals, dating ca. 750–720 BCE.[194] By the mid-sixth century BCE, examples of snake bracelets show that the snakes are now more realistic in appearance, with the addition of incised scales, a coiled shank, and plastically rendered heads.[195] Several simply decorated bronze bracelets with snake-head terminals were found in Late Classical graves at Olynthos.[196] In the Hellenistic period, one terminal formed the snake head while the other formed a coiled tail.[197] The earliest known examples with a coiled tail in known contexts are from Kralevo, Bulgaria, and Tuch el-Karamus, Egypt, dating to the third century BCE.[198] The one complete, once gilded, snake bracelet from the Sanctuary (**234**) has a mostly unravelled coiled tail, indicating that it is also likely Hellenistic in date. The bracelet's uncoiled length (43.5 cm) suggests that it was worn around the upper arm, perhaps in two coils, rather than on the wrist.[199] All five bracelets are decorated with punched semicircles imitating a snake's scales.

234. Bronze, hammered. Inv. 981. Tr. 96.13.6.10. S of Altar. **Figs. 6.12 and 6.22**
L 16.3; 43.5 (unravelled); W 0.9; Th. 0.15; Wt. 15.7
Intact, though mostly unravelled. Minor surface corrosion. Long, narrow band of bronze sheet, in the form of a snake. The well-preserved, realistic looking snake head has a narrow snout, indented eye, incised scales, and traces of gilding. The shank, forming the snake's body, bends below the head and is folded over about 8 cm from the tip, tapering to a narrow point of unravelled twisted metal, forming the tail. The shank is punched with rows of semicircular scales for about 6 cm behind the snake's head, thereafter flat until it tapers to form the tail.
Early third (?) century

235. Bronze fragment, hammered. Inv. 999 and Inv. 1001. Tr. 96.13.6.11. S of Altar. **Figs. 6.12 and 6.22**
L 10.08 ; W 0.6; Th. 0.1; Wt. 3.8
Good condition with surface corrosion. Two joining pieces. The shank has one overlapping fold. One end terminates in a small, flattened snake head that is bent backwards over the shank. The snake head lacks the realistic features of that on **234**. Head and shank are punched with semicircular scales.

236. Bronze fragment, hammered. Inv. 1108. Tr. 96.8.5.6. West Annex. **Figs. 6.12 and 6.22**
L 6.5; W 0.7; Th. 0.15; Wt. 1.2
Fair condition with surface corrosion. The band is punched with a scale pattern to the point where it bends upwards. One end is flattened into a very rudimentary snake head with no distinguishing features, while the other end is broken off evenly.

237. Bronze, hammered. Inv. 2747. Tr. 99.1.6.12. E of Terrace Wall. **Figs. 6.12 and 6.22**
L 5.3; total L 11.1; W. 0.6; Th. 0.2; Wt. 2.6
Fair condition with surface corrosion and cracks. One end is broken off, while the other end terminates in a simply rendered snake head with scales, now bent

backwards over the unravelled shank. Scales in the form of overlapping semicircles are preserved on the upper part of the band below the head.

238. Bronze fragment, hammered. Inv. 3336. Tr. 96.15.5.5. Refuse Pit outside Bldg A. **Fig. 6.12**
L 7.4; W 1.0; Th. 0.2; Wt. 3.5
Fair condition with surface corrosion. Broken at one end. The other end has a small hole pierced through it, and the semi-circular scale pattern stamped on both sides comes to an end just before the hole. The rectangular fragment is wider than the other examples.

Distribution of bracelets

With the exception of one fragment found in the refuse pit (Tr. 96.15 Level 5) near the West Annex of Building A, and another found outside the west wall of the West Annex (Tr. 96.8 Level 5), the other complete snake bracelet and snake bracelet fragments were discovered to the south (Tr. 96.13 Level 6) and east (Tr. 99.1 Level 6) of the Altar.

Hair rings (239–41)

Three pieces of furled sheet bronze may have been dedicated as votive hair offerings. Although now flattened, they once formed a circular shape that could have held locks of hair. Over 100 such objects were found in the Sanctuary of Artemis Hemera at Lousoi, as well as at other sanctuaries.[200] Adolescent girls cut and dedicated locks of hair to Artemis in a rite of passage before marriage. Apparently a lock could be dedicated to Athena, in appreciation for finding a husband.[201] Girls also cut and dedicated their hair to Athena at Argos.[202]

There may be other examples of hair rings in the Sanctuary, such as **89** and **90**, which are included with earrings because of their dimensions and decoration; however, most pieces of bronze sheet are in very poor condition, so their function is questionable.

239. Bronze, hammered. Inv. 2113. Tr. 96.13 (scarp cleaning). S of Altar. **Figs. 6.13 and 6.22**
Dim. 2.3 × 4.0; Th. 0.4; Wt. 2.3
Fair condition, with surface corrosion and splitting. Originally cylindrical in shape, and tapering towards one side, now flattened and split along a fold. The lower edge is decorated with two rows of incised lines.

240. Bronze band, hammered, folded over twice, with rounded ends, apparently preserved whole. Inv. 163. Tr. 95.6.5.7. N of Temple. **Fig. 6.13**
L est. 7.3, W 2.4; Wt. 5.6
Fair condition with surface corrosion. Wide band has been folded in two and flattened, with no evidence of decoration.

241. Bronze, hammered. Inv. 1845. Tr. 96.7.2.2. City Wall. **Fig. 6.13**
PL 4.4; W max. 2.8; Wt. 2.1
Fragile condition with surface corrosion. Thin, originally circular bronze sheet, cut into a shape that is wider in the centre and tapers to broken and bent ends. The long edges are now jagged and bent. No visible decoration.

Distribution of hair rings

None were discovered in secure contexts: two were located south of the Altar (Tr. 96.4 Level 6, 96.13 scarp), one was found outside the northwest wall of the Temple (Tr. 95.6 Level 5), and one was found near the Hexagonal Artillery Tower along the City Wall (Tr. 96.7 Level 2).

Diadems (242–3)

Repoussé decorated bands are found commonly in Archaic sanctuaries in southern Greece and South Italy. They have been identified as types of women's jewellery, including diadems, armbands, and finger rings. The repoussé decoration is generally simple, consisting of rows of dots, or ovules, but guilloche patterns are also found. They were especially popular at the Timpone della Motta site near Francavilla Marittima.[203] They are also very common at the Argive Heraion.[204] An example from the Korykian Cave decorated with a row of repoussé dots along both edges is 13.2 cm long, tapers to a point, and has a nail hole at the end exactly like **243**.[205] Many of these are folded, which leads one to suppose that this was done deliberately.

242. Bronze band, not decorated. Five pieces. Not yet conserved. Either these pieces represent two separate bands, or else the band diminishes in width and then increases again, since two of the pieces narrow to half the maximum width. Inv. 3164. Tr. 00.4.7.7 (City Wall). **Fig. 6.13**
L 2 largest pieces a) 16.3 b) 8.4; Max. W 2.0; Wt. 16.8
Similar ones are found quite commonly as dedications in sanctuaries. Papadopoulos (2003, 92 nn. 349–54)

gives references to others from Peloponnesian sanctuaries.

243. Band decorated with a row of small raised dots along both edges. The band narrows over its length. Folded over two times, broken at one or both ends. One possible nail hole. Inv. 2987. Tr. 00.4.4.4 (City Wall). **Fig. 6.13**
Est. L 8.2; W 3.5 to 2.9; Wt. 4.4

Fibulae (244–6)

In contrast to more than three dozen pins found in the Sanctuary, only two or three fibulae were found: a knob bow-hinged fibula (**244**), a plain bow fibula (**245**), and a spiral fragment possibly from a spectacle fibula (**246**).[206] Fibulae, like safety pins, were used to fasten the loose edges of a garment together, either at the shoulders, chest, arms, or hips. They also decorated the garment, so in this respect they functioned as jewellery.[207] First used in Bronze Age Greece, fibulae became popular during the Geometric period, but were rare in mainland Greece during the Archaic and Classical periods.[208] Fibulae typically have an arched bow, with one end forming the catch and the other ending in a sharp point to penetrate cloth fabric. Spectacle fibulae consist usually of two horizontal wire spirals joined together by double loop; one end of one spiral is straight to form the pin while the end of the inner coil of the other spiral curves up to form the catch.

Type A: Knob bow (244)

The hinged bow fibula with three large fluted knobs is very similar to fibulae from Lousoi, dated to the fourth century BCE by Brulotte.[209] It should be noted that the Lousoi fibulae are usually included in a small group of seventh-century BCE fibulae from Olympia, Argos, and Perachora.[210] It has been proposed that a Peloponnesian workshop was responsible for this small group.[211] These fibulae were no doubt influenced by the design of numerous imported Phrygian fibulae of contemporary date found in a number of Peloponnesian sanctuaries,[212] but they lack the distinctive palmette-shaped catch-plate of the Phrygian type.[213] Nevertheless, assuming that the fourth-century date of the Lousoi fibulae is correct, a similar date for the Stymphalian example would suit.

244. Bronze, solid cast. Inv. 1276. Surface. Outside NE corner of Bldg A. **Figs. 6.13 and 6.22**
L 4.1; W 2.5; Wt. 12.2
Pin and coil spring are missing, but part of the catchplate and most of the large heavy bow are preserved. The bow, round in section, is decorated by three fluted beads, bound by single reels, in the middle and at the ends. One end of the hinge has a hole through it for insertion of the pin.

Type B: Plain bow (245)

245 differs from other plain bow fibulae in that the lower end of the arched bow curves upward into a large loop, rather than the usual downward curving coil. No apparent parallels are known for this fibula type.

245. Bronze, cast and hammered. Inv. 2834. Tr. 96.3. Surface. Altar. **Figs. 6.13 and 6.22**
L 4.4; Max. W 1.4; Th. 0.1 (pin); Wt. 1.6
Well-preserved, intact simple bow. Narrow arched bow with a large upward-curving spiral terminates in a flattened catch-plate having a partially rolled outer edge. The pointed end of the pin rests on the catch-plate.

Type C: Spectacle fibula (?) (246)

The small, bronze wire spiral disk fragment is included in this section, since it may have once been part of a miniature spectacle fibula. The popular, larger, spectacle fibula type, found in Peloponnesian sanctuaries at Argos, Sparta, Perachora, and Lousoi, seems to have been in use from the eighth to the sixth centuries BCE, although examples from Olynthos are dated c. 500 BCE and possibly even to the fifth century.[214]

246. Bronze fragment, cast. Inv. 1586. Tr. 96.11 L 6 P 7. Temple. **Figs. 6.13 and 6.22**
D 1.5; Th. 0.3; Wt. 1.7
Poor condition. Round spiral disk made of thin, coiled wire; one tiny fragment is broken off. 3¾ coils are preserved. The small size suggests that it is either part of a young girl's spectacle fibula or a miniature votive.[215]

Distribution of fibulae

With the exception of the spiral disk fragment from a possible spectacle fibula, found in the northeast quadrant of the Temple (Tr. 96.11 Level 6), the two other fibulae were surface finds, one near the Altar (Tr. 96.3) and the other outside the northeast corner of Building A.

Appendix I: Suspension wires for pyramidal earrings

Inv. no.	Dimensions D	Find spot
1036	1.7	Tr. 97.2.5+96.15.5
1042	1.3	Tr. 97.2.5+96.15.5
1049	1.6	Tr. 97.2.5+96.15.5
1086	1.93	Tr. 97.4.3
2748	1.8	Tr. 99.6
3304	1.45	Tr. 96.15.4
3306	0.8	Tr. 96.15.5
3318	2.6	Tr. 96.15.4
3464	1.2	Tr. 96.15.5
3465	1.42	Tr. 96.15.5
3584	1.5	Tr. 96.15.5
3585	1.5	Tr. 96.15.4

Many of the pyramidal earring pendants found in the Sanctuary are separated from their suspension wires. These wires are mostly circular in shape, although the lower part is flattened with a V-shaped end, where it was attached by a rivet to the pendant.

Appendix II: Non-finger rings and rings with broken circuits

The following iron and bronze rings are too large, too thick, or too small to be finger rings and were likely used for other functional purposes. It is impossible to determine their original use, although Robinson classified some bronze rings found at Olynthos as handles on vases.[216] At Corinth, plain rings were used on looms to hold down warp threads.[217] Others may have been inserted in the holes of loomweights to attach threads.

Inv. no.	Metal	Dimensions D	Max. Th.	Wt.	Find spot
321	B	0.9	0.2	0.5	Tr. 95.4+1.2.4
572	B	0.9	0.2	0.2	Tr. 96.13.2
610	B	0.94	0.14		Tr. 95.6
650	B	1.5	0.2	0.3	Tr. 96.9.4
746 (missing)	I	1.6			Tr. 95.4+1.2
905	B	1.8	0.2	1.5	surface find
906	B	1.6	0.3	1.1	Tr. 96.14.1
1013	B	2.3	0.3		Tr. 96.11.4
1074	B	2.0	0.2	1.0	Tr. 97.3.2
1148	B	0.93	0.15		Tr. 96.3.3B
1173	B	1.4	0.2	0.6	Tr. 96.3.3B
1199	B	0.9	0.2	0.4	Tr. 97.4.7
1204	B	1.4	0.2		Tr. 97.4.7
1271	B	1.7	0.2	0.7	Tr. 97.5.4
1277	B	2.2	0.3	3.0	Tr. 97.6
1643	B	1.5	0.2	1.0	Tr. 97.4.7
2101	B	2.0	0.5		Surface. Temple
2399	B	1.1	0.2		Tr. 99.8.3
2606	B	1.6	0.2		Tr. 99.1B.2
2932	B	2.0	0.4	3.8	Tr. 00.2.2
2983	I	4.1	1.9		Tr. 00.4.4
3092	B	1.5	0.2		Tr. 96.5.0
3105	B	0.9	0.15		Tr. 00.3.5
3591	B	1.2	0.1		Tr. 96.15.5
3769	B	2.4	0.3		Tr. 96.15

Appendix III: Bronze shafts

Several fragments of slender bronze shafts were found in the Sanctuary, belonging either to clothing pins or parts of needles or bodkins.[218]

Inv. no.	Dimensions L	Max. Th.	Wt.	Find spot
63	7.7	0.3	2.4	Tr. 95.4.4
211	6.25	0.3	1.8	Tr. 96.4.2
238	9.5	0.3		Tr. 96.4.2
416	3.5	0.1		Tr. 95.2.4
428	5.3	0.17	0.5	Tr. 95.4+1.2
434	3.7	0.1		Tr. 95.4+1.2
667	12.9	0.3	4.4	Tr. 95.4+1.2.4
753 (16 small pins)	0.8–1.7	0.2		Tr. 95.4+1.2
1031	6.4	0.25	1.9	Tr. 97.2.5+96.15
1037	4.9	0.3	1.3	Tr. 97.2.5+96.15
1103	16.3	0.3	5.1	Tr. 96.8.6
1191	6.5	0.25	1.0	Tr. 96.3.1
1588	12.75	0.45	8.1	Tr. 96.11.6
2168	6.3	0.6	2.1	Tr. 99.3.3
2847	4.1	0.5	1.8	Tr. 00.1.2

Appendix IV: Jewellery votives from the refuse pit (Tr. 96.15 Levels 5, 6)

Jewellery type	Cat. no.	Inv. no.	Material
Earring Type A.I		3342	bronze
Earring Type B	**34**	3409	bronze
Earring Type C	**36**	3440	bronze
Earring Type E	**59**	3332	bronze
Earring Type E	**60**	3334	bronze
Earring Type E	**61**	3341	bronze
Earring Type E	**62**	3463	bronze
Earring Type E	**63**	3467	bronze
Earring Type E	**64**	3525	bronze
Earring Type E	**65**	3586	bronze
Earring Type E	**66**	3669	bronze
Earring Type E	**67**	3394	amber
Earring Type E	**68**	3583	bronze
Earring Type L.IV	**96**	3617	bronze
Suspension loop (App. I)		3304	bronze
Suspension loop		3306	bronze
Suspension loop		3318	bronze
Suspension loop		3464	bronze
Suspension loop		3465	bronze
Suspension loop		3584	bronze
Suspension loop		3585	bronze
Ring	**110**	3620	silver and gold
Ring	**101**	3581	silver
Ring	**138**	3438	bronze
Ring/earring		3591	bronze
Snake bracelet fragment	**238**	3336	bronze
Bead Type G	**170**	3595	bone

Appendix IV: (*Concluded*)

Jewellery type	Cat. no.	Inv. no.	Material
Bead Type G	**171**	3621	bone
Bead Type G		3331	bone
Bead Type G		3339	bone
Bead Type G		3387	bone
Bead Type G		3398	bone
Bead Type G		3521	bone
Bead Type G		3582	bone
Bead Type G		3594	bone
Bead Type G		3646	bone
Bead Type I	**173**	3461	bronze
Pin Type G	**206**	3520	bronze
Pin Type H	**209**	3436	bronze
Pin Type H	**210**	3622	bronze
Button	**237**	3578	bone

DISCUSSION

This sizeable collection is surprising inasmuch as it comes from a small, unpretentious sanctuary within a modest Arkadian city that was pillaged and destroyed in antiquity. Moreover, the large number of such jewellery votives indicates that jewellery was a very popular dedication, presumably by local women, to the female deity or deities of this Sanctuary, whether Athena, Eileithyia, or another. Also surprising are the number of almost unique pieces, such as the pyramidal earring made of rare amber (**67**), the equally rare lion-head finials for pins (**208–11**), the glass ball pinhead (**191**), the fibula (**245**) with no apparent parallel, the complete, though unravelled, snake armlet (**234**), the bronze ring with separate floral attachments (**138**), and the bronze earring with spiral finial (**37**). The dedicators' tastes appear to be varied and sophisticated, even for those of lower status.

Chronology

Documented contexts for jewellery are not as prevalent as they are for other artifact types, such as pottery and figurines. The most reliable source of comparanda for these finds of jewellery can be found in contemporary burials of the Peloponnese and mainland Greece with controlled contexts. Parallel pieces with no contexts other than the notation "said to be from," so common to museum collections, are also included in the Catalogue for the sake of thoroughness, although their value is regrettably very limited.

The poor preservation of the Sanctuary, in particular the disturbed nature of the stratigraphy, makes it difficult to date the jewellery votives with any precision. For example, Trench 99.1 is a deep trench southeast of the Altar filled with material from the Sanctuary, which because of clean-up operations or natural erosion made its way down the hill slope over top of a small rectangular room.[219] Some cultivation has also been attested in the area through the first half of the twentieth century, contributing to the disturbance. Basically, no single artifact can be dated from the small quantity of identifiable sherds in any given stratum, since the artifact may be an heirloom, as often is the case with pieces of fine jewellery. Likewise, post-destruction looting, as well as plant and animal activity, may have contributed to contamination, particularly of the upper strata. The pottery from all levels within the western part of the Temple (Tr. 95.4+1), where many pieces of jewellery were found, is mostly fourth and third century in date;[220] however, a mould-made Megarian bowl from the first half of the second century BCE, found deep in the mudbrick burn layer (Tr. 95.4+1 L 2), indicates that the fill is mixed. Nevertheless, this bowl does provide a terminus post quem for the destruction of the Temple. In addition, the jewellery discovered in the northeastern part of the cella (Tr. 96.11 Levels 4 and 5) was found in two levels of mixed fill with pottery ranging in date from the fourth to the second centuries BCE.[221] The jewellery found near the Altar (97.3 Level 2) and in trenches south and east of this structure (Tr. 97.4 Levels 2, 4, and 6, Tr. 96.13 Levels 4 and 5) also came from levels with pottery that suggest a Late Classical/Hellenistic date for their use.[222]

A 2003 informal study of the pottery finds from selected trenches in the Sanctuary revealed at least three phases of cultic activity, one phase of collapse and abandonment, and a residual phase.[223] There are very few sealed deposits, but the votive refuse pit, located in Trench 96.15 Levels 5 and 6, was sealed by a layer of closely packed stones and the floor of the West Annex. It has been dated ca. 400–300 BCE. [224] The deposit was placed against the west wall of Building A before the addition of the West Annex, thought to be ca. 300 BCE. Phase 5, which includes the votive material from this refuse pit, is the earliest phase examined in the pottery report from the Sanctuary (the latest phase was numbered Phase 1). A date ca. 300 BCE for the latest pottery in Phase 5 provides a terminus ante quem for the jewellery from the pit, consisting mostly of earrings and beads (see Appendix IV). This material, along with drinking and cooking vessels, miniatures, and terracotta figurines, indicates that cultic activity in the Sanctuary was flourishing at the time.

Small amounts of jewellery were found in levels with ceramic material dating after ca. 300 BCE, designated as Phase 4 of the Sanctuary.[225] These include a lunate earring (**28**), bronze finger ring (**97**), pin with pomegranate finial (**203**), and hair ring (**241**), all found east of the Altar (Tr. 96.4 Levels 5 and 6); three suspension loops for earrings[226] from Trench 96.15 Level 4 in the area west of Building A; and a lunate earring (**19**), three pyramidal earrings (**55–7**), a spiral (**71**) and plain circuit (**87**) earring, a bone tubular bead (**176**), seven suspension loops for earrings, and a bronze ring,[227] all found in the test trench to the south of the same floor (Tr. 97.2+96.15 Level 5). The jewellery votives, along with the pottery, attest to the continuing cultic activity within the Sanctuary, although the jewellery from the area of the West Annex of Building A could indicate another place where the clean-up of votive debris from the Temple was deposited.

Very little jewellery was found in places where Phase 3 to Phase 1 pottery occurred in the Sanctuary. A few pieces were found north and east of the Altar and above the floor in the West Annex of Building A in levels with pottery representing Phase 3 cultic activity, dating after ca. 220–200 BCE.[228] These pieces include a bone disk (**155**) and a bronze pinhead (**185**) found north of the Altar (Tr. 96.3 Levels 3, 4); an iron ring (**123**) and bone disk (**154**) found east of the Altar (Tr. 96.4 Levels 3, 4); a gold ring (**140**) from Trench 97.2 + 96.15 Level 4; and a large pyramidal earring (**52**), a bronze ring (**113**), a bone button (**231**), and a snake bracelet fragment (**236**) from Trench 96.8 Level 5 in the West Annex. Only one object, the glass eye-bead (**161**), was found in a trench (Tr. 95.2 Level 4 Pail 9) in Building A with pottery representing Phase 2, dating after the mid-second-century BCE collapse of the roof of the building.[229] One pyramidal earring (**53**) was found in a trench (Tr. 95.2 Level 1) in Building A, which had ceramic material ranging in date from the Late Classical period to the first century CE, representing Phase 1 of the Sanctuary. The pottery was from a level of disturbed topsoil, suggesting only that there was some residual activity in the Sanctuary at this date.

According to the ceramic evidence from the Sanctuary, as well as similar types of jewellery from graves and sanctuaries in the Peloponnese and mainland Greece, most of the jewellery votives in the Sanctuary should be fourth century BCE in date, with some fifth-century or possibly even earlier examples preceding (**97–8**, **102**, and perhaps some of the pins). As mentioned previously, only a small number of terracotta figurines and vases, some metal objects including iron spits, and the Archaic kore found in the Temple, ca. 490 BCE, can be assigned to the fifth century or earlier.[230] These objects provide little evidence for an earlier, Archaic phase for the Sanctuary. There was a noticeable tapering off of votives during the third and second centuries.

Materials

Only four pieces of gold jewellery (**140, 183, 223, 226**) were found in the Sanctuary, suggesting that the site was thoroughly looted during or after the time it was destroyed, apparently in the mid-second century.[231] The gold rosette (**223**) and gold sheet fragment (**226**) were likely torn from larger pieces such as wreaths, necklaces, or diadems. Likewise only six pieces of silver jewellery were found: a plain silver earring (**88**), a plain silver ring with gold sheet (**141**), a ring bezel (**110**), two medallions with gold overlays (**224–5**), and one bezel with a gold inlay (**115**).

Most jewellery, in the form of earrings and rings, is bronze (approximately 65% of the total collection). Judging from the numerous finds in sanctuaries, tombs, and houses, bronze or copper alloy was the most common material used in making jewellery in the Classical period.[232] Since bronze jewellery shone brightly, almost like gold when new, it was used for everyday wear and purchased by the lower classes, who could afford the less costly but only slightly less impressive imitations. Aristophanes, when mentioning that rings cost as little as three obols[233] or a drachma,[234] is likely referring to bronze rings. Gilding is found on three bronze pieces: a snake armlet (**234**), a lion-head earring (**81**), and a twisted wire hoop earring (**77**).[235] This use of a thin overlay of gold on bronze or silver jewellery began as early as the Bronze Age. The technique appears to have been especially popular during the fourth century.[236] Covering an inferior metal in gold made expensive-looking jewellery affordable to women outside the wealthier classes.

Nearly 14% of the jewellery is made of iron, mostly finger rings with bezels, and pins. This percentage is surprisingly high, since iron corrodes so readily. Approximately 12.5% of the jewellery is carved of bone, a common and inexpensive material used for manufacturing beads and buttons, perhaps in imitation of ivory. About 4% of the collection was of glass, used mostly for beads and ring insets, while the remaining pieces consist of a few stone and clay beads and one earring of amber (**67**), a particularly rare material for jewellery in the fourth century.[237]

There is no evidence in the Sanctuary for the manufacture of jewellery votives, although a large lump of copper or copper alloy,[238] found in Trench 96.13 Level 6, as well as a few slag fragments and a possible piece of a crucible, suggest that at least a small amount of casting took place in or near here. Bronze metal-working is attested at other Peloponnesian sanctuaries, such as those of Zeus at Nemea,[239] during the second half of the fifth century BCE, Poseidon at Isthmia,[240] during the fifth–early fourth centuries BCE, Zeus at Olympia, beginning in the late Geometric period, and Athena Alea at Tegea, also Geometric in date.[241] These reports, however, mention little archaeological evidence for jewellery production, with the exception of some silver ring fragments found at Isthmia.[242] It is believed that itinerant craftsmen worked temporarily at the Panhellenic sanctuaries, for the duration of a festival, and then departed home.[243] At Olynthos, Robinson proposed that the bronze finger rings had been made locally by skilled craftsmen.[244] It is not hard to imagine a similar scenario at Stymphalos, with bronze jewellery produced locally.

On the other hand, some types of bronze jewellery from the Sanctuary could very well have been manufactured at nearby Peloponnesian sites such as Lousoi and Mantinea, since the types are similar to ones found there. For example, the pins with ribbed biconical knobs (**198–200**), pomegranate finials (**203–4**), and lion-head finial (**209**) closely resemble examples found at a sanctuary in Mantinea, while the knob-bow fibula (**244** and mini-shieldlike buttons (**227–32**) are similar to ones found in the sanctuary of Artemis Hemera at Lousoi. For the most part, the jewellery votives from the Sanctuary at Stymphalos are similar in type to those found in other Peloponnesian sanctuaries and sites, such as Corinth, Perachora, Argos, Isthmia, Nemea, Olympia, and Halieis. Some votives, in the form of earrings, ring bezels, and pins (**32–4, 99, 101, 115, 208–11**), also can be compared in type and iconography to jewellery found at the Korykian Cave, near Delphi. It is not surprising since, as the crow flies, this site is about 75 kilometres directly north of Stymphalos across the Corinthian Gulf.

The few surviving pieces of gold from the Sanctuary were likely made at larger, wealthier Greek towns like Athens, where skilled jewellers tended to reside, satisfying the needs of the aristocratic class. Athenian goldsmiths, working in small workshops in semi-residential areas near the Agora and possibly on the Acropolis, also melted down old votives to make new ones.[245] The gold rosette (**223**) resembles those found on necklaces and diadems from Thessaly and Macedonia. A Macedonian goldsmith living in Athens or an Athenian goldsmith trained by a Macedonian one could just as easily have made the piece;[246] however, there appears to be no evidence for any Athenian workshops by the end of the first quarter of the fourth century, if not earlier, and the rosette from Stympahlos is most likely fourth century in date. Dyfri Williams suggests, as a possibility, that the economic downturn at Athens led skilled craftsmen to seek greener pastures in South Russia, South Italy, and Asia Minor, where flourishing workshops are found in the second quarter of the fourth century.[247]

The fragmentary, gilded silver medallion (**225**) depicting Eros embracing Psyche or possibly Aphrodite was also created by a skilled craftsman, familiar with the same artistic styles as are found on contemporary vases and mirrors. Unfortunately, nothing similar to this medallion has been found which might help suggest its place of manufacture, although its superior quality also suggests either a Macedonian or maybe even an East Greek origin. Perhaps this fine-quality jewellery (**223** and **225**) was brought to Stymphalos by returning mercenaries, who had the money to pay for gilded silver and gold objects as gifts for their wives or for their daughters' dowries or wedding gifts.[248] Two other objects from the Sanctuary are obvious imports: the large glass eye-bead (**161**) from Carthage or the Near East, and the Illyrian double-shafted pin (**217**) from northern Greece.[249]

Technique

Bronze earrings, rings, and fibulae were cast in a mould (of metal, stone, clay, or plaster) for the sake of economy and uniformity.[250] For example, solid pyramidal earring pendants were made through the lost wax technique in a mould, like the terracotta mould found on the Pnyx at Athens.[251] The pattern of beaded wire seen on pyramidal earrings **52** and **54** was made by incising lines in the wax and using a semicircular punch to create the bead shapes.[252] The bronze lunate earrings were likely cast in moulds, rather than with punches as were the gold earrings of this type.[253] Several lunates have a visible ridge on either side of their contoured form, being flattened slightly while the bronze was still warm. Moulds were also used for making lion-head earrings.[254] Formers and punches were used for making beads for necklaces. Fibulae and pinheads were mould-made, while the iron shafts of pins, as well as the iron finger rings, would have been forged and hammered.

Engraving, detailed incising, and other decorative techniques, such as beaded (**99**, **111**) and hatched (**100**) borders, gold inlay (**115**), and gilding (**77, 81, 224–5, 234**), were added to the signet rings, earrings, medallions, and bracelet after they were cast or hammered, as with the two gilded silver medallions (**224–5**). Hammered gold sheet was used for the fragment from a possible diadem (**226**) and the rosette (**223**), also made with twisted gold wire.

Six ring bezels show evidence of gold or silver studs, or a hole or deep impression where a stud was once placed: **115** has a gold stud, **102** and **105** have silver studs, **98** has a deep impression, and **103** and **101** have holes. These studs were probably amuletic in function, although the gold stud on **115** could also represent Athena's (?) shield. Apparently rings with gold studs acted as charms to ward off evil.[255]

A few pieces of jewellery have traces of solder to show where two pieces of metal had been joined. The four-sided top fragment of a pyramidal earring (**68**) has traces of silver-coloured solder used to join the suspension loop to the base. A bronze ring (**138**) has a little solder still where the floral decorations were attached.[256]

Bone beads (**149–59, 166–71, 176–7**), a pendant (**179**), pinheads (**207, 211**), and buttons (**227–33**) were hand-carved; no two pieces are exactly alike. It is unclear what type of animal bone was used to carve them (tests for animal identification are destructive and thus impractical). The glass and bronze gems (**216–22**) were made in a mould, while the glass beads (**161–2**) were wound and cut from a rod.

Iconography

Themes depicted on rings and medallions from the Sanctuary are mainly mythological, including deities, heroes, and hybrid and mythical creatures. This is typical for jewellery from other Classical and Hellenistic sites as well. Snakes and lions are popular animal motifs, and floral decoration is also found.

The bezels of bronze and gilded silver rings show varied themes, reflecting the personal tastes of the votaries or the choices of the makers. Impressions have been helpful for interpretation; most of the bronze bezels are very worn; even so, close parallels for many of the motifs have been difficult to find. The iconography includes a variety of mythological themes, as well as scenes, mainly of women, from daily life. The motifs of women, together of course with the size of the rings, suiting women's fingers, support the notion that the dedicators were predominantly female. A few bezels portray mythical or hybrid creatures such as Pegasos (**99**, possibly **112**), a popular choice on Corinthian coins as well, a triton (**97**) from the marine world, and a siren or harpy (**102**). The theme of human-bird hybrids was apparently long-lived at Stymphalos. Pausanias (8.22.7) records that behind the Temple of Artemis were plaster statues of females with bird legs.

Herakles was another popular mythological figure well known to the Stymphalians. This hero par excellence might be seen in the well-muscled figure carrying shield and club on the bronze ring **106.** Herakles' fifth (or sixth) legendary labour was to rid Lake Stymphalos of its nuisance birds. In addition, a Medusa with projecting tongue is portrayed on a gilded silver bezel (**110**), another popular motif on jewellery from the Classical period.

A few of the bezels likely depict deities, although their poor condition makes precise identifications difficult. For example, a small silver bezel with a large gold stud (**115**) portrays a seated and draped female deity, likely Aphrodite, holding a winged Eros, or possibly Athena holding a winged Nike. A similar motif, likely of a seated Aphrodite holding a winged Eros, is engraved on another bronze bezel (**116**), while a kneeling/running Eros is likely the figure depicted on the bronze bezel **111**. Aphrodite might also be the figure portrayed on the gilded silver medallion **225**. Representations of female deities predominate on jewellery, and Aphrodite, the goddess of love, is the most popular.[257] A female figure, likely a goddess, perhaps indeed Eileithyia, is depicted holding an object in each of her hands on the only glass bezel (**136**) found in the Sanctuary.[258] If it is a goddess and not a worshipper performing some cultic ritual, a good comparison exists with a coin of nearby Aigion depicting a female wearing a polos and holding two torches. The figure has been identified as the goddess of childbirth, Eileithyia.

Other engravings on bezels include a standing woman, possibly holding an infant (**100**), and a woman seated on the lap of a male (**101**), as well as women in other poses such as dancing (**105**), standing (**98, 117, 136**), and seated (**107**). One silver ring (**103**) and one bronze one (**118**) have undecorated bezels.

The two gilded silver medallions (**224–5**) also portray mythical figures. **224** depicts a human head, perhaps of a male or female deity, although a gorgon or maenad is also possible. The other medallion (**225**), very fragile and fragmented, portrays a couple embracing; the male figure is most likely Eros, while the female figure represents either Psyche or Aphrodite.

Snakes were popular, found in bracelets (**234–8**), a ring (**137**), pin (**212**), ornamenting rings (**108, 138**), and earrings (e.g., **52, 54, 77–8**). They were favoured both for their long narrow shape and their links to the Underworld. The snake, evoking awe, fear, and fascination, is a creature with a wide range of meanings, many of them chthonic, in antiquity. It is connected not only with the dead, buried in the earth, but also with life and fertility, since seeds germinate in the ground. Its ability to shed its old skin for a new one also made it symbolic of eternal life and renewal.[259] Snakes were believed to be protective spirits for the household. Coiled snake bracelets, armlets, and rings were the perfect shape for encircling an arm or finger.[260] Snakes were probably as common around Stymphalos in antiquity as they are today both on the acropolis and by the lake.

The lion, a fierce symbol of power, was another popular animal found on the earrings (**81–4**) and pins (**208–11**) of women. Williams and Ogden have suggested that powerful creatures such as lions functioned as sympathetic magic for the opposite gender.[261]

Decoration in the form of fruits, nuts, flowers, and buds is also found. Pomegranates, symbols of fertility and an attribute of Aphrodite, decorate the heads of pins (**203–7**). The bronze acorn pendant (**178**) was used to decorate a lunate earring (**26**), while the bone acorn pendant (**179**) likely came from a necklace, since its string hole is discoloured green from the bronze wire that it was once strung with. Acorns, the nuts of the oak tree sacred to Zeus, were a favoured form of pendant. Floral decoration on jewellery includes the gold rosette (**223**) from a diadem or necklace and the bronze ring with rosette engraved on its bezel (**108**). Small four-petal flowers were attached separately on a bronze finger ring (**138**). Three spiral earrings have narrow budlike terminals (**73–5**) and two pinheads are in the form of buds (**201–2**). One very small gold leaf-shaped droplet (**183**) may have also been a pendant for a necklace.

The Jewellery as Votive Offerings

Votive offerings were one of the three primary means, along with prayers and sacrifices, which ancient Greeks used to initiate and continue an intimate relationship with their gods.[262] Plato (*Laws* 909e–910a) notes that dedications of "whatever happens to be on hand at the moment" were made by women for many reasons, such as times of danger or suffering, sickness, or fortuity. Jewellery was one of the few possessions that Greek women would always have "on hand" as a dedication in answer to a vow or a prayer. This jewellery was likely acquired through dowries and wedding gifts.[263] It was customary for Greek women to make dedications at defining moments in their lives: puberty, marriage, and childbirth.[264] Jewellery votives, along with other votive types, were considered to be an expression of gratitude, a "thank-offering" (χαριστήριον), once the prayer to the deity was granted; in short, they expressed relationships of reciprocity between the gods and their worshippers.[265]

The pieces of jewellery from the Sanctuary are best regarded as offerings by votaries to the cult's deities, whether Athena Polias, Eileithyia, or others, such as Aphrodite and Artemis. These include many common items of adornment worn by women during the Late Classical and Hellenistic periods. This sizeable collection of jewellery, along with other votives closely associated with women, such as terracotta figurines of draped females, loomweights, and needles for making clothes, suggests a strong, if not a predominant, involvement by women in activities within the Sanctuary. As Williams and Schaus note, this Sanctuary generally lacks the warlike dedications, aside from the numerous projectile points of dubious votive character and several shield fragments, typically found in other sanctuaries of Athena, such as those in Archaic Ionia.[266] Because Stymphalian men were often absent in their role as mercenaries, women were perhaps left as the main devotees of the cult, as the votives seem to reflect.[267]

Unfortunately, no certain representations of Athena are preserved on any of the jewellery, unless **115** shows Athena, to lend support to the belief that a cult of Athena was indeed located in the acropolis Sanctuary.[268] Apparently a lock of hair could be dedicated to Athena, in appreciation for finding a husband.[269] Girls at the age of puberty also cut and dedicated their hair to Athena at Argos.[270] This rite indicates an intermediary stage between childhood and motherhood. A similar function might be proposed for the hair rings (**239–41**) discovered in the Sanctuary at Stymphalos.

The only other female deity possibly to be identified in the jewellery is Aphrodite, on the ring bezels **115** and **116** and the medallion **225**. It is not uncommon to find representations of one deity, especially in the form of statues and small votive figurines, within the sanctuary of another.[271] Perhaps one of the five aniconic pillars located to the northwest of Building A once represented Aphrodite, although there is no evidence to support this claim, and the ring and medallion with possible depictions of this deity were found southeast and east of the Altar, respectively, rather than near the stelai.[272]

The jewellery provides no inscribed, but one possible visual piece of evidence (**136**) for the worship of Eileithyia, goddess of childbirth, in support of the three artifacts with her name discovered during the recent excavations.[273] As a goddess of this Sanctuary, she is believed by Schaus to have had kourotrophic aspects, as suggested by the fragments of a "temple boy" statue found in the Temple and two terracotta figurines of young naked males.[274] Nevertheless, the great amount of women's jewellery found here and the few examples of hair rings also provide a clear iconographical message that this deity, as well as perhaps others in this Sanctuary, was worshipped as a kourotrophos. One (**236**), if not all, of the snake bracelets may very well have been dedicated to Eileithyia, since it was found near one of the aniconic stelai. Snake bracelets associated with Eileithyia and Artemis were very popular votives at Olympia. Of over 130 found there, nearly 50 were discovered around the altar of Artemis, indicating the importance of the snake in her cult as a helping and healing divinity.[275] In addition, these bracelets from Olympia may have been associated with the birth-cult of Sosipolis, a local infant deity and hero, who saved the Eleans from attacking Arkadians by changing into a snake and frightening them off, and with Eileithyia, his foster-mother and a goddess whom Artemis is closely identified with also at Sparta.[276] Both Eileithyia and Artemis are virgin, kourotrophic goddesses of childbirth: women prayed to Artemis to help them through the trauma of giving birth, whereas Eileithyia was a more hands-on deity, personally assisting women in labour. Thus, the snake bracelets found in the acropolis Sanctuary at Stymphalos might also have been dedicated to Eileithyia with similar motives of gratitude for giving birth safely.

Although considered foremost as a warrior goddess, Athena also has kourotrophic aspects to her nature, supporting the evidence for a predominantly female cult at Stymphalos. Pausanias (5.3.2) reported that pregnant women from Elis, who had formerly been unable to conceive, built a temple to Athena the Mother – an expression somewhat contradictory to her normal nature, considering this deity's perpetually virgin state.[277] However, like Eileithyia in the Sosipolis myth, Athena was also a surrogate mother, in this case, of the autochthonous Athenian king, Erichthonios, conceived by Gaia after Athena was nearly raped by Hephaistos.[278] More evidence for Athena as a kourotrophic deity is found in Euripides' play *Ion*. In this play, Kreousa puts her son Ion in a basket with gold snakes intending to bury him. Euripides (24–6) explains the addition of these serpents as the etiological origin of the Athenian custom of adorning children with golden snakes: it was meant to remind Athenians of Erichthonios, whom Athena placed in a basket with two guardian snakes.[279] Athenian infants may not have worn snake jewellery, but they did wear an amulet cord strung with lunate and circular pendants, seen especially on later fifth-century BCE miniature choes.[280] This amulet cord was believed to act as protection against the dangers associated with the first years of an infant's life, especially sickness and disease. Castor suggests that these cords worn by mortal infants indicate that their Athenian mothers were invoking Athena in her kourotrophic guise to protect their children in the same manner as she protected Erichthonios.[281] Although no pendants of this type were found in the Sanctuary at Stymphalos, dedications of snakelike jewellery would have been equally appropriate for Athena, as a protector of children, as for Eileithyia.

Of interest are the 21 miniature earrings, including lunates and those with triple band decoration (**12, 14, 18, 32–4**), pyramidals[282] (**39, 42, 44, 45, 49, 50, 57, 61, 63**), lion heads (**82–3**), and plain circuits with collars (**93–5**). There is no visual or literary evidence to determine exactly at what age girls had their ears pierced, but very young girls might have worn these small earrings. Most likely ear piercing occurred well before marriage, at least by the early teens.[283] It is possible that young females who survived infancy began by wearing small hoops and suspension loops with pendants, which were then dedicated along with all their other childhood belongings at the time of marriage.[284] Another alternative view is that small pieces of jewellery may have been worn by young brides, who married at thirteen or fourteen years of age.[285] It is also possible that these small earrings were dedicated as a thank-offering by mothers for the safe birth of their daughters or their recovery from sickness. As mentioned above, Athena's kourotrophic aspects are also found in Athens in the myth of Erichthonios, but evidence now for Eileithyia also provides an object for these miniature votives.

On the other hand, these miniature earrings may not have been real jewellery, but *simulacra*, tiny models of the real thing, such as the miniature fibulae found in sanctuaries at Glanitza, Lousoi, Argos, and Tegea.[286] Thus the miniature bronze earrings could have been made near the Sanctuary expressly for dedication to the deity, rather than being worn for personal adornment first before being offered as votives.[287] Indeed, one of a tiny pair of earrings (**32**) has a preserved hoop with no visible signs of wear, even today. In addition, the tiny wire spiral (**246**), possibly once part of a spectacle fibula, can be included here as a possible miniature votive. Other miniature votives found in the Sanctuary include a bronze figure of a bull and dozens of clay vessels, especially kotylai.

Some jewellery pieces found in the Sanctuary seem to have been dedicated by male votaries. These include eight iron rings with bezels (**120–2, 125–6, 128, 133, 135**), one bronze ring with plain bezel (**118**), and possibly the silver and gold ring engraved with the adjective ΚΑΛΟΣ (**115**). The iron and bronze rings are quite large, with outer diameters of their hoops ranging from 2.2 to 2.9 cm. Nonetheless, because rings were sometimes worn on the thumb or index finger or on the second or third joint of a finger, it is difficult to determine either whether a small ring had been worn by a woman or child or a large ring by a man.[288] Spartan males wore iron rings (Pliny *HN* 23.9) and men wore finger rings in the Classical period, judging from dedications found in the inventory lists on the Athenian acropolis.[289]

Of significance is the silver ring with the word ΚΑΛΟΣ inscribed along the outer edge of its bezel (**115**), the only piece with writing in the collection. The adjective *kalos*, meaning "handsome" or "beautiful," recalls the practice of praising a youth or male of any age, quite often named, and written on Attic pottery during the late sixth and fifth centuries BCE.[290] The only other ring bezel known to me with a *kalos* inscription depicts a standing nude male youth, likely an ephebe.[291] In this example the inscription describes the youth in the scene. The inscription on the Stymphalian bezel may very well refer to the depiction of the small winged figure held in the goddess's hand, if this figure does indeed portray Eros.[292] Although the ring bezel is small and feminine in appearance, one cannot rule out the possibility that a male votary dedicated it.

The numerous bronze earrings and rings from the Sanctuary indicate that they were a type of votive offering readily available for dedication by Stymphalian women of less conspicuous means. It is ironic that we know more about the jewellery votives and tastes of less privileged women simply because the votives, not being made of precious materials, were passed over during periodic clean-up of the Sanctuary or looting at the time of final destruction in antiquity. The few jewellery items of gold suggest only that there were wealthier female votaries who worshipped here alongside their less advantaged counterparts.

Placement of Jewellery Votives

The placement of the jewellery votives within the Sanctuary at Stymphalos is worth considering, although, as previously noted, the Sanctuary was destroyed and no doubt looted in antiquity. Unlooted temples are rare, although a recently discovered Archaic temple on Kythnos, dedicated possibly either to Hera or Aphrodite, had an unplundered adyton filled with approximately 1500 gold, silver, bronze, and iron artifacts, terracotta figurines, and painted vases. Final publication of this discovery will be unusually valuable, since the artifacts were in their original place of display.[293] The distribution of jewellery votives within the Sanctuary at Stymphalos, however, allows for general comments about where these offerings once were displayed or stored. Generally, votives were meant to be visible not only to worshippers and visitors in the sanctuary but also to the deity to whom the dedications were made.[294] Jewellery would have been among the showpieces (αγάλματα) of a sanctuary. These showpieces were often also found in the form of an ornament for the place of worship, an image or a tiny bronze vase.[295]

At Stymphalos, heavy concentrations of jewellery, such as pyramidal and lion-head earrings and bronze and iron finger rings, were found in the northwestern end of the cella, including near the off-centre square base perhaps for a cult statue (Tr. 95.4), located in the northwest quadrant. It seems obvious that these votives were placed there to be nearest to the focal point of the Temple, as well as to be seen by other worshippers. These dedications likely would have been placed on a table[296] or a bench, of which no remains are preserved, or possibly on the square base set in the Temple floor.

Some of the more precious jewellery might have adorned statues. For instance, the gold rosette (**223**), likely torn from a wreath or a diadem, was found towards the back of the Temple, close to an aniconic pillar, and only three metres from the main concentration of marble kore fragments. Although it is possible that the Stymphalian cult statue was aniconic rather than anthropomorphic in form,[297] this need not prevent it from having been adorned with jewellery, like the olivewood statue of Athena Polias in the Erechtheion on the acropolis at Athens, which according to ancient sources was very old.[298] This cult statue's stance and appearance are still highly debatable.[299] Aside from its being clothed in the Panathenaic peplos, Athenian inventory inscriptions describe the wide array of gold jewellery that once adorned this statue in the fourth century BCE: a diadem, earrings, neckband together with five necklaces, and a bracelet.[300] Whether the custom of adorning the cult statue of Athena Polias with jewellery was copied at other sanctuaries is unknown. Alternatively, jewellery may have adorned the kore found within the Temple, as at least one hole on a chest fragment of the statue suggests. Indeed, the kore may have served as the cult statue.

In addition, the presence of large, carved bone buttons in the Temple, found near the statue base for the possible cult statue (Tr. 95.4) and in the West Annex of Building A (Tr. 96.8), where weaving apparently was done in the Stymphalian Sanctuary,[301] might provide evidence for the possible dedication of a robe for the kore, if it indeed did serve as the cult statue. The annual custom of making a new peplos for the cult statue of Athena Polias, by a group of select young aristocratic Athenian women, played an important part in her cult.[302] Athena was not only their patron deity, she was also goddess of weaving. Thus, it is reasonable to suggest that the women involved in this small sanctuary at Stymphalos wove a robe for their cult statue as well.

A much smaller concentration of jewellery was found in the Temple pronaos (Tr. 96.11), especially in the northern half of the room. This jewellery includes earrings, beads, pins, buttons, a finger ring, and a fibula. Since the Temple is situated on sloping ground, with heavy rain and other disturbances, the jewellery might have shifted over time to places east or southeast of the cella. On the other hand it could also have been placed on a table or bench beside the north wall of the pronaos for display purposes.[303] Two bronze earrings (**35, 85**) and an iron pin (**192**) were discovered near or in the grave of a young girl in the pronaos, presumed to date between the fourth and sixth centuries CE, although the jewellery resembles types of Late Classical date. Most likely, the jewellery was discovered while the grave was being dug and was reburied along with the body. The few other pieces of jewellery in the Temple were discovered along the south wall. Some may have been displayed on an interior wall, hung on a peg or nail in the mudbrick walls.[304]

Surprisingly, only five jewellery votives, consisting of a ring (**108**), pin (**185**), bead (**155**), lunate earring (Inv. 912, not catalogued), and fibula (**245**), were found in Trench 96.3, containing the remains of the Altar, located east of the Temple. The fibula (**245**) of uncertain type and date was found on the surface. Altars were a common place to display votives; however, the sloping terrain of the acropolis Sanctuary likely assisted in shifting votives away from the Altar's immediate vicinity towards the south and east where more jewellery in fact appeared in a number of trenches (96.4, 97.4, 97.5 baulk, 96.13, 99.9, 97.3). Archaeological evidence for the placement of votives on altars is attested at the sanctuary of Artemis Orthia at Sparta, where the burnt debris of thousands of lead figurines was found on the east side of the "Greek Altar," dating from the end of the eighth century BCE to the end of the fourth century BCE.[305] In addition, much jewellery was found around the altar of Artemis at Olympia southeast of the Temple of Zeus.[306] Many rings in the large collection excavated from the sanctuary of Pan and the Nymphs at the Korykian cave, near Delphi, were found outside the mouth of the cave, also surrounding the altar.[307]

Of note is the sealed deposit of discarded votives found in the 2000 season of excavation outside the west wall of Building A, between this structure and the Temple, in Trench 96.15 Levels 5 and 6. Forty-one pieces of jewellery were found along with votive cups and fragments of terracotta figurines.[308] The votives were likely placed there at the end of the fourth century BCE, since no ribbed kantharos bowls of third-century date were found. Several types of jewellery were found in this deposit: silver and gilded silver rings (**103**, **110**), bronze lion-head pins (**209–10**), bronze pyramidal earrings (**59–68**), and bone beads (**170–1**).[309] Rarer finds include the amber pyramidal earring fragment (**67**), snake bracelet fragment (**238**), and ring with floral attachments (**138**).

This deposit represents a refuse pile, filled with broken pottery, figurines, and other objects brought together in a periodic clean-up of the Sanctuary. The items apparently represent a random selection from those left as gifts to the goddess, eventually brushed aside, walked on, or dropped, though some may have been stored together by type, e.g., pyramidal earrings, or material, e.g., bone beads, and thrown out at the same time. Nearly half the preserved finds from the dump are earrings, suggesting that they had been stored together in one place, likely the Temple, since rooms within Building A yielded very few remains of jewellery votives. Approximately 20 more pieces of jewellery, mostly earrings, were also found in the immediate vicinity above the stones sealing the deposit, as well as in nearby Trench 97.2. Perhaps these votives were part of another, slightly later clean-up of the Sanctuary, prior to building the West Annex, which were thrown out in a place already known to have contained votives no longer stored or on display. Gold and silver objects in the deposit are surprising, but in the sweeping of the Sanctuary grounds, they may simply have been overlooked in the piles of dirt.

Only one pin (**190**) was found in Trench 99.5, one of three trenches containing the five aniconic pillars, located to the north of the Temple and west of Building A, but 13 pieces of jewellery were excavated from Trench 96.8 immediately south of these pillars. This jewellery includes lunate (**30**), pyramidal (**52**), spiral (**73**), and silver (**88**) earrings, bronze (**113**) and iron (**129**) rings, bone beads (**157, 169**) and buttons (**231, 233**), and a snake bracelet fragment (**236**).[310] The location of these votives suggests that they were dedicated to a divinity represented by one of the pillars, most likely a female one.[311] They might have been placed on one of the large flat fieldstones situated in front of four of these pillars and serving as offering tables.[312]

Eleven jewellery votives, including rings, earrings, and pins, were also discovered in fill above a small rectangular room (Tr. 99.1) located southeast of the Altar (Building B).[313] Whether this room was also used as a storage facility for votives is uncertain, since the number is not large enough to make a persuasive case. These objects may simply have made their way down the sloping ground of the Sanctuary to their place of discovery.

The collection of jewellery votives from the small Sanctuary on the acropolis at Stymphalos is significant for its size (around 325 pieces) and variety of types. The site is remote even for travellers today; however, women there adorned themselves and made dedications of jewellery common enough in current fashion, such as the lunate and pyramidal earrings in the earlier part of the fourth century BCE and the lion-head earrings of the later fourth/beginning of the third centuries BCE. On the other hand, the discoveries of pins presumably from the Late Classical period may indicate a conservative trend in clothing with the Doric peplos still being worn by some of the local women. The finds of buttons, on the other hand, show that the later method of fastening clothes, either chitons or peploi, was also used.

Although most of the gold jewellery was likely looted in antiquity when the Sanctuary was destroyed, the pieces made of bronze and iron that were overlooked provide important additions to the corpus of Late Classical jewellery made of these materials from graves and other sanctuaries in the Peloponnese and mainland Greece. The sheer number of jewellery items found in some sanctuaries attests to their popularity as votive offerings. For example, nearly 800 Archaic pins were dedicated to Hera at Argos,[314] more than 800 bronze and iron finger rings were found in the sanctuary of Pan and the Nymphs in the Korykian cave near Delphi,[315] over 1200 pieces of jewellery (Geometric to Roman Periods), many of them fibulae, were discovered in the sanctuary of Athena Itonia, Philia, Thessaly,[316] and almost 1800 fibulae and pins were found in the Archaic sanctuary of Artemis Enodia at Pherai, Thessaly.[317] The rich collections from these sanctuaries are among the most important for studying jewellery types. Each example represented an offering thought to be particularly agreeable to the tutelary divinities of these sanctuaries.

Excavations from the sanctuary of Zeus at Olympia also uncovered large numbers of bronze jewellery, over 1300 pieces in total, ranging in date from Sub-Mycenaean to Roman. There are fewer finds of some types of Classical period jewellery from this much-visited, large Panhellenic sanctuary than from the much smaller, remote acropolis Sanctuary at Stymphalos: only 86 earrings from Olympia are Archaic to Classical in date,[318] compared to 94 bronze earrings discovered at Stymphalos. In addition, only 34 finger rings were discovered at Olympia from the fifth/fourth century BCE,[319] in comparison to the 54 finger rings found at Stymphalos. On the other hand, the dedications of snake bracelets from the altar of Artemis in the southeast part of the sanctuary at Olympia are much more numerous (114), likely because of the healing nature of this cult and its connection to the snakelike boy hero Sosipolis and to Eileithyia.

As for the two other Panhellenic sanctuaries in the Peloponnese, about 120 pieces of jewellery have been published from the sanctuary at Poseidon at Isthmia, ranging in date from the Protogeometric to the Byzantine periods, of which only 20 pieces are from the Classical/Hellenistic periods.[320] Finds of Classical period jewellery from the sanctuary of Zeus at Nemea are mentioned sporadically in the excavation reports and appear to be few in number.[321]

Closer to Stymphalos, the sanctuary of Artemis at Lousoi also has various types of Archaic and Classical jewellery votives, such as fibulae, earrings, and pins, although much remains to be published, it seems, so it is difficult to know exactly how much jewellery was found.[322] Likewise jewellery was discovered at the sanctuary of Demeter and Kore at Corinth, but only the unpublished pins in Kilian-Dirlmeier's study can be used for comparative purposes.[323] Since Corinth was destroyed about the same time as Stymphalos, in the mid-second century BCE, there are actually very few finds of Classical and Hellenistic period jewellery from the main excavations of the town site.[324]

Thus the numerous finds of jewellery from the acropolis Sanctuary at Stymphalos are a significant addition to the corpus of jewellery from Peloponnesian sanctuaries and sites. It may be partly explainable by the practice of Stymphalian men hiring themselves as mercenaries, for more jewellery votives from the Classical period were found at Stymphalos than at other larger and more prestigious sanctuaries. The absence of men, who left to serve as mercenaries or find other work, left local women in greater control of this cult, but when the men returned home, they likely brought with them some of the finer jewellery votives that were found in this Sanctuary. Indeed, there is a wide variety of jewellery types, partly because these pieces were overlooked during looting of the Sanctuary and partly because of accidents of preservation.

7

Miscellaneous Small Finds

Gerald P. Schaus

A great variety of objects are catalogued here by material and use. Some are easily recognized from similar objects at other sites; others are not. Since iron objects are generally well preserved at the site, some objects are described, and an illustration provided, even though they cannot be identified, nor for the moment their use determined with any probability. It is hoped that all may be better understood in the future. This especially applies to many of the objects classified as "utilitarian," and to those listed under "Varia" at the end of the catalogue.

In the normal detritus of a sanctuary site, there are objects of a ritual nature, used in cult practice. There are also gifts left behind as votives to honour the deity or deities worshipped in the sanctuary, and there are artifacts of purely practical use, connected with the architecture of the site or common daily needs of people at the sanctuary. They have nothing in common other than that they were found within the confines of the sanctuary or its immediate vicinity. In general these last have little to add to the larger questions of the sanctuary's history, cult practices, and community interactions. They are, however, important as a whole, since they fill gaps in our overall knowledge of the site and its visitors, contacts with outside areas, local craft accomplishment, levels of wealth, and aspects of both cult practice and daily life.

CATALOGUE

D	diameter
Est.	estimated
H	height
Inv.	inventory number
L	length
Max.	maximum
Min.	minimum
MPD	maximum preserved dimension
MPL	maximum preserved length
MPW	maximum preserved width
P	preserved
Th.	thickness
Tr.	Trench year.trench number.level number.pail number
W	width
Wt.	weight

All measurements are in centimetres, except weights, which are in grams.

Marble (?) alabastron

Alabastra receive their name from the material they were made of in Egypt, that is, alabaster, a finely textured, compact form of gypsum, in part stalagmite and in part travertine, which is translucent and may have shades of yellow, pink, brown, and grey in narrow bands. The alabastron shape, however, can be found much earlier in faience, at least by the time of the Eighteenth Dynasty. Such vases of alabaster normally have very thin walls, allowing more light through. They were made first in Egypt and commonly used as funerary offerings to hold ointments and perfumes. Alabastra made of glass were found at Assur and Nimrud in Assyria in seventh-century contexts.[1] Probably through the port of Naukratis, finished vases, and soon also perhaps the raw alabaster, were sent to Greece, where alabastra became popular as grave gifts and votives in sanctuaries, and were imitated by vase makers in clay, as well as by glass makers.[2] The colour of the alabastron from Stymphalos (lack of any pink, yellow, or brown shade, and the coarse grey grain), relative lack of translucence, thickness of the wall, and unusual vertical rather than horizontal grain suggest either a cheap form of alabaster or, more likely, an imitation in marble.[3]

1. Large thick-walled alabastron with small lug handles below the neck, missing mouth/rim, neck, and wall fragments including most of its bottom. Reconstructed from 31 pieces. Coarse grey and white marble (?). The grain runs vertically rather than horizontally. Some lime encrustation. **Figs. 7.1 and 7.18**
Inv. 867, 869, 1931, 1932. Tr. 95.1.8.13. Temple.
PL 19.8; D neck 2.9; Max. D wall 6.7; Max. Th. wall 1.6. Handles are located 4.3 cm below the base of the neck and rise 0.45 above the wall surface.
The alabastron shape tends to become taller and slimmer over time with narrower distinct neck. Compare Jacopi 1932, 65 fig. 66 (top centre) from the late seventh century with p. 170 fig. 202 (bottom left and right) from the fourth (?) century. For two very elongated alabaster alabastra, see Jacopi 1931, 391 fig. 448 (stray finds). A virtually complete one is in the Nemea museum with separate piece for the neck/mouth. Four alabaster alabastra were found at Perachora, judged to be fifth century on the basis of their slimmer shape, Dunbabin 1962, 517 (brief comments on manufacture) nos. E1–E4; and one from Corinth with vertical grain like the Stymphalos example, Davidson 1952, 61 no. 832. Another group came from the acropolis at Lindos, Blinkenberg 1931, 672 nos. 2860–2. At least 40 alabaster alabastra came from the Demeter Sanctuary at Cyrene, ranging in size from as small as 10 cm in length (see Warden 1990, 55–6 nos. 403–13 fig. 8 pl. 41); 10 more were published from Delos, all with the grain going horizontally, Zapheiropoulou 1973, 614 figs. 18–19.

The shape of the Stymphalos vase is rather tall and slim, but without the rim or the full length preserved, a comparison cannot be made with others in the table of proportions worked out for the Metapontum alabastra, Carter and Toxey 1998, 759–60. Its date is probably fourth century, if not a little earlier. At Metapontum, a new type (Type B) is introduced in the late fourth century.

Marble pyxides

Fine delicate vases made of marble must have been expensive to make and much admired, serving as models for similar vessels in clay and glass.[4] Although the shape of the lidded container found at Stymphalos is commonly referred to as a "pyxis," by the Roman period the Attic name was likely "kylichnis," and outside Attika it may have been "libanotis" from its use as a container for incense.[5] Besides incense and physicians' medicines, it was commonly used by women to hold jewellery and cosmetics. Inventory lists mention kylichnides made of various other materials besides marble, including bronze, ivory, silver, and wood.[6]

Weinberg makes a good argument for the manufacture of marble pyxides of the same type as **2** in Crete, along the southern coast of the west part of the island, based on finds of marble pyxides, as well as copies of the type done locally in glass.[7] The glass copies, she suggests, were produced between the third and first centuries BCE.[8] Although apparently aware of Weinberg's argument for the manufacture of marble pyxides on Crete, Coldstream published an unusual number of similar objects from the Demeter Sanctuary at Knossos as being of alabaster.[9] The material is described as white and translucent with fine crystals, which may apply equally to marble as to alabaster. Two of the Stymphalos lids (**3–4**) have small diameters and probably come from smaller pyxides like **2**. The more carefully finished lid (**5**) has a larger diameter, and a group of fine ridges near its outer edge. It may have fitted over a wider, lower pyxis, like one from Delos.[10]

2. Pyxis. Thin disk base with a shallow ridge on the upper surface between the outer edge of the base and the pyxis wall, thin vertical wall with shallow ridge on the exterior near the lip. Broken into about 20 pieces, restored, some pieces missing, others too small to replace. **Figs. 7.1 and 7.18**
Inv. 3758. Tr. 96.8.3.3. West Annex
H 2.6; D base 8.85; Th. of base at ridge 0.45; D wall 6.6; Th. wall at ridge 0.4
For five examples, some with traces of colour when found, from a tomb in Herakleion with similar flat, spreading base, vertical walls, and a ridge near the lip, see *ArchDelt* 24 (1969) B2 *Chron.*, 419–20 pl. 428. This tomb was dated to the end of the second century BCE on the basis of its pottery. Others in the National Museum, Athens and one from Naxos are published in Zapheiropoulou 1973, 628–9 figs. 36–8, while Weinberg 1959, 20 figs. 24–6 has two in Boston and one in Brussels. For a profile drawing of another in Berlin, said to be of alabaster, *AA* (1940) col. 628 fig. 10. Four more are in the Metropolitan Museum, New York, of which two are on tall stems and two with concave walls sit on low feet (inv. 1978.11.14a,b.–17a,b.). These are dated to the late fifth–early fourth century BCE.

3. Pyxis base fragment. Similar to **2** with a shallow ridge on the upper surface between the outer edge of the base and the pyxis wall. Broken at the start of the thin vertical wall. **Figs. 7.1 and 7.18**
Inv. 2405. Tr. 99.1.5.7. E of Terrace Wall
MPD 3.35; Th. at ridge 0.8
The ridge on the upper surface is closer to the pyxis wall than on **2**.

4. Pyxis lid rim fragment. Narrow ridge near the rim and deeper, wider ridge near the centre of the upper side, wide raised ridge to hold the lid in place on the under side. Broken, about one-sixth preserved. **Figs. 7.1 and 7.18**
Inv. 2498. Tr. 99.1.5.8. E of Terrace Wall
D rim est. 11.0; MPD 5.5; Th. at under side ridge 0.7
A pyxis lid in Boston is close in its placement of two ridges on the top surface, but they are larger in size, Caskey 1939, 80 fig. 13. Of the five pyxides from the tomb in Herakleion (above **2**), four have lids representing three different basic shapes (a. shallow conical, b. shallow conical with a horizontal spreading lip, and c. stepped with large ridges). This suggests more variation in the lids than in the pyxides themselves. The four pyxides in the Metropolitan Museum all have different lids (above **2**). **4** may belong to the shallow conical type, but the pattern of ridges is different. For alabaster (?) pyxides with similar lids from fifth-century contexts at Makri Langoni on Rhodes, see Jacopi 1931, 107 fig. 96 tomb 27, and 137–8 tomb 47 fig. 132.

5. Pyxis (?) lid rim fragment. Raised upper rim, short vertical lower rim, one ridge preserved on the under side wall. The upper side has six joining ridges (5 thin low ones + 1) decorating a slightly concave surface before it rises to a convex curve that bends down towards the centre. **Figs. 7.1 and 7.18**
Inv. 2717. Tr. 99.1.5.8. E of Terrace Wall
MPD 5.1; Th. double rim 0.8; Th. inner ridge 0.8
The shape is very unusual for a pyxis lid, with its concave-convex wall, upper and lower rims, and group of six low ridges near the rim. For a somewhat similar treatment of the rim, see the two "saucers" from Knossos, Coldstream 1973, 165 nos. 272–3 fig. 42.

6. Cylindrical (?) knob broken at its bottom, with a deep wide hole and two shallow channels.
Inv. 886. Surface cleaning, southeast of the Temple (SF 1997.2)
D 3.6; Th. 2.2
Compare the knobs on pyxis lids of the two pyxides with low feet in the Metropolitan Museum (above **2**).

Glass

Very little glass was found in the Sanctuary. Most examples were small fragments from the bodies of thin-walled vessels, totalling less than 50 in number. There were also a half-dozen ring bezels of glass, one of which was carved, several glass beads, and a small globe with wire perhaps from an earring. (See Young, chapter 6, pp. 119, 122, 126–7, 130.) The most interesting piece is a slightly curved, thin glass "eye" with wide circular shape, pronounced tear duct, and sharp corner angle, which appears to be stylistically early. It does not suit as an inlaid eye for a marble or bronze sculpture of the human form, since the shape is too circular and the tear duct is too pronounced, but it is closer to the shape of animal eyes, especially horses (see below).[11] Otherwise, it may be an inlay for a piece of jewellery, although parallels are difficult to find.

Only a very small number of rim and base fragments from glass vessels are catalogued here to provide at least a notion of the material in the Sanctuary. Two fragments of badly melted glass were also found. The core-wound fragments (**7–8**) are the only vessels which certainly belong to the period of use of the Sanctuary. Four vessels of blown glass (**9**, **11**, **14**), including the one-third complete plate (**10**), were found inside the Temple, and a fifth (**12**) was found just outside it. Two other small fragments (**15**) were also found inside the Temple; they had melted, possibly from the same fire as produced the ash around the plate. These may be Medieval in date, and are unexpected, since little other Medieval material has been identified from the Sanctuary, except for a twelfth-century coin of Manuel I (Weir, chapter 4 above, **II-97**). The plate was covered in black ashy earth, and since it is quite complete despite its very thin, fragile walls, it must have been broken and lost in a fire that took place inside the Temple, presumably by much later, casual visitors, well after the destruction of the Sanctuary.

Remarkably little glass was found at Corinth in the Greek period.[12] In the Roman, there are large amounts from the first and second centuries, during the provincial capital's most prosperous times.[13] It was in the Medieval period (eleventh and twelfth centuries) that Corinth became especially rich in glass, with the establishment of two glass-making factories there, but both went out of production at the time of the Norman conquest of Corinth.[14]

7. Alabastron (?), straight-sided wall fragment, core made. Dark blue opaque glass, with white threads (8 preserved) combed to create a festoon pattern. **Fig. 7.1**

Inv. 4633. Surface find (July 2003)
PH 4.1; PW 3.0; Th. 0.4
7 and **8** are the only inventoried examples of core-wound glass from the site. Comb strokes may go in either direction on similar vessels, so its upside is unclear. A good selection of such vessels is illustrated in colour in Kunina 1997, 247–53 nos. 1–38 colour pls. 1–19. For a similar vessel, though with combing alternatively up and down, see Bergman and Oliver 1980, 40 no. 10 from the late fourth century, and later alabastra with comb strokes upward only, Hayes 1975, 13 no. 28 pl. 2 (with refs.) dated second–first century BCE; Nenna, 1999, 28 no. 21 pls. 1 and 60 (in colour) – late second to early first century BCE; Hellenistic examples from Knossos are in Price 1992, 417, 438 nos. 1–8 pl. 336. For a good discussion of the type, see Grose 1989, 109–31 and 95–108 (colour plates). Similar decoration continues as late as the fourth century CE, Whitehouse 2001, 216–17 no. 785.

8. Wall fragment, core made. Dark blue glass, two yellow horizontal threads. Surface badly preserved. **Fig. 7.1**
Inv. 4571. Surface find
MPD 1.9; Th. 0.4

9. Small bowl, rim, three joining fragments. Colourless glass with translucent deep violet band along the rim; some patches of light violet have seeped into the colourless glass of the wall. Many small bubbles. Plain out-turned lip, steep-sided wall. The line of the lip is irregularly finished. **Fig. 7.1**
Inv. 4574. Tr. 95.4+1.2.3. Temple
MPD 6.85; D rim est. 12.0; Th. wall 0.1
The lip is turned out almost to 90°, and is too broad to allow for drinking, so this is more likely a dish than a drinking cup. The shape is similar to Nenna 1999, 47 no. B79 pl. 3 ("coupe" – made in mosaic glass) and 77 no. C106 pl. 15 ("bol conique à lèvre évasée" – colourless). The violet colour here is likely produced from manganese, with a thread of violet glass being marvered into the rim surface. Whitehouse (2001, 137–8) discusses objects decorated with marvered trails, noting that the technique is found in only two periods, the first century CE (ending in the third quarter of the century), where it is found on ribbed bowls (Isings form 17) and toilet bottles, and the fourth century and later, where it occurs on a wider variety of shapes. Examples in the Corning Museum that continue to the sixth century CE are illustrated in Whitehouse 2001, 211–17, nos. 776–85, mostly with opaque white and red trails, none of which are close to **9**. Since the shape of the Stymphalos piece is different from ones dated to the first century CE, according to Whitehouse, it seems that it must belong later, perhaps much later, in the Medieval period. At Corinth in the eleventh or twelfth century, a thread of blue glass is added to the rim of ribbed beakers and mould-blown cups; see Weinberg 1975, 137–40 figs. 22, 26. The use of added blue threads, at the rim and elsewhere, continued through the late fourteenth century in southern France, Foy 1989, 210, 229–31 figs. 81, 83. The Stymphalos piece uses violet rather than blue, and again it is marvered into the surface.
Medieval?

10. Shallow dish or plate with low out-turned wall, no offset lip, but the edge of the rim has shallow scallops. Flat bottom, no base. Transparent almost colourless glass. Eighteen fragments, many joining to give three larger pieces, complete profile. **Figs. 7.10 and 7.18**
Inv. 758. Tr. 95.4+1.2 Pails 2 and 4 Temple
MPD a) 10.4 b) 11.2 c) 7.9; D rim est. 17.0; H 1.1;
Th. wall/floor 0.06
Much black ashy soil adheres to the surface from burning. Oxidized glass film.
A similar plate with vertical rim from medieval Corinth (eleventh–twelfth century?) has its rim folded inward at intervals. I know of no parallels from the Roman period where the same is done. Davidson 1952, 110 no. 707 pl. 57.

(Fragments of **10** were found in Pails 2 and 4. Pail 4 material included the bronze patera **18** and vase base **21** found in the midst of intense burnt material in the NW corner of the Temple. It seems likely that these glass fragments were not properly distinguished in a later pit (Pails 2 and 3) from the Pail 4 material with burning. The same applies to **11**, which was found close to **10** in Pail 4 material.)
Medieval?

11. Dish or plate rim fragment. Blown, small bubbles. Everted rim, low wall tapering in to the floor, no base. The floor rises towards the centre. Colourless glass with greenish tint. **Fig. 7.1**
Inv. 788. Tr. 95.4+1.2.4. Temple
MPD 4.9; D rim est. 12.0; Th. wall 0.1
From a small deposit of twelve glass fragments inside the Temple, some of which belonged to **11**. At least two and more likely three vessels are represented in the deposit.

12. Dish rim fragment. Shallow with lipless rim. Colourless glass with violet tint. **Fig. 7.1**
Inv. 4634. Tr. 95.5.1.1. S of Temple
MPD 2.2; Th. 0.16

13. Cup base fragment. Blown. Low tubular base and the start of a sharply out-turned wall. Colourless glass with greenish tint. **Fig. 7.1**
Inv. 4572. Tr. 99.1.2.2. E of Terrace Wall
MPD 3.75; D base est. 13.0; Th. base 0.5
For the shape, cf. Price 1992, 430 no. 201 pl. 345. The tubular ring is common in the Early Roman imperial

period, see Rütti 1991, pls. 178–80; Nenna 1999, 117 nos. D18–19 pl. 35 for example. Similar cups with tubular bases are dated ca. 50–150 CE. A second hollow ring base fragment was found in Tr. 95.1.2.4, a little smaller in size. The tubular ring base, however, is not confined to the Roman period; it is common enough in material from the eleventh- and twelfth-century glass factories at Corinth; see Davidson 1952, figs. 12, 17.
Roman or later

14. Very thin-walled miniature vase with narrow collar at one end (neck?). Steep-sided wall. Transparent, pale blue. **Fig. 7.2**
Inv. 766. Tr. 95.1 wall cleaning. Temple
MPD 2.3; D rim est. 0.9; Th. wall 0.03
The size suggests a type of toilet bottle, though one expects the rim to turn outward with a suitable lip; compare Davidson 1952, 82, 104–5 fig. 11.

15. Two wall fragments, perhaps one with rim. Misshapen from a fire. Translucent, white, greenish tint. **Fig. 7.2**
Not inventoried. a) Tr. 95.1.2.4, b) Tr. 95.4+1.2.2. Temple
MPD a) 3.1 b) 3.3
Both pieces have been subjected to intense heat. There is evidence to suggest two occasions for fire inside the Temple. The earlier included burnt rafters and severe burning of some sculpture fragments. The later was more confined to a pit or pits, like a camp or cooking fire, and included black ashy material around some of the glass.

16. Object in the shape of an eye with tear duct and corner angle, thin, cut (?) glass, transparent, very pale green, with many small bubbles. If an eye, it is close to life-size. **Fig. 7.2**
Inv. 44. Tr. 95.1.7.12. Temple
L 2.5; W 1.5; Th. 0.2
Most likely an inlay, but it is unclear to what. The shape has an Archaic appearance, similar to eyes on Attic eye cups, with a circular shape, and pronounced tear duct, though not the same exaggerated outside corner. Eyes on Archaic human sculpture are more almond shaped, and although some inlaid eyes in sculpture are about as thin as this, the shape precludes it from fitting the Archaic kore from the Temple. For a thin inlaid eye in a kore, Sturgeon 2006, 57 fig. 19 (Acropolis 682). On the other hand, if this is indeed an eye, the shape would suit a horse, or perhaps a Gorgon, much better than a human. Compare inlaid eyes of horses in Delphi, *JdI* 108 (1993) 425 fig. 13, and Athens, Brouskari 1974, 52 (Acropolis 1340) fig. 92, and for an inlaid eye at Olympia identified as from an animal, Bol 1978, 135 no. 424 pl. 70. For a suspected association of inlaid eyes with the divine, including those of animals, see Ridgway 1993, 321 note 7.39.

17. Lump of slag (?) or molten glasslike material. Misshapen and badly pock-marked. Dark blue. **Fig. 7.2**
Inv. 4573. Tr. 00.3 surface find. S of Terrace Wall
MPD 2.9
Possibly a blue glass object caught in an intense fire.

Bronze vases and mirrors

As one expects in sanctuaries, bronze objects are popular items of dedication. Vases and mirrors, though generally sturdy and long-lasting, are also items of value to looters, and this may have led to parts of such objects being left behind, like handles and attachments.

The patera or phiale found in the northwest corner of the Temple was overlooked by salvagers, protected to some extent by the Temple walls. It was surrounded by an area where the most intense burning occurred. This is also where the least disturbance of the destroyed Temple is found. The nail hole punched through the phiale suggests that it was hung from the Temple wall, perhaps on a vertical beam in the mudbrick wall. It was thus made unusable as a ritual implement, and instead became a dedication to the deity.

18. Phiale or patera. Complete. Some surface corrosion; round nail hole in its floor punctured from inside. Cast bronze. Shallow bowl with flat floor rising quickly to an offset thickened rim. Raised line and groove on the floor around the omphalos. **Figs. 7.2, 7.3, and 7.18**
Inv. 3736. Tr. 95.4+1.2.4. Temple
D bowl 11.35; H 1.5; Th. wall 0.2; D omphalos 2.4; H to diameter 1:7.6
Williams et al. 1997, 49, 51 fig. 8 top (profile), pl. 10. More than 200 such phialai, mostly sixth century in date, were thrown into a sacred pond, presumably after pouring libations, at the Hera Limenia temenos at Perachora, Payne et al. 1940, 120–1, 148–56 pls. 51–7, 133–5, especially pp. 120–1, 152–3 for a discussion of the pond and the use of phialai for sacred purposes, and p. 150 for references to phialai from other temple sites. Sixty-eight Archaic phialai, all of thinly hammered sheet bronze (or copper), have been catalogued from the Timpone della Motta sanctuary, along with a good discussion of their manufacture, Papadopoulos 2003, 38–53 figs. 55–69 Table A. Many of them had holes punched through their floors for suspension, and several had holes through their mesomphalos to destroy their usefulness.

Five bronze phialai mesomphaloi dated to the Archaic period were found at Isthmia, Raubitschek 1998, 21–3 nos. 85–8 pls. 17–18 with discussion. One (no. 88) of these had two holes through its wall, presumably to hang as a dedication. **18** is unusual in being solid cast rather than hammered sheet. Its form and proportions of height to diameter (1:7.6) are more typical of fifth- and fourth-century phialai, like one in the Votonosi treasure, Vocotopoulou 1975, 759–61 no. 12 fig. 20. A solid cast phiale from the Demeter Sanctuary at Aghios Sostis near Tegea (Athens NM 14924) is similar in profile to the Stymphalos one, but with a mesomphalos. It is dated to the sixth century and has an inscription saying that Demarete dedicated it. A bronze cymbal in Athens from the Asklepieion at Epidauros with a dedication inscription likewise has a hole through the centre for hanging or to ruin its usefulness or both (Athens NM 10870).

Two mesomphalic phialai were found in House A v 9 at Olynthos, and dated to the first half of the fourth century; Robinson 1941, 183–4 nos. 571–2 pls. 39–42. No. 572 is especially close in shape to **18**, with a thickened rim which projects both outward and inward and is flat on top. Its proportions are 1:7.35. Both of the Olynthos phialai have a loop and ring for hanging, presumably from a nail in the house wall. In the fourth century, phiale proportions become as much as 1:10, though this is not the norm. In the Hellenistic period, proportions are mostly in the range of 1:6 to 1:7. See Luschey 1939, 38–40 nn. 249–50.

19. Shallow bowl, with rim which turns outward, then angles upward, no base. Part of the rim/wall is missing. (In its preliminary publication, it was reported to have traces of a silver alloy on the interior surface as if plated. This turned out to be remains of lead-tin solder.) **Figs. 7.2, 7.3, and 7.18**
Inv. 2092. Tr. 96.5 ext.2.2. City Wall near Hexagonal Tower
H 4.0; D rim 18.6; Th. wall 0.1
Williams et al. 1997, 51, 65 fig. 8 bottom (profile)
Found close to the iron strigil (**67**, see below), in a context representing either fill behind the foundation of the City Wall after its construction, or destruction debris with the Wall's collapse. Bronze bowls are fairly common, but the profile of the upper wall and rim of **19** is unusual. For a simple example from Corinth, Davidson 1952, no. 531 fig. 1 bottom; and from Isthmia, Raubitschek 1998, nos. 44–5, 47–50 pls. 10–11.

20. Shallow, thin-walled two-handled dish. Hammered sheet. Flat bottom, short vertical rise to a horizontal outturn, before the convex wall rises steeply to a plain rim. One bronze loop (omega) handle is preserved with recurved ends, now detached from the dish, leaving part of one hole for attachment. A small piece of the second handle is also preserved. Both holes for attachment of the second handle have parts of corroded iron straps acting as clips or cotter pins in the wall. The dish wall is fragile and cracked in places with pieces missing, including a large segment where the second handle was attached. **Figs. 7.2 and 7.19**
Inv. 1291. Tr. 97.4.6.9. S of Terrace Wall
D rim 8.6; D base 5.3; W base to angle of lower wall 1.05; H 2.5
The iron clips or cotter pins are short bands rather than mere wires. A cap or washer on the exterior must have helped hold the pins in place. Compare Papadopoulos 2003, 132–3 nos. 462–5 fig. 167 "bronze omega-shaped staples" with references to others. For an example from Dodona of an omega handle with the cotter pins still attached, Carapanos 1878, pl. 46 no. 9. For omega handles see below **28**, and for cotter pins, Robinson 1941, 246 nos. 977–82 pl. 65.

21. Base for a small vase (kantharos?). Cast. Some surface corrosion. Thickened vertical base rises to a sharp upper edge turned inward; within this "rim" a slightly convex floor surface rises in the centre to within 0.2 cm of the level of the base's "rim." On the underside, the ring base curves up to the flat "floor," and in the middle is a three-part "disk," made up of a convex element surrounded by a ridge, then a plain convex element, and a button at the centre. **Figs. 7.2, 7.3, and 7.19**
Inv. 2509. Tr. 95.4+1.2.4. Temple
D 4.05; Th. rim 0.59; D disk on underside 1.4; Wt. 27.3
Williams et al. 1997, 49 pl. 10 (left).
Although found lodged beneath the phiale **18**, there is no reason to associate the two. Ring bases for bronze vases are common; most are hollow rings, though sometimes with lead filling; see Payne et al. 1940, 160–1 pl. 64. Diameters vary considerably; larger ones are thought to be from amphoras and hydriai, smaller ones from oinochoai, kotylai, and cups. Of five found near the bottom of a well (third century BCE) at Nemea, a small solid one is attributed to a kantharos, Stephen G. Miller 1979, 80 no. BR 650 pl. 24a. One at Isthmia has the same raised elements in the middle of the underside though not the incurved rim on the upper side, Raubitschek 1998, 41 no. 176 pl. 33.

22. Everted flat rim (?) of a thin-walled vessel, possibly a small dinos or mixing bowl. Cast and hammered. Two joining fragments. Some surface corrosion, and encrustation.
Inv. 2525. Tr. 99.1.5.9. E of Terrace Wall
MPL 6.4; MPW 1.4; Max. Th. 0.16; D rim est. 23.0
Incised line near the outer edge of the rim. Inscription on the rim facing outward using the incised line as a baseline. **Fig. 7.4**
ΕΛΕΙΘΥ[---]
Letter forms: E: verticals extend below the lowest horizontal, Θ: horizontal stroke at centre, Y: V-shaped. The letters are neatly incised and well spaced.
From 'Ελείθυα or 'Ελείθυια, name or epithet of a goddess

E.g. ’Ελειθυ[ίαι] (“to Eleithuia”) [15]
A number of bronze mixing bowls with similar rims were identified at Isthmia, said to be made by casting and then hammering the walls, leaving the rims thicker and so better preserved; see Raubitschek 1998, 13–14; note especially p. 16 no. 48 pl. 11 for an inscribed rim (Archaic). A raised edge just at the break on the right edge suggests the location of a handle (?) attachment interrupting the inscription.

See also the Corinthian red-figure sherd, inv. 503 with a graffito (Schaus, chapter 10 below, p. 218, **6**), and a silver coin of Sikyon with the letters epsilon-lambda (Weir, chapter 4, pp. 64, 74, **II-51**), likely dedications to the same goddess. Other objects from the Sanctuary with a possible connection to this goddess include a glass bezel with a standing female figure holding long objects (torches?) in her hands (Inv. 690, Young, chapter 6, p. 119, **136**) and a loomweight (Inv. 2909) with an inscribed epsilon (Inv. 2909, Surtees, chapter 12, p. 242, **29**). For a brief discussion of Eileithyia worship see p. 14.

23. Vase (?) rim fragment. Slightly concave upper surface turns sharply down to a simple edge. **Fig. 7.4**
Inv. 2806. Tr. 99.1.4.4. E of Terrace Wall
PL 4.3; H 0.75; D rim est. 9.5; Wt. 5.0
The profile suits that of a bronze door boss, but its estimated diameter is much larger than even the biggest of about 140 such bosses recovered at Olynthos, Robinson 1941, 260–76 nos. 1037–1170 (no. 1044 is 6 cm in diameter).

24. Movable handle from a large vase, probably a situla or lekanis, rectangular in section, with sharply curved end. About half preserved. There is no room for a lotus bud tip, as **25**. **Fig. 7.4**
Inv. 3381. Tr. 00.4.8.11. City Wall
PL 11.65; W 0.75; Th. 0.45; Wt. 29.1
These sturdy handles are found at least as early as ca. 500 BCE on bronze pails: e.g., Gauer 1991, 110–11, 266–67 nos. E1-3 fig. 3 pls. 94–6, and many others fig. 29 pls. 103–8, and situlae, e.g. Brizio 1899, pls. 4.13, 5.14 (duck head at end). A lekanis handle is also possible, as Vocotopoulou 1975, 733–6 no. 2 fig. 4 (Votonosi), who (1975, 736) argues for a Corinthian manufacture. Three situla handles, of which one has curved-back ends like **24**, came from a late fourth–early third-century level of a well at Nemea, but they have a sharp narrowing of the handle just where it attaches to the vessel, Stephen G. Miller 1979, 80 pl. 24b.

25. Movable handle. Wide curving, rectangular in section, ending in a lotus bud tip. Broken, bent in several directions. **Fig. 7.4**
Inv. 3324. Tr. 96.15.5.5. Refuse pit –West Annex area
L est. 14.6; W 0.5; Th. 0.2; Wt. 13.7
From a similar large handle as **24.**

26. Movable handle tip in the shape of a lotus bud, bent. **Fig. 7.4**
Inv. 159. Tr. 96.6.1.2. Pillar Shrine area
L 4.0; Max. D 1.4; Wt. 27.1
Broken at a point where the handle was attached to a large vase by a loop attachment.

27. Cup kantharos (?) handle. Tear-drop wall attachment, wide out-curved handle looping up to a thickened, pointed finger-hold. Broken at one loop, and part of the wall attachment is missing. Much lead tin solder preserved on the underside of the wall attachment and flecks on the upper surface. **Fig. 7.4**
Inv. 310. Tr. 96.4.4.7. Altar area
MPD 8.05; PL wall attachment 3.1; Wt. 16.8
Similar handles appear on cups and cup kantharoi from the Votonosi treasure dated to the fourth century, Vocotopoulou 1975, 764–7 nos. 15–18, figs. 24–7 (cup kantharoi), 768–9 no. 20 fig. 29 (cup). A complete handle of this type was found at Dodona, Carapanos 1878, pl. 46.12. For less elegant pottery comparisons in Athens, see Sparkes and Talcott 1970, pls. 26, 28, cup kantharoi and cup skyphoi.
Second half of the fourth century

28. Handle (omega loop). Horizontal loop handle with recurved ends (one is broken), lotus bud (or “acorn”) tip; loop is square in section. **Fig. 7.4**
Inv. 982. Tr. 95.2.4.8. Building A
H 3.45; PW end to end 2.7; Max. Th. 0.38; Wt. 5.4
For omega handles (probably also **20** and **29**) see, for example, Warden 1990, 54–5 nos. 394–7, the most common type for metal vessels, being fitted into rings or as **20** into cotter pins; e.g., Blinkenberg 1931, 219 nos. 712–13 pl. 29. A hundred were catalogued at Olynthos, Robinson 1941, “Swinging Handles” Type I, 207–21 nos. 668–769 pls. 56–9, esp. p. 208 n. 70 for a discussion of the attachment.
Similar handles are also very common on bronze mirror covers; see Schwarzmaier 1997, e.g., pls. 5, 17, 38, 40–3. The range of proposed dates of these is over a century, 370–270 BCE, with most ca. 330–280 BCE.

29. Movable handle (omega loop?). Lotus bud tip fragment. **Fig. 7.4**
Inv. 162. Tr. 96.3.2.2. Altar area
PL 3.45; Max. Th. 0.47; Wt. 2.6
As **28,** but from a much larger vessel, possibly a situla. For earlier variants of the type, see Gauer 1991, fig. 29.

30. Horizontal loop handle, round in section. **Fig. 7.4**
Inv. 2490. Tr. 99.1.5.9. E of Terrace Wall
MPD 2.86; Th. handle 0.37; Th. at wall attachment 0.8; Wt. 5.8

Perhaps from a kylix or skyphos (kotyle) drinking vessel, as Raubitschek 1998, 37, 39 no. 158 pl. 30. Compare DeCou 1905, 288 nos. 2050–3 pl. 119; very close to Robinson 1941, 202, nos. 633, 635 pl. 53 "stationary handle" Type II.

31. Handle, double curved with grooves at one end, other end broken. **Fig. 7.4**
Inv. 1622. Tr. 95.3.6.11. North Annex
MPD 4.2; Th. 0.3; Wt. 6.0
Misshapen form suggests considerable force was applied to separate the handle from its vessel.

32. Handle, small loop with flattened ends and remains of holes for attachment. **Fig. 7.4**
Inv. 669. Tr. 96.8.3.4. West Annex
PL 2.8; PW end to end 2.1; Wt. 0.9

33. Handle, small loop with inward curving ends, one side now bent straighter. **Fig. 7.4**
Inv. 323. Tr. 96.3.3.5. Altar area
PL 3.2; W loop 1.6; Max. Th. 0.3; Wt. 2.8
Similar to the omega handles but with ends curved inward. The ends were meant for insertion into decorated cylinders like **38** and **39** which were soldered to the surface of bronze objects like mirror covers, vessels, or furnishings. Compare **34**. A good drawing of the type is Carapanos 1878, pl. 46.10. Three of these handles were found in a well at Nemea at a level of the late fourth or early third century BCE, Stephen G. Miller 1979, 80 pl. 24b. A similar loop handle is in the Nemea Museum along with two iron (?) loops still attached to non-decorated cylinders. At Olynthos, the type is quite rare. Robinson adds it to his "Swinging Handles" Type IIa, Robinson 1941, 222–3 nos. 774–5 pl. 60. At Isthmia, such handles are identified as bronze mirror handles for box mirrors belonging to the fourth century, Raubitschek 1998, 111 n. 15 (references), 115 nos. 396–7 pl. 62. Several were found at Olympia in Classical period contexts, Gauer 1991, 292 nos. Var 25, 31, 33, 36 pl. 29. Two others are seen in the Votonosi treasure with their cylinders, Vocotopoulou 1975, 776 nos. 27–8 fig. 36 a, c. For other examples attached to the covers of bronze mirrors, see Schwarzmaier 1997, passim (e.g., nos. 72, 101, 106, 181, 236, 243), where dates range from ca. 360 to 220 BCE.

34. Handle and attachment. Small oval loop handle with ends bent into a small tubular attachment decorated with narrow raised fillets. Part of the loop is missing. **Fig. 7.5**
Inv. 619. Tr. 95.4 + 1.2.4. Temple
Max. D 2.9; Th. loop 0.28; L attachment 1.3; Th. attachment 0.34; Wt. 2.8
A close parallel is in the Votonosi treasure, Vocotopoulou 1975, 776 no. 29 fig. 36e, suggested to be from a mirror or phiale. There are many other examples of this common type; e.g., Gauer 1991, 199 nos. Le 176–7, pl. 25 "high Archaic."

35. Ivy leaf attached to a small movable ring on a single-loop hinge. Lead tin (solder) covers one side of the leaf, with specks on the other side of the leaf, on the hinge, and on the ring near the hinge. Incised grooves along the central spine of the leaf on the side with the solder. **Fig. 7.5**
Inv. 301. Tr. 96.3.3.6. Altar area
D ring 1.7; Th. ring 0.24; L leaf 2.0; W leaf 1.65; Th. leaf 0.03; Wt. 3.3
The leaf part was soldered and perhaps also riveted to a larger object; stumps of rivets appear to be preserved. Very similar is one from Kalapodi, Felsch 2007, no. 2184 pl. 61. For earlier examples of leaves with rings though without the loose pivot, see Gauer 1991, pls. 99 and 107.1a. Cf. Robinson 1941, 124–5 nos. 422–5 ("pendants") pl. 25, and p. 227 no. 810 pl. 64 (Type IIc, "swinging handle"). See also "ring pulls" below, nos. **126–9**.

36. Silver rosette decoration and bronze ring. **Fig. 7.5**
Inv. 583, 584. Tr. 95.4+1.2.4. Temple
Rosette: D 3.2, Th. 0.5; Wt. 2.2. Bronze ring: D 2.85, Th. 0.65. Connecting band: L 0.8, W 0.5, Wt. of ring and connecting band 15.6
36 consists of three pieces: a silver rosette, a thick bronze ring, and part of the hoop attaching the ring to the rosette. The rosette is in poor condition, now bent; the bronze ring is in fair condition with surface corrosion and cracks. The band connecting the ring to the rosette is broken and badly corroded.

The rosette was hammered from a very thin sheet of silver. It is decorated with fourteen long narrow concave petals, divided by raised straight lines. The central hole has a diameter of 0.45 cm; one of the petals has a jagged hole of larger diameter where the ring was attached. The rosette was found still attached to the bronze ring. A similar silver rosette from the Archaic period, but with twelve petals, was found at Isthmia, Raubitschek 1998, 75 no. 293 pl. 44. The silver rosette or perhaps the connecting band on **36** was soldered or riveted to a metal surface like a mirror cover, or a box lid or drawer, and the bronze ring was able to swing up to fit a finger in opening the object. The rosette at Isthmia was judged to be too delicate to attach to a wood or metal surface itself, but perhaps was attached to a softer material, like cloth or leather. (I am grateful to A. Young for comments on this piece.)

37. Handle spool, thickened ends with depressions for placement of ring handle, convex middle interrupted by a ridge inside a groove, reels at both ends; the underside is flattened where it was attached to the vase (?) wall. **Fig. 7.5**

Inv. 23. Tr. 95.3.1.2. North Annex
L 3.75; Max. Th. 0.5; Wt. 3.4
The flattened side was soldered to a curved surface and the ends of a loop handle like **34** were inserted into the depressions at the two ends. Compare the mirror covers, Schwarzmaier 1997, no. 34 pl. 7 (from Akarnania, ca. 330 BCE), no. 181 pl. 16 (in New York, ca. 310 BCE), no. 188 pl. 18 (in New York, ca. 290–280 BCE). One from Olympia is very close in shape, Gauer 1991, 292 no. Var 27, pl. 29.3a.

38. Cylindrical handle spool, concave along its length, flattened on its underside but not curved noticeably. Ten single reels. Indentations at both ends. **Fig. 7.5**
Inv. 156. Tr. 96.6.4.9. Pillar Shrine area
L 4.2; Max. D 0.9; Min. D 0.6; Wt. 15.4
Larger spools with little perceptible curve where they are attached are probably from large vases like dinoi. They are very common, so for example, Blinkenberg 1931, 219 no. 714 pl. 30 with references to ones at Olympia, Delphi, Athens Acropolis, Argive Heraeum, and elsewhere, and Robinson 1941, 243 n. 202 (with references) pls. 64–5 nos. 966–73. Ten were found at Isthmia and dated to the sixth and early fifth century, Raubitschek 1998, 15, 18–20 nos. 63–70, 73–4 pls. 15–16. Some without indentations at the end were simply added along the rim of the vessel as decoration (below **39–43**); see Raubitschek 1998, 18–19 no. 63; Payne et al. 1940, 161 pls. 59.2, 66.19–24 for discussion and references to others with handles in position. At Olympia, where many were found, the ones with single reels spread out along the length of the cylinder, like **38**, are dated to the "Archaic" or "High Archaic" period; see Gauer 1991, 195, 198 nos. Le 123, 155, 163–5 pls. 23–4 (chronology chart p. 177). Others with both single and double raised reels are from the Archaic sanctuary at Timpone della Motta near Francavilla Marittima, Papadopoulos 2003, 28–33 with comments on their metal analysis. If **38** is also as early as the Archaic period, it may be from an heirloom left in the Sanctuary.
Archaic?

39. Cylindrical spool with 4+2+2+2 reels. No indentations on the ends, and no flattened side. **Fig. 7.5**
Inv. 949. Tr. 97.1.2.2. S of Bldg. A
L 3.8; D 0.75; Wt. 12.2

40. Decorative spool, slightly flat on one side where it was soldered to an object, no holes on the ends for inserting a ring pull. Six reels between beads. **Fig. 7.5**
Inv. 3683. Tr. 95.7 baulk scarp cleaning
L 2.3; D or W 0.7; Wt. 4.8

41. Small cylindrical spool with 1+2+2+2 reels. Carelessly made. No indentations at the ends for a ring handle. **Fig. 7.5**
Inv. 888. Tr. 96.13.4.7. S of Altar Terrace
L 1.3; D 0.3; Wt. 0.9

42. Small cylindrical spool with 1+2+2+2+1 reels, flattened on one side where it was soldered for attachment, no indentations on the ends. **Fig. 7.5**
Inv. 1043. Tr. 97.2 (96.15).5.5. West Annex
L 1.5; D. 0.3; Wt. 1.3

43. Small cylindrical spool. 2+2+2+2+2 reels. No indentations at the ends and no flattened side. **Fig. 7.5**
Inv. 26. Tr. 95.1.4.8. Temple
L 1.5; D 0.35; Wt. 1.6

44. Cast palmette appliqué, finished on the upper surface but rough on the underside. No evidence for attachment, broken at the base. **Fig. 7.5**
Inv. 352. Tr. 96.3.3.5. Altar area
PL 3.4; W palmette 1.8; Th. 0.2; Wt. 6.3
The palmette is very close to one from Olynthos, including the band with X's between the spiral tendrils, Robinson 1941, 201 no. 630 pl. 53, "Stationary Handles, Type I." The base of the palmette was better preserved as far as a nail hole, indicating its method of attachment. Robinson believed that such palmette appliqués were used to decorate bronze vases, Robinson 1941, 43–4, no. 27, figs. 7–8, pl. 6; no. 571a pl. 39. Also similar, but with larger fronds for the palmette, is one from Nemea, Stella G. Miller 1984, 184 pl. 41c, and one from Foce del Sele, Zancani Montuoro 1965–6, 149 no. 16 pl. 43c. Palmettes commonly decorated cylinder handle anchors, but these are thicker, as Gauer 1991, pls. 37–45.

Bronze mirror attachments

Small animal figures, most often hares, dogs, foxes, and cocks, interspersed with rosettes, regularly decorate the rims of bronze caryatid mirrors of the "standing Doric" type (ca. 490–420 BCE).[16] Congdon attributed caryatid mirrors to nine workshop centres, of which she locates five in the Peloponnese, including a Corinthian, "Sikyonian," "Argive," and "Argo-Corinthian." A beautifully preserved mirror in New York shows them at their best.[17] Another, on display in the National Archaeological Museum in Athens (NM Inv. 7579), decorated with cocks, hares, dogs, and rosettes around the rim, is dated ca. 455 BCE and attributed to Argive workmanship.

From the acropolis sanctuary at Stymphalos come two bronze hares, a fox, and a cock which are very similar to ones on these mirrors, especially ones attributed to north Peloponnesian workshops. The fox (**47**), cock (**48**), and one of the hares (**45**) can be compared with the animal attachments on a mirror in Baltimore (Walters

54.1165) which Congdon attributes to her "Corinthian B" school and dates ca. 465–460 BCE.[18] The same hare and the fox are comparable as well to those on a mirror in Berlin (Antiken Sammlung Inv. MI 10161), attributed by Congdon to her "Argo-Corinthian B" or "Argive B" school, and dated ca. 460 BCE.[19] The cock can best be compared with ones on a mirror in Athens (NM Inv. 15214), though it lacks the incised detail.[20] This is dated in the second quarter of the fifth century and is said to show "Sikyonian" influence. As for the second hare from the Sanctuary (**46**), it is more difficult to compare because of the unusual ears, which are perked up and curve forward, although the shape of a hare on Boston MFA Inv. 98.667 is not far off.[21] The two hares, however, are sufficiently different from each other that they must have been attachments on two different objects, perhaps indeed two such caryatid mirrors. If, in fact, these animals are from mirrors, then it is worth noting that mirrors have been associated with the goddess Aphrodite, and the individual animals attached to mirrors may have their own associations: for example, hares – Artemis and Aphrodite, dogs – Artemis, cocks – Aphrodite, Athena, Hermes, but foxes – no association.[22] Both full-size and miniature votive mirrors were found in the sanctuary on Mt Kotilo in Arkadia where Artemis and Aphrodite were worshipped.[23] It is likely that the bronze rosettes **49a–b** were also attachments for these mirrors, although they are sometimes found on vases as well. The bronze base **21** might have held one of these mirrors instead of a kantharos or other small vase, although normally the mirror stands are more elevated.[24]

Dogs chasing hares are a popular motif in seventh-century vase painting (Protocorinthian and Wild Goat for example) for symposium vessels. It is less obvious why they decorated women's mirrors, and why the mirror edge is conceived of as a kind of hunting ground.

45. Running hare. Ears are more carefully rendered. Stretched front legs and thickened back feet create two solid resting surfaces. **Fig. 7.5**
Inv. 3137. Surface find
L 2.6; H 1.2; Wt. 6.0
Second (?) quarter of the fifth century

46. Running hare. Long high ears, short nose, and perked tail, flat beneath the stretched front feet, thickened back feet to give firm attachment surfaces. **Fig. 7.5**
Inv. 327. Tr. 96.4.3.5. Altar area
H 2.6; L 2.9; Wt. 8.5
Williams et al. 1997, 48 fig. 7 (mistakenly reported as being from the nearby monastery site of Zaraka; corrected in Williams and Schaus 2001, 91 n. 54.)
The interior of the long, slightly curved ears is scooped out.
Second (?) quarter of the fifth century

47. Running fox or dog. Pointed snout, erect ears, and bushy tail (broken) suggest a fox. The front legs stretch out further than the back. Little detail. **Fig. 7.5**
Inv. 2133. Tr. 96.6 scarp cleaning
L 2.7; H 1.6; Th. 0.6
The fox on a British Museum mirror (Walters 1899, no. 243 pl. IV) has its back leg stretched out more than the Stymphalos animal, and its tail runs along the upper part of the leg. Two similar animals with bushy tails on a mirror in New York are called hounds, but the ears are shorter, Mertens 1987, 59 fig. 40.
Second (?) quarter of the fifth century

48. Standing cock. Eyes and wings are discernible surface details. The tail is a solid mass. Wide legs/feet create a solid but thin base. **Fig. 7.5**
Inv. 3388. Tr. 96.15.5.5. Refuse pit – West Annex area
H 2.8; W 2.3; Th. 0.7; Wt. 8.1
See Warden 1990, 6–8, 12–13 for mostly Archaic ones from Cyrene, and a reference to a fourth-century one in the New York art market. The Stymphalos example is stiff and lacking details compared to Archaic ones. A somewhat similar cock, though with head forward, has a base which does duty for its legs, Payne et al. 1940, 138 pl. 44.7. See also Davidson 1952, 66 no. 502.
Second (?) quarter of the fifth century

49. Two concave rosettes on a vertical stem that is square in section. **Fig. 7.5**
a) Inv. 197. Tr. 95.6.5.7. N of Temple (three of the petals are damaged)
D 1.65; rivet: L 0.5, W 0.5, Wt. 1.6.
b) Inv. 959. Tr. 96.13.5.8. S of Altar area
D 1.65; rivet: L 0.8, W 0.35, Wt. 2.2.
For similar rosettes set along the upper edge of a mirror rim on either side of a siren, see Mertens 1987, 59 fig. 40 (Early Classical); Congdon 1981, nos. 83, 90 pls. 77, 86; and for the placement of a rosette at the bottom of a mirror just above the head of a standing woman as mirror stand, see McClees 1924, fig. 81; Congdon 1981, no. 68 pl. 62. They can also be found on vase handles, as Gauer 1991, 240 no. P27 pl. 62 (from a basin, Early Classical, Corinthian).
Fifth century

Other bronze animals

50. Snake (?). Squared "head" which narrows at the "nose," V-groove on the upper surface, badly oxidized, long

body (shaft) curved semi-regularly, narrowing towards the end, round in section. Two pieces; the second, smaller piece is now missing. Flattened surface under the head for attachment (?). **Fig. 7.5**
Inv. 932. Tr. 96.13.4.7. S of Altar area
PL a) 18.2, b) 3.8; Max. Th. 0.4; W "head" 0.7; Wt. 19.6
Although the "head" and wavy "body" are snakelike, features like eyes and mouth are not clearly visible, and the head is more square than other bronze snakes. Compare, for example, Comstock and Vermeule 1971, 61 no. 63, or the many snake heads from bronze vase handles and projections at Olympia, Gauer 1991, fig. 1. None of the snakes from vases attach right at the head or have a tapering body. Nor would **50** seem to be a snake-headed pin, such as ones from Olympia, which are smaller, and have sharp double bends just below the head; see Philipp 1981, 88 nos. 266–7 pls. 5, 35. A better possibility is a plain snake-headed bracelet or arm band. There are many more decorative ones at Olympia, some of which loop around to attach at the head, although none is especially close to the Stymphalos piece; see Philipp 1981, pls. 52–7. For others at the Timpone della Motta sanctuary, Papadopoulos 2003, 76–9 fig. 99. Compare also a bronze snake with inscribed plate attached to its middle from Pergamon, Boehringer 1959, 165 fig. 31. Less likely is a strand of long hair broken off a large bronze statue, such as strands in the Olympia museum, which are more regularly wavy often with thin grooves down their length.

51. Standing bull figurine. Raised head, tail extended back and down. Short horns, proper left eye and ear, pizzle, scrotum, and tail knot are visible details. Surface corrosion, hole in the proper left leg (casting fault). **Fig. 7.5**
Inv. 4549. Surface find
L nose to tail 4.5; H 2.6; W shoulders 0.9
There is no evidence for attachment to another object like **45–8,** but a similar bull in Athens (National Museum 6408) is an attachment to a round handle of a large bronze vessel, Gauer 1991, 191 no. Le 76 pl. 7.2

A number of bull figurines from the Corinthia generally are earlier in date and more carefully rendered, as Davidson 1952, 65–6 nos. 497–8; Payne et al. 1940, 136 pl. 43.5–7; Raubitschek 1998, nos. 1–7 pls. 1–2. For a much larger and more detailed bull, but with similar squared tail and incised lines for eyes and horn, see Comstock and Vermeule 1971, 56 no. 57 from the Kabeirion, Thebes ca. 490 BCE with references to others. Such bronze figurines were very common at Olympia in the early period, Furtwängler 1890, pls. 10–13, but they continue down into the Classical, pl. 46 (though none are particularly close to the Stymphalos bull). The stiff upper part of the tail and bushy knot at the end are observed regularly by the Late Archaic–Early Classical period, see Stephen G. Miller 1980, 180 pl. 35c (incised bronze plaque from Nemea).

This little votive left by a worshipper, presumably in lieu of a live bull, follows a well-established tradition. It was common to sacrifice female animals to female deities, and male to male. To find a bull figurine in a sanctuary so far known to be devoted to female deities (Athena, Eileithyia) may be significant, but since there are at least five aniconic stelai, it is likely that at least one of them represented a male divinity.

Decorative bronzes

Shield decorations

At least four distinctly different bronze rosettes were found in the Sanctuary, and if they all come from shields and were left as votives, it suggests that dedications of hoplite equipment may have been more common than suspected up to now in the Sanctuary.[25]

52. Medallion decorated with an impressed rosette, outlined petals, dots at the end between each petal, fragments missing along the edge. Two iron rivets attach a bronze loop strap. The rivets end in round washers. Rivets and washers are badly corroded. **Fig. 7.6**
Inv. 3608. Tr. 97.5 baulk.6.7. E of Terrace Wall
D medallion 3.8; L rivet 1.3; Wt. 5.6
Such rosette medallions are not uncommon. One hundred and twelve are catalogued in the publication of the Argive shields from Olympia, Bol 1989, 21–3, 122–6 pls. 20–2. A very similar medallion from Olympia, with the iron rivets and bronze strap going between them still well preserved, was published in Furtwängler 1890, 148 pl. 45 no. 930, as a clasp from a small chest (*kästchen*). With the discovery of examples still in place on the inside of shields (Bol 1989, pl. 20 no. A147, pl. 22 no. A102; Kunze 1956, pls. 18–19 [A105]), it is clear that these are shield decorations. Bol (1989, 21) noted that larger ones were placed where the shield handholds were attached, while others were often equipped with a clasp which would hold a tassel, as seen on vase paintings. Dozens were found in the Argive Heraion, some with incised rosettes and dot borders, DeCou 1905, pls. 99–101. For an example from the Tria Goupata cave above Lafka to the west of Stymphalos, see *ArchDelt* 49 (1994) B1, pl. 57c. Others are from Perachora, Payne et al. 1940, pl. 48.9, and Alipheira, Orlandos 1967–8, 101 fig. 67. An example with the ring which fits into the bronze strap but without the decorative rosette is Furtwängler 1890, pl. 45 no. 931. See also Carapanos 1878, pl. 49.9, for a bronze disk decorated with an enclosed rosette, with one rivet and the bronze strap looped outwards. Several more came

from the Sanctuary of Athena Itonia at Philia, including one with the strap and rivets in place in the rosette ornament, Kilian-Dirlmeier 2002, 90 nos. 1406–12 pl. 90, and from the Artemis Sanctuary at Kalapodi, Felsch 2007, 370 nos. 2094–6 pl. 57. A group of eight disks decorated with embossed rosettes was found corroded together at Cyrene, Warden 1990, 42 no. 268 pl. 28. For a similar disk (3.7 cm) in gold from the Korykian Cave, decorated with rosette petals around the outside but a Gorgoneion in the centre, see Rolley 1984, 272 no. 50 fig. 21. Another group from Francavilla Marittima has one with a cotter pin still in place in a central hole, as well as one disk with a running Gorgon in repoussé, Papadopoulos 2003, 56–8 nos. 144–7 figs. 73–5. For very similar examples from tomb 44 at Atella, dated to the second half of the fourth century BCE and identified as decorative elements of a coffin, see Bottini ed. 1994, 201.

The type, decorated with rosettes, begins in the seventh century and continues into the Classical period or later; see Bol 1989, 21.

53. Medallion, about three-quarters preserved, puncture hole. Thin disk decorated with an impressed rosette of which ten raised outlined petals are preserved; a row of raised dots between lines around the outer edge. Trace of corroded iron (from rivets) on the surface. **Fig. 7.6**
Inv. 3138. Tr. 00.4.7.7. City Wall
D medallion 3.2; Th. 0.03; Wt. 1.4
Similar to **52**.

54. Medallion (disk appliqué), in six joining pieces, small pieces missing. Hole in the centre. Thin disk decorated with an impressed rosette, narrow raised petals, row of raised dots around the outer edge. **Fig. 7.6**
Inv. 464. Tr. 95.4 + 1.2.4. Temple
D 6.05; Th. 0.04; Wt. 5.0
Larger in size than **52** and **53**, and with no evidence of iron rivet attachments.

55. Medallion in two fragments, about one-third preserved. Thin disk decorated with an incised rosette and a row of tiny dots and one of larger dots impressed along the outer edge. **Fig. 7.6**
Inv. 3271. Surface find
MPD a) 4.5 b) 2.78; Th. 0.03; Wt. 2.0

56. Decorated disk, in ten small fragments, three with curved edges. Possible rosette or leaf pattern. Corroded surfaces. Cotter pin. **Fig. 7.6**
Inv. 1270. Tr. 97.5.4.7. E of Terrace Wall
MPD disk frags. 1.6; H cotter pin 1.25
Cotter pins are quite common, for example to hold loop handles (see **20**), or ring pulls, as Robinson 1941, pl. 61, and for others see p. 246 nos. 977–82 pl. 65; Warden 1990, 44 nos. 292–3 pl. 30; Blinkenberg 1931, 204 pl. 26 no. 637 (second row far left); Raubitschek 1998, 152–3 nos. 582–3 pl. 88 (misunderstood as T-rivets or staples), and compare 117 no. 421A–B pl. 65.

Other decorative bronzes

57. Band fragment in five joining pieces, one nail hole preserved in the corner piece. Decorated with a row of small raised dots along both edges, then a row of larger dots, then ovules and a row of outlined large dots down the middle. **Fig. 7.6**
Inv. 603. Tr. 96.10.3.3. City Wall, round tower
MPD two largest pieces a) 2.6 b) 2.5
Decorative treatment of such bands varies considerably and tells little. Compare, for example, from the Arkadian sanctuaries at Lousoi, Reichel and Wilhelm 1901, 56 fig. 102–4, and Alipheira, Orlandos 1967–8, 99–100 figs. 64–5, and from other sites, DeCou 1905, no. 1782 pl. 103; Kilian-Dirlmeier 2002, no. 2937 pl. 173; Warden 1990, 29 no. 166 fig. 3 pl. 22; Rolley 1984, 273–5 nos. 53–5 figs. 25–6 (Korykian Cave). Olympia has a fair collection of such bands (personal communication, S. Bocher, who is gathering examples from other sites), and the sanctuary at Timpone della Motta has quite an impressive number, identified mostly as finger rings, but some of the larger pieces as bracelets or armlets; see Papadopoulos 2003, 92–103 nos. 262–337 divided up into nine types based on decoration (with references to many other sites). The row of ovules is not a common pattern on these bands (one example at Timpone della Motta, Papadopoulos 2003, 94 no. 272 fig.118 c–d).

58. Band with two light folds lengthwise to create three zones of decoration. The central zone has a row of raised dots; the side zones have a row of half-circles and along the edge a row of small raised dots. Broken at both ends. **Fig. 7.6**
Inv. 3338. Tr. 96.15.5.5. Refuse pit – West Annex area
MPL 4.8; MPW 4.9; W central zone 1.4; Wt. 5.9
A thin band such as this must have been attached to another material to add a decorative touch, though there is no evidence of attachment preserved. Some of the decorated bands from the Sanctuary may be from belts, or diadems, of which ones in bronze were quite common, or arm bands. Compare, for example, Raubitschek 1998, 54–60 figs. 6 and 7 (mostly Archaic period examples), commonly decorated with small dots along the edge and larger dots on the interior of the bands; Philipp 1981, 203–4 nos. 749–53 pl. 47 (Armbänder).

59. Sheet fragment, rectangular or perhaps slightly tapering. Folded over once and a corner folded over in the other direction. Decorated with dots along the edge, and with

a repoussé circle and dot in the middle. Broken at both ends. **Fig. 7.6**
Inv. 2654. Tr. 97.5 baulk.4.5. E of Terrace Wall
PL 3.8; W at main fold 1.9; Wt. 2.3

60. Band in three pieces. Flattened and folded in two with a hole in the centre of each end. The outer edges have a row of tiny punched dots. **Fig. 7.6**
Inv. 1846. Tr. 96.4.6.9. Altar
L 2.6; W 2.0; Th. 0.2; Wt. 1.2

61. Lotus flower with small holes through the tips, two pieces, folded over and cracked. **Fig. 7.6**
Inv. 3152. Tr. 00.4.7.7. City Wall
MPL a) 3.4 b) 2.8
Tiny nails must have kept this decorative piece in place against a more solid material. Cf. a lotus bud (?) from Isthmia, Raubitschek 1998, no. 289 pl. 44.

62. Leaf-shaped attachment with hole in its centre, broken at the base. Sheet hammered. **Fig. 7.6**
Inv. 1035. Tr. 97.2.5.5. S of West Annex
PL 3.6; W 1.55; Wt. 1.9
Compare the attachment for hand holds on bronze shields, as Bol 1989, pl. 19, esp. D64 (with a single nail or rivet hole), or the attachment for a ring pull, Felsch 2007, no. 2185 pl. 61. There must have been many other uses of such attachments – for example, on bronze vases.

63. Leaf. Shaped like an olive leaf, slightly curled over at the stem end. **Fig. 7.6**
Inv. 2305. Tr. 99.10.1.1. N of North Annex
L 3.9; W 1.6; Wt. 1.4
This may have broken off a bronze olive wreath rather than being a decorative attachment for a hinge, for example, since there is no deliberate hole for a tack, and its inside end seems to narrow too much to secure a hinge or other object.

Strigils

One almost complete iron strigil and perhaps as many as four other fragmentary ones of bronze and iron were found in or close to the Santuary proper.[26] It is not certain that the complete one was part of the Sanctuary debris, but the fragmentary ones were likely to be. One was found in an area where many young goat horns occurred, presumably the remains of sacrificed animals. Another occurred in the West Annex area of Building A, and a third just south of the Altar Terrace. The fourth was a surface find. Strigils are usually associated with male athletics, but women may also have used them for cleaning the skin during bathing.

64. Bronze handle fragment from a tubular strigil (?). Made from a long narrow sheet which was rolled over lengthwise. Broken at both ends and down the middle and partly flattened into an oval in its diameter. It seems to taper somewhat, though this may be partly due to preservation. **Fig. 7.6**
Inv. 3529. Surface find (SF 2000.362)
L 4.2; W (rather than diameter) tapers 1.5–1.1; Wt. 4.5
Tubular strigils were an early form of this instrument used by athletes to scrape oil and dust from their bodies after exercise. This type may have been developed in Corinth in the Late Archaic period. It appears in Corinthian graves from the first half of the fifth century. Tubular strigils were made by rolling lengthwise a narrow sheet of bronze which had its two sides cut back for about two-thirds of its length. The uncut sides were rolled until they touched to create the handle, while the blade was created where the two cut-back portions of the sheet were rolled to make only a half-tube with the exposed edges being used for scraping. For this development and for examples from Isthmia, see Raubitschek 1998, 122–3, 129 nos. 460–3 fig. 26 pl. 73. Raubitschek (122) says that the blade is made by not rolling the sides as close together, but clearly strips had to be cut from the sides to create the shape. The short tubular handle is thought to have had a wooden or bone extension inserted into it; see Davidson 1952, 181, 183 no. 1317 pl. 81. The diameters of the tubular handles at Isthmia are very small, 1.0 to 1.5 cm, similar to this example from Stymphalos.

65. Bronze strigil (?) with a narrow handle which widens into a rounded concave spoon section. Broken at both ends. **Fig. 7.6**
Inv. 1848. Tr. 96.13.2.5. S of Altar
MPD 5.3; W handle 1.2; PW spoon 3.0, D est. 3.5; Wt. 6.7

66. Bronze strigil (?) fragment. The handle narrows in width before it reaches the wider concave spoon section. Broken at both ends. **Fig. 7.6**
Inv. 1100. Tr. 96.8.6.7. West Annex
MPD 3.9; W handle 1.4 to 0.9; Th. 0.1; Wt. 2.7

67. Iron strigil with long loop handle and narrow spoon; the handle is broken but complete, the spoon is broken into four pieces with parts missing. The handle continues up from the spoon in a single piece, then loops sharply back down to the underside of the spoon where it attaches. **Fig. 7.6**
Inv. 245. Tr. 96.5 extension.4.6. City Wall near Hexagonal Tower
L 21.0; L handle 10.5; W 3.5; Th. est. 0.2
Williams et al. 1997, 65.
At Isthmia, one of the Panhellenic Games sites, almost 100 strigils (slightly more made of iron than of bronze)

were left as dedications in the sanctuary, Rautbitschek 1998, 121 nos. 460–75 and pp. 173–4 Appendix J, fig. 26 pl. 73. Ones from Corinth are consistently similar to the Stymphalos example, Davidson 1952, 180–1, 183 nos. 1310–17; Blegen, Palmer, and Young 1964, pls. 80–1. Many bronze strigils were found at Perachora, of which the two best are Payne et al. 1940, pl. 80.15–16. Two strigil handles of iron came from the same site, ibid., pl. 86.30–1. A bronze strigil from Nemea similar to the Stymphalos one of iron came from a pit with mixed fifth- to late fourth-century material, Stephen G. Miller 1980, 196 pl. 47c. Dozens of strigils were found at Olynthos, mostly in graves, both male and female, made of iron and bronze; see Robinson 1941, 172–88 nos. 517–69 pls. 32–6, and p. 172 n. 49 for references to examples elsewhere. Women are sometimes shown using a strigil in bathing scenes, as on an Attic red-figure stamnos, Caskey 1939, 79 fig. 10. For an iron strigil with dedicatory inscription on the handle, see Carapanos 1878, 107–8 pl. 26.8,8 bis.

68. Part of the handle and spoon of an iron strigil, flattened and broken at both ends. Corroded surface, one edge of the spoon is folded over. **Fig. 7.6**
Inv. 1458. Tr. 97.9.5.5. SE of Terrace Wall
PL 11.3; PL handle 7.3; W handle 1.35

Hinges

These useful devices to allow the easy opening and securing of lids, doors, and other objects take a wide variety of forms, but basically depend on a pivot point and easy movement of parts. Both bronze and iron hinges probably belonging to small boxes are represented at Stymphalos, both plain and decorated with simple patterns.[27]

69. Two bronze hinge sections, each with two plates and two curved extensions to grab the hinge rod. The upper plate is scalloped along one edge with nail holes in each of the five half-rounds; the underside has matching nail holes of which some still have parts of nails; between the bronze plates are parts of the iron lid of a small box (?). **Fig. 7.7**
Inv. 3251 and 3278. Tr. 00.4.7.7 and 8. City Wall
PL a) 7.0, b) 7.2; PL extensions 2.0; L hinge 6.3; W hinge 2.3; Wt. a) 28.9, b) 36.2
Seven bronze hinges were preserved at Olynthos, and assumed to belong to wooden boxes and chests, Robinson 1941, 299–301 nos. 1301–7 pl. 86. Only one of them, no. 1306, has something approaching the scalloping of **69**. Closer, though, is a hinge from Dodona, Carapanos 1878, 99 pl. 53 no. 24, one of three found there. Judging from the bends in the bronze nails of **69**, about 1 cm distance from the bottom of the iron cover through which they penetrate, there must have been a wooden interior for this box. So, the bronze nails presumably acted to keep the iron sheeting attached to interior wooden boards.

70. Fragmentary bronze sheet with two half-rounds along one edge, a small hole through the middle of each, and a curled edge (for a hinge?) at about 90° to the other edge. The curled edge is divided in two by a "V" cut, and there are two holes along this edge as well, with room for a third, now missing. **Fig. 7.7**
Inv. 3684. Surface find
MPD 7.3
Almost exactly the same shape of bronze sheet was found at Philia except that the curl for the hinge was placed at 180° to the two half-rounds, and the spacing for the nail holes close to the hinge suggests only two were there, rather than possibly three on the Stymphalos fragment. A second piece with two half-rounds also came from that site, but was found separately; see Kilian-Dirlmeier 2002, 169 nos. 2941–2 pl. 173. These decorative bronze hinges held the lid for a small wooden box. Judging from these two examples, there were probably two or three pairs of half-rounds, each with nail holes set well apart from the hinge edge, though not exactly at the compass points.

71. Bronze band with tight curve at the end to wrap around a solid rod (hinge), decorated with two rows of small closely spaced squares; three irregular holes puncture the surface of which one may be a nail hole, broken at one end. **Fig. 7.7**
Inv. 3590. Tr. 96.15.5.5. Refuse pit – West Annex area
PL 4.5; W 1.85; W at curved end 1.3
It seems likely that such bronze bands, here with a hinge, decorated wooden boxes, perhaps for cosmetics or jewellery.

72. Bronze hinge decoration in the shape of a heart (said to have silver solder surface, but not shiny). **Fig. 7.7**
Inv. 1022. Tr. 96.13.6.12. S of Altar area
L 1.8; W 1.4; L loop for hinge 0.8; Wt. 0.8
The loop to receive a metal rod for the hinge is a simple bend over the upper part of the heart-shaped object. This may have been soldered onto a bronze box lid or other light object.

73. Iron plate in six pieces, with five small bronze pins in place. Three of the plate pieces, including a corner one, have extensions which probably are hinge grips. The pins have round caps and all have bent tips well below the level of the bottom of the plate (by ca. 0.7 cm), suggesting another material, like wood, that they penetrated before their tips were bent to secure them safely in place, as **69**. Badly corroded. **Fig. 7.7**

Inv. 171. Tr. 96.3.3.5. Altar area
Max. PL 2 joining pieces 5.3; Th. plate 0.3; D pin head 0.95; L pin 1.8

74. Triangular iron sheet with two extensions curled tightly to grip a hinge rod. One edge has an incurled rim which curves away from the hinge like a partial collar. Two pieces; the second preserves no original edges. Corroded. **Fig. 7.7**
Inv. 3451. Tr. 97.4 surface cleaning
L hinge 5.25; MPD a) 8.35 b) 6.9
The angle of the collar edge at about 75° to the hinge is odd, but may make sense if this is a hinged door to a circular object like a lantern.

Bronze door bosses

Door bosses (also called "door attachments" and "studs") are found commonly in three main shapes, a tall pointed one, a shorter pointed one, and a simple domed or rounded one, and they come in two or three sizes, varying from over 5 to less than 3 cm in diameter.[28] Lehmann notes at Samothrace that the "battens and meeting stile were attached by bronze bossed iron nails of square or round section."[29] In other words, the shorter horizontal cross boards (battens) were nailed to the longer vertical boards (stiles) to create a sturdy door leaf. Presumably the bronze boss provided a decorative exterior and protected the iron shank from rusting. Sixty bosses from a two-leaved exterior wooden door leading into a Macedonian tomb at Langaza were found along with remnants of the wood.[30] A single door leaf with 27 bosses still in situ was found at Lousoi, to the west of Stymphalos.[31] This had three double rows of bosses, each double row having a different kind of boss. One coin was found in the level with the door before the collapse of the roof tiles. It was identified as Sikyonian and dated 196–160/150 BCE. Mitsopoulos-Leon calculated the dimensions of the door leaf at Lousoi as at least 2.53 m high, and 0.51 m wide.[32]

Another door panel with three double rows of similar large bronze bossed nails and part of the iron lock (?) was found in a Roman-period house on the Lower Town Site at Stymphalos in 2001. Two of the double rows of five bosses were parallel to each other, while the third double row was found nearby but at a different angle and must represent a violent breaking of the door into two parts.[33]

Remains of another door were found at the entrance to the Edificio Quadrato at Foce del Sele. It has been restored with two door leaves having three bosses on each of three levels on each leaf, for a total of 18 bosses.[34]

More than 130 bronze bosses were found at Olynthos.[35] Robinson divided them into three types, plain rounded, rounded with an offset edge, and knobbed. Generally they come in two sizes, under 2.5 cm in diameter, and above 4.5 cm in diameter. Only one large one, no. 1170, is of the tall knobbed variety. Robinson observed their decorative use for doors, and the likelihood that they were soldered over the iron spike once it had been driven in, since the boss would be damaged otherwise.[36] This soldering has been remarkably strong, since in many cases the bronze boss itself has been ripped apart in trying to detach it from its placement. He also noted that they were not used solely on doors, but also on chests, other furniture like stools, window shutters, and perhaps even on shields. Besides wood, they may have decorated leather.[37] The short pointed or button type was found at Lindos, Locri Epizephyrii, Syracuse, and the Argive Heraion.[38] At Delos, 121 bosses ("cabochons") were divided into seven categories by size and shape.[39] There are two diameters for the Type A ones (ca. 6 and 2.6 cm), two of the Type B (6.3 and 2.7 cm), and three of the Type C (6, 5, and 2.9 cm). Some show that the iron nail was soldered to the bronze head. It is said that these certainly come from several wooden doors ornamented with decorative nails, and these nails were concentrated in area "μ" where there were commonly found burnt (calcined) wooden planks perhaps once from armoires for holding papyrii (library). In the Demeter Sanctuary at Cyrene, similar bronze bosses with conical heads were identified as dress pins. They are smaller (2.4 and 1.6 cm) in size.[40] In the Demeter Sanctuary at Knossos, again similar bronze bosses were suggested tentatively to be miniature cymbals, but at least one of them has iron in the central hole on the underside. Others from there are decorated with dot rows and rosettes, so they must have had another purpose.[41] The "pins" from the same site with bronze hemispherical heads and plain, often iron, shanks should belong in the same class as the bosses.[42]

Similar ones to the small domed type were also found at Corinth.[43] It would be reasonable to assume that the Stymphalos examples were made in Corinth, a well-known bronze-working centre, or perhaps another city along the coast..

75. Small conical boss with tip broken off; the stump of the iron nail is preserved. Bent rim. **Fig. 7.7**
Inv. 2391. Tr. 99.1.5.7. E of Terrace Wall
D boss 2.95; PH boss 1.25; Th. of rim 0.36; Wt. 11.3

76. Small conical boss with part of the iron nail. **Fig. 7.7**
Inv. 421. Tr. 96.7.2.2. City Wall
D rim 3.1; H boss 1.7; Th. rim 0.35; Wt. 13.1
In profile the boss dips from the rim, then rises in a central cone to a small knob. The iron nail is square in section.

77. Large boss with "button" knob, part of the iron nail shaft. **Fig. 7.7**
Inv. 2973. Tr. 00.4.3.3. City Wall
D rim 4.38; H boss 1.8; Wt. 31.8

78. Small rounded boss with iron nail shaft preserved in three pieces. **Fig. 7.7**
Inv. 1265. Scarp cleaning in Tr. 97.6. Pillar Shrine area
D rim 2.85; H boss 0.65; Wt. total 10.3; just disk with stump of shaft 9.5

79. Small rounded boss, broken in two pieces. **Fig. 7.7**
Inv. 1266. Scarp cleaning in Tr. 97.6. Pillar Shrine area
D rim 3.1; Wt. 6.3

80. Small rounded boss, part of the iron shaft. **Fig. 7.7**
Inv. 3457. Tr. 00.6.3.3. N of North Annex
D rim 2.9; W of inset border 0.4; H from top to broken shaft 1.4; Th. rim 0.2; Wt. 11.5

81. Small rounded boss, fragmentary, broken in two pieces. **Fig. 7.7**
Inv. 1185. Tr. 97.4.5.7. S of Terrace Wall
D rim 3.4; Wt. 9.7

82. Large rounded boss broken in two pieces. **Fig. 7.7**
Inv. 1347. Tr. 97.8.1.1. W of Temple
D est. rim 5.8; Wt. 28.5

Stamped roof tiles

Twelve stamped roof tile fragments from the Sanctuary, of which eleven have readable letters, are supplemented by eleven other stamped tiles from other parts of the city. Of the ones from other parts of the city, nine have names (an uninventoried piece is double stamped, the second stamp being upside down), one is a ligature, and one, a pattern. Most of these were found in the Artillery Bastion (Stym IV) just above the Sanctuary on the height of the acropolis, and of these, most were from a tile fall inside the Bastion that probably came from a layer of tiles that covered the mudbrick upper walls of the Bastion. Where they could be judged, only one stamp from the Sanctuary was placed on a convex surface. The rest came from the concave side of pan tiles.

One stamp from the Sanctuary and three from the Bastion apparently preserve the same name: TIMAIOΣ. Only one of these, inv. 2683, a surface find from the Bastion, preserves the full stamp, but a second, inv. 2279, also from the Bastion, preserves the first four letters, and **84** from deep in the destruction material inside the Temple (the only stamped tile found in the Temple) preserves the last four letters. Inv. 2317 only has the last three letters, but all three tiles which preserve the last letters have a small iota, a small omicron, and a spreading sigma. The omicron in all three is filled in rather than hollow (that is, a large dot rather than a circle). Both inv. 2317 and **84** have a sigma whose upper arm reaches the top rounded corner of the stamp, but the former has a thicker iota and it also has evidence of dark red paint over its surface. Furthermore, **84** and 2317 are made of similar hard, pinkish-orange clay with dark red and white inclusions, while inv. 2683 and 2279 have buff to yellow clay with grey inclusions. These differences of stamps and clay do not mean that the name on them is not the same in all four cases. It is possible that these four stamped tiles originated in the Sanctuary, or that the Temple roof tile and those on the Bastion wall are indicative of construction work at the same time.

Other complete or almost complete names on stamps from Stymphalos include ΛΑΕΡΤΑΣ (inv. 2371 – Bastion),]ΙΣΧΥΠΑΣ (inv. 2162 – Bastion), ?]ΦΙΛΙΑΣ (**83** – Sanctuary), and ΘΩΡΑΙ[(inv. 1601 – Bastion).

Miller argued that at Nemea the stamped tiles represented not the tile maker but the person or group to be credited with the roof construction, since the three types found there had ΔΑΜΟΙΟ (a form of "damosios"), NEMEIOU (crediting the demos of Nemeias), and genitive forms of the name ΣΩΣΙΚΛΕΣ (or a nickname, ΣΩΚΛΕΣ), who is named as "architect" (ΣΩΚΛΗΣΑΡΧΙΤΕΚΤΩΝ) on stamped tiles at the Argive Heraion.[44] Two stamps on Corinthian roof tiles support this idea. One cover tile is stamped KORINTHIΩN, crediting the building to the Corinthian people, and the other appears on tiles found both at the South Stoa and the Theatre, and is thought to credit the magistrate ΞΕΝΟΛΑΟΣ.[45] All the stamped roof tiles from the Demeter sanctuary at Corinth were Roman in date, most having the abbreviated name of the colony stamped on them, along with an abbreviated form of what is thought to be the maker's name.[46] In a way, then, the Corinth stamps fit Miller's proposed crediting of building projects to a person or group; in this case, the city. One Corinthian tile maker, Damostratos (Δαμόστρατος), is known from the building inscriptions of the Sanctuary of Asklepios at Epidauros.[47] He was contracted to provide tiles for at least two of the dwelling houses on the lower slopes of Mt Kyon, northeast of the sanctuary. This does not tell us, however, whether he stamped his name on the tiles. His name does not appear on any of the few stamped roof tiles preserved from pre-146 BCE Corinth.[48]

Most of the rest of the stamped tiles in the Sanctuary are from Building A. **90** and **91** may be related, with a possible omicron-iota ending, though the stamps are otherwise quite different, and neither is very readable. **87** begins with lambda-alpha, with faint letters and stamp with rounded corners, very much like Inv. 2371 from the Bastion, which has the full name – ΛΑΕΡΤΑΣ. It is interesting to see that very likely a second type of stamped tile is found at both the Sanctuary and the Bastion above it. The other stamps preserve a rather wide range of letters and types.

The letter forms are not particularly distinctive or datable. The appearance of a lunate sigma, on **92** (possibly also on **91**), is worth noting. This letter form appeared on an inscription at Stymphalos that has been dated ca. 303–300 BCE, but it is not likely to have been found on a roof tile stamp any earlier than that, and more likely later.[49] The very short cross stroke for the theta on **85** is also seen on the inscribed bronze rim, **22**.

The fabric of these roof tiles is not consistent. Some are made of fine, hard, pinkish-orange clay with red and white inclusions, while with others the clay is soft and powdery, orange or brown in colour, with quite different inclusions. At least two of them (**85** and **94**) are covered with red paint, similar to tiles from the theatre at Corinth, but without clay analysis, it is difficult to say which tiles were made locally and which were imported. There was at least some production of roof tiles locally, since a small stack of misfired tiles, vitrified in a mass, was found at Stymphalos (now on display in the Environmental Museum of Stymphalos).

83. Complete (?) stamp. Well-preserved stamp and thick-stroked letters.]ΦΙΛΙΑΣ (the phi is not completely clear; the four-stroke sigma is cramped and has irregular curves in the arms). The stamp is placed diagonally across the tile. Fine, hard, pinkish-orange clay. No visible inclusions. **Fig. 7.8**
Inv. 1069. Tr. 95.2.4.9. Building A
MPD tile 33.2; L stamp 8.6; W stamp 2.7; H letters 1.2 to 1.8

84. Partial stamp. Well-preserved stamp, clear letters.]ΑΙΟΣ (tall alpha and four-stroke sigma, short iota and omicron; solid omicron). Hard, pinkish-orange clay, with some dark red and white inclusions. Right upper corner is rounded, while the lower corner of the stamp is squared. **Fig. 7.8**
Inv. 3757. Tr. 95.4 + 1.2.3. Temple
MPD tile 12.4; PL stamp 6.5; W stamp 2.4; H letters 0.8 to 1.8

85. Partial stamp. Well-preserved stamp with squared corners, clear letters. ΘΕΑṆ[(theta with a dot for the cross stroke, curved upper and lower strokes of the epsilon). Fine, hard pinkish-orange clay, large white inclusions. Good dark red paint covering the surface. **Fig. 7.8**
Inv. 1401. Tr. 97.9.3.3. Room SE of Terrace Wall
MPD tile 19.5; PL stamp 6.0; W stamp 3.1; H letters 1.25 to 1.95
No similarities with **86,** which also begins with theta.

86. Partial stamp. Well-preserved stamp with rounded corners, one partial letter. Θ[. (theta with a dot for the cross stroke). Hard pinkish-orange clay with sandy white/grey/red inclusions. **Fig. 7.8**
Inv. 2229. Tr. 99.1.3.3. E of Terrace Wall
MPD tile 14.6; PL stamp 1.7; W stamp 2.1

87. Partial stamp. Clear stamp with rounded corners, but rather faint letters. ΛΑ[. **Fig. 7.8**
Inv. 92. Tr. 95.7.3.6. Building A
MPD tile 11.2
Possibly from a tile with the stamp ΛΑΕΡΤΑΣ, like one found with a well-preserved complete stamp at the acropolis Bastion, inv. 2317; see fig. 7.8. Watrous (1982, 162) comments on this name, which is given to one of the giants of the north frieze on the Siphnian Treasury at Delphi. He notes that the name is Eastern, and that it helps to characterize the giant as "barbarian," but Odysseus' father has the same name in Homer (Ionic vocalization "Laertes," *Od.* 1.179, 9.19–20).

88. Partial stamp. Squared corners, poorly preserved letters. Ḳ]Α[. (the first letter is not clear, and seems more like a ligature, the second letter is more clear). Soft orange clay with large pebbly inclusions. **Fig. 7.8**
Inv. 93. Tr. 95.7.3.6. Building A
MPD tile 11.6; PL stamp 4.0; PW stamp 3.2; PH letters 1.7
This is the only stamp on the convex surface of a tile. It was found in the same trench and level as **87**, and has the same second letter, alpha, but the first letter cannot be a lambda. For an example of ligatures on a second-century BCE roof tile from Megalopolis, Lauter 2002, 380 fig. 12 a, b (Δ + Α and Η + Κ).

89. Partial stamp. Well-preserved stamp, with thin-stroked "wobbly" letters. Ị]ΗΣ[. (the four-stroke sigma has a horizontal upper stroke but a diagonal lower stroke).

Hard light brown clay with white and dark brown inclusions. **Fig. 7.8**
Inv. 94. Tr. 95.3.5.9. North Annex
MPD tile 7.3; PL stamp 4.9; PW stamp 2.8; H letters 1.4

90. Partial stamp. Deeply stamped with rounded corners, but poorly preserved, small thick-stroked letters. ?]Α̣Μ̣Ο̣Ι. It is difficult to be certain that the stamp is to be read this way rather than reversed, in which case the first letters may be ΚΥ̣Α̣Ν[Hard, pinkish-orange clay with small red and white inclusions. **Fig. 7.8**
Inv. 1141. Tr. 95.2.4.9. Building A
MPD tile 16.5; PL stamp 6.9; W stamp 2.9; Max. PH letters 1.6
One might like to read "Damoi," but the letter before the possible alpha seems to have a vertical stroke close beside the alpha, so a delta does not seem likely.

91. Partial stamp. Shallow impression with rounded corner, thick-stroked letters, poorly preserved.]Χ̣Ο̣Ι̣ or]Κ̣Ο̣Ι̣ or]Χ̣Ο̣Ϲ̣ or]Κ̣Ο̣Ϲ̣. Only the small omicron seems to be sure. The last letter may be a lunate sigma. Rather soft powdery pinkish-orange clay, dark orange and white inclusions. **Fig. 7.8**
Inv. 1140. Tr. 95.2.4.9. Building A
MPD tile 22.1; PL stamp 3.3; W stamp 2.7; Max. PH letters 1.6

92. Partial stamp. Shallow stamp with square corners, small, clear but shallow letters. .]ΙΜΟϹ. The small solid omicron and lunate sigma are distinctive. Powdery, light brown clay, small white and large dark red inclusions. **Fig. 7.8**
Inv. 874. Tr. 95.2.3.6. Building A
MPD tile 21.0; PL stamp 5.0; W stamp 2.3; H letters 0.7 to 0.9

93. Partial stamp with a square corner, preserving only the last letter clearly. .]Σ (spreading sigma). **Fig. 7.8**
Inv. 98. Tr. 95.9.3.4. North Annex
MPD tile 32.0

94. Partial stamp. Deep but indistinct stamp with rounded corners. No letters can be discerned. Hard light red clay with many red inclusions. Dark red paint. **Fig. 7.8**
Inv. 2867. Tr. 96.10 surface. City Wall
MPD tile 22.3; PL stamp 4.5; W stamp 2.7

Terracotta Perirrhanteria (Louteria)

Large shallow basins with thick down-turned rims, decorated with horizontal grooves and occasionally red and black paint, were made of coarse clay but finished in a fine slip, except in the middle of the basin itself where instead "grog" was left to strengthen the surface. Most if not all the examples from Stymphalos must have come from Corinth.[50] The basins are formed in a mould,[51] and set on top of a tall column support with wide-spreading base to reach a convenient height for use in washing one's hands, and perhaps face. In a sanctuary context, its use is presumed to be for worshippers to cleanse themselves ritually. This use provides the term "perirrhanterion," as opposed to "louterion" for common bathing.[52] Such perirrhanteria were common products of the Corinthian potters from as early as the seventh century, but they continued to be exported as late as the fourth century.[53] In the Athenian Agora, Corinthian examples of the shape were found in three fabrics, including the common Corinthian tile fabric, and two others – Corinthian red and the so-called Sandy Class.[54]

Evidence in the Sanctuary at Stymphalos of the column supports is only preserved as part of the heavy wide-spreading base. For **96** the support is simply round, but a large terracotta fragment (inv. 967) found near the lakeside houses (Stym I) had Doric flutes decorating its exterior surface, like one from the Dema house.[55] Four bases from perirrhanteria were found in the Sanctuary, two of which are similar in shape, but the other two are significantly different. This may suggest that perirrhanteria lasted quite long and were only replaced when needed, perhaps as special orders. **98** and **99**, a base and part of a basin with rim respectively, may belong together based on decoration and fabric.

These vessels for ritual purification were commonly located near the entrance of the sanctuary, for example at Lindos,[56] or the entrance of a temple, for example at the Poseidon temple at Isthmia.[57] At Stymphalos, a stone base was excavated in situ at the right side of the first step leading up to the entrance of the Temple.[58] The base had a shallow round cutting set into the top of the block to a depth of 2.0 cm; its diameter is 0.405; there is no evidence for clamps. Normally the base for a statue would have a deeper cutting, and an indication of the method for securing the statue to the base, for example with clamps. Since the location of the base in the Sanctuary is suited for a worshipper to turn to the right and wash him- or herself before climbing four more steps to the entrance to the Temple, it seems probable that a perirrhanterion was set on the base, though perhaps not a stone one as might be found in wealthier sanctuaries, but rather a terracotta one such as those produced in Corinth, and used at Isthmia or in Corinth's Demeter Sanctuary.[59] The only significant problem with this idea is that none of the three preserved perirrhanterion bases is exactly the right diameter for the preserved cutting. Dating of similar perirrhanteria at Corinth suggests a fifth-century date, with the latest in the fourth century. The same is true for a well-dated example from the Dema house.[60]

95. Double base fragment. Three pieces of which two join. The lower part is a thick square base, while the upper part is a wide-spreading round base having a vertical rise, then at a sharp carination it inclines in a straight line to a thickened band of clay at the join of the base to the missing support column. An oval clamp (?) hole is partially preserved in the middle of the inclined upper base. Stamped pendant lotus and palmette chain along the top edge of the upper base. Buff to pink clay with many dark red, black, and white inclusions. Buff slip over the surface, possibly some traces of black paint on the exterior. Burnt in a fire on the bottom resting surface. **Figs. 7.9 and 7.20**
Inv. 1511 and 1654. Tr. 97.8.2.3 (W of Temple) and Tr. 97.12.3.3 (S of Temple)
PL square base 27.0; PW square base 12.5; H of square base section 6.6; D round base section 47.0; PH 19.0; L of clamp (?) hole ext. 4.5, int. 3.0
For the shape, with a square base and round shaft, see Iozzo 1987, nos. 120 (KN 162), 121 (C-65-324), and 122 (C-70-595). The first of these is also decorated with stamps, but early ones (triangles, running spirals, and spiral hooks), Weinberg 1954, 128 n. 121 pl. 30.f. The second was found in a context dated between the fifth and fourth centuries. The third of the three is painted with a dolphin using shading for details, dated to the end of the fifth–early fourth century, Iozzo 1987, 410 pl. 82. Several of the stands from the Demeter Sanctuary at Corinth have stamped patterns, such as rosettes, palmettes, ovules. None are similar to the anthemion pattern on **95,** perhaps because they are earlier in date, Pemberton 1989, nos. 661–5, 669–70, 674 pls. 60–1; Iozzo 1987, 388–98 nos. 64–89 passim. Pemberton (1989, 76) suggests that the use of red and black paint began at the end of the sixth or early fifth century, while the use of stamped decoration may have ended in the earlier fifth. It should be cautioned that dating evidence for this at Corinth is not strong.

One important consideration is that the stone base with round cutting at the foot of the Temple stairs has similar upper dimensions to the square base of this perirrhanterion (close to 50 cm sq. for the stone, and an estimated 47 cm sq. for the perirrhanterion), but the stone base has the round cutting, which would have no purpose if this perirrhanterion were used here. One possibility is that **95** was in use at the Temple first, and when it was damaged, it was replaced with a new perirrhanterion having a round base that was set on the stone with the round cutting. The lotus flowers all have the same fault in the lotus pattern stamp with a chip missing from beside the right petal.
Perhaps fifth century

96. Thick, low, wide-spreading base; narrow resting surface on its outer edge, and the beginning of the round support column. A hole at the top of the domed underside of the base may be to allow for proper firing. Eleven joining fragments. Light orange clay with coarse dark brown inclusions. Powdery, light brown clay on the surface from a thick slip. **Figs. 7.9 and 7.20**
Inv. 2511 and 1673. Tr. 99.1.5.10 (E of Terrace Wall) and Tr. 97.4.5.8 (S of Terrace Wall)
D base 32.5; PH 10.2; D column 13.5; D firing hole 4.0
This shape seems to be an earlier type, though here without decoration; compare Iozzo 1987, nos. 66–71. The diameter of the base is smaller than that of the cutting in the square stone base beside the Temple stairs by about 8 cm.

97. Thick, low, wide-spreading base, and the beginning of the round support column. Seven joining pieces. Soft, light orange clay. **Fig. 7.9**
Inv. 1602. Tr. 97.12.3.3. S of Temple
D base 51.0; D int. column 18.5; PH 6.5; H at base rim 2.5

98. Thick-walled base rising steeply from a narrow plain resting surface then angling in towards the missing support column. 4 + 2 grooves on the inclined upper part. Fifteen fragments, many joining. Orange-brown clay with medium-size brown inclusions. Trace of red paint in one groove. **Fig. 7.9**
Inv. 2794. Tr. 99.1.4.5. E of Terrace Wall
D base ca. 44.0; PH 14.8
Same fabric, perhaps from the same perirrhanterion as **99**. Pemberton (1989, 77 no. 666 pl. 60) believes that a similar basin with shallow grooves at Corinth belongs to the fourth century. The round cutting in the square base beside the Temple is 4 cm too small to hold this base.

99. Thick, broad out-turned rim fragment which drops vertically to give a wide outside face divided by six ribs. The grooves between the raised ribs are decorated alternately with fugitive black and red paint. Coarse dark orange clay with large medium brown inclusions. Fine light brown powdery clay slip on the surface. **Figs. 7.9 and 7.20**
Inv. 1571. Tr. 97.9.5.5. Room E of Terrace Wall
D rim est. 60.0; W rim 6.5; H rim outside face 5.7; MPD 16.7
See **98** for the fabric. Compare Iozzo 1987, 375 nos. 41–2 fig. 2, and nos. 126, 131 fig. 6. These broadly range in date from the mid-fifth through fourth century BCE.

100. Basin with thick out-turned rim which drops vertically to a wide outside face divided by three raised ribs and ending in a slightly flaring lower edge. Many fragments, some joining. Soft, powdery beige clay slip on the surface, light orange clay in the core with dark red, grey, brown, and some large white inclusions. The floor of the basin lacks any clay slip; the surface is full of coarse gritty particles ("grog"). Possible dull dark brown paint on the upper surface and outside face of the rim. **Figs. 7.10 and 7.20**
Inv. 0123, 1166, and 2248. Tr. 95.8.3.8. W of Temple
D rim est. 55.0; W rim 3.6; H rim outside face 4.7; MPD a) 36.0 b) 20.6 c) 19.5
For similar rims at Corinth, see Iozzo 1987, 375 nos. 40, 44 fig. 2, which date roughly from the mid-fifth through early fourth century. Iozzo (357) notes that the floors of basins were covered in a layer of "grog" to protect them from wear in the Classical period.

101. Thick broad out-turned rim fragment which drops vertically to a wide outside face divided by two preserved grooves, broken at the lower edge. Soft, fine, beige clay on the surface, coarser below with white, dark brown, and some larger red inclusions. Dark reddish-brown paint on the upper rim surface. **Figs. 7.10 and 7.20**
Inv. 1428. Tr. 97.8.2.2. W of Temple
D rim est. 55.0; W rim 7.3; PH rim outside face 4.8; MPD 19.5
For the downward sloping rim upper face, compare Iozzo 1987, 379 no. 46 fig. 2 pl. 69, which was found in a fifth-century well deposit at Corinth.

102. Thick broad out-turned rim fragment which drops vertically to an outside face divided by two preserved grooves, broken at the lower edge. Fine light brown clay with a few small grey and dark red inclusions. Black ash and burnt surface on under side. **Fig. 7.10**
Inv. 4552. Tr. 99.1.5.12. E of Terrace Wall
W rim 5.5; MPD 11.7

103. Plain, thickened flat rim and shallow basin wall fragment. Light orange clay with grey and black inclusions. Fine buff slip preserved on the flat upper surface of the rim and upper basin wall. Red paint on the rim, now mostly worn off. The underside of the basin is only roughly finished. **Figs. 7.10 and 7.20**
Inv. 3713. Tr. 00.6.2.2. N of North Annex
D rim est. 52.0; W rim 4.5; MPD 31.2
Unlike the other rim fragments with wide outside faces decorated with grooves, this rim simply narrows to a rounded edge without decoration. It is not clearly from a perirrhanterion as opposed to a simple shallow basin for common usage. At Corinth, plain rims are found on early basins, dated ca. 600 BCE, Iozzo 1987, 359 no. 4 pl. 63.

Stone Objects

A variety of stone objects were found in the Sanctuary, including two fragments from stone mills (**104–5**), a bead or spindle whorl (**106**), a white marble fragment (**107**) possibly from a vase (compare the marble pyxides **2–6**), and a sampling of chipped flint or chert bladelets (**108**).

104. Hand mill. Corner fragment of the upper stone of an "Olynthus" mill with rim, part of the sloping side of the hopper, the edge of the slot for the lever, and part of the lower grinding surface with herringbone striations. No evidence for the feeder slit. Dark grey volcanic stone. **Figs. 7.10 and 7.19**
Inv. 1402. Tr. 97.5.4.8. E of Terrace Wall
For the "Olynthos mill," see Frankel 2003; also Moritz 1958, 42–52 for development of the hopper mill from the Classical handmill; Runnels 1981, 119–22, 217, 330 fig. 14 for a description and discussion of the hopper mill; and White 1963, 200–1 n. 17 for the use of lava for mills for its hardness and abrasive surface, with ancient references. The ventral surface of **104** shows some signs of wear in the polishing of the surface. The herringbone furrows help lead the ground grain towards the edge of the grinding slab for collecting. This herringbone pattern on the underside is similar to that on a mill from the Mahdia shipwreck (dated to the second half of the second century or first half of the first century BCE), Frankel's Type IIIg, and the shape with lever slot on the short side (regular, not butterfly hopper) aligned with the feeder slit is Frankel's Type II4 or II5; see Frankel 2003, 12–13 figs. 8g and 10, II4, II5; for the Mahdia wreck hand mill, see Baatz 1994, 97, 99–100 figs. 4–6. Frankel (2003, 7, 18) notes the first appearance of the Olynthos mill in Greece in the fifth century BCE. It came into widespread use by the fourth century. Runnels (1981, 122) dates the hopper mill from the fifth to the first centuries BCE, with its greatest period of use in the fourth century. See his figs. 24–6 for hopper mills from Athens (Agora) and Halieis, and pls. 23–5 for hopper mills from Corinth and Halieis. For grain mills including hopper mills from Olynthos, Robinson and Graham 1938, 326–34 pl. 80, and fig. 34 for a reconstruction drawing of the use of the hopper mill. Millstones have also been found in shipwrecks, including the Serçe Limanı wreck, dated ca. 280–275 BCE, Pulak and Townsend 1987, 41–2. Other hopper mills from Delos and elsewhere are discussed, along with the drawing from a mould-made bowl showing its use, in Deonna 1938, 126–9 figs. 153–6, pls. 49–50. At least 15 finished hopper mills were found in the fourth-century Kyrenia shipwreck; see Runnels 1981, 125–6. These were made of vesicular andesites

probably from the island of Nisyros (note Strabo, 10.5.16, 488 for production of millstones on that island). Runnels believes that millstones in the Argolid and Attika were produced either on Aigina or Poros during the Greek period. One expects that Stymphalos, with its connections to the Argolid, probably got its millstones from the same locations. Andesite quarries for millstones are also found in the Methana peninsula.

A mortar, perhaps for grain, was mentioned in the Sanctuary of Kynthian Zeus on Delos, provoking the question by Deonna (1938, 103) whether it was a dedication or had a practical use in the sanctuary. The same question can be asked of the millstone in the Sanctuary at Stymphalos. Both **104** and **105** were found with coarse fill on the east side of the Terrace Wall below the Altar court.

105. Hand mill. Fragment with herringbone pattern on the flat surface of an Olynthos mill. Medium grey volcanic stone. **Fig. 7.10**
Inv. 2335. Tr. 99.1.5.5. E of Terrace Wall
PL 20.6; Max. PW 4.3
Certainly a different stone from **104**, but it may belong to the lower stone of the same mill since the herringbone pattern is close though not the same (there is no line joining the angles of the pattern on **104**, Frankel 2003, 16).

106. Bead or spindle whorl (?). Small conical object with round hole drilled through the centre, dark grey stone, broken in half and missing edge fragments. **Fig. 7.10**
Inv. 687. Tr. 96.15.1.1. S of West Annex
MPD 1.9; D hole 0.45
The hole may be too small for this to be a spindle whorl. One of two spindle whorls from Perachora of similar shape has thread lines worn into the surface to confirm its identification, Dunbabin 1962, 518 nos. F1–2, pl. 194. Warden suggested the identification of another one from Cyrene as a bead rather than a whorl, Warden 1990, 49–50 no. 361 pl. 37. Compare also from Lindos, Blinkenberg 1931, nos. 346–403 pls. 13–14; and Knossos, Coldstream 1973, 114, 120–1 nos. 42–52 pl. 80 (believed to be Minoan).

107. Small fine white marble fragment with three shallow grooves on one side, finished smooth on three other sides, broken at two ends. **Fig. 7.10**
Inv. 2417. Tr. 99.6.4.4. E of Terrace Wall
L 1.65; PW 1.65; Th. 0.6
Possibly from a three-reed strap handle or other part of a marble vase (though without close parallels), rather than a fragment of sculpture.

108. Chipped bladelet. Three faciae lengthwise, secondary chipping along one edge. Grey chert with red mottling. Fragment. **Fig. 7.10**
Inv. 35. Tr. 95.4+1.1.2. Temple
L 1.8

Other bladelets:
Inv. 2839. Tr. 00.1.1.1. E of Bldg. A. PL 3.05; beige and red
Inv. 2175. Tr. 99.3.3.3. Bldg. A. PL 1.3; grey
Inv. 2148. Tr. 99.3.3.3. Bldg. A. PL 1.7; grey
Inv. 565. Tr. 96.4.4.7. Altar. PL 2.8; Max. W 1.0; grey
Inv. 622 from Stym I. 96.18.1.1. PL 1.73; Max. W 0.71; grey

Finished flakes:
Not inventoried. Tr. 96.15.5.5. S of West Annex. PL 2.1; red
Inv. 2093. Stray. PL 3.74; Max. W 1.62; red
Inv. 0566. Tr. 96.5ext. 2.3. City Wall. PL 2.88; Max. W 1.66; brown
Inv. 0567. Tr. 96.95.1.9.15. PL 3.33; Max. W 2.1; Th. 0.59; double-edged point, broken at both ends; mauve and white

Most such bladelets and flakes cannot be dated. Bladelets found a use in sickles, while the flakes finished on one edge might suit a threshing sled. The double-edged point could have been used as a scraper. Early Bronze Age celts were found in Stym X, lower on the acropolis ridge (see fig. 1.2a–b), suggesting the presence on the acropolis of much earlier inhabitants. This might offer a better explanation for the bladelets and flakes, since they would seem to have little use in the Classical and Hellenistic cult practices. On the other hand, a selection of similar flint bladelets and blades was published recently from a house at Tria Platania in Macedonia, Adam-Veleni, Poulaki, and Tzanavari 2003, 241–2 nos. 336–45 (colour photos), dated by their context to the late fourth–early third century BCE, although also identified in the catalogue is a Palaeolithic stone knife of imported flint reused by Hellenistic occupants of a house at Komboloi, ibid. 240 no. 331.

Worked bone

Only a few worked bone objects were found in the Sanctuary.[61] Among them were apparently appliqués to decorate small boxes or furniture, but it is not clear how they were attached since most do not have holes for tacks. A couple of bone objects had more practical functions; with their sharpened points they may have been needles or even styli.

120 a–f includes five astragaloi – three of goats (Capra hircus), two of sheep (Ovis aries), and one bovine (Bos taurus). The goat and one sheep astragalos have a hole drilled through them, presumably to allow them to be strung together, probably not as jewellery but as a way to keep them safely. They may have been used either for astragalomancy or games. The surfaces are polished slightly from wear or handling. This is a relatively common votive, most likely given by a woman, to the goddess.

109. Carved object in the shape of an amphora or acorn. Flat on the underside, slightly convex upper decorated side. Broken in three pieces and mended, some chips missing from the upper end and the lower tip. Very careful carving. Raised line (or two?) along its upper edge, a pair of thin raised lines a little way below, then a broad undecorated zone, two more pairs of thin raised lines, followed by three rows of half-leaves before it narrows to an undecorated point. **Fig. 7.11**
Inv. 2423. Tr. 99.5.2.2
PL 4.5; W 2.4; Th. 0.3; Wt. 3.3
The shape is puzzling, but it may be meant to represent an amphora. Miniature amphoras at Delos and Rheneia made of lead, or in one case a stone mould for making such amphoras, have somewhat similar patterning around their lower walls. See Deonna 1938, 340 pls. 1.6, 80.849–54. For a bronze pendant which is also amphora-shaped (without handles) but has three rows of "leaves" in the upper half of its body, see Raubitschek 1998, 69–70 no. 265 pl. 40.
The half-leaves near the base remind one of the imbricate leaf pattern on mould-made bowls, as Edwards 1975, 158–61 nos. 786–92 pl. 65.

Pieces of carved and polished bone (nothing of ivory can be identified certainly in the Sanctuary) were occasionally used to decorate wooden boxes or perhaps furniture. Their method of attachment is not always clear. The flat undecorated underside of **109** suggests such a use for it, and other pieces, such as **112** and **113**, may have similar uses. **113** is undecorated, but the two small holes along one edge suggest that it was nailed to a larger object of wood. See Davidson 1952, 132 nos. 942–62 pls. 68–9. Compare also a bone pendant from the Sanctuary shaped like an acorn, Young, chapter 6 above, **179**.

110. Worked bone. Almost axe-blade shaped, broken at the narrower end where there is a slight reduction in thickness on both sides. Some knife marks are still visible on the upper (?) edge.
Furniture decoration (?). **Fig. 7.11**
Inv. 2402. Tr. 99.1.5.7
PL 4.5; W Max. 1.8; W Min. 0.7, Th. Max. (at narrower end) 0.4, Min. (at wider end) 0.2; Wt. 2.8

111. Worked bone. As **110**, but part of the "sharper" end has broken off, and it has broken at the narrower end where it becomes thinner, just as **110**. **Fig. 7.11**
Inv. 2324. Tr. 97.5.6.11
PL 4.0; PW Max. 1.5; W Min. 0.7; Th. Max. (at narrower end) 0.6. Min. (at wider end) 0.1; Wt. 2.4

112. Flat rectangular object. Badly burnt and warped (?). Many thin cut marks scored across the convex (inner?) surface, with a single careful groove lengthwise on the concave polished (outer) surface. Small chips from two corners. **Fig. 7.11**
Inv. 201. Tr. 95.4+1.2.3
L 5.5; W 1.0, Th 0.2; Wt. 2.1

113. Thin rectangular plaque. Two joining pieces preserving one side and parts of two other sides. Two small holes drilled through the piece close together near one edge. Broken along the full length of the other side. **Fig. 7.11**
Inv. 475. Tr. 95.4+1.2.3
L 3.6; PW 3.1, Th. 0.1; D holes 0.1; Wt. 2.9

114. Rectangular "bead." Complete (?), with a hole in one end, and a narrow groove carved around the outside of the other end. **Fig. 7.11**
Inv. 1163. Tr. 97.2 + 96.15 (no level or pail number on bag)
L 1.2; W 0.8; Th. 0.5; Wt. 1.0
This does not have a hole through it for stringing, just a hole which stops at the one end. It may have served as the head of a pin.

115. Carved and polished cylinder. Fair condition with pitting; broken on one end and a split on the other. Two narrow carved grooves around the circumference of one of the ends. A round hole pierces the short axis rather than lengthwise; another hole also pierces the end with the two narrow carved grooves of decoration. **Fig. 7.11**
Inv. 2192. Tr. 99.2.3.3. In front of Temple
L 2.3; D 0.7; Wt. 1.6.
This object might have been in imitation of a musical instrument such as an aulos, though one that is not hollow so no air could be blown down its length; it resembles an aulos fragment found in the Korykian Cave, although much smaller in size.[62]

116. Short tubular object, half preserved with a hole pierced through it; both ends are smooth. Polished shiny ext. surface; porous rough interior surface. Burnt black. **Fig. 7.11**
Inv. 1569. Tr. 95.1.2.3
PL 1.7; D 1.5; Th. 0.4; Wt. 1.6
This and likely also **117** are pieces from bone hinges similar to ones found at Corinth, Delos, and elsewhere. Wooden rods would join several of these hinges

lengthwise, and short wooden plugs would extend from chest lids or from the chests themselves into the lateral holes to allow the lids to pivot securely on the rods. See Davidson 1952, 128–9 nos. 872–4 pl. 64; Deonna 1938, 242–4 pl. 78.

117. Worked fragment, as **116**, from a short tubular object, about one-quarter preserved.
Not burned black, but perhaps calcined or bleached by the sun. **Fig. 7.11**
Inv. 688. Tr. 96.9.2.2
PL 1.55; Th. 0.3; Wt. 1.4

118. Point fragment. Pin or needle. Broken at one end and the tip may be missing part at the other. **Fig. 7.11**
Inv. 2326. Tr. 97.2 + 96.15.4.4
PL 2.2; W 0.4; Wt. 0.4
Bone needles are common at Corinth, but not until the Roman period; see Davidson 1952, 173–4 pl. 78–9, and see pl. 147a and b for stages in the production of such bone implements. Bone pins are also very common, and like needles are found mostly in Roman and later contexts, Davidson 1952, 278–80 pls. 118–20.

119. Thick point. Very coarse carving with the knife taking long strokes off the sides and ends. One side was sharpened to a point but it has broken at the tip. **Fig. 7.11**
Inv. 3277. Tr. 00.4.7.8
PL 8.2; W 0.6; Wt. 6.0
Without the other end being preserved, it is impossible to identify its use certainly. It is quite thick, and rather carelessly carved, but compare a spatulate instrument from Roman Corinth, Davidson 1952, 182, 184 no. 1336 pl. 82.

120. **a)** Goat astragalos with drilled hole through the centre. **Fig. 7.11**
Not inventoried. Tr. 00.3.4.4. S of Terrace Wall
L 3.1; Max. W 1.6; D hole 0.56
b) Goat, left astragalos with drilled hole. **Fig. 7.11**
Not inventoried. Tr. 00.3.4.4. S of Terrace Wall
c) Goat astragalos with drilled hole.
Inv. 300. Tr. 96.11.3.5
L 2.7; Max. W 1.5; D hole 0.6
d) Sheep, right astragalos with drilled hole.
Inv. 2325. Tr. 96.13.6.11. S of Altar area
L 2.8; W 1.8; Th. 1.7; Wt. 3.7
e) Sheep, right astragalos without a hole.
Inv. 2323. Tr. 96.8.6.7
L 3.0; W 1.6; Th. 1.4; Wt. 3.2
f) Cow, mid-left astragalos, cut straight on both sides. **Fig. 7.11**
Not inventoried. Tr. 99.1.6.12. E of Terrace Wall
Presumably cut this way to carve it into a usable object, or cut away from the astragalos to use the adjacent piece of the bone in bone-working.
(I am grateful to D. Ruscillo for comments on these worked bone pieces.)

Astragaloi are found commonly in sanctuary contexts. For a selection and references, see Deonna 1938, 332–4 pls. 93.820–4, 94.825, some pierced; Amandry 1984, 347–80. Amandry gives a lengthy discussion and lists of the hundreds of astragaloi found in the Korykian cave. Almost 2,900 are listed which have holes bored through them, pp. 349–56, 359–62. Further discussion of astragaloi is found in Poplin 1984, 381–93. Two published bone examples from the Demeter Sanctuary, Cyrene, likewise are pierced possibly for suspension, while other examples are in bronze, also pierced, Warden 1990, 65–6 nos. 492–9 (bronze), 500–1 (bone). For examples in other materials, see Robinson 1941, 503 nn.73–5, to which can be added a lead-weighted bone example from Torone, Cambitoglou et al. 2001, 720 no. 17.100 fig. 170 pl. 95. Warden (1990, 66) discusses the uses of astragaloi, including gaming pieces, for divination and as votives.

121. Cylindrical worked bone, mid-diaphysis of a mammal long bone. Worked on the edge to produce a notch, perhaps so it might interlock with another worked bone or other material. Fragment. **Fig. 7.11**
Not inventoried. Tr. 00.2.3.3
L cylinder 1.7; MPD 2.4
For two other similar fragments, see **116** and **117**.

122. Flat, polished bone, six fragments, from thick cortex bones, bovine or equid. Numerous, closely spaced, diagonal cut lines on one side of two of the pieces, and more careful decorative (?) diagonal crosses cut in another piece. Others are plain, without cut marks, perhaps to be used as inlay. **Fig. 7.11**
Not inventoried. Findspot: **122b** with careful diagonal crosses: Tr. 99.5.2.2 (Pillar Shrine); other fragments: Tr. 97.5.6.11 (E of Terrace Wall); Tr. 96.8.3.4 (West Annex); Tr. 99.1.5.8–11 (E of Terrace Wall); Tr. 99.6.6.6 (E of Terrace Wall); Tr. 97.5.3.4 (E of Terrace Wall).
Dimensions of larger pieces: PL a) 3.1, b) 5.35, c) 1.6; PW a) 0.91, b) 1.5, c) 1.0;
Max. Th. a) 0.35, b), 0.39, c) 0.14
Two boxes decorated with pieces of carved bone were found in a tomb near Thessalonika dating to the second half of the fourth or beginning of the third century, Kotzias 1937, 886–8, figs. 21–2, drawings XII–XIII. Included were large flat rectangular pieces, and fragments with incised figures. Two similarly shaped and polished pieces of bone were found at Torone, of which one was suggested to be a gaming piece, Cambitoglou et al. 2001, 720 nos. 17.98–9 fig.

170 pl. 95 with references to others at Corinth and Delos. These have more regular cuttings on them.

123. Worked piece of horn (?). Complete. Cut straight at both ends. **Fig. 7.11**
Inv. 486. Tr. 96.6.4.10
L 2.4; W 1.7; Th 1.1; Wt. 3.4

Miscellaneous worked bone fragments

Needle, mammal bone. Fragment of the end with an oval hole carved through it. **Fig. 7.11**
Not inventoried. Tr. 97.5.3.4. E of Terrace Wall
PL 1.9
Point – mammal bone – Tr. 97.2.4.4. S of West Annex
Sawn deer (Dama dama) mid-metatarsus cut at both ends – Tr. 96.8.3.4. Pillar Shrine area
Polished mammalian longbone fragment – Tr. 96.15.6.6. S of West Annex
Sawn cattle mid-rib (Bos taurus) – Tr. 99.10.1.1. N of North Annex

Utilitarian objects – bronze

Styli

Two objects can be identified as styli, one on the basis of its spatulate end, and the other on the basis of its pointed end and beaded shaft. The spatulate end served to erase writing on a wax tablet by smoothing out the wax.[63]

124. Small stylus. Complete. Part of the point is lost, the shaft has been bent, minor damage to the spatulate end. **Fig. 7.12**
Inv. 319. Tr. 96.3.3.5
PL 4.2; W head 1.0; Th. shaft 0.2; Wt. 0.8
Most styli are larger than this, but perhaps it suited a woman or child.

125. Point and part of the shaft. The shaft is square in section, but decorated with a beaded pattern where four sides of each "bead" are emphasized with a flat circle around a raised centre. The point is round in section, set off from the shaft by a reel and tapering slowly to the tip. **Fig. 7.12**
Inv. 1355. Tr. 97.5.4.7
PL 3.2; Th. Max. 0.35; Wt. 2.7
The shafts of bronze styli at Olynthos were regularly decorated in different ways, probably to help grip them. See Robinson 1941, pl. 114 esp. nos. 1725, 1727, 1731–4. None had the decoration of the Stymphalos example.

Ring Pulls

(See also **34–6**, for rings with decorative attachments.)

126. Small ring with iron strap looped around and across. Grooves along the ring. The iron strap doubles back around the ring to attach to it. **Fig. 7.12**
Inv. 579. Tr. 96.1.10.12. Temple
D ring 1.7; Th. ring 0.4; W of iron strap 0.45; Wt. 3.3
Such rings have been identified as "ring pulls" suitable for drawers or lids of furniture by Warden 1990, 45 nos. 299–300. At Olynthos, Robinson grouped such rings having attached pins with his "swinging handles" Type III – "Ring handles," Robinson 1941, 229–43, nos. 817–964 pls. 61–3. Cotter pins are commonly still attached to confirm the suggested use. A number of bronze rings with cotter pins were thought to be from pyxis lids at Isthmia, Raubitschek 1998, pls. 20–1 nos. 95–101; and for similar examples elsewhere, see DeCou 1905, nos. 947–8 pl. 88, nos. 2081–6 pl. 121; Kourouniotes 1910, 322 fig. 43; Blinkenberg 1931, 204 no. 637 pl. 26; Davidson 1952, 132 no. 903 pl. 67. It is easy enough to mistake such "ring pulls" for belt buckles, although belt buckles generally are larger, cf. for example two sizes of buckles from late Christian graves at Nemea, Stephen G. Miller 1988, 3 pl. 3d.

127. Small ring with bronze strap looped around and across. **Fig. 7.12**
Inv. 2215. Tr. 99.1.3.3. E of Terrace Wall
D ring 1.6; Th. ring 0.17; L of strap 1.6; Wt. 1.1

128. Small ring, square in section, with bronze strap looped around and across. The strap ends are bent sharply. **Fig. 7.12**
Inv. 427. Tr. 96.1.9.10. Temple
D ring 1.55; Th. ring 0.4; est. L of strap 2.7; Wt. 3.8

129. Small ring with bronze strap looped around and away. The strap widens where it loops around the ring. **Fig. 7.12**
Inv. 1046. Tr. 97.2 + 96.15.5.5. S of West Annex
D ring 1.7; L of strap 1.6; Wt. 1.7

Other bronze utilitarian objects

130. Ring. A break in the circle of the ring seems deliberate. **Fig. 7.12**
Inv. 3769. Tr. 96.15 surface. S of West Annex
D 2.3; Th. 0.25
This is one of several dozen found at the site. They are very common elsewhere. At the Demeter Sanctuary in Cyrene, Warden (1990, 39–40) noted 458 bronze rings, almost all being plain (only four were catalogued) and measuring between 6.0 and 2.0 cm or less in diameter.

He discussed the question whether they were votives or utilitarian objects. At the Argive Heraion, 550 rings were counted, DeCou 1905, pls. 90–2; at Olynthos, 147 were catalogued, Robinson 1941, 229–43 pls. 61–3; Kalapodi yielded over 500 plain bronze rings (Type A), Felsch 2007, 174–7 pls. 40–44.

130 is probably too small to be used in conjunction with a loomweight to hold a group of threads, which is one of several uses suggested for these rings. For other rings from the Sanctuary, see Young, chapter 6 above, Appendix II.

131. Ring. Iron rust clings to one side. **Fig. 7.12**
Inv. 2101. Surface cleaning
D 1.95; Th. 0.3; Wt. 3.8

132. Tweezers. Complete but bent at the handle so that one arm is straighter and the other more bent than originally. Formed from a single strip of bronze, rectangular in section, it has been curved in a circle in the middle to form two arms which angle outward and then back inward approx. 1 cm from the tips. **Fig. 7.12**
Inv. 903. Surface find
L 6.15; W 0.47; Max. distance between arms 2.05; Wt. 4.0
Simple tweezers like this were used by women for cosmetic purposes, including dipilation, and so have been presumed to be votives left by women, but this association is not a certain one. Seven bronze tweezers were found among the houses of Olynthos, Robinson 1941, 355–6 nos. 1713–19 pl. 113 (no. 1717 is closest to **132**). They were common dedications in the Diktaian cave, for example, where 5 complete and 50 partial ones were found, Hogarth 1899–1900, 111 fig. 45. Another 10 were found at Olympia, Furtwängler 1890, 68 nos. 493–6 pl. 25. At Kalapodi, 17 examples were found divided into 5 types from the Late Geometric to Archaic period, Felsch 2007, 206–7 (with references to many others), 355–6 nos. 1940–56 pl. 49. Felsch (2007, 207), however, notes that they are more commonly found in graves, and are not a common votive in sanctuaries, nor necessarily to be associated with women's toiletries. The examples from Kalapodi have wider arms. For surgical and cosmetic tweezers and dipilatories in the British Museum, see Walters 1899, 313 no. 2320 fig. 57 (surgical, tips end in teeth), 317–18 nos. 2394–8, 2403–18 figs. 71, 73. Some early Roman tweezers have much more solid, straight arms, such as Mitten 1975, 168 no. 51; even later, perhaps Byzantine, is Davidson 1952, 194 no. 1465 pl. 88. Cf. also Comstock and Vermeule 1971, 432 no. 627, acc. no. Res. 08.37.

133. Needle (?), solid cast, broken at one end and bent. **Fig. 7.12**
Inv. 238. Tr. 96.4.2.4. Altar area
PL est. 10.5; Max. Th. 0.2; Wt. 3.0
A complete needle was found in a small building (Stym XIV) beside the road leading to the Pheneos Gate at Stymphalos (inv. 4244 – L 15.7 cm). Examples from other sites are not rare, e.g., Cyrene, Warden 1990, 49 nos. 354–5. On the other hand, this may be just another pin shaft, which, when missing its end, cannot be classified as to type. See Raubitschek 1998, "straight pins" 44–7; Raubitschek merely groups such shafts into a list with find spots, Appendix D, p. 167 (22 listed).

Other fragmentary needles may have been found and simply treated as bronze shafts; see Young, chapter 6 above, Appendix III.

134. Narrow hollow tube, perhaps a needle. In fair condition with surface corrosion. **Fig. 7.12**
Inv. 2129. Tr. 96.4.(cleaning). Altar
L 11.0 cm; D 0.35 cm; Wt. 6.3

135. Needle (?). Broken and slightly bent at the thicker end. It comes to a point at the tapered end. The shaft is square in section. **Fig. 7.12**
Inv. 63. Tr. 95.4.4.4. Temple
L 7.7; W 0.3 thick end; Wt. 2.4

136. Needlelike object but tapered to a point at both ends. Bent twice. **Fig. 7.12**
Inv. 2494(?). Tr. 99.13.1.1
L 6.0; Th. 0.25; Wt. 1.9

137. Spindle hook. Hollow tube ending in a small hook. **Fig. 7.12**
Inv. 601. Tr. 96.13.2.4. S of Altar area
PL 2.1; Max. Th. 0.3; Wt. 0.2
Such hooks are found commonly, though not in large numbers, in both cultic and domestic contexts. At Stymphalos, taken in conjunction with the evidence for weaving, it may have been used in textile production. At Nemea, three "crochet hooks" were associated with Early Christian occupation in the stadium, Stephen G. Miller 2001, 124, 129 n. 305 figs. 229–30. For ones at Corinth, Davidson 1952, 173 nos. 1223–8 pl. 78. For others from Isthmia, Raubitschek 1998, 116 nos. 401 (iron), 402–4 (bronze) pl. 63, and p. 111 nn. 19–20 for spinning hooks from Lindos, Delos, and Olynthos. For Cyrene, Warden 1990, 48 no. 345 pl. 36, and p. 49 n. 32 for examples from Olympia. For Sardis, Waldbaum 1983, 62–3, 152 with other references. For Kalapodi, Felsch 2007, 245, 386 no. 2292 pl. 65. One of the five hooks from the Diktaian Cave still had a rivet to hold the wooden handle in place, Hogarth 1899–1900, 111 fig. 46.

138. Fish hook, broken at the upper end. The shaft has a narrow oval cross-section except at the upper end

where it was flattened and would have had an "eye" to attach it to a line. The bend of the hook is somewhat squared; the tip ends in a point with a sharpened tang. **Fig. 7.12**
Inv. 3155. Tr. 00.4.7.7. City Wall
PL 2.9; hook L 1.8
Twenty bronze fish hooks, dated from Archaic to Classical, were found at Isthmia, of which 19 came from a single deposit in the Sanctuary, Raubitschek 1998, 121 n. 15 nos. 453 (19) and 454 pl. 71. Several also were found at Corinth, Davidson 1952, 190 nos. 1447–9 pl. 88. A passage in *Anth. Pal.* 6.5 records fish hooks and lead-weighted fishing nets as dedications. One found at Nemea in mixed fill in the sanctuary of Zeus has the notches at the top end presumably for helping to hold the attached fishing line, Stephen G. Miller 1976, 184 pl. 33a. All of these are more rounded than the Stymphalos one. Another from Nemea has the same rather angled bend to the hook, but a smaller barb, Stella G. Miller 1984, 184 pl. 41b. For a sampling from Delos, both from religious and non-religious contexts, see Deonna 1938, 201 n.10, pl. 69.551–3, and for almost 100 fish hooks from Olynthos, Robinson 1941, 365–74 nos. 1788–1882 pls. 117–19. For recent discussions, based on ones from Torone, see Joyner et al. 2001, 730–1 nos. 18.20–3 fig. 171, and on over 40 from Olympia, see Baitinger and Völling 2007, 57–62 nos. 172–212 pl. 16 with references to many others in both sanctuaries and elsewhere. Fish hooks are not datable based on shape, since there is little or no change over time. For a possible fishing net weight in lead, see **213**, and for two lead bodkins which might have been used for fishing nets, see **219**.

139. Three small conical caps. **Fig. 7.12** (only two shown)
Inv. 1188 and 1296. Tr. 96.11.4.5. Temple
D a) 1.1 b) 1.03 c) 1.08; H 0.7; Wt. one "cap" 0.7, second "cap" 0.4
These caps were found within the Temple grave whose last occupant was a child (female, to judge from the little earrings and tiny bead necklace), but as many as five other burials preceded this one, and the burial was covered over with soil that must have come from the Temple vicinity. There are no holes for suspending these caps, but exactly the same was found for three similar bronze rounded domes from the sanctuary at Francavilla Marittima. See Papadopoulos 2003, 87–8, 207 nos. 246–8 fig. 110, with a reference to an unpublished piece of body armour from a grave at Liatovouni in Epeiros that had two groups of 14 such bosses on each shoulder. All three of the hemispheres from Timpone della Motta (Francavilla Marittima) were tested with an X-ray florescent spectrometer (as were all the other bronze objects in Papadopoulos' study) for their metal content, but the solder on the inside of two of them was also scanned. The solder or "alloy filler" was found to be pewter, composed of 53% lead and 47% tin. This solder explains the method by which they were attached to another metal surface.

140. Screen fragments. Three pieces of bronze sheet with holes deliberately punched through, perhaps from a strainer or lantern or cheese grater. **Fig. 7.12**
Inv. 954. Tr. 96.13.5.8. S of Altar area
MPD a) 2.1; Wt. 0.7
140–3 are similar in having deliberately punched holes, but their purpose is not clear. Strainers for wine lees, for example, are one possibility, but **140** seems more likely to be from the exterior wall of a lantern or perhaps a cheese grater. Cf. Warden 1990, 50 nos. 365–6, and see his nos. 17 and 402. Some similar examples, however, are not clearly part of a walled object; see Blinkenberg 1931, no. 693 pl. 29; Brizio 1899, pl. 4 fig. 5. Recently, Felsch 2007, nos. 2294–8 pl. 65 (frags.). Cheese may be grated into wine.

141. Screen fragment. A piece of bronze sheet with large punched holes, broken off then folded over twice. **Fig. 7.12**
Inv. 2840. Tr. 00.1.2.2. E of Building A
MPD 3.05; Wt. 3.6
More likely used as a strainer or sieve than a cheese grater, cf. Payne et al. 1940, pl. 81.11 (cheese grater) and 12 (sieve). Where the punctured holes were left sharp, Robinson was inclined to identify such sheets as graters, though they are not very sturdy; see Robinson 1941, 191–4 n. 18 (references to others) nos. 600–12 pls. 48–9.

142. Screen fragment. A piece of square-cut bronze sheet with parts of four straight rows of large square holes punched through. **Fig. 7.12**
Inv. 97. Surface cleaning
PL 3.5; PW 2.3; MPD 3.95; Wt. 2.2.
Judging from the neat rows and large size of the holes, this seems more likely to be from a lantern than a sieve.

143. Screen fragments with small square holes in rows. **Fig. 7.12**
Inv. 1578. Tr. 95.9.9.9
MPD a) 3.1, b) 3.0; Wt. of the four largest pieces 3.3
It is conceivable that this was from a cheese grater, but in a sanctuary context, there are other appropriate uses for such objects, whether to shield a flame in a lantern or catch wine lees.

144. Triangular plate with two large holes at the enlarged base. The tip is bent. **Fig. 7.12**
Inv. 2652. Tr. 99.1.5.10. E of Terrace Wall
PL 4.5; Max. W 4.35; D holes 0.9

It is difficult to tell whether the bent broken end came to a point or whether it was extended across to a second plate with two more nail holes (compare for example, Fürtwangler 1890, 97 no. 678 fig., or 165 no. 1011 fig.). If it is the latter, then this may be part of a handle, presumably attached to a wooden backing.

145. Plate attachment. Rectangular plate with four nail holes in the corners for attachment to a wooden (?) object. Part of one corner is broken off. **Fig. 7.13**
Inv. 3062. Tr. 00.3.4.4. S of Terrace Wall
L 3.4; W 1.9; Wt. 2.7
For similar attachments, see Warden 1990, 43–4.

146. Part of a plate attachment. Rectangular plate with two nail holes in the corners for attachment. Part of a bronze nail (?) adheres to the upper surface of the plate. **Fig. 7.13**
Inv. 2964. Tr. 00.2.4.4. S of Temple
PL 1.8; W 2.4; Wt. 2.6
As **145.**

147. Reinforcement band, slightly curved, one large hole at each end; complete in four pieces. **Fig. 7.13**
Inv. 312. Tr. 96.6.5.11. Pillar Shrine area
L 4.2; W 1.2; Wt. 2.6
Although similar to **148**, this is a shorter piece and the holes may not have been for similar pegs, but rather for rivets which would join to a second band with the same dimensions. Its use is unknown, though horse trappings or attachments to wood are possibilities. Compare Robinson 1941, pls. 138–9 for similar pieces.

148. Peg through a curved bronze band with holes for two more pegs – in three pieces. The peg "handle" is set diagonally to the length of the band. **Fig. 7.13**
Inv. 305. Tr. 95.4+1.2.4. Temple
L peg 2.4; L peg shaft 1.0; PL band a) 5.3, b) 2.8, c) 1.35; Th. peg handle 1.27; Max. W peg handle 1.5; Wt. total 20.8
The peg acts as a rivet, securing the bronze band to another object below. There is no clear reason to explain why the peg has such a triangular extension above the surface of the band, other than to create a more pleasing appearance. For curved iron bands with rivets through them used to produce a frame for a bronze shield, see Georgescu 2005, 277–9, figs. 38–9.

149. Peg (as **148**). Perhaps from the same object. Fig. **7.13**
Inv. 158. Tr. 95.4+1.2.2. Temple
L 2.13; L peg shaft 0.95; Th. peg handle 1.2; Max. W peg handle 1.0; Wt. 5.2

150. Reinforcement clamp, with two small oval bronze plates joined at each end by bronze rivets. Complete. **Fig. 7.13**
Inv. 651. Tr. 95.4+1.2.3. Temple
L plates 4.5; W 1.8; L rivets 1.5; Wt. 9.4
Used to join two objects together, presumably thin lengths of wood. A good variety of these support or reinforcement clamps were found at Olynthos, including ones with two plates, normally with just two nails through them, Robinson 1941, 301–9 nos. 1308–51 pls. 87–9. Others in bronze with two or four rivets came from Bassai, Kourouniotes 1910, 328–9, fig. 53, 1; from Timpone della Motta, Papadopoulos 2003, 129–30 nos. 450–4 fig. 161, and the Artemis Temple at Kalapodi, Felsch 2007, 388 no. 2327 pl. 66.

151. Two small oval plates, now twisted, joined with an iron rivet, two empty holes in both plates. **Fig. 7.13**
Inv. 2188. Tr. 99.94.3.3.3. Building A
L plate a) 2.45, b) 2.2; W 1.85; Wt. 1.3
Similar but smaller than **150** and using an iron rivet.

152. Oval plate, one hole preserved. Broken at one end. **Fig. 7.13**
Inv. 170. Tr. 95.4+1.2.3. Temple
PL 4.9; W 2.1; Wt. 2.9

153. Small oval plate, two holes, one small rivet or nail. **Fig. 7.13**
Inv. 1357. Tr. 97.7.2.2. Pillar Shrine
L 1.7; W 1.0; Wt. 0.6

154. Disk with two small pins and two holes. **Fig. 7.13**
Inv. 921. Tr. 96.10.5.5. City Wall
D 2.3; PL pin 0.62; Wt. 1.0

155. Nail. Complete. Square shaft; small head. **Fig. 7.13**
Inv. 260. Tr. 96.2.2.2. Altar area
L 4.8; D head 0.65; Th. shaft 0.2; Wt. 1.2
For a discussion of bronze and iron nails and tacks, see Munaretto and Schaus, chapter 8 below.

156. Nail. Missing part of its square shaft. **Fig. 7.13**
Inv. 278. Tr. 96.4.2.2. Altar area
PL 2.4; D head 0.7; Th. shaft 0.2; Wt. 0.8

157. Nail. Complete except for tip and part of the head. Shaft is square in section. **Fig. 7.13**
Inv. 261. Tr. 95.4+1.2.2. Temple
PL 3.7; D head 0.8; Th. shaft 0.2; Wt. 1.2

158. Three nails, one complete and the other two missing parts of their shafts. The shafts are square in section. **Fig. 7.13**
Inv. 756. Tr. 95.4+1.2.2. Temple
Complete nail: L 5.3; D head 0.8; th shaft 0.25; Wt. 1.7. Second nail: PL 3.4; D head 0.75; Th. shaft 0.25. Third nail is in two pieces: PL a) 1.2, b) 1.9; D head 0.75

159. Three small nails. Two are complete or almost complete, one is just a shaft. Shafts are square in section. **Fig. 7.13**
Inv. 754. Tr. 95.4+1.2.4 (or 5?). Temple
L a) 3.5, b) 3.1, c) 2.4; D head a) 0.7, b) 0.6; Th. shaft of all three 0.2; Wt. a) 1.3

160. Tack with long thin shaft and off-centre head where shaft is attached. Like several bronze nails/tacks above, it is from the Temple. **Fig. 7.13**
Inv. 678. Tr. 95.4+1.2.4. Temple
L 2.4; D head 0.6; Th. shaft 0.1; W 0.3

161. Tack with large head. Two pieces. Shaft is square in section, as with all these bronze nails/tacks. **Fig. 7.13**
Inv. 755; Tr. 95.4+1.2.4. Temple
PL of two pieces together 2.7; D head 1.5; Th. shaft 0.2; Wt. 1.8
A second small tack was found with this larger one, with L 1.2, D head 0.5, Wt. 0.3, and several other very narrow shaft fragments that do not seem to belong to either of these two.

162. Tack with long shaft. **Fig. 7.13**
Inv. 262. Tr. 96.4.2.2. Altar area
PL 3.0; D head 0.5

163. Small tack with small head. **Fig. 7.13**
Inv. 251. Tr. 95.6.5.7. N of Temple
L 2.1; D head 0.3; Wt. 0.3

164. Tack. Complete, with rounded head. **Fig. 7.13**
Inv. 1438. Tr. 95.9.8.8. North Annex
L 0.9; D head 0.7; W shaft 0.1; Wt. 0.3.

165. Tack. Almost complete (broken tip) with disk head. **Fig. 7.13**
Inv. 279. Tr. 95.4+1.1.4. Temple
PL 1.3; D head 0.8; Wt. 0.7

166. Group of twelve or so tiny pin shafts. **Fig. 7.13**
Inv. 753. Tr. 95.4+1.2.4. Temple
L 1.7 to 1.0; Th. Max. 0.14; Wt. group total 1.4
These were found together inside the Temple cella, but there was nothing to suggest what they belonged with.

167. T-staple with a square iron washer, badly corroded. **Fig. 7.13**
Inv. 2737. Tr. 99.13.3.3. S of Altar area
L shaft 1.8; PL T-arm 2.6; W washer 1.4
These T-staples are common, but rarely are found together with the iron washer which kept the intervening material tightly in place. For an example of one of these T-staples that had not been used, and so the end was not bent, see Carapanos 1878, pl. 52.16. Most commonly they are found bent, and so sometimes are seen as h-shaped in their original form, as Robinson 1941, 329 nos. 1544–52 pl. 96. More examples, dated to the Classical period, are Raubitschek 1998, 152, nos. 578–81 pl. 88, and Cambitoglou et al. 2001, 750–1 no. 18.79 fig. 173, pl. 97. Kilian-Dirlmeier (2002, 117) makes the suggestion that because so many were found at Thermopylai, they may have been used in the production of military equipment – for example, binding leather or wood to shields.

168. T-staple, square in section. Bent long arm. **Fig. 7.13**
Inv. 3068. Tr. 00.4.5.5. City Wall
L shaft est. 4.6; L T-arm 4.3, Wt. 3.0

169. T-staple, with all three ends sharpened. Bent long arm. **Fig. 7.13**
Inv. 556. Tr. 96.4.2.2. Altar area
H 1.4; L T-arm 2.3; Wt. 1.2

170. T-staple. Bent from use. **Fig. 7.13**
Inv. 353. Tr. 96.8.2.2. Pillar Shrine
H 1.6; L T-arm 3.1; Wt. 1.1

Utilitarian objects – iron

Obeloi – roasting spits

One hundred and thirty iron obeloi were recently published from Olympia, representing only a portion of the finds from that site since 1875. Many of them were recovered from wells.[64] This is one of the largest collections of iron spits in Greece and provides both a range in the shape of the grip ends and an indication of chronological development. Six types of grip ends were distinguished, although just four were found with more than one example, and just two were found in substantial numbers. The four types were a) round or oval grip end (7), b) half-moon or sickle-shaped grip (48), c) lancet- or lozenge-shaped grip (17), and d) triangular grip (5). Dating indications suggest that spits with the oval or round grip end (Type a) are the earliest, lasting through the last quarter of the sixth century. Type b spits begin in the second quarter of the sixth and last until the third quarter of the fifth at Olympia. Spits with lancet- or lozenge-shaped grip ends (Type c) are not well dated at Olympia but may continue from the seventh through the early fifth century. Type d spits with triangular grip ends are also poorly dated, though one came from an early fifth-century context.

It is difficult to confirm whether the Stymphalos spits fall easily into these types and general dating, since most material from the site has come from fourth-century or later contexts. A few objects from the Sanctuary are from the first quarter of the fifth century, but nothing earlier as yet is certain (except for the early Bronze Age (?) stone objects). Heirlooms and conservatism in the Arkadian mountains may explain the spits with round or grip end.

171. Obelos fragment. Bent rod, square in section, with an oval thickening near one end. **Fig. 7.14**
Inv. 550. Tr. 96.6.1.2. N end of West Annex
PL 34.5; Max. PTh. (rod) 1.0; Max. Th. oval knob 2.3; Th. ("handle" end) 1.3
Irregular thickness along the length of the rod cannot be accounted for just by oxidation of the surface. It must have been rough and irregular when originally used.

171, 175, and **176** may be identified as spits with round or oval grip heads. They belong with the "Type a" spits at Olympia, Baitinger and Völling 2007, 68–9 nos. 233–9 pl. 18, of which the latest examples (from Paestum) date to the last quarter of the sixth century. Of the hundreds of bronze spits from the Argive Heraion, just one has a similar handle into which the shaft was inserted, DeCou 1905, no. 2688 pl. 33.

Spits are common in some sanctuaries, whether as votives or for cooking meat – for example, at Sparta, where they were also used as a form of money, Dawkins, ed. 1929, 391–3; and at the Argive Heraion, where both iron and bronze spits were numerous, Waldstein et al. 1902, 61–2 fig. 31 (bundle of iron spits); DeCou 1905, 300–23 nos. 2273–2711 (bronze). At Perachora they seem to have been used as roasting spits, Payne et al. 1940, 187–9 pl. 86.9–15. Payne (188) comments that the bronze spits, found for example at the Argive Heraion, are not the same as iron spits used to roast meat at the temple. Their use is uncertain, but the knobs along them make them less than useful to spit the pieces of meat. At Nemea, examples with half-moon projections were found with material from the sixth and first half of the fifth century BCE, Stella G. Miller 1983, 79 pl. 23f; Stella G. Miller 1984, 181 pl. 37d.
Archaic?

172. Obeloi. Two long, thin iron rods, square in section. **Fig. 7.14**
Inv. 2646 and 2647. Tr. 99.1.5.10. E of Terrace Wall
Pres L 31.0 and 33.8; Max. PTh. 0.8
These two may have joined to form one long spit.

173. Obelos. Long, thin rod, with a thicker half and a thinner half, narrowing almost to a point. **Fig. 7.14**
Inv. 2675. Tr. 99.1.5.11. E of Terrace Wall
L 52.8; Max. PTh. 1.5
It is probably significant that **172** and **173** were found close to each other in a trench just to the north of the Tile-lined Basin Room and just east of the Altar. **175, 176,** and **178** were found in nearby trenches.

174. Obelos. As **172**. **Fig. 7.14**
Inv. 993. Tr. 97.2.3.3. S of West Annex
PL 38.0; W 0.8

175. Obelos handle (?). Sturdy half-oval knob, thick bar, rectangular in section, narrowing to a long shaft, square in section. Bent double, badly corroded. **Fig. 7.14**
Inv. 740. Tr. 96.4.3.5. Altar area
L handle 10.65; W knob 2.2; Est. L shaft 15.0; Th. shaft 0.5

176. Thick disk on a long shaft, broken. Badly corroded surface. **Fig. 7.14**
Inv. 3538. Tr. 97.5 baulk.5.5. E of Terrace Wall
L 10.1; D disk 3.1; Th. disk 0.6
Compare Type a spits at Olympia, Baitinger and Völling 2007, 68–9 nos. 233–9 pl. 18.

177. Two fragments of a small obelos (?). A long shaft (rectangular in cross-section) widens sharply then gradually tapers in. Both broken at their ends. Corroded. **Fig. 7.14**
Inv. 3200. Tr. 00.4.7.8. City Wall
PL a) 6.3; Max. W a) 2.1; PL b) 6.3; W narrow band 0.9

Based on its size and the shape of the "head," **177** fits more comfortably as a small Type c spit with lancet-shaped grip end, cf. Baitinger and Völling 2007, 71–2 pl. 25. The shafts are normally square in section and the ends are normally wider, but compare ibid., no. 302 – shaft 0.9 by 0.55 cm, and no. 304 – maximum width 2.2 cm.

The long shaft with a widened flat head (grip?) is similar in shape to so-called spatulas at Olynthos, but these are made of bronze, their shafts are round in section, and the heads are more angled, Robinson 1941, 352–4 nos. 1689–1704 pl. 112. The same is true for the examples from Delos, Deonna 1938, pl. 74. Especially close is a bronze one in Isthmia, Raubitschek 1998, no. 383 pl. 61, and for two others including an iron one, ibid., 110 n.10 (with references to others at Olympia, Dodona, and Corinth) nos. 382, 385 pl. 61. A bronze spatula from Nemea has a more gradually widened "spoon" section, Stephen G. Miller 2001, 112 fig. 201.

178. Obelos fragment. Shaft ending in a lozenge-shaped tip. The shaft is bent and the surface is badly corroded. **Fig. 7.14**
Inv. 173. Tr. 96.4.2.3. Altar area
PL 10.2; Th. shaft 0.5; L lozenge tip 1.8; W lozenge tip 0.8

Compare Type c obeloi from Olympia with a lancet head grip, which occur in seventh- and sixth-century contexts, Baitinger and Völling 2007, 71–2 pl. 25. See also **187**.

Hook keys (Haken Schlüssel)

179. Shaft, square in section, bent in a hook at one end at about a 90° angle to the tight ring curl at the other end. Corroded. **Fig. 7.14**
Inv. 551. Tr. 96.8.4.5. Pillar Shrine area
PL est. 8.9; Th. shaft 0.4; D curl 1.0
179–82 have similar circular rolls at the ends of their shafts, a common feature of ancient keys. The bend in the shaft in a different direction from the curl at the end can be found commonly in hook keys ("picklocks"), such as those at Olympia, where over a hundred were identified; for a full discussion, see Baitinger and Völling 2007, 117–32 nos. 501–603 pls. 45–53. Many have small hooks or completely rolled-over ends, one of which, like **179**, is at 90° to the direction of the rolled end, ibid., no. 527 pl. 48. Because examples of these keys have dedication inscriptions on them, and because they are found on sites like Olympia and Foce del Sele in larger numbers than there could possibly be buildings for them to be used, it has been suggested that they were in fact left in sanctuaries as votive gifts, and in particular for female deities, like Hera and Artemis among others, including perhaps Eileithyia.[65] A Lakonian-type key was found beside the altar of Zeus on Mt Lykaon, which, because it was found on top of the mountain by the altar rather than close to a building, D. Romano suggests is a votive dedication.[66]

Large keys with two sharp bends are regularly depicted in Greek art from the sixth century onward being held by women who are identified as *kleidouchoi* or "key bearers" and who had a priestly function, being given the responsibility for the security of the temple and its treasures. The key came to be a symbol of feminine priesthood.[67] The appearance of examples at Stymphalos, either left as votives or still having a utilitarian function, is significant particularly in light of the female deities worshipped here.

180. Shaft, square in section, ends in a ring loop. Broken shaft. Corroded. **Fig. 7.14**
Inv. 419. Tr. 95.8 scarp cleaning. W of Temple
PL 4.6; Th. shaft 0.65; D loop 1.4

181. Shaft, rectangular in section, narrowing at one end and curled tightly to produce a small hole. Corroded. **Fig. 7.14**
Inv. 534. Tr. 96.5 ext. 4.6. City Wall
PL 8.55; Max. W shaft 0.9; Th. 0.35; D curl 1.1

182. Bar narrowing at the end and curled tightly to produce a small hole. Badly corroded. **Fig. 7.14**
Inv. 671. Tr. 96.13.2.4. S of Altar area
PL 5.0; D curl 0.9; Max. PW 1.0

Other iron objects

183. Door handle. Main hand grip, square in section, slightly curved with a globular addition in the centre, two side arms at right angles to the main grip, each with a disklike thickening one-third along their length. One side arm had broken. Badly corroded. **Fig. 7.14**
Inv. 3642. Tr. 97.5 baulk.6.6. W of Terrace Wall
L grip 9.15; W grip 1.05; Th. central glob. 1.75; L arm 12.7; D disk 2.1
Good parallels of the same size and shape but in bronze were found at Olympia, Fürtwangler 1890, 146 no. 915 fig., and Olynthos, Robinson 1941, 249 n. 4 (references) no. 988 pl. 65 (pins through holes at the end held this handle in the door). A common term for door handle is δακτύλιον; see Burford 1966, 330 for its use in the Epidaurian building inscriptions, but this takes its origin from anything that is ring-shaped (Liddell and Scott, s.v. δακτύλιος), which in the case of **183** does not apply. Somewhat similar in size and shape are rectangular bronze handles for chests and basins (?), e.g., from Isthmia, Raubitschek 1998, 20 nos. 80–4 pls. 16–17; Corinth, Davidson 1952, nos. 895 and 901, pls. 66–7; and Olympia, Fürtwangler 1890, 147 no. 921 fig.

184. Implement resembling a latch handle. Broad flat strap with perpendicular projection (pivot?) narrows to half its width, then bends at 90° and continues to narrow to a squarish end. The narrow end and tip of the projection may be broken off. Badly corroded. **Fig. 7.14**
Inv. 1515. Tr. 97.9.5.5. Room S of Terrace Wall
Total L est. 15.0; L before bend 10.9; Max. W 1.6; Min. W 0.5; L projection 2.6
Use unknown

185. Handle (?). Long shaft, square in section, ending in a loop ring band at one end (accidental break and loop?), and a hook at the other. A separate piece of iron loops around the shaft close to the end with the hook. Badly corroded. **Fig. 7.15**
Inv. 739. Tr. 96.6.2.5. Pillar Shrine area
PL 16.0; Th. shaft 0.4
The shape is similar to handles from a situla (or "bucket"), of which many bronze ones are preserved, but not many iron ones. Cf. Baitinger and Völling 2007, 115–16 nos. 490–6 pls. 43–4. The iron loop still attached to the end of **185** may be the iron ring or loop which has pulled away from the situla.

186. Curved bar with nail or hook (?) at one end, broken at the other end, corroded. **Fig. 7.15**
Inv. 3162. Tr. 00.4.7.7 City Wall
MPD 7.0; Th. 0.3; L nail 1.0
Similar to another iron bar from the Sanctuary, inv. 2845 (Tr. 00.1.2.2 [E of Bldg. A], L 8.5 cm, W 0.9 cm), which is less curved and ends in a hook. For an iron fitting of similar shape, see Kilian-Dirlmeier 2002, 155 no. 2575 pl. 161.

187. Implement ending in a leaf- or lozenge-shaped tip. The shaft is split lengthwise and a ball-shaped accretion sits on the shaft. Badly corroded. **Fig. 7.15**
Inv. 670. Tr. 96.13.2.4. S of Altar area
PL 4.1; Th. shaft 0.75
For an iron shaft with a lozenge-shaped end, see **178**.

188. Disk with small central hole. About half preserved. **Fig. 7.15**
Inv. 633. Tr. 96.13.2.4. S of Altar area
D est. 4.8; Th. 0.2; D hole 0.6

189. Band in two non-joining fragments, decorated with grooves. Corroded. **Fig. 7.15**
Inv. 307. Tr. 96.8.3.3. Pillar Shrine area
MPD a) 2.95 b) 3.55; Th. 0.15
Bronze rather than iron strips decorated simply with horizontal ridges or grooves were found at Isthmia, and are suggested to be furniture appliqués, Raubitschek 1998, 147 nos. 552–4, pl. 86.

190. Small ornament (?), ring attached to a curved segment of wire. **Fig. 7.15**
Inv. 317. Tr. 96.10.1.1. City Wall
MPD 1.65

191. Socket (?) fragment from sheet iron. The socket is crimped to fit tightly against the object it is to hold. Part is badly crumpled. **Fig. 7.15**
Inv. 87. Tr. 95.6.1.2. N of Temple
D socket 4.1; L of socket 2.6
Parallels are difficult to locate for this object, but one possibility is that it belonged to a socketed fireplace shovel, so that the socket would hold a wooden handle, and the shovel part is missing. Compare Baitinger and Völling 2007, 92–4 nos. 377–80 pls. 30, 78. Less likely would seem to be socket choppers (Tüllenbeile), since the chisellike end would not be apt to break away from the socket part. See Baitinger and Völling 2007, 16–18 nos. 13–21 pl. 3.

192. Loop handle (?) with two rivets securing the two sides of the loop together. Broken and bent at the second rivet. Badly corroded surface. **Fig. 7.15**
Inv. 2791. Tr. 99.1.6.12. E of Terrace Wall
PL 8.0; Max. W 2.5; W at loop 0.7; Wt. 18.5
Although the loop handle is common for strigils, this one is much more sturdy and held together with rivets, which indicates a different use. The long rivets may have passed through a thick piece of wood in between the two sides of the iron loop.

193. Knife blade with tang for handle attachment. Badly corroded but complete. **Fig. 7.15**
Inv. 2935. Tr. 00.4.2.2. City Wall
L 21.9; L blade 16.1; L tang 5.8; Max. W blade 1.6; Max. Th. blade 0.3; Wt. 36.5
Such knife blades are not uncommon; they are also not closely datable. This one was found outside the Sanctuary, close to the City Wall, but not far away from the Tile-lined Basin Room south of the Terrace Wall where butchering of sacrificed animals may have taken place (see Schaus, chapter 2 above). Their use in the Sanctuary may be connected with the killing and butchering of sacrificial animals, although other uses are certainly possible. Besides the four blades catalogued at Isthmia (Raubitschek 1998, 101–2 nos. 370–3 pl. 60), Raubitschek lists another 39 blade fragments in her Appendix I, p. 172. She also notes a passage from Euripides, *Suppliants* 1197–1209, where Athena dictates that knives used in sacrifices should not be reused. At Nemea, two knife blades were found in the stadium, but in fifth- to sixth-century CE levels, Stephen G. Miller 2001, 129, 131 figs. 239–40. A small number of iron knives were found at Corinth, from Roman-Byzantine levels, Davidson 1952, 203 nos. 1567–73 pl. 93. From Olympia, 70 knives were published recently, divided into three main groups but with several variants, Baitinger and Völling 2007, 100–10 nos. 402–71 pls. 35–40. A first type includes those with sickle-shaped blades (16 examples), which seem to last until the end of the Archaic period. The second type has blades with a slight bow in their top edge (14 examples), which last at least into the Hellenistic period. The third main type has a straight top edge (31 examples) but may have a narrow or a wide blade. These continue through the sixth and first half of the fifth century. For Bassai, see Kourouniotes 1910, 318 fig. 39A. Over 50 knife blades from the Late Geometric through the Archaic period came from the Athena Itonia sanctuary at Philia, all of the same general type with both straight and somewhat bowed top edges, Kilian-Dirlmeier 2002, 71–2 nos. 1061–1112 pls. 68–72. About 30 blades or fragments came from the Cyrene Demeter Sanctuary, Warden 1990, 46–7 nos. 319–26 fig. 6 and pl. 33. From a non-sanctuary site, a good selection of iron blades was found at Olynthos, but only one has the tang for the handle still well preserved, Robinson 1941, 335–9, esp. no. 1606 pl. 102.

194. Bladelike object. **Fig. 7.15**

Inv. 37. Tr. 95.3.1.4. North Annex
PL 4.7; W 0.9; Max. Th. 0.45
The shape is like a knife blade, but it appears to be too narrow for a blade, and too thick especially along the non-cutting edge.

195. Implement. Thick shaft, square in section, with a diagonal split creating a forklike projection. The shaft is broken at its blunt end and also at a continuation of the shaft beside the diagonal split. Corroded. **Fig. 7.15**
Inv. 324. Tr. 96.6.2.3. Pillar Shrine area
PL shaft 6.95; Max. Th. shaft 0.75; PL projection 2.3; Max. Th. projection 0.35
It is difficult to say exactly what this object was. Two objects from Philia in Thessaly have a similar arm branching off the main bar, and are identified there as lamp hooks (Lampenhaken), Kilian-Dirlmeier 2002, 133 nos. 1975–6 pl. 118. Examples of "bifurcated probes" or forks are not close to **195** because of the shaft continuation, and three-tine forks tend to have wider spreading side tines. For examples, see Mitten 1975, 167, 171 nos. 50, 54; Davidson 1952, 187 nos. 1377–83 pl. 84. The thickness of the main shaft is closer in size to the iron spits, with short arms that split off the ends, found at Olympia; for example, compare Baitinger and Völling 2007, no. 278 pl. 24. Another possibility, though, is a kind of meat hook or "Fleischgabel," which likewise had a use in cooking and was used from the Archaic to the Byzantine periods; see Baitinger and Völling 2007, 96–9 nos. 390–401 pls. 32–4.

196. Implement. Long, thick shaft, rectangular in section, becomes thin and bends sharply before break. Both ends broken. **Fig. 7.15**
Inv. 1558. Tr. 97.9.5.7. Room S of Terrace Wall
PL 15.0; Max. W 1.7; Th. 0.6
Unknown use

197. Perhaps a handle or decorative pin. The head is curled tightly, the shaft (square in section) curves and then straightens and narrows to a point. A bulbous projection is set on the upper shaft. **Fig. 7.15**
Inv. 2596. Tr. 99.9.4.4. SE of Terrace Wall
L 7.8; W head to straight shaft 2.6; Th. 0.6
The curl at the head is tight and must be deliberate. The purpose of the bulbous protrusion is unclear, but if this is a pin, it presumably prevented the shaft from penetrating deeper into material or kept something in its place. The thickness of the shaft, though, is greater than would be normal for clothing pins. For rolled-head pins in the Peloponnese, see Kilian-Dirlmeier 1984, 206–7 pl. 84, esp. no. 3404 from Mantineia (iron). An example from Bassai may have a very small protrusion on the upper shaft; see Kourouniotes 1910, 326 fig. 50. Cf. pins with rolled heads from the Athena Sanctuary at Philia, Kilian-Dirlmeier 2002, 11 nos. 51–6 pl. 8, and the same from Olympia, Philipp 1981, pls. 35–6. These are of bronze, however, and they all lack the protrusion on the shaft.

198. Eyelet (?) formed by a rod looped in a circle at its centre and the two ends brought together and bent down. Badly corroded. **Fig. 7.15**
Inv. 3065. Tr. 00.4.5.5. City Wall
PL 5.95; D eyelet 2.6
Such eyelets are a common method of attaching a ring handle to a wooden cover or lid, as, for example, on a wooden sarcophagus lid at Montefortino, Brizio 1899, 671 pl. 4.15. Another example is Blinkenberg 1931, 204 no. 636 pl. 26 (bronze).

199. Eyelet, perhaps from a key or spike with ring head, cast. Corroded. **Fig. 7.15**
Inv. 2976. Tr. 00.2.3.3. S of Temple
L 4.0; D 2.15
At Cyrene (Warden 1990, 45 nos. 301–2 fig. 6 pl. 31), these are called ring bolts, supposing that a ring is bolted into wood which can then be used to open doors, or perhaps have a rope attached to it for pulling. One example at Cyrene is close to **199** in size. Similar objects at Olynthos are identified as part of a key, Robinson 1941, pl. 165, though others are spikes with ring heads (pl. 168). Many keys at Olympia have a ring at the end, but only one example has a roughly similar shaft, Baitinger and Völling 2007, no. 608 pl. 54. None of these suggestions need be correct, however. Very similar objects in bronze have been found in Olympia and other sites in the Peloponnese and identified as ring-headed pins, Kilian-Dirlmeier 1984, 284–5 nos. 4904–13 pl. 113. Given the other examples of iron jewellery in the Sanctuary, there is no reason to exclude this as a pin on the basis of its material.
A smaller one is inv. 167 from Tr. 95.6.5.7 (N of Temple), D 1.6.

200. Clamp with two rivets. The larger plate has bent ends, and the heads of the bolts are still clearly visible. The smaller plate is curved; no distinct bolt heads. The shafts of both bolts are square in section. **Fig. 7.16**
Inv. 3273. Tr. 00.6.2.2. N of North Annex
L bolts 9.65; PL larger plate 6.7; W larger plate 3.5; PL smaller plate 5.5; W smaller plate 2.6; Th. bolt shaft 0.8
Iron clamps with two rivets were quite common at Isthmia; like some bolts with washers, they were associated with wooden parts of carts or chariots. They must have had a wider range of uses, though; see Raubitschek 1998, 101–2, nos. 351–8 figs. 18–20, and 26 others listed in Appendix H, p. 171. At Olympia likewise there were quite a number of these clamps or reinforcements, but normally with five rivets between

the two plates. A good argument was made for their use in joining together parts of wooden wheels, specifically chariot wheels, since they were found close to the presumed location of the hippodrome, Baitinger and Völling 2007, 173–7 nos. 725–39 pls. 62–3. One of the Penteskouphia plaques clearly shows eight clamps with five rivets on each on a wagon with a cross-strutted wheel (as opposed to one with spokes), ibid., 174 fig. 5. No explanation is offered, though, for the difference between clamps with five rivets and those with two, which is certainly significant if both types are suggested to have the same use. This example from Stymphalos, with two rivets, is much larger in the length of its rivets. Whatever object it clamped must have had pieces of wood that were about 10 cm in thickness.

201. Oval reinforcement with two iron rivets driven through; both rivets are curved and broken; the plate is missing a section. Badly corroded. **Fig. 7.16**
Inv. 2437. Tr. 99.10.3.4. N of North Annex
PL reinforcement 5.4; PW reinforcement 3.0; L nail a) 4.5, b) 3.2
Perhaps like a two-plate clamp, but there is room for at least three nails on the preserved plate.

202. Rectangular reinforcement with rounded corners, two holes for nails or rivets. Badly corroded. **Fig. 7.16**
Inv. 306. Tr. 96.6.5.11. Pillar Shrine area
L 5.0; W 2.5

203. Rectangular plate with rounded corners, central oval opening, broken. Bent tack driven through the plate. **Fig. 7.16**
Inv. 3213. Tr. 00.5.3.3. E of Building A
PL 5.0; W 3.05; Th. 0.6; L tack 1.55

204. Thick bolt with round head and square iron plate (washer). Corroded. **Fig. 7.16**
Inv. 2663. Tr. 99.9.5.5. SE of Terrace Wall
L bolt 5.4; Th. bolt 1.2 × 0.9; D bolt head 2.5; L plate 3.6; W plate 3.0
A similar object was found at Torone, Cambitoglou et al. 2001, 753, no. 18.87, pl. 98, where it was classified as a rivet. The Torone object had two round iron washers on either end of a thick shaft (rectangular in section), but of about the same size as **204**. The one at Torone was found in a possible Late Roman context, though the lower levels of this context were Late Classical.

205. Bolt with round head and part of a square plate (washer). Corroded. **Fig. 7.16**
Inv. 3044. Tr. 00.3.4.4. S of Terrace Wall
L bolt 6.45; Th. bolt 0.8; D bolt head 2.8; L plate 2.05; W plate 1.9
The bolt must have been driven through a wooden object, or a hole drilled for insertion, then the washer put on and the bolt end hammered down, perhaps being bent over the washer to secure it. At Isthmia, similar iron bolts, including one with a washer, were associated with fixtures used on chariots; see **200**. There is nothing to suggest a similar use at Stymphalos. See Raubitschek 1998, nos. 341–5 p.101, pls. 57–8.

206. Round washer (?), broken, corroded. **Fig. 7.16**
Inv. 2962. Tr. 00.2.3.3. S of Temple
D 4.0; Th. 0.4; D hole 1.25

Other round washers:
Inv. 2360. Tr. 99.10.2.3. N of North Annex. Max. D 3.8
Inv. 2824. Tr. 99.1.4.5. E of Terrace Wall. Max. D 3.4
Inv. 735. Tr. 95.4+1.2.4. Temple. Max. D 3.2

Square and round iron plates with large holes through them for spikes or bolts, occasionally with the plate or "washer" still in place on the spike, are quite common at Stymphalos, but not found commonly in publications of other sites. A couple of examples, in two sizes, were found at Dreros, Marinatos 1936, 275–6 figs. 39–40. Several thin bronze disks with holes through the centres found at Olynthos may have functioned more or less as washers, reinforcing the area around a spike driven into wood, Robinson 1941, nos. 1209–12 pls. 78–9. Raubitschek (1998, fig. 33 and pl. 87) demonstrates several other uses of such reinforcing plates with staples, cotter pins, or nails.

207. Square washer, concave from use, corroded. **Fig. 7.16**
Inv. 3462. Tr. 96.15.5.5. S of West Annex
L 2.9; W 2.7; Th. 0.35; D hole 0.9

Other square washers:
Inv. 313. Tr. 95.1.10.16. Temple. Max. L 2.8
Inv. 2787. Tr. 99.7.6.12. Building A. Max. L 4.0
Inv. 3093. Tr. 00.3..4. S of Terrace Wal). Max. L 3.5

Iron "miniature shields"

208. Disk, slightly rounded with offset flat rim. **Fig. 7.16**
Inv. 1617. Tr. 97.12.3.3. S of Temple
D 5.35
The lack of evidence for a nail shaft in the centre of the underside, as well as the size and a distinct offset "rim," suggests that this is not an iron boss, but rather a miniature shield, left as a dedication in the Sanctuary. Similarly shaped disks in bronze have been identified as miniature votive shields, for example, Papadopoulos 2003, 61–2 nos. 161–4 fig. 79 with references including bronze ones from the older temple

at Bassai, Kourouniotes 1910, 316–17 figs. 36–7, and Blinkenberg 1931, 392 no. 1566 pl. 63, with references to others from Olympia, Sounion, and Crete (add from Dreros, Marinatos 1936, 277–8 fig. 41). A larger (9.7 cm D) miniature shield made of iron has been identified at Olympia with the same offset rim; see Baitinger and Völling 2007, 201–2 no. 808 pl. 71 with references for miniature weapon dedications (p. 201 n. 1004).

209. Disk with raised rim on one side. **Fig. 7.16**
Inv. 3611. Tr. 00.6.4.4. N of North Annex
D 3.5; Th. rim 0.88
No indication of a nail shaft in the centre of the underside and because of the raised rim, it is not from a nail.

Lead Objects

210. Weight. Triangular in shape, flat on one side, rounded on the other, with a small hole at the apex of one corner. **Fig. 7.16**
Inv. 2110. Tr. 99.3.1.1. Building A
H 3.9; W 2.45; Th. 0.86; Wt. 51.1

211. Weight. Narrow pyramidal shape with hole just below the apex and triangular impression on one of the sides with the hole. **Fig. 7.16**
Inv. 36. Tr. 95.2.1.1. Building A
H 2.65; W base 1.05; Th. base 1.0; Wt. 18.5
A similar weight at Perachora (Payne et al. 1940, 180 pl. 85.13) was suggested to be a loomweight. Lead disks at Isthmia weigh 20, 40, or 80 grams, and a conical weight is 46 grams. These may have been used on balance scales, though they do not conform to a known measure of weight, Raubitschek 1998, 112 nos. 406–12 pl. 64 fig. 24; see esp. p. 156 for a discussion of these and other lead objects and their apparent differences in weights by 10-gram units. Clearly **211** and **212** were meant as weights, and were hung from strings, but their identification as loomweights is doubtful simply because they weigh so little. **210** at 51 grams may provide enough tension on a couple of threads to be practical. Its shape is odd for a loomweight, however. For a conical and a pyramidal lead weight both with strings for hanging, and both dated to the third century BCE, see Raubitschek 1998, 111–12, nos. 405–405A pl. 63 (no weights given). No. 405 is conical and 405A is pyramidal. A pyramidal and a conical one in lead were also found at Miletus, 6.4 and 5.4 cm in height respectively, Voigtländer 1982, 169 nos. 419–20 fig. 60 pl. 34.4–5. It is worth noting that there is only one pyramidal loomweight of clay from the Sanctuary. A lead loomweight at Corinth is halfway between conical and pyramidal, Davidson 1952, 163, 172 no. 1212 pl. 77. It is 6.6 cm high, and therefore may have enough weight to be useful. The Heraion at Foce del Sele produced seven small pyramidal lead weights, Zancani Montuoro et al. 1965–6, 159 pl. 45b. For further bibliography and discussion, see Deonna 1938, 155–6.

212. Weight. Narrow pyramidal shape with hole just below the apex. **Fig. 7.16**
Inv. 157. Tr. 96.1.1.1. City Wall
H 3.1; W base 1.0; Th. base 1.0; Wt. 17.7

213. Weight. Disk shape with groove around the edge for attachment to a line/net. **Fig. 7.16**
Inv. 68. Tr. 95.7.4.9. Building A
D 1.9; Wt. 14.9
If this is a weight for a fishing net, it is less common than the tubelike ones found at Isthmia and elsewhere, but it would provide some company in the Sanctuary for the bronze fish hook, **138**.

214. String weight, rectangular head. One side has broken. **Fig. 7.16**
Inv. 955. Tr. 96.13.5.8. S of Altar area
PH 1.2; Head 1.4 × 1.2; PWt. 7.1

215. Pottery repair attached to the wall of a large Corinthian basin with wide out-turned rim. A large section of the rim is painted black. The lead repair holds a fragment of the adjoined piece with half the hole drilled through it, though the clamp has been bent. **Fig. 7.16**
Inv. 3149. Tr. 00.4.7.7. City Wall
MPD sherd 12.4; W rim 3.6; Max. L clamp 3.5
The repair on this basin gives an idea of the quality of the vase that was chosen for repair rather than tossing away as refuse. Lead repair clamps on large vases are quite common on Greek sites. Two examples are catalogued here. At least 14 other lead pottery repairs of different sizes have been found in the Sanctuary area. Lead had a low melting temperature, so it could be poured into holes drilled into adjoining fragments and connected with a low oval strip of lead on either side of the pottery break. It was also relatively cheap, a by-product of refining ores of other metals, such as silver. Such lead repair clamps are ubiquitous in Greece and hardly need comparisons; for a recent publication, see Raubitschek 1998, 157 n. 18 (references) no. 612 pl. 93. Warden's suggestion of iron and bronze pottery repair clamps at Cyrene raises the possibility of other materials besides lead being used, but no certain examples are found at Stymphalos, Warden 1990, 43–4 nos. 282–4 pl. 29.

216. Pottery repair, broken at one end, with at least one plug missing. **Fig. 7.16**

Inv. 736. Tr. 96.7.2.2. City Wall
PL 9.65; Max. W 1.8; H plugs 1.6; Th. plugs 0.7

217. Nail, rectangular head, broken shaft. **Fig. 7.16**
Inv. 2885. Tr. 00.3.1.1. S of Terrace Wall
PL 2.6; head 1.95 × 1.6
Payne (1940, 181, 186) suggested that some bronze nails from the Hera Limenia sanctuary show no traces of hammering and may be dedications by builders, and the lead nail (ibid., pl. 85.5) may likewise be a dedication since it is not a useful metal for driving into hard materials, similar to the cheap lead votives so common at Sparta.

One possible identification of this object is to carry or seal a curse. The material, lead, was commonly used for curse tablets (defixiones), and came to be appreciated in itself as appropriate for curses; see Gager 1992, 4. As for the object, a nail, normally the nail is driven through a lead sheet with the curse inscribed on it, but nails by themselves may have had symbolic meaning, not just to add pain to the curse, but to fix or bind it; see Gager 1992, 18, 53 no. 5 (second or third century CE).

218. Tubular shaft. A long narrow piece of lead, round in cross-section, which varies in diameter, but is thickest towards the middle of the shaft. **Fig. 7.16**
Inv. 2849. Tr. 00.2.1.1. S of Temple
L 10.7; Th. 0.55
Unknown use, but possibly just a form of ingot.

219. Two bodkins. Long narrow objects with eyelets at both ends. Both bent in two. One has its end broken off, both have one eyelet damaged. One of the complete eyelets is round, while the other is almost rectangular. **Fig. 7.16**
Inv. 2452. Tr. 99.1.5.8. E of Terrace Wall
L est. a) 9.8, b) 11.5; W eyelet 0.4; Th. stem 0.15
The bodkins were found close to a large iron nail. It is possible that they were bent double deliberately and left as votives in the Sanctuary. These are strange objects, since they are made of lead, which would seem less practical than bronze or even iron. Five similar objects, made of bronze and varying between 9 and 13 cm in length, were found at Olynthos, Robinson 1941, 361–2 nos. 1745–9 pl. 115. They must have had a special use, presumably in penetrating a coarse material, such as sackcloth, and pulling through a thick thread perhaps like a drawstring or tape.

Varia

220. Greave (?) fragment. Large sheet of bronze formed from four large joining pieces, three large non-joining ones, and many small fragments. The joining fragments have slightly curled edges. The shape has narrowing sides, then an angle inward and down to a point. **Fig. 7.17**
Inv. 3252. Tr. 00.4.7.8. City Wall
PL 4 joined pieces 17.5; Max. PW 12.5; MPD largest non-joining piece 11.0
The only evidence for a method of attachment is possible holes, well spaced apart, which may be visible along the broken edges. The piece with the more rounded edge may be misplaced, and even turned the wrong way up. S. Bocher (personal communication) suggested that it is half of a leg greave, noting that they tend to break along the centre line where there is a slight fold to help allow for opening when being put on. The curve of this edge and the somewhat rough edge to it may argue in favour of a break along a fold. **221** may belong with this.

221. Bronze spade-shaped sheet fragment with one or two holes along the edge. **Fig. 7.17**
Inv. 1383. Tr. 97.5.4.8. E of Terrace Wall
MPD 5.5; Wt. 6.3
This may belong with **220**, although it was found quite apart in a trench east of the Terrace Wall. The holes presumably were used to attach the object. If it does not belong, then it is difficult to identify. A variety of pieces made of sheet bronze are grouped together as "cut ornaments" at the Argive Heraion, DeCou 1905, nos. 1828–32 pls. 105, 108. What is called a bronze clasp at Isthmia has the same basic shape, ivy-leaf like, and three rather than just two rivets for attachment, Raubitschek 1998, 146 no. 543 pl. 84.

222. Bronze sheet with shallow impressed circle in the middle, perhaps other shallow impressed and raised lines, broken edges all around. **Fig. 7.17**
Inv. 2833. Tr. 96.4 surface cleaning. Altar area
MPD 7.7; Wt. 5.3
The shallow lines look deliberate, especially the circular one. Without more preserved, however, it is impossible to tell if this is from a decorated shield, for example, or other significant object with relief decoration.

223. Bronze sheet fragment, bent over. The surface of the bronze is shiny and well preserved. **Fig. 7.17**
Inv. 2569. Tr. 97.5 baulk.3.3. E of Terrace Wall
L 5.1; W Max. 2.4; Wt. 2.8
Perhaps another piece from the greave (?), **220**.

224. Bronze sheet fragment. Curled at one end, broken at the other, and along one edge. The preserved edge is thickened outward slightly to create a border. **Fig. 7.17**
Inv. 311. Tr. 96.13.4.7. S of Altar area
PL 5.4; PW 2.2; Wt. 4.4

225. Bronze fragment of unknown use. Flattened oval knob at the end of a strap that becomes wider but less thick and divides into two separate straps. **Fig. 7.17**
Inv. 325. Tr. 96.3.4.7. Altar area
PL 3.2; Max. W 0.6; Wt. 3.4
The surface on both sides is very rough and unfinished, suggesting that it was not meant to be seen.

226. Bronze hemispherical object with a round hole in the middle, narrow flat border along the outside edge. **Fig. 7.17**
Inv. 328. Tr. 96.4.3.5. Altar area
D ca. 3.5; Wt. 3.9
The bronze is thin and must have been subject to damage if used for anything but light tasks. Identification is difficult, but at Isthmia eleven bronze "tops" believed to be from lekythoi were found with a distinct rim, concave "wall," and small hole where they were presumed to have broken from a narrow neck; see Raubitschek 1998, 26 nos. 104–13 pl. 21. Another two mouths from lekythoi were found at Perachora, Payne et al. 1940, 158 pl. 61.3–4. Most of these are close in size to **226.** This seems a more likely identification than, for example, as a bracelet decoration, compare DeCou 1905, pl. 89 nos. 973–4, or belt decoration, compare Raubitschek 1998, inv. no. 5075B pl. 37 (no. 216 sub, p. 57).

227. Small bronze oval disk with groove lengthwise down the middle, and remains of tin solder on the same side as the groove. **Fig. 7.17**
Inv. 329. Tr. 96.9.1.1. Altar area
L 1.7; W 1.3; Th. 0.17; Wt. 2.1
The side with the groove and tin solder would seem to be the inner side attached to some other object, but the other side is undecorated, so difficult to understand regarding use.

228. Small thin bronze disk attachment, with narrow border; three small holes pierce the border. **Fig. 7.17**
Inv. 3310. Tr. 96.15.4.4. S of West Annex
D 1.2; Wt. 0.2
Similar and close in size to a "miniature shield" with four small holes around the rim, from the Diktaian Cave, Hogarth 1899–1900, 109 fig. 41. One from the Timpone della Motta sanctuary at Francavilla Marittima is twice as big, with a small loop "handle" attached to its convex side, but with the same three holes pierced along the rim, Papadopoulos 2003, 134 no. 466 fig. 168.

229. Large lump of copper or copper alloy (not slag). One side is smooth while four other sides have rough edges from fracturing. **Fig. 7.17**
Inv. 980. Tr. 96.13.6.10. S of Altar area
PL 3.4; PW 2.8; Wt. 108
This lump, along with a fragment or two of iron slag (?) in a shallow crucible shape (**230**) and a piece of molten glass (**17**), are all that remains to suggest some small amount of manufacturing in the Sanctuary area.

230. Large lump of smithing hearth or slag cake, shaped like a thick mushroom cap, or shallow crucible. Lumpy rust-orange corroded surface, almost bubbly lavalike texture where a small piece has broken off the edge. **Fig. 7.17**
Not inventoried. Tr. 95.8.3.11. Behind Temple
PD 9.0
Although no other evidence for smithing has been found in the Sanctuary, this one example of slag cake suggests it must have been done in the vicinity. Its find spot behind the Temple where objects can be dumped and trapped between the Temple's west wall and a sharp rise in the bedrock is worth noting, since there is no space for a smithing hearth directly behind the Temple. Such slag cakes are normally formed on the hearth wall below the blowing hole. They vary in size, but generally average 200 to 500 g. For a description of their formation, see "Bloom refining and smithing slags and other residues," *Historical Metallurgy Society*, Archaeology Datasheet No. 6 http://hist-met.org/hmsdatasheet06.pdf, consulted 15 June 2011. For a report on examples found at Segontium, see Michael Heyworth, "11 The metal slag." http://ads.ahds.ac.uk/catalogue/adsdata/cbaresrep/pdf/090/09011001.pdf.

231. Stalactite fragment. Small, hollow cylindrical object of white crystalline stone, narrowing to a point at the bottom. The wall is a uniform thickness except at the bottom where it thickens. The exterior surface is smooth but has two shallow horizontal ridges. **Fig. 7.17**
Inv. 3759. Tr. 96.5 ext.2.3
PL 4.3; PW 2.2; Th. wall 0.2 to 0.3
The thickness of the wall is quite uniform, and its curve is regular until it becomes narrower near the bottom. Water dripping through the local limestone forms drips of lime deposit within fractures of the rock. Although it is natural, **185** is out of place in the Sanctuary and may have been brought to the site deliberately. A large chunk of a stalactite was left in the Heraion on Samos, presumably as a votive (on display in the Samos museum).

8

Constructing the Sanctuary: Iron Nails for Building and Binding[1]

Monica Munaretto and Gerald P. Schaus

INTRODUCTION

In a very careful publication of the fourth-century BCE country house at Vari, in Attika, the British excavators listed various wooden elements believed to be used once in the structure, including upright column shafts and their cushion blocks, lintel beams and possible cross-struts securing them to the walls, wall plates at the top of the mudbrick walls, a timber framework for the tile roof consisting of tie-beams, inclined rafters, and ridge poles, and sheathing of planks or reeds between the rafters and the tiles, as well as wooden doors and window frames.[2] They also noted, however, that the woodwork was "lost without trace."[3] In fact, the unusual attention to detail in their study is impressive both for the construction of this house and for a second one they excavated and published near the Dema Wall, also in Attika; however, no mention is made at all of nails, and no nail is reported to have been found at either site.[4] Yet, nails are as common a "trace" as is available of the original woodwork associated with ancient building, not to mention as evidence for furnishings such as benches, tables, and chests, even if the information they provide may be limited.[5] Care in plotting distribution of specific types of nails across a site should yield some information about use of those types if they can be associated with a given building, or even a given part of a building. The distance from the head of a nail to the place where it is bent may provide some knowledge of the thickness of the wooden elements into which the nail was driven.[6] So many nails have significant bends in them towards their tapered ends that clearly it was common practice for builders to choose sufficiently long nails that they were driven all the way through the wood, and then the sharp exposed end was deliberately bent over to keep it out of the way, but also to tighten the grip on the two wooden elements through which the nail was driven (see fig. 8.1.1). Drying out of the wood, or rotting at the nail hole, would not affect the join of the two wooden elements as much if the nail was sharply bent over at the surface of the lower or inside wooden element. Preservation of a small amount of wood is sometimes assisted by the corrosion of a nail. The iron oxide (or copper oxide for bronze nails) actually inhibits rot in the wood, allowing for identification of the wood species at times, as at Kommos.

Samples of wood were found, preserved with the help of metal corrosion within the bosses of the door on the lower town site at Stymphalos. A preliminary examination of the samples suggests that the wood was oak (probably white oak), but also with some yew, perhaps used as strips over top of the main oak boards of the door.[7] The mountains surrounding Stymphalos still have impressive mature forests on their middle and upper slopes. The most common species by far is the fir or silver fir (ἐλάτη). The same species is mentioned by Theophrastus (*HP* 4.1.3) as thriving on the top of Mt Kyllene and other mountaintops and cold positions (no doubt including Kyllene's neighbours, Mt Oligyrtos and Mt Apelauron). Furthermore, while Theophrastus (*HP* 4.1.2) notes that the silver fir grows especially tall in places where it receives no direct sunlight, its wood in these conditions is not so dense and so not used for expensive work, such as doors. He implies that where the silver fir does not grow in these unusual circumstances, its wood would indeed be used for such purposes. Theophrastus (*HP* 5.1.5–8) gives a detailed description of both the silver fir and the pine (η πεύκη), and notes both the density of the former and the fact that it provides timber of the greatest length and straightness, suitable for yard-arms and masts. It was said to be durable, and used also for floor beams, roof beams, and doors.[8] The builders at Stymphalos surely made use of this readily available, dense wood instead of importing lumber from more distant and costly sources. A fourth-century inscription from Delphi lists providers of wood from Sikyon and its transport by sea.[9] Presumably this wood originated from the same source as the Stymphalians had at hand, the mountains lying between Sikyon and Stymphalos, first among which is Kyllene.

Many sites have yielded at least a few nails, and many others no doubt have produced quantities of nails which were largely ignored and never published.[10] Publication of nails has taken various forms, so, for example, in central/southern Greece, nails from the Korykian Cave are divided into two types.[11] The first (at least 82 examples) have a domed head ("skull cap") with diameters between 1.3 and 1.9 cm, and short shafts, about 2.5 cm; the second, with broad flat head and longer shaft (max. pres. is 3.6 cm), are more like tacks than real nails or spikes to hold wooden building material together. At Isthmia, Raubitschek divided the preserved nails by length and material into six groups: iron door bosses (5 mushroom heads, 18 flat heads); bronze nails (31 of 3.5 to 10 cm); iron nails (87 of 3.5 to 10 cm); iron spikes (27 of more than 10 cm); iron tacks (15 of less than 3.5 cm); and bronze tacks (22 of less than 3.5 cm).[12] At Corinth, four types of metal bosses (3 of bronze, 1 of iron) are represented, while a variety of nails and tacks are published as representative of the many finds over the years.[13]

On Crete, another collection of bronze and iron nails, from Archaic to Roman in date, came from the Greek sanctuary at Kommos on Crete, totalling 105 catalogued examples (60% bronze, 40% iron), divided into four types: nails (26 bronze, 21 iron), iron spikes (17), bronze "pinlike" (16), and "tacklike" (18 bronze, 3 iron).[14] A fair number of these had the remains of wood still attached to the nail, revealing information about the types of wood (all conifers) and the direction of the grain (angle of nail driven into wood). Shaw makes an important contribution by discussing the significance of the nails for construction in the sanctuary at Kommos. From Classical and Hellenistic contexts at Knossos, besides nails of bronze and lead (3+1) and studs of bronze, lead, and iron (3+1+1), the 59 catalogued iron nails were divided into three groups by shaft diameter size (6 of 5–6 mm, 15 of 7–8 mm, 34 of 9–10 mm, 1 of 4 mm, and 3 had square shafts).[15]

In northern Greece, at Olynthos, a large quantity of nails and bosses was found in domestic contexts of the fourth century.[16] These include 57 bronze spikes (7 to 21 cm), 36 bronze nails (2 to 5 cm), 32 bronze tacks (1.5 to 3.5 cm), many iron nails, some better called "spikes," and others found in the cemetery, likely used for coffins: 54 spikes (approx. 6 to 20 cm). A good variety of iron and bronze nails are also published from Torone.[17] These are divided first by material, then by the shape of the head, and last by the length and shape of the shank, without assigning any type numbers. Across the Aegean, at Sardis, the large collection was divided into five types according to the shape of the head, including "round and domed," "round and flat," "square and flat," "rectangular and flat," and "T-shaped, split and spread."[18] Finally, it is worth mentioning the large group of nails (about 100) on display at the museum at Vergina with finds from the royal burials. Despite the apparent lack of wooden roofing over the tomb or heroon structures, there were large spikes, medium-sized nails, and smaller "tacks" in the pile on display. Not all of them might have come from furniture within the tombs, one presumes. Andronicos mentions the "remains of blackened, rotting and disintegrating timber" in Tomb II, though this may be from a wooden couch and table in front of the stone sarcophagus,[19] and an iron hammer left behind on the floor of the so-called Prince's Tomb.[20] The spikes and iron hammer suggest that some building materials were left in the tombs after the burials took place.

Excavations in the acropolis Sanctuary at Stymphalos yielded almost 600 iron nails that were recorded in the field notes as small finds and measured in their trenches; about half of them were eventually inventoried. These represent about two-thirds of the total number found at the site over five seasons of digging (1995–7, 1999–2000).[21] There was a much smaller sample of bronze nails, including bronze bosses with iron shafts, and two lead tacks.[22] The unexpected number of nails is indicative both of the common use of nails in construction of the Sanctuary and the favourable conditions for preservation of iron objects on the acropolis. Further evidence for good preservation of iron here can be seen in more than 200 projectile points found scattered across the Sanctuary, as well as the iron finger rings and other iron objects.[23] It must be assumed, of course, that these 600 or so nails are only a portion, perhaps half at best, of the total number originally used in the Sanctuary's structures. Iron nails in this quantity have not been published from so concentrated an area in Greece previously, though Kommos provides a good comparison.

There is a wide range in size and shape for the nails in the acropolis Sanctuary. An attempt has been made here to develop a typology as others have done, based on the shape of the head, and the size of the shank, to see if information can be gained about their use, based on size and shape, and on their distribution across the site. Distribution, however, must be considered cautiously. While the site was destroyed and abandoned in what is likely a single event, there was very clearly a substantial movement of materials on the hillslope after that event, likely from a variety of causes, but certainly from later visitors, including local salvagers who made a concerted effort to reuse building materials.

The nails have been organized into five types based on the maximum diameter of the nail head and the length and width of the shaft or shank (see fig.8.1.1). Of 584 nails recorded as small finds and considered for the present study, 352 fit within the typology.[24] A sixth group has been identified as more likely "bolts" than nails.

TYPOLOGY

The six "nail" types are differentiated first on the size and shape of the head. Each is broken down further to reflect variations within the type. Nails without their heads intact were excluded from the six types, but can be classified separately by shaft length and width.

Group I includes those with large heads. These are better termed "bosses," commonly found as decorative elements on wooden doors, windows, and furniture. Group II has regular or mid-sized discoid heads, and Group III small discoid heads. Group IV includes all tacks, and Group V consists of nails with bent-over or curled heads. Three measurements were taken of nearly 300 nails, including the maximum diameter of the head, the thickness of the stem 1 cm below the head, and the length of the nail. The reason for a measurement of the thickness of the stem at a distance of 1 cm from the head is explained in the publication of the nails from Inchtuthil (where the measurement was taken a half-inch [1.27 cm] from the head).[25] In a well-preserved nail, the die size can be determined at this point, since a die is used to hold nails here while the head is being forged. Illustrations of the distinctive types have been included in figures 8.1 and 8.2.

CATALOGUE

Inv. inventory number
SF small find number
D diameter of head
L preserved length
W width at point 1.0 cm below head

All measurements are in centimetres.

Type I (large heads)

Fifty-four nails are grouped within this type, comprising 15% of the total classified. The group is divided into two main sub-types (A–B) based on the shape of the nail head, while shank size provides distinguishing subsets within the two major head types. The heads vary from mushroomlike (A) to flat round or flat square in shape (B), and range in diameter from 2.4 cm to 5.8 cm. Type I nails have shanks measuring 0.4 to 1.0 cm in die width and a variety of lengths. The longest measures 10.35 cm. Nearly half of the nail shafts are broken and thirteen are bent.

I.A.1 Large rounded head, mushroomlike, thick die width (2–3 examples)
Two were found together in the same context near the City Wall.
Inv. 263. SF 1996.127. **Fig. 8.1.2a**
D 4.0; W 1.1; L 6.1
West Annex. Tr. 96.6

I.A.2 Large rounded head, mushroomlike, medium die width (5 examples)[26]
Inv. 270. SF 1996.286. **Fig. 8.1.2b**
D 4.45; W 0.75; L 6.0
Altar area. Tr. 96.3
Inv. 957. SF 1997.52. **Fig. 8.1.2c**
D 4.7; W 0.7; L 7.2
S of Altar area. Tr. 96.13

I.B.1 Large flat head, thick or medium die width (11 examples)[27]
Inv. 2735. SF 1999.385. **Fig. 8.1.3a**
D 3.2; W 0.9; L 3.9. Broken
E of Altar Terrace Wall. Tr. 97.5B

I.B.2 Large flat head, narrow die width (28 examples)
Inv. 47. SF 1995.43. **Fig. 8.1.3b**
D 3.5; W 0.6; L 10.35
W of Temple. Tr. 95.8

I.B.3 Large rectangular or oval flat head, medium or narrow die width (5 examples)
Inv. 529. SF 1996.552. **Fig. 8.1.3c**
L head 3.25; W head 2.0; W 0.7; L 5.35
West Annex. Tr. 96.8

Group II (medium heads)

One hundred and forty-one examples in Group II constitute about 40% of the classified nails. These have medium-sized discoid heads and a range of die widths. In comparison to other groups, these nails generally have longer shafts. The sample group shows that heads here generally measure between 0.65 and 2.4 cm in diameter, and the shafts vary in thickness from 0.35 to 1.2 cm. The longest preserved length in Group II is 12.5 cm. Forty-five of these nails are clearly broken, and 52 are bent.

II.A Medium head, thick die width, long shank (8 examples)[28]
SF 1997.69. Not inventoried, **Fig. 8.1.4**
D 2.6; W 0.7; L 12.5. Bent
S of West Annex. Tr. 97.2

II.B Medium head, medium die width, long to medium shank (33 examples)[29]
Inv. 283. SF 1996.326. **Fig. 8.1.5a**
D 1.65; W 0.8; L ca. 10.1. Bent
Temple. Tr. 95.4+1
Inv. 2444. SF 1999.203. **Fig. 8.1.5b**
D 1.9; W 0.8; L 6.25. Bent
N of North Annex. Tr. 99.10.

II.C Medium head, medium die width, short shank (44 examples)
Inv. 268. SF 1996.71. **Fig. 8.1.6**
D 2.15; W 0.65; L 5.4
Altar area. Tr. 96.4

II.D.1 Medium head, narrow die width, long shank (12 examples)
Inv. 2102. No SF. **Fig. 8.1.7a**
D head 2.4; W 0.55; L 9.9
Temple

II.D.2 Medium head, narrow die width, short shank (41 examples)
Inv. 281. SF 1996.199. **Fig. 8.1.7b**
D 1.55; W 0.5; L 6.9
Temple. Tr. 95.4

II.E Medium square head (3 examples) **Fig. 7c**

Group III (small heads)

The nails from this group all have smaller nail heads than those in Groups I and II, ranging from roughly 0.55 cm to 1.5 cm in diameter. These 48 nails make up about 14% of the total sample. There are no heads in the sample measuring greater than 1.7 cm in diameter. The thickness of the nail shaft fits with other examples (0.25 to 1.8 cm), and the maximum length preserved is 9.0 cm, but most measure between 3 and 6 cm. Inv. 716 (**III.A**) tapers to a wedge or chisel end, rather than a tip. Nails with a similar end at Inchtuthil made up a small but noteworthy proportion of the nails there, and have been thought to be specifically used for securing wood to masonry. This is not likely the case at Stymphalos, since the rough fieldstone foundations would use mud mortar, rather than cement, and the orthostate courses in the Temple and Building A show no evidence of having nails in them.[30] Fourteen examples from this group are broken and 16 are bent.

III.A Small head, thick die width, short shank (almost no head, possibly broken) (4 examples)[31]
Inv. 716. No SF. **Fig. 8.1.8**
D 1.3; W 1.05; L 5.95
S of Altar area. Tr. 96.13

III.B Small head, medium die width (16 examples)
Inv. 2548. SF 1999.285. **Fig. 8.1.9**
D 1.4; W 0.7; L 5.4
S of Altar. Tr. 99.13

III.C Small head, narrow die width, short shank (24 examples)
Inv. 282. SF 1996.334. **Fig. 8.1.10**
D 1.15; W 0.55; L 3.5
West Annex. Tr. 96.8

III.D Small head, pinlike (3 examples)

III.E Small square head, short shank (1 example)
Inv. 3573. SF 2000.386. **Fig. 8.2.11**
D 1.55; W 0.4; L 4.1. Bent
E of Terrace Wall. Tr. 97.5B

Group IV (tacks)

There are 83 examples classified here as tacks, making up 23% of the total sample. Almost all have bent shanks. Many iron nails from the Sanctuary were not systematically examined; however, the field notebooks do normally differentiate between nails and tacks. In the unclassified group of iron nails, 36 small finds were identified as tacks, so that at least 119 of the 584 iron nails recorded in the Sanctuary field notes should be classified as tacks (i.e., 20%).[32] The small finds identified as tacks had heads with a maximum diameter measuring between 0.45 and 2.7 cm, and the maximum length preserved was 5.2 cm. The die width of the shank was usually rather narrow, ranging from only 0.2 to 0.75 cm. Twenty-eight of the classified tacks have broken shanks, and 42 were bent.

IV.A.1 Large mushroom head (2 examples)
Inv. 2111. SF 1999.8. **Fig. 8.2.12a**
D 2.7; W 0.3; L ca. 1.8. Bent.
Middle room of Building A. Tr. 99.3

IV.A.2 Medium mushroom head (3 examples)
Inv. 275. SF 1996.267. **Fig. 8.2.12b**
D 2.15; W 0.55; L 2.2. Bent
City Wall at Hexagonal Tower. Tr. 96.7

IV.A.3 Small mushroom head (3 examples)
Inv. 258. SF 1996.53. **Fig. 8.2.12c**
D 0.8; W 0.2; L ca. 2.8. Bent
Altar area. Tr. 96.4 IV.B

IV.B Large flat head (6 examples)
Inv. 267. SF 1996.93. **Fig. 8.2.13**
D 2.55; W 0.4; L ca. 1.9. Bent.
City Wall near Hexagonal Tower. Tr. 96.5 extension

IV.C.1 Medium flat or disk (often with raised rim) head (44 examples)
Inv. 284. SF 1996.281. **Fig. 8.2.14a**
D 1.4; W 0.25; L ca. 1.6. Bent
W of Temple. Tr. 95.8

IV.C.2 Medium size, thick disk head (16 examples)
Inv. 537. SF 1996.451. **Fig. 8.2.14b**
D1.8; W 0.9; L ca. 3.6
Altar area. Tr. 96.9

IV.D Medium to small square head (5 examples)
Inv. 2109. SF 1999.6. **Fig. 8.2.15**
Head 1.1 square; W 0.4; L 2.9. Bent
Middle room of Building A. Tr. 99.3

IV.E Small head, narrow die width (4 examples)
Inv. 2169. SF 1999.39. **Fig. 8.2.16**
D 0.4; W 0.15; L 2.0
Middle room of Building A. Tr. 99.3

Group V (folded head)

Group V includes nails that have a different head shape. The heads here were bent or folded over rather than the normal forged discoid heads with the shank attached near the middle of the disk.[33] There are 26 examples classified as Group V (roughly 7% of the 350 classified nails) with heads measuring 1.1 to 2.4 cm for their maximum length or diameter. The die widths range from 0.5 to 0.9 cm, and the maximum length of shank is 12.0 cm. Four nails of this type are broken and 11 have bent shafts.

V.A Folded head, with the head bent at least twice (5 examples)
Inv. 3580. SF 2000.382. **Fig. 8.2.17**
L head 1.8; L 6.5
W of Building A. Tr. 96.15

Inv. 288. SF 1996.307
L head 2.0.; W head 0.6; W 0.6; L 7.5
West Annex. Tr. 96.8

V.B Folded head, with long to medium shank (17 examples)[34]
Inv. 3446. SF 2000.304. **Fig. 8.2.18**
L head 0.55; L 7.85
E of Building A. Tr. 00.5

Inv. 532. SF 1996.579
L head 1.4; W 1.1; W 0.6; L 7.1
West Annex. Tr. 96.8

V.C Folded head, thick shank, rectangular profile (2 examples)
Inv. 2174. SF 1999.43. **Fig. 8.2.19**
L head 2.4; W head 0.8; W 0.8; L 5.5. Broken
E of Temple. Tr. 99.2

V.D Folded head, medium shank, rectangular profile (2 examples)
Inv. 2875. SF 2000.19. **Fig. 8.2.20**
W 0.2; L 5.7
Building A. Tr 97.9

Group VI (bolts)

A small number of so-called nails have heads similar to those of nails, but often thick shanks which are either round or square in section and have little or no taper. In almost every case the shanks are broken. These objects are very doubtful as nails, given the lack of taper and size of the shank, and instead may have been used more like bolts (γόμφοι, γόμφωσις), with heads at both ends to keep two pieces of wood or other materials together.[35] At Isthmia, an iron tire for a cart or chariot was found with several bolts still attached to affix the missing wooden wheel to it. Raubitschek suggests that some bolts were used with nave bands and other iron bands to reinforce or strengthen chariot and cart parts.[36] There must have been many other uses for such fixtures.

VI Large flat head, thick round shank, no clear taper.
Inv. 248. SF 1996.36. **Fig. 8.2.21**
D head 3.8; W 1.3; L 4.65. Broken
Altar area. Tr. 96.4

The unclassified nails

Two hundred and thirty-four other nails could not be classified, many of which were incomplete or lacking significant features. Field notes indicate their find locations and give brief descriptions to help place them in the context of the Sanctuary (see, e.g., "Group IV: Tacks" above); however, they offer little further information of significance. Thirteen of these nails were identified as spikelike and another ten were identified as peglike. In total, half (105) of the unclassified nails were found east of the Altar Terrace Wall, an area where much debris from the Sanctuary ended up.

NAIL TYPES AND FUNCTIONS

Group I (large heads)

The iron nails or bosses with large mushroomlike heads (I.A and I.B) are similar to ones found at Olynthos, Isthmia, and elsewhere, and commonly represented on red-figure vase depictions of doors, as well as on marble doors reproducing the fixtures of wooden doors, for example in Macedonian tombs.[37] They surely had a decorative purpose, since they could only have been more costly to produce and more difficult to use, compared to nails with large discoid heads. The disadvantage of rust forming on the iron heads and subsequent staining, even if the structure is somehow protected by an overhanging roof or ceiling, or a coating of pitch, may have been overcome to some extent through the use of similar, though often larger and more ornate, bosses of bronze though still having iron shanks.[38] In a passage describing a houseboat built for Philopator, Athenaeus (5.205.b), quoting Kallixeinos, notes that the bronze bosses (η ἐνήλωσις – literally, "the nailing") decorating the twenty doors around the portico had been treated with fire in order to give them a gilded appearance.

The projections extending from the centre of ornate bronze bosses could not have withstood hammering to set the shank into wood of any thickness, so the iron shank may have been driven home first, and then the bronze boss set over its exposed end.[39] This could not be done with the iron boss, since head and shank are one piece. Tacks with mushroom heads (Type IV.A) likewise must have served a decorative purpose, on a smaller scale. In addition to decoration, such fixtures functioned practically to attach battens to the vertical boards of doors and windows.[40] It was common to use two rows of five nails on each of the three main battens (top, middle, bottom), for a total of 30 nails or bosses, presumably because there were five vertical boards on a standard door with two nails fixing each batten to each board, or six nails per board, and if there were in fact two doors to close the doorway, as seen again in Macedonian tombs and vase paintings, then the number of bosses would double to 60. Thirty such bosses were found still in situ marking the remains of a broken door in a house at lake level at Stymphalos, with a different type of boss at each of the three levels (battens). This was almost exactly the same as another door panel found at Lousoi with 27 bosses still preserved in place.[41]

On this assumption, 60 bosses would decorate double doors leading into the Temple, and perhaps the same number on doors closing off Building A, so that as many as 120 bosses were used at a time, just for the doors. Others, perhaps smaller ones, might decorate windows.[42]

Group II (medium heads)

Nails in this group are suitable for use in construction and do not differ significantly from modern examples. Their frequency at Stymphalos (40% of the total classified) also suggests that they were standard for construction. For example, although few were found inside the main rooms of Building A, of 85 nails from the vicinity, 44 belong to Group II. In the adjoining West Annex area, another 32 nails from the group were found. In Building A and its two Annexes, as well as in the Temple, the main area where nails were needed is in constructing the ceiling and roof. Mudbrick walls were built on top of sturdy orthostate blocks in the Temple and main part of Building A, while in the North and West Annexes, mudbrick walls rested on low fieldstone foundations. There may have been vertical posts within these mudbrick walls to offer reinforcement and to help bear the weight of the heavy tile roof. The bronze phiale with a hole punched through its bottom found at the back of the Temple cella (inv. 3736 – chapter 7 above, **18**) provides the only evidence that such vertical posts existed, since the phiale would be fixed more easily against the

Temple wall if the nail holding it were hammered into wood rather than mudbrick.

Above the walls, solid boards or wall plates would be needed to sit firmly on top of the mudbricks and provide a base to distribute the weight of the heavy roof. A timber framework for the tile roof could then be constructed consisting of tie-beams, inclined rafters, and ridge poles, with sheathing of planks or reeds between the rafters and roof tiles. The most useful areas to employ nails are at the tops and bottoms of the inclined rafters, fixing them in place to the tie-beams and ridge pole. The roof tiles themselves sat in place without nails, though cross pieces on the roof must have kept them from slipping down the incline of the rafters.

Group III (small heads)

Nails from Group III were often bent, but their size makes them unsuitable for construction of any substantial architectural element, except perhaps window and door frames. Their average length in the sample is only 4.25 cm (fifteen are known to be broken). Nails of this length and type were more likely employed in the construction of furniture and fixtures. In addition, since a fair number of loomweights were found in clusters on the West Annex floor, and if they are indeed a sign of weaving there, the eight lighter-weight nails from Group III found in this room might have been used in a loom itself or in the room's other furnishings, such as tables, chairs, benches, chests, and shelves.

Group IV (tacks)

Compared to find spots of other nail types in the Sanctuary, very few tacks (Group IV) were found inside buildings. Of the 119 recorded, fewer than ten came from inside the Temple, or Building A or its annexes. The majority occurred instead to the south and east of Building A, or south of the Altar.

The tacks have been divided by head shape; it is assumed that different types had different purposes, though of course this may reflect only the preference of the builder. Those in Group IV.A, with rounded mushroomlike heads, were likely ornamental, as mentioned. Small nails or tacks could be used to hold hinges in place for lids, or appliqués as decoration on metal or wood furnishings.[43] Wooden components of furniture were commonly held together by wooden pegs or mortise and tenon joints instead of nails or tacks.[44]

In modern furniture making, mushroomlike tacks serve to hold upholstery or leather in place on a wooden frame, giving a smooth, rounded surface instead of the sharper outside edge offered by disk heads. But there is little evidence to suggest that the same use was made of these in antiquity; indeed cushions, mattresses, and loose covers took the place of upholstery and leather furniture covering.[45] If the tacks were indeed used in furniture, it is not surprising that few are found within the buildings, since usable pieces were portable and so would be objects of interest to looters or salvagers before the buildings collapsed. Although there is much evidence for burning within the Temple and thus the possibility of furnishings there being burnt, Building A and its annexes did not produce such evidence.[46] Tacks have also been identified as fixtures to close wooden boxes.[47] Representations of boxes on vases show small circular objects on their walls which probably represent metal tacks or studs.[48] Although perhaps unlikely, it has also been suggested that bronze nails in excellent condition may have been offered as votives by builders.[49]

Group V (folded head)

A dozen nails with folded-over heads were published from Olynthos, but their specific use is not known.[50] Both longer (over 10 cm) and shorter ones (5–8 cm) are found, and although they are not common, they occur with enough frequency that they must have been a regular feature of carpenters' equipment. Perhaps the type was a still-usable mistake by the blacksmith in forging nails.

NAIL DISTRIBUTION ACROSS THE SITE

It should be remembered first that very few nails were excavated in the 1995 season when efforts focused especially on the Temple and inside rooms of Building A. Secondly, nails were not recorded as small finds during the 1997 season, and many in the 1996 season were recorded but not inventoried. This affects distribution patterns in so far as it tends to weight finds more heavily towards the 1999 and 2000 seasons and trenches. In general, the distribution of nails across the site appears to be rather random, but there are a few exceptions. Relatively few were found within the two main buildings (Building A and the Temple), and where they occur, they are concentrated in a small area. Some trenches provided many iron nails, but not necessarily ones that could be associated with site architecture. Others produced only one or two examples. In trenches where large numbers are found, examples from Group II are most common, and they appear across the entire site. Distribution will be discussed in relation to specific features and areas: Temple, Building A, and the Altar Terrace Wall (see figs. 8.3 to 8.6).

The Temple

There are very few nails found within the Temple (see fig. 8.4). In total, 36 were recovered (Tr. 95.1, 95.4, including 95.4+1, 96.11, 95.6, 95.8, 96.14, 00.2), and of those, nearly half (16) were found in the northwest corner (Tr. 95.4 and 95.4+1). Of these, only six have been classified, fitting into Group II (those with regular or mid-sized heads), likely used for general construction. The use of wood in the interior of the Temple is likely, since the roof was made of terracotta tiles supported by wooden beams sitting on mudbrick walls possibly reinforced by vertical posts. This back corner of the Temple demonstrated the most burning of any area in the Sanctuary, with some stretches of blackened soil suggesting parts of beams that had fallen and been left to rot undisturbed. Finds of jewellery and terracotta figurines were also common in this corner of the cella.

The remainder of the Temple area contained 20 nails in total; one nail (tack) was discovered at the threshold of the Temple. Long trenches were excavated along the exterior of the Temple walls (north, west, and south sides) where only six nails were found.[51] It is important to keep in mind that there were other ways to secure roof beams, such as through cuttings to create joints or wooden pegs as is commonly used in modern timber frame construction. Another method was to bind elements together through sturdy ropes or cordage. It is possible that the Temple was viewed as a special building which required a different method of construction, although only the smaller number of nails in the vicinity is left to argue in favour of this possibility.

Building A

Twenty-five nails were found in the main rooms of Building A (see fig. 8.5). Only five were found in the southern half (Tr. 95.2 and 96.12). Twenty were found in the large Middle Room (northern portion) of the original building, with the highest concentration in the eastern half of this room. In the Middle Room (Tr. 95.7, 97.11, 99.3, and 99.7), seven nails are from Group II. The narrow trench 99.3 alone produced seven nails, four of which are tacks.[52] Only two were recorded from the North Annex (Tr. 95.3, 95.9, and 95.9 baulk), but in this early season, iron nails were saved but not commonly treated as small finds. In general, though, there were very few nails found within Building A, suggesting that the scavengers may have returned to search through the ruins, possibly removing timbers either for reuse or to search through floor material more easily.

Trenches excavated east of Building A in 2000 (Tr. 2000.1 and 2000.5) produced 28 nails. This includes ten tacks (Group IV), as well as six examples from Group II.

Eighty nails were recovered in and around the West Annex (Tr. 96.6, 96.8, 97.2, 96.15). Most likely they were used to build the roof and any other wooden architectural elements, but some have already been mentioned with regard to the furnishings, including a possible loom. Quite a number were found in the refuse pit (96.15) where debris from the Sanctuary was swept up and dumped. These may have come from some distance away in the clean-up. Of the nails that were classified, 32 belong in Group II (II.C occurring 14 times, II.D 10 times). Many of these have medium-sized heads, appropriate for general construction.[53]

North of Building A there is an area excavated in 1999–2000 which may be another extension to Building A. Here two trenches (99.10 and 2000.6) provided 25 nail samples. Of these, 17 have been classified, and again we find a prevalence of nails from Group II (seven in total found directly north of the North Annex).

Altar area and east of the Terrace Wall

The largest concentration of nails, by far, is in the southeast corner of the Sanctuary site, directly east of the Altar Terrace Wall and both north and west of the small room with the tile-lined basin in Building B (see fig. 8.6). Trench 99.1 alone produced 69 nails, and the adjacent 99.1baulk added another seven. Again, the largest number of examples comes from Group II (17 nails).[54] The reason for a high concentration of nails here is not clear; however, the site is on a slope, and a fair amount of debris, including nails, seems to have collected in this lower area east of the Altar over time. If we isolate the area directly east and southeast of the Terrace Wall, the total number of nails is 195 (33% of all the nails found on site).[55] Seventy-eight have not been classified, and of the remaining 117, 42 (35%) are from Type II (structural) and 41 (34%) from Type IV (tacks).

Assuming that the nails were driven into wooden objects, either structural elements or furniture, it appears that there was considerable disturbance after the destruction of the site, and that many wooden objects found their final resting place outside the buildings (Temple, Building A, Tile-lined Basin Room) where roofs had once protected them from the elements.

9

Pottery of Building A

Peter Stone

INTRODUCTION AND METHODOLOGY

Only the pottery from Building A, including the West and North Annexes, is presented here, since it provides important information about the use and history of this prominent building in the Sanctuary. Because the total volume of ceramic material in this deposit (and in the Sanctuary as a whole) is not great, and since almost all forms correspond to those published from other sites in the northeast Peloponnese, such as Corinth, Isthmia, and Argos, this study does little to expand formal typologies. Despite the limitation of the sample, the material from Building A is representative of that from the Sanctuary as a whole and is helpful in determining both the dates of activity in the Sanctuary and the use of different rooms in Building A. By extension, this study of the ceramics of Building A can contribute to an understanding of the use of space in Hellenistic ritual dining buildings and votive activity in Hellenistic sanctuaries. The mould-made bowls associated with Building A afford an opportunity to consider the use and possible meaning of Hellenistic decorative art in a specific, well-defined, context.

A summary of the evidence for dating and use of the pottery and an analysis of the "assemblages" from the different rooms of Building A are provided first. A detailed discussion of shapes, their chronology, and their comparanda from other sites is included. This is followed by a catalogue of examples of all identified shapes. Tables at the end encapsulate counts of each shape by fabric, as well as percentages of shapes within major sections of Building A, and the range of motifs from the mould-made bowls. (See fig. 9.8 for a plan of the building.)

Deposits are preserved within Building A that appear to represent two periods of its use. One of these, associated with the floor of the West Annex, is dated to the late fourth century. The other major deposition within Building A is attested on the floors of the North Annex, the Front Room, and the Southeast Room of the building and can be associated with the destruction of the building sometime in the second quarter of the second century or later.[1] Thus, on the floors of Building A are assemblages that elucidate, at least partially, its use in the Late Classical period and in the first half of the second century. In addition to these deposits, more material has been examined from the Middle Room of Building A, where there is evidence of deposition also dating to the second quarter of the second century or later; however, this material is much more fragmentary than that in the North Annex or the Front and Southeast Rooms and seems to have been subject to greater disturbance and admixture with earlier material. For this reason, the material from the Middle Room is excluded from statistical analysis and direct comparisons with the material from other rooms. While there is a little evidence to suggest that Building A was restored and reused briefly in the first or second century CE, no secure pottery evidence was found that could be associated with this reuse.[2]

CERAMIC EVIDENCE FOR THE DATING OF DEPOSITS

In an ideal situation, "independently" datable objects, such as coins or stamped amphora handles, present in some quantity, would help establish the date of the deposits associated with Building A. The practical reality is that only a few coins and no stamped amphora handles are attested.[3] Thus, it is necessary to compare the ceramics found in Building A with published material from dated contexts at other sites as an additional tool for determining dates for periods of activity in the structure. The implications for the chronology of Building A provided by excavated pottery are summarized here.

An extension of the floor level of the West Annex partially covers a refuse deposit of votive material which includes nothing that dates later than the fourth century. None of the ceramics associated with the floor of the West Annex need date later than the fourth century. Some of the forms represented, such as flaring-rim chytrai/cooking jugs and kotylai,[4] could date from as early as the seventh or sixth century or as late as the third century. The latest closely datable vessels are Attic kantharoi with moulded rim, dating to the mid-fourth century or later. Other vessel forms in the deposit such as Attic-type skyphoi and one-handlers were certainly very popular in the fourth century and into the third. The question that remains is approximately when the West Annex went out of use. Although the sample of material recovered from the floor of the West Annex is fairly small, there are some forms that are conspicuously absent. Most prominent among these are kantharoi of any form in Corinthian fabric. Such vessels are not attested at Corinth or Isthmia prior to the third century and are common in deposits elsewhere in the acropolis Sanctuary dated to the third and second centuries. Other forms that are present in third-century deposits elsewhere in the Sanctuary and at other sites in the Peloponnese but are "missing" on the floor of the West Annex are conical bowls, chytrai with flanged and thickened rim, and bowls/lekanai with moulded rim.[5]

Most of the vessel forms associated with the Hellenistic use of Building A, such as the various forms of kantharoi, and the chytrai and casseroles, are only datable broadly to the fourth or third century and the first half of the second century on the basis of their attestation in deposits at Corinth and Isthmia. Some of these forms, such as chytrai with flanged and thickened rim, do seem to occur generally later within this span, but most forms are of little help in establishing the date of the Hellenistic destruction of the building with any precision.

A few forms provide definite evidence for a second-century date for the destruction of Building A, rather than the later third. The deep rolled-rim plates attested in the destruction deposits in Building A are unattested in deposits dated earlier than the second century at Corinth and are unattested at Isthmia, a site that was destroyed very early in the second century, possibly by Philip V ca. 198 BCE.[6] The presence of more plates and saucers of all types than bowls for food in the destruction deposits is also in keeping with a trend, noted in Athens, towards more plates than bowls later in the Hellenistic period.[7]

The numerous mould-made bowls found in association with the Hellenistic destruction of Building A provide a better indication of date. Mould-made bowls are present in Athens in deposits dating as early as the last quarter of the third century; however, they do not appear there in any number in deposits dated earlier than the second quarter of the second century.[8] Mould-made bowls are not common at Isthmia or Corinth in deposits dated to the late third or early second centuries.[9] Since mould-made bowls are very abundant in the North Annex, and several are also present in the Front Room and Southeast Room, it seems most plausible to assign a date at least in the second quarter of the second century, and possibly later. The presence in this deposit of only one conical bowl, a popular drinking vessel in the later third and early second centuries at Isthmia, also suggests that the material in the North Annex and the Front and Southeast Rooms dates later than the very beginning of the second century.[10]

Determining with any precision how late the deposits representing the Hellenistic destruction of Building A might be is somewhat more difficult. Although absent evidence speaks less strongly than what is present, it is still significant that forms that might suggest a date very late in the second century or in the first century are not attested among the collapse material from Building A. The deposits in the North Annex, Front Room, and Southeast Room do not contain Campana B and similar upturned-rim plates attested in the interim period (i.e., 146–44 BCE) deposit in Corinth published by Romano.[11] Also absent are vessels in Eastern Sigillata A or imitations of them. Eastern Sigillata A became common in Athens by the late second and early first centuries,[12] and was common at Corinth in the Early Roman period (after it was refounded under Caesar).[13] Another form that is "missing" from the Building A collapse deposit that is present in quantity in Greek assemblages (and particularly in the Argolid) dated to the late second and first centuries is the two-handled cup.[14] The absence of this form is particularly striking since there is such a large quantity of drinking vessels in the material associated with the collapse of Building A, and particularly in the North Annex. Overall, the ceramic evidence suggests a date for the Hellenistic destruction of Building A, in the second or third quarters of the second century. Such absence of evidence is problematic, though, since Stymphalos was fairly isolated and may not have received many imports, as the general dearth of imported amphorai at the site attests.

OVERVIEW OF THE ASSEMBLAGE FROM THE FLOOR OF THE WEST ANNEX[15]

It should be explained first that the West Annex is the last section of Building A to be constructed. It has to be later than the votive refuse pit outside this Annex to the south, since its floor level extends southward to cover over the refuse pit. It is also later than the North Annex, since the West Annex depends on the North Annex for part of its east wall. Since the material in the refuse pit seems to extend in date down to the end of the fourth century at least, the West Annex cannot have been built any earlier than this. It is also not likely that it was built, used for a time, and then destroyed and abandoned as a pile of rubble very shortly afterwards, as the floor deposits might suggest. Since there was no easily distinguishable floor surface, other than what could be marked immediately below the groups of loomweights found in and just outside the West Annex, and since a room presumably being used for weaving was just as likely to be well swept so that weavers were not constantly walking on sherds as they worked, it is possible that the pottery associated with the floor is misleading in dating the destruction of this Annex to the late fourth century.

Almost all of the fragmentary vessels found associated with the floor of the West Annex of Building A were meant for cooking, dining, drinking, and the service of drink. Several lamps are attested as well (tables 9.1–2, at the end of this chapter). Attic-type skyphoi and one-handlers in Corinthian and Attic fabric were represented, as well as kantharoi in Attic fabric and kotylai in Corinthian fabric. Such a combination of vessels would normally suggest that the room was used for the preparation and/or consumption of meals. If, however, we consider the other finds in the room, most notably the groups of loomweights, the idea of a kitchen or dining room seems less likely than its use for weaving with an upright loom.[16] It is possible, though perhaps also a secondary function, that the West Annex was used for the storage of items used elsewhere or dedicated in Building A or the Sanctuary. Storage rather than dedication seems preferable, since the assemblage includes some very mundane cooking vessels that one might expect to see discarded in a sanctuary after use, but not deliberately dedicated. Also, unlike fourth-century deposits beneath the floor of the West Annex and outside of it, there are few miniature votive vessels.[17] The sample of material from the West Annex is small, but suggests that it could have served secondarily as a pantry for the storage of items used for preparing and eating meals within the Sanctuary besides its possible use for weaving. The West Annex was too small (it is only about 3 m wide) to host group dining or drinking activities.

OVERVIEW OF THE ASSEMBLAGES ON THE FLOORS OF THE NORTH ANNEX, FRONT ROOM, AND SOUTHEAST ROOM

The sample of material from the floors of Building A is much larger than that on the floor of the West Annex. This greater quantity, and the fact that material is represented in multiple rooms of contemporary date, allows a more nuanced interpretation of Building A's function in the second century than was possible for the West Annex. As in the West Annex, many of the vessels in these rooms are fairly well preserved and/or reconstructible, suggesting that they were possibly used within these rooms or very close by. Particularly significant is that in both the North Annex and the two southern rooms the proportions of fragmentary vessels corresponded well to their more complete counterparts in both function and in form.[18] The concentrations of vessels serving specific complementary functions in the North Annex and the Southeast Room, in particular, also suggests that these vessels were in fact used and discarded or left behind within these rooms (see chart 9.1; tables 9.4–7).[19] This deposition is similar in conception to what Ault and Nevett refer to as "primary refuse,"[20] i.e., items that are well preserved and were left near their place of use although not necessarily as the result of one event that seals the deposit as a "snapshot." Such deposition is in contrast to that noted by the excavators of the dining rooms at the Demeter Sanctuary at Corinth, where material used throughout the Sanctuary was intermixed in all of the ritual dining buildings.[21]

The North Annex of Building A contained an overwhelming majority of vessels for drinking, serving drink, and lamps (see chart 9.1, tables 9.3–5), most of them concentrated in or around a fire pit in the centre of the room. Relatively few vessels for the preparation or consumption of meals or other purposes were attested. In contrast, the southern rooms, and especially the Southeast Room, held a much greater number and proportion of vessels for the preparation of food and eating, a modest quantity of drinking vessels, and almost no vessels for the service of drink or lamps (see chart

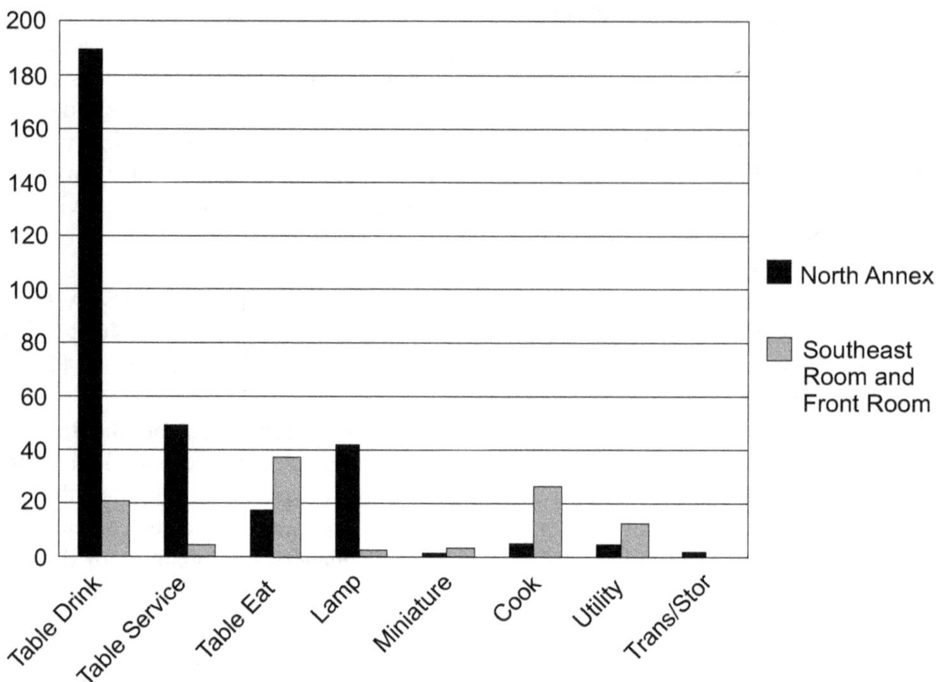

Chart 9.1. Vessels from the North Annex and combined Southeast Room and Front Room of Building A by functional class (absolute quantities)

9.1, and tables 9.3 and 9.6–7). The Southeast Room, which also had evidence for burning, can be interpreted as a kitchen for the preparation of meals, possibly to be eaten in the Front Room, the Middle Room, or, perhaps most likely, outside on the Altar Terrace or gentle slopes overlooking the valley.[22]

The quantity of drinking vessels and vessels for the service of drink in the North Annex clearly suggests some association with drinking, and corresponds nicely with the attestation of numerous drinking vessels in Greek sanctuaries in general.[23] The extremely high quantity of drinking vessels (almost 200, most of which are mould-made bowls) in such a relatively small space as the North Annex is curious when compared to the smaller quantity from the southern rooms of Building A. Since an estimated 15 to 18 people may fit comfortably in this room, it seems unlikely that large groups would have gathered in the confines of the North Annex at one time. Also, it would be a stretch to describe such a concentration of vessels near the hearth as merely a casual accumulation over time due to breakage, especially since many bowls were at least partially reconstructible (e.g., **11–14,** fig. 9.2).

The variety of forms and fabrics of the drinking vessels in the North Annex, and motifs and profiles of the mould-made bowls specifically, suggest that individuals brought these vessels to the Sanctuary and that they were not "standard equipment" manufactured or acquired systematically for use in the Sanctuary. It is possible that smaller groups of a few individuals repeatedly held drinking parties in or near the North Annex and left their drinking vessels behind, perhaps as token dedications.[24] A related, and not mutually exclusive, possibility is that individual visitors to the Sanctuary deliberately discarded these vessels after pouring out libations. Indeed, most of the miniatures that were dedicated in the Sanctuary in the fourth and third centuries were miniature drinking vessels.[25] The later drinking vessels are of course functional, rather than miniatures that simply evoke the idea of drinking.[26] Further support for the interpretation of the drinking vessels as votives is provided in and around the hearth in the North Annex by the concentration of lamps, which are often found in great numbers in sanctuaries from the Classical to Roman periods and must have been left as votives in many instances.[27] Of course, lamps also serve a utilitarian purpose, so they only offer tentative support for the idea of votive offerings.

The presence of large quantities of ceramic drinking vessels in a Hellenistic sanctuary context at which many metal objects have been found stands as a counterpoint to the suggestion that drinking vessels in the Hellenistic period were made primarily of metal.[28]

Almost all of the individual forms attested in the second-century collapse deposits of Building A have parallels in the domestic area at Stymphalos. There are few vessels obviously intended for votive use.[29] Bookidis has noted a similar trend in Hellenistic levels in the ritual dining buildings at the Sanctuary of Demeter and Kore at Corinth, where the ceramic material is essentially "domestic" in character.[30] However, as mentioned above, the concentration of large quantities of certain types of vessels, notably mould-made bowls and lamps, points to a pattern of deposition that is recognizably votive. A general comparison with quantified domestic assemblages from Halieis and New Halos,[31] for instance, shows that the concentration of lamps and drinking vessels in the North Annex is unusual for a domestic context.

The limited area of this concentration of drinking vessels and lamps at the Stymphalos sanctuary and the fact that it was only detectable after excavation suggest that it would be rather difficult to isolate similar phenomena on the basis of sherd scatters on the surface of a surveyed site. More comparative data from excavation and survey (preferably over the same area) of sanctuary sites is needed in order to determine the viability of identifying Hellenistic sanctuaries on the basis of survey evidence alone. The evidence from the Stymphalian sanctuary supports Bookidis' argument that we cannot use the same artifactual criteria to identify Archaic and Classical sanctuaries as those of the Hellenistic period.

It is intriguing that the decorated mould-made bowls comprise the most numerous single form, and are found in a fairly localized concentration within the North Annex (see table 9.4). If similar vessels were not found with regularity in domestic or other contexts both at Stymphalos and elsewhere, we might suppose that they had a cultic function. The hodge-podge of decorative motifs on the bowls (51 distinct motifs) and varied combinations of motifs (see table 9.8 and **11–14**, fig. 9.2, for an impression of the range and mixture of motifs) indicate that they were probably not made or selected for dedication on the basis of the content of their decoration.[32] Still, there is a much greater proportion of mould-made bowls among the drinking vessels in the North Annex than is the case at other Stymphalian contexts where they are attested. John Hayes has noted a similar predominance of mould-made bowls among the second-century fine wares recovered from the Sanctuary of Poseidon at Isthmia. These concentrations of mould-made bowls within the Sanctuary may indicate that "nicer" drinking vessels with some sort of decoration were preferred for dedication or "ritualized drinking" over undecorated ones in the northeast Peloponnese in the second century.[33]

The fact that many of the mould-made bowls were found in close association with a hearth or fire pit in the North Annex may be significant. Because the North Annex was not accessed from the main part of Building A but rather from the back of the Building, the deposit of material on the floor of this Annex need not have resulted from ritual activities centred on the Temple, the Altar, or the cooking/dining rooms of Building A. It seems more likely that the activity within the North Annex centred on the hearth or fire pit, and if the lamps are indicative of the time of day for the use of the mould-made bowls, it occurred at night.[34]

THE SECOND-CENTURY ASSEMBLAGE OF BUILDING A IN A REGIONAL CONTEXT

Most of the vessels recovered from Building A at Stymphalos find their closest comparanda at Corinth or sites near it such as Isthmia and Sikyon.[35] Indeed many of the table vessels occur in a fabric that is quite likely to have originated at Corinth, suggesting not only that there was a stylistic koine that extended from Corinth to northern Arkadia but also that Corinthian ceramics were regularly exported to Stymphalos in some quantity.

It is significant, though, that some vessel forms that are unattested or only occur sporadically at sites along the Gulf of Corinth are attested with some regularity at Stymphalos. The round-mouthed table juglets and simple everted-rim mugs/kantharoi, both present in some number in the North Annex of Building A, are not common at Corinth or Isthmia in Hellenistic contexts, but they do have close parallels at Nemea and sites in the Argolid such as Mycenae.[36] If these vessels are imports, it suggests that Stymphalos was connected to specific markets in the Argolid that Corinth and Sikyon may not have been. This is not meant to imply that Corinth did not receive any Argive products, since vessels do occur there in Argive fabric; however, it is possible that Corinth was not linked to the specific trading circuit(s) that supplied Stymphalos with round-mouthed table juglets and simple everted-rim mugs/kantharoi in the second century. It may be no coincidence that the round-mouthed table juglets perform the same function (i.e., single-serving pouring) as olpai, which are common at Corinth (and at least present at Sikyon) but not attested at Stymphalos. Such distribution suggests that local exchange in the northeast Peloponnese in the second century was somewhat fragmented, and that different market zones or economic circuits overlapped in a somewhat ad hoc manner. The choice of what imported vessels the inhabitants of Stymphalos used may have rested as much with the circulation of merchants in the area as it did with the personal preferences of the people of Stymphalos.

FABRICS

Petrographic and chemical analyses and sourcing studies of fabrics and clay beds at Stymphalos and the immediate region that could indicate the provenience of different fabrics have not been conducted. Still, several different fabrics were recognizable visually, some of which clearly correspond to better-known fabrics from farther afield, such as Attic, Corinthian, Argive, and blisterware. Attic fabric can range from orange brown to pink (Munsell 2.5YR 5–6/6–8, 5YR 6–7/4–6, 7.5YR 6–7/4–6). Corinthian and similar fabrics from the coastal region are very pale green to cream (Munsell 10YR 8/1–4, 2.5Y 8/1–4), soft, with no visible inclusions. Corinthian fabric does not hold a slip well under normal circumstances, and the acidity of the soil in the acropolis Sanctuary at Stymphalos has caused further deterioration of slip on vessels. Argive and visually identical fabrics are orange or brown-orange in colour (Munsell 7.5YR 7/6–8), and rather soft with slightly grainy breaks. Blisterware is another common fabric. In its canonical form, it is a clean and hard fabric ranging from a grey to a pinkish colour with an uneven surface texture (Munsell 2.5–5–7.5YR 6–7/2–8). At Stymphalos there is also a smooth version of what appears to be the same fabric, used for table vessels.[37] A soft semi-fine to coarse orange to brown fabric (Munsell 2.5–5–7.5–10YR 5–7/6–8) with frequent white inclusions was used for table, cooking, utility, and transport and storage vessels at Stymphalos. This fabric is referred to as North Peloponnesian orange.[38] Many cooking vessels also occurred in a gritty grey (Munsell 5YR 4/1–10YR 4/3) cooking fabric, and a few occurred in a soft powdery red fabric (Munsell 5YR 5/6, few Munselled examples) with few visible inclusions, and a hard smooth orange (Munsell 2.5–5YR 4–6/6–8, few Munselled examples) cooking fabric with white inclusions. On the basis of the distribution of fabrics in the deposits discussed here, it seems that the smooth orange-red cooking fabric became less common in relation to North Peloponnesian orange cooking fabric as the Hellenistic period progressed (see tables 9.2, 9.5, and 9.7). As is evident from the discussion above, most fabrics had a wide variation in colour, possibly the result of different firing conditions and the effects of the soil in the Sanctuary.[39]

SHAPES AND FORMS ATTESTED IN BUILDING A

The following section describes the shape and function of each of the forms identified at Stymphalos and discusses the attestation of these forms in dated deposits at other sites, especially those in the northeast Peloponnese. As is common in publications of ceramics from Mediterranean sites of antiquity, "shape" denotes a general shape suited to (a) discrete function(s) (e.g., bowl), and a "form" is a subset of a given shape with specific formal traits that allow it to be regularly distinguished (e.g., incurved-rim bowl). "Type," meaning a form that always occurs in a specific fabric or ware, is largely avoided here owing to the rather preliminary understanding of the fabrics of the region (see above).

Drinking vessels

Kotylai (**1**) are deep drinking vessels with a thin, rounded or angular foot that extends outward from the lower wall. The body of the vessel rises steeply in a continuous convex curve and terminates either in a vertical or a slightly inturned tapered rim. Two horizontal handles are attached at or below the level of the rim. A problem of identification is posed when only a portion of the rim is preserved, since the rim, and even the handle, can be similar in form to one-handlers, also quite common in the Sanctuary. Kotylai have been recovered from the floor of the West Annex in Corinthian or a similar fabric. No kotylai were recovered from the destruction deposits of Building A in the North Annex, Front Room, or Southeast Room.

Kotylai have a very long history in the northern Peloponnese. At Corinth, they are attested in the Demeter Sanctuary in contexts dating as early as the seventh century and were in use at least until the third century and perhaps even until the destruction of Corinth in 146 BCE.[40] It seems that their use during the later fourth century and Hellenistic period was restricted to cultic contexts at Corinth, since none were published by Edwards in his study of material from the area of the forum. They are also not published among the material of fourth- and third-century date from the Rachi settlement at nearby Isthmia. Examples of kotylai found in fourth- and third-century contexts at the Corinth Demeter Sanctuary are often quite small (although not miniature), suggesting that they were in fact intended for use in cult, rather than as everyday drinking vessels.[41] Most of the examples recovered from the West Annex at Stymphalos and deposits beneath it are of this smaller size, with a foot of less than 5 cm in diameter.

Attic-type skyphoi (**2–3**) are deep drinking vessels with an overall form similar to kotylai. The chief formal differences between skyphoi and kotylai are that skyphoi have a more substantial ring foot and are deeper, often with a constructed lower body that forms a "stem." Attic-type skyphoi have a plain straight or slightly everted rim with two horizontal handles attached at or slightly beneath it. In the West Annex, two Attic-type skyphoi are attested in Corinthian fabric and one in Attic or a similar fabric. Three additional examples are attested in the collapse deposits of Building A, two in Corinthian fabric, and one in an unknown soft, fine, orange fabric, possibly Attic. The examples in the collapse deposits may be residual.

Attic-type skyphoi were perhaps manufactured in Athens as early as the sixth century,[42] but they definitely occur in deposits both at Corinth and Athens in the fifth century.[43] At Corinth, they remained popular throughout the fourth century, and are found with decreasing frequency in deposits of the third century,[44] during which they were gradually replaced by kantharoi. Pemberton suggests that production of Attic-type skyphoi ceased in Corinth by the end of the third century.[45] At the Rachi settlement at Isthmia they are attested in deposits of the later fourth and third centuries.[46] At Berbati in the Argolid, examples are attested in association with material of fifth-century through Hellenistic date, although Penttinen interprets them as residual in Hellenistic contexts.[47] They are unattested at Lavda in Elis, a Peloponnesian site whose excavated contexts date primarily to the second century or later. The appearance of Attic-type skyphoi in contexts at other sites in deposits of fourth- and third-century date, but not second-century, suggests that the examples attested in the second century collapse deposit are most likely residual.

One-handlers (**4** (?)) have a simple ring foot with a convex underside, a body shaped like a broad, shallow bowl, and one horizontal handle. The rim can be slightly thickened and outturned, or tapered and inturned, like some kotyle rims. The form is equally suited for drinking or eating. Seven examples are attested in the West Annex floor deposit, six in Corinthian or similar fabric and one in Attic or similar fabric. The single example in the Building A collapse deposits is in Corinthian or similar fabric.

One-handlers are very common in deposits at Corinth dating to the fifth and fourth centuries, and examples are attested in deposits of third-century date at both Corinth[48] and the Rachi settlement at Isthmia,[49] where they seem to be replaced by kantharoi as the third century progresses.[50] In Elis one-handlers are attested in graves of the fourth and early third centuries.[51] At Athens they are uncommon after the early third century.[52] Their presence in the West Annex is in accord with this chronology; the single fragmentary example attested in the collapse deposits of Building A is probably residual.

Attic moulded-rim kantharoi (**5**) have a stemmed foot with moulding and conical underside, a convex lower wall, and a concave upper wall terminating in a "moulded" rim with a rounded flange protruding outwards. Two examples were attested in the West Annex deposit, both in Attic fabric, and none were preserved in the destruction deposits of Building A. No other examples of this form have been identified at Stymphalos to date. In Athens moulded-rim kantharoi were first produced in the second quarter of the fourth century and were the most popular drinking vessels there at the beginning of the Hellenistic period. They continued in use until the early third century there.[53]

Four other forms of kantharoi are likely to be attested among the Building A collapse material at Stymphalos: cyma or "Acrocorinth" kantharoi (**6–7**),[54] articulated kantharoi,[55] one-piece kantharoi,[56] and the kantharos with simple everted rim (**8–9**). These forms are most easily distinguished on the basis of the form of their foot; however, since most examples were fragmentary and no full profiles were preserved in the collapse deposits of Building A, the distinction in forms could not be precise. At present, all of these forms of kantharoi are only broadly datable to the third century and at least the first half of the second century.[57] Since all of them overlap in function as drinking vessels, determining the specific forms is not absolutely necessary to interpret the overall function of Building A, or its chronology. The variance in style that the kantharoi represent, however, does have a bearing on how the assemblages used in Building A in its final Hellenistic phase are interpreted. The variety of forms suggests that the items brought to the Sanctuary were not "standardized." Kantharoi occur in the Building A collapse deposits in Corinthian or similar fabric, Argive or similar fabric, and fine blisterware. Kantharoi are relatively common in several other locations at Stymphalos.

Simple everted-rim kantharoi/mugs warrant a more detailed description, since full profiles of this form have been recovered from Stymphalos (although not from Building A) and since it does not correspond exactly with any published form of kantharos or mug. Simple everted-rim kantharoi/mugs have a plain ring foot with flat resting surface and convex underside. There is no moulding on the foot or at most there are simple grooves on its outer face, and the foot meets directly with the convex lower wall. The upper body rises to a slightly outturned and tapering rim. One or two vertical loop handles are attached at the rim.[58] This form occurs exclusively in smooth blisterware fabric at Stymphalos, and in Building A is only attested in the collapse deposits. Several other examples of this form are attested at Stymphalos in other contexts.

The simple foot and overall shape of the body of simple everted-rim mugs/kantharoi have a general similarity to "Hexamilia" kantharoi and mugs from Corinth;[59] however, the handles of "Hexamilia" kantharoi are not attached directly to the rim on any published or inventoried example at Corinth.[60] In addition, all of the Hexamilia kantharoi inventoried in the Corinth storerooms have thicker walls and occur in a semi-fine to coarse fabric and not the hard, clean blisterware of the Stymphalian examples. Examples of the Hexamilia kantharos at Corinth also do not have an outturned rim, but rather a simple vertical tapered rim. Simple everted-rim kantharoi/mugs are also generally similar to one-handled mugs attested in a second-century deposit at Geraki in Lakonia,[61] although the foot on the Stymphalian examples is a true ring, and the carination of the body is less sharp. Closer parallels to the Stymphalian simple everted-rim kantharoi/mugs are on display at the Nemea museum, suggesting that they may be a product of Nemea or a site in the Argolid. At Stymphalos, simple-rim kantharoi/mugs are conspicuously absent among material recovered from the Terrace Wall fill deposit, the bulk of which dates to the late fourth and early third century (a deposit that contained numerous drinking vessels). They do occur regularly in contexts of late third- and second-century date at Stymphalos, indicating that they probably did not appear at Stymphalos until perhaps the second quarter of the third century or later.

Conical bowls (**10**) have a flat or slightly recessed base, and a wall that rises almost in a straight line before it tapers to form the rim. Often they are ribbed horizontally or display wheel ridging on the exterior. Although the fragmentary examples recovered from Building A at Stymphalos show no decoration, most examples of conical bowls published at Corinth and Athens have painted West Slope decoration or moulded decoration on the interior. It may be that at Stymphalos, where paint and slip have often been affected by the acidic soil, such decoration is simply not preserved. The conical shape with simple rim ideally suits its use for drinking. The only example attested in Building A comes from the collapse deposit and is in blisterware fabric.

At Corinth, Edwards dated conical bowls from the third quarter of the third century to the Mummian sack of 146 BCE, but he did so without the benefit of much contextual information.[62] Two examples were published from the Demeter Sanctuary at Corinth in deposits dated to the second half of the third century and ca. 200 BCE.[63] At the Rachi settlement at Isthmia, examples are attested in contexts dated to the second half of the third century.[64] Other examples are attested in deposits associated with the destruction of the site in the late third century.[65] Anderson-Stojanovich concluded that they were more popular there in the second half of the third century than in the first half,[66] and that they were the most common form of drinking vessel at the site when it was destroyed.[67] Similar vessels in Athens appeared as early as ca. 280 BCE and continued in use into the second century.[68] Conical bowls were most popular in the northern Peloponnese in the later third and early second century. The small number of conical bowls in the collapse deposit in relation to mould-made bowls may indicate that the latter replaced conical bowls during the second century.

Most mould-made bowls (**11–14**) attested in the Building A collapse deposits at Stymphalos are roughly hemispherical in shape with a medallion for a base and a wall that rises in a gentle "S" curve terminating in a slightly outturned rim (as in **11–13**).[69] This profile is similar to bowls published from Corinth, Argos, and Athens.[70] At least one example of a shorter bowl with a more angular profile terminating in a straight or inturned rim is also attested in the North Annex collapse deposit (**14**). This profile is characteristic of the "Ionian" or "Aegean" bowls published from Athens,[71] Delos,[72] and Corinth.[73] Since the example with a different, "Ionian" profile is also in a fabric otherwise unattested at Stymphalos, and bears a distinctive decorative scheme (see below), it seems that this is an actual import from Ionia or the Aegean islands.

The other bowls at Stymphalos occur in a fabric that appears identical to Corinthian, as well as smooth blisterware, Argive or similar fabric, North Peloponnesian orange, and other unknown fabrics of sporadic occurrence.[74] Identification of fabric has been complicated by the traces of burning found on several of the bowls from the North Annex, indicating that some were burned in fire(s), presumably in the hearth located within the room.[75]

The decoration of mould-made bowls is arranged in zones: medallion, calyx, wall, and rim. Some decorative elements are common in multiple zones or extend across multiple zones. The zones range from being marked only with a line in the profile (**11**) to having distinct bulges that divide them into "registers" (as in **12–13**). The single "Ionian" bowl is divided into a series of narrow horizontal rows of decoration that make the outer wall of the vessel appear "bumpy" in profile (**14**). Such a layout of decoration is similar to that on many of the Ionian bowls published from Delos,[76] and is not typical of the decoration of locally produced bowls published from Corinth, Athens, or Argos, which generally have taller and less rigidly divided decorated zones.

A range of decorative motifs in a variety of combinations was employed on the bowls found at Stymphalos, both in the Building A collapse deposit and on the site as a whole (see table 9.8).[77] The decorative elements fall into three broad classes: floral, figural, and geometric patterning. As has been demonstrated elsewhere, these decorative elements were often mixed with each other, and certain combinations of motifs were often repeated. For instance, bowls with rearing goats often have floral bases. The decoration of the bowls attested at Stymphalos, even when it includes figures, does not consist of narrative scenes and does not appear to have been specialized for use in a sanctuary.[78] The greatest concentration of mould-made bowls at Stymphalos by far is in the North Annex of Building A.

Although mould-made bowls are traditionally thought of as highly datable (even as a sort of "type fossil"), their precise dating has proved to be problematic.[79] Thompson placed the earliest examples in Athens ca. 275 BCE.[80] Edwards suggested that they were first produced "in Greece" ca. 250 BCE.[81] In 1982 Rotroff redated the advent of production for Attic bowls to the last quarter of the third century. She associated this production with the Egyptian metal vessels that may have been present at the celebration called the Ptolomeion, which occurred in Athens in 224/223 BCE.[82] Rotroff herself has since modified this view on the basis of new deposits, and the redating of several deposits. She now suggests that mould-made bowls were perhaps first produced in Athens in the final two decades of the third century,[83] but that they do not become common in Athenian deposits dated before ca. 180 BCE.[84]

Of course the chronology for mould-made bowls may be somewhat different in the Peloponnese from at Athens. Siebert correctly recognized in his 1978 study of the mould-made bowls in the Peloponnese (and especially Argos) that they may have gone into production elsewhere at a later date than they did in Athens. He placed the advent of production at most major Peloponnesian centres in the late third or early second century, a date which was later than that accepted at the time for the introduction of mould-made bowls in Athens.[85] Evidence from deposits excavated since then in the Peloponnese can help augment this assessment. At Isthmia, only a single sherd of a mould-made bowl is attested in sizeable deposits associated with the destruction of the site by Philip V probably very early in the second century.[86] The near absence of mould-made bowls suggests that they were not in general use at the Rachi settlement before it was destroyed. Recent unpublished seriation studies at Corinth suggest that they may not have been attested there before the second century either,[87] although they evidently did become popular before the Mummian destruction,[88] and several examples in Corinthian, Argive, and East Greek fabrics appear in the interim period deposit studied by Romano.[89] Mould-made bowls occur in second- or first-century contexts at Geraki in Lakonia,[90] and in a second-century domestic context at Lavda in Elis.[91] As in Athens, mould-made bowls did not become popular in the Peloponnese until sometime in the second century, and the available evidence suggests that they were not common at the very beginning of that century.

Attempts have been made to date the various motifs on bowls, such as long petals;[92] however, given the recent shifts in general chronology of the form and the possibilities of distinct motifs arising in specific regional workshops at different dates, it may be wisest to use caution in trying to pinpoint the dating of motifs.

A vessel similar in form to mould-made bowls and quite possibly inspired by them is the hemispherical bowl with incised decoration (**15**). The single example at Stymphalos occurs in an unknown sandy grey fabric, and has an incised "star" pattern not unlike that seen near the base of some net pattern mould-made bowls.

Vessels with similar incision in possible imitation of mould-made vessels are attested at Corinth. These vessels are quite elaborately painted.[93] The Stymphalian vessel shows no indication of paint, although the painted decoration may well have worn away in the acidic red soil of the Sanctuary. Edwards attributes a similar chronology to these vessels as he does to mould-made bowls, which makes sense if these vessels are indeed imitations of mould-made bowls.[94]

Vessels for table service

Round-mouthed table juglets (**16–18,** and note also **19**) are the only table service vessels attested in the West Annex floor deposit and are by far the most common table service vessels in the Building A collapse deposits. They consist of a slightly concave disk base and globular body that constricts to form a neck which is pulled out to form a simple, tapered rim. A single small strap handle is attached from the rim to the shoulder. Round-mouthed table juglets are of an appropriate size for a single serving of wine or water, and they were probably intended for an individual to mix wine to his liking.[95] Round-mouthed table juglets occur in the West Annex floor deposit in Corinthian or similar fabric and Attic or similar fabric. In the Building A collapse deposits they occur in Corinthian or similar fabric and smooth blisterware. They are attested at Stymphalos outside the Sanctuary, although not in great numbers.

Round-mouthed table juglets are not well attested at Corinth. Edwards only knew of one example and had very little context information with which to date it. Thus, he dated it broadly to the Hellenistic period.[96] An example of a round-mouthed table juglet is published from a fourth-century deposit at the Demeter Sanctuary at Corinth.[97] Juglets of similar form have been published from Messene and dated by Themelis to the fourth and third centuries.[98] They have also been published from Mycenae in contexts of third- and/or second-century date.[99] Similar juglets in Athens are first attested in the third century; however, they do not become common there before the mid-second century, and continue to be produced into the first century.[100] The nearest comparanda to the examples from Stymphalos are on display in the Nemea museum.[101] As their presence in fourth- and second-century contexts at Stymphalos suggests, it seems that round-mouthed table juglets had quite a long "life span" in the northern Peloponnese, or perhaps similar juglets occurred independently at different points in the Classical and Hellenistic periods.

Trefoil oinochoai (not illustrated) have a narrow trefoil mouth, a short neck, and a globular body on a concave disk base. A high, upswung handle is attached from the rim to the shoulder. The form is well suited to pouring, and, like the round-mouthed table juglet, is sized for a single serving of wine or water. The only example preserved in Building A comes from the collapse deposits and is in Corinthian or similar fabric. Given that there is only one, and only a small portion of its rim is preserved, it is possible that this trefoil oinochoe is only a residual occurrence. Very few examples of trefoil oinochoai have been identified at Stymphalos as a whole.

At Corinth, Edwards dates trefoil oinochoai from the fifth to the third centuries, and Pemberton notes them in contexts of similar date.[102] In Athens, larger trefoil "choes" were in use until ca. 275 BCE. Smaller trefoil "choes," similar to the example from the Building A collapse deposit, were used into the second century.[103]

Blisterware aryballoi (not illustrated) have a slightly concave, irregular base, a squat body, a short narrow neck, a narrow mouth, and a broadly splaying rim. A single small handle is attached from the rim to the shoulder of the vessel. These aryballoi are thus well suited for both storing and pouring liquids such as oil and perfume at a slow, steady rate. They only occur in blisterware. Two very fragmentary examples of "blisterware aryballoi" have been recovered from the collapse deposits of Building A (in blisterware), and none from the West Annex floor deposit.

At Corinth, Edwards dates blisterware aryballoi ca. 450–300 on stylistic grounds.[104] Pemberton publishes examples from a late fourth-century context and a mid-second-century context at the Demeter Sanctuary at Corinth.[105] They are also present in deposits dated to the late fourth or early third century at the Rachi settlement at Isthmia.[106] Since there are only two examples from the Building A collapse deposits, and they are poorly preserved, it is possible that they are residual or were incorporated into the mudbrick of the superstructure. Although they are not present in the material from the floor of the West Annex, blisterware aryballoi do appear regularly in other deposits of fourth- and third-century date in the acropolis Sanctuary at Stymphalos.

Table amphorai (**19**, unless it is a jug) have a moulded or slightly hanging rim, a broad mouth and neck, two handles attached at or just below the rim and at the shoulder, and a piriform body. Examples published elsewhere generally have a ring foot. The wide mouth makes it a good vessel for pouring or even dipping into a larger vessel for wine service. The one example identified in Building A collapse deposits was in Corinthian or similar fabric. At Stymphalos, table amphorai are only attested in the acropolis Sanctuary, and only four examples have been identified there.

Just one example of this form is published from Corinth in Corinthian fabric. It came from an unsecure context that provides little information for dating. Examples in imported fabrics were rare at Corinth as well.[107] It does not seem to have been a regular component of the Corinthian, or Stymphalian, table assemblages. This is worth noting, since table amphorai were a fairly common form in Athens, the Aegean, and the Eastern Mediterranean in the Hellenistic period.[108] The one example found in Building A collapse deposits, though it is in Corinthian or a similar fabric, is more similar in form to examples published from Athens than to the example published by Edwards from Corinth. At Athens, table amphorai of Hellenistic form were probably first produced ca. 275 BCE or earlier and continued to be used throughout the Hellenistic period.[109]

Table vessels for eating

Incurved-rim bowls (**20–1**), also known as echinus bowls, are attested in the West Annex floor deposit in Corinthian or similar fabric and in the Building A collapse deposits in Corinthian or similar fabric, blisterware fabric, and North Peloponnesian orange fabric. They have a simple or bevelled ring foot with a flat resting surface and slightly convex underside. The wall rises from the foot in a convex curve terminating in a rounded or tapering incurved rim. Incurved-rim bowls are very popular in most deposits at Stymphalos, which makes the relatively small quantity attested in the collapse deposits somewhat surprising.[110]

Edwards wrote that full-sized incurved-rim bowls first appeared in the late fifth century at Corinth, and smaller, salt-cellar-sized examples appeared in the first quarter of the fourth century. He claimed that production at Corinth continued into the second century.[111] Pemberton, who relied more on contextual information, suggested that the form first appeared in the early fourth century at Corinth and that its production continued until the late third century there;[112] however, at least one incurved-rim bowl has been found in a deposit dating to the second half of the second century at Corinth, suggesting that Edwards may have been correct in his original assessment.[113] At the Rachi settlement at Isthmia they are present in contexts of fourth- and third-century date.[114] At Lavda in Elis[115] and at Argos,[116] they occur in contexts of second-century date. In Athens, Rotroff notes that they were less common from the middle of the third century on,[117] although incurved-rim bowls are still attested in deposits of Sullan date.[118] Incurved-rim bowls were produced in the Roman period as well, and an example has been published from Corinth that Slane assigns to the Early Roman period.[119] Since so few incurved-rim bowls were attested in the Building A collapse deposit in comparison to earlier deposits at Stymphalos, it is possible that they had declined in popularity by the mid-second century at Stymphalos, just as they had in Corinth and Athens.

Semiglazed bowls (**22**) have a simple ring foot and convex lower wall that constricts and is pulled out in its upper reaches to form a concave upper wall terminating in a tapered, outturned rim. They are given the name "semiglazed" because most examples from Corinth are dipped in slip to about mid-wall on the exterior (the slip is only preserved in patches on the examples from Stymphalos). The simple outturned rim would work equally well for food or drink, but the absence of handles on the vessel, and the ring foot, which is not suitable for cupping, suggest that it would be most useful for food. No semiglazed bowls were found in the West Annex floor deposit. The two examples identified in the Building A collapse deposits at Stymphalos are in Corinthian or an identical fabric and blisterware. Very few other examples of this form have been recovered from Stymphalos.

At Corinth semiglazed bowls were very popular.[120] They appeared there as early as the fifth century, but did not become popular in contexts dated earlier than the mid-fourth century. Semiglazed bowls continue in use at Corinth until the Mummian sack in 146 BCE, according to Edwards and Pemberton.[121] At the Rachi settlement at Isthmia, semiglazed bowls are attested in contexts of fourth- and third-century date.[122] Anderson-Stojanovich notes that later examples generally have their greatest width at a lower point and have a more pronounced outturned rim.[123] Examples from the Building A collapse deposits of second-century date are rather low and broad, supporting her suggestion. Semiglazed bowls seem to have been more popular at Isthmia and Corinth than anywhere else, since the form was not popular at Athens or any other major Hellenistic site until the Late Hellenistic period.[124] It is also not attested at smaller excavated sites in the Northern Peloponnese, such as Lavda in Elis or Mycenae. The scarcity of semiglazed bowls at Stymphalos is in keeping with their rare appearance at sites aside from Corinth and Isthmia.

Plain-rim saucers (**23**(?), **27**)[125] have a simple ring foot, in at least one instance with a "fishplate" depression in the interior floor, and a convex wall that terminates in a simple rounded or tapered rim. The form is deep enough that it could have been used for either solid food or foods with a semi-liquid consistency. The only full profile of a plain-rim saucer from the Building A collapse deposit has a depression as on a hanging-rim fishplate in the centre of the floor.[126] Although there are several other plain-rim saucer rims attested in the Building A collapse deposits (unless they are from lids), there are no other feet of such small size with a fishplate depression (see **27**). It is thus unclear whether the example with the depression is anomalous at Stymphalos or not. This form is attested in the West Annex floor deposit in an unknown fabric and in the Building A collapse deposits in Corinthian or similar fabric, smooth blisterware, and North Peloponnesian orange fabric. Plain-rim saucers are quite common at Stymphalos in general.

Edwards dated saucers of this form (with or without depression) to the entire span of the Hellenistic period at Corinth.[127] Pemberton has published examples from the Demeter Sanctuary at Corinth in deposits dating from the last third of the fourth to the early second century.[128] They are also attested in an interim-period deposit at Corinth dated to the second half of the second century.[129] They occur in the well at the Rachi settlement of Isthmia in fill dated from the late fourth through the second quarter of the third century.[130] A plain-rim saucer was recovered from a third- or second-century context at Mycenae.[131] Plain-rim saucers are represented through most of the Hellenistic period in the northern Peloponnese, and are not attested in deposits of Sullan date in Athens, or Early Roman deposits at Corinth.

Offset-rim plates (**24**) have a simple or grooved ring foot, and a wall which turns up slightly to meet the offset rim. The two examples attested in Building A come from the collapse deposits and are in Corinthian fabric. Examples published at Corinth and Athens often have West Slope decoration on the rim; traces of incised West Slope decoration are visible on both examples from the Building A collapse deposits, despite all slip and possible paint being worn away. Few examples of offset-rim plates have been identified at Stymphalos in other contexts, and only one has been identified outside of the Sanctuary.

The only examples of offset-rim plates published by Edwards had relatively little context information, allowing him to assign them only broadly to the Hellenistic period.[132] Pemberton identified several in later third-century and second-century contexts at the Demeter Sanctuary at Corinth.[133] At the Rachi settlement at Isthmia, offset-rim plates are attested in contexts of third-century date, and in particular later third-century date.[134] At Geraki in Lakonia, they occur in a deposit of second- or first-century date.[135] In Athens, offset-rim plates are not attested in contexts dating earlier than the third quarter of the second century.[136] As with many of the forms under discussion here, they seem to be most common in contexts of late third- or second-century date in the northern Peloponnese.

Deep rolled-rim plates (**25, 27**) have a plain, somewhat heavy ring foot and either a plain floor or one with a groove and vestigial fishplate depression. They have a convex wall terminating in a slightly bulbous rolled rim, often with a groove on the inner lip. This groove was quite possibly meant to prevent semi-liquid food from sloshing out of the plate, which was actually quite deep and could have been used for the service of solid or runny foods. Some examples of rolled-rim plates from the Building A collapse deposit are burnt around the rim. Since they are also of an appropriate size to cover a casserole, it is possible that this burning is from use as lids for cooking vessels (either instead of or in addition to eating food). This form occurs only in the collapse deposit of Building A and is attested in North Peloponnesian orange fabric and Corinthian or similar fabric. Rolled-rim plates are attested in almost all excavated areas at Stymphalos.

At Corinth, deep rolled-rim plates are not attested in any contexts securely dated earlier than the second century,[137] and the latest is from the interim-period deposit of the second half of the second century.[138] None are published from the Rachi settlement at Isthmia, which was destroyed probably very early in the second century.[139] Deep rolled-rim plates are attested (with thickened rim but no groove) at Argos in tombs dated by Bruneau to the late second or early first century.[140] At Lavda in Elis an example occurs in a second-century domestic deposit.[141] Similar deep rolled-rim plates are dated by Rotroff to the second and third quarters of the second century and later in Athens.[142] Given this evidence, and the fact that deep rolled-rim plates do not occur in any of the examined deposits of secure third-century date at Stymphalos, it seems that deep rolled-rim plates were not present in the northern Peloponnese until sometime in the second century.

Hanging- or projecting-rim fishplates (**26–7**) have a simple ring foot, and can have either a plain floor or a fishplate depression in the interior floor and a wall that ranges from nearly perpendicular to the foot to a wall that rises quite steeply. The wall terminates in a rim that either hangs straight down or projects outwards and down at a diagonal (as in **26**, and all examples from the Building A collapse). Examples identified in the Building A collapse deposits occur in North Peloponnesian orange fabric.[143] Although fishplates are not common at Stymphalos, several other examples have been recovered from the Sanctuary and other areas of the city.

At Corinth, Edwards dated these plates from ca. 300 to the Mummian destruction of 146 BCE.[144] Fishplates were also attested there in the interim-period deposit of the second half of the second century.[145] In the Rachi settlement at Isthmia they were found in deposits of late fourth- and third-century date, although Anderson-Stojanovich noted that they were not very popular there.[146] Vessels with the shallow "vestigial" depression (or no depression), deeper overall form, and projecting rims, rather than the hanging rims seen on the examples from the Building A collapse, are found in contexts of second- and first-century date at Argos and Athens.[147] It seems that the fishplates recovered from the Building A collapse correspond with the second-century date of many of the other forms recovered from the collapse deposits of Building A.

Plates (or lids?) with bevelled rim (**28**) have a foot of unknown form (since it is only attested at Stymphalos in one example and no comparanda have been identified), a relatively steep wall, and a rim that is bevelled and projects slightly upwards/inwards. Like the other plates under discussion here, the form is deep enough that it could accommodate semi-liquid as well as solid foods. The only example attested in the Building A collapse was in an unknown orange fabric. There are no close parallels for this form.

Votive vessels

Miniature kotylai (**29**) have a flat, string-cut base and are roughly the shape of an inverted bell with two small pinched handles attached at or slightly beneath the rim. They were found both in the floor deposit of the West Annex in Corinthian fabric and in the Building A collapse deposit in both Corinthian and North Peloponnesian orange fabrics. Since they were made primarily to be dedicated, it is little surprise that the vast majority of them at Stymphalos were found in the Sanctuary.

Miniatures in general were very popular in Greek sanctuaries from the Archaic period until the late third century.[148] At Corinth, miniature kotylai are attested in deposits in the Demeter Sanctuary dating as late as the late fourth century.[149] Given this chronology, it is somewhat surprising that they occur in the Building A collapse deposits; however, the quantity recovered is very small in relation to the total number of vessels, and even these examples are fragmentary. It is entirely possible that the small fragments recovered from the collapse deposit were residual or built into the mudbrick walls of the superstructure.

Cooking vessels

Flaring-rim chytrai or round-mouthed cooking jugs (**30, 32,** and note also **34**) have a globular body that is constricted to form the neck and pulled back out to form a simple, tapered rim. The base is either rounded or given a slight concavity to allow it to sit upright. One vertical handle is attached at the rim and the shoulder. This form suits them well for cooking soups and gruels, boiling water, or fetching it.[150] Flaring-rim chytrai and/or cooking jugs are well attested in the West Annex floor deposit in smooth orange-red cooking fabric, but none are present in the collapse deposits of Building A. They are common throughout Stymphalos.

At Corinth, flaring-rim chytrai/round-mouthed cooking jugs are dated by Edwards from ca. 450 or 400 until the city's destruction in 146 BCE. He suggests that they increase in height over time.[151] They are present in deposits at the Corinth Demeter Sanctuary dating from the sixth century until the first half of the second century.[152] At the Rachi settlement, they are attested in deposits of the third century.[153] At Stymphalos, it seems that they had largely gone out of use prior to the time Building A went out of use, since there is a good quantity of pottery for cooking in the collapse deposits, yet just one of these jugs/chytrai (**34**) is present.

Flanged-rim chytrai (**36**) have a rounded bottom. Their body is globular in shape, and the "neck" and rim of the vessel are made separately and attached to the upper wall. On most examples the upper wall protrudes slightly past the point of rim attachment to form a slightly tapered or rounded flange. The "neck" is sometimes cupped, and the rim can be either plain (tapered or rounded) or thickened and angled. Almost all examples of flanged chytrai from the Building A collapse deposits at Stymphalos are of the latter variety. It seems likely, therefore, that these are generally later in date than examples of the form with simply tapered rims. Tapered-rim vessels occur much more frequently in deposits of earlier date at Stymphalos than they do in the Building A collapse deposits.[154] Usually one strap handle (but sometimes two) is attached at the rim and transition from the middle to upper body (shoulder); a horizontal handle is also positioned on the wall on some published examples. The flange and the cupping of the rim were meant to facilitate lids. Flanged-rim chytrai do not occur in the West Annex floor deposit, but several are present in the Building A collapse deposits in North Peloponnesian orange fabric. Flanged-rim chytrai are common in many areas of Stymphalos.

Edwards dates the only examples of flanged-rim

chytrai he published from Corinth to the mid-second-century Mummian destruction horizon, though he notes that the form seemed "very advanced." He dated a "stew pot" of essentially the same form, except for different handle configuration, to the third century.[155] Flanged chytrai with tapered rims are attested at the Demeter Sanctuary of Corinth perhaps as early as the sixth century; they continue in use in the Hellenistic period.[156] It is uncertain when the thickened-rim variety was first used in the Demeter Sanctuary, but Pemberton suggests that it is later in the period.[157] They continued in use at Corinth into the early Roman period.[158] Flanged-rim chytrai have been identified in contexts dating to the third century at Isthmia.[159] At Geraki in Lakonia a similar vessel is published as a cooking "jug" from a second- or first-century deposit.[160] In Athens chytrai with flanged and thickened rims are not very common, although examples have been found, some of which are imports.[161] That they are infrequent in Athens[162] is interesting, since they seem to be one of the most popular cooking forms in the northern Peloponnese over a long period of time.

The flanged-rim chytra with ledge rim (**37**) is like other flanged-rim chytrai except for a short ledge on the top of the rim. The single example at Stymphalos occurs in a hard and relatively smooth orange cooking fabric with some white inclusions and may be an import. It occurred in the Building A collapse deposit.

No close parallels for this form have been published, either from the immediate region of Stymphalos or from farther afield. It seems likely to be imported and was quite possibly produced at the same place as the bulging casserole with small ledge rim, to which it is similar in both fabric and rim form.

Most of the casseroles (**38–40**) recovered from the West Annex floor deposit and the Building A collapse deposits have the same overall form consisting of a broad rounded bottom (possibly mould-made),[163] and relatively straight sides terminating in a flanged, nearly vertical rim that is tapered, or more rarely thickened slightly. There is often a groove or slight bulging of the wall on the exterior just beneath the rim. On examples where handles are preserved, they are attached horizontally to the body or the rim. Casseroles occur in the West Annex floor deposit in a smooth orange-red and North Peloponnesian orange cooking fabric. In the Building A collapse deposits they occur in a smooth orange-red cooking fabric, North Peloponnesian orange, and a gritty grey cooking fabric with white inclusions.

Edwards dates casseroles in general from the early or mid-fifth century to the Mummian destruction.[164] Pemberton dates examples from the Demeter Sanctuary at Corinth to the fifth century and later.[165] Anderson-Stojanovich notes that casseroles with dramatically bulging walls became more popular at the Rachi settlement as the third century progressed.[166] No bulging-wall casseroles similar to those described by Anderson-Stojanovich occur in Building A at Stymphalos, though, even in the "late" collapse deposits. Furthermore, examples of non-bulging-wall casseroles are attested in a second-century domestic deposit at Lavda in Elis, which does not contain any bulging-wall casseroles.[167]

Bulging-wall casseroles with short ledge rims (not illustrated) are shaped like other casseroles except that their upper wall curves in to form a pronounced bulge beneath the rim attachment and they have a small ledge at the top of the rim. They occur in a hard, smooth cooking fabric with white inclusions. The two examples identified from Stymphalos both come from the acropolis Sanctuary.

No similar casseroles have been published from Corinth, and there are no published examples elsewhere in the Northern Peloponnese. As mentioned above, similarities in rim form and fabric to the flanged chytra with small ledge rim suggest it may have been produced at the same place as that form.

Cooking lids (**31, 33, 35, 41**) have simple tapered rims and simple wheelmade knobs to serve as handles. They occur in the West Annex floor deposit in North Peloponnesian orange fabric and a powdery red cooking fabric. In Building A collapse deposits they are attested in North Peloponnesian orange, gritty grey, and a powdery red cooking fabric. Cooking lids are common throughout Stymphalos. These lids are generic in form and do not display much change over time. Edwards dates them at Corinth from the sixth century until the Mummian destruction.[168]

Utility vessels

Bowls/lekanai with moulded rim (**42**) have a simple ring foot and a convex lower wall that rises to a carination at mid-wall, above which the upper wall is concave and terminates in a thickened rim with a groove on its face. More complete examples from other sites often have two horizontal handles attached to their upper wall. This form would be well suited for a variety of tasks from washing to cooking to mixing wine and water. Moulded-rim bowls/lekanai are not attested in the West Annex floor deposit. They occur in the Building A collapse deposit in North Peloponnesian orange fabric and in grey cooking fabric with white inclusions. All of the examples are very fragmentary, so it is possible that moulded-rim bowls/lekanai occur in the Building A collapse deposits residually.[169] This shape occurs with some regularity elsewhere at Stymphalos.

Edwards dated the examples of moulded-rim bowls/lekanai he published from Corinth to the mid-second century, and Pemberton published examples from deposits of late third- and second-century date.[170] They are also attested into the first century CE at Corinth.[171] At Isthmia they have been found in contexts as early as the early third century.[172] At Athens moulded-rim bowls/lekanai (Rotroff's lekane form 1) are found in deposits as early as the early third century and as late as the first half of the first century.[173] Although they occur in great quantities in Athens, it was not possible to trace any "development" of the form over time, aside from a tendency for later examples to have thicker walls and to be somewhat larger in size.[174]

Bowls/lekanai with projecting rim (**43**) have a simple or convex ring foot and convex wall that terminates in a rim that projects horizontally from the upper wall. Among published examples with this same rim form, the depth of the vessel can vary widely. Like moulded-rim bowls/lekanai, it has a generic form which would be useful for washing, mixing, or serving. In the West Annex floor deposit a single example in an unknown fabric is attested, and in the Building A collapse deposit, this form occurs only in North Peloponnesian orange fabric. Bowls/lekanai of similar form are found in several other areas at Stymphalos. Finding comparanda for such a "generic" form is somewhat difficult. Edwards does date similar vessels at Corinth to the mid-second century.[175]

Two examples of bowls with a short ledge rim (**44**) were identified in the Building A collapse deposits at Stymphalos in North Peloponnesian orange fabric. Since only the rim and a portion of the upper wall were preserved and no close comparanda were identified, it is impossible to determine what exactly the full form looked like, but it seems fairly certain that it was some sort of bowl or lekane. Given their fabric, it seems most likely that they were a type of utility vessel, though use for serving or eating food, or even as a casserole, is possible. Vessels of identical form have not been identified in any other context at Stymphalos so far.

A single amphora or thickened-rim jug rim is attested in the West Annex floor deposit and only two thickened-rim jugs or amphorai (not illustrated) were identified from the Building A collapse deposits. It is possible, then, that these are merely residual and that they should not be considered part of the functional assemblages of Building A. Jugs in general, however, do not preserve as well as many other vessel types because they are generally thin-walled and tall. The portion of the vessel that is most often preserved is the handle, a section of the vessel that is typologically indistinct.[176] Similar vessels, in a similarly fragmentary state, are attested from the domestic area of the lower site at Stymphalos (Stym I). Vessels with similar rims have been identified at Corinth, though they are not dated with any great precision there.[177]

Miscellaneous

An irregular vessel of uncertain form (**45**, not illustrated) in a hard, gritty purple cooking fabric was attested in the West Annex floor deposit. It has a short projecting rim around an irregularly shaped mouth and an even more irregular body. Though many sherds that must have belonged to this vessel were recovered, it was impossible to reconstruct a substantial portion of its profile. It is uncertain what function it may have served.

One very interesting vessel (**46**), largely complete, with no published comparanda known to me, was found in the Building A collapse deposits. In form it consists of a hemispherical bowl with an essentially plain, flattened rim and a piecrust moulding on the ring "foot." It is in an unknown fabric, but perhaps is local. No other examples of this form have been recognized at Stymphalos. Its shape suits it for a number of purposes, although the decorative waving of the "foot" is unusual. One vessel that is somewhat similar in shape is on display in the new Acropolis Museum (numbered there 163) in Athens, identified as a thymiaterion lid.

CATALOGUE

approx.	approximately
circum.	circumference
D	diameter
est.	estimated
ext.	exterior
H	height
int.	interior
Inv.	inventory number
m	metre(s)
max.	maximum
P	preserved
Th.	thickness

All measurements are in centimetres.

Find spots are indicated by trench, level, and pail numbers, so Tr. 96.95.9.3.3 means that the vase was found in 1996 in Trench 9 laid out in the 1995 season, Level 3, Pail 3.

Drinking vessels

1. Kotyle. Single sherd preserves approximately one-third circum. of the foot and small portion of the lower wall. Corinthian fabric (10YR 8/3) with traces of red on int. and ext., possibly applied in bands on ext. **Fig. 9.1**
Inv. 4902. Tr. 96.8.3.3. West Annex floor deposit
PH 1.3; D (est.) base 4.5; Th. wall 0.2

2. Skyphos, Attic-type. Three joining sherds preserve almost the entire foot and a portion of the lower wall. Corinthian fabric (2.5Y 8/4) with black on int. and ext. **Fig. 9.1**
Inv. 4890. Tr. 96.6.3.8. West Annex floor deposit
PH 4.7; D base 4.5; Th. wall 0.4.

3. Skyphos, Attic-type. Single sherd preserves the entire foot and portion of the lower wall. Unknown soft, fine orange fabric, possibly Attic (7.5YR 7/4) with worn brown-black slip on int. and ext. **Fig. 9.1**
Inv. 4801 Tr. 95.3.5.9. North Annex collapse deposit
PH 2.7; D base 3.6; Th. wall 0.4

4. One-handler (? or two-handled cup). Eight joining sherds preserve the entire foot, much of the lower wall, approx. one-third of the upper wall and rim, and entire handle. Corinthian fabric (10YR 8/4) with worn black slip on int. and worn red on ext. **Fig. 9.1**
Inv. 4896. Tr. 96.6.3.8. West Annex floor deposit
H 5.0; D (est.) rim 11.0; D base 4.7; Th. wall 0.3

5. Kantharos, moulded rim. Three joining sherds preserve slightly less than half circum. of the rim and upper wall, one entire handle spur. Attic fabric (2.5YR 7/4) with mottled black and brown slip, worn away in patches. **Fig. 9.1**
Inv. 4905. Tr. 96.8.3.3. West Annex floor deposit
PH 3.0; D (est.) rim 7.0; Th. wall 0.3

6. Kantharos, cyma, or similar. Two joining sherds preserve approx. one-quarter circum. of the rim and upper wall, beginning of a handle spur. Corinthian fabric (10YR 8/4) with very worn black slip on int. and ext. **Fig. 9.1**
Inv. 4802. Tr. 95.3.5.9. North Annex collapse deposit
PH 2.6; D (est.) rim 8.0; Th. wall 0.2

7. Kantharos, cyma or similar. Two joining sherds preserve approx. one-third circum. of the foot and part of the lower wall. Corinthian fabric (10YR 8/4) with traces of brown-black slip on int. and ext. **Fig. 9.1**
Inv. 4804. Tr. 96.95.9.3.3. North Annex collapse deposit
PH 1.3; D (est.) foot 4.2; Th. wall 0.3

8. Kantharos, simple everted rim. Two joining sherds preserve a small part of the rim and much of the upper wall, small part of the lower wall. Blisterware fabric (5YR 7/4) with slightly worn black slip on int. and ext. **Fig. 9.1**
Inv. 4803. Tr. 95.3.5.9. North Annex collapse deposit
PH 4.5; D rim not determined; Th. wall 0.2

9. Kantharos, simple everted rim. Three joining sherds preserve almost the entire foot and part of the lower wall. Blisterware fabric (7.5YR 7/6) with worn black slip on int. and ext. **Fig. 9.1**
Inv. 4806. Tr. 95.3.4.7 and 95.3.5.9. North Annex collapse deposit
PH 1.8; D base 3.4; Th. wall 0.4

10. Conical cup. Single sherd preserves entire foot and small part of the lower wall. Blisterware fabric (7.5YR 7/3) with no slip preserved. **Fig. 9.1**
Inv. 4779. Tr. 96.95.9.3.4. North Annex collapse deposit
PH 1.6; D base 2.9; Th. wall 0.3

11. Mould-made bowl. Twenty-three joining sherds preserve most of the body, approx. one-third circum. of rim. Unknown fabric (7.5YR 6/4) with streaky red-brown slip on int. and ext. **Fig. 9.2**
Inv. 116. Tr. 95.3.4.10. North Annex collapse deposit
H 6.5; D rim 12.0; D base 2.7; Th. wall 0.4
Decoration: floral medallion, imbricate fern with floral medallions on calyx, vine and ivy on wall, dots in the rim zone.

12. Mould-made bowl. Sixteen joining sherds preserve all of the lower half of bowl, approximately one-third circum. of the upper wall and one-quarter circum. of the rim. Unknown burnt fabric (10YR 6/2) with very worn black slip on int. and ext. **Fig. 9.2**
Inv. 1789, 1869, 2007, 2060, 2062. Tr. 95.9.3.4. North Annex collapse deposit
H 7.6; D (est.) rim 12.0; D base 2.2; Th. wall 0.3
Decoration: medallion illegible, net pattern and dots in groups of three on calyx and wall, made from a very worn mould.

13. Mould-made bowl. Nineteen joining sherds preserve nearly three-quarters of bowl with several gaps in wall and rim, three separately joining sherds preserve a small part of the rim to lower wall. Unknown fabric (10YR 8/4), possibly Corinthian with traces of red to black slip on int. and ext. **Fig. 9.2**

Inv. 2058. Tr. 95.9.3.4. North Annex collapse deposit
H 6.7; D (est.) rim 10.0; Th. wall 0.3
Decoration: medallion not sufficiently preserved, fern stamps and rosettes on calyx, standing women with juglets, Apollos with lyre, bacchants (?), and dots on wall, single scrolls in rim zone.

14. Mould-made bowl, Ionian. Nine joining sherds preserve approximately one-eighth circum. of the rim and almost half of the lower to mid-wall. Unknown fabric (10YR 6/8) with grey core (10YR 3/1), no slip preserved. **Fig. 9.2**
Inv. 1855 and 1865. Tr. 95.9–96.95.9. North Annex collapse deposit
PH 5.1; D (est.) rim 11.0; Th. wall 0.2
Decoration: acanthus or frond and spiral columns on calyx, grape or fig leaves alternating with "fleur de lis" – like motif on lowest wall register, bead and reel on middle wall register "blob" flowers, scrolls (very worn) in rim register.

15. Imitation mould-made bowl. Single sherd preserves entire base and portion of lower wall. Unknown burnt fabric (5YR 5/2) with traces of black slip on ext. **Fig. 9.2**
Inv. 1377. Tr. 97.95.9.6.6. North Annex collapse deposit
PH 1.7; D base 1.2; Th. wall 4.0
Decoration: incised net pattern.

Juglets/jugs

16. Round-mouthed table juglet. Two joining sherds preserve approx. one-third circum. of the rim and approx. one-sixth of the upper body. Attic or a very similar fabric (7.5YR 7/6) with well-preserved black slip on int. and ext. **Fig. 9.2**
Inv. 4903. Tr. 96.8.3.3. West Annex floor deposit
PH 3.7; D (est.) rim 6.0; Th. wall 3.0

17. Round-mouthed table juglet. Single sherd preserves approx. one-fifth circum. of the rim and shoulder. Blisterware fabric (5YR 6/8) with worn brown-black slip on int. and ext. **Fig. 9.2**
Inv. 4796. Tr. 96.95.9.3.4. North Annex collapse deposit
PH 2.2; D (est.) rim 8.0; Th. wall 0.2

18. Round-mouthed table juglet. Single sherd preserves approx. one-third circum. of the base and part of the lower wall. Blisterware fabric (5YR 6/4) with traces of red-brown slip on int. and ext. **Fig. 9.2**
Inv. 4798. Tr. 95.3.5.9. North Annex collapse deposit
PH 0.9; D (est.) foot 5.0; Th. wall 0.2

Amphora (?)

19. Table amphroa (or jug). Two joining sherds preserve approx. one-sixth circum. of the rim and neck. Corinthian fabric (10YR 8/4) with worn black slip on int. and ext. **Fig. 9.2**
Inv. 4783. Tr. 97.95.3.6.4. North Annex collapse deposit
PH 4.5; D (est.) rim 14.0; Th. wall 0.5

Other bowls

20. Incurved-rim bowl. Two non-joining sherds preserve approx. one-third circum. of the rim and upper wall. Blisterware fabric (5YR 6/6) with worn grey-brown slip on int., possibly slightly burnt. **Fig. 9.3**
Inv. 4799. Tr. 96.95.9.3.4. North Annex collapse deposit
PH 2.8; D (max. est.) 13.0; D (est.) rim 11.0; Th. wall 0.5

21. Incurved-rim bowl. Three joining sherds preserve the entire foot and most of the lower to upper wall almost to rim. Unknown burnt fabric (7.5YR 7/4) with worn black slip on int, and worn dull brown slip on the top half of ext. **Fig. 9.3**
Inv. 1397 and 4839 (inv. 1397 mistakenly inventoried with sherds of the semiglazed bowl, **22**, and the bowl with piecrust foot, **46**). Tr. 97.96.12.3.3. Southeast Room collapse deposit
PH 3.8; D base 4.2; Th. wall 0.2

22. Semiglazed bowl. Nineteen joining sherds preserve most of the vessel except small gaps in the body and rim. Blisterware fabric (5YR 7/6 and 5YR 6/2) with red-brown slip on most of the int. and ext. **Fig. 9.3**
Inv. 1397 and 4658 (inv. 1397 mistakenly inventoried with sherds of the incurved-rim bowl, **22**, and the bowl with piecrust foot, **46**). Tr. 96.12.3.3 and 96.12.4.4. Southeast Room collapse deposit
H 7.3; D rim 20.2; D foot 5.6; Th. wall 0.2

Saucer (?)

23. Plain-rim saucer (or lid). Seven joining sherds preserve the entire foot and approx. one-third circum. of the wall and rim, two additional non-joining rim fragments. Corinthian fabric (2.5Y 8/2) with traces of black slip on int. and ext. **Fig. 9.3**
Inv. 1946 and 2287 (several sherds from other saucers were inventoried along with 2287. Inv. 1946 duplicates a number assigned to a mould-made bowl from the North Annex). Tr. 96.12.4.4–5. Southeast Room collapse deposit
H 4.2; D (est.) rim 20.0; Th. wall 0.3

Plates

24. Offset-rim plate. Two joining sherds preserve approx. one-eighth circum. of the rim and start of the upper wall. Corinthian fabric (2.5Y 8/4) with no slip remaining. **Fig. 9.3**
Inv. 4836. Tr. 97.96.12.4.4. Southeast Room collapse deposit
PH 1.0; D (est.) rim 17.0; Th. wall 0.4
Decoration: incised vines on top of the rim.

25. Deep rolled-rim plate. Single sherd preserves a small part of the rim and upper wall. North Peloponnesian orange fabric (5YR 5/6) with traces of red-brown slip on int. and ext. **Fig. 9.3**
Inv. 4834. Tr. 96.12.3.3. Southeast Room collapse deposit
PH 2.3; Th. wall 0.6

26. Fishplate, projecting rim. Single sherd preserves approx. one-fifth circum. of the rim and upper wall. Slightly burnt North Peloponnesian orange fabric (5YR 6/6) with traces of red-brown slip on int. and ext. **Fig. 9.4**
Inv. 4800. Tr. 96.95.9.6.6. North Annex collapse deposit
PH 2.0; D (est.) rim 15.0; Th. wall 0.5

27. Fishplate. Four joining sherds preserve almost the entire foot and part of the lower wall. North Peloponnesian orange fabric (10YR 7/6) with traces of red-brown slip on int. **Fig. 9.4**
Inv. 4795. Tr. 95.9.3.4. North Annex collapse deposit
PH 2.9; D foot 7.0; Th. wall 0.7

28. Plate with bevelled rim. Sixteen joining sherds preserve approx. half circum. of the rim and wall. Unknown fabric (7.5YR 6/6), possibly North Peloponnesian orange with a slightly worn, streaky, metallic brown-black slip on int. and ext. **Fig. 9.4**
Inv. 1400 and 2318. Tr. 97.96.12.4.4–5. Southeast Room collapse deposit
PH 3.9; D rim 20.0; Th. wall 0.3

Miniatures

29. Miniature kotyle. Single sherd preserves the entire foot and part of the wall. Corinthian fabric (10YR 8/3) with traces of red-brown slip on ext. **Fig. 9.4**
Inv. 4842. Tr. 97.95.2.4.8. Front Room collapse deposit
PH 1.0; D foot 1.7; Th. wall 0.2

Cooking pots

30. Flaring-rim chytra/round-mouthed cooking jug. Four joining sherds preserve approx. one-third circum. of the rim and one-fifth circum. of the neck. Smooth orange-red cooking fabric (2.5YR 4/6) with much burning around the rim. **Fig. 9.4**
Inv. 4898. Tr. 96.6.5.11 and 96.8.3.4. West Annex floor deposit
PH 2.6; D (est.) rim 11.0; Th. wall 0.3

31. Cooking lid, chytra sized. Single sherd preserves approx. one-seventh circum. of the rim and wall. North Peloponnesian orange cooking fabric (5YR 6/8) with traces of burning around the rim. **Fig. 9.4**
Inv. 4911. Tr. 96.8.3.4. West Annex floor deposit
PH 0.9; D (est.) rim 10.0; Th. wall 0.4

32. Flaring-rim chytra/round-mouthed cooking jug. Single sherd preserves approx. one-quarter circum. of the rim and neck. Smooth orange-red cooking fabric (5YR 5/6). **Fig. 9.4**
Inv. 4901. Tr. 96.8.3.3. West Annex floor deposit
PH 3.8; D (est.) rim 9.0; Th. wall 0.4

33. Cooking lid, chytra or small casserole sized. Two joining sherds preserve approx. one-sixth circum. of the rim and a small part of the wall. The fabric is not identified, very burnt. **Fig. 9.5**
Inv. 4827. Tr. 97.96.12.4.4. Southeast Room collapse deposit
PH 1.3; D (est.) rim 15.0; Th. 0.2

34. Unlidded (?) chytra. Two joining sherds preserve approx. one-quarter circum. of the rim and upper wall. North Peloponnesian orange cooking fabric (5YR 5/8) with substantial burning on the ext. and lip. **Fig. 9.5**
Inv. 4824. Tr. 97.95.2.4.8–9. Front Room collapse deposit
PH 4.2; D (est.) rim 15.0; Th. wall 0.3

35. Cooking lid, chytra sized. Four joining sherds preserve approx. half circum. of the rim, most of the wall, and the entire knob. Soft powdery cooking fabric (5YR 5/6). **Fig. 9.5**
Inv. 4825. Tr. 97.96.12.4.4. Southeast Room collapse deposit
H 2.1; D rim 10.0; Th. wall 0.3

36. Flanged-rim chytra. Five joining sherds preserve approx. one-quarter circum. of the rim, one entire handle, and part of the wall. North Peloponnesian orange fabric (7.5YR 7/8). **Fig. 9.5**
Inv. 4680. Tr. 97.96.12.3.3. Southeast Room collapse deposit
PH 8.4; D (est.) rim 9.0; Th. wall 0.2

37. Flanged-rim chytra with ledge rim. Single sherd preserves approx. one-tenth circum. of the rim and part

of the upper wall. Unknown fabric (2.5YR 5/8). **Fig. 9.5**
Inv. 4562. Tr. 97.96.12.4. Southeast Room collapse deposit
PH 2.7; D (est.) rim 17.0; Th. wall 0.4

38. Casserole. Single sherd preserves approx. one-fifth circum. of the rim and wall. Gritty grey cooking fabric (ext. 7.5YR 5/6, int. 10YR 4/2) **Fig. 9.5**
Inv. 4819. Tr. 96.12.3.3. Southeast Room collapse deposit
PH 3.8; D (est.) rim 15.0; Th. wall 0.4

39. Casserole. Seven joining sherds preserve approx. one-fifth circum. of the rim and upper wall, much of the lower wall. Smooth red-orange cooking fabric (2.4YR 5/6). **Fig. 9.6**
Inv. 4860. Tr. 95.9.3.4. North Annex collapse deposit
PH 3.7; D (est.) rim 22.0; Th. wall 0.4

40. Casserole. Three joining sherds preserve approx. one-sixth circum. of the rim to lower wall. Gritty grey cooking fabric (5YR 4/2) with traces of burning on ext. **Fig. 9.6**
Inv. 4558. Tr. 96.12.3.3. Southeast Room collapse deposit
PH 5.0; D (est.) rim 21.0; Th. wall 0.4

41. Cooking lid, large casserole-sized. Three joining sherds preserve approx. one-eighth circum. of the rim and part of the wall. North Peloponnesian orange cooking fabric (2.5YR 5/6) with traces of burning around the rim. **Fig. 9.6**
Inv. 4826. Tr. 97.96.12.3.3. Southeast Room collapse deposit
PH 2.6; D (est.) rim 23.0; Th. wall 0.4

Bowls/lekanai

42. Bowl/lekane with moulded rim. Two joining sherds preserve a small part of the rim and upper wall. North Peloponnesian orange fabric (2.5YR 5/8). **Fig. 9.6**
Inv. 4828. Tr. 97.96.12.3.3. Southeast Room collapse deposit
PH 1.4; Th. 0.3

43. Bowl/lekane with projecting rim. Single sherd preserves approx. one-eighth circum. of the rim and small part of the upper wall. North Peloponnesian orange fabric (7.5YR 5/6). **Fig. 9.6**
Inv. 4794. Tr. 95.3.5.9. North Annex collapse deposit
PH 1.9; D (est.) rim 25.0; Th. wall 0.6

44. Bowl/lekane with short ledge rim. Single sherd preserves approx. one-eighth circum. of the rim and upper wall. North Peloponnesian orange fabric (2.5YR 6/6). **Fig. 9.6**
Inv. 4829. Tr. 97.96.12.4.4. Southeast Room collapse deposit
PH 1.5; D (est.) rim 27.0; Th.. wall 0.3

Miscellaneous

45. Unknown vessel. Four joining sherds preserve much of the rim and neck (?). Unknown gritty purple fabric (5YR 5/2). Not illustrated
Inv. 4912. Tr. 96.8.3.4. West Annex floor deposit
PH 3.6, irregular rim; Th. wall 0.3

46. Bowl with plain rim and piecrust foot. Twelve joining sherds, almost half of entire vessel. Unknown soft fabric (5YR 6/6) with traces of burning on int. (thymiaterion?). **Fig. 9.7**
Inv. 1397. Tr. 96.12.3.3. Southeast Room collapse deposit
H 9.0; D rim 24.0; D foot 19.5; Th. wall 0.6
Decoration: piecrust moulding around ext. of the foot.

TABLES

Table 9.1. West Annex floor identified table vessels, toilet vessels, lamps and votive vessels*

	Corinthian	Attic (or similar)	Blisterware	Unknown	Total
Table drinking					
Kotyle	3	–	–	–	3
Attic-type skyphos	2	1	–	–	3
One-handler	5	1	–	–	6
Moulded-rim kantharos	–	2	–	–	2
Table service					
Round-mouthed table juglet	2	2	–	1	5
Table eating					
Plain-rim saucer	–	–	–	1	1
Incurved-rim bowl	4	–	–	–	4
Toilet					
Pyxis	1	–	–	–	1
Pyxis lid	1	–	–	1	2
Lamp	2	–	1	1	4
Votive					
Miniature kotyle	3	–	–	–	3

* The counts in these tables represent non-joining sections of rim or base (whichever is more numerous for a given form) that are not obviously from the same vessel.

Table 9.2. West Annex floor identified cooking vessels, utility vessels, and transport/storage vessels

	Smooth red-orange	North Peloponnesian orange	Powdery red cook	Unknown	Total
Cooking					
Casserole	2	3	–	–	5
Flaring-rim chytra/jug	11	–	–	–	11
Lid	–	5	1	–	6
Utility					
Bowl/lekane with projecting rim	–	–	–	2	2
Transport/Storage					
Thickened-rim amphora or jug	–	–	–	1	1

Table 9.3. Vessels from the North Annex and combined Southeast and Front Rooms of Building A by functional class

	North Annex	South Rooms
Table drinking	190 (61%)	20 (19%)
Table service	49 (16%)	4 (4%)
Table eating	17 (5%)	37 (36%
Lamp	42 (13%)	2 (2%)
Miniature	1 (–%)	3 (3%)
Cooking	5 (2%)	26 (25%)
Utility	4 (1%)	12 (12%)
Transport/Storage	1 (–%)	0 (–%)

Table 9.4. North Annex identified table vessels, lamps, and votive vessels by fabric

	Corinthian	Blisterware	Argive	North Peloponnesian orange	Fabric not identified	Total
Table drinking						
Mould-made bowl	14	33	35	13	60	155
Various kantharoi	17	2	5	–	–	24
Simple everted-rim kantharos	–	7	–	–	–	7
Attic-type skyphos	1	–	–	–	1	2
Conical cup	–	1	–	–	–	1
Imitation mould-made bowl	–	–	–	–	1	1
One-handler	–	–	–	–	–	0
Table service						
Round-mouthed table juglet	25	18	–	–	2	45
Table amphora	1	–	–	–	–	1
Trefoil oinochoe	–	1	–	–	–	1
Blisterware aryballos	–	1	–	–	–	1
Table eating						
Hanging-/projecting-rim fish plate	–	–	–	12	1	13
Plain-rim saucer	–	–	–	–	–	0
Deep rolled-rim plate	–	–	–	–	–	0
Bevelled-rim plate	–	–	–	–	–	0
Incurved-rim bowl	1	1	–	–	–	2
Semiglazed bowl	1	–	–	–	–	1
Unknown bowl	–	–	–	–	1	1
Lamp	13	22			7	42
Votive						
Miniature kotyle	1	–	–	–	–	1

Table 9.5. North Annex identified cooking, utility, and transport/storage vessels by fabric

	North Peloponnesian orange	Gritty grey cook	Smooth red-orange	Powdery red cook	Fabric not identified	Total
Cooking						
Casserole	3	–	1	–	–	4
Casserole with short ledge rim	–	–	–	–	–	0
Flanged-rim chytra	1	–	–	–	–	1
Chytra with short ledge rim	–	–	–	–	–	0
Cook lid	–	–	–	–	–	0
Utility						
Projecting-rim bowl/lekane	4	–	–	–	–	4
Moulded-rim bowl/lekane	–	–	–	–	–	0
Ledge-rim bowl	–	–	–	–	–	0
Thickened-rim amphora or jug	–	–	–	–	–	0
Bowl with piecrust foot	–	–	–	–	–	0
Trans/Storage						
Pithos	–	–	–	–	1	1

Table 9.6. South Rooms identified table vessels, lamps, and votive vessels

	Corinthian	Blisterware	Argive	North Peloponnesian orange	Fabric not identified	Total
Table drinking						
Mould-made bowl	2	–	1	–	9	12
Various kantharoi	–	–	–	–	–	0
Simple everted- rim kantharos	–	1	–	–	–	1
Attic-type skyphos	–	–	–	–	–	0
Conical cup	–	–	–	–	–	0
Imitation mould-made bowl	–	–	–	–	–	0
One-handler	–	–	–	–	–	0
Table service						
Round-mouthed table juglet	1	2	–	–	–	3
Table amphora	–	–	–	–	–	0
Krater	–	–	–	–	–	0
Trefoil oinochoe	–	–	–	–	–	0
Aryballos	–	–	–	–	–	0
Table eating						
Hanging-rim fish plate	–	–	–	2	–	2
Plain-rim saucer	5	–	1	–	1	7
Deep rolled-rim plate	4	–	–	3	1	8
Bevelled-rim plate	–	–	–	–	1	1
Incurved-rim bowl	2	–	1	2	–	5
Semiglazed bowl	–	1	–	–	–	1
Unknown bowl	–	1	–	–	–	1
Lamp	–	–	–	2	–	2
Votive						
Miniature kotyle	–	–	–	1	–	1

Table 9.7. South Rooms identified cooking and utility vessels (no trans./storage vessels)

	North Peloponnesian orange	Gritty grey cook	Hard/smooth orange	Powdery red cook	Fabric not identified	Total
Cooking						
Casserole	2	9	–	–	–	11
Casserole with short ledge rim	–	–	1	–	–	1
Flanged-rim chytra	5	–	–	–	–	5
Chytra with short ledge rim	–	–	1	–	–	1
Cook lid	5	–	1	1	1	8
Utility						
Projecting-rim basin	–	–	–	–	–	0
Moulded-rim basin	2	1	3	–	1	7
Ledge-rim bowl	2	–	–	–	–	2
Thickened-rim jug	–	–	–	–	2	2
Bowl with piecrust foot	–	–	–	–	1	1

Table 9.8. Counts of identified motifs on non-joining sections of mould-made bowls from the North Annex (by vessel portion)*

Motif	Medallion	Calyx	Wall	Rim	Total
Narrow long petal	–	84	75	–	159
Wide long petal	–	3	4	–	7
Long petal with vertical mid-line	–	6	1	–	7
Net pattern, single line	–	49	1	–	50
Net pattern, double line with dots between	–	27	4	–	31
Letters	–	4	1	–	5
Nymphaea lotus	–	31	22	–	53
Rosette	2	8	27	3	40
Goat	–	1	8	–	9
Trophy	–	–	7	–	7
Dolphin	–	–	4	–	4
Dots	5	1	3	4	13
Bird	1	–	1	–	2
"Double Axe"	–	–	1	–	1
Grape bunch	–	–	2	–	2
Draped Apollo	–	–	1	–	1
Dancing figure	–	–	1	–	1
Palmette	–	–	2	–	2
Dog	–	–	2	–	2
Horse and rider	–	–	2	–	2
Eros	–	–	1	–	1
Dotted concentric semicircle	–	–	4	–	4
Woman with jug	–	–	1	–	1
Lyre player	–	–	1	–	1
Woman carrying something	–	–	1	–	1
Ivy and vine	–	1	2	–	3
Fig leaf	1	–	1	–	2
"Fleur de lis"	–	–	1	–	1
Bead and reel	–	–	1	–	1
"Blob" flower	–	–	1	–	1
Fern	2	41	–	–	43
Nymphaea caerulea	–	37	–	–	37
Acanthus	–	65	–	–	65
Frond	–	7	–	–	7
Torch	–	1	–	–	1
Unidentified figure	–	6	7	–	13
Feline	–	1	–	–	1
Spiral column	–	1	–	–	1
Dotted "clover"	2	–	–	–	2
Ivy leaf	2	–	–	–	2
Spiral	1	–	–	–	1
Blank	2	–	–	–	2
Flower	9	–	–	–	9
Wheel	3	–	–	–	3
Guilloche	–	–	–	44	44
Egg and dart	–	–	–	3	3
Egg and vertical line	–	–	–	1	1
Running spiral	–	–	–	24	24
Shield	–	–	–	2	2
Double scroll	–	–	–	1	1
Pinecone	1	1	–	–	2

* Special thanks are due to Erika Nitsch of Wilfrid Laurier University for her help in compiling this data. Many of the "sections" of bowls listed here are body fragments and were not factored into the total vessel count in order to maintain consistency with the quantification of forms as a whole, which was determined on the basis of counts of rims or bases (whichever was most numerous for a given form in a given fabric).

10

Select Pottery from the Sanctuary and Nearby City Wall Area

Gerald P. Schaus

A small selection of the pottery from the Sanctuary and nearby City Wall area is presented here for several reasons. First, a full study of the material is not yet ready, but because certain discrete pottery types are important for the history of the Sanctuary, it was thought worthwhile that at least some of them could be included in the present volume. Secondly, a careful study of the pottery from Building A with a discussion of its possible use has been presented by Peter Stone in the previous chapter. This includes an overview of the shapes with representative drawings and some statistical analyses. Not well represented in the Building A material, however, were coarse wares, including large storage pithoi and transport amphoras, as well as some of the earliest material from the site, the Attic and Corinthian black- and red-figured pottery. These shed light on significant aspects of the site's history and activities, which otherwise would be missing. Thirdly, some of the better-preserved, complete or mostly complete, vessels are presented, which should help balance the picture of the preservation of the material. Although these are few in number, taken together with the Building A material, they provide a better notion of the corpus as a whole. An impression of the range of fabrics is also improved by having these representative pieces available here. Finally, a small selection of the miniatures is presented. Miniature vases represent a significant percentage of the Sanctuary's ceramic material, and also offer insights into the types of dedications commonly left by the cult's participants.

It is clear from the pottery studied here, as well as that in Stone's chapter on pottery from Building A, that Corinth was the most important source of a wide variety of ceramic products at Stymphalos. Corinthian red-figure vases, including oversize skyphoi or calyx kraters made especially for dedication, many miniature vessels, again for dedication, some black-glaze pottery, transport amphorai, pithoi, and mould-made bowls are among the notable examples of pottery, but loomweights also seem to have come from Corinth, as well as lamps, terracotta figurines, perirrhanteria, and possibly also roof tiles. This is just part of a wider pattern of trade in Corinthian ceramic products, which has a long history, going back to the Late Geometric period, but which continued into the Late Classical and Hellenistic periods as well. One type, Corinthian red-figure, is rather easy to identify and so to trace its spread in the late fifth and fourth centuries. Herbert noted its presence at Perachora, Mycenae, the Argive Heraion, and Olympia, while McPhee added Aigosthenes, two sites in Boiotia, and also a couple in Italy.[1] Its appearance at Stymphalos, along with a rather wide array of other Corinthian products, is noteworthy but not especially unexpected, both because of the general dependence of Stymphalos on Corinth's ceramic industry, and because of the particular purpose these vases served as dedications in the acropolis Sanctuary.

CATALOGUE

D	diameter
H	height
L	length
MPD	maximum preserved dimension
P	preserved
Th.	thickness
W	width

All measurements are in centimetres unless otherwise indicated.

Corinthian red-figure[2]

One category of Corinthian pottery which demonstrates a strong inclination to imitate Attic is Corinthian red-figure. This style appears most commonly on shapes which likewise are borrowed from Attic, ones not normally found in the Corinthian repertoire. Both the contexts for this pottery and the themes depicted are also limited, as Pemberton notes.[3] Corinthian red-figure is not found in graves, but it does occur in contexts with ritual associations. Likewise the themes have little or no narrative, but instead simply depict women or divine figures. "The Classical techniques of red-figure and stamped black-glaze are produced in Corinth in very imitative examples, but also in very limited numbers … The Corinthian versions of both are also restricted in motifs, shapes, and even use (primarily ritual)."[4]

In this regard, the Sanctuary at Stymphalos is a reflection of the situation at Corinth, as are the terracotta figurines from the Sanctuary, which likewise have strong similarities with finds at Corinth. A dozen pieces of Corinthian red-figure have been found in the acropolis Sanctuary, many of which belong either to oversize skyphoi or calyx kraters. Herbert noted that the majority of red-figure pieces from Corinth's Demeter Sanctuary were from such oversize skyphoi, an impressive drinking vessel probably made and purchased specifically for dedication.[5] One of the Stymphalos fragments, with the naked torso of a bearded male, more likely Herakles than a satyr, comes from the workshop, if not the hand, of Herbert's Sketch Painter.[6] A date for it falls towards the end of the first quarter or early second quarter of the fourth century, according to evidence from deposits at Corinth.[7] Other pieces from Stymphalos may go back earlier, to around 400 BCE.

Closed vases

1. Wall fragment of a closed vase (pelike or oinochoe, perhaps). Burnt in a secondary fire. The clay has turned light grey, and the black paint has mostly flaked away, leaving a "shadow." **Fig. 10.1**
Inv. 3225. Tr. 00.4.7.7. City Wall, SE of Sanctuary
MPD 6.2; Th. 0.6
Ext. lines of an unidentifiable figure or floral, band of egg and dots pattern, painted below.

For this common ovule pattern as the lower border on red-figure pelikai, see Herbert 1977, nos. 3 and 6 pl. 1, and possibly nos. 7 and 14 pl. 2; and on oinochai, Herbert 1977, nos. 125–6 pls. 21 and 22, though other closed shapes also may have it.

2. Hydria (?), four joining wall fragments. Probably from a hydria, rather than an oversize skyphos. Fine pinkish-buff clay, black paint, flaked. Red miltos wash. **Fig. 10.1**
Inv. 801. Tr. 95.5.5.6. S of Temple
MPD 7.5; Th. 0.55
Ext. lower part of the tendril and parts of two spirals from a handle palmette, band of running (?) meander below.

For the floral, compare the right-hand tendril extending from a palmette below the handle of an Attic-type skyphos in Toronto (919.5.5 [C.421]) dated ca. 420–400 BCE, McPhee and Trendall 1986, 164–6 fig. 10. The addition of a band of meander below the palmette suggests a larger vase, such as a hydria, like Athens NM 12260 (see Herbert 1977, no. 121 pls. 18–19), which is by the same hand as the Toronto skyphos (Pelikai Painter), or an oversize Attic Type A skyphos, like Athens NM 1405 (see Herbert 1977, no. 160 pl. 26). A running meander is unusual; most Corinthian red-figure vases have a broken (McPhee's "stopt") meander or meander hooks.
Perhaps 420–390 BCE

3. Wall fragment of a closed vase. Fine, pinkish-buff clay, possible slip, lustrous black paint, adheres well. **Fig. 10.1**
Inv. 104. Tr. 95.9.1.1. North Annex – top soil
MPD 4.1; Th. 0.5
Ext. unidentified figures.
See Corbett's first of two Corinthian red-figure fabrics, Corbett 1962, 286; the same as **9** and **11**.

Calyx kraters

4. Calyx krater (?) wall fragment. Fine buff clay, black paint with a slight sheen, flaked in the decorated area leaving "shadows," red miltos wash. **Fig. 10.1**
Inv. 3279. Tr. 00.4.7.8. City Wall, SE of Sanctuary
MPD 7.4; Th. 0.5
A foot and part of a second belonging to a maenad (?) moving right, the lower edge of whose long chiton is ornamented with short vertical rows of dots between horizontal lines. Broken meander and saltire (diagonal cross) band between thin lines below.

Judging by the placement of the saltire square below the figure, which commonly centred this band, the composition held three or at most four figures with this one in the middle.

Compare the line of the chiton hem over the foot, as well as the pose of the foot, with that of the maenad on a calyx krater found in Boeotia, Boston 76.64, McPhee 1991, fig. 1. The ornate decoration of the hem on the Stymphalos vase is comparable in care to the maenad's chiton on the Boston vase, and two calyx kraters which McPhee attributes to the same hand, McPhee 1991,

fig. 3 (Athens NM 1380) and fig. 4 (Athens NM 1384). The pattern band below the scene, with broken meander and saltire square, is also found on the Boston vase. McPhee (1991) grouped Boston 76.64 with the two calyx kraters and two pelikes in Athens, along with several other vases in Corinth and Perachora as works by the same painter. Beazley (McPhee 1991, 332) had noted the same hand in four of these vases and had given him the name Dombrena Painter.
First quarter of the fourth century

5. Wall fragment of an open vessel (krater?). Fine, soft pinkish-buff clay. Black paint, adheres well. Red miltos wash. **Fig. 10.1**
Inv. 1843. Find spot – missing
MPD 3.0
Ext. relief lines depict folds of drapery of a figure (to left?).
Compare, for example, the draped figures on the reverse of Boston 76.64, and Athens NM 1384 (McPhee 1991, figs. 2 and 4 [right figure]), which face right, noting the circle about knee high which seems similar to that on **5**, but in the reverse direction.
Perhaps first quarter of the fourth century

6. Calyx krater (?) wall fragment with graffito. Fine, pinkish-buff clay, black paint with a slight sheen, thin, streaky, flaked. Possible red miltos wash. **Fig. 10.1**
Inv. 503. Tr. 96.4.4.7. Altar area
MPD 8.4; Th. 0.8
Int. painted. Ext. band of broken meander, otherwise painted. Graffito over the paint, ---ỊΘ̣UAI . Text: [---] ιθυαι. Εἰλείθυα/’Ελείθυα – name of a deity or epithet of a deity. Interpretation: [-?- Εἰλε]ιθύαι, [-?- ’Ελε] ιθύαι. [τᾶι? ’Ελε]ιθύαι perhaps. (My thanks to Molly Richardson for her helpful comments.)

The theta appears to be a crossed theta, although the dotted theta is established in cursive writing by the late fifth century in Arkadia; see Jeffery 1990, 207, 216 no. 37 pl. 41. In Sikyon, a diamond-shaped crossed theta came into fashion in the fifth century, Jeffery 1990, 138.

Feminine singular dative of a name, which one would expect to be a goddess. If the theta is read correctly, Eίλείθυια (Eileithyia), goddess of childbirth, is probable. There are many variations in the spelling of this name (see Liddell and Scott), but one of these, found in a fourth-century inscription from Astypalaea, is ’Ελείθυα (*IG* 12(3).192).

The thickness of the wall suggests a calyx krater with the meander band forming the base line of a figured scene.

Skyphoi

7. Two joining skyphos wall fragments and two non-joining surface chips. Black paint with a slight sheen, much flaked, red miltos wash. Traces of relief lines along the lower beard and the torso. **Fig. 10.1**
Inv. 3532. Tr. 00.6.3.3. N of North Annex
a) MPD 7.2, Th. 0.7; b) MPD 1.9
Int. thin, streaky black. Ext. a) naked male torso, frontal to three-quarters view to the left with the lower part of the bearded head in profile to right. An animal skin over the right shoulder is knotted at the lower neck with two ends hanging down on the upper chest. Dots may be visible on one leg of the skin where it comes across the man's chest to the knot. The man's right arm is extended out, broken at the hand but probably holding an object; part of a narrow horizontal object is badly preserved above (tray?). The left arm is broken at the shoulder but it was held away from the torso. b) surface chip preserving a "V-shaped" line, flesh of the naked male?

From an oversize Attic Type A skyphos; the profile is slightly concave. Similar bearded naked male figures in frontal or three-quarters view, wearing an animal skin and holding up a plate of fruit or offering tray in one hand (sometimes with a club or extinguished torch? in the other), have been suggested to be Herakles or a companion of Dionysos/satyr; see, for example, Herbert 1977, 10, 68–9 no. 161 pl. 27A (Athens NM 1405) (Herbert [1977, 10] says he is holding a club in the right hand, but later [p. 68] says an extinguished torch), and p. 50 no. 83 (C-71-368) pl. 14 (holding a box and a club?); McPhee 1983, 141 no. 9 pl. 34. Compare also the naked males on Herbert 1977, nos. 78 (C-37-2757) and 82 (C-46-116) pl. 14. For another rendering of Herakles, without a lion's skin, see McPhee 1991, 330 fig. 4 (Athens NM 1384). Specific myths are not commonly rendered in Corinthian red-figure (exceptions from Perachora include a scene of Marsyas and Apollo, and a possible Death of Sarpedon, Corbett 1962, 288–9 nos. 2792 and 2794 pl. 116), so even if Herakles is depicted rather than a satyr with a spotted leopard skin, it may have been a generic scene.
Comparable to work by Herbert's Sketch Painter
First half of the fourth century

8. Skyphos rim and wall fragment with one handle. Very fine buff clay, paint has fired dark red, flaked. Red miltos wash. **Figs. 10.1 and 10.5**
Inv. 4769. Tr. 97.4.6.9. S of Terrace Wall
D rim (est.) 28.0; Th. wall 0.6; W handle 9.6; Th. handle 1.6
Int. painted. Ext. below the lip is a band of egg and dots separated by thin vertical lines, reserved line, otherwise painted.

From an oversize Attic Type A skyphos, outturned rim and angled loop handle. Possibly from the same vase as **7**, though the two were found on opposite sides of the Sanctuary. The egg and dot pattern is common on these vases, but this example is done particularly

carefully, with solid half-circles along the baseline instead of "dots," and the eggs separated by thin vertical lines. Such thin lines separate "beads" on a pelike in Reading (RM 87-35-25, see McPhee and Trendall 1986, 162 fig. 3), but otherwise eggs are contiguous in Corinthian red-figure pattern bands.
First half of the fourth century

9. Rim and wall fragment from an Attic type skyphos. Corinthian (?). Very slightly everted rim, straight vertical wall. Fine light orange clay, shiny black glaze, adheres well, possible slip, red miltos wash. **Fig. 10.1**
Inv. 3663. Tr. 97.5 baulk.5.5. E of Terrace Wall
MPD 5.9; Th. 0.5
Band of tightly packed eggs and dots, head of a figure to right.
The shape of the rim is similar to the skyphos in Toronto (919.5.5 [C.421]), but here a band of eggs and dots has been added at the rim.
Perhaps ca. 400 BCE

Open vases

10. Wall fragment from an open vase. Fine, light orange clay, black paint fired brown on the interior, much flaked, red miltos wash. **Fig. 10.1**
Inv. 1659. Tr. 97.5.7.12. E of Terrace Wall
MPD 4.3; Th. 0.5
Int. painted. Ext. unidentified object(s) with part of a concentric circle or spiral pattern, other lines.

11. Wall fragment from an open vase. Light brown clay, buff slip, red miltos wash. Dull black paint has adhered very well. **Fig. 10.1**
Inv. 510. Tr. 96.4.2.2. Altar area
MPD 3.1
Ext. unidentifiable pattern, perhaps part of a handle floral.
This sherd is made from the first of the two Corinthian red-figure fabrics described by Corbett (1962, 286), i.e., with the addition of a slip which seems to have helped the paint adhere.

12. Wall fragment of an open vase. Buff clay, black paint with slight sheen. **Fig. 10.1**
Uninventoried. Find spot missing
MPD 2.9
Unidentified figure, with no inner markings preserved.

Corinthian miniatures[8]

Of the 50 or so inventoried miniature vases from the Sanctuary, 34 are kotylai (or skyphoi – the two shapes lose their distinctiveness by the fourth century). There is a three-handled, a one-handled, and a handleless example of the shape as well. Other shapes include a lekanis, a plate (or dish), a squat alabastron, two oinochoai, a fragmentary closed vase (hydria?), and a possible phiale. They are either plain or have banding and sometimes strokes in the handle zone as decoration, but little else. These are representative of hundreds of others which are preserved only as fragments in the context bags. They were inexpensive gifts to the deity or deities, though they might have had a function in ritual. They were important enough to be manufactured and transported to the site and given to the god(s) in hopes of divine favour. Only a representative sample is offered here.

13. Rim and wall fragment from a miniature (?) kotyle. The black paint has mostly flaked away, leaving a shadow of its decoration. **Fig. 10.1**
Inv. 2158. Surface find near West Annex area
MPD 3.4; Th. 0.2
Int. black. Ext. row of teardrop-shaped buds in the handle zone, band between two lines.
Unlinked buds become common in the handle zone by the late sixth century (Risser 2001, 25), and continue to the late fifth century BCE still neat and tightly packed together, as Risser 2001, 66 no. 172 pl. 12. After that they are more elongated, and widely spaced.
Fifth century

14. Group of three kotylai, broken but mended, complete; nested when found. Soil-encrusted. All three have distinct bases, though b) has a clear line to set off the base. **Fig. 10.1**
Inv. 3550. Tr. 96.15.5.5. Refuse pit, S of West Annex
a) H 3.3, D rim 4.3, D base 2.0; b) H 3.2, D rim 4.0, D base 1.9; c) H 2.8, D rim 3.8, D base 1.6
Ext. short vertical strokes in the handle zone, red band, black band on the lower wall and base.
For short vertical strokes in the handle zone of fourth-century miniature kotylai, see Risser 2001, 70 nos. 202–3. Pemberton (1989, 64) notes the disappearance of miniature kotylai in the Demeter Sanctuary at Corinth in the later fourth century.
These and many others were found in a sealed deposit of votive debris in this pit beside Building A, from the mid- to second half of the fourth century. Hundreds have been found in the Sanctuary as a whole, mostly as small fragments, but 31 whole or almost whole ones were inventoried besides the two below.[9] Of these, the largest has a height of 3.1 cm and a rim diameter of 5.8 cm. The smallest has a height of 1.6 cm and a rim diameter of 2.1 cm.

15. Complete kotyle. Soil-encrusted. **Fig. 10.1**
Inv. 3469. Tr. 96.15.5.5. Refuse pit, S of West Annex
H 1.6; D rim 2.8; D base 1.3
Ext. banding.

16. Complete kotyle. Paint fired red on the interior. **Fig. 10.1**
Inv. 2829. Tr. 96.11 scarp cleaning. Temple
H 2.0; D rim 3.4; D base 1.6
Ext. reserved handle zone, banding (red shadow?) below.

17. Three-handled cup, complete except two chips from the rim. The handles are short coils of clay attached carelessly below the lip without loops. Fine buff clay, no paint. **Figs. 10.1 and 10.5**
Inv. 2409. Tr. 99.10.3.4. N of North Annex
H 1.6; D. rim 2.8; D base 1.7
Compare Stillwell and Benson 1984, 313 nos. 1736–7 pl. 67. No. 1736 was found in the Terracotta Factory (Potters' Quarter), which Stillwell (1948, 46–7) believes was destroyed in an earthquake in the third quarter of the fourth century.
Fourth century

18. One-handled cup, complete. Traces of banding on the exterior, no paint on the interior. **Fig. 10.2**
Inv. 626. Tr. 95.4+1.2.3. Temple
H 1.7; D rim 2.7; D base 1.3
Two one-handled cups from the Terracotta Factory in the Potters' Quarter, Corinth, have similar bodies, but vertical rather than horizontal handles; see Stillwell and Benson 1984, 313 nos. 1733–4 pl. 67.

19. Handleless cup, complete. Fine, buff clay. Black paint, mostly flaked away. Slightly everted rim, concave upper body, and concave lower body separated by a sharp carination, no distinct base. **Figs. 10.2 and 10.5**
Inv. 630. Tr. 96.4.4.7. Altar area
H 1.7; D rim 2.9; D base 1.6
Int. and ext. painted.

The double concave wall profile is unusual, though a three-handled cup from Corinth is similar, Stillwell and Benson 1984, no. 1737 pl. 67.

20. Lekanis, missing part of one handle, and the lid. Buff, almost white clay, unpainted. Double rim to receive a lid. Simple horizontal loop handles. **Figs. 10.2 and 10.5**
Inv. 495. Tr. 95.4+1.2.4. Temple
H 2.4; D base 2.9; D outer rim 6.0; D inner rim 4.5
For the shape, see Risser 2001, 83–4. In the second half of the fifth century, it becomes lower and broader, and the foot contracts, as here. The profile changes from continuous curve to straight-walled with slight carination. The shape of **20** is close to two examples from fifth-century contexts in the Potters' Quarter, Stillwell and Benson 1984, 319 nos. 815, 817 pl. 69, both of which are unpainted. Plain examples, without paint, continue into the second half of the fourth century; see Pemberton 1989, 39, 41. In general, plain, unpainted miniatures become more common compared to decorated examples by the later fourth century, Pemberton 1989, 64.
About 450–350 BCE

21. Rim and neck of a trefoil mouth oinochoe, chip on the rim. Greyish-buff clay, black paint. **Figs. 10.2 and 10.5**
Inv. 3602. Tr. 00.5.6.6. E of Bldg. A
PH 1.6; W mouth 2.0; D neck 1.2
Painted on int. and ext. but mostly flaked on the ext.

22. Round-mouth jug. Complete. Handmade. Flat resting surface, cylindrical body, narrowing to a plain neck and rim. Vertical handle from the shoulder to above the rim, attaching at the rim. Soft, light-brown clay with some dark brown and white inclusions. **Fig. 10.2**
Inv. 1179. Tr. 96.8.6.7. West Annex
H 2.5; D (rim) 1.2; D belly 1.7.
Undecorated.

23. Two-handled jar. Complete except for the handles and a chip from the rim. Handmade. Rounded bottom, rounded body curving in to a wide neck and plain rim. The vertical handles from belly to rim rise above the rim. Soft dark red clay with small white inclusions. Rough surface. **Figs. 10.2 and 10.5**
Inv. 3598. Tr. 96.15.5.5. Refuse pit, S of West Annex
H 3.1; H (to handle stump) 3.2; D rim 2.5; D belly 3.8.
Probably locally made.

24. Unguentarium. Complete. Filled and covered with ashy material. Small flat resting surface, rounded body (sagging belly) tapering to a long narrow neck and outward thickened rim. Dark orange clay with small sandy inclusions. **Figs. 10.2 and 10.5**
Inv. 625. Tr. 95.4+1.2.4. Temple
H 5.8; D resting surface 2.0; D belly 3.8; D neck 1.5; D rim 2.1.
Carefully made on a wheel.

Black-glaze pottery

This is the most common type of fine ware in the Sanctuary overall, though the quality varies considerably, as well as the preservation. Most examples are in small fragments where the shape can only be guessed at. Below are a few representative examples chosen from among the better-preserved pieces.

Corinthian (?)

25. Large chous fragment. Corinthian (?). Wall and stump of one handle, six joining fragments, decorated with vertical fluting. Continuous convex curve; wide strap handle, almost triangular in section, is attached at the top of the ribbing, narrow vertical ribbing, beginning of the unribbed shoulder. Fine, pinkish-buff clay, thin semi-lustrous black glaze. **Fig. 10.2**
Inv. 3287. Tr. 00.5.2.2. E of Bldg. A
MPD 18.7; Th. wall 0.5; W base of handle 4.8
Ext. black, dipped with the line of darker paint at the base of the handle and across the top of the ribbing.
For the shape in Athens down to the fourth century, see Sparkes and Talcott 1970, 21–2 and no. 130 pl. 7 as an example with ribbing. For development of the shape in the Hellenistic period in Athens, Rotroff 1997, 125–7. The large chous is discontinued in Athens shortly after 300 BCE. For a rare Corinthian example of the shape with ribbing, see Pemberton 1989, 154 no. 386 fig. 3 pl. 44.
Fourth century

26. Echinus bowl fragments, over half preserved. Buff clay, black glaze. **Fig. 10.5**
Inv. 3226. Tr. 00.4.6.6. City Wall
H 2.2; D rim 8.0; D base 5.0
Int. and ext. painted.
For the shape, see Edwards 1975, 29–33 nos. 35–45 "saucer group," close to nos. 39–41 pl. 2, 44 (the profile for no. 42 on pl. 2 does not match the photograph of no. 42, pl. 44).
First half of the fourth century

North Peloponnesian or Argive (?)

27. Stemless cup fragment, about two-thirds preserved, with one handle stump. Small kylix with slightly thickened plain rim, horizontal round handle attached below the lip, low ring base. Fine, hard pinkish-buff clay, thin shiny black glaze. **Figs. 10.2 and 10.5**
Inv. 1872. Tr. 96.5 ext. 6.9. City Wall
H 5.7; D rim est. 14.0; Th. rim 0.6; H base 0.9; D base 5.2; Th. base 0.6
Int. black. Ext. black except reserved handle zone, lower wall and base. Drips of paint on the lower wall and base.
The shape is called a shallow kotyle in the Potters' Quarter, Corinth; see Stilwell and Benson 1984, 271 nos. 1485–7 pl. 62. Similar cups in the Agora are rare; see Sparkes and Talcott 1970, 267 no. 464 fig. 5 (shallower). The clay and thin, runny paint suggest an origin for the vase in the North Peloponnese.

28. Small bowl with projecting rim, missing pieces from the rim. Ring base, short convex body, wide horizontal rim. The interior bowl is hemispherical. Fine pink clay, thin black glaze, applied unevenly. **Figs. 10.2 and 10.5**
Inv. 574. Tr. 96.3.3.5. Altar area
H 3.7; D rim inside 6.7; D rim outside 11.0; W rim 2.1; D base 5.7
Int. and ext. painted black. The rim has deeply cut ovules stamped in a band between groups of four and two grooves.
Close parallels either in Athens or Corinth are difficult to find. In Athens, small bowls with projecting rims are shallow ones, and not decorated on their rims; see Sparkes and Talcott 1970, 299 no. 880 fig. 9 and no. 881 pl. 33; Rotroff 1997, 344–5 nos. 1045–9 fig. 64 pl. 78. At Corinth, likewise, the bowl is shallower, and the rim is not turned sharply horizontal (see Pemberton 1997, 62, 80 no. 74 fig. 8, pl. 19), though stamped palmettes occur on the rim without the grooves, and ovules and palmettes on the floor. In Campanian pottery, the shape can be more closely compared, with a deeper, almost hemispherical form, in vases which have been dated to the third century; see Morel 1980, 108, 179 nos. 1341c and 2532a pls. 15, 52.
350–275 BCE

29. Echinus bowl, mended from fragments, four-fifths complete. Convex ring foot, convex wall in a continuous curve to an inturned thin rim. Fine, powdery light brown clay (greyer in the core), brown glaze, mostly flaked away. Soil-encrusted. **Figs. 10.2 and 10.6**
Inv. 3322. Tr. 00.4.7.8. City Wall
H 6.5; D rim 12.5; D base 7.3
Int. and ext. once painted.
For echinus bowls at Corinth, see Edwards 1975, 29–31 esp. nos. 23–34 pl. 2. The trend over time is towards a narrowing of the foot. That on **29** is still quite wide.
Fourth or early third century

30. Echinus bowl, salt cellar group, complete. The shape is similar to **29** but much smaller and with sturdier walls. Soft, powdery, buff clay. Lustrous black glaze, much flaked away, fired brown to black. **Fig. 10.2**
Inv. 3163. Tr. 00.4.7.7. City Wall
H 3.1; D rim 5.2; D base 3.5
Int. and ext. painted.
For the salt cellar group at Corinth, see Edwards 1975, 30, 32–3 nos. 46–71 pl. 2. The same trend towards a narrower base in the third century suggests that the Stymphalos bowl may be no later than the early third century.
Fourth or early third century

31. Mould-made bowl, about half preserved, mended from fragments. Orange clay (5YR 6/8), soft and powdery, some small white inclusions and mica. Black glaze, mostly flaked away. **Figs. 10.2 and 10.6**
Inv. 496. Tr. 95.4+1.2.3. Temple
D rim est. 11.6

Medallion: eight-petalled rosette surrounded by two ridges. Calyx: fronds alternating with equally tall lotus petals (the fronds are stamped over top of the petals). Wall: warriors on horses galloping right, frond, rosette, and fluted column in the field. Rim: ridge separates wall from rim, otherwise plain. The warriors wear a chiton and helmet, and carry a shield and spear horizontally.

Edwards (1981, 190–205) carefully described eight fabrics from which mould-made bowls were made in a deposit from Corinth. None of them match the fabric of **31** closely enough to provide confidence in assigning it to one, but "Fabric D" has some similarities; see Edwards 1981, 203–4. Despite Edwards's noting that Corinthian bowls are made in several fabrics (Edwards 1986, 404), that of **31** still seems the wrong colour and unusually soft even for Corinthian, so it is only with hesitation that it is suggested as North Peloponnesian, or indeed Argive. For a list of production centres of mould-made bowls with references, see Künzl 2002, 77–9. For the calyx decoration with fronds alternating with leaves, compare, from Corinth, Edwards 1975, no. 795 pl. 66, which otherwise has little in common with **31**. For the galloping warrior figure, compare Edwards 1975, no. 841 pl. 71. The calyx decoration with alternating fronds and lotus petals is very common among Argive bowls, and the use of a column and rosettes in the field can also be found there in several examples (see Siebert 1978, nos. M41, M47, M49 pls. 26–7 for examples), but the description of Argive fabric is not especially close, nor is the horse and spearman found there. Two fragmentary bowls from the North Annex of the Sanctuary have the horse and rider motif; see Stone (chapter 9 above, table 8 "horse and rider"). The fluted column in the wall field is not found at Corinth, it seems, but does appear on an Athenian bowl in the Agora, Rotroff 1982, 90 no. 388 pl. 67. For dating, see the discussion by Stone (chapter 9 above).
200–146 BCE

Varia

32. Object in the shape of a penis, broken at the base. Buff clay (2.5Y 8/4, 2.5Y 2.5/1 surface), very fugitive black glaze. Corinthian (?). The foreskin covers the glans, but the vein below the penis is depicted prominently, so perhaps meant as erect (?). A hole perforated from the body, possibly through to the tip of the penis (filled with dirt now). Ext. black. **Fig. 10.3**
Inv. 3668. Tr. 97.5 baulk.6.7 (SF 2000.420). E of Terrace Wall
PL 5.5; W 2.5
A first thought in considering this object is that it came from an Attic eye cup or other drinking vessel with male genitalia either as a resting base or otherwise attached, but Attic examples are normally left in the colour of the clay, not painted black; see Boardman, "A Curious Eye Cup," *AA* 1976, 281–90 with references. Nor does **32** appear to be made of Attic clay. Another possibility is that it came from a terracotta statue, lifesize, such as the warrior from Olympia, Kunze 1956, 114–27 pls. 64–5, but again the Stymphalos object is painted black, and statues are not. The koroplast who shaped this object was careful in his work, observing the shape closely with foreskin and ventromedial corpus cavernosum. More interesting must be the thought of the dedicator who brought the vase of which this was a noteworthy part to the Sanctuary as a gift.

In an interesting discussion of two Chiot phallus cups (rhyta?) of ca. 600 BCE found at Naucratis and now in the British Museum, D. Williams (2006, 127) mentions, without references, perfume pots of Corinthian, Athenian, and East Greek origin in the shape of male genitalia, and likewise without reference some later vases in which cups with male genitals were offered to children apparently as feeding bottles. This might explain the hole pierced through the Stymphalos example, although Chian plastic female heads used as ornaments and lid handles also are sometimes pierced (for example, Schaus 1985, no. 537 pl. 31). It might also explain why this example is painted black, as the rest of the feeding bottle might be if it came from one.

Attic

The scraps of Attic are catalogued not for their intrinsic value, but because they demonstrate the presence of objects on the acropolis prior to the fourth century when the Sanctuary reached its height of activity. The appearance of a tiny amount of pottery as early as the marble statue of the kore is significant.

33. Wall fragment from a floral band cup. Pinkish-orange clay, dull black glaze. **Fig. 10.3**
Inv. 1844 (?). Find spot missing
MPD 3.2.
Int. black. Ext. three links of a chain, base of a floral, several dots.

"Floral band cup"; see Beazley 1932, 187, 189, who mentions them just briefly and gives a short list of some. Also called floral cups, palmette band cups, and cup-skyphoi with palmettes, they continue to about the mid-fifth century in various states of degeneracy. A good number were found in graves in the North Cemetery at Corinth; see Blegen, Palmer, and Young 1964, 153 (skyphoi of Hermogenean shape) and 155 (cup-skyphoi, Cracow Class and successors), esp. grave 281 (ca. 480–470 BCE).
First quarter of the fifth century

34. Two rim and wall fragments from a band cup or skyphos. Slightly everted rim. Fine pinkish-buff clay, slightly grey in the core. Lustrous black glaze. **Fig. 10.3**
Inv. 1665. Tr. 96.11.5.6. Temple
MPD a) 4.3, b) 4.8
Int. black. Ext. a) part of a palmette, dots, unidentified object, b) part of a palmette, dots

Parts of two handle palmettes; the dots must be abbreviated ivy branches, typical of fifth-century black-figure skyphoi and cups. Compare, for example, Moore and Philippides 1986, no. 1571 pl. 104.
First half of the fifth century[10]

35. Wall fragment from a cup (?) with part of the everted rim. Fine, pink clay, lustrous black glaze, red wash. **Fig. 10.3**
Inv. 799. Tr. 96.6 ext. 4.4. City Wall, SE of Sanctuary
MPD 3.1; Th. 0.3
Int. black. Ext. black rim, unidentified curved object.

36. Wall fragment of a small open vase. Fine pink clay, good black glaze. **Fig. 10.3**
Inv. 2313. Tr. 99.1.3.3. E of Terrace Wall
MPD 1.2; Th. 0.2
Int. black. Ext. three unidentified objects including a circle and dot (filler?).

37. Handle plate and stump of a round handle from a column krater. Fine pink clay, good black glaze. **Fig. 10.3**
Inv. 3750. Find spot missing
MPD 8.0
Attic black column kraters are extremely rare; see Sparkes and Talcott 1970, 54–5 no. 58 pl. 3; on the other hand, Attic black-figure column kraters normally are decorated on the handle plates; see Moore and Philippides 1986, 23–5. This leaves Attic red-figure column kraters, which become popular in the second quarter of the fifth, but continue into the third quarter. These often have their handle plates left undecorated, in black paint; see Moore 1997, 20–3. Corinthian kraters have thin glaze paint, but can be pink in their fabric, like Attic; however, they lack the handle plate in the fifth century; see Boulter 1953, 91.
Second or third quarter of the fifth century

38. Attic (?). Salt cellar: concave wall, missing a piece of the rim/wall and the base. Sharply concave wall in a continuous curve to both the thickened rim and the spreading ring base. Fine, powdery light brown clay, black glaze, much flaked. **Figs. 10.3 and 10.6.**
Inv. 789. Tr. 96.5 ext.7.10. City Wall
H 3.3; D rim 6.0; D base 6.2
Int. and ext. black.

For the development of the shape in Athens, see Sparkes and Talcott 1970, 136–7, nos. 934–8 fig. 9 pl. 34; Rotroff 1997, 166–7 fig. 65 ("saltcellar: spool"). The continuous curve of the body to rim and base lasts through the third quarter of the fourth century.
The colour of the clay and the badly flaking paint are closer to Corinthian, but this shape is not found normally in Corinthian.
Perhaps 400–325 BCE

39. Plate with rolled rim, half preserved. Thick, flat plate on a ring base, with a convex wall interrupted by a distinct groove and ridge, well before the start of the rolled rim. The clay is hard and fine, light orange-brown in colour; lustrous thick black glaze on the upper side, thin and duller on the underside where it fired more brown than black. **Figs. 10.3 and 10.6**
Inv. 3168. Tr. 00.6.1.1. N of North Annex
H 2.4; D rim 15.0; D base 8.5
The vase was probably dipped in black paint, with the upper side coated more carefully. Shallow grooves on the floor of the plate mark the decorated zone. Linked palmettes (one preserved on the floor chip) within rouletting. The palmette stamp has a noticeably taller central leaf, and possible tendrils (?) at the base.

For the shape, see Rotroff 1997, 142–5; also Sparkes and Talcott 1970, 30–1, and for a close example, p. 310 no. 659 fig. 10; for rouletting, ibid., 30–1, and the palmette stamps, ibid., 25–6.

The smaller size of the plate (15 cm rim diameter) suggests the second half of the fourth century, although the base is quite small proportionately.
350–300 BCE

40. Black-glaze strainer, wall/floor with ring base. Perforations through the floor. Careful stamped decoration. Three joining pieces of the lower wall, and ring base. **Fig. 10.3**
Inv. 3140. Tr. 00.6.1.1. N of North Annex
D base (est.) 4.1; PH 1.6; Th. wall 0.4
Int. reserved. Ext. black, stamped decoration in rows, "boxes," ovules, "boxes," double concentric circles. Two complete holes and three partially preserved holes through the floor within the ring of the base.

For strainers in the Athenian Agora, see Sparkes and Talcott 1970, 106, 272–3 nos. 527–31, pl. 31, and a one-handler made into a strainer, no. 768 pl. 30. The lack of paint on the interior may be compared to no. 528 in the Agora, which is painted on the interior except over the depression where the holes have been placed. It is difficult to find close comparisons for the stamped decoration, but the various types appear separately from the last quarter of the fifth to the first quarter of the fourth century; for example, Sparkes and Talcott 1970, no. 1198 pl. 47.

Transport amphoras[11]

Only five of the largest fragments are presented here. More remain to be studied in the storerooms; these, at least, give an idea of the consumption of wine or possibly oil for cooking and lamps in the Sanctuary. Two of the fragments may belong to the same amphora (**41** and **42**), since both appear to be of the Corinthian A' type. Another is a Type B amphora; whether it was made in Corinth, in the northern Peloponnese, Corfu, or elsewhere is a matter of debate. The fourth is an import from the north Aegean, possibly Thasos, which was renowned for its good wine and exported widely. As for the fifth, its identity at the moment remains unknown, but it provides another example of a type used in the Sanctuary.

Corinthian A'

41. Foot and lower wall. Short rounded knob with a ridge around its top, spreading lower wall. Hard orange clay with brown (mudstone?), black, and grey inclusions. **Figs. 10.3 and 10.6**
Inv. 2793. Tr. 99.1 baulk.4.5. E of Terrace Wall
MPD 20.5; PH 10.5; D knob 5.4; H knob 2.7
Very similar toes are found on both Corinthian A and A' amphorae from the fifth century; see Koehler 1978, 108–9, 362 no. 44 pl. 15 from a well deposit at Corinth dated 460–420 BCE (Type A). They continue into the fourth century in slightly different form, as her no. 51, and Koehler 1981, 456 fig. 1.b, pl. 99h (Type A'). The fabric of Type A' amphorae is similar to that of the fragment from Stymphalos, fine clay with large sharp inclusions. Somewhat smaller and more inclined to a point are toes found on Type B amphoras, produced in Korkyra, the northern Peloponese (Corinth?), and elsewhere. Two examples of B amphoras from the early fourth century can be seen in Koehler 1978, 36, 183 nos. 238bis and 239 pl. 40. For the development of Corinthian A and B amphorae, Koehler 1978, 9–49, with more recent comments, Koehler 1992, and see examples from the Tile Works at Corinth, Merker 2006, 108–11. For petrological study of the clays of Corinth, Whitbread 2003, and for his comments about the appearance of mudstone as inclusions in Corinthian A and A' amphoras but not B amphoras, see Whitbread 1995, 282.

If this is a Corinthian A' amphora, it may, like Corinthian A amphoras, have held olive oil rather than wine; see Koehler 1978, 5–6; 1981, 452.

From the spreading lower wall and shape of the toe, this should be early fourth century if not somewhat earlier.

42. Transport amphora neck, rim, part of one handle. Sharp-edged rim, spreading outward to an overhanging lower edge, small round vertical handle attached at the upper neck. Hard, light orange clay, some black and white inclusions. **Figs. 10.3 and 10.6**
Inv. 1341. Tr. 97.5.3.6 (database says L5P6, but bag says L3P6). E of Terrace Wall
7.5YR 7/6 PH 12.5; D rim (est.) 0.14; D handle 0.02
The shape of the rim is distinctive and is commonly described as triangular and pendent when it occurs on Greco-Italic amphoras, and also in Göransson's Cyrenaican 4 amphoras from the third century, especially the second half. See Will 1982; Vandermersch 1994, 80 ("bord champignon" or mushroom lip); Göransson 2007, 65–8 (Cyrenaican 4), 115–34 (Greco-Italic) esp. 129–34 (MSG VI). Especially close is an amphora from Teste Nègre in a local fabric of Marseille, but with an oval handle in section; see Bertucchi 1992, 128–9 fig. 65.1, 66.1. But the handle on the Stymphalos amphora is round in section rather than oval, and it is attached very close to the lower edge of the rim, which is unusual for the Greco-Italic type. Similarly close parallels for the triangular pendent rim can be found in fifth-century Corinthian A' amphoras; compare, for example, the ones from Metaponto, Morter and Leonard 1998, esp. p. 739 no. T 69.1, p. 746 nos. T 331-1 and T 350-9. The round rather than oval handles, placement of the handles close below the rim, and the shape of the neck are also better explained as Corinthian A' rather than as a Greco-Italic amphora. Although it was found some distance away, it is possible that **41** belongs to the same vessel. There were few clear surfaces to see if mudstone inclusions were also present.
Perhaps fifth or early fourth century

Corinthian B

43. Two handles, neck and shoulder. Handles rise up sharply from the neck to touch the lip, then curve sharply and are vertical to the shoulder. In section the handles are flattened ovals with pinched edges, thickening through the centre. Hard orange-brown clay changing to beige at the surface (slip?), no visible inclusions. **Figs. 10.3 and 10.6**
Inv. 1420. Tr. 97.4.6.9. S of Terrace Wall
5YR 6/6; W handles 4.2; H handles 14.2; Th. wall 0.7; D neck 9.7
The high arching handles attached to the neck and curving to the level of the rim are typical of Type B (Corinthian B) amphoras. The fabric, light orange becoming lighter on the surface and without inclusions, is also normal for this type. The shape of the strap handles in cross-section, with pinched edges, becomes common in the fourth century. A good example of this from Corinth is KP 1222, Koehler 1978, 191–2 no. 253

pls. 32, 40, which she dates to the late fourth–early third century. For a recent discussion of Corinthian B, or simply B amphoras, including origins, typology, and chronology, see Göransson 2007, 88–97.
Corinthian Type B amphora, fourth century probably

North Aegean, Thasian (?)

44. Foot. Tall narrow foot which widens at the bottom with a hollow on the underside. Hard orange fabric with white and black inclusions and some "mica" flakes. **Fig. 10.4**
Inv. 1139. Tr. 96.13.6.9. S of Altar area
2.5YR 6/8; PH 22.0; Th. foot 8.0
Amphoras from Thasos have a similar narrow foot, spreading at the base with a depression on the underside. Close examples belong to Grandjean's period 4 (ca. 340–250 BCE) although others are also found in his period 5 (after ca. 250), Grandjean 1992, 555 no. 44 fig. 6, 557 no. 47 fig. 7, 558 nos. 55–7 fig. 8 (period 4); 570 nos. 90–1 fig. 14 (period 5). The shape may fit most easily into Bon and Bon's Type II, though without more of it preserved and with numerous variations within this type, it is difficult to be certain, Bon and Bon 1957, 19. For a summary of Thasian amphoras and results of petrological analysis, Whitbread 1995, 165–97. Visual description of the clay gives a wide range of types, from dark red to pale ochre with mica whether large- or small-grained, into which the Stymphalos foot would fit easily, Bon and Bon 1957, 14; Whitbread 1995, 167. Mendean amphoras have similar-looking clay and have feet with a splay at their bottoms, but these generally are shorter with a more exaggerated splay than the Stymphalos foot. For a recent discussion of both Thasian and Mendean types with bibliography, see Göransson 2007, 136–45.
Probably North Aegean (Thasian?), fourth century BCE

Unidentified amphora

45. Rim, neck, beginning of the body, one strap handle and part of a second. Wide flaring mouth, with a vertically flared rim, thick strap handles from the top of the neck to the top of the shoulder, slight offset between the neck and body. Soft red clay, no visible inclusions or mica. Dark red slip. **Figs. 10.4 and 10.6**
Inv. 1510. Tr. 97.5.4.8. E of Terrace Wall
2.5YR 5/8; D rim (est.) 18.0; PH 18.5
The fineness of the fabric, the shape of the rim, and the red slip are not easy to parallel among transport amphoras. This may be better compared to storage/coarse-ware amphoras.
Assoc. pottery: late fourth century to 200–150 BCE

Pithoi[12]

There are two pithoi, found in the same trench, but clearly belonging to a smaller and a larger container, though not inventoried separately. The smaller one has been measured for the inventory record, but both are catalogued here. Fragments of one or two other pithoi, smaller in size, were also found in the Sanctuary area. These are clear indications of the storage of food in the vicinity, probably in Building A, or its annexes, of which the North Annex is more spacious.

The craft of the pithos maker was a specialized one, to judge by the study of such traditional clay crafts in earlier modern Greece.[13] A question arises about the transportation of large pithoi if they are made in one place and used in another. The large pithos from Stymphalos (**46**) is closely related to one from Corinth, and is made of the same fabric, so one presumes that it was made there and brought by wagon to Stymphalos despite its size and the difficulties of land travel with such bulky objects. It must have added substantially to its value when it finally arrived.

Neckless pithoi[14]

46. Rim and shoulder fragment. Thick rim of a pithos with tall vertical outer face, sharp turn to the shoulder. Light orange clay with many large brown and black inclusions, very coarse fabric. **Figs. 10.4 and 10.6**
Inv. 705. Tr. 96.6.2.1. Pillar Shrine area
D rim (est.) 42.0; W rim 7.0; H of ext. rim edge 5.7; Th. wall 1.9
The profile of the rim is similar to one found in the Dema house from the last quarter of the fifth century; see Jones, Sackett, and Graham 1962, 86 no. H fig. 11; Boggess 1972, no. 120 142–3 pl. 21. A whole miniature pithos with this rim shape came from Perachora, Dunbabin and Dunbabin 1962, 310 no. 3229 pl. 125.
Perhaps 425–375 BCE

47. Rim and foot, some wall fragments. (Other wall fragments of both pithoi may have been scattered on the site and misidentified as roof tile fragments.) Thickened rim, flat on top, flat ext. lip. Tall but simple stump-foot with bevelled resting edge and shallow raised underside. Hard light brown or buff clay with many dark, pebbly inclusions. **Figs. 10.4 and 10.6**
Inv. 2419. Tr. 99.10.3.4. N of North Annex
5YR 8/4; L rim 33; W rim 8.2; H rim 8.4; Th. bowl 2.5; Th. rim 2.0; D rim (est.) 52.0; Th. wall 2.0 to 2.3; H foot 5.2; D foot 12.0; PH 12.1; Th. wall 2.4
Small pithos with the upper surface of its rim 8.2 cm wide.

Compare the stump-foot on a Hellenistic pithos from Corinth, which has a thickened bevelled ring base, Boggess 1970, 74 fig. 3.

The foot fragment possibly belongs with another pithos, or else another foot, perhaps **50**, belongs with this rim fragment.

48. Two joining rim fragments and some wall fragments, including ones with a group of three raised horizontal lines and a curved line above or below made from applied clay strips. Thickened rim, flat on top, flat ext. edge. The heavy rim has a wide upper surface which slopes downward slightly to a vertical outer face. It continues below by inclining back to the join of the shoulder, where a narrow double ridge is found. The inner edge of the rim is bevelled where the upper and inside vertical edges of the rim meet. Buff clay on the surface, redder in the core, fired unevenly, many large brown (mudstone) and grey inclusions. **Fig. 10.4**
Not inventoried separately. Tr. 99.10.3.4. N of North Annex
PL rim 47.0; W rim (upper surface) 12.2; H outer rim edge 3.0; Th. wall 3.5; D rim (est.) 88.0.
From a larger pithos than **47**.
One of the largest pithoi from the Athenian Agora (P 19422) has the same rim diameter, Boggess 1972, 76 no. 123 pl. 22 (*Hesperia* 20 [1952] 180 fig. 6 pl. 64 b). The rim profile is very close to **47**, but the upper rim surface is more horizontal, and the outer edge is more vertical. The wall fragments decorated with a group of three horizontal lines have the same fabric and wall thickness as the other pithos wall fragments which seem to belong to this rim.

The pattern with a group of three raised horizontal lines and a curved or wavy line close above or below them is found on a Hellenistic pithos from a well in Corinth. The curved line is a continuous wavy or rounded zigzag set between two groups of three horizontal lines; see Boggess 1970. The shape of the rim is very similar, including the inside bevelled edge, and the raised narrow ridges where the rim meets the shoulder. The estimated diameter of the rim of the Stymphalos pithos is larger by 20 cm and the wall thickness is greater by about 1.0 cm, though the width of the top of the rim is almost exactly the same. The Corinth pithos had a coat of red slip applied carelessly over the area of decoration. It is possible that the Stymphalos pithos also was slipped in this area, though the heavy encrustation over the surface prevents certainty about this. The fabric of the two pithoi seems close, with both using mudstone as inclusions.

Boggess (1970, 78) points out two important points regarding the Corinth pithos. First, the decorated area was meant to be seen, and therefore, unlike many household pithoi, which are deeply sunk into the ground, this one was only meant to be partly sunken and partly exposed. Secondly, the fact that it was ornamented suggests that it was for use in a public building, such as a temple or clubhouse. This latter point would seem to apply as well to the Stymphalos example.

A date for the Corinth pithos could not be narrowed very closely. It was found in a well with destruction debris of the second century BCE, but it also contained material from as early as the fourth century.
400–150 BCE

49. Rim of a small pithos, with a raised line, groove at the join of rim to neck. Thickened rim, flat on top, flat ext. edge. Pinkish-brown clay in the core, almost buff at the surface. Fine brown and white inclusions. **Fig. 10.4**
Inv. 707. Tr. 96.4.3.5. Altar area
D rim (est.) 48.0; W rim 5.5; Th. rim edge 4.4
The rim profile is quite close to **47** though the ext. rim edge is more vertical.

50. Lower wall and foot. Small disk foot, shallow raised underside, wide-spreading wall. Buff to light brown clay with many pebbly inclusions. **Fig. 10.4**
Inv. 815. Tr. 96.6.4.2. Pillar Shrine area
MPD 31.0; Th. wall 2.5; H foot 3.9
The foot profile is similar to **47**, but the lower edge is not bevelled, nor is the disk as high.

If the find spot for the foot **(47)** is correct, then this foot (**50**) is from another pithos, but not from the much larger uninventoried pithos, either, whose wall thickness is greater.

11

Lamps

Hector Williams

Excavations in the area of the Sanctuary produced fragments of over 150 different terracotta lamps as well as a few complete ones; they date from the late fifth/early fourth century BCE to the early/mid-sixth century CE.[1] While most are not closely datable or from closed contexts, they do serve as an indicator of activity in the area through the centuries. The majority are wheelmade lamps of the mid-fourth to third century BCE, which were in use during the period of the Sanctuary's floruit. A striking feature of the collection is the diversity of types represented; indeed for some there are no exact parallels at other sites, although many of identifiable fabric appear to be Corinthian. It should be noted, however, that we know little about lamps from neighbouring Sikyon, and it is possible that future published work from that site will alter the picture at Stymphalos. A small number of lamps made in the first century and second/mid-third centuries CE indicate a renewed use of the area, perhaps by occasional worshippers or visitors. A single sixth-century CE fragment may be associated with early Christian graves in the area, but neither pottery, terracotta figurines, nor coins suggest any extensive activities after the mid-second century BCE.

In the ancient world, oil lamps were of course primarily lighting devices, but they could also be used as votives in sanctuaries and as offerings to accompany the dead, both pagan and occasionally Christian.[2] In some cases uses might be combined: cults like that of Demeter and Kore, which had nocturnal ceremonies, might well see their use both for practical purposes and as dedications.[3] At the Stymphalian Sanctuary, which seems to have had a residential aspect or at least one of dining, it is probable that the practical use predominated. Lamps as offerings often tended to run to similar or identical types, but there is little evidence for such homogeneity at Stymphalos except in the mid-second century BCE and the first century CE.[4] Often at sanctuaries there are multinozzled lamps and miniatures; only four lamps in the Sanctuary might indicate multiple nozzles (**34–7**) (and see **25**) and three are miniatures (**31–3**). Another less usual type is the so-called *Stocklampe*, a lamp with a conical tube running up from the base with which it might be fixed to a stick for carrying (**18–19**).

The fragmentary condition of most of the lamps from the Sanctuary makes a detailed study difficult; nozzles and base fragments tend to survive better, as do pieces of rim and top, but there is rarely a complete profile; indeed there are only two complete lamps. The soil conditions have also at times degraded surfaces and made them friable and thus difficult to clean fully. At times they have also left a heavy incrustation that is difficult to remove. The general lack of undisturbed stratigraphy, moreover, usually precludes their making any significant contribution to our knowledge of the chronology of local lamps, while the lack of change in profile of typical Late Classical/Early Hellenistic lamps means that dating is often limited to the range of a century or so. It seems likely that most lamps were broken in use and then cast away with other garbage. Ploughing of at least the upper thirty centimetres of much of the site (only by mule, according to local informants) until the early 1960s has inflicted further damage and disturbance on the area.[5] There are a sufficient number of lamps, however, to allow some areas of study and analysis. Careful excavation maximized the recovery rate of fragments, and the practice in antiquity of keeping anything used in a sanctuary inside its limits as the property of the divinity worshipped suggests that we have a relatively reliable sample of what was actually used at the site.[6] It is striking, however, that with the exception of the pit beside the west wall of Building A, there were no closed deposits of material such as might be buried during a clean-up of old offerings. It is also worth noting how relatively small in size the majority of fragments are.

One area that did add to such knowledge of the lamps in the Sanctuary, however, was the North Annex of Building A, in which a fire pit or hearth of the mid-second century BCE was found (dated by long petal moulded bowl sherds).[7] From it came remains of at least fifty wheelmade lamps, rather smaller in size than the usual; two sets of fragments (**15**) mended up into a complete profile that gives a good idea what the others might have looked like. Basically the lamp is reminiscent of the round-bodied lamps of the mid-fourth to mid-third centuries BCE, although the top is somewhat smaller. It may well be that this was a type popular elsewhere in Stymphalos at the time, although there are far more from the Sanctuary than, say, the housing area, a fact that suggests that they were especially intended for use in the Sanctuary. The relatively small size might have made them less useful in houses but more than adequate for a quickly burning votive offering; even today in Orthodox churches one can buy candles of different sizes to offer. Religious conservatism might have preserved the earlier form.

The lamps of Roman date form two distinct groups of the first and then of the second to mid-third centuries CE; it is likely, although not certain, that there was a gap in the use of the two types. There are at least eleven identifiable examples (**52–7**) of simple wheelmade lamps characteristic of the first century CE in the Corinthia (Broneer Type 16); most preserve only the distinctive stubby nozzles with large wick hole.[8] A complete one appeared in the upper levels of the Temple fill, suggesting that it had been left there, perhaps as a votive, at a much later time than the Temple's destruction. There is only one fragment of a mould-made lamp (**58**) of the type created in Italy and exported and copied widely throughout the Empire in the first century (Broneer Type 24 or 25); it is likely a product of the northern Peloponnese, if not Corinth itself.[9] There are nine small fragments (**59–66**) of the fine mould-made products of Corinth in the middle Empire (Broneer Type 27); they are easily identified by their fine unslipped buff fabric, their distinctive handles and nozzles, their rim patterns (panels/ovuli on shoulder and rays on disk and later vine and grape clusters on shoulder and rays on disk); we have not found any disks with the fine relief decorations for which these lamps are well known.[10] Dating is not close (ca. 100–250 CE), but the vine and grape cluster lamps probably come later in the series. There is also a single example of an early Christian lamp of ca. 500–550 CE, a local imitation of a North African lamp of the fifth century.[11] It might have been associated with late Roman burials in the pronaos of the Temple as a grave lamp; other lamps of the fifth and possibly early sixth century were found in several other areas of Stymphalos in cemeteries.

The pattern of survival is similar to that found elsewhere at Stymphalos, apart from the absence of "Ephesos lamps," of which two appeared in other parts of the city. This mould-made type, very popular in Greece and the Aegean, generally dates from the late second century BCE and into the early first century CE.[12] Similarly elsewhere there are only two or three "picture lamps," the common volute nozzle relief lamp that developed in Italy in the later first century BCE and was widely exported and copied in Greece through the next century. They appeared in the southeastern area of the city in the mid-first-century destruction level of the Roman houses, but they are few in number compared to the Broneer Type 16 lamps that are also found in that area. Because of their importance as chronological indicators of activity in the Sanctuary, all fragments of Roman date have been included, even very small ones.

CATALOGUE

D	diameter
Est.	estimated
H	height
Inv.	general site inventory number
L	length
MPD	maximum preserved dimension
P	preserved
Tr.	trench number.pail number.level number

All measurements are in centimetres unless otherwise indicated.

Profile drawings and photographs are by G. Schaus.

Surface finds were made by excavators while walking over the site, or by shepherds during the winter when heavy rains washed sherds out of scarps; occasionally the actual trench number can be recovered, but the information is not verifiable. In a few cases data on lamps apart from general find spot are missing because of extreme damage by a mouse infestation of the storerooms in 1997–8. Soil conditions in this area were very hard on lamps, sometimes encrusting them and sometimes softening their surfaces.

Late Classical/early Hellenistic wheelmade lamps

This category includes the earliest examples of lamps from the Sanctuary; their dating is based on lamps found in the Corinthia and in Athens, although it must be admitted that those lamps themselves are not closely dated. Indeed it is often difficult to date many lamps of the fourth to mid-third century BCE closer than to a century because there is so little development of the form. The strap handle (as in **1**), however, generally indicates an earlier date.[13]

1. Heavy lamp with globular body, groove around the filling hole, long nozzle and stumps of the strap handle across the back; round, slightly concave base. Intact except for the handle and a chip out of the nozzle. Light buff Corinthian clay, traces of dark brown slip. **Figs. 11.1 and 11.4**
Inv. 3379. Tr. 00.4.8.11. City Wall
L 8.5; D 6.5; H 3.5
First half of fourth century BCE

2. Front half of the lamp, preserving nozzle and full profile. Medium length nozzle with ovoid wick hole. Broad filling hole with narrow incurving rim. Round very slightly concave base set off by a groove. Medium orange clay, dark brown slip. **Fig. 11.1**
Inv. 627. Tr. 96.6.3.3. West Annex
PL 6.6; PD 5.9; H 3.2
Fourth century BCE

3. Nozzle and front third of lamp. Medium-sized nozzle carefully joined to the body; slightly incurving narrow rim and wide filling hole. Flat disk base set off from the body by a groove. Light buff Corinthian clay; poorly adhering dark brown slip. **Fig. 11.1**
Inv. 1584. Tr. 96.11.5.6. Temple
PL 5.8; PW 6.1; H 2.8
Fourth century BCE. (Some pottery from this level is as early as the mid-fifth century BCE, according to John Hayes.)

4. Fragment of the top and side. Small lamp. Low body with incurving wall and narrow rim; wide filling hole. Stub of the round horizontal handle. Medium orange clay, dark brown slip. **Fig. 11.1**
Inv. 1286. Tr. 97.4.5.7. Near Tile-lined Basin Room
MPD 3.6
Fourth century BCE?

5. Part of the side and top. Slightly curving sides; flat rim with double reserved groove around broad filling hole. Pale buff Corinthian clay; dark brown slip. **Fig. 11.1**
Inv. 3658. Tr. 97.5.5.5. E of Terrace Wall
PH 3.0; D est. 7.0
Fourth century BCE

Round-bodied lamps (RBL)

The round-bodied or round-shouldered lamp is the commonest found in the Greek world ca. 360–250 BCE, but it is a type that undergoes little change in that century. A globular body narrowing up to a top with small filling hole surrounded by one or more grooves, no handle but a small lug, often pierced, on one side (perhaps for hanging), a base foot, and a medium to long nozzle are the basic characteristics of the type.

6. Complete base and start of the lower body. Very thick base rising to slightly conical centre with slightly concave disk foot. Light orange clay, irregular dark to light brown slip; inside of disk foot reserved. **Fig. 11.1**
Inv. 685. Tr. 96.4.5.8. Altar area
MPD 7.7; MPH 3.3
Ca. 360–250 BCE

7. Fragment of the top and side of a small lamp. Inward-sloping disk separated from shoulder by channel; start of nozzle. Medium orange clay, dark brown slip. **Fig. 11.1**
Inv. 1376. Tr. 97.4.5.8. Near Tile-lined Basin Room
MPD 4.6
Ca. 360–250 BCE

8. Fragment of the top and side. Inward-sloping disk to small filling hole; round shoulder set off by a groove around the disk. Light grey clay (probably overfired or secondary burning), unslipped. **Figs. 11.1 and 11.4**
Inv. 1220. Tr. 97.5.2.4. E of Terrace Wall
MPD 3.7
Ca. 360–250 BCE

9. Joining fragments preserving the front half and all the base. Standard RBL with tapering nozzle and small wick hole. Groove around the top; narrow incurving rim around the filling hole. Slightly concave disk base set off from the body by a groove. Thick base rising to a slightly conical centre. Orange clay, dark brown slip. Possibly Attic. **Fig. 11.1**
Inv. 1557. Tr. 97.9.5.7. Tile-lined Basin Room
PL 9.6; D 6.3; H 4.4
Pottery from this level is not later than ca. 300 BCE.

10. Nozzle, part of the top and side. Medium-sized nozzle with elliptical wick hole. Start of the globular body; small disk and filling hole set off from the shoulder by

a groove. Made in a distinctive fabric with light orange clay, heavy grey/black slip. **Fig. 11.1**
Inv. 1670. Tr. 97.7 + 96.6. Pillar Shrine
MPL 5.3
Ca. 360–250 BCE

11. Nozzle and start of the body. Flat-topped nozzle flattened rather than round on the underside with elliptical wick hole. Light orange clay, dark brown slip. **Fig. 11.1**
Inv. 1881. Tr. 96.3.3.5. Altar area
MPL 3.3
Probably round-bodied.

12. Fragment of the top and side of a large lamp. Thick-walled body (1.1); start of the top with a deep groove around the edge and slightly raised collar around the filling hole. Orange clay, dark brown slip; possibly Attic. **Fig. 11.1**
Inv. 3657. Tr. 00.97.5 baulk.5.5. E of Terrace Wall
PH 4.3

13. Three joining fragments of the nozzle, body, and base. Top with groove around the edge offsetting the collar from the rim. Raised base, unslipped, slightly convex. Medium orange clay; dark brown slip, poorly preserved. **Fig. 11.1**
Inv. 1279. Tr. 1997.4.6.9. Near Tile-lined Basin Room
L 8.3; H 3.7

14. Fragment of the top and side. Incurving top around the filling hole; reserved groove around the disk. Globular body. Fine orange clay (Attic?), brown black slip.
Inv. 2963. Chance find in 2000 near the Temple
PL 5.6

14 bis. Fragment of the top and side. Grey clay, unslipped (blisterware?). **Fig. 11.1**
Inv. 2718. Tr. 99.1 baulk. E of Terrace Wall
MPD. 4.9

Another blisterware base fragment likely from this type was found in Trench 97.5.12.7.

Late round-bodied lamps

These represent a group found together in the destruction level of the North Annex of Building A along with long petal and other mould-made bowls of about the mid-second century BCE. They are in several fabrics and tend to be slightly smaller than the usual lamp.[14] They are so homogenous in size and appearance that it is likely they were made as offerings in the Sanctuary; perhaps religious conservatism dictated their style, which would not have been out of place more than a century earlier. There appear to be two types: one has the side smoothly curving down from the filling hole while the other has a "jog," a sharp angle, rising up from the filling hole before it continues down the side of the lamp; the filling holes are small and usually have a band or groove around the small disk into which they are set. There are very fragmentary remains – disk bases, rim and body sherds of at least 50 such lamps in the deposit in three fabrics: blisterware, standard Corinthian pale buff fabric, and unknown red fabrics. Unusual is the paucity of nozzles, with only seven fragments surviving.[15] Another such lamp that mended up complete came from the large artillery tower on the western side of the city (Stym V).

15. Joining fragments preserving much of the lamp. Round body with a groove forming a low collar around the filling hole; medium-length nozzle that splays out slightly with small ovoid wick hole. Round slightly raised base. No handle. Light orange clay, light brown slip. **Figs. 11.1 and 11.4**
Inv. 1878. Find spot data missing but likely as **16**
L 8.5; D 5.6; H 2.9
Mid-second century BCE

16. Joining fragments of the nozzle, body, and possibly base. Similar to **15**, but the nozzle is straight rather than splayed. Light orange clay, light brown slip. **Fig. 11.1**
Inv. 1765. Tr. 95.3.9.5. North Annex
PL 10.6; D 5.8

17. Two joining fragments preserving the start of the nozzle, top, and side. Round body with a groove forming a low collar around the filling hole; shorter nozzle than **15** but neatly joined to its rounded body. Light orange clay; brown slip. **Figs. 11.1 and 11.4**
Inv. 4546. Surface find
PL 5.8

Stocklampe

Known usually by its German name, this type first appears in the Late Archaic period and is especially popular in the northern Aegean and Black Sea region.[16] It is intermittently found in various forms over the next two centuries in the southern Greek world.[17] It always has a conical hole in the middle of the floor of the lamp, which could have taken a stick through it to carry the device. At Mytilene, for example, most of the Late Archaic lamps are an early form of the type, but the

Stymphalian examples with their much higher sides are typical of the fourth century BCE.[18]

18. Two non-joining fragments of the top, part of the nozzle and base. Round-bodied top; the nozzle is broad at the base and narrows towards the wick hole. The base has a slightly concave disk foot with conical tube rising in the centre. Pale yellow Corinthian clay; dark brown slip. **Fig. 11.2**
Inv. 2424. Tr. 99.1.7.5. E of Terrace Wall
PL top 4.7; PD base 4.3
Fourth century BCE

19. Part of the base, lower body, and central tube. Round base sloping slightly inward to the central tube. Orange clay; dark brown slip. **Fig. 11.2**
Inv. 1216. Tr. 97.4.4.6. Near Tile-lined Basin Room
MPD 6.1
This is a rare type at Stymphalos.
Fourth century BCE

"Mushroom"-shaped lamps

Examples of this very distinctive shape seem to appear otherwise only in the Corinthia, where a form appears occasionally in probable fourth-century BCE contexts at both Corinth and Kenchreai.[19] The Stymphalian lamps are quite small and may have been offerings. One (**21**) is shorter and less squat than the other with a larger filling hole, but their profiles show the relation. A third example (inv. 4243) was found at Stym XIV, an area near the southeast city wall. The presence of three of these lamps at Stymphalos suggests that the type may have been more common than previously known. There is also a question of date: one comes from the fire pit in the North Annex of Building A. As noted above, the lamps there are likely mid-second century BCE, although they look earlier, and it is possible that these two "mushroom-shaped" lamps are also later than they seem.

20. Complete. Mushroom-shaped upper body slightly in-turning around the filling hole; short nozzle with elliptical wick hole, flattened underside, set carelessly at a slight angle to the body; round slightly raised disk base. Orange/brown clay, possible traces of dark brown/black slip. **Figs. 11.2 and 11.4**
Inv. 628. Tr. 95.9.4.6. North Annex
L 8.4; D 5.7; H 2.7
Cf. Stym XIV inv. 4243 for a similar profile.

21. Complete. Small lamp with mushroom-shaped upper body; the top turns in slightly around the filling hole; short nozzle with elliptical wick hole and flattened underside; round slightly raised disk base. Orange clay, unslipped. **Fig. 11.2**
Inv. 499. Tr. 95.4+1.2.2. Temple
L 7.4; D 5.0; H 2.6

Large late Classical/Hellenistic lamps

This group of lamps is an amorphous one composed of different types that are larger in size than usual, especially the nozzle and the diameter of the disk. The date appears generally to be mid-fourth to mid-third centuries BCE.

22. Preserves chipped nozzle and part of the lower body. Flat spatulate nozzle with transverse elliptical wick hole. The body is broken off but appears to have been low. Light orange clay; dark brown slip with what looks like a medium orange self slip underneath. **Fig. 11.2**
Inv. 779. Tr. 96.4.5.8. Altar area
MPD 7.0; PH 3.2

23. Nozzle and body fragment. Very thick walls. Broad short nozzle with transverse elliptical wick hole; deep bowl-like body. Dark red/brown clay; traces of dark brown slip.
Inv. 1356. Tr. 97.4.7.11. Near Tile-lined Basin Room
PH 5.8

24. Nozzle, body and base fragment. Medium-size nozzle; start of a groove around the entire disk setting off the nozzle; low body with flat broad base. Dark grey/brown clay; lighter brown slip. **Figs. 11.2 and 11.4**
Inv. 1366. Tr. 97.5.4.7. E of Terrace Wall
PH 2.6; PL 6.2. Thick walls (max. 1.2)
Context pottery is fourth century BCE.

25. Fragment of the nozzle, upper body and rim of a very large, thick-walled lamp. Much burned around the top. Short nozzle joined smoothly to the top of the body; the rim curves in to a thick underroll of clay, leaving a broad filling hole. Dark red/brown clay; traces of brown slip. **Fig. 11.4**
Inv. 1656. Tr. 97.9.5.7. Tile-lined Basin Room
PH 4.7
Possibly from a multinozzled lamp.

26. Fragment of the top and side. Thin flat rim around a broad filling hole set off from the shoulder by a groove; slightly curving side with a small carination as it bends towards the base. Dark red/brown clay, dark brown slip.
Inv. 1663. Tr. 97.11.5.6. Middle Room of Building A
PH 2.5 D est. 14.0. Thin wall

27. Fragment of the rim, body and start of the nozzle. Double groove around rim. Thick wall. Light orange clay; dark brown/black slip inside and out.
Inv. 1064. Tr. 96.13.7.4. S of Terrace Wall
PH 2.9; PL 4.1
Looks early; probably Corinthian fabric imitating Attic.

28. Two joining fragments of the nozzle, top and body. Poorly preserved surface. Medium-sized nozzle; narrow rim with grooves at the inner and outer edges, broad filling hole. Low body. Coarse red/brown clay, unslipped. **Fig. 11.2**
Inv. 1065. Tr. 95.2.4.8. Front Room of Building A
PH 2.8; PL 6.2; D est. 11.0
Appears to be in the local cooking-ware fabric. Another nozzle fragment in a similar fabric but with thicker wall was found as a chance find at the site in 2004.

Lamps with watch-shaped profile

This shape appears first in Greece during the early third century BCE and becomes common around the central and eastern Mediterranean; generally they date to the first half of the century but may continue through to the end of the third century.[20] The profile is like a flattened cone or pocket watch. Interestingly, **30** is in a blisterware fabric very similar to the late round-bodied lamps (possibly dedications) above.[21] Its filling hole is also similar, but the flatter top and the lug on one side differentiate it from the later lamps.

29. Fragment of the top. Convex top with a broad shoulder and small filling hole surrounded by a groove; small lug at the edge of the fragment. Light orange clay; light green-beige slip. **Fig. 11.2**
Inv. 1767. Tr. 95.3.5.9. North Annex
MPD 4.7
One of the few later Hellenistic lamps from the Sanctuary.
Perhaps third century BCE

30. Non-joining fragments of the top. Light orange clay, traces of dark brown slip.
Inv. 4518. Tr. 99.1.5.7. E of Terrace Wall
MPD 7.2
Similar to **29**.

Another small disk fragment in blisterware was found in the fire pit the North Annex; if not residual, this piece brings the use of the type at least to the mid-second century BCE.

Miniature lamps

Miniature lamps are common in many periods and particularly as offerings in sanctuaries and graves. They are always wheelmade in this period and difficult to date stylistically; on grounds of context the Stymphalos examples appear to be Late Classical to Mid-Hellenistic in date.

31. Disk, part of the nozzle and body of a possible miniature lamp. Slightly sunken disk; start of the nozzle; rounded body. Medium orange clay, unslipped.
Inv. 2587. Tr. 99.1.5.9. E of Terrace Wall
MPD 2.4
Much smaller than **32–3**.

32. Nozzle and start of the body and filling hole. Simple V-shaped nozzle with ovoid wick hole. Pale buff Corinthian clay, traces of dark brown slip. **Fig. 11.2**
Inv. 1373. Tr. 97.6.3. Pillar Shrine area
PL 2.2
The nozzle was carelessly applied to a wheelmade body. Found in the Pillar Shrine area north of the Temple and possibly an offering left there.
Fourth century BCE

33. Complete (mended from fragments). Narrow rim sloping in to a large filling hole; possible vestigial lug on the right side of the rim. Flat round base; the nozzle is large in proportion to the body. Light orange clay, traces of brown slip. **Figs. 11.2 and 11.4**
Inv. 2099. Surface find
L 6.1; D 4.3; H 2.1

Multinozzled lamps

Multinozzled lamps, especially with more than three nozzles, generally are associated with sanctuaries, either as offerings or as illumination devices.[22]

34. Part of one nozzle, start of a second, section of the body and base. Short U-shaped nozzle; open top with thick carinated side; flat reserved base. Light buff Corinthian clay; dark brown/black slip. **Fig. 11.2**
Inv. 519. Tr. 95.5.5.6. S of Temple
MPD 5.3; H 3.2; D est. 18.0.
Likely late fifth to mid-fourth century BCE

35. Fragment with parts of nozzles and adjoining body. Very low body with thick wall; short U-shaped nozzle with small wick hole and beside it the root of a second nozzle (possibly twelve altogether originally). Pale buff Corinthian clay; dark brown slip. **Figs. 11.2 and 11.4**

Inv. 4545. Surface find. Tr. 01.1
MPD 4.8; PH 2.5
Fourth century BCE

36. Half of one nozzle and start of a second, edge of the body. Large U-shaped nozzle; groove around the outer edge of a narrow rim; wide filling hole. Pale buff Corinthian clay; brown to red mottled slip. **Fig. 11.2**
Inv. 3547. Tr. 00.97.5 baulk.5.5. E of Terrace Wall
MPD 5.1; PH 3.5
Coins and pottery from this level date ca. 350–300 BCE, but **36** is likely earlier.

37. Joining fragments of the top, nozzle and sides. Short U-shaped nozzle; groove around the narrow rim setting it off from the side; broad filling hole. Orange clay with grey core; dark brown slip inside and outside, spalling in places. **Figs. 11.2 and 11.4**
Inv. 2358. Tr. 99.1.5.6. E of Terrace Wall
MPW 7.1; PH 3.3; D est. 14.4
Low lamp.

Uncertain wheelmade type

38. Top fragment. Flat rim area with six small concentric grooves; low narrow collar around the depressed filling hole area; slight rim around a small filling hole. Fine orange clay and thin fabric, red/brown slip inside and outside.
Inv. 2098. Tr. 95.7.3.6. Middle Room of Building A
MPD 3.2

Nozzles

39. Nozzle and start of the body. Medium-size nozzle, heavily burned; small wick hole. Pale orange clay, unslipped.
Inv. 0919. Tr. 96.10.2.6. City Wall
PL 4.4
Probably from a round-bodied lamp.
Late Classical/early Hellenistic

40. Nozzle and start of the body of a small lamp. Battered and chipped short nozzle and body. Very pale buff Corinthian clay, dark brown slip. **Fig. 11.3**
Inv. 1882. Tr. 96.3.1.1. Altar area
PL 3.5; PH 2.5. Thick wall (max. 1.2)

41. Part of the nozzle and body. Medium-length nozzle, bevelled on the underside with a small ovoid wick hole. Slightly sunken flat disk with ridge around edge of body. Light orange clay; traces of dark brown slip.
Inv. 2357. Tr. 99.1.5.6. E of Terrace Wall
PL 4.9

42. Nozzle. Short nozzle with irregular ovoid filling hole; spatulate end that flares out slightly on both sides. Light orange clay; medium brown slip.
Inv. 2251. Tr. 99.2.3.3. E of Temple
PL 3.6
Similar to this is inv. 1881.

43. Nozzle. Small nozzle with large off-centre ovoid filling hole. Pale orange buff clay; dark brown slip, irregularly adhering to the clay.
Inv. 2233. Tr. 99.1.3.3. E of Terrace Wall
PL 2.7

44. Fragment of the nozzle and top. Medium-sized nozzle with a small filling hole; flat top with groove around the outer edge. Pale buff clay; trace of dark brown slip, Corinthian fabric.
Inv. 2977. Tr. 00.4.3.3. City Wall
PL 4.6
Late Classical/early Hellenistic context

45. Fragment of the nozzle and top. Medium-sized nozzle; the top of the lamp is slightly sunken with a rim around the edge. Broad filling hole. Pale buff clay; poorly preserved dark brown slip (typical Corinthian fabric). **Fig. 11.3**
Inv. 3041. Tr. 00.4.3.3. City Wall
PL 4.0
Late Classical/early Hellenistic

46. Fragment of the nozzle and top. Broad U-shaped nozzle with transverse oval wick hole. Plain flat rim and broad filling hole. Pale orange clay, dark brown slip.
Inv. 3408. Tr. 96.15.5.5. Refuse pit, W of Building A
MPW 3.9
Early to mid-fourth century BCE

47. Nozzle and start of the body; heavily burned. Long nozzle with elliptical wick hole which slopes slightly forward and is flattened underneath. An unusual feature of the nozzle is that the sides curve up to the top. Orange clay; brown slip. **Fig. 11.4**
Inv. 3533. Tr. 97.5 baulk.5.5. E of Terrace Wall
MPL 4.8
Context material dates ca. 350–300 BCE (coins and pottery), but it is possibly from a later round-bodied lamp.

48. Top and part of filling hole, and short nozzle. Probably a globular body. Orange clay; medium brown slip. **Figs. 11.3 and 11.4**
Inv. 1369. Tr. 96.12.4.4. Southeast Room, Building A
MPL 5.1
Perhaps fourth century BCE

49. Fragment of the lower part of the nozzle. Pale yellow clay; dark brown slip, inside and outside, Corinthian.
Inv. 1398. Tr. 97.8.1.1. W of Temple
PL 3.3
Short nozzle from a low lamp.
Fourth century BCE

50. Fragment of the nozzle and top. Short nozzle, bevelled underneath like **20**; large oval wick hole. Broad filling hole on top with a slightly inturned rim. Orange/brown clay, unslipped. **Fig. 11.3**
Inv. 512. Tr. 95.4+1.2.3. Temple
PL 5.2; W nozzle 2.5

51. Fragment of the nozzle and top. Tapering nozzle with slight bevelling under the wick hole. Flat round top with broad flat collar around the narrow filling hole. Orange clay, brown/black matt slip.
Inv. 1670 (?). Tr. 96.6 + 96.8. West Annex. Scarp cleaning
MPL 5.6

Early Roman wheelmade lamps (Broneer Type 16)

Broneer identified this lamp type some eighty years ago as a local one at Corinth starting in the Augustan period, but there have been occasional revisions to his dating scheme in the past two decades based on more recent work in the area of Corinth.[23] It marks one of the last appearances of wheelmade lamps in the Greek world until late antiquity. Rather than ending in the late Augustan or Tiberian period as Broneer suggested, the type seems to continue through the century and probably even into the second century (although the evidence appears tenuous for the late dating). Hundreds were found as dedications in the Palaimonian at the sanctuary of Poseidon at Isthmia in the early Roman period.[24] It is perhaps significant that five of these lamps came from the same context in the Temple (**52–4, 57,** and an uninventoried fragment) because it suggests there may have been more than casual use of the area in early Roman times.

52. Complete. Rectangular nozzle with flaring ends and large ovoid wick hole. Bowl-shaped body; concave disk with high edge; low set loop handle; slightly raised round base. Grey/brown clay with many white inclusions; traces of brown slip. **Fig. 11.3**
Inv. 62. Tr. 95.1.8.13. Temple
L 11.3; D 6.2; H 3.2

53. Joining fragments of the top and complete nozzle. Standard Type 16 nozzle that flares out slightly at the end; large oval wick hole; slightly concave disk. Red/brown clay, unslipped.
Inv. 1764. Tr. 95.1.8.13. Temple
PL 11.2; PD 6.3

54. Fragments of the top, body, and low flat base. Burned and sooty. Thinner fabric than usual. **Fig. 11.4**
Inv. 101. Tr. 95.4.4.4. Temple
MPD 3.0

55. Nozzle fragment. The nozzle has corners that flatten obliquely. Dark brown clay, unslipped. **Fig. 11.3**
Inv. 2096. Tr. 96.9.1.1. Altar area
PL 4.0

56. Joining fragments of the handle and body. Bowl-shaped body; sunken disk; loop strap handle. Medium orange clay, grey core; unslipped. Fine thin fabric. **Fig. 11.4**
Inv. 2719. Tr. 99.13.5.5. Altar, Terrace Wall
MPD 4.6

57. Many joining fragments of a burnt lamp including much of the disk, body, base, and handle. Medium orange clay, grey surface.
Inv. 4703. Tr. 95.4+1.2.2. Temple
PL 6.2
Similar to **56**.

(Other single nozzle fragments came from Tr. 95.4+1.2.3, Tr. 96.5 ext. 2.9, Tr. 97.7.5.6, and three fragments from Tr. 95.4+1.2.2.)

Early/Middle Roman mould-made lamp (Broneer Type 24 or 25?)

58 is typical of the thousands that were produced in various forms in the first and second centuries CE; it is the only one from the Sanctuary, however. It had an oval form and probably a rounded semi-volute nozzle but only simple leaf decoration on the shoulder.[25]

58. Fragment of the shoulder and disk. Broad shoulder with obliquely placed sharp oval leaves. Ridge around the plain sunken disk. Light orange clay, unslipped. **Fig. 11.3**
Inv. 4570. Tr. 99.1.3.3. E of Terrace Wall
MPL 5.5
Possibly a Corinthian imitation of an Italian type. Cf. Broneer 1930, no. 474 and no. 509 for the leaves.
Ca. 50–125 CE

Middle Roman mould-made lamps (Broneer Type 27)

This type is the most popular in Corinth in the second to mid-third centuries.[26] At Stymphalos, however, we have none of the fine moulded disk representations that mark some of the finest-quality lamps ever produced in the ancient world, nor do we have any signatures preserved from the many shops known. It is likely that the simple tops with ovuli around the disk, which is decorated with rays, are earlier than the types with vine leaves and clusters on the shoulder and rays on the disk. There is some question about the date and place of origin of the type, but Corinth is most likely for examples from Stymphalos.[27]

59. Fragment of disk and body. Pale yellow clay, unslipped. **Fig. 11.3**
Inv. 497. Tr. 96.5.ext.3.4. City Wall
MPD 2.2
The shoulder preserves part of a grape cluster; disk with rays and narrow framing ring.

60. Fragment of disk, rim and nozzle; very worn. Start of the nozzle; disk with rays; double groove around disk; possible ovuli on shoulder; air hole. Pale orange clay, unslipped. **Fig. 11.3**
Inv. 1282. Tr. 97.4.2.2. Near Tile-lined Basin Room
MPD 3.2

61. Handle and back of the body. Soft yellow buff clay, unslipped. **Fig. 11.4**
Inv. 2181. Tr. 99.3.3.3. Middle Room of Building A
MPD 4.3
Double groove on the handle; start of a pattern, probably ovuli, visible on the shoulder.
Perhaps second century CE because of the quality of the clay.

62. Two fragments preserving part of the shoulder and start of the nozzle. Pale yellow clay, unslipped.
Inv. 2274. Tr. 99.3.3.3. Middle Room of Building A
MPD 4.4
Vine leaf and grape cluster on the shoulder. Slightly blurred reproduction. Perhaps from the same lamp as **61**.

63. Lower back and handle and part of the base. Pale yellow clay, unslipped.
Inv. 25. Tr. 95.2.2.4. Front Room of Building A
MPD 3.7
Double groove down the back of the handle; circular groove around the base.

64. Two joining rim and disk fragments, start of the nozzle, very worn. Pale yellow clay, unslipped. **Fig. 11.3**
Inv. 2796. Tr. 99.9.1.1. E of Tile-lined Basin Room
PL 4.3
Framing ring around the disk with rays; vine cluster and leaf decoration on the shoulder.

65. Rim and disk fragment. Pale yellow clay.
Inv. 3017. Tr. 00.4.2.2. City Wall
PL 3.2
Possible trace of ovuli on the shoulder; rays on the disk.

66. Nozzle, rim, and disk fragment. Very worn. Light orange clay. **Fig. 11.3**
Inv. 1413. Tr. 97.9.2.2. Near Tile-lined Basin Room
MPD 3.3
The rim has traces of ovuli, groove around the disk, rays.

Two handles from lamps of this type came from Trench 99.1.2.2 (E of Terrace Wall) and Trench 99.13.5.5 (Altar, Terrace Wall area).

Early Christian mould-made lamp

Excavations at Stymphalos have uncovered five different areas of early Christian burials, including a multiple grave in the pronaos of the Temple.[28] Several graves included local late Roman lamps among their meagre contents, but the two imitation North African lamps that we have found have both been surface or near surface discoveries. Lamp shops in the area of modern Tunisia manufactured and exported vast quantities of fine redware lamps, especially from the early fifth century CE onward. The late Roman lamp industry at Corinth and elsewhere produced thousands of imitations of such lamps, often like our example, of very mediocre quality.[29] Such production went well into the third quarter of the sixth century.

67. Fragment of the disk and rim of a local imitation of a North African lamp. Brown clay, unslipped. **Fig. 11.3**
Inv. 1763. Tr. 95.2.1.1. Building A
MPL 5.3
Unclear traces of relief decoration are visible on the disk (probably not a Christian monogram); worn rosettes on the rim panel; clay webbing beside the handle.
Early to mid-sixth century CE

12

Loomweights

Laura Surtees

Loomweights comprise a large and distinctive group of artifacts found scattered throughout the Sanctuary on the acropolis. The presence of 99 loomweights in a Sanctuary which was dedicated, with some probability, to Athena, goddess of weaving, elicits questions on several levels as to their purpose. On their own, they indicate in a practical way the existence of weaving as an activity at Stymphalos, but because the loomweights were found in a cultic setting, they also require an investigation into possible religious uses or connotations for them. They cannot simply be accepted as tools in a practical manufacturing activity. Based on an analysis of the loomweights, their location and context, it may be argued that their presence in this Sanctuary at Stymphalos is a result of several activities, both ritual and practical. A full discussion follows the Catalogue.

INTRODUCTION

Shapes

Figure 12.1a shows a typical conical loomweight. Bases of loomweights are flat unless otherwise mentioned.

Type A: Conical shape with no space or division between the belly and base. The tip may be either pointed or rounded.
Type B: Conical shape, the belly protrudes outwards before sloping gradually into the base. The point of maximum diameter of the belly separates the weight into two distinct sections. The tip may be either pointed or rounded.
Type C: Conical shape with a distinct bevel dividing the belly from the base. The bevel is pronounced and the slope from the bevel to the base is sharp. The tip may be either pointed or rounded.
Type D: Elongated pyramidal shape with flat sides. The tip is flat.

For a discussion of these shapes see below, pp. 242–3 and figs. 12.4–5.

Size Groups

Group 1: Large: height 10–12 cm
Group 2: Medium: height 7–9.9 cm
Group 3: Small: height 5–6.9 cm
Group 4: Miniature: height 3–4.9 cm

Fabrics

I: Buff to yellowish green to white clay with fine grey inclusions. A soft fine powdery consistency.
II: Red to orange clay with grey and white fine to medium inclusions.
III: Light red powdery clay with grey and white small inclusions
IV: Pink or pinkish grey to reddish brown or brown clay with medium and large grey and white inclusions.

CATALOGUE

MPD Maximum preserved dimension
D Maximum diameter
B Diameter at the base
T.L.P Trench.Level.Pail
Wt. Weight (in grams)

All measurements are in centimetres, except weight.

Cat. no.	Inv. no.	T.L.P.	MPD	D	B	Wt.(g)	Profile	Fabric	Description
West Annex									
1	343	96.6.1.2	10.1	6.8	5.5	334	B.1	III	Complete. Symmetrical slope, slight gradual ridge
2	332	96.6.3.6	10.0	6.7	3.9	280	C.1	I	Complete with damaged base. Suspension hole filled with an organic material
3	339	96.6.3.6	4.6	3.0	2.2	24	C.4	I	Miniature loomweight. Complete. Pointed tip, small suspension hole, concave base
4	342	96.6.3.6	9.8	6.2	5.7	328	B.1	I	Fragment. Broken at tip, groove of suspension hole
5	345	96.6.3.6	9.4	7.2		326	1	IV	Fragment. Pointed tip and upper body, surface encrustation
6	346	96.6.3.6	9.6	7.0	4.7	304	C.2	I	Fragment. Broken at tip, fragment from neck and bevelled ridge not preserved, concave base, surface encrustation
7	348	96.6.3.6	10.1	6.7	4.6	326	C.1	I	Complete. Pointed tip, suspension hole only visible on one side
8	349	96.6.3.6	10.4	6.8	5.6	358	B.1	II	Complete. Pointed tip, surface encrustation, suspension hole filled with organic material
9	350	96.6.3.6	10.5	7.0	5.5	348	C.1	II	Complete. Pointed tip, lopsided slopes of the belly, small fragment broken on the side
10	351	96.6.3.6	10.2	7.0	5.4	352	C.1	II	Complete. Broken at tip but extant, surface encrustation covering the suspension hole
11	337	96.8.3.3	10.5	6.3	5.2	316	B.1	IV	Complete. Slight ridge at base, suspension hole filled and only visible on one side, chip on side
12	415	96.8.3.3	10.4	7.4	6.1	342	B.1	I	Complete. Broken tip but extant, large white inclusions in clay, suspension hole filled with organic material (stick)
13	453	96.8.3.3	11.4	7.1		348	B.1	II	Fragment. Pointed tip, partial base extant, flat sides, surface encrustation
14	485	96.8.3.3	10.8	6.7	5.0	332	B.1	IV	Complete. Pointed tip, surface encrustation, suspension hole filled with organic material, decorated with three incised vertical lines above the bevelled ridge, possible slip
15	531	96.8.3.3	10.8	6.8	5.1	332	B.1	II	Complete. Pointed tip, surface encrustation, suspension hole filled with organic material
16	585	96.8.5.6	11.2	7.5	6.1	428	B.1	II	Complete. Thin pointed tip, indented side, surface encrustation
17	940	97.2.3.3	10.2	7.3	5.8	364	C.1	II	Complete. Broken but extant pointed tip, symmetrical belly, slightly concave base with edge
18	941	97.2.3.3	11.2	8.2	5.5	476	C.1	II	Complete. Pointed tip, pronounced bevelled ridge, concave base with edge, dense surface encrustation
19	942	97.2.3.3	10.3	7.2	5.0	364	C.1	I/II	Complete. Rounded tip, concave base with edge, surface encrustation, suspension hole filled with organic material (stick)
20	943	97.2.3.3	10.5	7.4	6.0	434	C.1	II	Complete. Pointed tip, high belly bevelled ridge, surface encrustation
21	977	97.2.3.3	10.6	6.9	6.8	354	B.1	I	Complete. Pointed tip, asymmetrical sides of belly, surface encrustation
22	1158	97.2.4.4							Complete

South of Temple

23	1556	97.12.2.2	8.6	6.7	5.5	136	A.2	I	Fragment. Broken at tip with suspension hole groove visible, part of base extant
24	1579	97.12.2.2	10.2	6.9		140	B.1	III	Fragment. Round tip, elongated slopes of belly, slightly concave base with edge
25	1620	97.12.3.3	5.7			144		IV	Belly fragment
26	2906	00.2.2.2	9.1	7.4	6.4	348	C.2	III	Complete. Sides of belly slightly lopsided, well-defined bevelled ridge, flat base with distinct edge
27	2907	00.2.2.2	9.9	7.0	4.5	352	B or C.2	III	Complete. Rounded tip, warped base, chip in side
28	2908	00.2.2.2	10.8	7.0	6.0	446	C.1	IV	Complete. Pointed tip, surface encrustation, decorated with 2 or 3 incised vertical lines above the bevelled ridge
29	2909	00.2.2.2	11.3	7.7	6.2	464	C.1	I	Complete. Symmetrical belly, small depression in base, decorated with three incised vertical lines and one horizontal line above the bevelled ridge
30	2900	00.2.3.3	5.2	3.1	1.8	28	B	IV	Base fragment
31	3046	00.2.4.4	9.8	6.8	4.8	318	B.1	II	Complete. Pointed tip, slight bump on asymmetrical belly, concave base with edge, chip in side

East of Altar/Terrace Wall

32	1060	97.5.1.1	7.6	5.6		176	A.2	II	Complete. Chip fragment in tip, slipped
33	2572	97.5B.2.2	10.1	6.6	5.5	310	B.1	I	Complete. Pointed tip, evidence of wear on sides, surface encrustation
34	2643	97.5B.4.5	8.8	6.5		254	B.2	IV	Complete. Round tip, belly tapers inward, small depression in base, diameter of base is indistinguishable
35	2644	97.5B.4.5	7.2	5.5		84		IV	Fragment. Round tip, surface encrustation
36	3518	97.5B.5.5	10.4	6.9	5.2	310	B.1	I	Complete. Pointed pinched tip, indent on one side of belly
37	3572	97.5B.6.6	9.0	6.9		234	2	II	Fragment. Pointed tip, symmetrical belly, broken at base.
38	2164	99.1.2.2	6.1	5.2	2.7	66	B	II	Belly fragment
39	2180	99.1.2.2	6.5	5.3		132		IV	Neck and belly fragment. Groove of the suspension hole visible
40	SF 99.64	99.1.3.3							Body fragment
41	SF 99.237	99.15.5	7.4	7.4		190		III	Body fragment. Surface encrustation
42	2303	99.15.5	11.0	6.6		228	A.1	III	Fragment. Pointed tip, broken base
43	2340	99.15.5	9.7	5.2		132	1	III	Fragment. Pointed tip, symmetrical belly, partially extant base
44	2341	99.15.5	6.6	6.3		220	C	IV	Base fragment
45	2348	99.1.5.6	8.5	3.0		136		IV	Belly fragment, groove of suspension hole preserved, chips in side
46	2389	99.1.5.7	9.7	7.7	5.9	410	B.1	IV	Fragment. Rounded tip, deep indent on side, partially extant base, dense surface encrustation
47	2532	99.1.5.9	7.0	5.8		164	2	II	Fragment. Rounded tip, partially extant base, surface encrustation
48	2545	99.1.5.10	10.2	7.0	5.5	340	C.1	I	Complete. Pointed tip, asymmetrical belly, small depression in centre of base, dense surface encrustation

49	2546	99.1.5.10	10.6	7.0	5.0	346	C.1	II	Complete. Pointed tip. Slightly asymmetrical belly, small depression in centre of base. Conserved
50	2851	99.1.5.9.10.11.12	4.5	4.2		14		II	Fragment. Part of base extant
51	2674	99.16.12	8.1	6.4		200	1	II	Fragment. Rounded tip, surface encrustation
52	2342	99.8.2.2	8.4	6.6		222	C.2	IV	Fragment. Broken tip, symmetrical slope of belly, part of base preserved
53	2404	99.6.5.5	8.2	5.8		214	A.2	II	Complete. Rounded tip, surface encrustation
54	2610	99.9.4.4	9.9	6.6	4.0	320	C.2	II	Complete. Pointed tip, tapering inwards at base, suspension hole covered with heavy surface encrustation
55	334	96.4.3.5	6.0	4.3		66	A.3	I	Complete. Rounded tip, symmetrical sides, surface encrustation
56	347	96.4.3.5	6.6	3.6	3.3 4.7	100	D.3	IV	Complete. Flat tip, slight depression in base, burnt with minimal surface encrustation
57	336	96.4.4.7	10.4	7.7	5.3	358	B.1	III	Complete. Rounded tip, flat sides tapering towards rectangular base
58	1893	96.3.2.2	6.3	3.8		54		I	Fragment
59	338	96.3.3.5	11.1	7.2	4.7	346	B.1	III	Fragment. Rounded tip, uneven base, broken at base, chips in side

South of Altar

60	1000	96.13.6.11	5.5	6.2		142	A.1	I	Fragment. Semi-flat base, surface encrustation
61	1255	97.4.6.9	10.8	7.1	5.9	396	B.1	I	Complete. Pointed tip, asymmetrical belly, surface encrustation
62	1256	97.4.6.9	11.3	7.0	5.5	402	B.1	IV	Complete. Pointed tip, steep sloped belly, dense surface encrustation
63	1342	97.4.6.9	11.0	6.9	5.3	376	B.1	II	Complete. Pointed tip, flat base, slightly lopsided at base, minimal surface encrustation, decorated with 2–3 incised vertical lines above the bevelled ridge
64	1433	97.9.4.4	9.6	6.9	5.0	288	B.1	IV	Fragment. Slight depression in middle of the base, only one suspension hole visible, surface encrustation, half of weight extant
65	1536	97.9.5.5	10.0	7.4		304	C.1	I	Complete. Rounded tip, distinct bevelled edge, tapering of the sides towards the base, depression in base, concave base
66	1537	97.9.5.5	11.0	6.1		392	1	IV	Fragment. Pointed tip, partially extant base, black encrustation on the base, possible sign of burning or slip
67	1889	95.13.2.3	4.8	4.4	2.3	28		I	Fragment. Rounded tip
68	587	96.10.3.3	9.2	6.9	4.6	286	C.2	II	Complete. Rounded tip, tapered rectangular base with depression
69	897	96.10.5.1	8.6	7.0	4.2	282	B.1	III	Fragment. One side of weight extant including groove of suspension hole
70	902	96.10.5.1	7.3	7.3	5.7	300	A	IV	Fragment. Concave base with edge, partially extant, heavily pitted surface
71	895	96.5ext.10.1	10.0	6.9	5.8	328	B.1	III	Complete. Broken tip, symmetrical belly, surface encrustation
72	893	96.5ext.10.2	10.1	7.2	6.0	346	A.1	IV	Complete. Rounded tip, symmetrical belly, raised edge at base, surface encrustation
73	894	96.5ext.10.2	10.6	7.1		316	A.1	II	Fragment. Pointed tip, straight sloped sides, partially extant base, surface encrustation

74	896	96.5ext.10.2	11.7	7.7	6.0	402	B.1	III	Complete. Pointed tip, indent in belly, surface encrustation, cracked surface
75	3055	00.4.4.4	11.2	7.6		362	B.1	I	Complete. Flat tapering side of belly, minimal surface encrustation, possible thumb impression at tip
76	3056	00.4.4.4	9.1	7.4	5.1	354	B.1	I	Complete. Rounded tip, long straight slopes of belly, concave base with edge, heavy surface encrustation, decorated with 3 incised vertical lines above the bevelled ridge. Conserved
77	2981	00.4.4.4	8.7	5.4		122	1	II	Side fragment
78	2985	00.4.4.4	8.5	6.4	5.2	278	B.2	II	Complete. Conserved tip, chip in belly, slightly concave base with edge
79	3148	00.4.7.7	6.2	6.2		178		II	Belly fragment
80	1888	96.14.2.2	10.3	7.1	6.1	344	B.1	IV	Complete. Round tip, symmetrical belly, surface encrustation
81	0082	95.8.2.3	11.1	6.2	4.9	368	C.1	II	Fragment. Indentation on the sides, damaged base, surface encrustation
82	0083	95.8.3.11	7.2	5.6		160	A	IV	Fragment. Round tip, surface encrustation
83	331	95.5.5.6	10.1	7.6	5.5	446	C.1	III	Complete in 7 pieces. Lopsided belly with one flat side, concave base with edge, surface encrustation, suspension hole filled with organic material
84	1904	95.6.5.7	7.9	6.4	4.1	192	B.2	III	Fragment. Rounded tip, damaged belly and base
85	487	–	8.6	6.8	6.8	250	A.2	IV	Fragment. Pointed tip, flat triangular shape, surface damage at base, surface encrustation, evidence of burning
86	0085	95.2.1.1	9.7	5.0		125	1	IV	Fragment. Pointed tip, damaged base.
87	1897	94.4/95.7.1.1	3.5	3.1		14		IV	Tip fragment
88	1278	95.7.5.11	6.0	3.0	4.8	66	A	III	Fragment. Sides of belly lopsided
89	1900	95.9.3.4	3.9	3.9		28		III	Tip fragment. Rounded tip, broken at suspension hole
90	1364	95.9.7.7	6.2	5.9		110	A	III	Fragment. Partially extant base and tip
91	1208	97.6.1.1	6.5	6.4		96	C	III	Fragment. Slightly lopsided belly, small bump on the base, decorated with 2–3 incised vertical lines above the bevelled edge
92	1209	97.6.1.1	5.6	2.8		68	C	III	Fragment. Bump on the preserved base, evidence of burning
93	1354	97.7.1.1	4.9	3.4		40	B	IV	Base fragment
94	2244	99.5.2.2	5.8	4.2		54		III	Tip fragment
95	2247	99.5.2.2	10.5	6.8		302	B.1	III	Complete. Pointed tip, large inclusions in the surface, base conserved
96	2347	99.11.2.2	6.8	5.4		104	A or B	IV	Fragment. Flat base, surface encrustation
97	2359	99.10.2.3	8.5	6.8	5.8	276	A.2	III	Complete. Round tip, surface encrustation
98	3112	00.5.2.2	8.3	4.5		110		IV	Fragment. Groove of suspension hole preserved
99	Uncatalogued						B		Complete. Pointed tip, decorated with 3 incised vertical lines above the bevelled ridge. On display in Lafka Folklore Museum

DISCUSSION

Three main explanations for the deposition of loomweights in the Sanctuary at Stymphalos can be offered. First, random loss or debris in secondary contexts scattered throughout the Sanctuary. The original function of these objects is not determinable, since their apparently random scattering means they lack a primary context. They may once have been associated with a loom or been deposited as individual votive objects, but this evidence is now largely lost (unless the few inscribed marks have something to tell us).

The remaining loomweights can be divided into two groups: ones dedicated to the deity as votive gifts, and those which served as functional tools for weaving, possibly, though not conclusively, in a ceremonial rite related to the cult of the divinity, in this case perhaps Athena or Eileithyia.[1] Context and location of the loomweights are crucial criteria in determining their use in the Sanctuary.

On other sites, weaving equipment has been attested in both domestic and religious contexts. Items such as looms, loomweights, and spindle whorls have a practical function as tools for the production of cloth. In a domestic context, weaving was done on a daily basis by women of the household, and the appearance of weaving equipment is self-explanatory. On the other hand, loomweights and other weaving equipment at a religious site might have symbolic meaning and allude to the divine protection or patronage which this important daily activity had. It might also have a role to play within the ritual life of a cult – for example, offering a chance for the display of skills by girls and young women, and providing them with both validation of their role in society and an opportunity to be initiated into formal worship of the deity. Weaving was a fundamentally important task, and its value in society, both real and symbolic, perpetuated the notion of womanhood. The inclusion of women in celebrations of the religious sphere by means of weaving reinforced and legitimized the importance of women's role in ancient Greek society.

A relatively simple classification system has been developed in order to examine features of the loomweights from Stymphalos, including form, size, fabric, and markings, from both a qualitative and quantitative perspective. Furthermore, the acropolis Sanctuary at Stymphalos provides some evidence on the basis of distribution patterns that the loomweights were functional and therefore that weaving was part of ritual activity in the Sanctuary. Spatial distribution of loomweights within an architectural setting helps shed light on their use.[2] The depositional pattern and position of the loomweights help indicate whether the weights were in use at the time of their deposition, were being stored, were on display, or have since been disturbed. Evidence for the presence of looms, such as post holes or the charred remains of wooden beams, is sometimes visible in the soil, which may substantiate their presence, though, one hastens to add, no clear evidence was observed at Stymphalos.[3] The lack of systematic contextual analysis may well detract from an appreciation of the complexities of these objects and lead to assumptions about their function in purely practical domestic activities, despite evidence to the contrary. Therefore, stratigraphy, depositional patterning, and artifact characteristics, taken together, provide evidence for ancient practices and activities.

Excavations in the acropolis Sanctuary at Stymphalos yielded 99 loomweights. No bobbins were found, but two possible needles, one of bone (uncatalogued) and the other bronze (Inv. 238, Schaus, chapter 7 above, cat. **133**), have been identified, and two lead bodkins (Inv. 2452, Schaus, chapter 7 above, cat. **219**), a spindle hook (Inv. 601, Schaus, chapter 7 above, cat. **137**), and two possible spindle whorls (Inv. 687, Schaus, chapter 7 above, cat. **106**, and one uncatalogued) were found. Therefore, loomweights comprise by far the greater part of the assemblage of weaving equipment at the site. The lack of spindle whorls on the site may indicate, for example, that spinning of wool was done elsewhere in the town.

The Greeks wove on the warp-weighted loom, which had two upright vertical beams and two horizontal cross beams: one at the top to hold the cloth and one in the middle called the shed bar.[4] The loom either leaned against the wall or was supported at the base by upright wooden beams (fig. 12.1b).[5] The warp threads were hung from the top cross beam and attached to loomweights at the bottom holding the warp threads taut.[6] The tension of the threads needed to be consistent; thus a set of loomweights was required to which the threads were tied with their weight distributed equally among the threads.

Looms varied in size. The number and mass of loomweights required for a particular project varied according to the type and size of cloth being produced. On the basis of the length of preserved rows of loomweights or the distance between the preserved post holes from the loom, the widest recorded warp-weighted loom was 2.4 m and the smallest was 0.4–0.5 m.[7] The average width, however, was 1.2 m to 1.7 m.[8] Looms larger than 2 m would likely have caused difficulties in manoeuvring around the loom, even for two women working in unison.

Evidence for the average number of loomweights used on a loom derives both from groups of loomweights themselves and from depictions of looms. It remains unclear how many warp ends were attached to each loomweight. Davidson and Thompson estimated that twelve threads (0.026 m wide) were attached to a single loomweight. This would require 65–70 loomweights per loom for an average-sized cloth (ca. 1.75 m wide).[9] Such a large number of weights would be cumbersome, and crowding would increase the possibilities of tangling. Thus the method of staggering loomweights in parallel rows was adopted; this can be seen on a vase from Chiusi, and with finds from several sites, including Troy IIg.[10] Ethnographic studies have also demonstrated its practicality.[11]

More warp threads attached to a single loomweight increases the interval between loomweights, thus reducing the number, congestion, and possibility of breakage of loomweights. Rows or clusters of 10 to 40 loomweights have been found commonly on sites, indicative of the number required in a set.[12] The suspension hole of a loomweight, however, tends to be small, and, in order to accommodate numerous threads, an intermediary must have been used, as with modern looms. The intermediary, whether a ring, cord, long bar, or rod, was laced through the suspension hole and had the warp threads attached directly to it.[13] Depictions of weaving on the Amasis Painter's lekythos[14] and on a Corinthian aryballos[15] show this technique. Some intermediaries have been preserved, including a clay loomweight with bronze ring,[16] wooden rods in loomweights at Nemea,[17] and representations of loomweights with "sticks" stamped on loomweights at Corinth and the Pnyx in Athens.[18] Two loomweights (**12** and **19**) from the Sanctuary at Stymphalos had an organic material, perhaps a stick, embedded in the groove of the suspension hole.[19] This may be the remains of wooden rods similar to the loomweights at Nemea. The use of an intermediary reduced the number of weights required, although the weights had to be heavy to keep tension on a greater number of threads. Other aspects of the warp-weighted loom remain problematic, although variations between households and regions over time no doubt existed.

At Stymphalos, all the loomweights are perforated with a single suspension hole and are conical in shape, with the exception of a single pyramidal one.[20] All the loomweights appear to be handmade, which may account for the asymmetrical sides and other inconsistencies such as finger marks or dips and lopsided suspension holes.[21] Most of the loomweights were well fired, although a few exhibit cracked surfaces and chips indicative of poor firing. Small variations in size and shape occur, but in general the loomweights are similar. There are no traces of paint, decoration, or stamped impressions on any of the loomweights.

The only markings on the Stymphalos loomweights consist of incisions or worn grooves, found on seven loomweights (**14**, **91**, **28**, **29**, **63**, **76**, and one uncatalogued) (figs. 12.2–3). These are rather shallow, and surface encrustation renders them barely visible. The markings are all similar, consisting of three vertical lines, relatively symmetrical, on the belly of the loomweight just above or at the bevelled lower edge. **29** (fig. 12.3a) is unique in having a vertical line to the left of three horizontal lines.

The scarcity of marks on these loomweights means that the incisions were unlikely to be either manufacturer's or owner's marks. Their function remains problematic; however, one suggestion is that all seven of them were meant to have the same mark, and that this mark is most clearly seen on **29** but incised at 90° and the joining perpendicular line is missing for the other six.[22] The problem with this idea is that the other six have their three parallel strokes vertical to the loomweight base and do not have the linking perpendicular line. This is most clearly seen on a loomweight now in the Lafka ethnographic museum which was picked up as a surface find in the Sanctuary (see fig. 12.3b). The mark on **29** is an epsilon, even having the vertical line extend below the lowest of the horizontal strokes as with the epsilons on the bronze rim fragment (Inv. 2525, Schaus, chapter 7 above, cat. **22**). While this is hardly much to go on, nevertheless, given the consistent pattern of the other three dedication inscriptions on objects from the Sanctuary that name Eileithyia or seem to refer to her, it is possible that the "E" (epsilon) found on **29** again refers to Eileithyia, and that this loomweight at least, and possibly the others, was either a dedication to her, or left in the Sanctuary for the purpose of producing a garment for this goddess.[23]

The shapes of loomweights in the Sanctuary do not allow for chronological distinctions, as have been proposed at other sites, for example, Corinth or Olynthos.[24] Nor could they be compared convincingly to other typologies, since regional preferences and particularities are difficult to account for. In addition, the durability of weights means that a long period of use is possible, though it is difficult to estimate what an average span was. Many loomweights at Stymphalos, especially those from the Sanctuary, were in disturbed or secondary contexts, so dating is even less certain.

Nevertheless, the loomweights can be divided by shape into four main types (A–D, as listed above, p. 236, and see fig. 12.4). Type A is conical with sides sloping straight towards the base (with no outward curve at the belly), perhaps developing from the pyramidal tradition.[25] Otherwise, weights commonly have a low rounded or bevelled belly that tapers gently to a flat resting surface. This rounded or bevelled belly absorbed contact between weights and created a noticeable distinction between upper and lower parts of the weight (Types B and C, fig. 12.5). The bevelled ridge is set higher and becomes more defined in weights of Type C, which also tend to be elongated, with straighter sides. Only one truncated pyramidal loomweight (Type D, figs. 12.4 and 12.5) occurred at the Sanctuary. Most weights have a flat or slightly concave resting surface; all are able to stand upright.

These variations are difficult to explain other than as mere preference or tradition, since they seem to lack functional purpose.[26] Most loomweights at Stymphalos are Types B and C; thirteen belong to Type A, and one to Type D. A distinction between B and C can be made primarily on the basis of the angle of the belly ridge, although differences are not always clear. Finding weights of slightly different shape in the same context argues for the general insignificance of these variations. A suspension hole just below the top of each weight (1.5 cm to 2 cm below the tip) helped to distribute weight and reduced the risk of breakage at the tip itself.

The size, and therefore the mass, of a loomweight is its one essential characteristic. Tension determined the fineness and tightness of the cloth. Loomweights at Stymphalos vary from 4.6 cm to 11.4 cm in height (fig. 12.6). Most range between 8 and 11 cm. One miniature loomweight (4.6 cm) weighs only 24 g, and its usefulness in weaving is questionable. The lightness of this weight also strongly suggests that it may instead have been made specifically as a votive; however, it has also been noted that small loomweights may be paired with heavier ones to improve the weight distribution.[27] Two other small loomweights, both about 6 cm in height and 66–100 g in weight (one is pyramidal, Type D), are barely heavy enough individually to hold the threads taut, especially in comparison with other weights from the site.

Loomweights hung from threads on the same loom should have been closely similar in weight to provide equal tension on the cloth warp threads during weaving.[28] All loomweights at Stymphalos (including the fragments) have been weighed for comparison's sake. Complete ones range from 24 to 464 g; the average is 326 g with 40% of the loomweights weighing between 300 and 400 g. They tend to be heavier, in some cases considerably, than ones at other sites, for example Olynthos, Gravina di Puglia, San Giovanni, Halos, Ilion, and Narce in Etruria, although comparable ones found at the Silaris Heraion range between 325 and 425 g.[29] Uniformity of weight may be an indication of the quality of the workmanship as well as the consistency of the type of weaving practised.

The clay of the loomweights can be divided roughly into four fabrics, identified by colour, texture, and inclusions (see above, p. 236).[30] The weights are fairly consistent and evenly divided among the fabric types; however, fabric I is most distinctive based on colour, which is almost white or light buff with a greenish tinge, as opposed to more red, pink, and brown fabrics. No source of the clay for any of the types has been identified and therefore it is not possible to determine whether any of the clays were local. Fabric I is close in colour to Corinthian clay. No conclusive evidence for a kiln or potter's quarter has yet been found at Stymphalos. The presence of ceramic wasters in other parts of the city (Stym I and Stym X) suggests some local pottery manufacture, at least in the late Hellenistic and Roman period. It seems likely, therefore, that some loomweights were produced locally.

Distribution

The distribution pattern of loomweights (fig. 12.7) helps suggest their use in the Sanctuary. They were found strewn individually and in clusters with concentrations in certain locations (see, for example, figs. 12.8 and 12.9).

Finding fewer than four loomweights within any given room or defined outside area might well be the result of random loss or scattering during destruction or abandonment of the Sanctuary. Clusters of four or more loomweights are more indicative of sets, depending on the context.[31] Three main areas where the loomweight concentrations were densest are two outside areas: 1) east of the Altar and 2) south of the Temple, and an inside area: 3) within and near the West Annex of Building A (table 12.1). Other smaller clusters, not as concentrated, have been located throughout the Sanctuary; for example, the City Wall: these probably represent the accumulation of debris or the deposition of votives.

The second largest concentration of loomweights, after that of the West Annex, was found east of the Altar beyond the large Terrace Wall which abuts the

Table 12.1. Distribution count of loomweights by area

Areas in the Athena Sanctuary	Total
Building A	5
West Annex of Building A	22
West of Building A	6
East of Building A	1
North of Building A	1
Temple	1
Immediate periphery of Temple	5
South of Temple	9
Altar	5
South of Altar	8
East of Altar/Terrace Wall	23
City Wall	12
Unknown	1
Total	99

rough cobbled courtyard surrounding the Altar. Fourteen loomweights were found in trench 99.1 and another five in trench 97.5 (baulk). The mixture of material found in this context suggests that the deposition was at least partly votive in nature.[32]

Distinct strata could not be clearly distinguished in trench 99.1; the changing of levels tended to be at arbitrary depths, so levels generally are not representative of specific occupation phases. Preliminary analyses of the coins, figurines, and pottery provide tentative dates for the material from the fifth to the second century BCE,[33] although most of the pottery is from the fourth and third centuries. An abundance of pottery, including miniature votive vessels, fine, common, and coarse wares, was found here, as well as an assortment of other objects: iron nails and rings, bronze lunate earrings, iron projectile points, bronze coins, terracotta figurines, lamp fragments, perirrhanterion fragments, a silver lid, the rim of a stone vessel, a stone grain grinder, sheets of bronze with repoussé decoration, loomweights, plaster, miscellaneous metal, glass, and bone.

Many of the loomweights in this area were broken before deposition, so the average weight, including the fragments, was under 200 g, well below the average weight of 326 g for the entire site. The Terrace Wall separating this area from the Altar courtyard has not been securely dated; part of the fill beyond the wall is dated as late as the second century BCE.[34] Clearly this area, just below the Altar, offered a suitable and convenient location to dispose of rubbish and unwanted votives from the Sanctuary, which might account for the lack of well-defined strata and the diversity of the material within.

South of the Temple, a large quantity of material found in trenches 00.2 and 97.12 (figs. 12.7 and 12.9) seems more representative of an area of votive offerings. Perhaps such offerings had been displayed on tables or benches in and around the Temple, the remains of which have not survived.[35]

Finds include miniature votive cups, fine ware pottery, bronze rings, coins, terracotta figurines, loomweights, projectile points,[36] and various miscellaneous metal objects. The loomweights here might be representative of individual offerings or a dedicated set. The lack of architectural remains indicates the unlikelihood of weaving being done, since protection from the sun and elements was important.

On the other hand, the nine loomweights in this area might indicate an earlier or temporary area for weaving activity. In trench 00.2, five whole loomweights and one fragment were found; slightly to the west in trench 97.12, three more loomweight fragments were uncovered. Five of the loomweights are of similar shape and size; the profile group of the fragmentary one is inconclusive. The five complete loomweights in trench 00.2 average 10.2 cm in height, and belong predominantly to Type C, although Type B is also represented. They vary in weight from 318 g to 464 g.[37] Those from trench 97.12 seem smaller, though their fragmentary preservation makes comparisons difficult. The presence of the six loomweights in trench 00.2, on a hard-packed surface, possibly a floor or occupation surface, suggests the possibility of weaving. If so, one may ask how this area relates to the West Annex, where evidence for weaving is clearer. Pottery evidence from the floor of the West Annex suggests that that room had a short life, and if so, then an alternative area for weaving might be here, with temporary shelter provided by makeshift means.[38] This location and the associated materials, however, are ambiguous in suggesting weaving activity.

The primary context for weaving was in the West Annex of Building A,[39] where the largest concentration of loomweights, 19 altogether in several clusters, was found at floor level within and just outside the room, while 9 more occurred in the same vicinity.[40] This small room was built in the last phase of construction of Building A, which pottery evidence suggests was in the late fourth or early third century BCE. A low, narrow fieldstone foundation was laid on the north and west sides with the start of a return wall at the corner of the south side, where a door presumably was situated. The east side of the West Annex is formed by the west wall of Building A and part of its North Annex. The room is isolated from the rest of the building with no connecting door to Building A. The dimensions of the room are 4.8 m × 3.6 m, which would provide sufficient space for an average-sized loom with ample additional space for women to manoeuvre around it. Above the floor surface was a layer of yellowish decomposed mudbrick, approximately 15 cm deep, filled with roof tile debris. Immediately below the mudbrick deposition was the floor surface on which the loomweights rested.

All the loomweights were roughly the same size (on average 10.4 cm high) and of similar weight (on average 353 g).[41] Their form varies slightly; the group can be divided equally between Types B and C. Types A and D are both absent. They were found in three clusters within the room, not in a single straight line, perhaps as a result of disturbance during destruction of the room. It is worth noting that the two loomweights with organic material in their suspension holes, perhaps the remnants of wooden rods, were found here, suggesting they had been in use at the time of destruction.

Additional material was discovered along with the 19 loomweights. Pottery was not abundant, yet it corresponds with the change towards the use of table ceramics in this period. Within the room, tableware comprises the highest percentage of forms, followed by votive ware, including miniatures. Metal implements, primarily of iron and bronze, some of indistinguishable function, iron and bronze finger rings and earrings, lamp nozzles, two coins, and several projectile points were found in the same stratum as the loomweights. Nothing in the assemblage need argue for an alternate function for the room. These objects may have been used by the women weaving and represent loss or debris within the room. The presence of 19 loomweights within a defined space and on a floor surface with no other distinguishable function strongly suggests that they were part of a functioning loomweight set and that weaving was the primary activity in the room.

No epigraphical evidence has survived at Stymphalos to indicate the motives of the dedicator, if indeed some of these loomweights were dedications, but such weights were not uncommon as votives elsewhere, as seen both by their abundance in Greek sanctuaries and by their appearance in inventory lists and dedicatory inscriptions. Inscriptions sometimes provide evidence for the rational incentive and symbolism of weaving equipment as offerings.[42] Dedicating equipment in particular to the patroness of weaving, Athena, may emphasize the close relationship between the weaver and the goddess, and may symbolize women's life as well as their important economic role in Greek society. Loomweights, however, were inexpensive votives with little or no aesthetic or sentimental value but were token offerings by the dedicator. Other implements such as spindle whorls were more personal objects and often were decorated or of higher quality and may have been part of a woman's assemblage for a longer time and potentially have more sentimental value. The rarity of spindles, if not a function of the absence of spinning in the Sanctuary, and of other weaving equipment in the Sanctuary may suggest fewer religious dedicatory offerings of this nature and strengthens the hypothesis that the majority of the loomweights present in the Sanctuary were used for cultic weaving.

The discovery of 19 loomweights isolated in or very near a small room gives clear evidence for weaving here. Most likely fallen from a loom set up in the West Annex, these weights illustrate an activity within the Sanctuary that had a strong religious purpose. Documentation of such ritual practice, however, is scarce, especially in the archaeological record. The adornment of cult statues with garments or cloth is familiar from literary sources,[43] but evidence as to where the garment was woven is very unusual. Inventory and dedicatory lists from sanctuaries frequently record clothing among the dedications;[44] however, not all references to the clothing of a cult statue are associated with the ritual of weaving. The dedication of the woven garments often followed a procession to the cult statue, indicating that the clothing of the statue was secondary to the ritual of weaving and presentation of the sacred garment.[45] Homer (*Il.* 6.269–311) mentions a procession of women from the palace at Troy carrying a beautiful robe to be placed on the knees of the cult statue of Athena. In Alkman's *Partheneion* (*l.* 61), there is a description of the dedication of an object which an ancient commentator noted was a plough, but which might also be interpreted as a robe, to Artemis Orthia.[46] Additionally, evidence from Argos refers to the weavers of a garment for Hera at the Argive Heraion and possibly also for Athena at Argos.[47] The dedication of a cloth or robe was a common practice in Greek cult whether for a cult statue or simply to be hung as a dedication, as were the ritual activities of its production and display.

Evidence for the ritual act of weaving within a sanctuary precinct, however, is rare. Pausanias mentions that at Olympia a special robe for Hera was woven by 16 women, one from each of the districts of Elis. The weaving took place in a building in the marketplace built specifically for this purpose.[48] A chiton was woven annually by women at Amyklai for the image of Apollo. A separate room was assigned for this purpose.[49] Furthermore, a larger group of 22 loomweights was found in Room F, in a building across the road from the sanctuary of Athena Poliouchos on the acropolis of Halai.

Here the correlation between loomweights and sacred weaving was supported by a mid-third-century BCE inscription mentioning a group of officials called "petamnyphanterai" (πεταμνυφάντεραι), the weavers of the spreading cloth or weavers of hangings, who carried out weaving as part of the cult rituals.[50]

At Ilion (Troy), 15 terracotta loomweights and 4 spindle whorls were found together in a votive pit located below the sanctuary of Athena Ilias and may be the discarded material from cultic weaving materials from this sanctuary.[51] At Foce del Sele in southern Italy, 266 loomweights were found in a square building, the Edificio Quadrato, in the sanctuary of Hera. Although there is no consensus on the function of the building, the large quantity of weaving equipment within this building and its proximity to the Heraion suggested to Greco and de La Genière that it was used by women in the production of cloth associated with the cult.[52]

Elaborately decorated loomweights, dated by the excavator to the eighth century BCE, have been found in a sanctuary at the indigenous site at Francavilla Marittima in south Italy, which was later colonized by Greeks. Their presence in two rows on the floor of a building which became a temple in a later phase indicates the presence of a loom. It is suggested that women with special positions in the local society were involved in ceremonial weaving, in association with a goddess.[53] This indicates the significant role played by weaving in the lives of local women and in ritual practices prior to Greek colonization. The practice apparently continued after Greek contact. The primary deity presiding over this sanctuary in the Greek period was Athena.[54] A terracotta plaque of a goddess within a naiskos in the Museo Nazionale della Sibaritide has been associated with this same sanctuary at Timpone della Motta, and dated to the second half of the seventh century. The goddess has been identified as Athena, and the object on her lap is identified as a folded peplos.[55] Two other terracottas, from the sixth century, depict women holding what are taken to be cloths in their hands, which they perhaps wove as gifts for the goddess.[56]

In addition, the most detailed account of ritual weaving and the dedication of a garment for the gods is the peplos dedicated annually to Athena as part of the ceremonies of the Panathenaia festival in Athens. The peplos, used to clothe the cult statue, was woven by four specially selected young girls (arrephoroi) and women (ergastinai) from aristocratic families as part of the cult rituals. The ceremonial weaving began when the ergastinai set up a special loom at the Chalkeia festival, celebrated nine months prior to the Panathenaia festival.[57] The production of the peplos became part of the ritual, culminating in the dedication of the robe to Athena at the end of the Panathenaic procession.

Another peplos was woven every four years for the Greater Panathenaia and was openly displayed as a sail for the sacred ship in the Greater Panathenaia. This peplos was made in addition to one made to clothe the xoanon. The weaving of the sail peplos was done by professional male weavers who competed for the contract and honour of weaving it for Athena.[58] Mansfield emphasizes the distinction between professional weaving sponsored by the state and weaving with direct cult and religious affiliations.

The location of the weaving ritual is unknown. Presumably the professional weavers would have produced their cloth in their own workshops; however, since the arrephoroi and ergastinai held a religious office, it is plausible that the weaving occurred within a sanctuary, perhaps around or on the Acropolis where the arrephoroi resided.[59] It is possible that the ritual, connected with Hephaistos and Athena Ergane in the Chalkeia, occurred within the Agora, as at Olympia. Neither the literary nor the archaeological sources indicate where the loom was set up, so attempting to pinpoint the location of ritual weaving in connection with the Panathenaia is speculative.

It was, of course, common in the Greek world for ritual activity to occur within the precinct of sanctuaries, making it probable that auxiliary buildings within sanctuaries were the location of such cultic activities, including ritual weaving. Thus, the production and dedication of a peplos to clothe the cult statue, as evidenced in the literary and archaeological record, support a connection between ritual weaving and a location within or very close to sanctuaries.

It was clearly an honour for women to be chosen to participate in weaving a garment for a divinity. The task of weaving and the ceremonial presentation of the sacred cloth were important activities incorporated into cult ritual. Dressing the cult statue in elaborate woven garments may be associated with effigies, anthropomorphic statues, and semi-shaped statues as well as shapeless aniconic pillars representing both male and female gods. The garments themselves were visible manifestations of the care devoted to the deity. A strong correlation exists between the presence of weaving and the clothing of the cult statue and is likely connected with the integration and participation of women in sacred activities. Clothing of the cult statue, however, was an ancient tradition and cannot be seen as synonymous with ritual weaving.

The presence of weaving equipment and cloth as votives is found primarily in sanctuaries dedicated to Hera, Artemis, and Athena. At many sites, the deity associated with weaving is Athena, the patroness of handicrafts, particularly weaving. In fact, it is primarily through this activity that Athena was affiliated with the feminine world as manifested in her worship.

The ritual act of weaving garments for cult statues may have been rare. Mansfield suggests that the practice of communal weaving of garments for dedication as part of cult ritual may have been "synoikismic," where places that experienced synoikism may have used the practice to help unify the community – for example, at Athens, Argos, Olympia, and Sparta.[60] Stymphalos may offer another example, since the creation of a new town in the earlier part of the fourth century may have brought together peoples from the older site of Stymphalos, as well as other villages in the valley.

Weaving is also linked with the Athena Polias cult. In the sanctuary of Athena at Halai, the existence of officials specifically named as weavers indicates the importance of this task. Similarly in Athens, the arrephoroi are specifically dedicated to the task of weaving a ritual garment for Athena Polias which was then displayed publicly in a ceremonial procession around the city. Following the Athenian tradition, a similar festival and ritual, modelled on the Panathenaia and including the weaving of the peplos, were celebrated at Ilion in honour of the goddess Athena Polias. Such strong affiliations between the cult of Athena Polias and weaving may also exist at Stymphalos; however, it is worth keeping in mind that Eileithyia was also worshipped in the acropolis Sanctuary. When Pausanias (8.21.3) described the nearby city of Kleitor, he noted the temple of Eileithyia there, and added that Olen, a poet from Lycia, composed some hymns for the Delians, including one to Eileithyia, where she is called the fine weaver.[61] It bears noting as well that Pausanias (7.23.6) describes a cult statue of this goddess which he saw at Aigion, not so far from Stymphalos, made of wood (body) and marble (head, hands, and feet), which he says was covered from head to foot in a finely woven garment. It is possible that the same situation occurred at Stymphalos, and that the "finely woven" garment was made right in the Sanctuary. In either case, Athena or Eileithyia, the association with weaving is important.

It is clear then that evidence for cloth production as part of the cult activities in Stymphalos' Sanctuary on the acropolis is manifested in two ways: through votive offerings and through the ritual weaving of a sacred cloth. Scattered concentrations of loomweights, such as those found south of the Temple or east of the Altar, suggest the common practice of dedicatory offerings, made primarily by women to female deities, including Athena. The individual motives for the dedications are obscure, but the offerings may be viewed as symbolic gestures representing the value of weaving in Greek society and its importance as an economic, social, and religious activity in women's lives, bonding the dedicator to her deity. The loomweight would thus represent a bond between women and the goddess.

On the other hand, on the basis of context and arrangement, the cluster of 19 loomweights in the West Annex indicates the practice of weaving within the Sanctuary precinct itself. This small room was tucked away between the Temple, Building A, and the Pillar Shrine area, just out of sight of the Altar. Within this small room, evidence suggests that a loom was set up and used to weave cloths presumably used in the cult, perhaps as at Athens, as a sacred garment for the cult statue.

The Sanctuary on the acropolis at Stymphalos may have been established, or perhaps simply rejuvenated, by the move of the old town to its site on the ridge overlooking the lake. Stymphalos was allied with Athens in the fourth century, and the close relations of the two may have led to similarities in the worship of Athena Polias, including the well-attested annual ritual of weaving for the goddess.

13

Faunal Remains: Environment and Ritual in the Stymphalos Valley[1]

Deborah Ruscillo

INTRODUCTION

Since antiquity, the lake has been the centre of activity in the Stymphalos Valley. Bronze Age settlers were drawn to the lake and its natural resources as attested by polished stone celts going back at least to the third millennium BCE. As early as the Archaic period, the lake was made famous in myth by the sixth labour of Herakles, where the hero eradicated the troublesome Stymphalian birds from the area. The lower town site (Stym I), excavated by a team from the University of British Columbia in the 1990s, provides archaeological evidence for the habitation of the site during the late Classical, Hellenistic, and early Roman periods. In the thirteenth century CE, the location was known as *Zaraka* by the Cistercian monks who dwelled here, building an impressive abbey and compound.[2] The modern village of Stymphalia/Kionia is home to about 200 people, ensuring the continuity of life along the swampy edge of the lake. The known history and prehistory of human settlement here spans some five millennia, if not longer.

Humans have not been drawn to this valley solely for its water resources, however. The lush green environment has been home to an extensive array of fauna, many now extinct, including two or three species of deer, wild boar, lynx, otter, beaver, wolf, bear, and a host of sedentary and migratory birds. The varieties of freshwater fish, crustaceans, amphibians, and reptiles represented from excavations in the lower town site, the acropolis site, and the Cistercian monastery are impressive compared to other areas of Greece. Alas, many of these exotica have since become extinct or extirpated from the area due to environmental changes and overhunting by inhabitants through the centuries. In recent times, the lake has been overgrown with reeds because of fertilizers in the ground water from farming, making life for the aquatic species here increasingly difficult. Today, domestic animals exceed the local wild mammalian species, perhaps with the exception of rodents; the animal and crop farming in and around Stymphalos today has overshadowed the idyllic nature of the lake and its ecological balance.

The lake is an area of interest for environmentalists and ornithologists. Over 260 species of migrant and year-round species of bird live in the region of the lake and valley. The area is also rich in amphibian and reptile species; several species of salamander, newt, frog, toad, tortoise, terrapin, gecko, lizard, skink, and snake are also found here.

Countless empty gunshot shells found around the lake testify to the attraction of the area to hunters, who predominantly shoot certain species of birds, as attested by the number of birdshot shells, but hunt wild rabbit and hare as well. Bigger game, such as wild boar and deer, can no longer be found in the area.

Atop the acropolis of the town is the site of a Classical/Hellenistic temple and sanctuary. The site has a panoramic perspective of the lake and environs; its views and commanding position must have inspired awe in visitors here. The Sanctuary became popular in the fourth century and continued in use till the second century BCE, when it was largely destroyed, though some limited use may have continued into the Roman period.

THE FAUNAL SAMPLE FROM THE ACROPOLIS

Forty-four species of molluscs, crustaceans, amphibians, fish, reptiles, birds, and mammals were identified from the sample of over 11,380 specimens, weighing just over 30 kilograms. Preservation of bones in the sample was poor, owing to the location of the Sanctuary in the Stymphalian valley. The general humidity of the valley coupled with the erosion of the hilltop from the seasonal rains and winds provided an inhospitable environment for the preservation of organic materials. Other factors that contributed to the poor preservation of the bones were animal butchery, the use of bone as raw material for tools, the intentional breaking of bones to gain access to the marrow, rodent and canid gnawing, and heavy traffic in the areas in and around the Sanctuary during its occupation.

Of the 11,380 specimens, approximately 58% of the sample could not be identified beyond "class" (fish, avian, mammalian). More diagnostic specimens were identified to either genus or species. Sieving of the soil from the excavations produced bones of microfauna, including fish, amphibians, reptiles, birds, and small rodents, but these comprised a small percentage of the entire assemblage. Larger bones were washed in find groups using mesh bags dipped in buckets of water.[3] The results of the species identifications from this study can be viewed in table 13.1.

Mammalian bones were better preserved than those of other orders of animals. There is no doubt that fish were underrepresented in the sample, the site being in such close proximity to the lake. Samples from the medieval monastery, for example, produced many more fish and bird bones.[4] The frequency of avian and fish remains from Zaraka could be a reflection of food selection or recreation by the monks, i.e., fishing and falconry practices. The younger age of the bones warrants better recovery and preservation; the faunal sample from the monastery is about 1500 years younger than the sample from the acropolis.

In this assemblage, there are five specimens that have been brought to the site from a marine source: *Cerithium*, *Murex*, *Pecten*, *Tonna*, and Sparidae. Each of these species is represented by a single specimen. Three species are gastropods (*Cerithium*, *Murex*, *Tonna*), one is a bivalve (*Pecten*), and the other is a premaxilla from a sea bream (Sparidae family). Geological work in the Stymphalian valley shows that these specimens could not have been deposited naturally in local bedrock or overlying geological strata.[5] Rather, they have likely been deposited culturally by inhabitants at the site. The closest marine source is the Gulf of Corinth some 45 km north of the site. Lake Stymphalos has no rivers leading to the Gulf of Corinth or the Gulf of Argos to the east. The finding of scutes from the European stur-

Table 13.1. Species represented in the faunal sample from the acropolis, Stymphalos

Molluscs	
Bivalves	
**Pecten jacobaeus*	Scallop
Gastropods	
Clausilia	Door snail
**Cerithium vulgatum*	Common cerith
Euconulus fulvus	Tawny glass snail
**Murex trunculus*	Truncated dye snail
**Tonna galea*	Tun shell
Helicella	Heath snail
Helix aspersa	Common garden snail
Three unidentified species	Freshwater snails
Crustaceans	
Potamiscus sp.	Freshwater crab
Amphibians	
Rana sp.	Lake frog
Reptiles	
Snake	
Lacerta trilineata	Three-lined lizard
Testudo hermanni	Hermann's tortoise
Fish	
*Sparidae	Sea bream
Leuciscus cephalus moreoticus	Chub
Birds	
Aves sp.	Bird
Gallus gallus	Chicken
Grus grus	Common crane
Picidae	Woodpecker
Sturnus vulgaris	Starling
Turdus viscivorus	Mistle thrush
Rodents	
Lepus europaeus	European hare
Microtus guentheri	Guenther's vole
Microtus sp.	Vole
Orychtolagus cunnilicus	Wild rabbit
Rattus rattus	Black rat
Other mammals	
Bos taurus	Cattle
Canis familiaris	Dog
Canis lupus	Wolf
Capra hircus	Goat
Capreolus capreolus	Roe deer
Castor fiber/Lutra lutra	Beaver or otter
Cervus elaphus	Red deer
Dama dama	Fallow deer
Equus asinas	Donkey
Felis catus	Cat
Homo sapiens	Human
Martes foina	Beech marten
Ovis aries	Sheep
Sus scrofa	Pig
Vulpes vulpes	Fox

* = Species originating from a marine source

geon among the archaeological faunal remains from the medieval dump at the Zaraka monastery might initially suggest that there was a river nearby; sturgeon grow to an impressive size and therefore require large rivers in which to live and spawn. That this large river was located in the valley is highly unlikely; even in antiquity, the lake was landlocked with a subterranean outflow, believed by ancients to emerge near Lerna 50 km away:

> For once, when Cleomenes had sent to Delphi to consult the oracle, it was prophesied to him that he should take Argos; upon which he went out at the head of the Spartans, and led them to the river Erasinus. This stream is reported to flow from the Stymphalian lake, the waters of which empty themselves into a pitch-dark chasm, and then (as they say) reappear in Argos, where the Argives call them the Erasinus. (Hdt. 6.76.1; translation G. Rawlinson, *The Greek Historians*)

The lake is not large, spreading during the rainy season and shrinking in the dry summer months. Coring information has revealed that the lake has never been deeper than two metres.[6] Interestingly, there is a visible sinkhole on the southern edge of the lake which drains and controls the expansion of the waters.[7] The sturgeon and bream then must have been brought from other areas as a smoked or salted item. Other fish remains resemble those of the local species of chub (*Leuciscus cephalus moreoticus*), which is still extant in the lake. There are rumours that carp may also exist in the lake, but I have not been able to confirm this.

Other marine species occurring in the sample, specifically *Cerithium*, *Murex*, and *Pecten*, are commonly found in the sub-littoral and littoral shores of the sea, while Tonids and Sparids are found off shore. Dead specimens, of course, can be found washed up on beaches. It is probable that the marine molluscs were brought as souvenirs from the sea, though it is not clear whether the specimens were collected dead from the beach.

Potamiscus sp. is a freshwater crab that can still be found in the local water system. Their remains are typically represented by either the upper or lower part of the claw, perhaps the thickest part of the shell. Most of the freshwater and terrestrial species of gastropods are indigenous and are extant around the lake. There are currently three species of frog that live in Stymphalia; partial remains of a few bones seem to represent one species of amphibian.[8]

Of the many reptiles found in the valley, only three species are represented in the faunal assemblage, a snake, a three-lined lizard, and Hermann's tortoise. The snake and lizard are assumed intrusive, but the tortoise occurs more frequently and requires closer examination. The marginated tortoise (*Testudo marginata*) occurs in the valley as well, but not the common Greek tortoise (*Testudo graeca*).[9]

The bird remains found on the site represent both wild and domestic species. Chicken remains are the only ones that can be identified confidently as a domesticated avian species exploited primarily as a food source. Although many recreational birds, such as starlings and thrushes (*Sturnus*, *Turdus*), have been known to be selectively hunted and eaten by locals, it is difficult to determine whether these individuals were consumed for food. Woodpecker and crane (Picidae, *Grus*) are even less recognized in modern Greece as food items, though we know that Romans, for example, ate the latter (Apicius, Book IV, Ch. 2). Of course, all avian species can be eaten, but some of these remains could be incidental and intrusive; birds could die on site, or be caught by cats. A cat mandible was found in the Sanctuary assemblage, but it is unlikely that the cat was contemporary with the occupation of the site because the specimen was a surface find.

There is good evidence that both rabbits and hares were consumed by site occupants, while smaller rodents like rats and mice were likely intrusive. It is not clear whether rabbits were domesticated by site occupants or were hunted from feral populations. The black rat was probably a modern intrusion, since this species did not occur here in antiquity but was introduced in the historical period.

A single bone shaft of an otter or beaver was identified in the sample. Beaver and otter remains have been identified elsewhere in the valley (Stymphalos I and Zaraka, identified by the author). Beaver are now extinct in the Peloponnese while otter still occur. Otter (*Lutra lutra*) remains were also identified from the archaeological fauna of Lerna.[10]

A few domestic dog (*Canis familiaris*) bones were found in a variety of sizes. Wolf-sized canid bones were discovered in the assemblage. Rather than assuming that these were from a large breed of dog, one can expect the presence of wolf in the forested environment of the lake, perhaps hunted by inhabitants or even offered at the Sanctuary. Apollodorus gives the only account of wolves in the description of Herakles' sixth labour:

> The sixth labour he enjoined on him was to chase away the Stymphalian birds. Now at the city of Stymphalus in Arcadia was the lake called Stymphalian, embosomed in

a deep wood. To it countless birds had flocked for refuge, fearing to be preyed upon by the wolves. (Apollod. 2.5.6; Loeb translation)

The presence of two fox mandibles and long bones suggests that fox too may have been hunted. It is remarkable that these three canid species once inhabited the valley; fox and domestic dog are still found here.

Three individuals of beech marten were identified in the sample; this species is still common in the area. There is no clear evidence that this mustelid was placed in the archaeological record by humans, except by association in the same contexts as other wild animals such as hare, fox, wolf, otter, and deer.

Besides the remains of canids, there is evidence that perhaps three species of deer were hunted by inhabitants as well. Identifications from antler fragments provide an indication that roe deer (*Capreolus*), fallow deer (*Dama*), and red deer (*Cervus*) co-existed in the lush forests surrounding the valley; however, the central shaft of fallow and red deer antler can be similar during different stages of development, so *Dama* antler fragment identifications have been made cautiously. Likewise with long bone fragments; metric analyses of bones have shown that female red deer and male fallow deer overlap considerably, more so than male roe deer and female fallow deer.[11] In any case, the poor preservation of bones from this site did not warrant a metrical study of the archaeological bone. Thus, *Capreolus* and *Cervus* have been positively identified from the faunal remains, while the medium-sized species, *Dama*, has been identified tentatively.

The expected three species of domesticated bovids found on most Greek archaeological sites were identified (*Bos*, *Capra*, *Ovis*). These comprise the greater part of the sample from the acropolis in Stymphalos. Few specimens of cattle (*Bos*) were found, and almost all were from adults. Given the age of the cattle individuals and the osteological evidence of stress, particularly on the phalanges, cattle seem to have been exploited primarily for their use as beasts of burden. Cows could well have been exploited for their secondary products as well, and calving. From the culling age and sex profiles of sheep and goat, these domesticates seem to have been kept for meat (young males) and secondary products (older females).

There is evidence of both wild and domesticated pigs in the faunal remains from the Sanctuary. The frequency of pigs and their age profiles suggest a controlled culling pattern typical of herded animals. There are also fragments of large male tusks found, typical of wild individuals. Both seem to have been exploited by the inhabitants of the site.

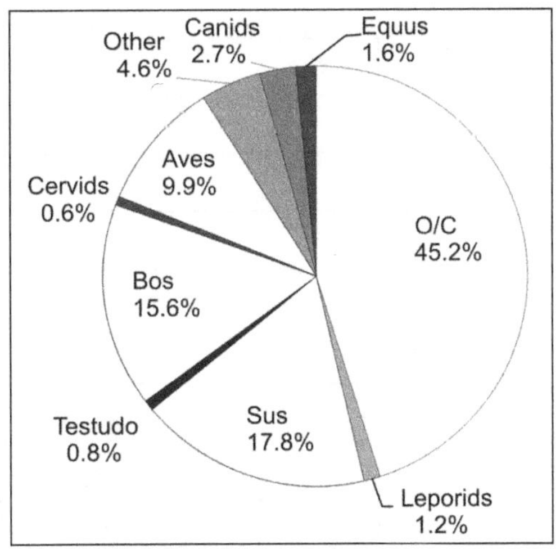

Chart 13.1. Summary of identifiable species from the acropolis site

STATISTICAL SUMMARY

All bone fragments were counted from each bag collected from excavations of the Sanctuary. Fragments smaller than 0.5 cm were not counted unless they were diagnostic. Of the specimens in the sample, 58.4% (6774) of the bones were unidentifiable. These can be said with certainty to be mammalian or avian remains, but genus could not be determined. The identifiable sample, i.e., 41.6% (4822), provides the species information. The frequency of species represented in the bone assemblage from the acropolis is summarized by chart 13.1. As is typical of most historical sites in Greece, bovids are predominant in the sample. Over 45% of the identifiable specimens are sheep or goat remains. Of these specimens, 14% could be further distinguished as either sheep or goat. From the diagnostic bovid remains, goats (225 specimens) were represented 2.5 times more than identifiable sheep remains (92). This statistic, if reflective of the whole sample, may represent a preference for goat over sheep for meat or sacrifice. Sheep may have been primarily kept for wool and milk, while goats were preferred for sacrificing or offering at the Sanctuary.

Chart 13.2 summarizes the age profile of the sheep and goats in the sample. Most of the specimens are between the ages of one and two years. The "Immature+"

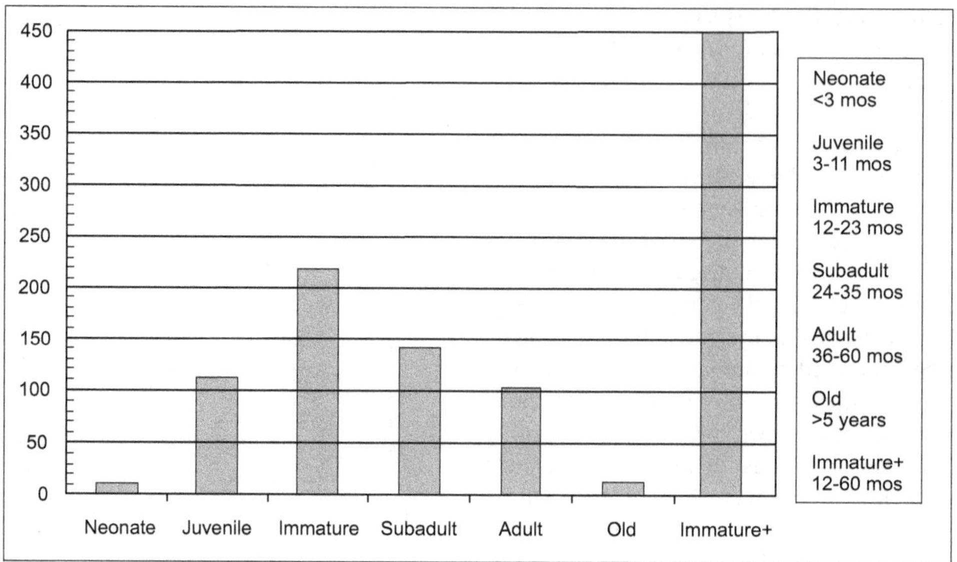

Chart 13.2. The age profile of sheep and goat specimens

category represents specimens that fall between the ages of 12 and 60 months, determined by the state of the cortical bone, which was neither juvenile nor very mature; no fusion data, dental eruption, or attrition data were available from these specimens. In general, the peak in the immature category usually indicates a meat-culling strategy for bovids. In the context of a sanctuary, the profile indicates younger animals being selected for offering to the deity.

Pig remains represent almost 18% of the sample. It is difficult to determine whether these specimens represent domestic or wild pigs (or both), simply because of the fragmentary condition of the bones. From the specimens that could be sexed, 16 males were identified compared to 13 females. In general, males are more visible in a bone assemblage because of their larger size in adulthood and canine morphological differences. The fact that 16 males exist in the sample presents a good case that wild boar were hunted. Males, save for one or two studs, are not usually herded because of their aggressive behaviour. Most male piglets are castrated within the first week of life and fattened for 6–24 months. The objective of castration is threefold: 1) without androgens, the individual becomes sluggish and gains weight more readily, 2) the meat has a less offensive smell, and 3) the individuals are more docile to herd.

Chart 13.3 indicates that pigs of all ages were slaughtered, which might be interpreted as random age killing, as in hunted individuals, rather than strategic culling of a domestic herd. No doubt some of these individuals were hunted, given the lush forest surroundings, which would have been suitable to sustain a healthy population of wild boar; however, the profile shows a peak configuration, spiking during the immature stage of growth (12–23 months old). Moreover, the broader group "Immature+" shown at the end of the columns in chart 13.3 was assigned to specimens from which age could not be accurately assigned, such as bone shafts. If the Immature+ individuals were added to the Immature, Subadult, and/or Adult groups, the representation of these ages would increase considerably, and the peak on the chart would become more impressive. Therefore, a culling pattern is present with a preference for individuals older than one year and younger than five. This pattern is typical of a meat strategy from herded animals. It is likely that domestic pigs were slaughtered for feasting or ritual use but occasionally hunted as well.

Cattle remains occurred regularly in all contexts and represent almost 16% of the sample. A large cattle skeleton, however, could produce many more fragments than a smaller animal. The MNI for the cattle remains is approximately 16 individuals across the whole site. The age of the remains is of older individuals.

Several cattle bones show stress indicators on selected elements which are consistent with animals used in traction.[12] Figures 13.4a and 13.4b show the distal and proximal phalanges from an old *Bos* individual with osteoarthritis perhaps from the stress of pulling weight, either as a draught animal or a beast of burden. The hooves of this individual must have been under consid-

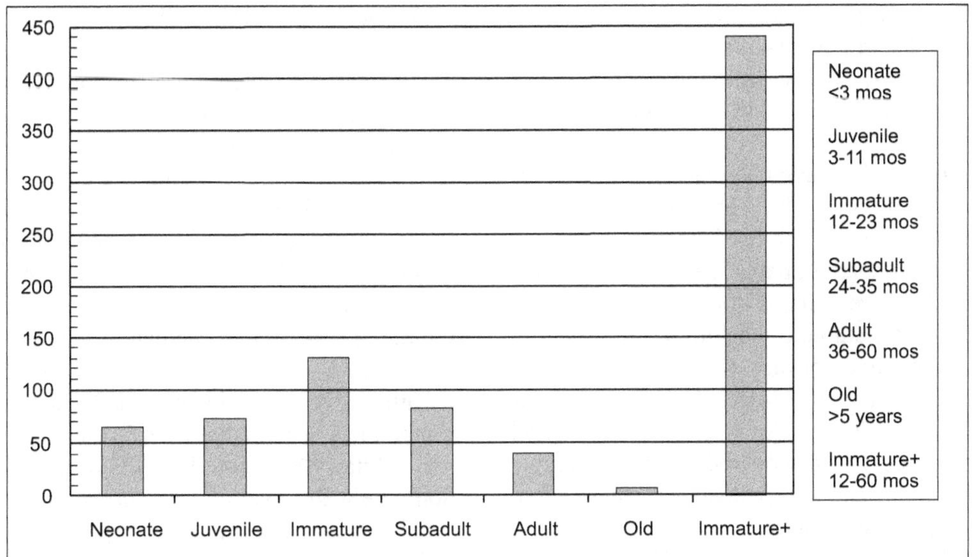

Chart 13.3. The age profile of pig specimens

erable strain for years during its life, enough to cause trauma to the phalanges.

Another interesting specimen in the assemblage was a horn core from a cattle cranium. A smooth indentation around the base of the horn core is typical of the friction groove created by a harness strapped on the head of the individual. Such marks are typically made by the harness of a yoke attached to the head for plough gear, for example. The combination of stress on the skeleton combined with the older age of the animals suggests that cattle were kept for traction and perhaps for secondary products, namely milk and dairy products and manure.

The fourth most frequently occurring taxa were avian. Surprisingly, about 10% of the sample comprised bird remains. Bird bones are rarely found in significant quantities from ancient sites, so it is remarkable that birds are so well represented in this poorly preserved sample. There must have been many more avian specimens that did not survive in the archaeological record for 453 bird bones to be extant among a sample 4800 bones.

Over 30% of the bird assemblage comprised chicken remains (*Gallus gallus*), indicating a preference for domesticated fowl for food and/or ritual. The other avian species in the assemblage were crane (*Grus grus*), mistle thrush (*Turdus viscivorus*), starling (*Sturnis vulgaris*), and a species of woodpecker (Picidae family). Three hundred and five avian bones were unidentifiable to family. As stated above, any bird species could be eaten, though specimens like the woodpecker, for example, could be intrusive in the sample either by natural death or deposition by a carnivorous animal; however, with the variety of bird species drawn to the waters of the lake and the surrounding trees, it is likely that wild birds would be exploited by inhabitants of the site, as they still are today. Their context in a sanctuary is particularly interesting and could help identify the deity to whom the Sanctuary was dedicated.

The presence of birds, leporids, and wild boar makes the low representation of cervid remains in the faunal assemblage perplexing. If the inhabitants of the site were indeed avid hunters, why then were deer remains (0.6%) so scarce? There are two possibilities: first, venison may not have been appropriate meat for consumption or sacrifice at the Temple, or secondly, the inhabitants preferred to hunt smaller game species. The deer remains are mostly red deer, though a medium-sized and smaller-sized cervid is extant in the sample, fallow and roe deer respectively. The MNI for deer is ten individuals.

In the leporid assemblage, both species *Lepus europaeus* and *Orychtolagus cunnilicus* are represented. In the valley, both species may have been hunted; *Orychtolagus* (rabbit) may have been from a feral population. Of course, rabbits could also have been domesticated. Hare and feral rabbits are still hunted in the area, and domestic rabbits are kept for food, though hunting has recently become more recreational than a necessity. Hare occurs in nine out of ten contexts studied below. Because leporids occur in all areas within the Sanctuary, it appears that their presence here is not accidental. There are over 30 Attic vases that depict hares and rabbits in different scenarios, though few are in ritual contexts. At Stymphalos, fragments of a kore holding a hare have been identified by Mary Sturgeon.[13] The leporid bones may then have a direct association with the deity at this site.

Some tortoise remains have been identified; they are commonly found around the hills in the valley. It is remarkable, however, that of the ten locations examined below in the faunal spatial analysis, eight contain tortoise remains. These are remains of Hermann's tortoise, a smaller species of testudinid reaching up to 35 cm in length. The marginated tortoise (*Testudo marginata*) also occurs in this region but does not appear in the sample; it is as if the specific species was selected. A burnt segment of carapace was discovered from the Temple interior. There is not enough evidence to suggest that this particular specimen was from a sacrificial victim; perhaps it was burnt along with rubbish. There are plenty of iconographic representations of tortoise carapace used as a base for the strings of a lyre.[14] It is possible that the shells were used as instruments or even bowls in the Sanctuary, and this is the reason why tortoiseshell parts are occurring so regularly. There were instances, however, when tortoises were offered to deities (see discussion below).

Canids represent 2.7% of the sample; this statistic was increased by the find of a complete dog skeleton found buried in the tower wall.[15] This statistic also includes wolf remains and fox remains. Though not usually hunted for food, these wild canids could have been hunted for their pelts,[16] or as sacrificial victims. As for domestic dogs (*Canis familiaris*), the remains could represent discarded remains of companions, or disturbed dog burials. Spatial analysis of the site, however, reveals that canid remains occur in nine of the ten contexts of the Sanctuary. Again, these species appear to be purposefully selected for the deity at the site.

Donkey (*Equus asinas*) was represented by several specimens at the site. The donkeys were mature in age and may or may not be directly associated with activities at the site. Though occurring relatively infrequently compared to other taxa in the assemblage (35 specimens total), donkey occurred in eight of the ten contexts at the site.

Within the "Other" category, there are another 22 species, including terrestrial and aquatic molluscs, fish, amphibians, reptiles, and some mammals, including hedgehog, cat, beech marten, mouse, and rat. Twenty-seven fragments of human remains likely originate from the burial just inside the northeastern corner of the Temple.[17]

SPATIAL DISTRIBUTION OF FINDS

The faunal data were divided into ten different locales by provenance. These locales were demarcated by trenches coinciding with architectural features. All other fauna from trenches that were excavated without a clear relationship to a particular building or feature were compiled into a broader, more general group "Sanctuary Grounds." The ten locales have been marked on the site plan in figure 13.1; they are 1) the interior of the Temple, 2) the area immediately outside the perimeter of the Temple, 3) the Pillar Shrine, 4) the West Annex of Building A, 5) the interior of Building A, 6) the area immediately around the Altar, 7) the terrace area in front of the Altar, 8) the interior of Building B, 9) the areas along the wall tower and within the towers, and 10) the remaining areas of the Sanctuary grounds. Each locale will be discussed separately and then an overview of the faunal remains will be offered to determine if they can help identify the deity to whom the Temple was dedicated.

1. The Temple interior

Faunal remains from the trenches excavated within the Temple produced an interesting variety of species, including human remains, likely from the multiple-use burial found in the northeast corner of the Temple. Table 13.2 summarizes the faunal finds.

Table 13.2. Summary of the fauna from the Temple interior

Species	No. of specimens	MNI	Comments
Aves	29		
Bivalvia	1	1	
Bos taurus	1	1	
Capra hircus	2	1	
Cerithium vulgatum	1	1	
Equus asinas	1	1	
Gallus gallus	19		
Homo sapiens	27	1	Neonate
Martes foina	2	1	
Ovis/Capra	10		1 burnt rib
Ovis aries	1	1	
Sus scrofa	32		
Testudo hermanni	1	1	Burnt
Turdus viscivorus	1	1	
Unidentifiable	208		
Total	336		

In this context from within the main Temple, the most notable aspect of this assemblage is the number of avian specimens. Avian bones (49) outnumber even the common bovid (13) and pig bones (32). One could argue that perhaps birds made nests in the Temple after abandonment, which might account for the occurrence of many avian individuals here, but around 40% of these birds are domestic chicken. Clearly, the fact that many birds occur here is not accidental; they must have been involved in the activities of the worshippers at the shrine, unless the small amount of medieval glass found inside the Temple indicates a kind of picnic spot on occasion at this later period.[18] Notable also are the two specimens of shells, at least one of them marine, as well as two of the only four beech marten specimens found on the site. The burnt tortoise carapace segment is possibly a remnant of a sacrificial victim.

2. The Temple exterior

Six hundred and sixty-three bones were excavated from the perimeter of the Temple exterior. It is difficult to determine whether these had any direct relation with the activities being performed within the Temple. This locale was created either to isolate bones from the excavation of the foundation trenches at the time of construction of the Temple, or to capture any specimens that may have been disposed of through a possible window that may have been constructed in the original building. Fauna, perhaps part of clean-out, have been found discarded through windows of other early Greek temples.[19]

Table 13.3. Summary of the fauna from the Temple exterior

Species	No. of specimens	MNI	Comments
Aves	4	1	
Bos taurus	49	1	4 butchered frs, 1 male
Canis familiaris	2	1	
Capra hircus	20	1	
Cervus elaphus	3	1	
Equus asinas	2	1	
Gallus gallus	3	1	
Helix aspersa	5	1	
Lepus europaeus	1	1	
Ovis/Capra	97	1	
Ovis aries	2	1	4 butchered frs, 1 female identified
Pecten jacobaeus	4	1	
Sus scrofa	32	5	2 butchered frs, 1 male identified
Testudo hermanni	2	1	
Unidentifiable	427		110 calcined juvenile mammalian bone pcs
Total	653		

Table 13.3 summarizes the fauna from this locale. Interestingly, the variety of fauna found in these trenches is similar to that within the Temple. With the exception of the human remains from the intrusive burial within the Temple, the species list from the exterior resembles that from the interior. Two marine species, *Cerithium* and a piece of a bivalve, were found within the Temple. These species were not found elsewhere on the site, yet another marine species *Pecten* was found here.

There are significant differences between the samples, however. Primarily, the sheer number of specimens is doubled in the exterior sample. This is not surprising considering that the Temple floor must have been swept from time to time; garbage would have been discarded outside the Temple once rituals or activities were completed. This may explain the 110 calcined juvenile (perhaps piglets, kids, and/or lambs) scraps found on the exterior of the Temple. Because they are calcined and very young, these animals may well have been holocaust sacrificial offerings, an idea supported by their provenance close to the Temple. The fact that other specimens of older animals were not found burnt indicates that juvenile individuals were selected for this type of ritual treatment, and not part of some general garbage dump burning. Suids were equally represented inside and out (32 specimens in each sample).

A remarkable, and perhaps most significant, difference between the samples is the amount of bird remains. There are seven times as many bird remains inside the Temple as outside. From inside the Temple, 49 avian specimens (including chicken) were recovered, while outside only 7 were found, despite the larger sample size. To support the significance of this observation, it is notable that bovids (sheep, goat, cattle) are represented ten times more outside than in (only 11 specimens inside, 126 outside). In other words, the common ritual offerings of bovids were *not* found in the Temple, but avian species were. This difference in the samples seems to suggest that birds were more commonly offered to the deity inside the Temple, while burnt sacrifice and communal feasting would have occurred outside the building.

3. The Pillar Shrine

Very few bones were found in this area close to the stelae. It does not appear that activities involving animals occurred here, though the locale may have been important for worship or perhaps even secular activities. Table 13.4 summarizes the scanty faunal remains found in relevant trenches in this locale.

Table 13.4. Summary of the fauna from the Pillar Shrine area

Species	No. of specimens	MNI	Comments
Aves	2	1	
Bos Taurus	5	1	
Canis familiaris	7	1	
Capra hircus	4	1	
Dama dama?	1	1	Female *C. elapus* premolar?
Equus asinas	2	1	
Gallus gallus	4	1	
Helicella sp.	3	1	
Lepus europaeus	1	1	
Ovis/Capra	46	3	2 female pubes identified
Ovis aries	13	3	
Sus scrofa	11	3	2 female teeth, 1 butchered mid radius
Unidentifiable	165		
Total	264		

Not only are there few remains here, but the preservation is especially poor. There are no burnt specimens and only one butchered pig bone. There is nothing remarkable about this sample, and it is doubtful that any of these bones were *in situ*. They resemble in composition dump similar to that found in other areas of the Sanctuary grounds (see subsection 10 below). If rituals were performed in this locale, it would more likely have been performed in the adjacent West Annex of Building A. Similar to the Temple interior, and perhaps just as interesting, this area seems to have been kept clean, swept periodically of all the debris that could have been brought in by traffic.

4. The interior of the West Annex of Building A

An extension of Building A seems to have been added on at a later stage of the Sanctuary. While its use is somewhat cryptic given the poor preservation of the architectural remains, the fauna present a compelling case for specific ritual activities involving birds, like those found on the interior of the Temple. Table 13.5 summarizes the fauna found from within the West Annex.

Table 13.5. Summary of the fauna from the West Annex of Building A

Species	No. of specimens	MNI	Comments
Aves	66	5	
Bos taurus	18	1	Butchered rib
Canis familiaris	9	2	
Capra hircus	25	2	Butchered prox right metacarpal
Dama dama	1	1	Phalanx
Equus asinas	7	1	
Gallus gallus	29	2	
Helicella sp.	3	3	
Helix aspersa	1	1	
Homo sapiens?	2	1	
Lacerta trilineata	1	1	
Lepus europaeus	2	1	
Leuciscus cephalus	1	1	
Microtus guentheri	14	1	
Martes foina	1	1	
Ovis/Capra	150	3	1 female; butchered and burnt frs.
Orychtolagus cunilicus	3	1	
Ovis aries	13	2	1 male, 1 female identified
Rana sp.	1	1	
Sus scrofa	86	4	3 male mandibular canines, burnt and butchered frs.
Testudo hermanni	15	1	
Unidentifiable	950		3 worked frs.; some burnt frs.
Total	1398		

This assemblage of bones resembles the sample from within the Temple and on the Terrace by the significant number of bird bones it contains (95). There are two notable differences, however. The sample is comprised of a predominance of bovid and suid remains (292);[20] these could be meal debris, even ritual meals. There are also two rib fragments of a human, perhaps misplaced from the burial in the adjacent Trench 99.2 at the northeast corner of the Temple. The other striking and unique characteristic of this sample is the occurrence of smaller fauna. They are Balkan green lizard (*Lacerta*), hare (*Lepus*), chub fish (*Leuciscus*), Gunther's vole (*Microtus*), beech marten (*Martes*), rabbit (*Orychtolagus*), toad (*Rana*), and tortoise (*Testudo*). As interpreted from the sample in Building A, some of these smaller species may have been intrusive, or they may not be accidental here; they could possibly be remains from the creations of medicinal concoctions, for example.[21] The impressive amount of bird remains in this poorly preserved sample suggests ritual significance for a specific deity worshipped here. The diversity of fauna found within this Annex testifies to its use in ritual activities, perhaps associated with the adjacent Pillar Shrine.

5. Building A interior

The original purpose of Building A is unknown; it has been suggested by Orlandos that it was the residence of the local priest(s) or priestess(es) (above, p. 3). The Southeast Room of the building had evidence for use as a kitchen (Trench 96.12). Table 13.6 summarizes the fauna found in trenches excavated within its walls.

Table 13.6. Summary of the fauna found within Building A

Species	No. of specimens	MNI	Comments
Aves	17	2	1 female identified
Bos taurus	36	2	2 butchered frs
Canis familiaris	8	2	
Canis lupus?	1	1	
Capra hircus	8	1	1 pathological phalanx
Equus asinas	13	1	Adult
Gallus gallus	3	1	
Gastropod	2	1	
Helicella sp.	1	1	
Helix aspersa	8	8	
Lepus europaeus	7	1	
Ovis/Capra	95	5	Mostly teeth and ribs
Snake	1	1	
Sturnus vulgaris	1	1	
Sus scrofa	83	5	3 male canine frs, 2 female teeth
Testudo hermanni	3	1	
Vulpes vulpes	4	1	
Unidentifiable	284		Some burnt frs
Total	575		

In Building A, there are significantly fewer bird remains than in the Temple, in its West Annex, and on the Terrace. There are, however, more bovid and suid remains (222), perhaps indicative of more meals for worshippers or residents of the building. The West Annex had a significant amount of bovid and suid bones as well, perhaps clean-out from the interior of Building A. There are also 13 equid bones, suggesting that this assemblage is just general dump, perhaps dredged up from the ground during the construction of Building A or dumped after the abandonment of the Sanctuary. There are remains of three canid species (dog, fox, and wolf). These could be the remains of hide removal, especially for fox and wolf pelts, and/or they could be ritual remains from offerings in the Sanctuary. Tortoise and snake remains could be natural intrusions into the sample, though such species were sometimes included in medicinal and ritual concoctions in antiquity, and could therefore have been culturally deposited. Snake occurs nowhere else at the site, and that it should be found indoors is perplexing. Tortoise remains have been found regularly in other contexts at the Sanctuary and probably had some involvement in the ritual activity at the site.

6. The Altar

The animal remains found around the Altar were in poor condition. Although these bones were found immediately around this structure, there is no compelling evidence that they are associated with the ritual use of the Altar. Very few bones of the 372 found in the area are burnt, and none were found *in situ* upon the Altar. There is nothing remarkable about this sample, and it should be examined as part of the Terrace sample below, since the entire Terrace surrounds the Altar feature. Table 13.7 summarizes the fauna from this locale.

Table 13.7. Summary of the fauna found around the Altar

Species	No. of specimens	MNI	Comments
Aves	1	1	
Bos taurus	29	1	Butchered mid scapula fr
Canis familiaris	2	1	
Capra hircus	3	2	Pathological dist right ulna
Capreolus capreolus?	1	1	
Gallus gallus	4	1	
Gastropod	1	1	
Grus grus	4	1	
Lepus europaeus	10	2	
Ovis/Capra	47	3	Butchered rib, burnt rib, proximal femur, female burnt pubis
Ovis aries	1	1	
Rattus rattus	1	1	
Sus scrofa	11	2	Male right manidular canine
Unidentifiable	257		Some burnt and butchered frs
Total	372		

If we were to make a connection between the ritual use of this Altar and the activities being performed in the adjacent Temple, the birds found here would be significant. The remains of the only crane individual are found here, which could be significant because of its context close to the Altar. Cranes are depicted on several Greek vases and are referred to in ancient texts; thus they must have been deemed an important bird by society at the time.[22] The famous Stymphalian birds have even been compared to the crane:

> These birds are of the size of a crane, and are like the ibis, but their beaks are more powerful, and not crooked like that of the ibis. (Paus. 8.22.5; Loeb translation)

It is intriguing, then, that remains of a crane should be found in a sanctuary in Stymphalos.

Some chicken and other unidentifiable bird bones were also present in this assemblage, which is interesting because of the consistent pattern of bird bone deposition found in ritually significant areas of the Sanctuary. Eighty specimens are bovids, yet only two of them are burnt. Pig, deer, dog, and hare were found unburnt in this sample as well, indicating that this bone assemblage probably has no direct connection to burnt sacrificial rituals on the Altar, but is perhaps linked to other ritual activity on the Terrace.

7. The Terrace

The Altar feature was erected upon a built terrace (see fig. 13.1) which was constructed presumably to level the ground directly in front of the Temple. It is reasonable to assume that the use of the Terrace with Altar coincided with the use of the Temple. Table 13.8 summarizes the fauna found at this locale.

Table 13.8. Summary of the fauna found on the Terrace

Species	No. of specimens	MNI	Comments
Aves	97	1	Mostly identifiable scraps
Bos Taurus	7	1	
Canis familiaris	2	1	
Capra hircus	4	2	
Gallus gallus	51	3	
Lepus europaeus	7	1	
Microtus sp.	1	1	
Ovis/Capra	62	4	4 butchered frs
Ovis aries	8	3	2 female and 1 male astragalus, 5 complete astragali
Potamiscus	1	1	
Sus scrofa	52	5	Burnt left mid humerus fr, 1 male right mandible canine
Testudo hermanni	1	1	
Unidentifiable	215		1 worked
Total	508		

The Temple interior and the West Annex samples had significant bird representation in otherwise poorly preserved assemblages. The Terrace sample is no different. There are 148 avian specimens in this sample – even more than bovids (81), which are typically dominant in Aegean faunal samples, including sanctuary assemblages.[23] Suids are represented moderately in this sample, consistent with their occurrence in other locales at the Sanctuary examined up until this point. The presence of dog and hare bones here is also typical compared with the contents of the faunal assemblages discussed so far.

8. Building B

The sample from this building was difficult to separate from the overlying built Terrace (see fig. 13.1). It is unclear whether Building B was a structure on the acropolis of the original Sanctuary, or if it is the remains of another unrelated construction predating the use of the acropolis as a sanctuary. The former seems more likely, though. This sample was separated from the other features on the site in order to discern if its contents were noticeably different from the other samples examined. Table 13.9 summarizes the fauna from this locale.

Table 13.9. Summary of the fauna from Building B

Species	No. of specimens	MNI	Comments
Aves	38	3	
Bos Taurus	185	2	Left worked astragalus, butchered frs
Canis familiaris	11	2	
Canis lupus?	3	1	

Table 13.9. (*Concluded*)

Species	No. of specimens	MNI	Comments
Capra hircus	76	6	2 females, 2 males, and 2 castrates identified; 1 worked astragalus; arthritic phalanx; butchered frs
Cervus elaphas	15	2	Butchered frs
Dama dama	1	1	
Equus asinas	1	1	
Gallus gallus	30	3	Butchered coracoids
Helicella sp.	1	1	
Helix aspersa	3	3	
Lepus europaeus	10	1	
Ovis/Capra	569	11	6 females, 2 males, 1 castrate; burnt and butchered pcs; dog chewed pc
Orychtolagus cunilicus	2	1	
Ovis aries	28	3	Osteoporotic metatarsus; butchered ulna and humerus; burnt astragalus
Picidae	1	1	
Sus scrofa	202	5	1 male, 2 females, arthritic radius, mp; butchered and burnt frs
Testudo hermanni	3	1	
Tonna galea	1	1	Marine species
Vulpes vulpes	2	1	
Unidentifiable	1536		3 worked frs
Total	2718		

The most immediate difference in this sample is the sheer number of bones. Despite the limited area of the excavations in Building B, the sample doubles that from excavations in the West Annex, for example, and resembles the sample in size and contents from the rest of the Sanctuary grounds (discussed below). The latter, however, comprises material excavated from twelve trenches, while the sample from Building B is only from five. It can therefore be considered a concentration of faunal remains, in relative terms, and possibly a dump. It is difficult to discern when this material was deposited; it is hard to imagine that Building B was in use while the faunal debris littered the floors. It is possible that it was dumped after the building went out of use and that these remains have no direct relation with the use of Building B. Initially, it appears that this locale had more to do with its position under the southeast edge of the Terrace. If the Terrace were periodically cleared of debris by sweeping it over the edge, the refuse would accumulate here in this locale, away from the Temple and its adjacent areas. This hypothesis can be tested by comparing the relevant samples. Three samples from the Temple interior, the Terrace, and Building B are considered in chart 13.4.

The three predominant taxa in the samples are compared: aves, bovids, and suids, i.e., bird species, sheep/goat and cattle, and pigs. The first two pie charts and represented samples are remarkably similar in composition – a predominance of avian species. Since we have assumed that the Terrace was in use at the same time as the Temple, the samples therefore reveal similar faunal selections for the activities conducted in both areas. In contrast, the sample from Building B shows different behaviour. A clear predominance of bovid bones is found here with meagre bird remains. If the debris from activities performed on the Terrace and Temple were swept off the edge, then one would expect that the composition of the sample there would be similar to the remains on the Terrace. This is not the case. The deposit in Building B is significantly different, and therefore was left there either during a different period of use of the acropolis or from different activities.

To explore this question further, another comparison of samples is made in chart 13.5. The similarity of composition between the faunal sample from the dump in Building B and the area on and around the Altar is remarkable, especially because the sample surrounding the Altar from the Terrace reveals a significantly different composition primarily comprising avian bones. The Building B deposit and the Altar samples show a predominance of bovid bones with moderate occurrences of suid and avian bones. If this similarity between these two locales is not coincidental, then this pattern seems to suggest either that the activities around the Altar are being echoed in the activities in Building B, or that the debris from the activities being performed on or by the Altar specifically is being collected and dumped over the edge of the Terrace. Furthermore, the similarities between the sample from the Terrace and within the Temple seem to indicate that the debris from the activities within the Temple is being swept out onto the Terrace. What we seem to be witnessing here are the remnants of very specific ritualistic behaviours. The animals being offered in the Temple are different from those being offered outside on the Altar. Neither place seems to be offering holocaust or burnt sacrifices, but rather blood sacrifices, because of the lack of burnt bones.

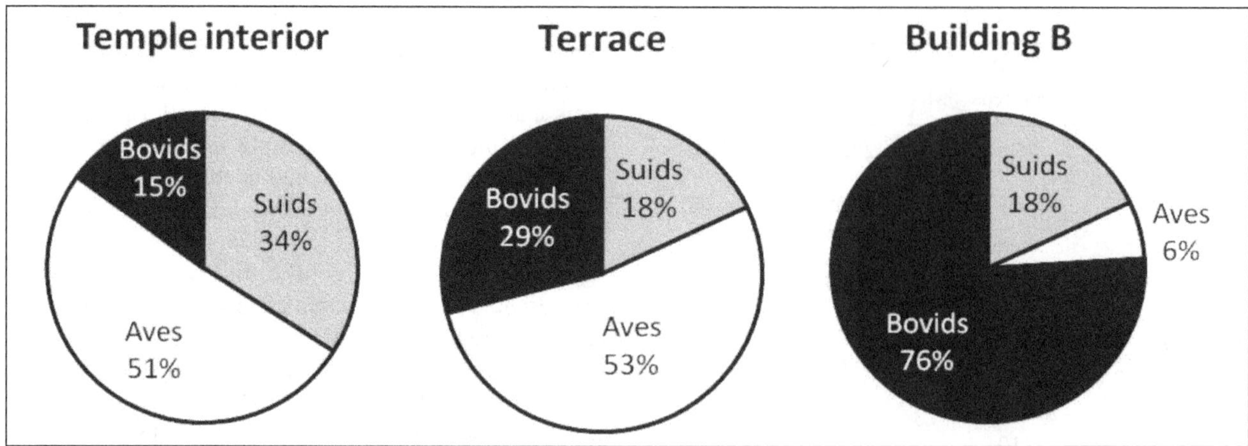

Chart 13.4. Comparison of predominant taxa in three different locales

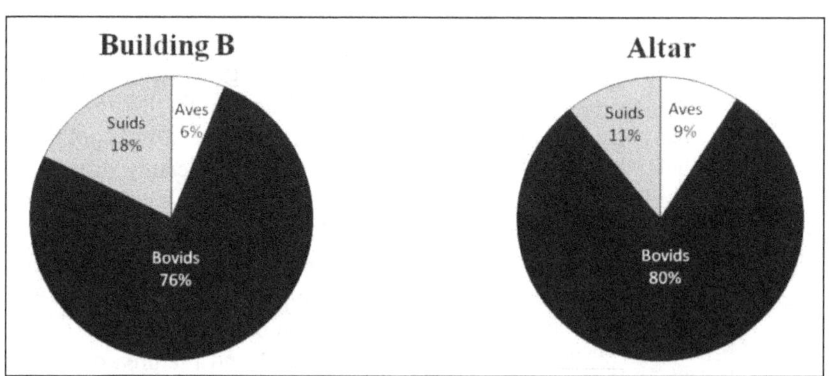

Chart 13.5. Comparison of predominant taxa in two locales

9. The Tower Wall

Excavations along the fortification wall, including two of its towers, provided a hearty faunal sample and an opportunity to compare the composition of this assemblage with others from the Sanctuary on the acropolis. Table 13.10 summarizes the fauna from this locale.

Table 13.10. Summary of the fauna from the Tower Wall

Species	No. of specimens	MNI	Comments
Aves	5	2	
Bos taurus	282	3	5 arthritic phalanges; butchered frs
Canis familiaris	20	2	
Canis lupus	3	1	
Capra hircus	39	4	1 female, 1 male; several butchered frs
Capreolus capreolus	1	1	Butchered glenoid
Equus asinas	3	1	
Gallus gallus	5	2	1 male burr
Lepus europaeus	3	1	
Lutra lutra	2	1	MC IV, phalanx
Ovis/Capra	332	5	1 burnt rib; several butchered frs; 1 male pubis
Ovis aries	5	1	
Potamiscus sp.	2	1	
Rattus rattus	3	1	
Sus scrofa	119	6	1 male canine; 1 male acetabulum; 1 female maxilla; several butchered frs
Testudo hermanni	9	1	
Vulpes vulpes	2	1	
Unidentifiable	843		Butchered juvenile frs
Total	1678		

In this sample, there is an overwhelming predominance of bovid remains (84%), followed by suid remains (15%). All other taxa are represented sparingly, including avian specimens. This sample is unique in that a large number of bovid remains are from cattle. Furthermore, in contrast to the sheep, goat, and pig bones, the cattle remains are 94% from non-meat-bearing bones (cranial bones, phalanges, metapodials, etc.), the result of primary butchery. The sheep, goat, and pig remains, on the other hand, are mainly meat-bearing elements. In general, the dump looks as if the contents are the result of meal preparation – there are more butchered pieces in this sample than others, for example, and there are many meat animals present here.

The cattle remains are from old adult individuals, perhaps slaughtered after their usefulness in fields or dairy had been fulfilled. The lack of long bones here suggests that either the animals were butchered close by and the meat carried away, or the animals were butchered, eaten, and the long bones kept to be used as raw materials for bone tools and other items. The latter seems more likely, considering that the long bones of the smaller ungulates are still present here, and because many pieces of worked bone have been found on the site.

10. The Sanctuary grounds

This assemblage of bones is a collection of fauna from areas that are not clearly associated with architectural features. These finds are from 12 different trenches, so it is not surprising that this sample is the largest of the ten locales. Table 13.11 summarizes the fauna from the miscellaneous areas on the acropolis.

Table 13.11. Summary of the fauna from the Sanctuary grounds

Species	No. of specimens	MNI	Comments
Aves	46	3	1 female identified, 2 butchered frs
Bos taurus	138	3	1 female pubis, butchered frs
Canis familiaris	10	2	Broken healed radius
Capra hircus	44	3	1 male, 1 female, 2 butchered frs, prox metatarsus with osteoporosis
Cervus elaphus	5	1	Antler frs, 2 burnt
Dama dama	2	1	
Equus asinas	5	1	2 burnt frs
Euconulus	1	1	
Felis catus	1	1	Rib – surface find
Gallus gallus	23	3	
Gastropoda	1	1	
Helicella sp.	2	5	
Helix aspersa	93	93	
Homo sapiens	3	1	Deciduous premolar
Lepus europaeus	11	2	2 frs could be *Orychtolagus*
Martes foina	1	1	Mandibular premolar
Ovis/Capra	454	6	2 male, 4 female, 2 castrates, 1 worn astragalus, canid chew, butchered frs
Orychtolagus cunnilicus	3	1	
Ovis aries	21	4	1 female identified, 1 astragalus with bored hole, butchered frs
Sparidae	1	1	Premaxilla
Sus scrofa	222	5	3 female, 2 male canines, butchered and burnt frs
Testudo hermanni	3	1	
Vulpes vulpes	17	2	
Unidentifiable	1899		Includes 6 worked pieces
Total	3006		

This sample is composed of more of the same species that have been identified from other contexts. Again, the three species of canids are present here, as well as specimens of tortoise, hare, rabbit, deer, and equid. The only Sparidae (sea bream) specimen was found here, as well as the only cat (*Felis*), which was a surface find and therefore probably fairly recent. There are a few human fragments in this sample as well (from Trench 96.13), probably misplaced from a burial either elsewhere on the site, or close by but unexcavated. Bovids are again predominant here. Three similar samples are examined together in chart 13.6

These three samples were chosen because of their likeness to each other. The likeness, however, is not surprising, given that these three samples seem to have similar taphonomic features; for example, these locales have not been strictly defined by architectural features. Even Building B remains are scanty and therefore may not contain the original contents from its period of use, as suggested by one hypothesis in the study above (subsection 8) of the spatial analysis. It can therefore be proposed that some or all of these areas are dumping

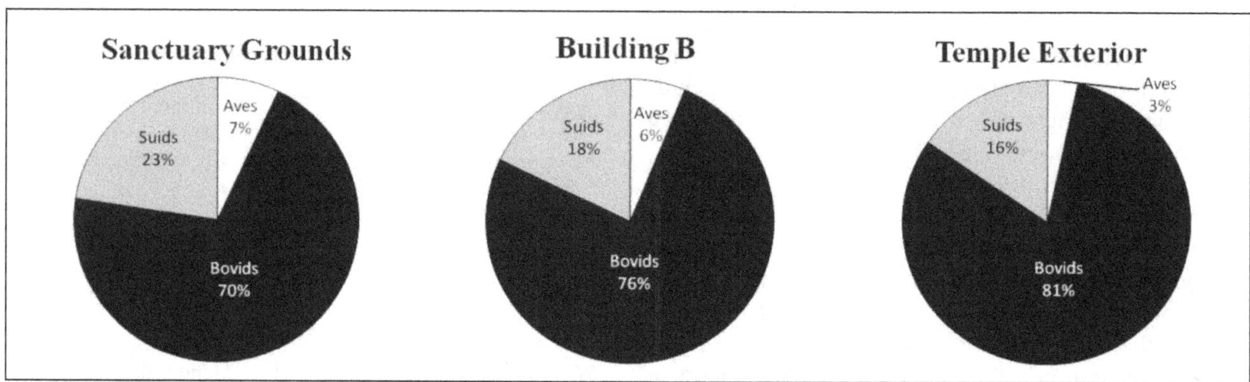

Chart 13.6. Comparison of predominant taxa in three different locales

grounds for general refuse. The sample excavated by the Tower Wall shows a predominance of bovids (84%) and considerably fewer avian remains (1%), as well. Perhaps it too can be grouped within the scope of the dumping grounds of the Sanctuary.

DISCUSSION: CAN THE FAUNAL REMAINS ILLUMINATE THE IDENTITY OF THE TEMPLE DEDICATION?

Identifying the deity to whom the Temple on the acropolis at Stymphalos was dedicated is somewhat perplexing. On the one hand, Orlandos' discovery in 1926 of an inscription reading ΠΟΛΙΑΔΟΣ by Building A ("the priests' house") clearly implies a connection with Athena Polias.[24] On the other hand, the frequent occurrence of avian, canid, leporid, cervid, and testudinid remains in "sacred" areas of the site, especially the Temple interior, the Terrace, and the West Annex of Building A, would suggest that the Sanctuary was dedicated to another deity, since these species are not typically offered to Athena.[25]

To determine to which deity the Sanctuary may have been dedicated using the faunal remains as evidence, it may be easier to begin by eliminating the deities with whom these fauna are not typically associated.[26] Having eliminated the gods and heroes to which only ruminants and suids are typically sacrificed, one is left with several possibilities, namely Aphrodite, Ares, Artemis, Asklepios, Eileithyia, Hekate, or Hera. This is not to suggest that bovids and suids were not sacrificed to these deities, but rather that wild species and/or birds or canids were acceptable offerings as well.

The animals that appear in seven or more contexts from the Sanctuary, not including ruminants and suids,[27] include avian species (aves and chicken appear in all ten contexts), testudinids (tortoise appears in nine), canids (dogs in nine, fox in four, and wolf in four), leporids (hare in nine, and rabbit in three), equids (donkey in eight), and cervids (fallow deer in four, red deer in three, and roe deer in two).

The presence of so many bird remains in all deposits is striking. Bird offerings could suggest a deity such as Aphrodite, for example, since any bird could be sacrificed to her. Specific birds named in ancient testimonia are the cock, dove, goose, partridge, and thrush.[28] Remains from the Sanctuary could very well represent most, if not all, of these species, even thrush from within the Temple proper. Furthermore, other appropriate victims to Aphrodite are bovids (cattle, sheep, and goat), pigs, and hares;[29] there are plenty of hare remains among the bovids and suids from nine of the ten locales investigated. Deer and equids have also been found at other sanctuaries dedicated to Aphrodite.[30]

The presence of other cervids, equids, and canids together also excludes the possibility that the Sanctuary was dedicated exclusively to Ares, Asklepios, Eileithyia, or Hekate. And then there is the matter of the tortoise remains. Although epigraphical evidence does not state that tortoises of any of these species are appropriate offerings for Hera, excavations of the Hellenistic sanctuary of Hera at Foce del Sele, after Poseidonia, yielded eggshells and the bones of goat, dog, cat, tortoise, poultry, and pigeons.[31] Pausanias refers to the three temples that were dedicated to Hera in Stymphalos:

> The story has it that in the old Stymphalos dwelt Temenos, the son of Pelasgos, and that Hera was reared by this Temenos, who himself established three sanctuaries for the goddess, and gave her three surnames when she was still a maiden, Girl; when married to Zeus he called

> her Grown-up; when for some cause or other she quarreled with Zeus and came back to Stymphalos, Temenos named her Widow. This is the account which, to my own knowledge, the Stymphalians give of the goddess. (Paus. 8. 22. 2; Loeb translation)

Pausanias continues by stating, "The modern city contains none of these sanctuaries."[32] The modern city to which Pausanias refers, however, must have existed in the second century CE during his lifetime. According to the pottery, statuary, and other finds at the acropolis Sanctuary, his writings occurred approximately 300 years after the Sanctuary was destroyed and largely abandoned; the Temple seems not have been functioning during the Roman period. Could this Sanctuary represent one of the three dedicated to Hera? Would the fauna perhaps represent specific sacrifices appropriate to one of the three "surnames" of the goddess that were locally acknowledged but not recorded? As far as we know, however, typical sacrifices to the goddess did not include cervids and equids. But neither were pigeons and tortoises known to be appropriate offerings to Hera, yet at Foce del Sele the zooarchaeological evidence shows otherwise.

Only one deity seems to fit the epigraphical accounts with all the species found in this Sanctuary: Artemis. A votive relief attributed to Artemis found in Aegina shows a deer and a tortoise in the sacrificial procession.[33] This is the only iconographic representation of a tortoise in a sacrificial procession for any deity. Furthermore, textual evidence also supports the sacrifice of "exotic" wild fauna to the goddess; during the festival of Artemis Laphria, any kind of wild animal is stated as suitable for sacrifice:

> For the people throw alive upon the altar edible birds and every kind of victim as well; there are wild boars, deer and gazelles; some bring wolf-cubs or bear-cubs, others the full-grown beasts. They also place upon the altar fruit of cultivated trees. (Paus. 7.18.12; Loeb translation)

With the exception of the bear bones, all of these kinds of animals are represented in the Sanctuary deposits, in addition to beech marten, fox, and otter. Zooarchaeological evidence from Lousoi in Arkadia from the sanctuary of Artemis Hemera also supports this pattern of unusual sacrificial fauna. Forstenpointner and Hofer report equids, dogs, cervids, hare, pigeons, partridge, pelican, and bustard from the bone assemblage at Lousoi.[34] The similarities between this faunal sample and the one from Stymphalos are striking, especially considering that Lousoi is not far from Stymphalos and similar in environmental characteristics and available fauna.

The presence of a sanctuary dedicated to Artemis is discussed in Pausanias:

> In Stymphalos there is also an old sanctuary of Stymphalian Artemis, the image being of wood, for the most part gilded. Near the roof of the temple have been carved, among other things, the Stymphalian birds. Now it was difficult to discern clearly whether the carving was in wood or in gypsum, but such evidence as I had led me to conclude that it was not of gypsum but of wood. There are here also maidens of white marble, with the legs of birds, and they stand behind the temple. (Paus. 8.22.7; Loeb translation)

This description does not suit the Temple on the acropolis, since it was destroyed long before Pausanias's visit. Instead, it is usually assumed that Pausanias was describing the large temple close to the Cistercian monastery, whose last remains were being dismantled when Heinrich Lattermann visited Stymphalos in 1910.[35]

One can never be certain of interpretations based on archaeological evidence; however, given that the fauna seem to correspond to that connected with the worship of Artemis, and that textual evidence identifies the presence of an active sanctuary to Artemis at Stymphalos still in the time of Pausanias, it seems reasonable to suggest that the acropolis Sanctuary could have had associations with this goddess as well. Moreover, the discovery of the marble kore holding a juvenile hare in her hand on the site supports this possibility.[36]

There are other aspects of the Sanctuary fauna that should be addressed. For example, there are areas where bovids, both cattle and sheep/goat, are more predominant and bird remains are scanty. These are the exterior perimeter of the Temple, the interior of Building B, and the general Sanctuary grounds. From the spatial analysis, these locations may be interpreted as secular areas. The ritually sensitive areas seem to have been the Temple interior, the West Annex of Building A, and the Terrace with the Altar. These are also the areas that would have been maintained to avoid the buildup of a great deal of debris. It appears as if the locales with the greatest amounts of bovid remains were areas where general dumping was more tolerated. It cannot be determined whether this debris would have all been from ritual activities, or from secular activities, or both.

Another aspect of the Sanctuary that should be addressed is the fact that Schaus has found convincing evidence that Eileithyia was worshipped here. There are few written testimonia to describe the rituals associated with this cult; we only know for certain that Eileithyia was a divine helper of women worshipped in the aid of childbearing. It is difficult to learn, however, what sort of offerings were made to Eileithyia from the limited information we have, so that we may check the applicability of our sample to this cult. We do have two ancient textual testimonials referring to appropriate offerings to Eileithyia, one from Ilion, which mentioned the sacrifice of a dog to the goddess, and the other a ewe during the festival of Eileithyia.[37] These do not conflict with the faunal findings on the acropolis; in fact, they fit rather neatly. Both dogs and sheep are found in almost all contexts at the site.

In the historical periods, Eileithyia became associated with the Olympian goddesses Hera and Artemis, and the eastern goddess Hekate. Hera was believed by some to have been the mother of Eileithyia.[38] Her position as mother of some Olympian gods gave her an association with childbearing and hope for expectant women, though her main patronage was generally to women and marriage. There is also an association between Eileithyia and Artemis, though not so much in a familial sense. Artemis is also associated with childbearing. In the *Orphic Hymn to Prothyraeia*, Eileithyia and Artemis are one and the same:

> For thou Eileithyia alone can give relief to pain, which art attempts to ease, but tries in vain. Artemis Eileithyia, venerable power, who bring'st relief in labour's dreadful hour. (Translation by Thomas Taylor)

The association with Hekate is more of a conflicting one. It is believed that the position and patronage of the eastern cult of Hekate conflicted with those of Artemis in her role in childbearing.[39] In Ephesus, there is a shrine to Hekate in the sanctuary of Artemis. She seems to have been absorbed by the Greek pantheon but kept in a marginal position. Perhaps the same conflict occurred with Eileithyia with the eastern introduction of Hekate, since both were pre-Olympian goddesses. With the widely accepted cult of Artemis, the beloved Eileithyia and Hekate were not replaced, but rather intertwined in the myths of the Theogony.[40] In Argos, the temples of Hekate and Eileithyia are opposite each other.[41] In one case, Hekate and Eileithyia seem to have merged to form *Eilioveia*, a cult figure to whom the Argives sacrificed dogs.[42]

It should be noted that dogs were considered appropriate sacrifices for Hera, Artemis, Hekate, and Eileithyia. The fecundity of dogs and their association with the Underworld seem to have made them an appropriate and relevant choice of offering for these dark and largely mysterious patronesses of childbearing. There are many remains of dogs found on this site, suggesting that the site may have been important in fulfilling the spiritual needs of expectant women. It seems possible that the fecundity of hares and rabbits was acknowledged in this way as well. If there were any doubt of the site's importance to childbearing themes, the discovery of the fragments of the "Temple Boy" statue at the site supports the faunal evidence.

The deities to whom the Sanctuary is dedicated are likely Artemis and/or Eileithyia. The faunal material, the statuary, the small finds, the ancient testimonia, and the fragmentary epipgraphical evidence[43] reveal a logical association of the site with these two goddesses. The available data can also exclude other deities. Because of their association, there is no reason why both could not be have been venerated at the site, perhaps as Artemis Eileithyia.

If we set aside the identification of the kore statue with the hare in hand as an effigy of Artemis herself, and assume that the ideological associations between Artemis and Eileithyia would warrant similar sacrificial offerings, then it would be plausible that the Sanctuary was dedicated mainly to Eileithyia, with Athena Polias as a lesser focus, based on the epigraphical evidence.

INTERESTING SPECIMENS

Many specimens found in the faunal assemblage deserve separate commentary. These bones have either been culturally modified, have an interesting context, or have some naturally unique interest in the sample from the acropolis.[44]

Knucklebones

Knucklebones are often found in sanctuary contexts because of their association with divination.[45] Figure 13.2 displays one of the two astragali which were found with holes bored through the middle. The holes could have been made for stringing a set of astragali up for transport and storage, though holed specimens from other Iron Age sites have been plugged with lead to provide more weight.[46] Several are required for either astragalomancy or for their use as gaming pieces. The astragalus presented in figure 13.2 is from the right leg of a male goat (Tr. 96.13, Pail 4), the other is from the right leg of a male sheep (Tr. 00.3). Both were recovered from the southern part of the excavated area near Building B. It could be a coincidence that the only two worked astragali from the site were found approximately six metres apart, or it could be that the building that once stood here housed an oracle of some sort.

There are 57 astragali found on the site from cattle, sheep, goat, donkey, pigs, and fox. Only sheep and goat astragaloi were usually used in divination in ancient Greece, and those were represented by 41 specimens. There seems to be no pattern of deposition of these astragali, and most do not show signs of polishing from handling. Sheep and goat astragali are equally represented.

Raw material for bone-working industries

Several pieces of cut bone were excavated mainly from the location by the Tower Wall where the majority of the debris from bone working was recovered. A few other pieces were found at different locations around the site. Figures 13.3a and 13.3b (Tr. 99.1, Pail 12) illustrate an example of a cut bone probably prepared for use as a bone tool. The specimen is a cut cattle astragalus shown in two perspectives. These cut marks are distinguished from common butcher marks for two reasons. First, the astragalus is not normally butchered completely through the bone; it is commonly severed from the distal tibia and discarded whole with the metatarsus and the phalanges because the lower leg does not bear any meat. Secondly, this specimen is cut several ways, as if to reduce it to a workable size for the object which the toolmaker had in mind.

Another fine example of industrial use of bones was a fallow deer metatarsus smoothly cut at both ends. The result was a fine tube, but the work was never completed (Tr. 96.8, Pail 4).[47]

Pathologies

A number of pathologies were identified from the site. Two have been illustrated in figures 13.4a and 13.4b, and in figures 13.5a and 13.5b. Figure 13.4a depicts the distal phalanges of an old cattle individual (Tr. 00.4, Pails 7 and 8). These arthritic specimens show hyperostosis and pitting of the periphery around the articular surface of the phalanges. These changes are caused by trauma to the hooves, probably due to the use of the cattle as draught animals.[48] Figure 13.4b shows the proximal phalanges from two different individuals of cattle; both reveal similar traumas as those in figure 13.4a. The specimen on the right, in particular, shows the trauma more clearly from the lipping on the upper left lateral surface, perhaps because an object was caught high up between the hooves.

Figures 13.5a and 13.5b show two different perspectives of the same pathological specimen, a wild boar's proximal left radius from an older individual (Tr. 99.1, Pail 8). The disfigurement of the "elbow" joint is caused by arthritic growth after a dislocation and relocation of the distal humerus. The specimen also shows butchery marks from a metal knife on the lateral side of the diaphysis (fig. 13.5b), suggesting that this specimen was probably hunted for food.

Other pathologies include a fractured and healed dog radius (Tr. 97.5, Pail 4), perhaps from a hunting accident, and two bovid metatarsi, one of a sheep and the other of a goat, with osteoporosis (Tr. 97.5, Pail 5 and Tr. 97.9, Pail 7). The osteoporosis has not been caused by age in either of these cases. These individuals were over two years of age, but probably younger than five. The osteoporosis was caused by malnutrition. Either their herders were not allowing them to graze long enough, or there were not enough nutrients to be found in the grazing fields, which can happen during long dry seasons. It is hard to imagine that a lake site would not have plentiful grazing grounds, so one is led to believe that the herders were not taking very good care of their animals. Several examples of arthritis due to wear from old age were identified, showing that some animals were kept until advanced maturity.

The pathologies from this site were useful in suggesting the use, treatment, and life histories of some animals in Stymphalos.

Burnt specimens

Some interesting burnt bone specimens were studied. Burnt bones are especially interesting in the context of a sanctuary site where sacrifices undoubtedly occurred. Figure 13.6 shows fragments of burnt deer antler (cf. *Cervus*). The presence of burnt antler suggests that the whole animal was sacrificed as opposed to being cut into pieces for meat. It could very well be that these remains are from the incineration of rubbish, but the occurrence of burnt antler even from a dump is rare. In the context of a sanctuary possibly having an association with Artemis, the presence of burnt cervid remains seems befitting.

The burnt antler fragments (fig. 13.6) were found just outside Building A (Tr. 2000.5) with another 208 bone fragments, only one of which was burnt. Incidentally, the other burnt fragment was a pubis from a juvenile sheep or goat individual. Juvenile specimens are common victims in sacrifices.

A concentration of burnt juvenile piglet bones was found south of the Temple (Tr. 2000.3). Most of these bones were highly fragmentary and could not be identified as to species. One hundred and ten juvenile bones were excavated in this context. Another concentration of juvenile bones was found just outside of the West Annex of Building A (Tr. 96.15). Here the preservation of the bones was slightly better, so it could be determined that the 434 calcined bones from this context were mainly piglets, with evidence of at least one lamb or kid. The MNI for the piglet remains is at least three individuals, though the range of sizes suggests more, perhaps five or six individuals.

From the spatial analysis, it was discovered that the Temple and the West Annex of Building A produced ritually significant fauna, suggesting that these two contexts were perhaps more sacred than other areas of the Sanctuary. That the two concentrations of calcined juvenile bones should be found outside these contexts supports this interpretation. Holocaust sacrifices would not be conducted indoors, but rather close to the sacred space. We know that piglets were common in fertility rites of women in antiquity, appropriate because of the fecundity of sows.[49]

Surprisingly few burnt specimens were found from the entire Sanctuary assemblage; of the 11,380 specimens, only 787 were found to be burnt, or 7% of the sample. In this collection of burnt bones, 544 specimens, or 70%, were found in only two trenches (Tr. 2000.2 and Tr. 96.15), and comprised juvenile individuals.

Canid gnaw marks

Several bones were identified with canid gnaw marks, presumably from domestic dogs. Figure 13.7 shows a mid ilium of a sheep or goat, an example of such gnawed bones (Tr. 97.5). The presence of gnawed bones suggests that some dogs were kept at the Sanctuary, or that feral scavengers perused the Sanctuary garbage. With so many canid individuals found from sacrificial deposits, it is interesting that some individuals may have been kept as pets at the Sanctuary.

Several bone specimens were also identified with rodent gnaw marks; these were likely gnawed after disposal.

Interesting contexts

One item that deserves mentioning is the very well preserved sheep skull seen in figure 13.8. What makes this specimen remarkable is not only its rarity of preservation among a sample of highly fragmentary bones, but the context in which it was found. This cranium was roughly but carefully cut in half in antiquity and then placed in a jar or pot. The complete jar was excavated with the sheep cranium *in situ*. Crania of animals are commonly butchered to extract the brain, considered a delicacy still in many parts of the world. The brain could have been extracted and then the remaining cranial piece could have been boiled to make a soup. Otherwise, the brain could have been exposed with the intention of boiling it for consumption as locals do today. The jar was found in Trench 2000.6 located just behind the north wall of Building A. It is possible that the cooking of this item was performed outdoors. The jar could also have been the container in which it was served to the diner. Considering the context in which it was found, it is unlikely that this specimen was a ritual offering.

CONCLUSION: UNDERSTANDING LIFE AND RITUAL IN THE ACROPOLIS SANCTUARY

The faunal sample from the acropolis Sanctuary at Stymphalos is an important assemblage in that it provides insights into the ritual lives of the worshippers at the site. The bones and most of the other material remains are in a poor state of preservation, making the reconstruction of daily life and religious rites in the Sanctuary a challenging task.

Since Orlandos' excavation of the site in 1924–6, it has been identified as a sanctuary of Athena Polias. From material remains discovered in the Sanctuary, evidence for the worship of Athena, Eileithyia, Artemis, and Aphrodite has been suggested.[50] The faunal remains have been able to support the supposition that Eileithyia, Artemis, or Aphrodite was worshipped at the site. The bone assemblage speaks more to the worship of Artemis than the other deities, based on the number of wild and exotic birds and animals found in the sacred contexts. The epigraphical evidence found on the site suggesting the worship of Eileithyia, however, cannot be ignored. Nor can the inscription found by Orlandos suggesting a connection with Athena, or the bezel ring and medallion with images of Aphrodite and Eros. The kore with the baby hare and the temple boy statuary are also important in identifying the deity.

These items appear in the Sanctuary for a reason; they are not casual objects left behind by confused worshippers. They are objects that were brought to the acropolis with intent and purpose. Frankly, there seems no real discrepancy in accepting that *all* these goddesses were worshipped at the site contemporaneously. As in modern Greek churches, the building may be dedicated to a specific saint, but the walls are lined with numerous divine images so that worshippers may come, pray, and pay homage to their own personal beloved saint. From an economic perspective, opening the scope of deities worshipped at a single location is "good for business."

Based on the faunal remains, specifically the birds, hares, rabbits, dogs, wolves, foxes, martens, donkeys, red, roe, and fallow deer, and tortoises, only one deity could be identified with all these fauna: Artemis. The kore holding the young hare in her hand found within the Temple has been associated with this goddess. Sacred areas within the Sanctuary where special ritual deposits have been recovered were the Temple proper, the West Annex of Building A, and the Terrace with the Altar. These include, however, other sacred objects inscribed in part with the name "Eileithyia."

It is possible that Artemis was worshipped at this location specifically for her association with Eileithyia. No doubt, the act of childbearing in antiquity was a harrowing experience. These and other deities were placated to ensure the safe delivery of babies and the recovery of their mothers. If we accept that Eileithyia was "replaced" by her Olympian associate in many parts of Greece and Asia Minor, then we might assume that Artemis and Eileithyia were often treated as one and the same. They then might share the same imagery, and the same sacrificial offerings.

The women of ancient Stymphalos had access to a variety of wild species with which to placate their goddesses. Whatever the need, be it the love of Aphrodite, the strength of Artemis, the ease of childbirth of Eileithyia, or the protection of Athena, all might have been sought at the acropolis Sanctuary in Stymphalos.

14

Human Skeletal Remains

Sandra Garvie-Lok

The two Late Roman/Early Byzantine graves recovered from the Sanctuary area are typical of the burials from this period recovered elsewhere at Stymphalos (fig. 14.1). While few individuals are represented, the remains are still of considerable interest because they offer insights into the health and social lives of the Late Roman/Early Byzantine population of the site.

GRAVE 1

Grave 1 (the Temple Grave) was recovered in 1997. A detailed description of the grave may be found in Schaus, chapter 2, pp. 24–5 (see fig. 2.29a–c). Briefly, the skeletal material excavated from the grave includes the largely complete remains of a young child, still in an articulated state. Also recovered were more fragmentary remains representing five additional individuals: an infant, an older juvenile, and three adults. While most of these remains were scattered above and around the articulated juvenile skeleton, the lower legs of one adult were still in situ. All of the bones were cleaned gently for study and photography using water and a soft brush. Where it was felt that the fragility of the bone might cause loss of important information through degradation in storage, elements were consolidated using a 5% solution of Paraloid B72 in acetone.

Grave 1 primary individual (osteology catalogue number ST-II-97-1-1): Preservation

While the articulated remains of the child are by far the most complete of those recovered from the tomb, their small size and fragility led to significant degradation after burial. Most of the cranium is present, but many elements are badly fragmented. The vertebral column was partially recovered, with most vertebral laminae present but most vertebral bodies absent. The ribs are well preserved and most are present; the sternum was not recovered. The bones of the shoulder and pelvic girdles are represented only by the diaphyses of the clavicles and a few other fragments. All long bone diaphyses are present, but most are in a fragmented and partial state. Most metacarpals and hand phalanges were recovered, along with some metatarsals and foot phalanges; no carpals or tarsals were recovered.

Grave 1 primary individual: Personal adornment and sex

The remains show some discolouration caused by the earrings the child was wearing when buried. In decay, the right earring created vivid green copper staining on some elements around the ear, including the right temporal, the right lateral part of the occipital, and the right ascending ramus of the mandible. The hyoid, the root of the right lower first incisor, and one of the metacarpals also show copper staining; this would have occurred after soft tissue decay allowed the earrings to move into contact with them. While this child is far too young to allow sex to be established using standard osteological techniques, the presence of the earrings identifies it as a girl.

Grave 1 primary individual: Age at death

Thanks to the presence of several indicators, the age of

this young girl can be estimated quite closely. The development of the deciduous lower canines agrees with an age at death of 1.5 to 2.5 years based on development in modern girls.[1] All second deciduous molars are fully erupted and slightly worn, indicating that they were in use for some time before death. Data for modern populations[2] indicate that this tooth generally erupts between 2.0 and 2.5 years of age. The development of the bones of the spine also suggests an age of at least 2.0 years.[3] Thus, while dental development indicates an age at death of 1.5 to 2.5 years, dental eruption and skeletal maturation suggest that death occurred in the latter half of this range, between 2.0 and 2.5 years.

Grave 1 primary individual: Description of pathological lesions

The remains display a number of pathological lesions. The first is on the anterior aspect of the right maxilla. It consists of an area of surface porosity around the infraorbital foramen, extending towards the alveolar border (see fig. 14.2). The pores do not penetrate deeply into the bone and are irregular in outline. The appearance of the lesion and its apparent limitation to the bone surface suggest a subperiosteal bone deposit formed in reaction to inflammation.[4] Its sharp-edged and disorganized appearance suggests a condition active at death.

The second lesion is on the temporal surface of the left zygoma. It consists of an area of fine, sharp-edged round to oval pores 1 mm and less in size, centred on the zygomaticotemporal foramen (see fig. 14.3). In contrast to the lesion on the maxilla, this surface appears less disorganized, with clearly defined pores penetrating a fairly smooth bone surface. Lesions are also seen on the right and left orbital roofs. These consist of raised areas bearing large, sharp-edged pores with a sinuous outline, which are confluent in places and penetrate deeply into the bone surface (see fig. 14.4). The appearance of the lesions is consistent with that of cribra orbitalia.[5] Although postmortem damage prevents a full assessment of the severity of the lesions, the preserved areas fall under Type 3 in Stuart-Macadam's classification system.[6]

The final lesions noted in this individual are defects in the root surfaces of three deciduous maxillary incisors and one deciduous mandibular incisor (see fig. 14.5). These are shallow depressions in the labial aspect of the root surface. They run immediately along the cementoenamel junction, undercutting the enamel slightly; the immediately adjacent enamel is unaffected and normal in appearance. The lesions extend 1–2 mm apically and terminate in a curved, sharply defined border. Their floors are darker in colour than the normal root surface and faintly striated. In location and appearance these lesions are consistent with clinical and palaeopathological descriptions of root-surface caries.[7]

Grave 1 primary individual: Interpretation of pathological lesions

The interpretation of the pathological lesions present in this young girl is briefly summarized here;[8] dietary and social implications are discussed further below. The presence of cribra orbitalia is a clear indicator of poor general health suffered for some time before death. However, when considered on its own it cannot be connected with one specific cause of ill health, as lesions of this appearance are reported to result from a number of health problems including anemia, scurvy, and infection, as well as thalassemia, the genetic anemia typical of Mediterranean populations.[9] Of these, thalassemia may be eliminated because it also causes other characteristic lesions including diploic expansion in the cranial vault, expansion of the facial bones, disruption of dental eruption, and changes in the ribs, vertebrae, and other postcranial elements,[10] none of which is seen in this individual. This leaves infection or nutritional problems as the likely cause of the lesion. The most usual diagnosis for such lesions of the orbital roof is anemia secondary to malnutrition or infection;[11] however, the other lesions present in this individual suggest that she might have been affected by scurvy instead of, or in addition to, anemia.

Scurvy, or vitamin C deficiency, is a disorder of nutritional origin that primarily affects the connective tissues.[12] Humans are incapable of synthesizing vitamin C and must obtain it from their diets. Vitamin C has a number of confirmed or suspected functions in the body, but the crucial one for the understanding of scurvy is collagen synthesis. In the absence of vitamin C, this synthesis is disrupted, and because collagens are crucial components of the bones, ligaments, tendons, and blood vessels, serious illness results. Human milk is high in vitamin C even when the mother's intake is inadequate, protecting nursing infants from scurvy.[13] However, if weaned to a diet with inadequate vitamin C, a child will develop scurvy after its tissue reserve pool of vitamin C is depleted. This can occur quite quickly due to the heavy demand placed on tissue vitamin C stores by rapid growth in the period between 6 months and 2 years of age, an age at which children are considered to be at peak risk of developing scurvy.[14]

The classic clinical symptoms of juvenile scurvy are loss of appetite and failure to thrive, irritability, and painful swellings caused by bleeding into the space between the bone and its surrounding periosteum.[15] Deposits of new bone form in reaction to this bleeding and may be visible postmortem or radiographically in the bones of the limbs and skull.[16] Juvenile scurvy is also characterized by a number of other symptoms resulting from defective collagen synthesis, including skin lesions and haemorrhage of the gums around the teeth, and by some symptoms reflecting other metabolic functions of vitamin C, such as anemia and an increased susceptibility to infection.[17] If proper vitamin C nutrition is not restored, juvenile scurvy can be fatal.

In recent years, great attention has been given to a complex of lesions of the skull which has been described in several archaeological populations and is proposed to be characteristic of juvenile scurvy.[18] Essentially, these consist of abnormal porosity in the surface of the temporal fossa and a few other characteristic locales. The lesions of this girl's left zygoma and right maxilla are an excellent fit to those descriptions. They are similar in appearance to the two types of abnormal porosity considered to result from scurvy, and the locations in which they are found are two of those considered to be typical of scurvy.[19] The presence of cribra orbitalia is also consistent with this diagnosis, as similar lesions are frequently found in individuals thought to be affected by scurvy.[20] The overall match of this child's lesions to those of scurvy is not perfect; cases attributed to scurvy in the literature typically also show abnormal porosity in the greater wings of the sphenoid,[21] which is not visible in this case. However, as it is considered possible for scurvy to affect the skeleton without causing lesions in the sphenoid,[22] this does not indicate that a diagnosis of scurvy should be rejected.

A diagnosis of scurvy is also supported by the unusual presence of root caries in this extremely young individual. The condition indicates the presence of gum recession, and is typically a disease of the middle-aged and old; both clinical and archaeological studies show it to be extremely rare in children.[23] A review of modern observations of oral scurvy suggests that in this particular case, gum recession may have been triggered by a combination of poor oral hygiene and the breakdown of gum tissues which is typical of scurvy.[24]

Thus, several of the pathological changes seen in this young girl's skeleton fit well with a diagnosis of scurvy. It is unclear whether this condition was present alone or in conjunction with anemia. As discussed above, lesions similar to cribra orbitalia are frequently found in individuals thought to be affected by scurvy; however, while these might be the direct result of scurvy,[25] it is also possible that they were caused by anemia secondary to scurvy. Anemia is a frequent complication of scurvy in modern clinical cases,[26] and was likely also associated with scurvy in past populations.[27] Given this, it is quite possible that this child suffered from both problems.

While it is not possible to say whether the death of this girl was a direct result of scurvy, the condition appears to have been active at death and would definitely have caused suffering. If it was not the direct cause of death, it may well have been an indirect cause of death, as the increased susceptibility to infection typical of scurvy would have made this girl more vulnerable to many other illnesses.

Grave 1 commingled remains (osteology catalogue ST-II-97-1-2)

These bones accompany the primary individual in Grave 1. They are quite poorly preserved and incomplete, and typical in appearance of the disturbed remains recovered from tombs used for several sequential burials (see "Grave 1 burial sequence," below). Despite poor preservation, it is possible to document the presence of five individuals: an infant, an adolescent, and three adults.

The infant remains were separated from the commingled bone on the basis of size and maturity. While very partial, they are consistent with the presence of a single infant. Recovered are portions of the frontal and right temporal, four ribs, parts of both clavicles and the right ulna, portions of one tibia and one humerus (side indeterminate due to damage), and a small amount of additional postcranial and vault material. Because no measurements were possible, a direct assessment of age could not be made; however, the overall size and morphology of the elements are closely similar to those of ST-II-99-2 (see below), suggesting that this infant, like that individual, died around the time of birth.

In addition to the infant remains described above, a few other subadult elements are present in the commingled bone. While quite partial, they are consistent with the presence of a single older juvenile. They include a partial set of permanent teeth, all found loose in the deposit and matched through similarities in size, morphology, and wear. The teeth are in excellent health and very lightly worn. Wear on the upper and lower second permanent molars shows that they had entered into occlusion before death. One developing third molar crown is present. A comparison of its stage of development to data for modern juveniles suggests an age at death of roughly 10 to 15 years,[28] which is in general agreement with recent eruption of the second permanent molars.[29] As the roots of most of the teeth have suffered postmortem damage, this age estimate cannot be narrowed further. Also present are a small selection of subadult postcranial elements consistent in their maturity and near-adult size with the age range suggested by the teeth. These include a partial left scapula with open epiphyses at the inferior angle and coracoid, a partial right radius with open proximal epiphysis, a distal left radial epiphysis, a distal carpal phalanx with its epiphysis open, and a partial vertebral body of near-adult size with an open epiphyseal plate. While only these elements could be securely assigned to this individual, the commingled remains described below as adult bone include a large amount of poorly preserved postcranial material, and given the near-adult size of this individual, it is likely that some bone from this individual is included in those fragments.

The rest of the commingled bone in the grave is adult. It includes material from throughout the body, generally quite poorly preserved and including a large number of comminuted long bone shaft fragments. The identifiable material is consistent with the presence of three adults. The dental remains are the most informative and allow some guesses as to the sex and rough age of the individuals present. The first is represented by a partial mandible with much of its dentition intact. The teeth are moderately worn, similar in wear to some individuals from other graves at Stymphalos who died in their thirties or forties. A gross carious lesion, which has destroyed about half of the tooth crown, is seen in the right first molar. The mandible is strong, deep-bodied, and typically male in morphology. The second individual is also represented by a partial mandible, more gracile than the first and possibly female. The teeth show light to moderate deposits of calculus but are otherwise healthy. Wear is somewhat lighter than that seen in the first mandible, suggesting a younger age at death. The third individual is represented by a small section of the left maxillary arcade and some loose teeth matched to it by wear and morphology. Wear and size distinguish these teeth from those of the first two individuals; the wear is quite heavy and suggests that this individual was older than the first two. The other cranial and postcranial material recovered is consistent with these suggestions, indicating the presence of one large, robust individual, likely male, and two more gracile individuals, both possibly female. Thus, the adult remains convincingly suggest the presence of three individuals: a likely male who died some time in middle age and two possible females, one of whom was younger than the male individual and one of whom was older. Based on robusticity, the lower legs recovered in situ may have belonged to the adult male.

Grave 1 burial sequence

In addition to the two Sanctuary graves, a number of other burials have been recovered in the course of Canadian excavations at Stymphalos.[30] These are grouped in four concentrations located along the city walls (Stym IV, Stym V) and in and around other structures within the city (Stym III, Stym IX). Datable material from some of these graves is fifth–sixth century CE; the nearby location and similar style of the others suggest that all should be considered together as cemeteries associated with a Late Roman/Early Byzantine community inhabiting the Stymphalos area. Examination of the remains from 21 of these graves and excavators' observations on grave architecture has allowed the typical construction and use sequence to be reconstructed. A grave was typically built for a single individual, who was interred in a supine position with the arms extended along the sides or crossed over the body. While graves varied in elaboration, it appears that the ideal was a built grave with walls and a cover, constructed of tile or stone gathered from surrounding disused structures. The fact that a few single juvenile burials were found in graves just large enough to hold them suggests that a grave was constructed to fit the size of its initial occupant. While some graves were not opened again, others were reopened later to allow additional individuals to be buried in them. The bones of the initial body were moved to allow the new body to be laid in the grave and replaced before the grave was closed. This process might be repeated several times. The condition of the disturbed remains found in these graves shows that during each opening and reuse, the bones of earlier burials tended to be broken up and many elements lost. The end result after several reuse episodes is a collection of badly fragmented and partial remains accompanying the final burial, which is found in situ and in far better condition.

Grave 1 is typical of these multiple-use graves. As described by Schaus (chapter 2, pp. 24–5), it is of an appropriate size to have accommodated one of the adults. Built initially for this individual, it was reopened on later occasions to admit the other two adults and the adolescent. The extensive fragmentation of the disarticulated remains suggests that the tomb was reopened several times, with enough time elapsing between burials to allow soft tissues to decay. Based on recovery of the lower legs in situ, the last of these individuals interred was likely the largest adult (probably male). As the infant died around the time of birth, it is unclear whether it was interred alone after being born or was in the womb of an adult woman whose pregnancy was near term. On its final opening, the tomb was used to inter the young girl whose remains were found in situ. The bones cleared from the space in which her corpse was laid were piled around and on top of her, and the grave was closed. Given the range of ages represented and the extended use period, it is possible that Grave 1 was a family tomb, a grave use pattern that has been suggested for contemporary burials elsewhere in the Peloponnese.[31]

GRAVE 2

Grave 2 (the Baby's Grave) was recovered from the Sanctuary area in 1999. A description of the grave may be found in Schaus (chapter 2, p. 31; see fig. 2.42a–b). The remains of a single infant were excavated from the grave. The recovery of the remains in situ, with many small elements of the skeleton intact, indicates that the grave was not significantly disturbed after the initial interment. All of the bones from the grave were cleaned gently for study using a soft brush; due to the delicacy of the remains and their fragile condition, water was used only where absolutely necessary to remove encrusted dirt preventing study. The remains are designated as ST-II-99-2 in the osteology catalogue.

Despite the undisturbed nature of the grave, most elements of this skeleton are in poor condition, showing postmortem breakage, abrasion, and chemical erosion. This reflects conditions of the burial environment, as well as the tiny size and fragility of the remains. Considering this, the remains are fairly complete. Most of the postcranial elements were recovered, although the right pubis, the left ulna, ischium and pubis, and most bones of the hands and feet are missing. The cranium is in poorer shape; the bones of the vault are largely present but extensively fragmented, and the face is represented only by the right zygoma, portions of the right and left maxillae and mandible, and three developing tooth crowns.

The size of this individual clearly indicates that death occurred very early in infancy. To obtain a more precise age estimate, a number of intact elements were measured (see table 14.1).[32] Comparison of these measurements to autopsy data on a series of modern fetuses and neonates[33] shows all of them to agree well with an age of 10 lunar months in utero (full term neonate). While a few of the measurements are small enough to fall also into the size range of 9.5 lunar month fetuses, most are not. Two deciduous first molar crowns were recovered; their development is consistent with that of a neonate or late-term fetus.[34] Thus, both size and tooth development agree with death around the time of birth. From the examination performed in the field, it is not possible to say whether this infant was stillborn or died shortly after birth. This question might be resolved by examining one of the developing tooth crowns in thin section; if birth was survived by more than 7–10 days, a neonatal line should be visible.[35]

Table 14.1. Measurements for Individual ST-II-99-2

Element	Measurement	Value (mm)
Right temporal (petrous part)	Length	38.0
	Width	18.1
Left temporal (petrous part)	Length	37.6
Left incus	Length	7.0
	Width	5.4
Sphenoid (body)	Length	11.2
Occipital (basilar part)	Length	12.3
	Width	16.3
Occipital (right lateral part)	Length	27.8
	Width	16.2
Atlas (left vertebral arch)	Length	15.2
Axis (left vertebral arch)	Length	17.0
Right humerus	Length	64.6
Left ulna	Length	62.2
Right radius	Length	55.4
Right ilium	Length	35.6
	Width	31.4
Left ilium	Length	35.4
	Width	31.9
Right ischium	Length	18.0
Right femur	Length	75.4
Right tibia	Length	66.5
Left fibula	Length	61.3

DISCUSSION: SOCIAL AND DIETARY IMPLICATIONS OF THE BURIALS

While small in number, the Late Roman/Early Byzantine burials from the Sanctuary provide some interesting insights into the beliefs and physical well-being of the population of the Valley of Stymphalos during this period. Of the two graves, one is a communal interment reused over a significant span of time for several burials, perhaps all within one family. The other is a single, undisturbed infant burial. These are typical of Late Roman/Early Byzantine graves recovered from Stymphalos; they are also closely similar to the Late Roman and Early Byzantine tombs documented at Isthmia.[36] The seven individuals represented by the remains include three adults, an adolescent aged 10 to 15 years, a toddler aged 2.0 to 2.5 years, and two infants who died around term. This profile is not unusual for a premodern population and reflects the many risks of a life lived without modern medical treatment. The recovered material suggests that the two stillborn or newborn infants were treated little differently in death from the older individuals. One was buried in the communal Grave 1, while the other was accorded single burial in Grave 2. This suggestion is tentative; it should be noted that the infant in Grave 1 might have been carried in the womb of an adult occupant, and that Grave 2 was placed in an anomalous orientation. However, a pattern of burial of young infants in a mode little different from that used for the rest of the population would be consistent with that seen in the rest of the site, and is of interest considering the many cultures in which burial patterns for extremely young infants differ from those for the rest of the population. Elsewhere in the Roman world, Watts has argued that the start of the Christian era in Britain is reflected in a shift in burial practices for infants, with a pagan tradition of differential burial replaced by a Christian tradition of inclusion in adult cemeteries. This shift is proposed to reflect the influence of Christian beliefs concerning the afterlife and the status of even the youngest infants as people to be protected and mourned.[37] Rife notes, however, that similar burial treatment of all age groups is general at Isthmia, and is present too early to be ascribed to the influence of Christianity. Instead, he argues that this burial pattern reflects the importance of the family as the basic organizational structure of the Isthmian rural economy, with children participating from a young age in economic activities such as herding. Under this system, even the youngest child would be seen as a full member of the family unit.[38] The similar burial pattern at Stymphalos, also a rural community, is consistent with this argument.

The diagnosis of scurvy in the young girl from Grave 1 is also significant for our understanding of life at Late Roman/Early Byzantine Stymphalos because it implies a long-term lack of foods rich in vitamin C, at least for this individual and possibly for the wider population. The richest sources of vitamin C are fruits and vegetables, especially citrus fruits. Organ meats also contain significant amounts of the vitamin, but meat, itself, has very little, as do the various grains.[39] Thus, the groups at highest risk for scurvy are those with limited or no access to fresh fruits and vegetables.

Scurvy has a long medical history, with illnesses matching its symptoms described by ancient Egyptian, Classical, Roman, and ancient Chinese authors.[40] The best-known historical cases of scurvy are those seen in sailors on extended ocean voyages consuming monotonous diets with no fresh fruits or vegetables. Outbreaks of scurvy were also often recorded in famines, in the members of long-term military expeditions, and in civilian populations whose normal diets were disrupted by war.[41] The association between scurvy, famine, and war continues today: in recent years several outbreaks of scurvy have been seen in refugee populations.[42] Given these facts, it might seem that scurvy in this young girl implies a famine or other severe disruption of local life. While this is possible, it is also possible that her condition reflects a general health problem in her community.

Far from being unique to conditions of war or famine, scurvy can present itself in times of peace and even plenty. It is documented in the modern United States, where the major risk factors are poverty, homelessness, social isolation (especially among the elderly), and extreme dietary habits due to personal tastes or psychological problems.[43] While these cases may be seen as marginal, studies on vitamin C consumption patterns show that consumption may be inadequate even within the general population. For example, a recent study of vitamin C intake found 17% of men aged 25 to 64 in the general U.S. population to be vitamin C deficient, though not to the stage of suffering clinical symptoms.[44] These findings highlight the way in which cultural factors such as food habits and the desirability ascribed to different foods can reduce vitamin C intake even when a sufficient supply of the vitamin is technically available.[45]

A further complication is the issue of storage and cooking. Because vitamin C is vulnerable to oxidation, significant losses can occur during storage and cooking, with the result that a food that is a good source of vitamin C when fresh and raw may lose most of its vitamin C before it is eaten.[46] This can become especially important in seasonal climates where fruits and vegetables cannot be harvested fresh throughout the year, and in cultures that cook their foods very thoroughly.

Due to such factors, scurvy was more common in historical populations than might be supposed. In premodern times it was a common winter ailment in Northern Europe owing to low availability of fresh fruits and vegetables; over 100 scurvy epidemics are recorded for this area between 1556 and 1857.[47] It has been argued that because this problem faced any grain-dependent agricultural population with periodically poor access to fruits and vegetables, scurvy was likely a fairly common ailment in archaeological populations.[48] Another known cause of scurvy in past populations was weaning. Juvenile scurvy in infants and toddlers as a result of weaning onto foods poor in vitamin C such as cereal mush or boiled milk is frequently documented in historical sources, and persisted into the twentieth century in some populations.[49] Given these facts, it is perhaps not surprising that skeletal lesions have been used to argue for the presence of scurvy in a number of archaeological populations throughout the world.[50]

Analogy to the modern and historical aspects of scurvy reviewed above suggests that while a catastrophic cause such as famine cannot be ruled out, the scurvy seen in this young girl may also indicate a general nutritional stress on the valley's population. It is possible that this was seasonal in nature; the valley does have fairly cold winters during which some key vitamin C sources such as garden vegetables may have been unavailable, and during which fires might often have been kept going in homes, encouraging food preparation techniques such as long, slow boiling which would significantly decrease the vitamin C content of foods. Given the age of this individual, however, the weaning scurvy seen in infants and toddlers fed a restricted diet of grain mush and well-cooked foods should also be considered.

Recently, Bourbou identified two cases of juvenile scurvy among proto-Byzantine remains recovered at Eleutherna on Crete.[51] This suggests that scurvy may not have been an unusual problem among Eastern Mediterranean populations of the Late Roman and Early Byzantine periods, and perhaps that the cause might lie in a cultural factor such as weaning practices. The other juvenile remains recovered from Stymphalos are currently being re-examined for signs of scurvy, and it is hoped that this, along with research on other populations, will clarify the significance of this individual case.

CONCLUSION

Although small, the assemblage of remains recovered from the Sanctuary's two Late Roman/Early Byzantine graves offers some intriguing clues about life in the Stymphalos valley in that period. Especially interesting is the possibility of infant scurvy at the site, as it suggests that infants were sometimes weaned onto diets poor in vitamin C, a practice that would have significantly affected health and survival in early childhood. Analysis of the Stymphalos burials as a whole will shed further light on this and other questions, and comparison to contemporaneous remains from sites such as Nemea, Corinth, and Isthmia promises to provide a more general picture of health and diet in the Corinthia in Late Roman/Early Byzantine times.

NOTES

Introduction

1 Williams 1983; Williams 1984; Williams 1985. On the geophysical methods employed, see R. Jones, Papamarinopoulos, and Williams 1988.
2 Among the volunteers, Amy Bennett, Shyla Brennan, Deirdre Bryden, Brett Campbell, Harry Edinger, Jennifer Fenton, Mehmet Fıcıcı, Michael Fontaine, Stacey Franklin, Jonathan Gibson, Amy Harrison, Bethany Hayward, Ian Hember, Allison Kennedy, Rajal Khan, Christie Lane, Tina Lykos, Adriana Manderich, Denise McGuire, Hugh Miller, Joyce Palmer, Richard Parker, Nadine Pierce, Lee Russell, Gerald C. Schaus, G. Jordan Schaus, Tara Turner, Maggie Smith, Alison Walters, Sharon Welke, Crystal Wright.

Chapter 1: Stymphalos

1 In some ancient authors, the name is given as "Stymphelos" (Ionic eta for alpha, e.g., Paus. 2.3.5, 5.10.9, 8.4.6, 9.11.6; Diod. Sic., 15.49.5), or "Stymphalis" (Her. 6.76). See J.G. Frazer, *Pausanias' Description of Greece* (London 1898) 271 (Paus. 8.22.1) for a list of other ancient authors mentioning the city. The name is also applied to the lake, the spring which feeds the lake originating near the old village of Kionia or Zaraka, now Stymphaleia, the stream, and even the mountain better known in antiquity as Kyllene or Zyrie. For a recent overview of this polis, see Hansen and Nielsen 2004. For a fuller background to the history, mythology, cults and sources, see *RE* 4, A, 436–53 s.v. "Stymphalos" (1931); *Der Neue Pauly* 11 (2001), 1062, s.v. "Stymphalos."
2 Frazer, *Description*, 268–70 (Paus. 8.22.1) provides a poetic description of the setting of the valley and lake.
3 A small celt of a fine green imported stone (Lakonia?) found in Stym X on the central terrace of the acropolis, and a somewhat larger one of grey stone from Stym XIV below the south edge of the acropolis, Williams et al. 2002, 171 and 183. A third one, larger and less well shaped, also came from Stym XIV.
4 Williams et al. 2002, 141.
5 Lattermann and von Gaertringen 1915, 75–7 fig. 3, pl. 13.2.
6 Williams et al. 2002, 170, visible in the upper middle of Plan 8, p. 161. Cf. Souyoudzoglou-Haywood 1999, 123 pl. 73d.
7 Orlandos investigated a tholos tomb 20 minutes' walk west of Stymphalos in 1928. This, however, is a Hellenistic tholos rather than a Mycenean one. Orlandos 1928, 121–3 figs. 1–3.
8 "And they that held Arcadia beneath the steep mountain of Cyllene, beside the tomb of Aepytus, where are warriors that fight in close combat; [605] and they that dwelt in Pheneos and Orchomenus, rich in flocks, and Rhipe and Stratia and wind-swept Enispe; and that held Tegea and lovely Mantineia; and that held Stymphalus and dwelt in Parrhasia, – all these were led by the son of Ancaeus, Lord Agapenor, [610] with sixty ships; and on each ship embarked full many Arcadian warriors well-skilled in fight. For of himself had the king of men, Agamemnon, given them benched ships wherewith to cross over the wine-dark sea, even the son of Atreus, for with matters of seafaring had they naught to do" (Homer, *The Iliad*, with an English translation by A.T. Murray, PhD in two volumes [Cambridge, MA: Harvard University Press; London: William Heinemann, 1924]). http://www.perseus.tufts.edu/hopper/text?doc=Perseus%3Atext%3A1999.01.0134%3Abook%3D2%3Acard%3D581
9 Curtius 1851, 217 n. 30 suggests that Pindar, *Ol. 6*, 88 refers to the Hera cult of old Stymphalos. Pindar's sixth

Olympic ode celebrates the victory of Hagesias, a citizen of both Stymphalos and Syracuse, in the mule chariot race most likely of 468 BCE. See Farnell 1932, 40.

10 See Pritchett 1998, 124 for references in ancient authors.

11 There was also a tradition that Trophonios, worshipped at Lebadeia in Boiotia, was born in Stymphalos; see Charax with the scholiast to Aristophanes, *Clouds* 508.

12 Mitsos 1946–7; for the dates see pp. 156–7, 172; *SEG* 25 (1971) 445. This period of refuge at Stymphalos may have significance, since there is some evidence for a revival of sorts in activity at the acropolis Sanctuary in the first half of the second century BCE. It may also have helped foster anti-Roman sentiment among the local people. For more on the cults of Stymphalos, see Sturgeon, chapter 3 below, pp. 48–9.

13 A narrow, metre-high stele found in the central part of the town north of the acropolis in 1983, Williams and Cronkite Price 1995, 13 n. 11; Williams and Schaus 2001, 77; see also a possible reference in Aeschylus to Hermes at Stymphalos made by a scholiast to Aristophanes' *Frogs*, Jost 1985, 102–3 n. 1.

14 Amandry 1971, 601–2 (ΔΑΜΑΤΡΟΣ ΣΤΥΝΦΑΛΟΙ); *SEG* XXXV, no. 371; Williams et al. 1997, 44.

15 *SEG* XI, no. 1111. Orlandos (1926, 134) describes the inscription as being found in 1926 in a small section of the acropolis temenos left undug after the 1924 season, near the "priests' house." He describes it as a fallen-over horos stone with measurements 0.56 × 0.29 × 0.21 m. On one side of the stone in "beautiful" fourth-century BCE letters, having a height of 0.035 m, was the single word inscription, ΠΟΛΙΑΔΟΣ. It was taken for safety to the house of Dem. Ath. Xernou in Kionia and has not been seen since. Orlandos believed that it gives us the real name of the goddess worshipped in the Temple, which previously had been assumed to be Hera, but see Schaus, chapter 2 below, pp. 13–14.

16 These will be discussed later, and for the kore, see Sturgeon (chapter 3 below, pp. 36, 43); Williams, Cronkite Price, and Schaus 1996, 80–3 figs. 4–5; Williams et al. 1998, 296–97 fig. 8; Williams and Schaus 2001, 85.

17 For both Dromeus and Hagesias, Olympic victors from Stymphalos, see Schaus 2007, 171–4.

18 Farnell 1932, 48. For a discussion of the three aspects of Hera, especially the unusual role as goddess separated from her husband, see Farnell 1896, 190–2.

19 See Ridgway 1970, 83–4.

20 Xen. *An.* 4.8.18 (a division of Arkadian hoplites and one of peltasts was in Cyrus's army); 6.2.10 (over half of Cyrus's Greek mercenaries were either Achaians or Arkadians).

21 The name "Agasias" is the same as the Olympic victor in the mule-chariot race, Hagesias, from Syracuse, and on his mother's side, from Stymphalos, honoured by Pindar (*Ol. 6*). Xen. *An.* 3.1.31; 4.1.27; 4.7.11–12; 5.2.15; 6.4.10; 6.6.5–34; 7.8.19.

22 For a discussion of Arkadian men as mercenaries, with perhaps as many as 10% of them serving by ca. 400 BCE, see Forsén and Forsén 2003, 267–8.

23 Xenophon only says that Iphikrates attacked walled towns in the region, not mentioning any by name, but Strabo, quoting a story in Eratosthenes, specifically talks about Iphikrates' siege of Stymphalos and his attempt to block the katabothros with sponges: διὸ δὴ καὶ Ἰφικράτη, πολιορκοῦντα τὸν Στύμφαλον καὶ μηδὲν περαίνοντα, ἐπιχειρῆσαι τὴν κατάδυσιν ἀποφράξαι σπόγγους πορισάμενον πολλούς, παύσασθαι δὲ διοσημίας γενομένης. Strabo 8.8.4 (Loeb ed.)

This story suggests both that the town was located on the plain within range of a backed-up lake, and that fortification walls had been built which may be affected by a flooded valley. This is more likely to coincide with the later date, 370/369 BCE, based on archaeological evidence for a foundation at the present location. See Woodhead 1957, 224 n. 4.

24 Walbank 1986; Woodhead 1957, 223–5.

25 Walbank 1986, 349, 351.

26 Walbank 1986, 352 n. 51.

27 Walbank 1986, 352 n. 51. One family tie between Athens and Stymphalos may well have developed between Xenophon, the Athenian, and Agasias, the Stymphalian, as mercenaries on the campaign to assist Cyrus in obtaining the Persian throne. Certainly, Xenophon praises the leadership qualities of Agasias towards the end of the campaign (above note 21).

28 Woodhead 1957, 225.

29 Williams and Gourley 2005, 219 n. 10; also Williams 2005, 398.

30 For a version of this idea, Williams and Schaus 2001, 85. The problem with this hypothesis, as pointed out by M. Sturgeon (below p. 43), is that there are not likely to have been any korai left in Athens after the Persian destruction, so the idea of a gift of a kore from Athens is rather unlikely. Instead, Sturgeon suggests that the kore must have been sent to Stymphalos before the Persian attacks, and to have been housed at old Stymphalos before the new Sanctuary on the acropolis was established.

31 Ἀπολλωνίδης γὰρ ὁ ταχθεὶς ὑπὸ Κασάνδρου στρατηγὸς ἐπὶ τῆς Ἀργείων πόλεως ἐξοδεύσας εἰς Ἀρκαδίαν νυκτὸς ἐκυρίευσε τῆς τῶν Στυμφαλίων πόλεως· Diod. 19.63.1 (Loeb ed.). An alternate translation is that Apollonides led out his men from the city of the Argives into Arkadia by night. This, however, does not seem to be important

information compared to the more significant observation that the city of Stymphalos was taken by a night-time assault.

32 Shipley 2005, for a recent discussion of the effect of Macedonian activity in the Peloponnese at this time. Weir, chapter 4 below, p. 72 note 37 for the capture of the northern Peloponnese by Demetrios Poliorketes.

33 Forsén and Forsén 2003, 269–71. Shipley 2005 argues against an overwhelmingly negative impact of the Macedonian presence in the Peloponnese, pointing out some evidence of positive developments in the late fourth to third centuries. This question will be examined more closely when all the evidence from the acropolis Sanctuary has been studied carefully.

34 Forsén and Forsén 2003, 270–1.

35 The taking of Stymphalos by siege, presumed to have occurred during the Mummian War, is never mentioned by an ancient author specifically. For a description, though of a somewhat earlier siege in the vicinity, see Polybius, 4.71–3, who records the taking of the town of Psophis by Philip V in 219/18 BCE. Scaling ladders and "missiles" (κλίμακας and βέλη) are key elements in the assault.

36 Paus. 7.16.9: "The walls of all the cities that had made war against Rome Mummius demolished, disarming all the inhabitants, even before assistant commissioners were dispatched from Rome, and when these did arrive, he proceeded to put down democracies and to establish governments based on a property qualification" (Loeb transl.).

37 ὁ δὲ πόλεμος ἔσχεν οὗτος τέλος Ἀντιθέου μὲν Ἀθήνησιν ἄρχοντος, Ὀλυμπιάδι δὲ ἑξηκοστῇ πρὸς ταῖς ἑκατόν, ἣν ἐνίκα Διόδωρος Σικυώνιος. (Paus. 7.16.10)

"This war came to an end when Antitheus was archon at Athens, in the hundred and sixtieth Olympiad, at which Diodorus of Sicyon was victorious." (Loeb ed. – Perseus Project website).

38 It is possible that some or all of these cities suffered from Roman attacks after the fall of Corinth, though Strabo is not specific about which wars caused their devastation.

39 Perhaps not coincidentally, Pausanias (8.22.8) gives a story of the neglect of Artemis' worship at Stymphalos in his own times and its consequences in the form of a flooding of the valley. For literary references, topography, mythology, and history of Stymphalos, see *RE* VII (4A) (1931) 436–53.

40 Williams et al. 1998, 277, 279–80; Williams et al. 2002, 145; Williams 2005, 399–400.

41 Campbell 1997, 177–80, 195–6.

42 For the glass, see Schaus, chapter 7 below, p. 150, "Glass"; for the coin, see Weir, chapter 4 below, p. 71, no. **II-97**.

43 H. Lattermann (*Archäologische Gesellschaft zu Berlin* [1914], 106) warned that local workers were continually destroying the structure. "Das sehr beachtenswerte Fundament des Artemistempels (neben dem sog. Katholikon ...) ist durch Peilungen an den eigentlichen Stadtplan angeschlossen worden; leider werden diese Reste, die wichtige Aufschlüsse versprechen, von den Bauern immer mehr zerstört." See Frazer, *Description*, 273, 275 for these remains, and references in earlier travellers, Leake, Curtius, and Vischer. It is appropriate here to explain some confusion in place names. The Cistercian monastery with possible Artemis temple column drums nearby has given both the name Zaraka to a collection of houses which is now part of Stymphaleia (explained by a local woman as being a northern section of the village), and the name Kionia to other parts of the neighbouring village. Zaraka or Saraka goes back as far as the thirteenth-century Medieval sources for the Cistercian monastery. Gell 1823, 384 says that it was at Zaraka that he saw the arches of an aqueduct, no doubt part of the Hadrianic aqueduct of which parts are still visible. Gell clearly gives the name then to the same hamlet around the spring called, by Frazer, Kionia. There is, however, more confusion in what is understood by Kionia. Today, Kionia is the group of houses, many now abandoned, to the west of the Cistercian monastery. This is where the so-called rock-cut "throne" (of presumed Mycenean date) is to be found, and also where a ravine empties which is dry now but must once have had a good flow of water. On the other hand, it is very clear from Frazer (1898, 269, 273), who visited the valley on 30 September 1895, that the name Kionia applied to present-day Stymphaleia. "The name is now transferred to the wretched little Albanian hamlet which stands some three-quarters of a mile away to the east (of the monastery) at the spring which is the chief source of the Stymphalian Lake."

This wonderful spring still bubbles copiously to the surface just below the main road towards the south end of the village of Stymphaleia. In antiquity it was named after the nymph Metopa, but in Frazer's day was called "Kephalovrysi" ("head" or "chief spring"). One further comment is that Frazer (1898, 273) could no longer find the column drums of two different diameters (3 feet and 18 inches) or the large blocks of marble and stone close to the monastery seen by Dodwell on his 1806 visit. Lattermann's observation of the destruction of the site by locals has already been mentioned, but one wonders if these column drums have any connection with the large column drums lying just east of the asphalt road towards the north end of Stymphaleia. These were found with a few marble roof tiles, which suggests that they have not been moved here from elsewhere.

44 Lattermann and von Gaertringen (1915, 74) express surprise that this simple fact had not been generally recognized previously. Early travellers may also have been misled by the rock-cut "throne" (Mycenean?) just above present Kionia, and perhaps also by the large Doric column drums and substantial foundation more than a kilometre to the northeast, at the other end of Stymphaleia.

45 Possibly near the hill of Aghios Konstantinos, where a cemetery and substantial columns have been located. A hill, called Aghia Triadha (see above) after a chapel along its ridge, just to the east of Lafka at the west end of the valley, has sections of a circuit (?) wall preserved on it, but few cultural remains, at least on the surface. The masonry of the wall looks Mycenean (periodic offsets, and cyclopean blocks).

46 See Martha 1883, 486–93, esp. 490.

47 Frazer 1898, 273.

48 Lattermann and von Gaertringen (1915, 74) mistakenly attribute this correction of Strabo to C.O. Müller, who visited the site in 1840, rather than to Dodwell.

49 For a preliminary report on excavations of the monastery, Campbell 1997. Final publication results are being prepared.

50 Dodwell 1819, 434.

51 Leake 1830, 110.

52 Leake 1830, 111.

53 Ross 1841, 54.

54 Curtius 1851, 203–5 with plan, pl. IV.

55 Vischer 1875, 498 note.

56 Bursian 1868–72, 197.

57 *Guides-Joanne, Grèce* 1891, 388.

58 Frazer 1898, 272.

59 Lattermann and von Gaertringen 1915, 71–90 pls. 13–14.

60 Lattermann and von Gaertringen 1915, 90 fig. 14 and pl. 14.3.

61 Orlandos 1926, 134. See above note 15.

62 For Orlandos' brief annual reports, see Orlandos, *Praktika* 1922–4, 1925–6, 1927, 1928, 1929, 1930; for the photograph and plan, see Orlandos 1924, 121 figs. 4 and 5. A summary of some of Orlandos' work is found in *JHS* 45 (1925) 225.

63 Papahatzis 1980, 260 fig. 243.

64 Preliminary reports on the excavations are in Williams and Cronkite Price, 1995, 12–18; Williams, Schaus, and Cronkite Price 1996, 76–88; Williams et al. 1997, 44–57; Williams et al. 1998, 285–97; Williams et al. 2002, 151–4. For the jewellery finds, see Young 2001, and for the summary of results, see Williams and Schaus 2001; also briefly Williams 2005, 401–2.

Chapter 2: The Sanctuary

1 Photographs of the site used in this volume are my own except where noted. Proper excavation photographs taken in the course of the campaign became inaccessible for use due to unfortunate circumstances in their storage at the project's base.

2 The earliest to suggest this seems to be Ludwig Ross (1841, 54). See above, p. 10.

3 The local limestone is hard, but rather brittle. It dissolves from rainwater, leaving holes in and through its exposed surfaces.

4 Orlandos 1925, 53. According to Pausanias (8.22.2) there were three sanctuaries to Hera at Stymphalos, but these were likely in the older location of the town (as discussed above).

5 Orlandos 1926, 134. Orlandos is not precise about the location of the find. On the one hand, he indicates that the discovery was made near the Temple excavated in 1924 (παρὰ τόν προπέρυσιν ἀνασκαφέντα ναὸν"); on the other, he states that there was a small unexcavated section of the "temenos" beside the "priests' house" which yielded the inscription. Taken together, one might suppose that the inscription came from the small area between the "priests' house" (Building A) and the Temple, very close to where we discovered the five stelai still in situ. Orlandos says that he worked both on the Temple and the "priests' house" in his "mikra anaskaphe" in 1924, but he could hardly have done much more than uncover sections of the walls of these two buildings, since no traces of his excavations were found during our own. It is difficult in the circumstances to be certain whether "temenos" here means the Temple itself or the Sanctuary as a whole.

6 For vertically inscribed horos stones from the Agora, Lalonde 1991, 22 no. H2 (sanctuary horos in the Agora) and 28 no. H31 (horos of the Kerameikos area) pls. 1–2, and 27 nos. H25–6 (horoi of civil establishments) pl. 2, which are inscribed both horizontally and vertically. These, however, are all inscribed on their wider faces, not on their narrower face like the Stymphalos stone. My thanks to M. Richardson for her helpful comments on these.

7 Lalonde 1991, nos. H25 and H26, pl. 2, and for wide spacing of horizontal lines, see H30, pl. 2.

8 Lalonde 1991, 23, 25; compare also H2 (53 × 23 × 13 cm), H5 (60 × 38 × 23 cm, broken at the bottom), H6 (55 × 20.5 × 16 cm, broken at the bottom).

9 For a good discussion of the epithet "Πολιάς" see Guettel Cole 1995, 301–5. "Πολιάς and Πολιεύς … were precisely defined terms narrowly used, Πολιάς only of Athena and Πολιεύς only of Zeus. Both titles originally

had a strict spatial reference and defined these two gods as guardians of the πόλις in its earliest meaning of 'acropolis'"(Guettel Cole 1995, 301).

10 Williams 1984, 179; *SEG* XXXVIII, no. 356; Williams and Cronkite Price 1995, 13 n. 11; Williams and Schaus 2001, 77.

11 The side of a herm is used for a kalos inscription on a red-figure amphora in Boston (MFA 68.163, *LIMC*, Hermes 93) written vertically; otherwise a couple of other herms are depicted with a caduceus on their sides (*LIMC*, Hermes 135, 136).

12 Inv. 27 is discussed in Weir, chapter 4, no. **II-51**, pp. 64, 74, and Inv. 503 and 2525 in Schaus, chapter 10, **6**, p. 218, and chapter 7, **22**, pp. 153–4. For the loomweight (Inv. 2909) and possibly several others with the letter "E" (epsilon) inscribed on it, see Surtees, chapter 12, **29**, pp. 238, 242. For a fifth object, a glass bezel with a goddess (?) holding two objects in her hands, which may be connected to Eileithyia, see Young, chapter 6 below, no. **136** (Inv. 690), p. 119.

13 Jost 1985, 39, 46, 524 ("Ilithyie"). For further discussion, see below, pp. 33–4 ("Pillar Shrine Area"). For a comprehensive discussion of religion in Arkadia, see Jost 1985, and for a more recent discussion of cults and sanctuaries in the region of Lousoi and Pheneos (northeast Arkadia), see Erath 1999, and Tausend 1999. Tausend (343–5) notes that the area of northern Arkadia from Psophis to Pheneos, including Kleitor, was occupied by an ethnically distinct people called the Azanes, and that their cults reflected some differences from their Arkadian neighbours.

14 Thanks are owed to Sarah Morris and Margaret Miles for alerting me to the Marmaria stelai.

15 Demangel 1926, 49–51 fig. 58; photo of the stelai in G. Roux, *Delphes, son oracle and ses dieux* (Paris 1976), pl. XVI fig. 29.

16 Roux 1976, pl. XVI fig. 29 caption; Demangel 1926, 49.

17 Demangel 1926, 49 nn. 6–7.

18 Orlandos 1924, 117–23, esp. 120–2 figs. 4–5; Orlandos 1926, 134.

19 A coin of Ptolemy III (Weir, chapter 4, p. 71, no. **II-94**) dated 246–221 BCE as well as two fourth-century coins of Corinth (Weir, chapter 4, p. 61, nos. **II-23–4**, 335–306 BCE) were found in Level 5 of this trench. A coin of Sikyon, dated ca. 330–200 BCE (Weir, chapter 4, p. 67, no. **II-72**) was found in Level 6, while one from Mantineia (Weir, chapter 4, p. 70, no. **II-90**), dated after ca. 370 BCE, and two from Histiaia (Euboia) (Weir, chapter 4, pp. 59–60, nos. **II-15–16**) dated 338–late third century BCE were found in Level 7. This suggests a depositing of Levels 7 to 5 from the fourth to the second half of the third century BCE.

Somewhat more complex stratigraphy was found in Trench 99.1, a large trench on the slope just to the east of the Altar Terrace Wall. This was excavated in a season when the author was not supervising work in the Sanctuary and no scarp drawings of the stratigraphy were left in the field notebook. Here Level 5, a deep layer of coarse fill, stones, tiles, and pottery, was taken in 6 pails (nos. 5–11), perhaps representing a destruction of the Sanctuary. Some iron projectiles were still found in the layer below (Level 6 Pail 12).

20 For Samothrace, see Lehmann and Spittle 1964, figs. 18–19, 24, and a restoration drawing opposite the title page. For the Artemis Temple at the Letoon, Metzger et al. 1979, 14 fig. 2 and pl. 3.a–b "l'édifice E"; Laroche 2003, 451; and des Courtils 2003, 147–8 figs. 54, 59, and restoration fig. 55.

21 Broneer 1967, 96–8; Lehmann 1967, 429–32.

22 Metzger et al. 1979, 14 n. 24 pl. 3a–b; des Courtils 2003, 147–8 figs. 54 and 59.

23 For the excavation of the cella, E. Hansen and le Roy 1976; and a later sondage, Laroche 2003, 451–2. See also now Hansen and le Roy 2012.

24 Des Courtils 2003, 141–5.

25 Des Courtils 2003, 145.

26 Laroche 2003, 451.

27 Three orthostate blocks from the pronaos cross wall are indicated on Orlandos' plan (above fig. 1.10), but they were no longer in situ when work began again in the mid-1990s.

28 *Archäologische Gesellschaft zu Berlin* 1914, 105–6.

29 Roux (1961, 23 pl. 2.2) commented on the poor quality of the limestone used for the temple of Apollo at Bassai with similar repairs needed.

30 For a summary of the various pieces of evidence for habitation on the site prior to the fourth century, see Hansen and Nielsen 2004, 530; while there is evidence for some occupation of the site prior to the fourth century, it is clear that much more intense activity can be traced only to the fourth century, perhaps its second quarter, Williams et al. 1997, 23; Williams 2005, 398.

31 Weir, chapter 4, p. 73, graph "Coin loss at Stym II by decade" with discussion.

32 Weir, chapter 4 below, no. **II-92**.

33 The sixth coin appeared in 2000 during trench cleaning. The coins are from Sikyon (3), Phlious, Chalcis, and Thessaly ("Ainianon"). The coin from Phlious may be the earliest, from the first half of the fourth century. Two of the Sikyonian coins are dated ca. 330 BCE, while the third may date ca. 330–251 BCE. The coin from Chalcis is perhaps the latest, with a suggested date of 338–305 BCE (see Weir, chapter 4, pp. 58–9, 62, 64–5, nos. **II-9,**

12, 35, 48, 49, 53). The coin from Thessaly had been dated ca. 400–344, but Weir now thinks this should be down-dated based on this hoard.

34 My thanks to Ben Gourley for an informative discussion about mudbrick architecture.

35 See, for example, the reconstructed roof of the fifth-century stone Temple of Athena Makistos near Skillous, in cross section, Nakasis 2004, Plans IX–X. For typical roof beam systems, Orlandos 1966, figs. 7–8; Dinsmoor 1950, fig. 20. For a general discussion of building materials, Fagerström 1988, 99–105.

36 For the Lakonian system of roof tiles, Winter 1993, 95–109. For some of the technical considerations of a terracotta roof, Schwandner 1990.

37 Cavanagh et al. 1996, 85. The prevalence of pan tiles and lack of cover tiles was also observed by the excavators at the temple of Zeus at Megalopolis, Lauter 2002, 380.

38 1997 field notebook, pp. 114–15, 130, and p. 140 for the second cover tile (from Tr. 97.12.2.2or3). A cover tile that was broken into 9 pieces and glued together is in the apothiki, not labelled, with a preserved length of 0.6 m, and a width that varies from 0.185 at its narrower end to 0.20 m.

39 Winter 1993, 109 describes the ridge tile as larger than the cover tiles and with a more complex shape to allow for overlap along the ridge beam. No tiles of this type, however, were identified on the site.

40 The temple of Athena Makistos has an unusual foundation in the centre of the west end of its stylobate which resembles the outline of the foundation for the stairs of the Stymphalos Temple, but it is a later accretion without function for the three-step krepidoma of this temple. See Nakasis 2004, 44 fig. 11, Plan 1.

41 Dinsmoor 1950, "Chronological List of Greek Temples" after p. 340.

42 Trianti 1984; Schattner 1990; Catling 1994, 269–75. A well-preserved temple or house model (fine white limestone or marble with partially restored façade, not labelled, but with the number 12[1] painted in red and immediately below in black at the back of its right side) is on display in the archaeological museum at Kavalla (see below).

43 Catling 1994, 273.

44 Geometric models from Argos, Chaniale Tekke, and Perachora have small openings high on the walls below the roof line; see Schattner 1990, 153–4 cat. 1, 3, 6 pls. 1–2, 4. A painted model from Thera belonging to the sixth century also has these openings, Schattner 1990, cat. 46 pl. 24.

45 For examples with antae, see Schnattner 1990, 50–1 cat. 19, pl. 9, pp. 57–60 cat. 23–4 pls. 12–14 (from Samos), and discussion pp. 140–2; and for examples with columns, pp. 22–3 cat. 1 pl. 1 (Argos), pp. 31–4 cat. 5–6 pls. 3.1–2, 4 (Larisa am Hermos, Perachora respectively), pp. 88–90 cat. 45–6 pls. 23–4 (from Sardis and Thera respectively). The Thera example has small columns resting on balustrades which extend across part of the front, creating an open porch.

46 Schattner 1990, cat. 19, 24, 26 pls. 9, 14, 16.1–2 (all three from Samos).

47 Schattner 1990, 52–3, 152 cat. 20 pl. 10.1–2.

48 Schattner 1990, cat. 47 pl. 25.

49 R.W.V. Catling, "Archaic Lakonian Architecture: The Evidence of a Temple Model," *BSA* 100 (1995) 317–24; Schattner 1990, 91–2 nos. 47–9.

50 Schattner 1990, 91–2 cat. 47–9; compare also Catling 1994, figs. 1–3 for the height to width of a narrow end of a model.

51 Schattner 1990, 205–7; Fagerström 1988, 156–7; but see Catling 1994, 274–5, who argues against the idea.

52 A temple identified as belonging to Asklepios excavated at Alipheira in southwestern Arkadia has a large base just at its entrance as well, but without any cutting. Its location, although on one's left when entering the temple, is suggestive of the same function. This temple is close to the same size (5.75 × 9.3 m) and same date (second half of the fourth century BCE) as the acropolis Temple at Stymphalos. See Orlandos 1967–8, 171–82 figs. 111, 115–16.

53 Blinkenberg 1941, 871–8 no. 487.

54 Eight examples have been catalogued; see Schaus, chapter 7, pp. 165–7.

55 The burials are discussed by Garvie-Lok, chapter 14 below.

56 See Garvie-Lok, chapter 14, pp. 270–2.

57 Oddly, the earrings are of Late Classical type (see Young, chapter 6, pp. 106–7, 112), but if they did belong to the little girl, they may have been of a long-lasting form.

58 Garvie-Lok, chapter 14 below, p. 273.

59 See Delattre 2008, 190–1 for a summary of the development of Christian belief regarding unbaptized children in the early to middle Byzantine period. My thanks to Chryssa Bourbou for her comments and references (in this and note 60) on this matter.

60 Tritsaroli and Valentin 2008, 96–97.

61 For a large Byzantine cemetery at Spata in Attica (199 individuals of whom 61 were subadults), see Tritsaroli and Valentin 2008, especially 103–6 for the youngest individual, est. one year old at death, who was buried apart in an agricultural activity area, with a north-south orientation (head to the north) and covered by a fragment of a beehive. In general, however, sub-adults were not

isolated in special funerary areas in Byzantine cemeteries, although they are sometimes found in greater concentrations in some places. See, for example, Tritsaroli and Valentin 2008, 103; Delattre 2008, 186–7; and note the discussion about burials at Isthmia of similar date in Garvie-Lok, chapter 14, p. 273.

62 Williams, chapter 11, pp. 234–5, nos. **52–66**; the complete lamp, no. **52**, is a Broneer Type 16. It was one of five found in the Temple (Williams, nos. **52–4, 57,** and an uninventoried lamp).

63 Williams, chapter 11, p. 235, no. **67**.

64 For the coins, see Weir, chapter 4, p. 71, nos. **II-95–7** (no. **II-97** Manuel I, dated 1143–80), and for some possibly Medieval glass, see Schaus, chapter 7, pp. 150–2.

65 Orlandos 1967–8, 182–99 figs. 123–9, with examples of other finely decorated altars.

66 See Hagerman, chapter 5 below.

67 I thank K. Sherwood Donahue, who is studying the figurines from the site.

68 See Stone, chapter 9, p. 194.

69 The Broneer Type 16 lamp fragment was found in pottery washing and was recorded on the Pail form. For the Type 27 lamps, see Williams, chapter 11, p. 235, cat. **61–3** (inv. 2181, 2274, 0025). For the coins, see Weir, chapter 4, pp. 63, 68, nos. **II-43** and **II-78**.

70 Weir, chapter 4, p. 68, no. **II-78**.

71 Several sherds with orange or red slip have been found in the Sanctuary, including a possible Eastern Sigillata A fragment from Trench 95.9 baulk. This, however, is very weak evidence for Roman-period occupation.

72 Tile fragments were separated into piles by size and counted. There were 428 tiles in the range of 10–30 cm^2, 320 of 30–90 cm^2, 270 of 90–200 cm^2, 75 of 200–300 cm^2, 44 of 300–400 cm^2, 15 of 400–600 cm^2, and 5 of 600–800 cm^2, for a total of 1157 tile fragments, with an approximate area of 11.2 m^2. Unbroken or otherwise reusable tiles must have been salvaged when the floor level was raised.

73 For the use of this room and a discussion of the loomweights, see Surtees, chapter 12, pp. 244–5.

74 The most interesting of the finds from this deposit was the jewellery, for which see Young, chapter 6, pp. 139, 145.

75 There was not much pottery recovered on or in the floor of the West Annex; see Stone, chapter 9, p. 195. Stone was aware of the problem of dating, and that some connection with the destruction of Building A and especially the North Annex around the mid-second century was a strong possibility, but he could find no support for this hypothesis in the recovered pottery.

76 For the grave's contents, see Garvie-Lok, chapter 14, p. 272.

77 For the orientation of infant burials, see above notes 58 and 60.

78 Schaus, chapter 1 above, p. 7, note 15.

79 Demangel 1926, 50 fig. 58.

80 Jost 1985, 232–3.

81 The type is best known from the representation of Hermes with his sculpted head on top and normally an erect phallus on the front side of a tall quadrangular pillar – the so-called herm. Examples of such pillars representing a variety of deities are on display in the Tegea museum; some of them have identifying and dedicatory inscriptions. See Rhomaios 1911 for a description of the collection in Tegea and others in Arkadia. Ten of the 18 examples in Tegea with a pyramid-shaped head had inscriptions. Rhomaios (158) rejects any influence on the Arkadian tetragonoi from either Egyptian obelisks or similar Phoenician examples of sacred stones (cippi). For a selection of such herms in sculpture and vases, see *LIMC* V, "Hermes" nos. 9–185. Pausanias (8.39.6) describes a statue of Hermes in Phigaleia that was clothed with a mantle, but which ended in a square shape rather than feet; and one in the old gymnasium at Megara (Paus. 1.44.2) that was in the shape of a small pyramid and was called Apollo Carinus (and here there was a sanctuary of the Eileithyiae). At Sikyon (Paus. 2.9.6), there was both a Zeus Meilichius shaped like a pyramid and an Artemis Patroa like a pillar ("kioni"), neither of which had any artistry, notes Pausanias. And at 8.48.6, Pausanias says that the form of the "tetragonal agalma" appears to him to be very dear to the Arkadians.

82 Rhomaios 1911, 154 fig. 11 and 156 fig. 12 respectively.

83 For the cave and the worship of Hermes on Kyllene, see Tausend 1999, 357–62; Kusch 1999.

84 Jost 1985, 377–8, 524. Jost discusses the relationship between the figure of Auge and Eileithyia. The spelling of "Eileithyia" has quite a number of variants, but the more common form in the Peloponnese seems to be "Eleuthia," at least in the Archaic period; see Pingiatoglou 1981, 53–61, 66–9. One votive relief from Lakonia from the Classical period has the upsilon after the theta; Pingiatoglou 1981, 60–1. For sanctuaries of this goddess in the Peloponnese, see Pingiatoglou 1981, 37–42, including ones at Kleitor, Pellene, and Corinth.

85 Jost (1985, 524) adds that this reference to weaving evidently associates her with Destiny.

86 Jost (1985, 524) objects to Baur's (1902, 29) conclusion from Pausanias that the hymn by Olen was sung at Kleitor and that the goddess was worshipped as the dispenser of destiny. Instead she says that Pausanias may merely be showing his erudition, since he (1.18.5) mentions a sanctuary of Eileithyia in Attica and again states that the

Delians sing a hymn by Olen. She concludes that at Kleitor, just as at Tegea and at Megalopolis, Eileithyia had her usual role.

87 See also Schaus, chapter 7, pp. 153–4, no. **22**. It is interesting that neither at Megalopolis nor at Delphi is Eileithyia associated closely with Artemis, since this is often the case elsewhere, especially in Boiotia. For a good discussion of Artemis-Eileithyia, see Vorster 1983, 70–2.

Chapter 3: Sculpture

1 I am grateful to Hector Williams, director of the Canadian excavations at Stymphalos, for asking me to study these sculptures, and to his colleagues, especially Professor Gerald P. Schaus, who directed the excavation of the acropolis temple, for consultation. I have had useful conversations with a number of people concerning some of the issues raised by this material, especially Nancy Bookidis, Catherine Keesling, Sonia Klinger, and Alexander Mantis, and I thank them for their insights. The reconstruction drawing is the work of Karen Hutchinson Sotiriou.

2 Williams et al. 1998, 287; Williams and Schaus 2001, 85.

3 Permission to conduct provenance testing on the Stymphalos sculptures was granted by the Archaeological Service. Y. Maniatis and D. Tambakopoulos, of the Laboratory of Archaeometry in the Institute of Materials Science at the National Centre for Scientific Research "Demokritos," visited Corinth in February 2007 and conducted analysis of two pieces, **1G** and **2G**. Three techniques were applied to each piece: measurements of maximum grain size under a stereoscopic microscope and qualitative examination of the marble crystalline features, electron paramagnetic resonance spectroscopy, and stable isotope analysis, followed by statistical analysis of the results. See Sturgeon, Maniatis, and Tambakopoulos 2012.

4 Williams et al. 1997, 47; evidence for earlier activity includes small amounts of fifth-century pottery, rim attachments for bronze caryatid mirrors, and undressed stones beneath the wall of the fourth-century temple; see pp. 20, 156–7, 222–3.

5 Williams and Cronkite Price 1995, 15; Williams, Cronkite Price, and Schaus 1996, 87; Williams and Schaus 2001, 83.

6 For later material found in the Temple, see pp. 150 (glass) and 234 (lamps); and for reuse of Building A after its mid-second-century BCE destruction, see p. 29.

7 Dionysos is associated with wild animals, but he is not represented with the proportions or modelling that characterize the Stymphalos hand.

8 Acropolis 615: Schrader 1939, 106–107, no. 56, pls. 82, 83, Attic, ca. 490–480 BCE; Richter 1968, 81, no. 125, figs. 401–4, ca. 500 BCE, island marble; Brouskari 1974, 69, ca. 490–480 BCE; Boardman 1991, 86, fig. 156, ca. 510–500. The dates cited here are those traditionally followed, except for those specifically addressed in Stewart's 2008 excellent treatment of Late Archaic sculpture chronology.

9 Acropolis 684: Schrader 1939, 104–6, no. 55, pls. 78–81; Richter 1968, 101, no. 182; Brouskari 1974, 68, 69, ca. 490 BCE; Stewart 2008, 2, 590, fig. 10.

10 Acropolis 671: Richter 1968, 70, 71, no. 111; Brouskari 1974, 74. Acropolis 615: Richter 1968, 81, no. 125; Brouskari 1974, 69, 70. Acropolis 685: Richter 1968, 100, no. 181; Brouskari 1974, 73. Acropolis 688: Richter 1968, 102, 103, no. 184; Brouskari 1974, 128, Pentelic; Stewart 2008, 407, 601, cat. no. 7.

11 Athens, NM 22: Marcadé 1950, 202, fig. 15; Hermary et al. 1996, 48, 49, no. 16; *LIMC* VI, 257, 258, no. 4bis, s.v. Leto (L. Kahil); Kaltsas 2002b, 73, no. 106; Karakasi 2003, 69, pls. 72, 226, 227. The holes on the Leto's chest are much larger than those of the Stymphalos figure.

12 Athens, NM 3687: Konstantinou 1931–2, pls. 5–7, fig. 4 for drawing of metal attachments; Boardman 1991, 85, fig. 149; Ridgway 1993, 91, 118 n. 3.74; Kaltsas 2002b, 74, no. 110, ca. 500 BCE.

13 On the metal jewellery found within the cella, see Young 2001, and Young, chapter 6 below.

14 For a drawing and discussion of this type of joining, see Rockwell 1993, 150, 151, drawing 47:1.

15 On cross-pin joins in korai, see, e.g., Acropolis Museum 670: Schrader 1939, 50, 51, no. 8; Claridge 1990, figs. 4, 7. Acropolis Museum 685: Schrader 1939, 97, no. 47, fig. 61; Claridge 1990, 142, fig. 7. Cf. also the right forearm of Antiope and the left shoulder of a torso from the west pediment of the Temple of Apollo at Eretreia, Archaeological Museum 18053 and 41: Touloupa 2002, 12–14, 17, nos. I.1 and I.4, pls. 6, 15, the cross-pin as a container for lead, 13.

16 Richter 1968, 85, 86, no. 138, figs. 441–4, ca. 530–520 BCE; reworked in antiquity.

17 Dickens 1912, 38, 39, lists the occurrences of right and left arm inserts; those with tenons only number 17 right, 5 left, and with tenon and dowel, 6 right, 3 left.

18 Athens, NM 2569: Alford 1978, 421–4, no. 74; Petrakos 1999, 277, fig. 187, Pentelic (Alford); Kaltsas 2002b, 61, no. 79, ca. 520 BCE; Sturgeon 2006, 54, 55, figs. 22a, b.

19 Herz 2000. Cf., e.g., a statue of Artemis on Paros, Archaeological Museum, Kleeman 1962; Rubensohn 1962,

55, 56, pls. 7, 8. On the characteristics of Parian marble, see Maniatis and Polikreti 2000.

20 On Archaic sculpture from Paros, see Pedley 1976; Kostoglou-Despini 1979; Zaphiropoulos 1986; Floren 1987, 160–72; Kokkorou-Alevra 1997, 2000; Zaphiropoulou 2000; Sturgeon 2006, 43, 44. On the distribution of sculptures in Parian marble, see Kokkorou-Alevra 2000, 143–50.

21 See, for example, kouros from Phigalia in Olympia, Floren 1987, 228, pl. 19:2; sphinx from Corinth, Walter-Karydi 1987, 57, figs. 64, 65; head of a youth from Corinth, Walter-Karydi 1987, 88, figs. 124, 125; legs from Isthmia, Sturgeon 1987, 70–3; and kouros from Tenea in Munich, Walter-Karydi 1987, 57, 59, fig. 68.

22 On outstretched hands, see Keesling 2003, 149–61; on fruits and birds, Keesling 2003, 144–49; Karakasi 2003, 124.

23 Compare, e.g., the hands, Athens, Acropolis 386: Schrader 1939, 162, no. 211, figs. 142, 143 (meat?, kidney?); Acropolis 379: Schrader 1939, 165, no. 221, fig. 145 (dove); Acropolis 372: Schrader 1939, 166, no. 223, fig. 146 (apple).

24 Berlin, Staatliche Museen 1750: Richter 1968, 46, no. 56; Kyrieleis 1995, 32, fig. 29. Torso, Samos, Vathy Museum P 149/ head Berlin, Staatliche Museen Sk 1874: Karakasi 2003, 16, pls. 8, 11.

25 Karakasi 2003, 38, 39.

26 See, e.g., Kyrkou 2003, on the terracottas from the Shrine of the Nymph on the south slope of the Acropolis, especially figs. 1–4, the reconstruction in fig. 21 (est. H 0.625 m), and references to other large terracottas, some of which stood as tall as 1.20 to 1.412 m (p. 48); Travlos 1971, 361–3; *LIMC* VIII, 202, s.v. Nymphe I (M. Kyrkou).

27 Hermary 1989, 336, nos. 666, 667 (horned deer, sixth century BCE), 337, no. 670 (flower, sixth century BCE), 369, no. 746 (bull, fifth century BCE); Nielsen 1992, 16, 17, nos. 3, 4 (flower, sixth century BCE), 23, no. 10 (calf, fifth to fourth century BCE); Karageorghis, Mertens, and Rose 2000, 118, 119, no. 184 (flower, early sixth century), 248, 249, no. 403 (draped male with bull mask, mid-third century); Keesling 2003, 147, 148.

28 For hares on grave stelai, see, e.g., two stelai in Athens from Larisa, Thessaly, Kaltsas 2002b, 97, no. 172 (NM 741), 98, no. 173 (NM 734), both from the mid-fifth century BCE; and a relief from Laurion, Attica, 165, no. 326 (NM 794), ca. 400 BCE.

29 Keesling 2003, 147, 148.

30 On terracotta figurines of Artemis holding a deer see, e.g., Klinger 2002, 2003.

31 See, for example, the dogs illustrated in Mainoldi 1984.

32 See, in general, *LIMC* II, 643, 644, nos. 224, 234, 242, s.v. Artemis (L. Kahil). The terracottas from Stymphalos include a running Artemis reaching into her quiver, Orlandos 1925, 53, fig. 3. K.D. Sherwood is preparing the terracotta figurines from the Canadian excavations at Stymphalos for publication.

33 Contrast, for example, a bronze crouching panther in the Mildenberg Collection, first half of fifth century BCE, with paws forward and elbows in (Kozloff 1981, 142, no. 120), with outward pointing elbows of a sleeping Molossian hound (Kozloff 1981, 196, no. 184; Perfahl 1983, fig. on 18).

34 Cf., e.g., a Greek terracotta dog in the Mildenberg Collection: Kozloff, Mitten, and Squaitamatti 1986, 30, 31, no. II, 135, ca. 500–450 BCE.

35 On felines, especially cats and cheetahs, see Ashmead 1977–8; Ashmead 1994; Donalson 1999; and Engels 1999; on leopards and panthers, see, e.g., Brown 1960, 170–6; Koch-Harnack 1983, 105–19, figs. 43–53.

36 Boston, Museum of Fine Arts 01.8055, which turns its head: Richter 1930, 9, pl. 9, fig. 30, seventh to sixth century BCE.

37 On the difficulty of distinguishing the type of feline, especially when the animal appears to be young, see Engels 1999, 174, 175.

38 So identified in Williams and Schaus 2001, 85. On the hare in ancient Greece, see, e.g., Keller 1909, 210–17, who notes the absence of the rabbit, 218; Richter 1930, 29, 30, figs. 152–7.

39 In bronzes, see Richter 1930, 30, 74, fig. 155, from the Athenian Acropolis, NM 6682; in terracottas, Higgins 1954, 259, no. 955, pl. 134, late fifth century, "from Tanagra." On vases, see, e.g., the red figure kylix in Copenhagen, National Museum 14268: *ARV*[2] 1583.2, Bérard 1989, fig. 122, ca. 500 BCE; kylix in London, British Museum E 46: *ARV*[2] 315.1, Bérard et al. 1989, fig. 121, ca. 500 BCE; coin: Richter 1930, 29, 30, fig. 154; Head 1968, 153; the hare is also used on coins of Rhegion (p. 109) and Croton (p. 99). Egyptian painting from Thebes, Keller 1909.

40 Berlin, Staatliche Museen 1750, H with plinth 1.67, H plinth 0.07, missing head: Blümel 1963, 42, 43, no. 34, figs. 94–8; it must have stood outdoors for many years, and so was not a cult statue; Richter 1968, 46, no. 56, figs. 186–9, possibly a dedication to Aphrodite; Freyer-Schauenberg 1974, 27–31, no. 7, pls. 7, 8; Karakasi 2003, 16, 166, no. 7, pls. 8, 9.

41 Vathy, Archaeological Museum P 149: Kyrieleis 1995, 32, figs. 27, 29 (with head Berlin, Staatliche Museen Sk 1874), pl. 8; Karakasi 2003, 16, no. 9a, pl. 11. On hand-held objects, see Freyer-Schauenburg 1974, 44; Kron

1986, 57–61; Karakasi 2003, 16, 48 and, on the meaning of the hare, associated with Aphrodite and Hera, 124. On hand-held offerings, see Schrader 1939, 159–67, where the objects held include meat, p. 162, no. 211, figs. 142, 143; Keesling 2003, 141–61, fruits and birds are commonly held by the Acropolis korai.

42 For the statue from Brauron, Archaeological Museum 60: Vorster 1983, 125, 222, no. 41, pl. 23:2, ca. 320 BCE; Ridgway 1990b, 338, pl. 175. See also the statue of a girl with a hare from the Ilissos area, Athens, NM 694: Kaltsas 2002b, 268, no. 559. Grave stelai from Thessaly in Athens, NM 741: Biesantz 1965, 13, 14, no. K19, pls. 10, 11, ca. 450 BCE; Kaltsas 2002b, 97, no. 172; NM 740: Biesantz 1965, 18, no. K29, pl. 4; Kaltsas 2002b, 98, no. 173, ca. 440 BCE.

43 Stele from Laurion, Athens, NM 794: Clairmont 1993, I, 256, 257, no. 1.200; Kaltsas 2002b, 165, no. 326.

44 Paris, Louvre MA 805: Clairmont 1993, I, 317, 318, no. 1.330a; Pfuhl-Möbius I, 20, no. 37, pl. 10, second quarter fourth century BCE. A hare also sits on a person's hand on a votive relief from Epidauros: Athens, NM 1426, *LIMC* II, 881, no. 204, s.v. Asklepios (B. Holtzmann); Comella 2002, 143, no. 145; Kaltsas 2002b, 227, no. 478; and on an early fourth-century funerary relief from Kasos in Rhodes, Pfuhl-Möbius I, 20, no. 36, pl. 10.

45 For depictions of hares on vases, see Koch-Harnack 1983, 63–98, 132, 226, figs. 1–31, 63, 64, 111. The bronze statuette of a hare found near the monastery at Stymphalos exhibits the typical conformation of a mature hare in a running position: Williams et al. 1997, 48, fig. 7 (drawing).

46 Cf., e.g., the kylix in Küsnacht, private collection: Bérard et al. 1989, fig. 118, Douris, ca. 490 BCE, where a hare, which is kept in a cage, rests on a youth's lap.

47 New York, MMA 07.286.110: Richter 1954, 3, 4, no. 4, pls. 6, 7; Richter 1968, 85, no. 138, figs. 441–4, H 0.69 m; Karakasi 2003, 124, pl. 124; the left hand originally held the garment.

48 For Apollo Philesios at Didyma by Kanachos of Sikyon, see *LIMC* II, 224, no. 332, for the Miletus relief, 224, no. 332a, s.v. Apollon (W. Lambrinoudakis).

49 London: Walters 1899, 19, 20, no. 209, pl. 1, probably from Etruria; Walters 1915, pl. 3.

50 Paris, Louvre: Collignon 1876, 291, 292, fig. on 292; Bielefeld 1962, 19, pl. 4:2.

51 Berlin, Staatliche Museen, Antiken-Abteilung 1845: Bielefeld 1962, 19, pl. 4:3.

52 Rome, Museo Nazionale, Palazzo Altemps 427220: de Lachenal 1980; cited with statue of a maenad or Artemis holding an animal once Ludovisi Collection, now U.S. embassy, Rome, Giuliano 1986, 164, no. VII, 14, inv. 61531 (B. Palma); Acquisizioni 1998, 82, 83 (M. De Angelis); De Angelis d'Ossat 2002, 100, 101.

53 In Compiegne, no. 1025: *ARV*[2] 1055.76, Schefold 1981, fig. 29; *LIMC* III, 494, no. 848, s.v. Dionysos (A. Veneri), Polygnotus Group, ca. 440–430 BCE. Besides Apollo, some male deities, such as Zeus and Poseidon, occasionally carry animals. See, e.g., *LIMC* VIII, 319, no. 27, pl. 324, no. 62, s.v. Zeus (M. Tiverios) for Zeus holding an eagle on his outstretched hand; and *LIMC* VII, 456, no. 97, s.v. Poseidon, 485, nos. 21, 22, 487, nos. 43–5, s.v. Poseidon/Neptunus (E. Simon) for Poseidon/Neptune holding a dolphin.

54 On Artemis holding a quadruped, see *LIMC* II, 664–6, 671, s.v. Artemis (L. Kahil).

55 British Museum, Sc 1560, Diana found in 1887 in Trastevere (Rome): Smith 1904, 21, 22, pl. 2, unrestored; *LIMC* II, 665, no. 562, s.v. Artemis (L. Kahil); Fullerton 1990, 29, 30, 35, no. IIB1, fig. 15, stag.

56 Rome, Villa Albani 662: *LIMC* II, 635, 636, no. 124, s.v. Artemis (L. Kahil); Helbig[4] IV, no. 3349, second century CE.

57 For Artemis holding a small fawn, see, e.g., *LIMC* II, 665, 666, 671, s.v. Artemis (L. Kahil), figurines from Thespiae (no. 578), from Delphi (no. 582), in Toronto (no. 587), from Brauron (665), early fifth century BCE. Lion, figurine from Brauron, Museum K 1881: *LIMC* II, 671, no. 663b, s.v. Artemis (L. Kahil), early fifth century BCE.

58 Panther, see, e.g., an Attic red-figure amphora in London, BM E256, from Vulci, late sixth century: *LIMC* II, 707, no. 1122, s.v. Artemis (L. Kahil); *ARV*[2] 168. Lion, on a Tyrrhenian amphora, lost: *LIMC* II, 707, no. 1116, s.v. Artemis (L. Kahil).

59 For Hera with lion, see an Attic red-figure cup in Berlin (Staatliche Museen F 2536) with the Judgment of Paris: *ARV*[2] 1287, 1; *LIMC* II, 136, 137, no. 1428, s.v. Aphrodite (A. Delivorrias), 440–430 BCE. For Aphrodite, cf. an Apulian red-figure squat lekythos in Taranto, Museo Archeologico 4530: Trendall and Cambitoglou 1978, 395, 2; *LIMC* II, 120, no. 1237, s.v. Aphrodite (A. Delivorrias), ca. 360 BCE, where the animal rests on the outstretched hand and forearm. For Demeter/Ceres, see the terracotta statue from Ariccia in Rome, Museo Nazionale 112343, which holds a piglet in its outstretched hand: Bianchi Bandinelli 1970, 32, fig. 37; Gallina Zevi 1977, 325, 327, no. 477, early third century BCE.

60 See Varro, *De Re Rustica,* 3.3.2; 3.12.1–6; Philostratus, *Imagines*, I.6.5.

61 See, e.g., the red-figure stamnos by the Dokimasia Painter, Oxford 1965.121: *ARV*[2] 414.34, Catling and Robertson 1966, 198, 201; Bérard et al. 1989, 71–87,

figs. 107–9, 112–19; for the hare as a symbol of the race, see Bérard et al. 1989, figs. 121, 122.

62 Athens, NM, Carapanos Collection 1031.

63 Blümel 1963, 42, 43, no. 34, figs. 94–8. The original significance of the south building is unclear, according to H. Kienast (personal communication).

64 Freyer-Schauenberg 1974, 27–31, no. 7, pls. 7, 8.

65 Toynbee 1973, 200–2. On hares, see the useful discussion in Bevan 1986, 184–93; for list of representations of hares found in various sanctuaries, Appendix 8.11, 414–16.

66 Paris, Cabinet de Médaille 428: *LIMC* II, 706, no. 1097a, s.v. Artemis (L. Kahil), ca. 370 BCE. Apollo holds the animal about the stomach, so that its rear legs are supported by his wrist.

67 Walters 1899, 23, no. 237; Jeffery 1963, 330, no. 15, ca. 500 BCE; drawing of hare in Ginge 1981, 11, fig. 1.

68 Schefold 1974, 74, 75, pl 16:1, 2; *LIMC* II, 651, no. 359, s.v. Artemis (L. Kahil).

69 The clearest distinction is made by the presence of horns and cloven hooves; when these are not present, hares may be distinguished by the location of the tail low on the rump and the long rear legs, but the small size of the figurines can make the identity of the animal uncertain.

70 See *LIMC* II, 665, 666, nos. 575–89, s.v. Artemis (L. Kahil); on the type, Higgins 1954, 247, no. 907, pl. 131. Figures holding hares: Higgins 1954, 45, 46, no. 49 (Camirus), 117, no. 386 (Halicarnassus), 355, no. 1305 (Taranto), 365, no. 1341 (Egnatia), 227, no. 852, male figure (Boiotia). Figures holding deer: Higgins 1954, 177, no. 662 (Athens), 238, no. 889 (Boiotia), 247, no. 907 (Corinth), 213, no. 798 (Boiotia), 292, no. 1075 (Olynthos), 390, no. 1476 (Cyrenaica). Corinth, *Corinth* XII, 30, nos. 92, 93, pl. 6, identified as rabbits; Higgins 1967, 81, 82, pl. 35:d, Corinthian. On Corfu: Lechat 1891; Dierichs 2004, 63, fig. 62; some stand 0.52 m tall. On Lousoi: Reichel and Wilhelm 1901, 37, fig. 25; Sinn 1992, 181–3, fig. 5.

71 Dierichs 2004, 63.

72 *LIMC* II, 667, nos. 612, 613, s.v. Artemis (L. Kahil); Lechat 1891, 48–54, 58–60, pls. 3, 6.

73 Kanoni terracottas: Lechat 1891, 32, no. 11 (1); 38, no. 23 (4); 38, no. 22, pl. 2:3 (20).

74 Jacobsthal 1931, 25, 26, nos. 16, 17, pl. 9, fig. 3; *LIMC* II, 675, nos. 711, 713, s.v. Artemis (L. Kahil).

75 See also Aelian, *De Natura animal*, XI: on Ikaros the hare is hunted only with her approval; Callimachus, *Hymn to Artemis*, Nisetich 2001, 27, 2–4: Artemis loves the slaughter of hares.

76 *LIMC* II, 664, 665, nos. 560 (from temple at Pyla, in Paris, Louvre AM 2759, H 1.06 m), 561 (from acropolis at Amathus, in Limasol, Museum 329/14), s.v. Artemis (L. Kahil). On the Pyla statue, see also Caubet 1976, 170, pl. 27:4–5. A limestone figure of Artemis from Pyla, third century BCE, holds an animal (hind) in the left hand, and so in some areas the tradition continues, Caubet 1976, 170, 171, pl. 28:1.

77 At Lousoi, for example, east of the temple a fragment of a large stone figure was found that is identified as part of a cult statue, Reichel and Wilhelm 1901, 35, fig. 23. Not enough remains (just part of the draped lower torso and groove for a metal belt) to identify the statue type. Both Lechat (1891, 35) and Dierichs (2004, 63) comment that some of the Corfu statuettes appear to be small versions of large-scale statues, such as the Lousoi figure.

78 Boston, Museum of Fine Arts 98.658: Kozloff and Mitten 1988, 62–5, no. 4, ca. 530–520 BCE (M. True), "like a miniature cult figure" (p. 63).

79 Berlin, Staatliche Museen 7644: Furtwängler 1913, 465, figs. 6, 7; Lamb 1929, 152, pl. 57:a; Mitsopoulos-Leon 1993, 34, fig. 2, ca. 470 BCE; the identification of the figure with Artemis Hemera has been debated. The attributes, now lost, do not appear in later photographs.

80 For a thorough discussion of this type, see M. True in Kozloff and Mitten 1988, 77–86.

81 On the marriageable age of young girls and their iconography, see, e.g, Sourvinou-Inwood 1988, 42–8, 51–9 ("budding breasts"); sexual maturity considered as age 14: Oakley and Sinos 1993, 10, 14, 132 n. 10.

82 Harrison 1991, 232. See also Neils and Oakley 2003, 265, no. 68, grave stele in Malibu of ca. 360 BCE, for a young girl with long hair and small, high breasts.

83 Acropolis 615: Richter 1968, 81, no. 125, fig. 401; Brouskari 1974, 69, 70, ca. 490–480 BCE. The wave patterns in Acropolis 684's hair are also similar, Richter 1968, 101, no. 182, figs. 578–82; Brouskari 1974, 68, 69, ca. 490 BCE.

84 Delphi: Coste-Messelière 1957, pl. 34; Palagia 2000, 348, for identification of the marble as Parian and the date. Corinth head, Corinth Museum BE 35: Krystalli-Votsi 1977, Walter-Karydi 1987, 88, figs. 124, 125. Acropolis 688: Richter 1968, 102, 103, no. 184, figs. 587–90; Brouskari 1974, 128.

85 Eleusis kore, Athens, NM 24: Karouzou 1968, 15, pl. 9:a; Richter 1968, 103, no. 185, figs. 591–4, ca. 490–480 BCE, who suggests that the holes behind the stephane were for the stephane's ends, not for hair locks; Kaltsas 2002b, 82, no. 139, Parian; Stewart 2008, 2, 589. Head of second kore from Eleusis, Athens, NM 60, "said to be Island marble": Richter 1968, 103, no. 186, figs. 595–6; Edwards 1986a, 309 n. 18, ca. 480 BCE; Stewart 2008, 2, 589, 590, fig. 9. Long front locks were added in marble

to some figures; cf., e.g., Acropolis 673 (Adam 1966, 47, 48, pl. 21:b) and 682 (Adam 1966, 86–9, pls. 36:a, c, 37: a).

86 Brother-sister stele, girl's head, Berlin 1531: Richter 1968, fig. 440; Boardman 1991, fig. 232.

87 Richter 1968, 103, no. 186, figs. 595, 596.

88 Acropolis 684: Schrader 1939, 104–6, no. 55, pls. 78–81 (island marble); Richter 1968, 101, no. 182. Acropolis 688: Schrader 1939, 62, no. 21, pls. 30–2 (Pentelic marble); Richter 1968, 102, 103, no. 184. Acropolis Charioteer relief, 1342: Brouskari 1974, 60, 68, fig. 127; Rolley 1994, 230, fig. 225 (island marble). Ilissos torso, NM 3687: Kaltsas 2002b, 74, no. 110.

89 Delos, in Athens, NM 22: Kokkorou-Alevra 2000, 148, 149, Parian; Kaltsas 2002b, 73, 74, no. 106.

90 Acropolis 686: Richter 1968, 99, 100, no. 180; Brouskari 1974, 127; Boardman 1991, fig. 160; Stewart 2008, 389 (on disassociating torso and legs), 407, 408 (cat. no. 6); 601 (dates mid-470s BCE).

91 Compare, e.g., the lower back of the kore, Acropolis 671: Richter 1968, 70, 71, no. 111, fig. 341; Brouskari 1974, 74, ca. 520 BCE; the lower ends of folds of Acropolis 615: Richter 1968, 81, no. 125, ca. 500 BCE; and Acropolis fragments, Schrader 1939, 155, no. 179, fig. 127, ca. 500 BCE, and 157, no. 182, fig. 131, early fifth century BCE.

92 Ohly 1976, the drapery of East V, 30, and the drapery associated with Athena, pls. 4, 5.

93 Nike, Acropolis 690: Brouskari 1974, 125, after 490 BCE; Boardman 1991, 86, 87, fig. 167; Rolley 1994, 187, fig. 169, Parian marble. Artemis on Paros: Kostoglou-Despini 1979, 3–13, on the date, 32–52, pls. 1–19; *LIMC* II, 632, no. 99, s.v. Artemis (L. Kahil), ca. 480–470 BCE.

94 Athens, NM 22: Richter 1968, 88–9, no. 148; Kaltsas 2002b, 73, no. 106, ca. 500 BCE.

95 Acropolis 684: Richter 1968, 101, no. 182; Brouskari 1974, 68, 69; Rolley 1994, 186, island marble. Ilissos torso, Athens, NM 3687: Kaltsas 2002b, 74, no. 110.

96 Athens, NM 1944, from Aegina: Ohly 1976, 26, pl. 10; Kaltsas 2002b, 81, no. 135 (no photo). Acropolis: Schrader 1939, 165, no. 221, fig. 145, with four creases, second half of the sixth century BCE.

97 Angelitos' Athena, Acropolis 140: Boardman 1991, 87, fig. 173, ca. 480 BCE. Eleusis maiden, Eleusis Museum 5235: Edwards 1986a, 311, 322. Propylaea kore, Acropolis 688: Richter 1968, 102, 103, no. 184, fig. 587. Xanthos: London, British Museum B 318: Metzger 1963, 51, pl. 35:2; Richter 1968, 109, figs. 652–4, ca. 470 BCE, fig. 652 (rear view).

98 See, e.g., two archaistic statues: Artemis from Pompeii, Naples, Museo Nazionale 6008: Fullerton 1990, 22–9, no. 2IIA1, fig. 10, first century BCE; and Athena from the Villa of the Papyri at Herculaneum, Naples, Museo Nazionale 101 (6007): Fullerton 1990, 46–9, 69, no. 3IA1, fig. 16, second half of first century BCE.

99 Siphnian Treasury: Floren 1987, 171–6, 339 (Master B on east, north, karyatids, as Parian, 171, and Master A on west, south, as Chian, 339); Ridgway 1993, 393–5 (Master B Attic/Cycladic), 411, 412 nn. 9.33, 9.34, with references.

100 For discussion of island sculptures in the late Archaic period, see note 20 above; Sheedy 1988, 370–3; Ridgway 1993, 138–41; Rolley 1994, 254–7; Kaltsas 2002a, 16–26.

101 Delos, Museum A 4092: Marcadé 1950, 204, fig. 16; *LIMC* II, 201, no. 100, s.v. Apollon (W. Lambrinoudakis). Kore, New York, Metropolitan Museum 07.306: Richter 1968, 89, no. 151.

102 Stele of Aristion from Velanideza, of Pentelic marble, Athens, NM 29: Boardman 1991, fig. 235; Kaltsas 2002b, 70, no. 100; Schmaltz 2005, as a recut relief.

103 Phrasykleia, Athens, NM 4889: cf. the soft, billowing quality of the material just above the belt and in the skirt about the hips, Kaltsas 2002a, 26, pls. 2–5. Nike from Paros: *LIMC* VI, 862, no. 131, s.v. Nike (A. Goulaki-Voutira).

104 For Acropolis korai nos. 684, 685: Richter 1968, nos. 182, 181 respectively. Charioteer relief: Brouskari 1974, 60, 68, fig. 127.

105 Delos, Museum A 4063: Karakasi 2003, pl. 67. Museum A 4064: Richter 1968, 88, no. 147; Karakasi 2003, pls. 218, 219.

106 Athens, NM 3687: Kaltsas 2002b, 74, no. 110.

107 On two Milesian korai, Berlin 1791 and 1577, see Richter 1968, 47, no. 57, p. 92, no. 161; Floren 1987, 381, pl. 32:4, 5; relief from Miletus, Richter 1968, no. 71; relief from Didyma, Richter 1968, no. 96.

108 Schrader 1939, 90, 91; Richter 1968, 76, no. 118.

109 For two marble hares dedicated in the Heraion by Karas, son of Bata, see *RE* I A (1920), 2197, s.v. Samos. On the significance for Aphrodite, see, e.g., P. Stengel, *HdA* V.3 (1920), 123, and n. 15, and above note 59.

110 Corinth SF-65-14: Bookidis and Fisher 1972, 317, pl. 63:a, b; Bookidis 1988; the animal would have been held against the torso with both arms (Bookidis, personal communication). Two other hares from terracotta statues were found in the same sanctuary, in fragmentary condition, Corinth S-1969-7, SF-69-20.

111 For the Isthmia sculptures, see Sturgeon 1996 and forthcoming.

112 Williams et al. 1997, 47.

113 See p. 282 n. 4. Fifth-century terracotta figurines and

pottery from the Sanctuary are noted in Williams et al. 1998, 287; fragments from an early fifth-century Attic floral band cup and a black-figure skyphos or band cup have been identified; and several bronze animals survive from caryatid mirror rims, likely from the late sixth or fifth century: cf. Congdon 1981, 16, nn. 48, 63, on animals attached to the edge of mirror disks, p. 105 on chronology.

114 Discussed with references to other probable early statues, Romano 1980, 435.

115 Williams et al. 1998, 287; Williams and Schaus 2001, 88.

116 Williams and Cronkite Price 1995, 2, 20, 21; Williams et al. 1997, 44; Williams et al. 1998, 295; Williams et al. 2002, 165.

117 Williams, Cronkite Price, and Schaus 1996, 82, 83. For the Merenda sculptures, see Kaltsas 2002a.

118 Cf., e.g., the Archaic statue bases reused in the Themistoklean wall, Athens, NM 3476, 3477: Kaltsas 2002b, 66–8, nos. 95, 96.

119 On sacrificial animals offered to Demeter, see Van Straten 1995, 78, 79 (pig), 20 (ox), 79 (ram), 180 (pregnant ewe); *Corinth* XVIII, iii, 9, 72, 78.

120 On the relationship between the gift and the giver, see Simon 1986, 371; and *AnthPal* 6.339, on a gift of a statue of Dionysos to Dionysos; 6.268k, on a hunter giving a statue of Artemis to Artemis, and 6.338, on a musician giving a statue to the Muses.

121 For the idol in the Centauromachy frieze from Bassai, in London, BM 524: Madigan 1992, 79–81, fig. 10, pl. 43.

122 Argos, in Athens, NM 3869: Eichler 1919, 31, fig. 23; Walter-Karydi 1987, 110, fig. 175a–c; Kaltsas 2002b, 115, no. 205, ca. 420–410 BCE.

123 Epidauros, Athens, NM 4680: Yalouris 1992, 25, no. 13, pl. 14; Kaltsas 2002b, no. 338: VI.

124 Also a loomweight has an incised epsilon on it. See Surtees, chapter 12, p. 242.

125 Williams and Schaus 2001, 90–2. It is possible that the names or images of deities were painted on these stelai. For two fragmentary inscriptions on vases and for discussion of the Poliados inscription, see Schaus, chapter 2, pp. 13–14.

126 For weaving in relation to Artemis, Athena, Hera, and Demeter, see Williams and Schaus 2001, 88, 89; with regard to Artemis, see Cole 2004, 214–21, 230; and see the votive relief from the Artemis Sanctuary at Echinos, in Lamia, on which clothing is depicted hanging on a line, Dakoronia and Gounaropoulou 1992; Van Straten 1995, 82, 83, fig. 88; to Athena, see Barber 1994, 239–44.

127 On Artemis as a kourotrophic deity, see, e.g., Vernant 1991, 198–202.

128 Morgan 1999, 422, citing miniature Corinthian kotylai (Williams 1996, 87); Late Archaic–early Classical terracottas found beneath paving around the fourth century altar (Williams et al. 1997, 55; Williams et al. 1998, 287); and the marble statue holding a hare.

129 The bronze hares from Stymphalos probably formed attachments to bronze mirrors, the bronze cock and fox: see Schaus, chapter 7, pp. 156–7; Williams et al. 1997, 48, fig. 7; Williams and Schaus 2001, 81, 90 n. 54. Cf. the bronze hare from the Athenian Acropolis, Athens NM 6682: de Ridder 1896, 166, no. 463, fig. 125; Richter 1930, fig. 155; on bronze mirror attachments, see Congdon 1981, 16, nn. 48, 63.

130 This point of interpretation is often debated. See, e.g., on the Acropolis korai as depictions of young women bearing offerings, Richter 1968, 3, 4, though not always clear, Stieber 2004, 138, and Karakasi 2003, 124, among others; as depictions of deities, Ridgway 1990a, 583–612; Ridgway 1993, 66, "mostly divine images"; Keesling 2003, 97–129. Schaus (2003) criticizes Keesling's 2003 thesis (pp. 149–58, esp. 158) that the outstretched hand indicates a cult statue, because the opposite has not been demonstrated, that humans are not represented in this way.

131 In Athens, NM 3980: Eichler 1919, 145–8, no. 2, figs. 83–5; Walter-Karydi 1987, 110, fig.175a–c. An Attic, Late Archaic funerary stele has also appeared in Argos: Whitley 2003a, 22, 23, fig. 36.

132 Once in Patras, now in the Aigion Museum: Mastrokostas 1986, pl. 58, ca. 480 BCE; Katsonopoulou 2000, 373–8, figs. 6, 7.

133 Tripolis, Archaeological Museum 3092: Spyropoulos 1993, 257, 258, figs. 1, 2, found in 1986.

134 On the Acropolis Athena, Acropolis 625: see Boardman 1991, 82, 83, 86, fig. 135; Floren 1987, 297–9, pl. 21:6; Keesling 1999, 523–32; Keesling 2003, 27, 33, fig. 10.

135 On Endoios: see Viviers 1992, 55–102.

136 Munich, Glyptothek 168: Richter 1970, 84, 85, no. 73, Parian marble; Floren 1987, 188, pls. 14:2, 15:1; Ridgway 1993, 54, 65, 114, with references. Two kouroi were found in 2010 at Corinth, *Greek Reporter*, 17 August 2011.

137 On Archaic Corinthian sculpture, see Bookidis 1997, 245, on the absence of female figures. On the Late Archaic head, Corinth BE 35: see Richter 1970, 157, no. 163a, ca. 490–480 BCE; Krystalli-Votsi 1977; Walter-Karydi 1987, 88, figs. 124, 125; Rolley 1994, 324, fig. 331. Early Classical head, Corinth S 2390: Morgan 1939, 266, fig. 10; Ridgway 1981, 426.

138 Archaic knee, Corinth S 614: Ridgway 1981, 423, pl. 91:a; legs from Isthmia: Sturgeon 1987, 70–3, nos. 4–13. In limestone, see the Isthmia kouros: Sturgeon 1987, 68–70, no. 3, and fragmentary sculptures from Corinth, Bookidis 1970.

139 Asine, in Nauplion: Renaudin 1921, 304, fig. 7; Floren 1987, 206 n. 10. Epidauros town, Athens, NM 63: Richter 1970, 98, 99, no. 91, island marble; Floren 1987, 206, pl. 16:3; Kaltsas 2002b, 60. Ligourio, Epidauros 172: Lambrinoudakis 1980, 483–6, pls. 220–22; Floren 1987, 206 n. 9. Phigaleia, Olympia, Museum 257: Richter 1970, 67, no. 41; Floren 1987, 228, n. 5, pl. 19:2; Ridgway 1993, 64, 65, possibly Apollo because the hands are forward, 77, 90 on the question of interpretation, worshipper or deity, 97 nn. 3.7, 8.

140 Athens, NM 2651: Raftopoulou 1993, 6–8, figs. 6, 7, just under life-size, of local stone.

141 Meligu, in Copenhagen, Glyptotek I.N. 1730: Giuliani 1979, 35, pl. 7:1; Floren 1987, 218 n. 35; Johansen 1994, 61, no. 17.

142 Sparta, Museum 3365: Ridgway 1993, 92, 119 n. 3.77. For a catalogue of Lakonian stone sculpture, see Herfort-Koch 1986, 74–8, nos. KS 1–KS 38.

143 The de Nion head: Pollini 2003. Corfu: Blackman 1998, 56, 57, figs. 80, 81, Parian marble.

144 See Sturgeon 1987, 18–26.

145 Kore fragments: Sparta, Archaeological Museum 1905: Wace 1904–5, 99–101, figs. 1, 2, upper torso with diagonal mantle; 102, 103, figs. 4, 5, back of head; Floren 1987, 217 n. 29. Aigies, in Gytheion, Archaeological Museum: Bonias 1993, the kouros of grey Lakonian marble from Taigetos; the female figure of white Dolian marble an archaizing work from the mid-fifth century BCE. Shield, Palagia 1993, of Parian marble.

146 Leontini head, in Catania, Museo Comunale: Richter 1970, 146, no. 184; Rolley 1994, 300, fig. 305; Lattanzi 2001, 8, figs. 21, 22. Leontini, in Syracuse, Museo Archeologico: Richter 1970, 146, no.183, Parian marble; Lattanzi 2001, 12, figs. 32, 33. Locri fragments, Reggio Calabria, Museo Archeologico: Lattanzi 2001, 11, figs. 30, 31. Metapontum kouros, in Potenza, Museo Archeologico: Richter 1970, 147, no. 187, Parian marble, probably from Temple of Apollo; Lattanzi 2001, 11, figs. 27–9. Megara Hyblaea, in Syracuse, Museo Archeologico: Richter 1970, 147, no. 186, Parian marble, from the cemetery. Terravecchia di Grammichele, Syracuse, Museo Archeologico: Richter 1970, 146, no. 185, Parian marble. Reggio Calabria, Museo Archeologico, storerooms: Lattanzi 2001, figs. 1–18.

147 Tarentum kore, Taranto, Museo Archeologico MAN no. 20923: Richter 1968, 95, no. 171, figs. 541–4; Floren 1987, 439 n. 273; Rolley 1994, 61, fig. 53, p.H 1.29 m, missing the head. Satiro, Berlin, Staatliche Museen: Richter 1968, 95, no. 172.

148 Keos, Athens, NM 3686: Richter 1970, 122, no. 144; Ridgway 1993, 152, 178 n. 4.78, 304; Kazamiakis 2000; Kaltsas 2002b, 58, no. 68. Aegina: Walter-Karydi 1987; Ohly-Dumm and Robertson 1988.

149 Aegina: Walter-Karydi 1987, 78, 114, nos. 41, 42, pl. 32.

150 Andros kore, Copenhagen, Glyptotek I.N. 1544: Richter 1968, 89, no. 152; Floren 1987, 182 n. 19, pl. 13:6; Johansen 1994, 56, 57, no. 13. Andros kouros, Andros Museum: Richter 1970, 108, no. 119; Floren 1987, 182 n. 20. Skyros, Skyros Museum: Lazaridis 1967, 287, pl. 186.

151 Istros kore, veiled head from a statuette: Alexandrescu Vianu 1990, 183, figs. 55, 56, ca. 540. Istros kouros, Bucharest, National Museum I 1689: Bordenache Battagilia 1969, 13, 14, no. 1, pl. 1; Richter 1970, 154, no. 86a; Alexandrescu Vianu 1990, 182, 183, figs. 1, 2; Alexandrescu Vianu et al. 2000, 428, 435, fig. 6, mid-sixth century BCE, possibly of marble from the Denizli 2 quarry. Both figures from Istros show strong similarities to Milesian sculptures. Olbia, Museum: Richter 1970, 143, no. 178. Odessa: Oksmann 1928, col. 82, fig. 1.

152 See, e.g., Trianti 1999; Kokkorou-Alevra 1999; recent excavations at Despotiko, near Antiparos, have yielded new Archaic sculptures; Kouragios 2009, 38–57.

153 For comments on the International Style, see, e.g., Ridgway 1993, 80–1, 128–9; on the blurring of regional styles in the Late Archaic period, Martini 1990, 216.

154 Williams and Schaus 2001, 85.

155 Cf., e.g., the sharp crease on the left side of the neck of a seated boy holding a puppy from Epidauros, Athens, NM 300: Kaltsas 2002b, 262, no. 548, mid-fourth century BCE. Notably, the Epidauros child has no hair, has a similarly shaped ear, and is seated. The god Asklepios, possibly shown as an infant on an Epidauros relief, adopts a pose similar to the statue with puppy, NM 1424: Karouzou 1968, 151; Kaltsas 2002b, 228, no. 479, late fourth century BCE.

156 Cf., e.g., Acropolis 674: Schrader 1939, 93–5, no. 44, pls. 62–6; Richter 1968, 81, no. 127, figs. 414, 416; Brouskari 1974, 70, ca. 500 BCE.

157 This feature is illustrated by a number of Acropolis korai, e.g., nos. 680, 684, 685, Schrader 1939, pls. 69, 80, 71, respectively; Richter 1968, 78, no. 122 (680), 101, no. 182 (684), 100, no. 181 (685); Brouskari 1974, 73 (680), 68, 69 (684), 73 (685).

158 Schrader 1939, pls. 64, 66; Richter 1968, no. 127, fig. 415.

159 Eschmun, 27 seated figures: Stucky 1993, 29–38, 83–8, nos. 98–124, pls. 23–30. Isthmia: Sturgeon 1987, 114–16, no. 25, ca. 330–320 BCE, probably from a sanctuary of Demeter.

160 Marble figures of this size are affixed to their bases by various means. With one seated/leaning boy from Sidon, two metal dowels still in the base once attached the statue to the plinth, Stucky 1993, 99. The "Little Refugee" from Nysa (Asia Minor) in Athens has three hook-shaped clamp cuttings in its plinth (NM 3485: Karouzou 1968, 185, pl. 67; Kaltsas 2002b, 297, no. 622, first century BCE), the boy from Lilaia (Lamia) has none (NM 2772: Kaltsas 2002b, 270, no. 563, third century BCE).

161 British Museum E 396: Neils and Oakley 2003, 72, 237, no. 37, attributed to the Manner of the Washing Painter, ca. 430–420 BCE; *ARV*[2] 1134,6.

162 Stucky 1993, 84, no. 101, pl. 24, the statue, L 0.525, W 0.41, D 0.19, the rectangular base, L 0.59, W 0.42, H 0.11 m; *ThesCRA* I, 430, no. 841, pl. 128.

163 Hadzisteliou-Price 1969, 96, 97; those in the Louvre: Hermary 1989, 69–111.

164 New York, MMA 74.51.2784: Beer 1994, 83, Appendix A, no. 2, pl. 197, Hellenistic; Karageorghis, Mertens, and Rose 2000, 262, no. 426.

165 Nicosia, Cyprus Museum, E 145: Beer 1994, 83, Appendix A, no. 3, pl. 198, Hellenistic.

166 New York, MMA 74.51.2750: Beer 1994, 57, no. 192, pls. 112, 113:a–b.

167 Ephesos, Vienna, Kunsthistorisches Museum I, 816, 2: Rühfel 1984, 258, fig. 110.

168 Lilaia boy, Athens, NM 2772: Karouzou 1968, 179, pl. 63; Vorster 1983, 161, 226, 227, 355, no. 67, pl. 6:4–5, ca. 300 BCE; Kaltsas 2002b, 270, no. 563, third century BCE. On the age, see Rühfel 1984, 227.

169 Nude boy, Athens Asklepieion, NM 2211: Vorster 1983, 202, 372, no. 123, pl. 9:2; Kaltsas 2002b, 270, no. 564, possibly Asklepios as an infant, fourth century BCE. Draped girl, Athens, NM 696: Bieber 1961, 137, fig. 542, ca. 300 BCE; Palagia 1982, 103 and n. 23, pl. 33:a; Kaltsas 2002b, 270, no. 565, ca. 310–300 BCE.

170 Brauron: Hadzisteliou-Price 1969, 105; Stucky 1993, 29, n. 198. Paros, Archaeological Museum A 260: Zaphiropoulou 1998, 82, fig. 94. Himeros: Lazaridis 1969, 170, pl. 62, H 0.41 m, third century BCE; Sinn 1992, 185, fig. 7, right; the Himeros child looks down at the bird that it holds.

171 Temple Boy from Lousoi, Sanctuary of Artemis, third century BCE: Reichel and Wilhelm 1901, 47, fig. 59, H 0.16, W 0.26, D 0.185 m, broken through abdomen; Sinn 1992, 185, fig. 7: left.

172 See, e.g., for Rhodes, Higgins 1954, a seated/leaning boy with both hands on the base, 93, nos. 257–9, from tomb of ca. 475–450 BCE; Gela: Higgins 1954, 314, nos. 1158, 1159, mid-fifth century BCE; Corinth, Asklepieion: *Corinth* XIV, 140, no. 24, pl. 54 (figurine), 141, pl. 55 (large, mould-made statuette, H 248 m) of an ill child, Beer 1987, p. 24; Corinth, Demeter Sanctuary: *Corinth* XVIII, iv, 68–73, nos. C227–C250, pls. 19–20; Cyrenaica: Burn and Higgins 2001, 244, nos. 2791, 2792, seated/upright boys, third–second centuries BCE.

173 Hadzisteliou-Price 1969, 97, 100, pl. 22, nos. 19 (Taranto, in Oxford, Ashmolean Museum, no. 1886.637), 20 (Selinus, in Palermo, Archaeological Museum).

174 Delphi: Rolley 1984, 264, 265, no. 5. *Corinth* XVIII, iv, 68, no. C234.

175 Robinson 1933, 75, no. 282, pl. 36.

176 Ephesos, in Vienna: Rühfel 1984, 258, 260, fig. 110; Aurenhammer 1990, 149–52, no. 132, pl. 91.

177 See, e.g., *Corinth* XVIII, iv, 68–73, nos. C227–C250, pls. 19, 20.

178 Williams et al. 1998, 292; Williams and Schaus 2001, 86, 87; a second terracotta depicts a standing boy.

179 Hadzisteliou-Price 1969, 106–110.

180 Williams, Cronkite Price, and Schaus 1996, 84; Williams et al. 1997, 53.

181 On deities or spirits thought to inhabit sculptures, see, e.g., Faraone 1992, 54–73; Kane 1998, 148–51, citing the Hermetic Dialogues, *Asclepius* 24a, *Hermetica* I.1, Scott 1924, 339.

182 On the find location of the Amphitrite torso, see Sturgeon 1987, 76, 99. O. Broneer (pers. com.) thought the villagers had buried the head in order to avoid being injured by its glance.

183 On the eye, see Sturgeon 1987, 157, no. 140.

184 On heads from the well, see Stroud 1965, 20, 21, pl. 10.

185 The temple measures L 11.6, W 6.0 m. Most sculptural pieces were found in a 4 × 4 m area in the southwest part of the cella (see fig. 3.45).

186 Williams 1996, 86; Williams et al. 1997, 50; Williams and Schaus 2001, 91–2. See Schaus, chapter 2, p. 17, figs. 2.12 and 2.13a–c.

187 The bedrock has two round holes and a square hole in its upper surface. Round holes are a typical feature of the hard limestone in this area, and the rectangular hole appears too irregular to be a cutting for a tenon.

188 J.G. Miller 1997.

189 Williams and Schaus 2001, 92.

190 Williams and Schaus 2001, 84–90.

191 Williams, Cronkite Price, and Schaus 1996, 49, pl. 7.

192 Young 2001, 123, 125.

193 For Archaic head decorations, see Ridgway 1990a, 605–12. For a wreath or diadem decorated with rosettes on

an archaistic figure, see, e.g., the Artemis from Pompeii, Naples, Museo Nazionale 6008: Fullerton 1990, 22–9, fig. 10. On the presentation of jewellery and garments to the cult image of Artemis on Delos, see, e.g., Romano 1980, 197–9, of garments to Artemis at Brauron, 89–91.

194 Paros Museum 757: Kleeman 1962, especially 207–9, 228, pls. 56–60; Rubensohn 1962, 37, of fine-grained Parian marble; *LIMC* II, 632, no. 100, s.v. Artemis (L. Kahil).

195 Williams et al. 1998, 285. On painted walls of the fourth century BCE, see, e.g., the "House of Many Colours" (Fii9) and house Avii4 at Olynthos, in each of which one major room had white baseboards and red walls; in addition, house Avii4 had a third colour above the baseboard, Cahill 2002, 85, 107.

196 Orlandos 1926, 134, assumed that the Poliados marker identified the deity of the Temple. The present location of this stele is unknown. See also Williams and Cronkite Price 1995, 12, 13.

197 Orlandos 1926, 134; Williams and Schaus 2001, 75. Zeus would also be possible; see *RE* 21, cols. 1363–5, s.v. Polias (Kruse), 1952. For discussion, see Schaus 2007 and in this volume, chapter 2, pp. 13–14.

198 Mitsos 1946–7, dated ca. 190–180 BCE; *SEG* 25, 1971, 445.

199 Martha 1883, 490.

200 Amandry 1971, 601, 602.

201 Congdon 1981, e.g., 16, nn. 48, 63.

202 Greek Anthology, W.R. Paton transl., Loeb ed. I (1927) 6,1; 18–20; 210–11. On scenes with wedding preparations, see, e.g., an Attic lebes gamikos, Athens NM 1454: Oakley and Sinos 1993, 18, figs. 28, 29, ARV^2 1038.1 and 1679; *Para* 443; Addenda 319.

203 Williams and Schaus 2001, 92, 93; Hadzisteliou-Price 1978, 114.

204 See Schaus, chapter 2, p. 14, this volume. On Eileithyia, see *LIMC* III, pp. 686–99, s.v. Eileithyia (R. Olmos); Pingiatoglou 1981.

205 Williams and Schaus 2001, 86, 87.

206 On the jewellery, see Young 2001.

207 On the identification of the basilica's deity, see Pedley 1990, 53, 54; for an illustration of the cippus, see Greco, Greco, and Pontrandolfo n.d., 46, fig. 34.

208 Animals appear to have been sacrificed and/or eaten near the temple site: see pp. 254–9; also Williams 1996, 87, 88; on their identification, see Williams and Schaus 2001, 89; R.H. Simms, *Database of Greek Animal Sacrifice*, http://www.emma.troy.ny.us/faculty/ bsimms/ mainmenu: the wild boar is not attested for Athena, and the pig and the goat are both unusual for that deity.

209 On the location and character of Artemis sanctuaries, see Cole 2004, 178–97; on Artemis cults in the Peloponnese, see Jost 1985, 393–424; on Arkadian sanctuaries of Artemis, Brulotte 1994, 35–105.

210 Despinis 2004, 263–99.

211 Despinis 2004, 303.

212 On Artemis as a kourotrophic deity, see Hadzisteliou-Price 1978, 121, 189, 190.

213 Richter 1968, 100, 101, no. 181; Brouskari 1974, 73, ca. 500–490 BCE.

214 Cf. the patterns on sleeves of Acropolis korai, Richter 1968, 73–80; Brinkmann 2004, esp. nos. 101–4.

215 Contrast the larger cuttings for marble plugs that secured locks on some Late Archaic korai, e.g., Athens, NM 22: Richter 1968, 88, 89, no. 148, and Acropolis 682: Richter 1968, 73–5, no. 116; Brouskari 1974, 67, 68, ca. 510–500 BCE.

216 Compare the patterns on the smooth portion of the sleeve of Acropolis 682, Richter 1968, 73–5, no. 116; Brinkmann 2004, no. 103.

217 In Acropolis 684, which also wears three garments, the epiblema is wrapped around the extended right arm, Richter 1968, 101, no. 182, figs. 579–82.

218 In addition to the pieces presented in this catalogue, 14 small bits of marble, some from drapery, some of indistinguishable shape, were found with the two statues and are housed in the Archaeological Museum of Ancient Corinth. An additional three small fragments of drapery that were discovered in the pottery lots are housed in the Storeroom in Stymphalia. I have examined them, and it is clear that they do not join the segments presented here.

219 On the Syracuse Aphrodite type, see *LIMC* II, 83, 84, no. 748, s.v. Aphrodite (A. Delivorrias); for the Aphrodite from Italica (87, no. 786), and the related figurine from Smyrna in Boston (86, no. 774).

220 Corinth S-89-6: Sturgeon 1998, 2.

Chapter 4: Coins

1 This study would not have been possible without both the unlimited access to the coins that I had from Hector Williams, director of the Stymphalos Project, and a research grant from the Social Sciences and Humanities Research Council of Canada (SSHRCC) (2001–4). I have also benefited from the assistance of undergraduate students, both those whom SSHRCC funded at Stymphalos, Morag Wehrle (2001), Monika Urbanski (2003), and Matthew Malott (2004), and a research assistant paid by the University of Windsor, Melissa Bradley (2005). I am especially grateful to two individuals for their help and suggestions along the way. In 2003,

Robert Knapp kindly gave me a draft copy of his and John Mac Isaac's manuscript of *Nemea, III* (here cited as Knapp and Mac Isaac 2005), which details the coins found at that panhellenic sanctuary near Stymphalos. Secondly, Orestes Zervos, numismatist at the Corinth Museum, where the Stymphalos coins of the 1994 through 1996 seasons are currently stored, was unflaggingly hospitable and generously accommodating of my work in his office in the summers of 2000 through 2004.

2 The following catalogue includes 85 coins of bronze (87%), 12 of silver (12%), and 1 of iron (1%). The proportion of silver coins in the Sanctuary is consistent with that found in Stymphalos as a whole (around 11%) but is very high when compared with other, comparable sites in the region. The possible significance of the abundance of silver is discussed on page 76 below.

3 Greek bronzes, as the small change of their day, apparently circulated more heavily, and thus wore out more quickly, than higher-denomination coins of silver or gold, though more or less precise quantification of the rate of wear by analogy with modern series has proved problematic (cf. Mac Isaac 1995). Nevertheless, it is usually safe to suppose that a bronze coin in EF condition cannot have circulated for more than a few years, and probably for less time than the same coin in VF grade.

4 Tr. = trench. The number following "Tr." in catalogue entries denotes the trench number, level number and pail number, so Tr. 97.5.4.7 denotes Trench 97.5, Level 4, Pail 7. SF = small find number (SF numbers began again at "1" each season), and Inv. = excavation inventory number. Trench numbers are often included on site plans and denote the years in which they were excavated. For instance, Trench 96.1 was the first trench opened in 1996; and trench 00.96.1 would be a year 2000 continuation of excavation in that same trench. Each trench was excavated in numbered levels from the surface down. For each trench there was a series of "pails." A change in level meant a change in pail, and there could be one or several pails for any given level. Pail numbers were continuous and did not restart with a change in level. Small finds were individual items that excavators felt deserved special attention and that received a unique number in the excavation catalogue for all of Stymphalos.

5 Price assigns his no. 316 to a Macedonian mint during Alexander's lifetime.

6 This coin is probably *SNG Copenhagen* no. 1142, which is the plain reverse variety, without any letters, monograms, or symbols.

7 Cf. Newell 1926, 48, no. 34, pl. IV.4 (=*Agora* XXVI, no. 504g): Tarsos mint: same monogram, no axe; and cf. Newell 1926, 150, no. 167, pl. XVII.6 (=*Agora* XXVI, no. 505): Carian (?) mint: same monogram, same axe, but head of Poseidon on obverse.

8 The hero may represent Phemios, the mythical king of the Ainianes (cf. Ajax the Lesser on staters of Opuntian Lokris, ca. 380–338 BCE). Compare *Agora* XXVI, 516: fourth- to third-century BCE bronzes with same types.

9 Kraay (1976, 113) favoured the higher dating of 379–371 BCE on the basis of examples in the Myron hoard that he dated to 350 BCE (*IGCH* no. 62), but most scholars have opted for the lower dating that suits a federal league reestablished after Chaironeia and perhaps centred on Thespiai.

10 For this very prolific emission, Picard (1979, 39) catalogues 370 specimens from 96 obverse and 115 reverse dies.

11 This coin most likely corresponds either to Picard's (1979) no. 38 (no reverse symbol) or no. 40 (crescent by eagle's tail).

12 Salamis bronzes are encountered at Olynthos in late fourth-century hoards, but no longer in a hoard of the 260s (*Agora* XXVI, 215).

13 The denomination of **II-17** follows *Agora* XXVI, no. 642. These chalkoi were evidently much scarcer (*Agora* XXVI, no. 642: 1 example) than the dichalka minted earlier in the fourth century (*Agora* XXVI, nos. 640–1: 54 examples).

14 Although the copious Pegasos/trident bronzes of Corinth were struck between the late fifth century BCE (Zervos 1980, 184, 203) and the late third century BCE (Price 1967b, 365–7), the examples from Stymphalos are consistently found in pottery contexts of the mid-, or late, fourth century BCE to early third century BCE. Compare *SNG Sweden II* nos. 1602–4, which are dated from the late fourth century BCE through ca. 275 BCE.

15 According to Mac Isaac (1988), the earliest bronze coins of Phlious repeat the same types of a somewhat earlier silver coinage (bull to left/ **Φ** framed by four pellets). He has dated the first bronzes to ca. 400–350 and consequently proposes ca. 425–400 for the silver prototypes (48). However, the presence of the silver trihemiobolon **II-35** in an apparent hoard along with **II-9**, **II-12**, **II-48**, **II-49**, and **II-53** suggests a lower, fourth-century date for at least this type. Although the bull's head is flatstruck and the silver has crystallized partially over the millennia, the coin exhibits very little actual wear (see for instance the very crisp-looking folds of skin around the bull's neck). A date simultaneous with Mac Isaac's Group 1 (i.e., ca. 400–350 BCE) would seem more apt. The other members of the hoard exhibit the same, or a very similar, degree of wear and are of fourth-century date themselves.

16 The denomination of Phliasian bronzes **II-36** through **II-43** follows Mac Isaac 1988.

17 I have followed the suggestions of Warren 1983, 1984, and 1998 for the denominations of the Sikyonian bronzes.

18 Warren's date for Group 2 (365/345–335/330 BCE) depends on the mid-fourth-century inception of the prolific Pegasos/trident bronzes (our **II-18** through **II-43**) that Martin Price had proposed (Warren 1983, 30, 32–3); however, the occurrences of the latter in late fifth-century contexts at Corinth (Zervos 1980, 184, 203, cf. Warren 1983, 33 n. 46), and of both sorts of coin together in a late fifth-century context at Nemea (Knapp and Mac Isaac 2005, 57–8), mean that Sikyon's Group 2 should be roughly contemporary with its Group 1.

19 Dating suggested by Warren 2000, 207.

20 The revised dating suggested by Warren (2000, 207–8) is consistent with the pottery contexts of **II-52** and **II-53**. Sikyon had certainly ceased minting these hemidrachms by the time it entered the Achaian League in 251 BCE and had probably ceased production ca. 280 BCE (*BCED Pel.* 82).

21 Warren (1983, 41) assigns type 4C.8 to the final phase of her Group 4C on the basis of stylistic similarities to her Groups 8.1 and 8.2 (first half of the second century BCE), and thus dates it to the late third century BCE. The archaeological confirmation for such a date is, in her words, "disappointingly inconclusive" (1983, 42), but is not necessarily contradicted by the stratigraphy at Stymphalos. Although the pottery contexts of two of the following examples suggest a date no later than the end of the fourth century BCE for Group 4C.8, they are not in fact sealed contexts: pottery from lower levels on the Temple's bedrock floor includes at least one second-century BCE mould-made bowl! I owe this important point to a personal communication from Gerald Schaus.

22 Revised chronology suggested by Warren (1998, 355–6).

23 Revised chronology suggested by Warren (1998, 356–8).

24 Revised chronology suggested by Warren (1998, 357).

25 Revised chronology suggested by Warren (1998, 358–9).

26 Revised chronology suggested by Warren (1998, 358–9).

27 Revised date given in Warren's unpublished work on the Achaian League bronzes, as cited by *Agora* XXVI, 235 n. 43.

28 I owe this attribution and its references to Knapp and Mac Isaac (2005), who record six such iron coins from the excavations at Nemea (nos. 1595–1600).

29 I gratefully owe this attribution to Orestes Zervos.

30 Caven 1990, 84–8.

31 Carthage: inv. 2270 (late fourth century BCE). Seleukos I: inv. 3605 (tetradrachm from Seleukeia-on-the-Orontes, ca. 300–295 BCE).

32 Out of the 2117 Greek coins found at Nemea, only two were Sicilian, both of them Syracusan bronzes of the fifth and fourth centuries BCE (Knapp and Mac Isaac 2005, nos. 3–4). From the Athenian Agora there were only eight Sicilian and three Italian coins out of 16,557 Greek coins (*Agora* XXVI, nos. 417–27). The only truly significant find of Syracusan bronzes in mainland Greece is the anomalous hoard *IGCH* no. 26, which consists of 51 fifth-century Sicilian bronzes, most of them Syracusan, that was discovered in 1964 at Chalkis in Euboia (published with illustrations by Franke 1966).

33 Newell 1926, 157; Tarn 1913, 66–7.

34 Knapp and Mac Isaac 2005, nos. 89–98. The 20 coins of Demetrios unearthed at Stymphalos come from all parts of the city, though five of them were found together in the Stym V.99 hoard in the foundations of an artillery tower (see note 49 below).

35 Kassander: Diod. Sic. 19.64.1. Demetrios: IG IV^2 1.68, l. 73. I owe these references to Knapp and Mac Isaac 2005, 16 n. 41.

36 Apollonides, Kassander's general, captured Stymphalos from Polyperchon in 315 BCE (Diod. Sic. 19.63.1). Philip V would return to the valley in 219 BCE to retake it from the Aitolian commander Euripidas (Polyb. 4.67–9). There is a numismatic analogy with the Athenian Agora. The great majority of the 16,557 Greek coins excavated there (91.5%) were, not unexpectedly, either Athenian (87%) or from states close to Athens, such as Megara (2%), the Boiotian League (1%), Chalkis (0.7%), or Corinth (0.8%). The appearance among the excavated coins of 259 bronzes of the Macedonian kings, in other words 1.6% of all the excavated coins, thus came as something of a surprise. Such coins would not normally have arrived in Attika in such numbers through the normal channels of trade, and the numismatist who published the Agora coins concluded that "many of the more than 250 Macedonian regal coins must have originally been used by Macedonian troops in the garrisons imposed on the Athenians from 317 to 307 and again from 296 to 229" (*Agora* XXVI, 166). At Corinth one also finds a relatively large number of Macedonian bronzes in excavation contexts, but this is readily explicable by Acrocorinth's being one of the four Macedonian garrisons that Philip V dubbed the "Fetters of Greece."

37 Sikyon: Strabo 8.382e; Diod. Sic. 20.102.1–4; Plut., *Demetr.* 39.1–2; Paus. 2.7.1; Polyaenus, *Strat.* 4.7.3. Capture of the northern Peloponnese: Diod. Sic. 20.103.1–7; Plut., *Demetr.* 25.1–2; Polyaenus, *Strat.* 4.7.8; Trogus, *Prologus* 15; Ath. 10.415a.

38 Plut., *Demetr.* 39.2–5; Polyaenus, *Strat.* 4.7.3 (cf. Tarn 1913, 66–7). Demetrios's capture of Thessaly and Boiotia

(Plut., *Demetr.* 39.1–2) and his foundation of Demetrias (Strabo 9.436b–c) that same year may have prompted a nervous Sparta to intervene at Thebes.

39 Newell 1926, 156–7.

40 In commenting on the nearly identical obverse iconography of contemporary issues by Tegea and Mantineia, Newell (1926, 158) pointed out that these cities "apparently found it to their advantage to imitate more or less closely the coins commonly in circulation among the troops of occupation."

41 Williams et al. 2002, 154.

42 See note 15 above.

43 The 1883 British Museum catalogue for Thessaly first used this dating, which has apparently remained uninvestigated and unchallenged ever since, for the following Thessalian peoples and poleis: the Ainianes, Halos, Atrax, Kierion, Krannon, Gyrton, Herakleia Trachinia, Lamia, the Malienses, Metropolis, the Oitaioi, Pelinna, Phalanna, Pharsalos, and Trikka. Head (1911, 291) writes of the Ainianes' coinage in particular that "the earliest coins of this people belong in style to the later period of fine art [i.e., 400–344 BCE]."

44 Martin (1985) is the seminal study of coinage and sovereignty in Thessaly and has persuaded most scholars that the two phenomena were not synonymous in Classical Greece. Other than a very rare obol of quite different type that was included in a hoard near Lamia of the fourth century BCE (*IGCH* no. 97), all other representatives of the Ainianes in hoards are hemidrachms (also known as triobols) that are identical to the example from Stymphalos and occur in hoards of the late third (*ICGH* no. 195) or mid-second century (*IGCH* nos. 261, 266, 270, 271, 2053). The coins travelled widely – findspots include Thessaly, Phokis, Aitolia, the northern Peloponnese, and even Calabria – but never in great numbers, since each of the hoards contains only one or two examples.

45 Warren 2000, 207 and n. 37.

46 Weir 2007, 13–20.

47 Approximately 12,500 coins were found in such a deposit, though admittedly of the Roman period, in the Sacred Spring of Sulis-Minerva in Bath (Walker 1988). For the spatial distribution of coins at Stym II, see p. 76.

48 A sealed votive pit discovered in Trenches 97.2 and 96.15 contained fourth-century pottery from a clean-up of the Sanctuary in about 300 BCE (Morris et al. 2003). No coins were found in the pit, but it provides a welcome analogue for the other clean-up hypothesized here.

49 For the attack, see note 36 above. The Stym V.99 hoard contains five bronzes of Demetrios Poliorketes (ca. 300–295 BCE), which are the latest certainly datable coins and thus support an early third-century BCE date for the great artillery tower that was built over the hoard. Two coins found in the foundations of the Pheneos Gate (Stym XIII) date ca. 360–325 BCE and ca. 400–350 BCE (inv. 3894 and 3976); and another coin found in the foundations of the Phlious Gate (Stym VIII) is a Corinthian piece struck between the late fifth and mid-third century (inv. 3653). It is quite possible that the whole city circuit was repaired and upgraded at about the same time. The pottery context for **II-15** and **II-16** certainly does not extend any lower than the late fourth century BCE.

50 Histiaia's loyalty vacillated between Athens and Macedonia in the fourth century BCE, but by the third century BCE the city was allied exclusively with the latter (*PECS* s.v. "Histiaia").

51 Price (1967a). I have not seen this dissertation but rely instead on Knapp and Mac Isaac's citations of it (2005, 96–108, nos. 428–84, 490–538, 540–707, 709–12).

52 Price 1967b; Williams and Fisher 1971; Bookidis and Fisher 1972, 294; Zervos 1980, 184, 203; Warren 1983, 33 n. 46; Warren 1984, 23.

53 See above note 15.

54 Knapp and Mac Isaac (2005) list 148 Phliasian pieces (nos. 1043–1190) out of 2117 Greek coins.

55 *IGCH* no. 171: out of the 3786 lower-denomination silver coins buried ca. 250/240 BCE, the Phliasian component is 82 triobols and 51 trihemiobols (3.5%). Nevertheless, this is the largest number of Phliasian coins ever discovered (cf. Mac Isaac 1988, 46–7).

56 *IGCH* no. 40: found in Arkadia (?), buried in the late fifth century, contains one Phliasian silver out of 91. *IGCH* no. 64: found in Corinth, buried ca. 338 BCE, contains one Phliasian bronze out of 57 silver and bronze coins. *IGCH* no. 67: found at Moulki (near Sikyon), buried ca. 350/325 BCE, contains two Phliasian silvers out of about 150. Other hoards from Thessaly (*IGCH* no. 57) and Delphi (*IGCH* no. 303) report one Phliasian coin apiece, but they are strays that prove the rule of an overwhelmingly local circulation.

57 For the recovery of nails from the Sanctuary, see p. 185.

58 A few dedicatory graffiti are known on Greek coins. All include some reference to the deity in the dative case and, space permitting, may also contain the dedicator's name in the nominative, and, very occasionally, the coin in the accusative (see Bicknell 1990 for a particularly chatty stater of Aigina). If **EΛ** (i.e., either 'Eλ- 'Eλ-, Eἰλ-, or Eἱλ-) represents the gift's divine recipient, then the possibilities include E(i)leithyia, the goddess of childbirth who is associated with Athena (e.g., on the Marmaria terrace at Delphi, Demangel 1923, 47–9 and 77–8), and Hellotia/

Hellotis, a cult title and festival of Athena at Corinth (Pindar, *Ol.* 13.40). For a punctured graffito dedication to Asklepios on a stater (ca. 350 BCE) of Stymphalos, perhaps by a Lakonian, see Dubois 1986, 190 (ΑΙΓΛΑΠΙΩ - Αἰγλαπιῶ); *SNG: Burton Y. Berry Collection*, part 2, no. 871 (American Numismatic Society, New York, 1962).

59 *BMC 11*, xxvi. The name is a rare one that is recorded only six times in the Archaic and Classical periods, and only in the Peloponnese, according to Oxford University's *Lexicon of Greek Proper Names* project (http://www.lgpn.ox.ac.uk). Thus any Phaënos of Argos who might turn up in the context of second-century Argos would very likely be our man.

60 *SEG* XXV 445 (=Burstein 1985, no. 71), l. 26. See note 85 below.

61 The iron disks from Stymphalos range in size from 13 mm to 25 mm and weigh between 1.0 g and 5.3 g. They were found in Trenches 94.2, 94.3, 94.4 (records for these 1994 finds are incomplete), 95.3 (Building A, inv. 129), and 95.4 (inside Temple, inv. 17). They are more likely heads from iron nails. By contrast, examples of six iron coins excavated at Nemea range between 20 mm and 30 mm and tip the scale between 11.7 g and 19.1 g; furthermore, all exhibit the forepart of a wolf on one side and a large A on the other (Knapp and Mac Isaac 2005, nos. 1595–1600).

62 The *locus classicus* is the courtesan Rhodopis's proud dedication of a great mass of iron spits at Delphi (Her. 2.135.3–4). See Schaps 2004, 82–8 for the place of this episode in the evolution of Greek money.

63 Mac Isaac 1988, 49, citing Price 1968, 100.

64 Besides **II-87** and the six examples from Nemea, only one other iron coin, now in the Numismatic Museum at Athens, can be connected with an excavation, namely that of the Apollo shrine at Epidauros (Mac Isaac 1988, 48 n. 19).

65 Knapp and Mac Isaac 2005, 57; Mørkholm 1991, 106–7, quoting Hackens 1968, 82–3. Five examples were excavated in the Athenian Agora (*Agora* XXVI, nos. 1007a–e), which makes this the single commonest Ptolemaic type to be found there. All the same, the 37 coins of the whole Ptolemaic dynasty from the Agora are proportionately much rarer there (*Agora* XXVI, nos. 1004–19, 0.2%) than the Ptolemy III bronzes at Nemea (nos. 1998–2012, 15 specimens, 0.7%) or at Stymphalos (17 specimens, 3.5%). The higher proportion for Stymphalos may be the result of the local men's greater involvement in mercenary service, which was a significant factor in the Arkadian economy.

66 One of the king's first actions overseas was to take control of Thrace in 243 BCE (Polyb. 18.51.5; Livy 33.40.5; App., *Syr.* 3b). The next year, Ptolemy accepted an invitation from Aratos of Sikyon to become leader, and doubtless a benefactor, of the anti-Macedonian Achaian League (Plut., *Arat.* 24.4–6; Paus. 2.8.5). We also hear that he provided large financial subsidies, apparently for some years, to King Kleomenes of Sparta to finance his erosion of Antigonid power in the Peloponnese, though Ptolemy stopped payment in 222 BCE to protest Kleomenes' open war with King Antigonos (Polyb. 2.63.1–5; Plut., *Cleom.* 32.4).

67 Mørkholm 1991, 106–7 opines that they were probably struck at Alexandria for circulation in Greece since their weights (three denominations of 17 g, 8.5 g, and 5.7 g) and obverse type (laureate bust of the king) would be idiosyncratic in Egypt. The date of this particular issue ought perhaps to be narrowed to the 220s BCE and Ptolemy's subsidy of specifically Spartan activities (Knapp and Mac Isaac 2005, 57, 173 n. 337).

68 See Mac Isaac 1995 for the potential longevity of bronze coins in circulation.

69 **II-1** (Syracuse); **II-44** through **II-46** (Sikyon); and **II-87** (Argos). For **II-1**, see p. 72.

70 **II-35** through **II-40** (Phlious, including one silver); **II-82** through **II-84** (Pellene); **II-87** (Hermione); **II-88** (Kleitor); **II-89** (Mantineia); and **II-90** (Arkadian League, 370–280 BCE).

71 See Weir 2007, 13–20 for the early third-century reconstruction of the western defences by the Macedonians.

72 Morris 2003: "The pottery assemblage from Phase 4 is similar to that of Phase 5 [i.e., fourth century BCE], with a high percentage of votive vessels and tableware and a minimal amount of cooking, service, toilet, and transport/storage vessels. Kantharoi appear in this phase however. Although the stratigraphical context of the pottery assemblage in the two phases is significantly different, the similarity of the assemblage in Phase 4 to a specifically votive deposit is suggestive of a similar type of activity taking place. Thus Phase 4 attests to the continuance of cultic activity at the sanctuary."

73 The Temple: Trenches 95.1, 95.4, and 96.1 inside the Temple contained 10 coins; and another 5 were found in 95.5, 95.6, and 99.2. The Altar: Trench 96.3 contained the Altar and 5 coins, 96.4 accounted for another 5, and another 2 came from 96.9 and 99.8.

74 **II-51**, a holed and graffitoed hemidrachm of Sikyon, was found in 95.5 along the Temple's south edge; and **II-90**, an obol of the Arkadian League, came from the Temple steps. Meanwhile, **II-52**, another hemidrachmon of Sikyon, was found just south of the Altar. All coins date approximately to the fourth century BCE.

75 Williams 2002, 154.

76 Trench 99.13: see p. 72 for the "hoard" of five silver coins; Trench 00.99.13, a continuation of 99.13 in the next year (**II-50**, Sikyon, late fourth century BCE); and Trench 00.3 (**II-10**, Boiotian League, late fourth century BCE).

77 See p. 73 for the possibility of a votive deposit to the south of the Altar.

78 At the panhellenic sanctuary of Nemea, 6% of its 2117 Greek coins were silver (Knapp and Mac Isaac 2005, 3–9). At the Athenian Agora, the figure was only about 1% (*Agora* XXVI, 4).

79 The census for all 492 coins excavated at Stymphalos, including Stym II, is Sikyon 38%, Corinth 16%, and Phlious 9%.

80 A few other cities in the Peloponnese are represented disproportionately by the Stym II corpus: Kleitor (one of two found at Stymphalos, **II-89**), Pellene (three of six found at Stymphalos, **II-82** to **II-84**).

81 Another piece of evidence, albeit indirect, for a votive deposit (see p. 73).

82 Schaus (2007) has pointed out that what was arguably the best-known representation of Herakles's Stymphalian labour in the Classical period, namely one of the metopes from the mid-fifth-century temple of Zeus at Olympia, seems to allude to the specific topography of Stymphalos: Herakles presents the dead birds to Athena, who is seated on a rocky ridge that resembles the acropolis where the Stym II Sanctuary is located.

83 It is a general principle that silver coins typically indicate trade connections, but that bronze coins are carried from place to place by travellers, i.e., unspent and unspendable outside their home jurisdictions. The idea for this kind of analysis came from Knapp and Mac Isaac 2005, 36–49.

84 See p. 72.

85 According to Pausanias (8.4.1–4), Arkas was the father of Elatos, the eponymous founder of Elateia, who was himself the father of Stymphalos, the eponymous founder of Stymphalos. In 198 BCE, Elateian refugees in the war between Philip V and Quinctius Flamininus benefited from this legendary relationship to settle among the Stymphalians for several years until they could return home (Polyb. 18.43.1; Livy 32.24.1–3; Paus. 10.34.3–4; *SEG* XXV 445 [=Burstein 1985, no. 71]).

86 Elis/Olympia: excavation catalogue no. 2383 (silver hemidrachm, 360–330 BCE, from a hoard closed in the 280s BCE), 2432, 3498 (silver obol, 360–330 BCE, very worn, from a Hellenistic context), 4178. Andros: excavation catalogue no. 4163. Chios: excavation catalogue no. 449. See note 87 below for Athenian coins.

87 Hellenistic Athenian issues: excavation catalogue nos. 41, 473, 910, 2143, 3365 (silver drachm, 229–200 BCE), 3559, 3688, 3872, 4282, 4494. Late Classical Athenian issues in Hellenistic contexts: excavation catalogue nos. 360 (silver hemidrachm, 393–350 BCE), 4290 (bronze, 330s–322/317 BCE).

88 A Pinarius Natta *denarius* of 149 BC (Crawford 1974: #208/1) from the mint of Rome was discarded here soon afterwards, Crawford 1985, 116–18.

Chapter 5: Weapons

* I would like to thank Professor H. Williams for allowing me to study the projectiles from Stymphalos, and Professor G.P. Schaus for his guidance and support. I would also like to thank Ben and Holly Gourley for their insights and comments and Peter Stone for his patient and informative response to many inquiries about the ceramics. Needless to say, any errors that remain are the responsibility of the author.

1 Similar artifacts have been recovered from several other sites within the confines of ancient Stymphalos, including excavations in the city's fortifications, the domestic quarter, and various public spaces; however, projectiles have been far more concentrated in the Sanctuary than in these other areas. The Artillery Bastion due west of the Sanctuary provides the only exception to this general rule. There, in a relatively small area, excavators discovered a cache of 32 sling bullets along with five projectile points indistinguishable from those found in the Sanctuary. See Williams and Cronkite Price 1995, 18, fig. 7; Williams, Cronkite Price, and Schaus 1996, 78–9; Williams et al. 1997, 53–7; Williams et al. 1998, 293, 295, and 310.

2 Many studies on Greek warfare have appeared in recent years (see, for example, Sabin, van Wees, and Whitby 2007), and much has been done on catapults (fundamental are Marsden 1969 and Marsden 1971; recent studies include Rihll 2007; Sáez Abad 2005), but not as much attention has been paid to the bolts, or "sharps" (Rihll's term), other than their lengths and the formulae for shooting them, no doubt because the tips or points or other details are not mentioned by ancient writers.

3 While the spear was not, strictly speaking, a "projectile" weapon, the spear head has been included in this assemblage because of its similarity in form and function to the projectile points. Seventeen ferrules were also recovered from the Sanctuary. Though originally identified as projectile points, upon further study they have been reidentified. They are catalogued in Appendix A to this chapter.

4 Fragments of mineralized wood were discovered within the socket of one catapult-bolt head, inv. 1616.

5 All dates are BCE unless stated otherwise.

6 This process has been reconstructed by Sim (1992, 111–12).

7 This is clearest in the assemblage from Dura-Europos (Rostovtzeff et al. 1936, 455, pl. 24), where points from the same calibre bolt showed measurable variation in dimension and mass.

8 Marsden 1969, 86. The shaft diameter may be deduced from measurements of the socket on the catapult points and the juncture between the tang and head on the arrowheads. Socketed projectiles were sometimes fitted to short wooden footings, or stelai, which were in turn fitted to hollow arrow shafts, often of reed. Tanged arrowheads might also incorporate footings/stelae. In both cases, the intention seems to have been to strengthen the juncture between the head and the shaft. See Coulston 1985, 267–8; also Rostovtzeff et al. 1936, 453–5.

9 The collection includes numerous shafts and heads (called "piles" by the excavators). They resemble very heavily built crossbow bolts. Their shafts are much thicker relative to their length than arrows and taper evenly from base to tip; their flights are wooden and arranged in such a fashion that the bolt could lie flat against the stock of the machine; they are tipped with heavy, socketed points fastened by small rivets or pins through the socket and into the stele. Rostovtzeff et al. 1936, pl. 34 no. 2. They were most likely bolts from a three- or three-and-a-half-span machine, perhaps a *cheiroballista*. This hypothesis rests on a comparison of Winter's (1997, 250) tables of bolt lengths with the dimensions of the intact bolt published by Rostovtzeff (Rostovtzeff et al. 1936, 455).

10 See Wheeler (1943, 75) and Manning (1985a, 170–7, V141–V249). The pieces from Hod Hill are particularly close to the Stymphalian examples in dimensions, with most falling between 6 and 9.5 cm. As Manning points out, mass is a problematic point of comparison due to the varying but omnipresent effects of corrosion. See also Bishop and Coulston 1993, 55–6, fig. 27, 81 fig. 44, and 139–40, fig. 99. For the pieces from Alesia, see *RA* 1864, pl. 22, especially the top six and bottom three pieces in the left-hand column. For those from Gimla, see Syon 1992. See also Ulbert 1984, no. 185.

11 The pieces from Dura averaged 10–12 cm in length and weighed 50–60 g (Rostovtzeff et al. 1936, 455).

12 Marsden 1969, 189–90.

13 A single, socketed iron projectile point from Kalapodi, described as a "Bolzenspitze" or "bolt point," may provide a much earlier date for this type of point, Schmitt 2007, 482 no. 395 pl. 96. It has a conical socket that runs directly into a pyramidal head, and was found in a sixth-century BCE level. (Thanks to G.P. Schaus for this reference.) This find suggests the important possibility that there may be no connection between the development of artillery and this style of point; however, unlike the majority of broadly similar points from Stymphalos, this piece does not appear to have a distinct neck between the head and the socket. Relatively speaking, it is also very long and slender in proportion, with a rectangular rather than square-sectioned head. It is not therefore entirely consistent with the later pieces identified as catapult-bolt heads. If an arrowhead, it is certainly a very unusual type for the period; it may be an "ad hoc" point, a javelin head, or perhaps even a ferrule.

14 For the original identification, see Reinders 1988, 259, no. 34.23 fig. 114. For the reassessment, see Hijmans 2003, 127–8; see nos. M38 and M50. None of the illustrated pieces (M38, M40, M47, M50) have a distinct neck separating the point from the socket.

15 A close look at the published dimensions (Hijmans 2003, 304–5) suggests that as many as half of these pieces could be catapult-bolt heads. In the absence of more illustrations this remains conjecture; however, the existing illustrations do suggest that the artifacts labelled as "ferrules" in fact comprise several distinct functional categories: a conclusion implied by the excavators themselves. Hijmans 2003, 128.

16 Robinson 1941, 393 no. 1983 pl. 123, but the possible socket would need autopsy to confirm. The controversy over the date of Olynthos' final abandonment, whether it occurred after Philip's siege in 348 or following Kassander's resettlement of the remaining Olynthians at Kassendreia in 316, now seems to have been settled. Cahill's (2002) reassessment of the site shows that limited habitation continued after 348. Rotroff (1997, 18–20) discussed how this may complicate assessments of the ceramic assemblages as a whole; however, Cahill (2002, 60–1) noted that there is no question that the material in the destruction layer – where the majority of the projectiles were found – does not date later than 348. Therefore the only complication with respect to dating the projectiles found at Olynthos is establishing whether they relate to the Persian siege of 479 or Philip's attack. Robinson 1941, 388.

17 Snodgrass 1967, 116–17; de Souza 2007, 452.

18 Hijmans 2003, 128. The publication provides no data on the mass of these pieces, so precise comparisons are impossible.

19 Robinson 1941, 416–18, no. 2174, pl. 129. Seventeen such objects were recovered from the Sanctuary. See Appendix A.

20 Compare Robinson 1941, nos. 2162, 2170–3, and 2175, pl. 129.

21 This is also borne out by the pieces recovered from the Sanctuary. Socket diameters range from 1.3 to 1.7 cm, that is, roughly twice the width of a typical arrow shaft as

reconstructed from the size of the bodkin and Cretan arrowheads. The catapult-bolt heads weighed almost twice as much as the next heaviest class of projectile point (Cretan) and twenty times as much as the smallest class (Scythian).

22 Identification of the pieces from New Halos is further complicated by the fact that they were all recovered from domestic contexts some distance from the fortifications: houses 1, 3, and 6. Hijmans 2003, 304–5. It is not easy to explain the presence of such pieces in private houses, unless they were salvage or scrap. No such problems appear in the case of Olynthos, where the artifact in question was found amid the debris of Philip's siege.

23 This statement pertains only to extant artifacts. Catapult bolts, as distinct from arrows, are attested in *IG* II^2 1422 no later than the late 360s. Marsden (1969, 65–6) dated this inscription to 371/0. P.J. Cole (1981, 219) later down-dated it to 363/2. Whatever its date, this inscription and others like it from the 350s (*IG* II 120 and 1440) provide no information as to possible differences between arrowheads and the heads of catapult bolts. While the shape and size of the head may have been a factor in the distinction between these types of projectiles, overall size, proportions, and/or flights may also have been distinguishing factors.

24 Marsden (1969, 174 and 180) concludes that the Romans relied on the Greeks as the source of machines and expertise as late as the first century.

25 Marsden 1969, 174–81. The pieces from Dura match the length prescribed for Hellenistic Greek three-span bolt-firing catapults with considerable precision – ca. 46.2 cm. Rostovtzeff et al. 1936, pl. 24. Winter (1997, 250–1) provides a useful table of calibres.

26 Diod.Sic. 14.42.1. He (14.50) recounts the siege in some detail. At one point he mentions the importance of bolt-firing catapults (14.50.4: τοῖς ὀξυβλέσι καταπέλταις). Projectile points dating to this siege were recovered in excavations conducted by Whitaker (1921, 154 and 168) whose "lance heads" could have been heads from catapult bolts. See Isserlin and du Plat Taylor 1974, 29, 62, 66, and 75. The latter (1974, 109) provide excerpts from Schliemann's unpublished diary relating his cursory investigations on the island in 1875, which mention his discovery of arrowheads from the siege. One he described as γλωχίνοι, another as leaf-shaped, a third as having the form of "a miniature lance," and a fifth as pyramidal without flutings. Marsden (1969, 100 n. 1) offers the suggestion that at least some of these came from catapult bolts. While this seems likely, the only published illustrations of projectile points from the site are of two bronze, "Scythian" type arrowheads (*Illustrated London News* 1963, 425–7). The presence of specially designed catapult-bolt heads at Motya would necessitate a revision of the proposed development of such artifacts presented here.

27 For little catapults, like hand-held crossbows, which existed from at least 200 BCE, see Rihll 2007, 91–105.

28 Marsden 1969, 60. Polyidos is credited with major advances in catapult design by Vitruvius (*De arch.* 10.13.3). In any case, the torsion catapult was in existence by 326, from an inscription listing an Athenian store with catapult equipment, *IG* II^2 1467; see Rihll 2007, 78–9.

29 Marsden 1969, 24 and 62.

30 Marsden 1969, 55–6. Diod.Sic.14.43.3. Marsden argues that from the context καταπέλται παντοῖοι should be taken as "catapult bolts of all kinds" rather than "catapults of all kinds." In either case it is not entirely clear if this statement refers to arrows or to bolts, or to missiles of different sizes, or to those with different styles of head, such as armour-piercing and fire-carrying. Earlier and later references to special missiles (14.42.2: "διόπερ ἀνυπέρβλητον φιλοτιμίαν εισφέροντες οἱ τεχνῖται πολλὰ προσεπενοῦντο βέλη καὶ μηχανήματα ξένα καὶ δυνάμενα παρέχεσθαι μεγάλας χρείας" "Consequently the workmen brought unsurpassable devotion to the devising of many missiles and engines of war that were strange and capable of rendering great service") and bolt-firing catapults (14.50.4), respectively, indicate a clear concern with designing missiles to suit the new machines.

31 Cole (1981, 219), interprets this (βέλος) to mean a catapult bolt. Plutarch, *Pel.* 2.3.

32 Marsden (1969, 65–6) favours the earlier date. Ober (1987, 571) supports his view. P.J. Cole (1981, 219) argued for the later date. See also Rouse (1902) 110 n. 15.

33 Notwithstanding the potential bolts recovered from Motya (above note 26).

34 Snodgrass 1967, 117.

35 Compare Olympia type II B 1. Baitinger (2001, 17–19) notes similar finds at Vergina, Megalopolis, Skilloundia/Mazi, Torone, Corinth, and Perachora. He rightly points out the similarity in form between the points from Olynthos and the examples from Olympia, but fails to take note of the difference in size.

36 Robinson 1941, no. 1983, pl. 123.

37 The shift from non-torsion to torsion was not complete until the third century. Marsden 1969, 60–3.

38 Bishop and Coulston 1993, 56; also Coulston 1985, 268–9. See also Magness 1992.

39 Robinson 1941, pl. 128, no. 2170; pl. 129, nos. 2174–75. Baitinger 2001, pl. 57, nos. 1210–11, pl. 58, nos. 1213–15. See also Stella G. Miller 1983, no. IL 505, pl. 41.

40 Hanson, 1989, 85–6 and 171–2. For examples of breast-

plates pierced by sauroteres, see also Snodgrass 1967, 56 and 80.

41 According to on-line discussion threads, some modern re-enactors have used the same utilitarian solution, adapting reproduction spear butts to serve as the heads of their artillery bolts and javelins. This striking coincidence may help account for the occasional confusion in distinguishing between these types of artifacts.

42 All measurements are maximum-preserved dimensions.

43 This and the following three pieces were never assigned catalogue numbers. They were, however, published in drawing form in Williams and Cronkite Price 1995, 19. They may be identified as follows: **79** top of the left-hand column; **80** bottom of the left-hand column; **81** bottom of the right column; **82** second from the bottom in the right-hand column.

44 Schmitt 2007, 483, pl. 97 nos. 397–404.

45 Bishop and Coulston 1993, 55–6. They postulate that such points might also have been suitable for arrows or javelins. In size, inv. no. 1190 seems closer to the catapult-bolt points than the javelin head and spear head from the Sanctuary.

46 Robinson 1941, 406; Snodgrass 1967, 82. A third arrowhead (inv. no. 1144) of this type was recovered from the Artillery Bastion west of the Sanctuary. It is distinguished by straight blades. For a nearly identical piece see Robinson 1941, no. 2121 pl. 125 and no. 2130, pl. 126; Baitinger 2001, nos. 433–40 pl. 12.

47 Athens: Broneer 1935, 113–16. Corinth: Davidson 1952, 199–201, no. 1520, pl. 91. Kalapodi: Schmitt 2007, Taf. 98 nos 418–20; Marathon: Erdmann 1973, 30–58 nos. CIa, CIIb1, and CIIb2. Nemea: Stephen G. Miller 1978, pl. 18, nos. BR 305–7, BR 391, BR 385, BR 390, BR 410, and BR 453; 1979, pl. 25, BR 524, BR 624; 1980, pl. 41, BR 662, BR 667, pl. 44 BR 731–3; 1981, BR 842, 869. Also Stella G. Miller 1984, BR 1143, BR 1153, BR 1157. Olympia: Baitinger 2001, pl. 12. Olynthos: Robinson 1941, 383, Type GIV nos. 2120–2, pl. 125, and Type GV no. 2130, pl. 126. Thermopylae: National Archaeological Museum, Athens.

48 Baitinger 2001, pl. 12, nos. 413 and 416, for Stymphalos, **84**. Robinson 1941, no. 2120, pl. 125, for Stymphalos, **84**.

49 These are from third-century CE contexts in Caerleon and Corbridge in Great Britain. Bishop and Coulston 1993, 138, nos. 2–3.

50 Stephen G. Miller 1977, pl. 6, no. BR 221 and pl. 7, nos. BR 77 and BR113. Baitinger 2001, pls. 4–5. See also Jacopi 1932, fig. 81, nos. 14411 and 14419. Note, however, that most of these pieces had long barbs springing from their sockets, a feature much easier to produce in a cast bronze arrowhead than in a forged iron one.

51 Walters 1899, 346.

52 Robinson (1941, 387) followed Walters (1899) in classifying these as Type D1.

53 Snodgrass 1964, 146–7.

54 Robinson 1941 nos. 1949 and 1960, pl. 121, Baitinger 2001, 10 pl. 2, nos. 31–2, 40 (all bronze and dated to the fourth century) and pl. 3 no. 50, which is iron and of similar date. Also for Olympia see Furtwängler 1890, 177–8, nos. 1093 and following, pl. 64. Snodgrass (1964, 146–7) discussed the development of the type, as did Robinson (1941, 383–91), who distinguished several subclasses. His Type D1 is the closest in shape to the Stymphalian pieces. See also Blinkenberg 1931, 194 no. 606 (Lindos); Chamoux 1955, 97, fig. 336b (Delphi); Payne et al. 1940, no. 20, pl. 82 (Perachora); Deonna 1938, figs. 239–40 (Delos); Schmitt 2007, Taf. 94, no. 364 (Kalapodi); Warden 1990, 51, citing *AfrIt* 4 (1931) 197 no. 17, fig. 21 (Cyrene).

55 Snodgrass 1967, 17, 29, and 40. Erdmann (1973) is the best source for examples from the Persian Wars.

56 Robinson 1941, 398.

57 Baitinger 2001, pl. 3 nos. 48–50. For the dates, see Baitinger 2001, 11. Robinson 1941, 388.

58 Stephen G. Miller 1977, pl. 7, IL 63, IL 70, and IL 77; 1978, pl. 18, IL 166, IL 211; 1980, IL 330, IL 332, pl. 44. For the date, late fifth or early fourth century, Miller 1977, 9–11; the former date was confirmed in Stephen G. Miller 1997, 65. See also Stella G. Miller 1984, 185, IL 475, IL 509, IL 511, pl. 42.

59 Robinson 1941, 388. While many of these are dated to the Persian sack of 479, others were found in contexts related to Philip's siege of 348.

60 Inv. no. 1374, recovered in 1997.

61 Walters 1899, 346. Robinson 1941, 392.

62 Although not illustrated, **149** and **156** have damaged tips, and **138** and **182** have bent tangs.

63 Robinson 1941, 392.

64 Baitinger 2001, 11–12, nos. 50–1, pl. 3.

65 Olympia: Baitinger 2001, 12; nos. 53–5, pl. 3. No. 53 was found in the well. Nemea, Stephen G. Miller 1977, IL 65–6 pl. 6, IL 97 and IL 99, pl. 5; 1978, IL 232 pl. 18, 1980, IL 328, pl. 44. See also Stella G. Miller 1984, 185, IL 480, IL 507, IL 510, IL 515, Il 518–19, pl. 42. All of these were originally identified as iron spear points, but they are clearly too small for this purpose. Though recovered from disturbed contexts, these points were found alongside numerous bronze arrowheads consistent with those found in secure contexts linked to the late fifth-century destruction. At Asea, two bodkin points were recovered during a survey of an unattributed sanctu-

ary. Both have been assigned to the "Classical" period. Forsén and Forsén 2003, 244 S60/ 35–6, fig. 146. For an ancient example from Corinth, see Davidson 1952, 199, no. 1512 pl. 91.

66 Schmitt 2007, 480, pls. 95 6, nos. 371 87. Nos. 385 and 386 were found in the fifth-century pit .

67 Coleman 1986, 96; D37–D42, pl. 38. For the date see pp. 6–8 and 68.

68 Robinson (1941, 392–7) "Type E," nos. 1972–2026. See nos. 1984–2004, pl. 123 and nos. 2008–26, pl. 124.

69 Schmitt 2007, 480, pls. 95–6 nos. 373–5. See p. 23 for a discussion of this context. There remains some question whether this is a destruction level, perhaps associated with Sulla's campaign in Greece, or a layer of fill material. In either case, the evidence from Kalapodi provides a vital link that suggests the continuity of this type of point from Late Classical through Roman periods.

70 For Roman examples see Bishop and Coulston 1993, 136, nos. 6, 8, 10. For the piece from Corinth, Davidson 1952, 201, no. 1532 pl. 93. The general type takes its name from a similarly shaped Mediaeval dagger. Such points were very common in the Mediaeval period. Rostovtzeff et al. 1936, 456, after Pope 1923, 53.

71 **190** and **191** were not assigned inventory numbers. **190** was, however, published in line drawing in Williams and Cronkite Price 1995, 19 (second from the top, right-hand column). **191** was recovered from the excavations in the Hexagonal Artillery Tower southeast of the Sanctuary.

72 Robinson 1941, 412–13 (Type A2), nos. 2145–7 and 2149 pl. 127.

73 Snodgrass 1967, 80. He noted that size is the key criterion by which javelin heads can be distinguished from spear heads. He also noted the importance of a slender blade and a proportionally long socket for throwing spears/javelins.

74 Baitinger 2001, 46–7, nos. 606, 610, and 614 pl. 21 and no. 625 pl. 22.

75 Baitinger (2001, 47) notes the lack of a typology for Olympia, and even more for Greece as a whole. He also stresses the difficulty of dating javelin heads stylistically, since they rarely receive meaningful attention.

76 Robinson 1941, 414 (Type B) no. 2154 pl. 128. Baitinger 2001, 42–8, nos. 746–50 pl. 28. Stephen G. Miller 1978, IL 174, and 225 pl. 81.

77 For surviving moulds see Bruneau 1968, 650 fig. 14 and Robinson 1941, 420 fig. 23.

78 Åström and Nicolaou 1980. Rihll (2007, 98) states that "lead slingshot seems to have been invented at the turn of the fourth century B.C." and Baitinger (2001, 31) says that "Bleigeschosse wurden nicht vor dem Ende des 5. Jahrhunderts verwendet," but neither apparently is aware of the evidence from Cyprus.

79 The most important contemporary examples are found in Robinson 1941, 421, nos. 2176–2380 pls. 120–4. See also Davidson 1952, 199–200 nos. 1525–7 pl. 91; Hellman 1982, 75–8 fig. 1; Foss 1975, 40–3 (including examples from Megalopolis, Aigilia, Knossos, Gortyn, Smyrna, and Hieropolis); Mylonas 1943, 87; Shear 1939, 225. For a more complete discussion and list of publications on ancient sling bullets, including a comprehensive discussion of their use, see Pritchett 1991, 44–53. His list includes Amphipolis, Argos, Athens, Corinth, Galatista, Kamiros, Kerkyra, Kosmas, Metropolis, Palairos, Pydna, Sikyon, and Thestia. Rihll (2007, 98–105) has an interesting discussion of the use of lead slingshot, especially for its delivery by "little catapults" rather than only by slings. For ones associated with Philip's attack on Torone in 349 BCE, see Cambitoglou et al. 2001, 723–6 nos. 18.1–18.11. For Olympia, Baitinger (2001, 31–2 pl. 13 nos. 493–7, especially two inscribed ones, nos. 496–7, perhaps associated with the battle near the Altis in 364 BCE) also provides a good discussion and many references to earlier studies and examples.

80 Pritchett 1991, 43, following Vischer 1878, 240–84.

81 Pritchett 1991, 48–9.

82 Cambitoglou et al. 2001, 725.

83 Jacopi 1932, 365 nos. XIV.9–11, fig. 110, showing a scorpion and spear head. Baitinger 2001, pl. 13 nos. 496–7, showing crossed thunderbolts; Rihll (2007, 3) mentions five in the British Museum with scorpions.

84 My thanks to G. Schaus for these suggestions.

85 Thanks to Dr Mary Richardson for her helpful suggestions regarding these inscriptions.

86 For the dating of the Bastion Deposit see Williams et al. 1998, 310–14, where initial pottery dating suggested that the sling bullets were associated with a late fourth-/early third-century destruction, and more recently, Williams and Gourley 2005, 249–50, where more careful analysis of the pottery by Peter Stone suggested that the cache of sling bullets was buried by the collapse of the Bastion dated to the late third/early second century.

The deposit in question certainly was not part of a stockpile of weapons. The only other projectiles (catapult-bolt head, inv. 1567, and bodkin arrowhead, inv. 1568) found in the same context were fragmentary and may have been discarded as rubbish. This deposit was recently mentioned and illustrated by Rihll (2007, 103), who mistakenly says that 130 catapult sharps (i.e., points) were also found in the acropolis tower (i.e., the Bastion), rather than the five actually found there, and who dates the deposit both to about the end of the third century (fig. 5.7 caption) and the mid-third century.

87 See pp. 98–101 for an extended discussion of this siege and others involving Stymphalos.

88 Diod. Sic. 19.63.4.

89 For Aristodemos see Diod. Sic. 19.57.4–5, 19.60.1, and 19.64.2–4. For Telesphoros see Diod.Sic. 19.74.1; 75.7. For Ptolemaios see Diod.Sic. 19.77.2; 87.3; and 20.19.2.

90 Diod. Sic. 20.103.5–6.

91 Plut. *Demetr*. 33.2; 35.1; 39.1.

92 See Weir, chapter 4, p. 72. This seems to confirm Shipley's recent suggestion (2005, 319) that the majority of poleis in the northern Peloponnese were garrisoned by "Macedonian" troops from the late fourth century to the reformation of the Achaian League.

93 Diod.Sic.19.64.4. Another possibility for API, though even less likely, is Aristonoüs of Amphipolis, who surrendered to Kassander's forces at Olympias' direction in 316 (Diod. Sic. 19.50.7–8).

94 Broneer 1935, 115.

95 This neglect extends to small metal artifacts more generally, especially iron. Hijmans 2003, 123.

96 Walters 1899; Richter 1915; Snodgrass 1967.

97 Bishop and Coulston 1993. See also Coulston 1985.

98 Robinson 1941. For Dura-Europos, Rostovtzeff et al. 1936; Nemea, Stephen G. Miller 1977–81; New Halos, Hijmans 2003; Olympia, Baitinger 2001; Pylos, Coleman 1986.

99 Figure 5.1 shows the distribution of projectile points across the Sanctuary.

100 **36** and perhaps **38** from Trench 97.7 should also probably be associated with this concentration of projectile points, since the area is contiguous with the western limit of Trench 96.8.

101 A ferrule (**201**) was found just beneath the floor in a level with much carbonized material.

102 Stone, chapter 9, pp. 194–5, and 2007, 24. Fragments of 14 drinking vessels, none of them dating later than ca. 300, were found associated with this floor. There were two coins found in this material, one Sikyonian, dated late fifth century, and the other from Pellene (**II-83**), dated ca. 350–300 BCE. Weir, chapter 4, pp. 64, 69. The destruction material above this floor was excavated as Trench 96.8.3.3 and 96.8.3.4. This material intruded on Trench 96.6. It may also have intruded into the eastern limits of Trenches 97.6 and 97.7, in which case catapult bolts **33**, **34**, **35**, **36**, and **38** should be added to the list of projectile points in this deposit.

103 Four ferrules (**208**, **211**, **212**, and **214**) were also found here.

104 A single jug fragment in Level 1 of Trench 00.6 was dated to the late third/first half of the second century. The balance of the material in this level was fourth century, as was all the diagnostic material recovered from lower levels (2–4).

105 P. Stone (personal communication) suggested this.

106 None of the five coins recovered from this fill material (inv. nos. 2449, 2488, 2522, 2611, and 2751) must date later than the first quarter of the third century. The latest are an issue of Demetrios Poliorketes dating 300–295 and a Sikyonian issue dated ca. 330–270. A further four catapult-bolt heads appeared in Pails 7 and 8 (**51–2**, **54–5**) from Level 5. Pails 6 and 8, however, produced a few sherds (Peloponnesian West Slope (?) and a mould-made bowl fragment) which seem to belong to the late third or even the second century. In the event that these scant ceramic remains are intrusions, the four projectile points in question might be considered part of the "lower" layer beyond the Terrace Wall. In the baulk (Trench 99.1 baulk) that was removed just south of Trench 99.1, several pieces of mould-made bowls and West Slope type ware were found in the lowest level (99.1 baulk Level 4 Pails 4 and 5) excavated. However, this material was separated from the lower levels of 99.1 proper by a wall enclosing a small room with a basin. No projectile points were found in the lower levels within this room.

107 Stone 2007, 25.

108 This is suggested by the overall consistency of ceramic finds and coins and the absence of any feature separating the trenches.

109 The detailed breakdown is as follows: Trench 97.4.5.8 – **156** (bodkin arrowhead); Trench 99.6.5 and 6 – **56** (catapult-bolt head), **166** (bodkin arrowhead); Trench 00.3.6 – **64** (catapult-bolt head), **187** (bodkin arrowhead); and Trench 96.13.4-6 – **26** (catapult-bolt head), **146,** and **148** (bodkin arrowheads), **195–6** (sling bullets).

110 Trench 97.5 and 97.5 baulk contained one sling bullet (**198**), five bodkin type arrowheads (**151, 155, 171, 173–4**), one Cretan arrowhead (**93**), and two catapult-bolt heads (**57**, **59**).

111 Stone 2007, 25–6. The sole coin recovered from these levels (Weir's **II-64**) is a Sikyonian issue of the third century; however, the presence of mould-made bowl fragments in the pottery assemblages of each context pushes the date of the layer well into the second century.

112 Trench 96.13 contained five bodkin arrowheads (**131**, **134**, **139–40**, and **143**). These were found in a thick fill with decomposed mudbrick (Levels 2 and 3), possibly from the nearby City Wall, which seemed to continue as deep as Level 4 Pail 7 in the eastern (lower) part of the trench, although only one mould-made bowl fragment

was identified in this material, in Level 2. Coins found in Trench 96.13 included Weir's **II-32** (inv. 900) dated ca. 410–248 (from Corinth), **II-55** (inv. 929) dated ca. 330–290, and **II-64** (inv. 657) dated ca. 270–200 (both from Sikyon). Trench 97.4 contained a catapult-bolt head (**32**). Trench 99.1 contained two bodkin arrowheads (**163–4**), six catapult-bolt heads (**47–8, 51–2, 54–5**), and one Type-H arrowhead (**86**). Trench 00.3 contained two bodkin arrowheads (**177** and **179**) and one Scythian arrowhead (**85**).

113 This surface, "roughly cobbled paving," is described above, p. 26, and in Williams and Schaus 2001, 80.

114 While it is possible to reconstruct the precise locations of the projectiles, which were recorded as small finds, the diagnostic ceramics were not identified until they had been cleaned.

115 Stone 2007, 29–30.

116 Trench 95.9 baulk. For the dating of mould-made bowls, see Rotroff 1982, 13 and Stone 2007, 53–5.

117 A ferrule (**75**) was also found on the floor level east of the hearth.

118 Stone 2007, 24–5. The attribution of this piece has been disputed. While it is far from the finest example of a catapult-bolt head in the collection, its identification poses no significant problems to the author.

119 See Williams et al. (1997, 53 and fig. 9) for a discussion of this tower and the location of **125**.

120 Inv. no. 1567. See Williams and Gourley 2005, 246–50 for the details of this structure.

121 See Williams and Gourley 2005, 249–50. It is important to bear in mind that the material from the collapse is not necessarily indicative of violent destruction. Although there was evidence of burning, it was localized in one relatively small area deep in the basement of the structure. Thus while the collapse could have been the result of violent action, it could also have been the end result of a gradual decay of the building after it was abandoned. Of course, one has to explain why it was suddenly abandoned, leaving behind the cache of sling bullets, and here we come back to a successful attack as one possibility.

122 *IG* II^2 120.36–7; 1412.28; 1414.19; 1422.8–9;1425; 1440.28; 1469.77–80 and 106–7; 1471.55–6; 1475.32. Cited in Cole 1981, 218.

123 There is some debate over the status of these pieces. Cole (1981, 219 n. 16) sees them as dedications. Ober (1987, 571 n. 9) considers them a military stockpile. Simon (1986, 255) takes the middle path, describing the Chalkotheke as a treasury as well as an arsenal. He notes that anything stored there would have been the property of Athena. See also Rouse 1902, 110.

124 These possibilities were first suggested by Williams and Cronkite Price (1995, 18).

125 Williams et al. 1998, 300–15.

126 The only other projectile recovered from the Temple was a bodkin arrowhead (**103**) from a disturbed context.

127 Building A and the North Annex: **4–5, 27, 40, 42, 110,** and **147**. The West Annex: **17, 30–1, 119, 127, 130,** and **133**.

128 See **16, 27, 38, 101, 118, 131, 135, 138, 156, 160, 165, 176,** and **180**.

129 Catapult-bolt heads **26, 51–2, 54–61,** and **64**; bodkin arrowheads **146, 148, 151, 155, 166, 169, 170–5,** and **187**; Cretan arrowhead **93**; sling bullets **195–6** and **198**.

130 See pp. 26–7, 29, as well as pp. 76 and 194.

131 On the frequency of such practices in Archaic sanctuaries see Simon (1986, 256). Many of the spear heads and some of the swords found at Kalapodi show similar damage. Schmitt 2007, spears 1, 2, 30, 81, 82 and swords 457, 462, 481, 483.

132 **16, 27, 42, 44, 60, 104, 131, 138, 160,** and **165** are illustrative.

133 For Olympia, see for example, Baitinger 2001, Bol 1989. Pritchett (1991, 258–61) offers some insights into the practice. For an older though still useful discussion see Rouse (1902, 95–148). Simon (1986, 234–62) offers an extensive list of sanctuaries with military dedications. To this list should be added the Sanctuary of Artemis and Apollo at Kalapodi, which contained more than 300 spear heads. They have been identified as dedications of war booty, Schmitt 2007, 424.

134 Kourouniotes 1910, 311–18 figs. 30–9.

135 Simon 1986, 255.

136 Williams, Cronkite Price, and Schaus 1996, 80. The best physical evidence for such involvement takes the form of foreign coins that have been interpreted as evidence of Stymphalian employment in the armies of Carthage, Syracuse, and Seleukos I. See Weir 2001, 4. For the city's most famous mercenary, "Aenias of Stymphalos," see Xen. *Hel.* 7.3.1. For the proverbial prevalence of mercenary employment among the Arkadians, see Xen. *Hel.* 7.1.23. See also Russell 1942, 104, 107–8; Braund 1994, 44; and Trundle 2004, 53–4.

137 An interesting possibility suggested by the presence of a sling bullet with the KA inscription in the Sanctuary is that the Macedonian garrison presumably installed after 315 (see below) may have patronized the acropolis Sanctuary. This supposition rests on two others: that the projectiles were votives and that the KA inscription in fact refers to Kassander, which has already been shown to be tenuous.

138 Simon 1986, 411.

139 Simon 1986, 234–52. This list includes only sanctuaries where spear heads and arrowheads were found. Simon lists several other possibilities where the patron deity is unclear or unknown. These include Glanitsa, Gortys, Larisa, and Messenia. Note that the preceding list contains two examples of military dedications in sanctuaries devoted to cults of Athena Polias. Lefkas yielded a miniature helmet dedicated to Athena Polias. The Tegean sanctuary of Athena Alea (also a *poliad* deity: Jost 1985, 363–4) yielded a miniature helmet, miniature shields, and arrowheads. Williams and Schaus 2001, 84 citing Preuner 1902, 363–4, and Voyatzis, 1990, 198–200. See also Simon 1986, 234–52.

140 Arrowheads along with spear heads are particularly well attested in Archaic sanctuaries, according to Simon (1986, 253). See his comprehensive list of such dedications (234–52).

141 Baitinger (2001, 92) suggests this practice had ceased by the mid-fifth century. In all, some 416 projectiles from Olympia should probably be considered dedications. This number is arrived at by subtracting the arrowheads which Baitinger linked firmly (53) and tentatively (20) to the fight in the Altis between the Eleans and the Arkadians in 364 from the total discussed in his publication.

142 Simon (1986, 237) suggests that some of the pieces from Old Smyrna, which are commonly linked to Alyattes' siege, might also be votive. The pieces from Larisa are another possibility, but the identity of the patron deity is not certain.

143 Jacopi 1932, 361, fig. 110.

144 Compare Ober (1987, 571) and Cole (1981, 219). Simon (1986, 255) persuasively describes the Chalkotheke as a treasury cum arsenal; see above note 123.

145 Williams and Schaus 2001, 84 citing *Altertümer von Pergamon* II, pl. 21.

146 Williams and Schaus 2001, 84. The latter is included in the Catalogue as **99**.

147 The logistics of transporting cumbersome battlefield trophies might also have discouraged their dedication as thank-offerings. Hanson 1989, 78–9 and 204–8.

148 Marsden 1969, 71–3; Ober 1987, 571–2.

149 Xen. *Hel.* 7.3.1. On the issue of identity see Whitehead 1990, 10–13.

150 Williams and Schaus (2001, 84) note the individuality of Athena worship in particular states and regions. According to Simon, there was an increasing concern with the suitability of offerings to the attributes of the deity following the Archaic period. Simon 1986, 418.

151 Schaus 2007, 169–71.

152 Reconstructions of the metope in question have traditionally placed a bow in Herakles' left hand. More recently scholars such as Beth Cohen (1994, 711) have been inclined to reconstruct a sling. Cohen's argument that the weapon should be restored as a sling due to a deliberate attempt by the artists to suppress the ancient association between Herakles and the bow is persuasive; yet it only underscores the potent traditional link between Herakles and the bow. An Attic black-figure amphora, London B631, dated ca. 550 and attributed to Group E, shows Herakles shooting the birds with a sling (Beazley Archive, 301062). A sixth-century Attic black-figure neck amphora (Paris F387, Beazley Archive 7590) similarly shows Herakles using a sling.

153 Strab. *Geo.*8.6.8. Apollod. *Lib.* 2.92. Apollonius Rhodius (*Argo.* 2.1052) indicates that Herakles tried and failed to kill the *Stymphalides* with his bow and only then resorted to the rattle gambit.

154 Williams and Schaus 2001, 84–5.

155 Williams and Schaus 2001, 84–7.

156 Simon 1986, 410 and 414.

157 Simon (1986, 254) cites Sokolowski 1955, no. 68; 1962 no. 124; 1969, no. 39; Plassart 1928, 140–3; and Plut. *Vit. Arat.* 21.

158 Forty-two projectiles have been recovered from military, domestic, and public spaces in other excavated areas within Stymphalos. These include examples of all types. The total is misleading, however, in that thirty-two of these projectiles came from a single cache of lead sling bullets in the Artillery Bastion west of the Sanctuary.

159 For examples see **12**, **20**, **22**, **33**, **38**, **90**, **114**, **118**, **131**, **133**, **139**, **146**, **155–6**, and **160**. However, if the damage to some of the points is to be taken as attempts at recycling following the end of the Sanctuary's occupation, one wonders why so many were abandoned after they had been laboriously pried out of debris. Even severe damage would not negate their scrap value, though it might make them less attractive to an army on the move.

160 Strabo, 8.8.4. "διὸ δὴ καὶ Ἰφικράτη, πολιορκοῦντα τὸν Στύμφαλον καὶ μηδὲν περαίνοντα, ἐπιχειρῆσαι τὴν κατάδυσιν ἀποφράξαι, σπόγγους πορισάμενον πολλοὺς παύσαςθαι δὲ διοσημίας γενομένης." ("And it was on this account, also, that Iphikrates, when he was besieging Stymphalos and accomplishing nothing, tried to block up the sink with a large quantity of sponges with which he had supplied himself, but desisted when Zeus sent an omen from the sky." Loeb transl.)

161 Schaus, chapter 1, p. 8, following Woodhead 1957, 224 n. 4 and Walbank 1986, 352 n. 51. While neither Woodhead nor Walbank takes a definite stand on this date, both clearly favour it.

162 Strabo 8.8.4. See Williams and Gourley 2005, 219.

163 On the foundation of the Sanctuary, see Sturgeon, chapter 3, p. 43. She suggests that the Archaic kore found in the Sanctuary may have been brought from an earlier Sanctuary, perhaps from the old city of Stymphalos implied by Pausanias (8.22.3).

164 Diod.Sic. 19.63.2. "Ἀπολλωνίδης γὰρ ὁ ταχθεὶς ὑπὸ Κασάνδρου στρατηγός ἐπὶ τῆς Ἀργείων πόλεως ἐξοδεύσας εἰς Ἀρκαδίαν νυκτὸς ἐκυρίευσε τῆς τῶν Στυμφαλίων πόλεως…" ("Apollonides, who had been appointed general over Argos by Kassander, made a raid into Arkadia by night and captured the city of the Stymphalians." Loeb transl.) Diodorus (19.63.4) subsequently relates Kassander's campaign from Kenchreai to Orchomenos later in 315. Stymphalos was probably still under Apollonides' control, but if it had rebelled when Apollonides was called back to suppress a rising in Argos, it may have been one of the two fortresses captured by Kassander during this campaign. In either case, it is likely that Kassander travelled through the territory of Stymphalos on this campaign.

165 Diod. Sic., 19.64.2. For Telesphoros, see Diod.Sic. 19.74.1–2. For Ptolemaios see Diod. Sic. 19.87.3

166 Plut. *Vit. Demetr.*25.1. "Δημήτριος δὲ παρελθὼν εἰς Πελοπόννησον, οὐδενὸς ὑφισαμένου τῶν ἐναντίων, ἀλλὰ φευγόντων καὶ προϊεμένων τάς πόλεις, προσηγάγετο τήν τε καλουμένην Ἀκτὴν καὶ Ἀρκαδίαν, πλὴν Μαντινείας…" ("And now Demetrios proceeded into Peloponnesus, where not one of his enemies opposed him, but all abandoned their cities and fled. He received into allegiance, Acte as it is called and Arcadia (except Mantinea)…" Loeb transl.) Diodorus (20.103.1–6) describes Demetrios' initial foray into Arkadia in 303. Plutarch (*Demetrios* 33.2) describes his return to the Peloponnese in 297 and subsequent campaigns in the area through 295 (*Demetrios* 35.1–2). Marsden (1969, 76) notes that Demetrios was the undisputed leader in artillery during this period. It is certain that he would have deployed a considerable artillery train in these campaigns.

167 See Schaus, chapter 2, p. 31.

168 The same might be said of the three projectiles recovered from beneath the layer of stones around the Altar. The date of this surface is uncertain, and while it may be tempting to connect it with the changes in the Sanctuary that appear to have occurred ca. 300, to do so would be speculation.

169 See Weir, chapter 4, p. 72.

170 Weir (2001, 5) initially suggested the connections among the coins, a Macedonian garrison, and the reconstruction of the fortifications. The connection to the projectiles is afforded by the inclusion of both a bodkin arrowhead and a catapult-bolt head in sealed construction fill within the Hexagonal Artillery Tower and the catapult-bolt head found between the foundation and superstructure of the Bastion that has been definitively associated with this reconstruction.

171 Though iron bodkin arrowheads have been dated as early as the late fifth century at both Olympia and Nemea, neither site produced any catapult-bolt heads. Nor could they have given the date of the catapult's invention.

172 The numbers for New Halos include the pieces reidentified as catapult-bolt heads above.

173 Plutarch (*Vit. Cleom.*, 26.3) describes a campaign that moved from Argos, through Phlious, to Oligyrtos, and then to Orchomenos.

174 Plut. *Vit. Cleom.* 3.5; 4.1–2.

175 Plut. *Vit. Cleom.* 25–27.

176 Polyb., 4.69.1. "τῆς δέ πρωτοπορείας τῶν Μακεδόνων ἐπιβαλούσις ἐπὶ τὴν ὑπερβολὴν τὴν περί τὸ καλούμενον Ἀπέλαυρον, ἣ πρόκειται τῆς τῶν Στυμφαλίων πόλεως περὶ δέκα στάδια, ἅμα συνεκύρησε καὶ τὴν τῶν Ἠλείων πρωτοπερείαν συμπεσεῖν ἐπὶ τὴν ὑπερβολήν." ("As the advanced guard of the Macedonians was coming over the hill near the pass called Apelaurus, about ten stades before you come to Stymphalus, it so happened that the advanced guard of the Eleans converged on the pass also." Loeb transl.)

177 Polyb., 2.55.8. "τοῦτο δέ ποιῆσαί μοι δοκεῖ διὰ τὸ κατὰ τὰς τῶν καιρῶν περιστάσεις παρὰ μόνοις Μεγαλοπολίτας καὶ Στυμφαλίος μηδέποτε δυνηθῆναι μήθ' αἱρετιστὴν καὶ κοινωνὸν τῶν ἰδίων ἐλπίδων μήτε προδότην κατασκευάσασθαι." ("I believe him to have acted so, because the Megalopolitans and Stymphalians were the only peoples from among whom in the varied circumstances of his career he could never procure himself a single partisan to share in his projects or a single traitor." Loeb transl.)

178 Weir 2001, 5. A potential fifth reason to link the projectiles to this period comes from the sling bullets. As we have seen, the KA inscription on one of the bullets from the Sanctuary is linked to a deposit of bullets found in the Artillery Bastion, twelve of which bore this same inscription. Nineteen of the bullets from the Artillery Bastion carried an ARI inscription, which could be an abbreviation of Aristomachos of Argos, who was general of the Achaian League's forces in 228. Plut. *Vit. Cleom.* 4.4. Of course linking these pieces to Aristomachos voids any exclusive association between the collection and Kassander.

179 Pausanias, 7.16.9. "πόλεων δέ, ὅσαι 'Ρωμαίων ἐναντία ἐπολέμησαν, τείχη μὲν ὁ Μόμμιος κατέλυε καὶ ὅπλα

ἀφῃρεῖτο πρὶν ἢ καὶ συμβούλους ἀποσταλῆναι παρὰ Ῥωμαίων·" ("The walls of all the cities that had made war against Rome Mummius demolished, disarming the inhabitants, even before commissioners were dispatched from Rome …") Pausanias 7.16.10 may indicate that the struggle against the Achaian league lasted for some time: "ὁ δὲ πόλεμος ἔσχεν οὗτος τέλος Ἀντιθέου μὲν Ἀθήνησιν ἄρχοντος, ὀλυμπιάδι δὲ ἑξηκοστῇ πρὸς ταῖς ἑκατόν, ἣν ἐνίκα Διόδωρος Σικυώνιος." ("This war came to an end when Antitheus was archon of Athens, in the hundred and sixtieth Olympiad, at which Diodorus of Sicyon was victorious [i.e., 140]".) W.H.S. Jones, translator of the Loeb edition, considered this date an error. The other possibility is that the war to subjugate the Achaian League lasted almost six years after the sack of Corinth, i.e., to 140, as Schaus noted (Williams et al. 1997, 53). In either case, Mummius would not have been present at the "demolitions," as Pausanias suggested, or at least not all of them; he had returned to Rome in 142 to celebrate his triumph.

180 Baitinger 2001, 19; Stephen G. Miller 1977, 9–10; 1979, 82; 1980, 186; and 1981, 51.

181 Of course, if the projectiles were dedications, this is moot.

182 Weir, chapter 4, p. 77 and note 58.

183 The nearest thing to corroboration comes from the debris associated with the collapse of the Artillery Bastion on the acropolis; however, as we have seen, this evidence is ambiguous (above note 121). Although remains of projectiles have been recovered from sites within Stymphalos other than those already mentioned, nowhere else are concentrations high enough to provide a definitive indication of military action. The list is as follows: Stym I, 13; Stym V, 1; Stym VII, 6; Stym VIII, 1; Stym IX, 1, Stym X, 3; Stym XV, 1.

184 Roman examples of javelin butts are published by Manning (1995a, 140, pl. 66 S65–S83). These are quite similar to the pieces from Stymphalos. Compare these with ones from Olynthos (Robinson 1941, 416–18, pls. 127–9 nos. 2162–3 and 2171). Of these, the closest to the Stymphalian examples is no. 2162.

185 Hijmans 2003, 128. See fig 3.34, M40.

186 This and the following piece were never assigned inventory numbers. They were, however, published as line drawings in Williams and Cronkite Price 1995, 19. The first of the present pieces corresponds to the one at the top of the right-hand column in the 1995 publication. The second is second from the bottom in the left-hand column.

Chapter 6: Jewellery

* I would like to thank Dr Hector Williams, University of British Columbia, and Dr Gerald P. Schaus, Wilfrid Laurier University, for enabling me to undertake this project. I am especially indebted to Dr Schaus for his insightful editing comments. The observations from Dyfri Williams and Alexis Castor were also much appreciated. I am very grateful to site conservator Lisa Bengston for her dedicated work on the jewellery, and illustrators Ans Hom, Giles Spence Morrow, and Taryn Webb for their careful drawings. Also many thanks are due to students from Wilfrid Laurier University who helped in the final preparations, especially to Lianne Maitland, Erika Nitsch, and Nizar Ghazal, as well as Ashley Kirby, Michele Gamble, Roxane Bruder, Victoria Waqué, and, from the University of Waterloo, Anne Leask and Colin Wallace. My apologies to any whose names I may have overlooked. The author gratefully acknowledges financial support for this research from two grants received from Wilfrid Laurier University.

1 Other jewellery pieces not included in the Catalogue can be found in Appendices I–IV, as well as in endnotes to individual Catalogue entries, where appropriate.

2 Boardman 1996, 3–4.

3 The terracotta statue of Aphrodite, from a tumulus at Çanakkale, demonstrates the quantity and variety of jewellery a woman could wear, including a pendant necklace, a tie breast-chain, a coiled snake bracelet on her left upper arm, an open hoop bracelet on her left wrist, a broad hoop bracelet on her right upper arm with a decorated band and disk, a spiral snake band on her left thigh, and a twisted hoop on her ankle, all made of gilded terracotta: see Naumann-Steckner 1998, 95–7, col. pl. 13 (end of the second century BCE?).

4 Inv. 1083; SF 1996.493, found beside **38**; and SF 1996.639.

5 Inv. 912, 947, 1016, 1032, 1107, 2520, 2539, 3207, 3342, 3682, 3770.

6 Williams and Ogden 1994, 34.

7 For a discussion of the development of this type, see Hadaczek 1903, 5–6, 21–5, who suggests that the lunate earring type originated in the Greek east. For Mycenaean examples of gold lunate earrings from Cyprus, see Marshall 1969, xxxiii, 22–4, nos. 292–346, pl. 3.

8 Lefkandi: Popham and Lemos 1996, pl. 79, no. A15 (Toumba Grave 79a; ca. 875 BCE; pair of bronze earrings).

9 Ephesus: Marshall 1969, 71–2, nos. 934–46, pl. 9; Higgins 1980, 119, pl. 21E; Musti et al. 1992, 246–7, no. 62, F, G.

10 Higgins 1980, 125, 159. This type still existed in Roman times, although in the modified form of a flat crescent, see Marshall 1969, xxxiii, 288, nos. 2451–62.

11 Eretria: Williams and Ogden 1994, 57, no. 9 ("said to come from a tomb at Eretria"; now in the British Museum; 420–400 BCE; gold pair). Derveni: Themelis and Touratsoglou 1997, 127–8, fig. 26 (Grave Z8; last quarter of the fourth century BCE; gold pair). Homolion, Thessaly: Stella G. Miller 1979, 7–10, pls. 2a–c, 3a–b (Grave A; ca. late fourth century BCE; gold pair); Theocharis 1961–2, 176, pl. 198a (ca. 400 BCE); Stella G. Miller 1979, 17, pl. 10a–b (Grave B; late fourth century BCE; gold pair). Vrasta, Thrace: *Gold of the Thracian Horsemen* 1987, 208, no. 345; Stella G. Miller 1979, 8, n. 25 (tumulus; first half of the fourth century BCE). Thasos, Soultou plot: Sgourou 2001, 340, 354, no. 33; fig. 22 (Grave S-VI; early to mid-fourth century BCE; pair of gilded earrings). Kul Olba: Williams and Ogden 1994, 146, nos. 88–9 (burial chamber; ca. 350 BCE; gold pair and single gold earring). Great Bliznitza: Williams and Ogden 1994, 190, no. 122 (tomb of the "Priestess of Demeter"; ca. 330–300 BCE; gold pair). Taranto: De Juliis 1984, 154, no. 67 (tomb III; ca. 350–300 BCE; gold pair).

12 Of the 42 lunates, 11 have only half a section preserved: Inv. 912, 947, 1016, 1032, 1107, 2520, 2539, 3207, 3342, 3682, 3770. They are included in counts for the sake of completeness and for discussion of distribution, but they are excluded from the Catalogue.

13 Perachora; Sanctuary of Hera Limenia: Payne et al. 1940, 178, no. 28, pl. 79 (seventh-century BCE levels). Lousoi, Sanctuary of Artemis Hemera: Reichel and Wilhelm 1901, 54, fig. 87–8 (sixth/fifth centuries BCE). Corinth: Davidson 1952, 250, pl. 107, no. 2001 ("Greek period"); Potters' Quarter: Stillwell 1948, 125, no. 50, pl. 49 (probably sixth century BCE); North Cemetery: Blegen, Palmer, and Young 1964, 275, no. 427.4, pl. 79 (Grave 427; late fifth century BCE: bronze pair). Mantinea: Karagiorga 1963, 90, pl. 103 (fourth century BCE). Olynthus: Robinson 1941, 86, no. 299, pl. 17 (Child's Grave 563; found beside the ear of the skeleton; based on the find of a squat lekythos in the same grave, the date given, "fourth century BCE," has been revised to the second or third quarter of the fourth century BCE: see Rudolph 1995, 202, n. 2); 87, no. 303–4, pl. 17 (Child's Grave 191; fourth century BCE). Korykian Cave, Sanctuary of Pan and the Nymphs: Rolley 1984, 270, nos. 33–4, fig. 12 (Archaic period).

14 Above note 12.

15 Two unpublished pairs of gilded terracotta lunates, with disks and acorn-shaped pendants, are in the Archaeological Museum, Chania, Crete.

16 Williams and Ogden 1994, 57, no. 9 ("said to come from a tomb in Eretria"; 420–400 BCE); 87, no. 38 ("said to be from Kalymnos"; 450–400 BCE); 211, no. 144 ("said to be from Taranto"; ca. 350 BCE); this latter type is represented in Tarentine graves on the Via Oberdan and Via Crispi: see De Juliis 1984, 151–2, nos. 60–1 (mid-fourth century BCE). An Archaic lunate earring, allegedly from the Athenian acropolis, has a pendant in the form of a plaque decorated with human figures in sixth-century style: see Hadaczek 1903, 24, fig. 45; Miller-Collet (1998, 26, n. 5) notes that the true provenance of this earring cannot be verified. See also note 15 above for unpublished examples from Chania.

17 Korykian Cave, Sanctuary of Pan and the Nymphs: Rolley 1984, 269–70, fig. 12, nos. 31–2 (sixth–fifth centuries BCE). A silver pair of unknown provenance is more elaborately decorated with granulation and filigree: see Hackens 1976, 55, no. 14.

18 Olynthos: Robinson 1941, 84–5, nos. 296–97, pl. 17 (Grave 239; late fifth or fourth century BCE); Robinson (p. 85) notes that similar specimens from Cumae, Italy are sixth century BCE in date: cf. Hadaczek 1903, 21, fig. 38. Korykian Cave, Sanctuary of Pan and the Nymphs: Rolley 1984, 269–70, no. 35, fig. 12 (no date given). Halai: Goldman 1940, 476, nos. 1–2, fig. 147 (grave; late fifth–early fourth century BCE, based on the date of similar-looking silver fibulae found in the same grave). Chalkidike: Amandry 1953, 51, fig. 28, no. 1; 53, fig. 29, nos. 10–11, 13–14 (from Trilophon-Mesimeri cemetery, no date given).

19 The date of the Lousoi fibulae of this type has been revised from the seventh to the fourth century BCE: see Brulotte 1994, 57.

20 A pair of gold earrings has wire terminals in the form of spirals, although this example is from a Protogeometric grave on Skyros: see Vlavianou-Tsaliki 1998, 122, no, 638, pl. 37.

21 Sanctuary of Hera Limenia, Perachora: Payne et al. 1940, 124, 176–8, pl. 79, nos. 1–11 (seventh century); Dunbabin 1962, 442, A306, pl. 188 (bone). Argos: Amandry 1953, 29–33, nos. 42–4, pl. 10 (grave; seventh century; gold earrings surmounted by sphinx and *potnia*, with small balls decorating the entire cone, in the manner of a bunch of grapes).

22 Higgins 1980, 128; Hadaczek 1903, 17–18, regards the pyramidal type as East Greek in origin and also notes that this type occurs on Sicilian coins dating from 600–466 BCE. A late fourth-century coin from Lokris depicts the head of a woman wearing a pyramidal earring: see Marshall 1969, 180, fig. 58. This earring type is also found on Archaic statues and vases, such as those adorning the

ears of the Berlin Kore, ca. 570–560 BCE: see Deppert-Lippitz 1985, fig. 63. A dancing figure on an Oltos kylix from Tarquinia (ca. 520/10 BCE) wears an earring comprised of a disk with a pyramidal pendant: see ibid. 124, fig. 71. A silver diadrachm, ca. 400 BCE, portrays the head of Hera wearing pyramidal and rosette earrings: see Seltman 1949, fig. 320.

23 Isthmia, Lambrou cemetery: Clement 1969, 119, pl. 108a (Grave 68 II 64; ca. fifth/fourth centuries BCE; pair). Halai: Walker and Goldman 1915, 425, fig. 2 (grave; late fifth century BCE). Halieis, altar: Jameson 1969, 321 (late fifth century BCE).

24 Apparently disks with rich floral and figural adornments were added to pyramidal earrings during the second half of the fourth century BCE: see Rudolph 1995, 201–2. For examples from uncontrolled contexts, see Marshall 1969, 180–2, nos. 1664–5, 1670–3 ("said to be from Kyme"; fourth–third centuries BCE); Williams and Ogden 1994, 96–7 nos. 49–50 (330–300 BCE); Marshall 1969, nos. 1666–7 ("said to be from Cyprus"; fifth–fourth centuries BCE); Williams and Ogden 1994, 241, no. 176 (330–300 BCE); Amandry 1953, 141, nos. 286–7 (Collection Stathatos; fourth century BCE); Bromberg 1990, 50, no. 25 (Benaki Museum gold pair; late fourth century BCE); Rudolph 1995, 199–202, no. 50 ("said to be from the eastern Mediterranean"; 350–275 BCE); Alexander 1928, 21, pl. 2 (Taranto; fourth century BCE); Deppert-Lippitz 1996, 72, no. 54 ("said to be from Magna Graecia"; late fourth century BCE).

25 Ano Komi: Touratsoglou 1998, 32–3 (tomb; late fourth century BCE; found with a coin of Philip II; gold pyramidal earring with a five-petal rosette). Amphipolis: Koukouli-Chrysanthaki 1979, 94, no. 381, pl. 53 (Grave 70; second half of the fourth century BCE; gold pair). Great Bliznitza: Williams and Ogden 1994, 181, no. 116 (Third Woman's Burial; 330–300 BCE).

26 Olynthos: Robinson 1941, 80, 82, no. 265, pl. 17 (Grave 370; late fifth/early fourth centuries BCE); no. 269, pl. 17 (Child's Grave 563; based on a squat lekythos in the same grave; the date given, "fourth century BCE," has been revised to second to third quarter of the fourth century BCE: see Rudolph 1995, 202, n. 2); no. 270, pl. 17 (Child's Grave 150; late fifth/early fourth centuries); no. 282, pl. 18 (Grave 31; ca. 375–350 BCE). The date of Olynthos' final abandonment has been discussed by Rotroff (1990), who noted that it was occupied for another 30 years after Philip's destruction in 348 BCE.

27 Corinth, North Cemetery: Blegen, Palmer, and Young 1964, 253, no. 364.3, pl. 79 (Grave 364; pair, third quarter of the fifth century BCE); Sacred Spring: associated with a cult: Williams, 1969, 62 no. 16 (with a list of 7 others) pl. 18h. Argos: Papaspyridi-Karouzou 1933–5, 43–4, fig. 22 (Grave 5; ca. 470–460 BCE); House of D. Boukara: Kritzas 1973, 127 (Grave 3; ca. late fifth/early fourth centuries BCE). Lousoi, Sanctuary of Artemis: Reichel and Wilhelm 1901, 54, fig. 91 (fifth century BCE). Olympia: Philipp 1981, 123–5, pl. 7, nos. 416–21 (Archaic/Classical). Unfortunately, the contexts of these earrings do not offer a precise chronological correlation with other finds in the sanctuary. Korykian Cave, Sanctuary of Pan and the Nymphs: Rolley 1984, 269–70, nos. 36–7, fig. 12 (fourth century BCE). Galixidi: Schwarzmaier 1997, 274–5 (grave; 330–320 BCE); Petrakos 1972, 375. Athens, Pnyx: Davidson and Thompson 1943, 102–3, no. 5 (earring), no. 6 (terracotta mould for pyramidal earring), fig. 46 (Third Period fill; ca. 425–325 BCE). Another good fourth-century example of unknown provenance is in Boston: see Comstock and Vermeule 1971, 200, no. 255.

28 Three could not be located: Inv. 1083; SF 1996.493, found beside **38**; and 1996.639; they are included in the total number discovered, but are excluded from this catalogue. 1996.639 was a miniature votive, only 1 cm in size. A bronze pyramidal earring (Inv. 1018) was found along the west road in the lower town site, along with pottery dating to the late fourth/early third century BCE: see Williams et al. 1998, 265.

29 See above, notes 26 and 27.

30 A gold pyramidal earring of unknown provenance in the Benaki Museum, Athens, has a more elaborate suspension hook, resembling a coiled snake: see Bromberg 1990, 41, 107, pl. 16 (first half of the fourth century BCE).

31 A pair of gold pyramidal earrings, "said to have been found in Greece," in the British Museum have spiral-beaded wires around their tapered, inverted cones: see Hockey 1998, 147, fig. 20.2 (ca. 400–350 BCE); Williams and Ogden 1994, 60. no. 12.

32 Strong 1966, 1, 11, 21–3; Hackens and Winkes 1983, 212; Pliny, *NH* 37.2, 11, 44. An amber pendant was found in a Geometric deposit in the sanctuary of Hera Akraia at Perachora: see Payne et al. 1940, 77. Also found at Perachora were amber intaglio seals and amber bows on bronze fibulae: see Dunbabin 1962, 439, 523–5 pl. 187, A242, 252, 259. Similar Late Geometric fibulae were discovered in the Sanctuary of Artemis Orthia at Sparta: see Dawkins 1929, 198, pl. 82, a, b, e, f, i, k. Ten spherical amber beads from the seventh century BCE were found in the Idaian Cave on Crete: see Sakellarakis 1988, 184–7, figs. 22–3; also p. 187 for references to amber beads from other Greek sanctuaries around the Mediterranean.

33 Strong 1966, 9. An amber bead was found in an Early Classical female burial at Pydna, Macedonia: see Tsigarida 1998, 48, no. 3 (Grave 51; first quarter of the fifth century BCE)

34 Late Archaic bronze wire earrings with beads in the form of thin amber disks were apparently common in central Italy: see Strong 1966, 90, no. 108.

35 The semicircle decoration and the bead pattern is the same on both **54** and the bronze pair with silver wires in the British Museum: see Williams and Ogden 1994, 10, fig. 1; Hockey 1998, 147–8, fig. 20.1 (ht. of pendants 1.5 cm).

36 Bronze solders with a high tin content were used in the Classical/Hellenistic period to join bronze objects together. Over time, copper in the solder corrodes away, leaving the silver-coloured tin behind. (Lisa Bengston, personal communication.)

37 Philipp 1981, 120, fig. 41, no. 409.

38 Inv. 1036, 1042, 1049, 1086, 2748, 3304, 3306, 3318, 3464, 3465, 3584, 3585, of which half were found in the refuse pit (Tr. 96.15) in Building A.

39 Olynthos: Robinson 1941, 91–2, nos. 316–25, pl. 18 (either from houses or provenance unknown; no dates given). Corinth, North Cemetery: Blegen, Palmer, and Young 1964, 210, no. 250.3, pl. 79 (Grave 250; snake's head on one end).

40 For a discussion of the spiral or omega-shaped earring type, see Hadaczek 1903, 12–15.

41 For selected spiral earrings at Lefkandi showing the simplest forms with flaring ends, see Popham and Lemos 1996, pl. 53, nos. 21–2 (Toumba Grave 46; ca. 950 BCE; pair, gilded spirals; pl. 56, nos. 3–4 (Toumba Grave 49, ca. 900 BCE; pair, gilded spirals); pl. 58, nos. 23–4 (Toumba Grave 51; ca. 875 BCE; pair, gilded spirals). At Lefkandi this type also has conical terminals; for example see Popham and Lemos 1996, pl. 66, nos. 27–8 (Toumba Grave 59; ca. 875 BCE; gold spiral). Spiral earrings with similar conical finials were found in sanctuaries at Perachora, Argos, Tegea, and Olympia: Perachora, Sanctuary of Hera Akraia: Payne et al. 1940, 73, nos. 16–17, pl. 18 (bronze). Argive Heraion: Waldstein 1905, 43, no. 281, fig. 88 (clay with painted red crosses). Tegea, Athena Alea: Dugas 1921, 387, no. 168, fig. 20 (bronze). Olympia: Philipp 1981, 114, no. 394, pl. 7 (Geometric; bronze). At Lefkandi there were also spiral earrings with flat disks: see Popham and Lemos 1996, pl. 85, nos. 57–8 (Toumba Grave 80, ca. 750 BCE).

42 For attribution of the elongated spiral type to Rhodes, see Laffineur 1978, 145–6. Elongated Rhodian spirals have been found at Ialysos and Kameiros. Ialysos: Jacopi 1929, 96 no. 12, pl. 5 (Grave 56; seventh century BCE; gold spiral); 100 no. 3 (Grave 57; seventh century BCE; gold spiral); 103 no. 22, fig. 93 (Grave 58; seventh century BCE; pair, silver spirals). Kameiros: Marshall 1969, 96–7, nos. 1168, 1173–4, pl. 12; Higgins 1980, 113, pl. 18a; Jacopi 1932, 336, fig. 82 (bronze). For oval spirals from Rhodes, see Jacopi 1932, 340, fig. 86 (mostly seventh-century votive deposit; two gold, two gilded bronze, four bronze).

43 Olynthos: Robinson 1941, 88–9, nos. 307–8, 310, pl. 18 (Grave 108; second quarter of the fourth century BCE; three bronze spirals); no. 311, pl. 18 (Child's Grave 69; late fifth/early fourth century BCE; bronze pair). Pydna, Macedonia: Tsigarida 1998, 48–50, no. 3, fig. 6.4 (Grave 51; gold spirals with snake-head terminals; first quarter of the fifth century BCE), no 6, fig. 6.3 (Grave 78; silver pair with snake-head terminals; first half of the fifth century BCE); no. 12, fig. 6.4 (Grave 49; third quarter of the fifth century BCE; gold pair with budlike finials found by the head of the deceased). Sindos: Vokotopoulou 1985, 220–1, no. 353 (Grave 96; 450–440 BCE). Philia, Sanctuary of Athena Itonia: Kilian-Dirlmeier 2002, 120–1, pl. 113, nos. 1865–70 (six Classical period graves excavated in 1963–4). Tarrha, Crete: Weinberg 1960, 95, 101, no. 9, pl. 30a (Grave 7b; called "hair rings"; silver pair found on either side of the head of young female; mid-fourth century BCE). Knossos, Sanctuary of Demeter: Coldstream 1973, 138, no. 59, pl. 87 (Deposit H; found in a late fourth/third century BCE context; silver). Halai, Lokris: Walker and Goldman 1915, 425, fig. 2 (grave; later fifth century BCE; silver); For other examples of generic context, see Amandry 1953, 54–5, nos. 137–40, pl. 24 (Trilophon-Mésiméri necropolis, Chalkidike; two silver pairs); Deppert-Lippitz 1985, 178, fig. 124 (silver pair from Athens; late fifth/early fourth centuries BCE); Greifenhagen 1970, 47, nos. 2–3, pl. 39 (fourth century BCE). A pair of gold spiral earrings with budlike finials and a mould for making this type was found in Olbia: see Kalashnik 2004, 69–70, fig. 9, fig. 42.

44 A gold spiral of unknown provenance has a rosette at the top of the spiral: see Higgins 1980, 126, pl. 25H; Williams and Ogden 1994, 52, no. 5 (425–400 BC); Marshall 1969, 177, no. 1648, pl. 30 (fourth century). A silver spiral at Athens has a disk with the head of Athena in relief: see Hadaczek 1903, 14, fig. 23.

45 Pyramidal head finials: Knossos, Sanctuary of Demeter: Coldstream 1973, 138, no. 60, pl. 87 (Deposit J; late first century BCE to mid-second century CE). "Said to be from Kyme": Williams and Ogden 1994, 95, no. 47 (ca. 420–400 BCE; gold pair); Marshall 1969, 165–6, no. 1585–6, pl. 26). Nymphaion: Higgins 1980, 126, pl. 24C (fifth century BCE). This type is also shown on a coin

from Lycia (450–400 BCE): see Williams and Ogden 1994, 34, fig. 30. Animal-head finials: Amathus, Cyprus: see Williams and Ogden 1994, 232, no. 165 (tomb 256; 425–400 BCE; griffin's head finials). Knossos, Sanctuary of Demeter: Coldstream 1973, 138, nos. 57–8 (Deposit H; likely fourth century BCE; snake's head finials). The Dallas Museum of Art has unprovenanced spiral earrings with ram's head finials: see Deppert-Lippitz 1996, 69, no. 41 ("Greece"; second half of the fifth century BCE). Female-head finials: this variety was common in southern Italy: see Williams and Ogden 1994, 212, no. 145 ("said to be from Taranto"; 350–320 BCE); Marshall 1969, 178, no. 1652, pl. 30. The Dallas Museum of Art has an unprovenanced late fourth-century example: see Deppert-Lippitz 1996, 69, no. 43 ("Greece").

46 For example, Robinson (1941, 89–90) wonders whether some of the Olynthian spirals were used for holding hair in place. **73** is similar to omega handles from bronze vases, though the bends are more pronounced.

47 Castor 1999, 25. She also notes, "Because the form of the hoop is the same for both hair and ear ornament, some spirals may have served both functions."

48 Williams and Ogden 1994, 34, fig. 30, 95 (detail of silver stater from Lykia in the British Museum); Hadaczek 1903, 14, fig. 20.

49 A vase painting by the Michigan Painter (510–500 BCE) depicts a spiral earring hanging from a wire: see Deppert-Lippitz 1985, 129, fig. 81. The silver spirals from the fifth-century BCE grave at Halai hung from small hoops: see Walker and Goldman 1915, 425, fig. 2. A sculpted female head from Cyprus, ca. 600 BCE, is wearing multiple spiral earrings on the upper lobe, and lunate earrings through her lower lobes: see Hackens and Winkes 1983, 58; Leipen 1966, 50, fig. 163.

50 Olynthos: Robinson 1941, 84, nos. 290–1, pl. 17 (Grave 203; last quarter of the fifth century BCE; pair); nos. 292–3, pl. 17 (Grave 519; end of the fifth or fourth century BCE; pair). Similar earrings were found in the Sanctuary of Pan and the Nymphs, Korykian Cave: see Rolley 1984, 269–70, nos. 26–30 (no date given), and the Sanctuary of Athena-Itonia, Philia: see Kilian-Dirlmeier 2002, 113, no. 1753, pl. 107 (Grave 1964, Δ2/III; sixth/fifth centuries BCE).

51 For a discussion of the lion-head earring type, derived from Etruscan, Italic, or Achaemonid prototypes, see Pfrommer 1990, 146–57; Higgins 1980, 159–60; Deppert-Lippitz 1985, 222–4; Hadaczek 1903, 46–9. Deppert-Lippitz 1996, 62–3, suggests that "the animal-head earring is a genuine Greek creation, inspired by a long-established type of Greek animal-head bracelet."

52 Amandry 1963, 212, nos. 137–8, pl. 32 (child's grave, Stathatos Collection; last quarter of the fourth century BCE); Pfrommer 1990, 144, 248, no. FK 93, 370 no. OR 221; he dates this earring to the mid- to third quarter of the fourth century, based on a coin of Philip II found with the earrings. Other examples of gold lion's head earrings from Macedonia include: Akanthos: Pfrommer 1990, 370, OR 219; Rhomiopoulou 1973–4, 696, pl. 503b (grave; late fourth century BCE); Amphipolis: Pfrommer 1990, 371, OR 224 (Grave I; not before late third century BCE); Koukouli-Chrysanthaki 1979, 93, no. 371 (Macedonian Grave Γ; second half of the fourth century BCE); Lazaridis 1960, 71, pl. 57b. Kozani: Pfrommer 1990, 371, OR 225 (Grave 1; early third century BCE; pair); Kallipolitis and Feytmans 1948–9, 90–1, fig. 3 (found with a coin of Alexander III; 323–319 BCE or later); Touratsoglou 1998, 32–3. Derveni: Rhomiopoulou 1979, 73, no. 268 (Grave H; second half of the fourth century BCE); Tsigarida 2006, 144, 149, fig. 8. Sedes: Pfrommer 1990, 371–2, OR 235 (Grave C; late fourth century); Rhomiopoulou 1979, 80, no. 321, pl. 45 (Grave Γ, second half of the fourth century BCE; found with a coin of Philip II, dated 336–323 or later); Kotzias 1937, 882, fig. 14; Touratsoglou 1998, 32–3. Liti: Tsakalou-Tzanavari 1989, 307–8, fig. 5 (cist tomb; late fourth century BCE). Mieza: Misailidou-Despotidou 1990, 130, fig. 11 (cist grave; third quarter of the fourth century BCE; pair). Abdera: Kallintzi 1990, 565, n. 11 (Cist Graves III and IV; fourth century BCE). Pydna: Tsigarida 2006, 149, fig. 7 (Grave Πυ771; third quarter of the fourth century BCE).

53 Isthmia, Sanctuary of Poseidon: Raubitschek 1998, 68, no. 250, pl. 39 (fourth to third centuries BCE; gold); Broneer 1953, 194–5, fig. 1, pl. 60d. Perachora, Sanctuary of Hera Limenia: Payne et al. 1940, 185, no. 40, pl. 84 (post-Archaic; gold). Corinth, cemetery on the north slope of Acrocorinth: Robinson 1962, 119, pl. 45e (Grave 4; end of the fourth/beginning of the third centuries BCE; gold pair); Pfrommer 1990, 367, OR 171 (mid-third century BCE). Olympia: Philipp 1981, 133, no. 487, pl. 41 (end of the fourth/early third centuries BCE); Pfrommer 1990, 367, OR 172 (early third century). Ithaka: Hadaczek 1903, 46, n. 2; Pfrommer 1990, 367, OR 170 (second century BCE). "Said to be from Akarnania": Oliver 1977, 46, no. 15 (burial; late fourth/early third centuries BCE); Pfrommer 1990, 209, FK 7, 367, OR 169 (late fourth century BCE). Delos, Rhenaia: Pfrommer 1990, 367, nos. 173–6 (mid- to late third century BCE; gold); Deonna 1938, 300, pl. 88, fig. 764. Samothrace, South Necropolis: Dusenbery 1959, 166, fig. 4 (unmatched gold pair from inhumation burial; late fourth century). Chersonesos: Williams and Ogden 1994, 198, no. 132

(tomb; 300–280 BCE). Taranto: Bennett and Paul 2002, 160–1, no. 17 (tomb 1, Via Molise, Taranto; c. 325–300 BCE; gold pair). For gold examples from uncontrolled contexts, see Leipen 1982, 74–5 (Hellenistic); Amandry 1953, 212, nos. 300–3, pl. 53 (Collection Stathatos; fourth century BCE); Marshall 1969, 188–93, nos. 1728–9, pl. 31 (Kourion, Cyprus, fourth to third centuries BCE), 1730–3, pl. 31, 1734–64, 1765 (Crete), 1766–7, 1768, pl. 31 (Ruvo, ca. third century BCE), 1769, 1770, pl. 31 (Capua, fourth to third century BCE); Hoffman and Davidson 1965, 106, fig. 26 (Swiss Private Collection; late fourth/early third century BCE; gold pair); Greifenhagen 1970, 44, no. 1, pl. 22 (late fourth/third century BCE; pair), no. 4, pl. 22 (end of the fourth/third century BCE); Greifenhagen 1975, pl. 44, no. 1 (from Campania?; fourth century BCE); no. 2 (Pergamon; late fourth/third century BCE); no. 3 (Campanari; fourth/third century BCE); nos. 4–5 (Syria; third century BCE); no. 6 (Melos; third century BCE); Rudolph 1995, 129–30, no. 27.B.1–2 (Eastern Mediterranean; Early Hellenistic; gold pair), 172, no. 36.B.1–2 (Eastern Mediterranean; third century BCE; gold pair); Deppert-Lippitz 1996, 62–3, 70, no. 46 (Greece; late fourth–early third centuries BCE), nos. 47–8 (Magna Graecia; late fourth to third centuries BCE); Albersmeier 2005, 21 (Walters Art Museum; Greek, fourth–third century BCE); Ergil 1983, 25–6, nos. 27–31 (Asia Minor; fourth–third century BCE). See also the very extensive catalogue in Pfrommer 1990, 367–77, although Stella G. Miller 1996, 43, n. 31, notes that "caution should be exercised in consulting this work inasmuch as it relies indiscriminately on items from private collections and the antiquities market as well as provenanced material." Unprovenanced material has been included in this Catalogue too for stylistic comparisons and for the sake of thoroughness.

54 Isthmia: Raubitschek 1998, 69, no. 259, fig. 10 (Roman). Olympia: Philipp 1981, 133–5, nos. 488–91, pls. 7, 41 (Roman); Higgins 1980, 177. Also similar is a Byzantine silver hoop from Corinth: see Davidson 1952, 251, no. 2012, pl. 107.

55 Cyrene, Sanctuary of Demeter: Warden 1990, 31–2, nos. 188–90 (with granulated clusters), no. 191 (undecorated). A pair of gold earrings, said to have come from Tharros in Sardinia, are also similar, although they are more in the form of a hook and have a cagelike pendant: see Richter 1953, 156, pl. 128b (seventh to sixth century BCE).

56 Lousoi, Sanctuary of Artemis: Reichel and Wilhelm 1901, 53–4, fig. 90. Perachora, Sanctuary of Hera Limenia: Payne et al. 1940, 178, no. 27, pl. 79 (seventh century).

57 Inv. 912, not catalogued.

58 One very corroded bronze ring fragment (Inv. 2512; Tr. 99.1 L 5, Wt.. 0.5), with half of a preserved bezel, was not included in the Catalogue.

59 Raubitschek 1998, 61, n. 81.

60 Boardman 2001, 212–14.

61 There is little evidence for an Archaic or Early Classical phase of the Sanctuary. Only a small number of terracotta figurines and vases, and some metal objects including iron spits, can be assigned to the fifth century or earlier. Also included is the Late Archaic kore found in the Temple, ca. 500 BCE; see also p. 43.

62 Marshall 1968, xxxii–iv.

63 Ibid., xxxiii.

64 *LIMC* VII.1, s.v. "Tritones," 74, no. 19.

65 Korykian Cave, Sanctuary of Pan: Zagdoun 1984, 197, 28 a–b (first half of the fifth century BCE); Nemea, Sanctuary of Zeus: Stephen G. Miller 1981, 50, pl. 13d (last quarter of the fifth century BCE). Corinth: Kraay and Hirmer 1966, no. 485 (coin, ca. 420–400 BC); no. 487 (coin; ca. 325–308 BCE). Stymphalos: (coin; Inv. 3051; ca. 350–300 BCE).

66 See Boardman 2001, 226–7, 284, fig. 235 (found with a coin of Philip II).

67 Korykian Cave, Sanctuary of Pan: Zagdoun 1984, 223, no. 129 (second half of the fourth century BCE); 231, no. 173 (second half to late fourth century BCE); Marshall 1968, 174, pl. 27, no. 1092 (unknown provenance; silver with gold inset); Boardman 2001, 230–1, fig. 247 (late fourth/early third century BCE). This motif is also found on a fired clay sealing from a finger ring (?), from a late fifth-century BCE grave at Ur: see Boardman 2001, 234–5, fig. 276.

68 For sirens on Archaic Greek gems, see Walters 1926, pls. 8, 10, nos. 440, 455–6, 459, 487, 564. See also the Late Archaic name vase of the Siren Painter, Robertson 1992, 136, fig. 138. Private collections: Spier 1992, 32, no. 46 (hollow gold ring, ca. 500 BCE or slightly later); Boardman 2001, 398, pl. 1040 (private collection, Switzerland; mid-fifth century BCE; blue chalcedony scaraboid; siren holding a lyre); Wagner and Boardman 2003, 6, no 14, pl. 7.

69 For an example of a harpy on an Archaic Greek silver ring, see Chadour-Sampson 1997, 76–9, no. 14 (second half of the sixth century BCE). The harpy engraved on this ring has extended wings in frontal view on both sides of its profile body, like those of the hybrid figure on the Stymphalian bezel, whereas the wings of the sirens (above note 68) are depicted in profile above their bodies.

70 Thasos: Sgourou 2001, 347, 355, no. 58, fig. 38 (Soutou plot; found with early to mid-fourth-century black-glaze bowls).

71 For the gold ring in the Museo Nazionale, Taranto, see Richter 1968, 85, no. 260 (from the necropolis of Taranto). Apparently at the sanctuary of Artemis Orthia in Sparta, girls and young women danced ecstatically wearing a short chiton: see Lawler 1964, 92; Schol. On Euripides' *Hecuba* 934. The Stymphalian figure may represent a dancing maenad, although no Dionysiac attributes are depicted, nor does this figure have the long swirling drapery seen on other examples with secure or uncertain contexts, e.g., Korykian Cave, Sanctuary of Pan and the Nymphs, Zagdoun 1984, 212, no. 89 (first half of the fourth century BCE), 215, no. 95 (first half of the fourth century BCE); Spier 1992, 34, no. 52 ("Greek"; fourth century BCE); 36, no. 57 ("Greek"; fourth century BCE); Marshall 1968, 14, no. 64 (fifth–fourth century BCE); Chadour-Sampson 1997, 92–4, no. 18 ("Greek"; fourth century BCE).

72 Marshall 1968, 196, no. 1241, pl. 30. A glass ringstone from Berlin and a Nicolo ringstone from Copenhagen, dating to the first century BCE, also depict Herakles with his right hand resting on his club and his left hand on his shield: see *LIMC* IV. s.v. "Herakles," nos. 426–7.

73 A large oval gold bezel from a Swiss private collection depicts a standing woman, similarly dressed, holding a lifelike mask: see Hoffman and Davidson 1965, 257, fig. 16 ("from Greece"; third century BCE). This object on the Stymphalian bezel also seems larger than a mirror, as for example seen on an unprovenanced, fourth-century silver ring bezel: see Wagner and Boardman 2003, 80, no. 591, pl. 77 (private collection).

74 *LIMC* IV.1, s.v. "Gorgo, Gorgones," 325.

75 Gold disk: Hackens 1976, 62, no. 20 (provenance unknown). Terracotta-gilt disks: Sedes: Kotzias 1937, 892–3, fig. 28, no. 8 (Grave Γ, late fourth century BCE). Knossos, Sanctuary of Demeter: Coldstream 1973, 173, no. 331 (deposit H; early Hellenistic). Asia Minor: Maas 1985, 321, pl. 62.1 (late fourth century BCE). Piraeus: Kyparissis 1926, 82, 84 fig. 33 (from a small Late Classical tomb). Two examples of disks without provenance are in the British Museum: see Marshall 1969, 245, nos. 2150–1, pl. 42. A bronze gorgon-head medallion with protruding tongue was found in a Classical grave in the Sanctuary of Athena Itonia, Philia, Thessaly: see Kilian-Dirlmeier 2002, 117, no. 1797, pl. 111 (Grave 1964, Γ2/V). A rhomboid bezel on a silver ring from a grave in the cemetery at Akraiphia, Boiotia, also depicts a gorgon head: see Andreiomenou 1997, 84, 120, fig. 36 (Grave MAK/41; ca. 500 BCE).

76 For example, see *LIMC* III, s.v. "Eros," no. 617 (krater from the Gallipoli Museum; ca. 440 BCE).

77 A gold ring shows a flying Eros holding a wreath in both hands: see Williams and Ogden 1994, 73, no. 29 ("said to be from Kephallenia"; 330–300 BCE). An unprovenanced second-century BCE cornelian ring portrays a standing Eros holding a wreath and a palm branch for a victor: see Wagner and Boardman 2003, 12, no. 61, pl. 15 (private collection).

78 A iunx wheel is a disk, twisted on a double strand, which served as a love charm: see Boardman 2001, 222. A kneeling Eros holds a iunx wheel on a fourth-century bronze ring in the Ashmolean: see Boardman 1975, 96, no. 80. A fourth-century gilded bronze ring from Naukratis depicts a similar motif: see Boardman 2001, 298, pl. 723; *LIMC* III, s.v. "Eros," no. 524; Marshall 1968, 198, no. 1258, pl. 30. This motif is also depicted on Late Classical Attic red-figure vases, e.g. by the Diomed Painter: see Boardman 1989, fig. 364.

79 Williams and Ogden 1994, 252, no. 193 ("said to be from Beirut"; 400–350 BCE); Boardman 2001, 294, pl. 625; Walters 1926, 68, no. 560, pl. 10; Marshall 1968, 63, no. 350, pl. 10.

80 Boardman 2001, 299, pl. 717 (Victoria and Albert Museum; no provenance; first quarter of the fourth century BCE); *LIMC* II, s.v. "Aphrodite," no. 839; Jackson 2006, 219–20, no. 15, pl. 26A. For another unprovenanced example in silver, see Boardman and Vollenweider 1978, 32, no. 140, pl. 26 ("Western Greek"; mid-fourth century BCE).

81 Korykian Cave, Sanctuary of Pan and the Nymphs: Zagdoun 1984, 211, no. 91 (first half of the fourth century BCE; bronze); 236, no. 201 (second half of the fourth century; iron). Olympia, northwest of the Temple of Zeus: Philipp 1981, 161, no. 586, pls. 9, 42 (fourth century BCE; bronze). Knossos, Sanctuary of Demeter: Coldstream 1973, 140, no. 72, pl. 88 (early fourth century BCE; bronze). Halieis: Dengate 1976, 321, no. 193, fig. 7 (found in the necropolis, but without a secure grave context; first quarter of the fourth century BCE; silver). This motif is also found on gold Paphlagonian staters from Amastris, dating ca. 300–285 BCE: see *LIMC* II, s.v. "Aphrodite," no. 817.

82 For a discussion of this inscription, see p. 144.

83 e.g. *LIMC* II, s.v. "Athena," nos. 18 (marble statue Acrop. 625; 530–520 BCE), 20 (terracotta statuette, Athens Acrop; ca. 500 BCE), 21 (terracotta statuette, Athens Acrop.; ca. 500 BCE), 23 (terracaotta statuette; Gela or Agrigento; end sixth/beginning fifth centuries BCE), 25 (terracotta statuette from Capua; beginning of the fifth century BCE); 41 (red-figure Attic cup from Vulci; ca. 490–480 BCE); 49 (red-figure Attic cup; ca. 470–460 BCE).

84 This statue mentioned by Pausanias has been identified as Acropolis 625: see Viviers 1992, 62–7, figs. 38–9; Kees-

ling 2003, 27–8, fig. 10; Marx 2001, 221–54; *LIMC* II, s.v. "Athena," no. 18 (530–520 BCE).

85 *LIMC* II, s.v. "Athena," 959, no. 19 (terracotta seated figurine; ca. 500 BCE). There is also a terracotta relief (Athenian Acropolis 1337–8) of a seated Athena wearing a diadem, dating to the end of the sixth century BCE: see *LIMC* II, s.v. "Athena," no. 16; Hurwit 1999, 21, fig. 18. Descriptions of goddesses in Homeric poetry, including the epiphany of Demeter in the *Homeric Hymn to Demeter* (lines 275–81), stress the beauty of their hair and headgear. For the Athena Polias statue wearing a stephane, see Kroll 1982, 68 (*IG* II^2 1424, lines 11–16.). The sole Archaic marble Nike from the Acropolis (Acr. no. 693) with its head preserved is also wearing a stephane: see Keesling 2003, 144, fig. 43.

86 Hurwit 1999, 316.

87 Gold ring: Kalashnik 2004, 72, fig. 34 (found in an urn in a late fourth–early third-centuries BCE tomb belonging to the family of statesman Agasikles); Williams and Ogden 1994, 198, no. 133; Boardman 2001, 299–300, pl. 744. Coins of Lysimachus: Kraay and Hirmer 1966, figs. 580–2; Thompson 1968, 165, pls. 16–22, nos. 8–257.

88 An unpublished gold ring from the Collection of Batya and Elie Borowski, Jerusalem, dating ca. 400–375 BCE, depicts a bare-headed Athena, standing before her upright shield, holding a winged Nike figure in her extended right hand and her helmet in the left hand: see Benson 1995a, 177–8, fig. 32.

89 Wagner and Boardman 2003, 22, fig. 120 (from a private collection).

90 Sanctuary of Demeter and Kore, Corinth: silver band with gold bezel and gold stud (mid-fifth century BCE): see Bookidis 1972, 317. Unprovenanced silver rings with gold studs are also found in the British Museum: see Marshall 1968, 166, no. 1031 (ca. 500 BCE); 173, no. 1080; 1085 (fourth century BCE); 174, no. 1090 (fourth–third centuries BCE); also in the Metropolitan Museum: see Williams and Ogden 1994, 73, no. 28 ("said to be from Akarnania"; 350–300 BCE); and in Munich, see Chadour-Sampson 1997, 80–3, no. 15 ("Greek"; late fifth to mid-fourth century BCE). For rings with gold studs having an amuletic function, see Kunz 1917, 293; Marshall 1968, xxiii.

91 Coldstream 1973, 158, nos. 222–5 and three uncatalogued ones, fig. 39.

92 Marshall 1968 (1907), xxxiv–xxxv for references, and examples in the British Museum, ibid., 223, nos. 1454–8.

93 Lehmann and Spittle 1982, 403–4.

94 Plantzos 1999, 78, 124, esp. no. 317 pl. 50; see also Marshall 1968, 202, no. 1287 = BM 1234 (from Smyrna?).

95 Stern 2001, 373 no. 206 ("Mediterranean; probably Greek"; "probably second century BCE").

96 Glass rings, dating between 330 and 150 BCE, have oval bezels and massive hoops: see Higgins 1980, 169–70 (type 4).

97 Marshall 1968, xlvi, Type E ix (Late Hellenistic).

98 Perachora, Temple of Hera Akraia: Payne et al. 1940, 74, no. 8, pl. 18 (Geometric; D 1.8 cm); Sanctuary of Hera Limenia: Payne et al. 1940, 185, nos. 37–8, pl. 84 (Geometric; two gold rings, ranging in diameter from 1.7 to 1.8 cm). Sindos: Vokotopoulou 1985, 98, no. 152 (Female Grave 20; 510–500 BCE; gold ring; 2.2 cm in diam.). Knossos, Sanctuary of Demeter: Coldstream 1973, 130, nos. 1–2, pl. 83 (Deposit H; most pottery is Classical and Hellenistic in this votive dump; two gold rings, ranging in diameter from 1.0 to 1.6 cm).

99 Altar/Shrine to Hera, Argos: Blegen 1939, 413–14, fig. 4; Blegen describes the structure as an outlying altar to Hera, based on the remains of votive offerings similar to those found in the Heraion (likely Archaic, although the shrine continued into Classical times). Isthmia, Sanctuary of Poseidon: Raubitschek 1998, 63, no. 239, pl. 38 (date uncertain).

100 Williams and Ogden 1994, 35; Warden 1990, 17.

101 Nymphaion: Williams and Ogden 1994, 133, no. 76 (kurgan 17; 425–400 BCE). Pantikapaion: Williams and Ogden 1994, 152–5, no. 94 (1854 stone tomb; 400–380 BCE); 156, no. 95 (1854 stone tomb; ca. 400 BCE); apparently the jewellery provides the only evidence for dating this female burial, hence the different dates; 162, no. 102 (1840 stone tomb; ca. 350 BCE). Great Bliznitza: Williams and Ogden 1994, 182, no. 117 (burial; 330–300 BCE); 188, no. 121 (tomb of the "Priestess of Demeter"; 330–300 BCE); 191, no. 123 (tomb of the "Priestess of Demeter"; 330–300 BCE). Southern Russia: Deppert-Lippitz 1985, 166, no. 116 (tumulus; Karagodeuashkh; 340–330 BCE). For other examples of bead necklaces with uncertain provenances, see Williams and Ogden 1994, 54–5, no. 7 ("said to be from Akarnania"; 450–400 BCE); 74, no. 30 ("said to be from near Thessaloniki"; ca. 300 BCE); 99, no. 53 ("said to be from Kyme"; ca. 330–300 BCE); 112, no. 64 ("said to be from Madytos"; 330–300 BCE); 116, no. 68 (Asia Minor, perhaps from a tomb in Mytilene; ca. 330–300 BCE). See also Triossi and Mascetti 1997, 14; Rudolph 1995, 191, no. 45 (Eastern Mediterranean, ca. 350–275 BCE).

102 For examples of necklaces of gold beads and semiprecious stones, see Alexander 1928, 5, no. 1 (Cyprus, fifth–fourth centuries BCE); no. 3 (Cyprus, seventh–sixth centuries BCE).

103 Beck 1981.

104 Beads: Cyrene, Sanctuary of Demeter: Warden 1990, 18–19, nos. 59–62, pl. 14 (bone and silver). Buttons: Corinth: Davidson 1952, 296, nos. 2514–18, pl. 122 (Classical/Hellenistic). Athens, Pnyx: Davidson and Thompson 1943, 104, nos. 9–11 (ca. 425–325 BCE).

105 Thompson 1960, 237–8 (the shoemaker's shop was in existence ca. 450–410 BCE).

106 Perachora, Sanctuary of Hera Limenia: Dunbabin 1962, 518–19, nos. F 20, G 9–10, pl. 194.

107 One more poorly preserved blue stratified eye-bead (Inv. 189) was found in the town site, measuring 2.7 cm in diameter.

108 Tatton-Brown 1981, 143.

109 Eisen 1916, 1–27. England: Guido 1978, 45, 47 (Arras Type II: dark blue with many stratified eyes). Central Europe: Venclová 1983, 11–17; Venclová (p. 16) believes that local production of eye-beads in Central Europe began in the sixth century BCE and reached its peak in the second and first centuries BCE. Cyrene, Sanctuary of Demeter: Oliver 1990, 92–3, nos. 40–56, pl. 5 (sixth–fifth centuries BCE; nos. 52–3 are "Arras Type II" beads). Examples in Greece have been found in Corinth, Olynthos, and Knossos. Corinth: Davidson 1952, 292, nos. 2426–7, pl. 121 (fifth–fourth centuries BCE). Olynthos: Robinson 1941, nos. 2652–6, pl. 171 (from houses); no. 2657, pl. 171; no. 2669, pl. 171 (Grave 332); no. 2670, pl. 171 (Grave 360). Knossos, Sanctuary of Demeter: Coldstream 1973, 115–16, nos. 7–10 (Archaic to fourth century BCE). A third-century BCE glass bead factory was discovered in Rhodes, where eye-beads were made among other types: see Weinberg 1969, 143–51, especially p. 145, pls. 79a, c, 84c.

110 Tatton-Brown 1981, 154–5, nos. 451–5, pl. 29, fig. 18. For a similarly decorated rod-formed finial with stratified eyes, see Stern and Schlick-Nolte 1994, 195, no. 39 (Ernesto Wolf Collection; made in Carthage or on the Syro-Palestinian coast, fourth to third centuries BCE). Also included in the Ernesto Wolf Collection is a string of 65 eye-beads, dating from the sixth to the first centuries BCE, mostly yellow glass with blue and white stratified eyes of which the largest has two compound eyes: see Stern and Schlick-Nolte 1994, 198–9, no. 41 (Mediterranean). See also the classification of eye-beads in Beck 1981, 43, 45, no. A.8.b.1, fig. 34a (ca. 600 BCE; Type 46, Subgroup A).

111 It is worth noting that a bronze coin (Inv. 2270) of Carthage was found in an artillery tower (Stym V) of the western City Wall at Stymphalos and dated by R. Weir to the late fourth century BCE. Eye-beads found in the Rhodian glass bead factory are different in that they lack the fused-on orange-yellow and blue beads found on the Stymphalian example.

112 Venclová 1983, 12–15, fig. 2.2.

113 Corinth: Pemberton 1985, 295–6, fig. 6, pl. 83 (Grave 1963–9; late fourth century BCE). Epanomi: Tsimbidou-Auloniti 1989, 324, pl. 10 (Grave 1; fifth century BCE). See also Amandry 1953, 68, no. 198, pl. 29 (Collection Stathatos; Chalkidike, Trilophon-Mesimeri cemetery).

114 Perachora, Sanctuary of Hera Limenia: Dunbabin 1962, 519, no. G 11, pl. 194 (glass). Chios, Harbour Sanctuary: Boardman 1967, 239, no. 546, fig. 162 (glass) 540, no. 555, fig. 162 (amber; 6 examples; 690–630 BCE). Cyrene, Sanctuary of Demeter: Warden 1990, 20, nos. 70–7, pl. 15 (Archaic; 21 bronze, 3 silver, 1 gold, 4 faience, 1 terracotta).

115 Beck 1981, 10, fig, 11a (Division I, Group 23).

116 Corinth: Davidson 1952, 291, nos. 2418–20 (first or early second centuries CE); Perachora, Sanctuary of Hera Limenia: Dunbabin 1962, 514, D 832–7 (found with Protocorinthian and Corinthian pottery); Chios, Harbour Sanctuary: Boardman 1967, 239–40, nos. 549–50, fig. 162 (Period I, pre-690 BCE; glass); no. 570 (Period I; faience). Knossos, Sanctuary of Demeter: Coldstream 1973, 115, no. 2, fig. 25 (Deposit E; "probably Late Minoan"; glass), no. 11, fig. 25 (Deposit H; "probably Archaic"; glass); Cyrene, Sanctuary of Demeter: Oliver 1990, 19, nos. 63–8, fig. 7 (27 bronze, 12 carnelian, 39 terracotta, 6 faience, and 7 ivory; several others were not catalogued; Archaic).

117 Sedes: Kotzias 1937, 891–2, fig. 27 (Grave Γ; fourth century BCE). Rhodes: Weinberg 1969, 144, pl. 76 a–b.

118 Thasos: Sgourou 2001, 340, 342, 354, fig. 25 (Grave S-VI; early to mid-fourth century BCE). One hundred and sixty-four ivory beads were found near the pelvis of a young woman, likely once forming a beaded belt.

119 Argive Heraion: Waldstein 1905, 264, no. 1551, pl. 92 (Archaic). Olympia: Furtwängler 1890, nos. 440–4, pl. 24. Tegea, Sanctuary of Athena Alea: Dugas 1921, 386, nos. 161–2, fig. 42 (Archaic); Voyatzis 1990, 337, B182–3, pl. 132.

120 Olynthos: Robinson 1941, 54, nos. 49–50, pl. 9 (Grave 516; fifth century BCE).

121 Derveni: Themelis and Touratsoglou 1997, 59, fig. 62 (Grave A; last quarter of the fourth century BCE). Chauchitsa: Casson 1923–4, 4, 7–9, 11–12, 14, 25, pl. 4, nos. b–c (biconical beads found in Graves 1, 4–5, 8–10, 13–14, 16–17, 21–2; Iron Age). Cyrene, Sanctuary of Demeter: Warden 1990, 17, nos. 47–9, fig. 3, pl. 14 (Classical; 5 bronze and 1 stone). See Boardman and

Hayes 1966, 77–80 for a discussion of distribution; biconical beads and a number of variants have been found in Tocra, Cyrenaica, the Balkans, and Sicily.

122 Warden 1990, 17.

123 The following beads with flattened rims are included in the total number of beads for purposes of discussing their distribution, although they are not included in the catalogue: Inv. 3331, 3339, 3387, 3398, 3521, 3582, 3594, 3646; see also Appendix IV.

124 Sparta, Sanctuary of Artemis Orthia: Dawkins 1929, 199, pl. 85, i, k–n, s–t (Geometric; bronze). Aigina, Temple of Aphaia: Furtwängler, Fiechter, and Thiersch 1906, pl. 119, fig. 65. Knossos, Sanctuary of Demeter: Coldstream 1973, 118, no. 27, fig. 25 (Deposit H; Geometric). Chios: Lamb 1934–5, 150, pl. 32.3 (Geometric/Archaic; silver). Cyrene, Sanctuary of Demeter: Warden 1990, 20–1, nos. 78–83, pl. 16 (Archaic; 3 bronze, 2 silver, 1 gold, 1 ivory, and 1 faience).

125 Acorns, seeds of the oak tree sacred to Zeus, were a favoured form of pendant. Acorn pendants were a common adornment on fourth-century BCE necklaces from the north Pontic cities, as seen on a fragmentary necklace from Temir Gora, near Kerch, now in the Hermitage: see Miller 1979, 11, pl. 5a. A gold necklace from a mid-fifth-century tomb in Nymphaion, now in the Ashmolean, has 22 acorn pendants: see Deppert-Lippitz 1985, 144–5, fig. 93. An elaborate gold necklace from Amathus, Cyprus, has a carnelian acorn pendant with a gold cap: see Williams and Ogden 1994, 233, no. 166 (tomb 256, sarcophagus II; 425–400 BCE).

126 For example, from Homolion, Thessaly: Stella G. Miller 1979, 10–11, pl. 4a–b (Grave A, late fourth century BCE). For a gold necklace with amphora pendants from Melos, see Marshall 1969, 213, no. 1947, pl. 35 (fourth century BCE); Higgins 1980, xxvi, 165, pl. 49B (330–200 BCE).

127 Inv. 1357; H 1.2 ; D 0.6.

128 Williams and Ogden 1994, 11, fig. 2.

129 Marshall 1969, 249, no. 2191, pl. 42.

130 Vase paintings are helpful for the use of pins with clothing; for examples, see Jacobsthal 1956, 106–10, figs. 331–8.

131 Argive Heraion: Waldstein 1905, 207–39, nos. 52–807; Jacobsthal 1956, 15.

132 The evidence for pins dedicated with clothes is attested in the inventory list of the Temple of Mnia and Auzesia at Oia, Aigina (*IG* 4.1588), in a dedication by a woman named Hierokleia to Harpokrates at Delos (1442, A 52–3; 146/5 BCE), and in an epigram (*Anth. Pal.* 6.282): see Jacobsthal 1956, 96–7, 102, 105.

133 Kilian-Dirlmeier 1984, 298.

134 Robinson 1941, 360–1, nos. 1736–42, pl. 114 (from the South Hill or houses).

135 Furtwängler, Fiechter, and Thiersch 1906, 404. Herodotus (5.87–8) records a story in which Athenian women used their clothing pins to kill a man who was the only survivor from an Athenian attack on Aigina. As a result, women were punished by being made to wear the buttoned Ionic chiton, rather than the pinned Doric peplos. This change is seen in Athenian sculptural representations of garments during the sixth century BCE: see Lee 2005, 55–6.

136 An early Classical red-figure krater by the Niobid Painter depicts Pandora wearing a peplos fastened with pins: see Lee 2005, 60, fig. 5.4. Lee (62) suggests that representations of Early Classical period women wearing the peplos were solely for iconographic purposes to show the embodiment of traditional Greek values: a "good woman" was one who wove traditional garments such as the peplos. For an example of a pin depicted on a fourth-century BCE Etruscan stamnos, see Jacobsthal 1956, 109, no. 38, fig. 338. Records from the temple of Artemis at Delos, dating between 280/70 and 239 BCE, included both gold and silver gilt pins: see Jacobsthal 1956, 100–1. In addition, inventory lists from the Hellenistic Kabireion at Thebes include two gold pins: see Jacobsthal 1956, 103–4. For Hellenistic (early third–second centuries BCE) examples of gold pins decorated with Eros figures, see Jackson 2006, 239–40, pl. 32.

137 Omitted are Inv. 2725, 2892, 3730–2 and SF 1996.564 (Wt. of Inv. 2725 is 3.3; Inv. 2892 is 3.0; Inv. 3730 is 1.5; Inv. 3732 is 5.1). All are considered in discussing distribution.

138 Iron pins were rare even from the Geometric and Orientalizing periods: see Jacobsthal 1956, 87, 98–9. For a group of iron pins recently published from Kalapodi, see Felsch 2007, 113, 283–4 nos. 415–22, 424, 429 pl. 28; see also a detailed study of pins from the Peloponnese, Kilian-Dirlmeier 1984, esp. 208–80 for types from the Archaic period.

139 See Appendix III for a list of the bronze shafts in the Sanctuary; some may belong to clothing pins, while others are likely needles or bodkins.

140 Kilian-Dirlmeier 1984, 208–98, pls. 85–114. I have included unpublished examples from her catalogue for the sake of thoroughness.

141 Williams and Schaus 2001, 85. It is also possible that the kore statue was brought to the Sanctuary from elsewhere, perhaps from the older site of Stymphalos.

142 The pin (Inv. 2471) is preserved in three fragments, measuring 8.2 cm in length; diameter of finial: 1.1 cm.

143 Argive Heraion: Kilian-Dirlmeier 1984, 213, no. 3498;

Waldstein 1905, 231, no. 650, pl. 83 (seventh century BCE).

144 Perachora, Sanctuary of Hera Limenia: Kilian-Dirlmeier 1984, 213, no. 3493, pl. 86; Payne et al. 1940, 172–3, no. 5, pl. 74. Argive Heraion: Kilian-Dirlmeier 1984, 213, no. 3494, pl. 86; Waldstein 1905, 228, nos. 586–7. Mycenae, Agamemnoneion: Kilian-Dirlmeier 1984, 213, no. 3495, pl. 86; Cook 1953, 68, pl. 41.

145 Mantinea: Kilian-Dirlmeier 1984, 211, nos. 3424–5 (pair); Karagiorga 1963, 88–90. Also similar is a pin from the Temple of Aphaia, Aegina: see Furtwängler, Fiechter, and Thiersch 1906, 398, no. 52, pl. 14.

146 Sparta, Sanctuary of Artemis Orthia: Kilian-Dirlmeier 1984, 223, nos. 3629–30, pl. 87; Dawkins 1929, 200 (Lakonian I [700–635 BCE, now revised to 650–620 BCE] or II [635–600 BCE, now revised to 620–580 BCE]. For a discussion of the revised dates of the Sanctuary of Artemis Orthia, Sparta, see Boardman 1963, 1–4.

147 I would like to thank Dr David Whitehouse, Corning Museum of Glass, for looking at a picture of this object, but he was not able to suggest any parallels.

148 Corinth, gymnasium area: Wiseman 1967, 428, no. 23, pl. 91j (Grave 39; late fourth to early sixth centuries CE); Davidson 1952, 281, nos. 2272–3, pl. 116 (fourth–fifth centuries CE). Olympia: Philipp 1981, 34, 36, no. 2, pl. 26 (sub-Mycenaean), 103–6, nos. 330–57, pls. 6, 38 (late Roman; 1 silver, 26 bronze). Isthmia, Sanctuary of Poseidon: Raubitschek 1998, 46, 48–9, nos. 191, plate 35 (date uncertain), 192 (from mixed contexts, "either Roman or Byzantine"). Nemea: Stephen G. Miller 1981, 48, pl. 12d (grave; early Christian). An Archaic iron pin fragment from the Argive Heraion has a round finial, although it is "possibly not a pin but iron rod with knobs": see Waldstein 1905, 234, no. 700, pl. 83.

149 Another iron pin (SF 1996.564) with a globe and small crowning knob is now missing.

150 Kilian-Dirlmeier 1984, 263, nos. 4556–66, pl. 108.

151 Perachora, Sanctuary of Hera Limenia: see Payne et al. 1940, 175, no. 10, pl. 76.

152 Olympia, Temple of Zeus: Kilian-Dirlmeier 1984, 263, no. 4561, pl. 108; Philipp 1981, 65, no. 144, pl. 31 (Archaic). Halai: Goldman 1940, 421–2, no. 38, fig. 62.3 ("sixth century with a possible survival to the fifth").

153 Mantinea: Kilian-Dirlmeier 1984, 269, nos. 4682–3, pl. 110; Karagiorga 1963 , 88–90, pl. 103b. Raubitschek 1998, 46, n. 25, notes that Kilian-Dirlmeier did not provide a chronological development for her type E, pointing out that "a few type E may be as early as the 6th century BCE, while others date to the 4th century BCE."

154 Olympia: see Kilian-Dirlmeier 1984, 274, nos. 4749–50, 4753–4 pl. 111; Philipp 1981, 53, no. 82, pl. 29; 79–80, nos. 226–8, pl. 34. Corinth, Sanctuary of Demeter and Kore: Kilian-Dirlmeier 1984, 274, no. 4751, pl. 111 (reported in catalogue as unpublished). Perachora, Sanctuary of Hera Limenia: Kilian-Dirlmeier 1984, 275, nos. 4755–9, pl. 111; Payne et al. 1940, 174, nos. 23–7, pl. 76 (Archaic).

155 Almyri: Kilian-Dirlmeier 1984, 274, no. 4752, pl. 111 (grave; fifth–fourth century BCE; reported in catalogue as unpublished).

156 Williams and Ogden 1994, 42; Rudolph 1973, xi; Hoffman and Davidson 1965, 12.

157 Lousoi, Sanctuary of Artemis Hemerasia: Kilian-Dirlmeier 1984, 276, no. 4784, pl. 111; Reichel and Wilhelm 1901, 54–5. Perachora, Sanctuary of Hera Limenia: Kilian-Dirlmeier 1984, 276–7, nos. 4785–6, 4792–3, 4811, pl. 111; Payne et al. 1940, 174, nos. 20, 30, 35–7, 38, pl. 76. Olympia: Kilian-Dirlmeier 1984, 276, nos. 4787, 4789, pl. 111; Philipp 1981, 82, nos. 240–1, pl. 34. Mantinea: Kilian-Dirlmeier 1984, 276, nos. 4788, 4790–1, 4795, pl. 111; Karagiorga 1963, 90, pl. 103b. Argive Heraion: Kilian-Dirlmeier 1984, 276, nos. 4807–8, pl. 111; Waldstein 1905, 234–5, nos. 705, 718, pl. 83. Corinth, Sanctuary of Demeter and Kore: Kilian-Dirlmeier 1984, 277, no. 4809, pl. 22 (reported in catalogue as unpublished). Argos: Kilian-Dirlmeier 1984, 276, nos. 4796–8, pl. 112 (Grave 2: fifth century BCE); 4800–6, pl. 112 (Grave 5/1933: first half of the fifth century BCE); Papaspyridi-Karouzou 1933–5, 40, 43, fig. 22 (second quarter of the fifth century BCE). Two other examples are from Tiryns: see Kilian-Dirlmeier 1984, 276–7, nos. 4799, 4810, pl. 12 (reported in catalogue as unpublished). An unusual example from the Demeter Sanctuary in Cyrene has glass inlay and a socketed head: see Warden 1990, 34, no. 214 ("Hellenistic, or perhaps Roman").

158 Kilian-Dirlmeier 1984, 279–80.

159 An unadorned bronze pomegranate finial (Inv. 78) was found in the lower town, measuring 2.2 cm in height and 1.5 cm in diameter.

160 Sparta, Sanctuary of Artemis Orthia: Dawkins 1929, 227, pl. 136.4 (seventh century BCE). Archaic bone pendants of a very similar form, although with string holes, are found at the Sanctuary of Hera Limenia, Perachora: see Dunbabin 1962, 442, nos. 288–90, pl. 188.

161 Mantinea: Kilian-Dirlmeier 1984, 276, no. 4795, pl. 111; Karagiorga 1963, 90, pl. 103b.

162 Corinth, Sanctuary of Demeter and Kore: Kilian-Dirlmeier 1984, 277, no. 4809, pl. 112 (reported in catalogue as unpublished). Tiryns: Kilian-Dirlmeier 1984,

277, no. 4810 (reported in catalogue as unpublished). Perachora, Sanctuary of Hera Limenia: Kilian-Dirlmeier 1984, 277, no. 4811; Payne et al. 1940, 174, no. 38, pl. 76.

163 A pomegranate pinhead, likely from Tegea, has part of its chain preserved: see Kilian-Dirlmeier 1984, 276, no. 4783, pl. 111 (reported in catalogue as unpublished).

164 Halieis: Dengate 1976, 299–300, no. 46 (Grave 6; second quarter of the fifth century BCE); 297, no. 58 (Grave 8; second quarter of the fifth century BCE); 299, nos. 72–5 (Grave 11, second quarter of the fifth century BCE). Argos: Kilian-Dirlmeier 1984, 276, 4796–8, pl. 112 (Grave 2; fifth century BCE).

165 Argive Heraion: Kilian-Dirlmeier 1984, 279, no. 4856, pl. 112; Verdelis 1960, 82 (silver); Kilian-Dirlmeier 1984, 279, no. 4858, pl. 112; Waldstein 1905, 235, no. 720, pl. 84. Payne et al. 1940, 174, notes that there is an exact replica of the Argive lion's head pin at Perachora, but neither depicts it nor discusses it further. Corinth, Sanctuary of Demeter and Kore: Kilian-Dirlmeier 1984, 279, no. 4857, pl. 112 (reported in catalogue as unpublished). Mantinea: Kilian-Dirlmeier 1984, 279, no. 4859, pl. 112. Korykian cave, Sanctuary of Pan and the Nymphs: Rolley 1984, 266–7, no. 11, fig. 8 (no date given). Ioannina: Etouzougae 1994, 369, pl. 124a (grave; c. 475–425 BCE). See also Amandry 1953, 61, no. 163, pl. 26 (Collection Stathatos, Trilophon-Mésiméri cemetery, Chalkidike).

166 Blegen, Palmer, and Young 1964, nos. 250.5–6 pl. 79 (grave; late third or early fourth quarter of the sixth century BCE).

167 Kilian-Dirlmeier 1984, 280.

168 Mantinea: Kilian-Dirlmeier 1984, 279, no. 4859, pl. 112.

169 Olympia: Kilian-Dirlmeier 1984, 285, nos. 4918–20, pl. 113; Philipp 1981, 87–8, nos. 265–7, pls. 5, 35. Halieis: Dengate 1976, 321, no. 194, pl. 81 (found in the necropolis area, but without a secure grave context; a fourth-century BCE date is based on a snake spiral earring found on the floor of the temenos). A Late Archaic example was found in the Sanctuary of Athena Itonia, Philia, Thessaly: see Kilian-Dirlmeier 2002, 99, pl. 96, no. 1541.

170 For roll-top pins from the Bronze Age Peloponnese, see Kilian-Dirlmeier 1984, 59–61, nos. 146–76, pl. 5. For a ninth-century example from Lefkandi, see Popham, Sackett, and Themelis 1979–80, 148–9, no. 11, 245, pls. 223a, 242F (P tomb 21). Archaic roll-top pins have been found at Olympia, Phigaleia, Corinth, Mantinea, and Isthmia. Olympia: Kilian-Dirlmeier 1984, 206–7, nos. 3383–7, 3390–6, 3398–3403, 3406–7, pl. 84; Philipp 1981, 88–95, nos. 268–306, pls. 35–6. Phigaleia: Kilian-Dirlmeier 1984, 206, no. 3397A–B, pl. 84. Corinth, Sanctuary of Demeter and Kore: Kilian-Dirlmeier 1984, 206, no. 3389, pl. 84 (reported in catalogue as unpublished). Corinth: Kilian-Dirlmeier 206, no. 3388, pl. 84; Stillwell 1948, 122–3, no. 44, pl. 49. Mantinea: Kilian-Dirlmeier 1984, 207, nos. 3404–5, pl. 84. Isthmia, Sanctuary of Poseidon: Raubitschek 1998, 45, 48, nos. 184–5, pl. 34 (Archaic). Archaic roll-top pins appear also at Aegina, Chios, Halai, Thera, Olynthus, and Cyrene. Aegina, Temple of Aphaia: Furtwängler, Fiechter, and Thiersch 1906, 392, nos. 17–18, pl. 114. Chios, Harbour Sanctuary: Boardman 1967, 223–4, nos. 377–80, fig. 145 (eighth/seventh centuries BCE). Thera: Dragendorff 1903, 302, pl. 490a ("Schiff's grave," Archaic). Halai: Goldman 1940, 418, 421, nos. 34–5, figs. 61.1–2. Olynthos: Robinson 1941, 363–4, nos. 1755–62, pl. 115 (sixth to mid-fourth centuries BCE). Cyrene, Sanctuary of Demeter: Warden 1990, 33–4, nos. 204–6, pl. 24 (Archaic; others not catalogued). Roll-top pins from the Classical and Hellenistic periods have been found at Isthmia and Knossos. Isthmia, Sanctuary of Poseidon: Raubitschek 1998, 48, no. 186, pl. 34 (Classical). Knossos, Sanctuary of Demeter: Coldstream 1973, 147–8, nos. 127 (deposit F; late third–early second century BCE); 128 (deposit H; mixed fill; fifth century BCE–second century CE). Coldstream (148) notes that "roll pins survive into Classical times, but with narrower heads." For a Roman one from Isthmia, see Raubitschek 1998, 48, no. 188, pl. 34. For a general discussion, see Jacobsthal 1956, 122–4.

171 Robinson 1942, 88 (Grave 428). Robinson provided no date for this burial from the Riverside cemetery, although other graves date from the sixth to mid-fourth centuries BCE, whereas Kilian-Dirlmeier (1984, 207) suggests an Archaic date.

172 For distinguishing characteristics of the Trebenishte pin type, see Maier 1956, 67–8, fig. 1.12.

173 Olympia: Kilian-Dirlmeier 1984, 286–7, nos. 4925–7, 4929–40, pl. 113; Philipp 1981, 97–102, nos. 309–22, 325, pl. 37. Philipp classified all double loop pins from Olympia as the Glasinac type of Illyrian double loop pin, but only two examples from Olympia belong to this type (nos. 323–4). The Glasinac type has two loops joined by an upswinging loop, rather than a downswinging loop: see Maier 1956, 65, fig. 1.10. Nemea, Temple of Zeus: Kilian-Dirlmeier 1984, 287, no. 4928, pl. 113; Stephen G. Miller 1980, 179, pl. 35b (third quarter of the fifth century BCE). Patras: Kilian-Dirlmeier 1984, 247, nos. 4941–2, pl. 113; Comfort 1950, 124–5, fig. 3C (jewellery hoard; "late Hellenistic/Early Roman";

labelled as "hairpins"). See also Kilian-Dirlmeier 1984, 288 for examples found on the mainland, northern Greece, and Albania, to which can be added those from the Korykian Cave, and graves at Paxoi, Pydna, Sindos, Derveni, and Philia. Korykian Cave, Sanctuary of Pan and the Nymphs: Rolley 1984, 266–7, no. 16, fig. 9. Paxoi: Preka-Alexandri 1995, 447–8, pl. 150γ (Grave 1; fourth–third centuries BCE). Pydna: Tsigarida 1998, 48, no. 2 (Grave 91; first quarter of the fifth century BCE; silver); 50, no. 11 (Grave 47; third quarter of the fifth century BCE; silver). Sindos: Vokotopoulou 1985, 311, no. 524 (Female Grave 73; 440 BCE). Derveni: Themelis and Touratsoglou 1997, 90, 102, nos. 131–2 (Grave β; last quarter of the fourth century BCE). Philia, Thessaly, Sanctuary of Athena Itonia: Kilian-Dirlmeier 2002, 111, no. 1745 (Grave 1964, Γ2/VI); nos. 1746–7 (Grave Theocharis, BII; sixth to fourth centuries BCE), pl. 107. .

174 Several hundred small glass disks with convex upper surfaces, "usually called 'gems' or 'gaming pieces,'" were found in the excavations of a glass factory in Hellenistic Rhodes: see Weinberg 1969, 146, pl. 80b. Glass disks found at Corinth may have been "used as insets for jewelry": see Davidson 1952, 223, 226, nos. 1780–5 (mostly Hellenistic in date).

175 The rosette was taken to the Corinth museum for safe-keeping; autopsy was not possible, so its description is based on photographs and inventory records.

176 Williams et al. 1997, 49, fig. 7.

177 The rosettes on a late third-century BCE gold diadem, from the Erotes tomb, Eretria, were wired to the diadem by means of one or more strips of twisted wire: see Hoffman and Davidson 1965, 60, drawing, p. XI.

178 Vergina: Andronicos 1984, 192, 196–7, figs. 158–9; Ginouvés et al. 1994, 164, 170–1, fig. 143. Homolion: Stella G. Miller 1979, 10–12, pl. 4 a–b (Grave A). A fourth-century Italian necklace from the tomb of the Taranto Priestess has three-tiered rosettes with hanging pendants as part of its decoration: see Williams 1988, 77, pl. 31.3–4.

179 For examples of gold appliqués once sewn on clothing in the form of circles, rectangles, cut-outs, and florals, see Williams and Ogden 1994, 61, no. 14 ("said to be from Athens"; 400–350 BCE); 104, nos. 56–7 ("said to be from Kyme"; 330–300 BCE); 114–15, no. 67 ("said to be from Madytos"; 330–300 BCE); 130–31, nos. 72–4 (Seven Brothers, kurgan II; 450–425 BCE); 134–5, nos. 78–80 (Nymphaion, kurgan 17; 425–400 BCE); 150–1, nos. 90–2 (Kul Olba; ca. 350 BCE; 194–5, nos. 127–30 (tomb, Great Bliznitza; 330–300 BCE).

180 Several gold appliqués of human heads with wavy hair were found in a stone burial chamber in Kul Olba, dating ca. 350 BCE: see Williams and Ogden 1994, 151, no. 91 (perhaps Aphrodite, maenad, Dionysos, Apollo, or Orpheus), no. 92 (maenad or young Dionysos). See also Greifenhagen 1970, 39, nos. 8–9 (from Kertsch, first half of the fourth century BCE; young Dionysos), nos. 10–11 (Crimea; gorgon), pl. 16. See also Musti et al. 1992, 265, no. 132. The "beautiful Medusa" type was common in the Hellenistic period, although the Stymphalian medallion lacks the snakes intertwined beneath the chin, typically found on contemporary representations: see *LIMC* IV.I, s.v. "Gorgo, Gorgones," 328–9; Musti et al. 1992, 273, no. 147.13 (royal tomb, Vergina; mid-fourth century BCE). A fragment of a medallion, from a grave in the Sanctuary of Athena Itonia, Philia, Thessaly, depicting a squared-off nose, pursed lips, and rounded cheeks, similar to the Stymphalian example, was identified as a gorgon: see Kilian-Dirlmeier 2002, 116–17, pl. 111, no. 1797 (Grave 1964, Γ2/V, Classical Period).

181 *LIMC* II, s.v. "Aphrodite," 120, nos. 1241 (Campanian red-figure oinochoe, ca. 350 BCE; seated Eros embracing standing nude Aphrodite); 1242 (mirror; fourth century BCE; seated half-draped Aphrodite embracing Eros); 1244 (gold ring from Pyrgos; fourth century BCE; seated Aphrodite kissing Eros, who is standing between her knees). Boardman 2001, 224, pl. 737 dates the Pyrgos ring from the mid- to late fourth century BCE.

182 The story of Cupid and Psyche may be an adaptation of the Greek of "Aristophontes Atheneus" according to Fulgentius, *Mythographus* 3.6; see also *OCD* 2nd ed. "Apuleius" 88.

183 For example, a Late Classical Etruscan onyx scarab depicts Psyche with butterfly wings: see *LIMC* VII, s.v. "Psyche," no. 13; Richter 1968, 212, no. 869; Walters 1926, no. 657, pl. 11. For a discussion of the butterfly wings of Psyche and the winged soul, see Cavicchioli 2002, 46–7.

184 *LIMC* VII, 584, s.v. "Psyche," nos. 92 (terracotta statuette; first half of the third century BCE), 124 (Fourth Style wall-painting from Pompeii VII 2, 6; 68–79 CE), 129 (marble sarcophagus, Rome), 138b (terracotta lamp, Hermitage; first century CE), 141a–c (marble statues; Roman copies of Hellenistic prototypes: a) Capitoline Museum, Rome; b) Ostia Museum; c) Galleria degli Uffizi, Florence).

185 For examples of Eros and Psyche embracing, see *LIMC* VII, s.v. "Psyche," nos. 121a (terracotta statuette; from Amphipolis; second–first century BCE); 121b (terracotta statuette, Louvre); 122 (terracotta statuette; Kharayeb; third–second century BCE); 141a–c (see above note 184).

186 Williams and Ogden 1994, 206, no. 237 (330–300 BCE); Marshall 1969, 241, no. 2113, pl. 41 (early third century BCE).

187 Strip diadems are generally embossed with animal or mythical figures; for example, Williams and Ogden 1994, 93, no. 45 (said to be from Kyme; 330–300 BCE). See also Treister 2001, 181–2. Several sixth-century examples of taeniai have been found in male and female graves at Sindos; for examples, Vokotopoulou 1985, 78–9, no. 111 (Female Grave 22; c. 500 BCE; gold, 43 × 3.1 cm), 80, no. 116 (Female Grave 20; 510–500 BCE, gold, 32.2 × 3.5–3.7 cm), 123, no. 183 (Male Grave 25; c. 540 BCE; gold, 26 × 3 cm), 128, no. 201 (Male Grave 59; 530–520 BCE; gold, 51.8 × 2.5 cm).

188 The decline of pins is seen in the archaeological record: see Kilian-Dirlmeier 1984, 298. Several vases from the early fifth and fourth centuries BCE portray buttons as clothing fasteners: see Jacobsthal 1956, 111–12, fig. 339.

189 Elderkin 1928, 337–8; Jacobsthal 1956, 111.

190 Kotzias 1937, 887, fig. 22 (Grave Γ; late fourth century BCE).

191 Lousoi, Sanctuary of Artemis Hemera: Mitsopoulos-Leon 1994, 42–3, fig. 6 (found in a house with coins dating 196–160/150 BCE). Mantinea: Karagiorga 1963, 90, pl. 103g (no date given). Corinth: Davidson 1952, 299, nos. 2519–24, pl. 123 (first century). Delos: Deonna 1938, 239–40, figs. 261–4, pl. 77.640–2. Cyrene, Sanctuary of Demeter: Warden 1990, 30, nos. 172–4 (Roman). A slightly larger bone disk found on the Pnyx was tentatively suggested to be a button: see Davidson and Thompson 1943, 104 no. 12 fig. 46 (Hellenistic or Roman).

192 See also H. Williams et al. 1998, 295–6, pl. 7.

193 Deppert-Lippitz 1998, 91, notes that "the discrepancy between pictorial representations and archaeological evidence is irritating and hard to explain," and that "the material used (silver or silver- or gold-plated bronze) is not the reason for the rarity of Greek bracelets." A volute krater from Taranto by the Karneia Painter, ca. 410 BCE, depicts a maenad wearing snake bracelets: see Deppert-Lippitz 1985, 146, fig. 94. The Varvakion statuette of Athena (original before 438 BCE) also has a snake bracelet on her arm: see Pfrommer 1990, 127–8, pl. 18, no. 1, 349, SR22. The Çanakkale Aphrodite wears a coiled snake bracelet on her left upper arm: see Naumann-Steckner 1998, 95–6, col. pl. 13.

194 Spata: Deppert-Lippitz 1998, 91; Philadelpheus 1920–1, 136–7, fig. 10 (Grave 3).

195 Deppert-Lippitz (1998, 91) cites bronze and silver specimens from Volantsa, and an unpublished grave in the Kerameikos, Athens: see Philipp 1981, 237–8, no. 874, pls. 15, 53 (Volantsa), 224, n. 429 (Kerameikos; Grave Wpa 8).

196 Olynthos: Robinson 1941, 68–72, pls. 12–13, no. 181 (Grave 289; late fifth or early fourth centuries BCE), no. 183 (Grave 254; fourth century BCE), no. 184 (Grave 566), no. 185 (Grave 248; early fourth century BCE), no. 186 (Grave 266; fourth century BCE), no. 188 (Grave 267; fifth century BCE or possibly late sixth), nos. 189–90 (Grave 184), no. 191 (Grave 191; fourth century BCE), no. 192 (Grave 292), no. 195 (Grave 520), no. 200 (Grave 177; fourth century BCE), no. 201 (Grave 203; last quarter of the fifth century BCE), no. 202 (Grave 319), no. 204 (Grave 248; early fourth century BCE), no. 205 (Grave 200; fourth century BCE), no. 207 (Grave 69; late fifth or early fourth centuries BCE), nos. 209, 215, 220 (Grave 343; fifth century BCE), no. 210 (Grave 301), no. 217 (Grave 298; fourth century BCE), no. 221 (Grave 273; late fifth or early fourth century BCE), no. 222 (Grave 299; fourth century BCE), no. 225 (Grave 295). A fourth-century silver bracelet with snake's head terminals is inscribed with the letters KLETIOS, probably the signature of the jeweller: see Williams and Ogden 1994, 72, no. 26.

197 Deppert-Lippitz 1998, 92 (ca. 350–300 BCE).

198 Deppert-Lippitz 1998, 92. Kralevo: Pfrommer 1990, 127, fig. 18.4, 351, SR 41 (tomb; first half of the third century BCE; silver pair). Tuch el-Karamus: Pfrommer 1990, 126, 129–30, 132, 134–6, 348, SR 6 (temple hoard; second quarter of the third century BCE; gold). Several third- and second-century examples are also from Thessaly: see Amandry 1953, 83, no. 219–20, pl. 32, 116–18, nos. 255–61, pls. 45–6 (Collection Stathatos); Pfrommer 1990, 349, nos. SR15–19.

199 A pair of snake bracelets were found on the upper arms of a skeleton from a tomb at Patras: see Naumann-Steckner 1998, 96; Papapostolou 1977, 315, pl. 107 (Grave 44; second quarter of the third century BCE). A fragmentary first-century BCE marble statue of a girl named Mego, holding a covered, herm-shaped statue, from the Artemis Temple in the Asklepion at Messene, depicts a snake bracelet wound around her upper arm as well as on her wrist: see Connelly 2007, 149–51, figs. 5.17–18; Daux 1970, 622, fig. 3 (identified as priestess). The snake bracelet worn on the upper left arm of the Çanakkale Aphrodite has three complete coils: see Naumann-Steckner 1998, 95–6, col. pl. 13.

200 See Sinn 1988, 158, fig. 14. Similar hair rings have been found for example in the Sanctuary of Aphaia at Ai-

gina: see Sinn 1988, 158, fig. 13; Furtwängler, Fiechter, and Thiersch 1906, nos. 35, 38, 40–2, 53–4, pl. 116; at the Sanctuary of Artemis and Apollo at Kalapodi: see Felsch, Kienast, and Schuler 1980, 80–2, fig. 61; and at the Sanctuary of Minoa, Amorgos: see Marangou 1998, 19, fig. 7b.

201 Dillon 2002, 215; *Anth. Pal.* 6.276, 277 (hair dedicated to Athena); Oakley and Sinos 1993, 14; *Anth. Pal.* 6.280 (hair dedicated to Artemis); Herodotus 4.34 (hair dedicated to Artemis by Delian girls); Euripides, *Hipp.* 1423–7 (hair offered to Hippolytus).

202 Rouse 1975, 242; Statius, *Theb.* ii. 253.

203 See Papadopoulos 2003, 92–103 nos. 262–337 figs. 117–31 with references to ones from many other sites. S. Bocher (personal communication) was helpful in identifying the type from examples at Olympia.

204 DeCou 1905, pls. 102–3. Compare also from Cyrene, Warden 1990, 29 no. 166, pl. 22, fig. 3.

205 Rolley 1984, 275, no. 56, fig. 27.

206 One almost complete AUCISSA type fibula with a hinge and high-arched bow of Hellenistic date (Inv. 898) and fragments of a few others have been found in the town site at Stymphalos: see Williams et al. 1998, 278.

207 Muscarella 1967, 51.

208 See Blinkenberg 1926 and Kilian 1975 for discussions and examples of Greek fibulae from the Bronze Age to the Archaic period.

209 Lousoi: Reichel and Wilhelm 1901, 53, fig. 85 (one of three); Brulotte 1994, 57 for date. Similar fibulae were found in Classical graves in the Sanctuary of Athena Itonia, Philia, Thessaly: see Kilian-Dirlmeier 2002, 119, no. 1826 (Grave Theocharis, A2), no. 1836 (Grave 12.2 1962), no. 1837 (Grave 1996, Γ3), pl. 112.

210 Olympia: Philipp 1981, 316, nos. 1128–30, pl. 70 (seventh century BCE). Argive Heraion: Waldstein 1905, 247–8, nos. 906–9, 911–12, 914–15, pl. 88 (seventh century BCE). Perachora, Sanctuary of Hera Limenia: Payne et al. 1940, 171, no. 29, pl. 79 (seventh century BCE). See also Blinkenberg 1926, 221–2 (XII 13 q–s), 225 (XII 14 q). Other fibulae from the Argive Heraion were likely made in the same Peloponnesian workshop, although they have two large knobs rather than one in the centre and the bow is handlelike rather than arched: see Waldstein 1905, 247–8, nos. 910, 916–18, pl. 88; Blinkenberg 1926, 226, Type 15c.

211 Muscarella 1967, 26; Kilian 1975, 155; Philipp 1981, 315.

212 On the Phrygian knob bow type, see Muscarella 1967. This type was originally classified as Asiatic Type XII, 13 by Blinkenberg (1926, 207–8, 219–22). Caner (1983, 208–9) proposed that Gordion, Phrygia, was likely a production centre for exports of this type to the Aegean islands and Greek mainland. Examples of Phrygian fibulae have been found in the following Peloponnesian sanctuaries: Olympia: Philipp 1981, 311–12 nos. 1116–19 (eighth–seventh centuries BCE); Argive Heraion: Waldstein 1905, 244–6, nos. 883–97, pl. 87 (seventh century BCE); Isthmia, Sanctuary of Poseidon: Raubitschek 1998, 50–1, no. 200, pl. 36 (seventh century BCE). Raubitschek (53) notes that the crossbar of the catch-plate on an Isthmian fibula and two fibulae from Perachora (Payne et al. 1940, 171, nos. 21, 24, pl. 71) have more knoblike ends than the Phrygian imports, suggesting that these examples were local productions. Philipp (1981, 304) comments on the great difficulty in determining whether the fibulae were imports or locally made because so many have been published inadequately.

213 Muscarella 1967, 26.

214 Blinkenberg 1926, 253–62, Type XIV. Argive Heraion: Waldstein 1905, 240–1, nos. 817–20, 824, pls. 84–5. Sparta, Sanctuary of Artemis Orthia: Dawkins 1929, 198, pls. 81–2 (late Geometric). Perachora, Sanctuary of Hera Limenia: Dunbabin 1962, 433–7 (Protocorinthian; 60 specimens composed of two ivory or bone disks connected by a bridge). Lousoi, Sanctuary of Artemis: Reichel and Wilhelm 1901, 53, no. 83 (Geometric). Tegea, Sanctuary of Athena Alea: Dugas 1921, 365, nos. 145, 147, figs. 19–20. Olynthos: Robinson 1941, 96–9, nos. 326–33, pls. 19–20. For examples from Rhodes, Thera, and Crete, dating from the Geometric period, see Sapouna-Sakellarakis 1978, 110–14, nos. 1530–43, pl. 47.

215 A small spiral disk of uncertain date, found in a grave in the Sanctuary of Athena Itonia, Philia, Thessaly, and measuring 1.6 cm (including part of the wire end for joining to another spiral disk), was identified as a bronze spectacle fibula: see Kilian-Dirlmeier 2002, 170, pl. 174, no. 2966; two other miniature spiral disk fragments were also discovered in graves in the same sanctuary: see p. 170, pl. 174, nos. 2967 (1.3 cm), 2968 (1 cm). Miniature bow-shaped fibulae have been found in sanctuaries at Glanitza, Lousoi, Argos, and Tegea: see Metzger 1940–1, 30, no. 13; Reichel and Wilhelm 1901, 52, fig. 75; Waldstein 1905, 241, no. 830, pl. 85; Dugas 1921, 381, no. 139, fig. 42; see also p. 107, n. 284. Small spiral disks have also been found on Archaic bronze finger rings in the Sanctuary of Artemis Enodia, Pherai, Thessaly: see Kilian 1975, 173, 194, fig. 70, nos. 16–21, and in sixth-century graves in the cemetery of Akraiphia, Boiotia: see Andreiomenou 1997, 84, figs. 34 (Grave ΜΩΡ/20; ca. 560 BCE), 35 (Grave Μαρα/2; first half of the sixth century).

216 Robinson 1941, 229–43, nos. 817–946.

217 Davidson 1952, 147.

218 For examples of needles and bodkins, see Robinson 1941, nos. 1746–52, pl. 115 (from Olynthian houses); Raubitschek 1998, 117, nos. 416–18, pls. 64–5 (Isthmia, Classical period).

219 The jewellery found in Trench 99.1 includes **14, 86,** and **182** from Level 3; **215** from Level 4; **75, 116, 128,** and **225**, Inv. 2512 (bronze ring fragment) from Level 5; **200, 237** from Level 6.

220 The jewellery from Trench 95.4+1: **98** from Level 1; **1–7, 25, 38, 76, 81–3, 102, 114, 117, 120–1, 134–6, 143, 148, 150–2, 162, 188, 223, 227–8** from Level 2; **99** from Level 4.

221 The jewellery from Trench 96.11 Level 4: **35, 85, 192** (presumed to be replaced in an early Christian grave in the Temple, see above p. 126), and **224**; the pottery includes vessels with black glaze, miniatures, and a blisterware base. 96.11 Level 5: **39–44, 124, 166, 193–5, 230**; the majority of pottery is fourth century in date.

222 The jewellery from Trench 97.3 Level 2: **91, 119, 201**; among the pottery are Corinthian or similar fabric kantharoi and miniature cups. Trench 97.4 Level 2 (south of the Altar): **12, 183, 189** (Corinthian or similar kantharoi and a moulded acanthus sherd). 97.4 Level 3: **13, 104, 199** (Corinthian or similar kantharoi). 97.4 Level 5: **50** (Corinthian or similar kantharoi; early mid- to fourth-century lamps). 97.4 Level 6: **92, 219** (Corinthian or similar kantharoi, skyphoi, lekanes, blisterware, miniature cups). Trench 96.13 Level 4 (south of the Altar): **10, 49, 127, 218** (Corinthian or similar kantharoi and blister ware). 96.13 Levels 5–6: **94, 234– 5** (Corinthian or similar kantharoi and miniature kotyle fragments).

223 This very helpful study, revealing five phases at the Sanctuary, was conducted by a group of graduate students from the University of Minnesota, with Susan Morris leading the work on the Sanctuary pottery. The pottery was examined from two rooms of Building A (Tr. 95.2, 96.12), two areas north and east of the Altar (Tr. 96.3, 96.4), the votive refuse pit (96.15), and the floor of the West Annex of Building A (Tr. 96.8, 97.2 + 96.15). A more detailed study of pottery from Building A has now been carried out by Peter Stone: see chapter 9 below.

224 A date ca. 350–300 BCE for the ceramic material from the votive pit is based on the presence of Attic kantharoi and the absence of Corinthian fabric kantharoi. See p. 194.

225 A Corinthian fabric kantharos, found within the layer of stones sealing the votive pit, suggests a date after ca. 300 BCE for this level.

226 Inv. 3304, 3318, 3585.

227 Suspension loops: Inv. 1036, 1042, 1049, 3306, 3464, 3465, 3584; bronze ring: 3591.

228 The date for Phase 3 is indicated by the presence of mould-made bowls and overhanging-rim kraters.

229 Phase 2 was assigned to the thick tile layer over the floor in Building A (Tr. 95.2 and 96.12) from the collapse of the roof. A rim of an overhanging-rim krater is the latest datable material from the ceramic material from Trench 95.2 Level 4 Pail 9.

230 See also p. 126.

231 Williams and Schaus 2001, 81–3: based on finds of projectile points, sling bullets, and arrowheads, taken together with mould-made bowls, coins, and Pausanias' mention of the Roman destruction of the Achaean League.

232 Williams and Ogden 1994, 10. Bronze rings with bezels became very common in the fourth century BCE: see Boardman 2001, 378.

233 Aristophanes, *Thesm.* 425.

234 Aristophanes, *Plut.* 883 f.

235 The gilding on these bronze pieces is not readily visible to the eye, but can be seen under magnification.

236 Marshall 1968, xxxii, xxxiv.

237 Apparently amber was not used much for decorative purposes in Greece after the sixth century BCE, although there was always a small supply on hand: see Strong 1966, 9.

238 Inv. no. 980.

239 At Nemea, excavations uncovered evidence of a bronze-casting workshop, with furnace, tools, and bronze drippings: see Risberg 1992, 33; Stephen G. Miller 1977, 19–20.

240 At Isthmia, a number of bronze drippings, unfinished castings, and broken bronze fragments indicate that a bronze foundry was located there: see Risberg 1992, 33; Rostoker and Gebhard 1980, 347–63, esp. 350–2, 361.

241 Risberg 1992, 33–4; Heilmeyer 1969, 1–28; Østby 1994, 60. There is also evidence of mostly bronze metal working in sanctuaries at Delphi, Delos, the Heraion on Samos, Aigina, Bassai, Aeotos on Ithaka, and Philia in Thessaly, as well as a structure tentatively identified as a bronze-smith's workshop, east of the temple of Apollo at Eretria: see Risberg 1992, 33, nn. 5–10, 36–9, nn. 24–6, for discussion and bibliography.

242 Rostoker and Gebhard 1980, 350. Some twisted pieces of jewellery at Olympia might be examples of miscasts, and therefore evidence of jewellery production at Olympia: see Philipp 1981, 20. Some stone implements and tools from the Geometric sanctuary of Athena Itonia at Philia, Thessaly, were likely used for manufacturing

votives, weapons, dress pins, and knives: see Risberg 1992, 37; Kilian 1983, 145. At Itonia there was also manufacturing of giant fibulae for purposes of dedication as votives: see Kilian 1983, 147.

243 Risberg 1992, 39; Heilmeyer 1969, 25; Rostocker and Gebhard 1980, 361.

244 Robinson 1941, 133.

245 Williams 1998, 99–100. At Vani in Colchis, the remains of a goldsmith's shop were found, including a gold bar, a gold "drop," and bone tools: see Chqonia 1996, 49–50.

246 For the likelihood of a jewellery trading link between Macedonia and Athens, originating during the Archaic period, see Miller-Collett 1998, 22–9, esp. 25. Macedonia and Thrace were the predominant sources of gold during the Classical period, while silver was exploited in Attica and Thasos: see Higgins 1980, 8–9; Treister 1996, 24–7; Herodotus 6.46–7 (Thasos). Both gold and silver were mined on Siphnos until the mines flooded in the sixth century BCE (Herodotus 3.57).

247 Williams 2003, 234.

248 See below notes 263 (wedding gifts) and 267 (mercenaries).

249 For the possible origins of the glass eye-bead (**161**) and the Illyrian double-shafted pin (**215**), see p. 122 (**161**) and p. 130 (**215**).

250 For a diagram depicting the various stages in making a bronze signet ring using lost wax casting, see Ogden 1992, 50, fig. 35. First a wax model of the ring is made, then it is coated with clay or plaster, then the wax is melted and replaced with molten bronze, after which the mould is broken and the cast ring is recovered and finished by polishing.

251 This terracotta mould has a single pour channel for the pendant in the shape of a pyramidal earring: see Davidson and Thompson 1943, 103, no. 6, fig. 46. The pendant is first modelled in wax and coated with layers of clay "investment" or mould. The wax model was used to carve and form the decoration reproduced on the surface of the metal casting. When heated, the wax melted and drained out while liquid bronze was poured in the pendant-shaped channel: see Hockey 1998, 148.

252 Hockey 1998, 148.

253 Excavation conservator Lisa Bengston also suggested that some lunates were cast in a mould as one solid piece. Eight punchers or formers for gold lunate earrings came from late sixth/early fifth-century pillaged tombs in Lydia: see Treister 2001, 17, 90, figs. 17–18 (from Uşak); Öztürk 1998, 45 (dimensions range from 1.7 to 2.4 cm).

254 The British Museum has a picture of a chlorite mould for making lion-head earrings on display. Dating from ca. third–second centuries BCE, this mould was used for making wax models for metal casting or impressing thin sheet metal; see also Marshall 1969, 240, no. 2112.

255 Kunz 1917, 293; Marshall 1968, xxiii.

256 See above note 36 for bronze solders with high tin content. My special thanks to L. Bengston, for her observations and remarks.

257 Williams and Ogden 1994, 38.

258 My thanks to Taryn Webb for her work on this difficult object, including the drawing.

259 Salapata 1997, 250.

260 Williams and Ogden 1994, 41.

261 Williams and Ogden 1994, 41.

262 Van Straten 1981, 65.

263 At Athens, jewellery was likely given as gifts to the bride at the *epaulia*, on the day after the wedding, which was used for the presentation of gifts from friends and family of the bride. This presentation is depicted on a red-figure pyxis (ca. 360–350 BCE), showing women in a procession carrying various items, among them a chest, the type used to hold jewellery: see Oakley and Sinos 1993, 16–17, 38, fig. 117. See also Miller-Collett 1998, 22. Blundell (2001, 115) notes that the *anakalupteria*, "gifts to new brides from the husbands or relatives," were the most significant gifts a new bride would have received. A late fifth-century BCE red-figure nuptial lebes depicts a *nympheutria* fastening a necklace around a bride's neck; this necklace was likely a gift from the prospective bridegroom: see Sabetai 2008, 294–5, 316, no. 141.

264 Rouse 1975, 240.

265 Brulotte 1994, 11; Van Straten 1981, 72–4.

266 Williams and Schaus 2001, 84; Simon 1986, 253.

267 Williams and Schaus 2001, 85.

268 The identification of this Sanctuary as belonging to Athena Polias is based solely on a long-lost inscription with the word ΠΟΛΙΑΔΟΣ (see Orlandos 1926, 134), although its location near the peak of the acropolis is also suggestive. The cult of Athena Polias, foremost civic deity at Athens in her guise as guardian of the city, is known in other Arkadian sanctuaries at Megalopolis, Tegea, and Phigalia: see Schaus, chapter 1, p. 7, n. 15, fig. 1.8; Jost 1985, 362–3; Farnell 1896, 299. Unfortunately, there are no published finds of jewellery from these sanctuaries, for comparison's sake. Instead, some comparative evidence exists in the form of inscriptions, coins, and descriptions by Pausanias. Surprisingly, only one private dedication of a gold ring appears in the inventory lists of the Erechtheion at Athens, which housed the old cult statue of Athena Polias: see Harris 1991, 433, no. 62; *IG*

II^2 1424.9–10 (374/3); 1424a.360–1 (371/0); 1425.304–5 (168/7); 1428.172 (367/6); 1429.39 (c. 367/6). In contrast, the inventory lists of the Parthenon record dedications of various types of jewellery, including rings, earrings, necklaces, and wreaths of gold and silver, most notably the dedication of gold neckbands by Roxane, the Bactrian wife of Alexander the Great, in 319 BCE: see Harris 1991, 329, no. 416; *IG* II^2 1492. 54–7(305/4?); Dillon 2002, 18–19. Harris 1995, 1; Opisthodomos: 45, no. 5 (stone bracelets), no. 6 (gold rings), 51, no. 36 (chains, gilded wood and tin earrings, necklace, iron rings, no. 37 (dedicated by Kleito, gold rings with onyx, jasper, and glass and necklaces with gold pieces), 53–5, no. 43 (gilt wood earrings), nos. 47–58 (gold rings and earrings, silver earrings and rings, some with sealstones of sard, an ornamented headband). West cella: 94–6, nos. 32–40 (gold ring, belt, earrings, and necklaces, as well as gilt seals, and chains). East cella: 138, no. 130 (two gold bracelets dedicated by Polyphippe, daughter of Meleteon of Archarnai), 139, nos. 133–5 (gold jewellery set with stones, gilt wood necklaces, silver gilt necklace), no. 140 (two gold chains), 140, nos. 142–7 (onyx), no. 148 (gold ring dedicated by Axiothea), 141, no. 152 (gold ring dedicated by Platthis of Aegina), 142, no. 155 (gold ring dedicated by Phryniskos of Thessaly), no. 156 (earrings and gold rings dedicated by Glyke), nos. 157–61 (gold and silver rings with seals and sards), 143, no. 162 (signet dedicated by treasurers in 366/5 BCE), 163, 165 (gold and stone seals).

269 *Anth.Pal.* 6.59; Dillon 2002, 215; see also p. 134 above for possible examples of hair rings found at Stymphalos (**239–41**).

270 Rouse 1975, 242; Statius, *Theb.* ii. 251–6.

271 Brulotte 1994, 8–9; Alroth 1987, 9–19.

272 For a discussion of the Stymphalian stelai and other groups found elsewhere in Megalopolis, Mantinea, and Pherai, see Williams and Schaus 2001, 90–1, and Schaus, chapter 2, pp. 31–4.

273 The three inscribed artifacts include a coin ("EL"), a potsherd from a calyx krater? ("…ITHYAI"), and a bronze rim ("ELEITHY"). For the coin, see Weir, chapter 4, pp. 64, 74, no. **II-51**; for the drinking cup and bronze rim, see Schaus, chapter 10, p. 218, no. **6**; chapter 7, pp. 153–4, no. **22**.

274 Williams and Schaus 2001, 85–7; Sturgeon, chapter 5, p. 49.

275 Deppert-Lippitz 1998, 91; Philipp 1981, 22, 230–57, nos. 837–40, 843, 846–8, 851–5, 857, 860–4, 866–7, 894, 896, 900–3, 905, 908–10, 912, 914–16, 918, 921, 923–4, 926–30, 932, 937, 939, 954–5, 964, 966, 968–9, pls. 52–8. Snake-headed jewellery has been found in many female burials, e.g., bronze snake bracelets from Olynthos (see above note 196), and in sanctuaries to Artemis, Athena, Hera, and Demeter: see Bevan 1986, 2:463–5 for examples. As descendants of the Bronze Age earth-goddess, these female deities retained traits of their ancestry through their association with the snake.

276 See Pausanias (6.20.2; 6.25.4) for the myth of Sosipolis; he noted that Sosipolis shared a sanctuary with Eileithyia at the foot of the hill of Kronos at Olympia. The probable remains of this small temple are located west of the Treasury of the Sikyonians: see Pingiatoglou 1981, 40–1, fig. 2. See also Farnell 1896, 611–12; Philipp 1981, 22–4; Bevan 1986, 1:270–1. At Sparta, Eileithyia was worshipped in two places, one beside the Sanctuary of Artemis Orthia, and the other shared with Apollo Karneios and Artemis Hegemone: see Pingiatoglou 1981, 40, 42. At Lousoi, Sinn believes that Artemis was also worshipped as a kourotrophos because of the great amount of jewellery votives and hair rings, as well as a marble statue of a squatting boy: see Sinn 1992, 185.

277 Rouse 1975, 254.

278 On Erichthonios, see Castor 2006, 625–6; Price and Kearns 2003, 69, 198; Bevan 1986, 1:273. Athena's kourotrophic nature towards Erichthonios is shown on an Attic red-figure calyx krater ca. 410 BCE, by the Nicias Painter, where she caresses the side of Erichthonios' face, while receiving him from Gaia: see Reeder 1995, 251, 261, no. 71. Athena's gesture is a motherly action well suited to her character as protector of the welfare of Athenians.

279 Castor 2006, 625–6. According to the myth, Athena gave the basket with the infant Erichthonios for safekeeping to the daughters of Kekrops, the first autocthonous Athenian king. After disobeying Athena's orders not to look inside, some of these daughters were driven mad when they saw the contents and jumped off the Acropolis to their death: see Reeder 1995, 250.

280 For examples of male infants wearing amulets on miniature choes, see Neils and Oakley 2003, 285–6, nos. 96, 99. See also Van Hoorn 1951 and Hamilton 1992. No Attic amulets have been found, suggesting that they may have been made of perishable materials. For a survey of the archaeological and artistic evidence for children's amulets, see Dasen 2003, 275–89.

281 Castor 2006, 626.

282 Two of the suspension loops (Inv. 1042, 3306) in Appendix I are very tiny, suggesting that they were once attached to miniature pyramidal pendants.

283 A Tanagra terracotta figurine from Aigina, ca. 325 BCE, depicts a young teenaged girl wearing earrings, as well as a tiara: see Neils and Oakley 2003, 257, no. 60.

284 My sincerest thanks to Alexis Castor for her valuable observations about the evidence for girls wearing jewellery and miniature jewellery votives. I would also like to thank Dyfri Williams, formerly Reseach Keeper, Department of Greek and Roman Antiquities, British Museum for his thoughts on this topic. He also believes that small-sized jewellery dedications could have been worn by girls of premarital or newlywed status.

285 See Benson 1995b, 180, no 35, who describes a tiny fifth-century gold lunate earring in the Walters Art Gallery, Baltimore, as evoking "the youthfulness of the girl who wore it." See also jewellery as wedding gifts to a new bride (above note 263)

286 Glanitza: Metzger 1940–1, 30, no. 13. Lousoi, Sanctuary of Artemis Hemera: Reichel and Wilhelm 1901, 52, fig. 75. Argive Heraion: Waldstein 1905, 241, no. 830, pl. 85; Tegea, Sanctuary of Athena Alea: Dugas 1921, 381, no. 139, fig. 42.

287 Boardman (1996, 5), however, believes that jewellery created deliberately for dedication was rare, "since a dedicatory inscription can readily be added to an existing piece," whereas gilt clay jewellery was created specifically for the tomb, as a substitute for the real thing.

288 Davidson 1952, 227. At the cemetery in Olynthos, it was common to find skeletons with one bronze ring worn on the third finger of the left hand: see Robinson 1941, 133.

289 Iron rings with supposedly special magical qualities were worn by initiates in a mystery cult on Samothrace: see Lehmann and Spittle 1982, 403–4. For male dedications of rings on the Athenian Acropolis see Harris 1991, 330–1, nos. 423, 425–6.

290 Robinson and Fluck 1979, 1–14; Robertson 1992, 20–1, 67, 107.

291 The fourth-century BCE ring of burnt sard is said to be from Athens, but it could also be Italic with Hellenistic influences: see Iliffe 1929, 13–14. I am grateful to Paul Denis of the Royal Ontario Museum for this information. A fifth-century BCE silver ring from the sanctuary of Artemis Hemera at Lousoi has ΚΑΛΑ on its bezel, likely the gift of a female votary: see Sinn 1980, 33–4, fig. 10.

292 *Kalos* inscriptions on Greek vases can refer to mythological heroes and deities, e.g., Eros, when they are identified only by their attributes and the inscription is nearby: see Robinson and Fluck 1979, 6.

293 Many pieces of jewellery were found at Kythnos such as gold pendants, a gold twisted wire bracelet, gold, silver, and bronze finger rings, silver and bronze earrings, gold, silver, bronze, and iron pins, silver, bronze, and iron fibulae, and beads of carnelian, rock crystal, glass paste, and faience. Some of the beads date to the Bronze Age, though most of the finds are Archaic in date, with some possibly belonging to the early fifth century BCE: see Whitley 2003, 76; Lobell 2003, 12. A votive deposit was also found *in situ* in a temporary cult building (480–450 BCE) in the Sanctuary of Artemis at Kalapodi, in which a number of objects, including rings and pins, were found lying on a large poros block directly beside the remains of an altar: see Felsch, Kienast, and Schuler 1980, 89–96, figs 71–7; Brulotte 1994, 297–8.

294 As Brulotte 1994, 259, notes in his work on the placement of votives in Peloponnesian sanctuaries of Artemis, "regardless of the size or intrinsic value of the gift it remained essential for the worshipper that his or her offering be placed or displayed somewhere in the sanctuary where it would be seen not only by the divinity worshipped within but also by visitors entering the sacred precinct."

295 Van Straten 1981, 75.

296 Stone offering tables became common in Greek sanctuaries during the fourth century BCE. They likely were placed before the cult statue or by a nearby wall, judging from the archaeological evidence found in the Sanctuaries of Artemis at Epidauros, Kalapodi, and Messene: see Brulotte 1994, 297–9.

297 Williams and Schaus 2001, 92; Schaus, chapter 2, p. 32–3.

298 For ancient references see Kroll 1982, 65 (Pausanias I.26.6), 72–3 (Eusebius, *Praeparatio Evangelica*, x.9.15, Apollodorus III.14.16, Plutarch, *De daedalis Plataeensibus*, Philostratos, *Vita Apollonii* III.14).

299 For example, Ridgeway (1992, 122) writes that "evidence for the statue's pose is at best inconclusive," as to whether it was a seated or standing figure. According to Kroll 1982, 70, 73–6, pls. 11:1–12, some Hellenistic Athenian coins represent the Athena Polias image. These coins indicate that the statue had to some degree a realistic face, but its wooden body was likely aniconic or amorphous. Kroll suggests that the face, either in the form of a mask or carved directly onto the olivewood, was a late addition, like the arms, possibly the work of Endoios during the late sixth century BCE. Shapiro (1989, 25) compares the statue to a "*xoanon,* a crudely carved wooden statue, perhaps little more than a plank fashioned into roughly human form"; he also notes (25, n. 51) that "whether the earliest *xoana* were aniconic images has been much disputed."

300 Harris 1995, 209, no. 20; *IG* II^2, 1426.4–7 (375/4); 1424.11–16 (374/3); 1424a.362–6 (371/70); 1425. 306–12 (368/7); 1428.176–82 (367/6); 1429.42–7 (ca. 367/6); 1456.20.2 (after 314/3); Kroll 1982, 68. n. 18.

Miller-Collett (1998, 23) notes that her jewellery and clothing were presumably regularly replaced.

301 Several terracotta loomweights were discovered in and near the West Annex of Building A, leading the excavators to assume that this room once held a loom: see Surtees, chapter 12, pp. 244–5; Williams and Schaus 2001, 88; see 88–9, nn. 46–9, for references to other sanctuaries of Athena, as well as of Artemis, Hera, and Demeter, which have finds of weaving equipment.

302 Barber 1992, 112–17.

303 Benches for the placement of votives were found on either side of the door in the small shrine to Artemis at Olympia: see Brulotte 1994, 275.

304 For example, a third-century BCE inscription (*IG* VII 303) from the Amphiaraion at Oropos mentions ornaments that had fallen from the walls: see Brulotte 1994, 265.

305 Dawkins 1929, 249–84, pls. 180–6, figs. 118–22.

306 Philipp 1981, 20.

307 Amandry 1981, 91.

308 See Appendix IV.

309 Eight others were found in the refuse pit (see note 123).

310 Also a pyramidal (Inv. 1083) and lunate (Inv. 3682) earring are included, but are omitted from the catalogue because of their poor state of preservation.

311 Among a group of five tetragonal statues at Megalopolis commented upon by Pausanias (8.32.4) are the female deities, Athena Ergane and Eileithyia.

312 See Williams and Schaus 2001, 91.

313 **14**, **86**, and **182** from Level 3; **217** from Level 4; **75**, **116**, **128**, **225**, Inv. 2512 (bronze ring fragment) from Level 5; **200**, **237** from Level 6.

314 Waldstein 1905, 207–39, nos. 52–807.

315 Zagdoun 1984, 183–4 (the catalogue consists of 386 rings with bezels, mostly fifth/fourth century in date).

316 See extensive catalogue in Kilian-Dirlmeier 2002.

317 Kilian 1975, 168.

318 Philipp 1981, 116–33, nos. 400–86.

319 Philipp 1981, 155–66, nos. 576–613.

320 Raubitschek 1998, nos. 186, 191 (pins), 203–4 (fibulae), 230–1, 234–6, 244, 247a (rings; 247 is a lump of molten lead with impressions of sealstone), 250 (earrings), 267 (pair of bronze anklets), 272–6 (bronze and copper leaves), 278 (bronze flower), 279 (gilded terracotta bead).

321 For example see Stephen G. Miller 1981, 50, pl. 13d (two bronze rings); Stephen G. Miller 1980, 179, pl. 35b (bronze Illyrian type pin). See also Kilian-Dirlmeier 1984, 213, no. 3499a (Archaic pin).

322 Reichel and Wilhelm 1901, 51–5, figs. 75–86 (fibulae), 87–91 (earrings), 92–6 (pins). See also Mitsopoulos-Leon 1994, 42–3, fig. 6 (buttons); Sinn 1980, 33, fig. 10 (fifth-century BCE silver ring with inscription); Sinn 1988, 158, fig. 14 (about 100 bronze hair rings). Sinn is apparently preparing a catalogue of the jewellery for publication.

323 Kilian-Dirlmeier 1984, nos. 3700, 3926, 4006A, 4170, 4185, 4538–40, 4558, 4567, 4751, 4853, from the Archaic period for example. Bookidis mentions, in the preliminary report IV: 1969–70, finds of bronze jewellery, mostly simple or bezelled hoop rings and pendant earrings, as well as a gold leaf bracelet and a silver ring with gold studs: see Bookidis 1972, 317.

324 Davidson 1952, nos. 1811, 1991 (gold and glass rings), 2001–2 (bronze and gold earrings), 2055 (gold necklace), 2269 (bronze pin), 2426–7, 2456–8, 2503–6, 2511–12 (glass, bronze, and terracotta beads), 2514–18 (bone buttons). For more recent finds of jewellery at Corinth, see, for example, Pemberton 1985, 294 nos. 5–8 (rock-crystal bead, glass eye-bead, faience beads, funerary necklace from mid-third-century BCE grave 1963–10, Anapologa cemetery); Blegen, Palmer, and Young 1964, 220, no. 274.1 (bronze pins from Grave 274, North Cemetery, ca. 485–475 BCE), 222, nos. 278.1–2 (iron brooch and pins from Grave 278, North Cemetery, first quarter of the fifth century BCE), 253, nos. 364.2–4 (bronze earrings, pendants, and necklace from Grave 364, North Cemetery, third quarter of the fifth century BCE); Robinson 1962, 119 (lion-head earrings from Grave 4, Cemetery on north slope of the Acropolis, end fourth–beginning third centuries BCE; gilded terracotta beads from Grave 6, end fourth–beginning third centuries BCE).

Chapter 7: Miscellaneous Small Finds

1 Barag 1970, 154–6 figs. 44–7.

2 For a recent discussion of this vessel type with comments on dating problems, see Carter and Toxey 1998, 757–61, including a catalogue of 28 alabastra from Metapontum graves.

3 One of the alabastra at Perachora has walls 1.8 cm thick; see Dunbabin 1962, 517 no. E4. Fragments of two alabastra identified as being marble were found at Tarrha, on the southwest coast of Crete, in an area where Weinberg believed marble vases were being produced, Weinberg 1960, 102 nos. 17–18 pl. 31f; Weinberg 1959.

4 Caskey 1939. For the presumed imitation of marble vases in clay, see Coldstream, Eiring, and Forster 2001, 87 (exaleiptra) and 125 (pyxis). For glass imitations, Weinberg 1959, 18–19.

5 Milne 1939; Roberts 1978, 2–4.

6 Milne 1939, 249; Roberts 1978, 2–3. For examples of three types of marble pyxides, see Roberts 1978, 2–3, 7 nn. 12–14, 139 n. 17. Several marble pyxides were found at Lindos, but were not illustrated, Blinkenberg 1931, 672 nos. 2863–5, 740 no. 3181, and at Camirus, Torr 1885, p. x, pl. 1 (facing title page) fig. D (alabaster?). Other pyxides and lids were found in Cyrene, Warden 1990, 57 nos. 419–32 passim, figs. 9–10 pls. 42–3. For an alabaster object that is larger in size with thicker walls, see Warden 1990, 59 no. 453 pl. 46 ("offering table").

7 Weinberg 1959. She found fragments of a marble pyxis in a small excavation at Tarrha on the southwest coast of Crete, Weinberg 1960, 102 no. 19 pl. 31f.

8 Weinberg 1959, 21. The discovery of five such marble pyxides in a tomb at Herakleion from the second century BCE (see **2**) supports Weinberg's suggested date.

9 Coldstream 1973, 164–6 nos. 262–87 fig. 42 pl. 96, with a reference to a marble pyxis found at Tarrha by Weinberg. Some of the fragments identified as plates look as if they could be pyxis lids, and he compares what he identifies as a stopper of an unguent vase to the knob of a pyxis lid as identified by Weinberg.

10 Zapheiropoulou 1973, 605, 607 fig. 6 (Type C).

11 Cavities for inlaid eyes vary in depth and shape. Some include space for the entire eye, cornea, iris, pupil; others provide only for the iris and pupil. Some are deep and others are shallow, with a drill hole for a pin (?). The insets tend to be natural materials, like ivory, bone, marble, and other stones, though sometimes a white "paste" is described. Glass is sometimes used as well. The best-known early example of this is thought by some to be the "Antenor" kore, Acropolis 681, which still has part of one inlaid eye preserved, said to be purple glass, e.g., Richter 1968, 69–70 no. 110 figs. 336–40, but others have identified it as rock crystal, which fits better with the use of natural materials; see Brouskari 1974, 78 (in the Greek edition, p. 80 ὀρεία κρύσταλλο – "rock crystal"); Ridgway 1993, 149. For three examples of inlaid glass eyes at Olympia, Bol 1978, 95 nos. 223, 422–3 pls. 46, 70 of which one (p. 50 no. 223) is dated to the Hellenistic period. For the technique of inlaid eyes, Bol 1978, 93–8; Lahusen and Formigli 1993; and for discussion of such statues with references, Mattusch 1988, 183 nn. 112–13; Sturgeon 2006, 55–58; Palagia 2006, 123 n. 43.

12 Davidson 1952, 76–8, 93 nos. 581–4 (three core-wound and one mould-pressed pieces).

13 Davidson 1952, 76–83, 93–107 nos. 585–684. Davidson (p. 77) comments that Corinth has the largest amount of excavated glass from the Roman and Medieval period of any site in Greece to her time.

14 Davidson 1940; Davidson 1952, 77, 83–90, 107–22 nos. 685–815; Weinberg 1975.

15 I am grateful to Molly Richardson for her kind advice on these two inscriptions.

16 See Congdon 1981, 7, 16. For examples of hares from mirrors found at Corinth and Sikyon, Davidson 1952, 66 nos. 500–1 pl. 48; Walters 1899, 24–5 no. 243 pl. IV (fox pursues two hares – Corinth); Blegen 1937, 336 fig. 3 (two dogs pursue hare – Sikyon).

17 Mertens 1987, 59 no. 40 pl. (in colour).

18 Congdon 1981, 167–8 no. 55 pl. 51.

19 Congdon 1981, 174–5 no. 64 pl. 60.

20 Congdon 1981, 172 no. 61 pl. 57.

21 Congdon 1981, 172–3 no. 62 pl. 58, ca. 460 BCE "Corinthian A" school.

22 See Congdon 1981, 17–18, and for the associations of the animals, p. 16 n. 63.

23 On display in the National Archaeological Museum, Athens, inv. 13101/1 (full size), and inv. 13101/2–4 (miniature mirrors). From another Arkadian sanctuary come two other miniature mirrors (inv. 8622–3). All are dated to the sixth century BCE.

24 Most of the caryatid mirrors have three-(lion)footed stands, but compare Congdon 1981, no. 21 pl. 19 for one with a lower ring base.

25 For a discussion of weapons, such as arrows and catapult bolts, as votives, see Hagerman, chapter 5, pp. 97–8.

26 For a good discussion of the shape and development of the strigil, see Raubitschek 1998, 122–4 with references.

27 A good variety occurs at the Itoni sanctuary at Philia, Kilian-Dirlmeier 2002, nos. 1624–5 pl. 99, nos. 1782–5 pl. 110, nos. 2863–70 pl. 170.

28 The type with the longest projection varies most in style, but see for example Macridy 1911, 202 fig. 16 A–C, representing 60 bosses arranged in three double rows of five each on the three diazomata of the double-leaved door at Langaza.

29 Lehmann 1969, 56. For the appearance of the bosses on doors, see 190 fig. 149 (restoration of wooden doors, Tomb at Langaza), 150 (marble door, Vergina tomb), and pls. 103, 107–8 (restored on the Hieron), and references to others from Halae, Olynthos, Corinth, Aigina, Priene, and Delos and representations on Greek vases, see ibid., Text I, 56 n. 46; Text II, 244–5 nos. 160–1, pl. 34.1–2

30 Macridy 1911, 195, 198, 200–1 fig. 8 (restoration in wood), pl. IV (restored drawing). Oddly, the three types of door bosses were not found in equal numbers. Only 10 of Type A with the longest projection were found, while 14 of Type B (small projection) and 36 of Type C (rounded) were found. In addition, 19 smaller bosses of Type A and Type B were found, and restored as being alternately

single and double decoration along the vertical overlap of the two leaves.

31 Mitsopoulos-Leon 1994, 43 figs. 5–6. The monograph on small finds from the more recent excavations at Lousoi appeared too late to be consulted: Mitsopoulos-Leon 2012. Both rounded and high spiked bosses were found at Dodona, Carapanos 1878, pl. 43 nos. 8–9, Vokotopoulou 1973, pl. 32b; while all three main types were found at Olympia, Furtwängler 1890, 191–2 pl. 67 nos. 1214, 1218, and 1221. Three different boss types, like those at Lousoi, were also found in the archive house at Kallipolis in Aitolia, presumably from a wooden door, Themelis 1979, 262 fig. 17.

32 Mitsopoulos-Leon 1994, 43.

33 Williams et al. 2002, 145, 148–9 plan 3 (upper left for remains of the door with bosses) and ill. 4. The number of boss types may have been miscounted as four instead of three because the tips of some bosses were damaged (e.g., the top two bosses in ill. 4 are the same type, but the one on the left has lost its tip).

34 Zancani Montuoro et al. 1965–6, 44–6 fig. 5.

35 Robinson 1941 , 260–76 nos. 1037–1170, pls. 70–5. For a discussion of Greek doors and doorways based on finds from Olynthos, see Robinson and Graham 1938 , 249–63.

36 Robinson 1941, 260 n. 58.

37 Robinson 1941, 274.

38 For Lindos, Blinkenberg 1931, 203 no. 621a, with references to others.

39 Siebert 1976, 817 fig. 30.

40 Warden 1990, 35 nos. 220, 229 fig. 4 and pl. 25.

41 See Coldstream 1973, 143–5 fig. 33.

42 Coldstream 1973, 149–50 nos. 134–57.

43 Davidson 1952, 141 nos. 1017–19

44 Stephen G. Miller 2001, 164–8. See also Birge, Kraynak, and Miller 1992, 285, 303–4 nos. 46, 98–9.

45 Broneer 1954, 88 n. 43 for the former, and n. 44 for the latter.

46 See e.g. Bookidis and Stroud 1997, 449, 471–3 nos. 13, 86–91.

47 *IG* IV^2 1, 109 B.97, 148; D.113, dated ca. 290–270 BCE.

48 The names that appear on the Corinthian tiles include Λέων? – the stamp reads ΕΠΙΛΕΟΛΤΟC from the skene of the Theatre, Hellenistic? – Stillwell 1952, 35 n. 25; Ξενολᾶς – the stamp reads ΕΠΙΞΕΝΟΛΑ and is found in two different dies, one from the South Stoa and one from the Theatre, but since the name is rare, it must belong to the magistrate Xenolaos, Hellenistic – Broneer 1954, 88 n. 44; Stillwell 1952, 35 n. 25 fig. 7; and Φίλων, also appearing inscribed before firing on the base of a mouldmade bowl (Hellenistic? – Roebuck 1951, 136 no. 90), in conjunction with buildings that are fourth century or Hellenistic in date. I owe this information to James Herbst.

49 Taeuber 1981, 186–7. For roof tiles with the lunate sigma from Megalopolis, dating to the first half of the second century BCE, see Lauter 2002, 380, 382 n. 24 fig. 12 a,b.

50 Iozzo 1987; Pemberton 1989, 75–8. For a group of fourth-century terracotta louteria from Klazomenai, see Cevizoğlu 2007.

51 Sparkes and Talcott 1970, 37.

52 Ginouvès 1962, 77–99 (louterion), 299–310 pls. 40–1 (perirrhanterion), esp. pp. 307–9 for the use of the term. Fifty marble basins with inscriptions on their outside rims were dedicated on the Acropolis in Athens, presumably given primarily as dedications though perhaps also being used to hold purifying water; see Raubitschek 1949, 370–413.

53 Weinberg 1954; Sparkes and Talcott 1970, 368 no. 1872 fig. 16 pl. 89 (second half of the fourth century context).

54 Sparkes and Talcott 1970, 37; Merker 2006, 17–18 (where the inclusions are described as "shale or hornfels (mudstone) … irregular in shape and angular … in quantities identified … as sparse, moderate, or abundant").

55 Jones, Sackett, and Graham 1962, 86 fig. 4.F.

56 Blinkenberg 1941, 201–4 nos. 5–6 bassins à eau.

57 Broneer 1971, 11–12.

58 See Schaus, chapter 2, p. 24. A similar block with shallow round cutting is preserved in the wall of the Cistercian monastery at Zaraka. This monastery was built of reused blocks from the Classical city, and is situated close to the presumed location of the ancient Artemis sanctuary.

59 Pemberton 1989, 75–8, 188–90 nos. 661–74 pl. 60 for 14 representative examples and discussion. None of the pieces from the Demeter Sanctuary at Corinth come from a secure Hellenistic context.

60 Jones, Sackett, and Graham, 1962, 85 fig. 4.F.

61 Young, chapter 6, p. 132, **227** (inv. 0326) is a bone disk with a bronze tack found lying snugly over and within the disk, perhaps as a decorative attachment.

62 See Bélis 1984, 178–80, fig. 2C: fragment measures 11.13 cm in length and 1.85 to 1.95 cm in diameter. Other auloi fragments have been found in sanctuaries at Perachora and Sparta (Artemis Orthia); see Dunbabin 1962, 447–51, pls. 189–90; Dawkins 1929, 236–7, pl. CLXI.

63 Deonna 1938, 253–5 pl. 80; Robinson 1941, 357–9 nos. 1725–35 pl. 114; Davidson 1952, 185–6 nos. 1348–54.

64 Baitinger and Völling 2007, 66–87.

65 Baitinger and Völling 2007, 122–3. For others, Greco and de La Genière 1996, 232 nos. 174.50–3 fig., Zancani Montuoro et al. 1965–6, 151–8 pl. 44 from Foce del Sele; Comstock and Vermeule 1971, 435 no. 638 Boston MFA

01.7515 from Lousoi; Jameson 1974, 72 no. HM 556, pl. 14 from Halieis. For a good explanation with diagrams of wooden door locks which were opened with such keys, see Jacobi 1930; Dawkins 1902–3, 190–5.

66 Personal communication. See Kourouniotes 1904, 165 fig. 2.

67 See Connelly 2007, 92–104, figs. 1.1, 3.3, 4.4–16, 8.4–6; also Mantis 1990, 28–65 pls. 49–53 inter alia.

Chapter 8: Constructing the Sanctuary

1 Bronze, as opposed to iron, door bosses are treated in Schaus, chapter 7, pp. 162–3 (cat. **75–82**), although functionally they belong together with the door bosses discussed here. Only iron nails were undertaken by Munaretto for study initially, leading to their separation.

2 Jones, Graham, and Sackett 1973, 427–8. For a discussion of ancient Greek construction in wood, including literary sources, inscriptions, "petrification" of wooden elements in stone architecture, varieties and sources of wood, sizes and prices of wood, tools, carpenters as a trade, and the means of joining wood including the use of nails, see Orlandos 1966, 1–49 (nails p. 45).

3 Jones, Graham, and Sackett 1973, 424.

4 For the second house, Jones, Sackett, and Graham 1962. It is possible that the nails were carefully removed from the woodwork before the two houses were abandoned, as seems to have been done at the Roman legionary fortress at Inchtuthil, Manning 1985b, 289, but not to find any nails, even broken ones, may be a matter of preservation. See also Robinson and Graham 1938, vii, 230–1 n. 7 for woodwork in houses at Olynthos and possible removal of woodwork by salvagers as a cause of the reduced numbers of nails found, though hundreds, both iron and bronze, were still recovered.

5 Raubitschek 1998, 132 n. 7, and 134 n. 25, for "metal fixtures" generally as indicators of the original wood in structures; Robinson 1941, 323 for iron nails used in coffins; Shaw and Shaw 2000, 384–6 for specific uses in buildings.

6 The thickness of a wooden door closing a Macedonian tomb at Langaza was calculated as 3.6 cm this way; see Macridy 1911, 200 n. 3 fig. 13.

7 Williams et al. 2002, 148 n. 18. See Orlandos 1966, 13–20 for the descriptions in ancient authors of different varieties of wood and their uses.

8 See Orlandos 1966, 16 nn. 10–14 for references in ancient authors.

9 Bourguet 1932, 151–2 no. 36.

10 Roman sites are better known for their nails, including the conservatively estimated 875,428 nails (more likely over a million, Manning 1985b, 289), mostly unused, which were buried in a deep pit at the legionary fortress at Inchtuthil when it was abandoned; see Angus, Brown, and Cleere 1962; Pitts and St Joseph 1985, 109–13; Manning 1985b, 289–92. Six groups were distinguished based on the diameter, shape, and thickness of the head, the shape and length of the shank, the section of the shank half an inch from the head where a die held the shank when the head was forged, and the weight. Manning (1985b, 291) accepts that the 6 groups can be reduced to 2 types. Type A(i) has large nails (spikes) with pyramidal heads to withstand heavy pounding; Type A(ii) includes the vast majority, for regular use, ranging in length from 38 mm to 241 mm; and Type B has nails with round section and chisel-shaped end, perhaps for masonry use. The Group E (or Type A.ii) nails comprised 87% of the total at Inchtuthil, and were suggested to be used for securing wooden cladding to frames.
At Botromagno in Apulia, about 200 examples from the Republican period are divided into 3 main types, based on the shape and size of their heads (see Macnamara 1992, 244–5 figs. 114–15), and at San Giovanni di Ruoti, 546 nails, mostly Late Roman, were recorded, with discussion of their possible uses, Small 1994, 142–5. Nails are also discussed in Cleere 1958.

11 Rolley 1984, 277 no. 64 figs. 32 and 33.

12 Raubitschek 1998, 134–5, 175–81 App. K–L fig. 35.

13 Davidson 1952, 140–3 nos. 1014–23 (bronze bosses), 1024 (iron boss), and 1025–55 (28 bronze, 2 iron, 1 lead – spikes, nails, tacks etc.). See also Stillwell 1948.

14 Shaw and Shaw 2000, 373–86, and references to others on Crete, 412–13 nn. 22, 29.

15 Branigan 1992, 367.

16 Robinson 1941, 310–29 pls. 91–6.

17 Cambitoglou, Papadopoulos, and Jones 2001, 740–2 nos. 18.44–51 (iron), 742– 4 nos. 18.52–60 (bronze) fig. 172 and pl. 97.

18 Waldbaum 1983, 68 pls. 21–2, with reference to Cleere's typology for nails from a Roman villa on the Isle of Wight.

19 Andronicos 1984, 71, and caption for fig. 34 p. 74.

20 Andronicos 1984, 217. An iron spike may be visible in fig. 32 p. 71 at the bottom centre.

21 So many were being discovered in the 1996 and 1997 seasons that inventorying of them by the apothiki staff was sporadic in 1996, and recording of them as small finds on site was discontinued in 1997. Both recording as small finds and inventorying of the nails restarted in 1999.

22 See Schaus, chapter 7, pp. 162–3, 174–5, 182.

23 Projectile points, Hagerman, chapter 5 above; iron finger

rings, Young, chapter 6, 117–19; and other iron objects, Schaus, chapter 7, pp. 175–81.

24 No standard classification of nails has been established, so nail descriptions are commonly misleading. Length, width, size of head, and preservation are important factors to be considered. Spikes generally have a preserved length, or if broken, an estimated original length above 10 cm, but also have a shaft width over 0.7 cm. Tacks normally have a broad head over 1.5 cm in width and a preserved length, or if broken, an estimated original length, less than about 3.0 cm.

25 Manning 1985b, 291.

26 Cf. nails (bosses) from Corinth, Davidson 1952, 141–2 no. 1024 (Hellenistic) fig. 22 pl. 72, and Isthmia, Raubitschek 1998, 138 nos. 488–91 pls. 75–6, Appendix K, pl. 96.K1 ("iron boss for door" – Archaic to third century). For a marble door from a Lydian tomb which seems to copy these decorative mushroom-head bosses, see Macridy 1911, 203 fig. 15.

27 Cf. nails (spikes) from Olynthos, Robinson 1941, nos. 1486, 1489 pl. 95.

28 Cf. from Olynthos, Robinson 1941, no. 1487–8 pl. 95.

29 Cf. from Olynthos, Robinson 1941, no. 1490 pl. 95.

30 Pitts and St Joseph 1985, 112 n. 87 Group F.

31 Cf. one from Olynthos, Robinson 1941, no. 1529 pl. 95.

32 At Kommos, 25% of the collection was classified as tack-like nails, Type IV, though the majority were of bronze; see Shaw and Shaw 2000, 382–3.

33 Cf. a type at Olynthos described as "triangular hook-head," Robinson 1941, 323 nos. 1529–40 pl. 95, with a reference to two from Aigina.

34 Cf. from Olynthos, Robinson 1941, nos. 1530–2 pl. 95; Raubitschek 1998, no. 504 pl. 78 (spike – 23 cm) from the Classical Period.

35 The term is used commonly with shipbuilding. Iron bolts are specifically mentioned in an inscription from the Amphiareion, *Arch. Eph.* 1923, 45 line 30.

36 Raubitschek 1998, 100–1 nos. 336 (iron tire), 340–3 (bands), 344–5 pl. 56–7.

37 Raubitschek 1998, 134 publishes four from Isthmia, nos. 488–91 pls. 75–6, with references to doors on vases, and marble doors. See also Robinson 1941, 260ff; Robinson and Graham 1938, 257, 266 fig. 24; and Adam-Veleni, Poulaki, and Tzanavari 2003, 178–80 nos. 28–32 for a variety of bronze bosses ("studs") from houses in Macedonia with references, including an unpublished PhD dissertation in Greek by N.A. Haddad on doors and windows in Hellenistic and Roman architecture of the Greek land (University of Thessalonike, 1995).

38 For bronze examples, see Schaus, chapter 7, pp. 162–3. It was common to protect the wood in buildings by coating it with pitch, and this was especially true of doors; see Orlandos 1966, 20–1 n. 15. Maintaining a sheen on iron bosses would be much more difficult than doing the same for bronze bosses.

39 Robinson and Graham 1938, 257.

40 Raubitschek 1998, 134; Robinson and Graham 1938, 266 fig. 24. For a discussion of bosses and many examples from Olynthos, see Robinson 1941, 260–78 with references.

41 See Schaus, chapter 7, p. 162.

42 Robinson and Graham 1938, 266 fig. 24 for windows.

43 See Schaus, chapter 7, p. 175, nos. **160–5**. For a wooden chest with bronze fittings and many decorative bronze tacks from Pompeii, see Mols 1999, fig. 28. In a fine house at Kallipolis in Aetolia, small silver nails were found with heads in the shape of ivy leaves, Themelis 1979, 271 fig. 37.

44 Mols 1999, fig. 21 for the types of joints found in Greek furniture, including the use of nails for strengthening. For Greek furniture, see Mols 1999, 69–72 with references to studies on techniques, types of woods, appliqués, and tools; Richter 1966, 13–84 ills. 37–426, and for furniture fixtures at Isthmia and elsewhere, Raubitschek 1998, 144–7.

45 Shaw thought that a group of tacks at Kommos may have served this purpose, Shaw and Shaw 2000, 383.

46 For details regarding the value of furniture, see Raubitschek 1998, 145, where deductions are made based on the work of Pritchett. Evidence from painting indicates that Greek furniture, especially seating, was light and easily moved. See Richter 1966, 63, figs 180–1, 201, 233, 365, 348.

47 Raubitschek 1998, 146. Tacks used in pairs may have had a cord placed around their stems to secure the lid. For other methods to secure box and chest lids, see Richter 1966, 72–8.

48 See Richter 1966, 75–6, figs. 392–5; Mitsopoulos-Leon 1990, pl. 31.7.

49 Payne et al. 1940, 181.

50 Robinson 1941, 323, 327–8 nos. 1529–40.

51 For information regarding the use of wood and terracotta tiles in Archaic sanctuaries, see Broneer 1971, 6, 36–7, 40, 55, 62.

52 The use of tacks on furniture is also noted above. For other indoor use of wood, such as the shelf, the wardrobe, and the buffet, see Richter 1966, 78–84, figs. 386, 421, 423, 425, 426.

53 Group I = 9, II = 32, III = 8, IV = 4+2, V = 7.

54 Of the 76 nails from Trench 99.1/99.1B, 43 have been classified. Group I: 7, II: 17, III: 8, IV: 4, and V: 6.

55 This area includes Trenches 97.5/97.5B, 97.4, 97.9, 99.1, 99.6, 99.9/99.9B, and 00.3.

Chapter 9: Pottery of Building A

1 All dates are BCE. Little earlier material (i.e., fourth or third century) was recovered that could be associated with the use of the rooms of Building A proper, presumably because they were kept clean while the building was in use.

2 See Schaus, chapter 2, p. 29.

3 For the most part, the coins from Building A are only broadly datable. See Weir, chapter 4, passim, esp. p. 76.

4 For a more detailed discussion of the chronology of the forms discussed in this section, see the shape essays below.

5 Of course none of this "missing" evidence should be considered conclusive on its own. For instance, chytrai with flanged and tapered rims, a common form at Stymphalos and other sites in the northeast Peloponnese in the fourth century, are also not attested.

6 Anderson-Stojanovich 1996, 93–4.

7 Rotroff 2000a (1997), 377.

8 For a discussion of Athenian mould-made bowl chronology, see Rotroff 2005; 2006.

9 Although many of the mould-made bowls in the deposit appear in a fabric that is visually indistinguishable from Corinthian, the destruction of Corinth in 146 BCE is not used here as a terminus ante quem, since it is possible that other centres in the coastal region, such as Sikyon, produced vessels using fabrics that are visually indistinguishable from Corinthian. Indeed, mould-made bowls and other vessels in a fabric identified as Corinthian occur in an interim-period deposit at Corinth published by Romano. See e.g., Romano 1994, 64–8, fig. 2, nos. 3, 9, 11–13, pls. 14, nos. 1–6; 15, nos. 8–14.

10 It is tempting to suggest that mould-made bowls served as a "replacement" for these cups, which are generally similar in form, but at present this must remain a hypothesis.

11 Romano 1994, 60, 74–7, figs. 6, nos. 33–4; 7, nos. 35–6, pls. 18, no. 33; 19, nos. 34–6.

12 E.g., Rotroff 2000a (1997), 378, pl. 194, no. 1; Vogeikoff-Brogan 2000, 296–8, fig. 2, nos. 1–4. One possible piece of Eastern Sigillata A was identified in pottery from the Middle Room.

13 E.g., Slane 1986, 277–8, fig. 2, nos. 2–6, pl. 61, no. 7 (true Eastern Sigillata A), and Slane 1986, 279, fig. 4, no. 11 (local imitation of Eastern Sigillata A). Eastern Sigillata A and its imitations of Late Hellenistic or Early Roman date also occur with some regularity among the surface material collected by the Sikyon Survey Project, possibly indicating that it was available in the region in the Late Hellenistic period (personal study).

14 E.g., Bruneau 1970, 478–80, fig. 61.10, nos. 110–11; Abadie-Reynal 1995, 2, 7, fig. 5.

15 The quantities of vessels discussed in this section are derived from counts of whole profiles or of substantial, non-joining sections of rims or bases, whichever was more numerous for a given form in a given fabric. This methodology is similar to that employed by Berlin at Troy (2002), and generally similar to the quantification strategy of Ault used at Halieis (2005). The only substantial difference between my method and Ault's is that the count represents rims *or* bases, rather than rims *and* bases.

16 See Surtees, chapter 12, pp. 243–5.

17 For instance, the votive debris deposit in Trench 96.15 beneath the floor of the West Annex held 344 fragments of miniatures out of 472 vessels. Most of the miniatures were drinking vessels.

18 Ault (2005, 47) and Berlin (2006, 5) have noted similar correspondences between the function of reconstructable and fragmentary pottery found in a given context. However, this is not to imply that no residual material is present in these contexts, merely that it does not appear in sufficient quantity.

19 Additionally, the material discussed here was intermixed with or beneath the layers of tile material that represents the roof, indicating that the vessels represented were present in Building A prior to the collapse of the roof.

20 Ault and Nevett 1999, 48.

21 Bookidis et al. 1999, 16; Pemberton 1989, 402.

22 It is possible that meals would have been eaten indoors or outdoors depending on the season, just as they are in modern Greek tavernas.

23 E.g., Isthmia: Bookidis et al. 1999, 14.

24 For example, Hellenistic "guild" associations were known to meet for drinking parties at sanctuaries, Kane 1975, 325–9. The extent to which these meals were "ritual" or "religious" events at all is debatable.

25 For instance, the debris deposit beneath the West Annex (96.15) contained 316 miniature drinking vessels out of 344 total miniatures and 472 total vessels in the deposit.

26 Rouse (1902, 352) discusses the dedication of non-functional votives for the idea they represent, rather than any value they hold.

27 E.g., Berlin 2002, 136; Edlund-Berry 2001, 72–3; Broneer 1977, 92.

28 Rotroff (1997, 14–15) points out that ceramic drinking vessels remained an important component of assemblages in Athens.

29 The miniatures in the deposit are probably residual material of fourth- or third-century date, since they are not attested in quantity in deposits of later date.

30 Bookidis 2003 (1996), 255–6, *contra* Alcock 1994, 252, 258.

31 Ault 2005, 19–57; Beestman-Kruyshaar 2003, 249–94. These comparisons are only meant to give an impression of the "norm," since household assemblages can vary substantially across time and place, even within the Hellenistic period. Comparison with published quantified material from houses of the mid- to late Hellenistic period from the area of the Corinthia or northern Arkadia would allow the material from Building A at Stymphalos to be much better contextualized.

32 Pemberton (1989, 46) has noted a similar lack of iconographic unity among the mould-made bowls at the Demeter Sanctuary at Corinth.

33 Hayes in Gebhard and Hemans 1998, 60.

34 It is important to keep in mind that, as mentioned above, lamps are a very common dedication in Greek and Roman sanctuaries dedicated to a wide variety of deities and rituals.

35 Personal study.

36 See pp. 200, 202 for discussion.

37 This smooth form of blisterware may correspond to the "harder, pink" clay in which some mould-made bowls at Corinth are attested. Edwards 1981, 205. It is also visually identical to the fabric of several Hellenistic vessels displayed in the Nemea museum, so this "smooth blisterware" may be an Argive fabric.

38 John Hayes coined this term for the fabric while working at Stymphalos and Isthmia in the northern Peloponnese.

39 Kathleen Slane discusses variations of fabric colour and the possible reasons for them. Slane 1990, 3–4.

40 Bookidis et al. 1999, 14; Pemberton 1989, 25–6, 28.

41 Pemberton 1989, 26–7, fig. 6, nos. 113–14, 402.

42 Sparkes and Talcott 1970, 84.

43 Pemberton 1989, 28–9.

44 Edwards 1975, 66–71, pls. 13–14, nos. 357, 363–5, 367–8, 371; 50–1, nos. 311, 317, 347, 316, 336.

45 Pemberton 1989, 30.

46 Anderson-Stojanovich and Reese 1993, 264, 298; Anderson-Stojanovich 1997 (1994), 14–15, pl. 5, no. IP6533.

47 Hjohlman, Penttinen, and Wells 2005, 24, 27–8, 32, 35, nos. 10, 50, 52, figs. 7, no. 10; 16, nos. 50, 52.

48 Bookidis et al. 1999, 14; Pemberton 1989, 36–7, fig. 11, nos. 122–3.

49 Anderson-Stojanovich 1997 (1994), 14–15, pl. 5, no. IP805.

50 Anderson-Stojanovich and Reese 1993, 264, 278–9, fig. 7, nos. 28–30.

51 Georgiadou 2005, 51–3, fig. 5.

52 Rotroff 1997, 155–6.

53 Rotroff 1997, 83, 85, 245–6, fig. 6, nos. 36–9, 42–4, 46–7; pls. 4, nos. 36–41; 5, nos. 42–7.

54 For cyma kantharoi see Edwards 1975, 76–82, nos. 389–450, pls. 15, nos. 399–401, 404, 408; 52, nos. 400–1, 404, 408; 53, no. 399.

55 For articulated kantharoi see Edwards 1975, 83–6, nos. 458–514, pls. 16, nos. 460, 463, 466; 53, nos. 460, 463, 466.

56 For one-piece kantharoi see Edwards 1975, 74–6, pls. 15, nos. 378–80; 52, nos. 378–80.

57 Pemberton (1989, 34–5) discusses the chronology of Corinthian kantharoi.

58 Only one example from Stymphalos (from the Stym IX puppy burial) is sufficiently preserved to indicate whether it had one or two handles originally, and it has one handle.

59 Edwards 1975, 86–7, nos. 515–23, pls. 16, nos. 515, 519, 521; 54, nos. 515, 519, 521.

60 Personal study.

61 Langridge-Noti in Crouwel et al. 2002, 55–7, fig. 16, nos. 1a–h.

62 Edwards 1975, 90–2, pls. 17, nos. 532, 546; 40; 55, nos. 532, 534–5, 538–41.

63 Pemberton 1989, 39, fig. 12, nos. 187, 453, pls. 20, no. 187; 47 no. 453.

64 Anderson-Stojanovich and Reese 1993, 296, pl. 67, nos. 127–8; Anderson-Stojanovich 1996, 73–4, fig. 9, no. 21.

65 Anderson-Stojanovich 1996, 85–6, pl. 30, nos. 48–9.

66 Anderson-Stojanovich 1996, 87.

67 Anderson-Stojanovich 2000 (1997), 383.

68 Rotroff 1997, 112–13, 277–9, fig. 21, pls. 33, nos. 332–40; 34.

69 See Rotroff 1982, 4–5, and Rotroff 2000b (1997) for a basic description of methods of manufacture.

70 E.g., Rotroff 1982, pls. 73–87; Siebert 1978, pls. 95–7.

71 Rotroff 1982, 42, 90, pls. 67, 88, no. 391.

72 Laumonier 1977, pls. 131–4.

73 Romano 1994, 60, 67–8, fig. 2, nos. 11–13, pls. 15, nos. 11–12; 16, nos. 13–14.

74 A small fragment of a mould was excavated in Stym X, an area of the acropolis of unknown function to the east of the Sanctuary, suggesting that such vessels were produced at Stymphalos.

75 I have erred on the side of caution in not identifying fabrics which occur in only a very few examples.

76 E.g., Laumonier 1977, pls. 34, no. 373; 50, no. 1088; 73, no. 5676; 88, no. 5829.

77 For a full list of motifs and counts see table 9.8. A detailed description of all of the motifs has not been included in this study, since the motifs used on mould-made bowls in general have been more than amply described in

works by other scholars, most notably Rotroff's (1982) work on Athenian material and Siebert's (1978) study of mould-made bowls from the Peloponnese. In addition, a study of motifs attested on bowls from Stymphalos was done for an MA thesis by Knapp (2002).

78 There are no examples of Homeric bowls at Stymphalos, and while there are "hunt scenes" these generally consist of simple alternating stamps of hunters and hunted and are not considered here as "narrative." For the most part, the bowls with figured decoration seem to have it randomly applied in much the same manner as the large sample of mould-made bowls found near the Hellenistic race course at Corinth, Edwards 1981, 196.

79 For a more thorough discussion of the evolution of mould-made bowl chronology, see Rotroff 2006b.

80 Thompson, Thompson, and Rotroff 1987, 157.

81 Edwards 1975, 152.

82 Rotroff 1982, 12.

83 Rotroff 2006b, 360.

84 Rotroff 2005, 24; Rotroff 2006b, 363–7. As a result of this revised chronology for their rise in popularity, Rotroff suggests that deposits containing a high proportion of mould-made bowls should not be dated any earlier than ca. 175 BCE. Rotroff 2006b, 376.

85 Siebert 1978, 172–8.

86 Anderson-Stojanovich 1997 (1994), 17; Anderson-Stojanovich 1996, 72, pl. 17, no. 17. Anderson-Stojanovich (1996, 93–4) provides a tentative dating for the destruction of the Rachi settlement at Isthmia.

87 Sanders, personal communication.

88 E.g., Edwards 1975, 151–5; Edwards 1981 and 1986b.

89 Romano 1994, 64–8, fig. 2, nos. 3, 9, 11–13, pls. 14, nos. 1–6; 15, nos. 8–14.

90 Langridge-Noti in Crouwel et al. 2002, 58–60, nos. 6a–6d, fig. 17; Langridge-Noti in Crouwel et al. 2003, 20–2, fig. 6, nos. 1a–c.

91 Goester and van de Vrie 1998, 133–4, 154–5, fig. 13 nos. p464, p466, p467, p626–7; unfortunately, neither of these contexts has materials that date them very closely within the span of the century.

92 E.g., Edwards 1981, 191–3, 196–7.

93 Edwards 1975, 88–90, pl. 54, nos. 527–30.

94 Edwards 1975, 88–9.

95 See Rotroff's discussions of the popularity in the Hellenistic period of smaller table service vessels that would allow individuals to mix their own wine, Rotroff 1996, 18; Rotroff 1997, 15. This individual mixing is in contrast to the krater of the Classical period, which contained a common mixture prepared by the "symposiarch."

96 Edwards 1975, 56, pls. 10, no. 280; 49, no. 280.

97 Pemberton 1989, 15–17, fig. 3, no. 350.

98 Themelis 2004 (2000), 42, pl. 18, no. 8296 (and two other examples not numbered).

99 Rudolph 1978, 221–2, fig. 10, nos. 44–5.

100 Rotroff 1997, 132–3, 299–301, figs. 39, nos. 533–51; 40, nos. 552–5, pls. 51, nos. 533–5; 52, nos. 536–55; Rotroff 2000a, 377, pl. 192, no. 6; Vogeikoff-Brogan 2000, 301, 303, fig. 7, no. 20.

101 Personal observation.

102 Edwards 1975, 53–6, pls. 10, nos. 251, 255, 258; 48, nos. 251, 255, 258; Pemberton 1989, 15–18, fig. 3, no. 390.

103 Rotroff 1997, 125–7, 293–6, figs. 34, nos. 467–8; 35–6, pls. 46, nos. 467–9; 47–8.

104 Edwards 1975, 146–8, pls. 35, nos. 761, 775; 64, nos. 750–1, 754, 756, 768, 774–5.

105 Pemberton 1989, 15, 54, pls. 10, nos. 76–7; 44, nos. 387–8.

106 Anderson-Stojanovich and Reese 1993, 267, 281, nos. 43–4, fig. 9, pl. 61.

107 Edwards 1975, 44, pls. 6, no. 187; 47, no. 187.

108 Rotroff 1996, 18.

109 Rotroff 1997, 121–4, 285–92, figs. 24–33, pls. 39, nos. 407–11; 40–5; Lynch, personal communication.

110 Only nine examples of incurved-rim bowls are attested in this deposit out of a total of 413 vessels.

111 Edwards 1975, 30.

112 Pemberton 1989, 39–41.

113 Romano 1994, 69, fig. 3, no. 19, pl. 16, no. 19.

114 Anderson-Stojanovich and Reese 1993, 264, 271, 273, 276, 279–83, 286–7, 289, 297–8, nos. 19, 39–40, 48–9, 68–9, figs. 3, no. 5; 6, no. 19; 9, no. 40; 10, nos. 48–9; 13, no. 68; 14, no. 83, pls. 59, no. 19; 61, no. 48; Anderson-Stojanovich 1997 (1994), 15–16, pl. 6, nos. IP702, IP687; Anderson-Stojanovich 1996, 65, 74, 87–8, figs. 5, no. 2; 8, no. 20.

115 Goester and van de Vrie 1998, 133–4, 157, fig. 15, nos. p432, p658.

116 Kolia 2000, 390, pl. 205, no. 5.

117 Rotroff 1997, 156; Rotroff 2000a, 378.

118 E.g., Rotroff 2000a, 377–8, pl. 103, no. 10.

119 Slane 1986, 289, fig. 12, no. 69. Berlin and Heath (in Alcock et al. 2005, 197–8) emphasize that bowls of this same general form were produced widely in the Mediterranean throughout almost all of the Hellenistic and Roman periods. Thus, when incurved-rim bowls are found outside of an independently datable context, it is best to use caution in assigning a specific date range to them.

120 Edwards 1975, 28–9, pls. 1; 43, nos. 2, 6, 11.

121 Edwards 1975, 28; Pemberton 1989, 42.

122 Anderson-Stojanovich and Reese 1993, 264–5, 271, 273, 276, 282–3, 289, 297–8, nos. 4, 17, 47, 82, figs. 3, no. 4;

5, no. 17; 10, no. 47; 14, no. 82, pl. 58, no. 4; Anderson-Stojanovich 1997 (1994), 15–16, pl. 7, nos. IP 566, IP588; Anderson-Stojanovich 1996, 86, pl. 30, no. 53.

123 Anderson-Stojanovich and Reese 1993, 264–5.

124 E.g., Rotroff 1997, 159–60.

125 **27,** a plate or saucer foot, could be from several different forms.

126 Similar to Edwards 1975, 41–2, no. 135, pl. 5, which Edwards classifies as a fishplate with bevelled rim.

127 Edwards 1975, 42–4, pls. 5, nos. 158, 164, 168; 46, nos. 158, 164, 168.

128 Pemberton 1989, 47–9, fig. 15, nos. 94–5, 131–3, 162, 176, 195, 464–8.

129 Romano 1994, 69, pl. 16, nos. 16–18.

130 Anderson-Stojanovich and Reese 1993, 265, 278, 281, 297–8, figs. 7, no. 27; 9, no. 42.

131 Rudolph 1978, 216–17, fig. 5, no. 19.

132 Edwards 1975, 39–40, pls. 4, nos. 127, 129; 45, nos. 127–9.

133 Pemberton 1989, 49–51, fig. 16, nos. 177, 472–3, pls. 19, no. 177; 48, no. 472.

134 Anderson-Stojanovich 1997 (1994), 16–17; Anderson-Stojanovich 1996, 86, pl. 30, no. 50.

135 Langridge-Noti in Crouwel et al. 2002, 62, 64, fig. 19.

136 Rotroff 1997, 154, fig. 57, nos. 838–46.

137 Edwards 1975, 36–7, pls. 4, nos. 104–5; 45, nos. 104–5; Pemberton 1989, 50–2, fig. 16, nos. 189, 197, pl. 21, nos. 189, 197 (Pemberton refers to examples from the Demeter Sanctuary as "flat-rimmed plates").

138 Romano 1994, 70, pl. 16, no. 23.

139 Anderson-Stojanovich 1997 (1994), 17.

140 Bruneau 1970, 507, 509, 519, fig. 212, nos. 61.6, 188.6, 188.7.

141 Goester and van de Vrie 1998, 133–4, 155, 157, fig. 15, no. p508, fig.

142 Rotroff 1997, 148–50, 313–14, figs. 49, nos. 682–93; 50, nos. 694–700, pls. 61, nos. 685, 687; 62, nos. 689, 692, 694, 696, 700.

143 An example in the Middle Room of Building A, which is not under consideration here, does occur in Corinthian fabric.

144 Edwards 1975, 40–1, pls 5, nos. 131–2; 46 nos. 131–2.

145 Romano 1994, 70, 76–7, fig. 7, no. 38; pls. 16, no. 24; 20, no. 38.

146 Anderson-Stojanovich and Reese 1993, 266; Anderson-Stojanovich 1997 (1994), pl. 7, nos. IP685, IP701.

147 Bruneau 1970, 481, 507, 509, 519, fig. 212, nos. 61.5, 188.4, 188.5. Rotroff 1997, 148–50, 317, 319–20, figs. 51, no. 730; 53, nos. 756–63, pls. 65, no. 730; 66, nos. 756–8; 67, nos. 759, 761, 763.

148 E.g., Rotroff 1997, 15; Ekroth 2003.

149 Pemberton 1989, 64–6, pl. 52, nos. 561–8.

150 See Edwards 1975, 141.

151 Edwards 1975, 139–42, nos. 722–45, pls. 34, nos. 727, 733; 63, nos. 727, 733.

152 Pemberton 1989, 68, 72, fig. 23, nos. 151–2, 646, pls. 17, no. 152; 58, no. 646.

153 Anderson-Stojanovich 2004 (2000), 625, nos. IP490, IP564, IP7720.

154 Unfortunately, vessels were only tallied as "flanged" as opposed to "unflanged" prior to the 2006 season, so there is no statistical data at present to support this dating.

155 Edwards 1975, 122–3, pls. 27, nos. 651, 656; 61, nos. 651, 656. Since none of the examples from the Building A collapse deposits are complete, distinctions in form on the basis of handle placement would be a matter of guesswork.

156 Pemberton 1989, 69, 74, fig. 24, no. 109, pl. 14, no. 109.

157 Pemberton 1989, 74.

158 Slane 1990, 75, fig. 18, nos. 172–3; Slane-Wright and Jones 1980, 147, 153, fig. 4, nos. 71–2, pl. 30, nos. 71–2; Slane 1986, 281–2, 292–3, figs. 6, nos. 20–2; 15, no. 95, pls. 62, no. 23; 67, no. 97.

159 Anderson-Stojanovich 2004 (2000), 624, pl. 303, nos. IP 825, IP 6523.

160 Langridge-Noti in Crouwel et al. 2002, 63–5, fig. 20, nos. 12a–12b.

161 Rotroff 2006a, 166–7, 169, 174–5, 305, 308, figs. 72, no. 576; 76, nos. 604–5; 77, no. 606, pl. 65, nos. 605–6, charts 17–18.

162 Rotroff, personal communication.

163 Anderson-Stojanovich 2004 (2000), 623.

164 Edwards 1975, 124–6, pls. 29, nos. 667, 670–1; 62, nos. 667, 670–1.

165 Pemberton 1989, 68–9, 71, 74–5, fig. 24, nos. 112, 660, pls. 14, no. 112; 59, nos. 659–60.

166 Anderson-Stojanovich 2004 (2000), 624.

167 Goester and van de Vrie 1998, 133–4, 150–1, fig. 10, nos. p864, p894.

168 Edwards 1975, 129–31, pls. 31; 62, nos. 688–9, 692, 694–9.

169 Some coarse-ware sherds may have been discarded along with roof tile fragments during excavation. This may partially account for the relatively few joining coarse-ware sherds attested in the Building A collapse deposit. Bookidis et al. (1999, 15–16) note that coarse and cooking vessels were not as well preserved in the Demeter Sanctuary at Corinth as fine wares.

170 Edwards 1975, 134; Pemberton 1989, 68, 70, 72, fig. 23, no. 645, pl. 58, no. 645.

171 Slane and Jones 1980, 156, no. 104.

172 Anderson-Stojanovich 2004 (2000), 625, pl. 304, no. IP 7713.
173 Rotroff 2006a, 109–10, 231, 270–1, figs. 39, nos. 234–8; 40–1, pls. 33–4, chart 28.
174 Rotroff 2006a, 109–10; Rotroff, personal communication.
175 Edwards 1975, 134–5, pls. 33, nos. 705–6; 63, nos. 705–6.
176 For instance, handles of jugs and amphorai are often identical.
177 Edwards 1975, 112–13, pls. 24, no. 631; 60, no. 631.

Chapter 10: Select Pottery from the Sanctuary and Nearby City Wall Area

1 Herbert 1977, 1; McPhee 1983, 138 n. 7; McPhee 1991, 329, 332. For a workshop believed to be established by an emigrant potter from Corinth at one of its colonies in northwest Greece (perhaps Ambrakia) that produced an imitation of Corinthian red-figure, see Papadopoulos 2009, 238.
2 Important studies include Herbert 1977; McPhee 1983; McPhee and Trendall 1986; McPhee 1991. For a description of the fabric, see Herbert 1977, 1–2; McPhee 1983, 137.
3 Pemberton 2003, 172.
4 Pemberton 2003, 177.
5 Attic Type A skyphos, see Herbert 1977, 66.
6 Rather than the student whom Herbert calls the Student Sketch Painter; see Herbert 1977, 9–11. The distinguishing characteristics of the younger painter are not clear to me, nor, it seems, to McPhee (below note 7).
7 Two very similar oversize skyphoi (Attic Type A) in the National Museum, Athens, are assigned by Herbert (1977, 12) respectively to the Middle Sketch Painter (Athens, NM 1412) and the Student Sketch Painter (Athens, NM 1405), though both are dated to the second quarter of the fourth century (p. 10: "probably dating to the second quarter of the 4th century" and "at the time the two skyphoi were painted, in the second quarter of the 4th century"). Herbert (1986, 31) dates Athens NM 1405 late in the second quarter. At the same time, she (1977, 10) places the middle work of the Sketch Painter in the first quarter of this century, with it ending towards the end of the first quarter. It is difficult to see why she places the Athens skyphos (NM 1412) in the second quarter, since the painting is still of high quality (p. 10: "very finely drawn, comparable to the best work of the Sketch Painter"). McPhee (1983, 152) rejects the attribution of these vases to two separate painters, but assigns them to the second quarter of the fourth century, on the basis of comparisons with Attic skyphoi.
8 Risser 2001. Besides Risser, the miniatures at Corinth are discussed by others, including Pemberton 1989, 64–6, 168–77, who notes the increasing appearance of plain miniatures without any paint, and Benson in Stillwell and Benson 1984, 309–43. For the miniatures from Perachora, see Dunbabin and Dunbabin 1962, 290–313. Miniature vases of Corinthian manufacture travelled great distances, including to Magna Graecia and North Africa, indicating their demand even while they were surely among the cheapest of votives. For a detailed discussion of miniature vessels from the Sanctuary of Athena Alea at Tegea, with an overview of this vessel type from elsewhere in the Peloponnese, see Hammond 1998, especially 139–44 (Arkadia), 144–62 (Argolid), and 162–87 (Corinthia).
9 Inv. nos. 623, 624, 761, 1162, 1183, 1463, 1518, 1731, 1841, 2152, 2166, 2393, 2760, 2965, 3169, 3321, 3326, 3328, 3335, 3433, 3437, 3442, 3555, 3587, 3588, 3593, 3597, 3616, 3623, 3624, 3701.
10 My thanks to J. Perreault for his comments on this and Inv. 1844 (?).
11 I am grateful to Mark Lawall for looking at photographs of these amphoras from the Sanctuary and providing helpful comments.
12 Boggess 1972; Blitzer 1990.
13 Blitzer (1990) discusses all aspects of the making of pithoi (pitharia) around Koroni in Messenia in the nineteenth and twentieth centuries, as well as their distribution in the Mediterranean. Examples of the largest (Type 1) pithari were documented at many coastal sites in the Aegean and even to North Africa, Cyprus, and Palestine, but they also turned up inland at Sparta, Tripolis, and Megalopolis; see Blitzer, 703 fig. 7.
14 For the shape, especially the canted rim which belongs with the neckless pithos, see Boggess 1972, 73–84, 142–4 nos. 116–34. The type begins in the second half of the fifth century.

Chapter 11: Lamps

1 Lamps have been found at other areas of the city, especially in the housing district just east of the acropolis. While the majority are late Classical/Hellenistic, a few go back to the early/mid-fifth century BCE. Some are early Roman, while the latest are from the fifth to sixth century CE.
2 Bailey (1973) provides a useful introduction to Greek and Roman lamps, their chronology, and their uses. At least three early Christian graves elsewhere at Stymphalos included lamps with the dead, although generally Christians did not use grave offerings.

3 For a sanctuary of Demeter and Kore at Mytilene and its lamps, see Bailey and Williams (forthcoming).

4 There is a deposit of fragments, mostly of nozzles, bases, and tops, from about fifty lamps that are similar in shape, size, and fabric, from a context that dates to the mid-second-century BCE destruction of the Sanctuary in the North Annex of Building A (see below on late round-bodied lamps).

5 We find a similar pattern with the terracotta figurines from the Sanctuary; scarcely a single complete one survives and most are represented only by fragments that usually do not join.

6 The proximity of the ancient City Wall along the south side of the acropolis and the presence of several towers make it likely that at least a few lamps had been used for illumination in those structures and thus may not belong to the Sanctuary.

7 We have found a small fragment of a mould for the manufacture of such bowls elsewhere on the acropolis but as yet have no evidence for the local manufacture of lamps, although one would expect it.

8 Broneer 1930, 56–60 for the initial study; for the most recent discussion that moves their date considerably later than Broneer's, see Slane 1990, 9–10. Very large numbers of such lamps also appeared at the Sanctuary of Poseidon at Isthmia (Broneer 1977), where they were popular dedications in the Palaimonion. Numismatic and ceramic evidence from the fifteen areas that we have excavated at Stymphalos indicates little material later than the first half of the first century CE. Professor Sheila Campbell's team found a Severan coin in the nearby thirteenth-century Cistercian monastery of Zaraka, and we found several fourth-century CE coins in the housing area, but no contemporary pottery or other finds.

9 Broneer 1930, 76–8; unfortunately none of the nozzle, handle, or base survives to provide a clear indication of the type.

10 Broneer 1930, 90–102 for the first study of the type; for more recent discussions see Perlzweig 1959, Williams 1981, and Slane 1990. For a recent proposal – still debatable – that the type originated and was produced in Patras, see Petropoulos 1999. At Corinth the type of lamp that we have found at Stymphalos stops with the Herulian attack of 267 CE.

11 Such lamps have been found by the thousands in western North Africa, especially in Tunisia and Algeria, and in their final form appeared around 400–425 CE; by the end of the century, mediocre copies were appearing in Greece. See Broneer 1930, 118–20 for the initial discussion, Garnett 1975 for a large deposit from the late Roman "Fountain of the Lamps" at Corinth, Williams 1981, 76–80 for a relatively recent treatment of the type in Greece. The single early Christian grave in the pronaos of the Temple yielded neither pottery nor lamps, although both appeared in other late graves elsewhere at Stymphalos.

12 For discussions see Williams 1981, 7–8 and Bailey 1975, 89–92. There is still uncertainty about when the type begins and ends; such lamps are also difficult to date within the broad period that we know for their use. At Delos nearly a quarter of over 5000 published lamps belong to versions of this type, Bruneau 1965. At Athens Rotroff (1997, 511) now dates the deposits from where they occurred to 100 BCE–100 CE.

13 Howland 1958, 68.

14 For blisterwares see Edwards 1975, 144–50.

15 I am greatly obliged to Peter Stone, who has studied the pottery from Building A, for clarification of details about the large number of fragments of lamps from this deposit.

16 Howland 1958, 39–40.

17 For a good discussion see Scheibler 1976, 44–9.

18 Scheibler 1976, 46–7.

19 Williams 1981, 4 no. 2; Corinth L69-4 (unpublished).

20 Broneer 1930, 50–1; Howland 1958, 91–3.

21 For blisterware see Edwards 1975; there is a considerable number of fragmentary blisterware aryballoi, askoi, and a few other shapes at Stymphalos; according to Peter Stone (personal communication), it is possible in fact that the ware originated somewhere other than Corinth (e.g., Sikyon).

22 See, e.g., Howland 1958, 128–9.

23 Broneeer 1930, 56–60; Slane 1990, 9–10.

24 Broneer 1977, 26–8.

25 For the type see Broneer 1930, 80–3.

26 For discussion see Broneer 1930, 90–102; Broneer 1977, 64–72; H. Williams 1981, 35–41; and Slane 1990, 13–17.

27 Petropoulos (1999, 80–4) suggests Patras in the reign of Domitian; the case remains unproven.

28 Williams et al. 2002, 155–7. Four areas of the ancient site itself have produced graves, several of which had lamps of the fifth century CE in or near them, and a fifth area at the northern end of the modern village (about three km from the ancient site) produced several more graves, one of which had a coin of Justinian II – ca. 535 CE – in it.

29 Garnett 1975; Williams 1981, 76–80. Bussiere (2007) collects several thousand examples from Algeria in the most recent study of the type.

Chapter 12: Loomweights

1 See below, pp. 242, 245–7.

2 Comprehensive studies of artifactual assemblages (Ault

and Nevett 1999), including those associated with cloth production, have enhanced our knowledge of both domestic and manufacturing contexts. These studies provide comparable material for assemblages found in other kinds of contexts. By examining the location, orientation, and context of weaving equipment, particularly loomweights, we can gain a greater understanding of the textile industry and its significance in Greek society, both from a domestic and religious perspective.

3 Barber 1991, 93–4; Blegen (1963, 71–3) describes the preservation of the three or four rows of loomweights between two post holes at Troy, Level IIg. At the Early Bronze Age site of Aphrodisias in Turkey (Kadish 1971, 136), loomweights were found all pointing in the same direction as if they had fallen directly from the loom.

4 For the origins of the warp-weighted loom see Barber 1991; Barber 1994. Barber (1991, 91) argues for the movement of the warp-weighted loom technology into Europe from Anatolia early in the Neolithic period; its use was widespread in the Bronze Age. The first depiction of the warp-weighted loom was in Northern Italy in the fourteenth century BCE, and its use continued down to the early Roman period, being common in both Greece and Italy, perhaps used simultaneously with the vertical two-beam loom in some areas; Hoffmann 1964, 321–3.

5 Hoffmann 1964, 304–11; Barber 1991, 103, fig.12.3.

6 For discussions of the mechanics of the warp-weighted loom, see Barber 1991, 91–113; Barber 1992, 108–9; Hoffmann 1964; Crowfoot 1940, 41–4. Key aspects are discussed below.

7 Hoffmann (1964, 313–14) refers to a row of fallen loomweights measuring 2.44 m from the Sorte Muld house on Bornholm. Additionally, an extant cloth measuring 2.11 m wide was found, indicating a width for the loom of 2.5–3.0 m. Barber (1991, 387) records the smallest preserved loom width as 0.40–0.50 m from Robenhausen in Switzerland.

8 Barber (1991, 91–113, 387–9) collected the evidence for groups of excavated loomweights, which may represent weaving or the storage of weaving, on Neolithic and Bronze Age sites. This provides an interesting range for the width of looms and the number and mass of the loomweights. Later sites have yielded evidence for weaving, primarily in a domestic context. At Olynthos, Cahill (2002, 171) describes a ground floor room in Villa CC with 43 loomweights in a row 1.1 m in length. At Gordion, 21 loomweights were found in a row measuring 1.59 m, suggesting the width of the loom; DeVries 1980, 39.

9 In the Pnyx publication (Davidson and Thompson 1943, 69–70), mathematical calculations based on the pictorial and archaeological evidence were used to determine approximately the average number of weights per loom. Hoffmann (1964, 297–321) discusses the technology on the basis of the iconography of Greek vases. For discussions of weaving on vases, see Clark 1983; Carroll 1983; Crowfoot 1940.

10 Blegen 1963, 71–3; other sites (see Hoffmann 1964, 310–14; Barber 1991, 102–4) also yielded staggered or multiple rows of loomweights.

11 Much of Hoffmann's (1964) and Barber's (1991, 1994) research consists of ethnographic studies of weavers in Scandinavia.

12 Barber 1991, 104; Cahill 2002, 175. Commonly between 20 and 30 loomweights have been considered to be a "set," so that a group of 23 loomweights, dated to the fifth century BCE, found in a dump in the Tile Works at Corinth may have been such a complete set or close to one; see Merker 2006, 57.

13 Barber 1991, 104–5; Davidson 1952, 147.

14 New York, MMA, 31.11.10.

15 Corinth, Greece, Archaeological Museum, CP 2038.

16 Davidson and Thompson 1943, 68 fig. 30 (British Museum, from Italy).

17 McLauchlin 1981, 79–81.

18 For Corinth, see Davidson 1952, 147, 154, 157, nos. 1145, 1164, 1165, and 1153; for the Pnyx, Davidson and Thompson 1943, 68, 78, 92, W 139, and W 40.

19 The conservator identified it as an organic material which might be a stick or rod based on the shape and fibrous nature of the material; however, conclusive and detailed analysis has not yet been completed.

20 Excavations at Stymphalos have yielded several assemblages of weaving equipment. Loomweights from Stym I (Lower Town site) are from a later period and belong to a domestic context, so direct comparisons are not immediately relevant. A greater variety in the form of the loomweights was observed at Stym I. Discoid, pyramidal, conical, and tapered ones are found. Regarding the suspension hole, all the loomweights, except the discoid ones from Stym I, have one hole. The presence of two suspension holes in the discoid weights might have eliminated the need for an intermediary.

21 At Corinth, the loomweights are thought to be mouldmade and wheel-finished, with a fine slip over the surface and even a final polish; see Merker 2006, 59.

22 For further discussion on the use of markings, see Davidson and Thompson 1943, 7–8; Davidson 1952, 153; Tatton-Brown 1992, 220. Merker (2006, 60) suggests that marks helped the maker reassemble sets which were distributed around the kiln during firing.

23 This was a suggestion of G. Schaus.

24 Davidson 1952, 146–72; Merker 2006, 57–60; Wilson 1930, 118–28. The period of occupation on these sites is much greater than at Stymphalos, which may allow for further development of form. Regional variations and preferences must be considered as well in comparing these typologies; particular shapes may change accordingly. For a recent discussion of loomweights from a regional survey at Asea, in southeastern Arkadia, see Forsén and Forsén 2003, 236–9.

25 This development from the pyramidal to the conical is noted at Olynthos, at the Pnyx in Athens, and at Corinth. The pyramidal style is especially popular at sites in Asia Minor, as well as Olynthos and Halos.

26 A progression from A to B to C is proposed here as logical, but it has no foundation in the Sanctuary evidence. It does, however, coincide with variations over time observed at other sites, especially at Corinth. There appears to be a pattern of elongation and sleekness as the weight develops; however, both B and C were in use simultaneously, and the variation may not be the result of a temporal or stylistic development but rather idiosyncrasies of the loomweight maker. See Merker 2006, 58.

27 Hoffmann 1964, 42; Wallrodt 2002, 182–3.

28 The warp threads needed to remain taut. It is simplest if all the weights are equally heavy, although, as Barber (1991, 95–6) notes, differences in weight can be overcome by the number of threads attached to each loomweight.

29 Wilson 1930, 118–28; Burnier and Hijmans 2003, 121; Simpson 1994, 218–19; Wallrodt 2002, 182–3; Tatton-Brown 1992, 218–19.

30 Four main clay groups or nine sub-groups are represented at Stymphalos. Colour and composition were examined macroscopically. A Munsell chart was not used. See above, p. 236 for descriptions of the sub-groups.

31 Barber 1991, 104; Cahill 2002, 175.

32 It was generally regarded as sacrilegious to dispose of votive material as mere refuse or to reuse cult offerings. Large sacred dumps (*bothroi*) were often dug to dispose of votives, Rouse 1902, 342–3, 345–6; Van Straten 1981, 80; Simon 1986, 171, 173–4.

33 This date was determined in the preliminary examination of coins by Robert Weir and of terracotta figurines by Kathleen Sherwood.

34 Most of the finds are from the fourth and third centuries BCE.

35 Rouse 1902, 342–3; Van Straten 1981, 78.

36 The projectile points may be the result of a siege, though catapult bolts could also have been dedicated in the Sanctuary. Votive gifts to a particular deity serve as a reflection of the dedicator. Simon (1986, 411–12) argues that the attributes of the divinities may be connected to the offering.

37 The fragment is only 4.0 cm high and weighs 28 g, but it may have fitted into the group when whole.

38 Schaus (chapter 2, p. 31) has suggested that the floor of the West Annex may have been swept clean and that it had a longer existence than indicated by the pottery found in association with the floor.

39 Trench 96.6 extended from the North Annex along the west side of the west wall of Building A. Trench 96.6 was then dug as two parts when the wall of the West Annex was uncovered. A 3 m extension of trench 96.6 to the south was opened as trench 96.8, which extends all the way to the face of Building A. The following season, trench 97.2 was opened west of trench 96.15 to locate the south wall.

40 Two of the 9 were found in close proximity to the other 19, but belonged to different levels.

41 I have excluded from the sample the miniature loomweight (4.6 cm in height), since it is an anomaly and could not have been used in conjunction with the other weights. **1** is similar in size and weight but was found in a later stratum. The measurements of **22** were not taken *in situ*, since it was discovered in pottery washing. According to the pail form, this was thought to belong to an earlier stratum. Although these loomweights may be connected with the larger group, they have been excluded from the analysis of the entire group because of their location and context within the trench.

42 *Anth. Pal.* 6.39, 47, 48, 160, 247.

43 See Mansfield 1985, 442–52 for discussion of the care and adornment of cult statues.

44 Barber 1992, 106; *Anth. Pal.* vi. 286.

45 Mansfield 1985, 443–4.

46 Simon 1986, 268; Page 1951, 22 (translation), 78–9 (discussion of the term "φάρος"). There is confusion as to the meaning of this term. Despite Page (1951, 79), it appears to make better sense that the girls in the procession carried a robe to Artemis Orthia rather than a plough. The connection to a robe and weaving may be represented by the large number of loomweights found at the Artemis Orthia sanctuary. Few of these loomweights have been published.

47 Mansfield 1985, 445, 465–7.

48 Paus. 5.16.2; Paus. 6.24.10.

49 Paus. 3.16.2; Mansfield 1985, 467–8; Williams and Schaus 2001, 88.

50 Goldman 1915, 448; Goldman 1940, 479. According to Liddell and Scott, πεταμνυφάντεραι are the weavers of hangings, indicating tapestries or wall hangings rather than garments or cloth for the cult statue.

51 Wallrodt 2002, 185–8.

52 Greco and de La Genière 1996, 225–6, 231–2 nos. 174.22–49; Zancani Montuoro et al. 1965–6, 61, 73–82 pls. 16–17. The building was constructed by the Lucanians, but Greco and de La Genière (1996, 226) argue that the Lucanians were influenced by Greek customs in weaving a robe for the cult image of Hera.

53 Kleibrink 2006; Attema 2008, 80.

54 Maaskant-Kleibrink 1993, 20–2 fig. 15; Kleibrink 2006, 123–4, 178 figs. 38c, 49.5–49.11b; Attema 2008, 79–80 fig. 9.14–15, and compare the assemblage of weaving equipment from the Early Iron Age dwelling on Plateau I at the same site, Kleibrink 2006, 104 figs. 33.18 and 33.19.

55 Maaskant-Kleibrink 1993, 8–13 figs. 6, 11b; Kleibrink 2006, fig. 2; Attema 2008, 86 fig. 13.

56 Attema 2008, 86 fig. 14.

57 Mansfield 1985, 260–4, Barber 1992, 112–16; Lefkowitz 1996, 81; Neils 1992, 17–18; Parke 1977, 38–9.

58 Aristotle, *Constitution of the Athenians* 49.3, 60.1; Mansfield 1985, 5–7, 51–6, 77–8. For the Greater Panathenaia, it was male weavers who wove the sail peplos for Athena, suggesting that professional male weavers were more skilled for this important religious task. The names of male weavers Akesas (or Akeseus) and Helikon are preserved in the literary sources. See Mansfield for a summary of evidence and the names of male weavers (1985, 5–6, 21–2, 54–5, 84).

59 Pausanias (1.27.3) mentions that the arrephoroi lived close to the temple of Athena Polias, perhaps best narrowed to Building III on the Acropolis. It has been suggested that the arrephoroi wove the peplos in this building, in the rear chamber of the Parthenon, or in a building later replaced by the Parthenon. Mansfield 1985, 275–7, 283–5.

60 Mansfield 1985, 443–4.

61 See above, p. 33 n.86. As Schaus (chapter 2, p. 14 n.12) has noted, besides the loomweight **29,** three partial inscriptions have been found on objects from the Sanctuary (a bronze vase rim, inv. 2525; a silver coin, inv. 57; and a Corinthian red-figure sherd, inv. 503) which may be restored as Eileithyia (bronze rim: Ελειθυ[-?-] and Corinthian sherd: [--IΘUAI]), or an abbreviation of the name (silver coin: ΕΛ).

Chapter 13: Faunal Remains

1 I wish to express my gratitude to Dr Gerald Schaus, whose saintly patience allowed me the time to take care of my many other obligations while writing parts of this contribution. I would also like to thank Dr Hector Williams, who invited me to Stymphalos to study the faunal material from all sites excavated in the area, and the Malcolm H. Wiener Laboratory of the American School of Classical Studies at Athens, particularly its former director Dr Sherry Fox, for an associateship and space at the lab to study the archaeological remains. Dr Robert Lamberton, Mr Kostas Papakonstantinou, Dr Giorgios Catsadorakis, and Mr Evangelos Spinthakis offered their records and knowledge of contemporary species in the area.

2 "Faunal Remains from the Abbey at Zaraka in Corinthia" by Ruscillo is forthcoming in the publication of the excavations at Zaraka by Dr Sheila Campbell. The site was excavated under the auspices of the Pontifical Institute of Medieval Studies at the University of Toronto.

3 David Reese is to be credited with this expedient way of washing animal bone remains. The bones become clean enough to show the surface and other diagnostic characters, while the method reduces the amount of breakage that might occur if the specimens were to be washed individually. The mesh bag also allows many bones to be washed at once, saving the analyst precious time.

4 See note 2 above.

5 T. Brown, personal communication, 2009.

6 Schaus, personal communication, 2010.

7 From "The Stymphalia Archaeological Landscape Project" abstract, K. Walsh, T. Brown, and B. Gourley, University of York.

8 I am indebted to K. Papakonstantinou for reviewing the list of archaeological fauna and making useful notes and suggestions.

9 K. Papakonstantinou, personal communication, 2008.

10 Gejvall 1969, 41.

11 Ruscillo, unpublished data.

12 See bone pathologies presented in Bartosiewicz, Van Neer, and Lentacker 1997.

13 See Sturgeon, chapter 3 above.

14 A nice example is the lekythos Tampa 86.79.

15 Unfortunately, the date of the complete dog burial in the tower is somewhat obscure; a beloved companion could have been buried here even in the past century. The backfill would contain antiquities which may or may not coincide with the date of the burial.

16 A fox is seen to the right of the hunter in lekythos Harvard 1925.30.51; a hare is to the left of the hunter.

17 See Garvie-Lok, chapter 14, p. 268.

18 See Schaus, chapter 7, p. 150, for the glass objects.

19 Along the northern side of Temple B at Kommos on Crete, for example; see Shaw and Shaw 2000, 27.

20 Most of these unidentifiable mammalian specimens are presumed to be bovid and suid bones.

21 As interpreted in Mylona 2013.

22 For vase depictions, see, for example, London B 668, St Petersburg B 1818, Louvre E 817; for textual evidence, "The cranes escape the winter time and the rains unceasing and clamorously wing their way to streaming Okeanos, bringing the Pygmaioi men bloodshed and destruction" *(Homer, Iliad 3.3; translation R. Lattimore).*

23 See *ThesCRA* I, 2, p. 67, "La documentation archéozoologique."

24 See Williams and Schaus 2001.

25 *ThesCRA* I, 77–9.

26 Most of the ancient textual references to all major and minor gods of Magna Graecia, and the currently available published zooarchaeological evidence, can be reviewed in *ThesCRA* I, 57–95.

27 Cattle, sheep, goat, and pigs occur in all ten locales studied.

28 Kadletz 1975, 10–14.

29 Philostr. 1, 6, 5, 303, "an offering to the goddess of a live hare"; also, Plat. com. *PCG* VII 188, 8–10, states that "sixteen thrushes in honey and a dozen cakes in the form of hares" were offered to Aphrodite Koutrophos.

30 At Miletos, hare, red and fallow deer, and pigeon remains were found; at Tamassos in Cyprus the remains of horse, dogs, fallow deer, hare, and birds were identified.

31 *ThesCRA* I, p. 84.

32 Paus. 8.22.3.

33 *ThesCRA* I, 71, p. 94.

34 Forstenpointner and Hofer 1997, 683–90.

35 See Schaus, chapter 1, p. 9, note 43.

36 See Sturgeon, chapter 3, pp. 39–40.

37 *ThesCRA* I, 279.

38 Hesiod, Apollodorus, and Diodorus all state that Eileithyia was the daughter of Hera and Zeus.

39 Johnston 1991, 246.

40 Hesiod states that Eileithyia is the daughter of Hera and Zeus, and that Hekate was the sister of Leto, mother of the divine twins Apollo and Artemis. Therefore, Eileithyia and Artemis are half-sisters through their common father Zeus, and Hekate is their aunt.

41 Paus. 2.22.7.

42 Socrates Argivus, *ap.* Plut., *Mor.*, 277b.

43 There are several partial inscriptions which suggest that the Sanctuary was dedicated to Eileithyia; see Schaus, chapter 2, p. 14, note 12.

44 For worked bone pieces, see Schaus, chapter 7, pp. 168–71.

45 Similarly holed bovid astragali were found in the Demeter sanctuary in Mytilene, for example; see Ruscillo 2013. Russell (2012, 133–7) gives a comprehensive overview of astragali in game and ritual contexts.

46 See Gilmour 1997 for a thorough discussion.

47 A number of complete, but mostly broken and discarded, bone tools are catalogued by Schaus; see chapter 7, pp. 170–1.

48 See Bartosiewicz, Van Neer, and Lentacker 1997 for pathologies and osteological identifications of draught cattle.

49 See Ruscillo 2013 for further discussion.

50 See Schaus, chapter 1, p. 14 (also pp. 33–4), for a discussion of the Sanctuary dedication based on small finds in this volume.

Chapter 14: Human Skeletal Remains

1 Developmental stage Rc according to Moorees, Fanning, and Hunt 1963b, fig. 5.

2 Holman and Jones 1998, fig. 5.

3 Atlas unfused at posterior midline synchondrosis; axis and all other recovered vertebrae fused at posterior midline synchondroses but unfused at neurocentral synchondroses. See Buikstra and Ubelaker 1994, fig. 20; Ogden 1984, 171; Stewart 1979, 139.

4 Ortner and Putschar 1981, 129–38; Roberts and Manchester 1995, 5–6.

5 Aufderheide and Rodríguez-Martín 1998, 349–50; Stuart-Macadam 1989a, 187–8.

6 Stuart-Macadam 1989a, 187–8.

7 Banting 1993, table 1; Hillson 1996, 274–5; Katz et al. 1982, 266; Kerr 1990, 857; Lynch and Beighton 1994, 233–4, 237–8.

8 An in-depth discussion of the differential diagnosis was presented in conference (Garvie-Lok 2006) and will be published elsewhere.

9 Roberts and Manchester 1995, 167–73; see also Ortner and Putschar 1981, 251–63.

10 Ortner and Putschar 1981, 251–7.

11 Aufderheide and Rodríguez-Martín 1998, 348–50; Roberts and Manchester 1995, 167–73; Stuart-Macadam 1987a; 1987b; 1989b, 212–19; Walker et al. 2009.

12 Fain 2005, 125–6; McDowell 2000, 604–13, 624–6.

13 WHO 1999, 6–7.

14 Stuart-Macadam 1989b, 219.

15 Fain 2005, 125–6; McDowell 2000, 604–13, 624–6.

16 Ortner and Putschar 1981, 271–3.

17 McDowell 2000, 624; WHO 1999, 6, table 4.

18 Ortner and Ericksen 1997; Ortner et al. 1999, 2001.

19 Ortner et al. 1999, fig. 9; Ortner et al. 2001, 344, tables 2 and 5, fig. 3.

20 Ortner and Ericksen 1997, 217, fig. 8; Ortner et al. 1999, fig. 5.

21 Ortner and Ericksen 1997, 214; Ortner et al. 1999, 322; 2001, 344.
22 Ortner et al. 2001, 348.
23 Banting 2001, 991, 994; Katz et al. 1982, 270; Kerr 1990, 857–8; Thomson 2004, 91; Watt et al. 1997a, 614; 1997b, 815–16; Whittaker and Molleson 1996, 59.
24 Garvie-Lok 2006.
25 Ortner, Kimmerle, and Diez 1999, 325; Walker et al. 2009.
26 Fain 2005, 126; McDowell 2000, 624; Pimentel 2003, 331; WHO 1999, tables 3 and 4; see also case studies reported by Cohen and Paeglow (2001) and Weinstein, Babyn, and Zlotkin (2001).
27 Stuart-Macadam 1989b, 219.
28 Developmental stage Cr_c according to Moorees, Fanning, and Hunt (1963a, figs. 5 and 6); see also Harris and McKee (1990, tables 2 and 3).
29 Hurme 1949, table 1; Jaswal 1983, table 6; Stewart 1979, table 11.
30 Williams et al. 2002.
31 Rife 2012, 169–71.
32 Methods and terminology follow those outlined by Fazekas and Kósa (1978, 43–53).
33 Fazekas and Kósa 1978, 124–5, 152–3, 226, 263, 294.
34 Stage C_{oc} according to Moorees, Fanning, and Hunt (1963b, figs. 4 and 5). Those authors depict the age range for this developmental stage as ending roughly one month after birth. Because their data set covers only development after birth, no age for the commencement of the stage is provided.
35 Smith and Avishai 2005.
36 Rife 2012.
37 Watts 1989, 378–9.
38 Rife 2012, 209.
39 WHO 1999, table G.
40 Sauberlich 1997, 1–2.
41 Pimentel 2003, 29–30; Sauberlich 1997, 1–16.
42 WHO 1999, 1–4.
43 Akikusa, Garrick, and Nash 2003; Cohen and Paeglow 2001; Fain 2005, 124; McDowell 2000, 626; Pimentel 2003, 328; Weinstein, Babyn, and Zlotkin 2001; WHO 1999, 20–1.
44 Hampl, Taylor, and Johnson 2004, 871.
45 Hampl, Taylor, and Johnson 2004, 874; Richardson, Ball, and Rosenfeld 2002, 293; WHO 1999, 29–40.
46 WHO 1999, table I.
47 McDowell 2000, 599.
48 Roberts and Manchester 1995, 171–3.
49 Rajakumar 2001, 78.
50 E.g., Bourbou 2003; Buckley 2000; Janssens et al. 1993; Maat 2004; Ortner and Ericksen 1997; Ortner, Kimmerle, and Diez 1999; Ortner et al. 2001; see, however, Melikian and Waldron 2003.
51 Bourbou 2003, 306.

WORKS CITED

Abadie-Reynal, C. 1995. "Céramique et romanisation de la Grèce: Argos aux Ier s. av. et ap. J.-C." In *Hellenistic and Roman Pottery in the Eastern Mediterranean-Advances in Scientific Studies*, edited by H. Meyza and J. Mlynarcyk, 1–10. Warsaw: Research Center for Mediterranean Archaeology, Polish Academy of Sciences.

Adam, S. 1966. *The Technique of Greek Sculpture in the Archaic and Classical Periods. BSA* supp. 3. London: Thames and Hudson.

Adam-Veleni, P., E. Poulaki, and K. Tzanavari. 2003. *Ancient Country Houses on Modern Roads: Central Macedonia.* Athens: Archaeological Receipts Fund.

Agora XXVI = Kroll, J.H. *The Athenian Agora.* Vol. XXVI: *The Greek Coins.* Princeton: American School of Classical Studies at Athens, 1993.

Agrinion = Thompson, M. *The Agrinion Hoard.* Numismatic Notes and Monographs 159. New York: American Numismatic Society, 1968.

Akikusa, J.D., D. Garrick, and M.C. Nash. 2003. "Scurvy: Forgotten but Not Gone." *Journal of Paediatrics and Child Health* 39: 75–7.

Albersmeier, S. 2005. *Bedazzled: 5000 Years of Jewelry: The Walters Art Museum.* London: D. Giles.

Alcock, S.E. 1994. "Minding the Gap in Hellenistic and Roman Greece." In *Placing the Gods: Sanctuaries and Sacred Space in Ancient Greece*, edited by S.E. Alcock and R. Osborne, 247–61. New York: Oxford University Press.

Alcock, S.E., A.M. Berlin, A.B. Harrison, S. Heath, N. Spencer, and D.L. Stone. 2005. "Pylos Regional Archaeological Project, Part VII: Historical Messenia, Geometric through Late Roman." *Hesperia* 74: 147–210.

Alexander, C. 1928. *Jewelry: The Art of the Goldsmith in Classical Times.* New York: Metropolitan Museum of Art.

Alexandrescu Vianu, M. 1990. "Die Steinskulptur von Histria." In *Histria: Eine Griechenstadt an der rumänischen Schwarzmeerküste*, edited by P. Alexandrescu and W. Schuller. *Xenia: Konstanzer althistorischer Vorträge und Forschungen* 25, 179–232. Konstanz: Universitätsverlag Konstanz.

Alexandrescu Vianu, M., M. Pentia, L. Nedelcu, N. Herz, and Z. Sharp. 2000. "Imported Antique Marble in Dobroudja." In *Paria Lithos: Parian Quarries, Marble and Workshops of Sculpture: Conference 1997*, edited by D.U. Schilardi and D. Katsonopoulou, 427–35. Athens: D.U. Schilardi.

Alford, H.L. 1978. "The Seated Figure in Archaic Greek Sculpture." PhD diss., University of California, Los Angeles.

Alroth, B. 1987. "Visiting Gods – Who and Why." In *Gifts to the Gods: Proceedings of the Uppsala Symposium 1985*, edited by T. Linders and G. Nordquist. *Boreas* supp. 15: 9–20. Uppsala: Academia Upsaliensis.

Amandry, P. 1953. *Collection Hélène Stathatos: Les bijoux antiques.* Strasbourg: Institut d'Archéologie de l'Université de Strasbourg.

– 1963. *Collection Hélène Stathatos: Les objets antiques et byzantins.* Strasbourg : Institut d'Archéologie de l'Université de Strasbourg.

– 1971. "Collection Paul Canellopoulos (I)." *BCH* 55: 585–626.

– 1981. *L'antre corycien I. BCH* supp. 7. Athènes: École Française d'Athènes; Paris: Boccard.

– 1984. "Os et coquilles." In *L'antre corycien* II. *BCH* supp. 9. Paris: Diffusion de Boccard.

Anderson-Stojanovich, V.R. 1996. "The University of Chicago Excavations in the Rachi Settlement at Isthmia, 1989." *Hesperia* 65: 57–98.

– 1997. "A Third-Century BC Deposit from the South Slope Cistern in the Rachi Settlement at Isthmia." In *Δ 'Επιστημονική Συνάντηση για την Ελληνιστική Κεραμική: Χρονολογικά Προβλήματα, Κλειστά Σύνολο-Εργαστήρια,* edited by S. Drougou et al. (1994), 13–19. Athens: Εφορεία Προϊστορικών και Κλασικών Αρχαιοτήτων.

– 2000. "Corinthian West Slope Pottery from Isthmia." In *Ε' Επιστημονική Συνάντηση για την Ελληνιστική Κεραμική* (1997), 381–5. Athens: Εφορεία Προϊστορικών και Κλασικών Αρχαιοτήτων.

– 2004. "Dinner at the Isthmus. Hellenistic Cooking Ware from the Rachi Settlement at Isthmia." In *ΣΤ' Επιστημονική Συνάντηση για την Ελληνιστική Κεραμική* (2000), 623–30. Athens: Εκδοση του Ταμείου Αρχαιλογικών Πόρων και Απαλλοτριώσεων.

Anderson-Stojanovich, V.R., and D. Reese. 1993. "A Well in the Rachi Settlement at Isthmia." *Hesperia* 62: 257–302.

Andreiomenou, A. 1997. "Observations on the Bronze Jewelry from the Cemetery of Akraiphia (820–480 BC)." In *Recent Developments in the History and Archaeology of Central Greece*, edited by J. Bintliff, 81–134. *BAR-IS* 666.

Andronicos, M. 1984. *Vergina: The Royal Tombs and the Ancient City.* Athens: Ekdotike Athenon.

Angus, N.S., G.T. Brown, and H.F. Cleere. 1962. "The Iron Nails from the Roman Legionary Fortress at Inchtuthil, Perthshire." *Journal of the Iron and Steel Institute* 200: 956–68.

Archäologische Gesellschaft zu Berlin. 1914. "Sitzung vom 9. Juni 1914." *AA*: 99–107.

Ashmead, A. 1977–8. "Greek Cats: Exotic Pets Kept by Rich Youths in Fifth Century B.C. Athens, As Portrayed on Greek Vases." *Expedition* 20(3): 38–47.

– 1994. "Etruscan Domesticated Cats: Classical Conformists or Etruscan Originals?" In *Murlo and the Etruscans: Art and Society in Ancient Etruria*, edited by R.D. De Puma and J.P. Small, 144–64. Madison: University of Wisconsin Press.

Åström, P., and I. Nicolaou. 1980. "Lead Sling Bullets from Hala Sultan Tekke." *OpAth* 13: 29–33.

Attema, P. 2008. "Conflict of Coexistence? Remarks on Indigenous Settlement and Greek Colonization in the Foothills and Hinterland of the Sibaritide (Northern Calabria, Italy)." In *Meetings of Cultures in the Black Sea Region. Between Conflict and Coexistence*, edited by P. G. Bilde and J.H. Petersen, 67–99. Black Sea Studies 8. Aarhus: Aarhus University Press.

Aufderheide, A.C., and C. Rodríguez-Martín. 1998. *The Cambridge Encyclopedia of Human Palaeopathology.* Cambridge: Cambridge University Press.

Ault, B.A. 2005. *Halieis.* Vol. 2, *The Houses: The Organization and Use of Domestic Space.* Bloomington: Indiana University Press.

Ault, B.A., and L. Nevett. 1999. "Digging Houses: Archaeologies of Classical and Hellenistic Greek Domestic Assemblages." In *The Archaeology of Household Activities: Dwelling in the Past,* edited by P. Allison, 57–77. New York: Routledge.

Aurenhammer, M. 1990. *Forschungen in Ephesos, Österreichischen archäologischen Institut in Wien*, X, i: *Die Skulpturen von Ephesos, Idealplastik* I. Vienna: Verlag der Österreichischen Akademie der Wissenschaften.

Baatz, D. 1994. "Die Handmühlen." In *Das Wrack: der antike Schiffsfund von Madia*, edited by G. Hellenkemper Salies, H.-H. von Prittwitz, and G. and G. Bauchhenss, 97–103. Köln: Rheinland-Verlag.

Bailey, D.M. 1973. *Greek and Roman Lamps*. London: British Museum Press.

– 1975. *A Catalogue of the Lamps in the British Museum* I: *Greek, Hellenistic and Early Roman Pottery Lamps*. London: British Museum Press.

Bailey, D.M., and E.H. Williams. *Greek and Roman Terracotta Lamps from Mytilene*. Forthcoming.

Baitinger, H. 2001. *OlForsch* XXIX: *Die Angriffswaffen aus Olympia*. Berlin: Walter de Gruyter.

Baitinger, H., and T. Völling. 2007. *OlForsch* XXXII: *Werkzeug und Gerät aus Olympia*. Deutsches Archäologisches Institut. Berlin: Walter de Gruyter.

Banting, D.W. 1993. "Diagnosis and Prediction of Root Caries." *Advances in Dental Research* 7: 80–6.

– 2001. "The Diagnosis of Root Caries." *Journal of Dental Education* 65: 991–6.

Barag, D. 1970. "Mesopotamian Core-Formed Glass Vessels (1500–500 B.C.)." In *Glass and Glassmaking in Ancient Mesopotamia*, edited by A.L. Oppenheim, R.H. Brill, D. Barag, and A. von Saldern, 131–99. Corning: Corning Museum of Glass; London and Toronto: Associated University Presses.

Barber, E.J.W. 1991. *Prehistoric Textiles: The Development of Cloth in the Neolithic and Bronze Ages with Special Reference to the Aegean*. Princeton: Princeton University Press.

– 1992. "The Peplos of Athena." In *Goddess and Polis: The Panathenaic Festival in Ancient Athens*, edited by J. Neils, 103–17. Princeton: Princeton University Press.

– 1994. *Women's Work: The First 20,000 Years: Women, Cloth, and Society in Early Times.* New York: Norton.

Bartosiewicz, L., W. Van Neer, and A. Lentacker. 1997. *Draught Cattle: Their Osteological Identification and History*. Koninklijk Museum voor Midden-Afrika, Annalen, Zoologische Wetenschappen, vol. 281.

Baur, P.V.C. 1902. *Eileithyia*. Columbia: University of Missouri.

Beazley, J.D. 1932. "Little-Master Cups." *JHS* 52: 167–204.

BCD Pel. = Walker, A., and BCD. *Coins of Peloponnesos:*

The BCD Collection. Zurich: LHS Numismatics, auction sale 96, 8–9 May 2006.

Beck, H. 1981. Reprint. *Classification and Nomenclature of Beads and Pendants*. York, PA: George Shumway. Original edition 1973.

Beer, C. 1987. "Comparative Votive Religion: The Evidence of Children in Cyprus, Greece and Etruria." In *Gifts to the Gods: Proceedings of the Uppsala Symposium 1985*, edited by T. Linders and G. Nordquist, 21–9. Boreas supp. 15.

– 1994. *Temple-Boys: A Study of Cypriote Votive Sculpture*. Part 1: *Catalogue*. *SIMA* 113. Jonsered.

Beestman-Kruyshaar, C. 2003. "Survey of the Distribution of the Types of Vessels in the Six Houses." In *Housing in New Halos: A Hellenistic Town in Thessaly, Greece*, edited by H. Reinder Reinders and W. Prummel, 284–94. Exton, PA: A.A. Balkema Publishers.

Bélis, A. 1984. "Fragments d'auloi." *L'antre corycien II*. *BCH* supp. 9, 176–81. Athens: École Française d'Athènes; Paris: Boccard.

Bennett, M., and A. Paul. 2002. *Magna Graecia: Greek Art from Southern Italy and Sicily*. New York and Manchester: Hudson Hills Press.

Benson, C. 1995a. "Gold Ring with Athena." In *Pandora: Women in Classical Greece*, edited by E. Reeder, 177–8. Princeton: Princeton University Press.

– 1995b. "Gold Boat Earring." In *Pandora: Women in Classical Greece*, edited by E. Reeder, 180. Princeton: Princeton University Press.

Bérard, C., et al. 1989. *A City of Images: Iconography and Society in Ancient Greece*. Translated by D. Lyons. Princeton: Princeton University Press.

Bergman, S.M., and A. Oliver, Jr. 1980. *Ancient and Islamic Glass in the Carnegie Museum of Natural History, Pittsburgh*. Pittsburgh: Carnegie Institute.

Berlin, A. 2002. "Ilion before Alexander: A Fourth Century B.C. Ritual Deposit." *Studia Troica* 12: 131–65.

– 2006. *Gamla I: The Pottery of the Second Temple Period*. IAA Reports 29. Jerusalem: Israel Antiquities Authority.

Bernheimer, G.N. 2001. *Glories of Ancient Greece: Vases and Jewelry from the Borowski Collection*. Jerusalem: Bible Lands Museum.

Bertucchi, G. 1992. *Les amphores et le vin de Marseille, VIe s. avant J.-C.–IIe s. après J.-C. Revue archéologique de Narbonnaise* supp. 25. Paris: Editions de CNRS.

Bevan, E. 1986. *Representation of Animals in Sanctuaries of Artemis and Other Olympian Deities*. 2 vols. *BAR-IS* 315.

Bianchi Bandinelli, R. 1970. *Rome: The Center of Power*. New York: Thames and Hudson.

Bicknell, P. "Turtle Tattle." *Numismatic Chronicle* 150: 223–5.

Bieber, M. 1961. *The Sculpture of the Hellenistic Age*. 2nd ed. New York: Columbia University Press.

Bielefeld, E. 1962. "Ein altanatolisches Motiv bei Kanachos?" *IstMitt* 12: 18–43.

Biesantz, H. 1965. *Die thessalischen Grabreliefs: Studien zur nordgriechischen Kunst*. Mainz: Philipp von Zabern.

Birge, D.E., L.H. Kraynak, and S.G. Miller. 1992. *Excavations at Nemea*. Vol. 1: *Topographical and Architectural Studies: The Sacred Square, the Xenon, and the Bath*. Berkeley: University of California Press.

Bishop, M., and J.C. Coulston. 1993. *Roman Military Equipment from the Punic Wars to the Fall of Rome*. London: Batsford.

Blackman, D. 1998. "Archaeology in Greece 1997–98." *AR* 1997–8: 1–128.

Blegen, C.W. 1939. "Prosymna: Remains of Post-Mycenaean Date." *AJA* 43: 410–44.

– 1963. *Troy and the Trojans*. London: Thames and Hudson.

Blegen, C.W., H. Palmer, and R.S. Young. 1964. *Corinth* XIII*: The North Cemetery*. Princeton: American School of Classical Studies at Athens.

Blegen, E.P. 1937. "News Items from Athens." *AJA* 41: 333–8.

Blinkenberg, Chr. 1926. *Fibules grecques et orientales*. Copenhagen: A.F. Host and Son.

– 1931. *Lindos: Fouilles de l'acropole, 1902–1914*. Vol. 1: *Les petites objets*. Texte et planches. Berlin: Walter de Gruyter.

– 1941. *Lindos. Fouilles de l'acropole, 1902–1914*. Vol. 2: *Inscriptions*. Berlin: Walter de Gruyter; Copenhagen: G.E.C. Gad.

Blitzer, H. 1990. "ΚΟΡΩΝΕΪΚΑ: Storage-Jar Production and Trade in the Traditional Aegean." *Hesperia* 59: 675–711.

Blümel, C. 1963. *Die archaisch griechischen Skulpturen der Staatlichen Museen zu Berlin*. Abhandlungen der Deutschen Akademie der Wissenschaften zu Berlin. Berlin.

Blundell, S. 2001. *Women in Ancient Greece*. Cambridge, MA: Harvard University Press. Original edition 1995.

BMC: The numbering in the BMC references is not continuous but restarts for each issuing authority. Thus a reference of BMC 10 nos. 20–3 for a coin of Mantineia refers to numbers 20 through 23 on the list of Mantineian coins in the volume BMC 10.

BMC 2 = Poole, R.S., ed. *Catalogue of Greek Coins in the British Museum: Sicily*. London: Trustees of the British Museum, 1876.

BMC 7 = Gardner, P. *Catalogue of Greek Coins in the British Museum: Thessaly to Aetolia*. London: Trustees of the British Museum, 1883.

BMC 8 = Head, B.V. *Catalogue of Greek Coins in the British

Museum: Central Greece. London: Trustees of the British Museum, 1884.

BMC 10 = Gardner, P. *Catalogue of Greek Coins in the British Museum. Peloponnesus (Excepting Corinth)*. London: Trustees of the British Museum, 1887.

BMC 11 = Head, B.V. *Catalogue of Greek Coins in the British Museum: Attica, Megaris, Aegina*. London: Trustees of the British Museum, 1888.

BMC 12 = Head, B.V. *Catalogue of Greek Coins in the British Museum: Corinth, Colonies of Corinth, etc*. London: Trustees of the British Museum, 1889.

Boardman, J. 1963. "Artemis Orthia and Chronology." *BSA* 58: 1–7.

– 1967. *Excavations in Chios: 1952–1955. Greek Emporio*. *BSA* supp. 6. London: British School of Archaeology at Athens.

– 1975. *Intaglios and Rings*. London: Thames and Hudson.

– 1989. *Athenian Red Figure Vases: The Classical Period*. London: Thames and Hudson.

– 1991. *Greek Sculpture: The Archaic Period. A Handbook*. London: Thames and Hudson.

– 1996. "The Archaeology of Jewelry." In *Ancient Jewelry and Archaeology*, edited by A. Calinescu, 3–13. Bloomington and Indianapolis: Indiana University Press.

– 2001. Reprint. *Greek Gems and Finger Rings*. London: Thames and Hudson. Original edition 1970.

Boardman, J., and J. Hayes. 1966. *Excavations at Tocra 1963–1965: The Archaic Deposits II and Later Deposits*. *BSA* supp. vol. 10. London: British School of Archaeology at Athens.

Boardman, J., and M.L. Vollenweider. 1978. *Catalogue of the Engraved Gems and Finger Rings in the Ashmolean Museum*. I: *Greek and Etruscan*. Oxford: Oxford University Press.

Boehringer, E. 1959. *Neue deutsche Ausgrabungen im Mittelmeergebiet und im vorderen Orient*. Deutsches Archäologisches Institut. Berlin: Gebr. Mann.

Boggess, E.M. 1970. "A Hellenistic Pithos from Corinth." *Hesperia* 39: 73–8.

– 1972. "The Development of the Attic Pithos." PhD diss., Bryn Mawr College. Ann Arbor: University Microfilms.

Bol, P.C. 1978. *OlForsch* IX: *Grossplastik aus Bronze in Olympia*. Deutsches Archäologisches Institut. Berlin: Walter de Gruyter.

– 1989. *OlForsch* XVII: *Argivische Schilde*. Deutsches Archäologisches Institut. Berlin, New York: Walter de Gruyter.

Bon, A.M., and A. Bon. 1957. *Études thasiennes* IV: *Les timbres amphoriques de Thasos*. Paris: École Française d'Athènes.

Bonias, Z. 1993. "Γλυπτά από τις Αιγιές Λακωνίας." In *Sculpture from Arcadia and Laconia: Proceedings of an International Conference Held at the American School of Classical Studies at Athens, April 1992*, edited by O. Palagia and W. Coulson, 177–87. Oxford: Oxbow Books.

Bookidis, N. 1970. "Archaic Sculptures from Corinth (From the Notes of Edward Capps, Jr.)." *Hesperia* 39: 313–25.

– 1972. "The Sanctuary of Demeter and Kore on Acrocorinth. Preliminary Report IV: 1969–1970. *Hesperia* 41: 283–317.

– 1988. "Classicism in Clay." In *Acts of the XII International Congress of Classical Archaeology, 1983*, III, 18–21. Athens.

– 1997. "Archaic Corinthian Sculpture: A Summary." In *Corinto e l'Occidente: Atti del trentaquattresimo convegno di studi sulla Magna Grecia, Taranto, 7–11 ottobre 1994*, edited by A. Stazio and S. Ceccoli, 231–56. Taranto: Istituto per la Storia e l'Archeologia della Magna Grecia.

– 2003 (1996). "The Sanctuaries of Corinth." In *Corinth* XX: *The Centenary: 1896–1996*, edited by C.K. Williams and N. Bookidis, 247–59. Princeton: American School of Classical Studies at Athens.

Bookidis, N., and J.E. Fisher. 1972. "The Sanctuary of Demeter and Kore on Acrocorinth: Preliminary Report IV: 1969–1970." *Hesperia* 41: 283–331.

– 1974. "The Sanctuary of Demeter and Kore on Acrocorinth: Preliminary Report V: 1971–1973." *Hesperia* 43: 267–307.

Bookidis, N., J. Hansen, L. Snyder, and P. Goldberg. 1999. "Dining in the Sanctuary of Demeter and Kore at Corinth." *Hesperia* 68: 1–54.

Bookidis, N., and R.S. Stroud. 1997. *Corinth* XVIII, iii: *The Sanctuary of Demeter and Kore, Topography and Architecture*. Princeton: American School of Classical Studies at Athens.

Bordenache Battaglia, G. 1969. *Sculture greche e romane del Museo Nazionale di Antichità di Bucarest*, 1. Bucharest: Casa editrice dell'Accademia.

Bottini, A., ed. 1993. *Armi: Gli strumenti della guerra in Lucania*. Bari: Edipuglia.

Boulter, C. 1953. "Pottery of the Mid-Fifth Century from a Well in the Athenian Agora." *Hesperia* 22: 59–115.

Bourbou, C. 2003. "Health Patterns of Proto-Byzantine Populations (6th–7th centuries AD) in South Greece: The Cases of Eleutherna (Crete) and Messene (Peloponnese)." *International Journal of Osteoarchaeology* 13: 303–13.

Bourguet, É. 1932. *Fouilles de Delphes*. III: *Épigraphie*. Fasc. V: *Les comptes du IVe siècle*. École Française d'Athènes. Paris: Éditions de Boccard.

Branigan, K. 1992. "Metalwork and Metallurgical Debris." In L.H. Sackett et al., *Knossos from Greek City to Roman Colony: Excavations at the Unexplored Mansion II*,

363–78. British School of Archaeology at Athens. Supp. vol. 21. Oxford: Thames and Hudson.

Braund, D. 1994 "The Luxuries of Athenian Democracy." *GR* 41: 41–8.

Brinkmann, V. 2004. *Bunte Götter: Die Polychromie der archaischen und frühklassischen Skulptur.* Munich: Staatliche Antikensammlungen und Glyptothek.

Brizio, E. 1899. "Il sepolcreto gallico de Montefortino presso Arcevia." *MonAnt* 9: 617–791.

Bromberg, A.R. 1990. *Gold of Greece: Jewelry and Ornaments from the Benaki Museum.* Dallas: Dallas Museum of Art.

Broneer, O. 1930. *Corinth* IV, ii: *Terracotta Lamps.* Cambridge, MA: Harvard University Press.

– 1935. "Excavations on the North Slope of the Acropolis in Athens, 1933–4." *Hesperia* 4: 109–88.

– 1953. "Isthmia Excavations, 1952." *Hesperia* 22: 182–95.

– 1954. *Corinth* I, iv: *The South Stoa and Its Roman Successors.* Princeton: American School of Classical Studies at Athens.

– 1967. Review of *Samothrace* IV, ii: *The Altar Court* by Karl Lehmann and Denys Spittle. Bollingen Series. New York: Pantheon Books in *AJA* 71: 96–8.

– 1971. *Isthmia* I: *Temple of Poseidon.* Princeton: American School of Classical Studies at Athens.

– 1977. *Isthmia* III: *Terracotta Lamps.* Princeton: American School of Classical Studies at Athens.

Brouskari, M. 1974. *The Acropolis Museum.* Athens: Commercial Bank of Greece.

Brown, W.L. 1960. *The Etruscan Lion.* Oxford: Clarendon Press.

Brulotte, E.L. 1994. "The Placement of Votive Offerings and Dedications in the Peloponnesian Sanctuaries of Artemis." PhD diss., University of Minnesota.

Bruneau, P. 1965. *Les lampes. Exploration archéologique de Délos.* Fasc. 26. Écoles Française d'Athènes. Paris: E. de Boccard.

– 1968. "Contribution à l'histoire urbaine de Délos à l'époque hellénistique et à l'époque impériale." *BCH* 92: 633–709.

– 1970. "Tombes d'Argos." *BCH* 94: 437–531.

Buckley, H.R. 2000. "Subadult Health and Disease in Prehistoric Tonga, Polynesia." *AJPA* 118: 481–505.

Buikstra, J.E., and D.H. Ubelaker, eds. 1994. *Standards for Data Collection from Human Skeletal Remains.* Arkansas Archaeological Survey Research Series 44. Fayetteville: Arkansas Archaeological Survey.

Burford, A. 1966. "Notes on the Epidaurian Building Inscriptions." *BSA* 61: 254–334.

Burn, L., and R. Higgins. 2001. *Catalogue of Greek Terracottas in the British Museum* III. London: British Museum.

Burnier Y., and S. Hijmans. 2003. " Loomweights." In *Housing in New Halos: A Hellenistic Town in Thessaly, Greece,* edited by H.R. Reinders and W. Prummel, 118–23. Lisse: A.A. Balkema Publishers.

Bursian, C. 1868–72. *Geographie von Griechenland.* Vol. 2: *Peloponnesos und Inseln.* Leipzig.

Burstein, S.M. 1985. *The Hellenistic Age from the Battle of Ipsos to the Death of Kleopatra VII.* Translated Documents of Greece and Rome, vol. 3. Cambridge: Cambridge University Press.

Bussiere, J. 2007. *Lampes antiques d'Algerie.* Montangac: Editions Morgoil.

Cahill, N. 2002. *Household and City Organization at Olynthus.* New Haven: Yale University Press.

Calciati, R. 1986. *Corpus Nummorum Siculorum: La monetazione di bronzo.* Vol. 2. Milan: Edizione G.M.

Cambitoglou, A., O.T. Jones, G. Joyner, and B. McLoughlin. 2001. "The Metal Objects." In *Torone* I: *The Excavations of 1975, 1976, and 1978,* edited by A. Cambitoglou, J.K. Papadopoulos, and O. Tudor Jones, 721–63. Text I and II and Illustrations. ΒΙΒΛΙΟΘΗΚΗ ΤΗΣ ΕΝ ΑΘΗΝΑΙΣ ΑΡΧΑΙΟΛΟΓΙΚΗΣ ΕΤΑΙΡΕΙΑΣ ΑΡ. 206–8. Athens: Η εν Αθήναις Αρχαιολογική Εταιρεία.

Cambitoglou, A., J.K. Papadopoulos, and O.T. Jones, eds. 2001. *Torone* I: *The Excavations of 1975, 1976, and 1978.* Text I and II and Illustrations. ΒΙΒΛΙΟΘΗΚΗ ΤΗΣ ΕΝ ΑΘΗΝΑΙΣ ΑΡΧΑΙΟΛΟΓΙΚΗΣ ΕΤΑΙΡΕΙΑΣ, ΑΡ. 206–8. Athens: Η εν Αθήναις Αρχαιολογική Εταιρεία.

Campbell, S.D. 1997. "The Cistercian Monastery of Zaraka." *EchCl* n.s. 16.1: 177–96.

Caner, E. 1983. *Fibeln in Anatolia I. Prähistorische Bronzefunde.* XIV.8. Munich: C.H. Beck.

Carapanos, C. 1878. *Dodone et ses ruines.* Paris: Librarie Hachette.

Carpenter, T.H. 1991. *Art and Myth in Ancient Greece.* London: Thames and Hudson.

Carroll, D.L. 1983. "Warping the Greek Loom: A Second Method." *AJA* 87: 96–8.

Carter, J.C. 1998. *The Chora of Metaponto: The Necropoleis.* Vol. 2. Institute of Classical Archaeology. Austin: University of Texas Press.

Carter, J.C., and A. Parmly Toxey. 1998. "Alabastra." In J.C. Carter, *The Chora of Metaponto. The Necropoleis.* Vol. 2, 757–69. Institute of Classical Archaeology. Austin: University of Texas Press.

Caskey, L.D. 1939. "Greek Marble Vases." *BMFA* 37: 74–80.

Casson, S. 1923–4. "Excavations in Macedonia – II." *BSA* 26: 1–29.

Castor, A.Q. 1999. "*Enotia*: The Contexts of Greek Earrings, Tenth to Third Century B.C." PhD diss., Bryn Mawr College.

– 2006. "Protecting Athena's Children: Amulets in Classical Athens." In *Proceedings of the XVIth International Congress of Classical Archaeology, Boston, August 23–26, 2003*, edited by C. Mattusch, A. Donohue, and A. Brauer, 625–27. Oxford: Oxbow Publishers.

Catling, H., and M. Robertson. 1966. "Antique Vases (Ashmolean Museum, Oxford)." *BurlMag* 108: 57, 196–201.

Catling, R.W.V. 1994. "A Fragment of an Archaic Temple Model from Artemis Orthia, Sparta." *BSA* 89: 269–75.

Caubet, A. 1976. "La collection R. Hamilton Lang au Musée du Louvre: Antiquités de Pyla." *RDAC*: 168–77.

Cavanagh, W., J. Crouwel, R.W.V. Catling, and G. Shipley. 1996. *Continuity and Change in a Greek Rural Landscape: The Laconian Survey.* Vol. 2: *Archaeological Data. BSA* supp. vol. 27. London: British School at Athens.

Caven, B. 1990. *Dionysius I, War-Lord of Sicily*. New Haven and London: Yale University Press.

Cavicchioli, S. 2002. *The Tale of Cupid and Psyche: An Illustrated History*. New York: George Braziller.

Cevizoğlu, H. 2007. "Basins and High Stands of the Classical Period at Klazomenai: A Preliminary Report." *IstMitt* 57: 235–47.

Chadour-Sampson, B. 1997. *Antike Fingerringe: Die Sammlung Alain Ollivier/Ancient Finger Rings: The Alain Ollivier Collection.* Munich: Prähistorische Staatssammlung München Museum für Vor- und Frühgeschichte; Norwich: Balding and Mansell.

Chamoux, F. 1955. *Fouilles de Delphes* V. Paris: E. de Boccard.

Chqonia, A. 1996. "Colchian Jewelry from the Vani City Site." In *Ancient Jewelry and Archaeology*, edited by A. Calinescu, 45–50. Bloomington and Indianapolis: Indiana University Press.

Clairmont, C. 1993. *Classical Attic Tombstones.* Kilchberg, Switzerland: Akanthus.

Claridge, A. 1990. "Ancient Techniques of Making Joins in Marble Statuary." In *Marble: Art Historical and Scientific Perspectives on Ancient Sculpture*, edited by M. True and J. Podany, 135–62. Malibu: J. Paul Getty Museum.

Clark, L. 1983. "Notes on Small Textile Frames Pictured on Greek Vases." *AJA* 87: 91–6.

– 1984. "Small Textile Frames: An Addendum." *AJA* 88: 65.

Cleere, H.F. 1958. "Roman Domestic Ironwork, As Illustrated by the Brading, Isle of Wight, Villa." *Bulletin of the Institute of Archaeology* 1:55–74.

Clement, P.A. 1969. "Lambrou Cemetery." *ArchDelt* 24, B'1: 119.

Cohen, B. 1994. "From Bowman to Clubman: Herakles and Olympia." *Art Bulletin* 76: 695–715.

Cohen, S.A., and R.J. Paeglow. 2001. "Scurvy: An Unusual Cause of Anemia." *Journal of the American Board of Family Practice* 14: 314–16.

Coldstream, J.N. 1973. *Knossos: The Sanctuary of Demeter. BSA* supp. 8. London: British School of Archaeology at Athens.

Coldstream, J.N., L.J. Eiring, and G. Forster. 2001. *Knossos Pottery Handbook: Greek and Roman.* British School at Athens Studies 7. London.

Cole, P.J. 1981. "The Catapult Bolts in IG 2^2 1422." *Phoenix* 35: 216–19.

Cole, S.G. 2004. *Landscapes, Gender, and Ritual Space: The Ancient Greek Experience.* Berkeley: University of California Press.

Coleman, J.E. 1986. *Excavations at Pylos in Elis. Hesperia* supp. 21. Princeton: American School of Classical Studies.

Collignon, M. 1876. "Séance du 22 mai." *RA* 32: 291–8.

Comella, A. 2002. *I relievi votivi greci di periodo arcaico e classico: diffusione, ideologia, committenza.* Bari: Edipuglia.

Comfort, H. 1950. "A Hoard of Greek Jewelry." *AJA* 54: 121–6.

Comstock, M., and C. Vermeule. 1971. *Greek, Etruscan and Roman Bronzes in the Museum of Fine Arts, Boston.* Meriden, CT: Meriden Gravure Co.

Congdon, L.O.K. 1981. *Caryatid Mirrors of Ancient Greece: Technical, Stylistic and Historical Considerations of an Archaic and Early Classical Bronze Series.* Mainz: Philipp von Zabern.

Connelly, J.B. 2007. *Portrait of a Priestess: Women and Ritual in Ancient Greece*. Princeton: Princeton University Press.

Cook, J.M. 1953. "The Agamemnoneion." *BSA* 48: 30–68.

Corbett, P.E. 1962. "Late Corinthian Vases. Imitations of Attic, B. Red Figure." In *Perachora: The Sanctuaries of Hera Akraia and Limenia, Excavations of the British School of Archaeology at Athens, 1930–1933.* Vol. 2: *Pottery, Ivories, Scarabs, and Other Objects from the Votive Deposit of Hera Limenia*, edited by T.J. Dunbabin. Oxford: Clarendon Press.

Corinth = *Corinth: Results of Excavations Conducted by the American School of Classical Studies at Athens*. American School of Classical Studies at Athens.

Corinth II = R. Stillwell. *The Theatre*. Princeton: American School of Classical Studies at Athens, 1952.

Corinth VII, iii = G.R. Edwards. *Corinthian Hellenistic Pottery.* Princeton: American School of Classical Studies at Athens, 1975.

Corinth VII, iv = S. Herbert. *The Red-Figure Pottery*. Princeton: American School of Classical Studies at Athens, 1977.

Corinth VII, v = M.K. Risser. *Corinthian Conventionalizing*

Pottery. Princeton: American School of Classical Studies at Athens, 2001.

Corinth XII = G.R. Davidson. *The Minor Objects.* Princeton: American School of Classical Studies at Athens, 1952.

Corinth XIV = C.A. Roebuck. *The Asklepieion and Lerna.* Princeton: American School of Classical Studies at Athens, 1951.

Corinth XV, iii = A.N. Stillwell and J.L. Benson. *The Potters' Quarter: The Pottery*. With contributions by A.L. Boegehold and C.G. Boulter. Princeton: American School of Classical Studies at Athens, 1984.

Corinth XV, i = A.N. Stillwell. *The Potter's Quarter*. Princeton: American School of Classical Studies at Athens, 1948.

Corinth XVIII, ii = K.W. Slane. *The Sanctuary of Demeter and Kore: The Roman Pottery and Lamps*. Princeton: American School of Classical Studies at Athens, 1990.

Corinth XVIII, iii = N. Bookidis and R.S. Stroud. *The Sanctuary of Demeter and Kore: Topography and Architecture.* Princeton: American School of Classical Studies at Athens, 1997.

Corinth XVIII, iv = G.S. Merker. *The Sanctuary of Demeter and Kore: Terracotta Figurines of the Classical, Hellenistic, and Roman Periods.* Princeton: American School of Classical Studies at Athens, 2000.

Coste-Messelière, P. de la. 1957. *Fouilles de Delphes* IV: *Monuments figurès: Sculpture*, IV, *sculptures du Trésor des Athéniens.* Paris: E. de Boccard.

Coulston, J.C. 1985. "Roman Archery Equipment." In *The Production and Distribution of Roman Military Equipment: Proceedings of the Second Roman Military Equipment Research Seminar*, edited by M.C. Bishop, 220–366. *BAR-IS* 275. Oxford: BAR.

Crawford, M.H. 1974. *Roman Republican Coinage.* Cambridge: Cambridge University Press.

– 1985. *Coinage and Money under the Roman Republic: Italy and the Mediterranean Economy*. London: Methuen & Co.

Crouwel, J.H., M. Prent, S.M. Thorne, R.T.J. Cappers, S. Mulder, T. Coster, E. Langridge-Noti, and L. van Dijk-Schram. 2002. "Geraki: An Acropolis Site in Laconia: Preliminary Report on the Eighth Season." *Pharos* 10: 1–82.

Crouwel, J.H., M. Prent, E. Langridge-Noti, and J. van der Vin. 2003. "Geraki: An Acropolis Site in Laconia: Preliminary Report on the Ninth Season." *Pharos* 11: 1–34.

– 2004. "Geraki: An Acropolis Site in Laconia: Preliminary Report on the Tenth Season." *Pharos* 12: 1–30.

Crowfoot, G.M. 1940. "Of the Warp-Weighted Loom." *BSA* 37: 36–47.

Curtius, E. 1851. *Peloponnesos, eine historisch-geographische Beschreibung der Halbinsel.* Vol. 1. Gotha: J. Perthes.

Dakoronia, F., and L. Gounaropoulou. 1992. "Artemiskult auf einem neuen Weihrelief aus Achinos bei Lamia." *AM* 107: 217–27.

Dasen, V. 2003. "Les amulettes d'enfants dans le monde gréco-romain." *Latomus* 62: 275–89.

Daux, G. 1970. "Notes de lecture." *BCH* 94: 595–623.

Davidson, G.R. 1940. "A Mediaeval Glass-Factory at Corinth." *AJA* 44: 297–324.

– 1952. *Corinth* XII. *The Minor Objects.* Princeton: American School of Classical Studies.

Davidson, G.R., and D.B. Thompson. 1943. *Small Objects from the Pnyx: I. Hesperia* supp. 7. Princeton: American School of Classical Studies at Athens.

Dawkins, R.M. 1902–3. "Notes from Karpathos." *BSA* 9: 176–210.

Dawkins, R.M., ed. 1929. *The Sanctuary of Artemis Orthia at Sparta*. London: Macmillan and Co.

De Angelis d'Ossat, M., ed., 2002. *Scultura antica in Palazzo Altemps: Museo Nazionale Romano.* Rome: Electa.

DeCou, H.F. 1905. "The Bronzes of the Argive Heraeum." In Charles Waldstein, *The Argive Heraeum*, vol. 2, 191–339. Boston, New York: Houghton, Mifflin and Co.

De Juliis, E.M., ed. 1984. *Gli ori di Taranto in età ellenistica: Catalogue of the Exhibition, December 1984 to March 1985, Milan.* Milan: A. Mondadori.

De Lachenal, L. 1980. "Su una statua di Menade." *BdA* 65 (5): 1–6.

Delattre, V. 2008. "Les sépultures de nouveau-nés au Moyen-Age: l'hypothèse d'un sanctuaire à répit précoce à Blandy-les-Tours (France, Seine-et-Marne)." In *Nasciturus, infans, puerulus vobis mater terra: la muerte en la infancia*, edited by F. Gusi Jener, S. Muriel, and C. Olària, 183–210. Diputació de Castelló, Série de prehistòria i arqueològia (SIAP).

Demangel, R. 1926. *Fouilles de Delphes* II. *Le sanctuaire d'Athéna Pronaia (Marmaria): Topographie du sanctuaire.* Paris: E. de Boccard.

Dengate, C. 1976. "A Group of Graves Excavated at Halieis." *ArchDelt* 31, A': 274–324.

Deonna, W. 1938. *Le mobilier délien.* 2 vols. *Exploration archéologique de Délos*. Fasc. 18. Paris: E. de Boccard.

Deppert-Lippitz, B. 1985. *Griechischer Goldschmuck.* Mainz am Rhein: Philipp von Zabern.

– 1996. *Ancient Gold Jewelry at the Dallas Museum of Art.* Dallas: Dallas Museum of Art.

– 1998. "Greek Bracelets of the Classical Period." In *The Art of the Greek Goldsmith*, edited by D. Williams, 91–4. London: British Museum Press.

de Reffye, V. 1864. "Armes d'Alise." *RA* 10: 337–49.

De Ridder, A. 1896. *Catalogue des bronzes trouvés sur l'Acropole d'Athènes. BÉFAR* 74. Paris.

des Courtils, J. 2003. *The Guide to Xanthos and Letoon: Sites Inscribed on the UNESCO World Heritage List.* Istanbul: Yayinlari.

de Souza, P. 2007. "Naval Battles and Sieges." In *The Cambridge History of Greek and Roman Warfare*, vol. 1, edited by P. Sabin, H. van Wees, and M. Whitby, 434–60. Cambridge: Cambridge University Press.

Despinis, G.I. 2004. "Die Kultstatuen der Artemis in Brauron." *AM* 119: 261–315.

DeVries, K. 1980. "Greeks and the Phrygians in the Early Iron Age." In *From Athens to Gordion: The Papers of a Memorial Symposium for Rodney S. Young. University Museum Papers I*, edited by K. DeVries, 33–49. Philadelphia: University Museum, University of Pennsylvania.

Dickens, G. 1912. *Catalogue of the Acropolis Museum* I: *Archaic Sculpture*. Cambridge: Cambridge University Press.

Dierichs, A. 2004. *Korfu-Kerkyra: Grüne Insel im ionischen Meer von Nausikaa bis Kaiser Wilhelm II.* Mainz: Philipp von Zabern.

Dillon, M. 2002. *Girls and Women in Classical Greek Religion.* London and New York: Routledge.

Dodwell, E. 1819. *A Classical and Topographical Tour through Greece, during the Years 1801, 1805, and 1806.* 2 vols. London: Rodwell and Martin.

Donalson, M.D. 1999. *The Domestic Cat in Roman Civilization.* Studies in Classics 9. Lewiston: Edwin Mellen Press.

Dragendorff, H. 1903. *Thera* II. Berlin: G. Reimer.

Dubois, L. 1986. *Recherches sur le dialecte arcadien.* Vol. 2: *Corpus dialectal.* Bibliothèque des cahiers de l'Institut de Linguistique de Louvain, 34. Louvain-la-Neuve: Cabay.

Dugas, C. 1921. "Le sanctuaire d'Aléa Athéna à Tégée avant le IV siècle." *BCH* 45: 335–435.

Dunbabin, A.D.D., and T.J. Dunbabin. 1962. "Miniature Vases." In *Perachora: The Sanctuaries of Hera Akraia and Limenia.* Vol. 2: *Pottery, Ivories, Scarabs and Other Objects*, edited by T.J. Dunbabin, 290–313. Oxford: Clarendon Press.

Dunbabin, T.J., ed. 1962. *Perachora: The Sanctuaries of Hera Akraia and Limenia*. Vol. 2: *Pottery, Ivories, Scarabs and Other Objects.* Oxford: Clarendon Press.

Dusenbery, E.B. 1959. "A Samothracian Necropolis." *Archaeology* 12: 163–70.

Edlund-Berry, I.E.M. 2001. "Miniature Vases as Votive Gifts at Morgantina (Sicily)." In *Ceramics in Context: Proceedings of the Internordic Colloquium on Ancient Pottery Held at Stockholm, 13–15 June 1997*, edited by C. Scheffer, 71–5. Stockholm: Almqvist and Wiksell.

Edwards, C.M. 1981. "Corinth 1980: Molded Relief Bowls." *Hesperia* 50: 189–210.

– 1986a. "The Running Maiden from Eleusis and the Early Classical Image of Hekate." *AJA* 90: 307–18.

– 1986b. "Corinthian Moldmade Bowls: The 1926 Reservoir." *Hesperia* 56: 389–419.

Edwards, G.R. 1975. *Corinth* VII, iii: *Corinthian Hellenistic Pottery*. Princeton: American School of Classical Studies at Athens.

Eichler, F. 1919. "Die Skulpturen des Heraions bei Argos." *ÖJh* 19–20: 1–153.

Eisen, G. 1916. "The Characteristics of Eye Beads from the Earliest Times to the Present." *AJA* 20: 1–27.

Ekroth, G. 2003. "Small Pots, Poor People? The Use and Function of Miniature Pottery as Votive Offerings in Archaic Sanctuaries in the Argolid and Corinthia." In *Griechische Keramik im kulturellen Kontext: Akten des Internationalen Vasen-Symposions in Kiel vom 24.bis 28.9, 2001*, edited by B. Schmaltz and M. Söldner, 33–7. Münster: Scriptorium.

Elderkin, K. 1928. "Buttons and Their Use on Greek Garments." *AJA*: 32: 333–45.

Engels, D. 1999. *Classical Cats: The Rise and Fall of the Sacred Cat.* London and New York: Routledge.

Erath, G. 1999. "Heiligtümer und Kulte Nordostarkadiens. Der archäologische Befund." In *Pheneos und Lousoi: Untersuchungen zu Geschicte und Topographie Nordostarkadiens*, edited by Klaus Tausend, 238–46. Frankfurt am Main: Lang.

Erdmann, E.H. 1973. "Die sogenannten Marathonpfeilspitzen in Karlsruhe." *AA* 88: 30–58.

Ergil, T. 1983. *Earrings: The Earring Catalogue of the Istanbul Archaeological Museum*. Istanbul: Ali Riza Baskan.

Etouzougae, A. 1994. "Νομός Ιωαννίνων." *ArchDelt* 49, B'1: 363–70.

Fagerström, K. 1988. *Greek Iron Age Architecture: Developments through Changing Times*. Göteborg: P. Åström.

Fain, O. 2005. "Musculoskeletal Manifestations of Scurvy." *Joint Bone Spine* 72: 124–8.

Faraone, C. 1992. *Talismans and Trojan Horses: Guardian Statues in Ancient Greek Myth and Ritual.* Oxford: Oxford University Press.

Farnell, L.R. 1896. *The Cults of the Greek States*, vol. 1. Oxford: Clarendon Press.

– 1932. *The Works of Pindar*. Vol. 2: *Critical Commentary*. London: Macmillan & Co.

Fazekas, I.G., and F. Kósa. 1978. *Forensic Fetal Osteology*. Budapest: Akadémiai Kiadó.

Felsch, R.C., ed. 2007. *Kalapodi. Ergebnisse der Ausgrabungen im Heiligtum der Artemis und des Apollon von Hyampolis in der antiken Phokis.* Vol. 2: *Zur Stratigraphie des Heiligtums* (Felsch). *Die Bronzefunde* (Felsch). *Die Angriffswaffen* (Schmitt). Deutsches Archäologisches Institut. Mainz am Rhein: Philipp von Zabern.

Felsch, R.C., H. Kienast, and H. Schuler. 1980. "Apollon und Artemis oder Artemis und Apollon? Bericht von den Grabungen im neu entdecken Heiligtum bei Kalapodi 1973–1977." *AA*: 38–122.

Floren, J. 1987. *Die griechische Plastik* I: *Die geometrische und archaische Plastik.* Munich: C. H. Beck.

Forsén, J., and B. Forsén. 2003. *The Asea Valley Survey: An Arcadian Mountain Valley from the Palaeolithic Period until Modern Times.* Sävedalen: Paul Åströms Förlag.

Forstenpointner, G., and M. Hofer. 1997. "Kulturhistorische und landschaftsmorphologische Ergebnisse aus der Untersuchung der Tierknochenfunde von Lousoi in Arkadien." *Anthropozoologica* 25–6: 683–90.

Foss, C. 1975. "Greek Sling Bullets in Oxford." *AR* 1974–5: 40–4.

Foy, D. 1989. *Le verre medieval et son artisanat en France méditerranéenne.* Paris: Centre National de la Recherche Scientifique.

Franke, P.R. 1966. "Leontinsche φυγάδες in Chalkis?: Ein Hortfund Sizilischen Bronzemünzen des 5 Jahrhunderts v. Chr. aus Euboia." *AA*: 395–407.

Frankel, R. 2003. "The Olynthus Mill, Its Origin, and Diffusion: Typology and Distribution." *AJA* 107: 1–21.

Frazer, J.G. 1898. *Pausanias's Description of Greece, Trans. with Commentary*, vol. 4. London: Macmillan & Co. Reprint, Trinity College, Cambridge, 1965.

Freyer-Schauenburg, B. 1974. *Samos* XI: *Bildwerke der archaischen Zeit und des strengen Stils.* Bonn: In Kommission bei R. Habelt.

Fullerton, M. 1990. *The Archaistic Style in Roman Statuary. Mnemosyne* supp. 110. Leiden: Brill.

Furtwängler, A. 1890. *Die Bronzen und die übrigen kleineren Funde von Olympia: Olympia IV.* Berlin.

– 1913. "Neue Denkmäler antiker Kunst II." In *Kleine Schriften* II, edited by J. Sieveking and L. Curtius, 453–86. Munich: Beck.

Furtwängler, A., E. Fiechter, and H. Thiersch. 1906. *Aegina: Das Heiligtum der Aphaia.* Munich: K.B. Akademie der Wissenschaften.

Gager, J.G., ed. 1992. *Curse Tablets and Binding Spells from the Ancient World.* New York and Oxford: Oxford University Press.

Gallina Zevi, A. 1977. *Roma medio repubblicana.* Rome: L'Erma di Bretschneider.

Garnett, K. 1975. "Late Roman Corinthian Lamps from the Fountain of the Lamps." *Hesperia* 44: 173–206.

Garvie-Lok, S. 2006. "Signs of Scurvy in a Late Roman Child from Stymphalos, Greece." Paper presented at the 34th annual meeting of the Canadian Association for Physical Anthropology, 25–8 October, Peterborough, Ontario, Canada.

Gauer, W. 1991. *OlForsch* XX: *Die Bronzegefässe von Olympia*, Teil 1. Berlin and New York: Walter de Gruyter.

Gebhard, E.R., and F.P. Hemans. 1998. "University of Chicago Excavations at Isthmia: II." *Hesperia* 67: 1–63.

Gejvall, N.-G. 1969. *Lerna, a Preclassical Site in the Argolid: The Fauna.* Athens: American School of Classical Studies at Athens.

Gell, W. 1823. *Narrative of a Journey in the Morea.* London: Longman, Hurst, Rees, Orme, and Brown.

Georgescu, C. 2005. "Les boucliers votifs et autres revêtments décorés archaïques en bronze et en fer." In P. Alexandrescu et al., *Histria. Les résultats des fouilles* VII: *La zone sacrée d'époque grecque (fouilles 1915–1989)*, 271–326. Bucharest and Paris: Editura Academiei Române; Diffusion de Boccard.

Georgiadou, A. 2005. *Totenkult und elische Grabkeramik spätklassischer und hellenistischer Zeit.* Thessaloniki: University Studio Press.

Gilmour, G.H. 1997 "The Nature and Function of Astragalus Bones from Archaeological Contexts in the Levant and Eastern Mediterranean." *OJA* 16: 167–75.

Ginge, B. 1981. *The Erotic Hare: A Hare-Shaped Etruscan Plastic Vase in the Odense University Classical Collection.* Odense: Odense University.

Ginouvès, R. 1962. *Balaneutiké: Recherches sur le bain dans l'antiquité grecque.* Bibliothèque des Écoles Françaises d'Athènes et de Rome 200. Paris: E. de Boccard.

Ginouvès, R., I. Akamatis, M. Andronicos, A. Despinis, et al. 1994. *Macedonia: From Philip II to the Roman Conquest.* Princeton: Princeton University Press.

Giuliani, L. 1979. *Die archaischen Metopen von Selinunt.* Mainz: Philipp von Zabern.

Giuliano, A., ed. 1986. *Museo Nazionale Romano: Le sculture* I, vi: *I marmi Ludovisi disperse.* Rome: De Luca.

Goester, Y.C., and M. van de Vrie. 1998. "Lavda: The Excavation 1986–1988." *Pharos* 6: 119–78.

Gold of the Thracian Horsemen: Treasures from Bulgaria. 1987. Catalogue of the Exhibition, 30 May to 4 October 1987, Palais de la Civilisation. Montreal: Editions de l'Homme.

Goldman, H. 1915. "Inscriptions from the Acropolis of Halae." *AJA 19*: 438–53.

– 1940. "The Acropolis of Halae." *Hesperia* 9: 381–514.

Göransson, K. 2007. *The Transport Amphorae from Euesperides: The Maritime Trade of a Cyrenaican City 400–250 BC.* Acta Archaeologica Lundensia. Series in 4°. No. 25. Lund: Almqvist & Wiksell.

Grandjean, C. 1990. "Le monnayage d'argent et de bronze d'Hermioné, Argolide." *RN* ser. 6, 32: 28–55.

Grandjean, G. 1992. "Contribution à l'établissement d'une typologie des amphores thasiennes: le matériel amphorique du Quartier de la Porte du Silène." *BCH* 116: 541–84.

Greco, C., G. Greco, and A. Pontrandolfo. N.d. *Da Poseidonia à Paestum.* Paestum.

Greco, G., and J. de La Genière. 1996. "L'Heraion alla Foce del Sele: continuità e trasformazione dall'età greca all'età lucana." In *I Greci in Occidente. Poseidonia e i Lucani*, edited by M. Cipriani and F. Longo, 223–32. Naples: Electa.

Greifenhagen A. 1970. *Schmuckarbeiten in Edelmetall. I. Fundgruppen.* Staatl. Museen Preuss. Kulturbesitz Antikenabt. Berlin: Mann.

– 1975. *Schmuckarbeiten in Edelmetall. II. Einzelstücke.* Staatl. Museen Preuss. Kulturbesitz Antikenabt. Berlin: Mann.

Grose, D.F. 1989. *The Toledo Museum of Art: Early Ancient Glass: Core-Formed, Rod-Formed, and Cast Vessels and Objects from the Late Bronze Age to the Early Roman Empire, 1600 B.C. to A.D. 50.* Toledo: Toledo Museum of Art; New York: Hudson Hills Press.

Guettel Cole, S. 1995. "Civic Cult and Civic Identity." In *Sources for the Ancient Greek City-State. Symposium August, 24–27 1994. Acts of the Copenhagen Polis Centre*, vol 2, edited by M.H. Hansen, 292–325. Historisk-filosofiske Meddelelser 72. Royal Danish Academy of Sciences and Letters. Munksgard, Copenhagen.

Guides-Joanne, Grèce. 1891. Vol. 2, *Grèce continentale et îles.* Paris: Librairie Hachette.

Guido, M. 1978. *The Glass Beads of the Prehistoric and Roman Periods in Britain and Ireland.* London: Thames and Hudson.

Hackens, T. 1968. "À propos de la circulation monétaire dans le Péloponnese au IIIe siècle av. J.-C." In *Antidorum W. Peremans Sexagenario ab Alumnis Oblatum*, edited by L. Cerfaux, W. Peremans, and A. Tourhoudt, 69–95. Louvain-la-Neuve: Publications Universitaires de Louvain.

– 1976. *Catalogue of the Classical Collection: Classical Jewelry.* Providence: Museum of Art, Rhode Island School of Design.

Hackens, T., and R. Winkes, eds. 1983. *Gold Jewelry: Craft, Style and Meaning from Mycenae to Constantinopolis.* Louvain-La-Neuve: Institut supérieur d'archéologie et d'histoire de l'art, Collège Erasme.

Hadaczek, K. 1903. *Der Ohrschmuck der Griechen und Etrusker.* Vienna: Alfred Hölder.

Hadzisteliou-Price, T. 1969. "The Type of the Crouching Child and the 'Temple Boys'." *BSA* 64: 95–111.

– 1978. *Kourotrophos: Cults and Representations of the Greek Nursing Deities.* Leiden: Brill.

Hainzmann, M. 1997. "Fundmünzen aus Aigeira I: Lokale Prägungen." In *Numismatic Archaeology, Archaeological Numismatics*, edited by K.A. Sheedy and Ch. Papageorgiadou-Banis, 40–6. Oxbow Monograph 75. Oxford: Australian Archaeological Institute at Athens.

Hamilton, R. 1992. *Choes and Anthesteria: Iconography and Ritual.* Ann Arbor: University of Michigan Press.

Hammond, L.A. 1998. "The Miniature Votive Vessels from the Sanctuary of Athena Alea at Tegea." UMI Microform 9974708. PhD diss., University of Missouri.

Hampl, J.S., C.A. Taylor, and C.S. Johnson. 2004. "Vitamin C Deficiency and Depletion in the United States: The Third National Health and Nutrition Examination Survey, 1988 to 1994." *American Journal of Public Health* 94: 870–5.

Hansen, E., and C. Le Roy, 1976. "Au Létôon de Xanthos: Les deux temples de Léto." *RA* series 7, 1976. II: 317–29.

Hansen, M.H., and T.H. Nielsen, eds. 2004. "Stymphalos." In *An Inventory of Archaic and Classical Poleis,* 529–30. Oxford: Oxford University Press.

Hanson, V.D. 1989. T*he Western Way of War: Infantry Battle in Classical Greece.* New York: A.A. Knopf.

Harris, D. 1995. *The Treasures of the Parthenon and Erechtheion.* Oxford: Clarendon Press.

– 1991. "The Inventory Lists of the Parthenon." PhD diss., Princeton University.

Harris, E.F., and J.H. McKee. 1990. "Tooth Mineralization Standards for Blacks and Whites from the Middle Southern United States." *Journal of Forensic Sciences* 35: 859–72.

Harrison, E.B. 1991. "The Dress of the Archaic Greek Korai." In *New Perspectives in Early Greek Art*, edited by D. Buitron-Oliver, 217–39. Washington, DC: National Gallery.

Hayes, J.W. 1975. *Roman and Pre-Roman Glass in the Royal Ontario Museum.* Toronto: Royal Ontario Museum.

Head, B.V. 1911. *Historia Numorum.* London: Clarendon Press.

– 1968 rev. ed. (1911). *Historia Numorum: A Manual of Greek Numismatics.* Chicago: Argonaut.

Heilmeyer, W.D. 1969. "Giessereibetriebe in Olympia." *JdI* 84: 1–28.

Hellman, M.C. 1982. "Collection Froehner: balles de fronde grecques." *BCH* 106: 75–87.

Hendy, M.F. 1969. *Coinage and Money in the Byzantine Empire 1081–1261.* Washington: Dumbarton Oaks Center for Byzantine Studies.

Herbert, S. 1977. *Corinth* VII, iv: *The Red-Figure Pottery.* Princeton: American School of Classical Studies at Athens.

– 1986. "The Torch-Race at Corinth." In *Corinthiaca: Studies in Honor of Darrell A. Amyx*, edited by M.A. Del Chiaro and W.R. Biers (assoc. editor), 29–35. Columbia: University of Missouri Press.

Herfort-Koch, M. 1986. *Archaische Bronzeplastik Lakoniens. Boreas* supp. 4.

Hermary, A. 1989. *Musée du Louvre: Catalogue des antiquités de Chypre: Sculptures*. Paris: Editions de la Réunion des Musées Nationaux.

Hermary, A., et al. 1996. *Sculptures déliennes*. Athens: École Française d'Athènes; Paris: de Boccard.

Herz, N. 2000. "The Classical Marble Quarries of Paros: Paros-1, Paros-2 and Paros-3." In *Paria Lithos: Parian Quarries, Marble and Workshops of Sculpture: Conference 1997*, edited by D.U. Schilardi and D. Katsonopoulou, 27–33. Athens: D.U. Schilardi.

Higgins, R.A. 1954. *Catalogue of the Terracottas in the Department of Greek and Roman Antiquities, British Museum*. 2 vols. London: British Museum.

– 1967. *Greek Terracottas*. London: Methuen.

– 1980. *Greek and Roman Jewellery*. London: Methuen and Co. Original edition 1961.

Hijmans, S. 2003. "The Metal Finds." In *Housing in New Halos: A Hellenistic Town in Thessaly, Greece*, edited by H.R. Reinders and W. Prummel, 123–38. Utrecht: HES Publishers.

Hillson, S. 1996. *Dental Anthropology*. Cambridge: Cambridge University Press.

Hjohlman, J., A. Penttinen, and B. Wells. 2005. *Pyrgouthi: A Rural Site in the Berbati Valley from the Early Iron Age to Late Antiquity: Excavations by the Swedish Institute at Athens 1995 and 1997*. Sävedalen: Paul Åstroms Förlag.

Hockey, M. 1998. "Examination and Cleaning of a Bronze Pair of Earrings." In *The Art of the Greek Goldsmith*, edited by D. Williams, 147–8. London: British Museum.

Hoffman, H. and P.F. Davidson. 1965. *Greek Gold: Jewelry from the Age of Alexander*. Mainz: Philipp von Zabern.

Hoffmann, M. 1964. *The Warp-Weighted Loom: Studies in the History and Technology of the Ancient Implement*. Oslo: Universitetsforlaget.

Hogarth, D.G. 1899–1900. "The Dictaean Cave." *BSA* 6: 94–116.

Holman, D.J., and R.E. Jones. 1998. "Longitudinal Analysis of Deciduous Tooth Emergence: II. Parametric Survival Analysis in Bangladeshi, Guatemalan, Japanese, and Javanese Children." *AJPA* 105: 209–30.

Howland, R. 1958. *The Athenian Agora* IV: *Greek Lamps and Their Survivals*. Princeton: American School of Classical Studies at Athens.

Hurme, V.O. 1949. "Ranges of Normalcy in the Eruption of Permanent Teeth." *Journal of Dentistry for Children* 16: 11–15.

Hurwit, J. 1999. *The Athenian Acropolis: History, Mythology and Archaeology from the Neolithic Era to Present*. Cambridge: Cambridge University Press.

Iliffe, J.H. 1929. "Minoan and Greek Gems." *Bull. ROMA* 8 (January): 13–14.

Illustrated London News. 1963. "A Phoenician Colony in Sicily" *Illustrated London News* 21, September 1963.

Iozzo, M. 1987. "Corinthian Basins on High Stands." *Hesperia* 56: 355–416.

Isserlin, B.S.J., and J.P. Taylor. 1974. *Motya: A Phoenician and Carthaginian City in Sicily*. Leiden: Brill.

Jackson, M. 2006. *Hellenistic Gold Eros Jewellery: Technique, Style and Chronology*. *BAR-IS* 1510. Oxford: Archaeopress.

Jacobi, H. 1930. "Der keltische Schlüssel und der Schlüssel der Penelope, ein Beitrag zur Geschichte des antiken Verschlusses." In *Schumacher-festschrift zum 70. geburtstag Karl Schumachers, 14. oktober 1930*, edited by Direktion des römisch-germanischen Zentralmuseums in Mainz, 213–32. Mainz: L. Wilckens.

Jacobsthal, P. 1931. *Die melischen Reliefs*. Berlin: H. Keller.

– 1956. *Greek Pins and Their Connexions with Europe and Asia*. Oxford: Clarendon Press.

Jacopi, G. 1929. *Clara Rhodos* III: *Scavi nella necropolis di Jalisso 1924–1928*. Bergamo: Instituto Storico-Archeologico di Rodi.

– 1931. *Clara Rhodos* IV: *Esplorazione archeologica di Camiro – II*. Bergamo: Istituto Storico-Archeologico di Rodi.

– 1932. *Clara Rhodos* VI–VII: *Esplorazione archeologica di Camiro – II*. Bergamo: Istituto Storico-Archeologico di Rodi.

Jameson, M.H. 1969. "Excavations at Porto Cheli and Vicinity, Preliminary Report, I: Halieis, 1962–1968." *Hesperia* 38: 311–81.

– 1974. "A Treasury of Athena in the Argolid (*IG* IV, 554)." In *ΦΟΡΟΣ: Tribute to Benjamin Dean Meritt*, edited by D.W. Bradeen and M.F. McGregor, 67–75. Locust Valley, NY: J.J. Augustin.

Janssens, P.A., A. Marcsik, C. de Meyere, and G. de Roy. 1993. "Qualitative and Quantitative Aspects of Scurvy in Ancient Bones." *Journal of Paleopathology* 5: 25–36.

Jaswal, S. 1983. "Age and Sequence of Permanent-Tooth Emergence among Khasis." *AJPA* 62: 177–86.

Jeffery, L.H. 1963. *The Local Scripts of Archaic Greece*. Oxford: Clarendon Press.

– 1990. *The Local Scripts of Archaic Greece: A Study of the Origin of the Greek Alphabet and Its Development from the Eighth to the Fifth Centuries B.C.* Revised edition with corrections and supplement by A.W. Johnston. Oxford Monographs on Classical Archaeology. Oxford. Oxford University Press.

Johansen, F. 1994. *Ny Carlsberg Glyptotek, Catalogue:*

Greece in the Archaic Period. Copenhagen: Ny Carlsberg Glyptotek.

Johnston, S.I. 1991. *Restless Dead: Encounters between the Living and the Dead in Ancient Greece.* Berkeley: University of California Press.

Jones, J.E., A.J. Graham, and L.H. Sackett. 1973. "An Attic Country House below the Cave of Pan at Vari." *BSA* 68: 355–452.

Jones, J.E., L.H. Sackett, and A.J. Graham. 1962. "The Dema House in Attica." *BSA* 57: 75–114.

Jones, R., S. Papamarinopoulos, and H. Williams. 1988. "Geophysical Explorations at Ancient Stymphalos." *Geoexplorations* 26: 255–61.

Jost, M. 1985. *Sanctuaires et cultes d'Arcadie.* Études péloponnésiennes 9. École Française d'Athènes. Paris: J. Vrin.

Joyner, G., A. Cambitoglou, O.T. Jones, and B. McLoughlin. 2001. "The Metal Objects." In *Torone* I: *The Excavations of 1975, 1976, and 1978,* edited by A. Cambitoglou, J.K. Papadopoulos, and O. Tudor Jones, 721–63. ΒΙΒΙΟΘΗΚΗ ΤΗΣ ΕΝ ΑΘΗΝΑΙΣ ΑΡΧΑΙΟΛΟΓΙΚΗΣ ΕΤΑΙΡΕΙΑΣ, ΑΡ. 206. Athens: Η εν Αθήναις Αρχαιολογική Εταιρεία.

Kadish, B. 1971. "Excavations of Prehistoric Remains at Aphrodisias, 1968 and 1969." *AJA* 75: 121–40.

Kadletz, E. 1975. "Animal Sacrifice in Greek and Roman Religion." PhD diss., University of Washington.

Kalashnik, Y. 2004. *Greek Gold from the Treasure Rooms of the Hermitage.* Zwolle: Waanders Publishers.

Kallintzi, D. 1990. "Ανασκαφή ταφικού τύμβου στα Άβδηρα." ΤΟ *ΑΡΧΑΙΟΛΟΓΙΚΟ ΕΡΓΟ ΣΤΗ ΜΑΚΕΔΟΝΙΑ ΚΑΙ ΘΡΑΚΗ* 4: 561–71.

Kallipolitis, B.D., and D. Feytmans. 1948–9. "Νεκρόπολις κλασσικῶν χρόνων ἐν Κοζάνη." *ArchEph*: 85–111.

Kaltsas, N. 2002a. "Die Kore und der Kuros aus Myrrhinous." *AntP* 28:7–40.

– 2002b. *Sculpture in the National Archaeological Museum, Athens.* Los Angeles: J. Paul Getty Museum.

Kane, J.P. 1975. "The Mithraic Cult Meal in Its Greek and Roman Environment." In *Mithraic Studies: Proceedings of the 1st International Congress of Mithraic Studies,* vol. 1, edited by J.R. Hinnels, 313–51. Manchester: Manchester University Press.

Kane, S. 1998. "Two Limestone Goddesses from the Sanctuary of Demeter and Kore/Persephone at Cyrene, Libya." In *ΣΤΕΦΑΝΟΣ: Studies in Honor of Brunilde Sismondo Ridgway.* University Museum Monograph 100, edited by K. Hartswick and M.C. Sturgeon, 145–53. Philadelphia: University Museum.

Karageorghis, V., J. Mertens, and M.E. Rose. 2000. *Ancient Art from Cyprus: The Cesnola Collection in the Metropolitan Museum of Art.* New York: Metropolitan Museum of Art.

Karagiorga, Th. 1963. "Άρχαία Μαντίνεια." *ArchDelt* 18, B'1: 88–90.

Karakasi, K. 2003. *Archaic Korai.* Los Angeles: J. Paul Getty Museum.

Karouzou, S. 1968. *National Archaeological Museum Collection of Sculpture: A Catalogue.* Athens: General Direction of Antiquities and Restoration.

Katsonopoulou, D. 2000. "Pedimental Sculptures in Parian Marble from Keryneia of Achaea." In *Paria Lithos: Parian Quarries, Marble and Workshops of Sculpture: Conference 1997,* edited by D.U. Schilardi and D. Katsonopoulou, 373–8. Athens: D.U. Schilardi.

Katz, R.V., S.P. Hazen, N.W. Chilton, and R.D. Mumma, Jr. 1982. "Prevalence and Intraoral Distribution of Root Caries in an Adult Population." *Caries Research* 16: 265–71.

Kazamiakis, K. 2000. "Η Παρία Λίθος στην Κέα κατά τον 6° αι. π.Χ." In *Paria Lithos: Parian Quarries, Marble and Workshops of Sculpture: Conference 1997,* edited by D.U. Schilardi and D. Katsonopoulou, 405–8. Athens: D.U. Schilardi.

Keesling, C.M. 1999. "Endoios's Painting from the Themistoklean Wall: A Reconstruction." *Hesperia* 68: 509–48.

– 2003. *The Votive Statues of the Athenian Acropolis.* Cambridge: Cambridge University Press.

Keller, O. 1909. *Die antike Tierwelt,* I. Leipzig: W. Engelmann.

Kerr, N.W. 1990. "The Prevalence and Pattern of Distribution of Root Caries in a Scottish Medieval Population." *Journal of Dental Research* 69: 857–60.

Kilian, K. 1975. *Fibeln in Thessalien von mykenischen bis zur archaischen Zeit. PBF* XIV.2. Munich: C.H. Beck.

– 1983. "Weihungen aus Eisen und Eisenverarbeitung im Heiligtum zu Philia (Thessalien)." In *The Greek Renaissance of the Eighth Century B.C.: Tradition and Innovation. Proceedings of the Second International Symposium at the Swedish Institute in Athens, 1–5 June, 1981,* edited by R. Hägg, 131–46. Stockholm: Swedish Institute at Athens.

Kilian-Dirlmeier, I. 1984. *Nadeln der frühhelladischen bis archaischen Zeit von der Peloponnes. PBF* XIII.8. Munich: C.H. Beck.

– 2002. *Kleinfunde aus dem Athena Itonia-Heiligtum bei Philia (Thessalian).* Mainz: Vorlag des Römisch-Germanischen Zentralmuseums.

Kleeman, I. 1962. "Ein Weihgeschenk an die delische Artemis in Paros." *AM* 77: 207–28.

Kleibrink, M. 2006. *Oenotrians at Lagaria near Sybaris. A Native Proto-Urban Centralized Settlement.* London: Accordia Research Institute.

Klinger, S. 2002. "On Women with Deer in Black-Figure Vase-Painting." *NumAntCl* 31: 11–43.

– 2003. "Artemis Holding a Deer: The Iconography of the Motif on a Red-Figure Oinochoe in Kiel." In *Griechische Keramik in kulturellen Kontext: Akten des Internationalen Vasen-Symposions in Kiel vom 24.bis 28.9, 2001*, edited by B. Schmaltz and M. Söldner, 142–4. Münster: Scriptorium.

Knapp, J. 2002. "Moldmade Bowls from the Athena Sanctuary at Stymphalos." MA thesis, University of British Columbia.

Knapp, R.C., and Mac Isaac, J.D. 2005. *Excavations at Nemea* III: *The Coins*. Berkeley and London: University of California Press.

Koch-Harnack, G. 1983. *Knabenliebe und Tiergeschenke: Ihre Bedeutung im päderastischen Erziehungssystem Athens*. Berlin: Mann.

Koehler, C.G. 1978. "Corinthian A and B Transport Amphoras." PhD diss., Princeton University.

– 1981. "Corinthian Developments in the Study of Trade in the Fifth Century." *Hesperia* 50: 449–58.

– 1992. "A Brief Typology and Chronology of Corinthian Transport Amphoras." In *Grecheskie amfory* [*Les amphores grecques. Les problems de l'evolution du métier et de la commèrce dans l'antiquité*], edited by V.I. Kats and S. Iu. Monakhov, 265–79 (Russian, English summary, 279). Saratova: Saratova University.

Kokkorou-Alevra, G. 1997. "Ionian Sculpture of the Archaic Period on Dorian Rhodes." In *Sculptors and Sculpture of Caria and the Dodecanese*, edited by I. Jenkins and G.B. Waywell, 150–6. London: British Museum.

– 1999. "Ο απόηχος της αρχαϊκής παριανής γλυπτικής σε ένα γυναικείο κεφάλι στο Μουσείο της Τριπόλεως." In *ΦΩΣ ΚΥΚΛΑΔΙΚΟΝ: Τιμητικός τόμος στη μνήμη του Νίκου Ζαφειροπούλου*, edited by C. Stampolidis, 254–61. Athens.

– 2000. "The Use and Distribution of Parian Marble during the Archaic Period." In *Paria Lithos: Parian Quarries, Marble and Workshops of Sculpture: Conference 1997*, edited by D.U. Schilardi and D. Katsonopoulou, 143–53. Athens: D.U. Schilardi.

Kolia, E. 2000. "Κλειστό σύνολο ελληνιστικής κεραμικής από το οικόπεδο I. Κολιγλιάτη στο Αργος." In *Ε' Επιστημονική Συνάντηση για την Ελληνιστική Κεραμική* (1997), 387–92. Athens: Εφορεία Προϊστορικών και Κλασικών Αρχαιοτήτων.

Konstantinou, I. 1931–2. "'Ο Κοῦρος τοῦ Ἰλισσοῦ." *ArchDelt* 14: 41–56.

Kostoglou-Despini, A. 1979. *Προβλήματα τῆς παριανῆς πλαστικῆς τοῦ 5ου αἰώνα π. X.* Thessaloniki.

Kotzias, N. 1937. "'Ο παρὰ τὸ ἀεροδρόμιον τῆς Θεσσαλονίκης (Σέδες) Γ.': τάφος." *ArchEph*: 866–95.

Koukouli-Chrysanthaki, H. 1979. "Eastern Macedonia." In *Treasures of Ancient Macedonia*, edited by K. Ninou, 86–98. Athens: Archaeological Museum of Thessalonike.

Kouragios, G. 2009. *Despotiko*. Athens: Ministry of Commercial Shipping and Island Policy.

Kourouniotes, K. 1904. "Ἀνασκαφαὶ Λυκαίου." *ArchEph*: 153–214.

– 1910. "Τὸ ἐν Βάσσαις ἀρχαιότερον ἱερὸν τοῦ Ἀπόλλωνος." *ArchEph*: 271–332.

Kozloff, A.P. 1981. *Animals in Ancient Art from the Leo Mildenberg Collection.* Cleveland: Cleveland Museum of Art in cooperation with Indiana University Press.

Kozloff, A.P., and D.G. Mitten, eds. 1988. *The Gods Delight: The Human Figure in Classical Bronze*. Cleveland: Cleveland Museum of Art in cooperation with Indiana University Press.

Kozloff, A.P., D.G. Mitten, and M. Squaitamatti. 1986. *More Animals in Ancient Art: From the Leo Mildenberg Collection.* Mainz: Philipp von Zabern.

Kraay, C.M. 1976. *Archaic and Classical Greek Coins*. Berkeley and London: University of California Press.

Kraay, C., and M. Hirmer. 1966. *Greek Coins*. New York: H.N. Abrams.

Kritzas, Ch. 1973. "Αργολίδος-Κορινθίας 1971–72." *ArchDelt* 28, B'1: 80–135.

Kroll, J.H. 1982. "The Ancient Image of Athena Polias." In *Studies in Athenian Architecture, Sculpture, and Topography: Presented to Homer A. Thompson*, 65–76. Princeton: American School of Classical Studies at Athens.

Kron, U. 1986. "Eine archaische Kore aus dem Heraion von Samos." In *Archaische und klassische griechische Plastik: Akten des internationalen Kolloquiums vom 22.–25. April 1985 in Athen*, I, edited by H. Kyrieleis, 47–65. Mainz: Philipp von Zabern.

Krystalli-Votsi, K. 1977. "Αυστηρορρυθμικὸ κεφάλι κούρου από τήν Κόρινθο." *ArchEph* 1976: 182–93.

Kunina, N. 1997. *Ancient Glass in the Hermitage Collection.* The State Hermitage. St Petersburg: ARS Publishers.

Kunz, G.F. 1917. *Rings for the Finger*. Philadelphia and London: J.B. Lippincott Co.

Kunze, E. 1956. *V. Bericht über die Ausgrabungen in Olympia*. Berlin: Walter de Gruyter.

Künzl, S. 2002. *Ein Komplex von Formschüsseln für megarische Becher. Die "Mainzer Werkstatt"*. Römisch-Germanisches Zentralmuseum: Forschungsinstitut für Vor- und Frühgeschichte. Band 32. Mainz.

Kusch, H. 1999. "Die 'Hermes-Höhle.' Eine Kultstätte am Ziria." In *Pheneos und Lousoi: Untersuchungen zu Geschicte und Topographie Nordostarkadiens*, edited by Kl. Tausend, 253–61. Frankfurt am Main: Lang.

Kyparissis, N. 1926. "Ανασκαφή Ταμπουρίων Πειραιῶς και Κερατσινίου." *ArchDelt* 10: 82–5.

Kyrieleis, H., ed. 1986. *Archaische und klassische griechische Plastik: Akten des internationalen Kolloquiums vom 22.–25. April 1985 in Athen*, I. Mainz: Philipp von Zabern.

– 1995. "Eine neue Kore des Cheramyes." *AntP* 24: 7–37.

Kyrkou, M. 2003. "Κοροπλαστικές αποκλίσεις στον αρχαϊκό Κεραμεικό." In *ΕΠΙΤΥΜΒΙΟΝ Gerhard Neumann*. Benaki Museum supp. 2, edited by D. Damaskos, 31–55. Athens: Benaki Museum.

Lahusen, G., and E. Formigli. 1993. "Der Augustus von Meroë und die Augen der römischen Bronzebildnisse." *AA* 108: 655–74.

Laffineur, R. 1978. *L'orfèvrerie rhodienne orientalisante*. Paris: D. de Boccard.

Lalonde, G.V. 1991. "Horoi." In G.V. Lalonde, M.K. Langdon, and M.B. Walbank. *The Athenian Agora* XIX: *Inscriptions: Horoi, Poletai Records, Leases of Public Land*, 1–52. Princeton: American School of Classical Studies at Athens.

Lamb, W. 1929. *Greek and Roman Bronzes*. New York: Dial Press.

– 1934–5. "Excavations at Kato Phana in Chios." *BSA* 35: 139–63.

Lambrinoudakis, V. 1980. "Δείγματα μνημειῶδους ἀρχαϊκῆς πλαστικῆς ἀπὸ τὴν Ἐπίδαυρο." In *Stele: Τόμος εις Μνήμην Νικολάου Κοντολεόντος*, edited by P. Kanellopoulos et al., 473–86. Athens: Friends of Nikolaos Kontoleon.

Laroche, D. 2003. "II. Travaux au Letoon." In J. des Courtils and D. Laroche, "Xanthos et le Letoon: Rapport sur la campagne de 2002." *Anatolia Antiqua* 11: 443–56.

Lattanzi, E. 2001. "Il cosidetto kouros di Reggio Calabria." *BdA* 115: 1–22.

Lattermann, H., and F. Hiller von Gaertringen. 1915. "Stymphalos." *AM* 40: 71–90.

Laumonier, A. 1977. *La céramique hellénistique à reliefs I: ateliers ioniens. Exploration archéologique de Délos*. Fasc. 31. Paris: D. de Boccard.

Lauter, H. 2002. "'Polybios hat es geweiht … ' Stiftungsinschriften des Polybios und des Philopoimen aus dem neuen Zeus-Heiligtum zu Megalopolis (Griechenland)." *AntW* 33.4: 375–86.

Lawler, L.B. 1964. *The Dance in Ancient Greece*. London: A. & C. Black.

Lazaridis, D. 1960. "Ἀνασκαφαὶ καὶ ἔρευναι εἰς Ἀμφίπολιν." *Prakt*: 67–73.

– 1967. "Skyros." *ArchDelt* 22 (2): 287.

– 1969. *Οδηγός Μουσείου Καβάλας*. Athens: Konstantinides and Michalas.

Leake, W.M. 1830. *Travels in the Morea*. 3 vols. London: J. Murray. Reprint 1968 Amsterdam: A.M. Hakkert.

Lechat, H. 1891. "Terres cuites de Corcyre (Collection de M. Constantin Carapanos)." *BCH* 15: 1–111.

Lee, M. 2005. "Constru(ct)ing Gender in the Feminine Greek Peplos." In *The Clothed Body in the Ancient World*, edited by L. Cleland, M. Harlow, and L. Llewellyn-Jones, 55–64. Oxford: Oxbow Books.

Lefkowitz, M.R. 1996. "Women in the Panathenaic and Other Festivals." In *Worshipping Athena: Panathenaia and Parthenon*, edited by J. Neils, 78–91. Madison: University of Wisconsin Press.

Lehmann, K., and D. Spittle. 1964. *Samothrace* IV, Part II: *The Altar Court*. New York: Bollingen Foundation.

Lehmann, P. Williams. 1967. "Letter to the Editor." *AJA* 71: 429–32

– 1969. *Samothrace* III. Text I and II, and plates. *The Hieron*. Bollingen Series LX.3. Princeton: Princeton University Press.

Lehmann, P., and D. Spittle. 1982. *Samothrace* V: *The Temenos*. Princeton: Princeton University Press.

Leipen, N. 1966. *The Loch Collection of Cypriote Antiquities: Lionel Massey Memorial Exhibition, Royal Ontario Museum, Oct. 18–Dec. 26, 1966*. Toronto: University of Toronto Press.

– 1982. "Timeless, Gleaming Gold: Ancient Greek and Roman Jewellery in the Royal Ontario Museum." *Canadian Collector* 17.4: 74–9.

Lesperance, P., S. Morris, P. Stone, and G. Toteva. 2003. "Final Report on the Pottery Finds, Stymphalos." Unpublished report.

Lisle, R. 1955. "The Cults of Corinth." PhD dissertation, Johns Hopkins University.

LIMC II.1-2. 1984. s.v. "Aphrodite" (A. Delivorrias et al.).

LIMC II.1-2. 1984. s.v. "Athena" (P. DeMargne).

LIMC III.1-2. 1986. s.v. "Eros" (A. Hermary).

LIMC IV.1-2. 1988. s.v. "Gorgo, Gorgones" (I. Krauskopf).

LIMC IV.1-2. 1988. s.v. "Herakles" (O. Palagia).

LIMC VI.1-2. 1992. s.v. "Leda" (L. Kahil and N. Icard-Gianolio).

LIMC VII.1-2. 1994. s.v. "Psyche" (N. Icard-Gianolio).

LIMC VII.1-2. 1997 s.v. "Tritones" (N. Icard-Gianolio).

Lobell, J. 2003. "Inner Sanctum Discovery." *Archaeology* 56: 12.

Luschey, H. 1939. *Die Phiale*. Bleicherode am Harz: Verlag Carl Nieft.

Lynch, E., and D. Beighton. 1994. "A Comparison of Primary Root Caries Lesions Classified According to Colour." *Caries Research* 28: 233–9.

Maas, M. 1985. "Ein Terrakottaschmuckfund aus dem Zeitalter Alexanders d. Gr." *AM* 100: 309–26.

Maaskant-Kleibrink, M. 1993. "Religious Activities on the 'Timpone della Motta,' Francavilla Marittima, and the Identification of Lagaría." *BABesch* 68: 1–47.

Maat, G.J.R. 2004. "Scurvy in Adults and Youngsters: A Review of the History and Pathology of a Disregarded Disease." *International Journal of Osteoarchaeology* 14: 77–81.

Mac Isaac, J.D. 1988. "Phliasian Bronze Coinage." *ANSMN* 33: 45–54.

– 1995. "Coins and the Field Archaeologist: Numismatic Finds as Artifacts." *ArchNews* 20: 21–5.

Macnamara, E. 1992. "The Metalwork." In *An Iron Age and Roman Republican Settlement on Bottromagno, Gravina di Puglia. Excavations of 1965–1974.* Vol. 2: *The Artifacts*, edited by A.M. Small, 230–48. British School at Rome, Archaeological Monographs 5. London.

Macridy, Th. 1911. "Un tumulus Macédonien à Langaza." *JdI* 26: 193–215.

Madigan, B.C. 1992. *The Temple of Apollo Bassitas* II: *The Sculpture*, edited by F.A. Cooper. Princeton: American School of Classical Studies at Athens.

Magness, J. 1992. "Masada: Arms and the Man." *Biblical Archaeology Review* 18: 58–67.

Maier, F. 1956. "Zu einigen bosnisch-herzegowinischen Bronzen in Griechenland." *Germania* 34: 63–75.

Mainoldi, C. 1984. *L'image du loup et du chien dans la Grèce ancienne: d'Homère à Platon.* Paris: Editions Ophrys.

Maniatis, Y., and K. Polikreti. 2000. "The Characterization and Discrimination of Parian Marble in the Aegean Region." In *Paria Lithos: Parian Quarries, Marble and Workshops of Sculpture: Conference 1997*, edited by D.U. Schilardi and D. Katsonopoulou, 575–84. Athens: D.U. Schilardi.

Manning, W.H. 1985a. *Catalogue of the Romano-British Iron Tools, Fittings and Weapons in the British Museum.* London: British Museum.

– 1985b. "The Iron Objects." In *Inchtuthil: The Roman Legionary Fortress*, edited by Lynn F. Pitts and J.K. St Joseph, 289–92. Britannia Monograph Series 6. London: Society for the Promotion of Roman Studies.

Mansfield, J.M. 1985. "The Robe of Athena and the Panathenaic Peplos." PhD diss., University of California, Berkeley.

Mantis, A.G. 1990. *Προβλήματα της εικονογραφίας των ιερειών και των ιερέων στην αρχαία Ελληνική τέχνη.* Athens: Ταμείο Αρχαιολογικόν Πόρον και Απαλλοτριώσεων.

Marangou, L. 1998. "The Acropolis Sanctuary of Minoa on Amorgos: Cult Practice from the 8th Century B.C. to the 3rd Century A.D." In *Ancient Greek Cult Practice from the Archaeological Evidence*, edited by R. Hägg, 9–26. Stockholm: Svenska Institutet i Athen.

Marcadé, J. 1950. "Notes sur trois sculptures archaïques récemment reconstituées à Délos." *BCH* 74:181–215.

Marinatos, Sp. 1936. "Le temple geométrique de Dréros." *BCH* 60: 267–85.

Marsden, E.W. 1969. *Greek and Roman Artillery: Historical Development.* Oxford: Clarendon Press.

– 1971. *Greek and Roman Artillery: Technical Treatises.* Oxford: Clarendon Press.

Marshall, F.H. 1968. *Catalogue of the Finger Rings, Greek, Etruscan and Roman in the Departments of Antiquities, British Museum.* London: British Museum. Original edition, 1907.

– 1969. *Catalogue of the Jewellery, Greek, Etruscan, and Roman, in the Departments of Antiquities, British Museum.* London: British Museum. Original edition, 1911.

Martha, J. 1883. "Stèle avec inscriptions trouvèe au lac Stymphale." *BCH* 7: 486–93.

Martin, T.R. 1985. *Sovereignty and Coinage in Classical Greece.* Princeton: Princeton University Press.

Martini, W. 1990. *Die archaische Plastik der Griechen.* Darmstadt: Wissenschaftliche Buchgesellschaft.

Marx, P.A. 2001. "Acropolis 625 (Endoios Athena) and the Rediscovery of its Findspot." *Hesperia* 70: 221–54.

Mastrokostas, E.I. 1986. "Αποθραύσματα υστεροαρχαϊκών εναετίων γλυπτών εκ Κερυνείας Αχαίας." In *Archaische und klassische griechische Plastik: Akten des internationalen Kolloquiums vom 22.–25. April 1985 in Athen*, I, edited by H. Kyrieleis, 139–41. Mainz: Philipp von Zabern.

Mattusch, C.C. 1988. *Greek Bronze Statuary, from the Beginnings through the Fifth Century B.C.* Ithaca: Cornell University Press.

McClees, H. 1924. *The Metropolitan Museum of Art: Daily Life of the Greeks and Romans, As Illustrated in the Classical Collections.* New York: Metropolitan Museum of Art.

McDowell, L.R. 2000. *Vitamins in Animal and Human Nutrition.* 2nd ed. Ames: Iowa State University Press.

McLauchlin, B.K. 1981. "New Evidence on the Mechanics of Loomweights." *AJA* 85: 79–81.

McPhee, I. 1983. "Local Red Figure from Corinth." *Hesperia* 52: 137–53.

– 1991. "A Corinthian Red-Figured Calyx-Krater and the Dombrena Painter." *OJA* 10: 325–34.

McPhee, I., and A.D. Trendall. 1986. "Six Corinthian Red-Figure Vases." In *Corinthiaca: Studies in Honor of Darrell A. Amyx*, edited by M.A. Del Chiaro and W.R. Biers (assoc. editor), 160–7. Columbia: University of Missouri Press.

Melikian, M., and T. Waldron. 2003. "An Examination of Skulls from Two British Sites for Possible Evidence of Scurvy." *International Journal of Osteoarchaeology* 13: 207–12.

Merker, G.S. 2006. *The Greek Tile Works at Corinth: The*

Site and the Finds. Hesperia supp. 35. Princeton: American School of Classical Studies at Athens.

Mertens, J. 1987. *Introduction to Greece and Rome: The Metropolitan Museum of Art*. New York: Metropolitan Museum of Art.

Metzger, H. 1940–1. "Le sanctuaire de Glanitsa (Gortynie)." *BCH* 64–5: 5–33.

– 1963. *Fouilles de Xanthos* II: *L'acropole lycienne*. Paris: Klincksieck.

Metzger, H., E. Laroche, A. Dupont-Sommer, and M. Mayrhofer. 1979. *Fouilles de Xanthos* VI: *La stèle trilingue du Létôon*. Institut français d'études anatoliennes d'Istanbul. Paris: Librarie C. Klincksieck.

Miller, J.G. 1997. "Temple and Image: Did All Greek Temples House Cult Images?" Paper read at the 98th Annual Meeting of the Archaeological Institute of America, 27–30 December 1996, New York; abstract in *AJA* 101: 345.

Miller, Stella G. 1979. *Two Groups of Thessalian Gold.* Berkeley, Los Angeles, and London: University of California Press.

– 1983. "Excavations at Nemea, 1982." *Hesperia* 52: 70–95.

– 1984. "Excavations at Nemea, 1983." *Hesperia* 53: 171–92.

– 1996. "New Developments in the Archaeology of Northern Greek Jewelry." In *Ancient Jewelry and Archaeology*, edited by A. Calinescu, 35–44. Bloomington and Indianapolis: Indiana University Press.

Miller, Stephen G. 1976. "Excavations at Nemea, 1975." *Hesperia* 45: 174–202.

– 1977. "Excavations at Nemea, 1976." *Hesperia* 46: 1–26.

– 1978. "Excavations at Nemea, 1977." *Hesperia* 47: 58–88.

– 1979. "Excavations at Nemea, 1978." *Hesperia* 48: 73–103.

– 1980. "Excavations at Nemea, 1979." *Hesperia* 49: 178–205.

– 1981. "Excavations at Nemea, 1980." *Hesperia* 50: 45–67.

– 1988. "Excavations at Nemea, 1984–1986." *Hesperia* 57: 1–20.

– 2001. *Excavations at Nemea.* Vol. 2: *The Early Hellenistic Stadium.* Berkeley: University of California Press.

Miller-Collett, S.G. 1998. "Macedonia and Athens: A Golden Link?" In *The Art of the Greek Goldsmith*, edited by D. Williams, 22–9. London: British Museum Press.

Milne, M.J. 1939. "Kylichnis." *AJA* 43: 247–54.

Minon, S. 2007. *Les inscriptions éléennes dialectales (VIe–IIe siècle avant J.-C.)*. Geneva: Librarie Droz.

Misailidou-Despotidou, B. 1990. "Από το νεκροταφείο της αρχαίας Μίεζα." *ΤΟ ΑΡΧΑΙΟΛΟΓΙΚΟ ΕΡΓΟ ΣΤΗ ΜΑΚΕΔΟΝΙΑ ΚΑΙ ΘΡΑΚΗ* 4: 128–41.

Mitsopoulos-Leon, V. 1990. "Bronzekästchen für Artemis." In *EYMOYSIA: Ceramic and Iconographic Studies in Honour of Alexander Cambitoglou*, edited by J.-P. Descœudres, 137–40. Mediterranean Archaeology supp. 1. Sydney: Meditarch.

– 1993. "The Statue of Artemis at Lousoi: Some Thoughts." In *Sculpture from Arcadia and Laconia: Proceedings of an International Conference Held at the American School of Classical School at Athens, April 1992*, edited by O. Palagia and W. Coulson, 33–9. Oxford: Oxbow Books.

– 1994. "Lousoi." *ÖJh* 63: 40–4.

– 2012. *Das Heiligtum der Artemis Hemera in Lousoi: Kleinfunde aus den Grabungen 1986–2000.* Sonderschriften. Österreichisches Archäologisches Institut. Vienna.

Mitsos, M. 1946–7. "Inscription de Stymphalos." *RÉG* 59–60: 150–74.

Mitten, D. 1975. *Catalogue of the Classical Collection: Museum of Art, Rhode Island School of Design, Providence, Rhode Island: Classical Bronzes.* Providence.

Mols, S.T.A.M. 1999. *Wooden Furniture in Herculaneum: Form, Technique and Function.* Circumvesuviana 2. Amsterdam: J.C. Gieben.

Moore, M.B. 1997. *The Athenian Agora* XXX: *Attic Red-Figure and White-Ground Pottery*. Princeton: American School of Classical Studies at Athens.

Moore, M.B., and M.Z.P. Philippides. 1986. *The Athenian Agora* XXIII: *Attic Black-Figured Pottery*. Princeton: American School of Classical Studies at Athens.

Moorees, C.F.A., E.A. Fanning, and E.E. Hunt, Jr. 1963a. "Age Variation of Formation Stages for Ten Permanent Teeth." *Journal of Dental Research* 42: 1490–1502.

– 1963b. "Formation and Resorption of Three Deciduous Teeth in Children." *AJPA* 21: 205–13.

Morel, J.-P. 1980. *Céramique campanienne: Les forms.* Rome: École française de Rome.

Morgan, C. 1999. "Cultural Subzones in Early Iron Age and Archaic Arkadia?" In *Defining Ancient Arkadia: Acts of the Copenhagen Polis Centre,* 6, edited by T.H. Nielsen and J. Roy, 382–456. Copenhagen: Royal Danish Academy of Sciences and Letters.

Morgan, C.H., II. 1939. "Excavations at Corinth, 1938." *AJA* 43: 255–67.

Moritz, L.A. 1958. *Grain-mills and Flour in Classical Antiquity*. Oxford: Clarendon Press.

Mørkholm, O. 1991. *Early Hellenistic Coinage: From the Accession of Alexander to the Peace of Apamea (336–188 BCE)*. Cambridge: Cambridge University Press.

Morris, S., et al. 2003. "Stymphalos 2003 Study Season: Report on Pottery Finds." Unpublished report for the Stymphalos Project.

Morter, J., and J.R. Leonard. 1998. "Storage Amphorae." In J.C. Carter, *The Chora of Metaponto. The Necropoleis.*

Vol. 2, 731–47 (with appendix by Harry Iceland, "Petrographic Analysis," 748–55). Institute of Classical Archaeology. Austin: University of Texas Press.

Muscarella, O. 1967. *Phrygian Fibulae from Gordion*. London: William Clowes and Sons.

Musti, D., et al. 1992. *L'oro dei Greci*. Novara: Instituto Geografico de Agostini.

Mylona, D. 2013. "Dealing with the Unexpected: Unusual Animals in an Early Roman Cistern Fill in the Sanctuary of Poseidon at Kalaureia, Poro." In *Bones, Behaviour and Belief: The Zooarchaeological Evidence as a Source for Ritual Practice in Ancient Greece and Beyond*, edited by G. Ekroth and J. Wallensten, 149–66. *SkrAth* 4°, 55. Stockholm: Swedish Institute at Athens.

Mylonas, G. 1943. "Excavations at Mecyberna, 1934, 1938." *AJA* 47: 78–87.

Nakasis, A. 2004. *Ο ναός της 'Αθηνάς Μακίστου* (Archaiologikon Deltion, publication no. 87). Athens: Υπουργείο Πολιτισμού. Ταμείο 'Αρχαιολογικῶν Πόρων και 'Απαλλοτριώσεων.

Naumann-Steckner, F. 1998. "Greek Jewellery and Its Representation." In *The Art of the Greek Goldsmith*, edited by D. Williams, 95–8. London: British Museum Press.

Neils, J. 1992. "The Panathenaia: An Introduction." In *Goddess and the Polis: The Panathenaic Festival in Ancient Athens*, edited by J. Neils, 13–27. Princeton: Princeton University Press.

Neils, J., and J. Oakley. 2003. *Coming of Age in Ancient Greece: Images of Childhood from the Classical Past.* New Haven: Yale University Press in association with the Hood Museum of Art, Dartmouth College, Hanover, NH.

Nenna, M.-D. 1999. *Les Verres. Exploration archéologique de Délos.* Fasc. 37. École Française d'Athènes, Paris.

Newell, E. T. 1926. *The Coinages of Demetrius Poliorcetes*. Oxford: Oxford University Press.

Nielsen, A.M. 1992. *The Cypriote Collection: Catalogue, Ny Carlsberg Glyptothek*. Copenhagen: Ny Carlsberg Glyptothek.

Nisetich, F. 2001. *The Poems of Callimachus.* Oxford: Oxford University Press.

Oakley, J., and R. Sinos. 1993. *The Wedding in Ancient Athens.* Madison: University of Wisconsin Press.

Ober, J. 1987. "Early Artillery Towers: Messenia, Boiotia, Attica, Megarid." *AJA* 91: 569–604.

Ogden, J. 1992. *Ancient Jewellery: Interpreting the Past.* Berkeley and Los Angeles: University of California Press.

Ogden, J.A. 1984. "Radiology of Postnatal Skeletal Development XII. The Second Cervical Vertebra." *Skeletal Radiology* 12: 169–77.

Ohly, D. 1976. *Die Aegineten* I: *Die Ostgiebelgruppe.* Munich: Beck.

Ohly-Dumm, M., and M. Robertson. 1988. "Aigina, Aphaia-Tempel XII: Archaic Marble Sculptures Other Than Architectural." *AA*: 405–21.

Oikonomides, M.. 1993. "Iron Coins: A Numismatic Challenge." *Rivista Italiana di Numismatica e Scienze Affini* 95: 75–8.

Oksmann, E. 1928. "Antike Skulpturen in Odessa." *AA*: 82–94.

Oliver, A. 1977. *Silver for the Gods: 800 Years of Greek and Roman Silver*. Toledo: Toledo Museum of Art.

– 1990. "Part II: Glass." In *The Extramural Sanctuary of Demeter and Persephone at Cyrene, Libya. Final Reports. Vol. IV*, edited by D. White, 87–109. Philadelphia: University Museum, University of Pennsylvania.

Orlandos, A.K. 1924. "'Ανασκαφαὶ εν Στυμφάλῳ." *Prakt*: 117–23.

– 1925. "'Ανασκαφαὶ ἐν Στυμφάλῳ." *Prakt*: 51–5.

– 1926. "'Ανασκαφαὶ ἐν Στυμφάλῳ." *Prakt*: 131–6.

– 1927. "'Ανασκαφαὶ ἐν Στυμφάλῳ." *Prakt*: 53–6.

– 1928. "'Ανασκαφαὶ ἐν Στυμφάλῳ." *Prakt*: 120–3.

– 1929. "'Ανασκαφαὶ ἐν Στυμφάλῳ." *Prakt*: 92.

– 1930. "'Ανασκαφαὶ ἐν Στυμφάλῳ." *Prakt*: 88–91.

– 1966. *Les matériaux de construction et la technique architecturale des anciens Grecs*. Première partie, translated by V. Hadjimichali. École Française d'Athènes. Travaux et mémoires, fasc. 16. Paris: Éditions de Boccard.

– 1967–8. *'Η 'Αρκαδικῆ 'Αλιφείρα καὶ τὰ μνημεῖα τῆς.* ΒΙΒΛΙΟΘΗΚΗ ΤΗΣ ΕΝ ΑΘΗΝΑΙΣ ΑΡΧΑΙΟΛΟΓΙΚΗΣ ΕΤΑΙΡΕΙΑΣ, 58. Athens.

Ortner, D.J., W. Butler, J. Cafarella, and L. Milligan. 2001. "Evidence of Probable Scurvy in Subadults from Archaeological Sites in North America." *AJPA* 114: 343–51.

Ortner, D.J., and M.F. Ericksen. 1997. "Bone Changes in the Human Skull Probably Resulting from Scurvy in Infancy and Childhood." *International Journal of Osteoarchaeology* 7: 212–20.

Ortner, D.J., E.H. Kimmerle, and M. Diez. 1999. "Probable Evidence of Scurvy in Subadults from Archaeological Sites in Peru." *AJPA* 108: 321–31.

Ortner, D.J., and W.G.J. Putschar. 1981. *Identification of Pathological Conditions in Human Skeletal Remains.* Smithsonian Contributions to Anthropology 28. Washington: Smithsonian Institution Press.

Østby, E. 1994. "Recent Excavations in the Sanctuary of Athena Alea at Tegea (1990–93)." In *Archaeology in the Peloponnese: New Excavations and Research*, edited by K. Sheedy, 39–64. Oxford: Australian Archaeological Institute at Athens.

Öztürk, J. 1998. "Lydian Jewellery." In *The Art of the Greek Goldsmith*, edited by D. Williams, 41–7. London: British Museum Press.

Page, D.L. 1951. *Alcman: The Parthenion*. Oxford: Clarendon Press.

Palagia, O. 1982. "A Colossal Statue of a Personification from the Agora of Athens." *Hesperia* 51: 99–113.

– 1993. "A Marble Athena Promachos from the Acropolis of Sparta." In *Sculpture from Arcadia and Laconia: Proceedings of an International Conference Held at the American School of Classical School at Athens, April 1992*, edited by O. Palagia and W. Coulson, 165–75. Oxford: Oxbow Books.

– 2000. "Parian Marble and the Athenians." In *Paria Lithos: Parian Quarries, Marble and Workshops of Sculpture: Conference 1997*, edited by D.U. Schilardi and D. Katsonopoulou, 347–54. Athens: D.U. Schilardi.

– 2006. "Classical Athens." In *Greek Sculpture: Function, Materials, and Techniques in the Archaic and Classical Periods*, edited by O. Palagia, 119–62. Cambridge: Cambridge University Press.

Palagia, O., and W. Coulson, eds. 1993. *Sculpture from Arcadia and Laconia: Proceedings of an International Conference Held at the American School of Classical School at Athens, April 1992.* Oxford: Oxbow Books.

Papadopoulos, J.K. 2003. *La dea di Sibari e il santuario ritrovato: Studi sui rinvenimenti dal Timpone Motta de Francavilla Marittima.* Vol. II.1: *The Archaic Votive Metal Objects. Bollettino d'Arte.* Special Volume. Rome.

– 2009. "The Relocation of Potters and the Dissemination of Style: Athens, Corinth, Ambrakia, and the Agrinion Group." In *Athenian Potters and Painters*, vol. 2, edited by J. Oakley and O. Palagia, 232–40. Oxford and Oakville: Oxbow Books.

Papahatzis, N.D. 1980. *Παυσανίου 'Ηλλάδος Περιήγησις, Βιβλία 7 και 8, 'Αχαϊκὰ καί 'Αρκαδικά.* Athens: ΕΚΔΟΤΙΚΗ ΑΘΗΝΩΝ.

Papapostolou, I. 1977. "'Ελληνιστικοί τάφοι τῆς Πάτρας I." *ArchDelt* 32, A': 281–343.

Papaspyridi-Karouzou, S. 1933–5. "'Ανασκαφὴ Τάφων τοῦ 'Αργους." *ArchDelt* 15: 16–53.

Parke, H.W. 1977. *Festivals of the Athenians*. London: Thames and Hudson.

Payne, H., et al. 1940. *Perachora: The Sanctuaries of Hera Akraia and Limenia: Excavations of the British School of Archaeology at Athens 1930–1933.* Vol. 1: *Architecture, Bronzes, Terracottas.* Oxford: Clarendon Press.

Pedley, J.G. 1976. *Greek Sculpture of the Archaic Period: The Island Workshops.* Mainz: Philipp von Zabern.

– 1990. *Paestum: Greeks and Romans in Southern Italy.* London: Thames and Hudson.

Pemberton, E. 1985. "Ten Hellenistic Graves in Ancient Corinth." *Hesperia* 54: 271–307.

Pemberton, E.G. 1989. *Corinth* XVIII, i. *The Sanctuary of Demeter and Kore: The Greek Pottery.* Princeton: American School of Classical Studies at Athens.

– 1997. "Corinthian Black-Glazed Pottery with Incised and Stamped Decoration." *Hesperia* 66: 49–97.

– 2003. "Classical and Hellenistic Pottery from Corinth and Its Athenian Connections." In *Corinth* XX: *Corinth, the Centenary: 1896–1996*, edited by C.K. Williams II and N. Bookidis, 167–79. Princeton: American School of Classical Studies at Athens.

Perfahl, J., ed. 1983. *Wiedersehen mit Argos und andere Nachrichten über Hunde in der Antike.* Mainz: Philipp von Zabern.

Perlzweig, J. 1959. *The Athenian Agora* VII: *Lamps of the Roman Period.* Princeton: American School of Classical Studies at Athens.

Petrakos, B. 1972. "Γαλαξείδι." *ArchDelt* 27, B': 375.

– 1999. *Ο δήμος του Ραμνούντος* I: *Τοπογραφία*. Athens: Archaeological Society in Athens.

Petropoulos, M. 1999. *Τα εργαστήρια τών ρωμαϊκών λυχναρίων τής Πάτρας κάι τό λυχνοματέιον*. Athens: Ministry of Culture.

Pfrommer, M. 1990. *Untersuchungen zur Chronologie früh- und hochhellenistichen Goldschmucks*. Tübingen: E. Wasmuth.

Pfuhl-Möbius = E. Pfuhl and H. Möbius, *Die ostgriechischen Grabreliefs,* 2 vols. Mainz: P. von Zabern, 1977-9.

Philadelpheus, A. 1920–1. "'Ανασκαφὴ παρὰ τὸ χωρίον Σπάτα." *ArchDelt* 6: 131–8.

Philipp, H. 1981. *Bronzeschmuck aus Olympia. OlForsch* XIII. Berlin: Walter de Gruyter.

Picard, O. 1979. *Chalcis et la confédération euboíenne: Étude de numismatique et d'histoire (IVe–Ie siècle)*. Paris: École Française d'Athènes.

Pimentel, L. 2003. "Scurvy: Historical Review and Current Diagnostic Approach." *American Journal of Emergency Medicine* 21: 328–32.

Pingiatoglou, S. 1981. *Eileithyia.* Wurzburg: Königshausen & Neumann.

Pitts, L.F., and J.K. St Joseph. 1985. *Inchtuthil: The Roman Legionary Fortress*. Britannia Monograph Series 6. London: Society for the Promotion of Roman Studies.

Plantzos, D. 1999. *Hellenistic Engraved Gems*. Oxford: Clarendon Press.

Plassart, A. 1928. *Les sanctuaires et les cultes du Mont Cynthe. Exploration archéologique de Délos*. Fasc. 11. Paris: École Française d'Athènes.

Pollini, J. 2003. *The de Nion Head: A Masterpiece of Greek Sculpture.* Mainz: Philipp von Zabern.

Pope, S.T. 1923. *A Study of Bows and Arrows.* Berkeley: University of California Press.

Popham, M.R., and I.S. Lemos. 1996. *Lefkandi III: The Toumba Cemetery*. Plates. London: British School at Athens.

Popham, M.R., L. Sackett, and P.G. Themelis, eds. 1979–80. *Lefkandi I: The Iron Age: The Settlement, the Cemeteries*. 2 vols. *BSA* supp. 11. London: British School at Athens.

Poplin, F. 1984. "Contribution ostéo-archéologique à la connaissance des astragals de l'antre corycien." *L'antre corycien II, BCH* supp. 9, 381–93. Paris: Diffusion de Boccard.

Powell, B.B. 1995. *Classical Myth*. Englewood Cliffs, NJ: Prentice Hall.

Preka-Alexandri, K. 1995. "Παξοί." *ArchDelt* 50, B'2: 447–8.

Preuner, E. 1902. "Inschriften aus Leukas." *AM* 7: 363–4.

Price, J. 1992. "Hellenistic and Roman Glass." In L.H. Sackett et al., *Knossos from Greek City to Roman Colony: Excavations at the Unexplored Mansion* II, 415–62. British School of Archaeology at Athens. Supp. vol. 21. Oxford: Thames and Hudson.

Price, M.J. 1967a. "Greek Bronze Coinage c. 450–150 B.C.: Its Introduction, Circulation and Value, with Particular Reference to the Series of Corinth." PhD diss., Cambridge University.

– 1967b. "Coins from Some Deposits in the South Stoa at Corinth." *Hesperia* 36: 348–88, pls. 74–5.

– 1968. "Early Greek Bronze Coinage." In *Essays in Greek Coinage Presented to Stanley Robinson*, edited by C.M. Kraay and G.K. Jenkins, 90–104. Oxford: Oxford University Press.

– 1991. *The Coinage in the Name of Alexander the Great and Philip Arrhidaeus*. Zurich and London: Swiss Numismatic Society and British Museum Press.

Price, S., and E. Kearns, eds. 2003. *The Oxford Dictionary of Classical Myth and Religion*. Oxford: Oxford University Press.

Pritchett, W.K. 1991. *The Greek State at War*. 5. Berkeley: University of California Press.

– 1998. *Pausanias Perigetes,* vol. 1. Amsterdam: J.C. Gieben.

Pulak, C., and R.F. Townsend. 1987. "The Hellenistic Shipwreck at Serçe Limanı, Turkey: Preliminary Report." *AJA* 91: 31–57.

Raftopoulou, E.G. 1993. "Sur certains archetypes de themes iconographiques du centre du Peloponese." In *Sculpture from Arcadia and Laconia: Proceedings of an International Conference Held at the American School of Classical School at Athens, April 1992*, edited by O. Palagia and W. Coulson, 1–12. Oxford: Oxbow Books.

Rajakumar, K. 2001. "Infantile Scurvy: A Historical Perspective." *Pediatrics* 108: 76–8.

Raubitschek, A.E. 1949. *Dedications from the Athenian Akropolis: A Catalogue of the Inscriptions of the Sixth and Fifth Centuries BC*. Edited with the collaboration of Lilian H. Jeffery. Cambridge, MA: Archaeological Institute of America.

Raubitschek, I.K. 1998. *Isthmia* VII: *The Metal Objects (1952–1989)*. Princeton: American School of Classical Studies at Athens.

Reeder, E.D. 1995. "Containers and Textiles as Metaphors for Women." In *Pandora: Women in Classical Greece*, edited by E.D. Reeder, 195–297. Princeton: Princeton University Press.

Reichel, W., and A. Wilhelm. 1901. "Das Heiligthum der Artemis zu Lusoi." *ÖJh* 4: 1–89.

Reinders, H.R. 1988. *New Halos, a Hellenistic Town in Thessalía, Greece*. Utrecht: HES Publishers.

Reinders, H.R., and W. Prummel, eds. 2003. *Housing in New Halos: A Hellenistic Town in Thessaly, Greece*. Lisse: A.A. Balkema Publishers.

Renaudin, L. 1921. "Le site d'Asine (argolide)." *BCH* 45: 295–308.

Rhomaios, K. 1911. "'Αρκαδικοὶ ἑρμαῖ." *ArchEph*: 149–59.

Rhomiopoulou, K. 1973–4. "Νεκροταφεῖον ἀρχαίας 'Ακάνθου ('Ιερισσὸς)." *ArchDelt* 29, B'3: 693–7.

– 1979. "Thessalonike and Surroundings – Chalkidike (Central Macedonia)." In *Treasures of Ancient Macedonia*, edited by K. Ninou, 58–85. Athens: Archaeological Museum of Thessalonike.

– 1979. "Thessaly-Pieria." In *Treasures of Ancient Macedonia*, edited by K. Ninou, 31–7. Athens: Archaeological Museum of Thessalonike.

Richardson, T.I.L., L. Ball, and T. Rosenfeld. 2002. "Will an Orange a Day Keep the Doctor Away?" *Postgraduate Medical Journal* 78: 292–4.

Richter, G.M.A. 1915. *The Metropolitan Museum of Art: Greek, Etruscan and Roman Bronzes*. New York: Metropolitan Museum of Art.

– 1930. *Animals in Greek Sculpture: A Survey*. Oxford: Oxford University Press.

– 1953. *The Metropolitan Museum of Art: Handbook of the Greek Collection*. Cambridge, MA: Harvard University Press.

– 1954. *Catalogue of Greek Sculptures: Metropolitan Museum of Art*. Cambridge, MA: Harvard University Press.

– 1966. *The Furniture of the Greeks, Etruscans and Romans*. London: Phaidon Press.

– 1968. *The Engraved Gems of the Greeks and the Etruscans*. London: Phaidon Press.

– 1968. *Korai: Archaic Greek Maidens*. London: Phaidon Press.

– 1970. *Kouroi: Archaic Greek Youths*. 3rd ed. London: Phaidon Press.

Ridgway, B.S. 1970. *The Severe Style in Greek Sculpture*. Princeton: Princeton University Press.

– 1981. "Sculpture from Corinth." *Hesperia* 50: 422–48.

– 1990a. "Birds, 'Meniskoi,' and Head Attributes in Archaic Greece." *AJA* 94: 583–612.

– 1990b. *Hellenistic Sculpture* I: *The Styles of ca. 331-200 B.C.* Madison: University of Wisconsin Press.

– 1992. "Images of Athena on the Acropolis." In *Goddess and Polis: The Panathenaic Festival in Ancient Athens*, edited by J. Neils, 119–42. Princeton: Princeton University Press.

– 1993. *The Archaic Style in Greek Sculpture*, 2nd ed. Chicago: Ares Publishers.

Rife, J. 2012. *Isthmia IX: The Roman and Byzantine Graves and Human Remains*. Princeton: American School of Classical Studies at Athens.

Rihll, T. 2007. *The Catapult: A History.* Yardley, PA: Westholme Publishing.

Risberg, C. 1992. "Metal-Working in Greek Sanctuaries." In *Economics of Cult in the Ancient Greek World: Proceedings of the Uppsala Symposium 1990*, edited by T. Linders and B. Alroth, 33–40. Acta Universitatis Upsaliensis. *Boreas* 21. Uppsala: S. Academiae Upsaliensis.

Risser, M.K. 2001. *Corinth* VII, v: *Corinthian Conventionalizing Pottery*. Princeton: American School of Classical Studies at Athens.

Roberts, C., and K. Manchester. 1995. *The Archaeology of Disease*. 2nd ed. Ithaca: Cornell University Press.

Roberts, S.R. 1978. *The Attic Pyxis.* Chicago: Ares Publishers.

Robertson, M. 1992. *The Art of Vase-Painting in Classical Athens*. Cambridge: Cambridge University Press.

Robinson, D.M. 1933. *Excavations at Olynthus* VII: *The Terra-cottas of Olynthus.* Baltimore: Johns Hopkins University Press.

– 1941. *Excavations at Olynthus* X: *Metal and Minor Miscellaneous Finds*. Baltimore: Johns Hopkins University Press.

– 1942. *Excavations at Olynthus* XI: *Necrolynthia: A Study in Greek Burial Customs*. Baltimore: John Hopkins University Press.

Robinson, D.M., and E.J. Fluck. 1979. *A Study of the Greek Love-Names*. New York: Arno Press.

Robinson, D.M., and J.W. Graham. 1938. *Excavations at Olynthus* VIII: *The Hellenic House: A Study of the Houses Found at Olynthus with a Detailed Account of Those Excavated in 1931 and 1934.* Baltimore: Johns Hopkins University Press.

Robinson, H.S. 1962. "Excavations at Corinth, 1960." *Hesperia* 31: 95–133.

Rockwell, P. 1993. *The Art of Stoneworking: A Reference Guide*. Cambridge: Cambridge University Press.

Roebuck, C. 1951. *Corinth* XIV: *The Asklepieion and Lerna.* Princeton: American School of Classical Studies at Athens.

Rolley, C. 1984. "Autres objets de metal." *L'antre corycien* II. BCH supp. 9, 261–80.

– 1994. *La sculpture grecque* I. Paris: Picard.

Romano, I. Bald. 1980. "Early Greek Cult Images." PhD diss., University of Pennsylvania.

– 1994. "A Hellenistic Deposit from Corinth: Evidence for Interim Period Activity." *Hesperia* 63: 57–104.

Ross, L. 1841. *Reisen und Reiserouten.* Erster Teil: *Reisen im Peloponnes.* Berlin: G. Reimer.

Rostoker, W., and E.R. Gebhard. 1980. "The Sanctuary of Poseidon at Isthmia: Techniques of Metal Manufacture." *Hesperia* 49: 347–63.

Rostovtzeff, M.I., A.R. Bellinger, C. Hopkins, and C.B. Welles, eds. 1936. *The Excavations at Dura-Europos: Preliminary Report of Sixth Season of Work, October 1932–March 1933*. New Haven: Yale University Press.

Rotroff, S.I. 1982. *The Athenian Agora* XXII: *Hellenistic Pottery: Athenian and Imported Moldmade Bowls.* Princeton: American School of Classical Studies at Athens.

– 1990. "Athenian Hellenistic Pottery: Toward a Firmer Chronology." In *Akten des XIII. Internationalen Kongresses für klassische Archäologie, Berlin 1978*, 173–8. Deutsches Archäologisches Institut. Mainz: Philipp von Zabern.

– 1996. *The Missing Krater and the Hellenistic Symposium: Drinking in the Age of Alexander the Great.* Broadhead Classical Lecture 7. Christchurch, NZ: University of Canterbury Press.

– 1997. *The Athenian Agora* XXIX: *Hellenistic Pottery: Athenian and Imported Wheelmade Table Ware and Related Material.* Parts 1 and 2. Princeton: American School of Classical Studies at Athens.

– 2000a. "A Sullan Deposit at the Athenian Agora." In *Ε' Επιστημονική Συνάντηση για την Ελληνιστική Κεραμική* (1997), 373–80. Athens: Εφορεία Προϊστορικών και Κλασικών Αρχαιοτήτων.

– 2000b. "Moulds: Production and Preparation – Use and Spread." In *Ε' Επιστημονική Συνάντηση για την Ελληνιστική Κεραμική* (1997), 496–501. Athens: Εφορεία Προϊστορικών και Κλασικών Αρχαιοτήτων.

– 2005. "Four Centuries of Athenian Pottery." In *Chronologies of the Black Sea Area in the Period c. 400–100 B.C.*, edited by V. Stolba and L. Hannestad, 11–30. Aarhus: Aarhus University Press.

– 2006a. *The Athenian Agora* XXXIII: *Hellenistic Pottery: The Plain Wares*. Princeton: American School of Classical Studies at Athens.

– 2006b. "The Introduction of the Moldmade Bowl Revisited: Tracking a Hellenistic Innovation." *Hesperia* 75: 357–78.

Rouse, W.H.D. 1902. *Greek Votive Offerings*. Cambridge: Cambridge University Press.

– 1975. *Greek Votive Offerings*. New York: Arno Press. Reprint.

Roux, Georges. 1961. *L'architecture de l'Argolide aux IVe et IIIe siècles avant J.-C.* Paris: E. de Boccard.

Rubensohn, O. 1962. *Das Delion von Paros.* Wiesbaden: F. Steiner.

Rudolph, W. 1973. *Ancient Jewelry from the Collection of Burton Y. Berry.* Bloomington: Indiana Art Museum.

– 1978. "Hellenistic Fine Ware Pottery and Lamps from above the House of the Idols at Mycenae." *BSA* 73: 213–34.

– 1995. *A Golden Legacy: Ancient Jewelry from the Burton Y. Berry Collection at the Indiana University Art Museum.* Bloomington and Indianapolis: Indiana University Press.

Rühfel, H. 1984. *Das Kind in der griechischen Kunst: von der minoisch-mykenischen Zeit bis zum Hellenismus.* Mainz: Philipp von Zabern.

Runnels, C.N. 1981. "A Diachronic Study and Economic Analysis of Millstones from the Argolid, Greece." PhD diss., Indiana University.

Ruscillo, D. 2013. "Thesmophoriazusae: Mytilenean Women and Their Secret Rites." In *Bones, Behaviour and Belief: The Zoological Evidence as a Source for Ritual Practice in Ancient Greece and Beyond*, edited by G. Ekroth and J. Wallensten, 181–95. *SkrAth* 4° 55. Stockholm: Swedish Institute at Athens.

Russell, A.G. 1942. "The Greek as Mercenary Soldier." *GR* 11: 103–12.

Russell, N. 2012. *Social Zooarchaeology: Humans and Animals in Prehistory.* Cambridge: Cambridge University Press.

Rütti, B. 1991. *Die römische Gläser aus Augst und Kaiseraugst.* 2 vols. *Forschungen in Augst.* Band 13/1. Augst: Römermuseum.

Sabin, P., H. van Wees, and M. Whitby, eds. 2007. *The Cambridge History of Greek and Roman Warfare.* 2 vols. Cambridge: Cambridge University Press.

Sabetai, V. 2008. "Birth, Childhood and Marriage." In *Worshiping Women: Ritual and Reality in Classical Athens*, edited by N. Kaltsas and A. Shapiro, 288–333. New York: Alexander S. Onassis Public Benefit Foundation (USA).

Sáez Abad, R. 2005. *Artillería y poliorcética en el mundo grecorromano. Anejos de Gladius* 8. Madrid: Ediciones Polifemo.

Sakellarakis, J.A. 1988. "Some Geometric and Archaic Votives from the Idaian Cave." In *Early Greek Cult Practice: Proceedings of the Fifth International Symposium at the Swedish Institute at Athens, 26–29 June, 1986*, edited by R. Hägg, N. Marinatos, and G. Nordquist, 173–93. Stockholm: Swedish Institute at Athens.

Salapata, G. 1997. "Hero Warriors from Corinth and Lakonia." *Hesperia* 66: 245–60.

Sapouna-Sakellarakis, E. 1978. *Die Fibeln der griechischen Inseln: Prähistorische Bronzefunde* 14.4. Munich: C.H. Beck.

Sauberlich, H.E. 1997. "A History of Scurvy and Vitamin C." In *Vitamin C in Health and Disease*, edited by L. Parker and J. Fuchs, 1–24. New York: Marcel Dekker.

Schaps, D.M. 2004. *The Invention of Coinage and the Monetization of Ancient Greece*. Ann Arbor: University of Michigan Press.

Schattner, T.G. 1990. *Griechische Hausmodelle: Untersuchungen zur frühgriechischen Architektur. AM* 15. Beiheft. Berlin: Gebr. Mann Verlag.

Schaus, G.P. 1985. *The Extramural Sanctuary of Demeter and Persephone at Cyrene, Libya. Final Reports II. The East Greek, Island and Laconian Pottery.* Philadelphia: University Museum.

– 2003. Review of Keesling 2003. *Mouseion* 3(2): 212–15.

– 2007. "Connections between Olympia and Stymphalos." In *Onward to the Olympics: Historical Perspectives on the Olympic Games*, edited by G.P. Schaus and S. Wenn, 167–78. Waterloo: Wilfrid Laurier University Press.

Schefold, K. 1974. "Grabungen in Eretria 1973." *AntK* 17: 69–75.

– 1981. *Die Göttersage in der klassischen und hellenistischen Kunst.* Munich: Hirmer.

Scheibler, I. 1976. *Kerameikos. Ergebnisse der Ausgrabungen.* Vol. 11: *Die griechische Lampen.* Berlin: Walter de Gruyter.

Schilardi, D.U., and D. Katsonopoulou, eds. 2000. *Paria Lithos: Parian Quarries, Marble and Workshops of Sculpture: Conference 1997.* Athens: D.U. Schilardi.

Schläger, H. 1965–6. "Ricostruzione." In P. Zancani Montuoro et al. 1965–6. "L'Edifio Quadrato nello Heraion all Foce del Sele." *AttiMGrecia* n.s. 6–7: 47–56.

Schmaltz, B. 2005. "ΕΡΓΟΝ ΑΡΙΣΤΟΚΛΕΟΣ ΑΡΙΣΤΙΟΝΟΣ." *AM* 120: 163–71.

Schmitt, H.-O. 2007. "Die Angriffswaffen." In *Kalapodi: Ergebnisse der Ausgrabungen im Heiligtum der Artemis und des Apollon von Hyampolis in der antiken Phokis.* Vol. 2, edited by R.C.S. Felsch, 423–551. Deutsches Archäologisches Institut. Mainz am Rhein: Philipp von Zabern.

Schrader, H., ed. 1939. *Die archaischen Marmorbildwerke der Akropolis, Die Koren* (E. Langlotz); *Rundwerke außer den Koren, Reliefs* (W.H. Schuchhardt); *Giebel, Friesfragmente* (H. Schrader). Frankfurt: Klostermann.

Schwandner, E.-L. 1990. "Uberlegungen zur technischen Struktur und Formentwicklung archaischer Dachterrakotten." *Hesperia* 59: 291–300.

Schwarzmaier, A. 1997. *Griechische Klappspiegel: Untersuchungen zu Typologie und Stil*. Berlin: Mann.

Scott, W., transl. 1924. *Hermetica*. Oxford: Clarendon Press.

Segre, M. 1994. *Iscrizioni di Cos*. I–II. Rome: L'Erma di Bretschneider.

Seltman, G. 1949. *Masterpieces of Greek Coinage: Essays and Commentary.* Oxford: B. Cassiver.

Sgourou, M. 2001. "Jewellery from Thasian Graves." *BSA* 96: 328–55.

Shapiro, H.A. 1989. *Art and Cult under the Tyrants in Athens*. Mainz am Rhein: Philipp von Zabern.

Shaw, J.W., and M.C. Shaw, eds. 2000. *Kommos: An Excavation on the South Coast of Crete.* Vol. 4: *The Greek Sanctuary*. Princeton: Princeton University Press.

Shear, T.L. 1939. "The American Excavations in the Athenian Agora: Sixteenth Report." *Hesperia* 8: 201–46.

Sheedy, K. 1988. "An Archaic Sphinx from Siphnos." *BSA* 83: 363–73.

Shipley, G. 2005. "Between Macedonia and Rome: Political Landscapes and Social Change in Southern Greece in the Early Hellenistic Period." *BSA* 100: 315–30.

Siebert, G. 1976. "Délos: Le quartier de Skardhana." *BCH* 100.II: 799–821.

– 1978. *Recherches sur les ateliers de bols à reliefs du Péloponnèse à l'époque hellénistique*. École Française d'Athènes. Paris: Diffusion de Boccard.

Sim, D. 1992. "The Manufacture of Disposable Weapons for the Roman Army." *Journal of Roman Military Equipment Studies* 3: 105–19.

Simon, C. 1986. "The Archaic Votive Offerings and Cults of Ionia." PhD diss., University of California, Berkeley.

Simpson, C.J. 1994. "Articles Associated with Textiles." In *Excavations of San Giovanni di Ruoti.* Vol. 2: *The Small Finds*, edited by A.M. Small and R.J. Buck, 34–7. Toronto: University of Toronto Press.

Sinn, U. 1980. "Ein Fundkomplex aus dem Artemis-Heiligtum von Lusoi im Badischen Landesmuseum." *Jahrbuch der Staatlichen Kunstsammlungen in Baden-Württemberg* 17: 25–40.

– 1988. "Der Kult der Aphaia auf Aegina." In *Early Greek Cult Practice: Proceedings of the Fifth International Symposium at the Swedish Institute at Athens, 26–29 June, 1986*, edited by R. Hägg, N. Marinatos, and G. Nordquist, 149–59. Stockholm: Swedish Institute at Athens.

– 1992. "The 'Sacred Herd' of Artemis at Lusoi." In *The Iconography of Greek Cult in the Archaic and Classical Periods. Kernos* supp. 1, edited by R. Hägg, 177–87. Athens and Liège.

Slane, K.W. 1986. "Two Deposits from the Early Roman Cellar Building, Corinth." *Hesperia* 55: 271–318.

– 1990. *Corinth* XVIII, ii: *The Sanctuary of Demeter and Kore: The Roman Pottery and Lamps*. Princeton: American School of Classical Studies at Athens.

Slane-Wright, K.W., and R.E. Jones. 1980. "A Tiberian Pottery Deposit from Corinth." *Hesperia* 49: 135–77.

Small, A.M. 1994. "The Building Materials." In *The Excavations of San Giovanni de Ruoti.* Vol. 1: *The Villas and Their Environment*, edited by A.M. Small and R.J. Buck, 123–47. Toronto: University of Toronto Press.

Smith, A.H. 1904. *A Catalogue of Sculpture in the British Museum* III. London: British Museum.

Smith, P., and G. Avishai. 2005. "The Use of Dental Criteria for Estimating Postnatal Survival in Skeletal Remains of Infants." *Journal of Archaeological Science* 32: 83–9.

Snodgrass, A.M. 1964. *Early Greek Armour and Weapons, from the End of the Bronze Age to 600 B.C.* Edinburgh: Edinburgh University Press.

– 1967. *Arms and Armour of the Greeks.* London: Thames and Hudson.

– 1971. Review of *Greek and Roman Artillery: Historical Development* by E.W. Marsden. *CJ* 21: 106–8.

Sokolowski, F. 1955. *Lois sacrées de l'Asie Mineure.* École Française d'Athènes. Paris: E. de Boccard.

– 1962. *Lois sacrées des cités grecques*. École Française d'Athènes. Paris: E. de Boccard.

– 1969. *Lois sacrées des cités grecques. Supplément*. École Française d'Athènes. Paris: E. de Boccard.

Sourvinou-Inwood, C. 1988. *Studies in Girls' Transitions: Aspects of the Arkteia and Age Representation in Attic Iconography.* Athens: Kardamitsa.

Souyoudzoglou-Haywood, C. 1999. *The Ionian Islands in the Bronze Age and Early Iron Age, 3000–800 BC*. Liverpool: Liverpool University Press.

Sparkes, B.A., and L. Talcott. 1970. *The Athenian Agora* XII, i and ii: *Plain and Black Pottery from the 6th, 5th and 4th Centuries BC*. Princeton: American School of Classical Studies at Athens.

Spier, J. 1992. *Ancient Gems and Finger Rings: Catalogue of the Collections: The J. Paul Getty Museum*. Malibu, CA: J. Paul Getty Museum.

Spyropoulos, T. 1993. "Νέα γλυπτά αποκτήματα του Αρχαιολογικού Μουσείου Τριπόλεως." In *Sculpture from Arcadia and Laconia: Proceedings of an International Conference Held at the American School of Classical School at Athens, April 1992*, edited by O. Palagia and W. Coulson, 257–67. Oxford: Oxbow Books.

Stemmer, K., ed. 1995. *Standorte: Kontext und Funktion antiker Skulptur.* Berlin: Freunde & Förderer der Abguss-Sammlung antiker Plastik.

Stern, E.M. 2001. *Roman, Byzantine and Early Medieval Glass 10 BCE–700 CE: Ernesto Wolf Collection.* Ostfildern: Hatje Cantz.

Stern, E.M., and B. Schlick-Nolte. 1994. *Early Glass of the Ancient World 1600 B.C.–A.D. 50.* Ostfildern: G. Hatje.

Stewart, A. 2008. "The Persian and Carthaginian Invasions of 480 B.C.E. and the Beginning of the Classical Style." Part 1: "The Stratigraphy, Chronology, and Significance of the Acropolis Deposits." *AJA* 112: 377–412. Part 2: "The Finds from Other Sites in Athens, Attica, Elsewhere in Greece, and on Sicily." Part 3: "The Severe Style: Motivations and Meaning," *AJA* 112: 581–615.

Stewart, T.D. 1979. *Essentials of Forensic Anthropology, Especially as Developed in the United States.* Springfield: Charles C. Thomas.

Stieber, M. 2004. *The Poetics of Appearance in the Attic Korai.* Austin: University of Texas Press.

Stillwell, A.N. 1948. *Corinth* XV, i: *The Potter's Quarter.* Princeton: American School of Classical Studies at Athens.

Stillwell, A.N., and J.L. Benson. 1984. *Corinth* XV, iii: *The Potters' Quarter: The Pottery.* With contributions by Alan L. Boegehold and Cedric G. Boulter. Princeton: American School of Classical Studies at Athens.

Stillwell, R. 1952. *Corinth* II: *The Theatre.* Princeton: American School of Classical Studies at Athens.

Stone, P. 2007. "Ritual Dining, Drinking and Dedication at Stymphalos: A Case Study of the Influence of Popular Culture on Religion." Unpublished MA thesis, University of Cincinnati.

Strong, D.E. 1966. *Catalogue of Carved Amber in the Department of Greek and Roman Antiquities.* London: Trustees of the British Museum.

Stroud, R.S. 1965. "The Sanctuary of Demeter and Kore on Acrocorinth: Preliminary Report I: 1961–1962." *Hesperia* 34: 1–24.

Stuart-Macadam, P. 1987a. "A Radiographic Study of Porotic Hyperostosis." *AJPA* 74: 511–20.

– 1987b. "Porotic Hyperostosis: New Evidence to Support the Anemia Theory." *AJPA* 74: 521–6.

– 1989a. "Porotic Hyperostosis: Relationship between Orbital and Vault Lesions." *AJPA* 80: 187–93.

– 1989b. "Nutritional Deficiency Diseases: A Survey of Scurvy, Rickets, and Iron-Deficiency Anemia." In *Reconstruction of Life From the Skeleton*, edited by M.Y. İşcan and K.A.R. Kennedy, 201–22. New York: Alan R. Liss.

Stucky, R.A. 1993. *Die Skulpturen aus dem Eschmun-Heiligtum bei Sidon. Antike Kunst* supp. 17. Basel.

Sturgeon, M.C. 1987. *Isthmia* IV: *Sculpture* I: *1952–1967.* Princeton: American School of Classical Studies at Athens.

– 1996. "The Palaimonion Group: New Roman Statuary at Isthmia." Paper read at the 97th Annual Meeting of the Archaeological Institute of America, 27–30 December 1995, San Diego, Abstract *AJA* 100: 399.

– 1998. "Hellenistic Sculpture at Corinth. The State of the Question." In *Regional Schools in Hellenistic Sculpture*, conference at the American School of Classical Studies, Athens, March 1996, edited by O. Palagia and W.D.E. Coulson, 1–13. Oxford: Oxbow Books.

– 2006. "Archaic Athens and the Cyclades." In *Greek Sculpture: Function, Materials, and Techniques in the Archaic and Classical Periods*, edited by O. Palagia, 32–76. Cambridge: Cambridge University Press.

– Forthcoming. "New Isthmian Sculptures and the Palaimonion." In *"The Bridge of the Untiring Sea": The Corinthian Isthmus from Prehistory to Late Antiquity*, edited by E.R. Gebhard and T.E. Gregory. *Hesperia* supp.

Sturgeon, M., Y. Maniatis, and D. Tambakopoulos. 2012. "Provenance Investigation of Two Marble Sculptures from Ancient Stymphalos." In *Interdisciplinary Studies on Ancient Stone: Proceedings of IX ASMOSIA Conference* (Association for the Study of Marbles and Other Stones in Antiquity), 2009, Tarragona, Spain, edited by A. Gutierrez Barcia, P.L. Mercadal, and L.R. de Llanza, 279–86. Tarragona: Institut Català d'Arqueologia Clàssica.

Svoronos, I. 1904. *Τα νομίσματα του κράτους των Πτολεμάιων*. Athens: P.D. Sakellariou.

Syon, D. 1992. "Gamla: Portrait of a Rebellion." *Biblical Archaeological Reports* 18: 20–37.

Taeuber, H. 1981. "Sikyon statt Aegeira: Neue Beobachtungen zur Stele von Stymphalos (IG V/2, 351–357)." *ZPE* 42: 179–92.

Tarn, W.W. 1913. *Antigonos Gonatas.* Oxford: Clarendon Press.

Tatton-Brown, V. 1981. "Rod-formed Glass Pendants and Beads of the 1st Millennium BC." In *Catalogue of Greek and Roman Glass in the British Museum*, vol. 1, edited by D.B. Harden, 143–55. London: British Museum Publications.

– 1992. "Loomweights, Bobbins, and Spindle-Whorls." In *An Iron Age and Roman Republican Settlement on Botromagno, Gravina di Puglia: Excavations of 1965–1974.* Vol. 2: *The Artifacts,* edited by A.M. Small, 218–26. London: British School at Rome.

Tausend, K. 1999. "Heiligtümer und Kulte Nordostarkadiens." In *Pheneos und Lousoi: Untersuchungen zu Geschicte und Topographie Nordostarkadiens*, edited by K. Tausend, 343–62. Frankfurt am Main: Peter Lang.

Themelis, P. 1979. "Ausgrabungen in Kallipolis (Ost-Aetolien). 1977–8." *AAA* 12: 245–79.

– 2004. "Ονοματολόγιο σκευών και αγγείων." In *ΣΤ' Επιστημονική Συνάντηση για την Ελληνιστική Κεραμική*

(2000), 715–24. Athens: Έκδοση του Ταμείου Αρχαιλογικών Πόρων και Απαλλοτριώσεων.

Themelis, P. and I. Touratsoglou. 1997. *Οι Τάφοι του Δερβενίου*. Athens: ΤΑΠ.

Theocharis, D. 1961–2. "'Ομόλιον." *ArchDelt* 17, β: 175–9.

Thompson, D.B. 1960. "The House of Simon the Shoemaker." *Archaeology* 13: 234–40.

Thompson, H., D. Thompson, and S.I. Rotroff. 1987. *Hellenistic Pottery and Terracottas*. Princeton: American School of Classical Studies at Athens.

Thompson, M. 1968. "The Mints of Lysimachus." In *Essays in Greek Coinage Presented to Stanley Robinson*, edited by C.M. Kraay and G.K. Jenkins, 163–82. Oxford: Clarendon Press.

– 1968. *The Agrinion Hoard*. Numismatic Notes and Monographs 159. New York: American Numismatic Society, 1968.

Thomson, W.M. 2004. "Dental Caries Experience in Older People over Time: What Can the Large Cohort Studies Tell Us?" *British Dental Journal* 196: 89–92.

Torr, C. 1885. *Rhodes in Ancient Times*. Cambridge: Cambridge University Press.

Touloupa, E. 2002. *Τὰ ἐναετία γλυπτά τοῦ ναοῦ τοῦ Ἀπόλλωνος Δαφνηφόρου στὴν Ερέτρια*. Library of the Archaeological Society in Athens 220. Athens.

Touratsoglou, I. 1998. "Dated Gold: The Evidence from Hellenistic Macedonia." In *The Art of the Greek Goldsmith*, edited by D. Williams, 30–8. London: British Museum Press.

Toynbee, J.M.C. 1973. *Animals in Roman Art and Life*. Ithaca: Cornell University Press.

Travlos, J. 1971. *Pictorial Dictionary of Ancient Athens*. New York: Praeger.

Treister, M.Y. 1996. *The Role of Metals in Ancient Greek History*. Leiden, New York, Köln: E.J. Brill.

– 2001. *Hammering Techniques in Greek and Roman Jewellery and Toreutics*. Leiden: E.J. Brill.

Trendall, A.D., and A. Cambitoglou. 1978. *The Red-Figured Vases of Apulia* I. Oxford: Clarendon Press.

Trianti, I. 1984. "Hausmodelle aus Mazi." *AM* 99: 112–19.

– 1999. "Νέα αρχαϊκά γλυπτά από τη Θήρα." In *ΦΩΣ ΚΥΚΛΑΔΙΚΟΝ: Τιμητικός τόμος στη μνήμη του Νίκου Ζαφειρόπουλου*, edited by C. Stampolidis, 190–201. Athens: Goulandris Foundation, Museum of Cycladic Art.

Triossi, A., and D. Mascetti. 1997. *The Necklace from Antiquity to Present*. London: Thames and Hudson.

Tritsaroli, P., and F. Valentin, 2008. "Byzantine Burial Practices for Children: Case Studies Based on a Bioarchaeological Approach to Cemeteries from Greece." In *Nasciturus, infans, puerulus vobis mater terra: la muerte en la infancia*, edited by F.G. Jener, S. Muriel, and C. Olària, 93–113. Diputació de Castelló, Sèrie de prehistoria i arqueologia (SIAP).

Trundle, M. 2004. *Greek Mercenaries, from the Late Archaic Period to Alexander*. London: Routledge.

Tsakalou-Tzanavari, K. 1989. "Ανασκαφική έρευνα στο νεκροταφείο της αρχαίας Λητής." *ΤΟ ΑΡΧΑΙΟΛΟΓΙΚΟ ΕΡΓΟ ΣΤΗ ΜΑΚΕΔΟΝΙΑ ΚΑΙ ΘΡΑΚΗ* 3: 307–12.

Tsimbidou-Avloniti, M. 1989. "Τάφοι κλασσικών χρόνων στην Επανωμή." *ΤΟ ΑΡΧΑΙΟΛΟΓΙΚΟ ΕΡΓΟ ΣΤΗ ΜΑΚΕΔΟΝΙΑ ΚΑΙ ΘΡΑΚΗ* 3: 319–29.

Tsigarida, B. 1998. "Fifth-Century BC Jewellery from the Cemetaries of Pydna, Macedonia." In *The Art of the Greek Goldsmith*, edited by D. Williams, 48–54. London: British Museum Press.

– 2006. "Couronnes, diadèmes, colliers et boucles d'oreille de Macédoine centrale à l'èpoque de Philippe II et d'Alexandre le Grand." In *Les ors des mondes grec et "barbare"*, edited by G. Nicolini, 139–52. Paris: A. et J. Picard.

Ulbert, G. 1984. *Cáceres el Viejo: Ein spätrepublikanisches Legionslager in Spanisch-Extremadura*. Mainz: Philipp von Zabern.

Vandermersch, C. 1994. *Vins et amphores de Grande Grèce et de Sicile, IVe–IIIe s. avant J.-C.* Études I. Naples: Centre Jean Bérard.

Van Hoorn, G. 1951. *Choes and Anthesteria*. Leiden: E.J. Brill.

Van Straten, F.T. 1981. "Gifts for the Gods." In *Faith, Hope and Worship: Aspects of Religious Mentality in the Ancient World*, edited by H.S. Versnel, 65–151. Leiden: E.J. Brill.

– 1995. *"Hiera Kala": Images of Animal Sacrifice in Archaic and Classical Greece*. Religions in the Graeco-Roman World 127. Leiden.

Venclová, N. 1983. "Prehistoric Eye-Beads in Central Europe." *JGS* 25: 11–17.

Verdelis, N. 1960. "Ἀρχαιότητες Ἀργολιδοκορινθίας." *ArchDelt* 16, B': 79–82.

Vernant, J.-P. 1991. "The Figure and Functions of Artemis in Myth and Cult." In *Mortals and Immortals: Collected Essays*, edited by F.I. Zeitlin, 195–206. Princeton: Princeton University Press.

Vischer, W. 1875. *Erinnerungen und Eindrucke aus Griechenland*. Basle: Schweighauser.

– 1878. "Antike Schleudergeschosse." *Kleine Schriften* 2: 240–84. Leipzig: S. Hirzel.

Viviers, D. 1992. *Recherches sur les ateliers de sculpteurs et la cité d'Athènes à l'époque archaïque: Endoios, Philergos, Aristoklès*. Brussels: Académie royale de Belgique.

Vlavianou-Tsaliki, K. 1998. "Πρωτογεωμετρικοί τάφοι στη Σκύρο. Συμβολή στην ΠΓ κεραμική." *ArchDelt* 53, A': 113–46.

Vocotopoulou, J. 1975. "Le trésor de vases de bronze de Votonosi." *BCH* 99: 729–88.

Vogeikoff-Brogan, N. 2000. "Late Hellenistic Pottery in Athens: A New Deposit and Further Thoughts on the Association of Pottery and Societal Change." *Hesperia* 69: 293–333.

Voigtländer, W. 1982. "Funde aus der Insula westlich des Buleuterion in Milet." *IstMitt* 32: 30–173.

Vokotopoulou, I. 1985. *Σίνδος. κατάλογος τῆς ἔκθεσης*. Athens: Ταμεῖο Ἀρχαιολογικῶν Πόρων καί Ἀπαλλοτριώσεων.

– 1967. "Νομὸς Ἰωαννίνων " *ArchDelt* 22, B'2: 342–9.

– 1973. *Ὀδηγὸς Μουσεῖου Ἰωαννίνων*. Athens.

Vorster, C. 1983. *Griechische Kinderstatuen*. Köln.

Voyatzis, M.E. 1990. *The Early Sanctuary of Athena Alea at Tegea and Other Archaic Sanctuaries in Arcadia*. Göteborg: Paul Åströms.

Wace, A.J.B. 1904–5. "Laconia II: Geraki, Sculptures." *BSA* 11: 99–105.

Wagner, C., and J. Boardman. 2003. *A Collection of Classical and Eastern Intaglios, Rings and Cameos: Studies in Gems and Jewellery I. BAR-IS* 1136. Oxford: Archaeopress.

Walbank, M.B. 1986. "Athens and Stymphalos: I.G. II^2 144+." *Hesperia* 55: 319–54.

Waldbaum, J. 1983. *Archaeological Exploration of Sardis*. Vol. 8: *Metalwork from Sardis: The Finds through 1974*. Cambridge, MA: Harvard University Press.

Waldstein, C. 1902. *The Argive Heraeum*. Vol. 1: Boston, New York: Houghton, Mifflin and Co.

– 1905. *The Argive Heraeum*. Vol. 2: Boston and New York: Houghton, Mifflin and Co.

Walker, A.L., and H. Goldman. 1915. "Report on Excavations at Halae of Locris." *AJA* 19: 418–37.

Walker, D.R. 1988. *Roman Coins from the Sacred Spring at Bath*. Oxford: Oxford University Committee for Archaeology.

Walker, P.L., R.R. Bathurst, R. Richman, T. Gjerdrum, and V.A. Andrushko. 2009. "The Causes of Porotic Hyperostosis and Cribra Orbitalia: A Reappraisal of the Iron-Deficiency-Anemia Hypothesis." *AJPA* 139: 109–25.

Wallrodt, S.J. 2001. "Late Classical Votive Loomweights from Ilion." *AJA* 105: 303.

– 2002. "Ritual Activity in Late Classical Ilion: The Evidence from a Fourth Century B.C. Deposit of Loomweights and Spindlewhorls." *Studia Troica* 12: 179–96.

Walter-Karydi, E. 1987. *Alt-Ägina* II, 2: *Die Äginetische Bildhauerschule*. Mainz: Philipp von Zabern.

Walters, H.B. 1899. *Catalogue of the Bronzes, Greek, Roman, and Etruscan, in the British Museum*. London: British Museum.

– 1915. *Select Bronzes, Greek, Roman, and Etruscan, in the British Museum*. London: British Museum.

– 1926. *Catalogue of the Engraved Gems and Cameos in the British Museum*. London: Printed by order of the Trustees.

Warden, P.G. 1990. "Part I: The Small Finds." In *The Extramural Sanctuary of Demeter and Persephone at Cyrene, Libya. Final Reports*, vol. 4, edited by D. White, 1–86. Philadelphia: University Museum, University of Philadelphia.

Warren, J.A.W. 1983. "The Autonomous Bronze Coinage of Sicyon. Part I." *NC* 143: 23–56, pls. 5–8.

– 1984. "The Autonomous Bronze Coinage of Sicyon. Part II." *NC* 144: 1–24, pls. 1–3.

– 1998. "Updating (and Downdating) the Autonomous Bronze Coinage of Sikyon." In *Studies in Greek Numismatics in Memory of Martin Jessop Price*, edited by R. Ashton et al., 347–61. London: Spink.

– 2000. "The Silver Coins of Sikyon in Leiden: Analysis and Some Comments on the Coinage." In *Pour Denyse: Divertissements numismatiques*, edited by S. Hurter and C. Arnold-Biucchi, 201–10. Bern: n.p.

Watrous, L.V. 1982. "The Sculptural Program of the Siphnian Treasury at Delphi." *AJA* 87: 159–72.

Watt, M.E., D.A. Lunt, and W.H. Gilmour. 1997a. "Caries Prevalence in the Permanent Dentition of a Mediaeval Population from the Southwest of Scotland." *Archives of Oral Biology* 42: 601–20.

– 1997b. "Caries Prevalence in the Deciduous Dentition of a Mediaeval Population from the Southwest of Scotland." *Archives of Oral Biology* 42: 811–20.

Watts, D.J. 1989. "Infant Burials and Romano-British Christianity." *ArchJ* 146: 372–83.

Webster, G. 1958. "The Roman Military Advance under Ostorius Scapula." *ArchJ* 115: 49–98.

Weikart, S. 2002. *Griechische Bauopferrituale: Intention und Konvention von rituellen Handlungen im griechischen Bauwesen*. Berlin: Verlag im Internet GmbH.

Weinberg, G.D. 1959. "Glass Manufacture in Ancient Crete." *JGS* 1: 11–21.

– 1960. "Excavations at Tarrha, 1959." *Hesperia* 29: 90–108.

– 1969. "Glass Manufacture in Hellenistic Rhodes." *ArchDelt* 24: 143–51.

– 1975. "A Medieval Mystery: Byzantine Glass Production." *JGS* 17: 127–41.

Weinberg, S.S. 1954. "Corinthian Relief Ware: Pre-Hellenistic Period." *Hesperia* 23: 109–37.

Weinstein, M., P. Babyn, and S. Zlotkin. 2001. "An Orange a Day Keeps the Doctor Away: Scurvy in the Year 2000." *Pediatrics* 108: 55–9.

Weir, R. 2001. "The Story of an Arcadian Polis: Coins from the Excavations at Stymphalos." Paper read at the 2001 meeting of the Archaeological Institute of America, San Diego.

– 2007. "The Stymphalos Hoard of 1999 and the City's Defences." *AJN* 19: 9–32.

Wheeler, M. 1943. *Maiden Castle, Dorset: Reports of the Research Committee of the Society of Antiquaries of London* 12. Oxford: University Press for the Society of Antiquaries.

Whitaker, J.I.S. 1921. *Motya, a Phoenician Colony in Sicily.* London: G. Bell.

Whitbread, I.K. 1995. *Greek Transport Amphorae: A Petrological and Archaeological Study.* Fitch Laboratory Occasional Paper 4. Athens: British School at Athens.

– 2003. "Clays of Corinth. The Study of a Basic Resource for Ceramic Production." In *Corinth: The Centenary 1896–1996. Corinth* XX, edited by Ch. Williams II and N. Bookidis, 1–13. Athens: American School of Classical Studies.

White, D. 1963. "A Survey of Millstones from Morgantina." *AJA* 67: 199–206.

Whitehead, D. 1990. *How to Survive under Siege: Aineias the Tactician; Translated, with Introduction and Commentary.* Oxford: Clarendon Press.

Whitehouse, D. 2001. *Roman Glass in the Corning Museum of Glass.* Vol. 2. Corning, NY: Corning Museum of Glass.

Whitley, J. 2003. "Archaeology in Greece 2002–2003." *AR* 49: 1–88.

Whittaker, D.K., and T. Molleson. 1996. "Caries Prevalence in the Dentition of a Late Eighteenth Century Population." *Archives of Oral Biology* 41: 55–61.

WHO. 1999. *Scurvy and Its Prevention and Control in Major Emergencies.* Geneva: World Health Organization.

Will, E.L. 1982. "Greco-Italic Amphoras." *Hesperia* 51: 338–56.

Williams II, C.K. 1969. "Excavations at Corinth, 1968." *Hesperia* 38: 36–63.

Williams, C.K., and J.E. Fisher. 1971. "Corinth 1970: Forum Area." *Hesperia* 40: 1–53.

Williams, D. 1988. "Three Groups of Fourth Century South Italian Jewellery in the British Museum." *RömMitt* 95: 75–95.

– 1998. "Identifying Greek Jewellers and Goldsmiths." In *The Art of the Greek Goldsmith,* edited by D. Williams, 99–105. London: British Museum Press.

– 2003. "Gilded Pottery and Golden Jewellery." In *The Macedonians in Athens 322–229 B.C.,* edited by O. Palagia and S.V. Tracy, 226–35. Oxford: Oxbow Books.

– 2006. "The Chian Pottery from Naukratis." In *Naukratis: Greek Diversity in Egypt: Studies on East Greek Pottery and Exchange in the Eastern Mediterranean,* edited by A. Villing and U. Schlotzhauer, 127–32. British Museum Research Pub. No. 162. London: British Museum.

Williams, D., and J. Ogden. 1994. *Greek Gold.* New York: H.N. Abrams.

Williams, H. 1981. *Kenchreai, Eastern Port of Corinth* V: *The Lamps.* Leiden: Brill.

– 1983. "Stymphalos: A Planned City of Ancient Arcadia." *EchCl* n.s. 2: 194–205.

– 1984. "Investigations at Mytilene and Stymphalos, 1983." *EchCl* n.s. 3: 174–83; appendix by Thomas Boyd, 183–6.

– 1985. "Investigations at Stymphalos, 1984." *EchCl* n.s. 4: 215–24.

– 2005. "The Exploration of Ancient Stymphalos, 1982–2002." In *Ancient Arkadia: Papers from the Third International Seminar on Ancient Arkadia, Held at the Norwegian Institute at Athens, 7–10 May* 2002, edited by E. Østby, 397–411. Papers from the Norwegian Institute at Athens 8. Athens: Norwegian Institute at Athens.

Williams, H., and S.-M. Cronkite Price. 1995. "Excavations at Stymphalos, 1994." *EchCl* n.s. 14: 1–22.

Williams, H., S.-M. Cronkite Price, and G. Schaus. 1996. "Excavations at Stymphalos, 1995." *EchCl* n.s. 15: 75–98. (For article authorship, op.cit. n.s. 16: x)

Williams, H., and B. Gourley. 2005. "The Fortifications of Stymphalos." *Mouseion* 5: 213–59.

Williams, H., and G. Schaus. 2001. "The Sanctuary of Athena at Ancient Stymphalos." In *Athena in the Classical World,* edited by S. Deacy and A. Villing, 75–94. Leiden: Brill.

Williams, H., G. Schaus, S.-M. Cronkite Price, B. Gourley, and H. Lutomsky. 1997. "Excavations at Ancient Stymphalos, 1996." *EchCl* n.s. 16: 23–73.

Williams, H., G. Schaus, S.-M. Cronkite Price, B. Gourley, and C. Hagerman. 1998. "Excavations at Ancient Stymphalos, 1997." *EchCl* n.s. 17: 261–319.

Williams, H., G. Schaus, B. Gourley, S.-M. Cronkite Price, K. Donahue Sherwood, and Y. Lolos. 2002. "Excavations at Ancient Stymphalos, 1999–2002." *Mouseion* 2: 135–87.

Wilson, L.M. 1930. "The Loom-weights." In *Olynthus* II: *Architecture and Sculpture: Houses and Other Buildings,* edited by D.M. Robinson, 118–28. Baltimore: Johns Hopkins University Press.

Winter, F.E. 1997. "The Use of Artillery in Fourth-Century and Hellenistic Towers." *EchCl* n.s. 16: 247–92.

Winter, N.A. 1993. *Greek Architectural Terracottas from the Prehistoric to the End of the Archaic Period.* Oxford: Clarendon Press.

Wiseman, J. 1967. "Excavations at Corinth: The Gymnasium Area, 1966." *Hesperia* 36: 402–28.

Woodhead, A.G. 1957. "Greek Inscriptions." *Hesperia* 26: 221–36 ("Athens and Stymphalos," 223–5).

Wroth, W. 1908. *Catalogue of the Imperial Byzantine Coins in the British Museum*. London: Trustees of the British Museum.

Yalouris, N. 1992. *Die Skulpturen des Asklepiostempels in Epidauros*. *AntP* 21. Munich: Hirmer.

Young, A. 2001. "The Jewelry from the Sanctuary of 'Athena,' Stymphalos: Preliminary Findings." *Mouseion* 1: 111–26.

Zagdoun, M.A. 1984. "Bagues et anneaux." *L'antre corycien II*. *BCH* supp. 9, 183–257. Athens: École Française d'Athènes; Paris: Boccard.

Zancani Montuoro, P., et al. 1965–6. "L'edificio quadrato nello Heraion alla foce del Sele." *Atti e memorie della Società Magna Grecia* n.s. 6–7: 23–195.

Zapheiropoulou, P. 1973. *Vases et autres objets de marbre de Rhénée*. *BCH* supp. 1, *Études déliennes*, 601–36. Athens: École Française d'Athènes; Paris: Éditions de Boccard.

Zaphiropoulos, N.S. 1986. "Αρχαϊκές κόρες της Πάρου." In *Archaische und klassische griechische Plastik: Akten des internationalen Kolloquiums vom 22.–25. April 1985 in Athen*, I, edited by H. Kyrieleis, 93–106. Mainz: Philipp von Zabern.

Zaphiropoulou, P. 1998. *ΠΑΡΟΣ*. Athens.

– 2000. "Parische Skulpturen." *AntP* 27: 7–35.

Zervos, O. 1980. "Coins Excavated at Corinth, 1978–1980." *Hesperia* 55: 183–205.

ILLUSTRATIONS

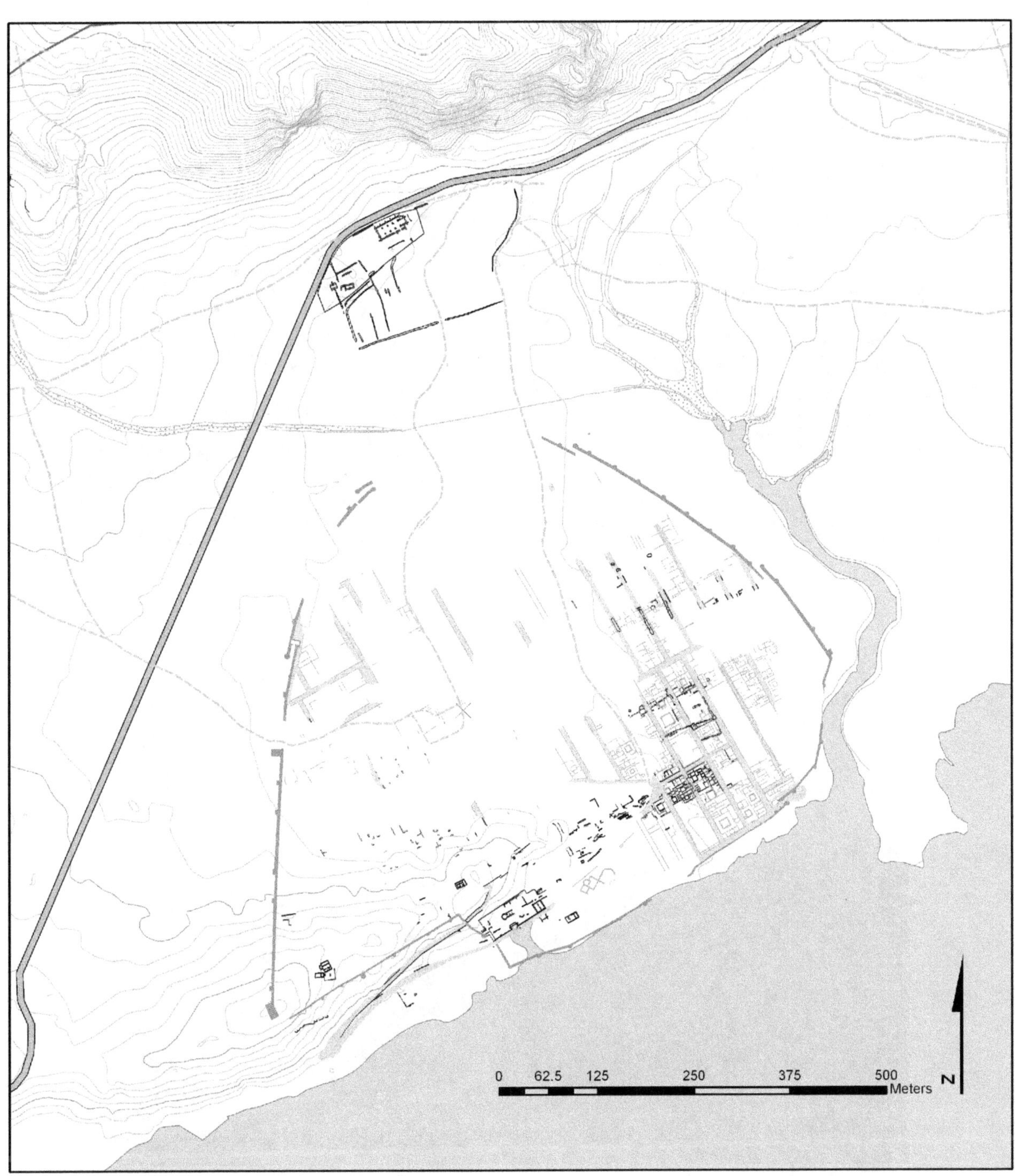

1

0.1. Plan of Stymphalos. Acropolis Sanctuary at lower left. (B. Gourley)

1a

1b

1.1a. Central part of the Stymphalos valley including the lake and low acropolis from the north

1.1b. The acropolis of Stymphalos just above the lake, with Mt. Kyllene in the background.

1.2a–b. Early Bronze Age stone celts from the acropolis, Stymphalos

1.3. Fragmentary Mycenean drinking cup, Stymphalos

1.4a–b. Views of the "throne" near Kionia

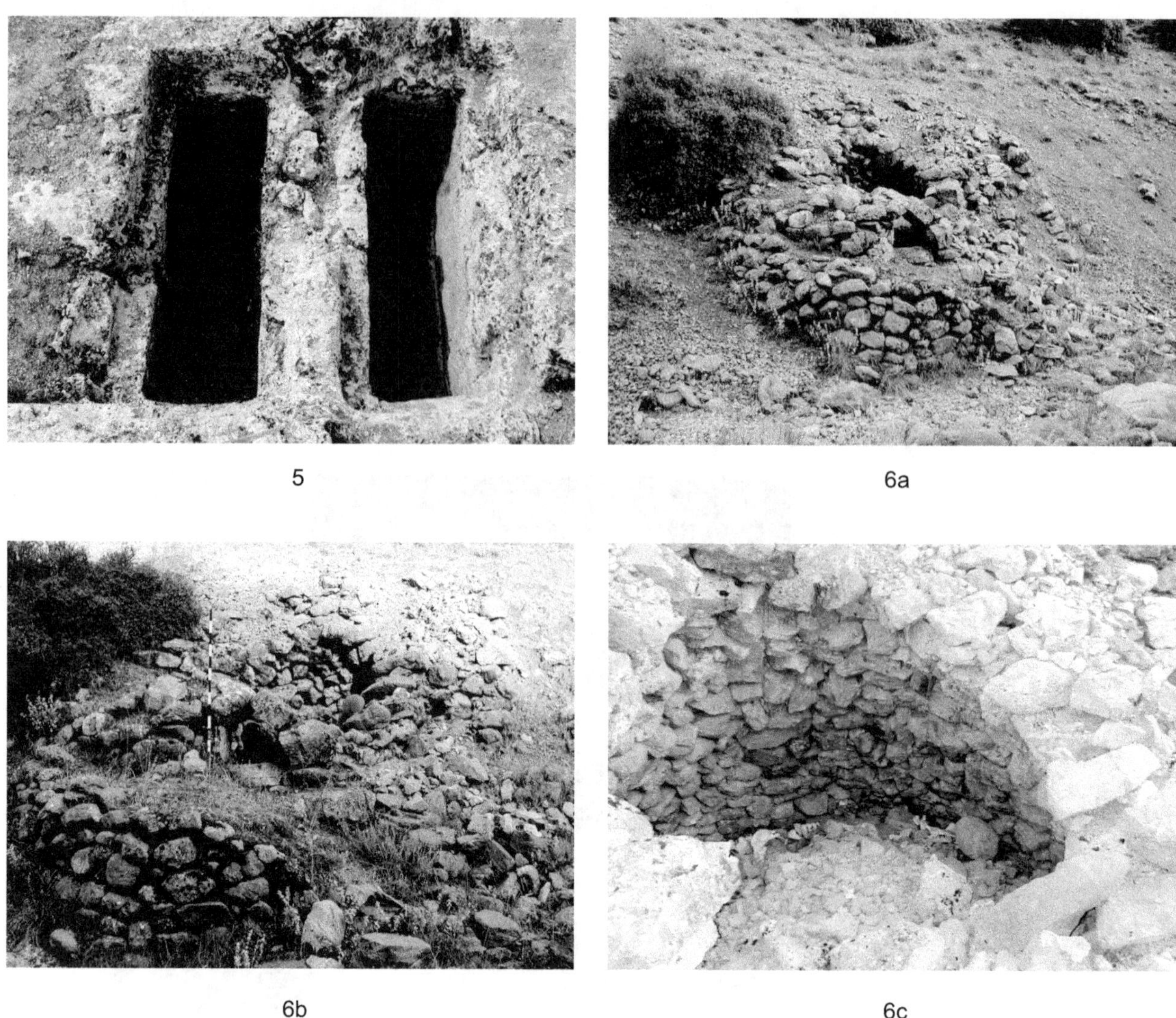

5

6a

6b

6c

1.5. Two shafts cut into bedrock towards the east end of the acropolis ridge

1.6a–c. Tholos tomb near Lafka

7

8

1.7. Cyclopean wall on Aghia Triadha hill near Lakfa.

1.8. Entry in Orlandos' field notebook with measured drawing of the POLIADOS inscription, and note that it was moved to the house of Ath. Xernou in Kionia (courtesy of the Archaeological Society at Athens)

1.9a–c. Orlandos' photographs of the Temple: 9a from the NW; 9b from the SW; 9c from the SE (courtesy of the Archaeological Society at Athens)

1.10. Orlandos' (1924, 121 fig. 5) plan of the acropolis Temple.

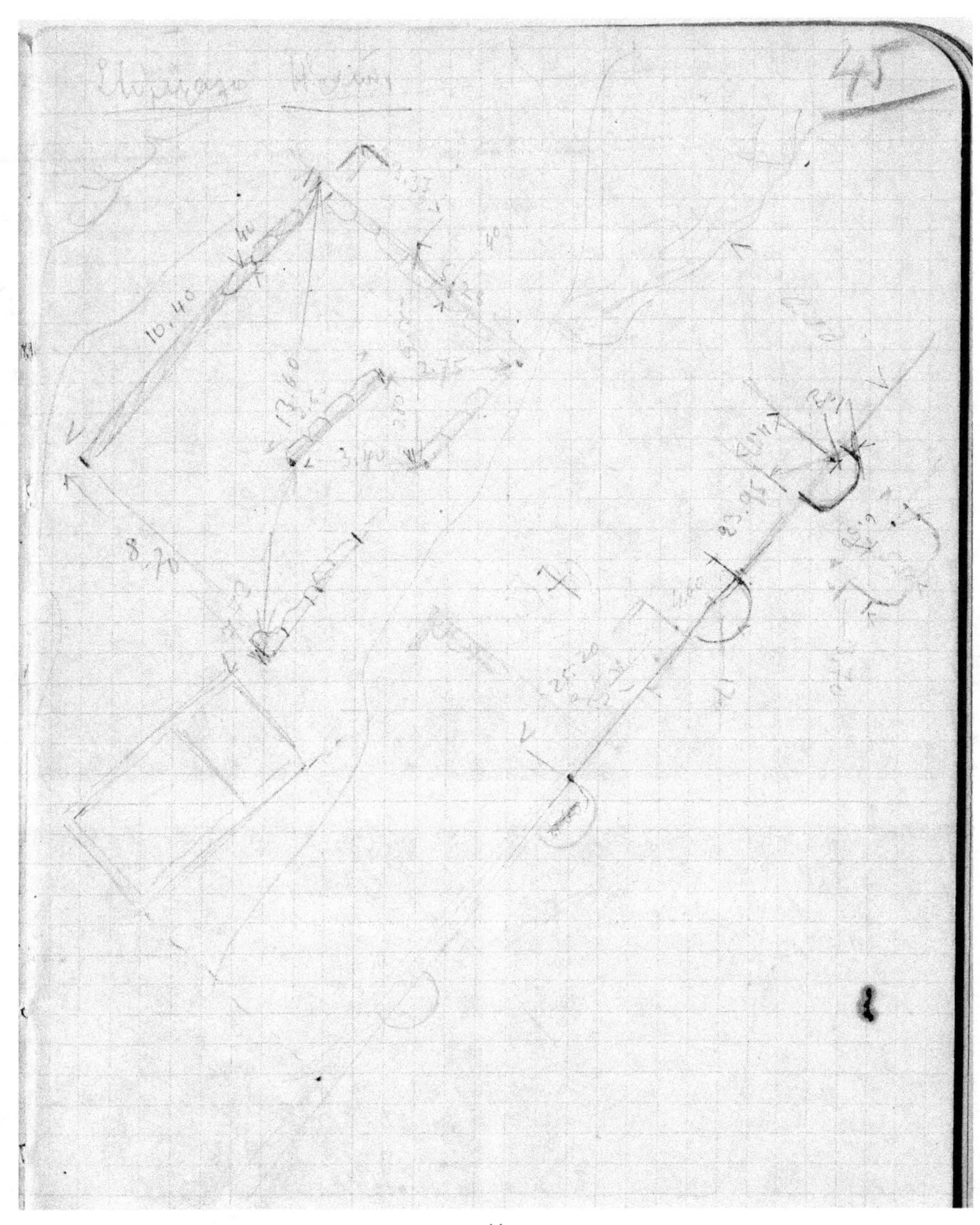

11

1.11. Orlandos' notebook plan of the Sanctuary (courtesy of the Archaeological Society at Athens)

2.1. Acropolis Sanctuary from the east (B. Gourley)

2.2a. Air view of the Sanctuary looking westward (B. Gourley)

2.2b. Air view of the Sanctuary looking northward (B. Gourley)

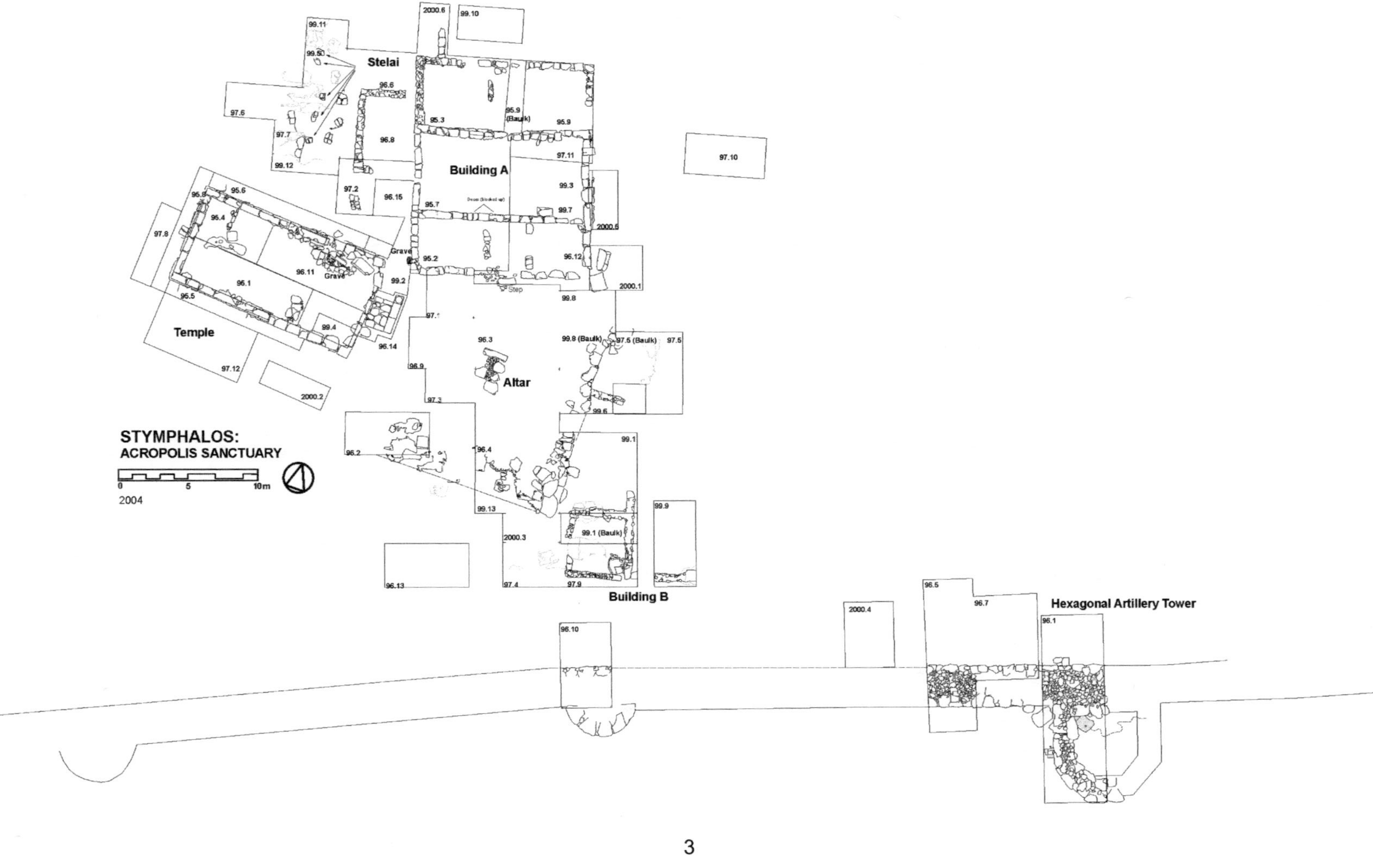

2.3. Plan of the Sanctuary and City Wall on the acropolis of Stymphalos (B. Gourley)

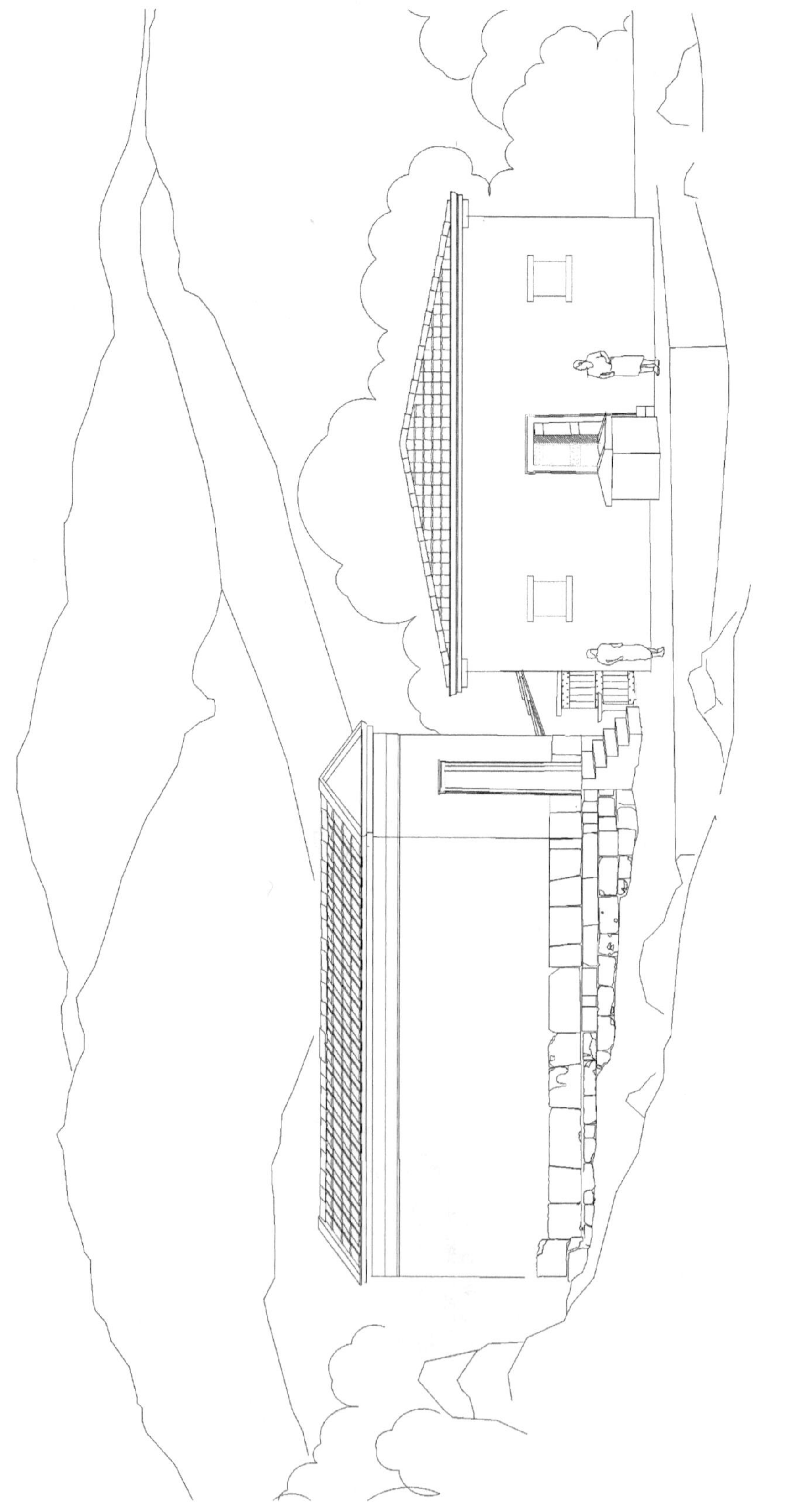

4

2.4. Reconstruction drawing of the Sanctuary from the south (B. Gourley)

5

6

2.5. Summer sunrise from the Sanctuary

2.6. Air view of the Temple, Altar and Building A (B. Gourley)

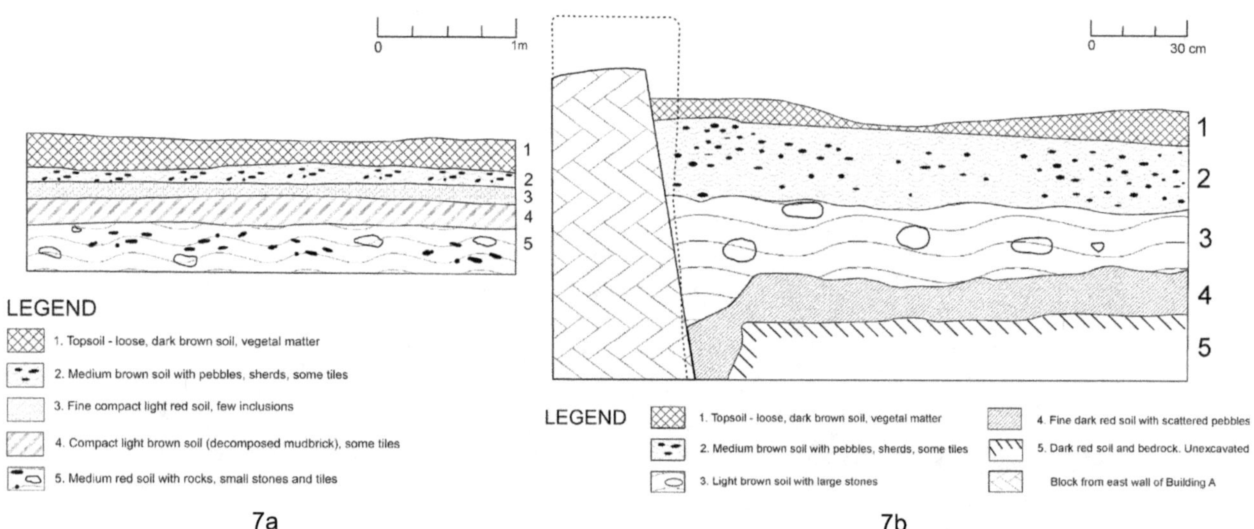

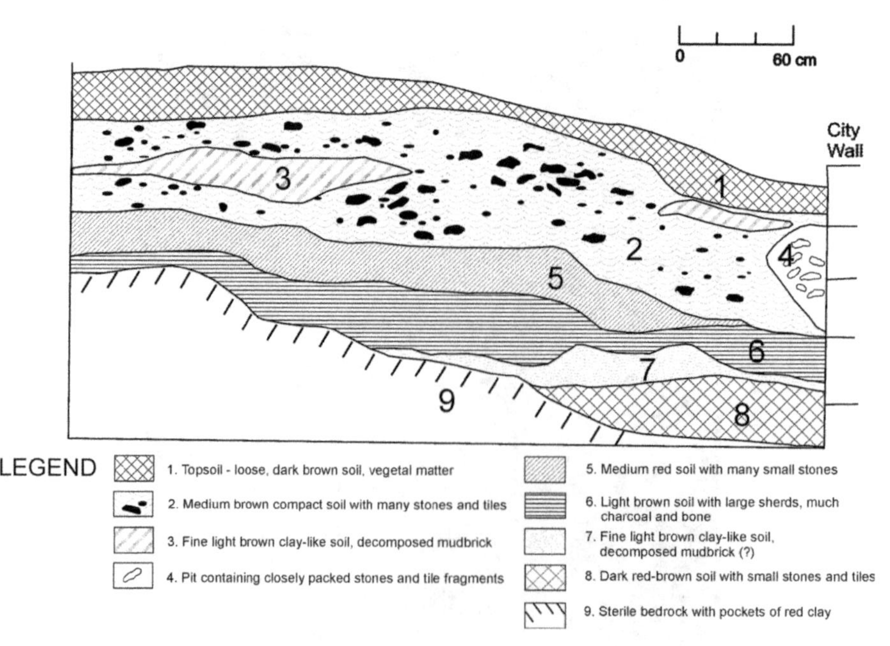

2.7a–c. Scarp drawings from Trenches 97.9, 00.5 and 00.4

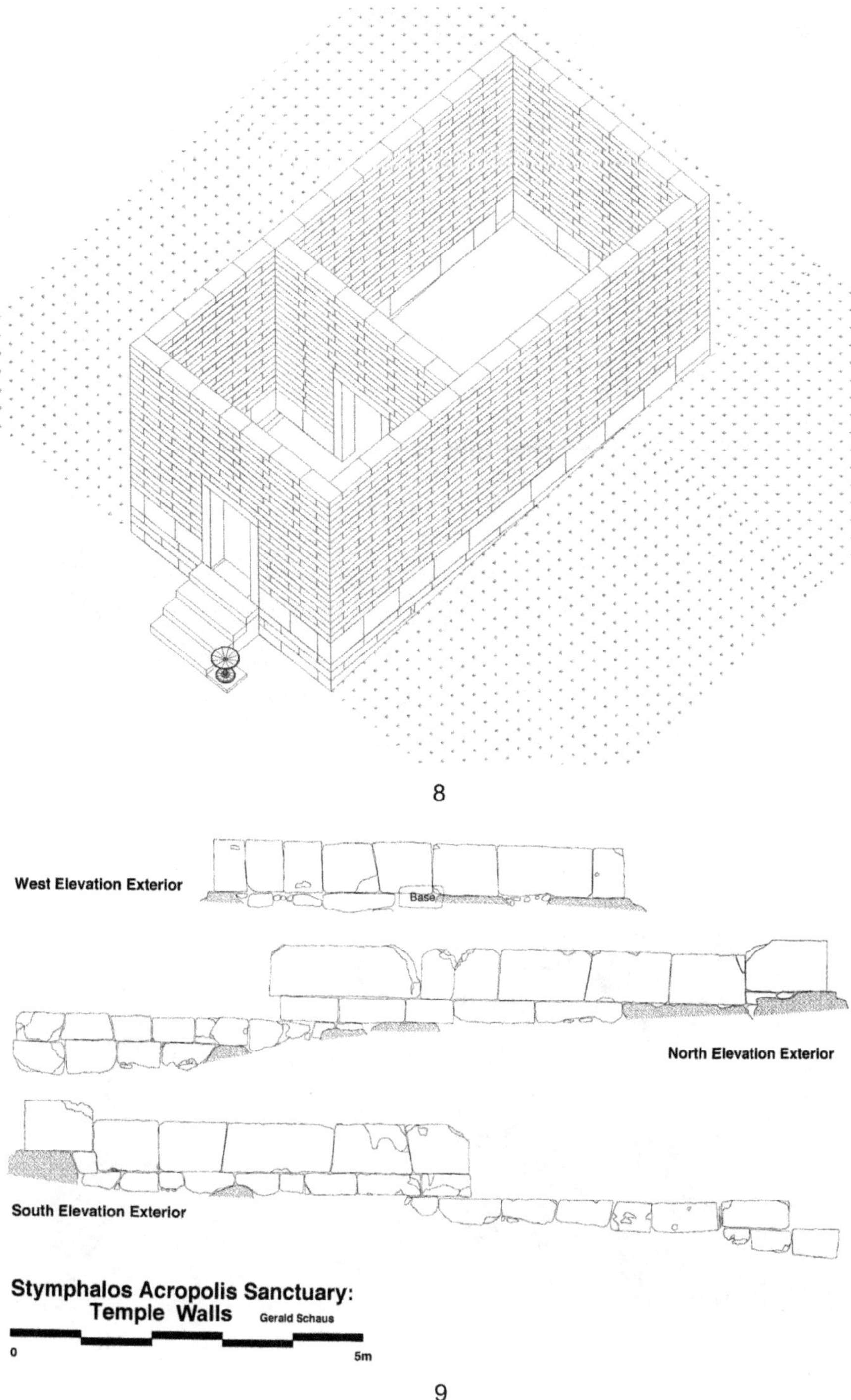

2.8. Reconstruction of the Temple walls and stairs from the northeast (D. Meadows)

2.9. Elevation drawings of the Temple walls

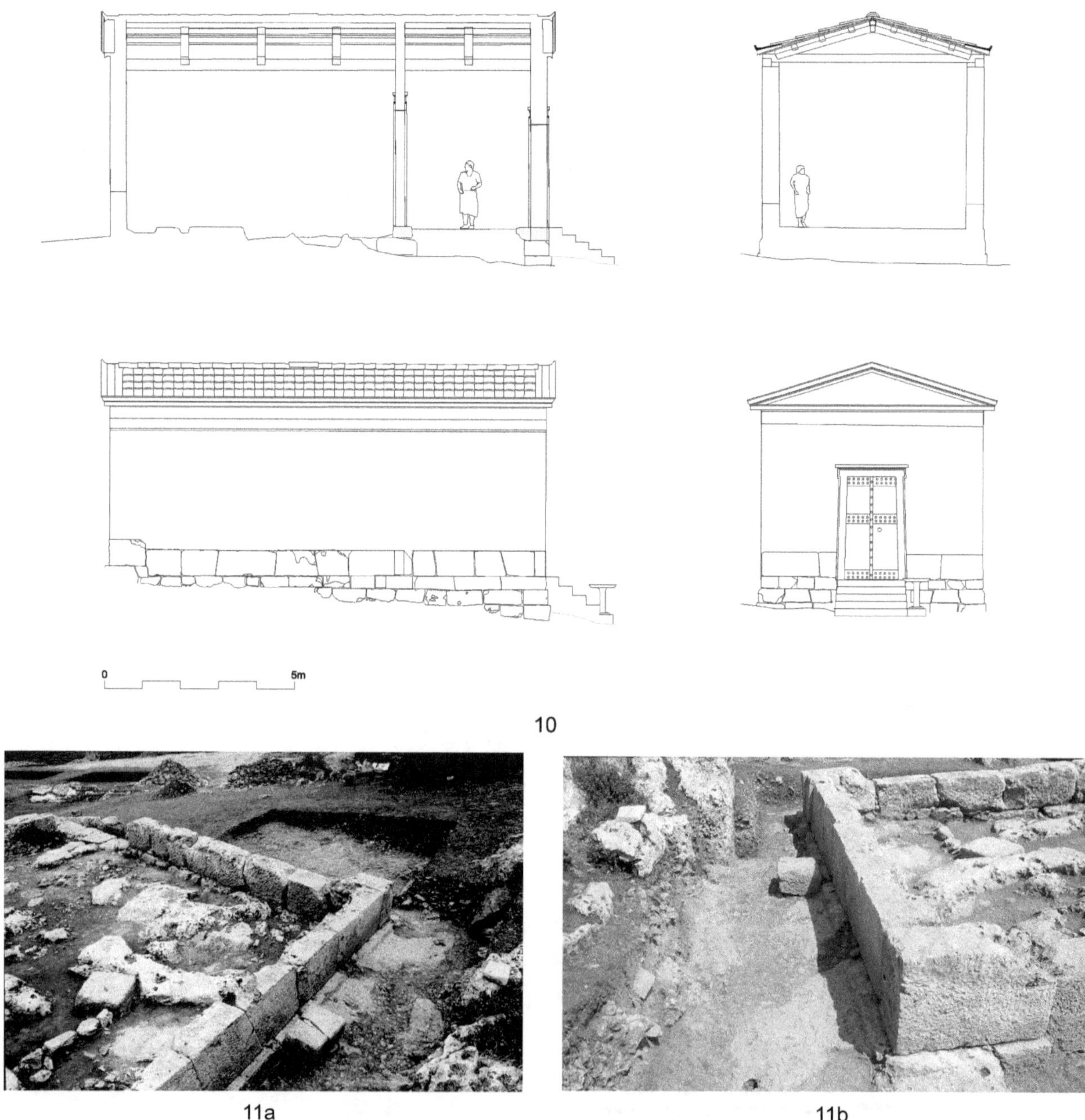

2.10. Temple. Reconstructed views and cross-section (B. Gourley)

2.11a–b. West end of the Temple from the northwest and south

2.12. Interior view of the Temple looking east

2.13a–c. Ashlar block beside bedrock outcrop within the cella

14

15a

15b

16a

16b

2.14. Dark burn areas within the cella, starting level with the ashlar block

2.15a–b. Bronze patera uncovered within the burnt soil in the northwest corner of the cella

2.16a–b. Mould-made bowl fragment amid burnt earth beside the ashlar block

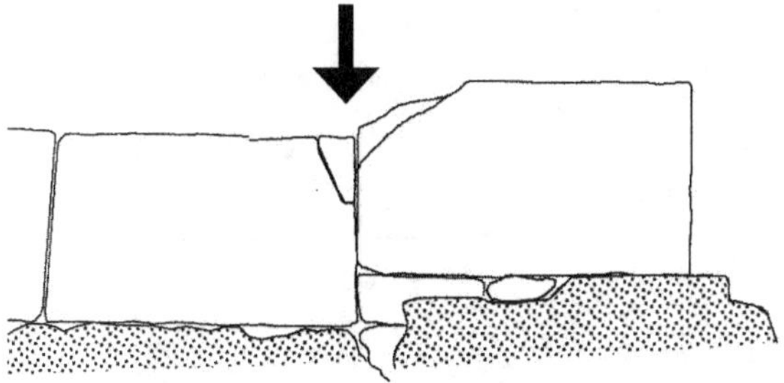

17a

17b

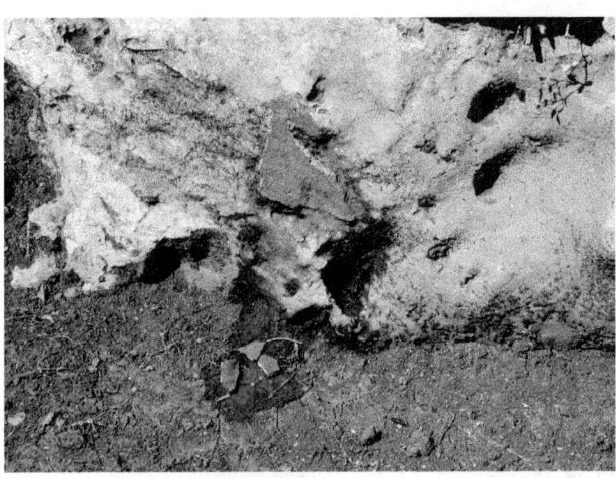

18a

18b

2.17a–b. Top right corner repair of the second orthostate block

2.18a–b. Red-painted lime plaster attached to a rough block of the string course, and other fragments found inside the cella

19a

19b

20

2.19a. A block of the pronaos wall is preserved in situ near the top left

2.19b. Ashlar block of the pronaos wall (left centre)

2.20. Fragments of burnt clay with surface striations

21a

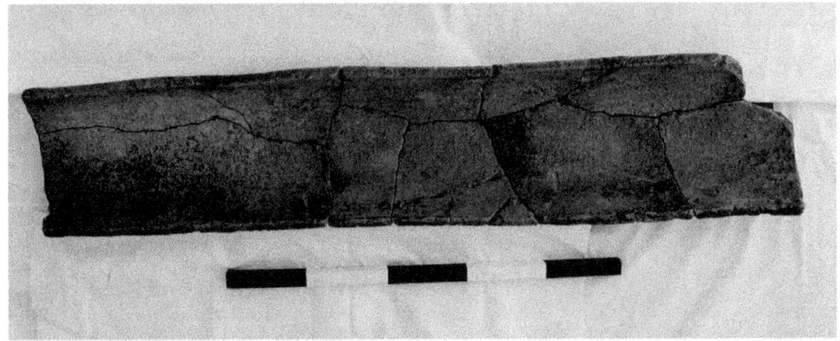

21b

22

2.21a–b. Cover tile found outside the west end of the Temple

2.22. Complete pan tile from Building A

2.23a–b. Thick pan tile from the West Annex

2.24a–c. Thick flat pan tile with deep inset along its lower ledge

2.25a–d. Views of the foundation for the Temple staircase and perirrhanterion (2.25c placement of the setting line for the second step)

2.26. Block (centre right) lying now over the Altar with a thickness (0.18–0.20) suitable for the Temple threshold or as a step

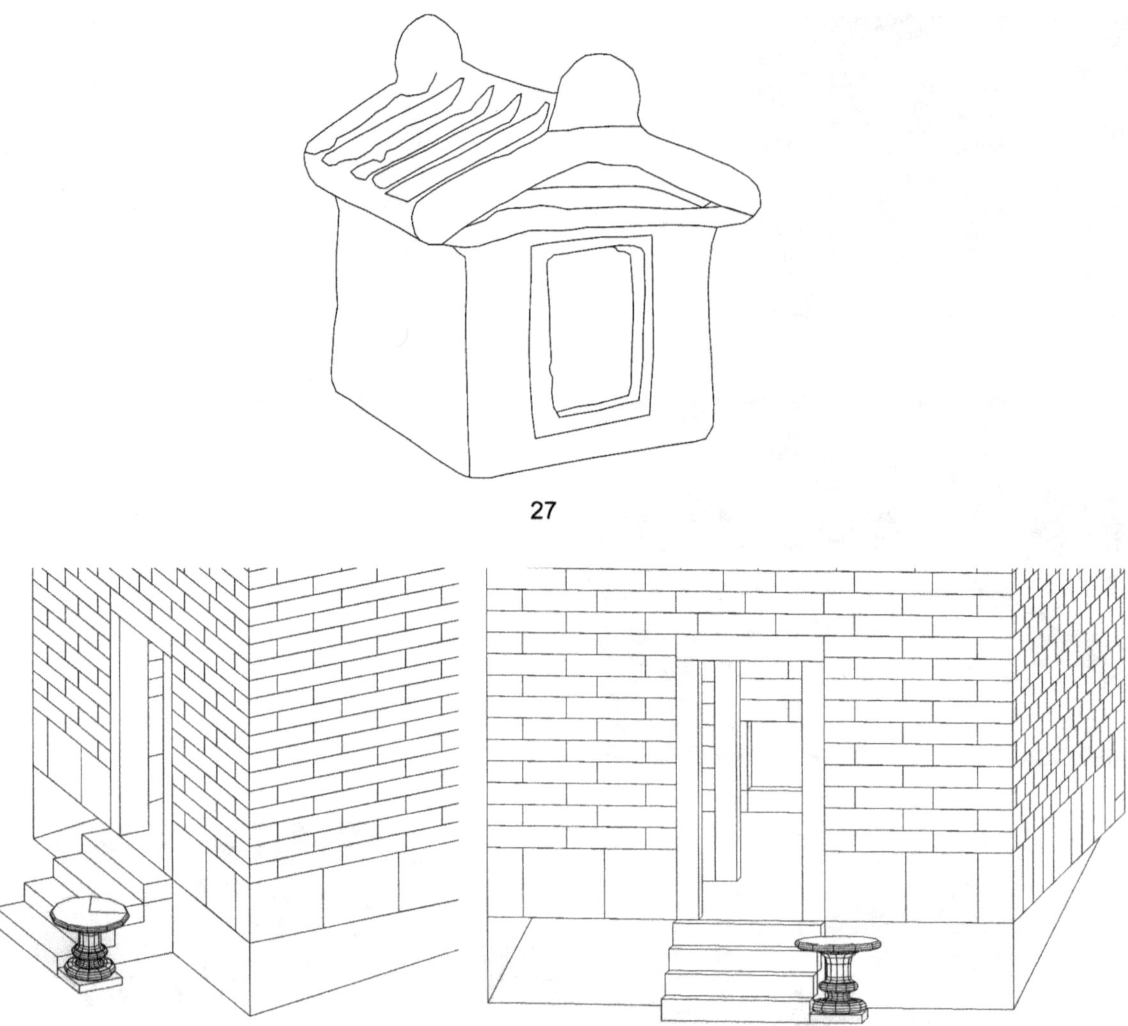

2.27. Terracotta temple model from Skillous. Olympia museum

2.28a–b. Temple stairs and perirrhanterion (David Meadows)

29a

29b

29c

2.29a–c. Grave in the Temple pronaos

30a

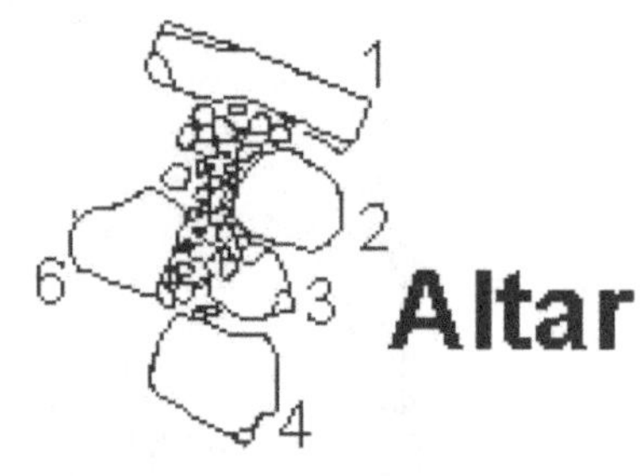

30b

30c

30d

2.30a. Altar area from the east

2.30b. Altar blocks

2.30c. Altar from the west, Block 5 (arrows)

2.30d. Traces of the rocky "paving" (right) amid bedrock outcrops

31a

31b

31c

2.31a–b. Section of rocky "paving" beside Block 1 of the Altar

2.31c. Irregular sections of rocky "paving" west of the Altar

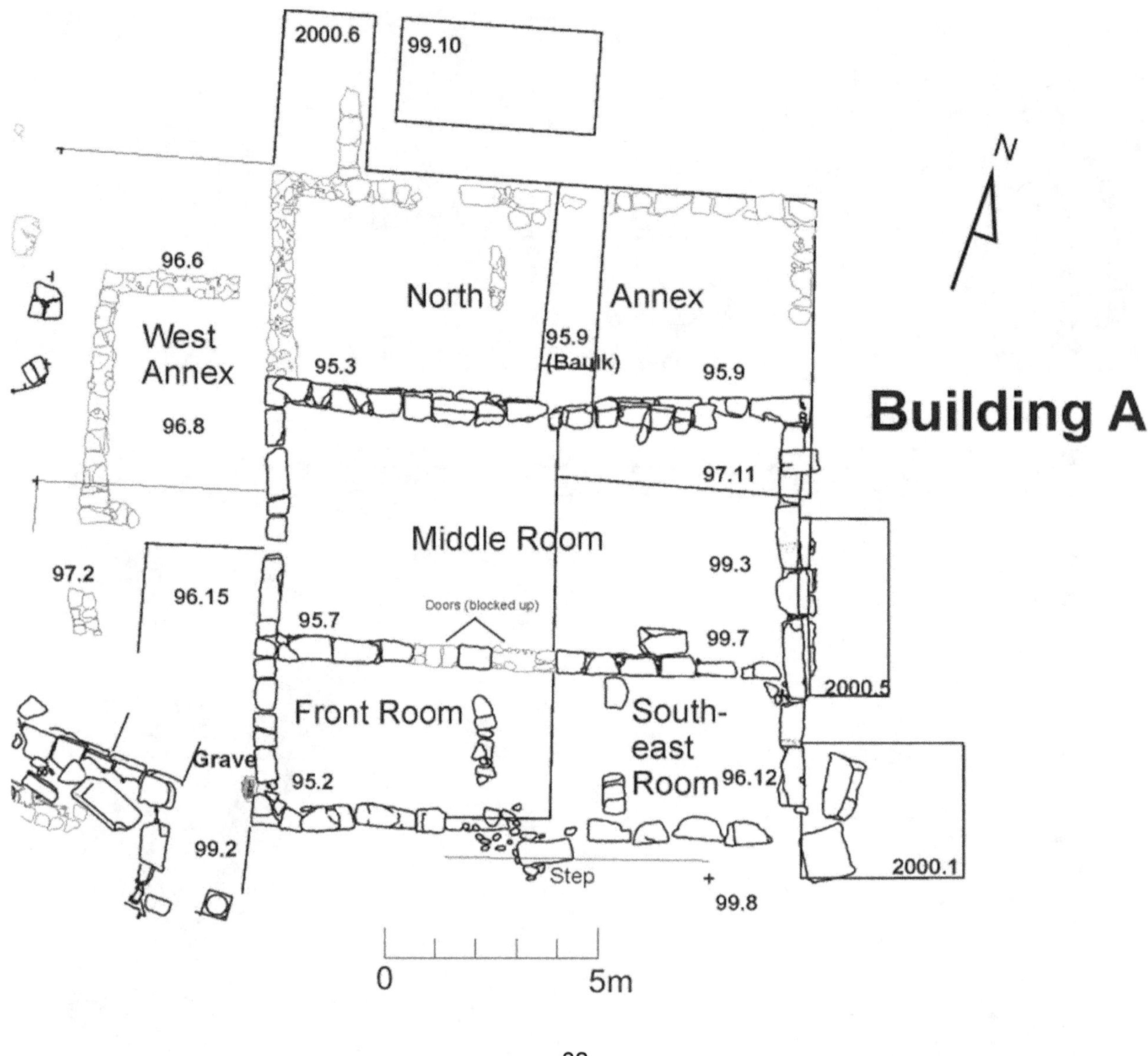

2.32. Building A rooms and annexes (B. Gourley)

33a 33b

34a 34b

2.33a–b. Entrance into Building A from the south (Altar Court area)

2.34a–b. Two views of the Southeast Room with broken tiles on the floor surface

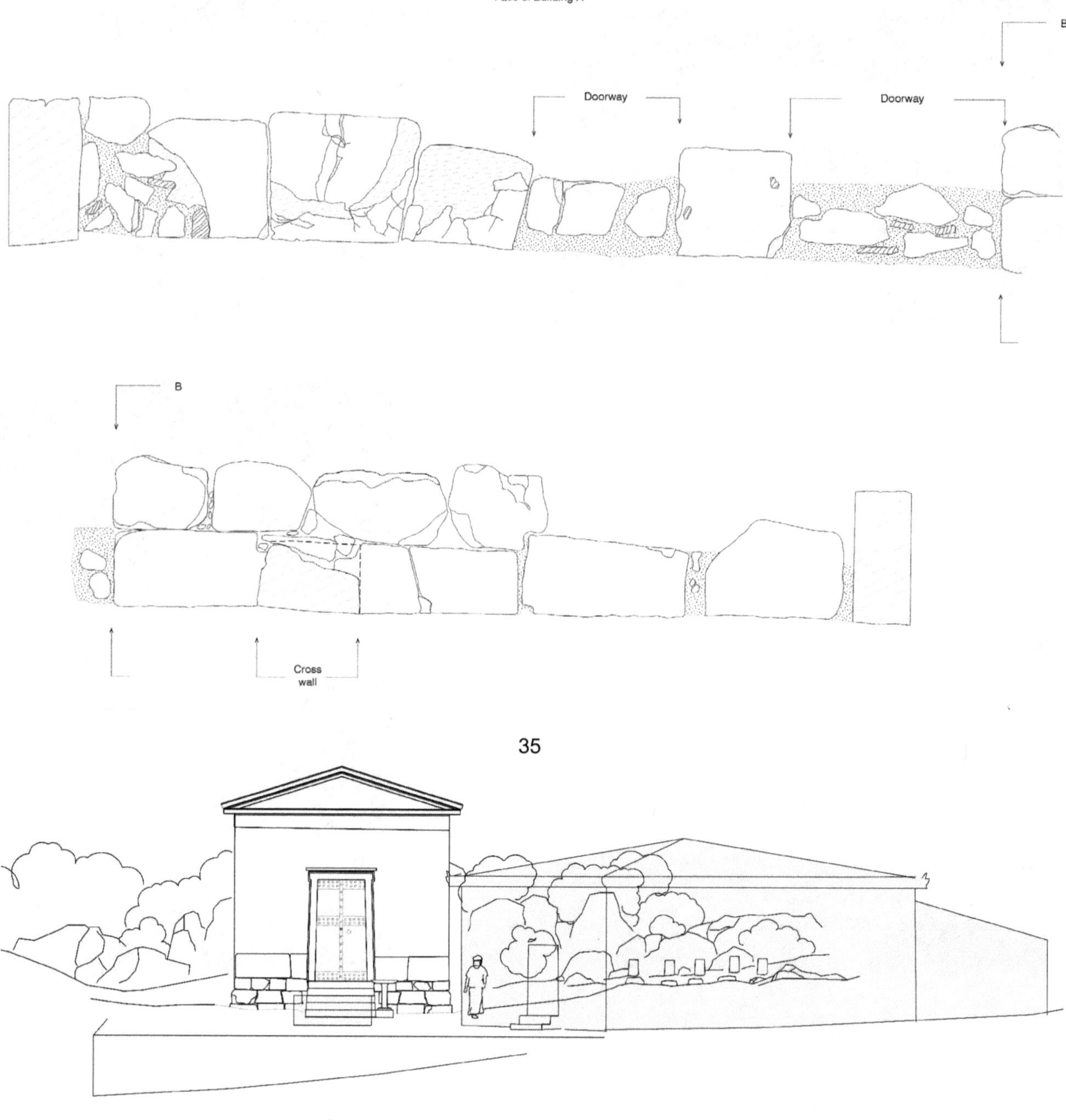

2.35. Elevation drawing of the middle wall (south face) of Building A (G. Schaus)

2.36. Temple and Pillar Shrine with Building A in outline (B. Gourley)

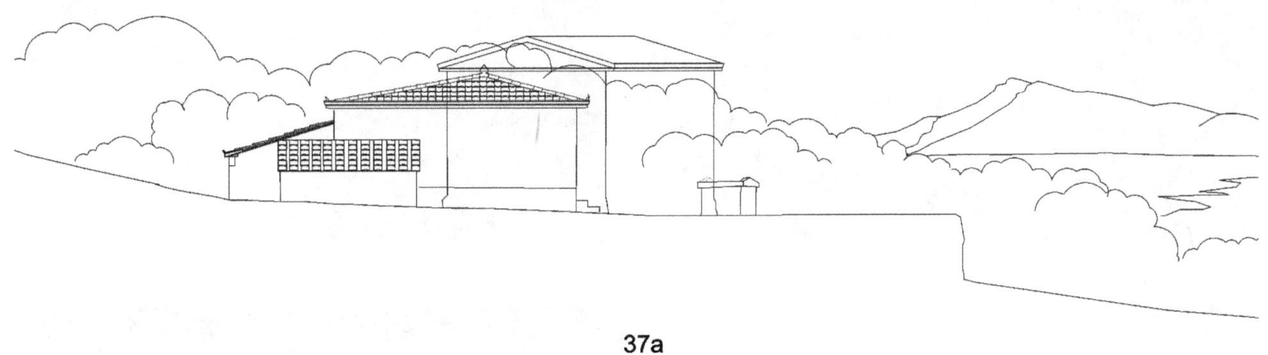

37a

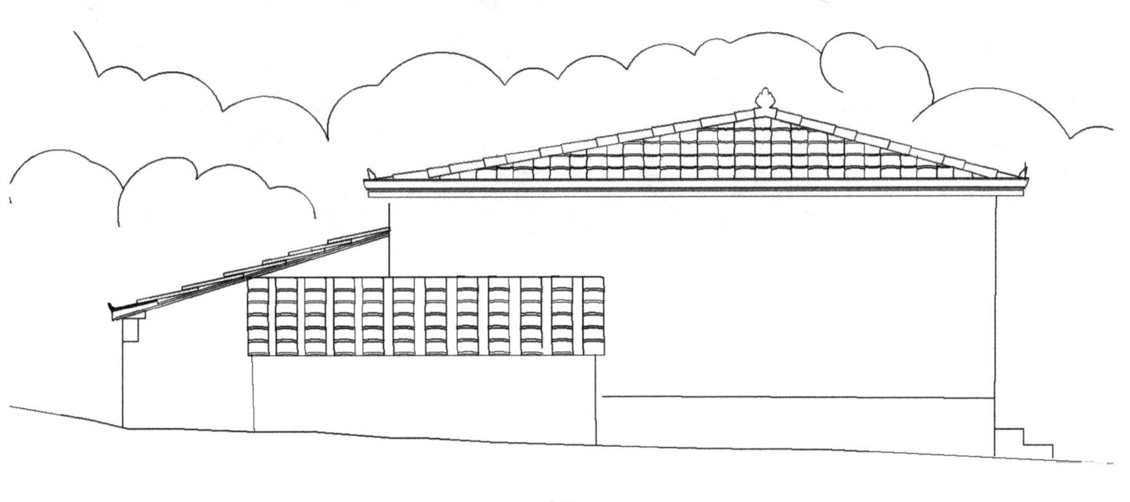

37b

2.37a. Building A with North and West Annexes from the west (Temple in outline) (B. Gourley)

2.37b. Reconstructed roof lines of Building A with North and West Annexes (B. Gourley)

2.38a–b. Layer of broken roof tiles in the Front Room, Building A

2.39. Evidence of burning (charcoal) on the floor surface below the broken tile layer

2.40. North Annex of Building A, from the northeast

41a
41b
41c

2.41a–b. Cluster of five loomweights on the floor, north end of the West Annex

2.41c. Cluster of three loomweights at the south end of the West Annex

42a

42b

2.42a–b. Infant burial between Building A and the Temple

43

2.43. Pillar Shrine area (right) north of the Temple (B. Gourley)

2.44a–b. Remains of three upright rectangular pillars in situ with three fieldstones in front

2.44c–d. Row of five upright pillars with fieldstones (one bedrock outcrop) in front of each

45

46

47

2.45. Pillar 6 in Trench 99.10

2.46. Stele in the Marmaria area, Delphi, with inscription to Zeus Polios

2.47. Broken stele with a pediment-like upper section, west of the Temple

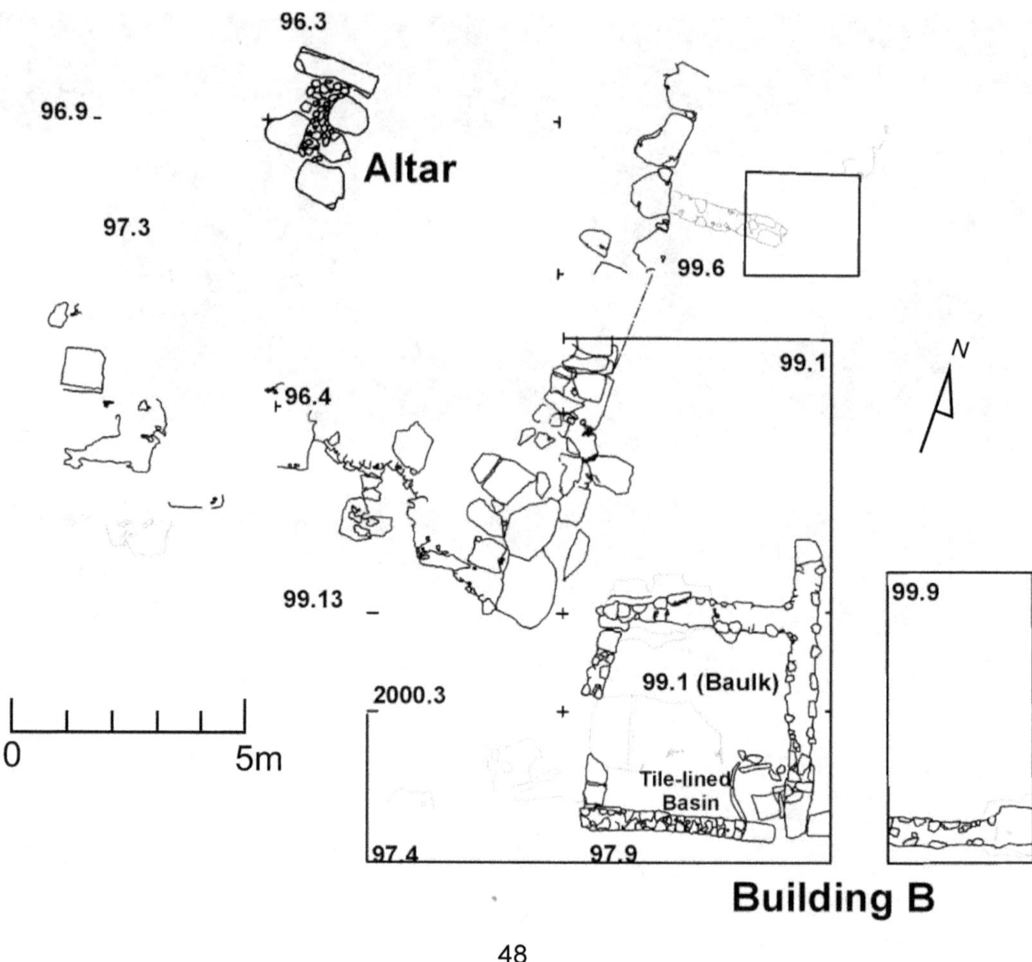

2.48. Altar Court and Building B with the Tile-lined Basin Room

49a

49b

49c

2.49a–c. Views of the Tile-lined Basin before and after excavation

50

2.50. Channel cut through bedrock outcrop south of the Temple

3.1. Kore from Stymphalos, reconstruction drawing, front (K. Sotiriou)

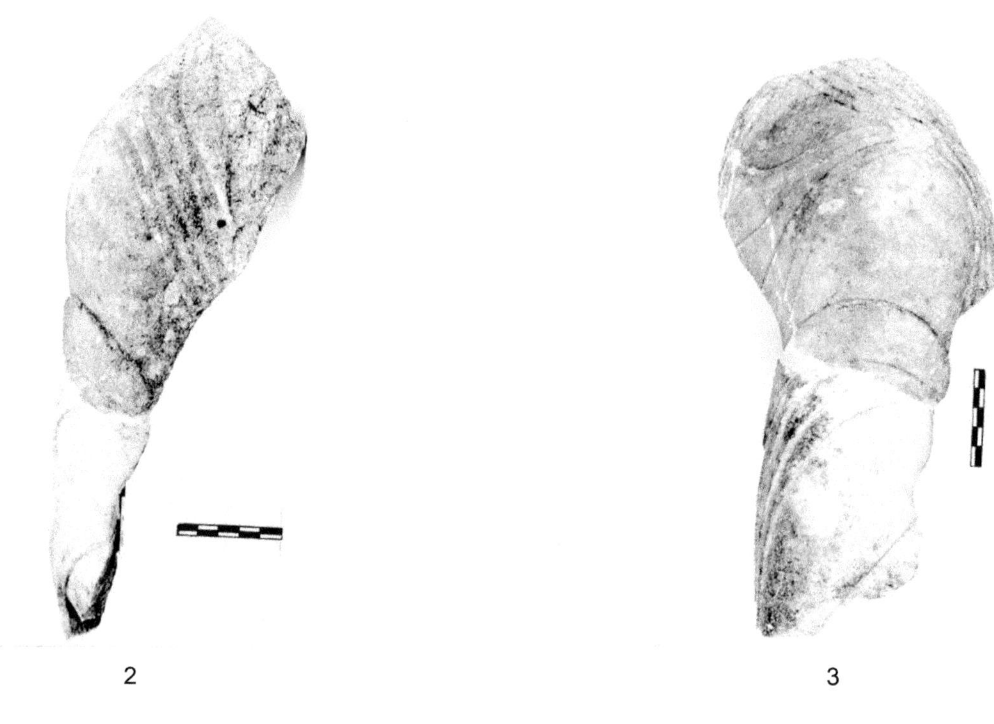

3.2. Right shoulder and upper arm, **1A**, front

3.3. **1A**, three-quarter view

3.4. **1A**, rear view

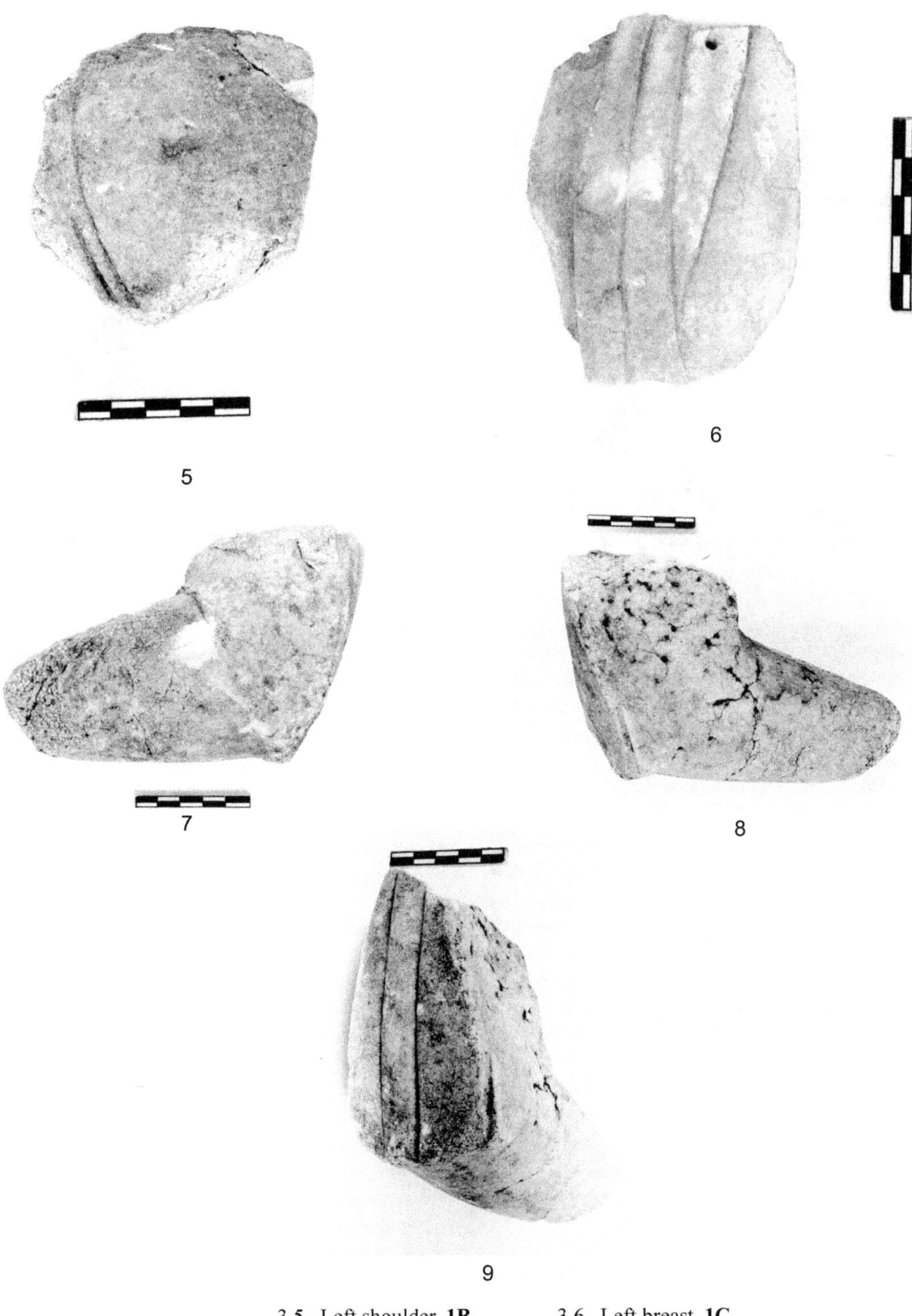

3.5. Left shoulder, **1B** 3.6. Left breast, **1C**

3.7. Left arm, **1D**, outside 3.8. **1D**, inside

3.9. **1D**, back

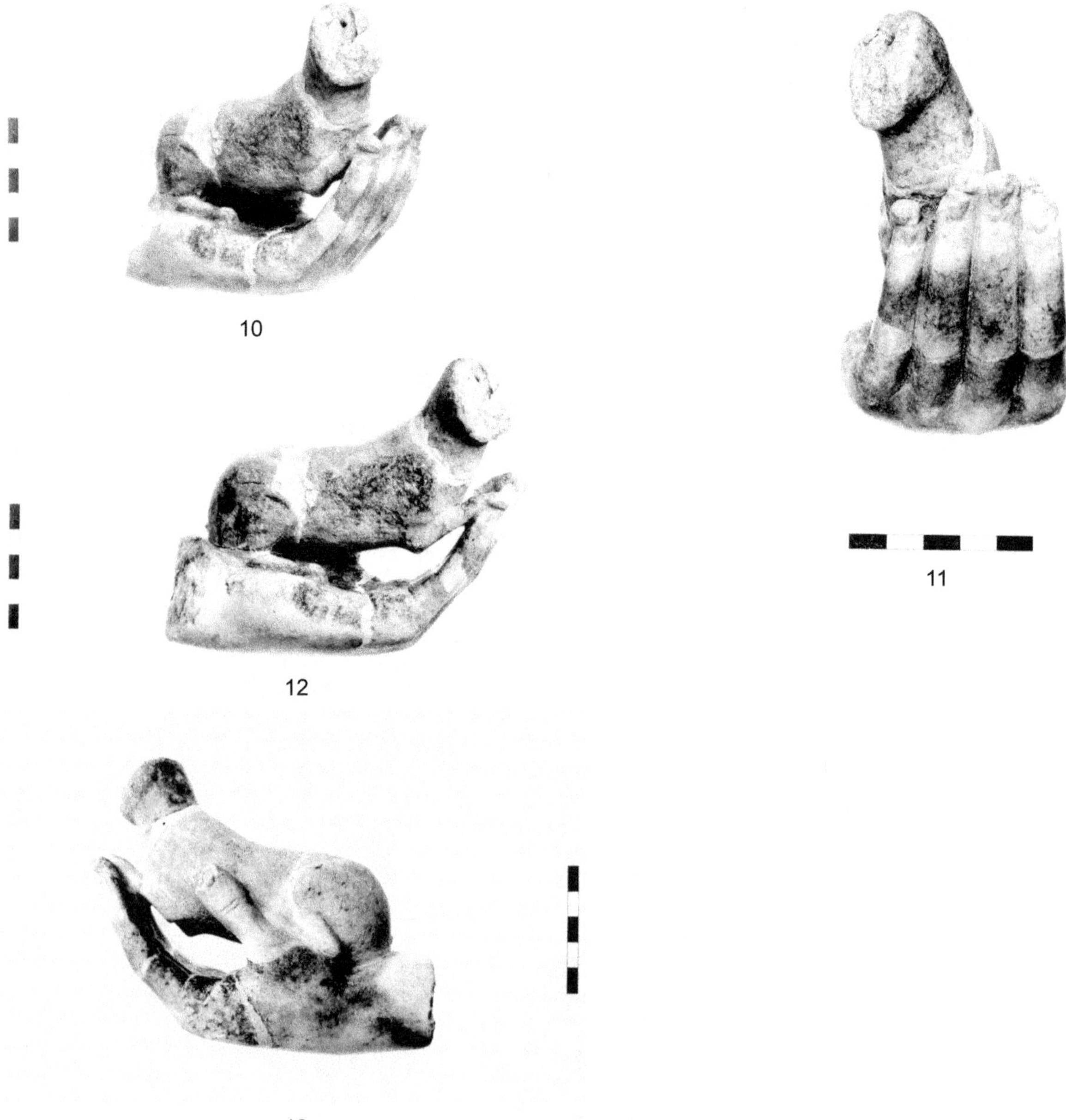

3.10. Left hand holding animal, **1E**, three-quarter view

3.11. **1E**, front

3.12. **1E**, right side

3.13. **1E**, left side

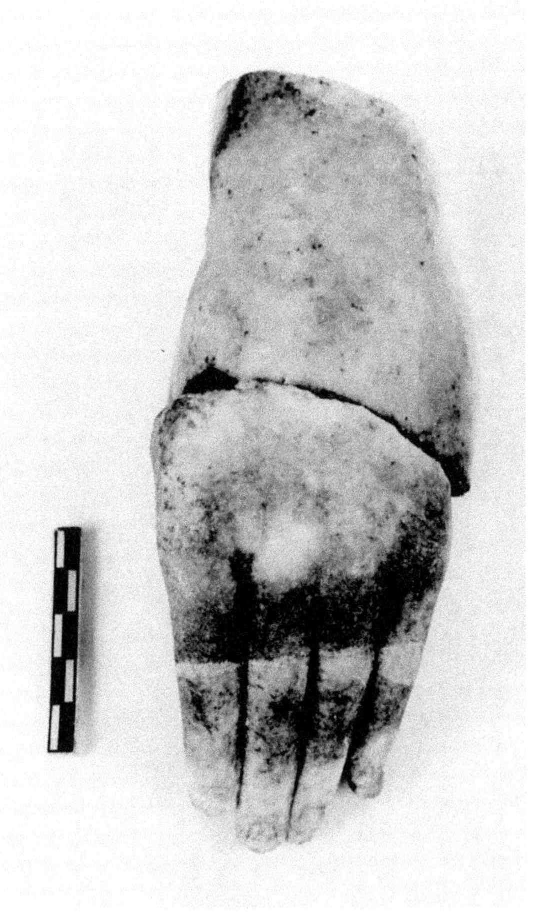

14

15

3.14. **1E**, back of hand

3.15. **1E**, palm of hand

16

17

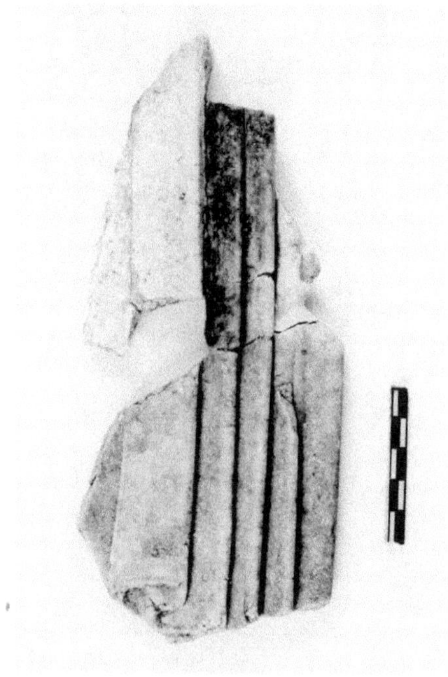

18

3.16. Fragment of hanging drapery, **1F**

3.17. Segment of two swallowtail folds, **1G**

3.18. Segment of hanging drapery, **1H**

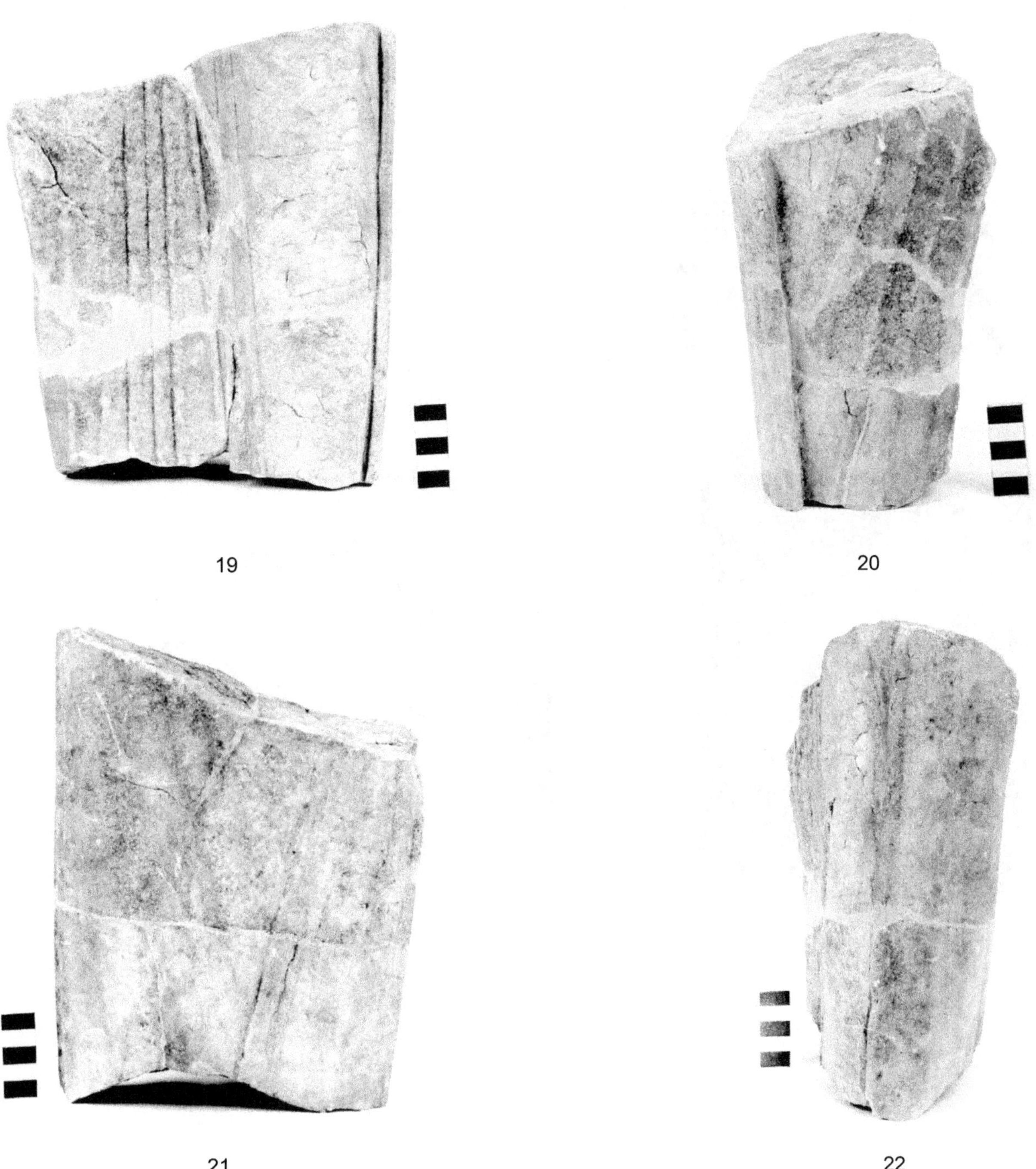

3.19. Draped legs, **1I**, frontal view

3.20. **1I**, right side

3.21. **1I**, rear view

3.22. **1I**, left side

3.23. Fragment of hanging drapery, **1J**

3.24. **1J**, back

3.25. Fragment of hanging drapery, **1K**

3.26. Fragment of hanging drapery, **1L**

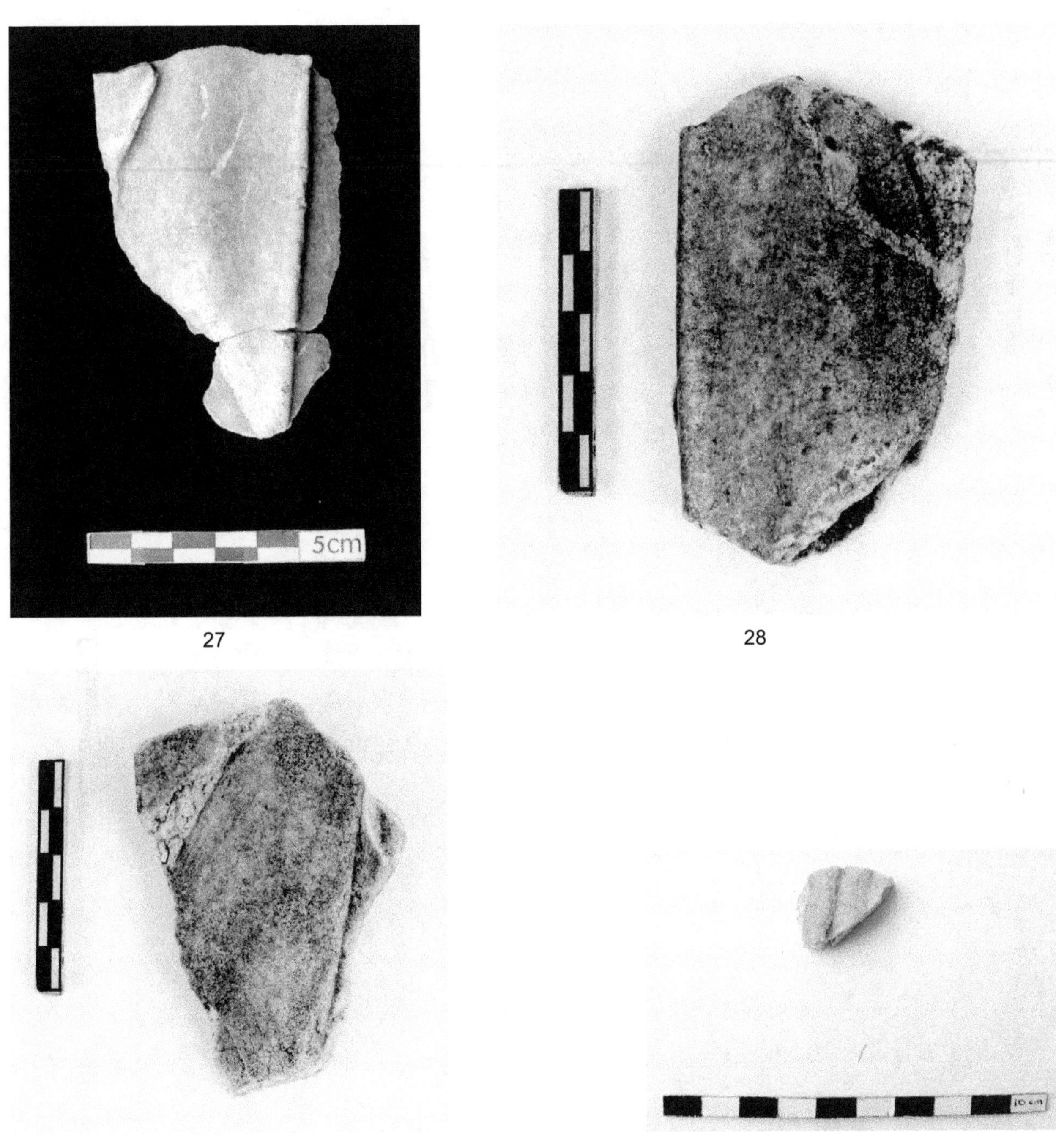

3.27. Fragment of mantle, **1M**

3.28. Small segment of overlapping fold, **1N**

3.29. Small segment of overlapping fold, **1O**

3.30. Fragment, possibly drapery, **1P**

3.31. Statue of a male child, “Temple Boy,” **2**: Head with left ear, **2A**, front

3.32. **2A**, left side

3.33. **2A**, right side

3.34. Fragment of head or torso, **2B**, front

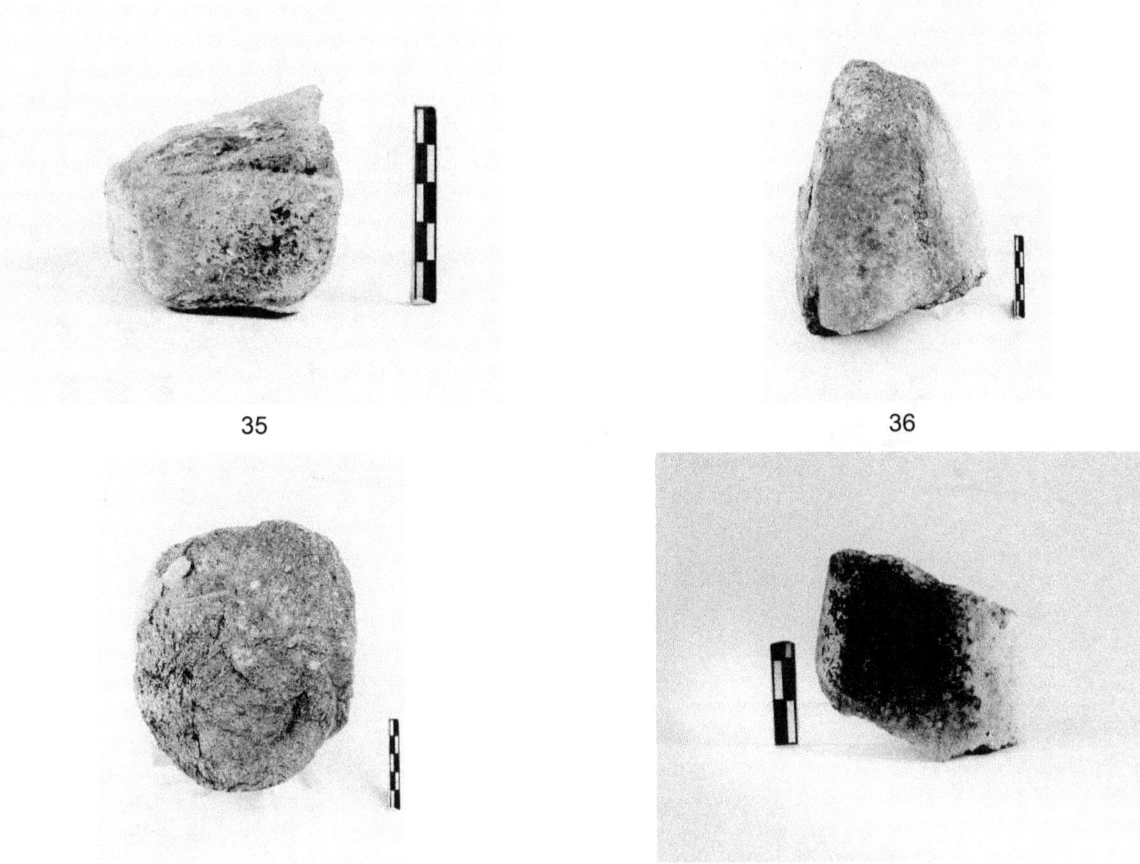

35

36

37

38

39

3.35. **2B**, back

3.36. Buttocks and left thigh, **2C**

3.37. **2C**, back

3.38. Fragment of a limb, **2D**

3.39. Fragment of curved skin, **2E**

40

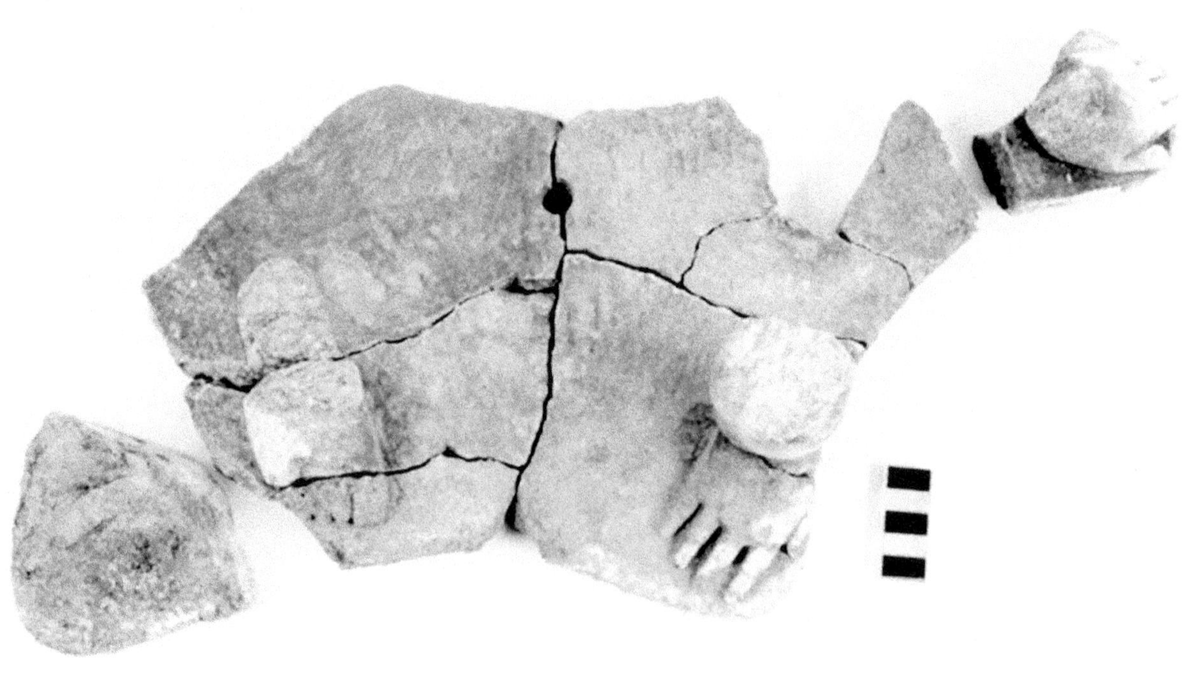

41

3.40. Plinth fragment, **2F**; Right arm, right hand, right foot on plinth, **2G**; Left hand on plinth, **2H**, frontal view

3.41. **2F**, **2G**, **2H**, from above

42

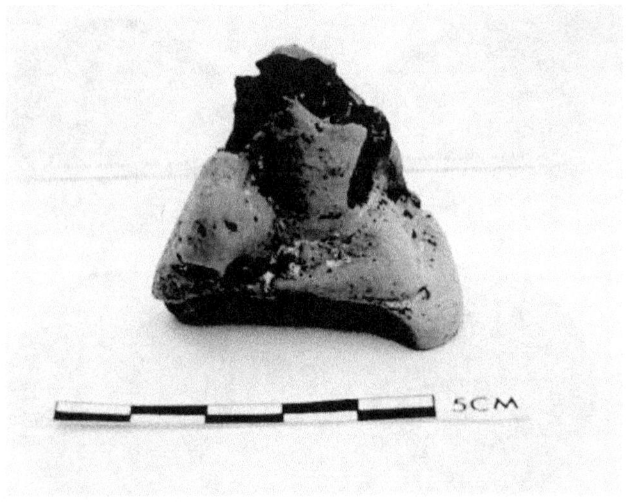

43

44

45

3.42. Fragmentary figurine of Aphrodite, **3**

3.43. Terracotta figurine of a temple boy from the Sanctuary, with one knee up and one to the side

3.44. Terracotta figurine of an Eros type from the Sanctuary

3.45. Sculpture fragments in the Temple

4.1. Syracuse (**II-1**), Macedonia (**II-5**, **6**), Thessaly (**II-9**), Boiotia (**II-10**), Opuntian Lokris (**II-11**), Chalkis (**II-12**), Histiaia (**II-16**), Salamis (**II-17**)

4.2. Corinth (**II-18**), Phlious (**II-35**, **38**, **42**), Sikyon (**II-46**, **47**, **49**, **51**, **57**)

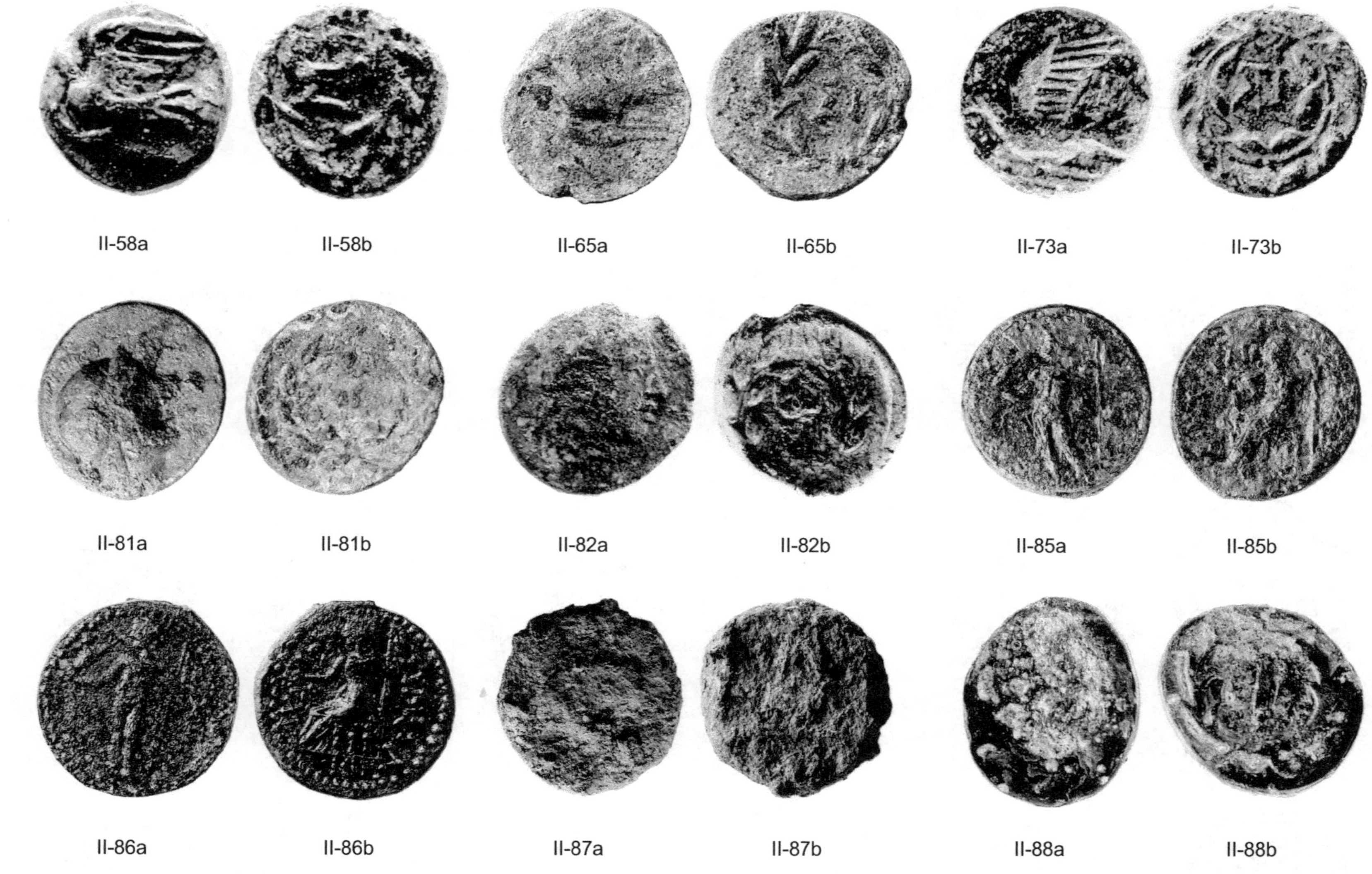

4.3. Sikyon (**II-58**, **65**, **73**), Aigeira (**II-81**), Pellene (**II-82**), Achaian League (Argos) (**II-85**), Achaian League (Stymphalos) (**II-86**), Argos (**II-87**), Hermione (**II-88**)

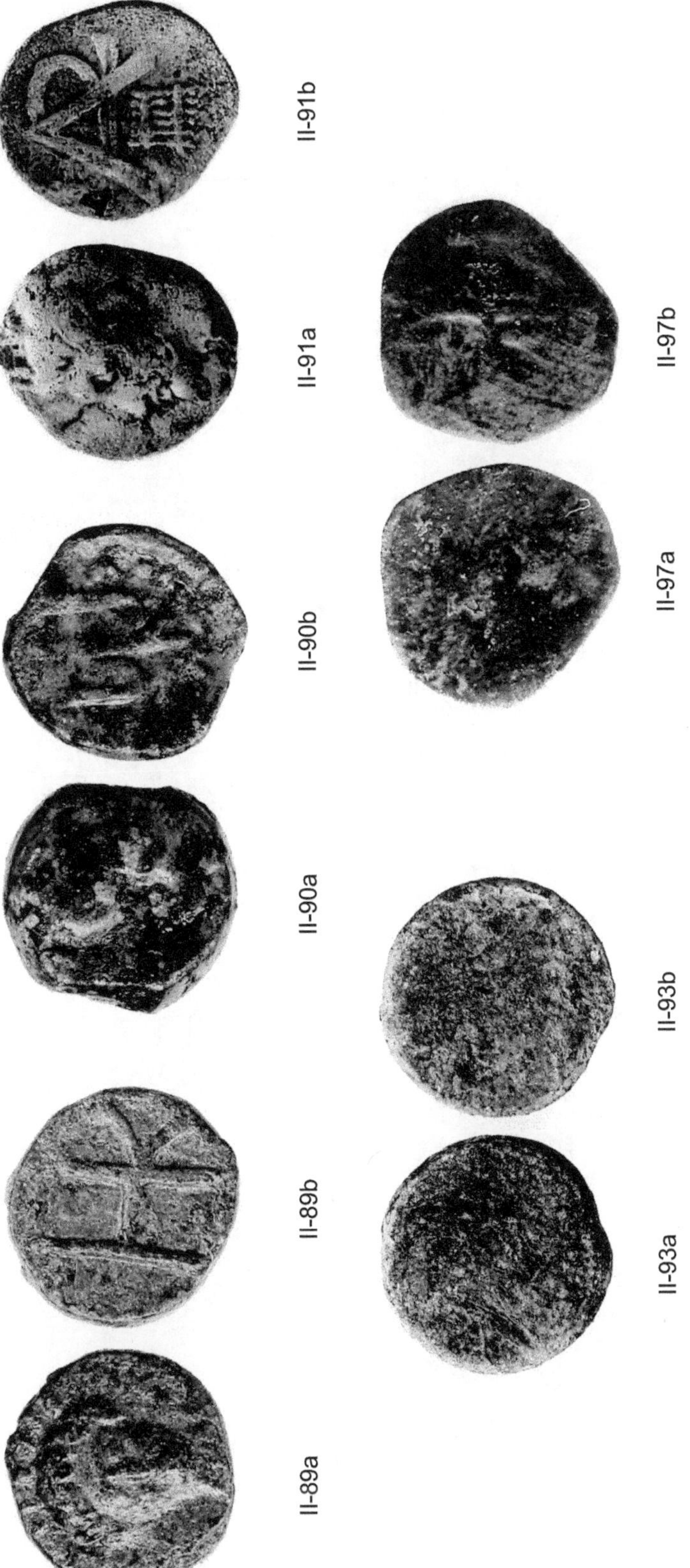

4.4. Kleitor (**II-89**), Manteinia (**II-90**), Megalopolis (**II-91**), Ptolemy III (**II-93**), Manuel I (**II-97**)

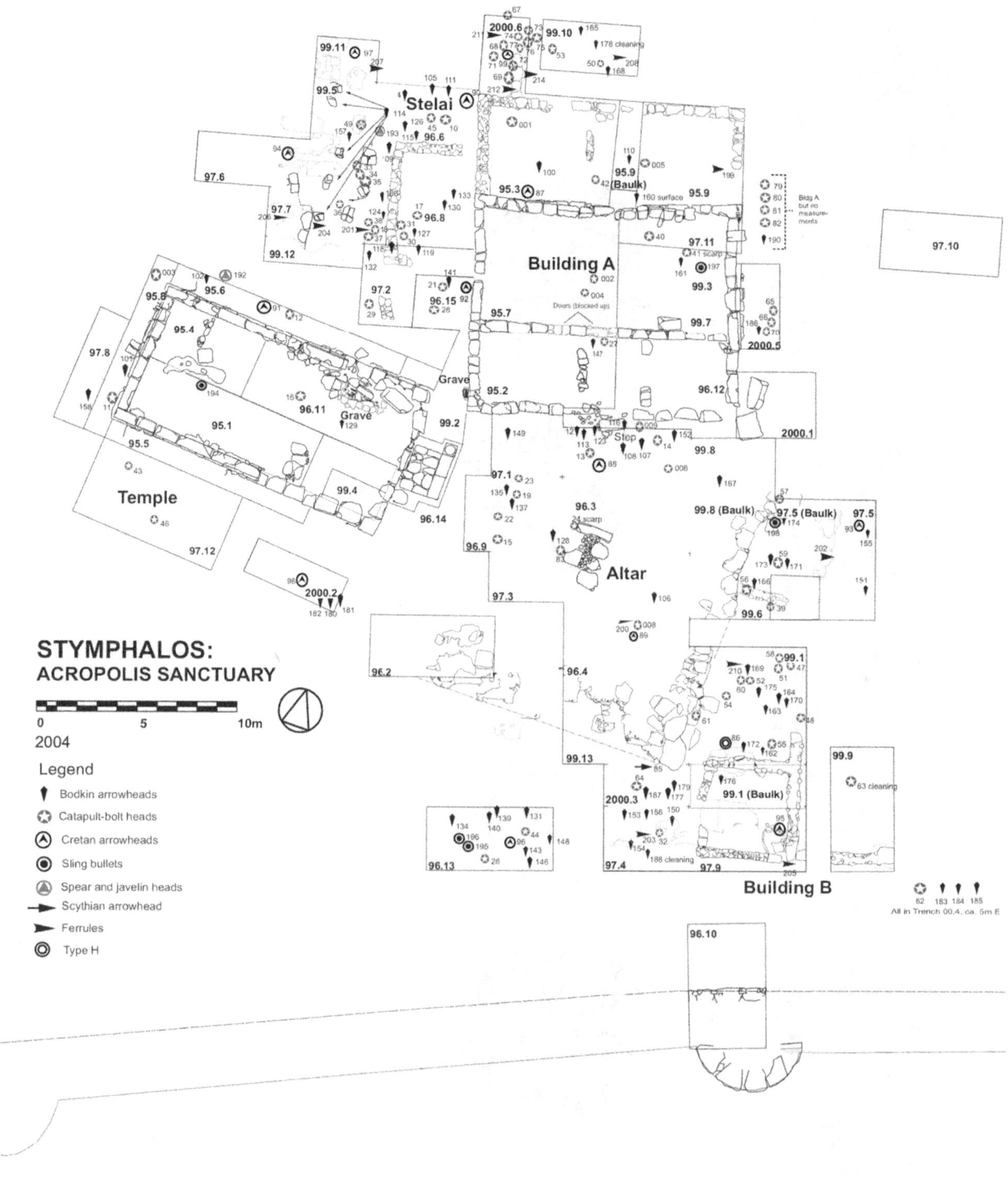

5.1. Distribution of the projectile remains in the Sanctuary

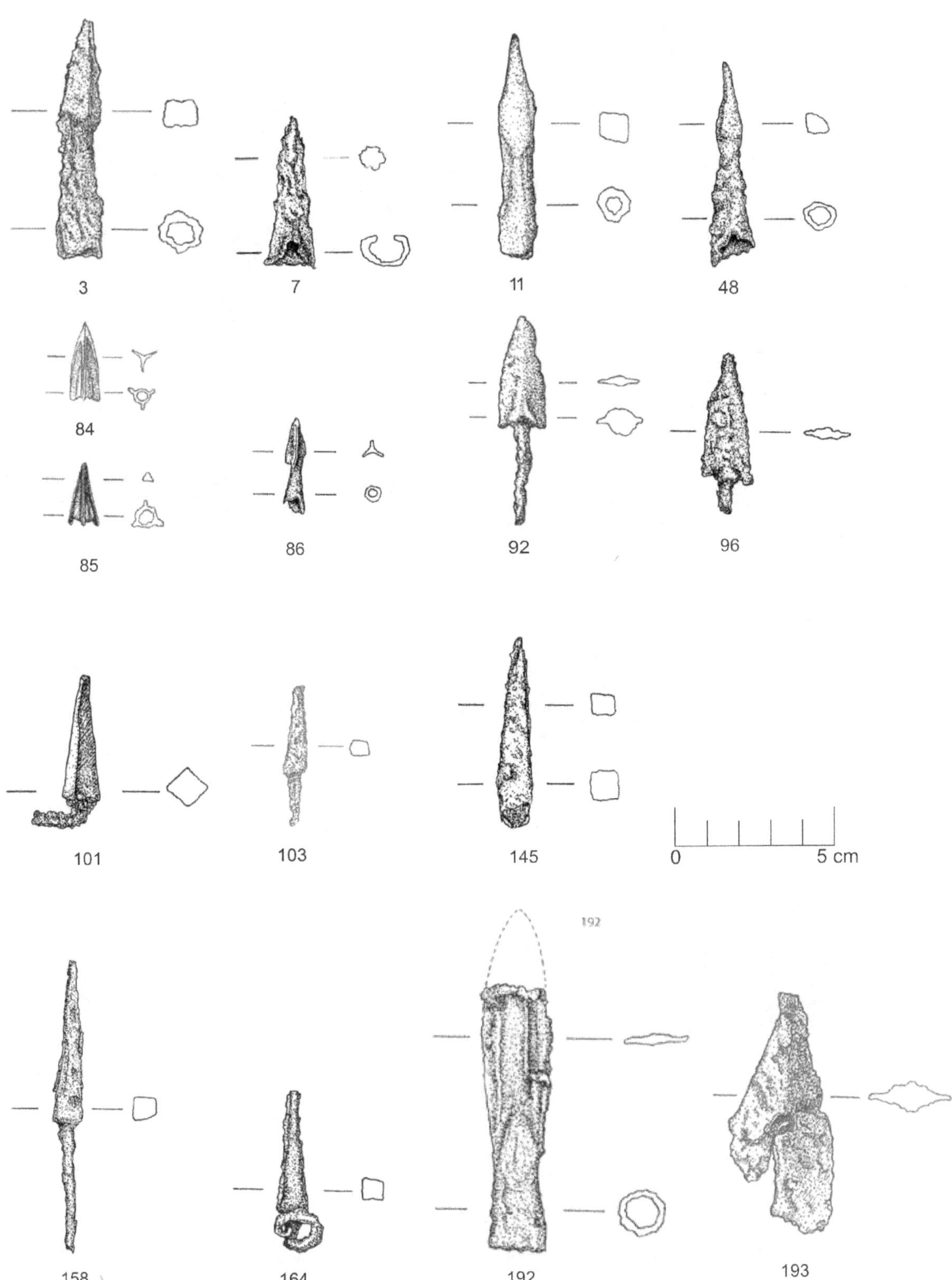

5.2. Catapult bolts (**3**, **7**, **11**, **48**), Scythian (**84**, **85**), Type H (**86**), Cretan (**92**, **96**), and bodkin arrow heads (**101**, **103**, **145**, **158**, **164**), javelin head (**192**), spear head (**193**) (drawings by G.S. Morrow)

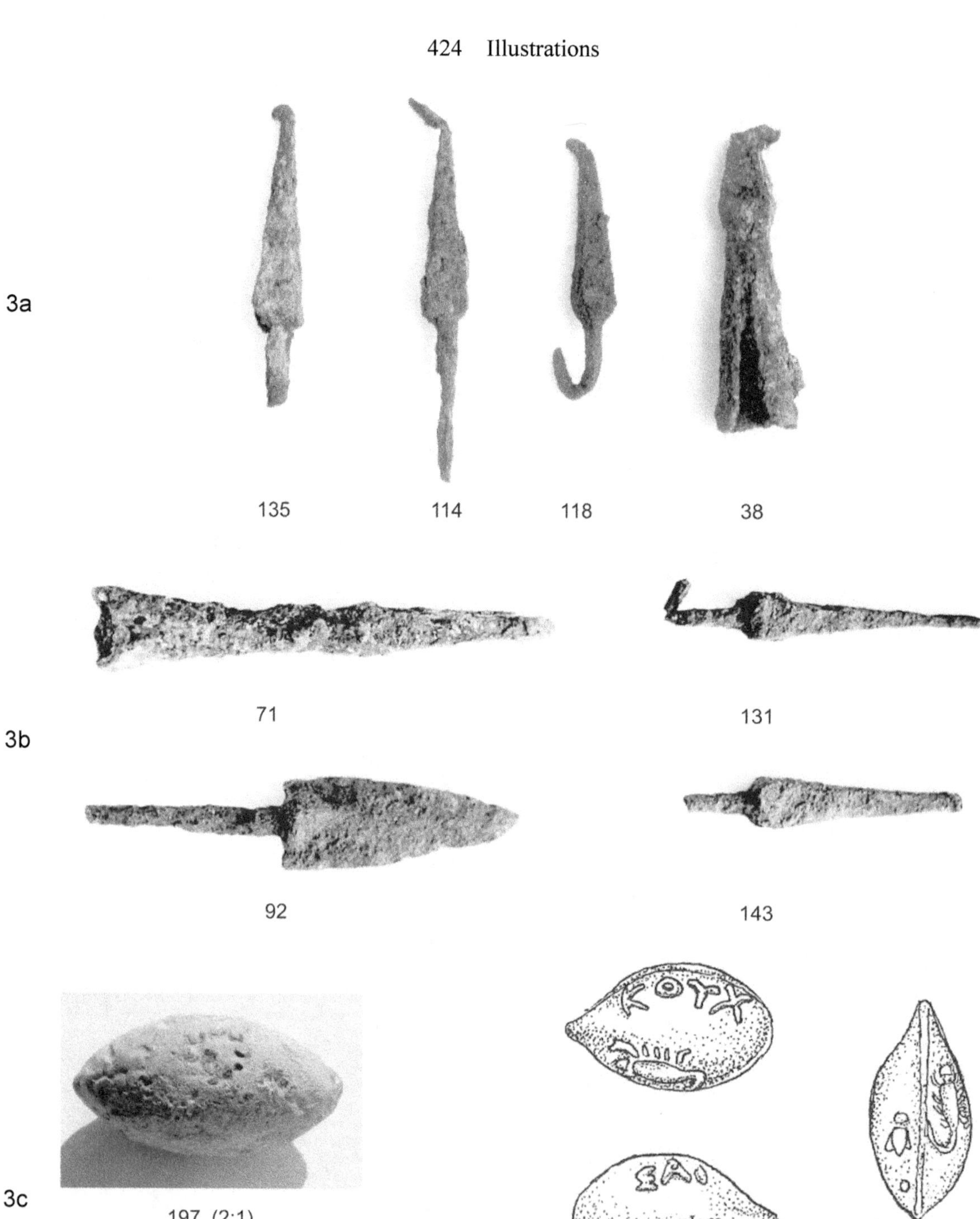

5.3a. Projectile points with bent tips (**135**, **114**, **118**, **38**), and bent tang (**118**)

5.3b. Catapult bolt (bodkin head with socket, **71**), Cretan (**92**) and bodkin arrowheads (**131**, **143**)

5.3c. Lead sling bullets (**197**, **198**)

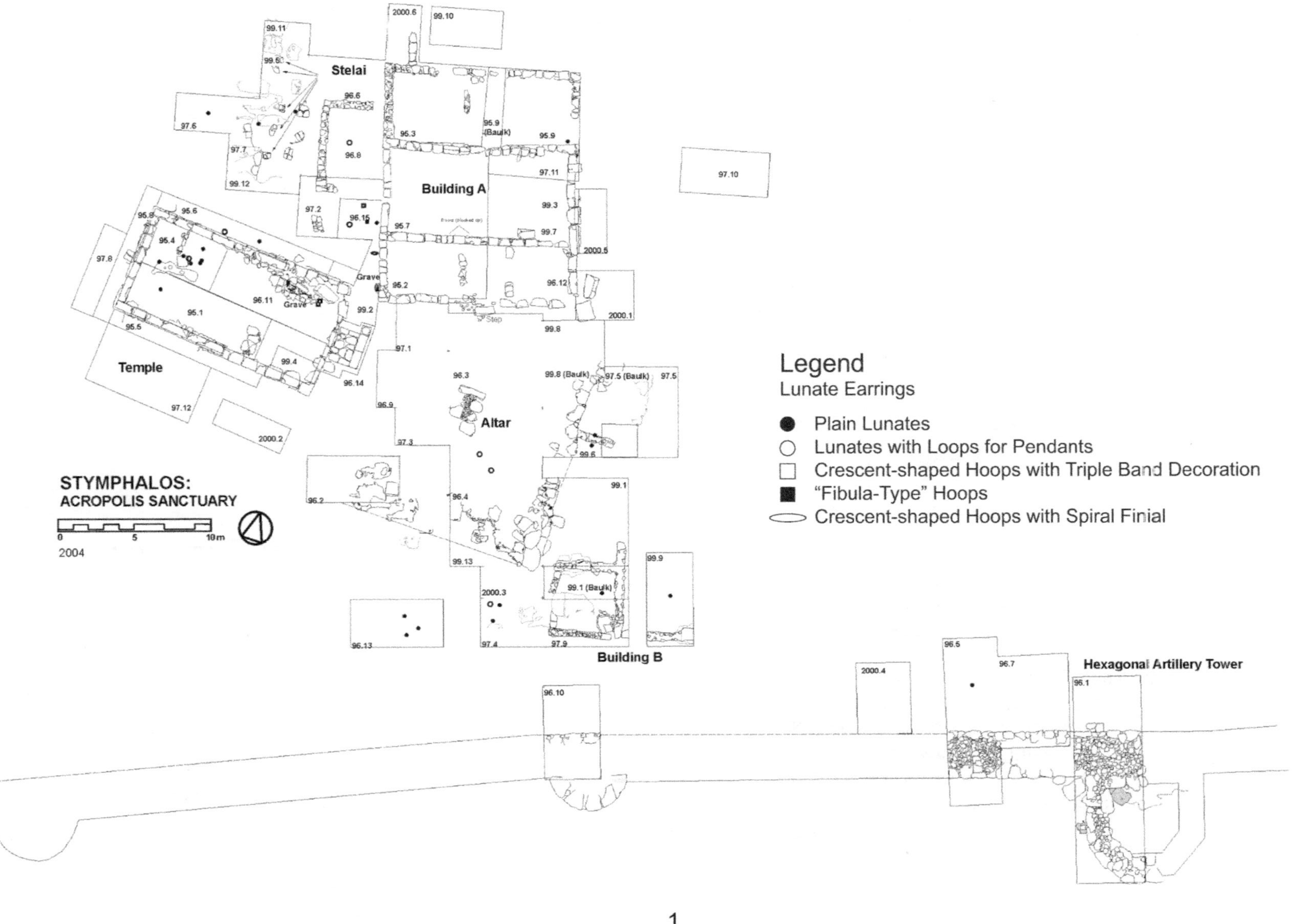

6.1. Distribution plan for lunate earrings

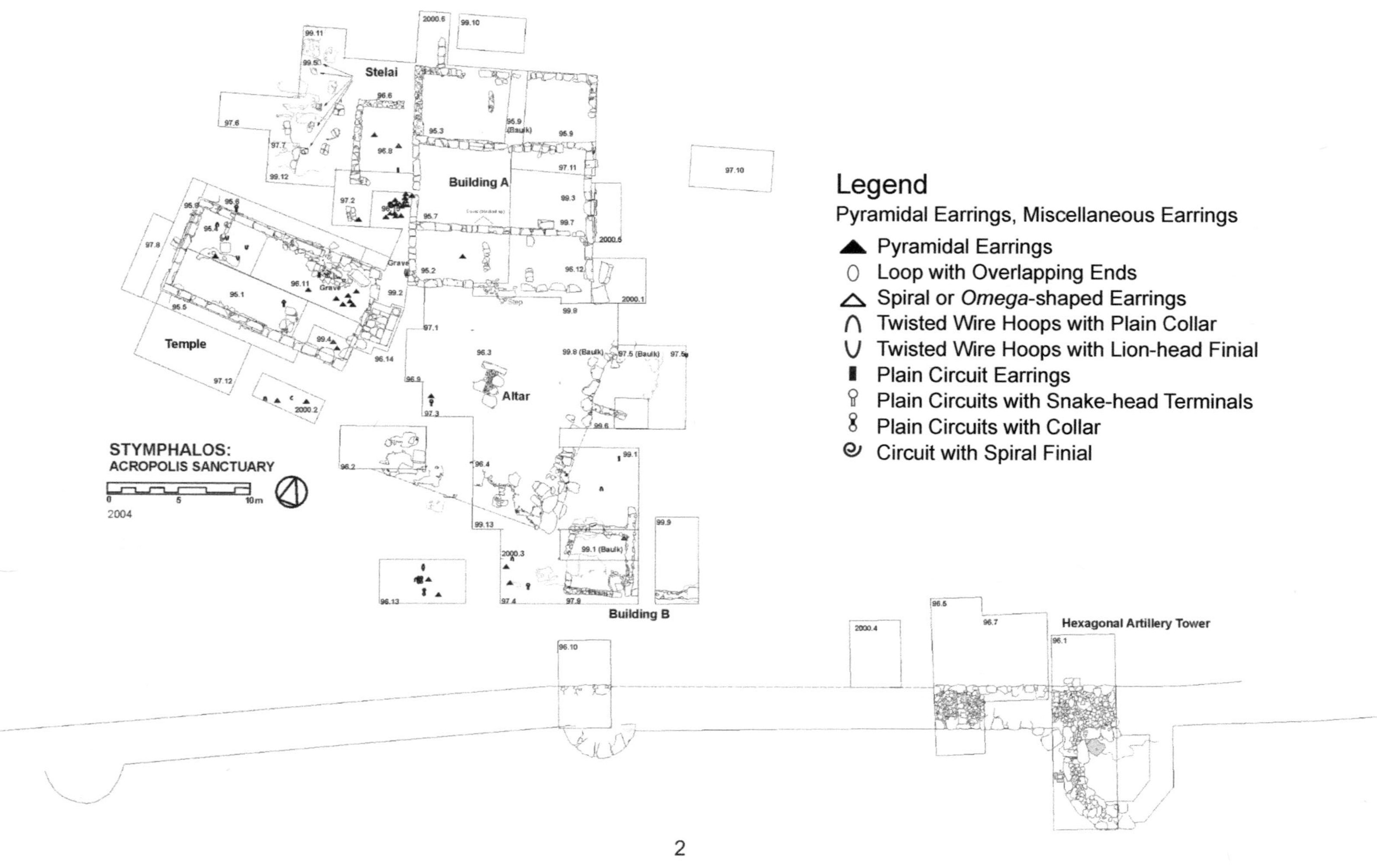

6.2. Distribution plan for pyramidal earrings

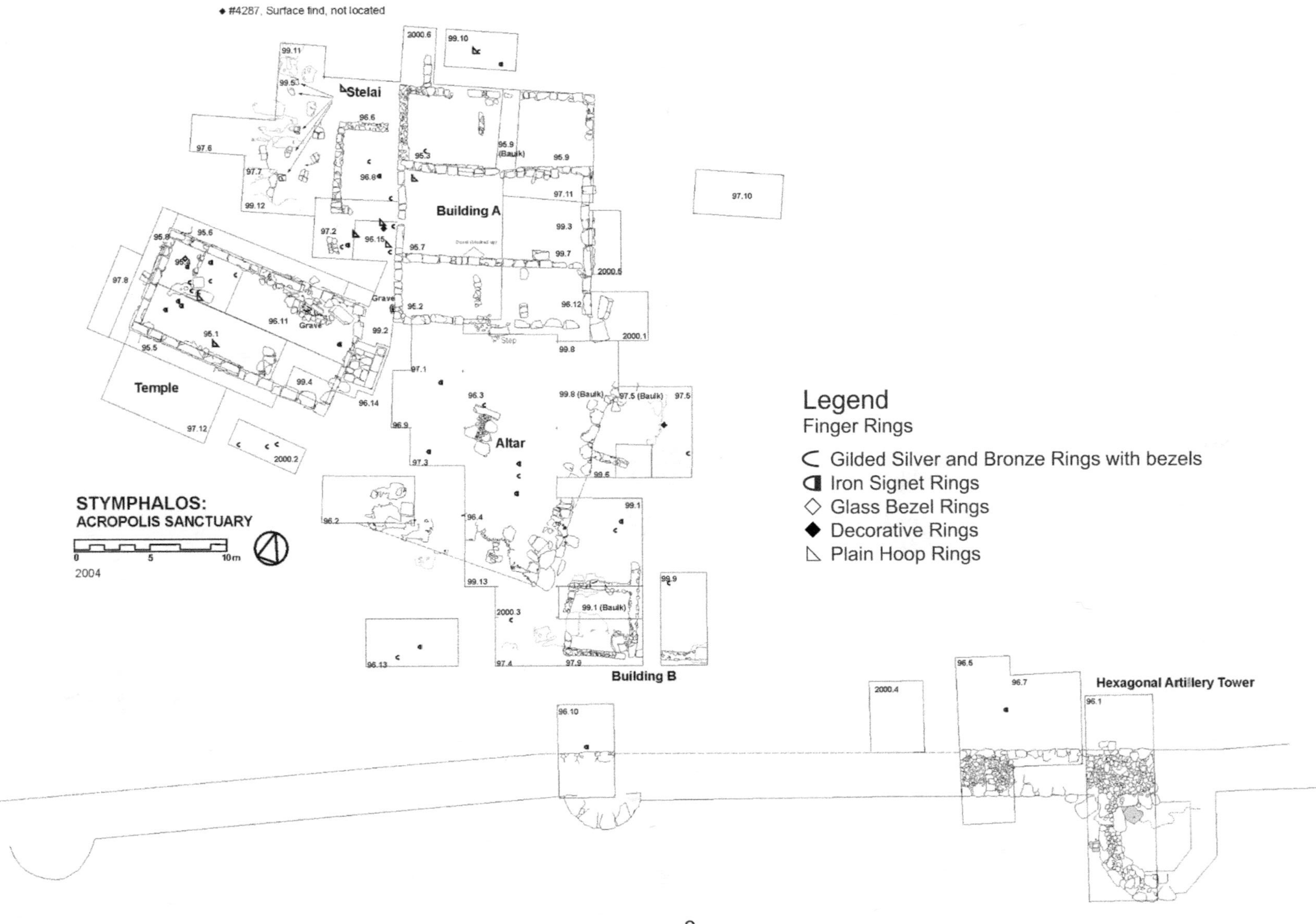

6.3. Distribution plan for finger rings

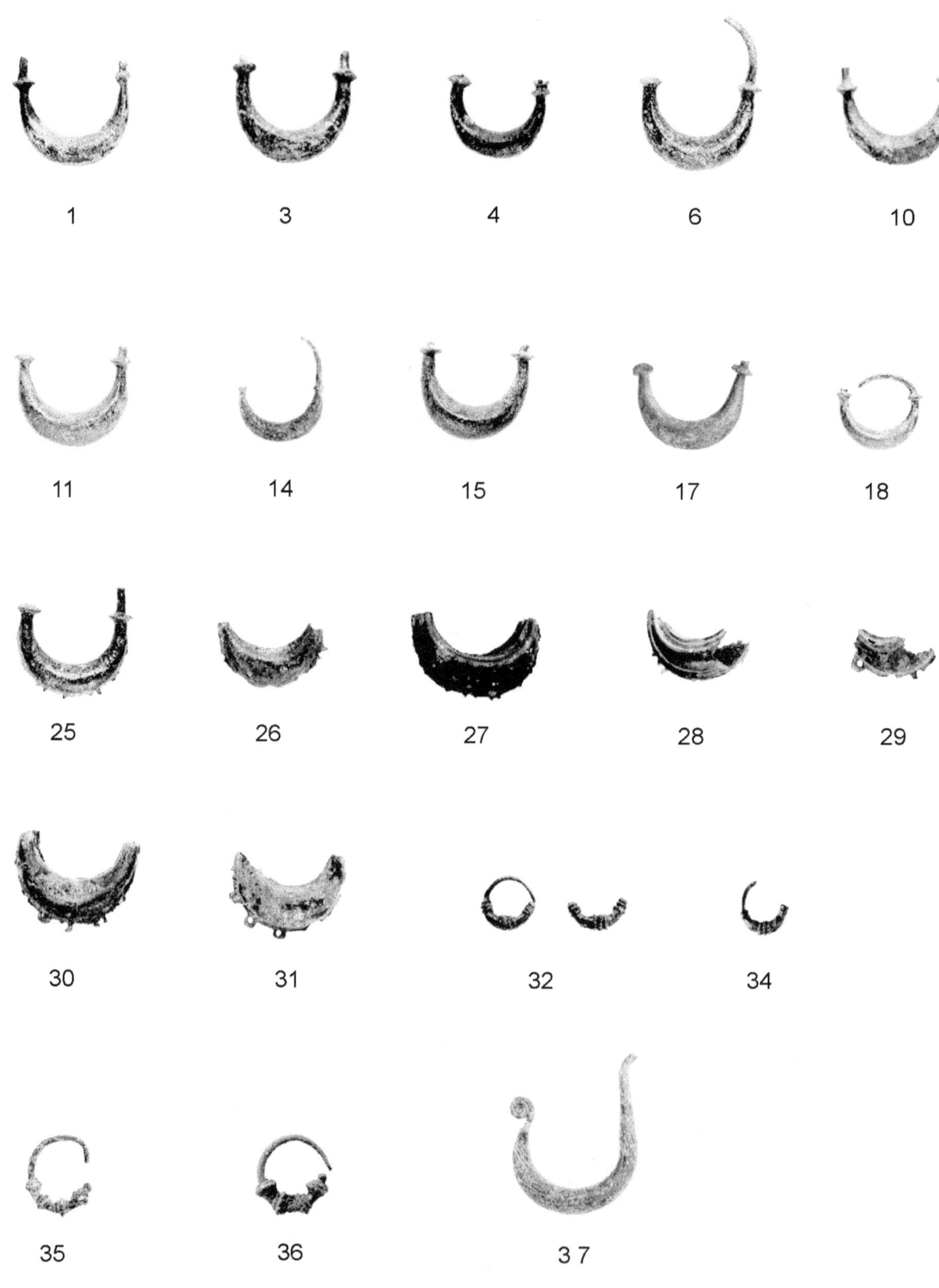

6.4. Earrings (**1**–**37**)

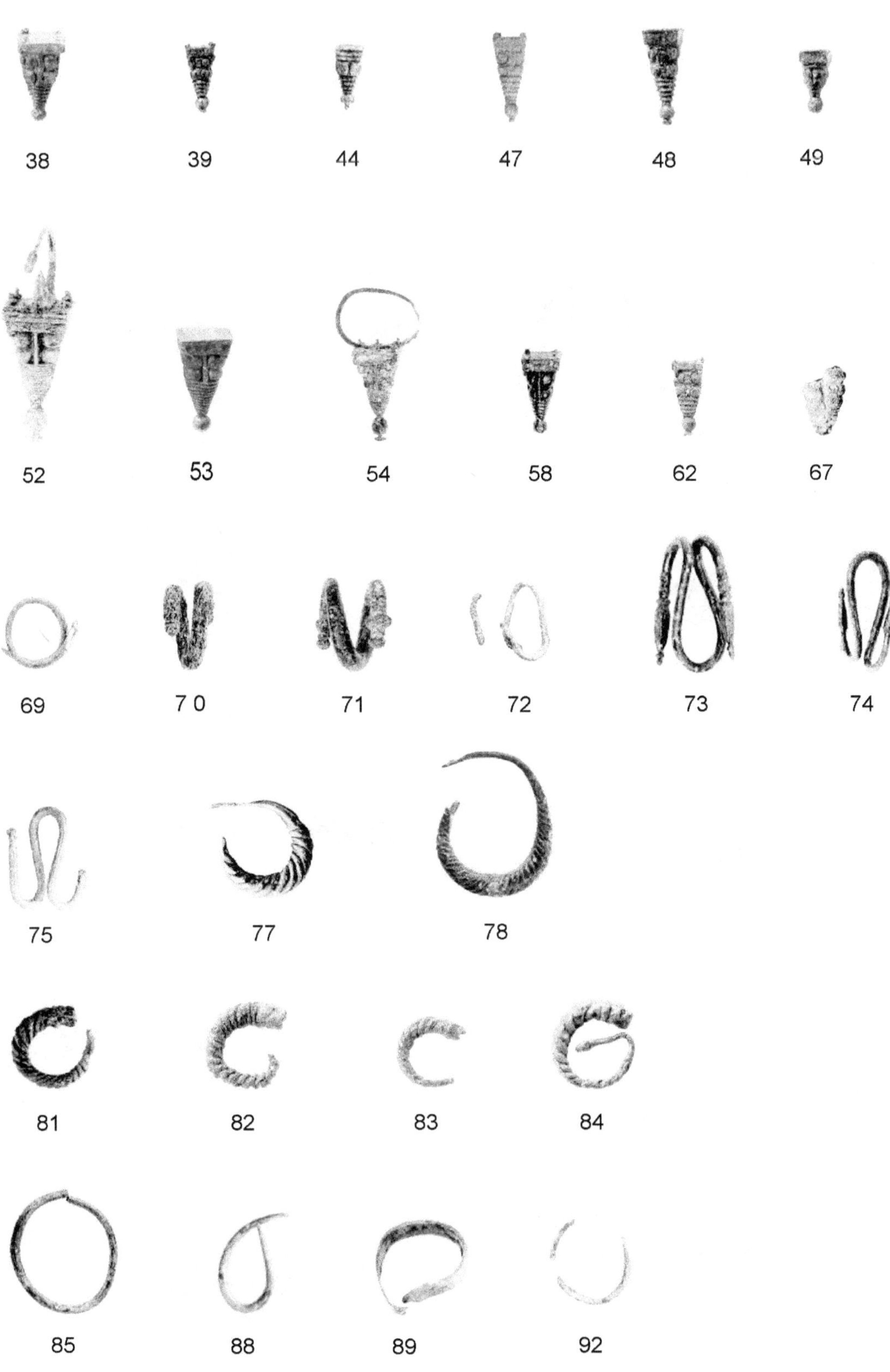

6.5. Earrings (**38–92**)

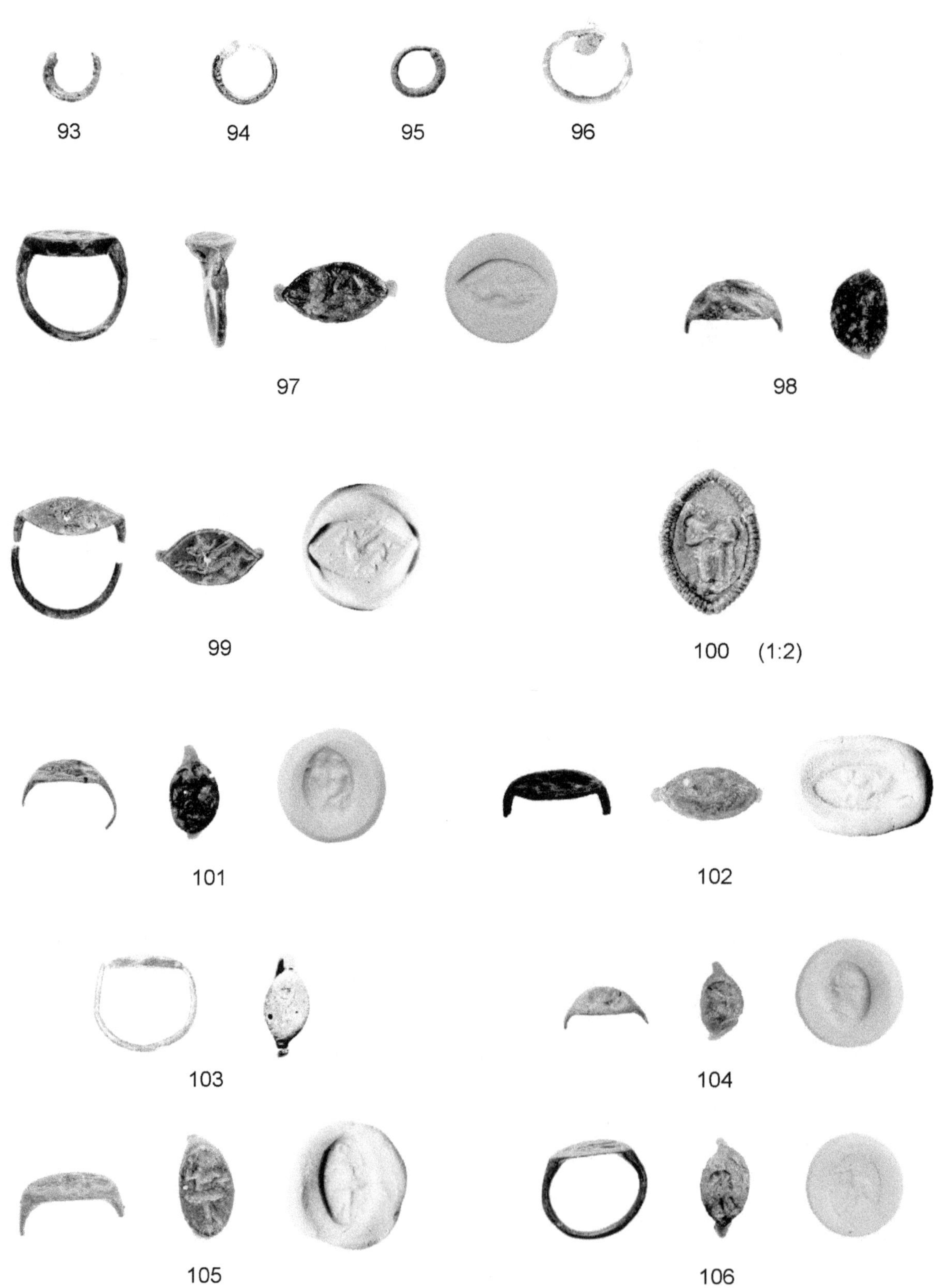

6.6. Earrings (**93–6**), finger rings (**97–106**)

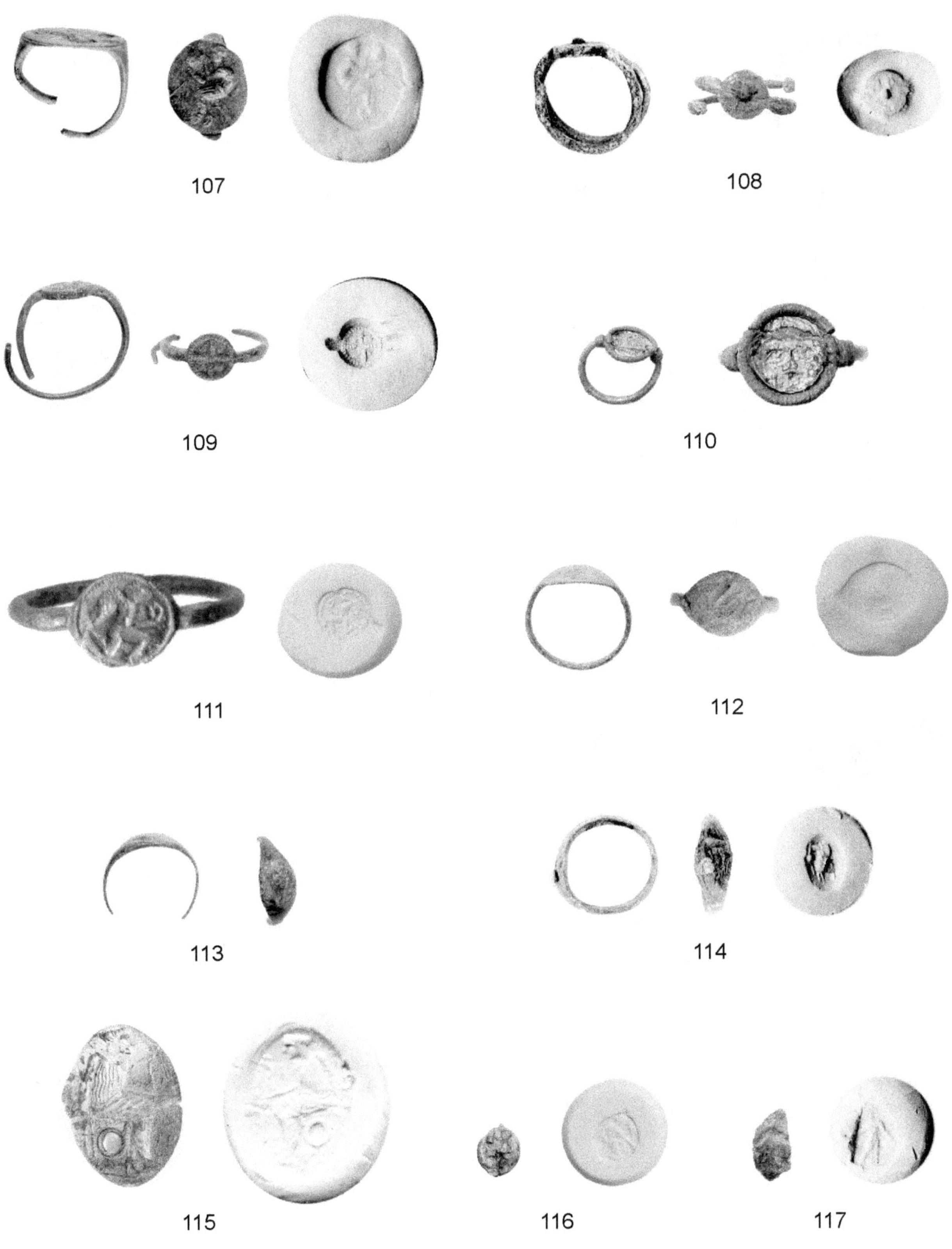

6.7. Finger rings (**107–17**)

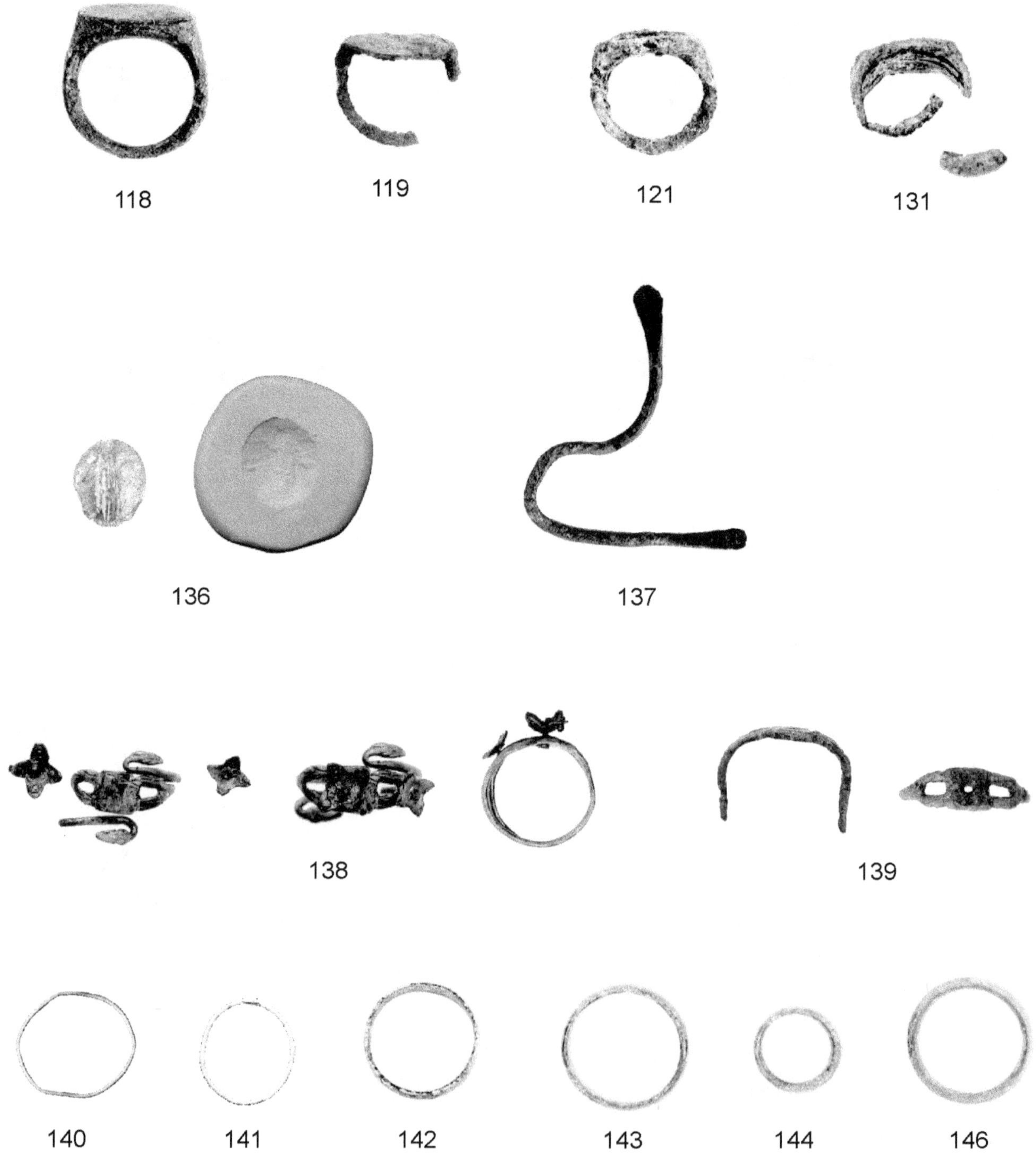

6.8. Finger rings (**118–39**), plain hoops (**140–6**)

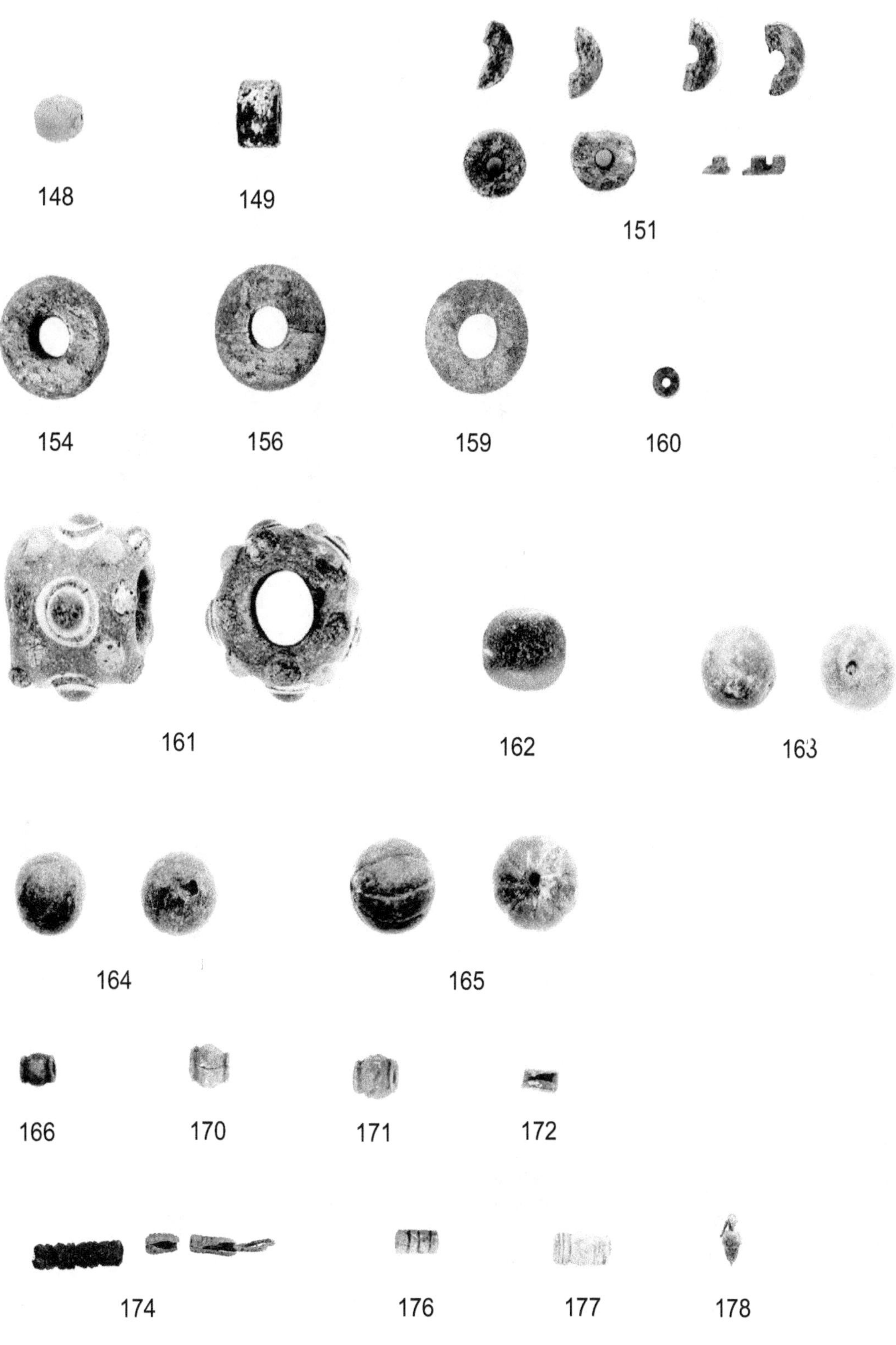

6.9. Beads (**148**–**77**), pendant (**178**)

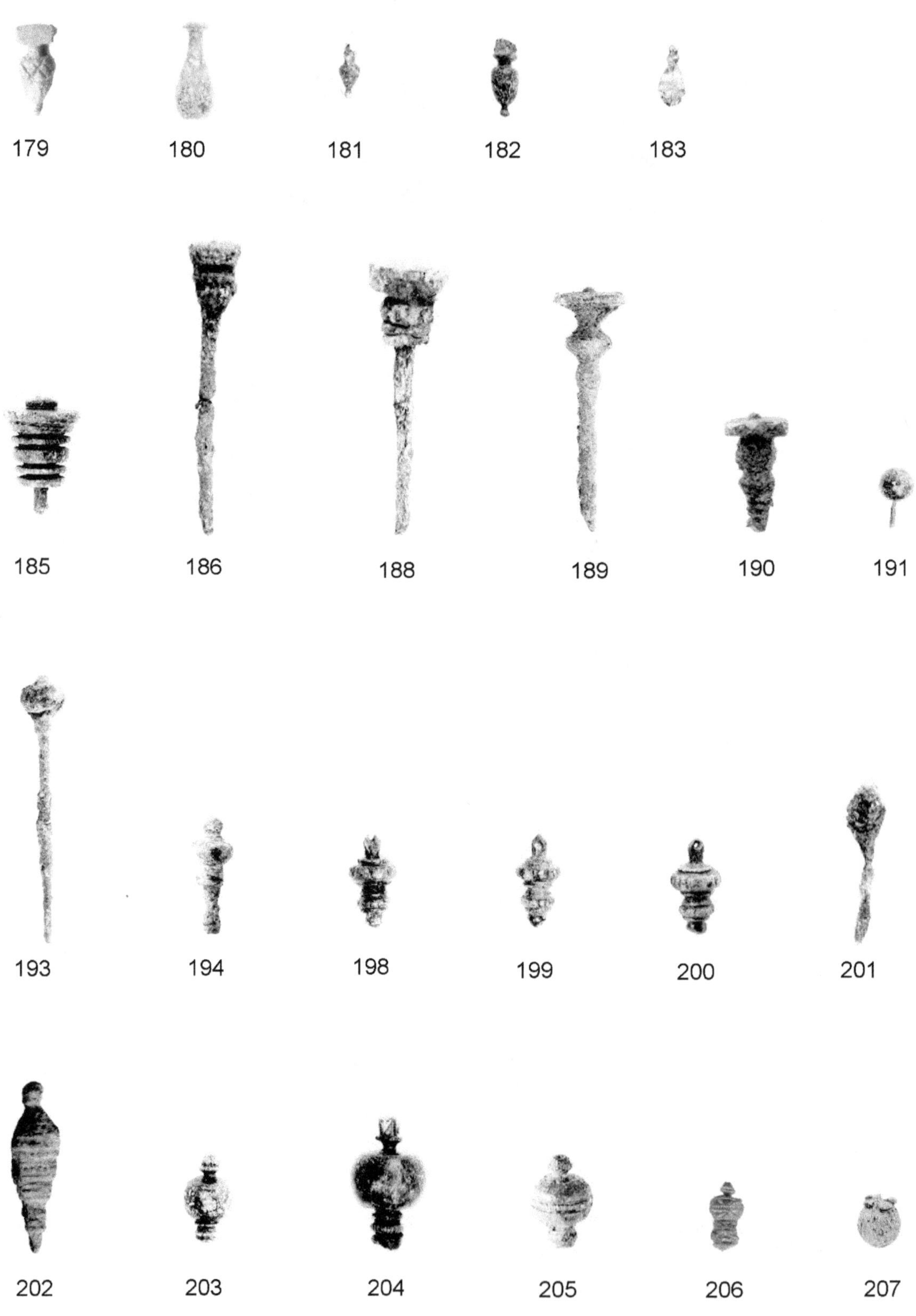

6.10. Pendants (**179–83**), pins (**185–207**)

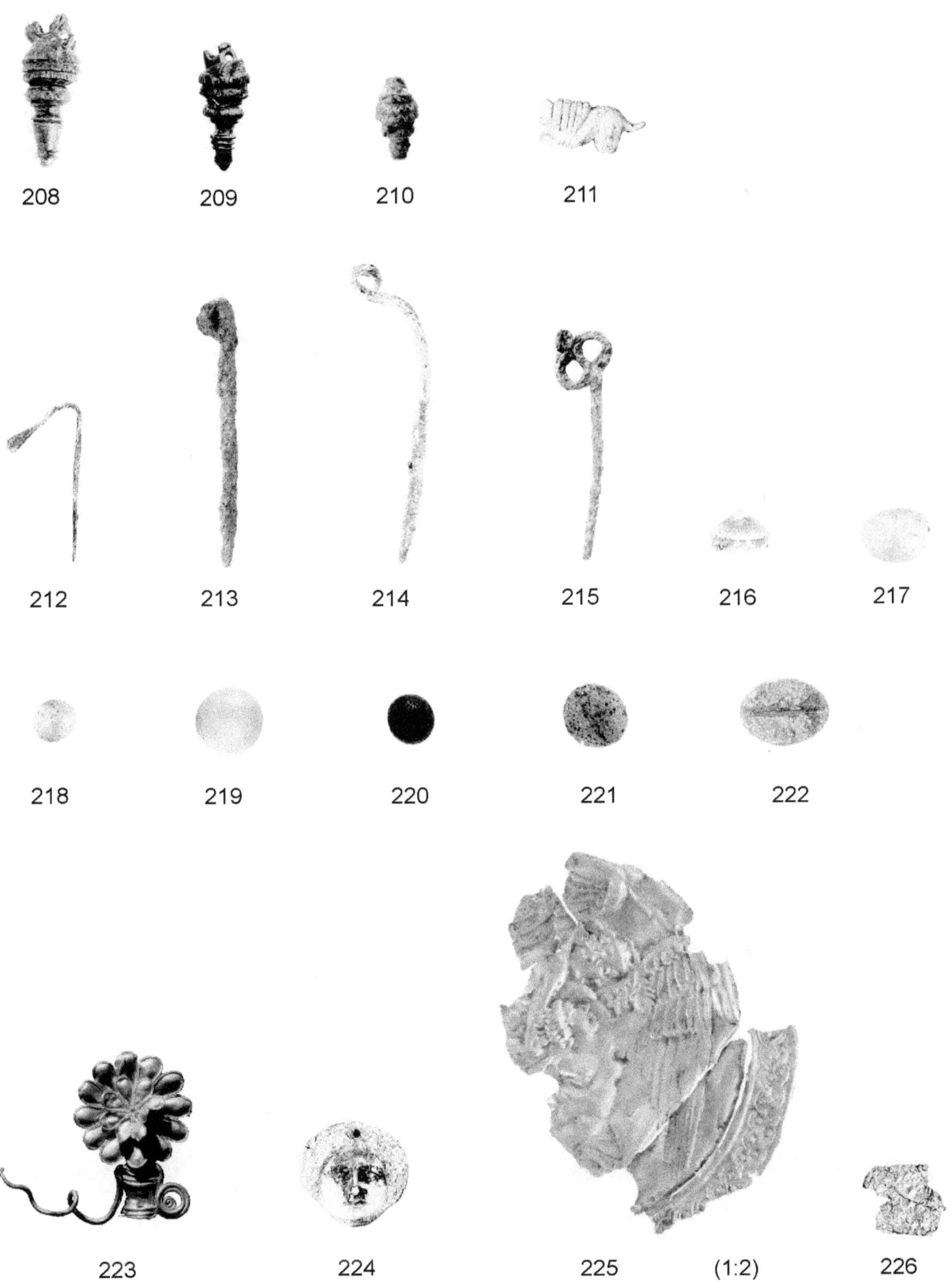

6.11. Pins (**208–15**), gems or gaming pieces (**216–22**), rosette attachment (**223**), medallions (**224–5**), gold sheet (**226**)

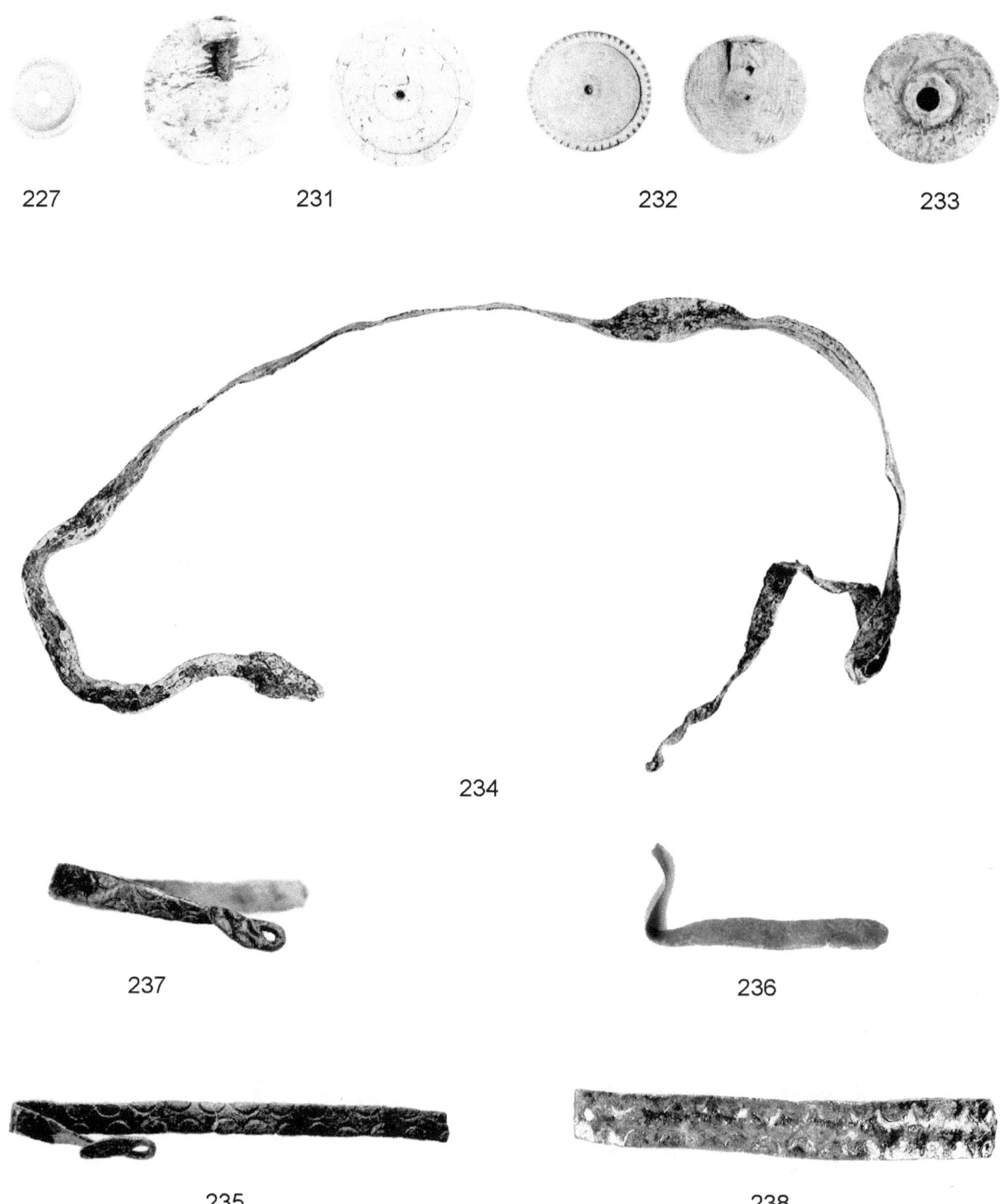

6.12. Buttons (**227**–**33**), snake bracelets (**234**–**8**)

6.13. Hair rings (**239–41**), diadems (**242–3**), fibulae (**244–6**)

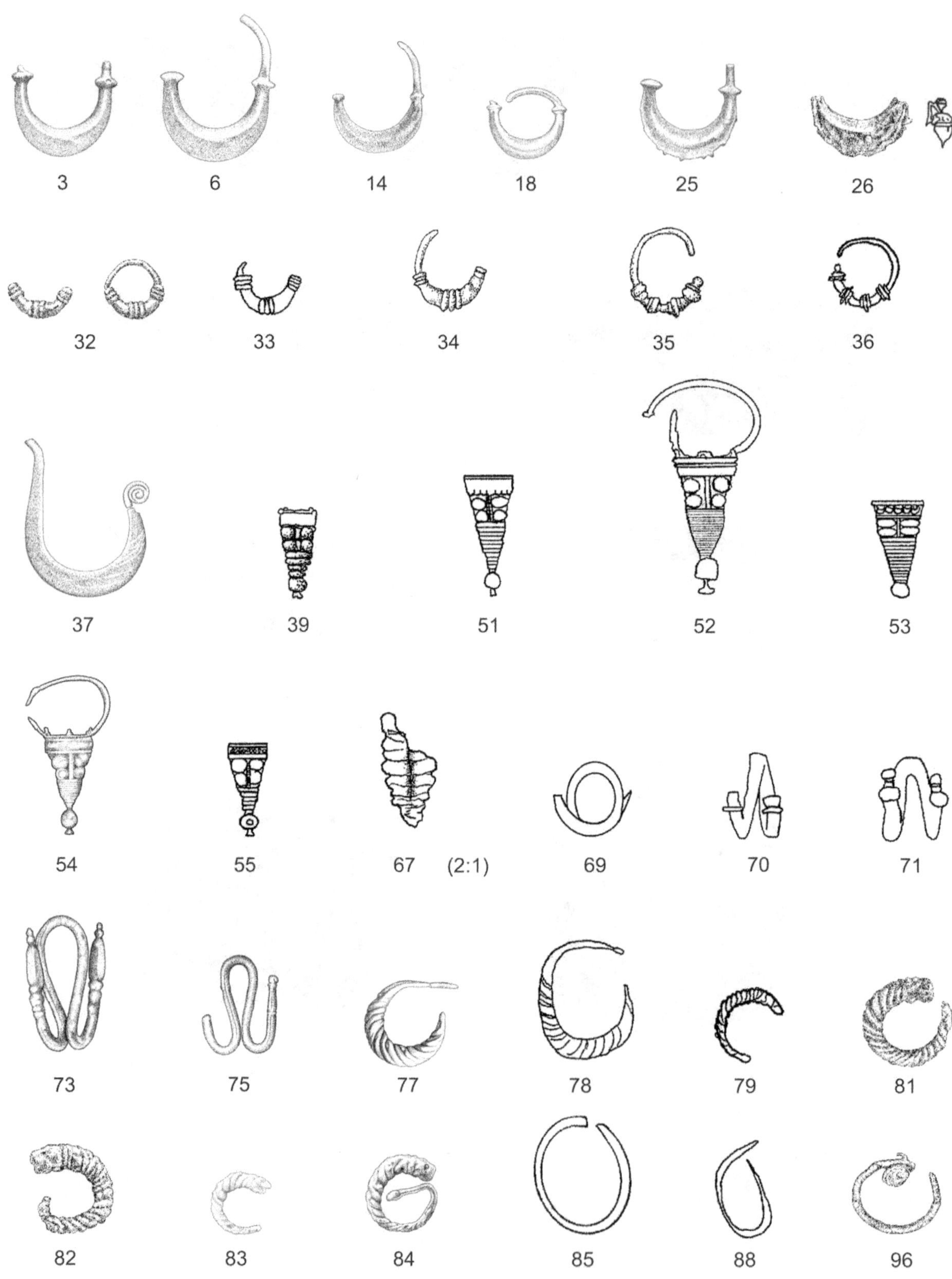

6.14. Earrings (**3**–**96**)

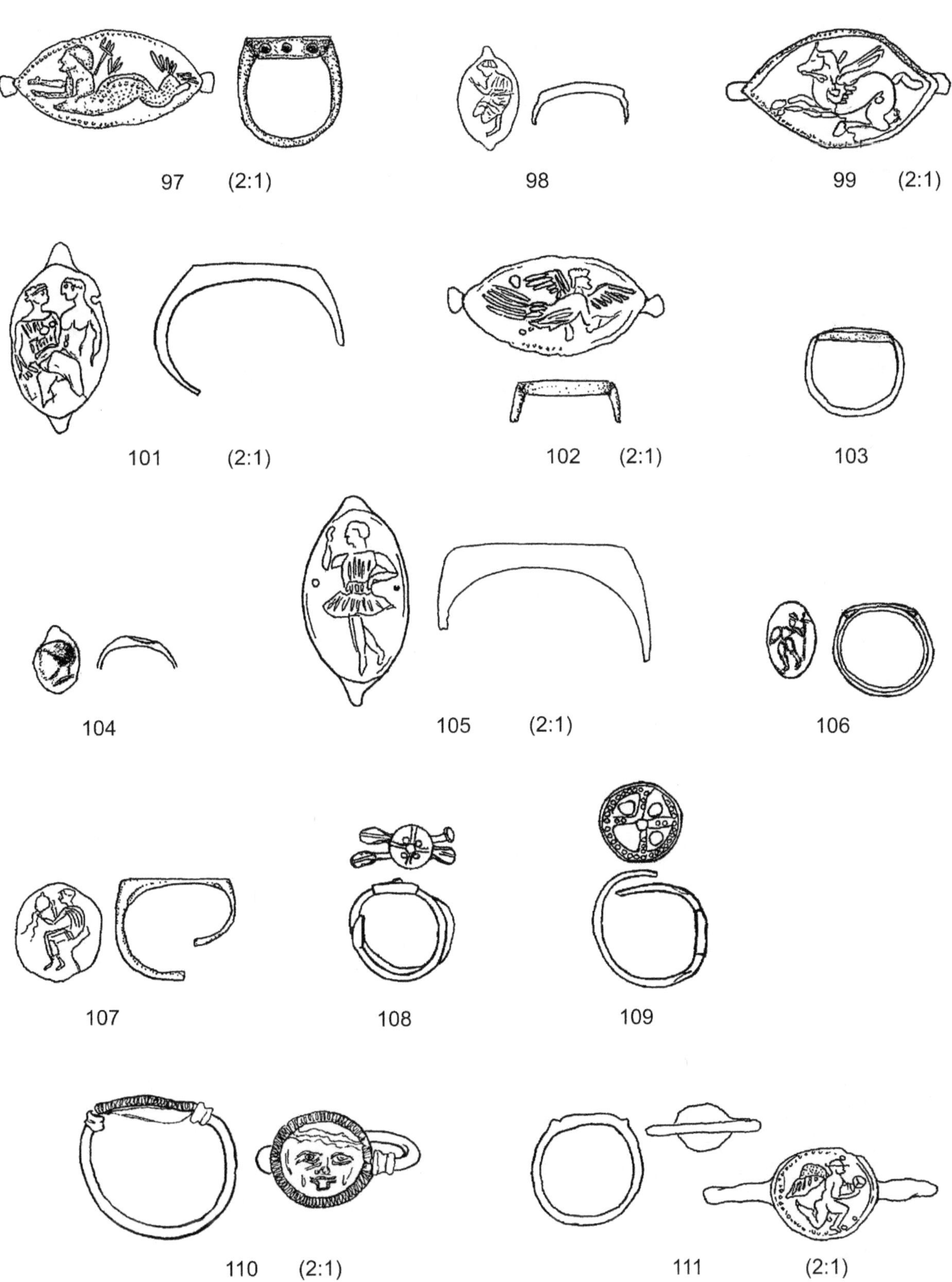

6.15. Finger rings (**97–111**)

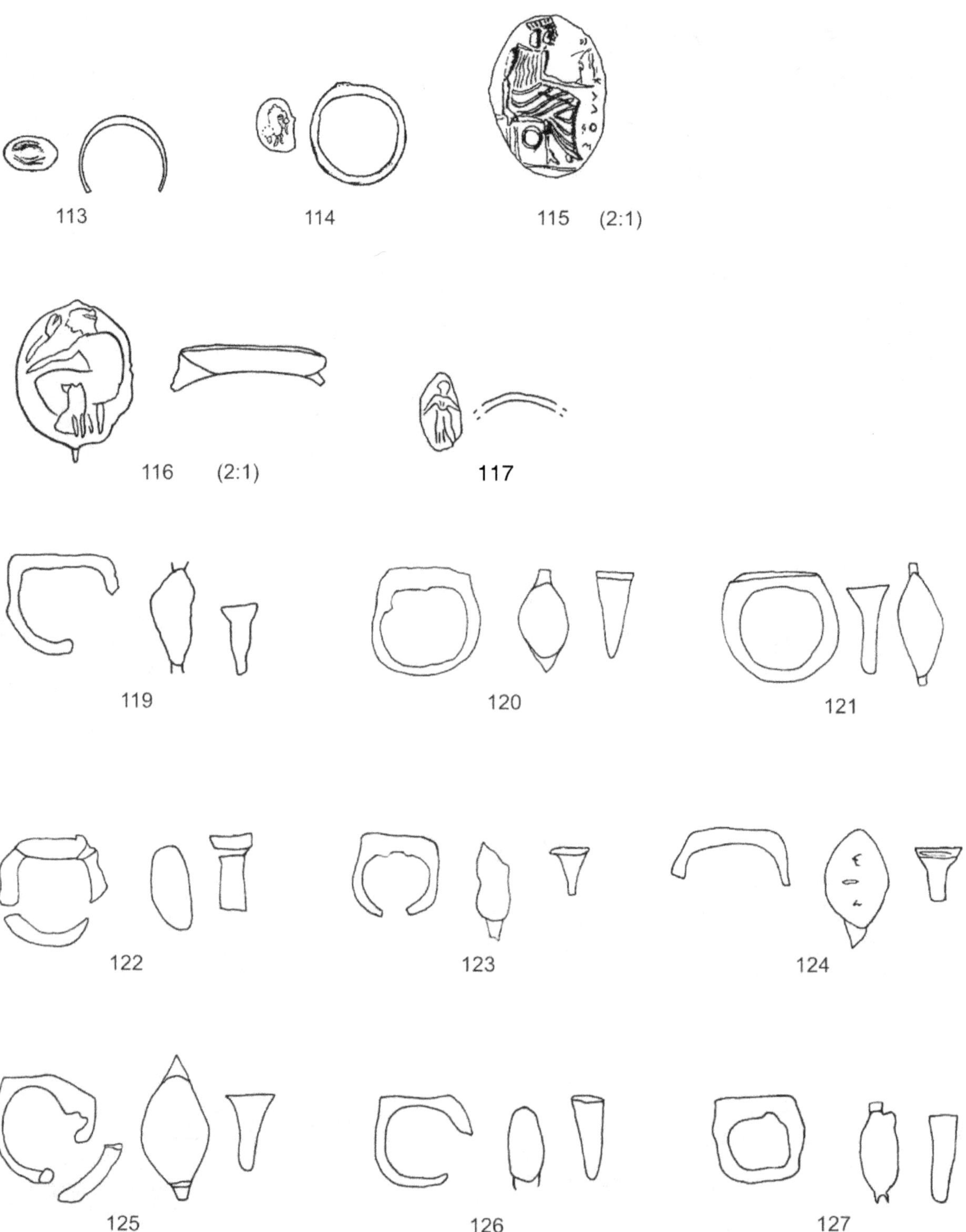

6.16. Finger rings (**113–27**)

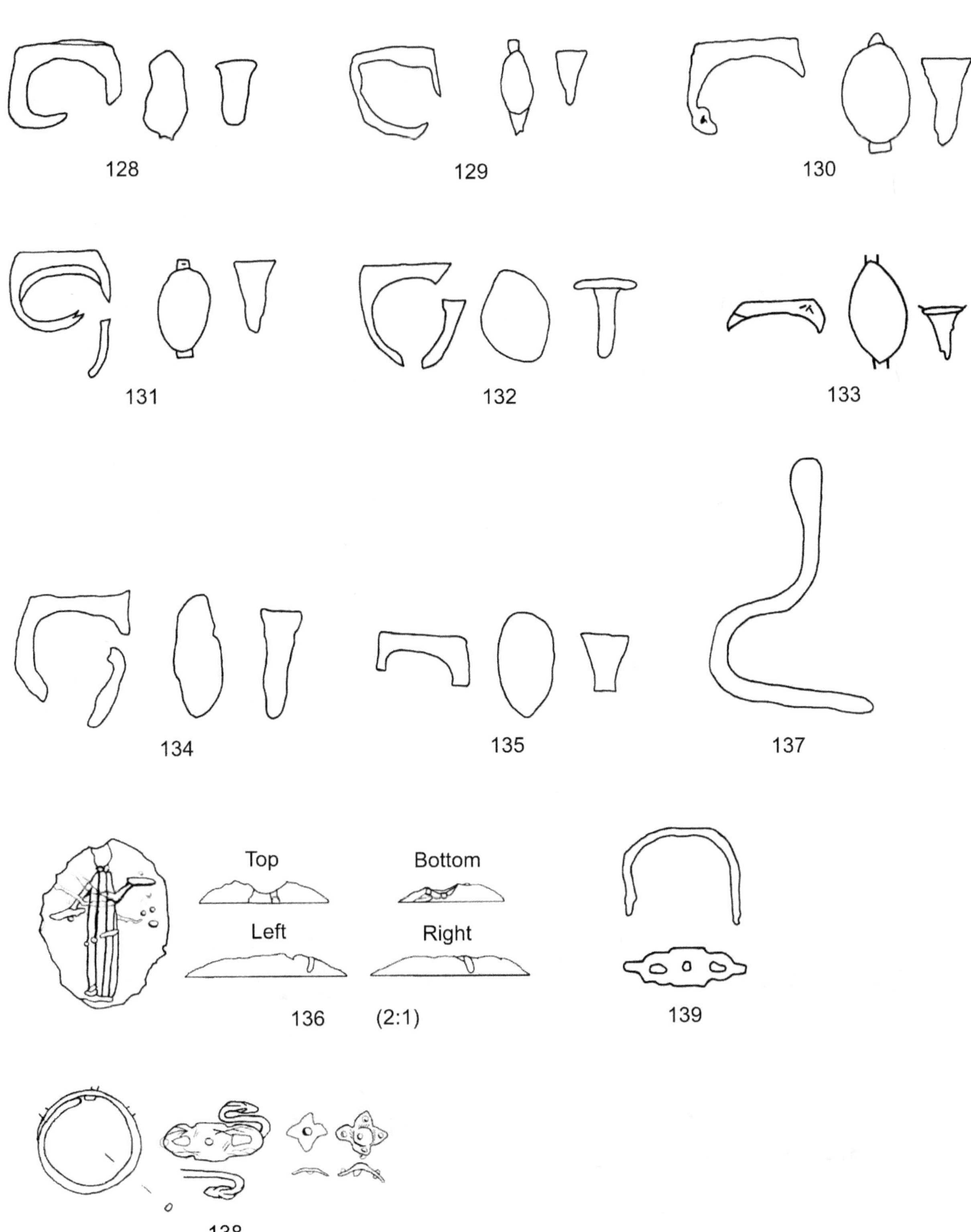

6.17. Finger rings (**128–39**)

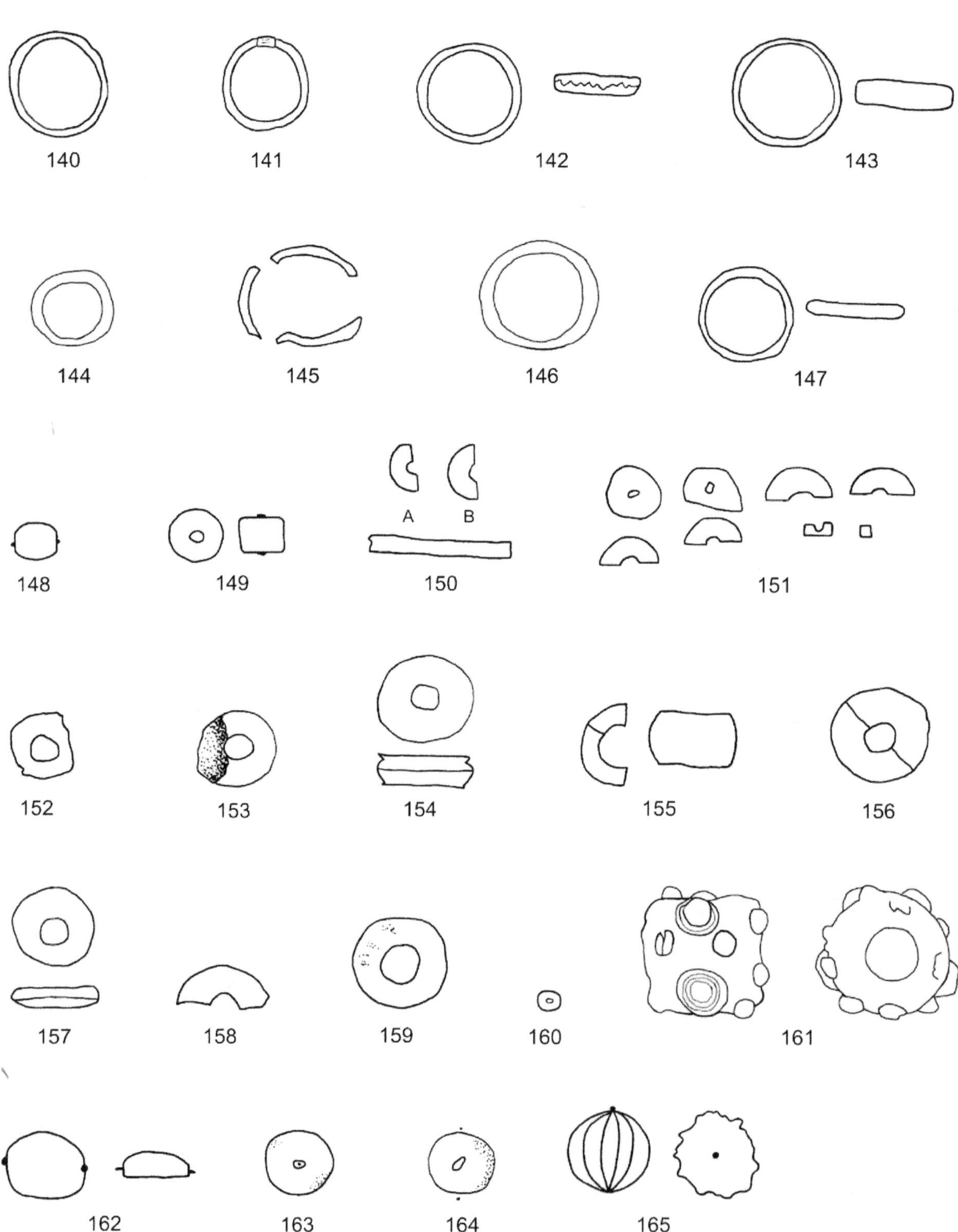

6.18. Plain hoops (**140–7**), beads (**148–65**)

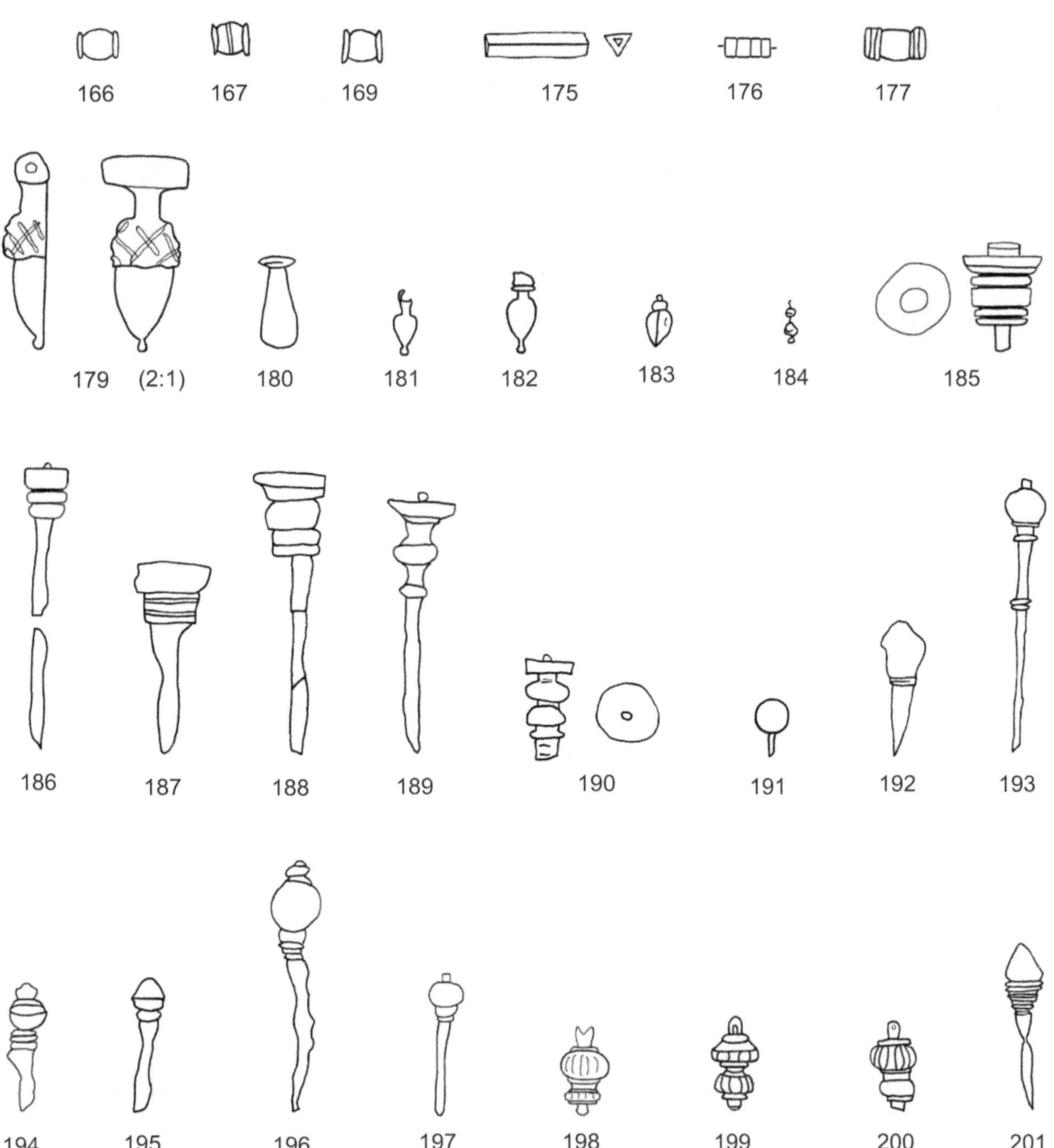

6.19. Beads (**166–77**), pendants (**179–84**), pins (**185–201**)

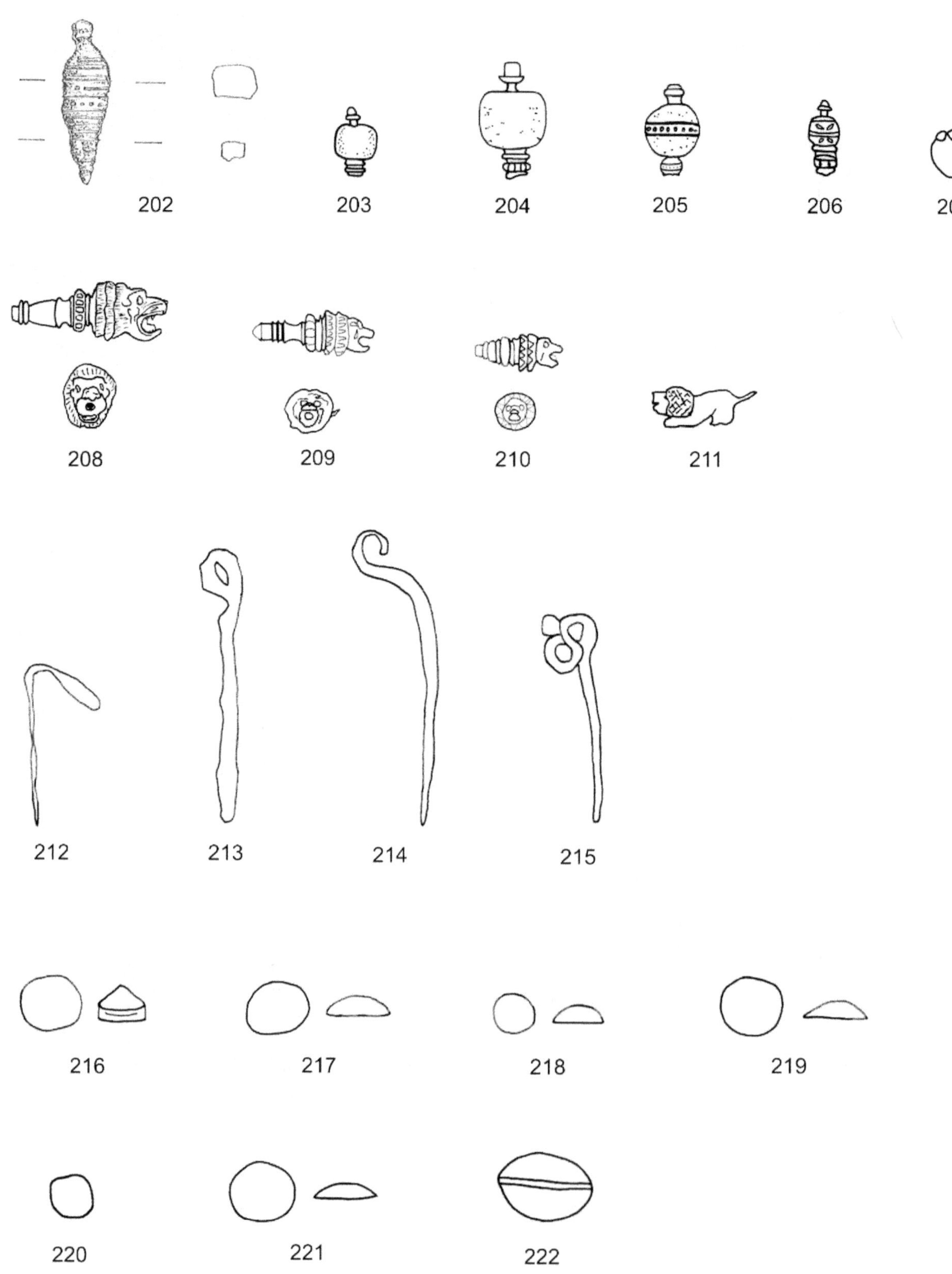

6.20. Pins (**202–15**), gems or gaming pieces (**216–22**)

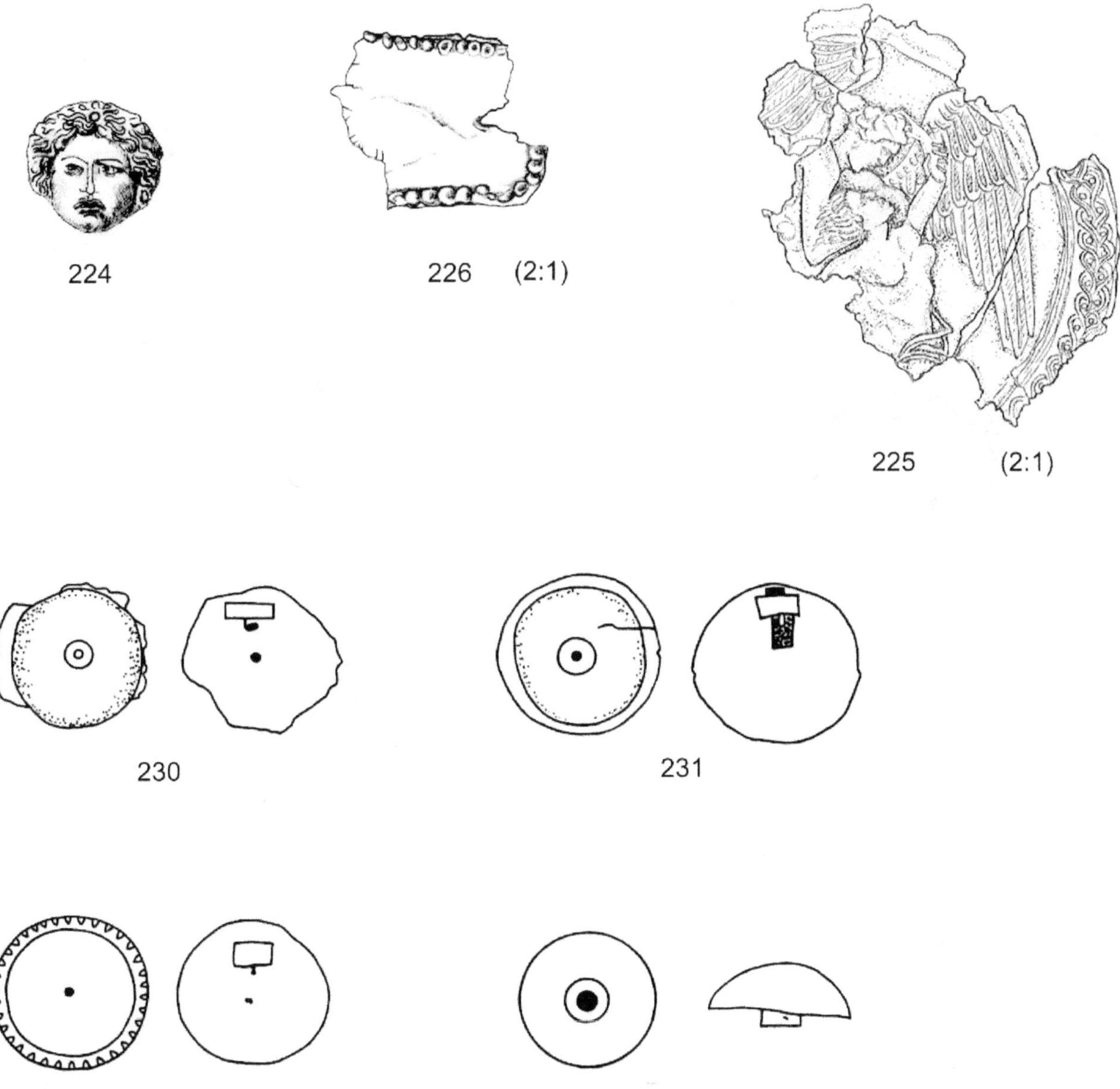

6.21. Medallions (**224–5**), gold sheet (**226**), buttons (**230–3**)

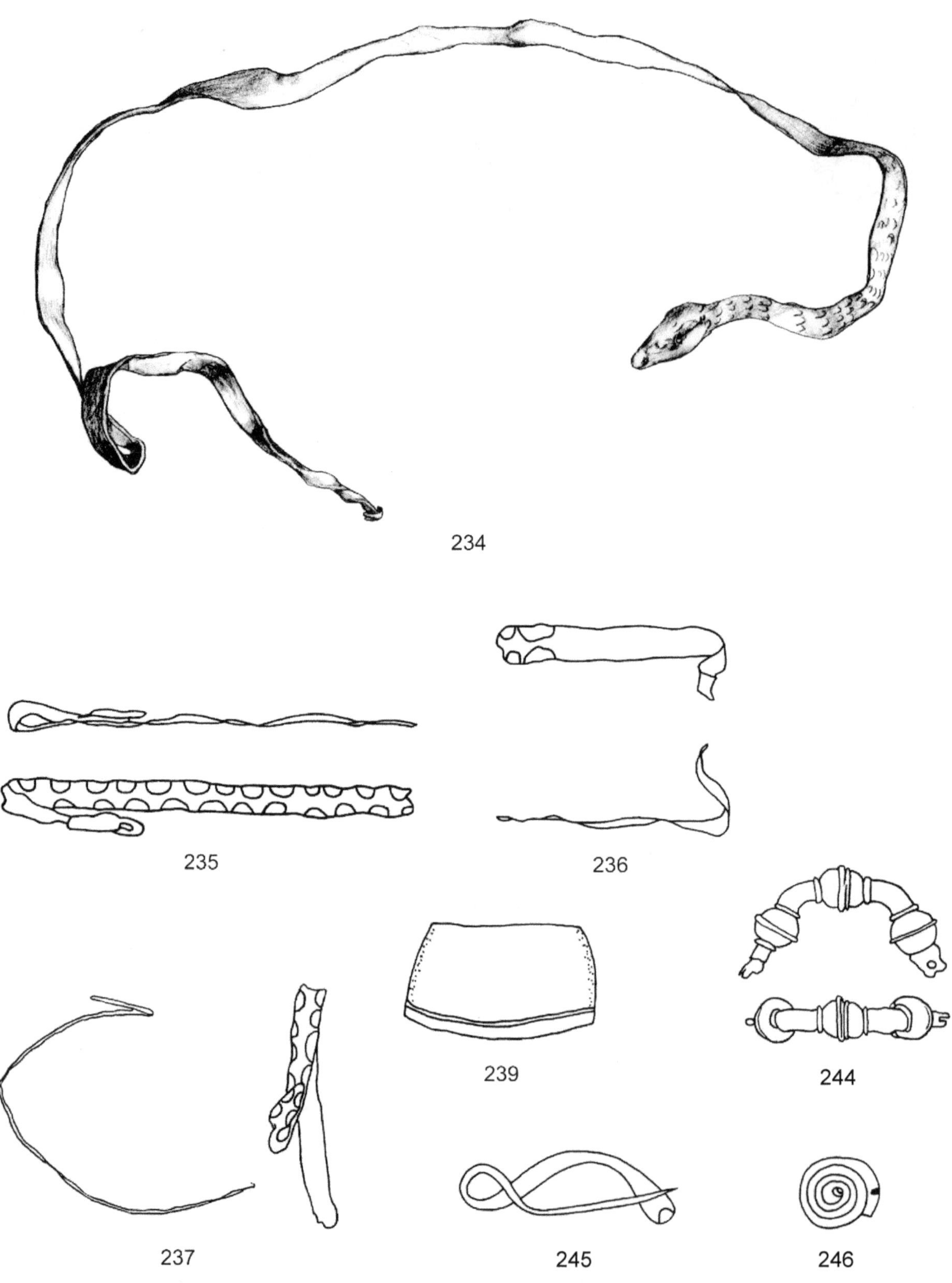

6.22. Snake bracelets (**234–7**), hair ring (**239**), fibulae (**244–6**)

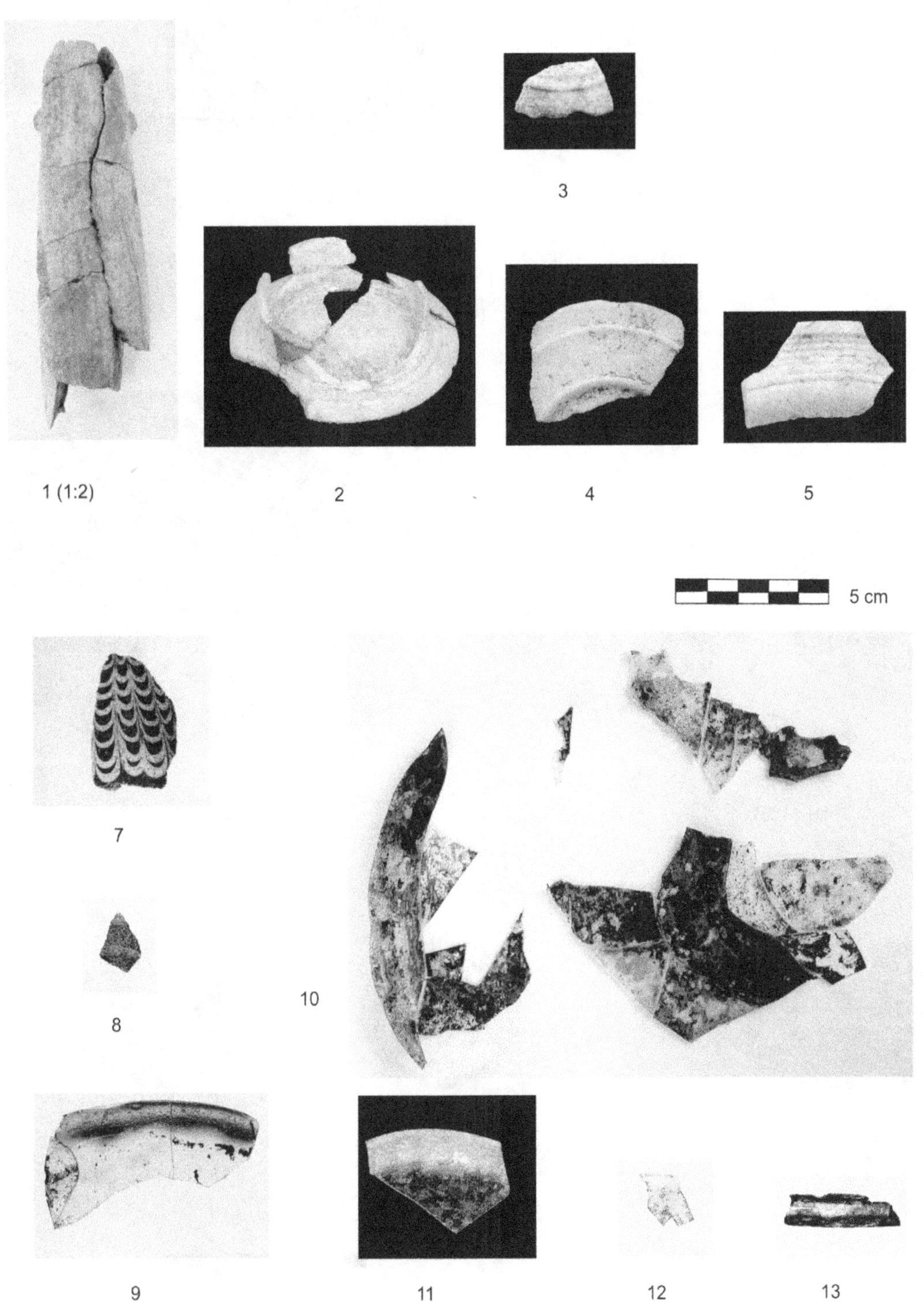

7.1. Stone vessels (**1**–**5**), glass objects (**7**–**13**)

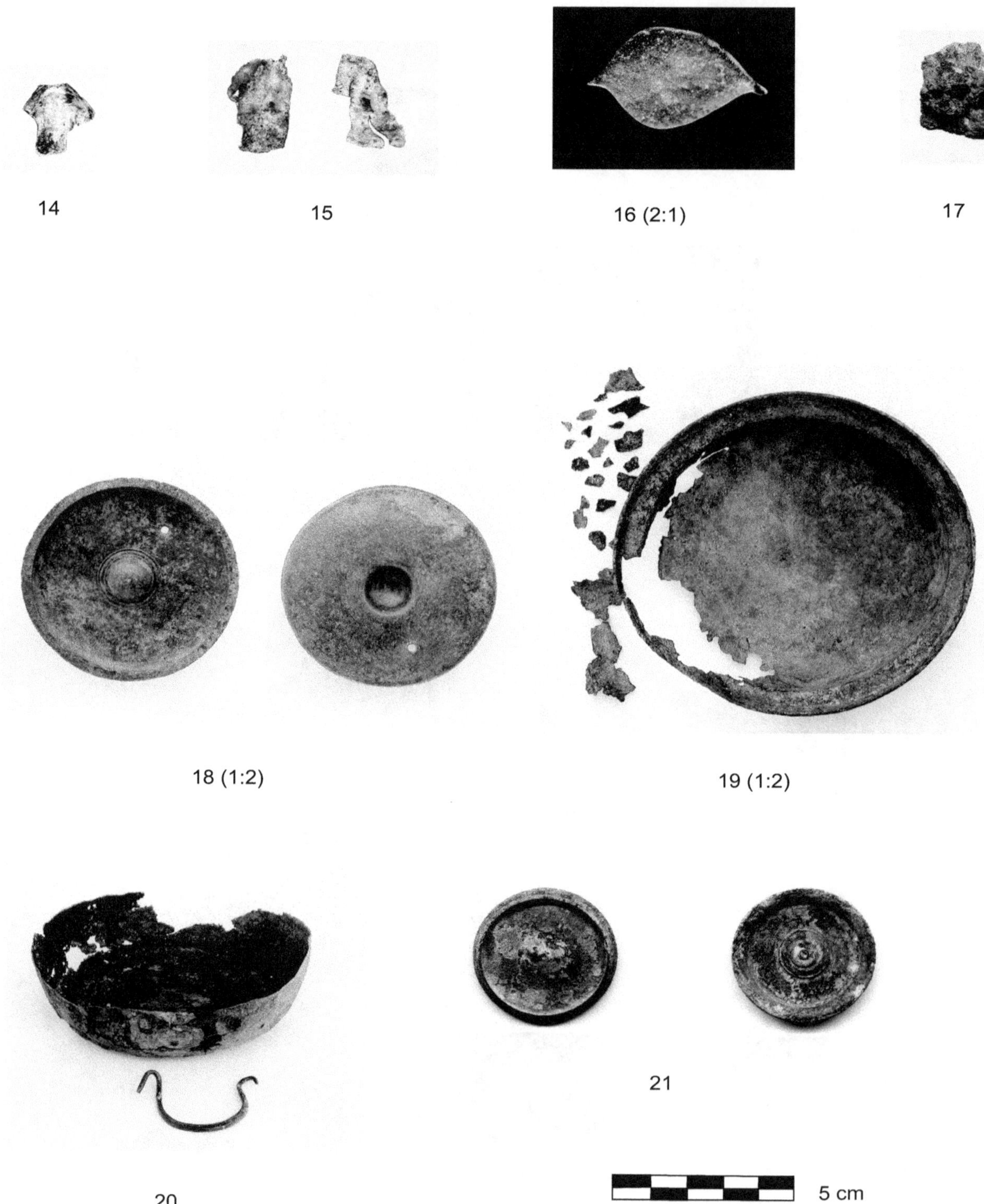

7.2. Glass objects (**14–17**), bronze vases (**18–21**)

18

Temple, NW corner, burnt area:
18 in situ, 21 found directly below

Bronze phiale (18) and base (21)
as excavated within burnt area

19

Bronze dish (20) below loomweight
Tr. 97.4 (south of Altar Terrace)

7.3. Bronze vases (**18–21**)

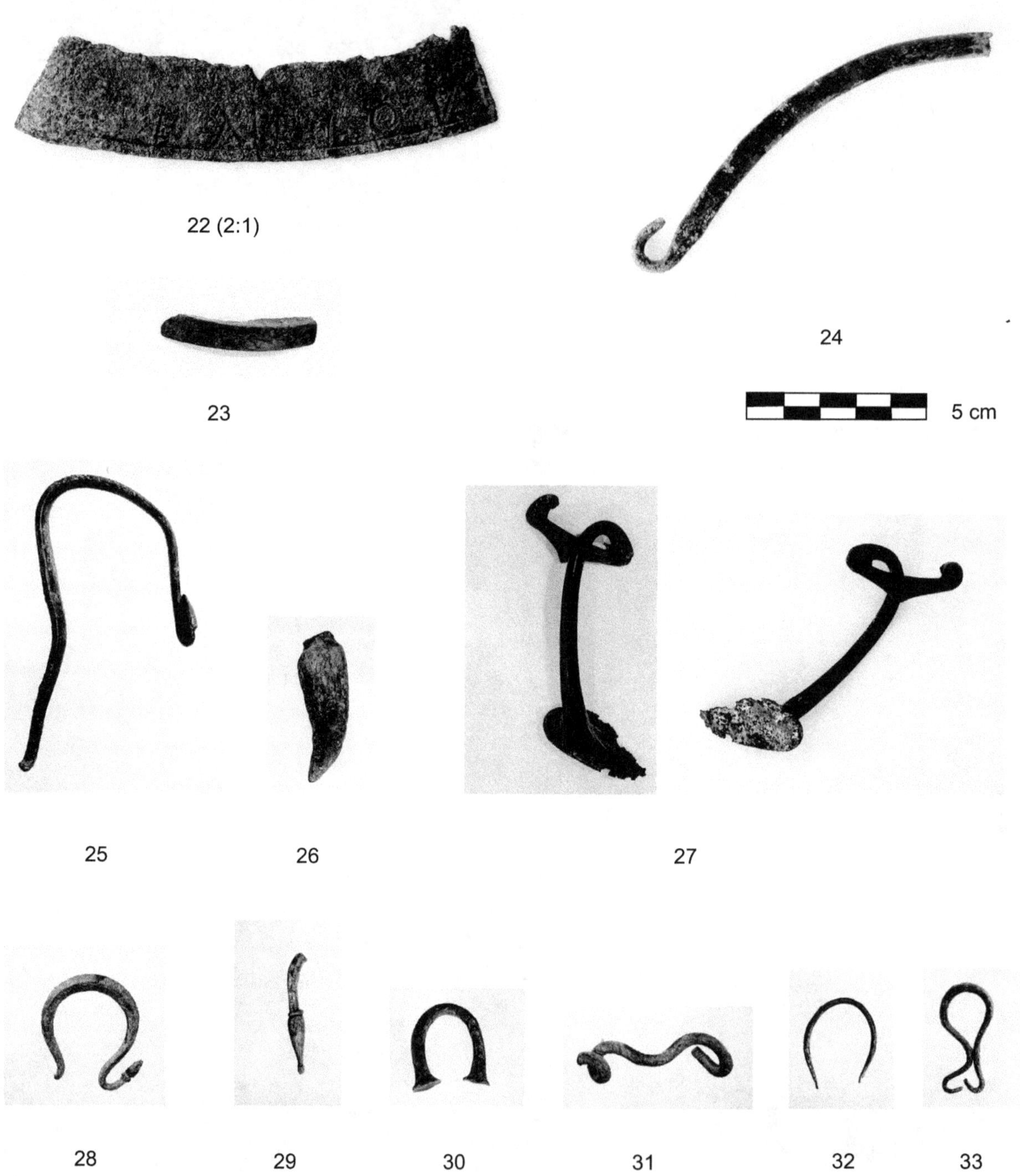

7.4. Bronze vases (**22–3**), bronze handles (**24–33**)

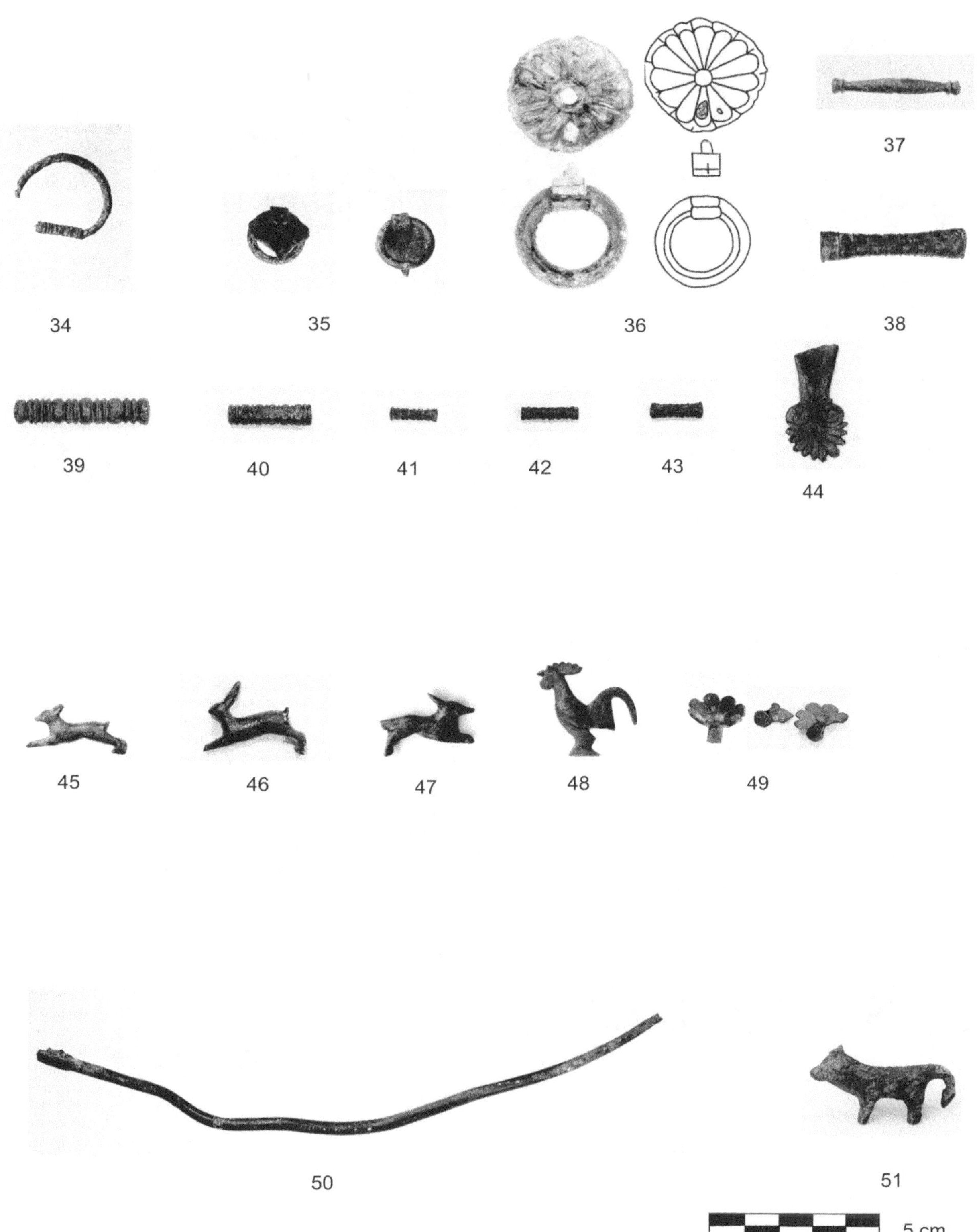

7.5. Bronze handles and spools (**34–43**), bronze mirror attachments (**44–9**), other bronze animals (**50–1**)

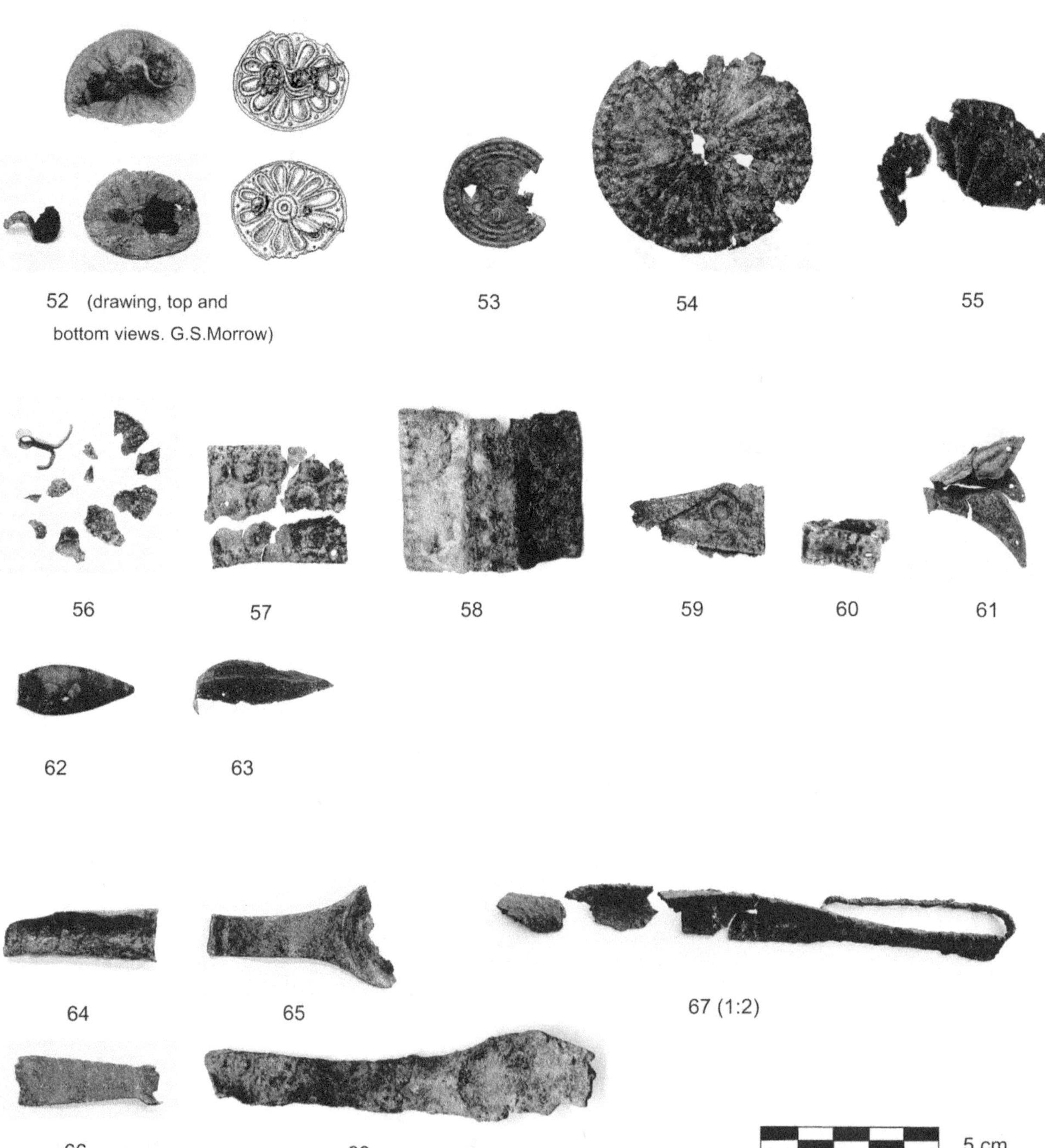

7.6. Decorative bronzes (**52–63**), strigils (**64–8**)

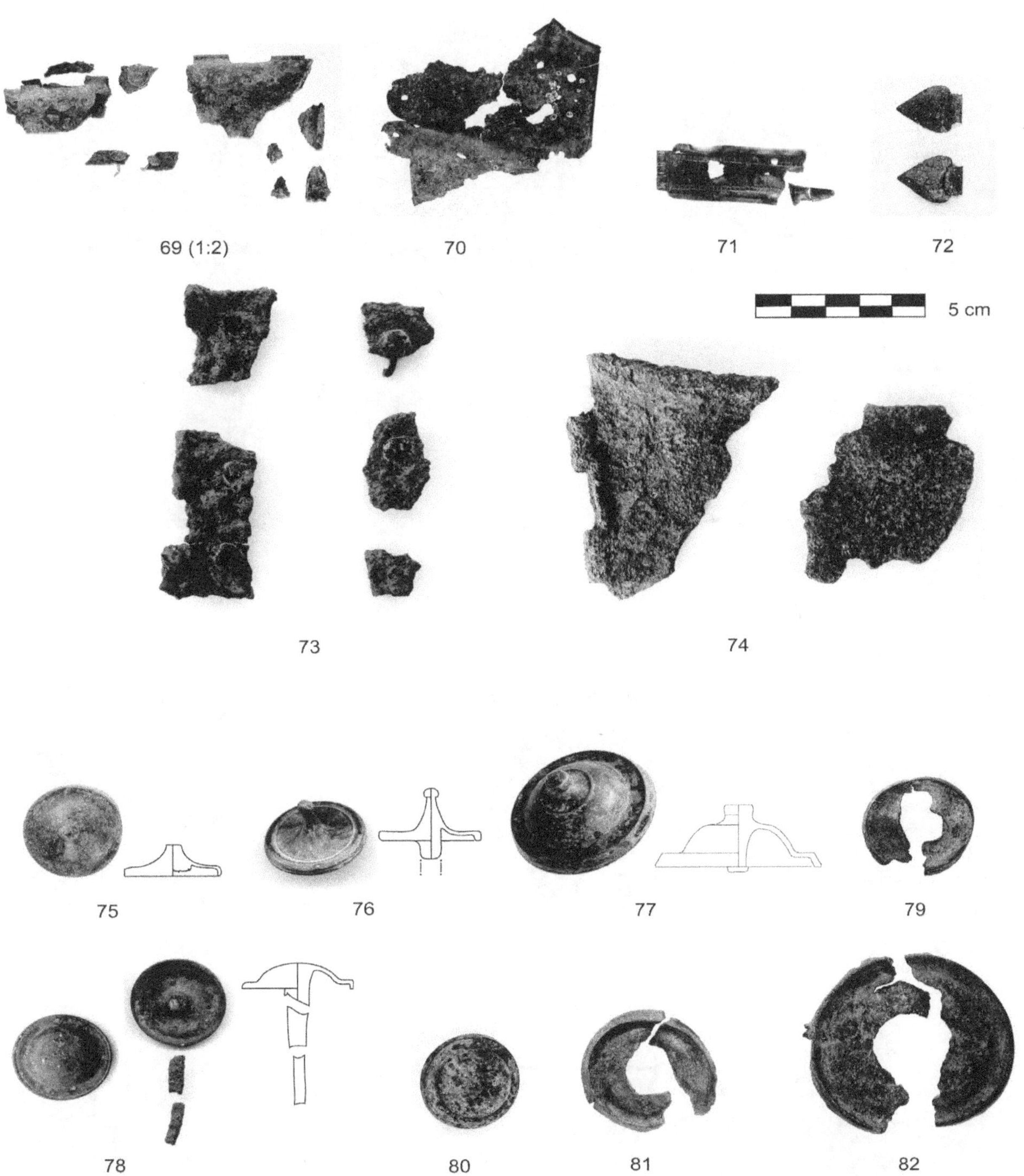

7.7. Hinges (**69–74**), bronze door bosses (**75–82**)

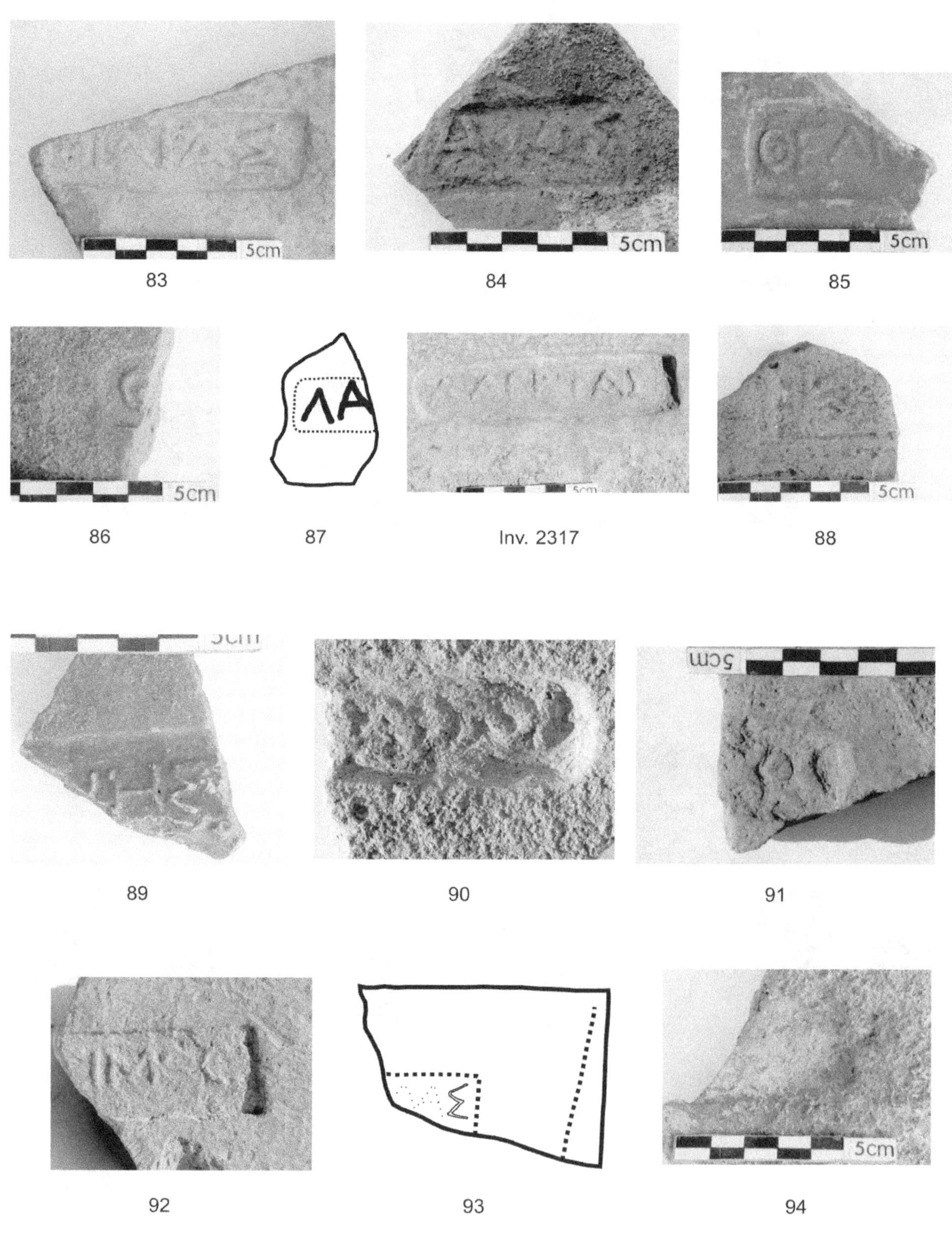

7.8. Stamped roof tiles (**83**–**94**)

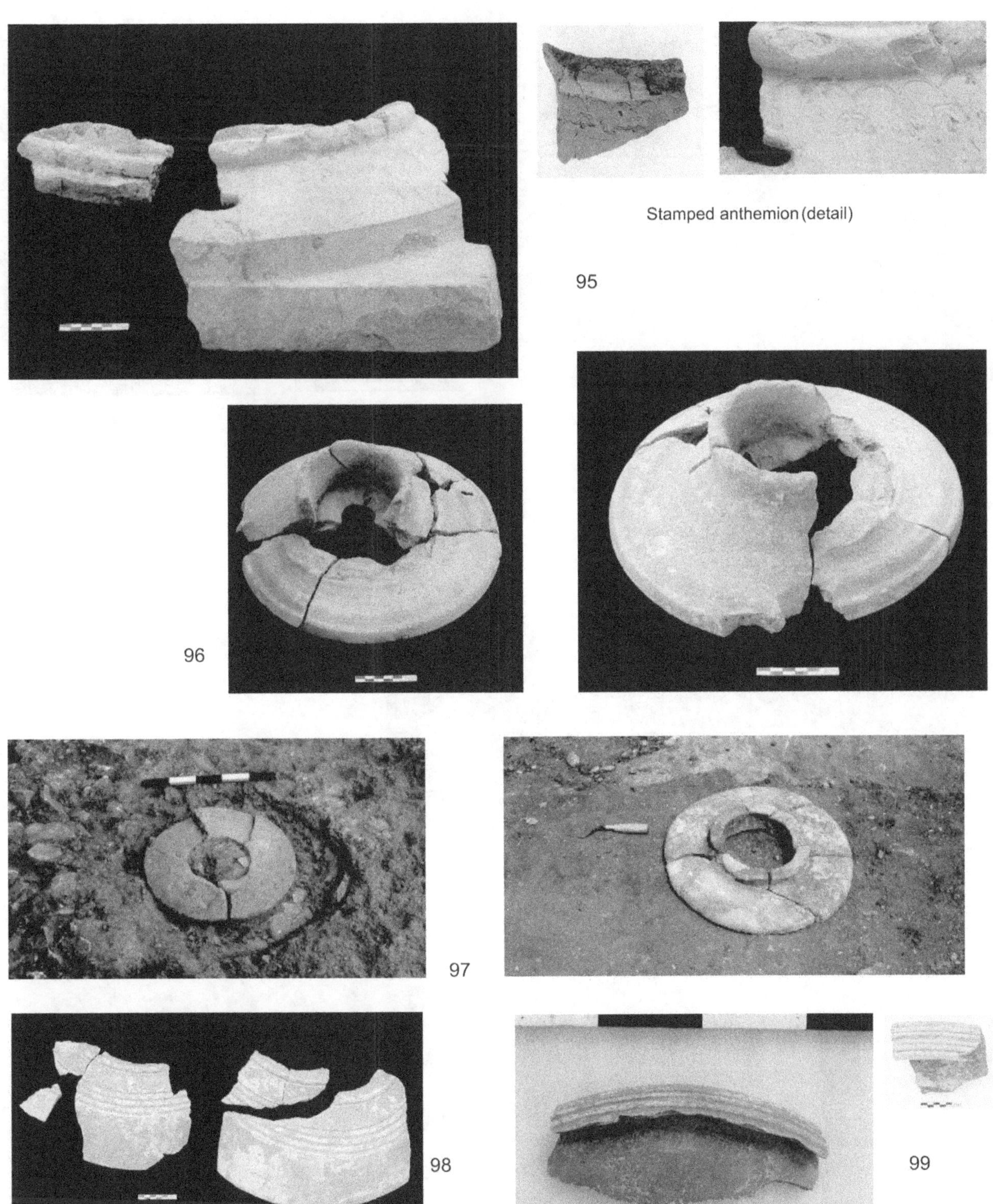

7.9. Terracotta perirrhanteria (**95–9**)

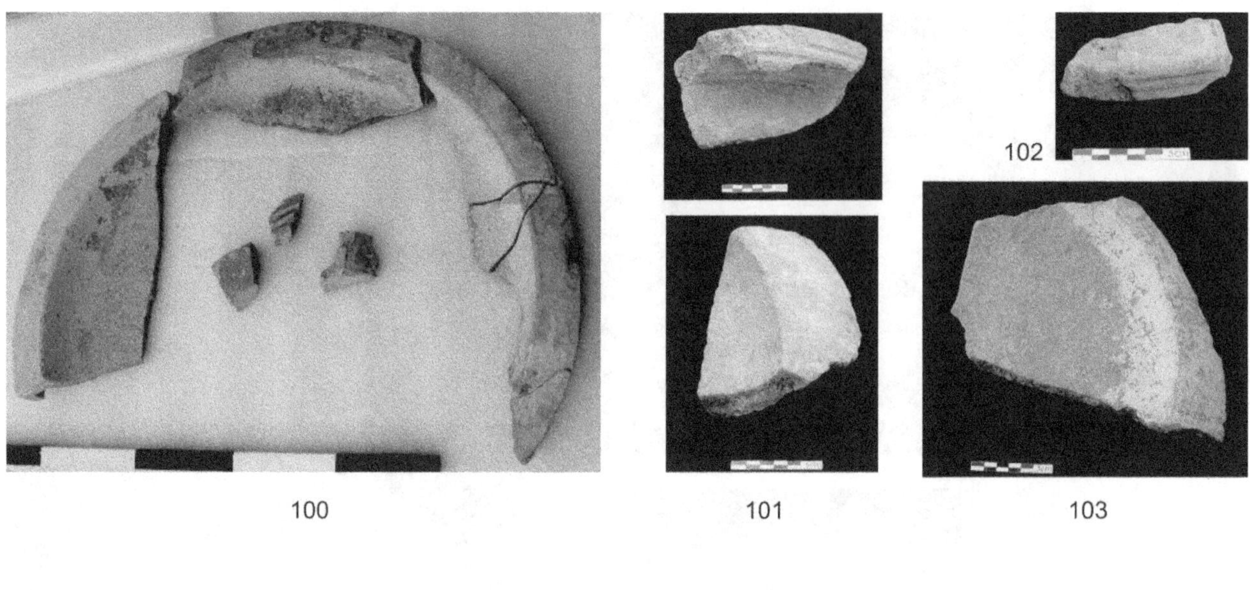

7.10. Terracotta perirrhanteria (**100–3**), stone objects (**104–8**)

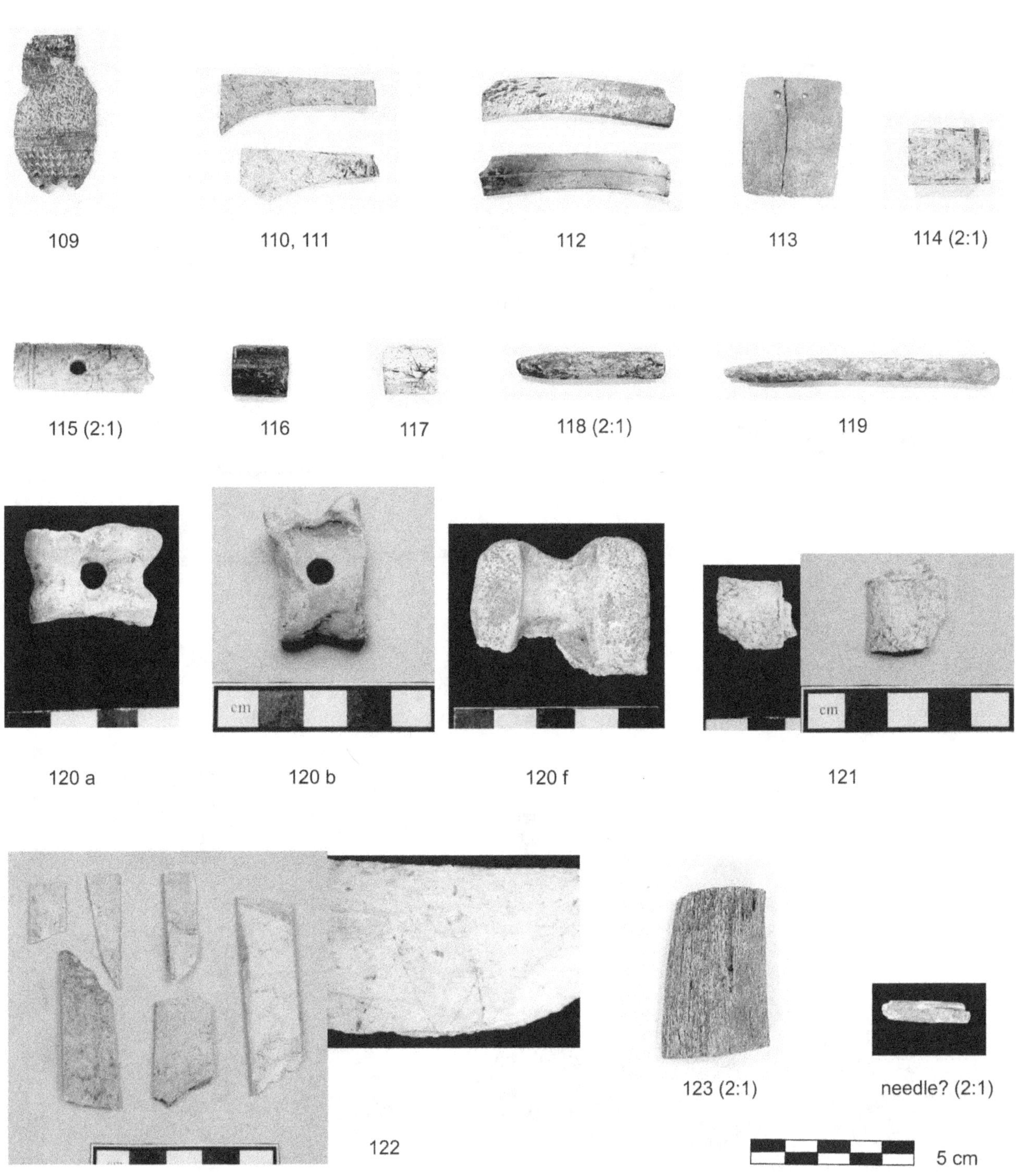

7.11. Worked bone objects (**109–23**)

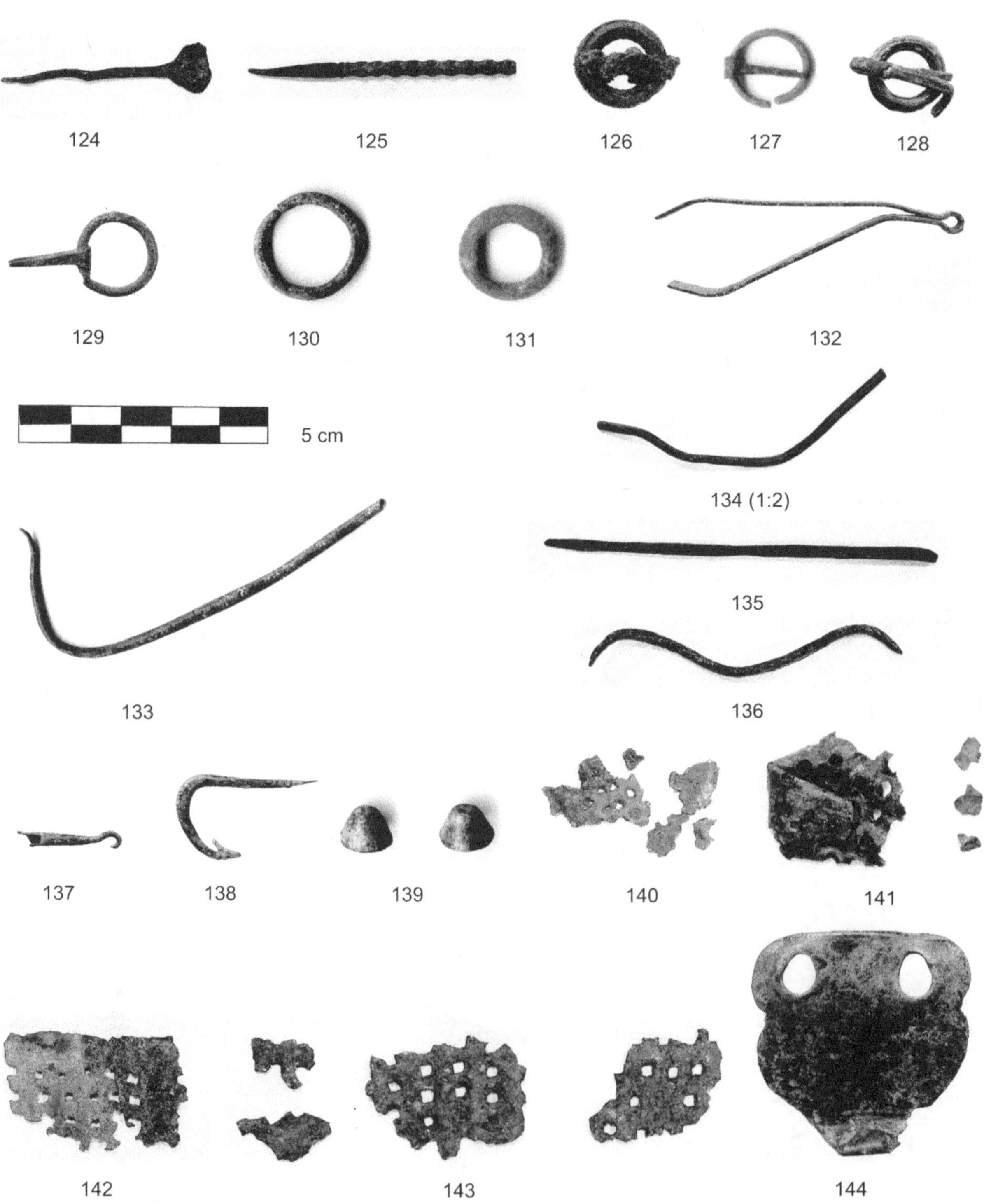

7.12. Utilitarian bronzes (**124–44**)

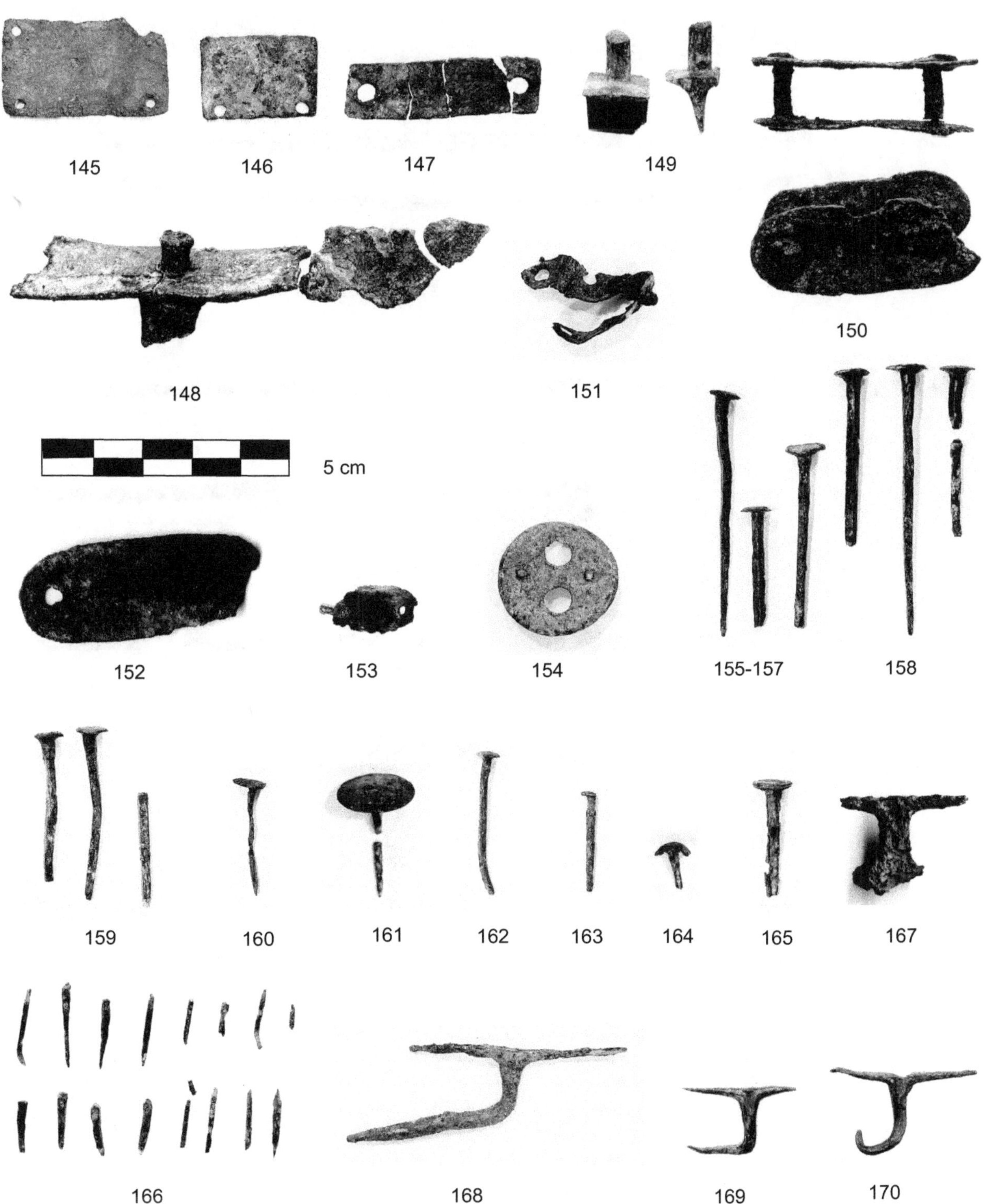

7.13. Utilitarian bronzes (**145–54**), bronze nails and tacks (**155–70**)

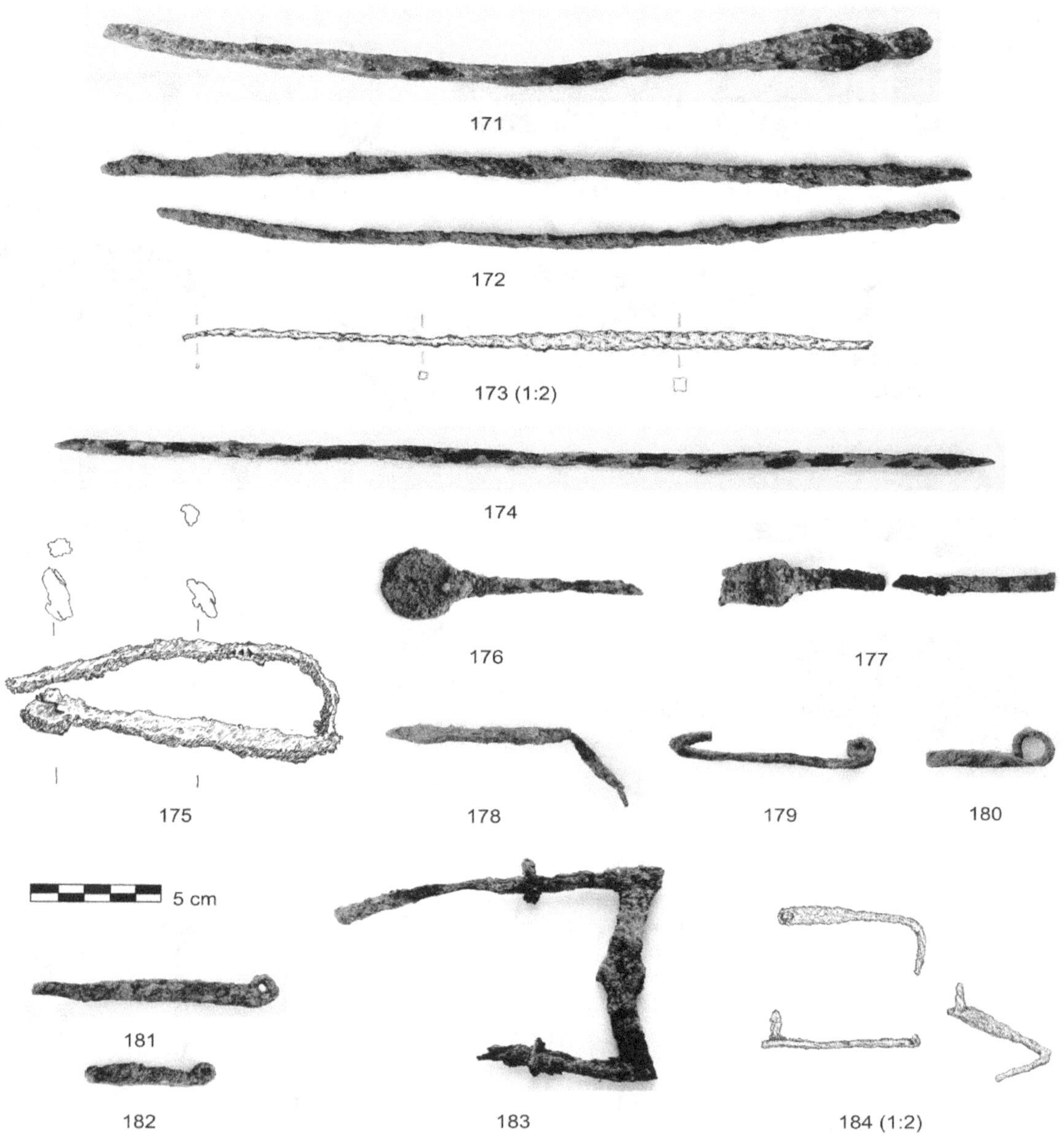

7.14. Iron obeloi (**171–8**), iron hook keys (**179–82**), iron door handle (**183**), iron object (**184**)

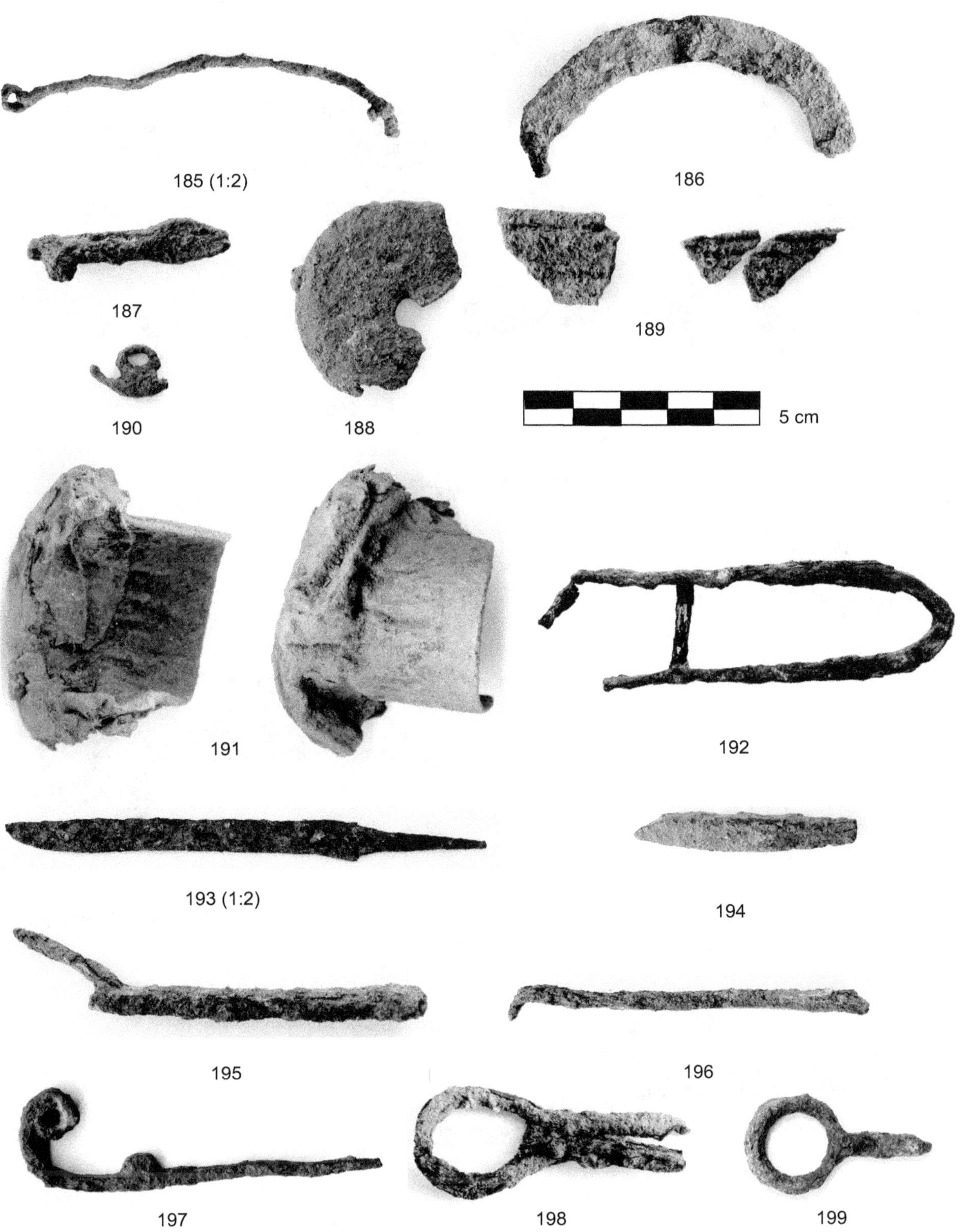

7.15. Iron objects (**185–99**)

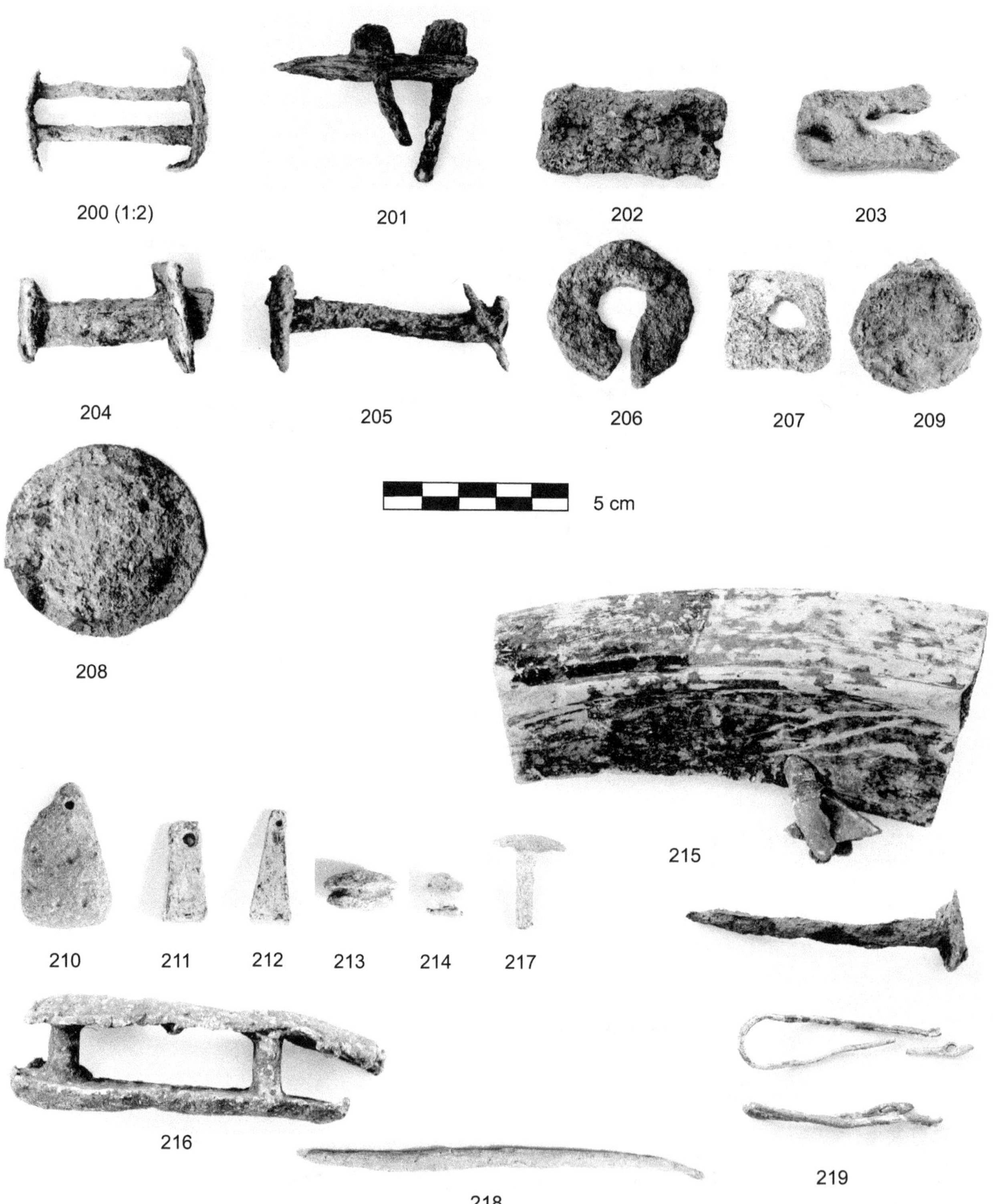

7.16. Iron objects (**200–9**), lead objects (**210–19**)

7.17. Varia (**220–31**)

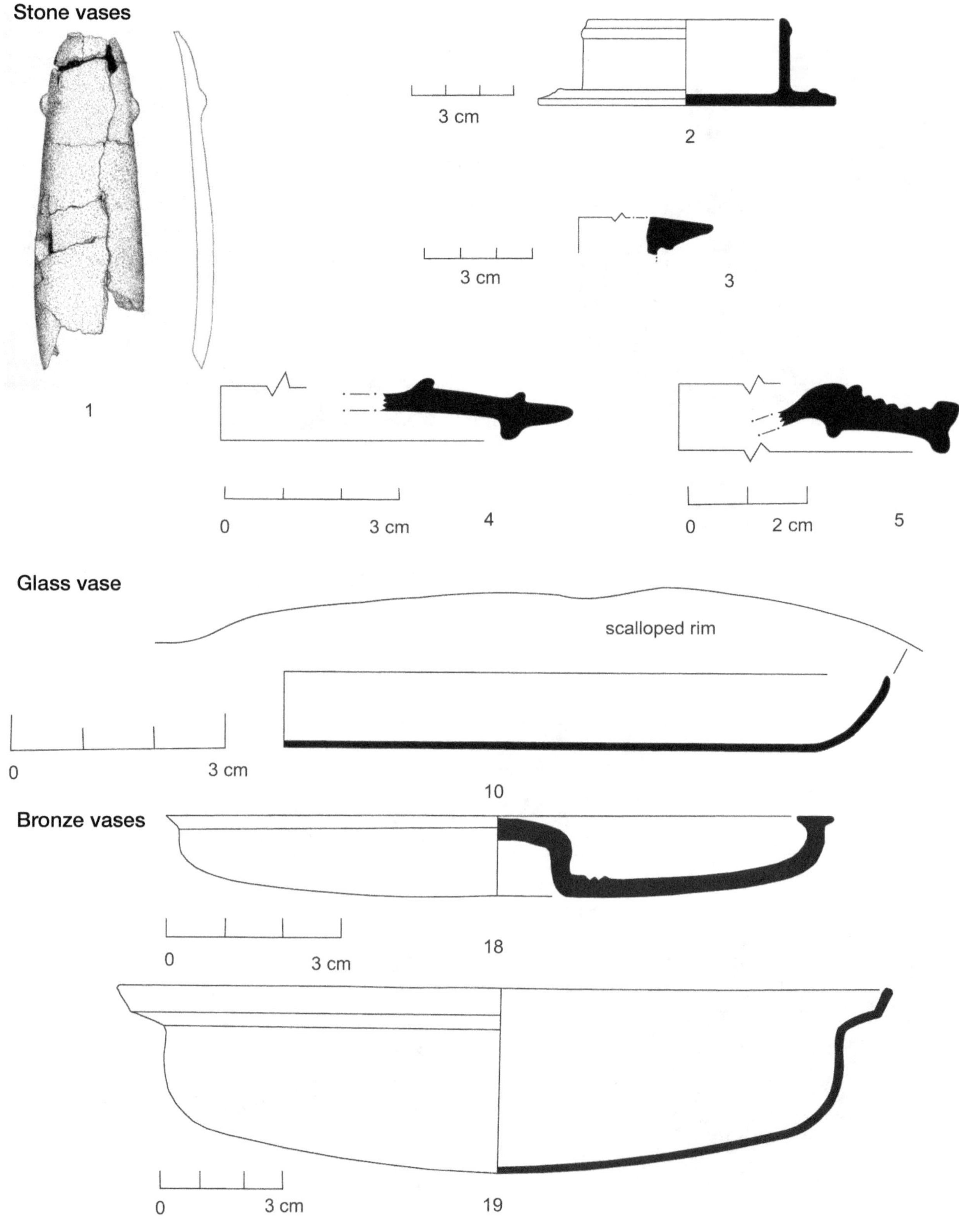

7.18. Stone vases (**1–5**), glass vase (**10**), bronze vases (**18–19**)

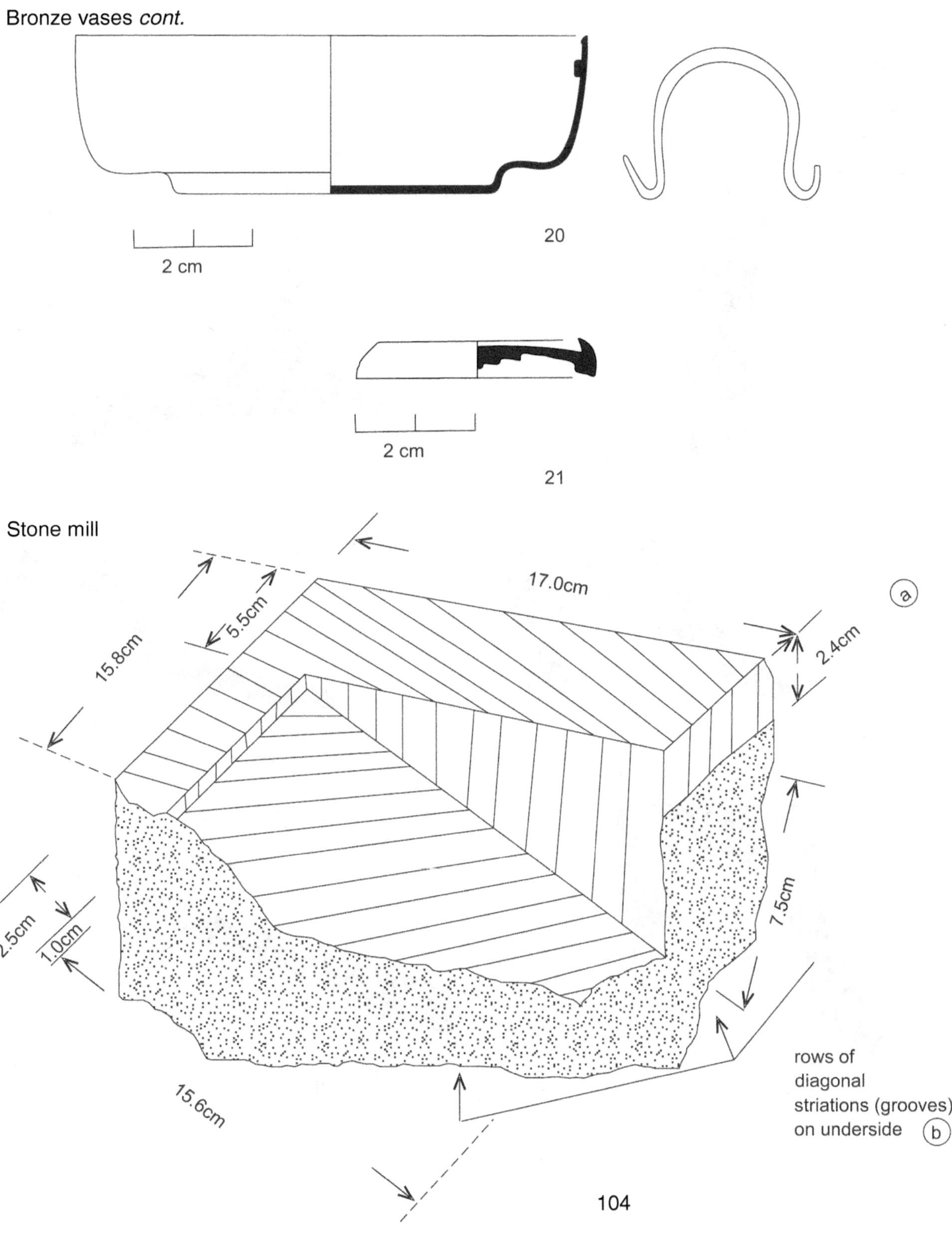

7.19. Bronze vases (**20–1**), stone mill (**104**)

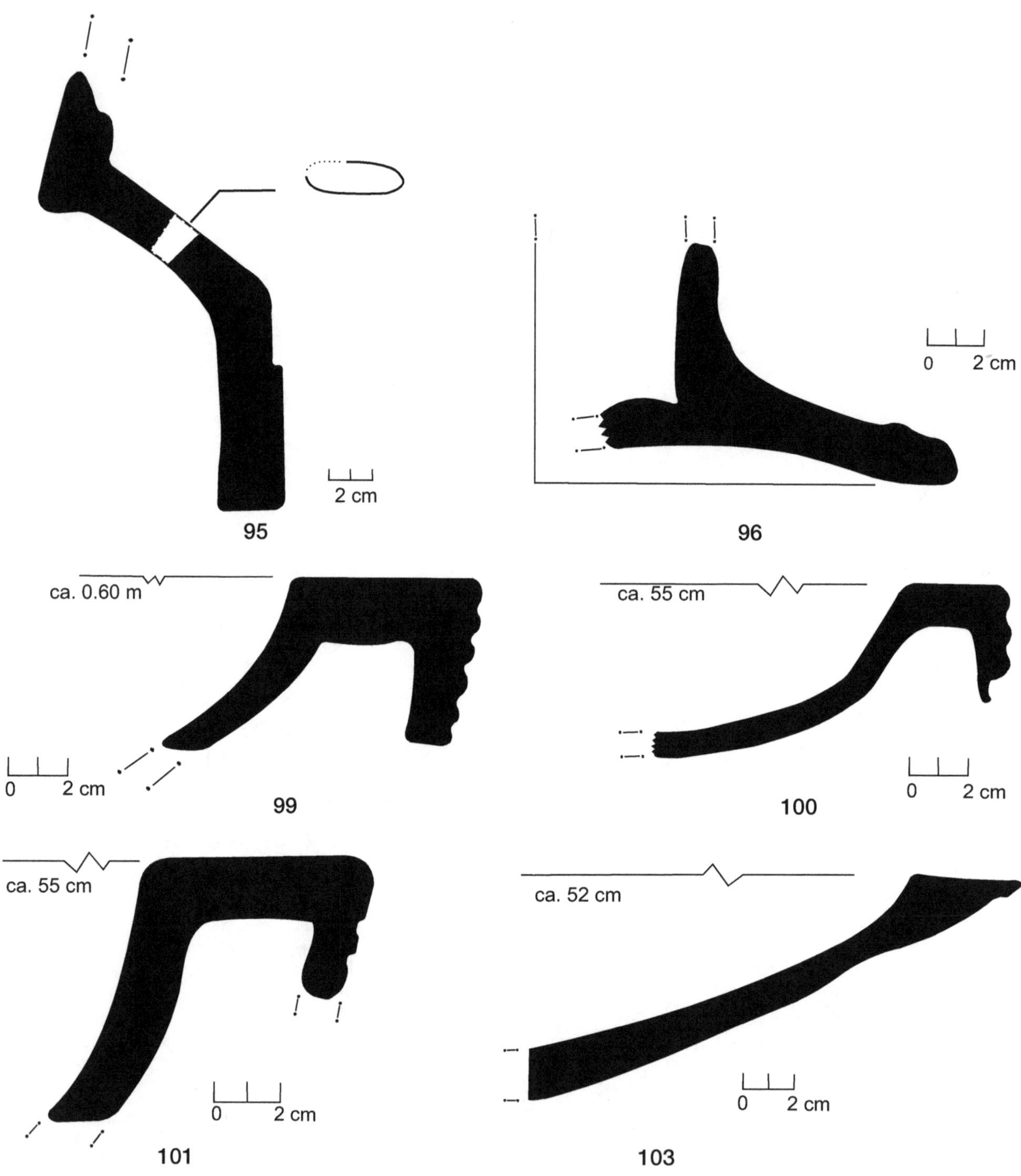

7.20. Terracotta perirrhanteria (**95**–**103**)

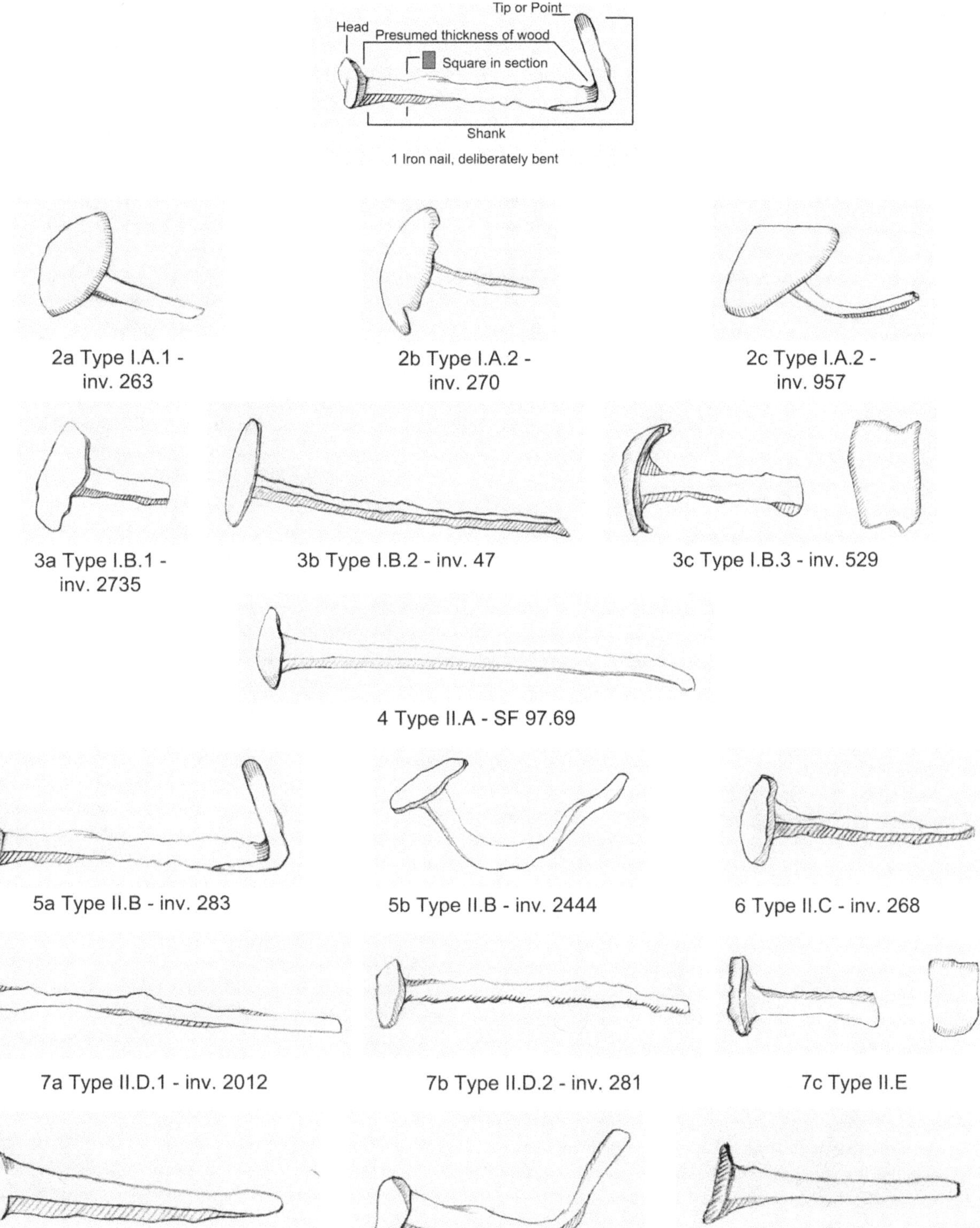

8.1. Iron nails Types I to IIIC

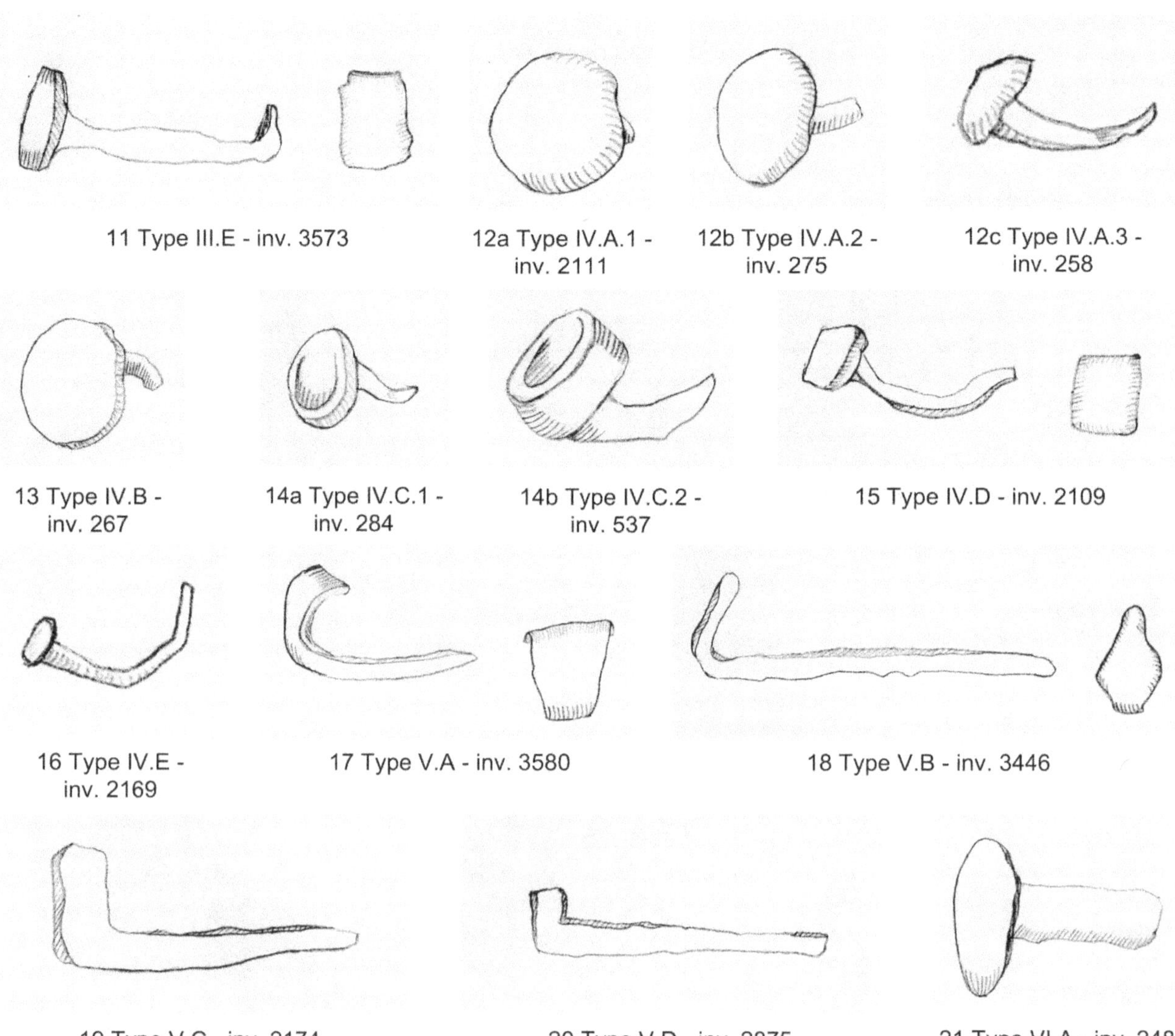

8.2. Iron nails Types IIIE to VI

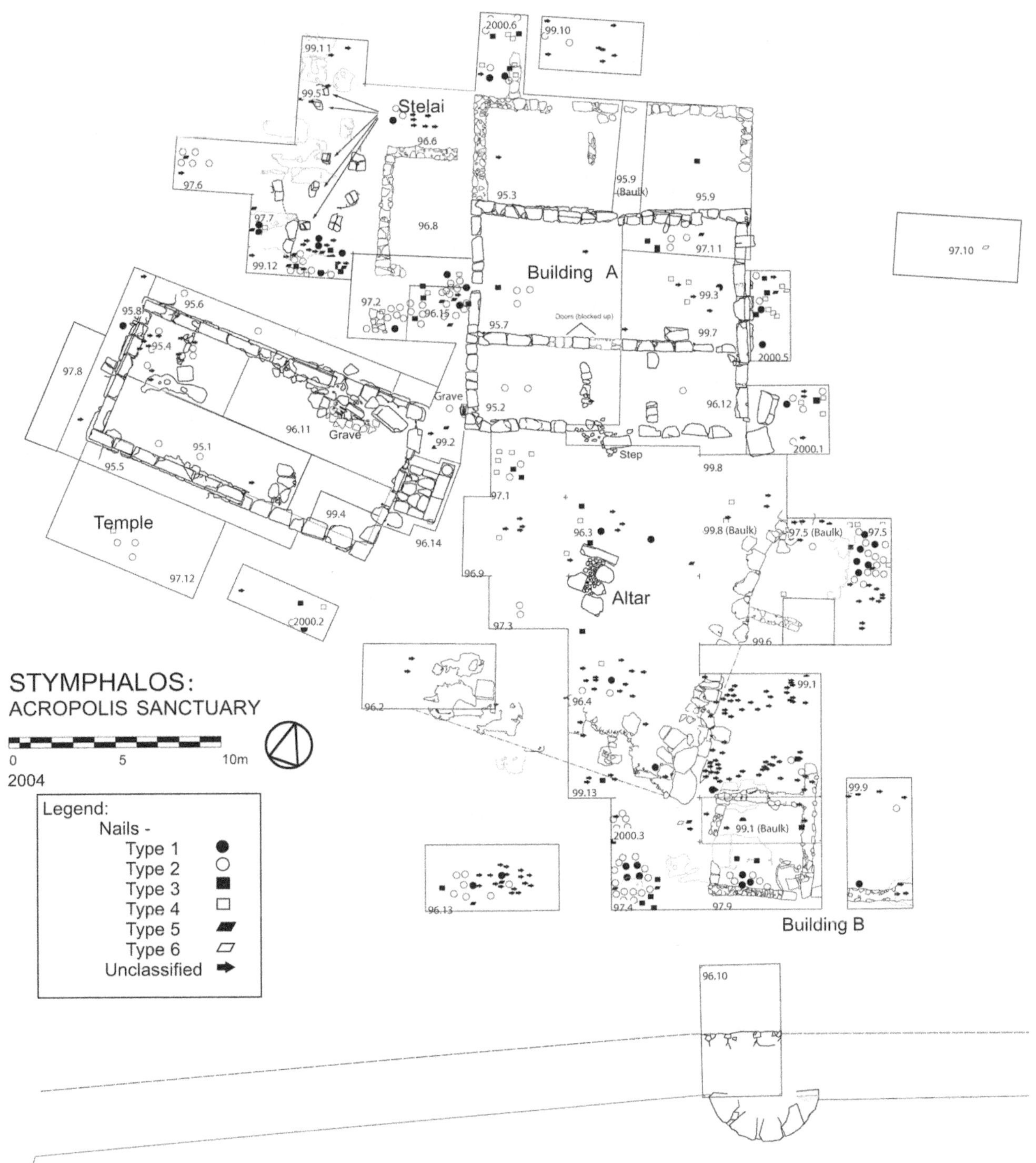

8.3. Nail distribution in the Sanctuary area

8.4. Distribution of nails in the Temple area (**23**)

8.5. Distribution of nails around Building A (**24**)

8.6. Distribution of nails in the Altar area and east of the Terrace Wall (**25**)

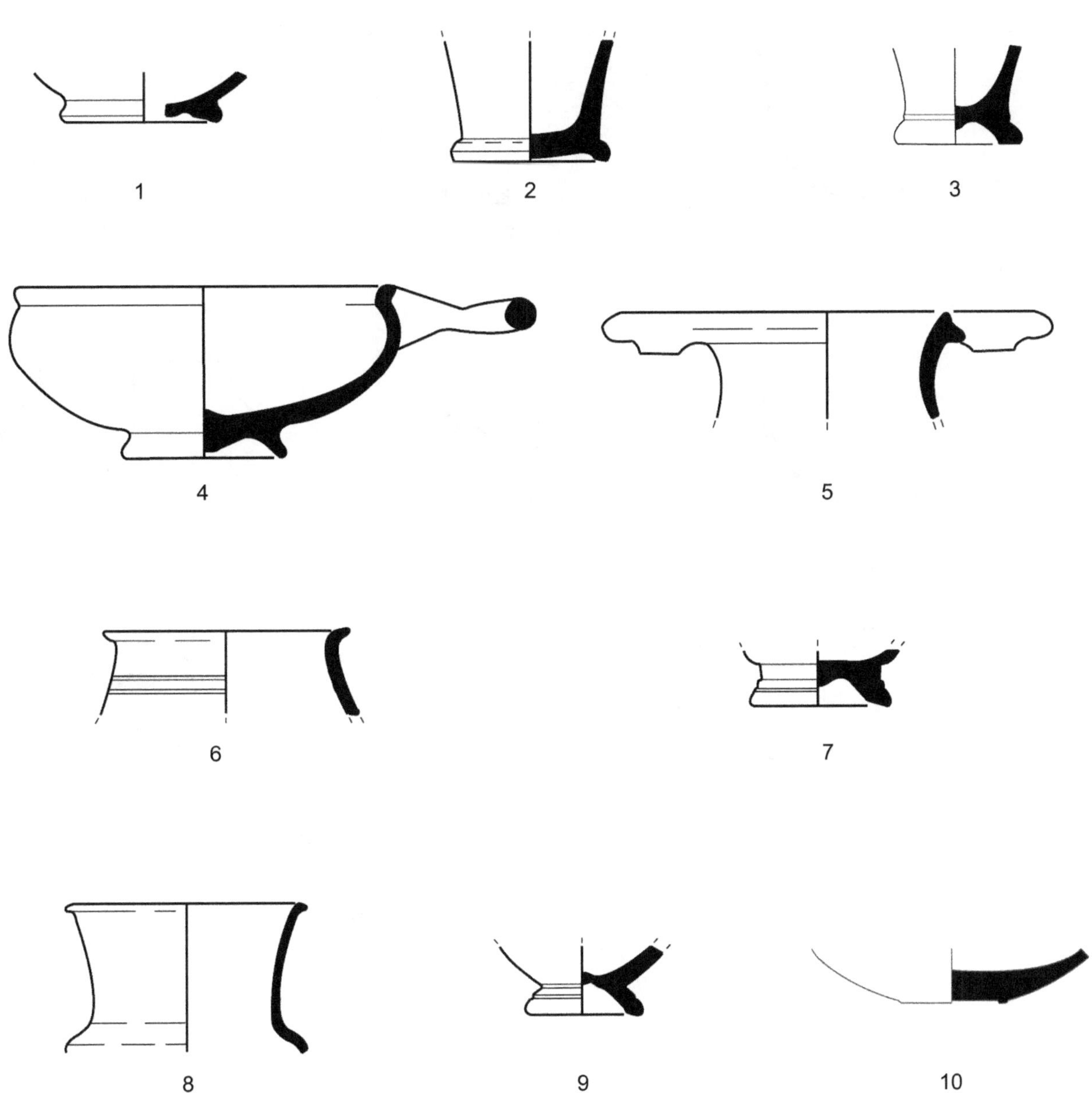

9.1. Drinking vessels from Building A: **1**. Kotyle from the West Annex floor deposit, inv. 4902 (1:2); **2**. Attic-type skyphos from the West Annex floor deposit, inv. 4890 (1:2); **3**. Attic-type skyphos from the North Annex collapse deposit, inv. 4801 (1:2); **4**. One-handler (?) from the West Annex floor deposit, inv. 4896 (1:2); **5**. Moulded-rim kantharos from the West Annex floor deposit, inv. 4905 (1:2); **6**. Cyma kantharos or similar from the North Annex collapse deposit, inv. 4802 (1:2); **7**. Cyma kantharos or similar from the North Annex collapse deposit, inv. 4804 (1:2); **8**. Simple everted-rim kantharos from the North Annex collapse deposit, inv. 4803 (1:2); **9**. Simple everted-rim kantharos from the North Annex collapse deposit, inv. 4806 (1:2); **10**. Conical bowl from the North Annex collapse deposit, inv. 4779 (1:2)

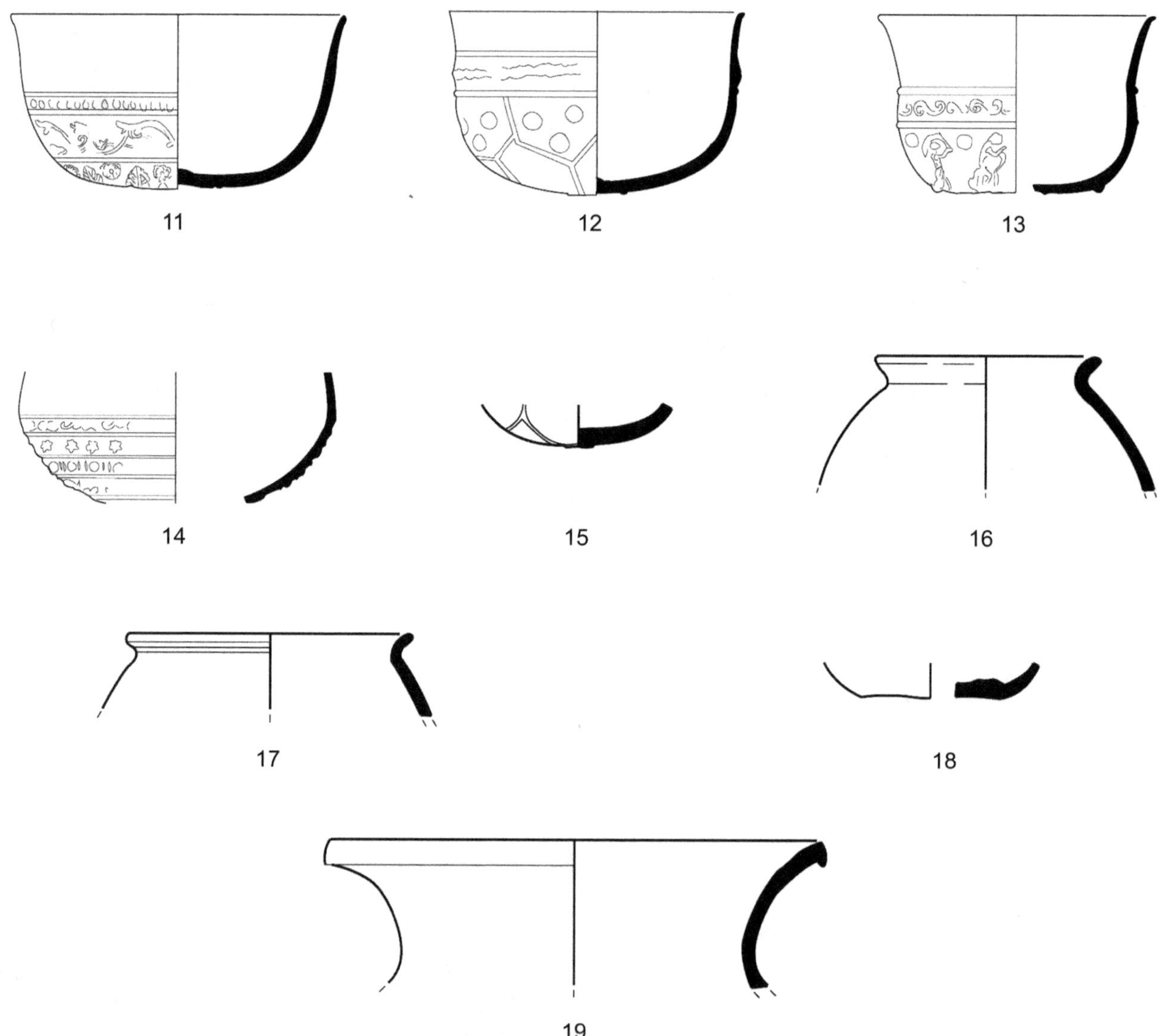

9.2. Mould-made bowls, imitation mould-made bowl, and table service vessels from Building A: **11**. Mould-made bowl from the North Annex collapse deposit, inv. 116 (1:2); **12**. Mould-made bowl from the North Annex collapse deposit, inv. 1789, 1869, 2007, 2060, 2062 (1:2); **13**. Mould-made bowl from the North Annex collapse deposit, inv. 2058 (1:2); **14**. Mould-made bowl from the North Annex collapse deposit, inv. 1855, 1865 (1:2); **15**. Imitation mould-made bowl from the North Annex collapse deposit, inv. 1377 (1:2); **16**. Round-mouthed table juglet from the West Annex floor deposit, inv. 4903 (1:2); **17**. Round-mouthed table juglet from the North Annex collapse deposit, inv. 4796 (1:2); **18**. Round-mouthed table juglet from the North Annex collapse deposit, inv. 4798 (1:2); **19**. Table amphora (or jug) from the North Annex collapse deposit, inv. 4783 (1:2)

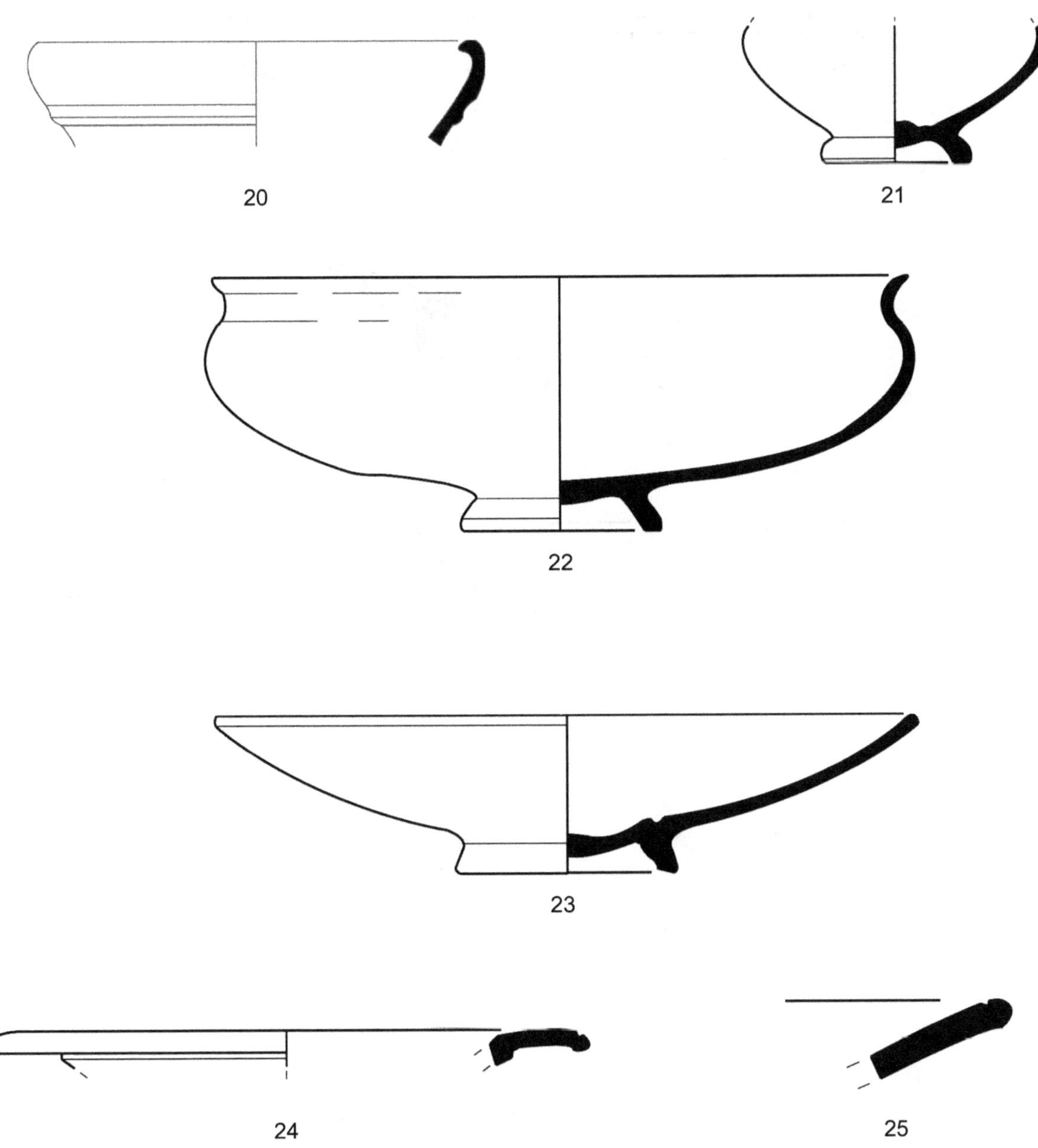

9.3. Table vessels for eating from Building A: **20**. Incurved-rim bowl from the North Annex collapse deposit, inv. 4799 (1:2); **21**. Incurved-rim bowl from the Southeast Room collapse deposit, inv. 1397 and 4839 (1:2); **22**. Semiglazed bowl from the Southeast Room collapse deposit, inv. 1397 and 4658 (1:2); **23**. Plain-rim saucer (or lid) from the Southeast Room collapse deposit, inv. 1946 and 2287 (1:2); **24**. Offset-rim plate from the Southeast Room collapse deposit, inv. 4836 (1:2); **25**. Deep rolled-rim plate from the Southeast Room collapse deposit, inv. 4834 (1:1)

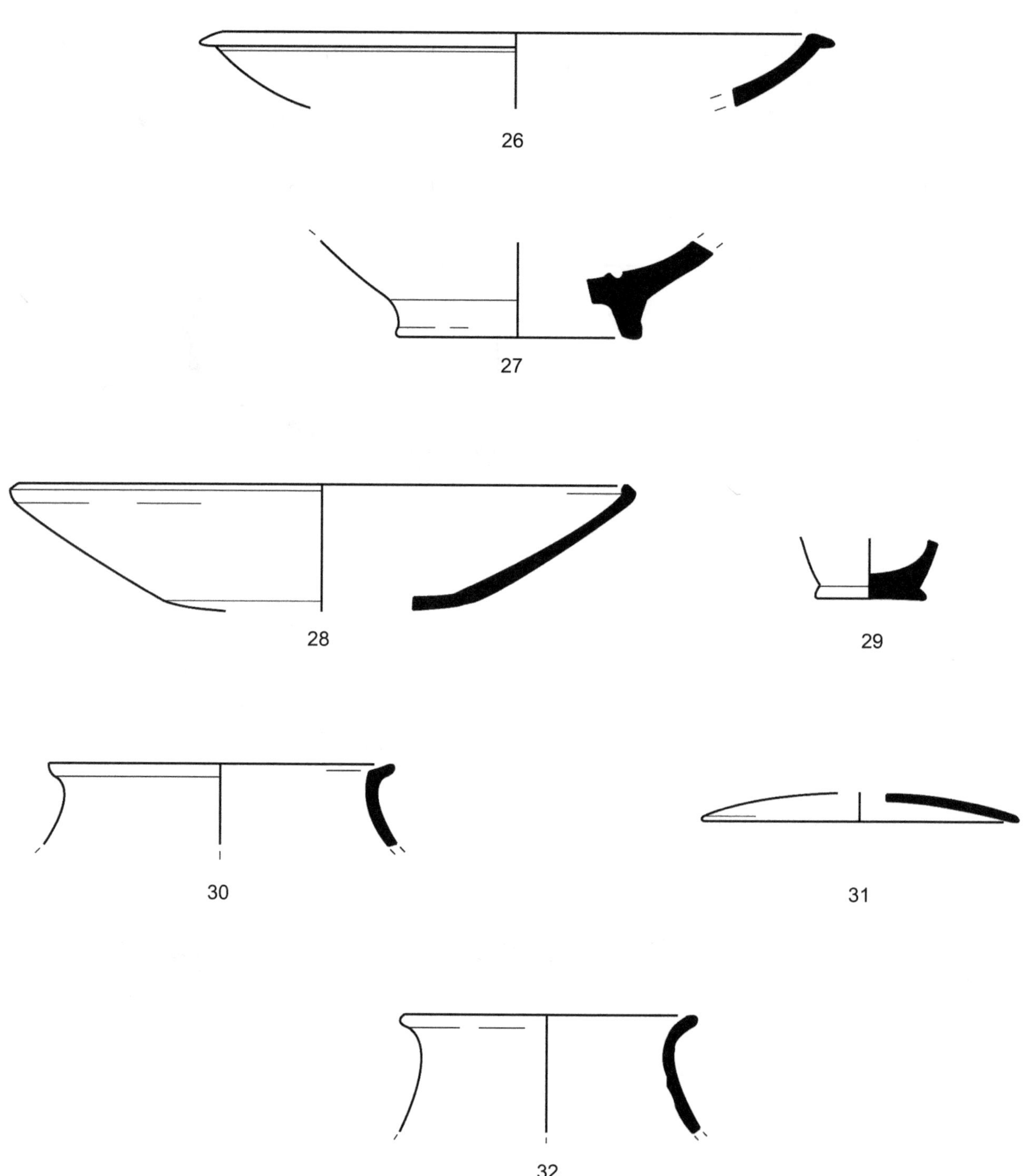

9.4. Table vessels for eating, miniature kotylai, and chytrai/jugs from Building A: **26**. Projecting-rim fishplate from the North Annex collapse deposit, inv. 4800 (1:2); **27**. Fishplate from the North Annex collapse deposit, inv. 4795 (1:2); **28**. Plate with bevelled rim from the Southeast Room collapse deposit, inv. 1400, 2318 (1:2); **29**. Miniature kotyle from the Front Room collapse deposit, inv. 4842 (1:1); **30**. Flaring-rim chytra/round-mouthed cooking jug from the West Annex floor deposit, inv. 4898 (1:2); **31**. Chytra-sized cooking lid from the West Annex floor deposit, inv. 4911 (1:2); **32**. Flaring-rim chytra/round-mouthed cooking jug from the West Annex floor deposit, inv. 4901 (1:2)

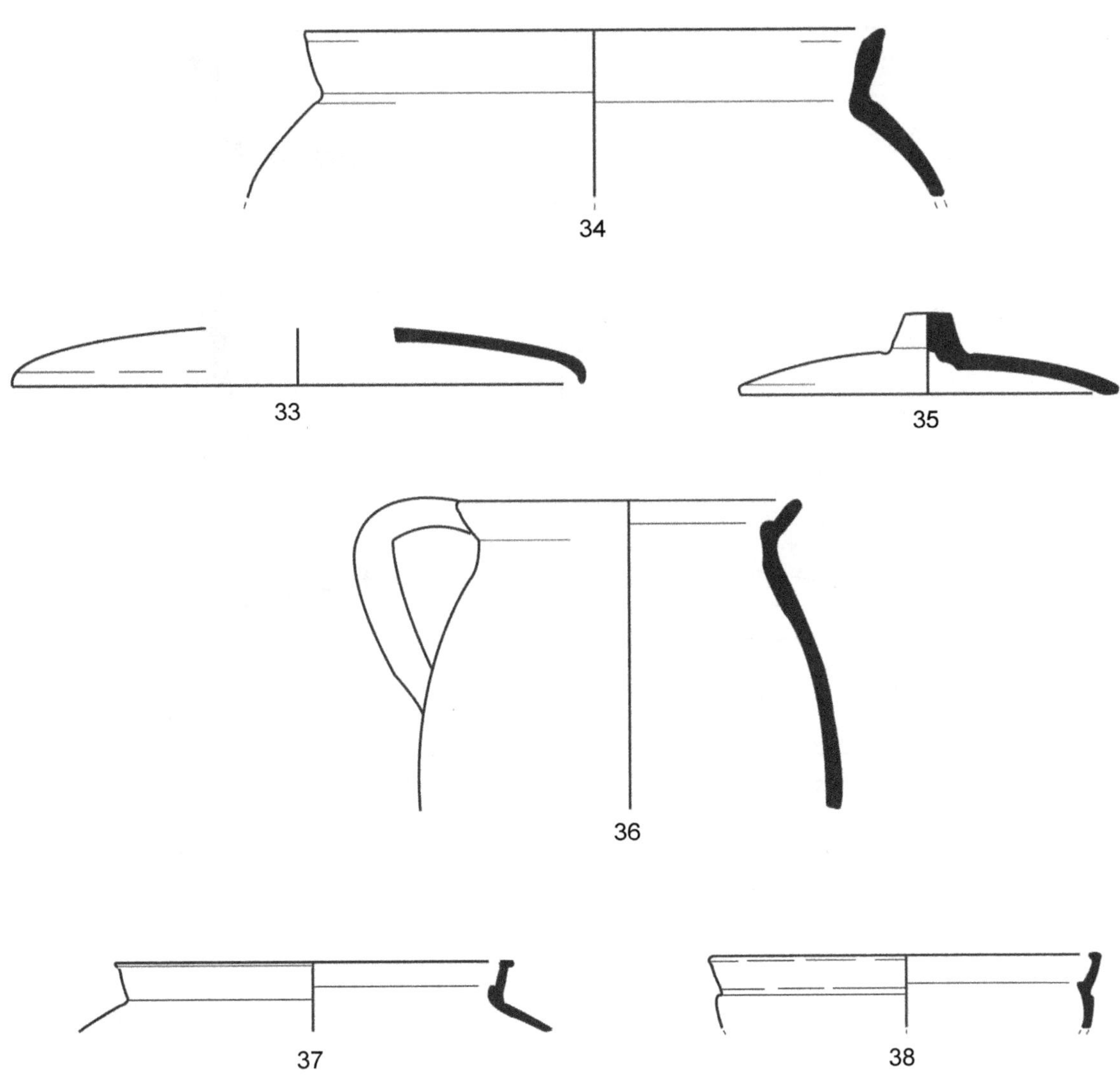

9.5. Chytrai and casseroles from Building A: **33**. Chytra or casserole-sized cooking lid from the Southeast Room collapse deposit, inv. 4827 (1:2); **34**. Unlidded (?) chytra from the Front Room collapse deposit, inv. 4824 (1:2); **35**. Chytra-sized cooking lid from the Southeast Room collapse deposit, inv. 4825 (1:2); **36**. Flanged-rim chytra from the Southeast Room collapse deposit, inv. 4680 (1:2); **37**. Flanged-rim chytra with ledge rim from the Southeast Room collapse deposit, inv. 4562 (1:2); **38**. Casserole from the Southeast Room collapse deposit, inv. 4819 (1:2)

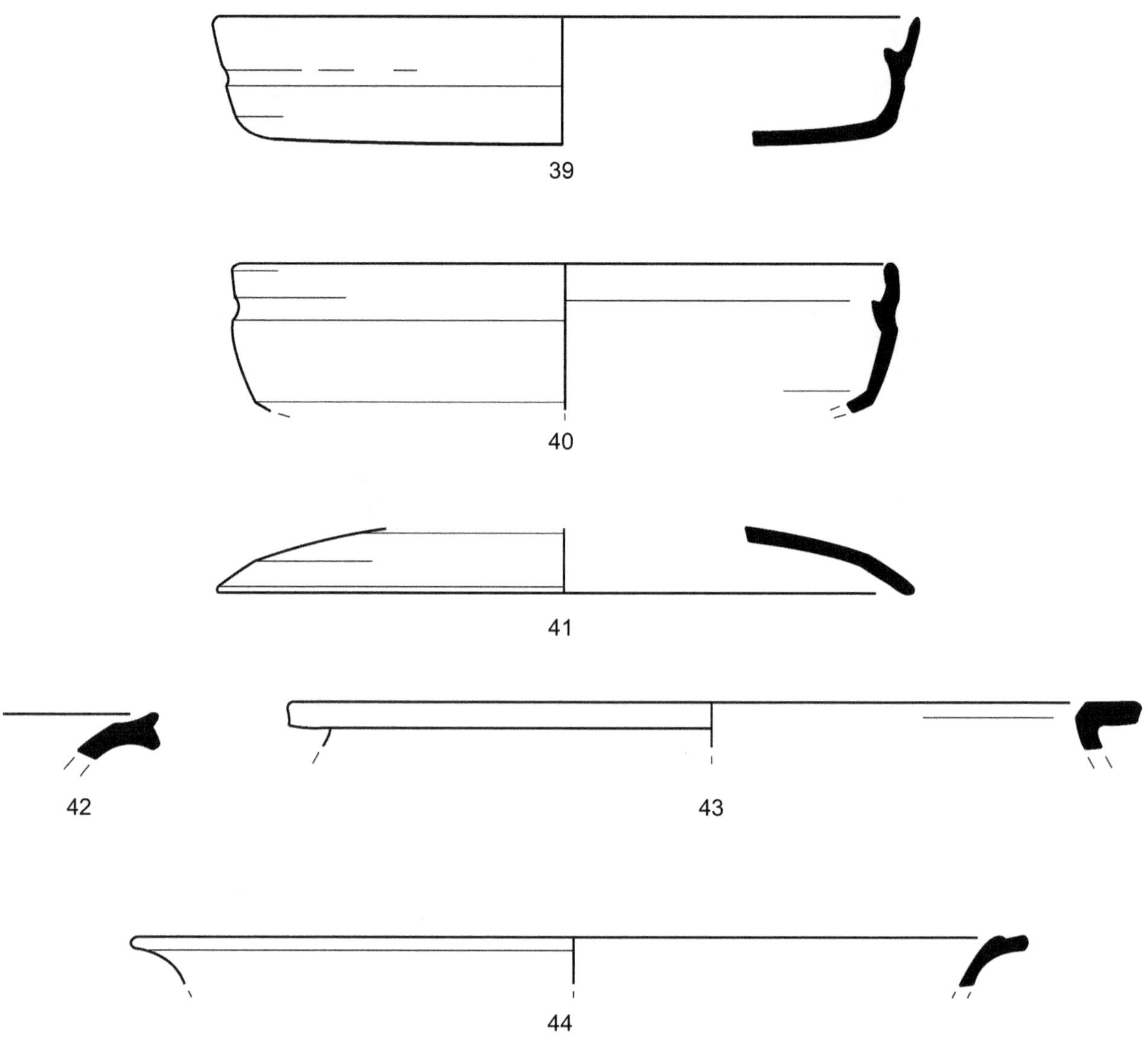

9.6. Casseroles and utility vessels from Building A: **39**. Casserole from the North Annex collapse deposit, inv. 4860 (1:2); **40**. Casserole from the Southeast Room collapse deposit, inv. 4558 (1:2); **41**. Large casserole-sized cooking lid from the Southeast Room collapse deposit, inv. 4826 (1:2); **42**. Bowl/lekane with moulded rim from the Southeast Room collapse deposit, inv. 4828 (1:2); **43**. Projecting-rim bowl/lekane from the North Annex collapse deposit, inv. 4794 (1:2); **44**. Bowl/lekane with short ledge rim from the Southeast Room collapse deposit, inv. 4829 (1:2)

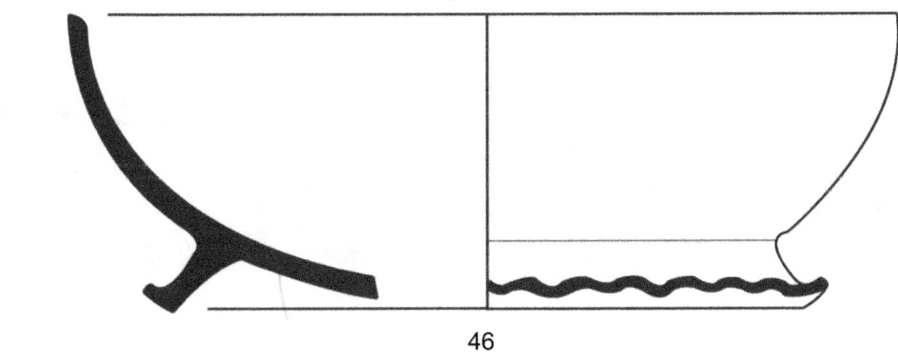

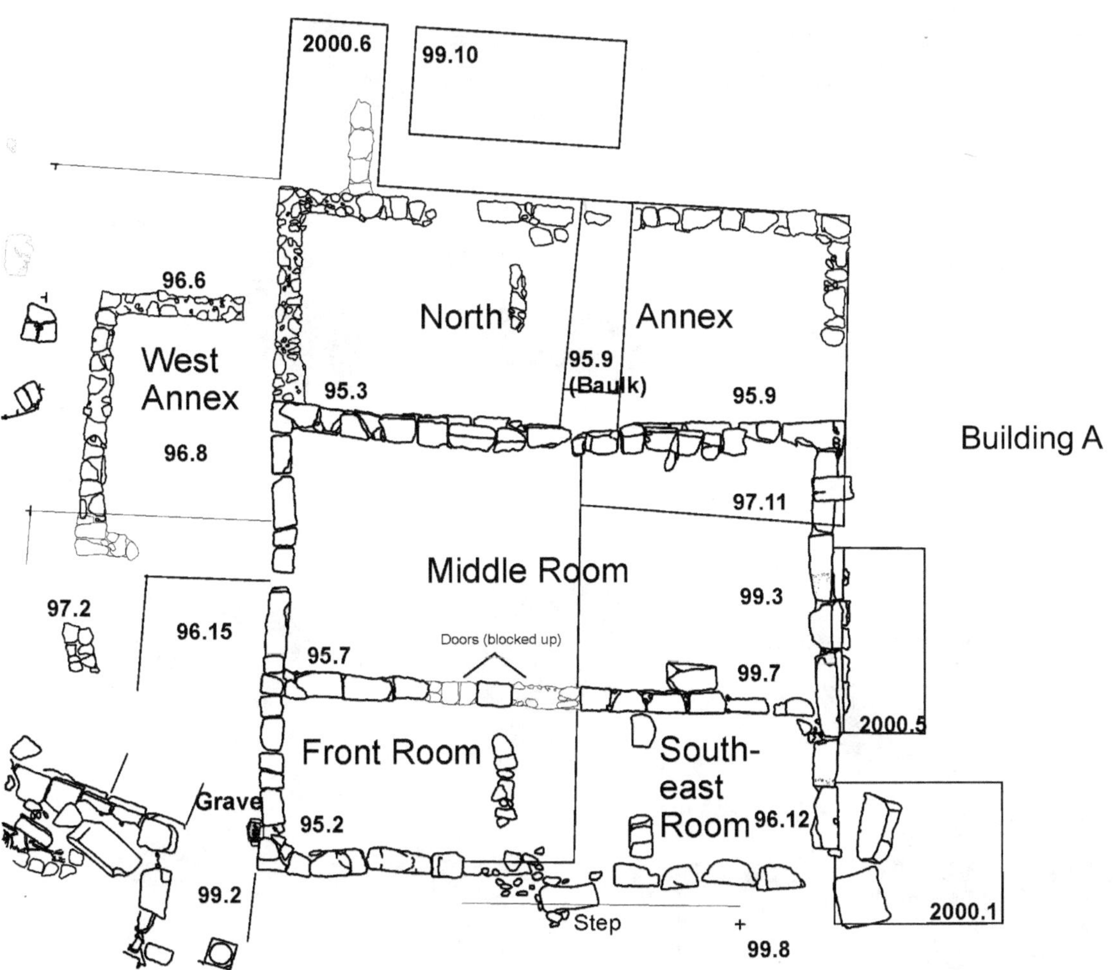

9.7. Unidentified vessel shape from Building A: **46**. Bowl with plain rim and piecrust foot from the Southeast Room collapse deposit, inv. 1397 (1:2)

9.8. Plan of Building A with Annexes

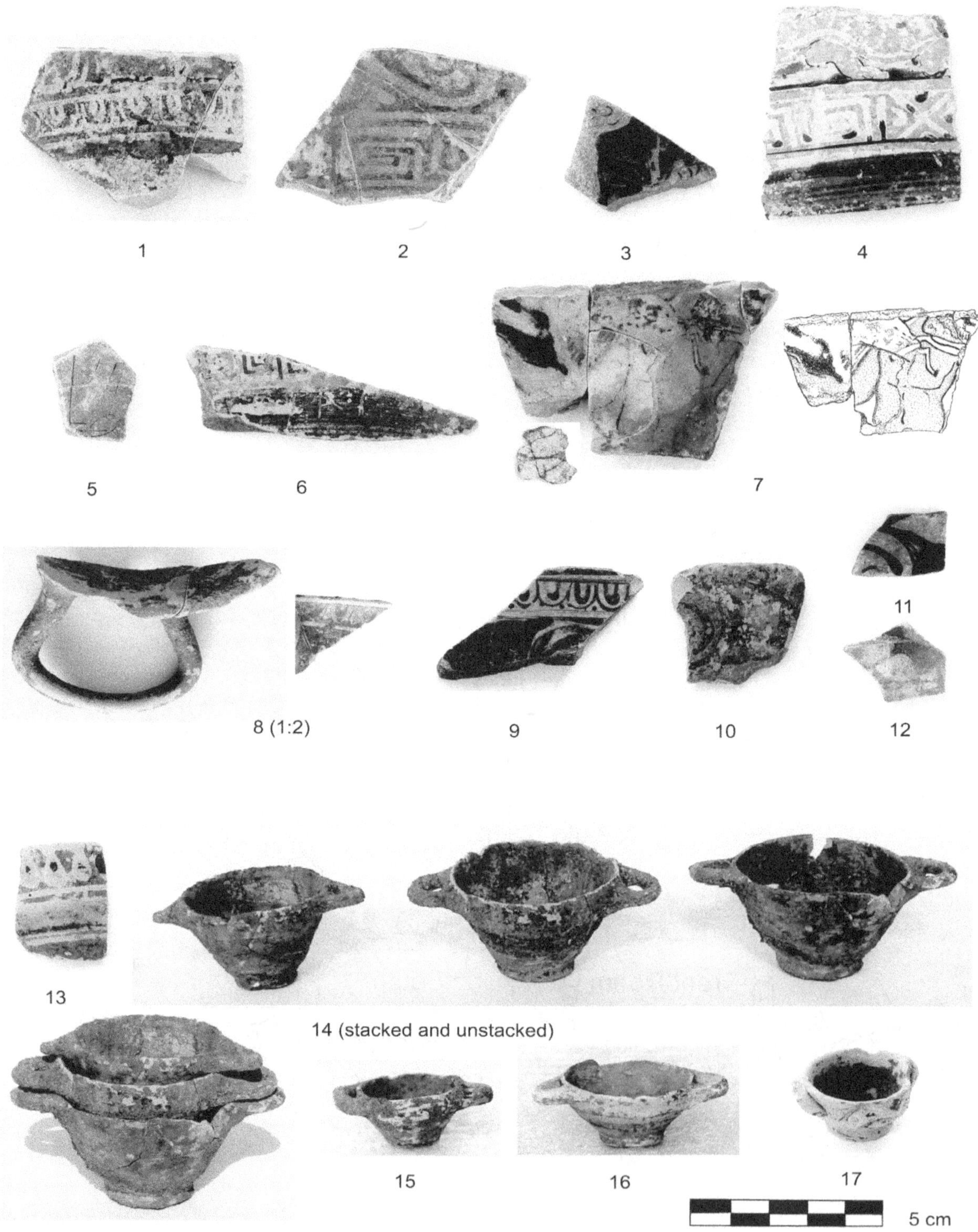

10.1. Corinthan red figure (**1–12**), miniature vases (**13–17**)

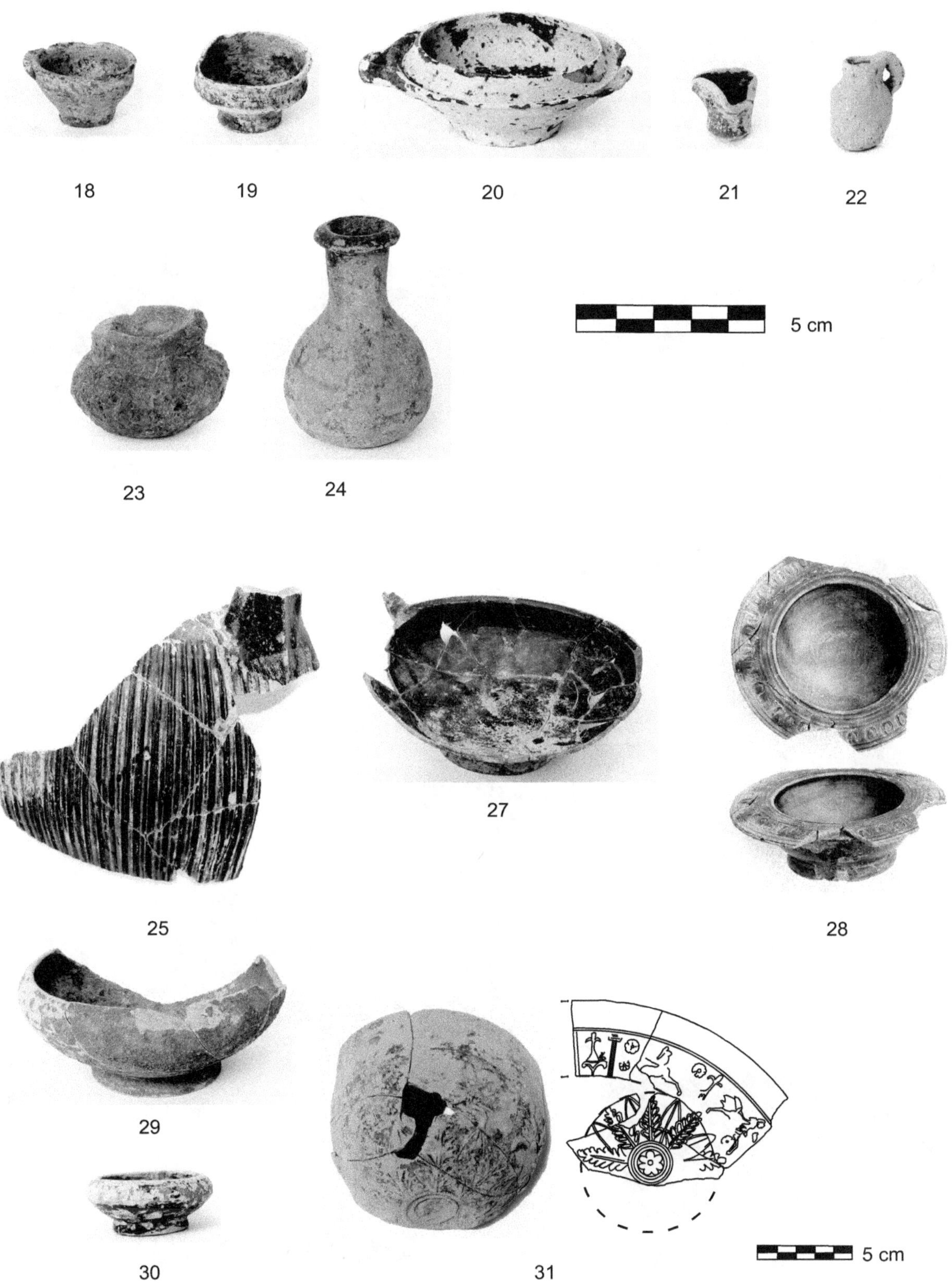

10.2. Miniature vases (**18–24**), black glaze and other pottery (**25–31**)

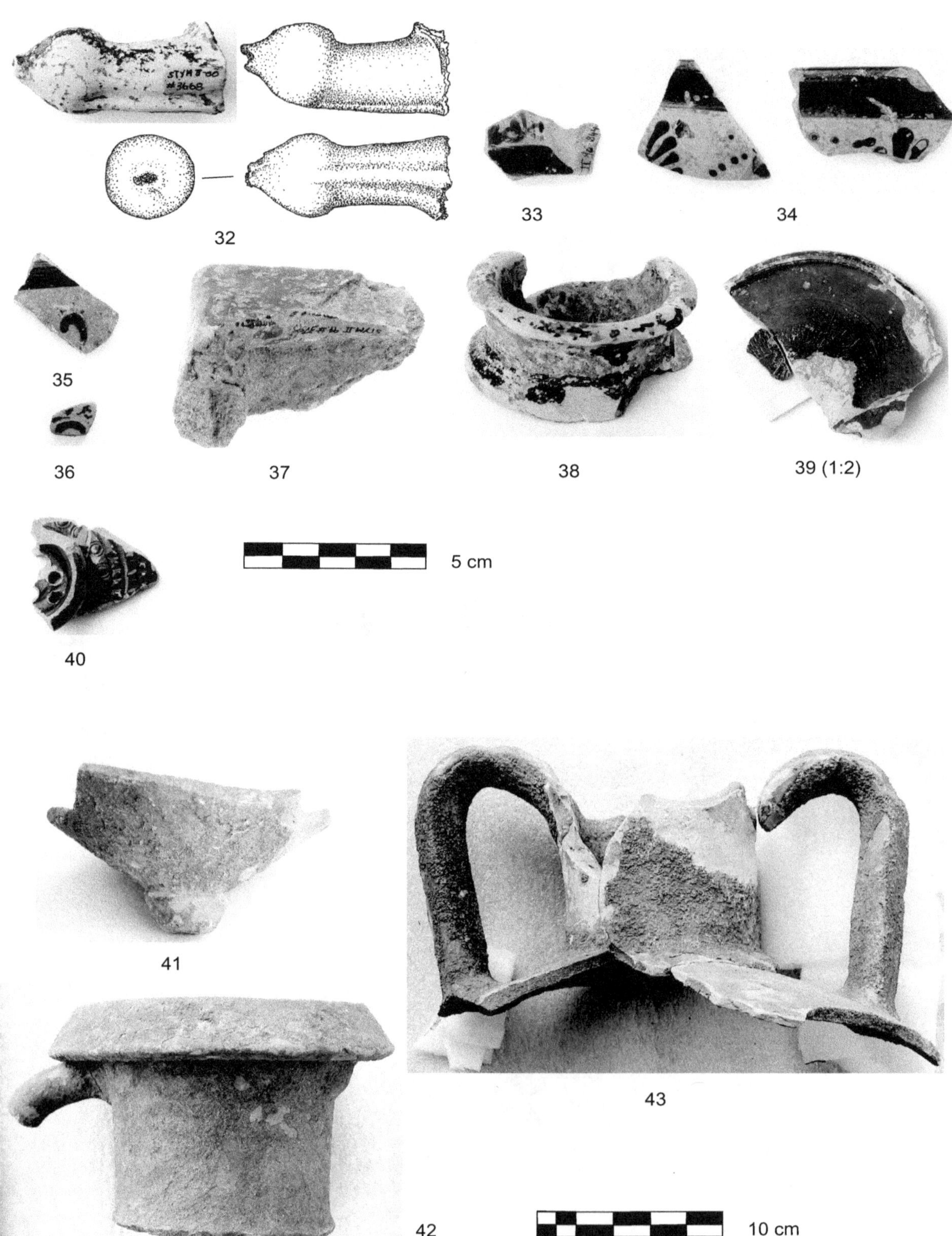

10.3. Varia (**32–40**), transport amphoras (**41–3**)

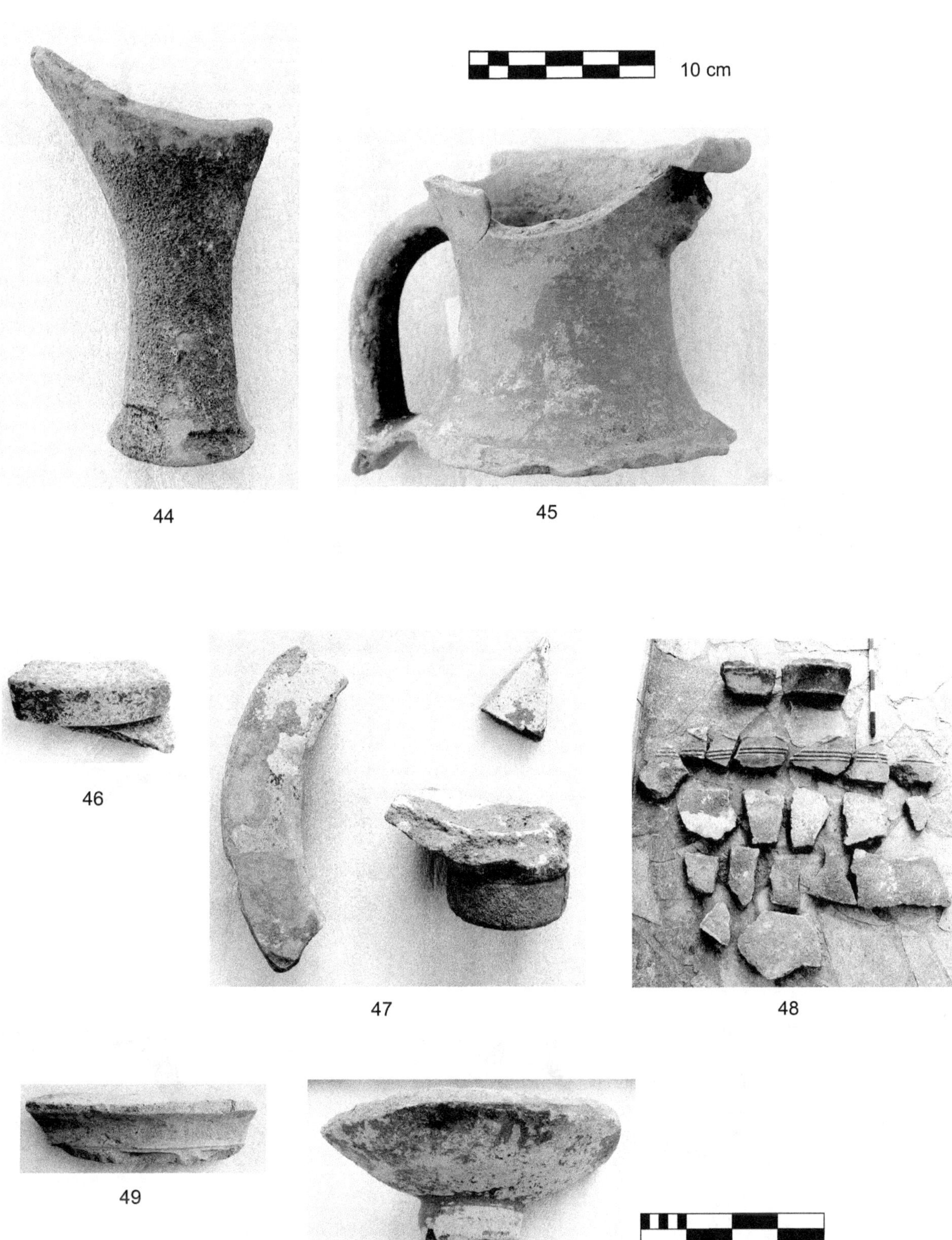

10.4. Transport amphoras (**44–5**), pithoi (**46–50**)

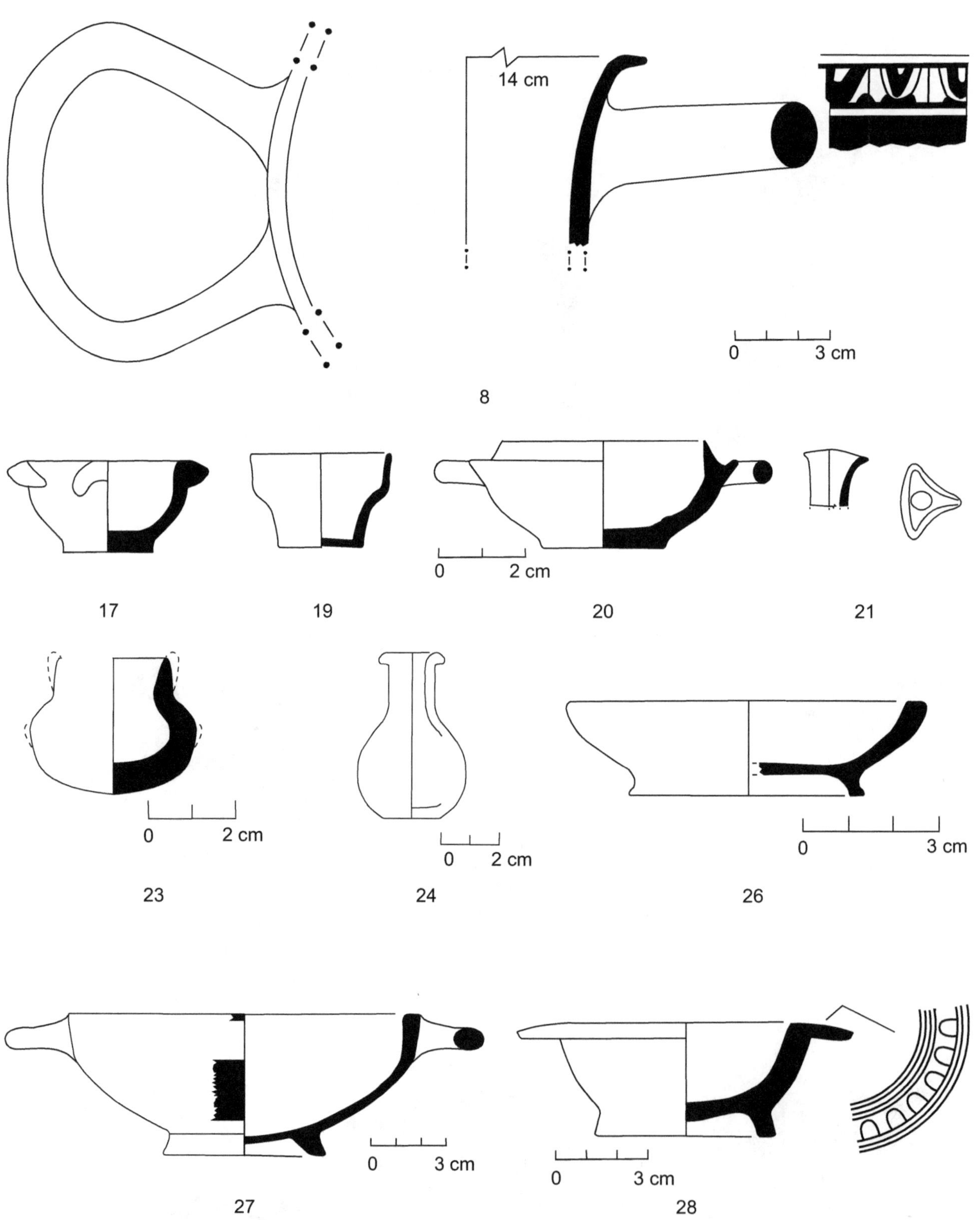

10.5. Corinthian red figure (**8**), miniature vases (**17–24**), black glaze pottery (**26–8**)

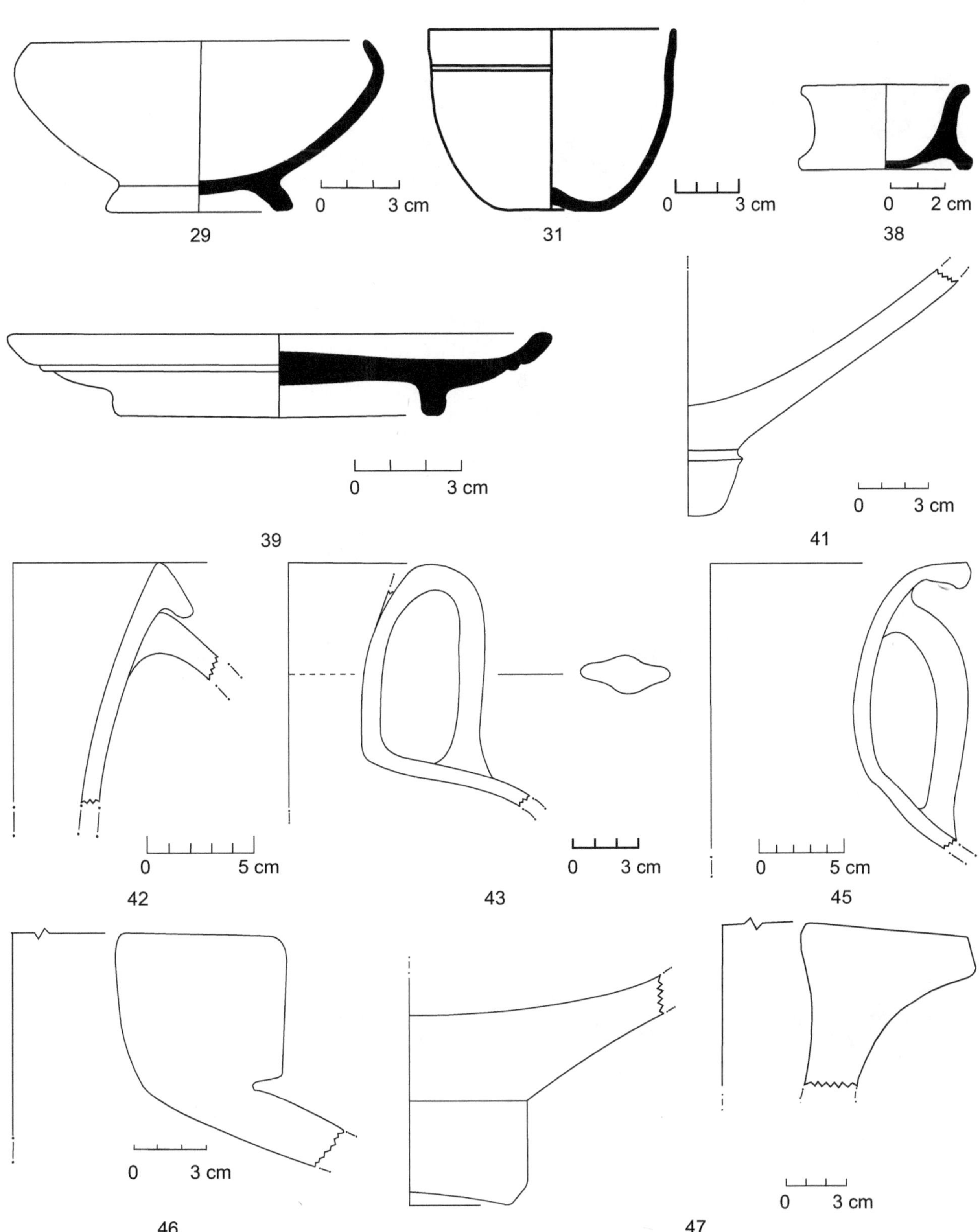

10.6. Black glaze and other pottery (**29–39**), transport amphoras (**41–5**), pithoi (**46–7**)

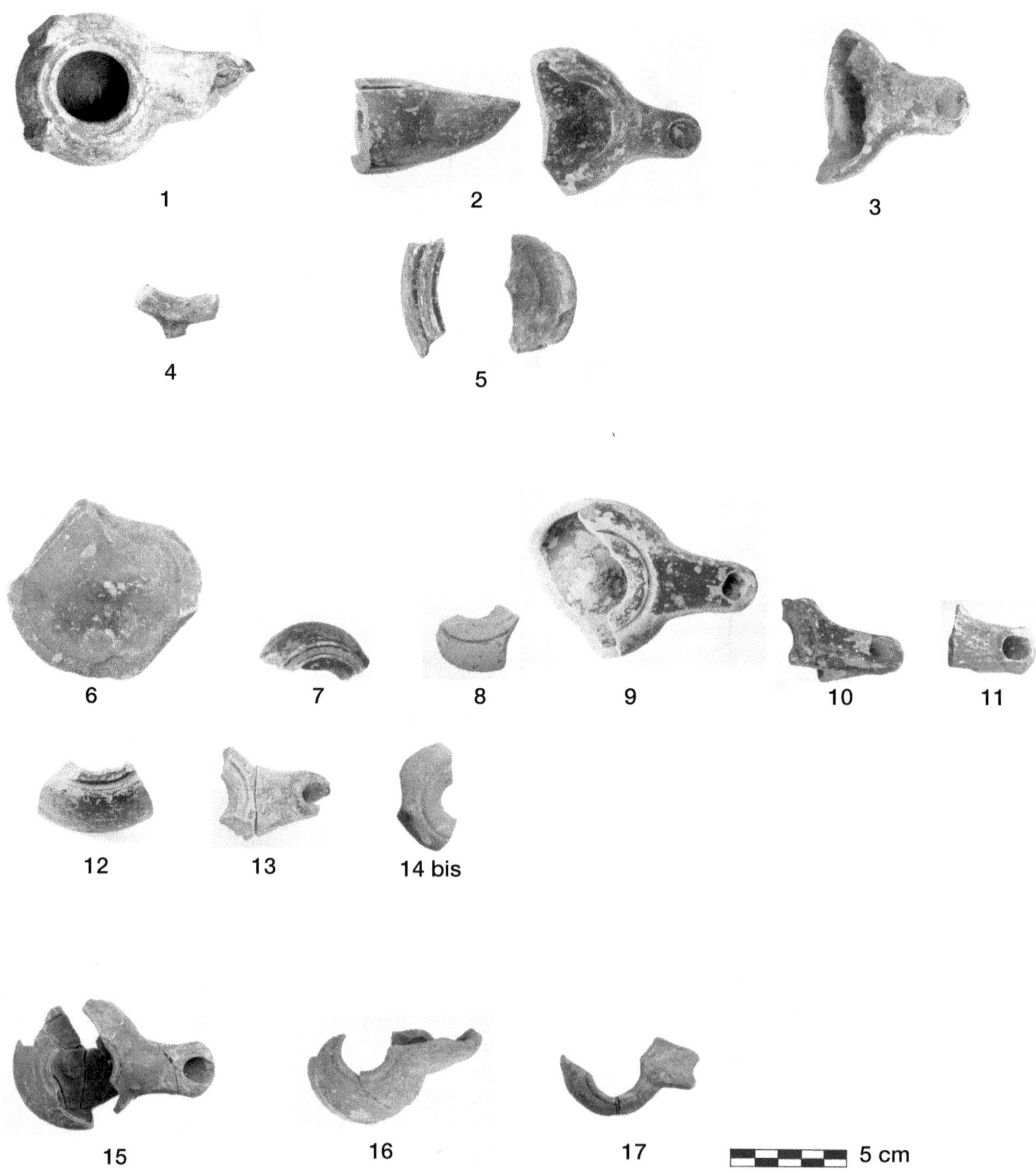

11.1. Lamps. Late Classical–early Hellenistic wheelmade (**1**–**5**), round-bodied (**6**–**14 bis**), late round-bodied (**15**–17)

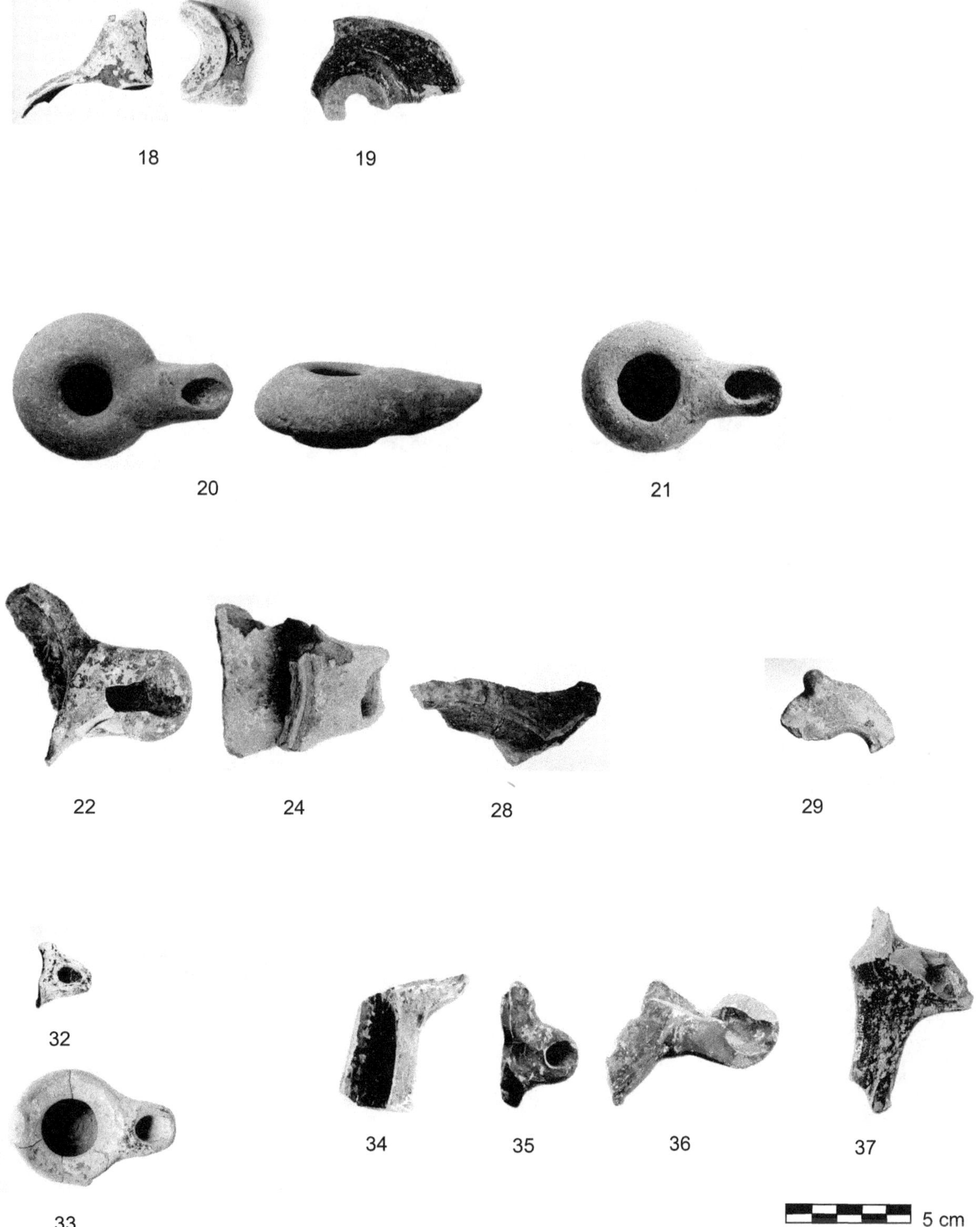

11.2. Lamps. Stocklampe (**18–19**), "mushroom"-shaped (**20–1**), large late Classical–Hellenistic (**22, 24, 28**), watch-shaped profiles (**29**), miniature (**32–3**), multinozzled (**34–7**)

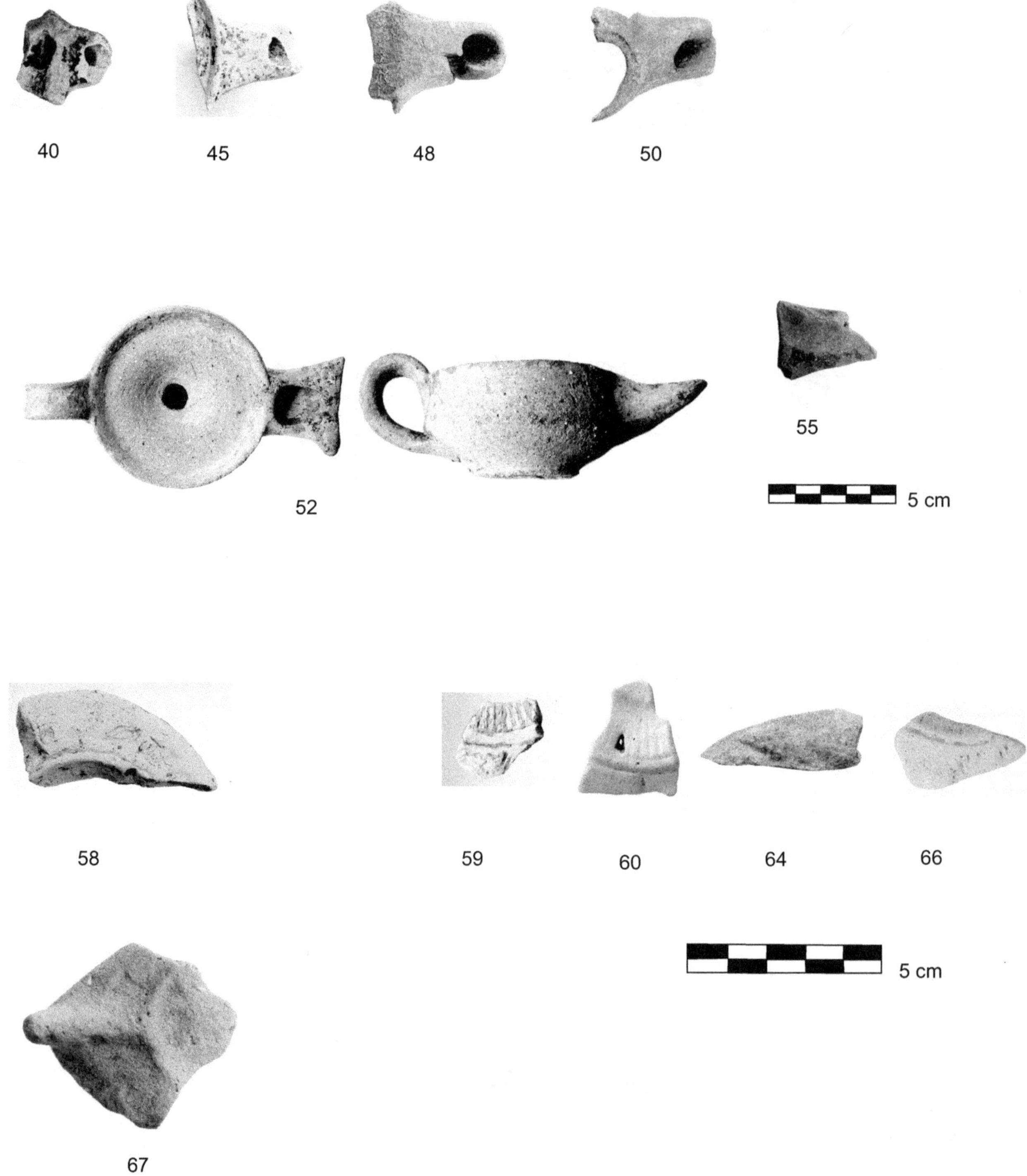

11.3. Lamps. Nozzles (**40, 45, 48, 50**), Early Roman wheelmade (**52**, **55**), Early/Middle Roman mould-made (**58**), Middle Roman mould-made (**59, 60, 64, 66, 67**), Early Christian mould-made (**67**)

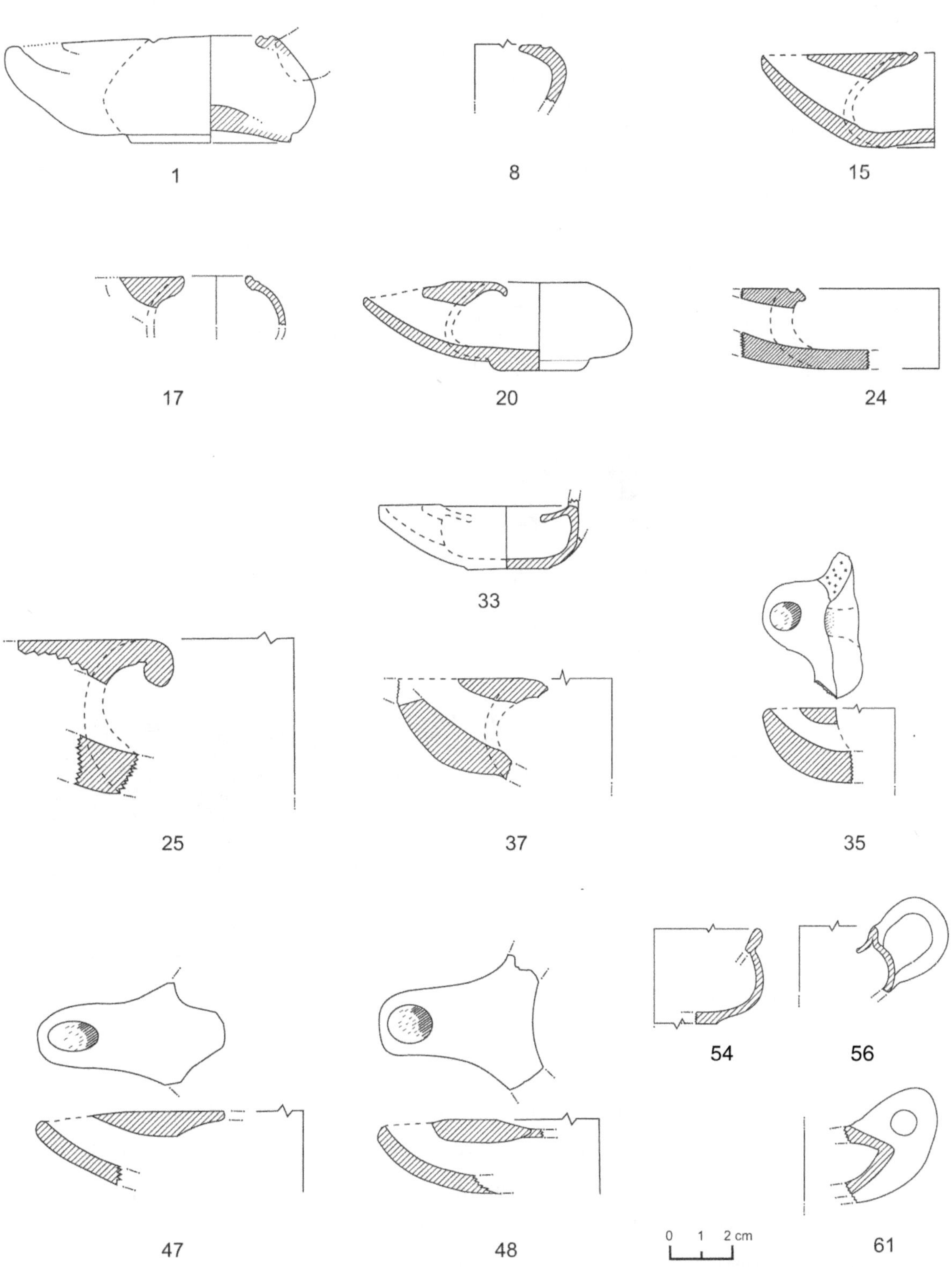

11.4. Lamp profiles (**1–61**, passim) (G. Schaus)

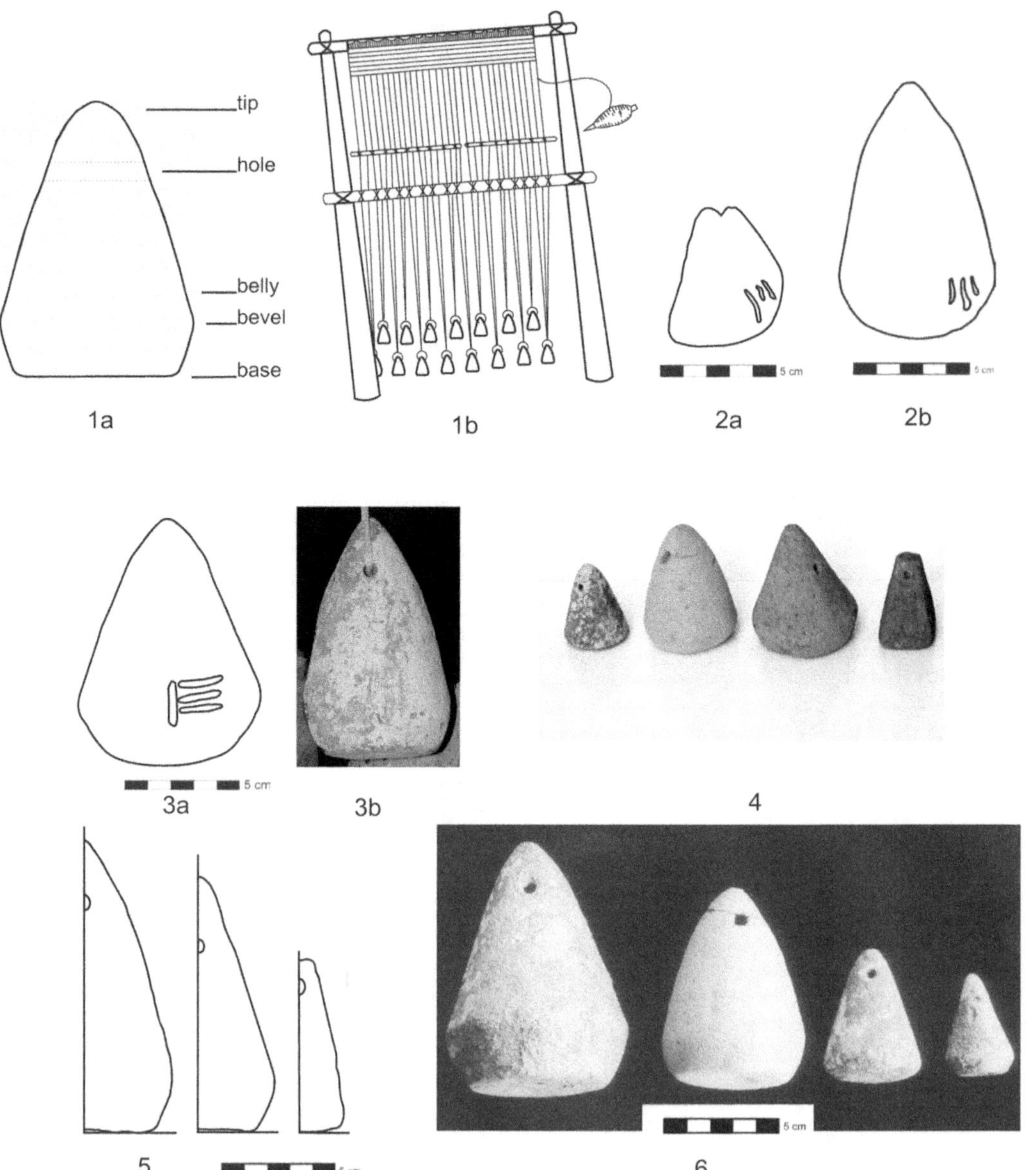

12.1a. Typical conical loomweight. Fig. 12.1b. Greek warp-weighted loom

12.2a–b. Loomweights with vertical incised lines on the belly above a bevelled edge (**63** and **91**)

12.3a. Loomweight (**29**) with incised epsilon mark

12.3b. Loomweight found in the acropolis Sanctuary, Stymphalos, now in Lafka

12.4. Four main types by shape left to right: A (**55**) small conical; B (**78**) convex conical, slightly raised belly; C (**26**) conical with bevelled belly; and D (**56**) pyramidal.

12.5. Profiles of types B (**28**), C (**26**) and D (**56**).

12.6. Loomweights from 11.4 cm to 4.6 cm in height. Groups by size: 1 (**29**), 2 (**78**), 3 (**55**) and 4 (**3**).

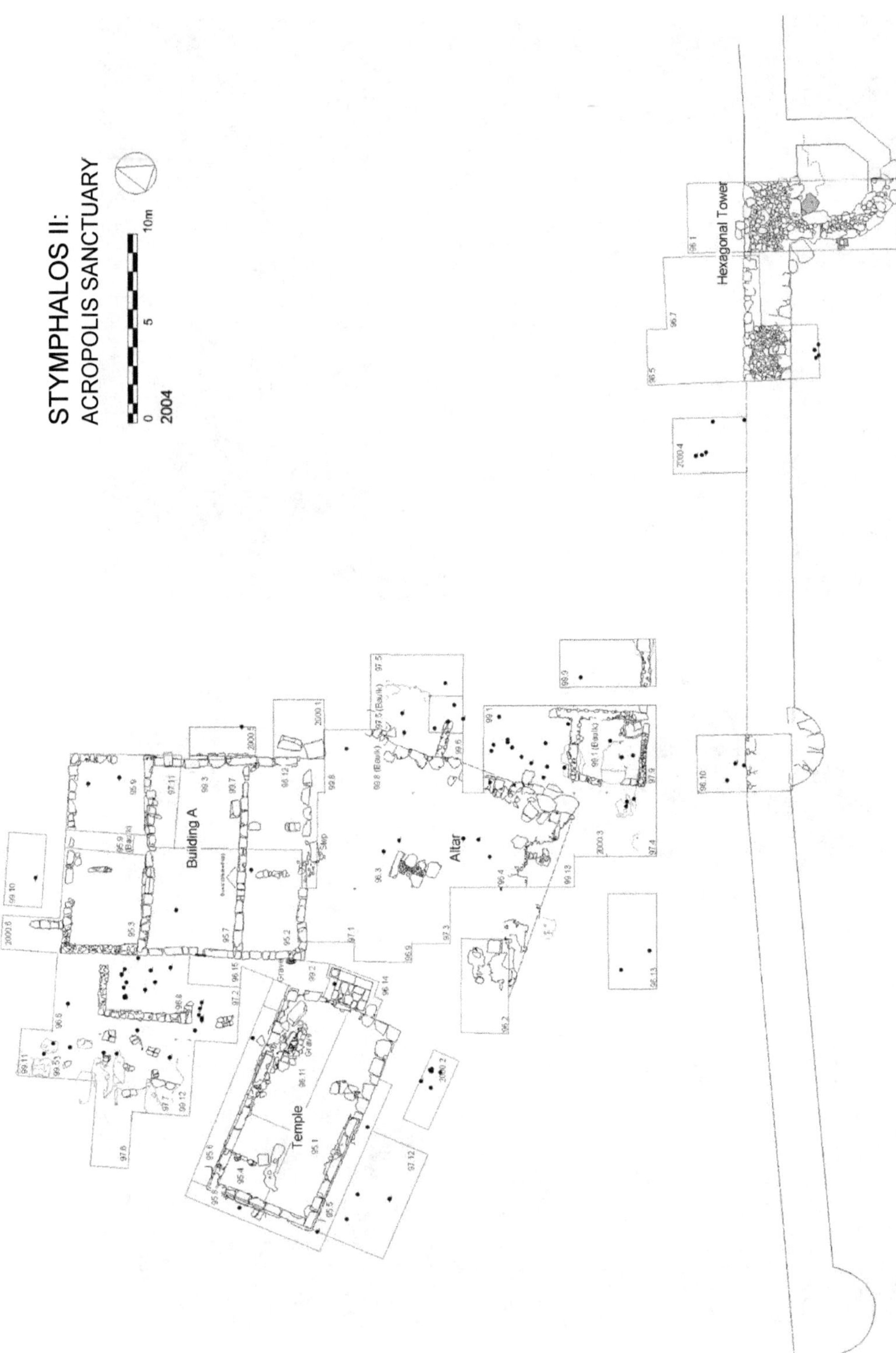

12.7. Distribution of loomweights in the Sanctuary

8

9

12.8. Five of nineteen loomweights found on a level of the West Annex area

12.9. Cluster of three loomweights with a fourth (incised with mark "E") a short way off, in Tr. 00.2 just south of the Temple

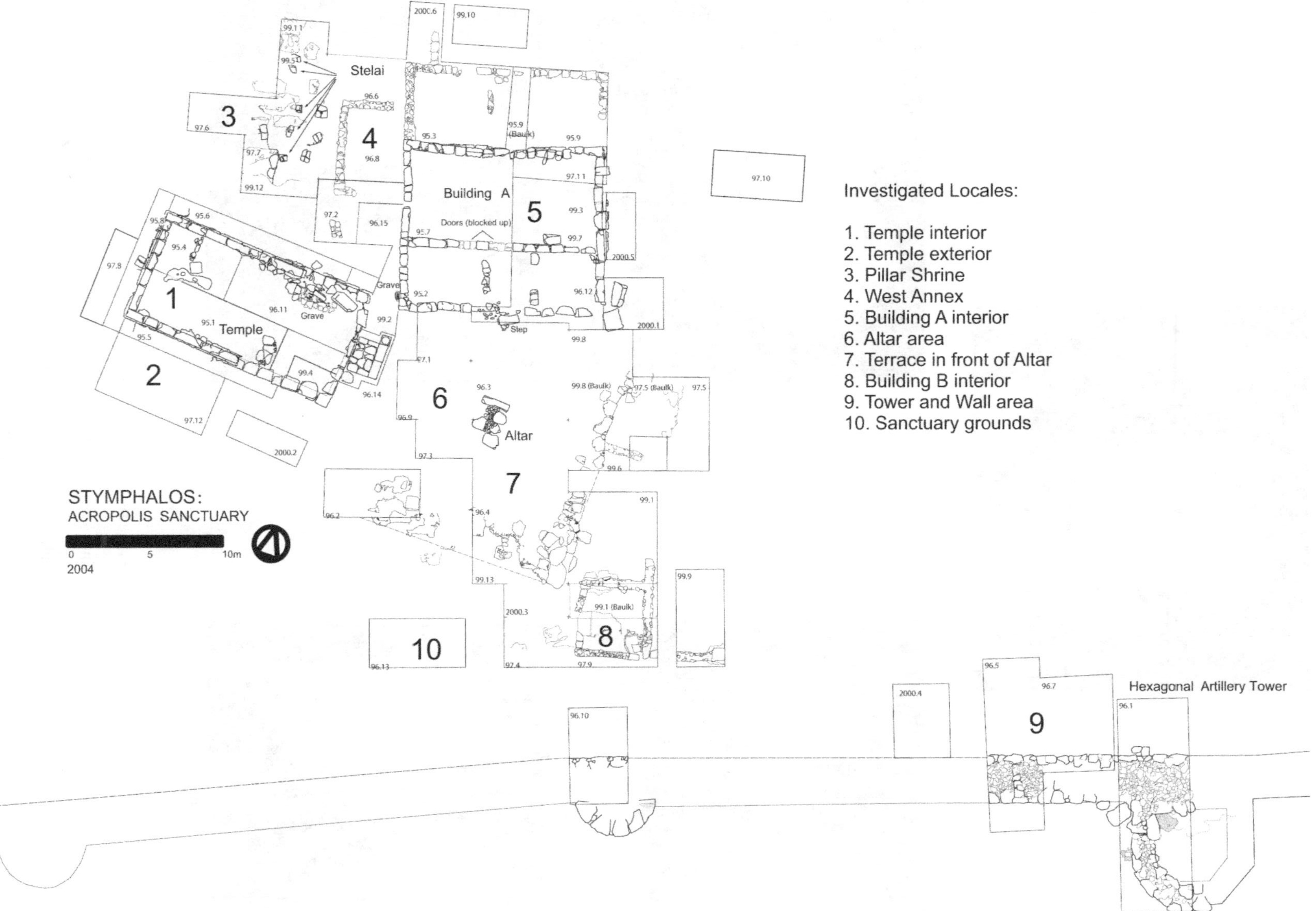

13.1. Ten areas of faunal investigation

2

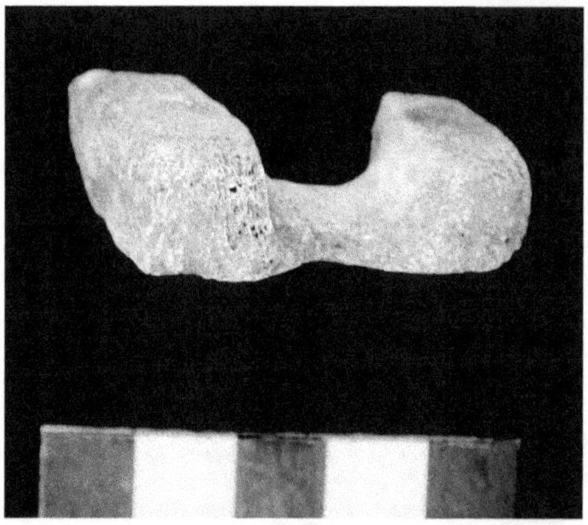

3a

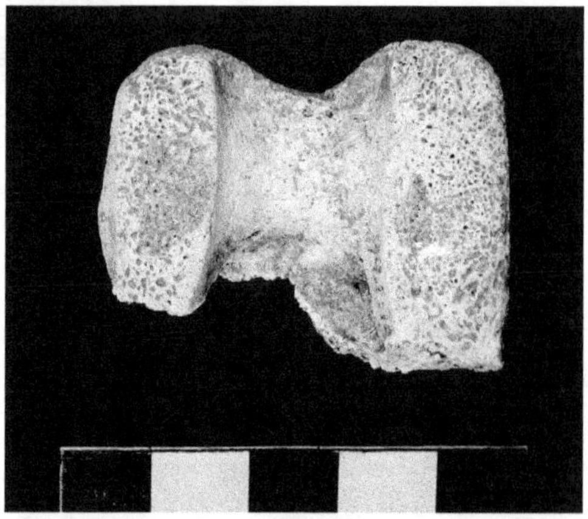

3b

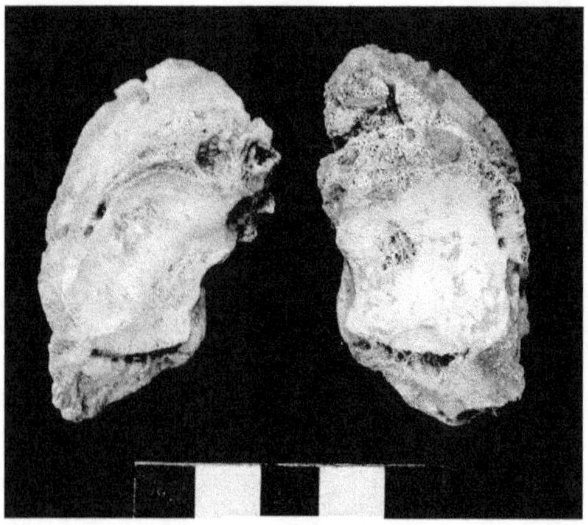

4a

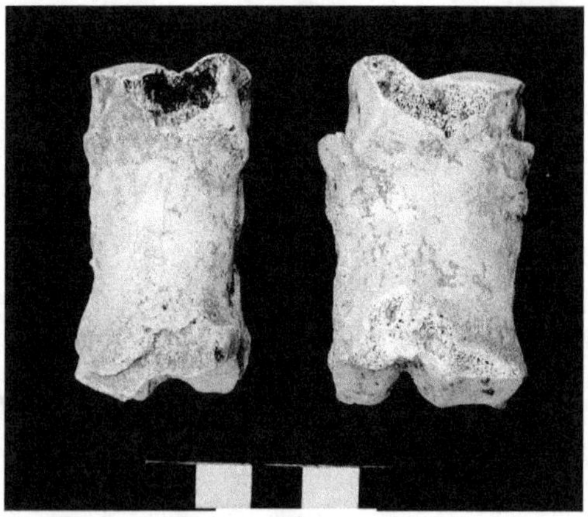

4b

13.2. Astragalus with bored hole

13.3a–b. Worked cattle astragalus, front and side views

13.4a. Cattle distal phalanges with hyperostosis and pitting

13.4b. Proximal phalanges with trauma

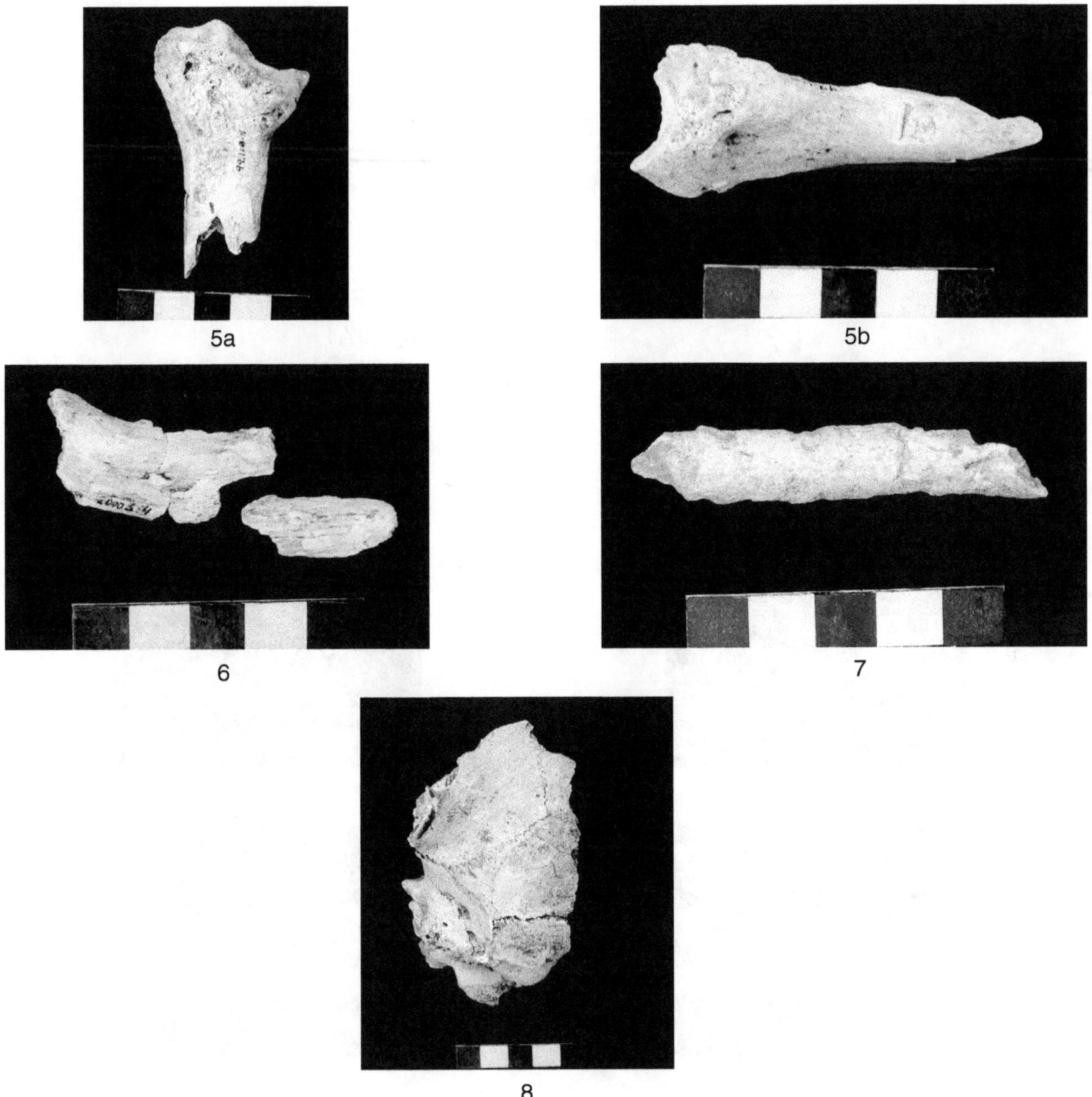

13.5a. Wild boar proximal left radius with arthritic growth

13.5b. Side view with butchery marks

13.6. Burnt deer antler

13.7. Mid ilium of a sheep or goat with gnaw marks

13.8. Sheep cranium, cut and found in a pottery jar

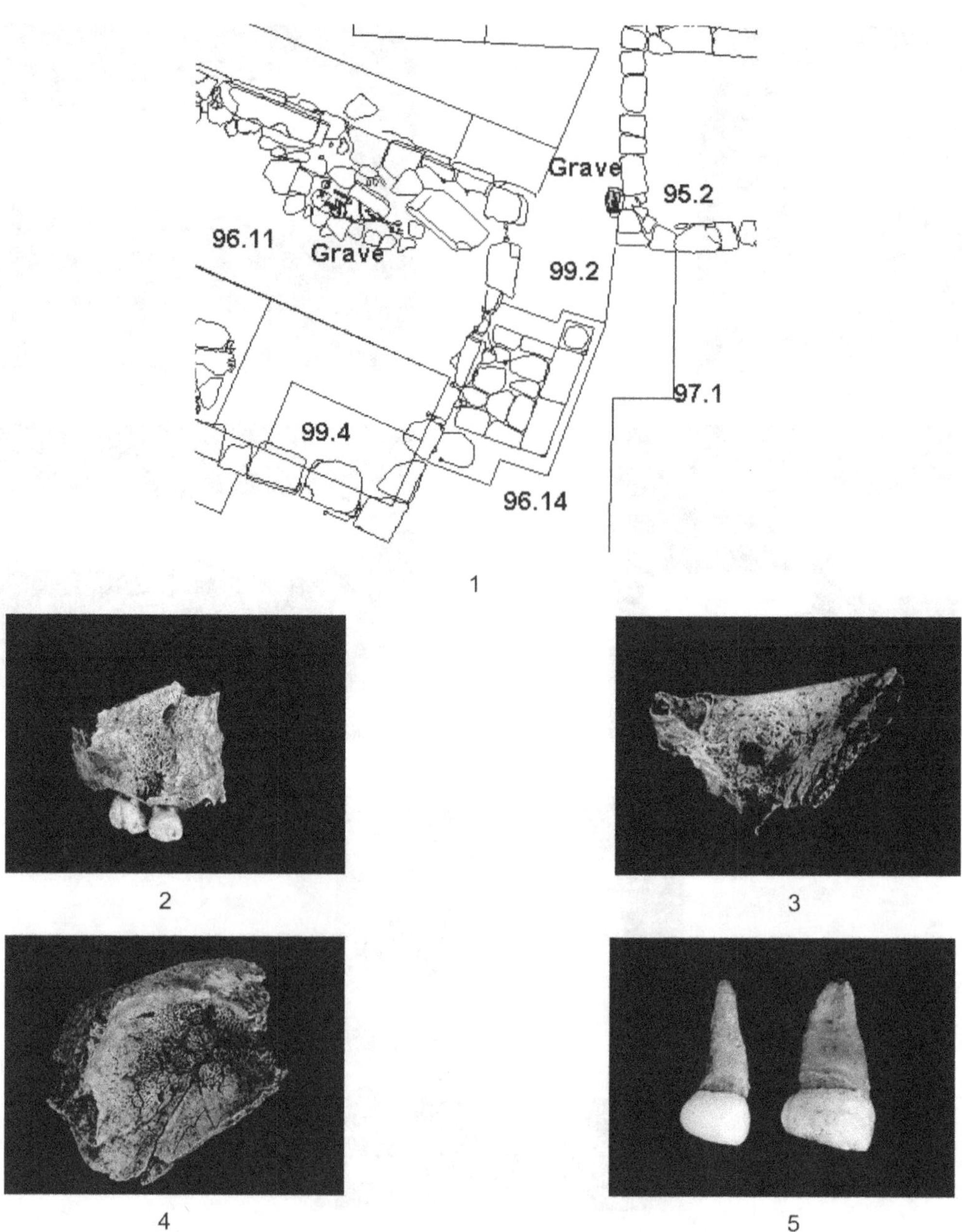

14.1. Graves 1 and 2 in and near the Temple

14.2. ST-II-97-1-1, anterior aspect of right maxilla; superficial porosity around and below the infraorbital foramen. The large defect immediately above the alveolar border between the deciduous molars is post-mortem damage

14.3. ST-II-97-1-1, temporal aspect of left zygoma; increased porosity centred around the zygomaticotemporal foramen

14.4. ST-II-97-1-1, right orbital roof; cribra orbitalia

14.5. ST-II-97-1-1, right maxillary deciduous incisors; root caries

Index

PHOENIX SUPPLEMENTARY VOLUMES SERIES

1 *Studies in Honour of Gilbert Norwood* edited by Mary E. White

2 *Arbiter of Elegance: A Study of the Life and Works of C. Petronius* Gilbert Bagnani

3 *Sophocles the Playwright* S.M. Adams

4 *A Greek Critic: Demetrius on Style* G.M.A. Grube

5 *Coastal Demes of Attika: A Study of the Policy of Kleisthenes* C.W.J. Eliot

6 *Eros and Psyche: Studies in Plato, Plotinus, and Origen* John M. Rist

7 *Pythagoras and Early Pythagoreanism* J.A. Philip

8 *Plato's Psychology* T.M. Robinson

9 *Greek Fortifications* F.E. Winter

10 *Comparative Studies in Republican Latin Imagery* Elaine Fantham

11 *The Orators in Cicero's* Brutus*: Prosopography and Chronology* G.V. Sumner

12 Caput *and Colonate: Towards a History of Late Roman Taxation* Walter Goffart

13 *A Concordance to the Works of Ammianus Marcellinus* Geoffrey Archbold

14 *Fallax opus: Poet and Reader in the Elegies of Propertius* John Warden

15 *Pindar's* Olympian One*: A Commentary* Douglas E. Gerber

16 *Greek and Roman Mechanical Water-Lifting Devices: The History of a Technology* John Peter Oleson

17 *The Manuscript Tradition of Propertius* James L. Butrica

18 Parmenides of Elea *Fragments: A Text and Translation with an Introduction* edited by David Gallop

19 *The Phonological Interpretation of Ancient Greek: A Pandialectal Analysis* Vít Bubeník

20 *Studies in the Textual Tradition of Terence* John N. Grant

21 *The Nature of Early Greek Lyric: Three Preliminary Studies* R.L. Fowler

22 Heraclitus *Fragments: A Text and Translation with a Commentary* edited by T.M. Robinson

23 *The Historical Method of Herodotus* Donald Lateiner

24 *Near Eastern Royalty and Rome, 100–30 BC* Richard D. Sullivan

25 *The Mind of Aristotle: A Study in Philosophical Growth* John M. Rist

26 *Trials in the Late Roman Republic, 149 BC to 50 BC* Michael Alexander

27 *Monumental Tombs of the Hellenistic Age: A Study of Selected Tombs from the Pre-Classical to the Early Imperial Era* Janos Fedak

28 *The Local Magistrates of Roman Spain* Leonard A. Curchin

29 Empedocles *The Poem of Empedocles: A Text and Translation with an Introduction* edited by Brad Inwood

30 Xenophanes of Colophon *Fragments: A Text and Translation with a Commentary* edited by J.H. Lesher

31 *Festivals and Legends: The Formation of Greek Cities in the Light of Public Ritual* Noel Robertson

32 *Reading and Variant in Petronius: Studies in the French Humanists and Their Manuscript Sources* Wade Richardson

33 *The Excavations of San Giovanni di Ruoti, Volume I: The Villas and Their Environment* Alastair Small and Robert J. Buck

34 *Catullus Edited with a Textual and Interpretative Commentary* D.F.S. Thomson

35 *The Excavations of San Giovanni di Ruoti, Volume 2: The Small Finds* C.J. Simpson, with contributions by R. Reece and J.J. Rossiter

36 The Atomists: Leucippus and Democritus *Fragments: A Text and Translation with a Commentary* C.C.W. Taylor

37 *Imagination of a Monarchy: Studies in Ptolemaic Propaganda* R.A. Hazzard

38 *Aristotle's Theory of the Unity of Science* Malcolm Wilson

39 Empedocles *The Poem of Empedocles: A Text and Translation with an Introduction, Revised Edition* edited by Brad Inwood

40 *The Excavations of San Giovanni di Ruoti, Volume 3: The Faunal and Plant Remains* M.R. McKinnon, with contributions by A. Eastham, S.G. Monckton, D.S. Reese, and D.G. Steele

41 *Justin and Pompeius Trogus: A Study of the Language of Justin's* Epitome *of Trogus* J.C. Yardley

42 *Studies in Hellenistic Architecture* F.E. Winter

43 *Mortuary Landscapes of North Africa* edited by David L. Stone and Lea M. Stirling

44 Anaxagoras of Clazomenae *Fragments and Testimonia: A Text and Translation with Notes and Essays* by Patricia Curd

45 *Virginity Revisited: Configurations of the Unpossessed Body* edited by Bonnie MacLachlan and Judith Fletcher

46 *Roman Dress and the Fabrics of Roman Culture* edited by Jonathan Edmondson and Alison Keith

47 *Epigraphy and the Greek Historian* edited by Craig Cooper

48 *In the Image of the Ancestors: Narratives of Kinship in Flavian Epic* Neil W. Bernstein

49 *Perceptions of the Second Sophistic and Its Times – Regards sur la Seconde Sophistique et son époque* edited by Thomas Schmidt and Pascale Fleury

50 *Apuleius and Antonine Rome: Historical Essays* Keith Bradley

51 *Belonging and Isolation in the Hellenistic World* edited by Sheila L. Ager and Riemer A. Faber

52 *Roman Slavery and Roman Material Culture* edited by Michele George

53 *Thalia Delighting in Song: Essays on Ancient Greek Poetry* Emmet I. Robbins

54 *Stymphalos: The Acropolis Sanctuary, Volume 1* edited by Gerald P. Schaus with contributions by Sandra Garvie-Lok, Christopher Hagerman, Monica Munaretto, Deborah Ruscillo, Gerald P. Schaus, Peter Stone, Mary Sturgeon, Laura Surtees, Robert Weir, Hector Williams, Alexis Young

www.ingramcontent.com/pod-product-compliance
Lightning Source LLC
La Vergne TN
LVHW082003060826
814660LV00031B/1270
* 9 7 8 1 4 8 7 5 2 0 4 2 7 *